shakespearean criticism

"Thou art a Monument without a tomb,
And art alive still shile thy Book doth
 live
And we have wits to read and praise to
give"

*Ben Jonson, from the preface
to the First Folio, 1623*

Mr. WILLIAM SHAKESPEARES

COMEDIES, HISTORIES, & TRAGEDIES.

Published according to the True Originall Copies.

LONDON
Printed by Isaac Iaggard, and Ed. Blount. 1623.

Frontspiece of the First Folio (1623). By permission of the Folger Shakespeare Library

Volume 53

shakespearean criticism

Excerpts from the Criticism of
William Shakespeare's Plays and Poetry,
from teh First Published appraisals
to Current Evaluations

Michelle Lee
Editor

Detroit
New York
San Francisco
London
Boston
Woodbridge, CT

STAFF

Lynn M. Spampinato, Janet Witalec, *Managing Editors, Literature Product*
Kathy D. Darrow, *Product Liaison*
Michelle Lee, *Editor*
Mark W. Scott, *Publisher, Literature Product*

Lisa Gellert, *Associate Editor*
Patti A. Tippett, Timothy J. White, *Technical Training Specialists*
Deborah J. Morad, Kathleen Lopez Nolan, *Managing Editors*
Susan M. Trosky, *Director, Literature Content*

Maria L. Franklin, *Permissions Manager*
Shalice Shaw-Caldwell, *Permissions Associate*

Victoria B. Cariappa, *Research Manager*
Corrine Boland, Tamara C. Nott, Tracie A. Richardson, *Research Associates*
Timothy Lehnerer, *Research Assistant*

Dorothy Maki, *Manufacturing Manager*
Stacy L. Melson, *Buyer*

Mary Beth Trimper, *Composition Manager*
Evi Seoud, *Assistant Production Manager*
Gary Leach, *Composition Specialist*

Randy Bassett, *Image Database Supervisor*
Robert Duncan, *Imaging Specialist*
Michael Logusz, *Graphic Artist*
Pamela A. Reed, *Imaging Coordinator*
Kelly A. Quin, *Imaging Editor*

Since this page cannot legibly accommodate all copyright notices, the acknowledgments constitute an extension of the copyright notice.

While every effort has been made to secure permission to reprint material and to ensure the reliability of the information presented in this publication, the Gale Group neither guarantees the accuracy of the data contained herein nor assumes any responsibility for errors, omissions or discrepancies. Gale accepts no payment for listing; and inclusion in the publication of any organization, agency, institution, publication, service, or individual does not imply endorsement of the editors or publisher. Errors brought to the attention of the publisher and verified to the satisfaction of the publisher will be corrected in future editions.

This publication is a creative work fully protected by all applicable copyright laws, as well as by misappropriation, trade secret, unfair competition, and other applicable laws. The authors and editors of this work have added value to the underlying factual material herein through one or more of the following: unique and original selection, coordination, expression, arrangement, and classification of the information.

All rights to this publication will be vigorously defended.

Copyright © 2000 Gale Group, Inc.
27500 Drake Road
Farmington Hills, MI 48331-3535

All rights reserved, including the right of reproduction in whole or in part in any form.
Gale Group and Design is a trademark used herein under license.

Library of Congress Catalog Card Number 86-645085
ISBN 0-7876-3148-5
ISSN 0883-9123
Printed in the United States of America

10 9 8 7 6 5 4 3 2 1

Contents

Preface vii

Acknowledgments xi

List of Plays and Poems Covered in *SC* xii

Race in Shakespeare's Works

Introduction	1
Overviews and General Studies	1
Race and Colonialism	11
Race and Gender	64
Titus Andronicus: Aaron	86
Further Reading	103

The Merchant of Venice

Introduction	104
Overviews and General Studies	105
Race	111
Disappointment	211
Elizabethan Culture and Values	214
Further Reading	232

Othello

Introduction	233
Race	233
Gender Issues	310

Language and Imagery 333

Social Background 350

Further Reading 357

Cumulative Character Index 359

Cumulative Topic Index 371

Cumulative Topic Index, by Play 391

Preface

Shakespearean Criticism (*SC*) provides students, educators, theatergoers, and other interested readers with valuable insight into Shakespeare's drama and poetry. A multiplicity of viewpoints documenting the critical reaction of scholars and commentators from the seventeenth century to the present day derives from hundreds of periodicals and books excerpted for the series. Students and teachers at all levels of study will benefit from *SC*, whether they seek information for class discussions and written assignments, new perspectives on traditional issues, or the most noteworthy of analyses of Shakespeare's artistry.

Scope of the Series

Volumes 1 through 10 of the series present a unique historical overview of the critical response to each Shakespearean work, representing a broad range of interpretations.

Volumes 11 through 26 recount the performance history of Shakespeare's plays on the stage and screen through eyewitness reviews and retrospective evaluations of individual productions, comparisons of major interpretations, and discussions of staging issues.

Beginning with volume 27 in the series, *SC* focuses on criticism published after 1960, with a view to providing the reader with the most significant modern critical approaches. Each volume is ordered around a theme that is central to the study of Shakespeare, such as politics, religion, or sexuality. The topic entry that introduces the volume is comprised of general essays that discuss this theme with reference to all of Shakespeare's works. Following the topic entry are several entries devoted to individual works.

Up until volume 48, published in October 1999, *SC* compiled an annual volume of the most noteworthy essays published on Shakespeare during the previous year. The essays, reprinted in their entirety, were recommended to Gale by an international panel of distinguished scholars.

Organization of the Book

An *SC* entry consists of the following elements:

- The **Introduction** outlines modern interpretations of individual Shakespearean topics, plays, and poems.

- Reprinted **Criticism** for each entry consists of essays arranged both thematically and chronologically. This provides an overview of the major areas of concern in the analysis of Shakespeare's works, as well as a useful perspective on changes in critical evaluation over recent decades. The critic's name and the date of composition or publication of the critical work are given at the beginning of each piece of criticism. Unsigned criticism is preceded by the title of the source in which it appeared. Footnotes are reprinted at the end of each essay or excerpt. In the case of excerpted criticism, only those footnotes that pertain to the excerpted texts are included.

- A complete **Bibliographical Citation** of the original essay or book precedes each piece of criticism.

- Critical essays are prefaced by **Explanatory Notes** as an aid to students using *SC*. The explanatory notes summarize the criticism that follows.

- Each volume includes such **Illustrations** as reproductions of images from the Shakespearean period, paintings and sketches of eighteenth- and nineteenth-century performers, photographs of modern productions, and stills from film adaptations.

- An annotated bibliography of **Further Reading** appears at the end of each entry and suggests resources for additional study. In some cases, significant essays for which the editors could not obtain reprint rights are included here.

Indexes

A **Cumulative Charater Index** identifies the principal characters of discussion in the criticism of each play and non-dramatic poem.

A **Cumulative Topic Index** identifies the principal topics in the criticism and stage history of each work. The topics are arranged alphabetically, by topic.

A **Cumulative Topic Index, by Play identifies the principal topics in the criticism and stage history of each work. The topics are arranged alphabetically, by play.**

Citing *Shakespearean Criticism*

When writing papers, students who quote directly from any volume in the Literary Criticism Series may use the following general format to footnote reprinted criticism. The first example pertains to material drawn from periodicals, the second to material reprinted from books.

Tetsuya Motohashi. "Body Politic and Political Body in *Coriolanus*," in *Forum for Modern Language Studies* XXX, no. 2 (April 1994): 97-112; reprinted in *Shakespearean Criticism,* vol. 50, ed. Kathy D. Darrow (Farmington Hills, Mich.: The Gale Group, 2000), 119-128.

Mary Hamer. "Authority and Violence," in *William Shakespeare: Julius Caesar* (Northcote House, 1998), 12-20; reprinted in *Shakespearean Criticism,* vol. 50, ed. Kathy D. Darrow (Farmington Hills, Mich.: The Gale Group, 2000), 230-34.

Suggestions are Welcome

Readers who wish to suggest new features, topics, or authors to appear in future volumes, or who have other suggestions or comments are cordially invited to call, write, or fax the Managing Editor:

Managing Editor, Literary Criticism Series

The Gale Group

27500 Drake Road

Farmington Hills, MI 48331-3535

1-800-347-4253 (GALE)

Fax: 248-699-8054 [000c]

Acknowledgments

The editors wish to thank the copyright holders of the excerpted criticism included in this volume and the permissions managers of many book and magazine publishing companies for assisting us in securing reproduction rights. We are also grateful to the staffs of the Detroit Public Library, the Library of Congress, the University of Detroit Mercy Library, Wayne State University Purdy/Kresge Library Complex, and the University of Michigan Libraries for making their resources available to us. Following is a list of the copyright holders who have granted us permission to reproduce material in this volume of *SC*. Every effort has been made to trace copyright, but if omissions have been made, please let us know.

COPYRIGHTED EXCERPTS IN *SC*, VOLUME 53, WERE REPRODUCED FROM THE FOLLOWING PERIODICALS:

ANQ: A Quarterly Journal of Short Articles, Notes, and Reviews, v. 7, 1994. Copyright © 1994 Helen Dwight Reid Educational Foundation. Reproduced with permission of the Helen Dwight Reid Educational Foundation, published by Heldref Publications, 1319 18th Street, NW, Washington, DC 20036-1802.—*Atlantis*, v. 9, Spring, 1984.—*CLA Journal*, v. XXXVIII, June, 1995; v. XL, March, 1997; v. XLI, June, 1998. Copyright, © 1995, 1997, 1998 by The College Language Association. All used by permission of The College Language Association.—*CLIO*, v. 22, Spring, 1993 for "Race and the Spectacle of the Monstrous in Othello" by James R. Aubrey. © 1993 by Robert H. Canary and Henry Kozicki. Reproduced by permission of the author.—*Critical Inquiry*, v. 13, 1987. Copyright © 1987 by The University of Chicago Press. Reproduced by permission.—*English Literary Renaissance*, v. 15, Autumn, 1985. Copyright © 1985 by English Literary Renaissance. Reproduced by permission.—*English Studies*, v. 73, June, 1992; v. 75, March, 1994. © 1992, 1994, Swets & Zeitlinger. Both reproduced by permission.—*The Journal of American History*, v. 79, 1992. Copyright © Organization of American Historians, 1992. Reproduced by permission.—*The Journal of Commonwealth Literature*, v. XII, 1977. Reproduced with the kind permission of Bowker-Saur.—*Judaism: A Quarterly Journal*, v. 43, 1994. Copyright © 1994 by the American Jewish Congress. Reproduced by permission.—*Literature & History*, v. 5, 1996. Reproduced by permission of Manchester University Press.—*Mosaic*, v. 27, 1994. © Mosaic 1994. Reproduced by permission.—*Papers on Language & Literature*, v. 32, Winter, 1996. Copyright © 1996 by The Board of Trustees, Southern Illinois University at Edwardsville. Reproduced by permission.—*PMLA*, v. 113, 1998. Reproduced by permission.—*Renaissance Drama*, v. XXIII, 1992. Copyright © 1994 by Northwestern University Press. Reproduced by permission.—*Shakespeare Quarterly*, v. 47, 1996; v. 48, 1997; v. 49, 1998. © The Folger Shakespeare Library, 1996, 1997, 1998. All reproduced by permission.—*Shakespeare Studies*, v. XX, 1988 for "Shakespeare's Jew: Preconception and Performance" by Marion D. Perret; v. XXIV, 1996 for "Allegorical Commentary in *The Merchant of Venice*" by Judith Rosenheim. © 1988, 1996 by Associated University Presses, Inc. All rights reserved. Both reproduced by permission of the respective authors.—*Shakespeare Survey: An Annual Survey of Shakespeare Studies and Production*, v. 48, 1995, for "Venetian Culture and the Politics of Othello" by Mark Matheson; v. 51, 1998, for "Race Mattered: Othello in Late Eighteenth-Century England" by Virginia Mason Vaughan; v. 51, 1998, for "Prejudice and Law in The Merchant of Venice" by B. J. Sokol. Copyright © Cambridge University Press 1995, 1998. All reproduced with the permission of Cambridge University Press and the respective authors.—*South Atlantic Review*, v. 55, November, 1990; v. 57, November, 1992. Reproduced by permission.—*Stanford Humanities Review*, v. 3, Winter, 1993. Reproduced by permission.—*The Yale Journal of Criticism*, v. 8, Fall, 1995. Copyright © 1995 by The Johns Hopkins University Press. Reproduced by permission.

COPYRIGHTED EXCERPTS IN *SC*, VOLUME 53, WERE REPRODUCED FROM THE FOLLOWING BOOKS:

Hall, Kim F. From *Things of Darkness: Economies of Race and Gender in Early Modern England.* Cornell University Press, 1995. Copyright © 1995 by Cornell University Press. All rights reserved. Reproduced by permission.—Hendricks, Margo. For "'The Moor of Venice,' or The Italian on the Renaissance English Stage," from *Shakespearean Tragedy and Gender.* Edited by Shirley Nelson Garner and Madelon Sprengnether. Indiana University Press, 1996. Copyright © 1996 by Indiana University Press. All rights reserved. Reproduced by permission.—Leininger, Lorie Jerrell. For "The Miranda Trap: Sexism and Racism in Shakespeare's Tempest," from *The Woman's Part: Feminist Criticism of Shakespeare.* Edited by Carolyn Ruth Swift Lenz, Gayle Greene, and Carol Thomas Neely. University of Illinois Press, 1980. Copyright © 1980 by the Board of Trustees of the University of Illinois. All rights reserved. Reproduced by permission.—Lyon, John. From *Harvester New Critical Introductions to Shakespeare: The Merchant of Venice.* Harvester/Wheatsheaf, 1988. Copyright ©

1988 John Lyon. All rights reserved. Reproduced by permission of Pearson Education Limited.—Moisan, Thomas. For "'Which is the merchant here? and which the Jew?': Subversion and Recuperation in *The Merchant of Venice*," from ***Shakespeare Reproduced: The Text in History and Ideology.*** Edited by Jean E. Howard and Marion F. O'Connor. Methuen, Inc., 1987. Copyright © 1987 by Thomas Moisan. All rights reserved.—Novy, Marianne. From ***Love's Argument: Gender Relations in Shakespeare.*** University of North Carolina Press, 1984. Copyright © 1985 University of North Carolina Press. Used by permission of the publisher.—Oz, Avraham. From ***The Yoke of Love: Prophetic Riddles in The Merchant of Venice.*** University of Delaware Press, 1995. Copyright 1995 by Associated University Presses, Inc. All rights reserved. Reproduced by permission.—Singh, Jyotsna G. For "Caliban Versus Miranda: Race and Gender Conflicts in Postcolonial Rewritings of *The Tempest,*" from ***Feminist Readings of Early Modern Culture: Emerging Subjects.*** Edited by Valerie Traub, M. Lindsay Kaplan, and Dympna Callaghan. Cambridge University Press, 1996. Copyright © Cambridge University Press 1996. Reproduced with the permission of Cambridge University Press and the author.

PHOTOGRAPHS APPEARING IN *SC*, VOLUME 53, WERE RECEIVED FROM THE FOLLOWING SOURCES:

Act III, scene ii, from William Shakespeare's *The Merchant of Venice,* from Boydell-Shakespeare Gallery, photograph. Special Collections Library, University of Michigan. Reproduced by permission.—Act III, scene iii, from William Shakespeare's *The Merchant of Venice,* from Boydell-Shakespeare Gallery, photograph. Special Collections Library, University of Michigan. Reproduced by permission.—Act V, scene i, From William Shakespeare's *The Merchant of Venice,* from Boydell-Shakespeare Gallery, photograph. Special Collections Library, University of Michigan. Reproduced by permission.—Irene Jacob as Desdemona, Kenneth Branagh as Iago, and Laurence Fishburne as Othello, in the film version of William Shakespeare's *Othello,* 1995, photograph by Rolf Konow. Castle Rock Entertainment. Courtesy of The Kobal Collection. Reproduced by permission.—Laurence Olivier as Othello and Maggie Smith as Desdemona, in scenes from the film version of William Shakespeare's *Othello,* 1965, photograph. BR Home Entertainment/Warner Brothers. Courtesy of The Kobal Collection. Reproduced by permission.—Eric Donkin as Arragon, Jane Casson as Merissa, and Maureen O'Brien as Portia, in a scene from the 1970 Stratford Festival production of William Shakespeare's *The Merchant of Venice,* 1970, photograph by Douglas Spillane. Courtesy of Stratford Festival Archives.— *Colm Feore as Salerio, Stephen Russell as Gratiano, Shaun Austin-Olsen as Solanio, and John Neville as Shylock, in a scene from the Stratford Festival production of William Shakespeare's The Merchant of Venice,* 1984, photograph by Michael Cooper. Courtesy of Stratford Festival Archives.—Seana McKenna as Jessica, and Keith Dinicol as Launcelot Gobbo in a scene from the Stratford Festival production of William Shakespeare's *The Merchant of Venice,* 1984, photograph by Michael Cooper. Courtesy of Stratford Festival Archives.— *Howard Rollins as Othello, Wenna Shaw as Desdemona, Scott Wentworth as Roderigo, Colm Feore as Iago, Goldie Semple as Emilia and Derek Boyes as Cassio, in a scene from the Stratford Festival production of William Shakespeare's Othello,* 1987, photograph by Michael Cooper. Courtesy of Stratford Festival Archives.—Powys Thomas as the Duke of Venice, William Needles as Barbantio, and Douglas Campbell as Othello, in a scene from the Stratford Festival production of William Shakespeare's *Othello,* 1959, photograph by Peter Smith & Co. Courtesy of Stratford Festival Archives.— *Paul Robeson as Othello, 1943, photograph.* AP/Wide World Photos. Reproduced by permission.

List of Plays and Poems Covered in SC

Volumes 1-10 present a critical overview of each play, including criticism from the seventeenth century to the present. Beginning with Volumes 11, the series focuses on the history of Shakespeare's plays on the stage and in important films. The Yearbooks reprint the most important critical pieces of the year as suggested by an advisory board of Shakespearean scholars. Beginning with Volume 27, each volume is organized around a theme and focuses on criticism published after 1960.

Vol. 1
The Comedy of Errors
Hamlet
Henry IV, Parts 1 and 2
Timon of Athens
Twelfth Night

Vol. 2
Henry VIII
King Lear
Love's Labour's Lost
Measure for Measure
Pericles

Vol. 3
Henry VI, Parts 1, 2, and 3
Macbeth
A Midsummer Night's Dream
Troilus and Cressida

Vol. 4
Cymbeline
The Merchant of Venice
Othello
Titus Andronicus

Vol. 5
As You Like It
Henry V
The Merry Wives of Windsor
Romeo and Juliet

Vol. 6
Antony and Cleopatra
Richard II
The Two Gentlemen of Verona

Vol. 7
All's Well That Ends Well
Julius Caesar
The Winter's Tale

Vol. 8
Much Ado about Nothing
Richard III
The Tempest

Vol. 9
Coriolanus
King John
The Taming of the Shrew
The Two Noble Kinsmen

Vol. 10
The Phoenix and Turtle
The Rape of Lucrece
Sonnets
Venus and Adonis

Vol. 11
King Lear
Othello
Romeo and Juliet

Vol. 12
The Merchant of Venice
A Midsummer Night's Dream
The Taming of the Shrew
The Two Gentlemen of Verona

Vol. 13
1989 Yearbook

Vol. 14
Henry IV, Parts 1 and 2
Henry V
Richard III

Vol. 15
Cymbeline
Pericles
The Tempest
The Winter's Tale

Vol. 16
1990 Yearbook

Vol. 17
Antony and Cleopatra
Coriolanus
Julius Caesar
Titus Andronicus

Vol. 18
The Merry Wives of Windsor
Much Ado about Nothing
Troilus and Cressida

Vol. 19
1991 Yearbook

Vol. 20
Macbeth
Timon of Athens

Vol. 21
Hamlet

Vol. 22
1992 Yearbook

Vol. 23
As You Like It
Love's Labour's Lost
Measure for Measure

Vol. 24
Henry VI, Parts 1, 2, and 3
Henry VIII
King John
Richard II

Vol. 25
1993 Yearbook

Vol. 26
All's Well That Ends Well
The Comedy of Errors
Twelfth Night

Vol. 27
Shakespeare and Classical Civilization
Antony and Cleopatra
Timon of Athens
Titus Andronicus
Troilus and Cressida

Vol. 28
1994 Yearbook

Vol. 29
Magic and the Supernatural
Macbeth
A Midsummer Night's Dream
The Tempest

Vol. 30
Politics
Coriolanus
Henry V
Julius Caesar

Vol. 31
Shakespeare's Representation of Women
Much Ado about Nothing
King Lear
Taming of the Shrew

Vol. 32
1995 Yearbook

Vol. 33
Sexuality in Shakespeare
Measure for Measure
The Rape of Lucrece
Romeo and Juliet
Venus and Adonis

Vol. 34
Appearance versus Reality
The Comedy of Errors
Twelfth Night
As You Like It

Vol. 35
Madness
Hamlet
Othello

Vol. 36
Fathers and Daughters
Cymbeline
Pericles
The Winter's Tale

Vol. 37
1996 Yearbook

Vol. 38
Desire
All's Well That Ends Well
Love's Labour's Lost
The Merry Wives of Windsor
The Phoenix and Turtle

Vol. 39
Kingship
Henry IV Parts 1 and 2
Henry VI Parts 1, 2, and 3
Richard II
Richard III

Vol. 40
Gender Identity
The Merchant of Venice
Sonnets
The Two Gentlemen of Verona

Vol. 41
Authorship Controversy
Henry VIII
King John
The Two Noble Kinsmen

Vol. 42
1997 Yearbook

Vol. 43
Violence
The Rape of Lucrece
Titus Andronicus
Troilus and Cressida

Vol. 44
Psychoanalytic Criticism
Hamlet
Macbeth

Vol. 45
Dreams
A Midsummer Night's Dream
The Tempest
The Winter's Tale

Vol. 46
Clowns and Fools
As You Like It
King Lear
Twelfth Night

Vol. 47
Deception
Antony and Cleopatra
Cymbeline
The Merry Wives of Windsor

Vol. 48
1998 Yearbook

Vol. 49
Law and Justice
Henry IV, 1 and 2
Henry V
Measure for Measure

Vol. 50
Social Class
Coriolanus
Julius Caesar
The Two Noble Kinsmen

Vol. 51
Love and Romance
Pericles
The Phoenix and Turtle
Romeo and Juliet
Sonnets
Venus and Adonis

Vol. 52
Morality
Richard II
Richard III
Timon of Athens

Vol. 53
Race
Othello
The Merchant of Venice

Future Volumes

Vol. 54
Beginnings and Endings
The Comedy of Errors
Love's Labour's Lost
The Two Gentlemen of Verona

Vol. 55
Feminist Criticism
All's Well That Ends Well
Much Ado About Nothing
The Taming of the Shrew

Vol. 56
Historical Revision
Henry VI, Parts 1, 2 and 3
Henry VIII
King John

Race

INTRODUCTION

Contemporary critical discussion of Shakespeare's works has frequently focused on the subject of race, particularly how racial "others" are represented in his dramas. Many commentators have focused on the importance of achieving a clear consideration of how Shakespeare and his Elizabethan contemporaries understood the term "race." Generally, scholars have observed that Shakespeare employed the word "race" in a genealogical sense, referring to noble bloodlines and royal succession. Nevertheless, many contemporary critics have located race as a central site of conflict in several of Shakespeare's works, including *Othello, The Merchant of Venice, Antony and Cleopatra, The Tempest,* and *Titus Andronicus*. To varying degrees, each of these works confronts the tensions between white, Christian Europeans, and cultural outsiders—blacks, Jews, Muslims, and Indians. In examining these conflicts, critics have generally argued that while Shakespeare presents an array of stereotypes, in many cases he succeeds in transcending these limited perceptions and offers a complex, if not always balanced, depiction of racial interaction.

In *Othello* and *The Merchant of Venice,* the dark-skinned Othello and Jewish Shylock dominate their respective plays—works pervaded by the drama of racial difference. While racial antagonism drives the plot of these powerful works, other plays approach the subject of race less directly, exploring the clash of cultures as an important motif. Among these works, *Titus Andronicus* features a significant element of racial discrimination, centered on the figure of Aaron. A black-skinned Moor, Aaron represents, on a superficial level, the Renaissance association of the color black with evil. Several critics, including Edward T. Washington (1995) and Jeannette S. White (1997), assert that Shakespeare's Aaron surmounts this stereotype, particularly in light of his compassionate love for his child. An ambiguous character, according to Washington, Aaron offers an evil exterior that masks his deeply hidden virtues.

Modern critics have also found the link between race and gender particularly intriguing in several of Shakespeare's plays. Lorie Jerrell Leininger (1980) observes the analogy between Prospero's oppression of his daughter Miranda and of his racially distinct slave Caliban in *The Tempest*. Leininger discusses Caliban's qualities as a lascivious Vice-figure who stands in contrast to Miranda and her inherent virtue. Kim F. Hall (1995) further explores the concept of a sexualized threat posed by a racial "other," discussing Caliban's attempted rape of Miranda and the danger to Roman imperial culture intimated by the sexually potent African queen Cleopatra in *Antony and Cleopatra*. Joyce Green MacDonald (1996) follows a similar line of inquiry by probing the symbolic import of a highly sexualized, black-skinned Cleopatra as an emblem of corruption and lustful desire.

Twentieth-century study of cultural imperialism has also proved a useful point of departure for the interpretation of Shakespeare's late drama, *The Tempest,* which has elicited a number of racially-inspired, anticolonial readings. Rob Nixon (1987) surveys the play's appropriation by African and Caribbean intellectuals of the postcolonial period, who have found in the racially-charged relationship between Prospero and Caliban a strong condemnation of European imperialism. This critical exploration is furthered by Jyotsna G. Singh (1996), who examines Caliban's recasting by modern proponents of decolonization as a cultural prototype of the oppressed New World revolutionary. Richard Takaki (1992) analyzes Caliban's connection to American history in the early age of English colonial expansion, associating Shakespeare's depiction of Caliban with Renaissance reports of "savages" in the Americas. Furthermore, Barbara Fuchs (1997) expands colonial interpretations of *The Tempest* to view in historical context the racial threats perceived by English imperialists in Ireland and the Islamic regions of the southern and eastern Mediterranean.

OVERVIEWS AND GENERAL STUDIES

Jonathan Crewe (essay date 1995)

SOURCE: "Out of the Matrix: Shakespeare and Race-Writing," in *The Yale Journal of Criticism,* Vol. 8, No. 2, Fall, 1995, pp. 13-29.

[*In the following essay, Crewe examines the "racializing potential" of Shakespeare's drama and poetry, arguing that "race is ubiquitous in Shakespeare's work."*]

At present, any attempt to discuss "Shakespeare and race-writing" in general will almost certainly appear misconceived. To suppose, for a start, that Shakespeare engages in something we might call race-writing is already to risk begging the question entirely. Even if the term "race" is granted, recent studies have rightly emphasized the heterogeneity and historical specificity of "racial" construction in the early modern period. These inhibiting considerations notwithstanding, I have posed the question of Shakespeare and race-writing in general terms. I have done so because it seems to me that prevailing historicist and/or cultural-studies categories make it difficult to precipitate the issue of "race" in Shakespeare broadly or fluidly enough to do justice to the phenomenon. Some further constriction may result from anxieties attendant on the discussion of so hurtful a topic as race. Without denying the sensitivity of the issue, I do not believe that these forms of constriction do any good. I shall proceed to argue, therefore, that insofar as Shakespeare can be seen to engage in "race-writing" at all, that writing is not confined to overtly racialized characters and situations in a handful of plays. On the contrary, "race" is ubiquitous in Shakespeare's work: ubiquitously prophesied; ever-present even when not deliberately foregrounded; constituted exorbitantly from the start.

Before elaborating on these remarks, I shall mention that they have not been prompted simply by consideration of Shakespeare's plays. Nor have they been exclusively prompted by recent discussion of Shakespearean and/or early modern racial construction.[1] An important instigation came from outside the field in the guise of Neil Jordan's film *The Crying Game*. Arguably, Jordan's film is one that seeks to realize the politically progressive potentialities of crossing in both the gendered and the racial senses of the term, the transvestite character Dil being the crossing figure in both those senses. Yet any assumption of progressive homology between the film's destabilizing sex-gender representations and its racial-ethnic ones would be questionable.[2] The ironic brilliance, articulateness, and political purposiveness of the film's gender-discourse are simply not matched in the film's racial/ethnic discourse. Perhaps it is because so many people now believe that sexuality and gender *are* culturally constructed and performed—or at least that the constructive-performative dimension is more consequential than the biological one—that Jordan's gender-bending *tour de force* could be produced as a mainstream film and received with broad public acclaim. As I have suggested, however, the film's racial/ethnic script remains fragmentary, relatively inarticulate, in comparison with its "performative" sex-gender script. Does this difference imply a lack of public conviction that race, too, is culturally constructed and performed? A strong residual belief that race is an intractable biological fact? Or does it imply a continuing deficiency in our critical discourses of "race"?

Consider the analogy apparently set up in the film between crossing (or passing) in gender terms and in racial/ethnic ones. Played by the "dark-skinned" Jaye Davidson, the gender-crossing transvestite character Dil can also be seen as a highly-eroticized racially or ethnically indeterminate figure, deconstructing the film's black-white polarities and constituting a valued third term. As an eroticized intermediary, Dil appears capable of negotiating racial/ethnic differences.[3] *The Crying Game* might thus be understood to promote ethnic plurality—and maybe "ethnicity" as such—in place of antagonistically "pure," reductive, racial identities (black man-white man; "nigger"-Irish). Some difficulties may be posed for this thesis, however, by the different ways in which Dil is seen by different viewing audiences.[4] A more serious difficulty arises from the apparent bodily coding—indeed, color-coding—of Dil as a figure of racial/ethnic indeterminacy or non-identity in the presence of sharply defined (black-white) bodily alternatives. In racial/ethnic terms, Dil does not represent a performative option so much as a particular look—one that leads bell hooks to characterize him/her as the type of the eroticized mulatta in an all too familiar racial schema. While I do not believe this characterization is necessarily correct, it raises a question about what Dil can stand for in the racial/ethnic context of the film.[5]

What, in fact, *can* Dil's racial/ethnic indeterminacy stand for if not the eugenic undoing of "pure" racial identity and hence antagonism? Failing any positive ethnic identification, to what can Dil's indeterminability attest if not a eugenic dream of benign mixture, with deracialization as its utopian telos? Yet no eugenic politics can be enunciated in film, or with reference to it, given both the current discrediting of racial eugenics and current reinvestment in ethnicity as distinct from race.[6] The film's discursive blockage on this subject is rendered virtually complete by the fact that any explicit eugenic idealization of Dil would be no less disturbing in its complicated invidiousness than is the abjecting disdain for persons of "mixed race" in strongly race-polarized and race-identified cultures.[7]

In short, although *The Crying Game* is an actively anti-racist film, it is also a film at once possessed and thwarted by racial consciousness. Such "passive" racialism, which is certainly not confined to *The Crying Game* alone at present, can be regarded as a troubling residue of Western racial construction at least since the actively formative (perhaps strictly reformative) early modern period. It is for participating momentously and overtly in such racial construction—among other things—that Shakespeare stands out among his English contemporaries. The study of Shakespeare's race-writing may thus enable us to recognize the extensiveness of the racial residue of Western cultural construction as a preliminary to further consideration of any "post-racial" identification or consciousness. It is on this premise that I wish to broach once again the broad question of Shakespeare's race-writing, concluding with an example from the sonnets as an important "racial" text.

Racial readings of Shakespeare are hardly new. In an essay titled "The Getting of a Lawful Race," however, Lynda Boose makes a case for reading the Shakespearean racial text more systematically and less anachronistically than has generally been done in the past from any point of view. These two requirements virtually mandate a fresh start in racial reading of Shakespeare, although it should be added that this fresh start has effectively been made by Shakespeareans working in postcolonial and cultural studies frames of reference. Some of the best new work appears in the very volume in which Boose issues her call for renovation.[8] Insisting, nevertheless, that such reading be properly historical, Boose establishes three caveats. First, racial categories and imaginary racial genealogies are fluid at the time Shakespeare is writing. To read these texts into stabilized modern racial categories is anachronistic. Second, to the extent that early modern racial categories *are* stabilized, or are in the process of being stabilized, they differ from modern ones. Categorical misalignments in racial readings of Shakespeare are thus also to be avoided. (These caveats resemble the one now widely accepted about the impropriety of applying modern categories of sexuality to Renaissance texts.) Third, racial categories are never constructed independently of other cultural-political categories, notably those of class, sexuality, gender and nationality. Crossing of categories can thus easily entail double or multiple crossing. For example, the speaker in *Micro-Cynicon: Sixe Snarling Satyres* (1599), by T- M- (Thomas Middleton?) alludes to a prostitute-figure anticipating Dil in *The Crying Game* as a "pale Checkquered black Hermaphrodite."[9] This strongly eroticized multicategorical figure resists any exclusively racial reading, apparently figuring instead a disturbingly magnetic indeterminability.

Boose focusses mainly on the formation of white racial ideology through an interplay between what might be called the Renaissance ethnographic Imaginary (comprising the essentially fictional constructions of race inherited from classical antiquity and the middle ages) and the empirical data of early modern inter-ethnic encounters, the latter occurring mainly under the impetus of European imperial expansion. As part of this discussion, she notes the formativeness of English colonial/racial construction of the Irish for later constructions of race that will, so to speak, be ever more elaborately color-coded and body-typed, thus technically becoming subject to empirical verification. The perniciousness of racial othering (and enslavement) arises not only from the power-differential governing these encounters but from their overwhelming predetermination by texts concerning the savagery, wildness or Plinian monstrousness of "other" races. (Clearly, idealization of racial others as noble or prelapsarian is another mode of imperious othering that does no service to its objects.) Yet this history, voluminous, complicated, and still in the process of being written, is not the whole story. I particularly want to focus here on the discursive *matrix* from which Shakespeare's race-writing is historically precipitated. The racializing potentialities of that matrix—what we might call its many proto-racial components—are as much responsible as any other immediate circumstance for Shakespeare's production of a racialized text.

The common, gendered term "matrix" is one I choose deliberately. In the first instance, I use it to designate the loose ensemble of logical categories and operations, rhetorical tropes, semantic units, grammatical and prosodic forms, and whatever other elements comprise the language-situation for Shakespeare and his contemporaries. Admittedly, the term "matrix" may, when used in this sense, seem barely distinguishable from "discourse." In use, the term may thus seem only to reiterate the post-structuralist point that language stands in a constitutive rather than a derivative or mimetic relation to social reality.

In fact, however, the term "discourse," even in Foucault's historically inflected usage, still adheres to its structuralist antecedents. Its use still recalls the structuralist model of language as a synchronic system, and it recalls more specifically the linearization of signifying utterance in structuralism, whether in terms of Saussure's single axis or Jakobson's coordinating axes. The systemic autonomy and unqualified originary status of language are likewise recalled, and have been dogmatically reiterated in a great deal of post-structuralist work. While "matrix" may still imply the constitutiveness of language, it does not invest language with primordial structural autonomy. Instead, a relatively unstructured, temporal grouping of elements—one capable of being troped, perhaps, as fecund, but also as "hysterically" mobile—is designated by the term. To the extent that structural binaries remain present in the matrix, their primordial constitutiveness is attenuated and their oppositional alignment is unsettled.

In *The Renaissance Notion of Woman,* for example, Ian Maclean refers Western gender-discourse (as we might also refer racial discourse) back to such primordial binaries as male-female; limited-unlimited; odd-even, etc., the series culminating in light-darkness; good-evil.[10] Obviously, these binaries cannot be regarded as neutral structural ones, but must rather be seen as value-laden residues of an unrecoverable but nonetheless real prehistory. In other words, their diachronic and culture-specific character is already manifest. Yet insofar as these binaries enter recorded (Western) cultural history, they do so within a loose, historically shifting, ensemble, not as fatefully determining structural poles. It is to this ensemble that the term "matrix" can be applied.

If there is a further justification for preferring the term "matrix," it is that it tropes linguistic constitutiveness *and* historical limitation in a way that appears to me reasonably consonant with Shakespearean practice. This consideration is not unimportant if, as I do, one attaches considerable heuristic as well as historical importance to Shakespeare's practice in race-gender representations. Insofar as "matrix" is irreducibly gendered, however, it remains unavoidably implicated in conflict between idealization of the prolific female source and misogynistic stigmatization of the female threat to masculine idealization.[11] Yet the term can still be usefully employed to designate the (admittedly very large) set of particulars constituting speech and writing as agencies of cultural production at any given moment; it is not therefore a term exclusively bound either to mythic engendering or biological procreation. To turn attention to the Shakespearean matrix as one in which a strong, widely dispersed, racializing potential exists is not to turn away from the historical specifics of Shakespearean racial construction, but rather to reconnect those specifics to the language-situation enabling such construction.

To indicate what I mean by the racializing potential of the matrix, I shall begin with an example from "The Rape of Lucrece." As one would expect, gender-conflict is strongly foregrounded in the poem, while categories of racial difference seem irrelevant given the implicit uniform "whiteness" of the poem's Roman characters.[12] Yet the moral terms of the poem are proto-racial as well. At Lucrece's death, her blood becomes a "purple fountain" bubbling from her breast, but as it spreads on the floor around her the mixed color purple begins to separate out into fractions:

> Some of her blood still pure and red remain'd,
> And some look'd black, and that false Tarquin stained.[13]

Lucrece's death is needed, in effect, to undo the internalized moral stain that is already tantamount to biological admixture. Only the most limited resemanticization would be needed to turn the "false" Tarquin who taints Lucrece's blood into an anxiously guilty yet sexually violent "colored" man, and Lucrece into the raped white woman. This resemanticization would still require Lucrece's noble death, not merely to uphold Roman honor in the abstract, but to forestall the birth of a child of mixed blood, an outcome strongly foreshadowed in the lines quoted above.

The initial purification-scenario, however, in which Lucrece's and Tarquin's blood separate out after flowing from the common purple source, proves revealingly insufficient. The red and the black components turn out not to be the only ones, while the diacritical antithesis between them in terms of purity and impurity requires further elaboration. Contemporary "experimental" knowledge of the bodily humors apparently supplied the basis for a further refinement:

> And as there are four elements out of which our bodies are compounded, so there are four sorts of humors answerable to their natures, being all mingled together with the blood, as we may see by experience in blood let out of one's body. For uppermost we see as it were a little skim like to the flower or working of new wine. . . . Next we may see as it were small streams of water mingled with the blood. And in the bottom we see a black and thicker humor, like to the lees of wine in a wine-vessel.[14]

Each of these blood-fractions represents one of the four humors, blood containing all of them in varying proportions.

One could argue that in "The Rape of Lucrece" this humoral observation, the empiricity of which is confirmed by its non-distinction from viticultural observation, undergoes moral allegorization as Lucrece's spilt blood composes itself into an emblem. I believe it would be more accurate to say, first, that a fateful empirical ligature is being produced here between humoral physiology and race, and, second, that unstably hierarchized physiological and moral elements are present in the matrix, along with a strong personifying agency that is also proto-racial:

> About the mourning and congealed face
> Of that black blood a wat'ry rigol goes,
> Which seems to weep upon the tainted place,
> And ever since, as pitying Lucrece' woes,
> Corrupted blood some wat'ry token shows,
> And blood untainted still doth red abide,
> Blushing at that which is so putrefied.[15]
>
> [1744-50]

As regards the previous diacritical antithesis between red and black, purity and impurity, it appears that untainted red blood is an irreducible oxymoron (it will "abide"). Yet the oxymoron will apparently be tolerable for ordinary moral and potentially procreative purposes (untainted blood can "abide" red). It is of this pure blood that the white woman will remain the primary vessel. Red blood cannot itself, however, be the signifier of purity. That at which it blushes is also its colored self. The signification of purity additionally requires that a completely untainted "wat'ry rigol" be separated out, and remain separated from, blood in any of its compromised colors. It is this colorless essence, of which the tears that forever bewail the tainted human condition also seem to be composed, that remains wholly antipathetic to any admixture with the blackness it also circumscribes.[16] Perhaps it is on this strange essence that the projection of a full-blown white racial ideology will eventually depend. Here, however, the only human face that materializes is the one into which the dark Tarquin-blood congeals. Essential purity has no picturable face, or, perhaps, human embodiment. This emblem's strange condensation of darkness, sexuality, loss, melancholia, death, sanctity and taint recurs in Sonnet 127, to which I shall turn in due course. It is in this knot or complex, however, that the human image is simultaneously precipitated and disavowed as black.

It is not only in this passage that a discourse of "color" is produced in the poem. Before the poem's tragic resolution transpires, another field of color has been negotiated through conventional Petrarchan troping of the red and the white:[17]

> When at Collatium this false lord arrived,
> Well was he welcom'd by the Roman dame,
> Within whose face beauty and virtue strived
> Which of them both should underprop her fame.
> When virtue bragg'd, beauty would blush for shame;
> When beauty boasted blushes, in despite,
> Virtue would stain that o'er with silver white.
> But beauty, in that white entituled,
> From Venus' doves, doth challenge that fair field;
> Then virtue claims from beauty beauty's red,
> Which virtue gave the golden age to gild
> Their silver cheeks, and call'd it then their shield,
> Teaching them thus to use it in the fight,
> When shame assail'd, the red should fence the white.
>
> [50-63]

Shakespeare is, as we know, among the English Renaissance writers who seek to reconstruct the figure of the Petrarchan woman as one in whom desire and chastity are reconciled, this reconciliation being solemnized through marriage. Such reconciliation under the aegis of "married chastity" represents an alternative to the old Petrarchan war between desire and chastity which is, on one hand, a gendered battle between male desire and female chastity, and on the other hand a civil war between desire and chastity in the woman herself.[18] In the woman's case, the red and white, respectively signifying the desire of her blood and her chaste spiritual purity, remain at odds. In "Lucrece," however, the alternative of reconciliation and interchange between desire and chastity, and between everything else those terms encode, is projected through an extraordinarily fluid, inventive, miscegenating blazon in which primary colors and significations are mingled, promising an end to the war of the sexes (and, of course, in the Elizabethan context, to the War of the Roses). Insofar as both race and gender are interchangeably constituted and color-coded, which is not to say that they are ever identically constituted, the blazon can provide a model for benign interchange and crossing as well as opposition. The apparent inability of this revisionary blazon to function as an effective model for nontragic resolution in the poem, or to resolve contradictions without revealing new ones, may simply reveal the power of countervailing imperatives of (racial) purity and (gendered) identity in the early modern period.[19] It is these highly reductive imperatives, to be written even or above all on people's bodies, that the protoracial discourse of "Lucrece" announces.

Local examples of racializing potential abound in the Shakespeare canon. Neither Macbeth nor, presumably, Shakespeare is thinking racially in the famous lines:

> Will all great Neptune's ocean wash this blood
> Clean from my hand? No; this my hand will rather
> The multitudinous seas incarnadine,
> Making the green one red.
>
> [II.ii.57-60]

Nor, presumably, is Lady Macbeth thinking racially when she says:

> Out, damned spot! out, I say!
> . . . . .
> What, will these hands ne'er be clean?
>
> [V.i.35, 43]

Yet the preternatural staining power of blood can be mobilized in Shakespearean and post-Shakespearean racial construction to signify the fatal effects of even the smallest admixture of bad/black blood; the characteristic exorbitancy of racialization—of racial discourse—is strongly anticipated in these hyperbolic locutions.[20] It is not just the indelibly tainting power of blood but its limitless dispersion that renders the dark woman-as-mother singularly threatening, as Boose has argued, to "white" patrilineal construction.[21]

Some examples of racializing potential are less local than this one. The strongly gendered Elizabethan language of cosmetic coloration, so well discussed by Frances Dolan in the context of misogyny, is already rife with anticipations of racialized "blackening," "whitening" and passing, while the cosmetic taint that impeaches female chastity also implies an underlying "darkness" equally capable of bearing race, class or gender implication.[22] (Thus the representation of the chaste woman, who must never be "colored," tinted, or tainted, becomes a virtual impasse for the male Elizabethan poet or painter.)[23] Racial actualization is already under way when Lysander blackens Hermia in *A Midsummer Night's Dream* by saying: "Away, you Ethiope" [III.iii.257] or "Out, tawny Tartar, out!" [III.ii.263]. Lysander's capacity to blacken Hermia arbitrarily and aggressively in this way implies a still-nascent power both of racial construction and "exposure." At the same time, Hermia's stereotypical characterization as the dark twin to the ideally fair Helena does not prevent Helena from seeing herself in competition with a *fair* Hermia [I.ii.227] for the Athenian beauty-prize. The fact that a dark beauty can be fairer than the fair depends, obviously enough, on the double and hence separable meanings of "fair" as blonde and as beautiful, implying the manipulable contingency of these characterizations. Yet the embeddedness of a small set of virulent Africanist or Orientalist tropes in the contemporary discursive matrix facilitates both a racial vectoring of representation and associative conjunction between logically disparate fields.[24]

The terms of cosmetic and bodily coloration merge, for example, with the terms of rhetorical coloration in the key racialized figure of Othello. Or, to put it differently, the figure of Othello materializes from a field in which, among other things, rhetorical, cosmetic, and bodily coloring become intermingled. Othello's bodily coloring seems almost complementary to the high rhetorical coloring he also manifests, while his denial of both these forms of coloring represents a paradoxically internalized cosmetology of passing. These denials notwithstanding, Othello's high "coloring" suffices to taint the chaste white woman (Desdemona), even or above all in his own mind.[25] Both the racist discourse of speakers in *Othello* and the play's racialized representation of Othello as "Moor" actualize a broad tainting potential of the play's matrix. In other words, Othello's emergence as a racialized character depends on a great deal more than the empirical contingency of Renaissance inter-ethnic encounters.

Examples of this kind could be multiplied almost indefinitely, and not only with respect to Shakespeare's overtly racialized characters or situations. Cumulatively, such examples project racial differences as deep-dyed ones, so to speak, while that projection in turn connects racialization via the discourse of purity to nameless archaic horrors of blood-taint. For Shakespeare, I would suggest, this racializing potentiality of the matrix, actualized as historical pressure and occasion dictate in such figures as Aaron, Tamora, Shylock, Jessica, Othello, Cleopatra and Caliban, is not exhausted by the production of these characters and situations.[26] The fact that the racializing potentiality is not localized, and cannot *be* bounded within a set of racial characters, means that it is indeterminable, always exorbitant. It is to this state of affairs that the sonnets testify as a "racial" text.

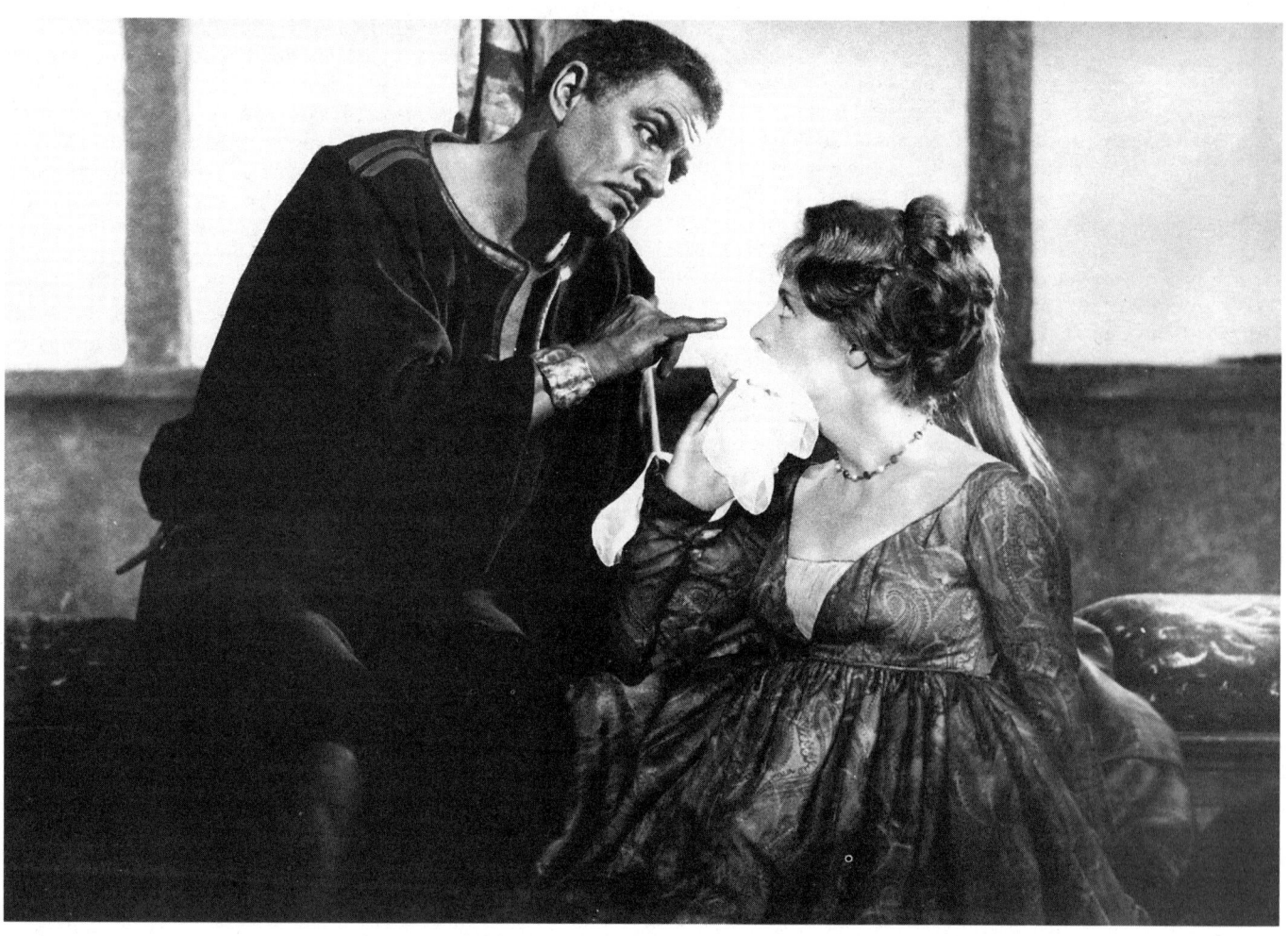

Laurence Olivier as Othello and Maggie Smith as Desdemona in a scene from the 1965 Warner Bros.-Seven Arts production of Othello.

A racial reading of the sonnets is strongly anticipated by Joel Fineman in *Shakespeare's Perjur'd Eye,* when he refers periodically to their "miscegenating" discourse.[27] In speaking of the sonnets as a script for miscegenation, Fineman is not speaking pointedly of them as a racial text. It is to an incongruous mixture of categories that he is primarily referring, heterosexuality already constituting a categorical mixture as opposed to the categorical purity of the male homoerotic bond. Yet on one hand Fineman cannot purge the term "miscegenation" of its latter-day racial meaning, which, according to the *OED,* dates from 1864, while on the other hand his application of the term to the sonnets makes them historically *anticipatory* of a racial discourse in which racial miscegenation will be tabooed or formally outlawed. In effect, Fineman's etymologically correct use of the term "miscegenation" hovers delicately between historical anticipation and retrospect. Boose, too, finds race not yet fully operative but unmistakeably emerging as *the* dominant European cultural category in the early seventeenth century.

In Fineman's terms, the sonnets constitute the Shakespearean master-code in which, among other things, modern Western subjectivity is decisively programmed. Fineman construes this subjectivity in Lacanian terms, making it first an effect of specular identification and then of symbolic reconstruction, the two phases corresponding roughly to the Young Man and Dark Lady sonnets respectively. No racial thematic is entailed in Fineman's reading, yet insofar as it is propped, like so many other sonnet-readings, on the imaginary master-narrative of the Young Man and the Dark Lady, it registers a strong racial-genetic potential. Fineman declines to thematize race because Lacanian subject-formation remains normatively if tacitly centered on the *white,* male, Western subject. For Lacan, just as there is explicitly "no woman," so there is implicitly no person of color, yet this constitutes erasure without prejudice, so to speak.[28]

What can be tacit for Lacan and Fineman, however, as well as being repressed in innumerable readings of the sonnets, is not tacit for Shakespeare, who problematically and momentously posits (or historically recognizes) the *fair* young man as the cultural ideal, with respect to whom all others will stand in abjected, specular or invisibly in-mixed relation. This prospect comes close to being fully enunciated in Sonnet 20 ("A woman's face with nature's own hand painted"). Although now practically read to death for its gender-ambiguity, the sonnet's preoccupation with color has largely escaped notice, as has the proto-racial implication of the line "a man in hue, all hues in his controlling." While "hue" may refer to a *male* appearance in the first instance, thus prophesying only gender-subordination, the normative fairness of this man is also implied, thus prophesying the subjection of all other "hues" to this one. However complicated, mixed, or self-alienated normative Western subjectivity may become, it will be vested in the specularized, white, male body.

Partly under the impetus of race-class-gender critiques as well as ethnic and multicultural politics, however, this state of affairs can no longer be taken for granted. What follows—or *has* already followed to a significant degree—is widespread reading of Shakespeare at, or somewhere between, two conceivable limits. At one end of the spectrum, Shakespeare is readable as a leading early modern promulgator of hegemonic Western race/class/gender norms, while at the other end he is read as profoundly and resistantly Other with respect to those same norms. At *this* end of the spectrum, Shakespeare's prolific, multipositional dramatizations, coupled with his personal "absence" or invisibility as author, make it possible for him to be critically relocated in the productive position of the black mother rather than the white father—to salutary effect, perhaps, on those still invested in Shakespeare as the canonical guarantor of white-male-universal Western culture.[29] That the theater should be the imagined locus of such "maternal" production is consistent with repeated troping of the theater, in Shakespeare and elsewhere, as countercultural and prolifically female (it is the scene of Cleopatra's triumph). In turning to Sonnet 127, however, I wish, instead of positioning Shakespeare in relation to these limits, to engage with his heuristic and self-reflexive troping of the racializing matrix.

> In the old age black was not counted fair,
> Or if it were, it bore not beauty's name;
> But now is black beauty's successive heir,
> And beauty slander'd with a bastard shame,
> For since each hand hath put on nature's power,
> Fairing the foul with art's false-borrow'd face,
> Sweet beauty hath no name, no holy bow'r,
> But is profan'd, if not lives in disgrace.
> Therefore my mistress' eyes are raven black,
> Her eyes so suited, that they mourners seem
> At such who, not born fair, no beauty lack,
> Sland'ring creation with a false esteem:
> Yet so they mourn, becoming of their woe,
> That every tongue says beauty should look so.

To begin by rehearsing some fairly common observations about this sonnet, it is strategically placed as the first of the so-called Dark Lady poems in the 1609 quarto sequence, following the truncated, twelve-line sonnet in rhyming couplets that ends the Young Man series. An important break and a transition are thus apparently marked; we might add that they are metrically re-marked in line 3 of the sonnet through the abrupt inversion and jarring caesura of "black/beauty's."[30] A modal shift from Petrarchan to anti-Petrarchan also coincides with the first appearance of the Dark Lady. This complex transposition and inversion of Petrarchan idealization seemingly includes a proto-racial critique of an entire value system predicated on an arbitrary coincidence between the "true," the "good" and the "fair."

These ordinary terms of approach to Sonnet 127 facilitate a racial reading. Rather than presenting a racial "character," however, Sonnet 127 seemingly enacts a struggle between romance precipitation and continuing repression of the powerful, racialized female character as a strong potentiality inherent in the matrix. Struggle occurs for many reasons. First, in Boose's terms, the black woman is the unrepresentable in white racial-genetic ideology. Bringing the black woman to consciousness and representation is thus a formidable counter-ideological undertaking. The degree to which the emergence of Cleopatra represents this "triumph" remains debatable, not only with reference to the play but to complex ongoing debate about the "blackening" and "whitening" of Cleopatra in Western cultural history.[31] Second, more is involved in Sonnet 127 than the substitution of one leading character (or addressee) for another in the sonnet sequence. An inversion of the figure-ground relation between fair young man and "colored" woman is also involved; an entire structure of representation (and of repression) is thus being painfully reconceived. Third, the emergence of the black woman entails a strongly reflexive turn to (troping of) the gendered matrix rather than the figures hitherto precipitated from it. The potentiating and simultaneously threatening relation of the matrix to its products comes dimly into view, as does the power of the matrix as the "tainted" source and ultimate undoing of all that is thought fair, good and true. In this moment of dawning recognition, the "normal" Petrarchan monotony of idealization and its discontents gives way to a state of volatile, highly charged ambivalence. Fourth, the emergence of the black woman subverts the narrative in which she is comprehended. In the "old days," we are told, "black was not counted fair," thus the emergence of "black beauty" as a historical novelty prophesies an epochal reversal and lamentable transvaluation of values. In a sense, however, these old days are no further back than the previous sonnet, and any contemporary reader of Sonnet 127 could have been aware that the female "black beauty" of the Song of Solomon may well have antedated the "fair" ideal of the previous sonnets. The coincidence between fair, true, and good is thus threatened with exposure as a latter-day imposition—and form of denial—given spurious originary status. A wholly false, supplanting cultural genealogy and value-system may therefore be represented by the fair young man, not by the stigmatized black woman. Finally, the entire order of visionary, specular optics in which the "I" is precipitated as a function of the "eye," and which, according to Fineman, constitutes pre-modern Western subjectivity, is undone, exposing a range of disconcerting alternatives. The mirror of identity becomes one of melancholy difference rather than sameness; or absorbs instead of reflecting; or confronts the beholder simultaneously with the lack of any identity and corresponding pathos of a shared, senselessly martyred dark humanity, from which the name of "beauty" is witheld; or, finally, becomes the mirror of a human mortality at once denied and projected onto the dark person as distinct from the immortally fair one.

The near-inconceivability for the speaker of everything being registered in this sonnet is made explicit in a number of ways that barely require commentary: it is enough to note the poem's scandalized citation of the purity-threatening universality of cosmetic color; the disappearance of nature; the indeterminability of the bastard; the rupture of true genealogy, and so on. Beyond the speaker's concern about these fetishes of the period, however, a deeper dislocation is implied in the poem by the persistence of logical and rhetorical forms that no longer make normal logical and rhetorical sense. "Therefore," which opens the sestet, is a logical ligature that makes no intelligible connection, and it is shortly followed by what seems like a failed rhetorical progression from "her eyes are raven black" to "her eyes so suited." The unexpected and baldly infelicitous repetition of "eyes" creates a sense of logical *and* rhetorical deficiency while apparently undermining any distinction between the eyes and something else in which, or to which, they might be "suited." If, on the other hand, the eyes are well-suited for the paradoxically funereal occasion of their debut, as is the black face that appears in Lucrece's spilt blood, they also seem to mark the point of disappearance between the suit and that which is suited, the costume and the wearer of the costume. The lady is being painted black-on-black, as black takes over everywhere. The double negative construction in the line "At such who, not born fair, no beauty lack" makes the affirmative virtually unrecoverable, both in the line and as an antecedent to "Slandering creation with a false esteem." Effects of this order are not containable by a merely antithetical conception of anti-Petrarchanism, which, as Fineman among others has pointed out, is anticipated from the start in Petarchanism. ("My mistress eyes are nothing like the sun" is more programmatically anti-Petrarchan yet considerably less charismatically dark than Sonnet 127.)

Sonnet 127 is not a text that produces a racial character—a "black woman" in any sense in which that term would now be understood—but it is certainly one that engages in reflexive thematization of the unbounded potentialities of the racializing matrix. Perhaps only tentative conclusions can accordingly be drawn from the poem. One such conclusion is that since race has not yet been fully hardened into a master category or yoked to a master-narrative of white racial supremacy, the poem holds both racialized "truth" and its momentous undoing in prophetic suspension. In the moment of anticipation, both "white" racial ideology and its dismantling—not merely its unmasking—are prophesied. Insofar as history can be said to have verified the ambiguous prophecy, however, it cannot yet be said to have produced closure or anything close to "post-racial" consciousness; the residues, the continuing impasses, and the threats of reversal remain in historical contention.

Another, related, conclusion is that racial consciousness persists in the present because it cannot be dissipated simply through attacks on racism, by critiques of overtly racialized texts and cultural situations, or even, for that matter, by postcolonial revision and cultural critique of the Shakespearean text. Indispensable and consequential though these remain, race-writing is too insidiously pervasive, too unconfined, to be fully encompassed in these ways; indeed, a dangerously premature sense of mastery or enclosure may be produced by critiques of racial ideology as such. To return to the Shakespearean text is not (redundantly) to begin the critical reckoning with race all over again, but rather to begin a critical reckoning with "post-racial" residues even more threatening when unrecognized than when seen in all their alarming magnitude.

Notes

1. Although their bearing remains only indirect here, I want to acknowledge the importance of the race-critiques produced by Kwame Anthony Appiah, notably "Illusions of Race" and "Topologies of Nativism," in *In My Father's House: Africa in the Philosophy of Culture* (New York: Oxford University Press, 1992), 28-72.

2. For one negative view of the film's racial representations, see Frann Michael, "Biology Notwithstanding . . . ," *Cineaste,* 20 (1993): 30-35.

3. I make no presumption about actor Jaye Davidson's ethnicity or his "racial" identity, to neither of which any reference is made in the film.

4. Since racial categories and perceptions are by no means universal, how Dil is seen may differ significantly between the U.S. and England (or Ireland), and may differ again between those English-language settings and their Latin counterparts.

5. bell hooks, "Seduction and Betrayal: *The Crying Game* meets *The Bodyguard*," *Outlaw Culture* (New York: Routledge, 1994), 53-62. While this characterization of Dil may partly explain the favorable U.S. reception of *The Crying Game,* I believe the term "mulatta" is misplaced with reference to any figure in a contemporary British film, that term belonging more recognizably to U.S. than to English racial discourse. Although the *mestiza* can be positively troped as a cultural figure in contemporary Latina writing, as, for example, in Gloria Anzaldua, *Borderlands = La frontera: The New Mestiza* (San Francisco: Spinsters/Aunt Lute, 1987), racial body-typing remains a form of literalism by no means transcended in *The Crying Game.*

6. The last flourishing of eugenics as a pseudoscience under the Third Reich served to discredit it almost

entirely. The eugenic complement to racialist thinking is evident in various historical guises, however, including prescientific ones. Insofar as race is taken, in one sense or another, as a natural fact, eugenics becomes the mode of cultural intervention and control. Intervention can take the form of "getting a lawful race," of aristocratic "breeding," or of maintaining pure "bloodlines." Genetic engineering has now reopened the prospect of eugenic manipulation, whether in science fiction or scientific fact. It is beyond the scope of this essay to explore the continuities and discontinuities between "race" and "ethnicity" in contemporary discourse, yet it seems fair to say that impulses towards positive ethnic identification tend to inhibit any final undoing of "race," as do suspicions of genocidal intent.

7. Repression rather than mere blockage might seem to be the operative term here, given bell hooks's observation that "Neil Jordan [has] repeatedly said that [his film] has nothing to do with race." "What's passion got to do with it?" *Outlaw Culture,* 43.

8. Lynda Boose, "'The Getting of a Lawful Race:' Racial discourse in Early Modern England and the Unrepresentable Black Woman," in *Women, "Race," and Writing in the Early Modern Period,* ed. Margo Hendricks and Patricia Parker (New York: Routledge, 1994), 35-54. My discussion of Shakespearean race writing "in general" is not meant to devalue or deny precedence to many important specific discussions, including, in this volume, ones by Jean Howard, Kim F. Hall, Margo Hendricks, and Jyotsna Singh. Nor is it meant to deny the multiplicity of specific "racial" types being constructed in this period (Irish, Jewish, Scottish, etc.). If I have focussed primarily on Boose's essay, it is because of the methodological principles it enunciates.

9. Quoted in Bruce Smith, *Homosexual Desire in Shakespeare's England: A Cultural Poetics* (Chicago: University of Chicago Press, 1991), 181.

10. Ian Maclean, *The Renaissance Notion of Woman: A Study in the Fortunes of Scholasticism and Medical Science in European Intellectual Life* (Cambridge: Cambridge University Press, 1980), 2-3.

11. My essay-title ("Out of the Matrix") recalls a chapter-title ("Escaping the Matrix") in Janet Adelman's *Suffocating Mothers: Fantasies of Maternal Origin in Shakespeare's Plays, "Hamlet" to "The Tempest"* (New York: Routledge, 1992). I believe my argument is broadly compatible with Adelman's, although her primary concerns are maternity and male gynophobia.

12. In *Titus Andronicus,* however, lawful Roman paternity and whiteness are not just assumed but actively constituted in doubly antithetical relation to Aaron's lawless paternity and blackness, and Tamora's racially othered (Gothic) maternity and femininity.

13. "The Rape of Lucrece" in *The Riverside Shakespeare,* ed. G. Blakemore Evans et al. (Boston: Houghton Mifflin, 1974) 1741 II: 1742-43. (All further references are to *The Riverside Shakespeare*).

14. Pierre de la Primaudaye, *The French Academy,* in William Shakespeare, *Hamlet,* A Norton Critical Edition, ed. Cyrus Hoy, 2nd. ed. (New York: Norton, 1992), 109.

15. Presumably following *OED,* "rigol" [l. 1745] is glossed as "ring, circle" in *The Riverside Shakespeare.* The *OED* definition seems primarily inferred from this passage, however, and one other in Shakespeare (*2 Henry IV,* IV.v.36) where the term is applied to the crown.

16. Samuel Purchas, *Purchas his Pilgrimage* (1613), reports that: "Some ascribe it [black skin color] (as Herodotus) to the blacknesse of the Parents sperme or seede." Cited in Boose, "The Getting of a Lawful Race," 43. It should be recalled, however, that geographical as well as genetic theories of racial (color) difference were widely entertained in the Elizabethan period.

17. Notoriously, the self-division of the woman tends to undermine her ideal integrity or wholeness in Petrarchan scenarios, while her spontaneous blushing "betrays" both her own desire and her complicity with her male assailant. The lines I have quoted, "Some of her blood still pure and red remain'd, / And some look'd black, and that false Tarquin stained," leave the question of sexual desire and agency in suspense. "False" can apply either as an adjective to Tarquin's character or as the adverb "falsely" to the staining of his character by Lucrece's accusation. Whether Lucrece has "black" blood herself, and is thus the passive, subsequently guilty, and ultimately suicidal sexual aggressor, or whether she is the blackened innocent, remains at least grammatically unresolved.

18. Roland Greene observes that "in English as well as other European languages, the matter of racial difference comes into the word *color* in the early modern period, especially through the history of international exploration" ("Petrarchism among the Discourses of Imperialism," in *America in European Consciousness: 1493-1750,* ed. Karen Ordahl Kupperman [Chapel Hill: University of North Carolina Press, 1995]: 147).

19. Rigorous logical opposition to forms of categorical merging, blurring or admixture, (i.e., logical opposition to miscegenation in its root sense), is a feature of Calvinist thought that has widely been regarded as racially (even genocidally) consequential in U.S. history. I simply note this widely held view, as well as the strongly Calvinistic strain in English reformation thinking. An iconoclastic dedication to pure whiteness or chastity is apparent in the work of major English poets from Spenser through Milton; perhaps Shakespeare is unusual in construing this dedication as fatal.

20. Indeed, the "one drop" criterion of racial impurity, familiar in the context of American studies, is anticipated in this memorably phobic locution. See, for example, Walter Benn Michaels, "The No-Drop Rule," *Critical Inquiry,* 20 (Summer, 1994): 758-69.

21. In Boose's view, Eurocentric racial ideology stringently delegitimizes any procreation between a black man and a white woman or vice versa, though interracial sexual encounters are variably coded and tolerated—even licensed as a mode of white male seigneurial right or white woman's romance. The tragedy of *Othello* conveniently (yet imperatively) precludes the generation of offspring between Othello and Desdemona, lawful marriage notwithstanding.

22. Frances Dolan, "Taking the Pencil Out of God's Hand: Art, Nature, and the Face-Painting Debate in Early Modern England," *PMLA,* 108 (March, 1993): 224-39.

23. The *locus classicus* for this impasse is the Proem to Book 3 of *The Faerie Queene,* in which it falls to the (male) author to depict chastity. For chastity to be credible, however, it must remain uncolored, untainted, and untinted, hence unpictured (it must in fact be de-picted), as must the perfectly chaste figure of Elizabeth I.

24. The virulence and/or exorbitant mobilization of these embedded tropes can be gauged from such instances as Francis Bacon's utopian *New Atlantis.* In that text, "the Jew" having been assimilated as rational skeptic affirming the all-white, "virgin" (*sic*) Christian patriarchy, the main symbolic threat remaining is "the Spirit of Fornication" that appears in the likeness of "a little, foul ugly Aethiop." Francis Bacon, *New Atlantis* and *The Great Instauration* in Crofts Classics, ed. Jerry Weinberger (Wheeling, IL: Harlan Davidson, 1989), 66. See also G.K. Hunter, "Othello and Color Prejudice," in *Interpretations of Shakespeare,* ed. Kenneth Muir (Oxford: Clarendon Press, 1985), 180-208, for an important discussion of the classical and patristic prehistory of early modern "race," and Karen Newman, "'And wash the Ethiop white': Femininity and the Monstrous in *Othello,*" *Shakespeare Reproduced: The Text in History and Ideology,* ed. Jean Howard and Marion F. O'Connor (New York: Methuen, 1987), 141-62.

25. The taint that unhinges Othello in the play has been identified by Stephen Greenblatt, "The Improvisation of Power," *Renaissance Self-Fashioning: From More to Shakespeare* (Chicago: University of Chicago Press, 1980), 222-54, as the sexual taint, discursively produced by a confessional Christian culture and materialized by the blood-spotted sheets of the marriage bed. In Greenblatt's view, Othello is anxiously at war with his own sexuality. That he should be especially or exemplarily so is, however, related to the hypersexualization of the black man already being effected in "white" early modern culture.

26. The political economy of this "dictation" is considered in broad terms by Vassilis Lambropoulos, *The Rise of Eurocentrism: Anatomy of Interpretation* (Princeton: Princeton University Press, 1993, and Samir Amin, *Eurocentrism,* tr. Russell Moore (New York: Monthly Review Press, 1989).

27. Joel Fineman, *Shakespeare's Perjur'd Eye: The Invention of Poetic Subjectivity in the Sonnets* (Berkeley and Los Angeles: University of California Press, 1986). It is all too easy to hear "miscegenation" as a pejorative term formed with the prefix "mis-" (as in *mistake, misbegotten, misconceived,* etc.) rather than as a compound noun formed from L. *miscere + genus.* Although the earliest *OED* citation identifies "miscegenation" as a pseudoscientific racist coinage dating from 1864, the term etymologically designates only a mixture of kinds, not necessarily a mismatch. Nineteenth-century racialization of logico-scientific terminology is, however, apparent in this coinage.

28. I am not accusing Lacan or Fineman of political incorrectness. Their claims are rigorously and unsentimentally developed, and have been found usefully provocative—more so than many conciliatory claims—by a number of feminists and cultural theorists. Franz Fanon's well-known appropriation of Lacan in *Black Skin, White Masks* is a case in point.

29. I am not aware of any professional work in which these limit cases are systematically argued, though the limits have been apparent. The "black mother" thesis has been propounded by Marjorie Garber in the semi-formal context of a talk at Dartmouth College. However salutary, this repositioning of Shakespeare is potentially invidious along lines suggested by Tania Modleski in *Feminism Without Women: Culture and Criticism in a "Postfeminist" Age* (New York: Routledge, 1991). Insofar as the white, male author-subject is presumed capable of assuming any cultural position and mastering its discourse, he can be taken to represent all "others," thus rendering their particular experience and even existence redundant.

30. By whom and under what circumstances they were so marked in the 1609 quarto we have no idea. I attach neither more nor less significance to the quarto sonnet-order than is skeptically allowed by Stephen Booth (ed.) in *Shakespeare's Sonnets* (New Haven: Yale University Press, 1977), 545-46. "Dark Lady" is of course a critical fabrication to which the objections are now obvious: the term is embarrassingly gentrifying and euphemistic.

31. Mary Hamer, *Signs of Cleopatra* (New York: Routledge, 1993), 5 ff, notes that the historical Cleopatra was ethnically Greek, not Egyptian, as

was the contemporary ruling class in Egypt. Cleopatra appears generally to have been represented as fair-skinned in the Western iconographic tradition surveyed by Hamer. Whether Shakespeare was unaware of Cleopatra's ethnicity or was blackening her in a process of denegation isn't clear, but her "tawniness" connects her via the lines I have already cited from *A Midsummer Night's Dream* to the "Ethiope," while her being "with Phoebus' amorous pinches black / And wrinkled deep in time" [I.V.28-29] strongly connects her to the sonnet-figure of the woman. The psychoanalytic trope of the sexualized woman as the "dark continent" rather than as a bounded character is strongly anticipated in all of this. Standard Elizabethan punning might further suggest the doubleness of this figure as both incontinent and all-encompassing (continent), doubly forestalling ideological enclosure while effortlessly containing its own contradictions.

RACE AND COLONIALISM

Rob Nixon (essay date 1987)

SOURCE: "Caribbean and African Appropriations of *The Tempest*," in *Critical Inquiry*, Vol. 13, No. 3, Spring, 1987, pp. 557-78.

[*In the following essay, Nixon focuses on the anticolonial interpretations of* The Tempest *set forth by African and Caribbean intellectuals of the period from the late 1950s to early 1970s.*]

> Remember
> First to possess his books.
>
> —*The Tempest*

The era from the late fifties to the early seventies was marked in Africa and the Caribbean by a rush of newly articulated anticolonial sentiment that was associated with the burgeoning of both international black consciousness and more localized nationalist movements. Between 1957 and 1973 the vast majority of African and the larger Caribbean colonies won their independence; the same period witnessed the Cuban and Algerian revolutions, the latter phase of the Kenyan "Mau Mau" revolt, the Katanga crisis in the Congo, the Trinidadian Black Power uprising and, equally important for the atmosphere of militant defiance, the civil rights movement in the United States, the student revolts of 1968, and the humbling of the United States during the Vietnam War. This period was distinguished, among Caribbean and African intellectuals, by a pervasive mood of optimistic outrage. Frequently graduates of British or French universities, they were the first generation from their regions self-assured and numerous enough to call collectively for a renunciation of Western standards as the political revolts found their cultural counterparts in insurrections against the bequeathed values of the colonial powers.

In the context of such challenges to an increasingly discredited European colonialism, a series of dissenting intellectuals chose to utilize a European text as a strategy for (in George Lamming's words) getting "out from under this ancient mausoleum of [Western] historic achievement."[1] They seized upon *The Tempest* as a way of amplifying their calls for decolonization within the bounds of the dominant cultures. But at the same time these Caribbeans and Africans adopted the play as a founding text in an oppositional lineage which issued from a geopolitically and historically specific set of cultural ambitions. They perceived that the play could contribute to their self-definition during a period of great flux. So, through repeated, reinforcing, transgressive appropriations of *The Tempest*, a once silenced group generated its own tradition of "error" which in turn served as one component of the grander counterhegemonic nationalist and black internationalist endeavors of the period. Because that era of Caribbean and African history was marked by such extensive, open contestation of cultural values, the destiny of *The Tempest* at that time throws into uncommonly stark relief the status of value as an unstable social process rather than a static and, in literary terms, merely textual attribute.

Some Caribbean and African intellectuals anticipated that their efforts to unearth from *The Tempest* a suppressed narrative of their historical abuse and to extend that narrative in the direction of liberation would be interpreted as philistine. But Lamming, for one, wryly resisted being intimidated by any dominant consensus: "I shall reply that my mistake, lived and deeply felt by millions of men like me—proves the positive value of error" (*PE*, p. 13). Lamming's assertion that his unorthodoxy is collectively grounded is crucial: those who defend a text's universal value can easily discount a solitary dissenting voice as uncultured or quirky, but it is more difficult to ignore entirely a cluster of allied counterjudgments, even if the group can still be stigmatized. Either way, the notion of universal value is paradoxically predicated on a limited inclusiveness, on the assumption that certain people will fail to appreciate absolute worth. As Pierre Bourdieu, Barbara Herrnstein Smith, and Tony Bennett have all shown, a dominant class or culture's power to declare certain objects or activities self-evidently valuable is an essential measure for reproducing social differentiation.[2] But resistance to the hegemony of such hierarchies is still possible. In this context, Lamming's statement exudes the fresh confidence of the high era of decolonization, in which a "philistinism" arose that was sufficiently powerful and broadly based to generate an alternative orthodoxy responsive to indigenous interests and needs.

For Frantz Fanon, decolonization was the period when the peoples of the oppressed regions, force-fed for so long on foreign values, could stomach them no longer: "In the colonial context the settler only ends his work of breaking in the native when the latter admits loudly and intelligibly the supremacy of the white man's values. In the period of decolonization, the colonized masses mock at these very values, insult them, and vomit them up."[3] From the late fifties onward, there was a growing resistance in African and Caribbean colonies to remote-controlled anything, from administrative structures to school curricula, and the phase of "nauseating mimicry" (in Fanon's phrase) gave way to a phase in which colonized cultures sought to define their own cultures reactively and aggressively from within.[4] In short, decolonization was the period when "the machine [went] into reverse."[5] This about-face entailed that indigenous cultural forms be substituted for alien ones—inevitably a hybrid process of retrieving suppressed traditions and inventing new ones. Both approaches were present in the newfound preoccupation with *The Tempest*: hints of New World culture and history were dragged to the surface, while at other moments the play was unabashedly refashioned to meet contemporary political and cultural needs.[6]

Given the forcefulness of the reaction against the values of the colonial powers, it may appear incongruous that Caribbean and African intellectuals should have integrated a canonical European text like *The Tempest* into their struggle; it made for, in Roberto Fernández Retamar's words, "an alien elaboration."[7] And this response may seem doubly incongruous given Shakespeare's distinctive position as a measure of the relative achievements of European and non-European civilizations. In discussions of value, Shakespeare is, of course, invariably treated as a special case, having come to serve as something like the gold standard of literature. For the English he is as much an institution and an industry as a corpus of texts: a touchstone of national identity, a lure for tourists, an exportable commodity, and one of the securest forms of cultural capital around. But the weight of Shakespeare's ascribed authority was felt differently in the colonies. What for the English and, more generally, Europeans, could be a source of pride and a confirmation of their civilization, for colonial subjects often became a chastening yardstick of their "backwardness." The exhortation to master Shakespeare was instrumental in showing up non-European "inferiority," for theirs would be the flawed mastery of those culturally remote from Shakespeare's stock. A schooled resemblance could become the basis for a more precise discrimination, for, to recall Homi Bhabha's analysis of mimicry in colonial discourse, "to be Anglicized is *emphatically* not to be English."[8] And so, in colonial circumstances, the bard could become symptomatic and symbolic of the education of Africans and Caribbeans into a passive, subservient relationship to dominant colonial culture.

One aspect of this passive orientation toward Europe is touched on by Lamming, the Barbadian novelist who was to appropriate *The Tempest* so actively for his own ends. Discussing his schooling during the early 1940s, Lamming recalls how the teacher "followed the curriculum as it was. He did what he had to do: Jane Austen, some Shakespeare, Wells's novel *Kipps,* and so on. What happened was that they were teaching exactly whatever the Cambridge Syndicate demanded. That was the point of it. These things were directly connected. Papers were set in Cambridge and our answers were sent back there to be corrected. We had to wait three to four months. Nobody knew what was happening till they were returned."[9] Given the resistance during decolonization to this kind of cultural dependency, those writers who took up *The Tempest* from the standpoint of the colonial subject did so in a manner that was fraught with complexity. On the one hand, they hailed Caliban and identified themselves with him; on the other, they were intolerant of received colonial definitions of Shakespeare's value. They found the European play compelling but insisted on engaging with it on their own terms.

The newfound interest in *The Tempest* during decolonization was, in terms of the play's history, unprecedentedly sudden and concentrated. However, in the late nineteenth and early twentieth century, *The Tempest's* value had been augmented by a prevalent perception of it as a likely vehicle first for Social Darwinian and later for imperial ideas. This tendency, which Trevor Griffiths has thoroughly documented, was evident in both performances and critical responses to the play.[10] A notable instance was *Caliban: The Missing Link* (1873), wherein Daniel Wilson contended that Shakespeare had preempted some of Darwin's best insights by creating "a novel anthropoid of a high type."[11] Amassing evidence from the play, Wilson deduced that Caliban would have been black, had prognathous jaws, and manifested a low stage of cultural advancement. Wilson's text shuttles between *The Tempest,* Darwin, and Linnaeus and is interlarded with detailed brain measurements of gibbons, baboons, chimpanzees, and a range of ethnic groupings.

Ironically, it was Beerbohm Tree's unabashedly jingoistic production of *The Tempest* in 1904 that elicited the first recorded response to the play in anti-imperial terms, as one member of the audience assimilated the action to events surrounding the Matabele uprising in Rhodesia:

> When the man-monster, brutalised by long continued torture, begins, 'This island's mine, by Sycorax my mother, which thou takest from me', we have the whole case of the aboriginal against aggressive civilisation dramatised before us. I confess I felt a sting of conscience—vicariously suffered for my Rhodesian friends, notably Dr. Jameson—when Caliban proceeded to unfold a similar case to that of the Matebele. It might have been the double of old King Lobengula rehearsing the blandishments which led to his doom: 'When thou camest first / Thou strok'dst me, and mad'st much of me; would'st give me'—all that was promised by the Chartered Company to secure the charter.[12]

Just as the Matabele uprising was a distant, premonitory sign of the anticolonial struggles to come, so, too, W. T. Stead's unorthodox response to *The Tempest* anticipated a time when the play would be widely mobilized and esteemed as an expression of "the whole case of the 'aboriginal' against aggressive civilisation."

But it was another forty-four years before any text provided a sustained reassessment of *The Tempest* in light of the immediate circumstances leading up to decolonization. That text was *Psychologie de la colonisation,* written by the French social scientist, Octave Mannoni. However much Third World intellectuals have subsequently quarreled with his manner of mobilizing the play, Mannoni's inaugural gesture helped to shape the trajectory of those associated appropriations which lay ahead and, concomitantly, to bring about the reestimation of *The Tempest* in Africa and the Caribbean. Mannoni's novel response enabled him to evolve a theory of colonialism with Prospero and Caliban as prototypes; conversely, his hypotheses about colonial relations, arising from his experiences in Madagascar, made it possible for him to rethink the play. This reciprocal process was not gratuitous but prompted by an early stirring of African nationalism: Mannoni is insistent that his theory only fell into place through his exposure to one of the twilight moments of French colonialism—the Madagascan uprising of 1947-48 in which sixty thousand Madagascans, one thousand colonial soldiers, and several hundred settlers were killed. In 1947 his ideas began to take shape, and, by the time the revolt had been suppressed a year later, the manuscript was complete. The occasional character of *Psychologie de la colonisation* is foregrounded in the introduction, which Mannoni closes by marking the coincidence of his ideas with "a certain moment in history, a crisis in the evolution of politics, when many things that had been hidden were brought into the light of day; but it was only a moment, and time will soon have passed it by."[13] The pressing horrors of the Madagascan crisis prompted Mannoni to find a new significance for *The Tempest,* encouraging him to weave a reading of Shakespeare's poetic drama through his reading of the incipient drama of decolonization.

Mannoni's account of the psychological climate of colonialism is advanced through an opposition between the Prospero (or inferiority) complex and the Caliban (or dependence) complex. On this view, Europeans in Madagascar typically displayed the need, common among people from a competitive society, to feel highly regarded by others. However, the Prospero-type is not just any white man, but specifically the sort whose "grave lack of sociability combined with a pathological urge to dominate" drives him to seek out uncompetitive situations where, among a subservient people, his power is amplified and his least skills assume the aspect of superior magic (*PC,* p. 102). Whether a French settler in Africa or Shakespeare's duke, he is loath to depart his adopted island, knowing full well that back home his standing will shrink to mundane dimensions. Mannoni found the Madagascans, on the other hand, to be marked by a Caliban complex, a dependence on authority purportedly characteristic of a people forced out of a secure "tribal" society and into the less stable, competitively edged hierarchies of a semi-Westernized existence. According to this theory, colonialism introduced a situation where the Madagascan was exposed for the first time to the notion and possibility of abandonment. Crucially, the colonist failed to comprehend the Madagascan's capacity to feel "neither inferior nor superior but yet wholly dependent," an unthinkable state of mind for someone from a competitive society (*PC,* p. 157). So, in Mannoni's terms, the Madagascan revolt was fueled less by a desire to sunder an oppressive master-servant bond than by the people's resentment of the colonizers' failure to uphold that bond more rigorously and provide them with the security they craved. What the colonial subjects sought was the paradoxical freedom of secure dependence rather than any autonomous, self-determining freedom. This assumption clearly shaped Mannoni's skepticism about the Madagascans' desire, let alone their capacity, to achieve national independence.

Mannoni values *The Tempest* most highly for what he takes to be Shakespeare's dramatization of two cultures' mutual sense of a trust betrayed: Prospero is a fickle dissembler, Caliban an ingrate. The nodal lines here, and those that draw Mannoni's densest commentary, are spoken by Caliban in the play's second scene. They should be quoted at length, for they are taken up repeatedly by subsequent Caribbean and African appropriators of *The Tempest.*

> When thou cam'st first,
> Thou strok'st me, and made much of me, wouldst give me
> Water with berries in't, and teach me how
> To name the bigger light, and how the less,
> That burn by day and night, and then I lov'd thee
> And show'd thee all the qualities o' th' isle,
> The fresh springs, brine-pits, barren place and fertile:
> Curs'd be I that did so! All the charms
> Of Sycorax, toads, beetles, bats, light on you!
> For I am all the subjects that you have,
> Which first was mine own king; and here you sty me
> In this hard rock, whiles you do keep from me
> The rest o' th' island.[14]

To Mannoni, it appears evident that "Caliban does not complain of being exploited; he complains of being betrayed." He "has fallen prey to the resentment which succeeds the breakdown of dependence" (*PC,* p. 106). This view is buttressed by an analogous interpretation of Caliban's revolt in league with Trinculo as an action launched "not to win his freedom, for he could not support freedom, but to have a new master whose 'foot-licker' he can become. He is delighted at the prospect. It would be hard to find a better example of the dependence complex in its pure state" (*PC,* pp. 106-7).

Such statements rankled badly with Caribbean and African intellectuals who, in the fifties, for the first time sensed the imminence of large-scale decolonization in their regions. In such circumstances, the insinuation that Caliban was incapable of surviving on his own and did not even aspire to such independence in the first place caused considerable affront and helped spur Third Worlders to mount adversarial interpretations of the play which rehabilitated Caliban into a heroic figure, inspired by noble rage to oust the interloping Prospero from his island. Fanon and Aimé Césaire, two of Mannoni's most vehement critics, found the "ethno-psychologist's" disregard for economic exploitation especially jarring and accused him of reducing colonialism to an encounter between two psychological types with complementary predispositions who, for a time at least, find their needs dovetailing tidily.[15] *Psychologie de la colonisation,* these critics charged, made Caliban out to be an eager partner in his own colonization. Mannoni, in a statement like "wherever Europeans have founded colonies of the type we are considering, it can safely be said that their coming was unconsciously expected—even desired—by the future subject peoples," seemed to discount any possibility of Europe being culpable for the exploitation of the colonies (*PC,* p. 86). Mannoni's critics foresaw, moreover, just how readily his paradigm could be harnessed by Europeans seeking to thwart the efforts for self-determination that were gathering impetus in the fifties.

Fanon and Césaire's fears about the implications of Mannoni's thesis were vindicated by the appearance in 1962 of *Prospero's Magic: Some Thoughts on Class and Race* by Philip Mason, an English colonial who sought to give credence to Mannoni's ideas by using them to rationalize resistance to colonialism in Kenya ("Mau Mau"), India, and Southern Rhodesia. The upshot of this effort was Mason's conclusion that "a colonial rebellion may be a protest not against repression but against progress, not against the firm hand but against its withdrawal" and that (for such is every "tribal" society's craving for firm authority) "countries newly released from colonialism . . . [will experience] a reduction of personal freedom."[16]

Prospero's Magic is an intensely autobiographical and occasional work. Its author, in siding with Mannoni, was also seeking to counteract the first fully fledged Caribbean appropriation of *The Tempest,* Lamming's recently published *Pleasures of Exile* (1960). The lectures comprising *Prospero's Magic* were delivered at the University College of the West Indies on the eve of Jamaica's independence and are based on Mason's more than twenty years as a colonial employee in India, Nigeria, and Rhodesia, where he witnessed the death throes—or as he terms it, the fulfillment—of British imperialism. Rereading *The Tempest* in the political atmosphere of 1962, he was discomfited by his recognition of the Prospero in himself. Circumstances had altered: "While many of us today find we dislike in Prospero things we dislike in ourselves, our fathers admired him without question and so indeed did my generation until lately" (*PM,* p. 92).[17] Mason tried to square his awareness that colonialism was becoming increasingly discredited with his personal need to salvage some value and self-respect from his decades of colonial "service." So he was at once a member of the first generation to acknowledge distaste for Prospero and personally taken aback by his own sudden redundancy: "With what deep reluctance does the true Prospero put aside his book and staff, the magic of power and office, and go to live in Cheltenham!" (*PM,* p. 96). Mason, for one, conceived of himself as writing at the very moment when the colonial master was called upon to break and bury his staff.

By the time Caribbeans and Africans took up *The Tempest,* that is, from 1959 onward, widespread national liberation seemed not only feasible but imminent, and the play was mobilized in defense of Caliban's right to the land and to cultural autonomy. "This island's mine by Sycorax my mother / Which thou tak'st from me" (1.2.333-34) are the lines that underlie much of the work that was produced by African and Caribbean intellectuals in the 1960s and early 1970s.[18] Those same two lines introduce Caliban's extended complaint (quoted at length above), the nodal speech Mannoni had cited as evidence that Shakespeare was dramatizing a relation of dependence, not one of exploitation. But, significantly, and in keeping with his very different motives for engaging with the play, Mannoni had lopped off those two lines when working the passage into his argument. On this score, Third World responses consistently broke with Mannoni: Caliban, the decolonizer, was enraged not at being orphaned by colonial paternalism but at being insufficiently abandoned by it.

The first Caribbean writer to champion Caliban was Lamming. His nonfictional *Pleasures of Exile* can be read as an effort to redeem from the past, as well as to stimulate, an indigenous Antillean line of creativity to rival the European traditions which seemed bent on arrogating to themselves all notions of culture. Lamming's melange of a text—part essay on the cultural politics of relations between colonizer and colonized, part autobiography, and part textual criticism of, in particular, *The Tempest* and C. L. R. James' *The Black Jacobins* (1938)—was sparked by two events, one personal, the other more broadly historical.[19] Lamming began his text in 1959, shortly after disembarking in Southampton as part of the great wave of West Indian immigrants settling in Britain in the fifties. But his circumstances differed from those of most of his compatriots, for he was immigrating as an aspirant writer. As such he was keenly aware of taking up residence in the headquarters of the English language and culture and, concomitantly, of being only ambiguously party to that language and culture, even though a dialect of English was his native tongue and even though—for such was his colonial schooling—he was more intimate with Shakespeare and the English Revolution than with the writings and history of his own region.

Lamming's reflections on the personal circumstances which occasioned *The Pleasures of Exile* are suffused with his sense of the book's historical moment. Writing on the brink of the sixties, he was highly conscious that colonial Africa and the Caribbean were entering a new phase. The political mood of the book is expectant ("Caliban's history . . . belongs entirely to the future" [*PE,* p. 107]), most evidently in his account of an envious visit to Ghana, the first of the newly independent African states. That trip sharpened his anguished sense of the British West Indies' failure as yet to achieve comparable autonomy. He recalls the intensity of that feeling in his introduction to the 1984 edition: "There were no independent countries in the English-speaking Caribbean when I started to write *The Pleasures of Exile* in 1959. With the old exceptions of Ethiopia and Liberia, there was only one in Black Africa, and that was Ghana. Twenty years later almost every rock and pebble in the Caribbean had acquired this status" (*PE,* p. 7). While looking ahead to Caribbean self-determination, Lamming was also writing self-consciously in the aftermath of an action one year back that had quickened nationalist ambitions throughout the area: "Fidel Castro and the Cuban revolution reordered our history. . . . The Cuban revolution was a Caribbean response to that imperial menace which Prospero conceived as a civilising mission" (*PE,* p. 7).

Lamming's relationship to decolonization is markedly distinct from Mannoni's. The Frenchman was in Madagascar as a social scientist observing and systematizing the psychological impulses behind an incipient struggle for national autonomy, while the Barbadian's reflections on decolonization are less distanced and more personal, as he declares himself to be Caliban's heir. Lamming's and Mannoni's different tacks are most conspicuous in their treatment of Caliban's pronouncement: "You taught me language; and my profit on't / Is, I know how to curse" (1.2.363-64). From that quotation Mannoni launches an analysis of the role in 1947-48 of the westernized Malagasies, some of whom had become so acculturated during study abroad that they could no longer engage with their countryfellows. The cross-cultural status of yet others who were less thoroughly assimilated but had become fluent in acrimony facilitated their rise to positions of leadership in the national resistance. Lamming, by contrast, takes up Caliban's remarks on language as one who is himself a substantially Europeanized Third Worlder, a West Indian nationalist living in England, and someone reluctant to segregate his theoretical from his autobiographical insights.[20] Much of the personal urgency of Lamming's text stems from his assimilation of Caliban's linguistic predicament to his own. As a writer by vocation, he is especially alert to the way colonialism has generated linguistic discrimination, to how, as a West Indian born into English, he is branded a second-class speaker of his first language.

Though Lamming addresses the question of the unlanded Caliban who declares "This island's mine," he dwells most obsessively on the educational inheritance which he finds enunciated in the speech "You taught me language." While the nationalist struggle provides a shaping context for *The Pleasures of Exile,* Lamming's Caliban is not just any colonial subject but specifically the colonized writer-intellectual, the marginal person of letters. Lamming's root frustration is the ostensible lack of parity between the possibilities for political and for cultural freedom. Come formal independence, the people may establish their own laws and governments, but won't Caribbean writers still lag behind, permanently shackled to the colonizer's language—whether English, French, or Spanish—since it is the only one they have? "Prospero lives in the absolute certainty that Language which is his gift to Caliban is the very prison in which Caliban's achievements will be realised and restricted. Caliban can never reach perfection, not even the perfection implicit in Miranda's privileged ignorance" (*PE,* p. 110).[21] That is, as long as Caliban is still bound to his former master's language, he is still partly condemned to live the life of a servant.

What holds for language holds equally for culture in general. If Caliban's accent sounds sour and deformed to the British ear, so too his knowledge of British traditions—no matter how relentlessly they have been drummed into him in Barbados—will be shown up as flawed and fragmentary. Yet on this score Lamming is unevenly pessimistic, for his very appropriation of *The Tempest* testifies to his faith in the Caribbean intellectual's capacity to scale the conventional heights of British culture. Instead of deferring slavishly to a British norm, Lamming manages—with Caliban's lines at the ready—to treat that norm as a pretext for and object of abuse. To write about Shakespeare is a strategy for commanding a hearing in the West, but he values this audibility primarily because it enables him to draw attention to his ostracism. He is only too aware of the implications of quoting Shakespeare to legitimate his "illegitimate" treatment of that same hallowed author:

> It is my intention to make use of *The Tempest* as a way of presenting a certain state of feeling which is the heritage of the exiled and colonial writer from the British Caribbean.
>
> Naturally, I anticipate from various quarters the obvious charge of blasphemy; yet there are occasions when blasphemy must be seen as one privilege of the excluded Caliban. [*PE,* p. 9]

Lamming seizes the outcast's prerogative to impiety in part to shake the insiders' monopoly of a text that draws and bears on Caribbean history. But this destructive impulse feeds a more positive one: the desire to mount an indigenous countertradition, with a reinterpreted Caliban from 1611 and the contemporary, about-to-be-liberated Antillean of 1959 flanking that tradition. So for all its dense, original analogies between *The Tempest* and the Caribbean of the late fifties, what is at stake in *The Pleasures of Exile* is something larger than the immediate, local value of a Shakespearean play: it is the very possibility of decolonizing the area's cultural history by replacing an imposed with an endemic line of thought and action. Within the context of this grand design, the initial gesture of annexing Shakespeare was pivotal, as it generated a Caliban who could stand as a prototype for successive Caribbean figures in whom cultural and political activism were to cohere. Lamming's reconstructed tradition runs through Toussaint Louverture, C. L. R. James, and Fidel Castro to the author himself who, like many of his generation of West Indian writers, immigrated to England to embark on a literary career but while there also pressed for his region's independence. That these particular figures should have been selected to brace the countertradition points to Lamming's conviction that—linguistic dilemmas notwithstanding—Caribbean culture and politics had been and should ideally continue to be allies in each other's decolonization.

In spirit, Lamming's dissident reassessment of one of the high texts of European culture had been matched by the Trinidadian James' reverse angle in *The Black Jacobins* on one of the most celebrated periods of European history, the French Revolution. *The Pleasures of Exile* is designed to make these two unorthodox gestures seem of a piece, through remarks such as "[there] C. L. R. James shows us Caliban as Prospero had never known him" (*PE*, p. 119). James' Caliban is Toussaint Louverture, leader of the first successful Caribbean struggle for independence, the Haitian slave revolt of 1791-1803. As the title of his book might suggest, James was concerned to dredge up a counternarrative, from a Caribbean perspective, of events which had been submerged beneath the freight of Eurocentric history. For Lamming, James' action and others like it were essential to the establishment of a Calibanic lineage; but once established, that lineage had still to be sustained, which would require one salvaging operation after another. This apprehension was borne out when, at the time of writing *The Pleasures of Exile*, Lamming discovered that James' book, out of print for twenty years, was in danger of sinking into neglect. So he set himself the task of doing in turn for James what James had done for Louverture: keeping afloat a vital, remedial tradition that was threatening to disappear.

During the era of decolonization, negritude proved to be one of the strongest components of this remedial tradition, and it was the negritudist from Martinique, Césaire, who came to renovate *The Tempest* theatrically for black cultural ends in a manner indebted to Lamming if fiercer in its defiance. These two writers' approaches coincided most explicitly in their determination to unearth an endemic lineage of cultural-cum-political activists; it is telling that within the space of two years, each man published a book resuscitating Toussaint Louverture and celebrating his example.[22]

Césaire's *Une Tempête* (1969) exemplifies the porous boundaries between European and Afro-Caribbean cultures even within the anticolonial endeavors of the period. As an influence on Césaire's response to Shakespeare, Lamming keeps company with Mannoni and the German critic, Janheinz Jahn. Mannoni had experience of French island colonies in both Africa and the Caribbean for, prior to his stint in Madagascar, he had served as an instructor in a Martinican school where Césaire had been his precocious student. More than twenty years later, in *Discours sur le colonialisme*, Césaire upbraided his former schoolmaster for not thinking through the implications of his colonial paradigm. And Césaire's subsequent, inevitably reactive adaptation of Shakespeare further demonstrated just how far he had diverged from Mannoni's motives for valuing *The Tempest*. More in keeping with the spirit of *Une Tempête* was Jahn's *Geschichte der neo-afrikanischen Literatur*, which appeared a few years before Césaire wrote his play. Jahn's pioneering study gave prominence to the Calibanesque in Mannoni and Lamming and, by designating the negritude writers (Césaire, Leopold Senghor, and Ousmane Diop) black cultural liberators à la Caliban, hinted at ideas that Césaire was to develop more amply. Notable among these was Jahn's attempt to counteract Lamming's dejected pronouncements about the confining character of Prospero's language by exhorting Caliban to free himself through cultural bilingualism—by recovering long-lost African strains and using them to offset the derivative, European components of his cultural identity. Jahn urged further that suitable elements of European culture be transformed into vehicles for black cultural values. Along these lines, negritude could be defined as "the successful revolt in which Caliban broke out of the prison of Prospero's language, by converting that language to his own needs of self-expression."[23]

Césaire has been quite explicit about his motives for reworking *The Tempest*:

> I was trying to 'de-mythify' the tale. To me Prospero is the complete totalitarian. I am always surprised when others consider him the wise man who 'forgives'. What is most obvious, even in Shakespeare's version, is the man's absolute will to power. Prospero is the man of cold reason, the man of methodical conquest—in other words, a portrait of the 'enlightened' European. And I see the whole play in such terms: the 'civilized' European world coming face to face for the first time with the world of primitivism and magic. Let's not hide the fact that in Europe the world of reason has inevitably led to various kinds of totalitarianism . . . Caliban is the man who is still close to his beginnings, whose link with the natural world has not yet been broken. Caliban can still *participate* in a world of marvels, whereas his master can merely 'create' them through his acquired knowledge. At the same time, Caliban is also a rebel—the positive hero, in a Hegelian sense. The slave is always more important than his master—for it is the slave who makes history.[24]

Césaire's perception of Prospero as "the man of methodical conquest" and his insistence on the slave as the preeminent historical agent become the touchstones for his radically polarized adaptation of Shakespeare. Forgiveness and reconciliation give way to irreconcilable differences; the roles of Ferdinand and Miranda are whittled down to a minimum; and the play's colonial dimensions are writ large. Antonio and Alonso vie with Prospero for control over newly charted lands abroad, and Shakespeare's rightful Duke of Milan is delivered to the island not by the providence of a "happy storm" but through a confederacy rooted in imperial ambitions. Prospero is demythologized and rendered contemporary by making him altogether less white magical and a master of the technology of oppression; his far from inscrutable power is embodied in antiriot control gear and an arsenal. Violating rather than communing with life on the island, he is, in Caliban's phrase, the "*anti-Natur.*"

Une Tempête self-consciously counterpoises the materialist Prospero with an animistic slave empowered by a culture that coexists empathetically with nature. Indeed, Caliban's culture of resistance is his sole weaponry, but it is more formidable than the shallow culture Shakespeare permits him, as Césaire plumbs the depths of the slave's African past to make him a more equal adversary.[25] Caliban's defiance is expressed most strongly through the celebration of the Yoruba gods Shango and Eshu; two of his four songs of liberation fete Shango, an African figure who has survived in Caribbean voodoo and Brazilian macumba. And in a critical irruption, Eshu scatters Prospero's carefully ordered classical masque, making the imported divinities seem precious, effete, and incongruous.

Césair's Caliban also goes beyond Shakespeare's in his refusal to subscribe to the etiquette of subjugation:

> CALIBAN: Uhuru!
> PROSPERO: Qu'est-ce que tu dis?
> CALIBAN: Je dis Uhuru!
> PROSPERO: Encore une remontée de ton langage barbare. Je t'ai déjà dit que n'arrive pas ça. D'ailleurs, tu pourrais être poli, un bonjour ne te tuerait pas![26]

This opening exchange between Caliban and his colonial overlord sets the stage for Césaire's conviction that the culture of slaves need not be an enslaved culture. Here he is more optimistic than Lamming, who saw Caribbean cultures of resistance as ineluctably circumscribed by the colonizer's language; one thinks particularly of Lamming in Ghana, casting an envious eye over children chatting in their indigenous tongue, a language that "owed Prospero no debt of vocabulary" (*PE*, p. 162). Even if Césaire's Caliban cannot throw off European influences entirely, his recuperation of a residual past is sufficient to secure his relative cultural autonomy. Crucially, his first utterance is "Uhuru," the Swahili term for freedom which gained international currency through the struggles for decolonization in the late fifties and sixties. And Caliban retorts to Prospero's demand for a *bonjour* by charging that he has only been instructed in the colonial tongue so he can submit to the magisterial imperatives, and by declaring that he will no longer respond to the name Caliban, a colonial invention bound anagramatically to the degrading "cannibal." Instead, the island's captive king christens himself "X" in a Black Muslim gesture that commemorates his lost name, buried beneath layers of colonial culture. The play supposes, in sum, that Caribbean colonial subjects can best fortify their revolt by reviving, wherever possible, cultural forms dating back to before that wracking sea-change which was the Middle Passage.

Césaire's remark that the slave, as maker of history, "is always more important than his master" has both a retrospective and an anticipatory force, pointing back to Louverture, Haiti, and the only triumphant slave revolt, and forward through the present to colonialism's demise. Césaire steeps his play most explicitly in the contemporary Afro-Caribbean struggles for self-determination when he stages, via Ariel and Caliban, the debate, ubiquitous in the late fifties and sixties, between the rival strategies for liberation advanced by proponents of evolutionary and revolutionary change. The mulatto Ariel shuns violence and holds that, faced with Prospero's stockpiled arsenal, they are more likely to win freedom through conciliation than refractoriness. But from Caliban's perspective Ariel is a colonial collaborator, a political and cultural sellout who, aspiring both to rid himself nonviolently of Prospero and to emulate his values, is reduced to negotiating for liberty from a position of powerlessness. The success of Caliban's uncompromising strategies is imminent at the end of the drama. When the other Europeans return to Italy, Prospero is unable to accompany them, for he is in the thrall of a psychological battle with his slave (shades of Mannoni here), shouting "Je défendrai la civilisation!" but intuiting that "le climat a changé." At the close, Caliban is chanting ecstatically, "La Liberté Ohé, La Liberté," and defying the orders of a master whose authority and sanity are teetering.[27]

Césaire, then, radically reassessed *The Tempest* in terms of the circumstances of his region, taking the action to the brink of colonialism's demise. He valued the play because he saw its potential as a vehicle for dramatizing the evolution of colonialism in his region and for sharpening the contemporary ideological alternatives open to would-be-liberated Antilleans. Césaire sought, from an openly interested standpoint, to amend the political acoustics of Shakespeare's play, to make the action resonate with the dangers of supine cultural assimilation, a concern since his student days that was accentuated during the high period of decolonization. This renovation of the play for black cultural ends was doubly impertinent: besides treating a classic sacrilegiously, it implicitly lampooned the educational practice, so pervasive in the colonies, of distributing only bowdlerized versions of Shakespeare, of watering him down "for the natives." *Une Tempête* can thus be read as parodying this habit by indicating how the bard might have looked were he indeed made fit reading for a subject people.

Césaire's play was published in 1969. The years 1968 through 1971 saw the cresting of Caribbean and African interest in *The Tempest* as a succession of essayists, novelists, poets, and dramatists sought to integrate the play into the cultural forces pitted against colonialism. During those four years, *The Tempest* was appropriated among the Caribbeans by Césaire, Fernández Retamar (twice), Lamming (in a novelistic reworking of some of the ideas first formulated in *The Pleasures of Exile*), and the Barbadian poet Edward Braithwaite. In Africa, the play was taken up during the same period by John Pepper Clark in Nigeria, Ngugi wa Thiong'o in Kenya, and David Wallace in Zambia.[28] Among these, Braithwaite and Fernández Retamar followed Lamming's lead, finding a topical, regional urgency for the play through articulating the Cuban revolution to Caliban's revolt. Braithwaite's poem, "Caliban," salutes the Cuban revolution against a backdrop of lamentation over the wrecked state of the Caribbean. The body of the poem, with its clipped calypso phrasing, knits together allusions to Caliban's song, "'Ban, 'Ban, Ca-Caliban," Ferdinand's speech, "Where should this music be?" and Ariel's response, "Full fadom five." But it is Caliban the slave, not the royal Alonso, who suffers a sea-change, falling "through the water's / cries / down / down / down / where the music hides / him / down / down / down / where the si- / lence lies." And he is revived not by Ariel's ethereal strains and, behind them, Prospero's white magic, but by the earthy music of the carnival and the intercession of black gods.[29]

But it was Fernández Retamar, a prominent figure in the cultural renovation of postrevolutionary Cuba, whose interest in the play was most specifically sparked by that nation's experience of decolonization. He first brought *The Tempest* glancingly to bear on the circumstances of his region in "Cuba Hasta Fidel" (1969); two years later he elaborated more fully on this correspondence. The second essay, "Caliban: Notes Towards a Discussion of Culture in Our America," at once passionately chronicles the accumulative symbolic significance of Caliban and commemorates those whose deeds and utterances bodied forth the author's conception of the Calibanesque. This sixty-five-page exhortative history draws together many of the issues deliberated by earlier writers:

> Our symbol then is not Ariel . . . but rather Caliban. This is something that we, the *mestizo* inhabitants of these same isles where Caliban lived, see with particular clarity: Prospero invaded the islands, killed our ancestors, enslaved Caliban, and taught him his language to make himself understood. What else can Caliban do but use that same language—today he has no other—to curse him, to wish that the "red plague" would fall on him? I know no other metaphor more expressive of our cultural situation, of our reality. ["C," p. 24]

Fernández Retamar proceeds to list thirty-five exemplary Calibans, among them Louverture, Castro, Césaire, and Fanon. And just as Lamming had singled out Louverture for special treatment, here José Martí, the late nineteenth-century Cuban intellectual and political activist who died in the struggle for Cuban independence, is commended at length for his fidelity to the spirit of Caliban.[30]

Fernández Retamar, as flagrantly as Lamming, makes it apparent how little interest he has in affecting any "scholarly distance" from *The Tempest*. Far from striving to efface his personality, affiliations, and the circumstances of his reading of *The Tempest*, he steeps his essay in occasion and function and speaks consistently in the first-person plural, a voice that inflects his words with a sense of collective autobiography. His interest is in the advantage to be derived from the play by a community who, from a European perspective, could possess at best an ancillary understanding of Shakespeare and, at worst, would be likely perpetrators of barbarous error.[31] Yet that very exclusion conferred on them a coherent identity: "For it is the coloniser who brings us together, who reveals the profound similarities existing above and beyond our secondary differences" ("C," p. 14). Oppositional appropriations of *The Tempest* could be enabling because "to assume our condition as Caliban implies rethinking our history from the *other* side, from the viewpoint of the *other* protagonist" ("C," p. 28). Put differently, having the nerve to push the play against the Western critical grain, marginalized Caribbeans were relieved of the struggle, unwinnable in Western terms, to gain admission to the *right* side. Their brazen unorthodoxy thus became instrumental in redefining the *wrong* as the *other* side, in opening up a space for themselves where their own cultural values need no longer be derided as savage and deformed.

Fernández Retamar's essay is synoptic yet retains a distinctively Cuban bent, illustrative of the diversity among the consistently adversarial readings of the play. For one thing, Cuba straddles the Caribbean and Latin America geographically and culturally, and Fernández Retamar's arguments are marked by this double affinity. His focus is hemispheric, and his Caliban, originally the victim of European conquistadors, now labors more directly under North American imperialism. And coming from a society where mulattos predominate, he instinctively defines "our America" as *mestizaje,* as culturally and ethnically mixed; the conflict between Prospero and Caliban is consequently seen in class rather than racial terms.[32] Where for the negritudist Césaire Caliban had most emphatically to be black and Ariel, the favored servant and counterrevolutionary, to be mulatto (a correspondence between race and privilege native to Martinique and much of the formerly French and British Caribbean), for Fernández Retamar, the Ariel-Caliban split is predominantly one of class. The lofty Ariel is representative of the intellectual who must choose between collaborating with Prospero and deliberately allying himself with Caliban, the exploited proletarian who is to advance revolutionary change.

Lemuel Johnson's volume of poems, *highlife for caliban* (1973), marks the decline of *The Tempest*'s value as an oppositional force in decolonizing cultures. Johnson writes out of the historical experience of Freetown, Sierra Leone's capital, a forlorn city of slaves who had been liberated by Britain and had resettled there. Their freedom is announced but scarcely felt as such. The backdrop to the poems is neocolonial: Caliban is now head of state, but his nationalist ideals have become corrupted and enfeebled by power. By the same token, he has experienced the gulf between formal independence and authentic autonomy, as his nation remains in Prospero's cultural and economic thrall and the final exorcism of the master seems improbable. This condition is psychologically dissipating, for "it is the neocolonial event that finally divests Caliban of that which had kept him whole—a dream of revenge against Prospero. But how shall he now revenge himself upon himself?"[33]

The Tempest's value for African and Caribbean intellectuals faded once the plot ran out. The play lacks a sixth act which might have been enlisted for representing relations among Caliban, Ariel, and Prospero once they entered a postcolonial era, or rather (in Harry Magdoff's phrase), an era of "imperialism without colonies."[34] Over time, Caliban's recovery of his island has proved a qualified triumph, with the autonomy of his emergent nation far more compromised than was imagined by the generation of more optimistic nationalists—politicians and writers alike—who saw independence in. Third Worlders have found it difficult to coax from the play analogies with these new circumstances wherein Prospero, having officially relinquished authority over the island, so often continues to manage it from afar.

With the achievement of formal independence, the anticolonial spirit of insurrection has been dampened and the assertive calls to reconstruct endemic cultures attenuated. By the early seventies the generation of more idealistic (and often more literary) leaders who bridged the periods pre- and postindependence was being replaced by a cohort of Third World leaders who in power have become preoccupied, as Edward Said has noted, primarily with technocratic concerns and defense.[35] Issues of national or racial identity have largely been superseded by issues of survival. In this climate, Shakespeare's play has been drained of the immediate, urgent value it was once found to have, and the moment has passed when a man like Lamming could assert so sanguinely that "*The Tempest* was also prophetic of a political future which is our present. Moreover, the circumstances of my life, both as a colonial and exiled descendant of Caliban in the twentieth century, is an example of that prophecy" (*PE*, p. 13). The play's declining pertinence to contemporary Africa and the Caribbean has been exacerbated by the difficulty of wresting from it any role for female defiance or leadership in a period when protest is coming increasingly from that quarter. Given that Caliban is without a female counterpart in his oppression and rebellion, and given the largely autobiographical cast of African and Caribbean appropriations of the play, it follows that all the writers who quarried from *The Tempest* an expression of their lot should have been men. This assumption of heroic revolt as a preeminently male province is most palpable in Fernández Retamar's inclusion of only one woman in his list of thirty-five activists and intellectuals who exemplify the Calibanesque.

Between the late fifties and early seventies *The Tempest* was valued and competed for both by those (in the "master"-culture's terms) traditionally possessed of discrimination and those traditionally discriminated against. On the one hand, a broad evaluative agreement existed between the two sets of feuding cultures, the colonizers and the colonized both regarding the play highly. On the other hand, the two groups brought utterly different social ambitions to bear on the play. Writers and intellectuals from the colonies appropriated *The Tempest* in a way that was outlandish in the original sense of the word. They reaffirmed the play's importance from outside its central tradition not passively or obsequiously, but through what may best be described as a series of insurrectional endorsements. For in that turbulent and intensely reactive phase of Caribbean and African history, *The Tempest* came to serve as a Trojan horse, whereby cultures barred from the citadel of "universal" Western values could win entry and assail those global pretensions from within.

Notes

1. George Lamming, *The Pleasures of Exile* (New York, 1984), p. 27; all further references to this work, abbreviated *PE*, will be included in the text.

2. See Pierre Bourdieu and Jean-Claude Passeron, *La Reproduction: Eléments pour une théorie du système d'enseignement* (Paris, 1970), and Bourdieu, *La Distinction: Critique sociale du jugement* (Paris, 1979); Barbara Herrnstein Smith, "Contingencies of Value," *Critical Inquiry* 10 (Sept. 1983): 1-35; Tony Bennett, *Formalism and Marxism* (London, 1979), "*Formalism and Marxism* Revisited," *Southern Review* 16 (1982): 3-21, and "Really Useless 'Knowledge': A Political Critique of Aesthetics," *Thesis 11* 12 (1985): 28-52.

3. Frantz Fanon, *The Wretched of the Earth,* trans. Constance Farrington (New York, 1968), p. 43.

4. Jean-Paul Sartre, preface, ibid., p. 9.

5. Ibid., p. 16.

6. Shakespeare's debt to the Bermuda pamphlets and other Elizabethan accounts of the New World has been extensively analyzed, often in relation to the evolution of British colonial discourse in the seventeenth century. See especially Frank Kermode, introduction to *The Tempest* (New York, 1954), pp. xxv-xxxiv; Stephen J. Greenblatt, "Learning to Curse: Aspects of Linguistic Colonialism in the Sixteenth Century," in *First Images of America: The Impact of the New World on the Old,* ed. Fredi Chiappelli, 2 vols. (Berkeley and Los Angeles, 1976), 2:561-80; Leslie A. Fiedler, "The New World Savage as Stranger: Or, ''Tis new to thee,'" *The Stranger in Shakespeare* (New York, 1972), pp. 199-253; Peter Hulme, "Hurricanes in the Caribbees: The Constitution of the Discourse of English Colonialism," in *1642: Literature and Power in the Seventeenth Century: Proceedings of the Essex Conference on the Sociology of Literature, July 1980,* ed. Francis Barker et al. (Colchester, 1981), pp. 55-83; Barker and Hulme, "Nymphs and Reapers Heavily Vanish: The Discursive Con-texts of *The Tempest*," in *Alternative Shakespeares,* ed. John Drakakis (London, 1985), pp. 191-205; and Paul Brown, "'This thing of darkness I acknowledge mine': *The Tempest* and the Discourse of Colonialism," in *Political Shakespeare: New Essays in Cultural Materialism,* ed. Jonathan Dollimore and Alan Sinfield (Ithaca, N.Y., 1985), pp. 48-71.

7. Roberto Fernández Retamar, "Caliban: Notes Toward a Discussion of Culture in Our America," trans. Lynn Garafola, David Arthur McMurray, and Robert Marquez, *Massachusetts Review* 15 (Winter/Spring 1974): 27; all further references to this work, abbreviated "C," will be included in the text.

8. Homi Bhabha, "Of Mimicry and Man: The Ambivalence of Colonial Discourse," *October* 28 (Spring 1984): 128.

9. Ian Munro and Reinhard Sander, eds., *Kas-Kas: Interviews with Three Caribbean Writers in Texas: George Lamming, C. L. R. James, Wilson Harris* (Austin, Tex., 1972), p. 6. For kindred treatments of the way British-centered curricula generated mimicry and cultural dependency in the former British West Indies, see Austin Clarke, *Growing Up Stupid Under the Union Jack: A Memoir* (Toronto, 1980), and Chris Searle, *The Forsaken Lover: White Words and Black People* (London, 1972).

10. Trevor R. Griffiths, "'This Island's Mine': Caliban and Colonialism," *Yearbook of English Studies* 13 (1983): 159-80. Although Griffiths does not tackle the question of value directly, his essay complements mine insofar as it focuses on how *The Tempest* was appropriated not in the colonies but in Britain. Griffiths' analysis treats both the heyday of imperialism and the subsequent retreat from empire. For discussion of how *The Tempest* was taken up from the seventeenth century onward, see Ruby Cohn, *Modern Shakespeare Offshoots* (Princeton, N.J., 1976), pp. 267-309. Cohn's account of the two adaptations of the play by the nineteenth-century French historian and philosopher Ernest Renan is especially comprehensive.

11. Daniel Wilson, *Caliban: The Missing Link* (London, 1873), p. 79.

12. W. T. Stead, "First Impressions of the Theatre," *Review of Reviews* 30 (Oct. 1904); quoted in Griffiths, "'This Island's Mine,'" p. 170.

13. [Dominique] O. Mannoni, *Prospero and Caliban: The Psychology of Colonization,* trans. Pamela Powesland (New York, 1964), p. 34; all further references to this work, abbreviated *PC,* will be included in the text. The centrality of *The Tempest* to Mannoni's theory was given added emphasis by the extended title of the English translation.

14. William Shakespeare, *The Tempest,* act 1, sc. 2, ll. 332-44; all further references to the play will be included in the text.

15. See Fanon, *Peau noire, masques blancs* (Paris, 1952), and Aimé Césaire, *Discours sur le colonialisme,* 3d ed. (Paris, 1955). See also the section, "Caliban on the Couch," in O. Onoge, "Revolutionary Imperatives in African Sociology," in *African Social Studies: A Radical Reader,* ed. Peter C. W. Gutkind and Peter Waterman (New York, 1977), pp. 32-43.

16. Philip Mason, *Prospero's Magic: Some Thoughts on Class and Race* (London, 1962), p. 80; all further references to this work, abbreviated *PM,* will be included in the text.

17. Though it is underscored by a different politics, Sartre makes a related remark in his preface to *The Wretched of the Earth:* "We in Europe too are being decolonized: that is to say that the settler which is in every one of us is being savagely rooted out" (Sartre, preface, p. 24).

18. For a thematic rather than a historical survey of the figure of Caliban in Third World writing, see Charlotte H. Bruner, "The Meaning of Caliban in Black Literature Today," *Comparative Literature Studies* 13 (Sept. 1976): 240-53.

19. See C. L. R. James, *The Black Jacobins: Toussaint Louverture and the San Domingo Revolution* (New York, 1963).

20. Given the antipathy between Trinidadian-born V. S. Naipaul and the more radical Lamming, and given Lamming's identification with Caliban, it is probable that Naipaul had the Barbadian in mind in his fictional *A Flag on the Island,* where the narrator parodies Caribbean celebrations of Caliban by citing a local autobiography, *I Hate You: One Man's Search for Identity,* which opens: "'I am a man without identity. Hate has consumed my identity. My personality has been distorted by hate. My hymns have not been hymns of praise, but of hate. How terrible to be Caliban, you say. But I say, how tremendous. Tremendousness is therefore my unlikely subject'" (Naipaul, *A Flag on the Island* [London, 1967], p. 154).

21. Cf. the remark by Chris Searle, another writer who reads Caribbean culture through the Prospero-Caliban dichotomy: "The ex-master's language . . . is still the currency of communication which buys out the identity of the child as soon as he begins to acquire it" (Searle, *The Forsaken Lover,* p. 29).

22. See Lamming, *The Pleasures of Exile,* and Césaire, *Toussaint Louverture: la révolution francaise et le problème colonial* (Paris, 1961).

23. Janheinz Jahn, *Neo-African Literature: A History of Black Writing,* trans. Oliver Coburn and Ursula Lehrburger (New York, 1969), p. 242.

24. Césaire, quoted in S. Belhassen, "Aimé Césaire's *A Tempest,*" in *Radical Perspectives in the Arts,* ed. Lee Baxandall (Harmondsworth, 1972), p. 176.

25. For the fullest discussion concerning Césaire's Africanizing of Shakespeare, see Thomas A. Hale, "Aimé Césaire: His Literary and Political Writings with a Bio-bibliography" (Ph.D. diss., University of Rochester, 1974), and "Sur *Une tempête* d'Aimé Césaire," *Etudes Littéraires* 6 (1973): 21-34.

26. Césaire, *Une Tempête: D'après "la Tempête" de Shakespeare—Adaptation pour un théâtre nègre* (Paris, 1969), p. 24.

27. Ibid., p. 92.

28. See Fernández Retamar, "Cuba Hasta Fidel," *Bohemia* 61 (19 September 1969): 84-97, and "Caliban: Notes Toward a Discussion of Culture in Our America"; Lamming, *Water with Berries* (London, 1971); Edward Braithwaite, *Islands* (London, 1969), pp. 34-38; John Pepper Clark, "The Legacy of Caliban," *Black Orpheus* 2 (Feb. 1968):

16-39; Ngugi Wa Thiong'o, "Towards a National Culture," *Homecoming: Essays on African and Caribbean Literature, Culture, and Politics* (Westport, Conn., 1983); David Wallace, *Do You Love Me Master?* (Lusaka, 1977). In Lamming's allegorical novel, Caliban resurfaces in the form of three West Indian artists who reside in London and collectively play out the dilemmas of colonizer-colonized entanglements during the era of decolonization. Clark's reflections turn on the relation between "the colonial flag and a cosmopolitan language." Clark both follows and reroutes Lamming's insights on this subject as, unlike his Caribbean predecessor, he approaches English from an African perspective, that is, as a second language. Ngugi's essay, published in 1972, was originally delivered at a conference in 1969. In it he assails Prospero for first dismantling Caliban's heritage and then denying that such a culture ever existed. Ngugi proceeds to sketch strategies for reaffirming the value of that damaged inheritance, notably by decolonizing language and education. Wallace's play was first performed in 1971. Regional nuances aside, *Do You Love Me Master?* is much of a piece with trends already discussed: aided by rioting prisoners, Caliban, a cursing Zambian "houseboy," drives the "bossman," Prospero, out of the country. In the final scene Prospero's stick, more truncheon than wand, is broken, and the crowd encircles the master shouting "Out, out!" and waves banners proclaiming freedom. The play incorporates songs in three African languages.

29. Braithwaite, "Caliban," *Islands,* p. 36.
30. The strong historical presence of Martí in the essay is redoubled by Fernández Retamar's invocation, from the same era, of José Enrique Rodó's *Ariel.* Published in 1900, this Uruguayan novel was written in direct response to the 1898 American intervention in Cuba. Rodó identifies Latin America with Ariel, not Caliban.
31. The European suspicion that colonized people would treat Shakespeare with, to invoke Fernández Retamar's phrase, "presumed barbarism" was starkly evident when the Parisian critics dismissed Césaire's *Une Tempête* as a "betrayal" of the bard. See Hale, "Sur *Une Tempête* d'Aimé Césaire," p. 21.
32. See Marta E. Sánchez, "Caliban: The New Latin-American Protagonist of *The Tempest,*" *Diacritics* 6 (Spring 1976): 54-61.
33. Sylvia Wynter, "Afterword," in Lemuel Johnson, *highlife for caliban* (Ann Arbor, Mich., 1973), p. 137.
34. Harry Magdoff, "Imperialism without Colonies," in *Studies in the Theory of Imperialism,* ed. Roger Owen and Bob Sutcliffe (New York, 1972), pp. 144-70.
35. See Edward Said, "In the Shadow of the West," *Wedge* 7/8 (Winter/Spring 1985), p. 10.

Ronald Takaki (essay date 1992)

SOURCE: "*The Tempest* in the Wilderness: The Racialization of Savagery," in *The Journal of American History,* Vol. 79, No. 3, December, 1992, pp. 892-912.

[*In the following essay, Takaki probes* The Tempest's *relation to the English colonization of America, interpreting Caliban as representative of a "savage" American Indian figure.*]

"O brave new world that has such people in't," they heard Miranda exclaim. It was 1611 and London theatergoers were attending the first performance of William Shakespeare's *The Tempest.* In the early seventeenth century, the English were encountering what they viewed as strange inhabitants in new lands. Those experiences determined the meaning of the utterances they heard. A perspicacious few in the audience could have seen that this play was more than a story about how Prospero was sent into exile with his daughter, Miranda, took possession of an island inhabited by Caliban, and redeemed himself by marrying Miranda to the king's son.[1]

Indeed, *The Tempest* can be approached as a fascinating tale about the creation of a new society in America. Seen in that light, the play invites us to view English expansion not only as imperialism but also as a defining moment in the making of an English-American identity based on race. For the first time in the English theater, an Indian character was being presented. What did Shakespeare and his audience know about the native peoples of America, and what choices were they making when they characterized Caliban? Although they saw him as a "savage," did they racialize savagery? Was the play a prologue for America?

The Tempest studied in relationship to its context can help us answer those questions. *Othello* also offers us an opportunity to analyze English racial attitudes, as Winthrop Jordan has demonstrated so brilliantly, but our play is a more important window for understanding American history, for its story is set in the New World. Moreover, the timing of that first performance of *The Tempest* was crucial: It came after the English invasion of Ireland but before the colonization of New England, after John Smith's arrival in Virginia but before the beginning of the tobacco economy, and after the first contacts with Indians but before full-scale warfare against them. In that historical moment, the English were encountering "other" peoples and delineating the boundary between *civilization* and *savagery.* The social constructions of both those terms were dynamically developing in three sites—Ireland, Virginia, and New England.[2]

One of the places the English were colonizing in 1611 was Ireland, and Caliban seemed to resemble the Irish. Theatergoers were familiar with the "wild Irish" on stage, for such images had been presented in the plays *Sir John Oldcastle* (1599) and *Honest Whore* (1605). Seeking to conquer the Irish in 1395, Richard II had condemned them as "savage Irish, our enemies." In the mid-sixteenth century, the government had decided to bring all of Ireland under its rule, and to that end, it encouraged private colonization projects.[3]

Like Caliban, the Irish were viewed as "savages," a people living outside of "civilization." They had tribal organizations, and their practice of herding seemed nomadic. Even their Christianity was said to be merely the exterior of strongly rooted paganism. "They are all Papists by their profession," claimed Edmund Spenser in 1596, "but in the same so blindly and brutishly informed for the most part as that you would rather think them atheists or infidels." To the English colonists, it seemed that the Irish lacked "knowledge of God or good manners." They had no sense of private property and did not "plant any Gardens or Orchards, Inclose or improve their lands, live together in settled Villages or Townes." The Irish were described as lazy, "naturally" given to "idleness," and unwilling to work for "their own bread." Dominated by "innate sloth," "loose, barbarous and most wicked," and living "like beasts," they were also thought to be criminals, an underclass inclined to steal from the English. The colonists complained that the Irish savages were not satisfied with the "fruit of the natural unlaboured earth" and therefore continually "invaded the fertile possessions" of the "English Pale."[4]

The English colonizers established a two-tiered social structure. According to sixteenth-century English law, "every Irishman shall be forbidden to wear English apparel or weapon upon pain of death. That no Irishman, born of Irish race and brought up Irish, shall purchase land, bear office, be chosen of any jury or admitted witness in any real or personal action." To reinforce this social separation, British laws prohibited marriages between the Irish and the colonizers. The new world order was to be one of English over Irish.[5]

The Irish also became targets of English violence. "Nothing but fear and force can teach duty and obedience" to this "rebellious people," the invaders insisted. The sixteenth-century English were generally brutal in waging war, but they seemed to have been particularly cruel toward the Irish. The colonizers burned the villages and crops of the inhabitants and relocated them on reservations. They slaughtered families, "man, woman and child," justifying their atrocities by arguing that families provided support for the rebels. After four years of bloody warfare in Munster, according to Edmund Spenser, the Irish had been reduced to wretchedness. "Out of every corner of the woods and glens they came creeping forth upon their hands, for their legs would not bear them. They looked anatomies of death; they spake like ghosts crying out of their graves." The death toll was so high that "in short space there were none almost left and a most populous and plentiful country suddenly left void of man and beast." The "void" meant vacant lands for English resettlement.[6]

The invaders took the heads of the slain Irish as trophies. Sir Humphrey Gilbert pursued a campaign of terror: He ordered that "the heads of all those . . . killed in the day, should be cut off from their bodies and brought to the place where he encamped at night, and should there be laid on the ground by each side of the way leading into his own tent so that none could come into his tent for any cause but commonly he must pass through a lane of heads. . . . [It brought] great terror to the people when they saw the heads of their dead fathers, brothers, children, kinsfolk, and friends." After seeing the head of his lord impaled on the walls of Dublin, Irish poet Angus O'Daly cried out:

> O body which I see without a head,
> It is the sight of thee which has withered up my strength.
> Divided and impaled in Ath-cliath,
> The learned of Banba will feel its loss.
> Who will relieve the wants of the poor?
> Who will bestow cattle on the learned?
> O body, since thou art without a head,
> It is not life which we care to choose after thee.[7]

The English claimed that they had a God-given responsibility to "inhabit and reform so barbarous a nation" and to educate the Irish "brutes." They would teach them to obey English laws and to stop "robbing and stealing and killing" one another. They would uplift this "most filthy people, utterly enveloped in vices, most untutored of all peoples in the rudiments of faith." Thus, although they saw the Irish as savages and although they sometimes described this savagery as "natural" and "innate," the English believed that the Irish could be civilized, improved through what Shakespeare called "nurture." In short, the difference between the Irish and the English was a matter of culture.[8]

As their frontier advanced from Ireland to America, the English began making comparisons between the Irish and the Indian "savages" and wondering whether there might be different kinds of "savagery."

The parallels between English expansionism in Ireland and that in America were apparent. Sir Humphrey Gilbert, Lord De La Warr, Sir Francis Drake, and Sir Walter Raleigh—all participated both in invading Ireland and in colonizing the New World. The conquest of Ireland and the settlement of Virginia were bound so closely together that one correspondence, dated March 8, 1610, stated: "It is hoped the plantation of Ireland may shortly be settled. The Lord Delaware [Lord De La Warr] is preparing to depart for the plantation of Virginia." Commander John Mason conducted military campaigns against the Irish before he sailed for New England, where he led troops against the Pequots of Connecticut. Samuel Gorton wrote a letter to John Winthrop, Jr., connecting the two frontiers: "I remember the time of the wars in Ireland (when I was young, in Queen Elizabeth's days of famous memory) where much English blood was spilt by a people much like unto these [Indians]. . . . And after these Irish were subdued by force, what treacherous and bloody massacres have they attempted is well known."[9]

The first English colonizers in the New World found that the Indians reminded them of the Irish. Capt. John Smith observed that the deerskin robes worn by the Indians in Virginia did not differ much "in fashion from the Irish mantels." Thomas Morton noticed that the "natives of New England [were] accustomed to build themselves houses much like the wild Irish." Roger Williams reported that the thick woods and swamps of New England gave refuge to the warring Indians "like the bogs to the wild Irish." Thus, in their early encounters, the English projected the familiar onto the strange, their images of the Irish onto the native people of America. Initially, "savagery" was defined in relationship to the Irish, and Indians were incorporated into this definition.[10]

The Tempest, the London audience knew, was not about Ireland but about the New World, for the reference to the "Bermoothes" (Bermuda) revealed the location of the island. What was happening on stage was a metaphor for English expansion into America. The play's title was inspired by a recent incident. Caught in a violent storm in 1609, the *Sea Adventure* had been separated from a fleet of ships bound for Virginia and had run aground in the Bermudas. Shakespeare knew many of the colonizers, including Sir Humphrey Gilbert and Lord De La Warr. One of his personal friends was the geographer Richard Hakluyt, author of widely read books about the New World. The future of Englishmen lay in America, proclaimed Hakluyt, as he urged them to "conquer a country" and "to man it, to plant it, and to keep it, and to continue the making of Wines and Oils able to serve England."[11]

The description of the play's setting evoked the mainland near the "Bermoothes"—Virginia. "The air breathes upon us here most sweetly," the theatergoers were told. "Here is everything advantageous to life." "How lush and lusty the grass looks! how green!" Impressed by the land's innocence, Gonzalo of *The Tempest* depicted it as an ideal commonwealth where everything was as yet unformed and unbounded, where letters, laws, metals, and occupations were yet unknown. Both the imagery and the language revealed America as the site of Prospero's landing: It was almost as if Shakespeare had lifted the material from contemporary documents about the New World. Tracts on Virginia had described the air as "most sweet" and as "virgin and temperate," and its soil as "*lusty*" with meadows "full of *green grass*." In *A True Reportory of the Wracke*, published in 1609, William Strachey depicted Virginia's abundance: "no Country yieldeth goodlier *Corn*, nor more manifold increase . . . we have thousands of goodly *Vines*." Here was an opportunity for colonists to enhance the "fertility and pleasure" of Virginia by "cleansing away her woods" and converting her into "goodly meadow."[12]

Moreover, the play provided a conclusive clue that the story was indeed about America: Caliban, one of the principal characters, was a New World inhabitant. "Carib," the name of an Indian tribe, had come to mean a savage of America, and the term *cannibal* was a derivative. Shakespeare sometimes rearranged letters in words ("Amleth," the name of a prince in a Viking tale, for example, became "Hamlet"), and here he had created another anagram in "Caliban."[13]

The English had seen or read reports about Indians who had been captured and brought to London. Beginning with Christopher Columbus, European visitors to the New World had brought back Indians. Columbus himself had displayed Indians. During his first voyage, he wrote: "Yesterday came [to] the ship a dugout with six young men, and five came on board; these I ordered to be detained and I am bringing them." When Columbus was received by the Spanish court after his triumphal return, he presented a collection of things he had brought back, including gold nuggets, parrots in cages, and six Indians. On his second voyage, in 1493, Columbus again sent his men to kidnap Indians. On one occasion, a captive had been "wounded seven times and his entrails were hanging out," reported Guillermo Coma of Aragon. "Since it was thought that he could not be cured, he was cast into the sea. But keeping above water and raising one foot, he held on to his intestines with his left hand and swam courageously to the shore. . . . The wounded Carib was caught again on shore. His hands and feet were bound more tightly and he was once again thrown headlong. But this resolute savage swam more furiously, until he was struck several times by arrows and perished." When Columbus set sail with his fleet to return to Spain, he took 550 Indian captives with him. "When we reached the waters around Spain," Michele de Cuneo wrote matter-of-factly, "about 200 of those Indians died, I believe because of the unaccustomed air, colder than theirs. We cast them into the sea."[14]

English explorers also engaged in the practice of kidnapping Indians. When Capt. George Waymouth visited New England in 1605, he lured some Abenakis to his ship; taking three of them hostage, he sailed back to England to display them. An early seventeenth-century pamphlet stated that a voyage to Virginia was expected to bring back its quota of captured Indians: "Thus we shipped five savages, two canoes, with all their bows and arrows." In 1614 the men on one of Capt. John Smith's ships captured several Indians on Cape Cod. "Thomas Hunt," Smith wrote, "betrayed four and twenty of these poor savages aboard this ship, and most dishonestly and inhumanely . . . carried them with him to Maligo [Malaga] and there for a little private gain sold . . . those savages for Rials of eight." In 1611, according to a biographer of William Shakespeare, "a native of New England called Epenew was brought to England . . . and 'being a man of so great a stature' was showed up and down London for money as a monster." In *The Tempest* Stephano considered capturing Caliban: "If I can recover him, and keep him tame, and get to Naples with him, he's a present for any emperor." Such exhibitions of Indians were "profitable investments," literary scholar Frank Kermode noted, and were "a regular feature of colonial policy under James I. The exhibits rarely survived the experience."[15]

To the spectators of these "exhibits," Indians personified "savagery." They were depicted as "cruel, barbarous and most treacherous." They were thought to be cannibals, "being most furious in their rage and merciless . . . not being content only to kill and take away life, but delight to torment men in the most bloody manner . . . flaying some alive with the shells of fishes, cutting off the members and joints of others by piecemeal and broiling on the coals, eating the collops of their flesh in their sight whilst they live." According to Sir Walter Raleigh, Indians had "their eyes in their shoulders, and their mouths in the middle of their breasts." In *Nova Brittania,* published in 1609, Richard Johnson described the Indians in Virginia as "wild and savage people," living "like herds of deer in a forest." One of their striking physical characteristics was their skin color. John Brereton described the New England Indians as "of tall stature, broad and grim visage, of a blacke swart complexion."[16]

Indians seemed to lack everything the English identified as civilized—Christianity, cities, letters, clothing, and swords. "They do not bear arms or know them, for I showed to them swords and they took them by the blade and cut themselves through ignorance," wrote Columbus in his journal, noting that the Indians did not have iron. George Waymouth tried to impress the Abenakis: He magnetized a sword "to cause them to imagine some great power in us; and for that to love and fear us."[17]

Like Caliban, the native people of America were viewed as the other. European culture was delineating the border, the hierarchical division between civilization and wildness. Unlike Europeans, Indians were allegedly dominated by their passions, especially their sexuality. Amerigo Vespucci was struck by how the natives embraced and enjoyed the pleasures of their bodies: "They . . . are libidinous beyond measure, and the women far more than the men. . . . When they had the opportunity of copulating with Christians, urged by excessive lust, they defiled and prostituted themselves." Caliban personified such passions. Prospero saw him as a sexual threat to the nubile Miranda, her "virgin-knot" yet unbroken. "I have used thee (filth as thou art) with humane care," Prospero scolded Caliban, "and lodged thee in mine own cell till thou didst seek to violate the honor of my child." And the unruly native snapped: "O ho, O ho! Would't had been done! Thou didst prevent me; I had peopled else this isle with Calibans."[18]

To the theatergoers, Caliban represented what Europeans had been when they were lower on the scale of development toward civilization. To be civilized, they believed, required denial of wholeness—the repression of the instinctual forces of human nature. Prospero, personification of civilized man, identified himself as mind rather than body. His epistemology relied on the visual rather than the tactile and on the linear knowledge of books rather than the polymorphous knowledge of experience. With the self fragmented, Prospero was able to split off his rationality and raise it to authority over the other—the sensuous part of himself and everything Caliban represented.[19]

But could Caliban, the audience wondered, ever become Christian and civilized? The sixteenth-century Spanish lawyer Juan Gines de Sepulveda had justified the Spanish conquest of Indians by invoking Aristotle's doctrine that some people were "natural slaves." The condition of slavery, Sepulveda argued, was natural for "persons of both inborn rudeness and of inhuman and barbarous customs." Thus what counted was an ascriptive quality based on a group's nature, or "descent."[20]

On the other hand, Pope Paul III had proclaimed that Indians as well as "all other people" who might later be "discovered" by "Christians" should not be deprived of their liberty and property, even though they were outside the Christian faith. Christopher Columbus had reported that Indians were "very gentle and without knowledge of . . . evil." He added: "They love their neighbors as themselves, and have the sweetest talk in the world, and gentle, and always with a smile." In the play, Gonzalo told theatergoers: "I saw such islanders . . . who, though they are of monstrous shape, yet, note, their manners are more gentle, kind, than of our human generation you shall find many—nay, almost any." Thus, Indians were not always viewed as brutish by nature: Already capable of morality and gentleness, they could be acculturated, become civilized through "consent."[21]

Indeed, Caliban seemed educable. Prospero had taught him a European language: "I . . . took pains to make thee speak, taught thee each hour one thing or other. When thou didst not, savage, know thine own meaning, but wouldst gabble like a thing most brutish." Defiantly, the native retorted: "You taught me language, and my profit on't is, I know how to curse. The red plague rid you for learning me your language." A Virginia tract stated that the colonists should take Indian children and "train them up with gentleness, teach them our English tongue." In the contract establishing the Virginia Company in 1606, the king endorsed a plan to propagate the "Christian Religion to such people" who as yet lived in "darkness and miserable ignorance of the true knowledge and worship of God." Three years later, the Virginia Company instructed the governor of the colony to encourage missionaries to convert Indian children. They should be taken from their parents if necessary, since the parents were "so wrapped up in the fog and misery of their iniquity." A Virginia promotional tract stated that it was "not the nature of men, but the education of men" that made them "barbarous and uncivil." Every man in the new colony had a duty to bring the savage Indians to "civil and Christian" government.[22]

In 1611 these cultural constructs of Indians were either the fantasy of Shakespeare or the impressions of policy makers and tract writers in London. What would happen to these images on the stage of history?

The first English settlement in the New World was in Virginia, the home of fourteen thousand Powhatans. An agricultural people, they cultivated corn—the mainstay of their subsistence. Their cleared fields were large—one-hundred-acre fields were not uncommon—and they lived in palisaded towns, with forts, storehouses, temples, and framed houses covered with bark and reed mats. They cooked their foods in ceramic pots and used woven baskets for storing corn; some of their baskets were constructed so skillfully they could carry water in them. The Powhatans had a sophisticated numbering system for evaluating their harvests. According to John Smith, they had numbers from one to ten, after which counting was done by tens to one hundred. There was a word for "one thousand." The Powhatan calendar had five seasons: "Their winter some call *Popanow,* the spring *Cattaapeuk,* the sommer *Cohattayough,* the earing of their Corne *Nepinough,* the harvest and fall of the leafe *Taquitock.* From September until the midst of November are the chief Feasts and sacrifice."[23]

In Virginia the initial encounters between the English and the Indians opened possibilities for friendship and interdependency. The first colonists arrived and set up camp in 1607. There were 120 of them. Then, John Smith reported, came "the starving time." A year later, only 38 still lived, hanging precariously on the very edge of survival. The New World had been depicted as a garden; the reality of America was something else. Descriptions of its natural abundance turned out to have been exaggerated. Many of the English were not prepared for survival in the wilderness. "Now was all our provision spent . . . all help abandoned, each hour expecting the fury of the savages," Smith wrote. Fortunately, in that "desperate extremity," the Powhatans brought food to the starving strangers.[24]

A year later, several hundred more colonists arrived; again they quickly ran out of provisions. They were forced to eat "dogs, cats, rats, and mice," even "corpses" dug from graves. "Some have licked up the blood which hath fallen from their weak fellows," a survivor reported. "One [member] of our colony murdered his wife, ripped the child out of her womb and threw it into the river, and after chopped the mother in pieces and salted her for his food, the same not being discovered before he had eaten part thereof." "So great was our famine," John smith stated, "that a savage we slew and buried, the poorer sort took him up again and ate him; and so did diverse one another boiled and stewed with roots and herbs."[25]

Hostilities soon broke out as the English tried to extort food supplies by attacking the Indians and destroying their villages. In 1608 an Indian declared: "We hear you are come from under the World to take our World from us." A year later Gov. Thomas Gates arrived in Virginia with instructions that the Indians should be forced to labor for the colonists and also make annual payments of corn and skins. The orders were brutally carried out. During one of the raids, the English soldiers attacked an Indian town, killing fifteen people and forcing many others to flee. Then they burned the houses and destroyed the cornfields. According to a report by Commander George Percy, they marched the captured queen and her children to the river where they "put the Children to death . . . by throwing them overboard and shooting out their brains in the water."[26]

Indians began to doubt that the two peoples could live together in peace. One young Indian told Capt. John Smith: "[We] are here to intreat and desire your friendship and to enjoy our houses and plant our fields, of whose fruits you shall participate." But he did not trust the strangers: "We perceive and well know you intend to destroy us." Chief Powhatan had come to the same conclusion; he told Smith that the English were not in Virginia to trade but to "invade" and "possess" Indian lands.[27]

Indeed, Smith and his fellow colonists were encouraged by their culture of expansionism to claim entitlement to the land. In *The Tempest* the theatergoers were told by Sebastian: "I think he [the king of Naples] will carry this island home in his pocket and give it his son for an apple." Prospero declared that he had been thrust forth from Milan and "most strangely" landed on this shore "to be the lord on't." Projecting his personal plans and dreams onto the wilderness, he colonized the island and dispossessed Caliban. Feeling robbed, Caliban protested: "As I told thee before, I am subject to a tyrant, a sorcerer, that by his cunning hath cheated me of the island." But the English did not see their taking of the land as robbery. In *Utopia* (1516), written almost one hundred years before English colonization of America began in earnest, Sir Thomas More had provided a rationale for the appropriation of Indian lands: Since the natives did not "use" the soil but left it "idle and waste," the English had "just cause" to drive them from the territory by force. In 1609 Robert Gray declared that "the greater part" of the earth was "possessed and wrongfully usurped by wild beasts . . . or by brutish savages." A Virginia pamphlet argued that it was "not unlawful" for the English to possess "part" of the Indians' land.[28]

But the English soon wanted more than just a "part" of Indian territory. Their need for land was suddenly intensified by a new development—the cultivation of tobacco as an export crop. In 1613 the colony sent its first shipment of tobacco to London, a small but significant four barrels' worth. The exports grew dramatically: 2,300 pounds in 1616, 19,000 the following year, 60,000 by 1620. The colonists increasingly coveted Indian lands, especially already cleared fields. Tobacco agriculture stimulated not only territorial expansion but also immigration. During the "Great Migration" of 1618-1623, the colony grew from 400 to 4,500 people.

In 1622 the natives tried to drive out the intruders, killing some three hundred colonists. John Smith denounced the "massacre" and described the "savages" as "cruel beasts," who possessed "a more unnatural brutishness" than wild animals. The English deaths, Samuel Purchas argued, established the colonists' right to the land: "Their carcasses, the dispersed bones of their countrymen . . . speak, proclaim and cry, This our earth is truly English, and therefore this Land is justly yours O English." Their blood had watered the soil, entitling them to the land. "We, who hitherto have had possession of no more ground than their [Indian] waste, and our purchase . . . may now by right of War, and law of Nations," the colonists declared, "invade the Country, and destroy them who sought to destroy us."

They felt they could morally sweep away their enemies and even take their developed lands. "We shall enjoy their cultivated places. . . . Now their cleared grounds in all their villages (which are situated in the fruitfulest places of the land) shall be inhabited by us."[29]

In their fierce counterattack, the English waged total war. "Victory may be gained in many ways," a colonist declared: "by force, by surprise, by famine in burning their Corn, by destroying and burning their Boats, Canoes, and Houses . . . by pursuing and chasing them with our horses, and blood-hounds to draw after them, and mastives to tear them." In 1623 Capt. William Tucker led his soldiers to a Powhatan village, presumably to negotiate a peace treaty. After he concluded the treaty, he persuaded the Indians to drink a toast, serving them poisoned wine. An estimated two hundred Indians died instantly; Tucker's soldiers then killed another fifty and "brought home part of their heads." In 1629, a colonist reported, the English forced hostile Indians to seek peace by "continual incursions" and by "yearly cutting down, and spoiling their corn." The goal of the war was to "root out [the Indians] from being any longer a people."[30]

What happened in Virginia, while terrible and brutal, was still based largely on the view that Indian "savagery" was cultural. Like the Irish, Indians were identified as brutal and backward, but they were not yet seen as incapable of becoming civilized because of their race, or "descent." Their heathenism had not yet been indelibly attached to distinctive physical characteristics such as their skin color. So far at least, "consent" was possible for Indians. What occurred in New England was a different story, however, and here again *The Tempest* was preview.[31]

Although the theatergoers were given the impression that Caliban could be acculturated, they also received a diametrically opposite construction of his racial character. They were told that Caliban was "a devil, a born devil" and that he belonged to a "vile race." "Descent" was determinative: his birthmark signified an inherent moral defect. On the stage, they saw Caliban, with long shaggy hair, personifying the Indian. He had distinct racial markers. "Freckled," covered with brown spots, he was "not honored with human shape." Called a "fish," he was mockingly told: "Thy eyes are almost set in thy head." "Where should they be set else? He were a brave monster indeed if they were set in his tail." More important, his distinctive physical characteristics signified intellectual incapacity. Caliban was "a thing of darkness" whose "nature nurture [could] never stick." In other words, he had natural qualities that precluded the possibility of becoming civilized through "nurture," or education. The racial distance between Caliban and Prospero was inscribed geographically. Prospero forced the native to live on a reservation located in a barren region. "Here you sty me in this hard rock," he complained, "whiles you do keep from me the rest o' the island." Prospero justified this segregation, charging that the "savage" possessed distasteful qualities "which good natures could not abide to be with. Therefore wast thou deservedly confined into this rock, who hadst deserved more than a prison." The theatergoers saw Caliban's sty located emblematically at the back of the stage, behind Prospero's "study," signifying a hierarchy of white over dark and cerebral over carnal.[32]

This deterministic view of Caliban's racial character would be forged in the crucible of New England. Five years after the first performance of *The Tempest,* Capt. John Smith sailed north from Virginia to explore the New England coast; again he found not wild men but farmers. The "paradise" of Massachusetts, he reported, was "all planted with corn, groves, mulberries, savage gardens." "The sea Coast as you pass shews you all along large Corne fields." Indeed, while the Abenakis of Maine were mainly hunters and food gatherers dependent on the natural abundance of the land, the tribes in southern New England were horticultural. For example, the Wampanoags, whom the Pilgrims encountered in 1620, were a farming people, with a political system of governance and representation as well as a division of labor with workers specializing in arrow making, woodwork, and leathercraft.[33]

The Wampanoags as well as the Pequots, Massachusets, Nausets, Nipmucks, and Narragansets cultivated corn. As the main source of life for these tribes, corn was the focus of many legends. A Narraganset belief told how a crow had brought this grain to New England: "These Birds, although they do the corn also some hurt, yet scarce one *Native* amongst a hundred will kill them, because they have a tradition, that the Crow brought them at first an *Indian* Grain of Corn in one Ear, and an *Indian* or French bean in another, from the Great God *Kautantouwits* field in the Southwest from whence . . . came all their Corn and Beans." A Penobscot account celebrated the gift of Corn Mother. During a time of famine, an Indian woman fell in love with a snake in the forest. Her secret was discovered one day by her husband, and she told him that she had been chosen to save the tribe. She instructed him to kill her with a stone axe and then drag her body through a clearing. "After seven days he went to the clearing and found the corn plant rising above the ground. . . . When the corn had born fruit and the silk of the corn ear had turned yellow he recognized in it the resemblance of his dead wife. Thus originated the cultivation of corn."[34]

These Indians had a highly developed agricultural system. Samuel de Champlain found that "all along the shore" there was "a great deal of land cleared up and planted with Indian corn." Describing their agricultural practices, he wrote: "They put in each hill three or four Brazilian beans [kidney beans]. . . . When they grow up, they interlace with the corn . . . and they keep the ground very free from weeds. We saw there many squashes, and pumpkins, and tobacco, which they likewise cultivate." Thomas Morton noted the Indian practice of "dung[ing] their ground" with fish to fertilize the soil and increase the harvest. After visiting the Narragansets in Rhode Island, John Winthrop, Jr., noted that, although the soil in that region was "sandy & rocky," the people were able to raise "good corn without fish" by rotating their crops. "They have every one 2 fields," he observed, "which after the first 2 years they let one field rest each year, & that keeps their ground continually [productive]." According to Roger Williams, when the Indians were ready to harvest the corn, "all the neighbours men and women, forty, fifty, a hundred," joined in the work and came "to help freely." During their green corn festival, the Narragansets erected a long house, "sometimes a hundred, sometimes two hundred feet long upon a plain near the Court . . . where many thousands, men and women" gathered. Inside, dancers gave money, coats, and knives to the poor. After the harvest, the Indians stored their corn for the winter. "In the sand on the slope of hills," according to Champlain, "they dig holes, some five or six feet, more or less, and place their corn and other grains in large grass sacks, which they throw into the said holes, and cover them with sand to a depth of three or four feet above the surface of the ground. They take away their grain according to their need, and it is preserved as well as it be in our granaries." Contrary to the stereotype of Indians as hunters and therefore savages, these Indians were farmers.[35]

However, many colonists in New England disregarded this reality and invented their own representations of Indians. What emerged to justify dispossessing them was the racialization of Indian "savagery." The Indians' heathenism and alleged laziness came to be viewed as inborn group traits that rendered them naturally incapable of civilization. This process of dehumanizing the Indians developed a peculiarly New England dimension as the colonists associated Indians with the devil. Indian identity became then a matter of "descent": Their racial markers indicated ineradicable qualities of savagery.

This social construction of race occurred within the economic context of competition over land. The colonists argued that only those who used the land were entitled to it. Native men, they claimed, pursued "no kind of labour but hunting, fishing and fowling." Indians were not producers. "The *Indians* are not able to make use of the one fourth part of the Land," argued the Puritan minister Francis Higginson in 1630, "neither have they any settled places, as Towns to dwell in, nor any ground as they challenge for their owne possession, but change their habitation from place to place." In the Puritan view, Indians were lazy. "Fettered in the chains of idleness," they would rather starve than work, complained William Wood of the Massachusetts Bay colony in 1634. Indians were sinfully squandering America's resources. Under their irresponsible guardianship, the land had become "all spoils, rots," and was "marred for want of manuring, gathering, ordering, etc." Like the "foxes and wild beasts," Indians did nothing "but run over the grass."[36]

The Puritan possession of Indian lands was facilitated by the invasion of unseen pathogens. When the colonists began arriving in New England, they found that the Indian population was already being reduced by European diseases. Two significant events had occurred in the early seventeenth century: Infected rats swam to shore from Samuel de Champlain's ships, and some sick French sailors were shipwrecked on the beaches of New England. By 1616 epidemics were ravaging Indian villages. Victims of "virgin soil epidemics," the Indians lacked immunological defenses against the newly introduced diseases. Between 1610 and 1675, the Indian population declined sharply—from 12,000 to a mere 3,000 for the Abenakis and from 65,000 to 10,000 for the southern tribes.[37]

Describing the sweep of deadly diseases among the Indians, William Bradford reported that the Indians living near the trading house at Plymouth "fell sick of the small pox, and died most miserably." The condition of those still alive was "lamentable." Their bodies were covered with "the pox breaking and mattering and running one into another, their skin cleaving" to the mats beneath them. When the sick Indians turned over, "whole sides" of their skin flayed off. In this terrible way, they died "like rotten sheep." After one epidemic, Bradford recorded in his diary: "For it pleased God to visit these Indians with a great sickness and such a mortality that of a thousand, above nine and a half hundred of them died, and many of them did rot above ground for want of burial."[38]

Leaders of the Massachusetts Bay colony interpreted these Indian deaths as divinely sanctioned opportunities to take the land. John Winthrop declared that the decimation of Indians by smallpox manifested a Puritan destiny: God was "making room" for the colonists and "hath hereby cleared our title to this place." After an epidemic had swept through Indian villages, John Cotton claimed that the destruction was a sign from God: When the Lord decided to transplant his people, he made the country vacant for them to settle. Edward Johnson pointed out that epidemics had desolated "those places, where the English afterward planted."[39]

Indeed, many New England towns were founded on the very lands the Indians had used before the epidemics killed them. The Plymouth colony itself was located on the site of the Wampanoag village of Pawtuxet. The Pilgrims had noticed that the village was empty and the cornfields overgrown with weeds. "There is a great deal of Land cleared," one of them reported, "and hath beene planted with Corne three or four yeares agoe." The original inhabitants had been decimated by the epidemic of 1616. "Thousands of men have lived there, which died in a great plague not long since," another Pilgrim wrote; "and pity it was and is to see so many goodly fields, and so well seated, without men to dress and manure the same." During their first spring, the Pilgrims went out into those fields to weed and manure them. Fortunately, they had some corn seed to plant. Earlier, when they landed on Cape Cod, they had come across some Indian graves and found caches of corn. They considered this find, wrote Bradford, as "a special providence of God, and a great mercy to this poor people, that here they got seed to plant them corn the next year, or else they might have starved." The pallid strangers probably would have perished had it not been for the seeds they found stored in the Indian burial grounds. Ironically, Indian death came to mean life for the Pilgrims.[40]

However, the Puritans did not see it as irony but as the destruction of devils. They had demonized the native peoples, condemning Indian religious beliefs as "diabolical, and so uncouth, as if . . . framed and devised by the devil himself." In 1652 Thomas Mayhew, who was a missionary to the Wampanoags of Martha's Vineyard, wrote that they were "mighty zealous and earnest in the Worship of False gods and Devils." They were under the influence of "a multitude of Heathen Traditions of their gods . . . and abounding with sins."[41]

To the colonists, the Indians were not merely a wayward people: They personified something fearful within Puritan society itself. Like Caliban, a "born devil," Indians failed to control their appetites, to create boundaries separating mind from body. They represented what English men and women in America thought they were not and, more importantly, what they must not become. As exiles living in the wilderness far from "civilization," the English used their negative images of Indians to delineate the moral requirements they had set up for themselves. As sociologist Kai Erikson explains, "deviant forms of behavior, by marking the outer edges of group life, give the inner structure its special character and thus supply the framework within which the people of the group develop an orderly sense of their own cultural identity. . . . One of the surest ways to confirm an identity, for communities as well as for individuals, is to find some way of measuring what one is *not*." By depicting Indians as demonic and savage, the colonists, like Prospero, were able to define more precisely what they perceived as the danger of becoming Calibanized.[42]

The Indians presented a frightening threat to the Puritan errand in America. "The wilderness through which we are passing to the Promised Land is all over fill'd with fiery flying serpents," warned the Puritan minister Cotton Mather in 1692. "Our Indian wars are not over yet." The wars were now within Puritan society and the self; the dangers were internal. Self-vigilance against sin was required, or else the English would become like Indians. "We have too far degenerated into Indian vices. The vices of the Indians are these: They are very lying wretches, and they are very lazy wretches; and they are out of measure indulgent unto their children; there is no family government among them. We have [become] shamefully Indianized in all those abominable things."[43]

To be "Indianized" meant to serve the Devil. Cotton Mather thought this had happened to Mercy Short, a young girl who had been a captive of the Indians and who was suffering from tormenting fits. According to Mather, Short had seen the Devil. "Hee was not of a Negro, but of a Tawney, or an Indian colour," she said; "he wore an high-crowned Hat, with straight Hair; and had one Cloven-foot." During a witchcraft trial, Mather reported, George Burroughs had lifted an extremely heavy object with the help to the Devil, who resembled an Indian. Puritan authorities hanged an Englishwoman for worshipping Indian "gods" and for taking the Indian devil-god Hobbamock for a husband. Significantly, the Devil was portrayed as dark-complected and Indian.[44]

For the Puritan, to become Indian was the ultimate horror, for they believed Indians were "in very great subjection" to the Devil, who "kept them in a continual slavish fear of him." Governor Bradford harshly condemned Thomas Morton and his fellow prodigals of the Merrymount settlement for their promiscuous partying with Indians: "They also set up a maypole, drinking and dancing about it many days together, inviting the Indian women for their consorts, dancing and frisking together like so many fairies." Interracial cavorting threatened to fracture a cultural and moral border—the frontier of Puritan identity. Congress of bodies, white and "tawney," signified defilement, a frightful boundlessness. If the Puritans were to become wayward like the Indians, it would mean that they had succumbed to savagery and failed to shrivel the sensuous parts of the self. To be "Indianized" meant to be de-civilized, to become wild men.[45]

But they could not allow this to happen, for they were embarking on an errand to transform the wilderness into civilization. "The whole earth is the Lord's garden and he hath given it to the sons of men [to] increase and multiply and replenish the earth and subdue it," asserted John Winthrop in 1629 as he prepared to sail for New England. "Why then should we stand starving here for the places of habitation . . . and in the meantime suffer a whole Continent as fruitful and convenient for the use of man to lie waste without any improvement."[46]

Actually, Indians had been farming the land, and this reality led to conflicts over resources. Within ten years after the arrival of Winthrop's group, twenty thousand more colonists came to New England. This growing English population had to be squeezed into a limited area of arable land. Less than twenty percent of New England was useful for agriculture, and the Indians had already established themselves on the prime lands. Consequently, the colonists often settled on or directly next to Indian communities. In the Connecticut Valley, for example, they erected towns such as Springfield (1636), Northhampton (1654), Hadley (1661), Deerfield (1673), and Northfield (1673) adjacent to the Indian agricultural clearings at Agawam, Norwottuck, Pocumtuck, and Squakheag.[47]

Over the years, the expansion of English settlement sometimes led to wars that literally made the land "vacant." During the Pequot War of 1637, some seven hundred Pequots were killed by the colonists and their Indian allies. Describing the massacre at Fort Mystic, an English officer wrote: "Many were burnt in the fort, both men, women, and children. . . . There were about four hundred souls in this fort, and not above five of them escaped out of our hands. Great and doleful was the bloody sight." Commander John Mason explained that God had pushed the

Pequots into a "fiery oven," "filling the place with dead bodies." By explaining their atrocities as divinely driven, the English were sharply inscribing the Indians as a race of devils. This was what happened during King Philip's War of 1675-1676. About a thousand English were killed during this conflict, and over six thousand Indians died from combat and disease. Altogether about half of the total Indian population had been destroyed in southern New England. Again, the colonists quickly justified their violence by demonizing their enemies. The Indians, Increase Mather observed, were "so *Devil driven* as to begin an unjust and bloody war upon the English, which issued in their speedy and utter extirpation from the face of God's earth." Cotton Mather explained that the war was a conflict between the devil and God: "The Devil decoyed those miserable savages [to New England] in hopes that the Gospel of the Lord Jesus Christ would never come here to destroy or disturb His *absolute empire* over them."[48]

Indians, "such people" of this "brave new world," to use Shakespeare's words, personified the devil and everything the Puritans feared—the body, sexuality, laziness, sin, and the loss of self-control. They had no place in a "new England." This was the view trumpeted by Edward Johnson in his *Wonder-Working Providence*. Where there had originally been "hideous Thickets" for wolves and bears, he proudly exclaimed in 1654, there were now streets "full of Girls and Boys sporting up and down, with a continued concourse of people." Initially, the colonists themselves had lived in "wigwams" like Indians, but now they had "orderly, fair, and well-built houses . . . together with Orchards filled with goodly fruit trees, and gardens with variety of flowers." The settlers had fought against the devil who had inhabited the bodies of the Indians, Johnson observed, and made it impossible for the soldiers to pierce them with their swords. But the English had violently triumphed. They had also expanded the market, making New England a center of production and trade. The settlers had turned "this Wilderness" into "a mart." Merchants from Holland, France, Spain, and Portugal were coming to it. "Thus," proclaimed Johnson, "hath the Lord been pleased to turn one of the most hideous, boundless, and unknown Wildernesses in the world in an instant . . . to a well-ordered Commonwealth."[49]

But all of these developments had already been acted out in *The Tempest*. Like Prospero, the English colonists had sailed to a new land, and like him, many of them felt they were exiles. They viewed the native peoples as savages, as Calibans. The strangers occupied the land, believing they were entitled to be "the lord on't."[50]

The English possessed tremendous power to define the places and peoples they were conquering. As they made their way westward, they developed an ideology of "savagery," which was given form and content by the political and economic circumstances of the specific sites of colonization. Initially, in Ireland, the English had viewed savagery as something cultural, or a matter of "consent." They assumed that the distance between themselves and the Irish, or between civilization and savagery, was quantitative rather than qualitative. The Irish as "other" were educable: They were capable of acquiring the traits of civilization. But later as colonization reached across the Atlantic and as the English encountered a new group of people, many of them believed that savagery for the Indians might be inherent. Perhaps the Indians might be different from the English in kind rather than degree; if so, then the native people of America might be incapable of improvement because of their race. To use Shakespeare's language, they might have a "nature" that "nurture" would never be able to "stick" to or change. Race or "descent" might be destiny.[51]

What happened in America in the actual encounters between the Indians and the English strangers was not uniform. In Virginia, Indian savagery was viewed largely as cultural: Indians were ignorant heathens. In New England, on the other hand, Indian savagery was racialized: Indians came to be condemned as a demonic race, their dark complexions signifying an indelible and inherent evil. Why was there such a difference between the two regions? Possibly the competition between the English and the Indians over resources was more intense in New England than in Virginia where there was more arable land. More important, the colonists in New England had brought with them a greater sense of religious mission than the Virginia settlers. For the Puritans, theirs was an "errand into the wilderness"—a mission to create what John Winthrop had proclaimed as "a city upon a hill" with the eyes of the world upon them. In this economic and cultural framework, a "discovery" occurred: the Indian other became a manifest devil. Thus savagery was racialized as the Indians were demonized, doomed to what Increase Mather called "utter extirpation." That process of cultural construction contributed to the making of a national identity.[52]

Over the centuries, the significance of this cultural construction of race grew even broader, more dynamic, and more inclusive. The play could harbor broader constructions, too, for Caliban's racial identity was ambiguous. Caliban could also have been African. "Freckled," dark-complected, a "thing of darkness," Caliban was the son of Sycorax, a witch who had lived in Africa. "Have we devils here?" declared Stephano in *The Tempest*. "Do you put tricks upon's with savages and men of Inde, ha?" As this reference to India suggests, Caliban could also have been Asian.[53]

Notes

1. William Shakespeare, *The Tempest,* ed. Louis B. Wright and Virginia A. Lamar (New York, 1971), 81. *The Tempest* has recently been swept into the storm over "political correctness." George Will issued a scathing attack on "left" scholars and their "perverse liberation" of literature, especially their interpretation of *The Tempest* as a reflection of "the imperialist rape of the Third World." Shakespeare specialist Stephen Greenblatt responded: "This is a curious example—since it is very difficult to argue

that *The Tempest* is *not* about imperialism." Such an authoritative counterstatement clears the way for a study of the play in relationship to its historical setting. See George Will, "Literary Politics: 'The Tempest'? It's 'really' about imperialism. Emily Dickinson's poetry? Masturbation," *Newsweek,* April 22, 1991, p. 72; and Stephen Greenblatt, "The Best Way to Kill Our Literary Inheritance Is to Turn It into a Decorous Celebration of the New World Order," *Chronicle of Higher Education,* June 12, 1991, pp. B1, B3. As Adam Begley has recently noted, Stanley Fish reminds us that "the circumstances of an utterance determine its meaning." See Adam Begley, "Souped-Up Scholar," *New York Times Magazine,* May 3, 1992, p. 52. The ideas on race and ethnicity presented in this article are further developed in Ronald Takaki, *A Different Mirror: A History of Multi-Cultural America* (Boston, forthcoming).

2. Winthrop Jordan, *White over Black: American Attitudes toward the Negro, 1550-1812* (Chapel Hill, 1968), 37-40. *Othello* was first performed in 1604, before the founding of Jamestown. Jordan overlooked the rich possibility of studying *The Tempest.*

3. Nicholas P. Canny, "The Ideology of English Colonization: From Ireland to America," *William and Mary Quarterly,* 30 (Oct. 1973), 585; David B. Quinn, *The Elizabethans and the Irish* (Ithaca, 1966), 161; Francis Jennings, *The Invasion of America: Indians, Colonialism, and the Cant of Conquest* (New York, 1976), 7. George Frederickson, *White Supremacy: A Comparative Study in American and South African History* (New York, 1971), 13, describes the conquest of Ireland as a "rehearsal."

4. Canny, "Ideology of English Colonization," 585, 588; Howard Mumford Jones, *O Strange New World: American Culture, the Formative Years* (New York, 1965), 169; Keith Thomas, *Man and the Natural World: A History of the Modern Sensibility* (New York, 1983), 42; Jennings, *Invasion of America,* 46, 49; James Muldoon, "The Indian as Irishman," *Essex Institute Historical Collections,* 111 (Oct. 1975), 269; Quinn, *Elizabethans and the Irish,* 76.

5. Muldoon, "Indian as Irishman," 284; Quinn, *Elizabethans and the Irish,* 108.

6. Canny, "Ideology of English Colonization," 593, 582; Jennings, *Invasion of America,* 153; Frederickson, *White Supremacy,* 15; Quinn, *Elizabethans and the Irish,* 132-33.

7. Canny, "Ideology of English Colonization," 582; Jennings, *Invasion of America,* 168; Quinn, *Elizabethans and the Irish,* 44.

8. Canny, "Ideology of English Colonization," 588; Jennings, *Invasion of America,* 46, 49; Quinn, *Elizabethans and the Irish,* 76; Shakespeare, *Tempest,* ed. Wright and Lamar, 70.

9. Quinn, *Elizabethans and the Irish,* 121; William Christie MacLeod, "Celt and Indian: Britain's Old World Frontier in Relation to the New," in *Beyond the Frontier: Social Process and Cultural Change,* ed. Paul Bohannan and Fred Plog (Garden City, 1967), 38-39; Jennings, *Invasion of America,* 312.

10. Quinn, *Elizabethans and the Irish,* 121; Muldoon, "Indian as Irishman," 270; MacLeod, "Celt and Indian," 26. See also Canny, "Ideology of English Colonization," 576.

11. Shakespeare, *Tempest,* ed. Wright and Lamar, 13, 81; Frank Kermode, "Introduction," in William Shakespeare. *The Tempest,* ed. Frank Kermode (London, 1969), xxvii; Robert R. Cawley, "Shakespeare's Use of the Voyagers in *The Tempest,*" *PMLA,* 41 (Sept. 1926), 699-700, 689; Frederickson, *White Supremacy,* 22; Shakespeare, *Tempest,* 13. See also Leo Marx, *The Machine in the Garden: Technology and the Pastoral Ideal in America* (New York, 1964), 34-75.

12. Shakespeare, *Tempest,* ed. Wright and Lamar, 27-28, 31; Cawley, "Shakespeare's Use of the Voyagers in *The Tempest,*" 702-4; Kirkpatrick Sale, *The Conquest of Paradise: Christopher Columbus and the Columbian Legacy* (New York, 1990), 102. For analysis of America imaged as a woman, see Carolyn Merchant, *Ecological Revolutions: Nature, Gender, and Science in New England* (Chapel Hill, 1989), 101; and Annette Kolodny. *The Lay of the Land Metaphor as Experience and History in American Life and Letters* (Chapel Hill, 1975).

13. Shakespeare, *Tempest,* ed. Wright and Lamar, xxxviii; Kermode, "Introduction," xxiv. For the anagram of Hamlet, see dedication to William Shakespeare at Kronborg Castle, Denmark.

14. Samuel Eliot Morison, ed., *Journals and Other Documents on the Life and Voyages of Christopher Columbus* (New York, 1963), 126; Sale, *Conquest of Paradise,* 126; Morison, ed., *Journals and Other Documents,* 238, 226-27.

15. Kenneth M. Morrison, *The Embattled Northeast: The Elusive Ideal of Alliance in Abenaki-Euramerican Relations* (Berkeley, 1984), 22-23; Leonard A. Adolf, "Squanto's Role in Pilgrim Diplomacy," *Ethnohistory,* 11 (Fall 1964), 247-48; Cawley, "Shakespeare's Use of the Voyagers in *The Tempest,*" 720, 721; Shakespeare, *Tempest,* ed. Wright and Lamar, 41, 40; Shakespeare, *Tempest,* ed. Kermode, 62.

16. William Bradford. *Of Plymouth Plantation: 1620-1647* (New York, 1967), 26; Frederickson, *White Supremacy,* 11; Roy Harvey Pearce, *Savagism and Civilization: A Study of the Indian and the American Mind* (Baltimore, 1967), 12; Colin G.

Calloway, ed., *Dawnland Encounters: Indians and Europeans in Northern New England* (Hanover, 1991), 33.

17. Shakespeare, *Tempest*, ed. Wright and Lamar, 70; Wilcomb Washburn, ed., *Indian and White Man* (New York, 1964), 4-5; Morrison, *Embattled Northeast*, 22-23. On the significance of the sword, see Riane Eisler, *The Chalice and the Blade: Our History, Our Future* (New York, 1988).

18. Shakespeare, *Tempest*, ed. Wright and Lamar, 85; Washburn, ed., *Indian and White Man*, 4, 5, 7.

19. Shakespeare, *Tempest*, ed. Wright and Lamar, 62, 18, 19.

20. Frederickson, *White Supremacy*, 9. The terms "descent" and "consent" are from Werner Sollors, *Beyond Ethnicity; Consent and Descent in American Culture* (New York, 1986), 6. Sollors minimizes the significance of race, arguing that it is "merely one aspect of ethnicity." Sollors, *Beyond Ethnicity*, 36. I take the opposite position here as well as in Ronald Takaki, "Reflections on Racial Patterns in America," in *From Different Shores: Perspectives on Race and Ethnicity in America*, ed. Ronald Takaki (New York, 1987), 26-38; and Ronald Takaki, *Iron Cages: Race and Culture in Nineteenth-Century America* (New York, 1979).

21. Sollors, *Beyond Ethnicity*, 36-37; Frederickson, *White Supremacy*, 8; Morison, ed., *Journals and Other Documents*, 92, 136; Shakespeare, *Tempest*, ed. Wright and Lamar, 57.

22. Shakespeare, *Tempest*, ed. Wright and Lamar, 19; Cawley, "Shakespeare's Use of the Voyagers in *The Tempest*," 715; Frederickson, *White Supremacy*, 12; Pearce, *Savagism and Civilization*, 9, 10.

23. James Axtell, *After Columbus: Essays in the Ethnohistory of Colonial North America* (New York, 1988), 190; Helen C. Rountree, *The Powhatan Indians of Virginia: Their Traditional Culture* (Norman, 1990), 44, 45, 46, 49, 60, 63.

24. Mortimer J. Adler, ed., *Annals of America*, vol. I: *Discovering a New World* (Chicago, 1968), 21, 26, 22.

25. Gary Nash. *Red, White, and Black: The Peoples of Early America* (Englewood Cliffs, 1974), 58; Adler, ed., *Annals of America*. 1, 26.

26. Cotton Mather, *Magnalia Christi Americana*, books I and II (Cambridge, 1977), 116; Frederickson, *White Supremacy*, 24; Sale, *Conquest of Paradise*. 277.

27. Jennings, *Invasion of America*, 66; Nash. *Red, White, and Black*, 57.

28. Merchant, *Ecological Revolutions*, 22; Shakespeare, *Tempest*, ed. Wright and Lamar, 29, 80, 52; Thomas More, *Utopia* (New Haven, 1964), 76; Thomas, *Man and the Natural World*, 42; Cawley, "Shakespeare's Use of the Voyagers in *The Tempest*," 715.

29. Jennings, *Invasion of America*, 78, 80; Sale, *Conquest of Paradise*, 295.

30. Nash, *Red, White, and Black*, 62, 63; Sale, *Conquest of Paradise*, 293, 294; Jennings, *Invasion of America*, 153.

31. Sollors, *Beyond Ethnicity*, 6, 36, 37.

32. Shakespeare, *Tempest*, ed. Wright and Lamar, 70, 15-16, 18, 19, 29, 50. For the location of Caliban's sty, see Shakespeare, *Tempest*, ed. Kermode, 63.

33. Howard S. Russell, *Indian New England before the Mayflower* (Hanover, 1980), 11; Adler, ed., *Annals of America*, 1, 39.

34. Eva L. Butler, "Algonkian Culture and the Use of Maize in Southern New England," *Bulletin of the Archeological Society of Connecticut* (no. 22, Dec. 1948), 6; Speck, "Penobscot Tales and Religious Beliefs," *Journal of American Folk-lore*, 48 (Jan.-March 1915), 75; Merchant, *Ecological Revolutions*, 72.

35. Russell, *Indian New England*, 10, 11, 166; Merchant, *Ecological Revolutions*, 80; Peter A. Thomas, "Contrastive Subsistence Strategies and Land Use as Factors for Understanding Indian-White Relations in New England," *Ethnohistory*, 23 (Winter 1976), 10; Roger Williams, *A Key into the Language of America* (Detroit, 1973), 170; Butler, "Algonkian Culture and the Use of Maize," 15, 17. For a study of the Abenakis as hunters, see Merchant, *Ecological Revolutions*, 29-68.

36. Johnson, *Wonder-working Providence*, 262; William Cronon, *Changes in the Land: Indians, Colonists, and the Ecology of New England* (New York, 1983), 55, 56; William Wood, *New England's Prospect*, ed. Alden T. Vaughn (Amherst, 1977), 96.

37. Alfred W. Crosby, "Virgin Soil Epidemics as a Factor in the Aboriginal Depopulation in America," *William and Mary Quarterly*, 33 (April 1976), 289; Dean R. Snow, "Abenaki Fur Trade in the Sixteenth Century," *Western Canadian Journal of Anthropology*, 6 (no. 1, 1976), 8; Merchant, *Ecological Revolutions*, 90.

38. Bradford, *Of Plymouth Plantation*, 270-71.

39. Roy Harvey Pearce, "The 'Ruines of Mankind': The Indian and the Puritan Mind," *Journal of the History of Ideas*, 13 (1952), 201; Peter Carroll, *Puritanism and the Wilderness: The Intellectual Significance of the Frontier, 1629-1700* (New York, 1969), 13; Johnson, *Wonder-working Providence*, 40.

40. Cronon, *Changes in the Land*, 90; Alfred W. Crosby, "God . . . Would Destroy Them, and Give Their Country to Another People," *American Heritage*, 29 (Oct./Nov. 1978), 40; Bradford, *Of Plymouth Plantation*, 65-66.

41. William S. Simmons, "Cultural Bias in the New England Puritans' Perception of Indians," *William and Mary Quarterly,* 38 (Jan. 1981), 70, 62.

42. Kai Erikson, *Wayward Puritans: A Study in the Sociology of Deviance* (New York, 1966), 13, 64. See also Pearce, *Savagism and Civilization,* 8.

43. Cotton Mather, *On Witchcraft: Being, the Wonders of the Invisible World* (New York, n.d.), 53. This treatise was originally published in 1692. Simmons, "Cultural Bias," 71.

44. Richard Slotkin, *Regeneration through Violence: The Mythology of the American Frontier, 1600-1860* (Middletown, 1973), 132, 142, 65.

45. Johnson, *Wonder-working Providence,* 263; Bradford, *Of Plymouth Plantation,* 205.

46. John Winthrop, *Winthrop Papers,* vol. II: *1623-1630* (Boston, 1931), 139.

47. Thomas, "Contrastive Subsistence Strategies and Land Use," 4.

48. Charles M. Segal and David C. Stineback, eds., *Puritans, Indians & Manifest Destiny* (New York, 1977), 136-37, 111; Sherburne F. Cook, "Interracial Warfare and Population Decline among the New England Indians," *Ethnohistory,* 20 (Winter 1973), 19-21; Simmons, "Cultural Bias," 67; Segal and Stineback, eds., *Puritans, Indians & Manifest Destiny,* 182.

49. Johnson, *Wonder-working Providence,* 71, 168, 211, 247-48; see Cronon, *Changes in the Land,* 166-67.

50. Shakespeare, *Tempest,* ed. Wright and Lamar, 76.

51. Shakespeare, *Tempest,* ed. Wright and Lamar, 70; Sollors, *Beyond Ethnicity,* 6-7, 36-37.

52. Perry Miller, in Miller, *Errand into the Wilderness* (New York, 1964), 1-15; John Winthrop, "A Model of Christian Charity," in Perry Miller, ed., *The American Puritans: Their Prose and Poetry* (New York, 1956), 79-84; Simmons, "Cultural Bias," 67. Miller's metaphor and theme originally came from Samuel Danforth's sermon, delivered on May 11, 1670, "A Brief Recognition of New England's Errand into the Wilderness."

53. Shakespeare, *Tempest,* ed. Wright and Lamar, 15, 41.

Margo Hendricks (essay date 1996)

SOURCE: "'Obscured by Dreams': Race, Empire, and Shakespeare's *A Midsummer Night's Dream,*" in *Shakespeare Quarterly,* Vol. 47, No. 1, Spring, 1996, pp. 37-60.

[*In the following essay, Hendricks examines Shakespeare's "figurative evocation" of India in* A Midsummer Night's Dream, *probing "the play's complicity in the racialist ideologies being created by early modern England's participation in imperialism."*]

> "There's no such thing as 'England' any more . . . welcome to India brothers!"[1]

In July 1991 I was engaged as a textual advisor for a production of *A Midsummer Night's Dream* performed by the Shakespeare Santa Cruz repertory company (hereafter SSC). In a camp rendering of Shakespeare's text, director Danny Scheie sought to illuminate what he viewed as the sexual politics of the text. Featuring a variety of pop-culture motifs (ranging from 1950s American teenage attire and behavior to Disney's *Snow White*), the production obstructed any possibility of seeing the play as merely a romantic idealization of courtly behavior (though it did reinforce the centrality of marriage as a solution to social discord). While segments of the production were noteworthy for their playful disruption of tradition (particularly in treating the young lovers), the production also exhibited disturbingly unexamined acceptance of some sexual and racial stereotypes in its treatment of Titania and Hippolyta. Knowing that a camp Titania and Hippolyta would prove crowd-pleasers, the director was untroubled by the implications for the construction of race and gender of casting a black male as Titania and costuming him in a pink tutu and pink wig, or presenting Hippolyta as a stereotypic Wagnerian Valkyrie (thick blond braids, horned helmet, spear, etc.).

The director made a more radical and problematic decision with the Indian boy. Whether the Indian boy appears onstage at all is generally of little consequence, since he has no lines and would function as little more than a stage prop, part of the spectacle of Oberon and Titania's first meeting in the play. The director of the SSC production, however, chose to have the Indian boy make an appearance.[2] Normally this choice would scarcely merit a review note, let alone an entire essay. Yet, like the directorial decisions behind the representations and interpretations of Hippolyta, Oberon, Titania, and Theseus, the appearance and casting of the Indian boy bore ideological significance worth examining. First, the director, in a break with both textual and theatrical tradition, cast an adult male as the changeling: the "boy" was in his early twenties, six feet tall, tanned, and naked except for a gold lamé loincloth. Second, in both the costume designer's drawings and on the stage, the Indian boy was culturally and racially marked: a turban (complete with feather), "Turkish" slippers, and jewelled dagger. The Indian boy appeared on the Santa Cruz stage as a veritable Sinbad, a rich oriental "trifle" accessible to the gaze of predominantly white audiences for six weeks.

At the end of its run, this postmodern production of Shakespeare's *A Midsummer Night's Dream* might have gone the way of other small-repertory-company productions of Shakespeare's comedy: the "part of the Indian boy played by" an inscription on the actor's résumé; favorable or unfavorable reviews; and, after strike, the cast and crew moving on to other endeavors. But this history was not to be. The following year, while teaching a class on gender and theater, I was asked by students who knew that I had worked on the production to arrange a screening of the videotape. The students had heard that it was a lively, funny, and brilliant interpretation of Shakespeare's play. As I watched the videotape of SSC's *A Midsummer Night's Dream*, I meditated on the image of the Indian boy: was anyone other than me troubled by the oriental fantasy created by the director's political production? Did any of my students comprehend the unmistakably racist denotations of the representation? More important, was this particular representation of the Indian boy a directorial whim, or was the director constrained by something in a centuries-old playtext which inhibited any other possible reading of the Indian boy?

The director's attempt to infiltrate Shakespeare's text and subvert the long history of its theatrical production, as well as his commitment to challenge audience expectations about casting, I would argue, worked to engender not a radical rewriting of Shakespeare's text but merely another supplemental history of it. For in the representation of the Indian boy (and, in a different way, the figure of Titania), directorial subversion was instrumental in reaffirming an aspect of orientalist ideology: like the odalisque who became a favorite topos of Impressionist painting, the Indian boy of SSC's production silently conjured the template of eroticism and exoticism adumbrated in the West's vision of India and the East.[3]

The SSC production of *A Midsummer Night's Dream* sought to offer what Leah Marcus calls a "localized" Shakespeare: an attempt "to create an edge of defamiliarization about what has become too well known, engineer a set of encounters between disparate cultural situations in order to open up ways for audiences to rediscover the plays at the point 'where remoteness and accessibility meet.'" That is, the production, in part novel and in part familiar, endeavored to reveal "the cultural otherness of what we thought we understood."[4] Yet, with contextualization, I want to offer an explanation as to why, in the SSC production, this "localizing" not only failed to "defamiliarize" but in fact colluded—and arguably could only collude—with an *a priori* racial ideology that imagines the Indian boy and what he signifies in early modern English culture.

The starting point for my reading of *A Midsummer Night's Dream* is a rudimentary query: what are we to make of the Indian boy? On the textual level the Indian boy is simply a plot device: he figures as the origin of the conflict between Oberon and Titania (a conflict that presumably begins in India). But why does he have to be Indian? Why not describe the boy as merely a changeling child? Or, if critical tradition is correct that all the fairies of *A Midsummer Night's Dream* are taken from English folklore, why not identify the changeling as the English boy? Obviously the dramatic structure and characterizations would not have been affected by such a change and, in fact, would have been made more definitively local. So once again it seems useful to ask: why does Shakespeare initially identify the child as "stol'n" from an "Indian king" and later expand on this identification with an elaborate narrative of the boy's maternal ethnic origins? Furthermore, what are we to make, culturally, of the fairies who fight for possession of him? Finally, what implications about race and early modern England's mercantilist and/or colonialist-imperialist ideology might we draw from Shakespeare's use of India?

Until recently explorations of early modern thinking about race meant recognizing early modern social discourse "to be about race . . . when it employs a category which [we are] able to identify as having a referent corresponding to that designated by [our] own understanding of the term 'race.'"[5] In other words, such works as *Othello, Titus Andronicus,* or *The White Devil,* with their inclusion of a "black" character as a pivotal figure in the dramatic narratives of white European societies, have been taken as definitive signposts of early modern representations of race and racist ideologies. But what if our inferences, our understandings, are inaccurate? What if, in attempting to sort out the significance of early modern English literature to a post-World War II global political economy, we have misread, or not read at all, some of the signs of racial thinking present in that literature? Is it possible that a too narrow definition misrepresents and engenders an under-reading of the complexity and ambiguity of the word *race* and of its social and cultural articulation in sixteenth-century England? To ask these and other critically imperative questions about the ideological implications of any Renaissance text is also to be concerned with how audiences (then and now) might construe the concept of race and its linguistic inflections.

In the whole of Shakespeare's dramatic canon the word *race* is employed only seventeen times, and generally it signifies genealogy. For example, in *2 Henry VI,* Suffolk tells Warwick

> Thy mother took into her blameful bed
> Some stern untutored churl, and noble stock
> Was graft with crab-tree slip—whose fruit thou art
> And never of the Nevilles' noble race.
>
> (3.2.212-15)[6]

We find the same signification when the word is used in *Richard III* ("Live, and beget a happy race of kings" [5.3.157]), *Antony and Cleopatra* ("Have I my pillow left unpressed in Rome, / Forborne the getting of a lawful race" [3.13.107-8]), and *Cymbeline* ("a valiant race" [5.4.83]). There are only three instances when *race* seems to connote something different. The first occurs in *Measure for Measure* when Angelo remarks "And now I give my sensual race the rein" (2.4.161), where he is clearly referring to his personality. The second takes place in *The Tempest* when Miranda says of Caliban "But thy vile race . . . had that in't which good natures / Could not abide to be with" (1.2.361-63), where *race* suggests type. And the third instance, somewhat ambiguous in its meaning, takes place in *Macbeth,* where Duncan's horses are called "the minions of their race. / Turned wild in nature" (2.4.15-16).[7]

In every usage there is a locus, an axis of determinism attendant upon a preconceived notion of fundamental distinctions, whether that locus is in a class-based concept of genealogy, in an essential nature, or in the ambiguity of ethnic typology. Race is envisioned as something fundamental, something immutable, knowable, and recognizable yet visible only when its boundaries are violated; thus race is also, paradoxically, mutable, illusory, and mysterious. Race is material (Duncan's horses) and immaterial (Angelo's nature). Race is language more than it is biology; yet without biology the language of race could not (and would not) exist.[8] Race is transmitted yet is viewed as essence. Race is ideology; race is ontology. Race is all this and nothing: a shaping fantasy.

It is this "shaping fantasy" in *A Midsummer Night's Dream,* a vision of race, which I intend to trace in my reading of Shakespeare's playtext. To begin with, I want to argue that literally and figuratively the playtext denotes cultural and temporal spaces that I shall refer to as "borderlands," spaces that are clearly marked for recognition. According to Gloria Anzaldúa, "Borderlands are physically present wherever two or more cultures edge each other, where people of different races occupy the same territory, where under, lower, middle and upper classes touch, where the space between two individuals shrinks with intimacy."[9] While the most obvious instances of this phenomenon in *A Midsummer Night's Dream* occur in the social interactions between humans and fairies, male and female, Athenian and Amazon, I believe a borderland also coalesces on an ideological level in the concept of race. This concept is neither wholly the older (and more feudal) idea based on class and lineage nor wholly the more modern idea based only on physical appearance (i.e., skin color, physiognomy). Rather, the idea of race in *A Midsummer Night's Dream* is an uneasy mixture—the miscegenation, if you will—of these two views. My argument is that the figurative evocation of Indian localizes Shakespeare's characterization of the fairies in *A Midsummer Night's Dream* and marks the play's complicity in the racialist ideologies being created by early modern England's participation in imperialism. Moreover, it is my contention that this racialist ideology is not unique to Shakespeare's playtext but endemic to most textual representations of India contemporary with it.

As a way of situating this hypothesis, I begin with the literary tradition behind Shakespeare's use of Oberon and this character's link with India, in particular the medieval romance *Huon of Bordeaux,* Edmund Spenser's *The Faerie Queene,* and Robert Greene's *Scottish Historie of James the fourth.* I then examine two sixteenth-century travel narratives about India. Both the medieval romance and the two travel narratives, I argue, ideologically and lexically imagine a geographic region that becomes such a commonplace that the mere mention of the word "India" is enough to conjure a particular image, one figured in terms of skin color, geography, sexuality, and religion, and which instantiates a cultural subtext in Shakespeare's portrayal of fairyland. The final sections of this essay explore the ideological significance of these images, Shakespeare's use of India, and the lexicon both presuppose. In ways similar to yet different from descriptions of the New World, early modern accounts of India are marked by an emerging taxonomy of gender and linguistic difference. It is not unusual for the writer of an English Renaissance narrative to digress from topographical, mercantile, or political description in order to address a culture's sexual practices and behavior, especially the actions of women. Furthermore, what is striking in such digressions is the intrusive presence of an emerging racial lexicon tied to physical appearance and hybridity. By drawing a link between this lexicon, travel narratives, and Shakespeare's Oberon/Titania/Indian boy/Bottom scenario, I want to highlight how dramatic invention intersects with lexical formulation in the reconceptualization of race. My argument, heuristically and philologically, endeavors to expand our understanding of the politics of race in early modern England. As Kim Hall suggests, modern concepts of "race are in large part the result of lingering notions of 'difference' that resided at the intersections of English travel and trade, plantation, empire, and science in the early modern period."[10]

I

Steven Mullaney has argued that a "map in the modern sense of the term is a guide to the present: a graphic index to the location of things in space, a traveler's aid which makes the passage from here to there less difficult."[11] *A Midsummer Night's Dream* might very well be considered a map of the sort Mullaney has described; in a number of its verbal and metaphoric expressions, the playtext offers a rather precise geographic index for identifying the location of spaces in the play. The comedy's action begins in Athens, moves to a wood outside the city (traditionally termed fairyland), and returns to Athens. One critic has argued, in a fine discussion of the anamorphic perspectives in *A Midsummer Night's Dream,* that the play compels us first to look straight on at Athens, then "shifts our perspective by obliging us to consider the forest, then brings Athens back in the third [perspective] and says, 'Look again'."[12] Yet the playtext's spatial layout is not so much a bipolar (Athens and Forest) as a tripolar configuration, with India sitting as the symbolic and ideological hub of departure and convergence for all the business of fairyland. That is, whatever exchange occurs, regardless of origin, is mediated through the discursive space that is India. Furthermore, "the routes of access" are "cultural and temporal as well as spatial."[13] It seems safe to assume that early modern audiences for *A Midsummer Night's Dream* came to the theater with a map for reading these local details of Shakespeare's dramatic world. The modern critic's dilemma is (and has been) how to reproduce that map so that its demarcations can be known more precisely.

Like a number of recent scholars, I have found extradramatic texts, travel narratives and medieval romances, useful in reading *A Midsummer Night's Dream* as Shakespeare's contribution to the literary invention of racial mapping.[14] I am not arguing that the play's audiences would have connected it directly to these texts. Rather, these works provide a means of recapturing a set of assumptions about India which were circulating in London at the time of the play's inscription, and with which Shakespeare's audiences could have been familiar. This familiarity did not necessarily require that all members of the audiences had read these narratives or even possessed the same degree of literacy.[15] For many Londoners knowledge of India (and Africa and the Americas) would have come orally, from seamen who served on the merchant and fighting ships traversing the Atlantic and Indian oceans.[16] These seamen were the most likely conduits for an image of India among those who could not read or, perhaps, afford to purchase the printed texts but who could afford to go to the theater.[17] In this manner the play's audiences might have been comprised not only of individuals acquainted with the medieval romance *Huon of Bordeaux*, Edmund Spenser's *Faerie Queene*, Robert Greene's *The Scottish Historie of James the fourth* (the literary sources for Shakespeare's depiction of Oberon), as well as manuscript and printed travel narratives, but also of people for whom India may have been the stuff of a sailor's tavern tale, a map made in the human imagination.

Let us begin to read our map of fairyland by turning to an index Shakespeare could have created for the lost traveler. Under the subject heading "Oberon," we might find the following citation: see Lord Berners, *Huon of Bordeaux*.[18] One of a number of medieval romances glorifying a culture no longer possible in late-sixteenth-century England, *Huon of Bordeaux* recounts the history of a young duke who unknowingly slays the son of Charlemagne and, for his crime, is sent to Babylon on a quest that Charlemagne believes will ensure Huon's death. Huon is told to return to Paris with a thousand bears, a thousand hawks, a thousand young men, and a thousand of Babylon's fairest maidens. He is also to bring Charlemagne a handful of the hairs and four of the teeth of Admiral Gaudys, Babylon's ruler. Huon's quest leads him to the East, where he meets Oberon, king of the fairies. Oberon, it turns out, is no ordinary fairy king, first, because he is mortal and, second, because his genealogy is notable. Oberon says that his father was Caesar (who was on his way to Thessally to wage war with Pompey when Oberon was begotten) and his mother "the lady of the privey Isle." Oberon, chronology notwithstanding, also claims as an older brother Neptanabus, king of Egypt, who is said to have "engendered Alexander the Great."[19]

Oberon explains that one fairy who was not invited along with the "many a prince and barons of the fair / and many a noble lady" to attend Oberon's birth delivered the following curse: though Oberon would be the "fairest creature that ever nature formed," at three years of age he would cease to grow.[20] After recounting his genealogy, Oberon informs Huon that he is also "king of Momur, the which is [about].iii. C. leagues from hence" (that is, from where they stand conversing, which is itself two days' ride from Jerusalem).[21] With Oberon's help, Huon successfully, though at times painfully, completes his quest and, in addition, wins the "fair" Esclarmonde. At the romance's conclusion Huon comes to Momur, where a dying Oberon, having called together all his subjects, including Arthur, Morgan le Fay, and Merlin (who in this narrative is Morgan le Fay's son), transfers the fairy kingship to Huon (despite Arthur's vigorous objections). Not only is Huon made king of the fairies, but he also takes up residence in Momur, which is "in the far-reaching district that was known to mediaeval writers under the generic name of India."[22]

Lord Berners's translation of this thirteenth-century *chanson de geste* went through at least three editions during the sixteenth century and, significantly, provided a source not only for Shakespeare but also for Edmund Spenser and Robert Greene.[23] The romance was also adapted in 1593 by the Earl of Essex's Men and performed, according to Henslowe, as "hewen of burdoche."[24] Though this playtext is lost to us, Spenser's and Greene's texts survive; in their depiction of Oberon, they continue the associations begun in *Huon of Bordeaux* of the fairy king with the East in general and India in particular.

Book 2 of Spenser's *Faerie Queene* is the only section of the poem where *Huon of Bordeaux's* imprint can be easily discerned, for included in the narrative of Sir Guyon's adventure is an account of his genealogy. Toward the end of canto 9, Spenser writes:

> Sir *Guyon* chaunst eke on another booke,
> That hight *Antiquitie* of *Faerie* lond,
> In which when as he greedily did looke,
> Th'offspring of Elues and Faries there he fond.[25]

Guyon's ancestry is derived from Elfe, the first man, created by Prometheus, and Elfe's union with "a goodly creature . . . whom he deemd in mind / To be no earthly wight" and names "*Fay*."[26]

As Sir Guyon continues to read, he discovers that "of these [Elfe and Fay] a mightie people shortly grew, / And puissaunt kings, which all the world warrayd / And to them selues all Nations did subdew." The first mention of India comes not with Oberon but with Elfin, whom Spenser describes as "him all *India* obayd, / And all that now *America* men call."[27] The genealogy ends with Oberon, son of Elficleos and the younger brother of Elferon. When Elferon dies, Oberon inherits the "scepter" and the "rich spoiles and famous victorie" with which his father had advanced the "crowne of *Faery*." And in his reign Oberon— "doubly supplide, in spousall, and dominion"—surpassed the achievement not only of his father but of his ancestor Elfin in establishing the Faeries' "power and glorie ouer all."[28]

Robert Greene's *The Scottish Historie of James the fourth, slaine at* Flodden. *Entermixed with a pleasant Comedie, presented by* Oboram *King of* Fayeries offers a more three-dimensional portrait of the fairy king and one a bit closer to that presented in *Huon of Bordeaux*. Though in some ways an ancillary figure in the drama (the presenter of "a pleasant Comedie"), Oberon comes to have a significant role in *The Scottish Historie of James the fourth*. He is the first character to appear onstage, and throughout the play he surfaces as Bohan's confidant and (to some degree) protector. Like his romance counterpart, Oberon is a catalyst for change, for transformation in the human world. He appears to Bohan ostensibly as an auditor of Bohan's storytelling, but as the play progresses, we recognize the fairy king as the symbolic intervention of fate in Bohan's affairs, rescuing Bohan from his despair and saving the life of Bohan's son.

Relevant here is not Oberon's role in the action of the play but what his representation signals. At the end of the first act, Oberon says,

> I tell thee Bohan, Oberon is king,
> Of quiet, pleasure, profit, and content,
> Of wealth, of honour, and of all the world,
> Tied to no place, yet all are tied to me.[29]

Despite his claim of being "tied to no place," Oberon does in fact tie himself to a specific locale. The dumb show Oberon paints for Bohan is marked by its Asiatic regionalism: the first scene depicts the defeat of Semiramis, "the proud Assirrian Queene," by Staurobates; the second treats of Cyrus's coronation and his death; and the third scene portrays the murder of Sefostris, a "potentate," by his "servants" (who, after slaying the king, continue to dine) at a banquet.

What is worth noting in these depictions of Oberon—in Spenser's brief genealogy, Greene's "pleasant Comedie," or the detailed narrative of *Huon of Bordeaux*—is the dense geographical umbra that stands at the imaginative center of the fairy king's literary history. Whether he appears in England, Scotland, or the outskirts of Jerusalem, Oberon enters each locale as an already "localized" (thus ethnic) entity. In other words, though all the world may be "tied" to Oberon while he claims to be "tied to no place," early modern writers insist that we recognize his claim as inaccurate, that we see him as clearly linked to the vast, undifferentiated region called India.[30]

By the time Shakespeare comes to write *A Midsummer Night's Dream*, images of an Asiatic or "Indian" Oberon are fairly well established as part of the literary imagining of the fairy king through the auspices of Spenser's and Greene's works. Undergoing something of a shift, however, was the *non*literary imagining of India. With the radical transformation of geographical knowledge produced by early modern mercantilism, Oberon's India gradually began to lose its quasi-mystical, quasi-mythical currency as a generic signifier of a distant imagined place and began to acquire a more precise delineation in terms of cultural and ethnic (or what we would call racial) taxonomies.[31] Though the mere mention of the word *India* still carried with it the figuration of an imaginative site of fabulous wealth, fantastic creatures, and other rarities in the English political consciousness, India also became representable as a real geographic and cultural space, capable of being partitioned, classified, conquered, and exploited. This transformation occurred through the early modern travel narrative.

II

The publication of travel narratives about India offered something of a corrective to the cultural mythology created by classical and medieval writers.[32] English (and other European) travelers no longer expected to find anthropophagi or Amazons in the East; these species now took up residence in the unexplored areas of Africa.[33] In addition, with the subdivision of the world into Old and New, and thus also an East and a West Indies, the ideological, literary, and cartographic topos of India had to be rewritten, had to be more precisely localized.[34] The "immense, unimaginable distance" adumbrated in medieval and classical accounts of India needed to be contained; and as ships set sail from England, Portugal, Spain, the Netherlands, France, and the Italian states, cartographers, soldiers, colonizers, and traders attempted, by producing more accurate demarcations of geographical space, to do just that.[35] Ultimately these inscriptions would set the stage for the modern ideology of race.

One narrative prototype for modern racial taxonomies is Richard Eden's *The History of Travayle in the West and East Indies, and other countreys lying eyther way, towardes the fruitfull and ryche Moluccaes*.[36] Eden's work contains a translation of Lewes Vertomannus's account of his travels in India. The text is meant to provide the reader with knowledge of the politics, customs, social relations, and physical appearance of the peoples of India, along with information about India's topography. Interwoven with Vertomannus's narrative is a familiar (to our way of thinking) polarization of racial differences, with Europe at one end of the spectrum and Africa at the other. Vertomannus begins by declaring his intent to convey an impression of "the fruitfulness and plentifulnesse" of India.[37] His text is replete with descriptions of the regional rulers' wealth and state. "Marvelous rich" becomes a refrain, as does the minute detailing of a ruler's household: the sultan of Cambia "progresses" through all of India, taking with him "four thousand tents and pavillions, also his wife, children, concubines, slaves, four or five of the most courageous horses, monkeys, parrots, leopards, hawks." Of the king of Narsinga, Vertomannus writes that his "horse with the furniture [i.e., trappings] is esteemed to bee worth as muche as one of our cities, by reason of innumerable jewelles of great price."[38] It is, however, in Vertomannus's description of the physical appearances of Indians that he employs the color-coded grid of what I will label modern racial distinctions. For example, he describes the people of Melacha as being of "blackish ashe colour. Their apparell is like to the Mahumetans of the citie Memphis. . . . They have very large foreheads, round eyes, and flatte noses." Of the people of Pego, he writes that the "inhabitants . . . are like unto them of Tarnassari [another Indian city] but of whiter color, as in a colder region, somewhat like unto ours." In general, however, the people he meets are reported to be "of weasel colour, enclining to blacknesse, as are the most part of these Indians, being in manner scorched with heate of the Sunne."[39]

The physical appearance and wealth of the Indians are not the only matters subject to scrutiny. India's inhabitants, like those of Africa and Europe, profess a variety of religions and include Christians, Jews, and Muslims as well as what Vertomannus and others call "Gentiles," that is, Hindus and Buddhists. And, somewhat surprisingly, given the internecine struggles of early modern Christian Europe over dogma, Vertomannus often discusses these belief systems with considerable detachment. In the course of relating the cultural and religious behavior of India's peoples, the writer reveals a Eurocentric bias when describing those practices that deal specifically with gender relations. It is here, in that most contested of ideological spaces, that the early modern European traveler develops the racial denotations that later become familiar images not only of India but also of Africa and the Americas.

In the account of his visit to Calcutta, Vertomannus describes what he perceives as an extraordinarily peculiar custom: the king's wife is deflowered by the "Archbishop," though Vertomannus claims that "only the king of Calecut keepeth this custom." As we read through Vertomannus's text, however, we discover that this practice occurs in the city of Tarnassarie as well, with one significant difference; instead of the king's wife being given to "the priests to be deflowered," she is given to a "white man, as to the Christians or Mahumetans, for he will not suffer the Idolaters to do this. The inhabitantes likewise have not to do carnally with their wives, before some white man, of what so ever nation, have first the breaking of them."[40]

This deviation from marital norms, as Vertomannus sees it, is not limited to the rulers of Indian cities but, on the contrary, is found at nearly every level of society. Among the gentlemen and merchants, to exchange wives is seen as a matter of courtesy and friendship. Even so, Indian women are judged to have more freedom than their European counterparts. Vertomannus says that it is not uncommon for a woman to be "married to seven husbands, of the which every of them hath his night by course appointed to lye with her: And when she hath brought forth a childe, she may give it or father it to whiche of them she listeth: Who may in no case refuse it."[41] The idea of such sexual freedom among women, of course, violated nearly every ideological code of the European traveler, and the early modern European travel narrative became the space where sexual freedom could be simultaneously presented and condemned. For instance, the Dutch traveler Jan van Linschoten reports that it is common for "the women slaves . . . [to] slip into some shoppe or corner . . . where their lovers meet them, and there in hast they have a sport, which done they leave each other: and if she chance to have a Portingal or a white man to her lover, she is so proud, that she thinketh no woman comparable unto her." Van Linschoten, unlike Vertomannus, elides all religious, ethnic, and class differences among the women of India to generalize that they "are verie luxurious [i.e., lecherous] and unchaste, for there are very few among them, although they bee married, but they have besides their husbands one or two of those that are called souldiers, with whome they take their pleasures."[42]

The narrative and geopolitical mapping produced by early modern travelers to India was not just a cartographic re-imagining of the world but an ethnographic interpretation of it. As part of the circulation of ethnographic taxonomies, maps were often reproduced in printed texts. In creating these maps and narratives, early modern travelers envisioned themselves as meaningful contributors to a new, global epistemology. More important, the narratives seemed authentic and accurate because the writers had visited the place described, had studied the indigenous peoples and their societies, and had published their findings in a written form that carried no taint of the "poetic."

Because the observer's status as a reliable informant is reified by this discursive strategy, even his reiteration of a medieval or classical fable acquires a veneer of authenticity. Hence, contrary to the writer's expressed aim, the narratives produce what might be termed a "'poetics of displacement'"; that is, cultural imagery which simultaneously defines Asia, Africa, and the Americas in terms an early modern European could comprehend and offers new metaphorical terrains for the construction of difference.[43] In effect, the written and oral narratives circulating in sixteenth-century England reproduced images of India as a region of "such treasure and rich Merchandize, as none other place of the whole world can afford,"[44] even as they constituted it ideologically as a site of gender, ethnic, religious, and political differences.

The India of early modern English narratives is, as Thomas Hahn has argued, an "'imaginative reality'": a place where "explorers . . . and their field of vision [were] framed by the imaginary [i.e., literary] landscape as much as by the real."[45] The poetic cartography of *A Midsummer Night's Dream* is a familiar one if we know how to read it. Like Africa and the Americas, India is a world where an Amazon and a fairy king can be lovers; a place where the visible signs of difference between Europeans and Indians can be remarked and similarities unacknowledged; a site where exoticism and difference are as conventional as trade and commodities—a place fit for exploration and exploitation. This is the India of *Huon of Bordeaux* and of the English Jesuit who, when "tolde that he could not want a living in the towne, as also that the Jesuites could not keepe him there without he were willing to stay," chose to reject the "Cloister, and opened shoppe, where he had good store of worke: and in the end married a Mestizos daughter of the towne, so that he made his account to stay there while he lived."[46] This is the India of Shakespeare's changeling boy.

III

At the beginning of Act 2, Puck informs one of the queen's fairies (and the audience) that Titania has a "lovely boy," allegedly the "stol'n" son of an "Indian king," whom Oberon desires to be a "Knight of his train, to trace the forests wild" (2.1.25). On a textual level Puck has little reason to establish the boy's identity beyond distinguishing him as a source of tension between the fairy queen and king; as I suggested earlier, the play's dramatic structure would not have been violated had this information been omitted or had Shakespeare identified the child as an English boy. Similarly, if the fairies are to be seen as English, there is no obvious reason for Shakespeare to specify India as Oberon's most recent place of resort. Titania demands,

> Why art thou here,
> Come from the farthest step of India,—
> But that, forsooth, the bouncing Amazon,
> Your buskined mistress and your warrior love,
> To Theseus must be wedded. . . .
>
> (2.1.68-72)

Though Titania answers her own question—"Why art thou here"—her words do not entirely explain Shakespeare's invocation of India.

Oberon is, of course, explicitly connected with India in the literary tradition from which Shakespeare draws. However, this explanation does not help us to address the query—why an Indian boy?—posed at the beginning of this essay. Perhaps another way to get at an answer is to examine Shakespeare's characterization in terms of his use of the lexicon engendered by early modern English mercantile activity in India. In this way we can make intelligible India's function as the center of linguistic and ideological exchanges between Athens and fairyland. Like Athens, India is an actual geographic place, and, like fairyland, it is still figured as a place of the imagination. This simultaneity permits the articulation of a racial fantasy in *A Midsummer Night's Dream* where Amazons and fairies signify an alien yet domestic paradox in an otherwise stable, homogeneous world.

When Titania offers Oberon the reason for her resistance to his wishes, in a poignant (and poetic) vision of female and mercantile fecundity, this vision is, in effect, a mapping of this reality:

> His mother was a votress of my order,
> And in the spicèd Indian air by night
> Full often hath she gossiped by my side . . .
> Marking th'embarkèd traders on the flood,
> When we have laughed to see the sails conceive
> And grow big-bellied with the wanton wind;
> Which she, with pretty and with swimming gait
> Following (her womb then rich with my young squire),
> Would imitate, and sail upon the land
> To fetch me trifles, and return again
> As from a voyage, rich with merchandise.
> But she, being mortal, of that boy did die,
> And for her sake do I rear up her boy;
> And for her sake I will not part with him.
>
> (2.1.123-37)

Titania's words in this scene vividly reproduce the idealized imagery in the writings of travelers to India. The votaress embodies what India could (and would) represent to Europe as, like the merchant ships, she returns "from a voyage, rich with merchandise," to bring Titania the exotic "trifles" of an unfamiliar world.[47]

Her speech "rich" with the language of English mercantilism, Titania evokes not only the exotic presence of the Indian woman's native land but also the power of the "traders" to invade and domesticate India and, aided by the "wanton wind," return to Europe "rich with merchandise." In Shakespeare's "poetic geography," India becomes the commodified space of a racialized feminine eroticism that (to judge by the written accounts of such men as Vertomannus and van Linschoten) paradoxically excited and threatened the masculinity of European travelers. This racial subtext, which complicates the "shaping fantasy" of *A Midsummer Night's Dream,* is not obvious when Titania and Oberon first appear onstage. Their initial exchange is accusatory and fraught with erotic tension that masks their far greater conflict.

In response to Titania calling Hippolyta his "buskined mistress and warrior love," Oberon retorts: "How canst thou thus, for shame, Titania, / Glance at my credit with Hippolyta, / Knowing I know thy love to Theseus?" (2.1.74-76). Oberon then lists the women Theseus has seduced and abandoned, apparently with Titania's aid.[48] Titania casually dismisses Oberon's accusation: "these are the forgeries of jealousy" (l. 81). The audience soon discovers what is really at the core of Titania's and Oberon's estrangement: she has refused to give him the child of her votaress, the "little changeling boy." As the text presents it, Titania's interest in the boy is sentimental, linked to her relationship with his mother and the promise the fairy queen made. Oberon's interest, on the other hand, is textually much more ambiguous. In fact, if both he and Puck are to be taken at their word, Oberon's interest in the Indian boy is primarily one of dominion: possession is linked to Oberon's political authority.

From the beginning both Oberon and Puck make clear that Oberon desires to have the boy as a "henchman" or "Knight of his train." Furthermore, Oberon's desire for the boy seems very much connected to desire for dominion over Titania. Hence I am inclined to view Oberon's quest for the boy less as the embodiment of fatherly love or pride than as the manifestation of a perceived prerogative to claim possession—to have "all . . . tied to" him. The paternal interest that many critics argue lies at the heart of Oberon's desire is not evident in his words.[49] One finds in his exercise of paternalism the very ideology that made it "the smart thing for titled and propertied families in England to have a black slave or two among the household servants."⁵⁰ Like the growing number of non-European (particularly African) children who were imported into England to serve as badges of status for England's aristocracy, the "changeling boy" is desired as an exotic emblem of Oberon's worldly authority. Oberon's desire to claim the Indian boy as his servant should not be trivialized; in another century or so Asian Indians would become the household fashion.

But why the insistence on possession of the Indian boy? Dramatically, both Oberon's and Titania's obduracy is crucial to the plot structure but not dependent on the changeling's being Indian. The answer is to be found in Shakespeare's rewriting of the figure of Oberon and in the larger problem that *A Midsummer Night's Dream* explores in some detail: gender relations. And, as we shall see, a changeling is not always a mere changeling.

The idea of change (or transformation) is central to the dramatic plot and to the specific resolution of the dissension between Oberon and Titania. In order to dissolve the stalemate, Oberon must produce willingness in Titania to "amend" their "debate"; that is, he must persuade her to change her mind about giving up the Indian boy. The flower, "love-in-idleness," itself a product of change, enables Oberon to achieve his desire—the changeling child. The curious thing about this situation, and one worth exploring, is why Oberon feels it necessary to provide Nick Bottom as a substitute for the Indian boy.⁵¹ Luce Irigaray suggests that men "make commerce *of* [women] . . . , but they do not enter into any exchanges *with* them," largely because "the economy of exchange—of desire—is man's business."⁵² Because there is no other male of equal rank and power with whom Oberon can negotiate an exchange, and because the object he desires is not a wife but a page, he is forced to rewrite the rules governing this "economy of exchange" so that a direct transaction with Titania can take place. Importantly, the objects of exchange must be equivalents, and thus Oberon must provide a changeling for a changeling.

When Nick Bottom reappears from the brake, his head transformed into that of an ass, Snout declares, "O Bottom, thou art changed. What do I see on thee?" (3.1.96). Peter Quince considers Bottom "monstrous" and later declares that Bottom has been "translated" (11. 86, 98). Puck's alteration of Bottom enacts a familiar literary emblem.⁵³ Bottom, intriguingly, is "translated" into neither centaur nor satyr; it is not his body that is altered but his head: "An ass's nole I fixèd on his head" (3.2.17). The alien(ness) Bottom represents is a mixture of the familiar and the foreign; with the exception of his head, Nick Bottom remains distinctly human. What is striking about Puck's trick and Oberon's exploitation of it is not only that it violates the sociocultural endogamy—the commerce that upholds patriarchal traffic in women—but that, in the substitution of the "translated" Nick Bottom for the Indian boy as the other male in the triangular relationship of desire, it irrevocably redefines both sexual and racial parameters in fairyland.

While the boy changeling may be viewed as the object of maternal affection, the adult changeling clearly invokes a different response in the fairy queen. In Titania's bower, Bottom, though subject to the fairy queen, clearly is not perceived as a mere child. On the contrary, as Titania's behavior indicates, Bottom becomes a substitute for Oberon as well. By employing Bottom as the erotic trap that permits him to "steal the boy," Oberon finds himself ensnared by the "hateful imperfection" of monstrous humanity that he has engendered: "For, meeting her of late behind the wood / Seeking sweet favours for this hateful fool, / I did upbraid her and fall out with her" (4.1.60, 45-47). For Oberon, who is initially pleased with Puck's prank, the "sweet sight" (1. 43) of Titania embracing a "translated" Bottom in her bower eventually loses its charm. Once central to Titania's erotic desires, Oberon finds himself displaced twice: first by a changeling and then, in Bottom, by a monstrous "changeling" to boot. And while Oberon may now possess the Indian boy, it appears that the new changeling has become for the fairy king more than the "fierce vexation of a dream" (1. 66).

Change, rather than dreams, is the defining trope of *A Midsummer Night's Dream*. Whether in the changed story of the lovers Apollo and Daphne or in the "little western flower," in Lysander's drug-induced change or in Hippolyta's weariness with the moon—"Would he would change!" (5.1.238)—change generates not something unintelligible and fundamentally alien but something that, because of its composition, is (paradoxically) differently the same. In effect, what is constituted is the hybrid. Even so, Hippolyta's moon, Hermia's Lysander, and the "little western flower" remain intelligible to all as moon, man, and flower despite their transformation. The change that Bottom and the Indian boy literally and symbolically register, on the other hand, is of a more particularized form—it is an ethnic (or racial) change that involves the forcible removal of a person from one culture to another and, in the case of Bottom, a change that produces a phenotypical transformation as well. And, not surprisingly, the ease with which change is accommodated, even accepted, produces general anxiety within fairyland.

At the center of this trope of change is a concept linked to the Spanish term *mestizaje*, or mixedness. The *Diccionario de Uso del Español* defines *mestizaje* as the "*cruzamiento de razas*" (crossbreeding of races) or the "*conjunto de mestizos*" (group of mestizos) and relates it to the verb *mestizar*, defined as "*adulterar la puerza de una raza por el cruce con otras*" (adulterating the purity of one race by mixing with others).⁵⁴ Both Bottom and the changeling child exemplify this hybrid state: in Bottom we see the *cruzamiento* of two species—human and equine (literally, the *mulatto*)—and in the Indian boy the possibility of human and fairy mixedness (the *mestizo*).

It is, of course, critically problematic to label Bottom and the Indian boy in the terms of a racial lexicon that is not employed in Shakespeare's play. Yet I believe such a move is both theoretically and heuristically appropriate given

Shakespeare's own framing of fairyland as a borderland between India and Athens. In this space, through his "translation" and incorporation into fairyland, Bottom becomes the figurative and literal instantiation of that newly engendered lexical hybrid, the *mulatto*. Similarly, while the Indian boy's enigmatic textual history must forever occlude the "facts" of his genesis (is Puck right when he declares the boy's father to be an Indian king, or is this merely one more of the mischievous sprite's fabrications?), Titania's narrative of the Indian boy's origins and her own behavior are so symptomatic of the accounts of Indian women by the travelers van Linschoten and Vertomannus that it is worthwhile linking these representations to the emerging linguistic taxonomy of cultural difference. Shakespeare's use of India calls attention to this parallel discourse; and if we look closely at its lexical and taxonomic matrices, we can shed light on the way race works in *A Midsummer Night's Dream*. As we shall see, the conflicting terrain of fairyland, with its easy violation of borders—both speciegraphical and geographical—adumbrates an ontological engagement with the linguistic complexities of *mestizaje*.

IV

Etymologically, *mestizaje*, *mestizo*, and *mestiço* trace their origins to the Latin *miscere*, as does the word miscegenation (*miscere* = to mix and *genus* = kind, sort, type). *Mulatto*, on the other hand, originates in the Latin word *mulus*, which describes the offspring born of an ass and a mare. Even so, *mulatto*'s semantic genealogy includes *miscere*, for what produces the offspring is the mixing of what are perceived to be two different species or kinds. *Changeling*, unlike *mestizo*, *mestiço*, or *mulatto*, only indirectly traces its lexical and semantic genealogy to the Latin *miscere*.[55] *Changeling*'s etymology originates in the Latin *mutare*, yet its semantic instantiations suggest a closer kinship to *miscere* and *translatio*.[56]

The lexicon of *mestizaje* was used politically and culturally to describe the offspring of a union between European males and non-European females (though with different configurations based on geography): the Spanish term *mestizola* referred principally to the offspring of Spanish men and American Indian women; *mestiço/a* described the offspring of Portuguese men and African or Asian Indian or American Indian women;[57] and *mulatto/a* identified the offspring of Spanish men and African women.[58] This racializing lexicon entered the English language largely via translations of Spanish and Portuguese travel narratives, though not until Richard Perceval and John Minsheu compiled their bilingual dictionaries was this lexicon codified as part of the English language.[59] Familiar modes of categorizing people (according to class or nationality) were no longer useful in the new world that European imperialism was beginning to create—a world suddenly comprised of hybrids, *mestizos*, and *mulattos*. Hence the appropriation of such words as *race*, *mestizo*, *mestiço*, and *mulatto* allowed the English to fill a cultural and lexical gap opened by the inadequacy of more familiar terms such as *changeling*.[60]

Predictably, what the new hybridity produced was not an orderly taxonomy but rather a state of lexical and cultural instability, mutability, and permeability. The Indian boy and the transformed Nick Bottom signal a new variant on the notion of race, a variant that silently but insistently calls attention to the details of its sociohistorical genesis. And while I would not insist that Shakespeare drew faithfully on the accounts of *mestizaje* in such narratives as those of Vertomannus or van Linschoten, I would point to the parallels between Shakespeare's account of the Indian boy's lineage and, for example, Vertomannus's terse report on the "deflowering" of the king of Calcutta's wife. Similarly, we find an analogy between Titania's refusal to give the Indian boy to Oberon and the obdurate Indian woman, who takes "pleasure in carrying [her *mestiço* child]. . . abroad . . . [and who] by no meanes will give it to the father, unlesse it should be secretly stollen from her, and so conveyed away."[61] Titania's unwillingness to give the boy to Oberon ("Set your heart at rest. / The fairy land buys not the child of me" [2.1.122]) may therefore be more than an example of maternal feelings; it may also echo the Indian woman's challenge to Eurocentric, patriarchal assumptions about control of the female body and about that body's ability to destabilize the idea of marking race solely through paternity. Generated in the face of such instability is an anxiety (exemplified in the behavior of both Oberon and the Europeans) about how best to handle such situations.[62] If we accept Nick Bottom in his "translated" state as emblematic of the *mulatto* and the Indian boy as emblematic of the *mestiço* child engendered in the deflowering of the king of Calcutta's wife, Oberon's vexation at the "sweet sight" of the *mulatto* in Titania's bower (and his earlier vexation with Titania's fondness for the *mestizo*) resonates with the European's growing anxiety about the definition of race in the borderlands.

The displacement of the changeling child and the substitution of the adult changeling foreground the problem of unregulated female sexuality and its effect on the existing concept of race. Nick Bottom might then signify a return to Irigaray's notion of "sociocultural endogamy," the other adult male in the "economy of desire," one who introduces an unexpected dimension into the equation. Just as the sexual relations of the Indian women expose as illusory the European notion of race within the borders of early modern India, so Oberon's knowledge of Titania taking pleasure in the transformed Bottom calls into question the possibility of sustaining absolute categories of difference. Oberon and his European counterpart each discover the general limits of patriarchal power and the specificity of his own fallibility. What we witness in India and fairyland is the fragmentation of patriarchal ideologies denoting race because women's erotic desires can displace and dispel the sexual continuum upon which race is constituted. It is for this reason that I find less than satisfactory the argument that "Fairy Land is an offstage kingdom, geographically and politically independent of any human territory."[63] Because fairyland is linked to India, a space of *mestizaje*, it sounds the discordant notes of shifting racial definitions even as it adumbrates a potential solution to the problems engendered by *mestizaje*. Furthermore, it is precisely because India has become the site where the concept of race (aristocratic genealogy) can easily be destabilized that race must be rewritten in order to posit an ideology capable of handling the superficial differences between Indians and Europeans.

The resolution, therefore, is not the eradication of the concept of race but its reformulation. The "new" idea of race, and its concomitant lexicon, must begin to reflect this possibility (*mestizaje*) and to contain it. Such containment is achieved, however, not by abandoning the imperial project but by redefining its lexical and ideological taxonomies when dealing with indigenous peoples. As we see in the descriptions offered by Vertomannus, van Linschoten, and others, the imperial project necessitates an essentialism (a "nature") that increasingly is linked to external appearance, in particular to skin color. Thus the image of the dark-skinned savage, the licentious and barbarous non-European, became the norm, instilling a sense of revulsion among Europeans for the sexual behavior that produces *mestizaje*. In words different from yet similar to those of the European travelers, Oberon insists that Titania look on the hybrid Bottom and abhor the image and reality of what she has hitherto embraced. Ironically, *this* changeling's genesis (or paternity) derives from Oberon, and Titania's relationship with the changeling therefore potentially violates two social taboos, incest and miscegenation—the former symbolically and the latter literally. Oberon's dilemma is resolved, even if temporarily, by the restoration of Bottom to his human appearance. The fact that Bottom and the Indian boy are the catalysts for a state of *mestizaje* in fairyland cannot be erased.

When viewed in the shifting context of early modern England's discourse of race, Oberon's "pity" may be tinged with a more complex emotion, as, in the moment of his victory, he discovers himself supplanted not only by a racially ambiguous male but by one of his own making. Though Bottom's expulsion from fairyland, as well as the Indian boy's expulsion from Titania's bower, may alleviate Oberon's vexation, it does not dispel the racial quandary their existence engenders. While Nick Bottom's return to both his human state and to Athens enacts the restoration of a class and gender hierarchy, it also leaves behind a new vision of a racial landscape, a "new world" where the image of humanity is not the European but a changeling—the *mestizola, mestiçola, mulattola*. More importantly, Shakespeare's two changelings in *A Midsummer Night's Dream* are haunted by the ghostly presence of the historical condition of *mestizaje* which occasions both Shakespeare's dramatic representation of Indian and the modern Western notion of race.

V

My analysis has suggested that Shakespeare's comedy continues the racial discourses constituted by travel narratives that represented India as a "territory to be conquered and occupied," displaying its people as "rich trifles" to sate the European appetite for exotic novelty.[64] At the same time, *A Midsummer Night's Dream* constitutes race as an ideological fissure, producing a problematic dichotomy between race as genealogy and race as ethnicity or physical appearance.

It is this fissure, only recently visible to political criticism, that the director of the SSC production of *A Midsummer Night's Dream* failed to discern in his interpretation of the playtext.[65] Indeed, productions of the play become trapped in a historical conundrum whenever there is a decision to cast the Indian boy and put him onstage. The director (and, by extension, the play's readers) cannot avoid the culturally predetermined orientalism built into Shakespeare's geographic allusion. Furthermore, given the cultural role played by Shakespeare's canon in modern English imperialism, the SSC director's decision becomes even more problematic precisely because the Indian boy's presence on the modern stage engenders a localized reading where past and present historical discourses occasionally merge but more often collide. Shakespeare's evocation of India marks an ideological space where the colonizing impulse imposes a mode of representation suitable to the dynamics of an imperial project. Until directors, actors, textual advisors, and scholars begin not only to rethink their assumptions about the ideological purpose of Shakespeare's Indian boy but also to acknowledge the complex and varied images of race in Shakespeare's play, productions of *A Midsummer Night's Dream* may be destined to rehearse endlessly a racial fantasy engendered as part of imperialist ideology: the fantasy of a silent, accepting native who neither speaks nor resists.

The Indian boy is the most silenced of the play's characters, never given words to express his desires, his self-perception. What if he, rather than Puck, had been given the final word: what would the changeling child have said? What if, after four hundred years, his voice were restored to him? What would he say to the hybrid Bottom? Would the Indian boy declare, as a young white reggae fan in Birmingham, England, did, that

> there's no such thing as "England" any more . . . welcome to India brothers! This is the Caribbean! . . . Nigeria! . . . There is no England, man. This is what is coming. Balsall Heath is the center of the melting pot, 'cos all I ever see when I go out is half-Arab, half-Pakistani, half-Jamaican, half-Scottish, half-Irish. I know 'cos I am [half Scottish/half Irish]. . . who am I? . . . Tell me who I belong to? They criticize me, the good old England. Alright, where do I belong? You know, I was brought up with blacks, Pakistanis, Africans, Asians, everything, you name it . . . who do I belong to? . . . I'm just a broad person. The earth is mine . . . you know we was not born in Jamaica . . . we was not born in "England." We were born here, man. It's our right. That's the way I see it. That's the way I deal with it.[66]

Somehow, giving our silent *mestizo* the voice of another *mestizo*, rather than that of an academic like myself, seems fitting. The words of this half-Scottish/half-Irish changeling stand as a vivid reminder that it was in the "antique fables," the "fairy toys" produced in the colonizing dreams of Europeans, that the "shaping fantasies" of modern imperialism began. These words are a reminder that it will be the *mestizos*—the racialized descendants of those who framed the lexicon and practices of modern imperialism—who, dealing with it, will write the final epilogue to the shaping fantasy of race.

Notes

1. Quoted in Akhil Gupta and James Ferguson, "Beyond 'Culture': Space, Identity, and the Politics of Difference," *Cultural Anthropology* 7 (1992): 6-23, esp. 10.

2. The Indian boy appears in a 1906 film version of the play, in Max Reinhardt's classic 1935 film, in two BBC video productions, and in the New York Shakespeare Festival's video production. In nearly all of these productions, the character's costume signifies ethnicity. Additionally, in the New York Shakespeare Festival's production a black actor plays the boy. Illustrations and paintings of Act 1, scene 2, also are eclectic when it comes to representing the Indian boy; for example, Fuseli includes the child while Boydell does not.

3. See Edward Said, *Orientalism* (New York: Random House, 1979). For a cogent engagement with Said's work, see Lisa Lowe, *Critical Terrains: French and British Orientalisms* (Ithaca, NY, and London: Cornell UP, 1991).

4. Leah S. Marcus, *Puzzling Shakespeare: Local Reading and Its Discontents* (Berkeley, Los Angeles, and London: U of California P, 1988), 40.

5. Frank Reeves, *British racial discourse: A study of British political discourse about race and race-related matters* (Cambridge: Cambridge UP, 1983), 8. Much work has been done, from a cultural-studies perspective, on theorizing race. Some of the best studies include: Kwame Anthony Appiah, *In My Father's House: Africa in the Philosophy of Culture* (New York and Oxford: Oxford UP, 1992); David Theo Goldberg, *Racist Culture: Philosophy and the Politics of Meaning* (Oxford: Blackwell, 1993); *The "Racial" Economy of Science: Toward a Democratic Future*, Sandra Harding, ed. (Bloomington and Indianapolis: Indiana UP, 1993); Donna Haraway, *Primate Visions: Gender, Race, and Nature in the World of Modern Science* (New York and London: Routledge, 1989); and the introduction to *The Bounds of Race: Perspectives on Hegemony and Resistance*, Dominick LaCapra, ed. (Ithaca, NY, and London: Cornell UP, 1991).

6. Quotations of Shakespeare plays other than *A Midsummer Night's Dream* follow *The Complete Works of Shakespeare*, ed. David Bevington, 4th ed. (New York: HarperCollins, 1992). Quotations of *A Midsummer Night's Dream* follow R. A. Foakes's New Cambridge edition (Cambridge: Cambridge UP, 1984).

7. This usage points to the ambiguity of the term, as in a few early modern dictionaries "horse" is one of the definitions given for *race*. The word *race* was also used to describe the quality of wine. This type of lexical ambiguity about nature and appearance, as David Scott Kastan reminded me, is also at play in the Prince of Morocco's use of the word *complexion*—"mislike me not for my complexion, / The shadowed livery of the burnished sun" (2.2.1-2)—in *The Merchant of Venice*.

8. See Donna Haraway's stunning essay "Universal Donors in a Vampire Culture—It's All in the Family: Biological Kinship Categories in the Twentieth-Century United States" in *Reinventing Nature,* William Cronon, ed., forthcoming.

9. Gloria Anzaldúa, *Borderlands/ La Frontera: The New Mestiza* (San Francisco, CA: Spinsters/Aunt Lute, 1987), preface [n.p.].

10. Kim F. Hall, "Reading What Isn't There: 'Black' Studies in Early Modern England," *Stanford Humanities Review* 3 (1993): 23-33, esp. 25. The parameters for engagement with the notion of race have been redefined by other recent work on the early modern period, including Ann Rosalind Jones and Peter Stallybrass, "Dismantling Irena: The Sexualizing of Ireland in Early Modern England" in *Nationalisms and Sexualities,* Andrew Parker, Mary Russo, Doris Sommer, and Patricia Yaeger, eds. (New York and London: Routledge, 1992), 157-71; *Women, "Race," and Writing in the Early Modern Period*, Margo Hendricks and Patricia Parker, eds. (New York and London: Routledge, 1994); Emily C. Bartels, "Making More of the Moor: Aaron, Othello, and Renaissance Refashionings of Race," *Shakespeare Quarterly* 41 (1990): 433-54; and Margo Hendricks, "Managing the Barbarian: *The Tragedy of Dido, Queen of Carthage,"* Renaissance Drama n.s. 23 (1992): 165-88.

11. Steven Mullaney, *The Place of the Stage: License, Play, and Power in Renaissance England* (Chicago and London: U of Chicago P, 1988), 6.

12. James L. Calderwood, "*A Midsummer Night's Dream:* Anamorphism and Theseus' Dream," *SQ* 42 (1991): 409-30, esp. 410.

13. Mullaney, 6.

14. See, for example, Peter Hulme, *Colonial Encounters: Europe and the native Caribbean, 1492-1797* (London and New York: Methuen, 1986); and John Gillies, *Shakespeare and the geography of difference* (Cambridge: Cambridge UP, 1994). Though not directly exploring questions of race, Stephen Greenblatt's *Marvelous Possessions: The Wonder of the New World* (Chicago and London: U of Chicago P, 1991) and Richard Helgerson's *Forms*

15. Yet I think we can, as Andrew Gurr suggests, assume that audiences of *A Midsummer Night's Dream,* comprised of nobles, artisans, apprentices, clerks, citizens, and day laborers, literate and illiterate Londoners, would represent a range of knowledge or awareness of what events, people, texts, and ideologies were being alluded to in the plays; see *Playgoing in Shakespeare's London* (Cambridge: Cambridge UP, 1987), esp. 80-85.

16. For example, Richard Hakluyt writes that in his "publike lectures [he] was the first, that produced and shewed both the olde imperfectly composed, and the new lately reformed Mappes, Globes, Spheares, and other instruments of this Art for demonstration in the common schools, to the singular pleasure, and generall contentment of my auditory" (*The Principal Navigations Voyages Traffiques & Discoveries of the English Nation,* 12 vols. [Glasgow: James MacLehose and Sons, 1904], 1:xviii). While there is, of course, no empirical means of verifying the direct influence of orality in the circulation of these images, I consider Hakluyt's words to be convincing evidence of the validity of my point. On the relationship between oral and literary knowledge, see Walter J. Ong, *Orality and Literacy: The Technologizing of the Word* (London and New York: Methuen, 1982).

17. See Gurr, 82-86.

18. John Bourchier, Lord Berners, *The Boke of Duke Huon of Burdeux,* ed. S. L. Lee (London: Early English Text Society, 1887). I have modernized the spelling of quotations from this text.

19. Lee, ed., 72-73.

20. Lee, ed., 73. Oberon's other gifts include a magic horn and cup and the power to acquire whatever he desires merely by wishing for it.

21. Lee, ed., 74.

22. Lee, ed., 1.

23. Editor S. L. Lee notes that it is difficult to determine the date of the second edition. He argues for 1570, however, because the colophon to the third edition (which Lee contends is "doubtless a reprint of the first") states "that the book was translated by Lord Berners 'in the year of our Lord God one thousand five hundred three score and ten'." The third edition was printed in 1601 by Thomas Purfoot, "to be sould by *Edward White*" (Lee, ed., lv-lvi).

24. See *Henslowe's Diary,* ed. Walter W. Greg (London: A. H. Bullen, 1904), 16. Henslowe also lists the play under the titles "hewen of burdockes" and "hewen."

25. Edmund Spenser, *The Faerie Queene,* ed. A. C. Hamilton (London and New York: Longman, 1977), II.ix.60.1-4.

26. Spenser, II.x.71.5-6.

27. Spenser, II.x.72.1-3 and 5-6.

28. Spenser, II.x.75.3-5, 8-9, and II.x.76.1. In Spenser's allegory, Oberon figures for Henry VIII and thus becomes the father of Tanaquill or Glorian (Elizabeth). A. C. Hamilton notes that in Roman history Tanaquill was the wife of the first Tarquin, ancestor of Sextus Tarquinius, whose rape of Lucretia is often figured as the genesis of the Roman Republic. Spenser's link of fairy and Roman through the figure of Oberon mimics the account of Oberon's lineage in *Huon of Bordeaux* and thus continues the mythologizing of England's racial history. For a brilliant discussion of the relationship between Tarquin's rape of Lucretia, republicanism, and Renaissance humanism, see Stephanie H Jed, *Chaste Thinking: The Rape of Lucretia and the Birth of Humanism* (Bloomington and Indianapolis: Indiana UP, 1989).

29. Robert Greene, *The Scottish History of James the Fourth,* ed. J. A. Lavin (London: Ernest Benn, 1967), 1.3. [chorus] 4-7.

30. See Thomas Hahn, "Indians East and West: primitivism and savagery in English discovery narratives of the sixteenth century," *Journal of Medieval and Renaissance Studies* 8 (1978): 77-114. Hahn argues that *India* variously referred to "all of Asia, as Samuel Purchas declared in the seventeenth century: 'The name of India, is now applied to all farre-distant Countries, not in the extreme limits of Asia alone; but even to whole America, through the errour . . . in the Westerne world, thought that they had met with Ophir, and the Indian Regions of the East'" (78).

31. See Hahn, 79-88.

32. For another useful study of the ethnography of travel writing in pre- and early modern Europe, see Mary B. Campbell, *The Witness and the Other World: Exotic European Travel Writing, 400-1600* (Ithaca, NY, and London: Cornell UP, 1988).

33. Here I am referring to Leo Africanus's *Geographical Historie of Africa* (London, 1600) and George Best's *A true discourse of the late voyages of discouerie . . .* (London, 1578).

34. See Gillies, passim.

35. Gupta and Ferguson, 10.

36. Richard Eden, *The History of Travayle in the West and East Indies, and other countreys lying eyther way, towardes the fruitfull and ryche Moluccaes* (London, 1577). Quotations from the narrative of Lewes Vertomannus follow this edition.

37. Vertomannus in Eden, 354^v.

38. Vertomannus in Eden, 382^r and 386^v.

39. Vertomannus in Eden, 403^v, 401^v, and 382^r.

40. Vertomannus in Eden, 388^v and 399^r.

41. Vertomannus in Eden, 390ʳ.
42. *John Hvighen van Linschoten. his Discours of Voyages into yᵉ Easte & West Indies. Devided into Foure Bookes* (London, 1598), 62 and 60.
43. James Clifford, *The Predicament of Culture: Twentieth-Century Ethnography, Literature, and Art* (Cambridge, MA: Harvard UP, 1988), 10.
44. Van Linschoten, "To the Reader."
45. Hahn, 91.
46. "The report of John Huighen van Linschoten concerning M. Newberies and M. Fitches imprisonment, and of their escape, which happened while he was in Goa" in Hakluyt, 5:512.
47. In an unpublished essay, Joan Pong Linton has noted that, within the early modern English lexicon, *trifles* was generally used to describe the type of exchanges between Native Americans and English sailors. For a different analysis of relations of exchange between the English and Native Americans, see Pong Linton, "*Jack of Newbery* and Drake in California: Domestic and Colonial Narratives of English Cloth and Manhood," *ELH* 59 (1992): 23-51.
48. One wonders whether this accusation might also imply that Titania is the real object of Theseus's love, that it is for love of her that he left the other women.
49. In this I diverge from Louis A. Montrose, who reads this conflict in terms of the psychology of the nuclear family, where Oberon's efforts are seen as an "attempt to take the boy from an infantilizing mother and to make a man of him" ("*A Midsummer Night's Dream* and the Shaping Fantasies of Elizabethan Culture: Gender, Power, Form" in *Rewriting the Renaissance: The Discourses of Sexual Difference in Early Modern Europe*, Margaret W. Ferguson, Maureen Quilligan, and Nancy J. Vickers, eds. [Chicago and London: U of Chicago P, 1986], 65-87, esp. 74). Allan Dunn also sees the play in terms of this psychology, though he reads this familial conflict from the changeling's point of view, in his "The Indian Boy's Dream Wherein Every Mother's Son Rehearses His Part: Shakespeare's *A Midsummer Night's Dream*," *Shakespeare Studies* 20 (1988): 15-32. It seems to me that both monarchs operate within a feudal ideology about social responsibilities and status. Thus the Indian boy elicits from the monarchs very different interpretations of their social roles.
50. Peter Fryer, *Staying Power: The History of Black People in Britain* (London and Sydney: Pluto Press, 1984), 9. See also Folarin Shyllon, *Black People in Britain 1555-1833*, published for The Institute of Race Relations (London: Oxford UP, 1977); and James Walvin, *The Black Presence in Britain* (London: Orbach and Chambers, 1971).
51. The substitution of Nick Bottom as the object of Titania's affections, his regression to an infantile state, and the sexual significance of this new relationship have long received critical attention. For an insightful examination of sexuality, bodily functions, and shame in *A Midsummer Night's Dream*, see Gail Kern Paster, *The Body Embarrassed: Drama and the Disciplines of Shame in Early Modern England* (Ithaca, NY, and London: Cornell UP, 1993), esp. 125-43.
52. Luce Irigaray, "Women on the Market" in *This Sex Which is Not One*, trans. Catherine Porter (Ithaca, NY, and London: Cornell UP, 1985), 172 and 177.
53. For a discussion of Apuleius's *The Golden Ass* and Ovid's *Metamorphoses* as sources for Shakespeare's representation of Bottom, see Foakes, ed., 9-10.
54. María Moliner, *Diccionario de Uso del Español*, 2 vols. (Madrid: Editorial Gredos, 1967), 2:402.
55. See, for example, Thomas Middleton's and William Rowley's *The Changeling*. In its common usage in early modern England, *changeling* referred to a person put in place of another and, in particular, to a child secretly substituted for another child by fairies. It was also used to describe dramatic and inexplicable shifts in human behavior.
56. *Translation*'s etymology originates with the Latin word *translatio*, which is derived from the union of *trans* and *ferre* (away from/across and to carry/to bear, respectively). *Translation* as Shakespeare uses it, however, seems to evoke a signification more akin to the semantics of *miscere*—that is, a mixing of two things to produce one—than to the notion of *translatio*, to carry or bear away. Peter Quince's use of the word *translated* insinuates this connection as it continues the pun created by Snout's use of the word *change*.
57. The Portuguese racial lexicon also included the term *castiço*: *castiço* referred to a Portuguese born in India, while *mestiço* described any Asian, African, or New World native who had a European ancestor.
58. The word *mulatto/a*, of course, immediately evokes an image of the animal, something the other two terms do not suggest. But, and this is crucial to our understanding of the link between language and sexual reproduction, the word *mulatto/a* also implies the inability to fix the idea of race, something the other two terms imply as well. I have generalized the gender of these relations not because Spanish and Portuguese women were absolutely uninvolved in the colonial process but because there is little evidence to indicate whether they were involved in miscegenous relations with native men.
59. In his 1623 *A Dictionary in Spanish and English*, John Minsheu offers his readers an "enlarged and amplified" version of Richard Perceval's 1594 *Biblioteca Hispanica*. Minsheu's aim was to provide "for the further profit and pleasure of the learner or delighted in this tongue." Minsheu's dictionary goes far beyond Perceval's not only in sheer number of

words but also in its inclusion of words that mark racial identity.

60. I give both the Spanish and Portuguese spellings for *mestizo* to resist the totalizing of Spanish and Portuguese cultures as homogeneous. While linguistically the two nations are quite similar, they are distinct entities. In both languages *mulatto* has the same spelling.

61. Van Linschoten, 62.

62. In 1510 Affonso de Albuquerque, viceroy of the Portuguese settlement at Goa, instituted a policy prohibiting marriages between Portuguese men and "the 'black women' of Malabar—in other words dark-skinned women of Dravidian origin, who were often termed 'Negresses' by the Portuguese" (C. R. Boxer, *Race Relations in the Portuguese Colonial Empire 1415-1825* [Oxford: Clarendon Press, 1963], 64-65).

63. Homer Swander, "Editors vs. A Text: The Scripted Geography of *A Midsummer Night's Dream*," *Studies in Philology* 87 (1990): 83-108, esp. 87. Swander's analysis is primarily concerned with the staging of the play rather than its internal geography. In an analogous discussion with different conclusions, Gary Jay Williams looks at a "semi-operatic adaptation" of *A Midsummer Night's Dream* performed in 1816. Williams argues that the "interesting and historically significant text of" this production is its "staging and the new pictorial scenery, whose vocabulary must be read in the light of empire," thus specifically recognizing the play's dependence upon a specific geographical and political "human territory" ("The Scenic Language of Empire: *A Midsummer Night's Dream* in 1816," *Theatre Survey* 34 [1993]: 47-59, esp. 47).

64. Patricia Parker, *Literary Fat Ladies: Rhetoric, Gender, Property* (London and New York: Methuen, 1987), 131.

65. Arguing that "the least interesting motivation behind the Indian Boy conflict would be the excuse that Oberon sincerely needs a page or 'henchman'," the director chose to highlight the sexual tensions of the play from a different angle (Danny Scheie, "Program Notes on *A Midsummer Night's Dream*" [Santa Cruz, 1991], 32).

66. Quoted in Gupta and Ferguson, 10.

Jyotsna G. Singh (essay date 1996)

SOURCE: "Caliban Versus Miranda: Race and Gender Conflicts in Postcolonial Rewritings of *The Tempest*," in *Feminist Readings of Early Modern Culture: Emerging Subjects,* edited by Valerie Traub, M. Lindsay Kaplan, and Dympna Callaghan, Cambridge University Press, 1996, pp. 191-209.

[*In the following essay, Singh studies postcolonial readings of* The Tempest, *which emphasize the role of Caliban as a prototype of the modern revolutionary due to his engagement in a power struggle with Prospero.*]

CALIBAN AND DECOLONIZATION

I cannot read *The Tempest* without recalling the adventures of those voyages reported in Hakluyt; and when I remember the voyages and the particular period in African history, I see *The Tempest* against the background of England's experimentation in colonisation . . . *The Tempest* was also prophetic of a political future which is our present. Moreover, the circumstances of my life, both as colonial and exiled descendant of Caliban in the twentieth century is an example of that prophecy.[1]

There is just one world in which the oppressors and oppressed struggle, one world in which, sooner than later, the oppressed will be victorious. Our [Latin] America is bringing its own nuances to this struggle, this victory. The tempest has not subsided. But *The Tempest*'s shipwrecked sailors, Crusoe and Gulliver, can be seen, rising out of the waters, from terra firma. There, not only Prospero, Ariel, and Caliban, Don Quixote, Friday and Faust await them, but . . . halfway between history and dream—Marx and Lenin, Bolivar and Marti, Sandino and Che Guevara.[2]

Since Caliban first appeared on the stage in Shakespeare's *The Tempest* in 1611, he has been theatrically reincarnated in many different forms. Most recently, Prospero's "misshapen knave" and "demi-devil" has been transformed into a third world revolutionary. Revisionary histories of colonialism—especially since the 1960s—frequently evoke the figure of Caliban as a symbol of resistance to colonial regimes in Latin America, the Caribbean, and Africa. These revisions interrogate the so-called "discovery" of the Americas to trace a history of the Caliban myth in the early encounters between the European colonizers and natives. Crucially, they challenge the veracity of Columbus' account of "cannibals" in his diary, suggesting that the term "cannibal"—for which Caliban is an anagram—is itself a deformation of the name *Carib,* an Indian warrior tribe opposed to the Europeans or a variant of another tribal name, *Kanibna.* Furthermore, they argue that while there is limited and conflicting evidence backing Columbus' association of caribs/cannibals with people who eat human flesh, the image of the cannibal easily elided with Shakespeare's Caliban, ideologically holding in place the European distinction between their own "civilized" selves and the "savage" others they encountered in the New World.[3] Cheyfitz lays down the boundaries of this revisionary reading as follows:

Whatever the actual linguistic case may be, however, we have cause to wonder, as Columbus himself apparently did from time to time, at Columbus' association of the cannibals with eating human flesh. He did not have any empirical evidence, and his assertion that the Arawaks themselves told him is contradicted by Columbus' own admission that neither the Indians nor the Europeans knew each other's language. If we try to imagine the use of gestures in this case, we have not gotten around the problem of translation, but only embedded ourselves more deeply in it . . . [however] after the association Columbus elaborated in his journal, cannibal . . . [became] a part of a diverse arsenal of rhetorical weapons used to distinguish what they conceive of their "civilized" selves from certain "savage" others, principally Native Americans and Africans.[4]

Such contemporary interrogations of the so-called originary moment of European colonialism in Columbus' "discovery" of the Americas have stirred considerable interest in earlier, native revisions of colonial history. Today, as we question Prospero's heroic qualities within the providential code that had previously designated the play a pastoral romance, we can also recognize why Caribbean and Latin American writers, in the wake of decolonization in the 1960s, imaginatively identify with Caliban in their rewritings of Shakespeare's play. Roberto Fernandez Retamar recalls a history of a variety of Latin American responses to *The Tempest* through this century—some of which valorize Ariel as a native intellectual—and argues that new readings from a genuinely non-European perspective were only enabled by the gradual emergence of "third world" nations.[5] Thus, writing in 1971, Retamar declares

> Our symbol then is not Ariel . . . but rather Caliban. This is something that we, the *mestizo* inhabitants of these same isles where Caliban lived, see with particular clarity: Prospero invaded the islands, killed our ancestors, enslaved Caliban, and taught him his language to make himself understood. What can Caliban do but use that same language—today he has no other—to curse him . . . I know no other metaphor more expressive of our cultural situation, of our reality . . . what is our history, what is our culture, if not the history and culture of Caliban?[6]

These identifications with Caliban, and an accompanying unease about his alien language, typify numerous Latin American and Caribbean responses, especially in their articulations of Caliban's revolutionary potential against Prospero's linguistic authority. The Barbadian writer George Lamming, while assuming his people's identification with Caliban, often returns to the impasse of the colonizer's language in his pioneering essay of 1960:

> Prospero has given Caliban language: with all its unstated history of consequences, an unknown history of future intentions. This gift of language meant not only English, in particular, but speech and concept as a way, a method, a necessary avenue towards areas of the self which could not be reached any other way . . . Prospero lives in the absolute certainty that Language, which is his gift to Caliban, is the very prison in which Caliban's achievements must be realized and restricted.[7]

Writing some years later, the Martinique writer and founder of the Negritude movement, Aimé Césaire, is more unequivocal in his play, *A Tempest,* casting Caliban as a successful revolutionary who persistently repudiates Prospero's (European) version of history:

> CALIBAN: . . . I am telling you [Prospero] . . . I won't answer to the name Caliban . . . Call me X. That would be best. Like a man without a name. Or, to be more precise, a man whose name has been stolen. You talk about history . . . well, that's history, and everyone knows it! . . . Uhuru.[8]

These and other such third world identifications with Caliban have clearly occasioned a paradigm shift among Western audiences and critics who in the past "tended to listen exclusively to Prospero's voice; [who] after all . . . speaks their language."[9] And in his stage manifestations too, Caliban has come a long way from appearing as the eighteenth-century primitive or the nineteenth-century Darwinian "missing link" to be accepted as a colonial subject or an embodiment of any oppressed group.[10] Undoubtedly, these anti-colonialist rewritings of Shakespeare's *The Tempest* question the play's seemingly aesthetic concerns, crucially relocating it within a revisionist history of the "discovery" of the Americas and the struggles for decolonization in this region. However, while these historicizations of Prospero's mistreatment of Caliban *make visible* the colonial contexts of Shakespeare's play, they often simply signal a *reversal* of the roles of the oppressor and the oppressed, typically demonstrated by Césaire in *A Tempest* when he depicts the relation between Prospero and Caliban as an endless and inevitable Hegelian struggle between the master and slave. Despite leaving open the possibility of a constant negotiation of power between the two men in alternating roles, the play does little to question the inevitability of hierarchical structures.

Therefore, ironically, Prospero refuses to return to Europe at the end of Césaire's play. He threatens a freed and defiant Caliban: "I will answer your violence with violence," but concludes almost tamely: "Well Caliban, old fellow, it's just us two now, here on the island . . . only you and me," while Caliban shouts: "Freedom Hi-Day, Freedom Hi-Day."[11] Finally, in his anti-colonial version of Shakespeare's play, Césaire leaves Prospero and Caliban at an impasse: locked in a continual, potentially violent struggle while sharing the otherwise uninhabited island.

In Lamming's reading of *The Tempest,* the writer also frequently lapses into psychologizing universals when defining the Prospero/Caliban polarity (in which Miranda has a peripheral role):

> [According to Lamming, while] Caliban is [Prospero's] convert, colonised by language, and excluded by language . . . Prospero is afraid of Caliban. He is afraid because he knows that his encounter with Caliban is largely his encounter with himself. The gift [of language] is a contract from which neither participant is allowed to withdraw . . . [yet] Caliban is a child of Nature . . . [and] Miranda is the innocent half of Caliban.[12]

In such formulations, Prospero is the dominant force in a natural psychic struggle between Self and Other, namely, between Prospero and Caliban—and Miranda as the object of desire functions to define and keep this rivalry alive.

Lamming and Césaire exemplify a tendency among the anti-colonial appropriations of *The Tempest* to reverse the roles of oppressor and oppressed. And more importantly, in doing so, they view the identities of the women—of Miranda and of the missing "native" woman, Sycorax—simply as an aspect of the Prospero/Caliban opposition rather than in terms of the complex *sexual ideologies* underpinning colonialism. I wish to look afresh at the relation between Miranda and Caliban, specifically at the way in which Shakespeare's play intersects with postcolonial reappraisals of it, which, I believe, do not adequately address the interactions between race, sexuality, and political struggle. At the center of my concerns lies the *gendering* of these postcolonial discourses of revolution in which Caliban as the prototype of a male revolutionary becomes a convenient, homogenizing symbol for decolonization. What these writers do not acknowledge is that their focus on Caliban "generates a self-conscious, self-celebrating male paradigm" that often posits a utopia in which women are marginalized or missing.[13] Retamar imagines such a male utopia in his vision of a tempest, "halfway between history and dream," which will unify the former oppressors and oppressed: Prospero, Caliban, and Ariel figure alongside Friday, Don Quixote, Marti, and Guevara, among others, but Miranda (as well as her dead mother) and Sycorax are missing.[14]

Postcolonial theorists (both in Western and non-Western locations) have frequently critiqued narratives of "discovery" for the way in which they gender "the New World as feminine, [while] sexualizing . . . its exploration, conquest, and settlement."[15] Some have also traced a history of this feminization of the various non-European cultures, whereby they exude a "full blown . . . sensuality" of a "sweet dream" in which the West had been wallowing for more than four centuries."[16] From these examples it is evident that critics resisting colonialism have been quick to note how gender is crucial in mapping the signification of power relations in the West—especially in relation to its native others. It is surprising, however, that in their rewritings of *The Tempest,* non-Western writers like Lamming, Césaire, and Fanon have created liberationist, third world narratives oddly oblivious to the dissonances between race and gender struggles. Thus, ironically, their anti-colonial discourse produces the liberated "Black Man" via the erasure of female subjectivity. For instance, they acknowledge Miranda, but only as the property of the European masters, and therefore, in this eyes, a desired object to be usurped and claimed in the service of resistance. It is Fanon's alienated black male who best expresses this contradiction in the agenda of decolonization, when he declares: "I marry white culture, white beauty, white whiteness. When my restless hands caress those white breasts, they grasp white civilization and dignity and make them mine."[17] Such assertive, and potentially forcible, claims on the European woman are never questioned by Fanon or others, while the possibility of a fruitful partnership with a native woman—a native mate for Caliban—is never given serious consideration.

In *The Pleasures of Exile,* for instance, "resistance and liberation are an exclusively male enterprise."[18] Lamming attempts to understand the relation between Miranda and Caliban who, in his version, share "innocence and incredulity" but differ in "their degree of being."[19] Ultimately, however, he privileges "Caliban's history . . .[which] belongs to the future."[20] Miranda, in contrast, is made to depend on her father's view of history and await her future within a patriarchal lineage, whereby "the magic of birth will sail [her], young, beautiful, and a virgin, into the arms of the King's only son."[21] Furthermore, and more crucially, as Paquet mentions in her foreword, "[finally] like Melville's Ishmael, Caliban is left alone on the island [without the promise of a mate]" and "Sycorax, as a symbol of a landscape and a changing human situation, is a memory, an absence, and a silence . . . [as] Lamming consciously postpones consideration of Sycorax and Miranda's mother as contributing subjects of Caribbean cultural history."[22]

Aimé Césaire's play, *A Tempest* (which I will discuss at length later), also celebrates Caliban's linguistic and political appropriations of Prospero's power, but once again, without radically altering the terms of a patriarchal power struggle in which the woman's presence is incidental or abstract: namely to perpetuate her father's noble lineage by marrying Ferdinand, the ruler of Naples. And Caliban's mother, the "native" Sycorax, figures in the play as a *symbolic* Earth Mother embodied in the natural elements of the island. As a result, while the experience of the play foregrounds a seemingly gender-neutral struggle between master and slave, it is, in effect, predicated on the marginalization of the female figures. Before analyzing the gender politics of Césaire's play any further, I would like to examine the discourse of sexuality in Shakespeare's *The Tempest* and explore how it offers the crucial nexus for Prospero's colonial authority. An analogy for Prospero's imposition of cultural and political organization on the sexuality of his subjects—Miranda, Caliban, and to a lesser extent, Ferdinand—can be found in the structure of the exchange of women as gifts in earlier, "primitive" societies—a structure which served as an idiom for both *kinship* and *competition* among men. In this I hope to show that while Césaire rewrites Shakespeare's play as a third world manifesto of decolonization, he leaves intact the intractable system of gender categories that are the centerpiece of Prospero's ostensibly benevolent mastery.

Desiring Miranda

MIRANDA:
Why speaks my father so urgently? This
Is the third man that e'er I saw; the first
That e'er I sighed for . . .
FERDINAND:
O, if a virgin
And your affection not gone forth, I'll make you the
Queen of Naples.[23]

(Shakespeare, *The Tempest,* 1.ii.445-49)

On the occasion of Ferdinand and Miranda's first meeting, arranged and controlled by Prospero, in act I, scene ii of Shakespeare's play, a curious and telling exchange takes place between the three of them. Miranda articulates her desire for Ferdinand by distinguishing him from the other two men she has known: her father and Caliban. Here, Miranda is unaware of her father's apparently "magical" control of this moment, even as she articulates her desire as a personalized, autonomous experience of sighs and longings. Ferdinand, however, does not look to his heart to understand his attraction for her; instead, he quickly reveals a connection between his sexual desire and the requirements of a patriarchal lineage: "if a virgin," he asks her, "I'll make you / The Queen of Naples." Prospero, the presiding deity, controls their feelings as he finds his power slipping—"this swift business / I must uneasy make" (I.ii.451-52)—while cautioning Miranda against her limited judgment: "Thou think'st there is no more such shapes as he, / Having seen but him and Caliban. Foolish wench! / To th' most of men this is a Caliban, / And they to him are angels" (I.ii. 479-82).

In eliding Caliban and Ferdinand in vague comparison to "most of men"—while rhetorically suggesting an identity and difference between them—Prospero points out how he uses Caliban as the less-than-human other in order to define gender (and racial) identity in conveniently elusive terms of what it is *not*. In this gesture, Prospero unwittingly reveals that not only does he fear Caliban's potential for miscegenation with Miranda, but that every man who desires his daughter is potentially a Caliban, unless that desire can be channeled to fulfill the demands of an aristocratic lineage.

While noting the dynamics of Prospero's fatherhood, critics often have observed the play's ambivalence toward motherhood. For instance, Coppèlia Kahn notes that "[Prospero's] only mention of his wife is highly ambivalent, at once commending and questioning her chastity before his daughter: 'Thy mother was a piece of virtue, and / She said thou wast my daughter (I.ii.56-57).'"[24] David Sundelson reiterates this point by suggesting that the "reverence for father Prospero does not extend to mothers. Whatever ambivalence toward them is hidden in Prospero's tale of expulsion, the one mother in the play is unmistakably demonic: Sycorax."[25] She is a "foul witch" (I.ii.263), a "damned witch . . . banished for mischiefs manifold, sorceries terrible / To enter human hearing" (I.ii.264-65). Sundelson then argues, "This demon mother's rage is 'unmitigable' (I.ii.276); only a father could end the torture."[26] Stephen Orgel also persuasively reads the effects of Prospero's ambivalence toward wives/mothers: "The absent presence of the wife and mother in the play constitutes a space that is filled by Prospero's creation of surrogates and a ghostly family: the witch Sycorax and her monster child Caliban . . . the good child/wife Miranda . . ."[27]

Caliban as the offspring of this "demon" mother serves appropriately as an other. Thus, Prospero's (and the play's) view of Caliban as a potential rapist illustrates how the discourse of sexuality underpins colonial authority. That Prospero assumes authority in terms typical of colonialist discourse is recognized by most postcolonial critics. As one critic states, "Colonialist discourse does not simply announce a triumph for civility, it must continually *produce* it [through a struggle with rather than an assimilation of its others]."[28] Hence, interpellated within Prospero's narrative of sexual and racial control, the identities of both Caliban and Miranda must constantly be *produced* in terms of sexual struggle in which, as Prospero's subjects, their sexuality comes under constant surveillance, even as one enables the repression of the other. Both race and gender conflicts come into play in this three-way dynamic, inhering within the same system of differences between colonizer and colonized, yet not without some *dissonances* within the systemic forces. Miranda, who knows no men (other than her father) between whom she can distinguish, responds unequivocally to Caliban's different appearance, which seems an inherent sign of his "villainy." In II.ii. she declares to her father: "'Tis [Caliban] a villain sir, / I do not love to look on" (I.ii.309). Yet, like a typical colonizer, she also reveals her civilizing impulses toward Caliban: "I pitied thee, / Took pains to make thee speak, taught thee each hour / One thing or another" (I.ii.353-55)—simultaneously holding out little hope of improvement for his "vile race."

Neither Prospero nor Miranda allow Caliban an identity as a desiring subject who wishes to gain sexual access to Miranda for the legitimate aim of "peopl[ing]. . . This isle with Calibans" (I.ii.350-51). However, given Prospero's manipulation of Ferdinand's "wooing," it is clear that he decides which man is to have access to his daughter. Though Miranda has a position of colonial superiority over Caliban, she nonetheless has a marginal role within a *kinship* system in which all the three males are bonded through their competing claims on her. According to Lévi-Strauss, Mauss, and others, one of the most striking features of this system among so-called primitive societies was the practice of giving and receiving gifts as a part of social intercourse; within this system, the gift of women was the most profound because the exchange partners thereby enacted a relationship of kinship.[29] Significantly, however, gift exchange could confer upon its participants a special solidarity as well as a sense of competition and rivalry. From the perspective of some feminist anthropologists, this system had far-reaching implications for women:

> If it is women who are being transacted, then it is men who give and take them who are linked, the woman being a conduit of a relationship rather than a partner to it. The exchange of women does not necessarily imply that women are objectified . . . But it does imply a distinction between gift and giver. If women are the gifts, then it is the men who are exchange partners. And it is the partners, not their presents, upon whom the reciprocal exchange confers its quasi-mystical power of social linkage . . . [Thus] women are *given* in marriage, *taken* in battle, exchanged for favours, sent as tribute, traded, bought, and sold.[30]

Several contemporary anthropologists recognize the danger of attributing a timeless universality to this concept of a kinship system. For instance, they point to the gender inflections of Lévi-Strauss' reasoning when he says that women should be exchanged as the way only of overcoming the contradiction by which the same woman is, on the one hand, the object of personal desire, and, on the other, the object of the desire of others and a means of binding others through alliance with them. Such a naturalized definition of a woman's role also, critics argue, does not account for some matrilineal, non-Western societies that neither hold proprietorial attitudes toward women nor use them as a means of social and sexual exchange. Despite these limitations of Lévi-Strauss' gendered language, the notion of the exchange of women is nonetheless useful in demonstrating, when applicable, how a specific cultural paradigm organizes and shapes female sexuality and subjectivity.[31]

It is apparent, then, that underlying the dynamics of Prospero's power struggle with Caliban and, to a lesser extent, with Ferdinand, over the two men's sexual claims to Prospero's daughter, lies the social grid of the kinship system. Thus, desiring Miranda makes the noble Ferdinand a suitable exchange partner for her royal father. She is to be the means whereby the royal descendents of the two men will be related by blood. Ferdinand makes apparent that this arrangement is, in effect, an exchange of Miranda's virginity (which her father must guard) for the throne of Naples. This is reinforced at the end of the play, when Ferdinand retrospectively asks *his* father's permission for his marriage to Miranda: "I chose her when I could not ask my father / For his advice" (v.i.190-91).

The marriage of Ferdinand and Miranda typically exemplifies the theory of reciprocity in kinship systems. Marriages are the most basic form of gift exchange, whereby the woman whom one does not take is offered up as a precious gift. Caliban, the seeming outsider among kin, nonetheless has a role within the system of gender differences underpinning gift exchanges among men. His desire for Miranda leads him to imagine a kinship with Prospero, even if it means *taking* her forcibly: "Would't had been done! / Thou didst prevent me; I had peopled else / This isle with Calibans" (I.ii.349-51). In this scenario, Caliban not only wishes to create a blood tie with Prospero, but also to use Miranda as a means of producing male children—a population in the image of Caliban rather than of Miranda. When Prospero prevents Caliban from violating the "honour of [his] child" (I.ii.348), he in turn assumes a proprietorial control over his daughter as a sexual gift, which he will later *give* to the royal Ferdinand.

A central feature of the traditional kinship structure is that *all* levels and directions in the traffic of women, including hostile ones, are ordered by this structure. Thus, gift exchange could be an idiom of rivalry and competition and marriage itself could be highly competitive.[32] In this context, while Prospero believes that Caliban exists outside of any civilized social forms, the latter is nonetheless Ferdinand's rival in desiring Miranda, and on the basis of this claim is bonded with the two other men; an acknowledgment and denial of his desire by Prospero ironically serves to legitimate Caliban's position as a rival within the structures of gift exchange. Prospero and Miranda may consider Caliban "a thing most brutish," but from his perspective, the colonizer has withheld from him the gift of woman in order to maintain the hierarchical boundaries between them. The basis of the power struggle between Prospero and Caliban, then, is an implicit consensus about the role of woman as a gift to be exchanged.

Miranda's role as a gift is further complicated by Prospero's implicit (and European) fear of a monstrous progeny that could result from a misplaced gift exchange with a man who is racially marked as other. In Prospero's eyes the imaginary "Calibans" who could "people" the isle would connect his lineage to that of Sycorax, whom *he* describes as the "damned witch" whose "sorceries terrible" banished her from "Argier" (Algiers). For Prospero (and for European audience), her magic is antithetical to his supposedly beneficent Art because she embodies an aberration of nature, both in terms of her sexuality (her impregnation by an incubus) and her racial identity as a non-European. While Prospero claims to know the history of her life, his only source is Ariel, and as one critic points out, "we have no way of distinguishing the facts about Caliban and Sycorax from Prospero's invective about them."[33] Given his demonizing rhetoric, it is not surprising that a fear of miscegenation is a crucial trope that structures Prospero's "plot" of selective inclusion and exclusion in which Miranda, Ferdinand, and Caliban figure as prominent characters.

We get a fuller sense of Sycorax's demonization if we consider *The Tempest*'s relation to the poetic geography of the Renaissance (derived from classical and medieval sources), in which European identity is frequently contrasted with images of otherness. According to John Gillies, Sycorax's mythic journey from Algiers to the New World is motivated not so much to find a new "howling wilderness" as to *make* one. Her adoption of "Setebos," a New World "devil" ("my Dam's god"), evokes associations with the name of the demonized god of the "heathen" Patagonian Indians. Thus, in her role as the non-Western other in the collective European imagination, she is like "Ham, progenitor of the Caananite, the Negro and other supposedly bestial and slavish races, . . . an outcast from the world of men, a wanderer beyond bounds and an active promoter of the degeneracy of her 'vile' race."[34]

Prospero's plot of a "happy end," however, does not accommodate the figure of Claribel, who haunts the margins of *The Tempest*. In fact, it is telling that Shakespeare's play, unlike Prospero's script, does not resolve the contradiction between the anxiety of miscegenation from Miranda's potential union with Caliban and the political imperative for a European like Alonso to give his daughter in a marriage across racial lines. References to the forced marriage of Claribel to the King of Tunis in North Africa, which appear early in the play, strike a discordant note in the emerging racial ideology that leads European audiences to rejoice at the play's "happy" marriage at the end—a marriage that preserves the purity of European lineage in the union of Naples and Milan.

That Claribel's match deviates from the cultural norm is made evident by Sebastian when he chides Alonso "That would not bless our Europe with your daughter / But rather loose her to an African" (II.i.129-30) and reminds him that his daughter was divided by her "loathness" for the Tunisian and "obedience" toward her father. Furthermore, Gonzalo's unexplained identification between Claribel and Dido, Queen of Carthage, complicates our view of the racial and gender politics involved in the match. For instance, the fate imposed upon Alonso's reluctant daughter is the one violently resisted by Dido who chose to die rather than marry an African King, Iarbus. According to Peter Hulme, to recall Carthage "is to bring to mind several centuries of punishing wars with Italy . . . when presumably Claribel has been a gift to fend off a dangerous new power in the central Mediterranean."[35] The references to Dido also evoke contradictory images: that of the widow, and "a model at once of heroic fidelity to her murdered husband and the destructive potential of erotic passion."[36] Overall, while the meanings of this allusion are multiple and remain ambiguous, references to North Africa encroach upon the boundaries of the imaginary Italian states of the Renaissance that defined their culture against "barbarians" like the offspring of the Algerian Sycorax, or in another instance, the "barbarian Moor." While images of the Tunisian queen do not intrude into Prospero's plan of social and sexual organization, they nonetheless open up an imaginary space for viewers (and readers) of the play to imagine the (impossible or repressed) possibility of miscegenation in the service of political expediency, even as the woman's subjectivity continues to be shaped by her status as a gift.

Some political, especially feminist, readings of Shakespeare's *The Tempest* try to open up the play to such dissonances that remain unaccommodated by the play's "happy" conclusion. One such strategy is to read an implicit affinity between Caliban and Miranda in relation to the overarching power of Prospero, whom they designate as a racist patriarch. While acknowledging that historically European women have been complicit with their men in producing the non-European man as a demonized Other and a potential rapist, they attempt to read against the grain of such polarizations. Lorrie J. Leininger's landmark essay, despite its essentialism, is useful in exploring a relationship between Miranda and Caliban, not in sexual terms, but in the context of a mutual recognition of the possibilities of resistance.[37] Thus, Leininger creates an imaginary riposte by Miranda to her father in which she both reveals and disrupts colonial hierarchy as well as the kinship system: "My father is no God-figure. No one is a God-father" (p. 291). Calling for respect for Caliban's non-European ancestry, she also refuses to be used as a means of his oppression:

> . . . men are reminded of Indians when they first see Caliban; he might be African, his mother having been transported from Algiers . . . I will not be used as the excuse of his enslavement . . . I need to join forces with Caliban—with all those who are exploited . . .[38]

Furthermore, Leininger's Miranda repudiates the value placed on her "virginity" both by the kinship system—as a gift exchanged or withheld—and by the colonial institutions based on the "protection" of European women: "I cannot give assent to an ethical scheme that locates all virtue symbolically in one part of my anatomy. My virginity has little to do with the forces that will lead to a good harvest or to greater social justice."[39] Such insights offered by feminist revisions of *The Tempest* make visible the structural contradictions in Miranda's subject-position as "the sexual object of both the Anglo-American male and the native other."[40] And while Miranda ultimately aligns herself to the colonizing father and husband, the play and Leininger also gesture toward an alliance, however problematic, in a childhood "prehistory" when Miranda taught Caliban language, or in a utopian, egalitarian future.

Such feminist possibilities and insights rarely figure in third world, postcolonial versions of the play. A call for decolonization and revolution in a play such as Aimé Césaire's *A Tempest* ironically shows that race and gender struggles occur in antithetical, rather than cooperative relationships. The play enacts a breakdown of colonial hierarchy, but leaves intact the system of kinship between men.

A POSTCOLONIAL "BRAVE NEW WORLD"

PROSPERO:
Good God, you tried to rape my daughter!
CALIBAN:
Rape! Rape! Listen you old goat, you're the one that put those dirty thoughts in my head. Let me tell you something: I couldn't care less about your daughter, or about your cave for that matter.[41]

Aimé Césaire's Caliban is clearly the protagonist of *A Tempest*. In this telling exchange between him and Prospero, he strongly repudiates the identity of a rapist that he claims *is produced* by his master. Caliban's almost perfunctory dismissal of any possibility of sexually desiring Miranda is put to question in II.i by her description of that "awful Caliban who keeps pursuing me and calling out my name in his stupid dreams" (p. 35). Except for these two moments that leave a lingering sense of ambivalence, the play largely leaves unexplored the issue of power and sexuality as it concerns the relationship between Prospero, Miranda, and Caliban. The latter moment, in effect, seems to deny his identity as a desiring subject, shrugging off "dirty thoughts" not of his own making to become a single-minded prototype of a third world revolutionary. Does his rejection of Miranda as a sexual prize signal a "brave new world" in which the patriarchal kinship bonds between men are dissolved?

Before responding to this rhetorical question, let me first establish *A Tempest*'s dramatic and political credentials. First published in French in the wake of decolonization in

1969, it revised the history of the Caribbean. Calling for a troupe of black actors performing their own version of Shakespeare's play, it was initially produced in Africa, The Middle East, and the Caribbean, as well as in France. It was translated into English by Richard Miller in 1985 and was introduced to New York audiences in a successful, though politically restrained, production in 1991. The spirit of the play derives from the Negritude movement, of which Césaire was one of the founders, with its aim being to reverse the political and linguistic oppression of blacks within colonialism.

Set in a colony—a prototype of a Caribbean or African setting—in the throes of resistance and unrest, the play initially focuses on Caliban's verbal attacks on Prospero's control over language and representation. Here Césaire is clearly sensitive to the way in which the name Caliban/cannibal appears in Shakespeare's play—and in colonial history—"through an imperial and colonial act of translation."[42] Thus, Césaire has Caliban declare his independence in Swahili, "Uhuru!" To which Prospero mutters, "Mumbling your native language again! I've already told you, I don't like it" (p. 11). He wants his native subject to "at least thank (me) for having taught you to speak at all. You, a savage . . . a dumb animal, a beast I educated, trained, dragged up from the Bestiality that still clings to you" (p. 11). Césaire's Prospero is the familiar proponent of the "civilizing mission"; thus, Caliban's rebellion is rightly aimed at Prospero's power of "naming" when he declares, "I don't want to be called Caliban any longer . . . Caliban isn't my name" (p. 15).

Accompanying Caliban's disruptions to the colonizer's language are intimations of an actual resistance movement (as Prospero tells Ariel in III.iii: "Caliban is alive, he is plotting, he is getting a guerilla force" [p. 50]), as well as of an impending black independence in Ariel's concluding resolve to sing "notes so sweet that the last / will give rise to a yearning / in the heart of the most forgetful slaves / yearning for freedom . . . and the lightened agave will straighten [into] / a solemn flag" (p. 60). Prior to his articulation of this "unsettling agenda," Ariel, who is labeled a "Mulatto," plays the historical part of those mixed races, often in the middle of the colonial hierarchy, more able to accept their somewhat limited oppression. Ariel declares that he and Caliban are "Brothers in suffering and slavery . . . and in hope as well . . . [but] have different methods" (p. 20); yet Ariel's vision of brotherhood includes Prospero, and for him any fight of freedom is for his master too—"so that Prospero can acquire a conscience" (p. 22).

The play does not end with an unequivocal victory leading to the expulsion of the colonizer. Rather, it posits a Hegelian dialectic in which Prospero and Caliban remain on the island, with Prospero declaring his power as well as a curious, almost natural bond. "Well Caliban, old fellow, it's just us two now, here on the island" (p. 68). Given this ending, *A Tempest* is commonly staged as a "political comedy" with a humorous rhetorical play on language.[43] However, one cannot overlook the political message of the play: to promote "black consciousness" and rewrite the script of colonial history. At least imaginatively, if not literally, the play creates a different kind of "brave new world" in which the struggle for political and cultural independence is in *process.*

Undoubtedly, Césaire's postcolonial vision (incorporating the philosophy of Negritude) challenges the categories of representation defining the non-European races as inferior and in need of civilization. But while it celebrates a revolution of brotherhood, it holds in place a kinship system in which women figure as gifts or objects of exchange. Caliban's somewhat ambivalent repudiation of Miranda seems to free him from hostility and rivalry toward Prospero and Ferdinand, but in another sense, his gesture can also be read as a symbolic rejection of a potential gift—a daughter who is to be given to some man in marriage. Unlike feminist critics such as Leininger, Césaire, in his revision of Shakespeare's play, makes no attempt to reconceptualize the relationship between Caliban and Miranda, or to suggest any possibilities of a shared resistance to the patriarch. Anxieties about possible miscegenation, so crucial to Prospero's demonization of Caliban in Shakespeare's play, are repressed by Césaire in his diminishment of Miranda's role. Caliban's summary dismissal of any desire to possesses Miranda sexually is a convenient structural device for mobilizing an all-male revolution—one which recapitulates the kinship structure in its most basic form, giving a minimal presence to Miranda.

Thus, a play celebrating the emerging freedoms of the 1960s does not change Miranda's fate. Her marriage is once again *arranged* in a gift exchange that will ensure future peace and stability in a growing nation that will now combine two European city states. Prospero articulates this to Ariel at the outset: "These are men of my race and of high rank . . . I have a daughter. Alonso has a son. If they were to fall in love I would give my consent. Let Ferdinand and Miranda marry, and may that marriage bring us harmony and peace. That is my plan. I want it executed" (p. 16). Though Prospero willfully stays on this island to continue his "civilizing mission," he ensures the consolidation of his kingdom through the alliance of Naples and Milan via the marriage of his daughter. Hence, while Césaire empowers Caliban to cry out unfailingly, "Freedom Hi-Day," we never find out how Miranda's "brave new world" turns out after all.

While Miranda's circumscribed role conveniently fulfills the requirements of a European patriarchy, it is telling that Césaire does not introduce a woman who can be Caliban's "physiognomically complementary mate." Writing in the context of the history of the Americas, and specifically from the perspective of Caribbean women, Sylvia Wynter criticizes Shakespeare's play for its absence of Caliban's mate:

> [The] question is that of the most significant absence of all, that of Caliban's Woman, of Caliban's physiogno-

mically complementary mate. For nowhere in Shakespeare's play, and in its system of image-making, one which would be foundational . . . to our present Western world system, does Caliban's mate appear as an alternative sexual-erotic model of desire . . . an alternative system of meanings. Rather there, on the New World island, as the only woman, Miranda . . . [is] contrasted with the ontologically absent, potential genetrix—Caliban's mate—of another population of human, i.e., of a "vile race" "capable of ill-will."[44]

Reading this absence historically, Wynter (citing Caribbean writers like Maryse Condé) suggests that "the nondesire of Caliban for his own mate, Caliban's 'woman' is . . . a founding function of the 'social pyramid' of the global order that will be put in place following upon the 1492 arrival of Columbus in the Caribbean."[45] In this first phase of Western Europe's expansion into the Americas, given the expanding slave trade out of the "Europe-Africa-New World triangular traffic," Caliban as "both the Arawak and African forced labour, [supposedly] had no need/desire for the procreation of his own kind."[46] It is ironic that these criticisms, revealing the limitations of Shakespeare's play, are also applicable to Césaire's revisionary version. Caliban's revolt can have little impact as long as the absence of a native woman as his sexual reproductive mate functions to negate the progeny/population group comprising the original owners/occupiers of the New World lands, the American Indians.

In conclusion, if Aimé Césaire's *A Tempest* is widely read as an allegory of decolonization, it fails to address adequately the relationship between liberation movements and the representations of sexual difference. Instead, it shows that if resistance movements are "imagined communities," then such imaginings are frequently based upon particular, and often disempowering, constructions of women's sexuality.[47] As gifts of exchange, or conduits of homosocial desire between men, women taking part in the movements for real national liberation could not escape the determinations of earlier kinship structures. Reflecting this historical trend, Césaire conveniently represents Miranda as the property of the colonizers, but more significantly, displaces the sexual, maternal identity of the "native" woman, Sycorax, onto the idealized abstraction of the Earth as Mother, while denying Caliban a potential union with a Caribbean woman. Finally, Césaire's call for a revolution lacks credibility as he prevents Prospero's former slave from peopling the isle with Calibans.

Notes

1. George Lamming, *The Pleasures of Exile* (1960) (Ann Arbor: University of Michigan Press, 1992), p. 13.
2. Roberto Fernandez Retamar, *Caliban and Other Essays*, trans. Edward Baker (Minneapolis: University of Minnesota Press, 1989), p. 55.
3. For fuller accounts of *The Tempest* and decolonization, see Eric Cheyfitz, *The Poetics of Imperialism: Translation and Colonization from The Tempest to Tarzan* (Oxford: Oxford University Press, 1991), pp. 42-58. To follow the production of the term, "Cannibal," see Peter Hulme, *Colonial Encounters: Europe and the Native Caribbean 1492-1797* (London: Methuen, 1986), pp. 1-3. Also see Roberto Fernandez Retamar, *Caliban and Other Essays,* pp. 6-21.
4. Cheyfitz, *The Poetics of Imperialism,* p. 42.
5. Retamar, *Caliban and other Essays,* pp. 6-21. Retamar offers a detailed history of the changing political images of Caliban in Latin American history through decolonization.
6. *Ibid.,* p. 14.
7. Lamming, *The Pleasures of Exile,* p. 14.
8. Aimé Césaire, *A Tempest: An Adaptation of The Tempest for Black Theatre,* trans. Richard Miller (New York: Ubu Repertory Theatre Publications, 1969), p. 15.
9. Francis Barker and Peter Hulme, "Nymphs and Reapers Heavily Vanish: The Discursive Con-Texts of *The Tempest*," in *Alternative Shakespeares,* John Drakakis, ed. (London: Methuen, 1985), p. 204.
10. Virginia Vaughan, "'Something Rich and Strange': Caliban's Theatrical Metamorphoses," in *Shakespeare Quarterly* 36.4 (Winter 1985): 390-405.
11. Césaire, *A Tempest,* pp. 67-68.
12. Lamming, *The Pleasures of Exile,* p. 15.
13. Sandra Pouchet Paquet, foreword to George Lamming, *The Pleasures of Exile,* pp. xxi-xxiv, offers a feminist critique of Lamming's postcolonial vision. Specifically, her focus on the missing Sycorax identifies the limitations of the postcolonial revisions of the original.
14. Retamar, *Caliban and Other Essays,* p. 55.
15. See Louis A. Montrose, "The Work of Gender in the Discourse of Discovery," in *New World Encounters,* Stephen Greenblatt, ed. (Berkeley: University of California Press, 1993), pp. 177-83, for a look at the ways in which the early colonial discourses were gendered, thus feminizing the "New Worlds." His analysis offers a useful model for a rhetorical analysis of the structure of colonial narratives.
16. Malek Alloula, *Colonial Harem* (Minneapolis: University of Minnesota Press, 1987), p. 3.
17. Frantz Fanon, *Black Skin White Masks* (1952), trans. Charles Lamm Markmann (New York: Grove Press, 1967), p. 63.
18. Paquet, foreword, Lamming, *The Pleasures of Exile,* pp. xxi-xxii.
19. Lamming, *The Pleasures of Exile,* p. 114.
20. *Ibid.,* p. 107.
21. *Ibid.*
22. Paquet, foreword, *ibid.,* p. xxii.

23. William Shakespeare, *The Tempest* (1610-11) (New York: Signet Classic/Penguin, 1987). All quotations are taken from this edition.

24. Coppèlia Kahn, "The Providential Tempest and the Shakespearean Family," in *Representing Shakespeare: New Psychoanalytic Essays,* Murray A. Schwartz and Coppèlia Kahn, eds. (Baltimore: Johns Hopkins University Press, 1980), pp. 217-43.

25. David Sundelson, "'So Rare a Wonder'd Father': Prospero's *Tempest,*" in *ibid.,* pp. 33-55.

26. *Ibid.*

27. Stephen Orgel, "Prospero's Wife," in *Rewriting the Renaissance: The Discourses of Sexual Difference in Early Modern Europe,* Margaret W. Ferguson, Maureen Quilligan, and Nancy Vickers, eds. (Chicago: University of Chicago Press, 1986), p. 51.

28. I base my analysis of the structure of colonial discourse on Paul Brown's formulation, in "'This Thing of Darkness I Acknowledge Mine': *The Tempest* and the Discourse of Colonialism," in *Political Shakespeare,* Jonathan Dollimore, ed. (Ithaca: Cornell University Press, 1985), pp. 48-54.

29. My application of the exchange of women in kinship systems is indebted to Gayle Rubin's feminist, anthropological analysis, "The Traffic in Women: Notes on a Political Economy of Sex," in *Toward an Anthropology of Women,* Reyna R. Reiter, ed. (New York: Monthly Review Press, 1974), pp. 171-77. For a fuller discussion of Mauss' and Lévi-Strauss's theories by Rubin, see pp. 177-75.

30. *Ibid.,* pp. 174-75.

31. Eleanor Burke Leacock, *Myths of Male Dominance* (New York and London: Monthly Review Press, 1981), pp. 229-41. Leacock discusses the gender inflections of Lévi-Strauss' formulations as well the tendencies of other anthropologists "to seek universals in relations between the sexes," pp. 231-33.

32. Rubin, "The Traffic in Women," pp. 172-74.

33. Orgel, "Prospero's Wife," p. 55.

34. John Gillies, *Shakespeare and the Geography of Difference* (Cambridge: Cambridge University Press, 1994), pp. 140-44. He locates Sycorax within the poetic geography of the period, by drawing on associations (made by Renaissance and earlier geographers and ethnographers) between her and other non-European others.

35. Hulme, *Colonial Encounters,* pp. 111-12.

36. Orgel, "Prospero's Wife," 51.

37. Lorrie Jerrell Leininger, "The Miranda Trap: Sexism and Racism in Shakespeare's *The Tempest,*" in *The Woman's Part: Feminist Criticism of Shakespeare,* Gayle Green, Ruth Swift Lenz, and Carol Thomas Neely, eds. (Urbana: University of Illinois Press, 1980), pp. 285-94.

38. Leininger, "The Miranda Trap," pp. 291-92.

39. *Ibid.,* p. 292.

40. Laura Donaldson, *Decolonizing Feminisms: Race, Gender, and Empire-Building* (Chapel Hill: University of North Carolina Press, 1992), p. 17.

41. Césaire, *A Tempest,* act I, scene ii, p. 13. All subsequent quotes will be taken from this edition. Page numbers are noted in parenthesis within the text.

42. Cheyfitz, *The Poetics of Imperialism,* p. 41.

43. D.J.R. Bruckner, Review of *A Tempest, New York Times,* October 16, 1991, p. B 1.

44. Sylvia Wynter, "Beyond Miranda's Meanings: Un/silencing the Demonic Ground of Caliban's Woman," in *Out of the Kumbla: Caribbean Women and Literature,* Carole Boyce Davies and Elaine Savoury Fido, eds. (Trenton, NJ: Africa World Press, 1990), p. 360.

45. *Ibid.,* pp. 360-61.

46. *Ibid.,* p. 361.

47. I am indebted to the "Introduction" to *Nationalisms and Sexualities,* eds. Andrew Parker, Mary Russo, Doris Sommer, and Patricia Yaeger (London: Routledge, 1992), p. 13, for this formulation of "imagined communities" derived from Bendict Anderson's useage. Several essays, under the section "Women, Resistance, and the State," examine the relationship between resistance movements and social constructions of women's bodies, pp. 395-424.

Barbara Fuchs (essay date 1997)

SOURCE: "Conquering Islands: Contextualizing *The Tempest,*" in *Shakespeare Quarterly,* Vol. 48, No. 1, Spring, 1997, pp. 45-62.

[*In the following essay, Fuchs extends typical colonialist interpretations of* The Tempest *to include the play's references to European imperialism in Ireland and the Islamic Mediterranean.*]

It is an axiom of contemporary criticism that *The Tempest* is a play about the European colonial experience in America. While this perspective has generated enormously enriched readings of the play, it runs the risk of obscuring the complicated nuances of colonial discourses in the early seventeenth century. When is America not America? When it is Ireland, or North Africa, or Europe itself, or the no-man's-land (really every man's *desired* land) of the Mediterranean in-between. Just as the formal literary elements of a text—metaphors, puns, patterns—may signify in multiple ways, context, too, may be polysemous. By exploring other contexts for the insistent colonial concerns of Shakespeare's island play, I hope to show how a multiple historical interpretation can unpack the condensed layers of colonialist ideology. This type of reading depends not only on recent *Tempest* criticism—what one might call the American readings—but on studies of England's colonial role in Ireland. My aim is, first, to provide descriptions of the contemporary colonial contexts in both Ireland and the Mediterranean, which I believe shed light on the play, and, second, to suggest the advantages for political criticism of considering all relevant colonial contexts simultaneously. If, as I will argue, the superimposition of those contexts on the play reflects the way colonialist ideology is "quoted" from one contact zone to another in the sixteenth and early seventeenth centuries, criticism that attempts to trace that ideology will gain from identifying precisely such layering of referents.[1]

My purpose in this essay is not to refute American readings of *The Tempest*; I agree with Peter Hulme that placing New World colonialism at the center of the play has made it a fundamentally more interesting and, at least for twentieth-century readers, a more relevant text.[2] Instead, by highlighting the historical and political dimensions of the contemporary Mediterranean world and England's colonial experience in Ireland, I hope to continue to historicize the colonialist discourse that American readings first brought to the fore. Even in highly suggestive and politically sophisticated readings of *The Tempest*, the Mediterranean often equals the literary, the *Aeneid*, the essentially European, functioning largely as a background to American *newes*[3]—what Hulme calls the first layer of a textual palimpsest.[4] The new transatlantic colonial discourse works itself out against this background of the *Aeneid* and classical Mediterranean travels. Yet this critical privileging of America as the primary context of colonialism for the play obscures the very real presence of the Ottoman threat in the Mediterranean in the early seventeenth century and elides the violent English colonial adventures in Ireland, which paved the way for plantation in Virginia.

Although twentieth-century historians can speak of the Ottoman Empire in the early seventeenth century as having "passed its peak,"[5] such a perspective was hardly available, as Samuel Chew points out, to contemporary observers of Islam's might.[6] As I hope to show, the sense of an Eastern empire encroaching on Europe pervades Shakespeare's play, making the European "center" of the text simultaneously the origin of colonial adventure and the target of another empire's expansionism. The general absence of Ireland from discussions of colonialism in the play is troubling, particularly since the devastation of a native population and its culture was more deliberate and vicious in England's first plantation than in its later ventures in Virginia. As Paul Brown has suggested, there are strong analogies between Prospero's island and Elizabethan Ireland, which locate them both "between American and European discourse."[7]

. . . . .

The Irish are the niggers of Europe, lads.

The Commitments

What are we to make of Roddy Doyle's equation—his rather tongue-in-cheek justification for an Irish band's focus on soul music? Doyle has found a parallel between the situation of African Americans within the U.S. and that of the Irish vis-à-vis postimperialist Europe. While his use of the ugly term *niggers* indicates the conflictive nature of such a comparison (in that the register of working-class/colonized solidarity fails to transcend racial prejudice, and in that the comparison problematically erases the presence in Europe of large black immigrant populations), Doyle's comparison also parodies the discursive strategies of quotation which contribute to colonization. By comparing them to another oppressed population, Doyle establishes the right of the Irish to soul; ironically, the colonization of Ireland itself depended largely on strategies of comparison which represented its conquest as a repetition of earlier imperialist ventures to Africa and the Americas. As Nicholas P. Canny has pointed out, the colonization of Ireland functioned as an apprenticeship for England's plantation in the Americas.[8] I propose to focus here on the discursive dimension of this education—what I term colonial quotation.

By *quotation* I mean the references by colonial writers to the works of earlier explorers and planters as well as the larger rhetorical maneuver of assimilating the unknown by equating it with the already-known. Such quotation does not overlap perfectly with the notion of *translatio imperii*—the westward translation of Rome's imperial tradition to the nascent European empires. However the quoted discourse may use *translatio imperii* as its particular justification.[9] The quotation of colonialist discourse from one instance to the next naturalizes expansion by bringing newly "discovered" lands and people under the conceptual domain of the already-known, the already-digested. Thus this particular kind of intertextuality advances a colonialist ideology.[10]

The equation between prior and ongoing colonial encounters may be achieved by literal textual quotation of authorities, by referring to the colonist's own previous experiences in another territory, or by reading a newly discovered culture as another manifestation of one already othered. Such a strategy underlies the remarkable encounter between Trinculo and Caliban in 2.2 of *The Tempest*, where the European does not know what the man/fish is but certainly knows what to *make of it*: a for-profit display like the multiple "dead Indians" in London fairs: "Were I in England now, as once I was, and had but this fish painted, not a holiday-fool there but would give a piece of silver. There would this monster make a man—any strange beast there makes a man" (ll. 27-30).[11]

The context of exhibition that Trinculo quotes serves to frame the new and bring it under his dominion. The irony, of course, lies in the fact that the man "made" by such exhibition would be not Caliban attaining human status but Trinculo made rich.[12] Although Trinculo claims to "let loose" his earlier opinion when he realizes that Caliban is alive, even calling him an "islander," the framework of exhibition is immediately reinstated by Stephano, who says he would take the monster home to present to a ruler or sell for profit (ll. 67-68, 74-75). Alive or dead, Caliban fulfills the role of spectacular other and, throughout the comic process of recognition by which Stephano and Trinculo discover him, occupies an abject position. His monstrosity corresponds quite neatly to the Europeans' expectations. For Caliban himself, of course, the situation is framed by Prospero's abusive treatment, which has scripted him as victim.

Caliban's cloak plays a central part in this complicated series of misrecognitions and discoveries, especially as a signal of the play's Irish context. The presence of the cloak does not prove such a context, but it suggests how English domination of Ireland might *take cover* in the text under precisely such details. The cloak, I would argue, is the only native artifact allowed Caliban. He first shrouds under it in order to escape detection by Trinculo, who he fears is a spirit in Prospero's service. Trinculo does discover him and immediately joins him under his "gaberdine" to seek protection from the storm.[13] There Stephano finds the two of them—a curious hybrid creature with four legs and two mouths, recalling Iago's characterization of Othello and Desdemona's marriage as a miscegenistic "beast with two backs." Such unhallowed combinations are precisely the issue here, as Trinculo unwittingly becomes monstrous in Stephano's eyes. Given England's anxiety over distinguishing savage from civilized, islander from colonizer in Ireland, it is possible to read this episode in Shakespeare's text as one of the indices of this colonial adventure.

The English conquest of Ireland was a messy affair. The twelfth-century Anglo-Norman conquest had provided England with a foothold in Dublin and the eastern counties—an area known as the Pale—while large portions of Ireland remained, literally and figuratively, beyond the Pale of English authority.[14] Cruel attempts to control the island during Elizabeth's rule were both enabled and impeded by this earlier conquest. Over the intervening four centuries the Old English settlers had become in cultural terms all but indistinguishable from the Irish, which hugely complicated English attempts to fight the colonial war on cultural turf by proscribing Irish custom, dress, and social institutions. One of the earliest English statutes in Ireland, enacted in 1297, had required the English to "relinquish the Irish dress," while the Statutes of Kilkenny in 1366 had expressly linked English adoption of the "manners, fashion, and language of the Irish enemies" to the decay of "the said land and its liege people, the English language, the allegiance due to our lord the king, and the English laws."[15] By the sixteenth century, despite such separatist legislation, Old English settlers had adopted many Irish ways. The imperfect allegiance of the Anglo-Irish nobility to Elizabeth and to her metropolitan power was reflected in their rather less ambivalent embrace of Irish culture.

The Irish mantle became a particularly loaded signifier of such cultural struggles.[16] In Spenser's *A View of the Present State of Ireland* (1596) the two interlocutors, Eudoxus and Irenius, propose several competing genealogies for such mantles. Irenius states that the Irish have such a custom "from the Scythians," to which Eudoxus responds with a long history tracing the mantle from Jews to "Caldees" and Egyptians, through Greeks and Romans. But Irenius—who is given an extensive last word on the matter—cuts that history short:

> I cannot deny but anciently it was common to most, and yet Sithence disused and laid away. But in this latter age of the world since the decay of the Roman Empire, it was renewed and brought in again by those northern nations, when breaking out of their cold caves and frozen habitation into the sweet soil of Europe, they brought with them their usual weeds, fit to shield the cold and that continual frost to which they had at home been enured; the which yet they left not off, by reason that they were in perpetual wars with the nations where they had invaded, but still removing from place to place carried always with them that weed as their house, their bed and their garment, and coming lastly into Ireland they found there more special use thereof, by reason of the raw cold climate, from whom it is now grown into that general use in which that people now have it; afterward the Africans succeeding, yet finding the like necessity of that garment, continued the like use thereof.[17]

The mantle—house, bed, and garment—becomes inextricably linked to Irish transhumance, the seasonal movement of people and their livestock in search of pastures, one of the practices that most disturbed the English and which they associated closely with barbarity and "enormities unto that commonwealth."[18] Yet this history looks forward, too, by projecting the mantle from the Irish to the Africans, despite the logic of climatic determinism. Irenius does not deny the mantle a genealogy but simply replaces the history of civil peoples with one of savagery, setting the stage for the kind of colonialist quotation that I shall analyze below.

The discussion of the mantle continues at some length, with Irenius paradoxically providing more examples of the usefulness of such garments the more he seeks to criticize them. The perspective from under the cloak differs greatly from that outside it—as Irenius says, "the commodity doth not countervail the discommodity. . . . for it is a fit house for an outlaw, a meet bed for a rebel, and an apt cloak for a thief."[19] One's appreciation of the mantle, then, will vary radically according to whether one is the persecuted or the persecutor. In Spenser's description the mantle becomes the reified signifier of Irish resistance, which cannot be fully penetrated by English authority, even with English ethnography leading the way. As Jones and Stallybrass argue, "The mantle represents Irishness as the refusal to adopt English order, English social categories, English style."[20] Moreover, as one of the prime signifiers of Irishness, the mantle served to assess the extent to which earlier settlers had "gone native": the adoption of the mantle was presumably the culminating move in such acculturation.[21] It is significant, then, that this problem is carefully avoided in Irenius and Eudoxus's discussion, as the latter moves quickly from the mantle to a warning about English use of the "glib," or long bangs over the eyes:

> Sure I think Diogenes' dish did never serve his master more turns, notwithstanding that he made his dish his cup, his measure, his waterpot, then a mantle doth an Irishman, but I see they be all to bad intents, and therefore I will join with you in abolishing it. But what blame lay you to then glib? Take heed, I pray you, that you be not too busy therewith, for fear of your own blame, seeing our Englishmen take it up in such a general fashion, to wear their hair so unmeasurably long that some of them exceed the longest Irish glibs.[22]

The Irish glibs, Irenius answers, are "fit masks as a mantle is for a thief." The subject of English mimicry of Irish fashions, however, has once again been carefully avoided. If, as Sir John Davies wrote, the Old English imitating Irish ways are "like those who had drunke of Circes Cuppe, and were turned into very Beasts," the real threat lay not in the power of the witch but in the fact that her colonist victims "tooke such pleasure in their beastly manner of life, as they would not returne to their shape of men againe."[23] The metaphor takes on an interesting resonance if read back into Spenserian allegory in Book II of *The Faerie Queene*. In the Bower of Bliss, Acrasia/Circe's cup threatens not so much the disarmed knight (who can, after all, be disenchanted) as it does Grill, who stubbornly insists on going—and staying—native, famously refusing to be saved back into civilization.

The cultural warfare so well exemplified by Spenser's diatribe was just one front of attack in the English conquest of Ireland. As the violence escalated from the 1560s to the early part of the seventeenth century, anti-Irish rhetoric became ever more virulent, precisely to justify the widening attacks against Irish civilian populations. Ireland did eventually provide large estates for English gentlemen, but only after a bloody and extended struggle such as the English had not expected. Throughout this conflict, Ireland and America were both considered attractive options for expansionist ambitions; when particularly frustrated in their Irish campaigns, colonizers like Humphrey Gilbert and Walter Ralegh turned to America instead. Similarly, when the earliest English settlements at Roanoke proved impossible to sustain, such veterans of the American voyages as Thomas Hariot and John White tried planting in Ireland as an alternative.[24]

The connection between these desirable colonies as expansionist sites was established rhetorically at a number of levels. The description of dress—to return to our discussion of Caliban's cloak—is one of the clearest instances of the quoting of a previous colonial experience in a new plantation. The English often perceived the Americas through an Irish filter. Thus Gabriel Archer described the natives' leggings in New England as "like to *Irish* Dimmie Trouses," and Martin Pring saw natives with "a Beares skinne like an *Irish* Mantle over one shoulder."[25] Even Powhatan's dress was described by one of John Smith's companions as "a faire Robe of skins as large as an Irish mantle."[26] As the comparisons expand beyond costume to other cultural practices, such as "wild" mourning, devil worship, and transhumance—all of which the English believed they had found on both sides of the Atlantic—it becomes easier to see how such comparisons contribute to the "othering" of a culture by assimilating it conceptually to one already subdued, if not conquered.[27] The resulting quotations function as the colonist's mirror image of miscegenation: instead of the confusion of racial boundaries that might actually threaten his dominion, he creates a purely rhetorical union of various colonial subjects. The others are insistently other but similar among themselves. I should stress, of course, that both the similarities and differences quoted belong to a constructed "text" of culture.[28]

Quoting from one colonial context to the other serves to domesticate the new—the American experience—and equate it with the already-advanced plantation of Ireland. Yet the considerable chronological overlap of European colonial experience in Ireland and America makes the temporal sequence more difficult to untangle. Although Ireland's subjection is the primary colonial context for England in the 1590s and early 1600s, that conquest is in turn justified by comparing the English role in Ireland to that of the Spaniards in America.[29] References to previous Spanish conquests introduce a kind of reciprocity in colonialist quoting, with Ireland as the middle term: the English quote the Spanish experience in America in order to justify England's role in Ireland, and then transfer that Irish experience to Virginia. Yet the process of quotation must reach increasingly farther back in history for additional terms to substantiate the comparison. Thus the similarity between the English situation in Ireland and the Spanish *Conquista*—a problematic one considering Elizabethan propaganda against Spain—is reinforced by allusions to the *Reconquista,* or expulsion of the Moors from Spain, to further buttress colonialist apologias. Davies justifies the forcible transplantation of the Irish in Ulster by referring to "the Spaniards [who] lately removed all the Moors out of Grenada into Barbary, without providing them any new seats there."[30] The end of the comparison gives away Davies's conscience: Spain was far more concerned with preventing the return of the Moors expelled from North Africa than with their resettlement. In Ireland what to do with a starving peasant population forcibly removed from its land was a question not easily addressed.

Nicholas Canny finds the main source for the English/Spanish connection in Richard Eden's translation of Peter Martyr's *De Orbe Novo* (1555), which was probably familiar to English notables in Ireland in the 1560s.[31] The Spanish conquest of the Americas became a model for the domination of savage peoples, so that the English comparison of their own role in Ireland to the Spanish conquests became closely imbricated with the construction of the Irish as barbarous. In this colonialist logic, once the Irish were thus characterized, they became appropriate subjects for the same treatment Native Americans had received at the hands of the Spanish. That the English reviled Spanish behavior, disseminating the infamous Black Legend of Spanish atrocities in the Indies, seems not to have impeded use of this model when the Irish situation made it expedient.[32] English characterizations of Irish savagery, based on the natives' supposed paganism and transhumance, proceeded apace: by 1560 Archbishop Matthew Parker could take such descriptions as a given, advocating the establishment of resident clergy in the north of England to prevent the inhabitants from becoming "too much Irish and savage."[33]

In constructing the Irish as savages, the English placed them within a temporal framework in which Ireland existed at a stage of social development long since surpassed by England. Ireland required civilizing by England in much the same way that England had required colonizing by Rome.[34] Sir Thomas Smith engaged in this rather partial relativism when he explained:

> This I write unto you as I do understand by histories of thyngs by past, how this contrey of England, ones as uncivill as Ireland now is, was by colonies of the Romaynes brought to understand the lawes and orders of thanncient orders whereof there hath no nacon more streightly and truly kept the mouldes even to this day then we, yea more than thitalians and Romaynes themselves.[35]

The recognition of one's own past in another by no means implies an acceptance of that other; it instead establishes a temporal dynamic in which that other must be made the same—forcibly brought up to date, so to speak. Here, England has already been civilized, having accepted the imposition of the Roman mold. This shapely civility then authorizes the imposition of a similar rule on Ireland, as *translatio imperii* becomes a kind of *translatio morum*.

English emphasis on the need to civilize the savage Irish partly replaces an earlier model of colonialist justification in which the Old English had argued that the Irish needed to be liberated from the tyranny of their own ruling class but were essentially fit subjects for English law and, indeed, desirable tenants or laborers.[36] It is possible to read these shifting constructions of the colonial subject in the two depictions of islanders in Shakespeare's text. Although Ariel need not be read as the co-opted native, as some modern rewritings of *The Tempest* insist, it *is* possible to view him as the colonizer's fantasy of a pliant, essentially accommodating, and useful subject. Of course, the play's ironic presentation of Prospero's fantasy shows the tensions inherent in this model. Ariel's gratitude is never as complete or as certain as Prospero would wish. Perhaps, the text suggests, a liberated native tends to interpret liberation in terms rather different from those of his or her enlightened liberator. In the lively prehistory of the play,

Prospero freed Ariel from Sycorax's tyranny—wonderfully literalized in the pine trunk that bound him; but it is unclear whether subjugation to the new magician on the scene really means more liberty for the sprite.

Caliban, meanwhile, recalls the second model developed by the English to justify colonization: the Irish subject in need of civilizing. Miranda's speech presents the colonizer's story of attempts to civilize the native and locates the supposed intractability of Caliban in his lack of language (1.2.350-61). Consider her description of his inability to express himself:

> I pitied thee,
> Took pains to make thee speak, taught thee each hour
> One thing or other. When thou didst not, savage,
> Know thine own meaning, but wouldst gabble like
> A thing most brutish, I endowed thy purposes
> With words that made them known.
>
> (ll. 352-57)

Emphasis on the impenetrability of Caliban's language—even he, according to Miranda, cannot understand it—evokes the English colonizers' frustration with Gaelic as a barrier to their penetration of the territory.[37] But Caliban cannot be "liberated" simply by being taught English. The end of Miranda's speech betrays the unspoken half of the colonialist argument: if the native's "vile race" makes him inherently unsuited to civilization, then violence is justified:

> But thy vile race—
> Though thou didst learn—had that in't which good natures
> Could not abide to be with; therefore wast thou
> Deservedly confined into this rock,
> Who hadst deserved more than a prison.
>
> (ll. 357-61)

Here the duplicitous logic of colonialist ideology is exposed: if one explanation for Caliban's subjection doesn't work, a more essentialist one will be found. Language is more useful than Caliban knows.

My point is not that the elements of colonialist discourse in the text do not apply to the Americas. It would be ridiculous to deny that the English experienced a similar or even greater disorientation when confronted with American languages and cultures than with Gaelic. Instead, I am attempting to display the layering of such contexts in the play, from the basic discourse of savagery developed by the English in Ireland to their eventual experiences in the Americas. To read only America in *The Tempest* is to ignore the connections that colonial quotation establishes between England's two main Western plantations, connections perhaps expressed most graphically in the instability of their geographic referents. In the first part of the seventeenth century, Ireland could be, as it was to Bacon, "the second island of the ocean Atlantic," or it could migrate to a completely different conceptual context, as in Fynes

Moryson's description of "This famous Island in the Virginian Sea."³⁸

. . . . .

This Tunis, sir, was Carthage.

(2.1.82)

Even within these pages it has not been possible to separate Irish and Mediterranean colonial contexts without postponing the insistent presence of the latter, as the English in Ireland compare themselves to the Spaniards expelling the Moors and the Irish mantle is sighted not only in America but in Africa. Our inability to describe simultaneously the bewildering number of ways in which early modern Europe experienced other civilizations prevents us from uncovering all the connections among those experiences, but a focus on one area of contact should not preclude consideration of others. Ann Rosalind Jones has tried to bring together multiple cultural encounters by exploring the often-made comparison of Vittoria Colombina's Moorish maid Zanche to the Irish in Webster's *The White Devil*.³⁹ The attribution to Zanche of both Irish and Moorish savagery is particularly evocative if we consider that two terms of the comparison represent, respectively, a newly established Western colony *of* England and an Eastern empire that was a threat *to* England. Such a conflation of attributes in the figure of the Moorish maid may suggest how the English import a gendered discourse into their cultural negotiations with the Moors in order to disable the Islamic threat.

Textual signs of English anxiety about Islamic power in the Mediterranean abound in the play, though critics generally relegate those signs to a literary register. When discussing the marriage of Alonso's daughter Claribel to the king of Tunis, Gonzalo points out that Tunis *is,* in a fundamental way, Carthage: "This Tunis, sir, was Carthage." Critics hastily explain *Carthage,* with its baggage of Virgilian associations, as though the mention of Tunis were self-explanatory.⁴⁰ While some recent criticism has explored the early seventeenth-century construction of Islam in the English theater,⁴¹ there are specific textual traces of the imperial Ottoman threat in *The Tempest.* Even though by the 1580s trade was established between England and the Turkish world, the perceived menace of Islam was still great. Writing his *Generall Historie of the Turkes* in 1603, Richard Knolles calls them "the greatest terrour of the world" and advocates the reading of his text because the Ottoman Empire "in our time so flourisheth, and at this present so mightily swelleth as if it would ouerflow all, were it not by the mercie of God."⁴² The threat of Islam existed on two fronts: southeastern Europe (which will not concern us here) and the Mediterranean. Knolles shows great respect for Ottoman power on both land and sea: "With the great Ocean [the Ottoman monarch] much medleth not, more than a little in the gulfes of Persia and Arabia: most of his territories lying vpon the Mediterranean and Euxine seas. . . . Now for these seas, no prince in the world hath greater or better means to set forth his fleets than hath he."⁴³

During the sixteenth century the Barbary Coast that figures so prominently in Shakespeare's play had come gradually under Turkish power.⁴⁴ In fact, Algiers, Sycorax's home before her banishment, had been captured by the Turks in the 1530s. Charles V led an expedition against it in 1541 but without success. Tunis itself had very recently been the site of a European struggle against the Ottoman Empire: captured by the Spanish in 1572, it was reconquered by the Turks in 1574.⁴⁵

Morocco had never been part of the empire, and a substantial diplomatic relationship developed between its rulers and Elizabeth, allied together against both the Spanish and the Turks.⁴⁶ After James's peace with Spain, England abandoned its rather fanciful plans for invading Spain with Morocco's help and instead considered invading Morocco. Writing to King James, Henry Roberts suggested that the campaign be carried out with "Irish solduars and they of the Out Isles," as "the countrey wilbee the better to bee ridd of them, for they bee but idle and will never fall to worke but steale as longe as they remaine in Ireland."⁴⁷ Once again the colonized—here proposed as mercenaries—return to English rhetoric as new conquests are envisioned.

The possibility of conquering Morocco, however remote, might account for the representation of non-Turkish Moors, in plays such as Heywood's *Fair Maid of the West,* as embodying a "dangerous but effeminate otherness that finally renders them safely inferior to their European visitors," as Jean Howard puts it.⁴⁸ But Howard makes race the main cause of such a representation, minimizing the difference between Turks and Moroccan Moors in terms of an expansionist imperative. I think that the difference in terms of an imperial threat is fundamental: isolated Morocco could be an ally or, treacherously, could be turned into a colony; under the Ottoman Empire the rest of North Africa remained a much greater threat. Thus England's willingness to consider Moroccan Islam a lesser threat than Spanish Catholicism: Morocco was not an expansionist power, or at least not in the direction of Europe.

The perceived threat from the Ottoman Empire itself, however, did not abate, even after the decisive victory at Lepanto. This 1571 naval battle was hailed as the triumph of Christendom over the Turks, but it was soon clear that the intra-European alliances necessary to mount a credible challenge to Ottoman power would not last. One textual record of the unusual place that Lepanto occupied in the history of the European struggle against Islam is King James's epic poem on the subject, written after the battle and republished when he acceded to the English throne.⁴⁹ The poem caught Richard Knolles's attention, and he dedicates his history to James, "for that your Majestie hath not disdained in your *Lepanto* or *Heroicall Song,* with your learned Muse to adorne and set forth the greatest and most glorious victory that euer was by any the Christian confederat princes obtained against these the *Othoman* Kings or Emperors."⁵⁰ Perhaps the most interesting signs of the European tensions that made the Lepanto victory unrepeatable appear in James's preface to the reader, where he provides an extensive set of justifications for a Protestant monarch's praise of the Catholic alliance: "And . . . I knowe, the special thing misliked in it, is, that I should seeme, far contrary to my degree and Religion, like a Mercenary Poët, to penne a worke, *ex professo,* in praise of a forraine Papist bastard. . . . " Although the extraordinary circumstances of the battle justify his praise of Don Juan of Austria "as of a particular man," James suggests, the reader should not extrapolate from that praise any sympathy for the Catholic League: "Next follows my invocation to the true God only, and not to all the He and She Saints, for whose vain honors, DON- IOAN fought in all his wars."[51] In James's ambivalent unwriting of the poem's epic praise, we see reflected the fragility of the European unity that had led to the great naval triumph.

In the years after Lepanto, as English trade with the Turks was gradually established, England developed a complex relationship to the Ottoman threat. While a healthy respect for the Turks' imperial might prevailed, Islam (especially in the Moroccan version) also became a term in an elaborate set of rhetorical constructions which played it off against Catholicism as a lesser, or merely equivalent, evil. An observer like Knolles, however, thought that Spain, given its American riches, was the most appropriate power to deal with the Turkish emperor:

> There remaineth only the king of Spaine, of all other the great princes either Christians or Mahometanes (bordering vpon him) the best able to deale with him; his yearely reuenewes so farre exceeding those of the Turkes. . . .[52]

Knolles suggests that the Spanish have the best chance of defeating the Turks but regrets that their resources are spread too thin over their many possessions "for the necessarie defence and keeping of his so large and dispersed territories."[53]

For England the situation vis-à-vis the Turks was further complicated by piracy in the Mediterranean. As the sixteenth century drew to a close, petty piracy gradually replaced large naval encounters.[54] English merchants were prey to Barbary pirates from Algiers or Tunis, but English piracy also flourished, glorified during Elizabeth's reign as privateering against the Spanish and alternately condemned and condoned once peace with Spain had been reached. When English pirates fell out of favor at home, they "turned Turk." Purchas locates the scandalous confusion of Moors and English renegades in Algiers, which he calls "the Whirlepoole of these Seas, the Throne of Pyracie, the Sinke of Trade and the Stinke of Slavery; the Cage of uncleane Birds of Prey, the Habitation of Sea-Devils, the Receptacle of Renegadoes of God, and Traytors to their Country."[55] But the figure of the English renegade seemed threatening, I conjecture, mainly because it shattered the carefully constructed mirroring of Barbary Coast pirates in English privateering. As long as this mirror image was maintained, the English could imagine a role for themselves in controlling the Mediterranean. Once English pirates became, effectively, outlaws and went over to the other side, England was at a disadvantage, having no official expansionist presence in such contested territory. This complicated background of piracy on the sea and traditional Islamic expansionism on land lies behind the Algiers described as Sycorax's birthplace in *The Tempest,* 1.2. Yet even that origin is made more complicated by the location of the main action of the play on an island somewhere between Tunis and Italy.

In some ways the Mediterranean islands themselves were the most volatile territories in the region. Malta had withstood the Turkish assault in 1565, but the Knights of St. John had moved there only when it proved impossible to defend Rhodes. Cyprus, too, was in Turkish hands, as even the victory at Lepanto had proved insufficient to reconquer it. All the islands were especially vulnerable, of course, to pirate raids. Any island imagined in the Mediterranean at the time of the play, then, would be understood to exist in a hotly contested space, permanently threatened by the Ottoman Empire if not directly under its control.

If one focuses on Tunis and the threat it posed to the Christian areas of the Mediterranean, the indecorous marriage that sets the royal party in *The Tempest* on their journey becomes ever more outrageous. If the marriage of Desdemona to Othello is controversial, it could at least be partly redeemed by the fact that Othello the Moor fights against the Turks on the side of Venice. To marry a daughter to the king of Tunis, while perhaps expedient in political terms, is a far more radical move than to pair her off in some convenient European alliance. To Lynda Boose's argument that "the black male-white female union is, throughout this period and earlier, most frequently depicted as the ultimate romantic-transgressive model of erotic love,"[56] I would add that the chastening tragic end of *Othello* cannot be discounted as one vision of such unions. The threat of violence to Christian women from irascible foreign husbands is well chronicled in Knolles, who tells the story of Manto . . . , a Greek lady taken prisoner by the Turks, who marries Ionuses Bassa, an official in Suleiman's army. After an initial interlude of married bliss, Bassa, "after the manner of sensuall men still fearing least that which so much pleased himselfe, gaue no lesse contentment to others also," becomes madly jealous.[57] Manto tries to leave him and return to her country but is betrayed by a eunuch, whereupon her husband kills her. This story could have served as a source for *Othello;* whether or not it did so, it highlights the dangers that Europe imagined for a woman married into the empire of Islam. Such a union would probably be more acceptable in European eyes when (as with Othello fighting for Venice or the Prince of Morocco coming to Belmont to woo Portia unsuccessfully in *The Merchant of Venice*) it involved the domestication of the foreign male rather than the removal of a European woman to North Africa or Asia Minor. As Sebastian points out, rubbing salt in Alonso's wounds:

> Sir, you may thank yourself for this great loss,

> That would not bless our Europe with your daughter,
> But rather lose her to an African,
> Where she, at least, is banished from your eye,
> Who hath cause to wet the grief on't.
>
> (2.1.121-25)

The description of Claribel's forced marriage recalls grim accounts of Christians captured by Barbary Coast pirates rather than stories of transgressive romance. Sebastian continues to insist upon the near-sacrificial nature of the union:

> You were kneeled to and importuned otherwise
> By all of us, and the fair soul herself
> Weighed between loathness and obedience at
> Which end o'th' beam should bow. . . .
>
> (ll. 126-29)

What does this marriage tell us, then, about the sexual politics of the play as a sublimated arena for imperial struggles? Knolles suggests the reason for the Claribel-Tunis union when he describes Naples as the European border of the Ottoman Empire. Alonso is thoroughly chastised for his decision to marry off his daughter (presumably to contain Islamic attacks on Naples), but the reproaches come from one who wishes him ill and would usurp his crown. The thoroughly negative characterization of the island conspirators somewhat relegitimizes the marriage, since it is mainly Sebastian who condemns it. Yet the most telling reaction to the supposed alliance with Tunis comes when Sebastian and Antonio discuss murdering Alonso for his crown. At this point Claribel entirely replaces her Moorish consort, as her femaleness is used to fix Islam firmly in Africa. When Antonio asks Sebastian who, after Ferdinand, is next in line to the crown of Naples, Sebastian answers "Claribel." Antonio then places Claribel at a further and further remove from the crown by insisting on the impossible distances that separate her from Europe:

> ANTONIO
> She that is Queen of Tunis; she that dwells
> Ten leagues beyond man's life; she that from Naples
> Can have no note unless the sun were post—
> The man i' th' moon's too slow—till newborn chins
> Be rough and razorable; she that from whom
> We all were sea-swallowed, though some cast again—
> And by that destiny, to perform an act
> Whereof what's past is prologue, what to come
> In yours and my discharge.
> SEBASTIAN
> What stuff is this? How say you?
> 'Tis true my brother's daughter's Queen of Tunis,
> So is she heir of Naples, 'twixt which regions
> There is some space.
> ANTONIO
> A space whose every cubit
> Seems to cry out, 'How shall that Claribel
> Measure us back to Naples? Keep in Tunis,
> And let Sebastian wake.'
>
> (2.1.244-58)

Sebastian's commonsense rejoinder about "some space" is perfectly reasonable, considering that the distance from Tunis to Naples, as Stephen Orgel points out, is three hundred miles.[58] But what interests me here is the incredible amplification of space that Antonio imagines, as he expands the Mediterranean into an immense ocean. His hyperbole not only makes the crossing impossible but also neatly obscures its possible agents. Although Antonio measures the length of the voyage by a man's lifespan, by the man in the moon's speed, and by the time it takes for a baby boy to reach manhood, the actual man Claribel has married is nowhere to be found in the passage. Presumably, however, the king of Tunis would support his royal consort's claims to a European throne; perhaps his interest in conquering that throne justified the marriage in the first place. Antonio's exclusive focus on the possibility of Claribel's return should thus be read as a strategy for containing the role of Islam in the play. In a perverse metonymy, the European woman, instead of her threatening husband, becomes "Tunis." Unlike "Norway," "Denmark," "Morocco," "Aragon," and other heroic national appellations, the name of "Tunis" signifies only an infinitely distant Claribel. Much as the Turks in *Othello* are conveniently drowned in a single line of dialogue—"News, friends: our wars are done; the Turks are drown'd" (2.1.202)—in order to allow the domestic action to proceed, Antonio's relocation of Claribel to faraway Tunis and his erasure of her husband define the power struggles within the play as essentially European, regardless of the place where they are occurring. Of course Alonso's party is itself an exception to the supposed impossibility of getting to Tunis. Antonio admits this but points to their being "sea-swallowed" on their return. And yet the very urgency of the conspiracies on the island would indicate that the Italians have little doubt they will eventually return home. The play's containment of "Tunis"—a pressing, contemporary imperial threat—by focusing on Claribel's distance rehearses the earlier containment of a historical empire, Carthage, through the jocund references to "Widow Dido" in 2.1.

In *The Tempest* gender does the work of imperialism rather than of discovery.[59] The containment of the Islamic threat to European sovereignty or Mediterranean expansion plays itself out once again in the peculiar story of Sycorax's banishment from Algiers. This expulsion functions as a screen for European fears of Islamic control of the Mediterranean islands. Sycorax—cast as too awful even for the rough society of Algiers—is banished, as Prospero (whose source for this knowledge is somewhat unclear) tells Ariel, "For mischiefs manifold and sorceries terrible / To enter human hearing" (1.2.264-65). Yet her banishment was a commuted sentence; her life was spared "for one thing she did"—that is, her pregnancy. This ascription of mercy to the Algerians, reflecting European law, effectively replaces the Barbary pirates or Ottoman galleys—whose power so impressed Knolles—with the flimsy bark of sailors on a charitable mission who deposited the pregnant Sycorax on the island. Again, the metonymic reduction of Islam to the figure of the witch is perverse, for what is at stake in the Mediterranean is not the "Satanic" side of Islam—which Sycorax might represent—but its military might. The rewriting of Islamic expansionism into an errand of mercy operates once again through a female figure—a type of containment far more subtle than the effemination Howard points to in Heywood's play, or even than the commonplace associations of the East with luxury and sensuousness. Here the female figures take the place of the threatening Moors, so that the latter are disarmed at a remove. By indirectly neutralizing the threat of Islam, the text of *The Tempest* prevents any direct engagement with its forces, addressing instead a female version, which is more easily conquered, at least in rhetoric. As the action of the play proves, Sycorax represents a temporary presence rather than an effective Islamic conquest of the island; her son Caliban loses it immediately to the Europeans. Moreover, this second instance of containment through figuration is presented by Prospero, who, whatever his colonialist failings, clearly represents a center of moral authority in the text. Thus it is not only conspirators who turn to the feminine as a strategy for ensuring European power: Prospero's story emasculates Algerian naval power just as Antonio and Sebastian's fantasies erase the king of Tunis.

The gendered dynamics of Mediterranean containment in the play recall the more common gendered colonialist trope of ravishing a newly discovered land. Clearly this particular island no longer has her maidenhead; she is thoroughly known by Caliban, who was familiar with her secrets even before Prospero arrived, and who showed Prospero "all the qualities o'th' isle" (l. 337). Instead of rhapsodizing the European rape of the island, then, the text provides as counter-metaphor another rape—Caliban's attempt on Miranda—as colonialist justification (ll. 347-48).[60] Caliban's attack on Prospero's daughter once more genders the colonizing impulse; here it is the defense of the European woman that justifies repression of the non-European.

The triad of female figures which I have considered (two of them absent, two largely submissive daughters) thus participates in the text's containment of Islamic expansionism and its more complex espousal of European colonialism. The rhetorical representation of the women, through hyperbole, metonymy, and the anti-metaphor of Miranda's near-rape, performs European imperial goals at the discursive level, and it is only by interrupting that performance through, for example, a consideration of the play's multiple contexts that the illusionism can be examined.

Thus the discursive work of gender functions as yet another set of colonialist strategies. Much like the use of quotation which I identified when discussing the connections between English experiences in Ireland and America, these rhetorical strategies in *The Tempest* make sense only when viewed from the perspective of multiple contexts. Europe's experience of being another empire's goal was closely bound up, temporally, materially, and rhetorically, with its burgeoning experience of empire-building; it is no wonder, then, that the multiple dimensions come together in a text as complex and polysemous as *The Tempest*. By purposely conflating and collapsing these contexts, I have attempted to give a political reading of the play which insists on what Richard Knolles would call "the four parts of the world," in order to prevent Shakespeare's island play from itself becoming isolated somewhere in the Americas.

Notes

I would like to thank Stephen Orgel and Patricia Parker for their kind suggestions for this essay.

1. I take the term "contact zone" from Mary Louise Pratt's *Imperial Eyes: Travel Writing and Transculturation* (London and New York: Routledge, 1992). Pratt uses this term to replace "colonial frontier," a term "grounded within a European expansionist perspective" (6-7).

   In her suggestive "Rogues, Shepherds, and the Counterfeit Distressed: Texts and Infracontexts of *The Winter's Tale* 4.3," (*Shakespeare Studies* 22 [1994]: 58-76), Barbara A. Mowat explores the "infracontexts" of *The Winter's Tale*. In my analysis of *The Tempest*, I will show how such superimposition of contexts serves colonialist ideologies. In discussing what I shall call "colonial quotation," I adhere to a wide definition of intertextuality as a relation between not only literary but also cultural texts. This notion of intertextuality recognizes that, as Roland Barthes argues, "The logic that governs the Text is not comprehensive (seeking to define 'what the work means') but metonymic; and the activity of associations, contiguities, and cross-references coincides with a liberation of symbolic energy" ("From Work to Text" in *Textual Strategies: Perspectives in Post-Structuralist Criticism*, Josué V. Harari, ed. [Ithaca, NY: Cornell UP, 1979], 73-81, esp. 76). Unlike Barthes, I perceive such symbolic energy as driving a particular ideological project.

2. See Peter Hulme, *Colonial Encounters: Europe and the native Caribbean, 1492-1797* (London and New York: Methuen, 1986), 106.

3. William C. Spengemann, in *A New World of Words: Redefining Early American Literature* (New Haven, CT, and London: Yale UP, 1994), points out that America "was in fact the source of the genre called 'newes'" (97).

4. See Hulme, 108-9.

5. Bernard Lewis, *Islam and the West* (New York: Oxford UP, 1993), 16.

6. See Samuel C. Chew, *The Crescent and the Rose: Islam and England during the Renaissance* (New York: Oxford UP, 1937), 100.

7. Paul Brown, "'This thing of darkness I acknowledge mine': *The Tempest* and the discourse of colonialism" in *Political Shakespeare: Essays in cultural materialism*, Jonathan Dollimore and Alan Sinfield, eds., 2d ed. (Ithaca, NY, and London: Cornell UP, 1994), 48-71, esp. 57.

8. See Nicholas P. Canny, "The Ideology of English Colonization: From Ireland to America," *William and Mary Quarterly* 30 (1973): 575-98.

9. For one approach to the role of translation in colonization, see Eric Cheyfitz, *The Poetics of Imperialism: Translation and Colonization from* The Tempest *to* Tarzan (New York and Oxford: Oxford UP, 1991).

10. In his "Broken English and Broken Irish: Nation, Language, and the Optic of Power in Shakespeare's Histories" (*Shakespeare Quarterly* 45 [1994]: 1-32) Michael Neill suggests how a different form of quotation might serve to *counter* colonialism. If, as he argues, Irish nationalism was produced by the same English nationalism that violently redefined and colonized Ireland, then perhaps the strategy of quotation need not work entirely to the conquerors' advantage.

11. Quotations of *The Tempest* in this essay follow the Oxford text (ed. Stephen Orgel [Oxford: Clarendon Press, 1987]).

12. I find Brown's identification of Trinculo with the "footloose Irish" (56) as a masterless barbarian unconvincing, given that Trinculo so clearly occupies the position of colonizer in this episode. This is not to suggest, however, that the text is not staging an anxiety about the *English* masterless classes.

13. In his introduction, Cheyfitz suggests that this reference to gaberdines links Caliban to the Jews (xii), although the main evidence in the *Oxford English Dictionary* for such a connection derives from Shakespeare's own usage in *The Merchant of Venice* (*Oxford English Dictionary*, prepared by J. A. Simpson and E.S.C. Weiner, 2d ed., 20 vols. [Oxford: Clarendon Press, 1989], 6:302). I would argue that the highly charged discourse about Irish coverings in the period provides a more immediate referent.

14. For a good summary of this history, see David Beers Quinn, *The Elizabethans and the Irish* (Ithaca, NY: Cornell UP, 1966), or Canny, *The Elizabethan Conquest of Ireland: A Pattern Established 1565-76* (New York: Barnes and Noble, 1976).

15. The preamble to the Statutes of Kilkenny, excerpts reprinted in A. J. Otway-Ruthven, *A History of Medieval Ireland* (London: Ernest Benn; New York: Barnes and Noble, 1968), 291.

16. For a suggestive account of the role of the Irish mantle in terms of gender dynamics, see Ann Rosalind Jones and Peter Stallybrass, "Dismantling Irena: The Sexualizing of Ireland in Early Modern England" in *Nationalisms & Sexualities,* Andrew Parker, Mary Russo, Doris Sommer, and Patricia Yaeger, eds. (New York and London: Routledge, 1992), 157-71. Neill also discusses the mantle as a site for English anxieties about the "inscrutable" Irish other (26).

17. Edmund Spenser, *A View of the Present State of Ireland,* ed. W. L. Renwick (Oxford: Clarendon Press, 1970), 51.

18. Spenser, 49.

19. Spenser, 51.

20. Jones and Stallybrass in Parker et al., eds., 166.

21. In discussing the contradictory English attitudes toward the mantle, Jones and Stallybrass note that "a miscegenation of clothes returns to haunt the colonizer" when a military supplier in Ireland suggests to Elizabeth that she provide her English troops there with an Irish mantle (Jones and Stallybrass in Parker et al., eds., 168). Although the authors read the episode as a sign of fragile English cultural identity, to adopt the mantle might also be to incorporate the enemy's tricks.

22. Spenser, 53.

23. Sir John Davies, *A Discovery of the Reasons Why Ireland Was Never Entirely Subdued* (1612), 182; quoted here from Jones and Stallybrass in Parker et al., eds., 163.

24. See Quinn, 109ff.

25. Samuel Purchas, *Purchas His Pilgrimes,* 4 vols. (London, 1625), 4:1647 and 1655.

26. John Smith, *Works. 1608-1631,* ed. Edward Arber (Birmingham: Privately Printed, 1884), 102; see also page 405.

27. Although I cannot address it here, such colonial quoting was also used to characterize African peoples newly encountered in the period, comparing them to the Irish.

28. Colonialism mediates English encounters with its several others, so that observation is never neutral or transparent. As Neill has shown, not only is ocular control essential to English domination in Ireland, but the construction of the Irish as different already brands them with a kind of guilt (26-27 and 6).

29. For a discussion of such triangulation, see Canny, "The Ideology of English Colonization."

30. Davies to Salisbury, 8 November 1610, quoted here from Davies, *Historical Tracts* (Dublin, 1787), 273-86, esp. 283-84.

31. See Canny, "The Ideology of English Colonization," 593-94.

32. The first translation of Bartolomé de las Casas's *Breve historia de la destrucción de las Indias* appeared in England under the title *The Spanish Colonie* (London, 1583). The English emulation of Spanish behavior is thus exactly contemporaneous with its condemnation. For an account of how this ambiguity played itself out in Ralegh's voyage to Guiana, see Louis Montrose, "The Work of Gender in the Discourse of Discovery" in *New World Encounters,* Stephen Greenblatt, ed. (Berkeley: U of California P, 1993), 177-217.

33. Matthew Parker, *Correspondence* (1833), quoted here from Quinn, 26.

34. This strategy for disarming criticism of colonialism has had a long life. Compare Joseph Conrad's evocation of a "primitive" London in *Heart of Darkness* (New York: Signet, 1978): after eulogizing the Thames as the artery of commerce and empire, Marlow says, "And this also has been one of the dark places of the earth" and proceeds to evoke the Roman arrival in Britain (67).

35. Sir Thomas Smith to Fitzwilliam, 8 November 1572; quoted here from Canny, *Elizabethan Conquest,* 588-89.

36. See Canny, *Elizabethan Conquest,* 580 and 589.

37. The English address the threatening incomprehensibility of the natives' language itself through the mechanisms of colonial quotation. The term *hubbub,* originally used to describe an Irish war cry or outcry, migrates to Virginia, where Henry Spelman hears the Indians making a "whoopubb" (Smith, cv). The *OED* itself incorporates the strategies of colonial quotation, defining *hubbub* as "a confused noise of a multitude shouting or yelling; esp. the confused shouting of a battle-cry or 'hue and cry' by *wild or savage races*" (7:459, my emphasis).

38. Francis Bacon, *The Letters and the Life of Francis Bacon,* 4th ed. (1868), and Fynes Moryson, *An Itinerary* (1617); both quoted here from Quinn, 121-22.

39. See Ann Rosalind Jones, "Italians and Others: Venice and the Irish in *Coryat's Crudities* and *The White Devil,*" *Renaissance Drama* 18 (1987): 101-19.

40. See, for example, Robert Wiltenburg, "The *Aeneid* in *The Tempest,*" *Shakespeare Survey* 39 (1987): 159-68; and John Pitcher, "A Theater of the Future: *The Aeneid* and *The Tempest,*" *Essays in Criticism* 34 (1984): 193-215. Orgel does mention Spain's repeated attempts to invade Tunis in the sixteenth century (40).

    It must be noted that the imperial name of Carthage itself travels far beyond the classical world. By the seventeenth century Cartagena was the name of both a city in Spain and a Spanish settlement in what is now Colombia. Orgel cites Richard Eden's mention of this West Indies harbor as "Carthago" in *The Decades of the New World* (London, 1555), a translation of Peter Martyr's *De Orbe Novo.*

41. See especially Lynda E. Boose, "'The Getting of a Lawful Race': Racial discourse in early modern England and the unrepresentable black woman"; Jean E. Howard, "An English Lass Amid the Moors: Gender, race, sexuality, and national identity in Heywood's *The Fair Maid of the West*"; and Particia Parker, "Fantasies of 'Race' and 'Gender': Africa, *Othello,* and bringing to light," all in *Women, "Race," and Writing in the Early Modern Period,* Margo Hendricks and Patricia Parker, eds. (London and New York: Routledge, 1994), 35-54, 101-17, and 84-100.

42. Richard knolles, *The Generall Historie of the Turkes,* 2d ed. (London, 1610), A4^v and A6^v.

43. Knolles, Aaaaaa6^r.

44. See, for example, Prospero's account of Sycorax (1.2.261-70) and the discussion of Claribel's marriage to the king of Tunis (2.1.68-84 and 244-58).

45. For a concise summary of these events, see Chew, 551-55.

46. For a detailed account of the history of Anglo-Moroccan relations, see Jack D'Amico, *The Moor in English Renaissance Drama* (Tampa: U of South Florida P, 1991), 7-40.

47. Henry De Castries, *Les Sources Inédités de L'Histoire du Maroc* (1918); quoted here from D'Amico, 38.

48. Howard in Hendricks and Parker, eds., 113.

49. For the poem's publication history and an account of the battle as the background for *Othello,* see Emrys Jones, "'Othello', 'Lepanto' and the Cyprus Wars," *SS* 21 (1968): 47-52.

50. Knolles, A3^r.

51. "Lepanto" in *The Poems of James VI of Scotland,* ed. James Craigie, 2 vols. (Edinburgh: William Blackwood and Sons, 1955), 1:198.

52. Knolles, Bbbbbb^r.

53. Knolles, Bbbbbb^r.

54. See Fernand Braudel's encyclopedic *The Mediterranean and the Mediterranean World in the Age of Philip II,* trans. Siân Reynolds, 2 vols. (London: Collins, 1973), 2:1186-95.

55. Purchas, quoted here from Chew, 344.

56. Boose in Hendricks and Parker, eds., 41.

57. Knolles, 557.

58. Orgel, ed., 2.1.245n.

59. I allude to Montrose's discussion of Ralegh in Guiana ("The Work of Gender" in Greenblatt, ed.).

60. In another variation on this theme, the natives' alleged sexual violence toward the Europeans' intended land was sometimes offered as a colonialist justification, as in Purchas's description of the vulnerable Virginia: ". . . howsoeuer like a modest Virgin she is now vailed with wild Couerts and shadie Woods, expecting rather rauishment then Mariage from her Natiue Sauages . . ." (4:1818).

RACE AND GENDER

Lorie Jerrell Leininger (essay date 1980)

SOURCE: "The Miranda Trap: Sexism and Racism in Shakespeare's *Tempest*," in *The Woman's Part: Feminist Criticism of Shakespeare,* edited by Carolyn Ruth Swift Lenz, Gayle Greene, and Carol Thomas Neely, University of Illinois Press, 1980, pp. 285-94.

[*In the following essay, Leininger discusses the oppression of women and non-whites—personified in the characters of Miranda and Caliban, respectively—in* The Tempest.]

Shakespeare's *Tempest* was first performed before King James I at Whitehall in November of 1611. It was presented a second time at the court of King James early in 1613, as part of the marriage festivities of James's daughter Elizabeth, who, at the age of sixteen, was being married to Frederick the Elector Palatine. The marriage masque within *The Tempest* may have been added for this occasion. In any case, the Goddess Ceres' promise of a life untouched by winter ("*Spring come to you at the farthest / In the very end of harvest!*" IV.i.114-15)[1] and all the riches the earth can provide ("*Earth's increase, foison plenty*") was offered to the living royal couple as well as to Ferdinand and Miranda.

Elizabeth had fallen dutifully in love with the bridegroom her father had chosen for her, the youthful ruler of the rich and fertile Rhineland and the leading Protestant prince of central Europe. Within seven years Frederick was to become "Frederick the Winter King" and "The Luckless Elector," but in 1613 he was still the living counterpart of Ferdinand in *The Tempest,* even as Elizabeth was the counterpart of Miranda. Like Miranda, Elizabeth was beautiful, loving, chaste, and obedient. She believed her father to be incapable of error, in this sharing James's opinion of himself. Miranda in the play is "admired Miranda," "perfect," "peerless," one who "outstrips all praise"; Elizabeth was praised as "the eclipse and glory of her kind," a rose among violets.[2]

What was the remainder of her life to be like? Elizabeth, this flesh-and-blood Miranda, might have found it difficult to agree that "We are such stuff / As dreams are made on; and our little life / Is rounded with a sleep" (IV.i.156-58). The future held thirteen children for her, and forty years as a landless exile. Her beloved Frederick died of the plague at the age of thirty-six, a plague spreading through battle camps and besieged cities in a Europe devastated by a war which appeared endless—the Thirty Years War, in which whole armies in transit disappeared through starvation and pestilence. The immediate cause of this disastrous war had been Frederick and Elizabeth's foolhardy acceptance of the disputed throne of Bohemia. Politically inept, committed to a belief in hierarchical order and Neoplatonic courtliness, the new king and queen failed to engage the loyalty of the Bohemians or to prepare adequately for the inevitable attack by the previously deposed king.

While the happiness of the young lovers in *The Tempest* depended upon their obedience to Miranda's father, the repeated political and military failures of Elizabeth and Frederick were exacerbated by their dependence upon the shifting promises of King James. Elizabeth experienced further tragedy when two of her sons drowned, the eldest at the age of fifteen in an accident connected with spoils from the New World, the fourth son in a tempest while privateering in the New World. There was no Prospero-figure to restore them to life magically.

The Princess Elizabeth, watching *The Tempest* in 1613, was incapable of responding to clues which might have warned her that being Miranda might prove no unmixed blessing: that even though Miranda occupies a place next to Prospero in the play's hierarchy and appears to enjoy all of the benefits which Caliban, at the base of that hierarchy, is denied, she herself might prove a victim of the play's hierarchical values. Elizabeth would be justified in seeing Miranda as the royal offspring of a ducal father, as incomparably beautiful (her external beauty mirroring her inward virtue, in keeping with Neoplatonic idealism), as lovingly educated and gratefully responsive to that education, as chaste (her chastity symbolic of all human virtue), obedient and, by the end of the play, rewarded with an ideal husband and the inheritance of two dukedoms. Caliban, at the opposite pole, is presented as the reviled offspring of a witch and the Devil, as physically ugly (his ugly exterior mirroring his depraved inner nature), as racially vile, intrinsically uneducable, uncontrollably lustful (a symbol of all vice), rebellious, and, being defined as a slave by nature, as justly enslaved.

Modern readers have become more attentive than Elizabeth could have been in 1613 to clues such as Prospero's address to Miranda, "What! I say, / My foot my tutor?" (I.ii.471-72). The crucial line is spoken near the end of the scene which begins with Prospero's and Ariel's delighted revelation that the tempest was raised through Prospero's magic powers and then continues with the demonstration of Prospero's ability to subjugate the spirit Ariel, the native Caliban, and finally the mourning Prince Ferdinand to his will. Miranda's concern is engaged when Prospero accuses Ferdinand of being a spy, a traitor and usurper; Prospero threatens to manacle Ferdinand's head and feet together and to force him to drink salt water. When Ferdinand raises his sword to resist Prospero's threats, Prospero magically deprives him of all strength. Miranda, alarmed, cries,

> O dear father,
> Make not too rash a trial of him, for
> He's gentle, and not fearful.
>
> (I.ii.469-71)

Prospero's response is,

What! I say,
My foot my tutor?

(I.ii.471-72)

Miranda is given to understand that she is the foot in the family organization of which Prospero is the head. Hers not to reason why, hers but to follow directions: indeed, what kind of a body would one have (Prospero, or the play, asks) if one's foot could think for itself, could go wherever it pleased, independent of the head?

Now it is true that Prospero is acting out a role which he knows to be unjust, in order to cement the young couple's love by placing obstacles in their way. Miranda, however, has no way of knowing this. Prospero has established the principle that stands whether a father's action be just or unjust: the daughter must submit to his demand for absolute unthinking obedience.

But might not being a "foot" to another's "head" prove advantageous, provided that the "head" is an all-powerful godlike father who educates and protects his beloved daughter? Some ambiguous answers are suggested by the play, particularly in the triangular relationship of Prospero, Miranda, and Caliban.

When Prospero says to Miranda,

We'll visit Caliban my slave, who never
Yields us kind answer,

Miranda's response is,

'Tis a villain, sir,
I do not love to look on.

(I.ii.310-12)

Miranda fears Caliban, and she has reason to fear him. The play permits either of two interpretations to explain the threat which Caliban poses. His hostility may be due to his intrinsically evil nature, or to his present circumstances: anyone who is forced into servitude, confined to a rock, kept under constant surveillance, and punished by supernatural means would wish his enslavers ill.[3] Whatever Caliban's original disposition may have been when he lived alone on the isle—and we lack disinterested evidence—he must in his present circumstances feel hostility toward Prospero and Miranda. Miranda is far more vulnerable to Caliban's ill will than is her all-powerful father.

Prospero responds to Miranda's implicit plea to be spared exposure to Caliban's hostility with the *practical* reasons for needing a slave:

But, as 'tis,
We cannot miss him: he does make our fire,
Fetch in our wood, and serves in offices
That profit us. What, ho! slave! Caliban!

(I.ii.312-15)

A daughter might conceivably tell her loving father that she would prefer that they gather their own wood, that in fact no "profit" can outweigh the uneasiness she experiences. Miranda, however, is not free to speak, since a father who at any time can silence his daughter with "What! My foot my tutor?" will have educated that "foot" to extreme sensitivity toward what her father does or does not wish to hear from her. Miranda dare not object to her enforced proximity to a hostile slave, for within the play's universe of discourse any attempt at pressing her own needs would constitute both personal insubordination and a disruption of the hierarchical order of the universe of which the "foot/head" familial organization is but one reflection.

Miranda, admired and sheltered, has no way out of the cycle of being a dependent foot in need of protection, placed in a threatening situation which in turn calls for more protection, and thus increased dependence and increased subservience.

Miranda's presence as the dependent, innocent, feminine extension of Prospero serves a specific end in the play's power dynamics. Many reasons are given for Caliban's enslavement; the one which carries greatest dramatic weight is Caliban's sexual threat to Miranda. When Prospero accuses Caliban of having sought "to violate / The honour of my child" (I.ii.349-50), Caliban is made to concur in the accusation:

O ho, O ho! Would't had been done!
Thou didst prevent me; I had peopled else
This isle with Calibans.

(I.ii.351-53)

We can test the element of sexual politics at work here by imagining, for a moment, that Prospero had been cast adrift with a small son instead of a daughter. If, twelve years later, a ship appeared bearing King Alonso and a marriageable daughter, the play's resolution of the elder generation's hatreds through the love of their offspring could still have been effected. What would be lost in such a reconstruction would be the sexual element in the enslavement of the native. No son would serve. Prospero needs Miranda as sexual bait, and then needs to protect her from the threat which is inescapable given his hierarchical world—slavery being the ultimate extension of the concept of hierarchy. It is Prospero's needs—the Prosperos of the world—not Miranda's, which are being served here.

The most elusive yet far reaching function of Miranda in the play involves the role of her chastity in the allegorical scheme. Most critics agree that the chastity of Miranda and Ferdinand in the fourth act symbolizes all human virtue ("Chastity is the quality of Christ, the essential symbol of civilization"[4]), while Caliban's lust symbolizes all human vice.

The first result of this schematic representation of all virtue and vice as chastity and lust is the exclusion from the field of moral concern the very domination and enslavement which the play vividly dramatizes. The exclusion is accomplished with phenomenal success under the guise of religion, humanism, and Neoplatonic idealism, by identifying Prospero with God (or spirit, or soul, or imagination), and Caliban with the Devil (or matter, body, and lust). Within the Christian-humanist tradition, the superiority of spirit over matter, or soul over body, was a commonplace: body existed to serve soul, to be, metaphorically, enslaved by soul. In a tradition which included the *Psychomachia*, medieval morality plays, and Elizabethan drama, the "higher" and "lower" selves existing within each person's psyche had been represented allegorically in the form of Virtues and Vices. A danger inherent in this mode of portraying inner struggle lay in the possibility of identifying certain human beings with the Vice-figures, and others (oneself included) with the representatives of Virtue. Such identification of self with Virtue and others with Vice led to the great Christian-humanist inversion: the warrant to plunder, exploit and kill in the name of God—Virtue destroying Vice.

It was "only natural" that the educated and privileged be identified with virtue and spirit, and that those who do society's dirty work, and all outsiders, be identified with vice and matter. Ellen Cantarow has analyzed the tendency of allegory to link virtue with privilege and sin with misfortune, making particular power relationships appear inevitable, "natural" and just within a changeless, "divinely ordained" hierarchical order;[5] Nancy Hall Rice has analyzed the manner in which the artistic process of embodying evil in one person and then punishing or destroying that person offers an ersatz solution to the complex problem of evil, sanctioning virulent attacks on social minorities or outcasts,[6] and Winthrop D. Jordan has discussed the tendency of Western civilization to link African natives, for example, with preconceived concepts of sexuality and vice. Jordan speaks of "the ordered hierarchy of [imputed] sexual aggressiveness": the lower one's place on the scale of social privilege, the more dangerously lustful one is perceived as being.[7]

Thus in *The Tempest*, written some fifty years after England's open participation in the slave trade,[8] the island's native is made the embodiment of lust, disobedience, and irremediable evil, while his enslaver is presented as a God-figure. It makes an enormous difference in the expectations raised, whether one speaks of the moral obligations of Prospero-the-slave-owner toward Caliban-his-slave, or speaks of the moral obligations of Prospero-the-God-figure toward Caliban-the-lustful-Vice-figure. In the second instance (the allegorical-symbolic), the only requirement is that Prospero be punitive toward Caliban and that he defend his daughter Miranda's chastity—that daughter being needed as a pawn to counterbalance Caliban's lust. In this symbolic scheme, Miranda is deprived of any possibility of human freedom, growth or thought. She need only *be* chaste—to exist as a walking emblem of chastity. This kind of symbolism is damaging in that it deflects our attention away from the fact that real counterparts to Caliban, Prospero, and Miranda exist—that real slaves, real slave owners, and real daughters existed in 1613 for Shakespeare's contemporaries and have continued to exist since then.

To return to one of those daughters, Miranda's living counterpart Elizabeth Stuart, at whose wedding festivities *The Tempest* was performed: it appears likely that King James's daughter and her bridegroom were influenced in their unrealistic expectations of their powers and rights as future rulers by the widespread Jacobean attempt to equate unaccountable aristocratic power with benevolent infallibility and possibly by the expression of that equation in *The Tempest*. In our own century the play apparently continues to reflect ongoing societal confusions that may seduce women—and men—into complicity with those who appear to favor them while oppressing others. Can we envision a way out? If a twentieth century counterpart to Miranda were to define, and then confront, *The Tempest's* underlying assumptions—as, obviously, neither the Miranda created by Shakespeare nor her living counterpart in the seventeenth century could do—what issues would she need to clarify? Let us invent a modern Miranda, and permit her to speak a new Epilogue:

"My father is no God-figure. No one is a God-figure. My father is a man, and fallible, as I am. Let's put an end to the fantasy of infallibility.

"There is no such thing as a 'natural slave.' No subhuman laborers exist. Let's put an end to *that* fantasy. I will not benefit from such a concept presented in any guise, be it Aristotelian, biblical, allegorical, or Neoplatonic. Three men are reminded of Indians when first they see Caliban; he might be African, his mother having been transported from Algiers. I will not be used as the excuse for his enslavement. If either my father or I feel threatened by his real or imputed lust, we can build a pale around our side of the island, gather our own wood, cook our own food, and clean up after ourselves.

"I cannot give assent to an ethical scheme that locates all virtue symbolically in one part of my anatomy. My virginity has little to do with the forces that will lead to good harvest or to greater social justice.

"Nor am I in any way analogous to a foot. Even if I were, for a moment, to accept my father's hierarchical mode, it is difficult to understand his concern over the chastity of his *foot*. There is no way to make that work. Neither my father, nor my husband, nor any one alive has the right to refer to me as his foot while thinking of himself as the head—making me the obedient mechanism of his thinking. What I do need is the opportunity to think for myself; I need practice in making mistakes, in testing the consequences of my actions, in becoming aware of the numerous disguises of economic exploitation and racism.

"Will I succeed in creating my 'brave new world' which has people in it who no longer exploit one another? I cannot be certain. I will at least make my start by springing 'the Miranda-trap,' being forced into unwitting collusion with domination by appearing to be a beneficiary. I need to join forces with Caliban—to join forces with all those who are exploited or oppressed—to stand beside Caliban and say,

> As we from crimes would pardon'd be,
> Let's work to set each other free."

Notes

1. This quotation and subsequent ones are from *The Tempest,* Arden Shakespeare, ed. Frank Kermode (Cambridge, Mass.: Harvard University Press, 1958).

2. "The eclipse and glory of her kind" is the closing line of Sir Henry Wotton's poem, "On His Mistress, The Queen of Bohemia," in *The Poems of Sir Walter Raleigh . . . with those of Sir Henry Wotton and other Courtly Poets from 1540-1650,* ed. John Hannah (London: Bell and Sons, 1892), pp. 95-96. "A rose among violets" is a paraphrase of the third verse of that poem; the compliment was often quoted.

3. That the spirit Ariel, the figure contrasted to Caliban in the allegorical scheme, is a purely imaginary construct for whom no human counterparts exist helps to obscure the fact that human counterparts for Caliban did indeed exist. A community of free blacks had been living in London for over fifteen years at the time of the writing of *The Tempest.* The first Indian to have been exhibited in England had been brought to London during the reign of Queen Elizabeth's grandfather, Henry VII. For a full discussion of the historical background see Chapter II of my dissertation, "The Jacobean Bind: A Study of *The Tempest, The Revenge of Bussy D'Ambois, The Atheist's Tragedy, A King and No King* and *The Alchemist,* the Major Plays of 1610 and 1611, in the Context of Renaissance Expansion and Jacobean Absolutism," University of Massachusetts/Amherst, 1975. For more on the effects of the ambiguity surrounding the definition of Caliban as an abstract embodiment of evil and as an inhabitant of a newly discovered island see Chapter III of the same work, which considers *The Tempest* in relation to seventeenth- and twentieth-century imperialism.

   Four critics, among others, who have dealt with the colonial aspects of *The Tempest* and have focused upon Caliban and his enslavement as moral concerns are O. Mannoni, *Prospero and Caliban: The Psychology of Colonization,* trans. Pamela Powesland (New York: Praeger, 1956); Philip Mason, *Prospero's Magic: Some Thoughts on Class and Race* (London: Oxford University Press, 1962), pp. 75-97; Roberto Fernández Retamar, "Caliban," *Massachusetts Review,* 15 (Winter-Spring 1974), 7-72; and Kermode, "Introduction," *The Tempest.* While Kermode observes that Shakespeare, and more generally Renaissance writers, held contradictory attitudes toward Indians, viewing them on one hand as inhabitants of a golden age, with no *meum* or *tuum,* and on the other hand as human beasts in whom one could place no trust, he nevertheless arrives at the conclusion that "the confusion of interests characteristic of the subject is harmoniously reflected in Shakespeare's play" (p. xxxi)—a "harmony" more likely to be acceptable to those who are at ease with the historical reality of conquest and enslavement than by those who, like Caliban's living counterparts, have been conquered, enslaved, or colonized. It is puzzling that even an article as sensitive as Harry Berger, Jr.'s "Miraculous Harp: A Reading of Shakespeare's *Tempest,*" in *Shakespeare Studies,* 5 (1969), 253-83, in its exploration of the contradictory elements in Prospero's character—his tendency to see himself as a god, his limited knowledge of human nature, his pleasure in dominating others, and his preference for, and success in, dealing with projected embodiments of pure evil—falls short of focusing upon the dramatization of enslavement itself as an ethical concern. I explore this question, posed in general terms, in my "Cracking the Code of *The Tempest,*" *Bucknell Review,* 25 (Spring 1979), issue on "Shakespeare: Contemporary Critical Approaches," ed. Harry R. Garvin and Michael D. Payne.

4. Irving Ribner, "Introduction" to Shakespeare's *Tempest,* ed. George Lyman Kittredge, rev. Ribner (Waltham, Mass.: Blaisdell, 1966), p. xv.

5. Ellen Cantarow, "A Wilderness of Opinions Confounded: Allegory and Ideology," *College English,* 34 (1972), 215-16.

6. Nancy Hall Rice, "Beauty and the Beast and the Little Boy: Clues about the Origins of Sexism and Racism from Folklore and Literature," Diss. University of Massachusetts/Amherst 1974, p. 207.

7. Winthrop D. Jordan, *The White Man's Burden: Historical Origins of Racism in the United States* (New York: Oxford University Press, 1974), p. 196.

8. See, for example, accounts of the 1562-68 slaving voyages of Sir John Hawkins (one with Sir Francis Drake) which appear in Richard Hakluyt's *Principall Navigations Voiages and Discoveries of the English Nation* (London, 1589; facs. rpt. Cambridge: Cambridge University Press, 1965), Part Two, 521-22, 526-29, 531-32, 553-54, 562-64.

Kim F. Hall (essay date 1995)

SOURCE: "Marriages of State: *The Tempest* and *Antony and Cleopatra,*" in *Things of Darkness: Economies of Race and Gender in Early Modern England,* Cornell University Press, 1995, pp. 141-60.

[*In the excerpt below, Hall evaluates the racial and sexual threat to imperial culture posed by Caliban and Cleopatra in* The Tempest *and* Antony and Cleopatra, *respectively.*]

Colonialist readings of *The Tempest* have shown the text to be a fertile ground for exploring issues of race, cultural contest, and authority in English encounters in the "new world."[1] They have been less attentive to roles of women in colonial structures. The threat of interracial desire, although only one element in the myriad contests over social control in the play, is key to the establishment of an ideal of patriarchal authority. Perhaps because of his indeterminacy (to which I shall return later), Caliban has been read alternatively as black African, Afro-Caribbean, and Native American; however, in all these permutations, he embodies and resists ideologies of dark and light even as he is continually read as dark other.[2] Ania Loomba proposes that "explicitly social-Darwinist, racist and imperialist productions indicated Caliban's *political* colour as clearly *black*" (143). The text itself locates Caliban on one side of a binarism in Prospero's final pronouncement on Caliban, "this thing of darkness I / Acknowledge mine" (5.1.275-76), and in clearly marking him as a slave who is associated with darkness and dirt: "thou earth" (1.2.314; Vaughan and Vaughan 15).[3] Caliban functions as a "thing of darkness" against which a European social order is tested and proved. Conversely, Miranda is the emblem of purity and integrity whose person is the grounds of this struggle: the contest for access to her reveals a concern over the purity of the aristocratic female body that symbolically assures the integrity of aristocratic bloodlines ("fair issue" [4.1.24]) and an orderly disposition of property (Loomba 83). In addition to the connection between Caliban and Miranda, the play features a series of attempted joinings or unions that momentarily disrupt categories of race, class, and gender. These unions generally draw attention to the increased fluidity of these categories in new world enterprise and particularly question the future of dynastic alliance and succession in an Atlantic economy.

In the first scene Prospero charges Caliban with the attempted rape of Miranda: "I have used thee—/ Filth as thou art—with humane care, and lodged thee / In mine own cell, till thou didst seek to violate / The honour of my child" (1.2.345-48). While Caliban's response indicates that he did indeed make advances to Miranda, modern minds conditioned by American racism are compelled to disrupt Prospero's fostering of Ferdinand's "seduction" in place of Caliban's "rape," for, as Susan Griffin reminds us, the rape threat is the prime image formed by the racist imagination:

> At the heart of the racist imagination we discover a pornographic fantasy: the specter of miscegenation. The image of a dark man raping a fair woman embodies all that the racist fears. The fantasy preoccupies his mind. A rational argument exists which argues that the racist simply uses pornographic images to manipulate the mind. But these images seem to belong to the racist. They are predictable in a way that suggests a more intrinsic part in the genesis of this ideology. (298)

Although it may seem anachronistic to impose such a race/sex dialectic on an early text, and possibly offensive to seem to "explain" Caliban's behavior, it is nonetheless true that interracial sex does become an issue in the Virginia colonies not twenty years after the first performance of *The Tempest*. In the first Virginia law case (*Re: Davis* 1630) involving race, a white, Hugh Davis, was publicly whipped for fornication with a black woman (Giddings 35-36).

Completely authorized by the play, Prospero's hostility toward Caliban is linked to his obsessive attempts to control his environment and his daughter's sexuality. Caliban's response, "O ho, O ho! Would't had been done! / Thou didst prevent me—I had peopled else / This isle with Calibans" (1.1.348-50), strikes at the heart of European fears of the putative desire of the native other for European women and thus functions to license Prospero's anxiety (Loomba 149). Caliban's threat "to people the isle" with his offspring clearly suggests that he would control the island by creating a new "mixed" race and rebuts Prospero on his own terms. Territorial claims are backed here by a need for patriarchal control over women.[4]

Miranda's response to Caliban is equally telling: the language lessons (which she implies brought about the attempted violation), rather than fostering communication, reveal an epistemic "difference" that serves only to heighten her sense of racial difference and her estrangement from Caliban:

> I pitied thee,
> Took pains to make thee speak, taught thee each hour
> One thing or other. When thou didst not, savage,
> Know thine own meaning, but wouldst gabble like
> A thing most brutish, I endowed thy purposes
> With words that made them known. But thy vile race—
> Though thou didst learn—had that in't which good natures
> Could not abide to be with . . .
>
> (1.2.352-59)

Miranda's tirade against Caliban's alien "ingratitude" does seem out of character for the dutiful daughter she is in the rest of the play.[5] Her claim that Caliban does not "know thine own meaning" replicates the play's central ethos, which cannot accept that his "gabbling" has value: just as Prospero's power is located in his book, "true" meaning (and power) lies in European, aristocratic language. Like many colonial travelers who denigrate the language of other cultures when confronted with meanings they do not accept, Miranda reads Caliban's native tongue as a nonlanguage and refuses to accept his use of her discourse on the grounds that it is corrupted with "uncivil" meanings. Her lessons, rather than reforming and "civilizing" him, only let him express his "savage" impulses in terms she cannot help but understand. He controls the language rather than be controlled by it. Caliban's "sin," as it were, is both linguistic and sexual; in saying, "My profit on't / Is I know how to curse," he subverts the language just as he is said to attempt to corrupt Miranda.

Caliban's rejected sexual advances signal his position in the web of economics, hegemonic control, and linguistic exclusion that is common to discourses of race. In arguing that race becomes the central trope for forming differences between "cultures, linguistic groups, or adherents of specific belief systems which—more often than not—also have fundamentally opposed economic interests" (5), Henry Louis Gates, Jr., also suggests that "literacy . . . is the emblem that links racial alienation and economic alienation" (6). Caliban's "difference" is produced out of just such a combination of linguistic exclusion and economic competition: his reply ("my profit on't / Is I know how to curse") articulates both economic and linguistic / racial alienation. Although writing is not directly an issue, access to a language of power is; curses (or spells), while seemingly powerful weapons for Sycorax, have no efficacy for Caliban. In this new linguistic economy, powerful curses and spells are located in Prospero's book. This triangulated linguistic community, with Prospero at the apex, serves to enforce both a racial hierarchy and patriarchal authority. Miranda, while teaching Caliban, performs the proper role of the woman within culture: she teaches a "mother language" to Caliban that is supposed to replace his original mother's tongue. However, neither Miranda's nor Caliban's relationship to language is powerful. Miranda's own mastery of language is still secondary to Prospero's: it is represented as purely oral, and she is frequently conjoined to silence in the beginning of the play. Juliet Fleming astutely notes that the vernacular and the oral are often associated with the feminine; more important, she contends that such mediated relationships to standardized languages are typical: "But while women (and foreigners) may be permitted to lend their assent to the new authoritative functions of English, they are not expected to use it authoritatively themselves; indeed the adequately 'ruled' English turns out to be the exclusive possession of men" (299).

So, too, the enforcing of a subject people's "assent" to a ruler's language is a key tool of colonial power. Caliban, typically, has been taught language as a tool of his own subordination; it is so tied into his labor as servant and guide that its use merely "profits" Prospero. We can see a similar ethos of language and national/ethnic competition in Spenser's *A View of the Present State of Ireland,* which is concerned in many ways with the legal, cultural, and economic ramifications of the union of cultures under imperialism. One of the fears that erupts from the discussion of the dubious lineage of Spaniards (seen as a mixed-race people) is the problematic purity of the Englishmen living in Ireland.[6] Miscegenation (which, like blackness in George Best, is dubbed an "infection" by Spenser) and assimilation show their first effect in language:

> Irenius: . . . and first I have to find fault with the abuse of language, that is, for the speaking of Irish amongst the English, which, as it is unnatural that any people should love another's language more than their own, so is it very inconvenient and the cause of many other evils. Eudoxus: It seemeth strange to me that the English should take more delight to speak that language than their own, whereas they should (me thinks) rather take scorne to acquaint their tounges thereto, for it hath been ever the use of the conquerer to despise the language of the conquered, and to force him by all means to learn his. So did the Romans always use, insomuch that there is almost no nation in the world but is sprinkled with their language. (67)

The discussion here shows a crucial connection between inscriptions of racial difference and colonial control. Cultural and political differences between the English, the Scottish, and the Irish are distilled to problematic linguistic differences, the overcoming and assimilation of which is the first step in an imperialist project.[7] Irenius replies to Eudoxus's concerns that so few can be influenced linguistically by linking language acquisition to social formations, particularly to domestic practices:

> I suppose that the chief cause of bringing in the Irish language, amongst them, was specially their fostering, and marrying with the Irishe, which are two most dangerous infections, for first the childe that sucketh the milke of the nurse must of necessity learn his first speech of her, the which being the first that is enured to his tongue is ever after most pleasing unto him, insomuch as though he afterwards be taught English, yet the smack of the first will always abide with him, and not only of the speech, but of the manners and conditions, . . . The next is the marrying with the Irish, which how dangerous a thing it is in all commonwealths, appeareth to every simplest sense, and though some great ones have used such matches with their vassals, . . . yet the example is so perilous as it is not to be adventured . . . (67, 68).

In this section of the *View,* fears of interracial alliance are very explicitly linked to fears of assimilation of the ruler by the ruled. This particular passage presents English fears of alternative social structures, such as Irish fosterage, and presents women as a chief danger. In some ways, fosterage is an even more powerful way of forming alliances between groups than marriage. Patricia Fumerton says of the Irish practice: "So strong was the bonding of fosterage that it cemented ties not only between the child and its foster parents but also between the foster parents and the natural parents" (46). This forming of bonds, which is not significantly different from Elizabethan practices of child exchange, is here a threat both because of the "unhealthy" mixture of Irish and English, and because of the ever-present danger of English assimilation. Women in this scenario become dangerous carriers of the infection of foreign difference, a danger so perilous that intermarriage needs to be avoided at all costs.

The connection between language and profit in Caliban's reply reverberates throughout *The Tempest*. The Europeans see Caliban as the conduit to the various means of new world wealth talked of in traveler's tales. Prospero makes Caliban a slave after he shows his knowledge of "every fertile inch o' th' island," taking the profit of both the island and Caliban's labor and leaving him with only the dubious gain of language ("my profit on't / Is I know how to curse"). Trinculo and Stephano immediately see the economic potential in Caliban. At first sight, Trinculo imagines putting Caliban on display: "Were I in England now, as once I was, and had but this fish painted, not a holiday-fool there but would give a piece of silver. There would this monster make a man—any strange beast there makes a man" (2.2.27-30). Trinculo's enterprise again demonstrates the ambiguous allure of economic involvement. In gaining wealth from possession of the native, the European is rhetorically made one with the other, just as the hunger for novelty allows a "monster" to "make a man." In Trinculo's formulation, he is created (made) by the native even as he makes him an object of exchange: "There would this monster make a man." Colonialism and class interact when Trinculo (who, unlike Ferdinand, is not "the best of them that speak this speech" [1.1.430]) unwittingly creates the very entanglement that imperialism dreads: "Any strange beast there makes a man. When they will not give a doit to relieve a lame beggar, they will lay out ten to see a dead Indian" (2.2.30-32).

This entanglement is itself ironically staged in the image of Trinculo and Caliban under the gabardine. Stephano associates the sight with foreign strangeness, crying, "Do you put tricks upon's with savages and men of Ind? Ha?" (2.2.56-57). Like Trinculo he instantly thinks of profit as well as of the monstrous mixture of Englishman and native: "This is some monster of the isle with four legs, who hath got, as I take it, an ague. Where the devil should he learn our language? I will give him some relief, if it be but for that. If I can recover him, and keep him tame, and get to Naples with him, he's a present for any emperor that ever trod on neat's-leather" (2.2.63-68). Significantly, Caliban's oddity or monstrosity is due in part to his ability to speak a master language, an ability that (at least in Trinculo's formulation) rewards him: "I will give him some relief." Trinculo sees yet another profit in Caliban, perhaps buying favor from an emperor in exchange for this new world oddity. The comic entanglement of the lower-class European and the native is reminiscent of colonial propaganda, which locates a dangerous blurring of the line between the civilized and the barbaric in the lower classes and which uses the threatening economic need of the lower classes as the impetus for colonial expansion.[8] Indeed, this coalition threatens Prospero's imperial project as much as the plot itself threatens his life. Prospero's much-noted hasty exit would then be read as a reaction to a class threat to aristocratic power. It also gestures toward an anxiety about class mobility enabled by colonial enterprise, an issue to which I will return at the end of this [essay].

Despite such class concerns, the proper disposition of both gender and race remains the central anxiety. Ferdinand's appearance on stage immediately after Prospero's dismissal of Caliban highlights interesting parallels between the noble European and the foreign "savage." Like Caliban, Ferdinand requires instruction from Miranda: "Vouchsafe my prayer / May know if you remain upon this island, / And that you will some good instruction give / How I may bear me here" (1.2.423-26). However, unlike Caliban, Ferdinand is "culturally sound" as well as of noble birth. His first thought upon seeing Miranda is that she "speaks his language": "My language! Heavens! / I am the best of them that speak this speech, / Were I but where 'tis spoken" (1.2.429-31). His characterization of his status as an epistemic connection rather than one of consanguinity signals an instant bond with Miranda. Linguistic compatibility, seen in other Shakespearean couples such as Romeo and Juliet and Beatrice and Benedick as a mere sign of sexual compatibility, takes on racial overtones in that racial and cultural difference are tied to rhetorical skill. The emphasis on linguistic prowess serves in some ways to efface crucial similarities between Ferdinand and Caliban. Prospero is, with good reason, equally concerned with regulating Miranda's courtship with Ferdinand, although his reaction to that courtship is qualitatively different from his reaction to Caliban. As David Sundelson points out, Ferdinand's reassuring reply to Prospero suggests both hidden rape fantasies and the possibility of abandonment (48), revealing a basic sexuality—common to both men—that must be contained by the father. These similarities in some ways suggest that the "real" difference between Caliban and Ferdinand is racial, not moral or sexual.

The pressures of imperialism insist on the control and regulation of female sexuality, particularly when concerns over paternity are complicated by the problems of racial and cultural purity. Prospero's manipulation of Ferdinand rewards him insofar as it creates a marriage of state that forms the basis for a new empire as well as a romantic attachment. Act 2 opens with a discussion of the marriage of Claribel, daughter of the king of Naples, in which Shakespeare provides an alternative glance at the way in which the traditional political marriage is endangered by European contact with less desirable others. The king of Naples arranges a political marriage between Claribel and the king of Tunis, a move he consequently regrets, because it has indirectly separated him from a daughter and a son. Once on the island, Alonso is roundly castigated by Sebastian for abusing his authority over his "fair daughter" (2.1.70) because he chose to "lose her to an African" (2.1.123):

> You were kneeled to and importuned otherwise
> By all of us, and the fair soul herself
> Weighed between loathness and obedience at
> Which end o' th' beam should bow. We have lost your son,
> I fear, for ever. Milan and Naples have
> More widows in them of this business' making
> Than we bring men to comfort them.
> The fault's your own.
>
> (2.1.126-33)

Sebastian's criticism, like Alonso's regret (Would I had never / Married my daughter there, for coming thence / My son is lost [2.1.105-7]), directly attributes Ferdinand's loss—and the loss of the royal bloodline—to the marriage. All sorts of privation are attributed to the wedding (in contrast to the bounty promised in Miranda's wedding masque): in Sebastian's condemnation, European families are ruptured and bloodlines broken because of this marriage. Prospero prospers not only because of his successful manipulation of the Ferdinand-Miranda alliance but also because of Alonso's disastrous decision to open up the sex/gender system to an African king. In refusing to open the sex/gender system to non-European outsiders, Prospero demonstrates his ability to preserve the integrity of the "fair" aristocratic body and, consequently, the state. Not only does he regain his kingdom, he becomes the father to a new dynasty.

The attention to paternal authority only throws into relief the very visible absence of mothers in the play. Typically, Prospero gives the maternal history of both Miranda and Caliban. Miranda's mother is mentioned in order to confirm the purity and insularity of Prospero's own bloodline:

> Prospero:
> Twelve year since, Miranda, twelve year since,
> Thy father was the Duke of Milan, and
> A prince of power—
> Miranda:
> Sir, are you not my father?
> Prospero:
> Thy mother was a piece of virtue, and
> She said thou wast my daughter; and thy father
> Was Duke of Milan, and his only heir
> And princess no worse issued.
>
> (1.2.53-59)

Ironically, her presence is evoked by Miranda's unwitting, yet witty, denial of her father's royal power. Prospero's reply ("She said thou wast my daughter") reveals an anxiety over inheritance and the woman's role in reproduction, a factor that had a particularly strong resonance for James, whose own claim to England's throne was particularly vexed because, as Stephen Orgel notes, "His legitimacy, in both senses [as designated ruler and son], thus derived from two mothers, the chaste Elizabeth and the sensual Mary" ("Prospero's Wife" 59). Caliban counters Prospero's attacks with an equally strong claim to an "empire" through his African mother's bloodline:

> This island's mine by Sycorax my mother,
> Which thou tak'st from me. When thou cam'st first
> Thou strok'st me and made much of me; wouldst give me
> Water with berries in't, and teach me how
> To name the bigger light and how the less,
> That burn by day and night; and then I loved thee,
> And showed thee all the qualities o'th' isle,
> The fresh springs, brine pits, barren place and fertile—
> Cursed be I that did so! All the charms
> Of Sycorax, toads, beetles, bats light on you!
> For I am all the subjects that you have,
> Which first was mine own king, and here you sty me
> In this hard rock, whiles you do keep from me
> The rest o'th' island.
>
> (1.2.331-44)

It is in response to Caliban's claim of property rights that Prospero charges Caliban with rape, a rhetorical move that reinforces Valerie Smith's point that "instances of interracial rape constitute sites of struggle between black and white men that allow privileged white men to exercise their property rights over the bodies of white women" (158). Although Smith is referring here specifically to the view of white women as property, historically claims of rape have worked to mystify property interests.

Caliban poses the ultimate threat to such a quest for social and political integrity. Not only is he made into a sexual threat against an aristocratic body, his own unfixed and ambiguous origins make him an embodiment of the miscegenative threat. Caliban himself is that site of anxiety provoked by the expansion of England. Peter Hulme persuasively suggests that the play is situated within a fundamental dualism, represented both geographically in the island and physically in Caliban:

> The island is the meeting place of the play's topographical dualism, Mediterranean and Atlantic, ground of the mutually incompatible reference systems whose co-presence serves to frustrate any attempt to locate the island on a map. Caliban is similarly the ground of these two discourses. As "wild man" or "wodehouse", with an African mother whose pedigree leads back to the *Odyssey*, he is distinctly Mediterranean. And yet, at the same time, he is, as his name suggests, a "cannibal" as that figure had taken shape on colonial discourse: ugly, devilish, ignorant, gullible and treacherous—according to the Europeans' descriptions of him. (108)

As I argue [elsewhere], Africa is a foundational presence in new world discourses. Hulme's formulation provides a necessary corrective to many colonialist readings that look only to new world materials as influential on the play. Alden and Virginia Vaughan note the surprisingly infrequent attempts to link *The Tempest* to discourses of Africa (51). Although it is not my intent here to embark on that project, thinking along Hulme's lines opens up the possibility for Caliban to occupy multiple sites of difference and might counter some of the unease that critics have felt with the imprecision with which one can identify the play as "colonialist." Meredith Skura, for example, bases a large part of her critique of what she calls "revisionist" readings of the play on a survey of new world materials and a conclusion that there was no stable colonialist discourse that Shakespeare could be said to draw on.[9] As a useful counter to Skura's argument, it would be helpful to combine Hulme's insight with Mary Louise Pratt's concept of the "contact zone," which is a colonial space "in which peoples geographically and historically separated come into contact with each other and establish ongoing relations, usually involving conditions of coercion, radical inequality, and intractable contact" (6). The island is a space of competing and conflicting discourses that are about the contact itself. There are any number of these "contact zones" in Renaissance travel literature, and it might be fruitful to think of those in relation to the play. For example, one might think about the infamous example of Sir Francis Drake, whose crew, on his third circum-navigation, impregnated a black woman named Maria and abandoned her on an island along with two black men.

Caliban embodies the contradiction and contest characteristic of border spaces, and in that position he contests Prospero's imperial visions. Just as Caliban verbally refuses Prospero's attempts to construct a seamless colonial narrative and critical attempts to construct a unified play of forgiveness and restoration, his "difference" itself is unsettled; it defies categories and is therefore, for the Europeans and contemporary critics, "unsettling." Even the seeming resolution seems to open up the issues of Caliban's birthright and inheritance once more:

> This misshapen knave,
> His mother was a witch, and one so strong
> That could control the moon, make flows and ebbs,
> And deal in her command without her power.
> These three have robbed me, and this demi-devil—
> For he's a bastard one—had plotted with them
> To take my life. Two of these fellows you
> Must know and own; this thing of darkness I
> Acknowledge mine.
>
> (5.1.268-76)

The terms originally used to control and disinherit Caliban ("misshapen knave," "bastard," "demi-devil") are here reproduced along with a discourse of theft and illegitimacy, which are used to license Prospero's moves to create a political dynasty. Both moves publicly establish Prospero's ownership in a proprietorial sense, suggesting that any "acknowledgment" or bond with a dark other can be safely made only within a context of ownership and control.

The play opens up another perspective on interracial union through the perplexing "widow Dido" jesting that precedes the breast-beating over Claribel's marriage. It is now a commonplace that the *Aeneid* is a crucial subtext for issues of dynastic politics and royal authority in *The Tempest* (Orgel, *Tempest* 39). The story of Aeneas, the founder of imperial Rome, and Dido, the African queen, provides yet another cautionary tale of the threat of female sexuality to colonial expansion when Dido's passion is read as diverting Aeneas from the task of empire. The bantering over Dido's status as widow represents conflicting Renaissance readings of the Dido story (Orgel, *Tempest* 42), which speak to the issue of proper marriage. Gonzalo's insistence on Dido as widow authorizes her union as a marriage (since one must be a wife to be a widow) and thereby legitimizes the foreign female's part in the creation of empire. In contrast, Antonio's jesting reduces Dido's importance: she becomes a mere dalliance on Aeneas's part and no significant threat to Aeneas's imperial project.

Gonzalo, in changing the subject from the king's doomed children, turns to an imaginative politics that paradoxically creates a "new" commonwealth with existing political structures. The proximity of the description of his "socialist" state to the issues of dynastic succession suggestively links changes in the European social order to the threat of miscegenation. Issues of racial difference are consequently collapsed into problems of economics, politics, class, and gender. Like Shakespeare's Cleopatra, Gonzalo's Dido competes for title of widow and a legitimate place in the imperial text and provokes the possibility of alternative dynastic structures that are not purely European.

Shakespeare's *Antony and Cleopatra* is the play that perhaps is most closely concerned with the ways an African queen threatens empire. Cleopatra's darkness makes her the embodiment of an absolute correspondence between fears of racial and gender difference and the threat they pose to imperialism. As Ania Loomba states, "Dominant notions about female identity, gender relations and imperial power are unsettled through the disorderly non-European woman" (125). In his tirade on Antony's "dotage" in the opening scene, Philo comments on both Cleopatra's sexuality and her darkness, claiming that Antony's eyes "now bend, now turn / The office and devotion of their view / Upon a tawny front" (1.1.4-6) and calling him "the fan / To cool a gipsy's lust" (1.1.9-10).[10] His language, typical of orientalist discourse, makes it clear that Shakespeare is at pains to have us see a black Cleopatra. For Shakespeare, as Leonard Tennenhouse notes, "Cleopatra is Egypt. As such, however, she embodies everything that is not English according to the nationalism which developed under Elizabeth as well as to the British nationalism later fostered by James" (144).

Although there seems to be no male tradition in England of a swarthy Cleopatra, Samuel Daniel's Cleopatra (1594) may provide some clues to the darkness of Shakespeare's. While Cleopatra is never described as physically dark in *The Tragedie of Cleopatra,* her deeds are "black"; in many ways, she is an outsider even within her own country. The chorus's lament suggests that her unruly behavior is a danger to her own community and estranges her from the rest of Egypt:

> And likewise [she] makes us pay
> For her disordered lust,
> Th' int'rest of our blood:
> Or live a servile pray,
> Under a hand unjust,
>
> . . . . .
>
> This have her riot wonne,
> And thus shee hath her state, her selfe and us undunne.
>
> (16v)

In Daniel's version, Cleopatra is very much the unruly *female* whose sexuality destroys not only Antony but Egypt as well. Although it is apparent in Shakespeare's *Antony and Cleopatra* that Cleopatra has lost Egypt to the Romans, there is no Egyptian censure for this, whereas in Daniel's *Cleopatra* her servants, rather than Antony's, turn traitor and repent. One reason for Cleopatra's lack of darkness may be that *The Tragedie of Cleopatra* begins after Antony's suicide, which tends to minimize the ominous specter of mixed-race children, a vision that would have been incompatible with the maternal role Daniel envisions for her.

. . . [There] seems to be an emerging female tradition of a dark Cleopatra. One most obvious reason for this phenomenon is that female writers in various ways identify with the Roman Octavia, an identification that makes Cleopatra a different threat than is found in the male tradition. In her *Salve Deus Rex Judaeorum,* Aemilia Lanyer makes Cleopatra black, but only in relation to the fair Octavia:

> Yea though thou wert as rich, as wise, as rare,
> As any Pen could write, or Wit devise;
> Yet with this Lady canst thou not compare,
> Whose inward virtues all thy worth denies:
> Yet thou a blacke Egyptian do'st appeare;
> Thou false, shee true; and to her Love more deere.
>
> (1427-32)

In describing Cleopatra, "as rich, as wise, as rare, / As any Pen could write," Lanyer zeroes in on the crucial matter of Cleopatra as text. Her literary appropriation is much like colonial appropriation in that she is the rich matter to be tamed and controlled for imperial growth. However, as Shakespeare's Octavius discovers, Cleopatra is a highly resistant text in her insistence on fashioning her own role in the empire. This resistance is perhaps due to her absolute identification with Egypt. Although her blackness and difference appear in proportion to her Dido-like threat to empire, the strong correlation between Cleopatra's sexual difference and her cultural difference makes it difficult to manipulate one against the other.

Egypt itself is a very malleable sign. Indeed, as with contemporary Eurocentric geography, many writers of the Renaissance did not locate Egypt on the African continent. Often in geographical and political discourses, Egypt is spoken of as though it is a separate continent, unconnected with Africa. Here Egypt is a focal point of East-West confrontation, claimed as African or "Asiatic" simultaneously, existing as a constantly claimed but ultimately unfixed signifier. Throughout Leo Africanus's *Geographical Historie,* for example, Egypt is alternately both an early cradle of Christianity and a bastion of "Mahommetism." With its mixture of religions and races, Egypt is itself like the threatening "infinite variety" attributed to Cleopatra. This absolute identification of Cleopatra with Egypt is most apparent in the association with the Nile. Her speech to Charmian is a case in point:

> "Where's my serpent of old Nile?"
> (For so he calls me). Now I feed myself
> With most delicious poison. Think on me,
> That am with Phoebus' amorous pinches black,
> And wrinkled deep in time?
>
> (1.5.25-29)

Here, we see three of the elements associated with the Nile: serpents, poison/pollution, and blackness. It has been suggested by many editors of the play that this link with the Nile is meant to suggest Cleopatra's fecundity and fertility; travel writings, however, offer a different, more negative understanding of the significance of the Nile. As I noted [elsewhere], travelers' tales of Africa's rivers, which regularly overflow their boundaries, had become a source of fascination for the English, and the geographical fact of inundation is regularly conflated with the sense of darker-skinned Africans as people who resist boundaries and rule. In his description of the Nile, Leo Africanus demonstrates how depictions of the Nile become inextricably connected with assessments of Egypt's political order: "Creatures therein contained are exceeding strange, as namely sea-horses, sea-oxen, crocodiles, and other such monstrous and cruel beasts, (as we will afterward declare) which were not so hurtfull either in the ancient times of the Egyptians or of the Romaines, as they are at this present: but they became more dangerous ever since the Mahumetans were lords of Egypt" (335). The Nile and its inhabitants become more dangerous as they move farther from the "civilized" world. Depictions of the Nile invariably involve unspoken comparisons with English rivers, and the inundations conjure up the specter of Western impotence and stagnation in the face of Egypt's "fat prosperity" (Daniel, L3v).[11]

Similarly, the Nile runs throughout *Antony and Cleopatra* as a sign of overwhelming sexuality and social disorder and associates Cleopatra with the kind of overflow and excess characteristic of the female grotesque. Antony, like the Renaissance traveler, regales the drunken triumvirate with tales of Egypt and the "flow o' th' Nile" (2.7.17), while Enobarbus tells the attendants tales of Cleopatra's "infinite variety." The play opens with an evocation of the flooding of the Nile as Philo proclaims, "This dotage of our general's / O'erflows the measure" (1.1.1-2). Antony's and Cleopatra's assertions "Melt Egypt in Nile. . . . Let Rome in Tiber melt" (1.1.33) also link this powerful image of inundation with the struggles of empire. The dark/light binarism, here acted out as a division of Egypt and Rome, is continually on the verge of dissolution. More than a wishing-away of worldly cares or a sign of Egyptian dispersal of symbols of order and measurement, the metaphors of excess bespeak an anxiety striking directly at the heart of Europe's primal fear: loss of identity in measureless expansion. Antony's absorption with Cleopatra is only the romantically reversed reading of Rome's political absorption. Although it is true that "the luxury and feasting of the Egyptian court image a natural plenty which is curbed by no Roman temperance," this natural plenitude, so seductive to a modern audience, is precisely what would have been threatening to a Europe struggling to control its own countrymen loosed into a foreign world of plenty (Kermode 1345).

This combination of unlicensed sensuality and economic exchange is perhaps best symbolized by Antony's gift of an "orient pearl" (1.5.41):

> "Say the firm Roman to great Egypt sends
> This treasure of an oyster; at whose foot,
> To mend the petty present, I will piece
> Her opulent throne with kingdoms. All the East,
> Say thou, shall call her mistress."
>
> (1.5.43-49)

Like Emilia's admonition of husbands that "pour our treasures into foreign laps" (*Othello* 4.3.88), Alexas's message from Antony evokes both male submission and sensuality: Antony pictures himself placing kingdoms at the foot of Egypt's throne (rather than Rome's) and delivering the treasures of the Orient to Cleopatra. The image of his message is suggestive of the imperial image of Elizabeth in the Ditchley portrait, in which she literally has kingdoms at her foot.[12] Unlike Elizabeth's virgin pearl, however, this "treasure of an oyster" continues the conflation of sexual and material exchange: oysters were long thought to be an aphrodisiac.[13] Similarly, Cleopatra's wealth and the sexual threat represented by her children underlie her contest with Octavius when she counters his perhaps false offer of protection for her children with an inaccurate accounting of her "money, plate, and jewels" (5.2.138). The fertility associated with Cleopatra is a threat to the Roman world; in this scene her illegitimate children become the battleground on which she struggles to maintain her stake in the empire.

Antony's affair with Cleopatra is perhaps not as damaging as his "going native" and falling into the plenitude and excess of Egypt. Cleopatra's court is a place of sexual misrule, and in Rome Antony is continually censured for sexual freedom, which is taken for granted in Egypt. In Octavius's eyes, Antony is humbled and effeminized; he uses an image of cross-dressing to denigrate the relationship further: he "is not more manlike / Than Cleopatra; nor the queen of Ptolomy / More womanly than he" (1.4.5-7). The descriptions of the court feature all sorts of transgressive behavior, which includes neglecting class as well as racial and sexual boundaries:

> Let's grant it is not
> Amiss to tumble on the bed of Ptolomy,
> To give a kingdom for mirth, to sit
> And keep the turn of tippling with a slave,
> To reel the streets at noon, and stand the buffet
> With knaves that smells of sweat.
>
> (1.4.16-21)

In descriptions of Antony's "dereliction of duty" (some of which sound not very much different from Harrington's scenes of license in James's court), we see that the Romans blame Antony not so much for the affair as for the behavior it provokes: "Mark Antony / In Egypt sits at dinner, and will make / No wars without-doors" (2.1.11-13).

The closing scenes of *Antony and Cleopatra* turn upon the manipulation of Cleopatra as an imperial text. Like "widow Dido" of *The Tempest,* she is subject to variant readings. Octavius wants finally to tame and display the previously unruly matter of Cleopatra:

> Know, sir, that I
> Will not wait pinion'd at your master's court,
> Nor once be chastis'd with the sober eye
> Of dull Octavia. Shall they hoist me up,
> And show me to the shouting varlotry
> Of censuring Rome?
>
> (5.2.52-57)

As her speech shows, Cleopatra proves well aware of Roman efforts to fix her position in the imperial picture. Octavius attempts to read her as the dangerous female subject, the strumpet who brought down Rome by causing Antony's downfall:

> Saucy lictors
> Will catch at us like strumpets, and scald rhymers
> Ballad's out a' tune. The quick comedians
> Extemporally will stage us, and present
> Our Alexandrian revels: Antony
> Shall be brought drunken forth, and I shall see
> Some squeaking Cleopatra boy my greatness
> I' th' posture of a whore.
>
> (5.2.214-21)

Cleopatra poses an alternative reading of her part in the imperial text. Refusing to be seen as a fatal dalliance, subject to conflicting interpretations, she inscribes herself as a wife. As in *The Tempest,* the issue of lawful marriage with the other is crucial. In chastizing Cleopatra, Antony bemoans the time diverted from creating legitimate children:

> Have I left my pillow unpress'd in Rome,
> Forborne the getting of a lawful race,
> And by a gem of women, to be abus'd
> By one that looks on feeders?
>
> (3.13.106-10)

Shakespeare here has Antony erroneously evoke the idea of a "lost" pure bloodline. Antony did produce children with Octavia, a fact obscured in Shakespeare's text, which is a crucial indication of character in North's translation of Plutarch and, later, for Dryden's in *All for Love*.

Although, as Stanley Cavell notes, Antony deliberately distances himself from any possibility of marriage to Cleopatra (22-24), he dies thinking of himself as a bridegroom: "My queen and Eros / Have by their brave instruction got upon me / A nobleness in record; but I will be / A bridegroom in my death, and run into't / As to a lover's bed" (4.14.97-101). Cleopatra, in turn, stages her death as an imperial marriage: "Husband, I come! / Now to that name my courage prove my title! . . . Peace, peace! / Dost thou not see my baby at my breast, / That sucks the nurse asleep?" (5.2.287-307). Her insistence on being seen as a legitimate wife threatens the closure of the imperial text. Reading these "other" mistresses as wives forces the acceptance of their mixed offspring and directly negates the Roman emphasis on noble deeds and pure bloodlines.

Egypt and Caliban's island are both liminal spaces in which the separations of dark and light, self and other, are momentarily broken down, and the anxieties over that collapse are displayed and explored. Both *Antony and Cleopatra* and *The Tempest* grapple with difficulties of maintaining cultural integrity and endogamous unions within imperial/colonial economies of desire. In doing so, the texts offer early hints at what will later become entrenched racial stereotypes. Rome is England's imagined forefather in empire, and *Antony and Cleopatra* provides an object lesson in imperial history; Antony becomes a warning against the dangers of overinvolvement with the reputed sexual excess of black women. *The Tempest,* looking forward to future colonization, offers the greater threat of the black man as rapist. Both images work less to control actual black sexuality than to shape an image of a white, male ruling class as rational, restrained, and powerful in the face of dangerous excess and unregulated sexuality. However, just as in the travel narrative, such warnings against the other have embedded in them a fascination with the other. Difference always escapes the desire for control. The model imperial powers, Octavius and Prospero, both fail in their attempts to control and order foreign others for their own use. Octavius is ultimately not able to restrain and display Cleopatra, and Prospero is forced to acknowledge his connection to a "thing of darkness."

Notes

1. For examples of what "new historicism" and cultural materialism have made of the colonial themes in this play, see Paul Brown, "'This thing of darkness I acknowledge mine': *The Tempest* and the Discourse of Colonialism"; Stephen Greenblatt, *Shakespearean Negotiations: The Circulation of Social Energy in Renaissance England;* Peter Hulme, *Colonial Encounters: Europe and the Native Caribbean, 1492-1797.* For discussions of postcolonial issues see especially Thomas Cartelli, "Prospero in Africa: *The Tempest* as Colonial Text and Pre-Text"; Ania Loomba, *Gender, Race, Renaissance Drama,* 142-58; and Rob Nixon, "Caribbean and African Appropriations of *The Tempest.*"

2. Alden T. and Virginia Mason Vaughan's *Shakespeare's Caliban* offers a wide-ranging reception history of the play.

3. A. and V. Vaughan also explore the intriguing possibility that the name Caliban derives from the Romany word *Cauliban,* which meant "'black' or things associated with blackness" (33-34). Line references to *The Tempest* are to the Oxford edition, ed. Stephen Orgel.

4. Stephen Orgel argues that the competing claims of Caliban and Prospero for the island represent the available ways of understanding royal authority under James I's reign ("Prospero's Wife" 58).

5. For a discussion of the critical commentary on these lines and the theater's attempts to resolve them, see Stephen Orgel's introduction to the Oxford edition of *The Tempest.* I will add that violent rejections of the other's sexual advances only serve, rather than disrupt, the interests of patriarchy. Although this may be a case of the "radically discontinuous" speech attributed to women (Belsey, *Subject of Tragedy* 160), it also true that women bear the responsibility of policing the borders of the state and rejecting differences that threaten patriarchal structures and are licensed to speak out in that capacity.

6. Spenser outlines one of the sources of this sense of Spain's mixed heritage when he suggests that Spain's current riches are the inheritance of a long history of invasion, particularly by Africans: "For the Spaniard that now is, is come from as rude and savage nations as they, there being as it may be gathered by course of ages and view of their own history (though they therein labour, much to ennoble themselves) scarce any drop of the old Spanish blood left in them: . . . And yet after all those the Moors and barbarians breaking over out of Africa, did finally possess all Spain, or the most part thereof, and tread down under their foul heathenish feet, whatever little they found there yet standing; the which though afterwards they were beaten out by *Ferdinand of Aragon* and Elizabeth his wife, yet they were not so cleansed, but that through the marriages which they had made, and mixture with the people of the land during their long continuance there, they had left no pure drop of Spanish blood; no, nor of Roman nor Scythian; so that of all nations under heaven I suppose the Spaniard is the most mingled, most uncertain and most bastardly" (43-44).

7. José Piedra analyzes the first grammar of a modern European language, Antonio de Nebrija's *Gramática de la lengua castellana,* as an arm of imperial rule: "Europe, Africa, and America became the grounds on which Spain planned to practice enslavement justified as a rhetorical brokerage of universal knowledge" (282). He further claims, "Nebrija provided the New World with the justification for a cohesive Hispanic Text; he unified 'otherness' under the grammatical self-righteousness of the colonial letter" (284).

8. See Chapter 1, pp. 53-54.

9. Skura's essay is itself quite fascinating in that it critiques attempts at historical specificity while at the same time insisting on ahistorical psychoanalytic paradigms (such as "man's timeless tendency to demonize 'strangers'" [45]) that re-inscribe the universality of Shakespeare. Ironically, the very materials she uses would seem to question the "timeless tendency to demonize strangers": although all colonial narratives are in some sense motivated fictions, the recurring trope of the friendly, welcoming native who suddenly turns hostile suggests that demonization is not the first response—unless one assumes that white Europeans are never strangers. So, too, Caliban's first response is not to demonize the "stranger" Prospero but to welcome him. Skura also claims that "Shakespeare was the first to show one of *us* mistreating a native, the first to represent a native from the inside, the first to allow a native to complain onstage, and the first to make the New World encounter problematic

enough to generate the current attention to the play" (58). This peroration contains a set of highly problematic and offensive assumptions that reveal the difficulties of her critical approach. Her references to the "universality of racial prejudice" (56) and "general psychological needs" (69) are specifically linked to her assertion that Shakespeare was the first to show one of *us* mistreating a native. These assertions, like her insistence on the universality (yet uniqueness) of Shakespeare, rely on the notion of a unified and universal white subject—in other words, herself. Who is included in the italicized "us" that we are shown in the play? Any reader of the play? Any literary critic? Any teacher? Am I, a black feminist critic of Shakespeare part of the "us" that Skura imagines? Like those who accept Prospero's narratives as the "truth," Skura assumes that all readers are potential Prosperos.

10. Although "gypsy" is usually glossed as a shortened form of "Egyptian," it typically carries connotations of darkness as well as associations with lechery and deceit. Sir Thomas Browne calls gypsies "Counterfeit Negroes" in the section "Of Gypsies" in his *Pseudodoxia Epidemica*. See also Alden and Virginia Vaughan's discussion of gypsies in *Shakespeare's Caliban: A Cultural History*, 33-36.

11. Ania Loomba suggests that the association of Cleopatra with eating also locates her as a racial other: "The recurrent food imagery reinforces her primitive appeal: she makes men hungry, she does not cloy their appetite (II. ii. 240-42); she is Antony's 'Egyptian dish' (II. vi. 122), she is 'salt Cleopatra' (II. i. 21). She is the supreme actress, artifice herself, and simultaneously primitive and uncultivated" (78). Cultural critic bell hooks sees the desire for the primitive in modern capitalist culture as rooted in an ethos of consumption: "When race and ethnicity become commodified as resources for pleasure, the culture of specific groups, as well as the bodies of individuals, can be seen as constituting an alternative playground where members of dominating races, genders, sexual practices affirm their power-over in intimate relations with the Other" (hooks, *Black Looks* 23).

12. For discussions of this portrait see Roy Strong, *Gloriana: The Portraits of Queen Elizabeth I*, 135-41. See also Andrew and Catherine Belsey, "Icons of Divinity: Portraits of Elizabeth I," 15-17. Ania Loomba draws a more sustained connection between the ways in which Elizabeth I and Cleopatra "evoked specifically Renaissance fears of female government" (76).

13. I thank Gwynne Kennedy, whose paper on the correspondence between Lady Mary Wroth and Lord Denny, "She 'thincks she daunces in a net': The Reception of Lady Mary Wroth's *Urania*," addresses the use of the oyster in the exchange of poems between Wroth and Denny.

Works Cited

Cavell, Stanley. *Disowning Knowledge in Six Plays of Shakespeare*. Cambridge: Cambridge University Press, 1987.

Daniel, Samuel. *Delia and Rosamond Augmented, Cleopara*. London, 1594.

Fleming, Juliet. "Dictionary English and the Female Tongue." In *Enclosure Acts: Sexuality, Property, and Culture in Early Modern England*, ed. Richard Burt and John Michael Archer, 290-325. Ithaca: Cornell University Press, 1994.

Fumerton, Patricia. *Cultural Aesthetics: Renaissance Literature and the Practice of Social Ornament*. Chicago: University of Chicago Press, 1991.

Gates, Henry Louis, Jr., ed. *Reading Black, Reading Feminist: A Critical Anthology*. New York: Penguin, 1990.

———. "Writing 'Race' and the Difference It Makes." In *"Race," Writing, and Difference*, ed. Henry Louis Gates, Jr., 1-20. Chicago: University of Chicago Press, 1986.

Giddings, Paula. *When and Where I Enter: The Impact of Black Women on Race and Sex in America*. New York: Morrow, 1984.

Griffin, Susan. "The Sacrificial Lamb." In *Racism and Sexism: An Integrated Study*, ed. Paula S. Rothenberg, 296-305. New York: St. Martin's, 1988.

Hulme, Peter. *Colonial Encounters: Europe and the Native Caribbean, 1492-1797*. New York: Methuen, 1986.

Kermode, Frank, et al., eds. *The Oxford Anthology of English Literature*. New York: Oxford University Press, 1973.

Lanyer, Aemilia. *The Poems of Aemilia Lanyer: Salve Deus Rex Judæorum*. Ed. Susanne Wood. New York: Oxford, 1993.

Loomba, Ania. *Gender, Race, Renaissance Drama*. Manchester and New York: Manchester University Press, 1989.

Orgel, Stephen. "Prospero's Wife." In *Rewriting the Renaissance: The Discourses of Sexual Difference in Early Modern Europe*, ed. Margaret W. Ferguson et al., 50-64. Chicago: University of Chicago Press, 1986.

Pratt, Mary Louise, *Imperial Eyes: Travel Writing and Transculturation*. New York: Routledge, 1992.

Skura, Meredith Anne. "Discourse and the Individual: The Case of Colonialism in *The Tempest*." *Shakespeare Quarterly* 40 (1989): 42-69.

Smith, Valerie. "Black Feminist Theory and the Representation of the 'Other.'" In *Changing Our Own Words: Essays on Criticism, Theory, and Writing by Black Women*, ed. Cheryl A. Wall, 38-57. New Brunswick: Rutgers University Press, 1989.

———. "Split Affinities: The Case of Interracial Rape." In *Conflicts in Feminism,* ed. Marianne Hirsch and Evelyn Fox Keller. New York: Routledge, 1990.

Sundelson, David. "So Rare a Wonder'd Father: Prospero's *Tempest.*" In *Representing Shakespeare: New Psychoanalytic Essays,* ed. Murray M. Schwartz and Coppélia Kahn, 33-53. Baltimore: Johns Hopkins University Press, 1980.

Tennenhouse, Leonard. *Power on Display: The Politics of Shakespeare's Genres.* New York: Methuen, 1986.

Vaughan, Alden T., and Virginia Mason. *Shakespeare's Caliban: A Cultural History.* New York: Cambridge University Press, 1991.

Joyce Green MacDonald (essay date 1996)

SOURCE: "Sex, Race, and Empire in Shakespeare's *Antony and Cleopatra,*" in *Literature & History,* 3rd Series, Vol. 5, No. 1, Spring, 1996, pp. 60-77.

[*In the following essay, MacDonald explores the implications of a black Cleopatra who uses her sexuality to thwart Roman imperial power.*]

In Act I of Shakespeare's *Antony and Cleopatra,* the Queen of Egypt, sweetly torturing herself with thoughts of her absent lover, implores Antony to

> Thinke on me,
> That am with Phoebus amorous pinches blacke,
> And wrinkled deepe in time.[1]

Along with Philo's disgusted observation as the play opens that Antony's formerly martial eyes 'now turne / The Office and Devotion of their view / Upon a Tawny Front' (I.1.6-8), Cleopatra's self-definition as 'blacke' assigns a clear racial difference from the Romans to the Egyptian queen.[2] Except for an appendix in Janet Adelman's 1973 study of Shakespeare's *Antony and Cleopatra,* however, sustained critical attention to the question of his Cleopatra's blackness has been rare.[3] Indeed, Michael Neill, its most recent editor, declares in his thoughtful discussion of the play that 'the issue of racial difference in *Antony and Cleopatra*' is 'relatively insignificant'.[4]

In part, I think, Neill's conclusion follows from his rejection of a previous tendency to read the play as offering an 'uncomplicated endorsement of racialist and sexist essentialisms' (86); several critics have exposed the operation of 'sexist essentialisms' in the play.[5] At the same time as his critical evaluation of the play is unwilling to attach too much significance to racial difference, however, Neill's stage history also points out that theatrical production has succeeded almost entirely in suppressing what the text does suggest about color and culture: 'it is a telling paradox of the play's stage history that, despite Shakespeare's clearly envisaging Cleopatra as a North African queen whose skin is either "tawny" or "black", there is no history of black Cleopatras as there has been, since the triumphs of Ira Aldridge in the mid-nineteenth century, a series of striking black Othellos' (65). Tracing the rarity of casting a black actress in the role of Cleopatra to 'the same Orientalism' (65) which gave audiences blackface and brownface Othellos, Neill notes that despite the increasing recent availability of such classically trained performers 'no major company has been willing to capitalize on this development to explore the play's treatment of racial and cultural otherness' (66). I am not certain whether 'racial otherness' here is the same thing as the 'racial difference' Neill elsewhere says does not significantly matter in the play, but I do agree with him that the casting of white Cleopatras constitutes a denial of representation.[6]

Most discussions of race or culture in *Antony and Cleopatra* present themselves in terms of orientalism, which has been characterized as 'a praxis of . . . male gender dominance, or patriarchy; the Orient was routinely described as feminine, its riches fertile, its main symbols the sensual woman, the harem, and the despotic—but curiously attractive—ruler'.[7] What I would like to do by discussing the Renaissance Cleopatra as an African woman is to differentiate racial from sexual difference as they both operate in a politics of imperialism.

In an earlier paper, I argued that Aldridge's performance as Othello unsettled the economy of white masculine superiority and erasure of black masculinity which marked antebellum productions.[8] Here, I would like to try to extend my inquisition into the performance of racial identity in Renaissance drama by entertaining another proposition: if we accept this Cleopatra's reference to her dark skin as literal, the way in which she explains its origins does indeed race as well as gender her subjectivity in ways which depart from the traditional portrayals of those other North African queens in whose company I believe, along with Neill, she properly belongs.[9] As a woman, and a 'blacke' woman at that, Cleopatra and her impromptu mythography signify all the more powerfully because of the scarcity of black women in early modern representations of race. Accepting the frequently shifting range of meaning attached to such designations of racial identity as 'black' in the period, critics such as Kim Hall and Lynda Boose still note the resistance of readers to accepting that Renaissance uses of 'black' could sometimes literally mean 'of African descent'.[10] Such resistance precludes asking questions about the possible representational places occupied by blackness, and perhaps particularly by black women, in the period's insistent sexualizations of imperial, social, and cultural value.[11]

As Adelman early pointed out and as a distinguished body of work on meanings attached to questions of racial identity in the Renaissance has detailed, 'race' in the period was understood to turn on questions of lineage, nation, or region as frequently as it was understood to refer directly to skin color.[12] However, this fullness of meaning, and its difference from modern understandings, should not blind us to the fact that the early-modern literature of Africa and Africans clearly attests that formulations of 'race' in Renaissance culture frequently explored precisely the difference in skin color that Shakespeare brings to our attention in *Antony and Cleopatra*.[13] To see race as an essential quantity in this play is to underestimate this rich and contradictory range of meaning, as well as to fail to appreciate how contested, how hybrid, notions of Roman and Egyptian identity were in the period the play dramatizes.[14] I want to look at the concept of Cleopatra's 'race' as it appears in her long textual tradition, and thus attempt to excavate its roles from broader attention to the play's orientalist and imperialist qualities. To speak meaningfully about Cleopatra's race is to include in one's use of the term an account of the ideological work race did (and does), work which was often enabled by and proceeded in tandem with the writing of other kinds of difference from a subject who is conceived of in this case as not only white, but also Roman (or English), not only male but also a heterosexual dominant male. As an African, a woman, and a queen determined to establish and maintain herself in power, Cleopatra embodies three potent sources of threat to the masculine and white project of establishing Roman empire.

Race in early modern Cleopatra texts signifies both as Neill's organizing fiction, and as a literal representation of cultural alterity according to the perspective of Roman (and/or masculine and/or white) dominance.[15] In the differences in the way Shakespeare's play and some other narratives of the bonds between Rome and Africa produce the links between race, empire, and sexuality, I believe we can see the reasons why the self-proclaimed 'blacke' skin of Shakespeare's queen is not incidental, but central, to the cultural and imperial story it tells.

In order to specify just how I believe the possibility of a 'blacke' Cleopatra contradicts other early modern refusals to identify foreign queens as racially different from their political opponents, I begin with the story of an antecedent African queen, Elissa of Carthage. As does the Cleopatra tradition, the story of Elissa's escape from her home in Phoenicia and her founding of a new empire in North Africa turns on a specifically historical moment of cultural confrontation. For example, Arthur Golding's translation of the classical historian Justin's *Abridgement of the histories of Trogus Pompeius* (1564), an important collection of Roman views of Hellenistic culture, tells us that her native city of Tyre was founded by the Phoenicians 'the yere before the destruction of Troye', thus contextualizing one story of empire within another held to be of particular significance to Britain.[16] Margo Hendricks has persuasively argued that Marlowe's depiction of Aeneas' repudiation of Dido (with whom Elissa was identified in the Renaissance) serves as a kind of allegorization not only of English imperial might generally but also of English defeat of the north Africans with whom their hated Spanish enemies were deeply conflated in the period.[17] Thus, looking backward to Ellisa's moment of the dissolution and foundation of mighty empires reveals a pattern of mastery whose racial inscriptions are articulated through its constructions of gender: male Aeneas over female Dido, the seed of Troy and Britain over that of Phoenicia and Carthage.

The account of Elissa's triumph and eventual death in Carthage provided in Golding's Justin insists on this mutual constitution of gender and race, although I believe it employs senses of 'race' which emphasize nationality and culture as well as more explicitly connect skin color to an essentialized notion of character. Fleeing from her evil brother-in-law Pygmalion, who has already murdered her husband Sychaeus, Elissa makes landfall in Cyprus. There, she and her followers see the local custom of having their young unmarried girls earn their 'marriage money' through prostitution and, in her role as leader of the expedition, she makes a quick decision: '*Elisa* commaunded her men to ravishe foureskore or thereaboutes that wer virgins . . . to the entent her younge men might have wives, and the city increase of issue' (fol. 88).

Like the Rome which later opposed it in the Punic wars, Carthage's posterity was assured through an act of imperial rape.[18] What matters in such rapes of state is not so much the act of sexual violence at its center (note the offhand numbering of 'foureskore or so' victims of kidnap and presumably forced intercourse), but the colonizing assumptions underlying the crime. Presumably Elissa and her followers act on their belief that marriage to a fugitive and a stranger would be better than an even sexual exchange with a countryman. This sense of sexual exclusivity will drive Elissa's own behavior: she will later claim loyalty to the memory of her dead husband as the prime reason for choosing suicide rather than marriage to Hiarbas, king of Mauretania. In the midst of this story of rape and possibly incest as well (Pygmalion's full intent toward her is never quite clear), Elissa remains determinedly chaste. This determination obviously differentiates her from the Cypriot virgins who freely commercialize sex as a customary prerequisite to marriage, but it also and perhaps more significantly works to remove her from the sexualized arena in which empires are founded and maintained. The legend of Elissa produces her as a kind of female worthy, a good woman who is free to devote herself to the posterity of her race precisely because she will deny herself children and sexual connection. Golding's Justin concludes the episode by informing us that 'As long as *Carthage* was unvanquished, she was worshipped for a goddess' (fol. 90).

If Elissa's sponsorship of the rapes at Cyprus thus suggests two ways—one biological, one cultural—in which constructions of female sexuality can matter to the colonialist project, her climactic encounter with the neighboring King Hiarbas of Mauretania clearly points to the colonizing of race by gender and nationality. Having heard of Elissa's extraordinary accomplishments at Carthage, Hiarbas is determined to have her for his wife, regardless of how she may view his proposal. His ambassadors, reluctant to present Hiarbas' demand of marriage as baldly to her as he presented it to them, necessarily 'wente to woorke wyth her craftely after the nature of Afres, declaringe that theyr kynge demaunded some personne, that could learn hym and his Afres more civill manners and trade of lyvynge, but he coulde fynde none that would vouchsafe to forsake his owne kinfolke, to go among such barbarous people that lived after the manner of brute beastes' (fol. 89). In effect, Hiarbas' 'Afres' force Elissa to live up to her civilizing mission: if she is as genuinely committed to spreading civilization as the foundation of Carthage suggests she is, then she must accompany them back to Mauretania, where her talents are so desperately needed. The deceitful 'Afres' here remove Elissa from her role as an imperial commodifier of foreign women's sexuality and put her in the same position as those maidens whom her followers kidnapped: they will decide how her sexuality ought to be used. Her decision to burn herself alive atop of a funeral pyre 'made to pacify the ghoste of her fyrst husbande' (fol. 90) rather than marry Hiarbas allows her to maintain her chastity and avoid the Cypriot women's subject position in this gendered and sexualized discourse of empire. As importantly, it permits her to escape a miscegenous bond with Hiarbas, through embrace of cultural controls on her body and her sexuality; in this way, rules of gender difference may be seen to underwrite one of the primary principles of racial difference. The refusal of a sexual bond with a cultural opponent makes a heroine of her; when the city is conquered, as she herself refused to be, then she will fall from the pantheon.

In Justin, race operates to associate Hiarbas' treacherous, deceitful 'Afres' with a particular culture or nationality, the 'barbarous' Mauretanians. He is comparatively muted on Elissa's 'race', emphasizing instead the identity of colonizer and conqueror she shares with the Romans who will follow her dominion in North Africa. For imperial purposes, this indirection, combined with the depth of her self-consecration to her lawful patriarchally-chosen husband, in effect 'races' her white; she functions like a continent, conquering Roman.

The legend of Elissa's discipline and heroism won a place for women in epic adventure precisely by decontaminating the idea of Woman of its negative sexual connotations, a necessary prerequisite to giving her an imperial identity, and by displacing the concept of racial difference onto her male Mauretanian adversaries. In Justin, racial difference in the modern sense of skin color signifies most powerfully in the conflicts between wouldbe colonizers and their opponents; Elissa herself is primarily textualized as a gendered and sexualized being. And yet the use she makes, or declines to permit to be made, of her sexuality also connotes a 'racial' identity, tracing the links between sexuality and colonial mastery outlined by Paul Brown.[19] In contrast to this displacement of blackness from the figure of the African queen—a displacement which enables the essentializing of her gender—Shakespeare's Cleopatra is both racially and sexually different from her Roman opponents. Her 'blacke' skin and her powerful sexuality together work to define the nature of the political challenge she presents to Rome's designs in Egypt.

The Renaissance saw the historical Cleopatra as a woman whose corruption was most immediately manifest in her use of her sexual power as a weapon over Roman heroes. This sexual power was explicitly presented as a challenge to the integrity of the family-based image of Roman society beloved of Renaissance classicists, who tended to reproduce late-republican Rome's concerns with lineage and family in the image of their own era's usage of the family as an instrument of political and sexual control.[20] Aemilia Lanyer, for example, imagines a Cleopatra who, while unquestionably beautiful, is so 'unaccompanied with virtue' that she provoked the split between Antony and Octavius:

> Beautie the cause *Antonius* wrong'd his wife,
> Which could be decided but by sword:
> Great *Cleopatraes* Beautie and defects
> Did worke *Octaviaes* wrongs, and his neglects.[21]

The Egyptian queen in the Countess of Pembroke's 1594 translation of Garnier's *Antonie* reproaches herself for causing Antony's desertion of the field at Actium:

> My face too lovely caus'd my wretched case.
> My face hath so entrap'd, so cast us downe,
> That for his conquest *Caesar* may it thanke,
> Causing that *Antony* one army lost
> The other wholy did to *Caesar* yeld.

She affirms to her maid 'Eras' that she is 'sole cause' of his disgrace: 'I did it, only I'.[22] Here, the heterosexual attraction which is disciplined to imperial purpose in other narratives of Roman progress in Africa is set free to become a disruptive force not only in matters of state, but in Antony's private household as well. These two female authors negotiate their way into writing by omitting the political issues at stake in Rome's struggle to bring Egypt within the forming empire, refusing the possibility of a multiply-formed identity for Cleopatra by essentializing her gender. Indeed, Pembroke's 'translation', while remaining generally faithful to Garnier's original, further simplifies the gender issues surrounding the queen by omitting his emphasis on her power to attract and thus eroding the grounds for considering the nature of Antony's relation with her.[23] While Lanyer's reproduction of Cleopatra within a precisely defining discourse of outlaw female sexuality makes no notice of Cleopatra's race, Pembroke believes she is white; at line 428 'Eras' here sympathetically wonders why the queen 'Water(s) with teares' the 'fair alablaster' of her face. She also seems to speak from within a dominant race's perspective as she begs her servant Euphron to take her and Antony's children to some distant exotic place where they will be safe—where, for example, 'Black *æthiopes* to neighbour Sunne do shewe . . . their freezed locks' (1862, 1861). As she speaks from within a partriarchal discourse of beauty and of family value, Pembroke's queen also speaks a European and white orientation of native and foreign, black and white. Her whiteness domesticates her to the dominant perspective Pembroke adopted and adapted in her own writings.[24]

While also featuring a white queen, Thomas May's translation of Lucan's *Pharsalia*, the Silver Age epic of the civil wars between Julius Caesar and Pompey and one of the fullest Renaissance accounts of Rome's political progress in Egypt, dilates on Pembroke's almost offhanded racing of Cleopatra. As is the question of Elissa's race in Justin's *History*, this Cleopatra's whiteness is more broadly opened explicitly to include a range of historical and cultural meanings rigorously excluded from the purview of Pembroke's Senecan concerns.[25] Indeed, May's translation prefaces its account of Caesar's ultimate triumph over Pompey with a scene of Caesar surveying the ruins of Troy, thus plainly orienting itself in relation to the master narrative of empires won and lost, of civilizations in conflict, of the necessity of firmly opposing matters of love and matters of war. Identifying himself as 'The greatest heire of all *Iulus* race', Caesar raises an altar to the ruins' mute evidence of Rome's heroic ancestry and vows that if Troy's shades will 'Prosper my course',

> thankefull Rome shall raise
> Troyes walls againe, your people Ile restore,
> And build a Roman Troy.[26]

Almost immediately after making this vow, Caesar receives the gift of Pompey's head, draped in an Egyptian mantle; King Ptolemy of Egypt, Pompey's ally and brother-in-law, has sold him to Caesar in exchange for his help in maintaining his own throne. The power of his own myths of origin and historical destiny thus initially seem dominant over any possible competing Egyptian design, but he is proven wrong, in Lucan's view, by the evidence of his affair with Cleopatra, which occupies most of the poem's tenth and final book:

> Our Capitall she with her Sistrum scarr'd,
> With Ægypt's base effeminate rout prepar'd
> To seize Rome's Eagles, and a triumph get
> Or captiv'd *Caesar;* when at *Lencas* fleet
> It doubtfull stood, whether the world that day
> A woman, and not Roman should obey.
>
> (10:S)

In Lucan's formulation of the fateful impropriety of Caesar's love, 'woman' is syntactically opposed to 'Roman', and not to 'man': for all practical purposes, 'Roman' *means* 'man', or at least did before Caesar's fateful encounter with Cleopatra. Here, gender anxiety is opened to include not only Celopatra's womanhood, but also Egyptian and Roman manhood. Cleopatra's lavish court culture in effect disrupts the identification with fathers' unforgiving *labor* which was the hallmark of the republican period, suggested here by Caesar's pious impulse at the sight of Troy's ruins. In May's Lucan, gender helps make the role of 'racial' difference in this imperial conflict between Roman and Hellenistic value visible. Indeed, Lucan often seems convinced that all the delicate political maneuvering designed to let Egypt enter the forming empire while saving its rulers' Ptolemaic face is a desperate compromise destined to result in the compromise and erosion of Roman value:

> We let thy Isis in Romes temples dwell,
> Thy deify'd dogs, and sorrow causing bell;
> Osiris, whom thou shewest, while thou weep'st,
> A man; our god in dust thou Ægypt keep'st.
>
> (Book 8, P2)

Political expediency had sometimes dictated that the natural order should be overthrown and men placed in a subject position to women, as English history had demonstrated, but at least obedience to great 'Eliza' had not entailed worship of such an obvious and overblown sexual ripeness; rather the contrary.[27] Nor had subjection to the rule of England's exemplary Eliza, so determined to resist the importunings of male suitors, threatened national sovereignty as Caesar's obsession with Cleopatra threatened Rome's identity as the conquering male in the imperial bond.

Lucan's Cleopatra is as sexually alluring as Lanyer's and Pembroke's, but with a major difference; she is a sexual agent, one whose sexuality is allowed to speak cultural as well as gender difference from the helplessly fascinated Caesar. He is moved despite himself by Cleopatra's distinctly unRoman view of the union between sexual and imperial projects as she implores him to enforce her late father's will, under whose terms she was left a coequal ruler of Egypt 'to enjoy / My brothers crowne, and marriage bed' (10: S).[28] Caesar, May notes, maintains enough control over himself to realize that granting Cleopatra political authority in Egypt would be disastrous to Rome's own best interests there,

> But beauty pleades, and that incestuous face
> Prevailes; the pleasures of a wanton bed
> Corrupt the judge.

Just as Lucan's Cleopatra owns her sexualized cultural difference in a way that is suppressed in Lanyer's or Pembroke's versions, the Roman history also allows Cleopatra's sexuality an imperial dimension which is absent from the women's texts. She invites Caesar to a rich feast, where the bounty of Egypt is summed up and made available in her body:

> Her snowy breasts their whitenesse did display
> Thorough the thin Sidonian tiffenay
> Wrought, and extended by the curious hand
> Of Ægypt's workmen.

Powerfully attracted by a foreign queen who has every intention of fueling his desire, Caesar is 'taught' by this spectacle 'The riches of the spoiled world to take' (10: S3). The territorial and personal ambition that were to become issues in the conspiracy against Caesar are here linked to his lust for what ought properly to have remained a mere object of acquisition but became instead a living emblem of an entire 'spoiled world'. The sexual element of early modern colonial discourse, so familiarly regarded as a social instrument for civilizing outlanders' savagery and bringing them peacefully into the frame of European civil order[29], is here strikingly turned against the would-be builder of empire. Cleopatra's sexual authority over Caesar embodies her country's resistance to Roman mastery.

Earlier in Lucan's account of Rome's first African encounters, Roman conquerors are shown in the act of civilizing and making productive the unnatural barrenness of Libya, 'Barren in all that's good', and yet sprouting monsters where the venom from Medusa's severed head dropped onto it. It took the Romans to show 'The Mauretanian men' how to make use of their sole natural resource, their country's rich forests of 'Citron wood'; until the Romans arrived, the Mauretanians had been 'contented with the shade' (Book 9: Q4). One race of men here easily masters another, but when the foreigner is both a woman and a queen, hierarchies of gender cancel hierarchies of race.

Other accounts of Egypt further articulate Lucan's suggestions of a link between sexuality, gender, and the Egyptian land.[30] Plutarch's essay 'Of Isis and Osiris' bases its analysis of Isis' place in Egyptian cosmology on her love for her brother and mate, Osiris. After Osiris, the chief god of Egypt, was murdered and dismembered by their half-brother Typhon, Isis found and reassembled the scattered pieces of Osiris' body, all except for his penis, which Typhon had thrown into the river Nile. Isis fashioned him another member, 'called *Phallus,* which she consecrated'; she built a temple wherever she found a part of his body, eventually burying his reassembled body in a special coffer and venerating it in commemorative ceremonies.[31] Plutarch's interpretation of this myth holds that the waters of the sacred river Nile represent Osiris' seed, and 'the body of Isis is the Earth or land of *Egypt*', (1059) made fruitful by the river's annual flood. Isis and Osiris were also identified with the moon and the sun, so that she also became the patron of the fertility of human women. Egyptians believed that during the new moon, Osiris lay buried in his special coffer, that the gaiety and civility he embodied were gone from the earth. As the moon waxed full, it provided proof that Isis had conquered the power of death through her special love, that she had conceived and was growing in pregnancy. As the special goddess of this pregnant moon, Isis both governed the mortal world of change and depended on the physical love of her brother and mate to fulfil her cosmic destiny. Plutarch characterizes her as 'the feminine part of Nature', who has 'an infinite number of names' (1065).

The goddess Isis and the Egyptian queens who identified themselves with her[32] were worshipped as the 'mother of the world' (1061), capable of bringing order and wholeness out of chaos and pain. The mysterious fruitfulness of the Egyptian soil and Shakespeare's queen who bodies it forth ('great *Caesar* . . . ploughed her, and she cropt', II.ii.232-33) rehabilitates the African soil on which the last of these imperial contests played itself out. Shakespeare's play accomplishes this reformation through recourse to a mythological tradition which not only assigns cosmic authority to a woman, but which locates that authority in a spiritual construction of her sexuality which lay clearly outside any construction available under terms of a more conventionally patriarchal culture, and which intimately identifies this entirely foreign sexual power with the landscape over which she rules.

To return to Shakespeare's 'blacke' Cleopatra after seeing the conjoined places occupied by 'race' (in its cultural and geographic senses), gender, and the imperial process in other accounts of Roman Africa and Egypt is, I hope, to be readier to accept that it matters that she is through her own declaration physically different from her Roman lover(s). Her dark skin, in the terms of the well-known proverb from the period about washing the Ethiop, is a literal emblem of the impossibility—or at least, extreme difficulty—of the task the Romans have set themselves in conquering Egypt. That Antony and Cleopatra are bound together across lines of race as well as of imperial purpose further illustrates the infirm status of the Roman identity for which Octavius lays down the guiding assumptions in the play, and to which the Hellenism of the historical Antony was perceived to pose such a potent threat.[33]

As well as sexually removing the perhaps already-alienated Antony from his solidarity with Rome, Cleopatra's deliciously offhand allusion to her sexual power, and the story of racial origins it engenders, also negates the patriarchal and dynastic terms under which Renaissance classicists conceived of Rome's 'right' to empire, denying colonialism's (hetero)sexual and masculinist constitution. The dark skin Cleopatra identifies as the result of Apollo's rough sexual play was most commonly reported as the result of a cosmic accident, when the chariot of the sun and the mighty winged horses which drew it veered out of their normal course under the poor management of Apollo's half-mortal son Phaeton. *The Countess of Pembroke's Ivychurch* is typical: the unruly horses 'note the vulgar people', and 'the bridles are the stay of governement'. Resolute rulers should 'spare the whip, reine them hard'.[34] Phaeton's sad story 'to the life presents a rash and ambitious Prince', 'altogether unfit for government; which requires mature advice, and supernaturall knowledge'. The horses he is too weak to control 'are the common people, unruly, fierce, and prone to innovation: who finding the weaknesse of their Prince, fly out into all exorbitancies to a generall confusion'.[35] Phaeton's presumption in imagining he could drive his father's horses is a prime example of the 'madnesse' resulting from the arrogance of the wellborn; the 'ruling of men, or guiding of a Kingdom, is *ars artium,* and a worke of no lesse difficulty then the ruling of Phoebus his charriot'[36]

In order to rewrite the origin of her dark skin as the result of an intentional coupling between herself and the sun god, Cleopatra erases Phaeton; only Phoebus has determined her color and racial identity, and only by his loving touch. Cleopatra's information that a god's desire for her and not any misfortune lies at the heart of the observable facts of racial difference refuses the authoritarian applications of the myth and recasts the place of female sexuality and agency in Roman productions of the imperial process. Her spontaneous myth of origins also sets aside the patrilineal basis of the activity of making empires ('heire of all *Iulus* race'), since she tells of an irregular union without issue. Instead of a story about why concentrating power in the hands of one strong authoritarian ruler is best, Cleopatra links her race to a story about masculine desire and masculine surrender. When Antony installs Cleopatra, her son by Julius Caesar, and 'all the unlawfull issue, that their Lust /. . . hath made between them' (III.vi.7-8) as rulers of Lower Egypt, refusing the value of the marriage of state with Octavius' sister, he refuses as well the authority of a precisely-defined patriarchal 'family' as an authorizing model for the conduct of public life.[37]

Octavius tries and fails to honour the ties between Roman men through the use of women—first Octavia, then, after Antony's death, Cleopatra. To include Cleopatra in his triumph would be to announce his defeat not only of the alternate, womanist order Antony and she tried to establish in Egypt, but also, perhaps, to renounce the power of his own identification with the man who was his 'Brother', his 'Competitor', his 'Mate in Empire' (V.i.42, 43). Regarding Antony both as his sturdily homosocial 'brother' and as his more ambiguous 'Mate', Octavius' grief and determination here suggest how subject to flux the play's apparently stable gender and racial hierarchies actually are.[38] Defeating Cleopatra and obliterating the proof of her power over Antony closes Egypt's tantalizingly open formulations of race and gender identity by firmly delimiting a masculine and unitary Roman body of state.[39]

Cleopatra's death and transumption to another plane of being is undertaken in conscious spite of the Roman masculinist order. The degree to which she succeeds in proclaiming the value of her lineage and her sexuality in creating a world that is independent of and opposite to Rome is perhaps nowhere indicated as strongly as in Antony's heartbroken reaction to the false news of her death in Act Four. Calling his manservant Eros, he vows to follow her:

> I come my Queene. *Eros*? Stay for me,
> Where Soules do couch on Flowers, wee'l hand in hand,
> And with our sprightly Port make the Ghostes gaze:
> *Dido,* and her *Aeneas* shall want Troopes,
> And all the haunt be ours. (IV.xiv.50-54)

Antony's fancy that the legend of his and Cleopatra's passion will eclipse Virgil's ultimate proof of the incompatibility of love and imperial duty shows Shakespeare in the act of unwriting the certainties of epic.[40] Dido, that other African mother of empire, who committed suicide out of the forlorn realization that her love could find no lasting place in Aeneas' dynastic heart, will be superseded by Cleopatra, whose death for love will compel admiration even among the shades in the underworld, and whose sacrifice will be rewarded with her married lover's eternal devotion. In this way, *Antony and Cleopatra,* more perhaps than any of the other Renaissance texts of African queens, allows room for contradiction of the masculine and white verities these texts reproduce. This Cleopatra's Roman lover is led by his love for her into a denial of the power of one of Rome's founding legends and all its burden of sexual fear; in an allusion as offhand as Cleopatra's explanation of her dark skin, he will refuse as well the foundational significance of racialized cultural conflict to the construction of a recognizably Roman identity.

Notes

1. I cite the New Variorum of *Antony and Cleopatra*, ed. M. Spevack, M. Steppat, and M. Munkelt, (New York, 1990); here, I.v.27-29. All subsequent references will be provided parenthetically in the text.

2. However, note also this Cleopatra's reference to the 'blewest veines' (II.v.29) in the hand she offers the messenger who brings her news of Antony's marriage to kiss. This imprecision about skin color and racial identity is common in Renaissance texts, as several observers have noted, so that characters who are supposed to be black often refer to themselves as 'Indians', for example. In this play, the meanings of race are further complicated by the etymology of the word 'gypsy' believed to have derived from 'Egyptian'; Philo goes on here to refer contemptuously to how Antony's great 'Captaines heart' has now become merely 'the Bellowes and the Fan / To coole a Gypsies Lust' (I.i.8, 9-10). The institutionalization of the slave trade in the mid-seventeenth century stabilized and narrowed notions of race around skin color to a far greater degree than is always observable earlier in the Renaissance.

3. *The Common Liar: An Essay on 'Antony and Cleopatra'* (New Haven, 1973), pp. 184-188. All subsequent references will be provided parenthetically in the text.

4. Michael Neill in the Oxford *Antony and Cleopatra* (Oxford, 1994), p. 87. All subsequent references will be provided in the text.

5. Linda T. Fitz, 'Egyptian Queens and Male Reviewers: Sexist Attitudes in *Antony and Cleopatra* Criticism', *SQ* 28 (1977), 297-316, traces the place of prejudiced and reductive attitudes toward women and gender in the modern history of the play's reception. Following Jonathan Dollimore's influential argument in *Radical Tragedy: Religion, Ideology and Power in the Drama of Shakespeare and his Contemporaries* (Chicago, 1984) that the sexual bond between Antony and Cleopatra 'is rooted in a fantasy transfer of power from the public to the private sphere', (216) that the play's apparent great binaries are actually ideological effects of the power relations in whose terms the lovers define themselves and their destiny, most recent critics resist reading gender in the play in firmly oppositional or absolute terms. See, for example, Jonathan Gil Harris, '"Narcissus in thy face": Roman Desire and the Difference it Fakes in *Antony and Cleopatra*,' *SQ* 44 (1994), 408-425; Clare Kinney, 'The Queen's Two Bodies and the Divided Emperor: Some Problems of Identity in *Antony and Cleopatra*', in Anne M. Haselkorn and Betty Travitsky (eds), *The Renaissance Englishwoman in Print: Counterbalancing the Canon* (Amherst, 1990), pp. 177-186; and Jyotsna Singh, 'Renaissance

Antitheatricality, Antifeminism, and Shakespeare's *Antony and Cleopatra*', *Renaissance Drama*. n.s. 20 (1989), 99-121.

6. While I don't particularly care whether the historical Cleopatra was 'white' or 'black' and note the growing consensus among biologists and ethnographers that 'race' is not a scientifically useful term, I do want to draw attention to what may be forcibly excluded from an understanding of *Antony and Cleopatra* by the refusal to explore the textuality of race in stories about the two of them. Other critics interested in the roles of racial ideologies in the Cleopatra traditions include John Henrik Clarke, 'African Warrior Queens', in Ivan Van Sertima (ed.), *Black Women in Antiquity* (New Brunswick, 1984), who calls the unexamined assumption that Cleopatra was white a prime example of 'the emergence of the doctrine of white superiority', pp. 126-127. Mary Nyquist's fascinating '"Profuse, Proud Cleopatra": "Barbarism" and Female Rule in Early Modern English Republicanism', *Women's Studies* 24 (1994), 85-87, argues the operation of early modern processes of 'orientalization and domestication' (85) in representations of Cleopatra. Ania Loomba, *Gender, Race, Renaissance Drama* (Oxford, 1989) is probably the most theoretically sophisticated discussion of the work of race in the gendering of Renaissance drama; see especially pp. 42-45 on the 'historical dependency between patriarchalism and racism' (45), and 124-127 on the reduction of 'Cleopatra's "infinite variety"' to both patriarchal and racist stereotypes' (127).

7. Edward Said, 'Orientalism Reconsidered', in Francis Barker *et al.* (eds), *Literature, Politics and Theory* (London, 1986), 225. Also see Said, *Orientalism* (London, 1978), and Edith Hall, *Inventing the Barbarian: Greek Self-Definition Through Tragedy* (Oxford, 1989). On orientalism in *Antony and Cleopatra*, see John Gillies, *Shakespeare and the Geography of Difference* (Cambridge, 1994), esp. pp. 112-123; M. P. Charlesworth, 'The Fear of the Orient in the Roman Empire', *Cambridge Historical Journal* 2.1 (1926), 1-16; and an unpublished paper by B. A. Kachur, 'Shakespeare and Orientalism on the Edwardian Stage', esp. 2-13 (Seminar on Nineteenth-Century Shakespeare, Shakespeare Association of America, 1994).

8. 'Acting Black: *Othello, Othello* Burlesques, and the Performance of Blackness', *Theatre Journal* 46 (1994), 231-249. Much of this paper's argument about the burlesques' treatment of miscegenous sexuality builds on Neill's observations in 'Unproper Beds: Race, Adultery, and the Hideous in *Othello*', *SQ* 40 (1989), 383-412.

9. The history of Rome's conflicts in Africa—the three Punic wars and its absorption of Egypt into the empire—as well as the founding of Rome itself are marked by fateful encounters between Roman heroes and foreign noblewomen. These women include Sophonisba, niece of the Carthaginian general Hannibal who opposed Roman legions under the leadership of Scipio Africanus in the second Punic War (218-201 B.C.) and whose marriage to the Romans' client prince Massanissa eventually forced her suicide; Dido, the queen of Carthage whose tragic love for Aeneas conflicted with his epic destiny to found a new Troy to the west of the old; and Cleopatra, queen of Egypt.

10. Lynda Boose, '"The Getting of a Lawful Race": Racial Discourse in Early Modern England and the Unrepresentable Black Woman', in Margo Hendricks and Patricia Parker (eds), *Women, 'Race', and Writing in the Early Modern Period* (London, 1994), esp. pp. 47-49; and two papers by Kim F. Hall, 'Sexual Politics and Cultural Identity in *The Masque of Blackness*', Janelle Reinelt and Sue-Ellen Case (eds), *The Performance of Power: Theatrical Discourse and Politics* (Iowa City, 1991), pp. 3-18, and 'Rethinking Difference: The Politics of Race in Shakespeare', presented at the Shakespeare Association of America, 1992. Also see an unpublished paper by Wendy Wall, '"Dark'ning Thy Pow'r to Lend Base Subjects Light": Writing and Race in Early Modern England'. Peter Erickson, 'Representations of Blacks and Blackness in the Renaissance', *Criticism* 35 (1993), 506-515, notes that in nonreligious Renaissance paintings, it is difficult to 'read' the spatial arrangement of black figures 'because they appear less hierarchically fixed, more capable of multiple scenarios' (506). Bell hooks continues this critique of representations of black people, especially black women, in a contemporary context in *Black Looks: Race and Representation* (Boston, 1992).

11. In an apparent contradiction on the significance of Cleopatra's race similar to Neill's, Adelman believes that it doesn't particularly matter what exactly Shakespeare meant to suggest by having Cleopatra call herself 'blacke', but that her nonwhite skin is meant to contribute to the creation of a sense of her 'ancient and mysterious sexuality' (188); while her sexuality would presumably be represented differently if she were white, Adelman also seems too hasty to refuse to ask what it might mean if Cleopatra and her sexuality were constructed as black. On early-modern links between sexuality, gender, and territoriality, see Louis Montrose, 'The Work of Gender in the Discourse of Discovery', *Representations* 33 (1991), 1-41. Margaret Ferguson has discussed how what she terms the 'erotics of imperialism' affect the treatments of racial and gender confrontation in the period in 'Juggling the Categories of Race, Class and Gender: Aphra Behn's *Oroonoko*', *Women's Studies* 19 (1991), 159-181, and 'Color it Black: English Fantasies of Transgressive Masculine Desire in Shakespeare's *Titus Andronicus* and Behn's *Abdelazar*'

(Shakespeare Association of America, 1994). Patricia Parker, *Literary Fat Ladies: Rhetoric, Gender, Property* (New York, 1987), argues that travel narratives link the Petrarchan motif of the blazon, 'the tradition of opening the "bosom of nature" to view, and the language of the feminized new land, opened to its developer' (142). Petrarchan style is important here, of course, because of its descriptive language of 'black' and 'white' as a way of discussing and evaluating the effects of feminine beauty.

12. Besides Loomba, *Gender, Race, Renaissance Drama,* see the essays collected in *Women, 'Race', and Writing in the Early Modern Period* and in special issues of *Renaissance Drama* 22 (1992), on the topic 'Renaissance Drama in an Age of Colonization' and *Theatre Journal* 46 (1994), 'Early Modern Reenactments'; Kim F. Hall, 'Acknowledging Things of Darkness: Race, Gender, and Power in Early Modern England', Ph.D. dissertation, University of Pennsylvania, 1990; Eldred Jones, *Othello's Countrymen: The African in English Renaissance Drama* (London, 1965); Antony Barthelemy, *Black Face: Maligned Race: The Representation of Blacks in English Drama from Shakespeare to Southerne* (Baton Rouge, 1987); and Jack D'Amico, *The Moor in England Renaissance Drama* (Tampa, 1991).

13. See, for one example, George Best's *A True Discourse of the Late Voyages of Discoverie, For the Finding of a Passage to Cathaya* (London, 1578), which traced Africans' blackness to 'some naturall infection of the first inhabitants of that Countrey', (30) a moral stain he roots in the decision of Noah's son Cham to have sexual intercourse with his wife while confined in the Ark against an express prohibition in the hopes of fathering a child who would become heir to the new world revealed after the Flood.

14. Gary Miles, 'How Roman Are Shakespeare's "Romans"?', *SQ* 40 (1989), esp. 261-270, is an important account of how the self-image of Roman politicians differed under republican and imperial regimes. Miles argues that as the empire grew, so too did the prizes to be won by contenders for power and the steps they were willing to take to secure that power: 'A new language and vocabulary had to be found by which to communicate the stature of the new breed of aristocratic statesman. The Romans found this new vocabulary in the Greek-speaking eastern Mediterreanean with its long history of royal dynasties', including the Ptolemies of Egypt (261). On the clashes between Egyptian hellenism and the high Roman style see also Robert S. Bianchi, 'Ptolemaic Egypt and Rome: An Overview', in *Cleopatra's Egypt: Age of the Ptolemies* (The Brooklyn Museum, 1988), pp. 13-20. Bianchi notes the split within Egyptian culture between the ruling Ptolemaic court's hellenistic influence and the pharaonic culture of the Egyptian people. Martin Bernal, *Black Athena: The Afroasiatic Roots of Classical Civilization,* 2 vols. (New Brunswick, 1987) further argues the influence of subsaharan African civilizations on that of Egypt, vol. 1, 240-243.

15. Here, I depart from Gillies' conclusions in *Shakespeare and the Geography of Difference.* While Gillies is highly aware of the degree to which ancient accounts of geography color Renaissance versions of nationality and culture, he is silent on the ways in which racial identity, in the broad senses I argue above, also figures in these versions. For him, for example, *Antony and Cleopatra* is a play whose 'ancient construction' of what he calls the 'exotic' (p. 102) primarily exists in its representation of Antony as a kind of moral (as well as geographical) adventurer; '[e]xoticism is hardly the reigning theme' here (p. 112). I would argue instead that perceptions of Cleopatra's 'exotic' stature—her identity as a queen of Egypt who conducts herself according to distinctly unRoman sexual, political, and cultural standards—dominate the play.

16. *Thabridgment of the histories of Trogus Pompeius, Collected and wrytten in the Laten tonge, by the famous historiographer Justine, and translated into English by Arthur Goldyng* (London, 1564): here, fol. 87. Justin's work, as Goldyng's title suggests, is actually a digest of Trogus; Justin's interest in highlighting important moments from Greek culture would have smoothly recommended itself to the synthesizing impulses of English classicism. All subsequent references will be provided parenthetically in the text. Richard Waswo, 'The History that Literature Makes', *NLH* 19 (1988), 541-564, and Patricia Parker, 'Romance and Empire: Anachronistic *Cymbeline*', in George M. Logan and Gordon Teskey (eds), *Unfolded Tales: Essays on Renaissance Romance* (Ithaca, 1989), pp. 189-207, discuss the importance of the Matter of Troy and the Matter of Rome in English Renaissance culture.

17. In 'Managing the Barbarian: *The Tragedy of Dido, Queen of Carthage*', *Renaissance Drama* n.s. 23 (1992), 165-188.

18. Comparing the rape of the Sabine women by Romulus' followers to the abduction of the Cypriots' daughters, Stephen Orgel (ed.), *The Tempest* (Oxford, 1987), alludes to an 'imperial mythology, in which rape is essential to the foundation of empire' (41).

19. In '"This Thing of Darkness I Acknowledge Mine": *The Tempest* and The Discourse of Colonialism', in Jonathan Dollimore and Alan Sinfield (eds), *Political Shakespeare: New Essays in Cultural Materialism* (Ithaca, 1985), pp. 48-71.

20. On the importance of lineage and family to pre-imperial Romans' self-definition, see Miles, 'How Roman Are Shakespeare's "Romans"?', 260.

21. I cite Susanne Woods (ed.), *The Poems of Aemilia Lanyer: 'Salve Deus Rex Judoeæorum,'* (New York, 1993), marginal gloss p. 59; lines 213-216.

22. I cite the reprint of Pembroke's *Antonius* included in the New Variorum of *Antony and Cleopatra;* here, lines 437-441, 455. All subsequent references will be provided parenthetically in the text.

23. See Kim Hall's discussion of Lanier's and Pembroke's Cleopatras in '"I Rather Would Wish to Be a Blackamoor": Beauty, Race, and Rank in Lady Mary Wroth's *Urania*', in *Women, 'Race', and Writing,* esp. 182-183.

24. Tina Krontiris, *Oppositional Voices: Women as Writers and Translators of Literature in the English Renaissance* (London, 1992), believes that the Countess of Pembroke's pursuit of 'safe' genres such as translation eventually became 'a kind of cultural trap for her, pushing her further into a conventional role', (67) although she does not pursue the link between gender and conceptions of race I have been arguing here.

25. On the Senecan style of the Pembroke circle's works on Cleopatra, see J. Leeds Barroll, *Shakespearean Tragedy: Genre, Tradition, and Change in 'Antony and Cleopatra'* (Washington, D. C., 1984), pp. 34-35; and Marilyn Williamson, *Infinite Variety: Antony and Cleopatra in Renaissance Drama and Earlier Tradition* (Mystic CT., 1974), pp. 132-134. Margaret McGowan, 'The Presence of Rome in Some Plays of Robert Garnier', in E. Freeman, H. Mason, M. O'Regan, and S. W. Taylor (eds), *Myth and Its Making in the French Theatre: Studies Presented to W. D. Howarth* (Cambridge, 1988), pp. 12-29, discusses Garnier's and other French classicists' perception of a special relevance in histories of Rome's civil wars to their own era of French history.

26. *Lucan's Pharsalia: Or The Civill Warres of Rome, betweene POMPEY the great, and JULIUS CAESAR. The whole tenne Bookes. Englished by Thomas May* (London, 1631); here, Book 9, R4. All subsequent citations will be provided parenthetically in the text. May was obviously fascinated by the conflict between Rome and Egypt. Not only did he translate the *Pharsalia,* but he also wrote an original seven-book continuation of the epic which took readers up to Caesar's assassination, and a play, *The Tragedy of Cleopatra Queene of Ægypt* (acted 1626, printed 1639), which explored Cleopatra's suicide.

27. On parallels between the legends of Cleopatra and of Elizabeth I, see Keith Rinehart, 'Shakespeare's Cleopatra and England's Elizabeth', *SQ* 23 (1972), 81-86, and Theodora Jankowski, '"As I am Egypt's Queen": Cleopatra, Elizabeth I, and the Female Body Politic', *Assays* 5 (1989), 91-110.

28. Keith Hopkins, 'Brother-Sister Marriage in Roman Egypt', *Comparative Studies in Society and History* 22 (1980), 303-354, notes the wide occurrence of sibling marriage in pre-Roman Egypt and suggests that the practice only came to an end 'under the double impact of Roman law and Christianity' (354), some years after the events dramatized in *Antony and Cleopatra.*

29. See Paul Brown, '"This Thing of Darkness I Acknowledge Mine"', 48-54.

30. See, for example, Michael Lloyd, 'Cleopatra as Isis', *Shakespeare Survey* 12 (1959), 88-94; Barbara J. Bono, *Literary Transvaluation: From Vergilian Epic to Shakespearean Tragicomedy* (Berkeley, 1984), pp. 191-213; Adelman, *Common Liar,* pp. 66-67; and Loomba, *Gender, Race, Renaissance Drama,* pp. 124-130.

31. *The Philosophy Commonly Called The Morals written by the learned philosopher Plutarch of Chæronea; tr. out of Greek into English, and conferred with the Latine translations and the French, by Philemon Holland,* 2nd ed. (London, 1657); here, p. 1053. All subsequent citations will be provided parenthetically in the text.

32. Jan Quaegebeur, 'Cleopatra VII and the Cults of the Ptolemaic Queens', in *Cleopatra's Egypt,* pp. 41-53, and Mary Hamer, *Signs of Cleopatra: History, Politics, Representation* (London, 1993), pp. 10-16, discuss the ways in which the queens of Cleopatra's line publicly represented themselves as divine. My thinking here on the links between female sexuality, territory and sovereignty was originally stimulated by Sondra Delaney, who shared with me her photographs of the temple of Hathor (a divinity often identified with Isis) at Dendera.

33. According to Plutarch's *Life* of Mark Antony, it was his custom to emphasize his family's claim of descent from 'one *Anton,* the sonne of *Hercules*', by trying to dress as this eastern god was frequently represented, with 'his cassocke gyrt downe lowe upon his hippes, with a great sword hanging by his side' (*New Variorum,* 399). See Gillies, *Shakespeare's Geography of Difference,* pp. 112-118, and Linda McJannet, 'Antony and Alexander: Imperial Politics in Plutarch, Shakespeare, and Some Modern Historical Texts', *College Literature* 20 (1993), 1-18, for more on Antony's hellenism; and Cynthia Marshall, 'Man of Steel Done Got the Blues: Melancholic Subversion of Presence in *Antony and Cleopatra*', *SQ* 44 (1993), 385-408, on the refusal or incapacity of Shakespeare's Antony to fill a proper Roman role.

34. Abraham Fraunce, *The Third part of the Countess of Pembroke's Ivychurch: Entituled, Amintas Dale* (London, 1592; rpt. New York, 1976), 36. The Phaeton-Apollo story appears in Ovid's *Metamorphoses,* Book I.

35. George Sandys, *Ovid's Metamorphoses English'd* (Oxford, 1622), p. 66, p. 67.

36. Alexander Ross, *Mystagogus Poeticus, Or The Muses Interpreter,* ed. John R. Glenn (London, 1647; rpt. New York, 1987), p. 493.

37. Plutarch's *Life* of Mark Antony reports that after the deaths of Antony and Cleopatra, their various children were disposed of according to Roman imperial design. His eldest son by his first wife Fulvia was executed by Octavius, perhaps to forestall the power of filial identification among the Romans; Octavia raised his children by Cleopatra and married their eldest daughter to the king of Mauretania. Octavius married his daughter to Octavia's son Marcellus by her first marriage; Octavia married one of her daughters to Caesar's most trusted lieutenant, Agrippa, and then, after Marcellus's death, persuaded him that his own daughter should be remarried to Agrippa, setting her own daughter aside in order to do so. Preserving the bloodline of her birth family, the Octavians, was obviously of highest priority to Antony's widow.

38. The term 'homosocial' derives from Eve Kosofsky Sedgwick, *Between Men: English Literature and Male Homosocial Desire* (New York, 1985); her discussion, pp. 32-36, of the triangulation of desire in Shakespeare's sonnets is relevant to the familial politics through which Octavius and Antony attempt to structure their relation: 'The Sonnets present a male-male love that . . . is set firmly within a structure of institutionalized social relations that are carried out through women: marriage, name, family, loyalty to progenitors and to posterity' (35). Jonathan Gil Harris, '"Narcissus in thy face"', also notes the relevance of Sedgwick to Octavius and Antony's situation, 419-420.

39. At I.ii.80-81; I.iv.5-7; and II.v.21-23, characters confuse Cleopatra with Antony or with other men. Holland's translation of 'Of Isis and Osiris' provides some discussion of this fluid gendering of the Egyptian queen: Egyptian authorities 'name the Moon, mother of the world; saying, that she is a double nature, male and female: female, in that she doth conceive and is replenished by the Sun: and male, in this regard that she sendeth forth and sprinkleth in the air, the seeds and principles of generation' (1061).

40. See Mihoko Suzuki, *Metamorphoses of Helen: Authority, Difference, and the Epic* (Ithaca, 1989), 258-263.

TITUS ANDRONICUS: AARON

Edward T. Washington (essay date 1995)

SOURCE: "Tragic Resolution in Shakespeare's *Titus Andronicus,*" in *CLA Journal,* Vol. XXXVIII, No. 4, June, 1995, pp. 461-79.

[*In the following essay, Washington argues that the figure of Aaron transcends the Renaissance representation of blacks "as stereotypical dramatic emblems of evil."*]

At the end of a tragedy the waters close over the wreckage of the tragic figures. Those who remain pay tribute to the fallen, inviting the sense that life shall move on, the community having learned something useful from the sad events. Most critics assert that in *Titus Andronicus,* the new alliance between the Andronici and the Goths, with Lucius in the lead and Lucius Jr. in the wings, represents the solution to Rome's dilemmas, the renewed life after tragic events.[1] But despite Lucius' alliance and coronation at the end, it is black Aaron and his child who signal new hope for this tragic world, thereby undermining the play's representation of blacks as stereotypical dramatic emblems of evil.[2]

I

Aaron's role as a barbarous black infidel is rendered ambiguous by his relative merits and by subtly subversive patterns of dramatic action in the text. Thus in a tragedy of blood that presents fourteen on-stage murders, we see only one slaying carried out by Aaron, the play's so-called arch-"fiend."[3] More significantly, while Roman and Gothic characters wage acts of cruel revenge that beget more killings, Aaron's single murder of the nurse[4] actually *saves* a life, that of his newborn son. In this latter scenario Aaron must also prevent the child's mother, Tamora, and halfbrothers, Demetrius and Chiron, from murdering their own flesh and blood: his success in doing so saves (temporarily) his Gothic step-family from falling prey to the self-destructive family in-fighting that erodes Rome's political stability.[5] Aaron not only preserves life, but he is also the only figure (except the black child and perhaps the midwife) to be threatened with death and not die. The Moor's ability to survive adverse situations provides some reason to suspect that his proposed execution at the end of the drama will progress no further than the attempt to hang him earlier on (V.i.47-48). In short, despite his instigations, his violent acts, and his confessions of wrongdoing, Aaron's role is aligned with patterns of family unity and survival that oppose the society's (and the play's) downward spiral toward dissolution and death.

Aaron's movement toward life is affirmed by food and devouring motifs. Rome is portrayed as a ravenous tiger, a famished "blood-drinking pit" (II.iii.224) that consumes all in its path. In this regard, we can hardly dismiss Titus' two banquet feasts, Aaron's reference to a survival diet as he flees with his son, and the Moor's final death sentence by means of starvation. Titus' first banquet is a light repast that aims to fit the Andronici for a long but ultimately victorious battle against their enemies, as Titus says: "So, so; not sit; and look you eat no more / Than will preserve just so much strength in us / As will revenge these bitter woes of ours" (III.ii.1-3). That Aaron also decides to eat sparsely during the course of his escape with his son suggests that lean feeding (in opposition to the voraciousness motif) is a metaphor for victory and survival in the play, as Aaron soliloquizes to the child: "I'll make you feed on berries and on roots, / And feed on curds and whey, and suck the goat, / And cabin in a cave, and bring you up / To be a warrior, and command a camp" (IV.ii.178-81). The link between plain fare and salvation is strengthened insofar as Titus' second banquet involves a hideously rich dinner of human heads that signals the continuation of revenge mayhem. Although this banquet sets the stage for the drama's most gruesome carnage, Aaron is not a guest at this final, bloody feast. Rather it is his lot to be partly buried in (i.e., only half-swallowed by) the earth, thereupon to die of starvation. Yet, too coincidentally, Aaron's execution by starvation parallels the leanness motif which also describes the play's movement toward survival. Given that Aaron's demi-burial allows his persuasive tongue to flourish, and given his earlier reprieve from hanging, we wonder if the Moor, in slimmer shape, might not wriggle his way out of even this seemingly final death sentence. That is, the theme of reduced appetite as a means to salvation suggests "new life" for Aaron at the end of the play.

Aaron's impulse toward life is further corroborated by language and action which define children as prisoners. Titus calls the tomb where his dead sons lie a "cell of virtue" (I.i.93) and an "earthy prison" (I.i.99). Not surprisingly, he treats his living children like prisoners or even slaves: Titus wills his daughter, Lavinia, to Saturninus at the same time that he bequeathes to the new emperor his sword, his chariot, and his Gothic prisoners (I.i.243-52); he disowns his sons for challenging his parental authority (I.i.294); Saturninus refers to Lavinia as one of Titus' "stock" (I.i.300). Hence in a further instance of unhealthy family relationships among the Romans, we find children in the role of captives. Aaron, on the other hand, sees his child as an important family member who deserves freedom, for he comments to Demetrius and Chiron:

> He is your brother, lords, sensibly fed
> Of that self blood that first gave life to you;
> And from that womb where you imprisoned were
> He is enfranchised and come to light.
>
> (IV.ii.122-25)

After refashioning his son's identity into that of a freedman, Aaron rebuts Tamora's directive to slay the child: "Tell the empress from me, I am of age / To keep mine own, excuse it how she can" (IV.ii.103-04). Being a mature adult and no child/prisoner, Aaron asserts that he is no captive, that he has freedom to nurture his son's life, not send it to an early grave (as is the practice in Rome). Aaron's final speech then gathers together the thematic threads that join him and the black child to the idea of salvation: "I am no baby, I, that with base prayers / I should repent the evils I have done" (V.iii.185-86). In these lines (which have little meaning outside the present context) Aaron declares to the Romans that he is no baby, no child that to them is a prisoner. It is Aaron's gritty claim of freedom and life for himself, not confinement and death. Moreover, if his statement is correct that babies are inherently capable of repentance (and since the only baby on stage is his), then should Aaron perish, the child's ability to repent could nevertheless lead to salvation. No comparable sense of survival and religious redemption, in form or content, occurs among the Romans as it does with Aaron and the black child. This seems to point to the blacks in this play as real or potential representatives of renewed life in a declining Rome.[6]

II

It is remarkable that in the midst of this Roman death chamber there is a birth, an event uncommon in Shakespeare and one much less suitable for tragedy than for comedy or romance. Aaron is the father and the only character willing to defend the infant's life in a society that slaughters its own children:[7] "[The child] shall not live," says Chiron, and Aaron replies, "He shall not die" (IV.ii.80-81). The normative critical response to the black child is that he is a reincarnated synthesis of two devils, Tamora and Aaron.[8] Yet in a play where the only things "hatched" are evil plots that lead to death, this child comes to life, and it is suggested that it will thrive. While some argue that the black child merely emblematizes the magnitude of tragic evil in Rome,[9] it should be noted that those in the play who would kill the child are villains who themselves succumb (save Lucius, who must be coerced into preserving life). That is, the callousness of the infant's would-be murderers encourages us to view the child as a positive entity, not only in the light of his survival but also in terms of his moral value.

Specifically, the black child is the only innocent character in the play, one who seeks no revenge and plots no murder: even the problem comedy pregnancies in *All's Well That Ends Well* and *Measure for Measure* are more ominous in their bourgeois contexts of sexual decorum than is Aaron's living child in this Roman wasteland. It might also be noted that the child's retreat from a dangerous Rome through the countryside toward salvation—and Aaron's statement that his son would be great someday—is a dramatic pattern that echoes the journey of the infant Moses out of Pharoah's hands.[10] This pattern also resembles the story of Romulus and Remus, whose trials led to the founding of Rome. Additionally, the child's emergence from a ruinous monastery wall suggests (with the extenuation of his life) a phoenix rising from the ashes. Each of these accounts involves a difficult sojourn through nature, the result of which is new, or improved, or extended life.

Further support for the view that the black child symbolizes salvation ensues from a few lines spoken by Aaron late in the play. After explaining to Demetrius and Chiron that they must accept a markedly new plan of action if they expect to survive the birth of the child, he whispers to his son: "Come on, you thick-lipp'd slave, I'll bear you hence; / For it is you that puts us to our shifts" (IV.ii.176-77). A motif exists in the play which reveals that the closer the Romans come to seeing the truth about their plight, the more radical become the shifting sands of character behavior and plot. (Similarly, as action and character behavior become more extreme, the closer the Romans come to seeing the truth.) For example, Saturninus' heightened anxiety exposes his incompetence and prompts the citizenry to shift their support from him to Lucius and the alien Goths. When Titus loses his wits, Tamora and the boys respond to his extremes by disguising themselves, in truth, as the villains they are; this is turn leads to recognition by Titus and to the extremely shocking and bloody end. Lastly, the blackness of the newborn child reveals the truth of Aaron and Tamora's relationship, which impels the Moor to shift from Rome. Aaron's subsequent capture results in a full confession of all the previously hidden truths. The real tragedy of this play, however, is that despite the gradual emergence of truth, no one has the wherewithal to use the facts to halt the revenge: Tamora's mania for retribution causes her to underestimate the truth in her choice of allegorical disguises; Titus and the Romans see the truth but continue to wreak havoc. Conversely, in light of the unending chaos in Rome, Aaron's departure (the shift brought on by the advent of the child) denotes foresight and an impulse toward life as the black character abandons a noxious environment to make a new start in a land more replete in healthy family support and friends. (Lucius also leaves Rome but returns to continue the revenge.) Just as Aaron attempts to jettison the revenge cycle, to gain life by leaving Rome, it appears that the black child is capable of breaking free as well—as Demetrius' singular rejection of Lavinia's plea for mercy confirms: "What, would'st thou have me prove myself a bastard?" (II.iii.148). As the play's acknowledged bastard, the black child, unlike Demetrius, appears to possess the potential for mercy that could break the chain of endless retribution in Rome.

As noted above, critics of *Titus Andronicus* tend to dismiss the idea that the blacks in this play represent anything other than evil and death, due mainly to the new configuration of Andronici and Goth that heralds a new society at the end.[11] Yet many doubts exist as to whether this new configuration entails a substantive change from the past. My argument is that it does not. To support this assertion we may begin by noting that Lucius, the new emperor, helped to initiate the feuding in this play by sacrificing Tamora's son Alarbus; and like other Romans he never realizes the degree to which vengeance and lack of mercy contribute to Rome's sorrows. Lucius never confesses, never repents, and it is stated that he is a soldier who perhaps rapes when he pillages (IV.i.107-11). Additionally, Lucius has problems communicating (which brings into question his leadership capabilities); he is inconsistent (e.g., his desertion to the Goths); and ultimately, he continues the revenge cycle with the sentences he imposes on Tamora and Aaron. Lucius does agree to nourish the black infant—yet he could be nursing his own demise should the child develop the leadership qualities hoped for by Aaron. The Goths agree to join forces with Lucius, but this alliance results from their belief that Tamora and Aaron had defected to the Romans (V.i.16), which they had not. The revelation of this truth could render the Goths a Trojan horse rather than a loyal ally to Rome. When we look beyond the elder to the youngest Lucius, the prospects for change do not improve. Clearly, little Lucius, named for his father, signals no change; this stasis is affirmed by the boy's vow to follow his father's violent ways, even as his grandfather Titus teaches him to revenge (IV.i.106-19). Then, too, there is the boy's heartfelt and noble desire to take Titus' place in the tomb. Despite genuine grief, however, young Lucius' sacrificial impulse only accentuates the misdirected death-oriented nature of the Roman society. In short, when Rome's future leader is hinted to be a violent, vengeful, death-desiring character (who, like his father, would storm a mother's bed-chamber to redress a wrong [IV.i.112]), the prospects for change in a declining Rome seem bleak.

Beyond the questions raised concerning weaknesses in the new Roman leadership, another issue which casts suspicion on the conventional tragic renewal concerns the functionary role of women. Of Titus' twenty-eight children and grandchildren, Lavinia is his only female descendant, and she dies without issue. Marcus is without wife as is Lucius. Tamora, the only woman to give birth (in a play filled with swollen tombs that resemble swelling wombs [II.iii.239-40]), dies. From a dramatic standpoint Rome's future lacks the female element necessary for regeneration. Ironically, the only other mention of a woman in *Titus Andronicus* is the wife of Muly, Aaron's black countryman, who has a child (possibly a daughter) about the same age as Aaron's son. (The female nurse and midwife are more or less placental beings who would suffocate a newborn life unless they are cut away.) What this census suggests is that Rome, unchanged by new leadership, moves toward sterility and death while the promise of life and the future lie with Aaron and/or his son, and/or his countrymen. As such, we can hardly dismiss these black figures as simplistic conventional emblems of evil that are subsumed in the end by a superior Roman (or Gothic) race.

III

References to darkness and blackness in this play adhere by and large to expected negative values: coffins are draped in black, criminal acts of "black night" (V.i.64) occur in "shaded" (II.iii.16) woods, illicit love is "raven-colored" (II.iii.183), and a "black fly" (III.ii.66-67) symbolizes evil. Dark images are also used to foreshadow the entrance of the "devil" (V.i.40) Aaron, to denote the perniciousness of Aaron's words and deeds and to describe Aaron's (or his child's) Moorish being. These uncomplimentary views of blackness are expressed primarily by white characters, but even Aaron seems to speak of blackness in pejorative terms: "Let fools do good, and fair men call for grace, / Aaron will have his soul black like his face" (III.i.204-05). Despite the text's espoused loathing of blackness (and corresponding embrace of whiteness), patterns exist in the language, action, and themes of *Titus Andronicus* that challenge the neatness of this conventional literary dichotomy, particularly with respect to Aaron's role as a conventional racial emblem of evil.

As alluded to earlier, one hedge against this hierarchical color dichotomy is the imputation of evil to the play's white characters.[12] These imputations suggest that whites are deficient in certain capabilities, attitudes, and moral virtues which the black characters in fact possess. The play uses inversion to foreground these uncomplimentary views of whiteness. For instance, Lavinia's temperament, virtue, and beauty define her as "Rome's rich ornament" (I.i.52), yet peevish and sensual sides to her personality (II.iii.66-70; 80-84) undermine her role as the city's "spotless" (V.ii.176) princess. Equally incongruous is the ritualistic dressing of the new emperor in the "pure white robe" (I.i.183) of election, for we discover rather quickly that Rome's leaders are enmired in political fractiousness, excessive religious zeal, and homicide. Thus it is no accident that Titus not only rejects the pure white robe of office early on, but also, in the end, arrays himself in the blood-daubed whites of a demented cook—a hideous translation of the white gown of leadership that was to signify his unsullied worthiness.

Another vagary in the conventional dichotomy of black and white involves the ways in which Aaron qualifies the standard meanings of the color emblems. While Aaron occasionally employs negative epithets of darkness, he never implies that such usage denotes inherent deficiencies in racial blacks. Aaron's reference to his son as a "tawny slave" (V.i.27) is an affectionate description since he obviously sets great store by the child. Similarly, when he alludes to criminal behavior that is as "black" as his face, or when he likens his own imperviousness to guilt to that of a "black dog (as the saying is)" (V.i.122), these similes of comparison (as the parenthetical comment denotes) simply acknowledge his skin to be the same color as the hue conventionally associated with depravity and evil. Conversely, the whites (including Tamora and her boys) see racial blackness literally as a metaphor for naturalistic evil. Aaron therefore is a "foul fiend" and a portent of evil "that comes in the night in the likeness of a coal-black Moor" (III.ii.78). A semantic confrontation between these divergent figures of blackness occurs when Lucius captures Aaron and must decide how to punish him. Having already asserted that Aaron's color defines his moral character (Lucius calls Aaron "the incarnate devil" and his child the "growing image of Aaron's fiend-like face" who is "too like the sire for ever being good" [V.i.40,45,50]), Lucius says: "Bring down the devil, for he must not die . . . presently" (V.i.145-46). But Aaron's response (especially given the cogency of his earlier remarks concerning idolotry and hypocrisy in Roman religious practices [V.i.73-85]) clearly provides a more rational assessment of the relationship between race and deviltry: "If there be devils, would I were a devil, / To live and burn in everlasting fire, / So I might have your company in hell" (V.i.147-49). According to Aaron, if deviltry exists, it harbors no racial preferences; and since evil exists among the whites in Rome, Aaron's statement disposes of Lucius' inference that deviltry is determined by racial blackness.

When the conventional values of black and white (i.e., evil and good) in the play are qualified, undercut, or overturned, they signal themes of misperception, poor comprehension, or religious hypocrisy—problems that constitute stumbling blocks to civility and order in Rome. Hence Romam (and Gothic) assumptions about Aaron's moral turpitude (and about the sinfulness of a child who has committed no evil) allow the white characters to dismiss qualities in the Moor that could otherwise be useful to them. Aaron's critique of Roman religious mores could help Lucius to comprehend the problems that stem from his murder of Alarbus, but Lucius hears only the ravings of a pagan fiend. Aaron's commitment to family unity and political alliance contrasts with Rome's factionalism, yet both Romans and Goths would continue to murder their own—in the case of Tamora and her boys, because their own is black. Aaron's enduring sexual relationship with Tamora is seen as despicable due largely to the Moor's blackness, but this racial dodge allows Demetrius and Chiron to gloss their own beastly sexual appetites and their rape of Lavinia. Then, too, Titus' glint of perception concerning family unity, mercy, and wise leadership is dashed by Marcus' scapegoating of Aaron via the witless metaphor of a black fly (III.ii.52-72). These misperceptions do not prove that Aaron is benign or wholly innocent; rather they show how conventional white racism (or conventional literary antiblackness) in *Titus Andronicus* reflects the restrictive (and hence destructive) vision of this Roman society. When Marcus labels Aaron the "chief architect and plotter of these woes" (V.iii.122), we know better that Rome's problems have their deepest roots in the psyches of the Roman leaders and in the fabric of the society as Shakespeare re-presents it dramatically. Consequently we have little reason to believe that the removal of Aaron and his child from the community will bring an end to Rome's sorrows.

IV

Having suggested several ways in which *Titus Andronicus* allows us to see redeeming qualities in its otherwise evil black characters, the larger question becomes: Is there a significant dramatic point to be made concerning the unanticipated virtues in Aaron and his child? To answer this question, we might first note that blackness or darkness constitutes one pole of a pair of antithetical entities which vies with its opposite for ascendency in the play. In addition to black and white, other prominent polarities include Roman and Goth, high and low, speech and silence, word and deed, reason and madness, love and hate, life and death. Shakespeare uses racial differences to highlight the theme of polarized conflict, and Aaron's blackness represents the evil that opposes Rome's "pure white" valor, piety, and nobility. Regardless of the degree to which this morality struggle holds true, a further dynamic is at work between opposing dramatic forces which illuminates a more complex meaning for blackness in *Titus Andronicus*.

In a recent essay on blackness in selected early modern texts, Joyce MacDonald argues that the polarized racial codes in *Titus Andronicus* remain rigidly dichotomized throughout the play: "The racialist discourse out of which

Shakespeare shaped [Aaron] posits an absolute gap between the racial selves it denominated as 'black' and 'white'"[13] I would argue, however, that while black and white racial images contend with each other throughout the play, there are times when this struggle abates to reveal a subtle, reconciling intermingling of antithetical poles—thereby bridging the "absolute gap" between black and white postulated by MacDonald. In Act IV, for example, Titus has seemingly lost both his power and his wits as he futilely endeavors to send complaint letters to the gods. As Marcus observes to his son: 'O Publius, is not this a heavy case, / To see thy noble uncle thus distract?" (IV.iii.24-25). Realizing that Titus has reached a dangerously low point, Publius (i.e., the public? the society?) suggests a plan of action to cure Titus, one which brings dark and light images together with sensitivity and compassion:

> Therefore, my lords, it highly us concerns
> By day and night t'attend him carefully,
> And feed his humour kindly as we may,
> Till time beget some careful remedy.
>
> (IV.iii.27-30)

Publius' remedy seems sound enough; however, as with the black fly incident, Marcus again blocks Titus' way to compassion and sanity when he proclaims Andronicus' miseries to be "past remedy" (IV.iii.31). Yet despite Marcus' dismissal of Publius' therapy, we find the "day and night" image of cure reinvoked at that critical point in the action when Titus realizes the truth about his misfortunes as he proclaims to Tamora when she appears as Revenge:

> I am not mad; I know thee well enough:
> Witness this wretched stump, witness these
>   crimson lines;
> Witness these trenches made by grief and care;
> Witness the tiring day and heavy night:
> Witness all sorrow that I know thee well
> For our proud empress, mighty Tamora.
>
> (V ii 21-26)

Here again the enjoinment of antithetical images of day and night, of light and dark, signal genuine progress toward sanity as Titus begins to recognize the immediate cause of his sorrows. As his perception of the truth improves (V.i.1-100), correspondingly the play's dialogue acquires several pairs of mingled opposites (e.g., right and wrong, talk and action, enemy and friend, day and night, etc.) that seem to clarion Titus' (and the play's) climactic moment of sight, truth, and remedy, as Titus observes insightfully to the disguised Tamora:

> In the emperor's court
> There is a queen attended by a Moor;
> Well shalt thou know her by thine own proportion,
> For up and down she doth resemble thee.
>
> (V.ii.104-07)

The black and white images in *Titus Andronicus* are just one of several binary sets that must move from a state of destructive conflict to harmonious reconciliation (or dialectical equilibrium) if Rome is to free itself from the cycle of revenge. The "day and night" as remedy motif suggests that while antithetical opposition is a given in the play, the society's leaders must redirect this conflict toward conciliatory solutions or suffer the ongoing consequences of dissension, violence, madness, and death. Because Titus does not fully comprehend how the adumbration of polar conflict can lead to peace in Rome, he continues to seek revenge. Thus as Titus prepares to execute Demetrius and Chiron for their rape of Lavinia, he also deconstructs the salubrious blend of conflictual signifiers that seemed to offer remedy earlier:

> Here stands the spring whom you have stain'd with
>   mud,
> This goodly summer with your winter mix'd:
>   . . . . .
> Hark, villains, I will grind your bones to dust,
>   . . . . .
> And make two pasties of your shameful heads.
>
> (V.ii.169-70; 186; 189)

If harmonious opposites become brutally antagonistic when Titus resumes revenge, we might wonder too about Lucius' ostensibly curative alliance with the Goths. That is, despite Lucius' treaty with his former enemy, he too continues to carry out revenge with his murder of Saturninus, his sentencing of Aaron to a torturous death, and his decision to deny Tamora a civilized burial—a decision "devoid of pity" (V.i.199), not unlike the one which led him to murder, mutilate, and burn Alarbus at the start of the play.

Aaron, on the other hand, does surprisingly well at joining opposites. It is he who beats back the antagonistic white view that the infant should die because of its heterogeneous racial origins. He also intimates that blacks are more open to such mixing: that is, Aaron's (black) countryman, Muly, and his "fair" (IV.ii.155) wife have a child who (unlike Tamora and Aaron's dark child) resembles his light-complexioned mother. Clearly the Moorish culture is more accustomed to mingling varied opposites and more accepting of the diverse products of mixed extremes. The Moors are also more keenly aware of the folly that ensues from myopic presumptions concerning the worth of combined opposites, as is evidenced when Aaron is overheard to comment to his child:

> Peace, tawny slave, half me and half thy dame!
> Did not thy hue bewray whose brat thou art?
> Had nature lent thee but thy mother's look,
> Villain, thou might'st have been an emperor.
>
> (V.i.27-30)

I would argue that no other character in the play exhibits as much concern for and insight into the nature of antithetical opposition (of any sort) as Aaron. His commonsense views on mixing and his defense of his biracial child encourage us to align his tolerance of enjoined opposites with Publius' day-and-night remedy for madness. If Publius is right in contending that a compassionate synthesis of light and dark brings forth cure, then with Aaron's compassion, the child of mixed racial origins may in fact represent a remedy for Rome rather than its endless woes.

V

As active as opposing characters, themes, and images are in *Titus Andronicus,* attracting and repulsing one another, their conflict is subsumed by an overriding truth that defines unabated conflict as destructive to civilized life. A civilized existence in Rome depends upon the recognition of relatedness even amidst a sea of potentially destructive difference. One way in which the play accentuates relatedness in spite of difference is through the idea of family. Mothers, brothers, sisters, uncles, aunts, sons, daughters, fathers, grandfathers, and stepfathers abound here; primogeniture is an emotional issue for parents and has particular import with regard to who will lead the state; marriages (and sexual relationships outside of marriage) create new family ties. Titus is called "father of my life" (I.i.253) by Saturninus; Lavinia asserts that Titus "gave . . . life" (II.iii.159) to Tamora when he pardoned her; Bassianus calls Titus the "father" (I.i.423) of Rome; and a peripheral messenger likens his sorrows for Titus to the sadness which he felt at the death of his own father (III.i.240). I would offer also that the competition for who will belong to whom (whether by virtue of war, desire, sexual relations, or marriage) creates a strong sense of relatedness that binds all members of the society together as a family. Even the culminating pact between the Romans and the Goths seems to echo the sudden and unlikely nuptials of Saturninus and Tamora. In addition to real and suggested familial bonds between and among the characters, the drama emphasizes commonality in its use of mirror plots: Tamora pleads for her son, and Titus pleads for his sons; Demetrius and Chiron argue over Lavinia as do Saturninus and Bassianus; both Aaron and Lucius have young sons; the clown is cut off when he petitions the court for the safe delivery of a family member; and Titus is similarly cut off from his sons by Saturninus. Along with the construed family ties, these mirror-like patterns seem to draw the characters together into a unified community that counterposes the dominance of polar conflict in the play.

Yet if it seems likely that familial and social unity provide solutions to Rome's giddy madness, then it is the Romans (or more generally the whites) who seem least equipped to see and act upon this truth. It is the whites who carry out all except one of the slayings, who demonstrate too little concern for the first-born sons of others, and who kill or seek to kill their own flesh and blood (as well as those who are different from themselves). Even when the white characters succeed in merging opposites, the harmony of the resulting union is suspect. Titus is able to mingle antithetical word-images of day and night, but he continues to seek revenge; Lucius joins with the Goths, but the alliance rests upon their mutual desire to "be aveng'd" (V.i.16); Saturninus mixes with Tamora but only for selfish and lascivious reasons, which highlight his character flaws and his weaknesses as a leader of Rome. Tamora has the ability to "gloze with all" (IV.iv.35), yet her fair words are deceitfully foul and destructive. Hence Tamora claims to have affection for Aaron, but her rejection of the black child exposes her deeper hatred of blackness and her disdain for new life. In the end, her unyielding appetite for revenge destroys her marriage to the Roman Saturninus and ultimately brings death to herself and her boys. In short, the forms of unity established by the play's white characters are unstable due to misperception, lack of foresight, immorality, racism, and the unwillingness to halt the revenge.

Despite the wrongs that Aaron has committed or engineered, the mixing he carries out constitutes the play's only substantive alliances between mighty opposites. Aaron engenders new life in a dying Rome through mixing, and then he preserves that life by orchestrating a double-mix between his biracial Gothic child and the white Roman society. While he makes little pretense of using fair words, in the end his foul words lead obversely to a fair end for his child in Rome. Most of Aaron's achievements derive from his witty ability to adapt to new and often dangerous situations with peoples and values that are antithetical to his presumedly static spheres of racial otherness: blackness, deviltry, beastliness, prurience, and treachery. With his good qualities, however, Aaron becomes, paradoxically, the character most fit to symbolize, if not actually to bring forth, the "day and night" solutions to a revenge-bound Rome; the one character sure to remain upright amidst the shifting sands of a declining empire; the character who does the most to get and preserve life in a place where death seems omnipresent.

The view that Aaron, despite his vices, is much more than a conventional black stereotype gains support from the Roman world that we find depicted in the play. Titus' Rome is not a glorious and wondrous antique city, but rather a "wilderness of tigers" (III.i.54), whose most prominent settings include the palaces of weak kings, the gloomy area around a family tomb, woods filled with more pits and plots than trees, ruined monasteries, and ruined family houses. In short, this Rome is an inverted green world that is more a wasteland of myopia, fractiousness, and death than a great civilization. If the values which made Rome great are turned upside down in this play, it is possible that Shakespeare's Aaron reflects and extends these inverted values by playing the part of a seemingly evil blackness that nevertheless harbors the seeds of hope in a dying Rome.

Notes

1. See, for example, Karen Cunningham, "'Scars Can Witness': Trials by Ordeal and Lavinia's Body in *Titus Andronicus*," *Women and Violence in Literature,* ed. Katherine Anne Ackley (New York: Garland, 1990) 154; William Slights, "Sacrificial Crisis in *Titus Andronicus*," *University of Toronto Quarterly* 49 (1979-80): 30; and Albert Tricomi, "The Mutilated Garden in *Titus Andronicus*,"

Shakespeare Studies 9 (1976): 103. For a counterview see Dorothea Kehler, "*Titus Andronicus*: From Limbo to Bliss," *Shakespeare Jahrbuch* 128 (1992): 131.

2. C. L. Barber and Richard P. Wheeler refer to Aaron as "the villainous root of all evil." ("*Titus Andronicus:* The Abortive Domestic Tragedy," *The Whole Journey: Shakespeare's Power of Development* [Berkeley: U of California P, 1986] 131); Eugene Waith deems Aaron (and by extension, his baby) "embodiment(s) of evil, [their] blackness readily seen as emblematic" (in his introduction to the new Oxford Shakespeare edition of *Titus Andronicus* [Oxford: Oxford UP, 1984] 64); Alan Summers calls Aaron "the contriver and symbol of nightmare disintegration and revolting barbarism" ("Wilderness of Tigers," *Essays in Criticism* 10 [1960]: 283).

3. William Shakespeare, *Titus Andronicus,* ed. J. C. Maxwell, Arden edition, (London: Methuen, 1953) V.i.45. Subsequent references will appear in the text.

4. Aaron threatens the life of the midwife, but we never see the act carried out and never hear that it has occurred.

5. In Act I, before Aaron speaks a word, we see many examples of family and political bickering among the Romans. Saturninus and Bassianus contend for the throne and for Lavinia's hand in marriage; Titus argues with his family over Lavinia's right to marry Bassianus; Titus slays his son Mutius; Titus and Saturninus argue variously over the proper respect due to an eldest son, an emperor, and a valiant warrior of Rome.

6. The time period to which the play belongs is the 4th century, A.D., during the waning years of the Empire. The turmoil, social dysfunction, and bleak outlook represented in the drama are generally considered to be Shakespeare's view of the Roman Empire in decline. See Robert Miola, *Shakespeare's Rome* (Cambridge: Cambridge UP, 1983) 60-64, and Robert Broude, "Roman and Goth in *Titus Andronicus,*" *Shakespeare Studies* 6 (1970): 27-30.

7. The Andronici execute Tamora's son, Alarbus; Titus kills his daughter Lavinia as well as his son Mutius; Tamora would have her own newborn baby slain.

8. In addition to Barber/Wheeler and Waith, cited above, see also Tricomi 94-97.

9. Charles Forker asserts that "[Aaron's] bastard child suggests the perpetuity of evil in the ecology of the tragedy" ("The Green Underworld of Early Shakespearean Tragedy," *Shakespeare Studies* 17 [1985]: 38). Joseph E. Kramer argues similarly that "the black baby is the visual embodiment of the past evil and the living embodiment of the prime malefactors" ("*Titus Andronicus:* The Fly-Killing Incident," *Shakespeare Studies* 5 [1969]: 16).

10. That Moses was the brother of the Old Testament figure Aaron gives further credence to this analogy.

11. In addition to Cunningham, Slights, and Tricomi, cited above, Bernard Spivak goes so far as to suggest that Aaron's role as a hybrid vice figure predisposes him to villainy that aims to destroy social harmony: "[Aaron] pours the sweet milk of concord into hell, his achievement this way being standard for the role of the Vice in any morality with political or social implications" (*Shakespeare and the Allegory of Evil* [New York: Columbia UP, 1958] 383).

12. The convention of the "white devil" in Renaissance drama indicates that black/white color symbolism could be manipulated to alter the circumscribed values that typically attended this moralized color dichotomy.

13. Joyce MacDonald, "'The Force of Imagination': The Subject of Blackness in Shakespeare, Jonson, and Ravenscroft," *Renaissance Papers* 1991: 74.

Jeannette S. White (essay date 1997)

SOURCE: "'Is Black So Base a Hue?': Shakespeare's Aaron and the Politics and Poetics of Race," in *CLA Journal,* Vol. XL, No. 3, March, 1997, pp. 336-66.

[*In the following essay, White contends that Aaron in* Titus Andronicus *subverts the Elizabethan notion that equates blackness with evil.*]

"Mislike me not for my complexion," the Prince of Morocco passionately implores Portia in the *Merchant of Venice*.[1] In sharp contrast, Aaron, Shakespeare's first Moor, who makes his unforgettable appearance in *Titus Andronicus,* cares little about how others perceive him, finding in his color no reason for embarrassment of self-loathing. No apologist, he is quite comfortable with his hue, never mind that the play's other characters find in his blackness a symbol of negation. A complex and compellingly suave character who revels in inflicting pain on others, he marches to the sound of no drumbeat except his own. Aware as is Morocco of the social stigma attached to non-whites, Aaron knows that overcoming his racial stereotype is well-nigh impossible in the color-conscious Roman society in which he finds himself. Conditioned to wedding darkness to wickedness like the Romans, Shakespeare's audience would have had no problems with equating a character of ebony shade to human depravity at its very worse. To the Elizabethans, in fact, blackness and evil were so synonymous that this notion spawned social attitudes predicated on the belief that black was always indicative of evil. As intelligent as he is shrewd, Aaron is fully cognizant of the fact that he is vilified because of his ethnicity and thus is predetermined to be Satan's ally. His color, in effect, predisposes him to ignoble deeds. This study proposes to show that "racial determinism" is very much a factor in *Titus Andronicus* and that it is the pernicious virus eating away at European society. Against such a scourge Aaron must continually wage his own battle, for his color is so inextricably linked to his destiny that it becomes the only barometer against which his personality and conduct are measured. In a very telling sense, the Moor's ends, as he well knows, are fated, but this awareness does not prevent him from constantly and consciously trying to subvert the established order as he perilously negotiates his space as subject and rejects his position as "other."

The abhorrence of things black was not in any sense unique to the Renaissance. Indeed, the ideology of blackness as detestable had its literary and linguistic antecedents in the ancient world,[2] where black became a powerful metaphor for every conceivable type of aberration. By extension, of course, dark-skinned people were tarnished because their complexion rendered them social undesirables, devoid of humanity. Writing in *Blank Darkness: Africanist Discourse in French*, Christopher Miller puts the allegorical significance of this much-maligned color succinctly into historical perspective:

> Discourse in color moves between a reef and a maelstrom. Blackness would appear to be a rock of negativity: from Sanskrit and ancient Greek to modern European languages, black is associated with dirt, degradation, and impurity, as if it were the perfect representation of an idea. In texts from the Ancients on, whether the speaker's attitude is positive or negative in regard to black people, *blackness* remains a powerful negative element. If black people are deemed blameless, it is usually in spite of their blackness. By actively forgiving and overlooking the color of their skin, one perceives an "inner" whiteness.[3]

In establishing the tradition, Classical writers had given powerful poetic expression to their society's assumption that dark skin was a conspicuous badge of dishonor. To Renaissance scholars looking to the antique world for models, such stellar literary lineage was of great importance in helping them to find their own distinct voices. Instrumental, too, in influencing the Elizabethans were the teachings of the early Church fathers as well as the plays of their Medieval forebears. In carrying on the practice, these two groups continued to perpetuate the color myth, attesting to how widespread was the belief that black was akin to sin.[4] With such precursors to guide them in the process of giving dramatic expression to a dominant social belief, Shakespeare and his contemporaries knew they had found the necessary tools to create a literature of their own—one that was essentially Renaissance in outlook. In short, they found in the works of the ancients and their more recent predecessors compatible ideas and endowed them with their own cultural traits. As expected, this merging of ancient and modern conventions aided them in fashioning their own fable of blackness as they brought their own individual visions to bear on the matter. In *Titus*, for example, Shakespeare expropriated the convention of disparaging blackness from its textual descendants to accommodate his own worldview. In so doing, he was able to articulate the racial attitudes of his own times by transforming and distilling the ancient themes to suit the purposes of the Elizabethan stage.

Winthrop D. Jordan points out in *White Over Black* that the English had long equated everything that was despicable and offensive with blackness. According to him, in their eyes "Black was an emotionally partisan color, the handmaid and symbol of baseness and evil, a sign of danger and repulsion."[5] Further illuminating these preconceptions, Jordan finds that whiteness and blackness stood distanced from each other at opposite poles, with the former representing fairness as opposed to the latter, which was closely allied to foulness. In this atmosphere he writes, "White and black connoted purity and filthiness, virginity and sin, virtue and baseness, beauty and ugliness, beneficence and evil, God and the devil" (7). By deliberately choosing as villain a black Moor,[6] the figure who customarily bears the ancestral curse of Ham,[7] Shakespeare was underscoring the precarious position of the "Other" in the England of his day. As a neophyte dramatist versed in feeling the pulse of his times, he chose to exploit a racial symbol that he knew would evoke negative responses. Surely it could not have been lost upon him that Aaron's dark skin, standing as it does in such striking visual contrast to the pale skin of the other characters, would have alerted his audience to the ominous presence of evil. Since in the Elizabethan conception, the Moor's color typified his state of grace, Aaron could not possibly have escaped all the unpleasant associations with degeneracy from the very outset. Not least among a host of unsavory traits that Moors were said to possess were grossness, brutishness, and debauched sexual natures, all highly suggestive of innate animalistic qualities. To a Renaissance play-going audience, such repulsive characteristics connected Moors to the demonic powers that inhabited the nether world. In a very real sense, then, since Aaron obviously is not made in God's image, he would be cast quite naturally in the mold of one of the damned, an ally of Satan himself, the proverbial Prince of Darkness. But if he is of the devil's party, he is quite unashamedly so, and he rides roughshod over all others in the play. No noble savage he! That he plays the barbarian in the midst to the hilt as if the Roman world were his personal stage is not all that surprising, given his understanding of his position as "Other" in a society that denies him any measure of humanity. Astute and calculating, he knows what is expected of him, how great a role his skin tone plays in defining who he is. Thus, as Gordon Ross Smith surmises, Aaron epitomizes "the well-known phenomenon of a person's becoming what he was thought by the people around him to be."[8]

By any standard, Moors on the Elizabethan stage were looked upon as strange creatures, startlingly different in appearance, socially and culturally dissimilar, the highly peculiar and suspect Other. Usually, such characters were perceived of as being ruthless, diabolical, and dangerous. If they were like Othello, the Noble Moor of Shakespeare's later play, the chance of integrating peacefully into an alien society was, at best, still a rather difficult feat to accomplish. Thus, although Othello desperately strives for grace, the prognosis is much the same as it is for Aaron. In essence, the racial malady that afflicts European society is so deadly that looking beyond color for healing is not possible. No matter how honorable Othello is, no matter how virtuous, dignified, noble and well-meaning, ultimately, he must lose his way. Because he is black, he cannot escape the curse that his contaminating color imposes upon him in a world not his own, and he must, thus, in the eyes of Venetian society, succumb to the dark powers within as if his hue dictated that his ends would be fated. It is as if he is, from birth, like Winterbourne in Henry James' *Daisy Miller*, "booked to make a mistake."[9] For his part, Aaron fully epitomizes the prototype, the inherently evil, vile, and villainous Moor whose soul could never be washed white. All too conscious that he is viewed as satanic, he opts to employ Lucifer's prerogative—to go fourth and sin as much as he pleases. Rather than striving for decency and goodness, which would be pointless in this deterministic venue, Aaron positions himself so that he can become an active player in charting his own course. In repudiating the limitations which Roman society places upon him, he knowingly decides not to become an unhappy prisoner of skin tone in an overwhelmingly hostile white environment. By striking out against his oppressors, Aaron is able to wreak havoc, and he does so with sadistic and sardonic pleasure.

As Shakespeare presents the situation, Aaron is even further removed from the realm of grace than other Moors on the English stage, in light of the fact that in *Titus* no character truly resides inside this charmed circle. Indeed, this exalted sphere is home to no one in this drama in which social, political, and familial structures have broken down, leaving no stabilizing influences. Framed as it is by this rupturing of society, the grim world of the play is one in which smoldering hostilities and horrifying acts of revenge hold sway, canceling out, in the process, dignity, goodness, honor, and decency. Thus, it is not alone the fact that Aaron's color makes him the symbol of depravity in his work; indeed, as Titus himself so aptly sums up the social climate, "Rome is but a wilderness of tigers."[10] In employing the jungle metaphor, Shakespeare is accentuating the fact that beasts in the guise of men prowl the imperial city, holding it at bay. There is no question that the Romans in *Titus Andronicus* were living in deeply troubled and troubling times. Undeniably, the world of the play is one in which discord reigns, much of it exacerbated by Titus' refusal to accept the throne offered him. More than anything else, it is this tragic error, coupled with his sanctioning of Saturninus as emperor, that sets in motion the political and familial chaos that will rend the fabric of Roman society. But to no one's surprise, it is in Aaron's fertile mind that revenge takes form and meaning. Entering the play in the unenviable position of monstrous Other, he is, quite clearly, the dram of evil that will pollute a Rome already tottering on the brink of anarchy. In this decadent city of predators, however, where fantastic horrors are commonplace, cynical Aaron is in no sense the only one who preys on others; rather, he is just one among the many transgressors against decency and humanity. If he seems like a coiled snake ready to spring, he is not the only serpent in the fallen Roman world. In point of fact, Shakespeare shows that in the den of hissing vipers that is Rome, there is no line of demarcation separating the civilized and the unenlightened inhabitants. Whether they be Romans, Goths or Moors, the characters all display debasing and dehumanizing traits: all ghoulishly relish revenge; all suffer from the spiritual malaise that afflicts Rome; all are in need of grace. In the largest view, the most arresting image that emerges is that of frenzied cannibals devouring each other. With no truly virtuous people to maintain the rather sordid cause of humanity in this jungle-world, so eerily populated by scavengers and vultures feeding on one another, Aaron certainly is no worse than the rest. He is, after all, the primitive Moor, who is supposed to behave this way!

Jack D'Amico argues in *The Moor in English Renaissance Drama* that in such distressing sociopolitical settings, outsiders are always natural targets of blame. He contends, rightly, that in common with other civilizations at risk, European societies could not accept reponsibility for the moral and social dilemmas with which they were faced. As a result, they had to find scapegoats—the strangers in their midst—to shoulder the burden for whatever was amiss in their world. In this way, he writes, they were able to absolve themselves of any accountability:

> The Moor as villain becomes a convenient locus for those darkly subversive forces that threaten European society from within but can be projected onto the outsider. The destructive forces of lust and violence are thus distanced by being identified with a cultural, religious, or racial source of evil perceived as the inversion of European norms.[11]

Along with the rest of Europe, Renaissance England was exposed to the hazards of complex and changing times. In coming to terms with the religious, social, philosophical, political, and intellectual currents astir in the era, Elizabethans had to deal with the anxiety that always comes from apprehensiveness of the new. Clearly, their perceptions of reality arose from ideological and cultural preconceptions that were due to a very large extent to their desire to define themselves and interpret their position on the world's stage. With the reemergence of the classics along with colonial expansion, the voyages of discovery, the slave trade, competition with other European neighbors, and commerce with other countries, the English people were reacting to novel ideas at the same time that they were encountering hitherto unheard-of realms. Unquestionably, the nervous tensions that resulted from the uneasy meeting with non-Caucasians, those mysterious "Other" humans, were a direct consequence of their extreme uncomfortableness in "this brave new world." This disquietude resulted from fear of the unfamiliar and having to look squarely at the issue of race. In this atmosphere where black was already taboo, no people could be more symbolic of the unknown than dark-skinned Africans, so emblematic of Western culture's long-held irrational fears. According to Jordan, this intersection of black and white was extreme enough to cause consternation by the very nature of abruptness:

> The powerful impact which the Negro's color made upon Englishmen must have been owing to suddenness

of contact. . . . England's immediate acquaintance with black-skinned peoples came with relative rapidity. While the virtual monopoly held by Venetian ships in European foreign trade prior to the sixteenth century meant that people much darker than Englishmen were not entirely unfamiliar, really black men were virtually unknown except as vaguely referred to in the hazy literature about the sub-Sahara which had filtered down from antiquity. Native West Africans probably first appeared in London in 1554. . . . The impact of the Negro's color was the more powerful upon Englishmen . . . because England's principal contact with Africans came in West Africa and the Congo where men were not merely dark but almost literally black: one of the fairest skinned nations suddenly came face to face with one of the darkest people on earth.(6)

Seeing their own white skin as the epitome of beauty, they naturally found people of black pigmentation and divergent facial features ugly (8). No effortless convergence of the twain here as the example of Aaron among the Romans illustrates so well.

By all indications, the shock of actually being in proximity to a race so dissimilar to their own spurred the Elizabethans to protective action. As a defense mechanism, they called upon their sense of nationalism and ethnic superiority to guide them to new self-definition. Not surprisingly, this state of affairs lent itself to the setting up of national barriers designed to keep nonnatives on the periphery of English society. In their quest to retain their national character and ethnic identity, they propagated the racial myths so prevalent in *Titus*. Noticeably, almost everyone in the play refers to Aaron's race with disdain,[12] holding him culpable for most of Rome's ills. Even before he ever says a word, he stands out conspicuously by color as a menacing figure whose sinister presence bodies ill. In her study "Making More of the Moor: Aaron, Othello and Renaissance Refashionings of Race," Emily Bartels comments that prior to his first pronouncement, Aaron, though wordless, speaks volumes:

> Tellingly, throughout the opening crisis the Moor stands beside Tamora, silent but threatening in his silence and blackness. After Saturninus' regime is securely in place, he gains a voice, and with it the capacity to contrive, control, and corrupt.[13]

As a Moorish character, Aaron is supremely qualified to epitomize the contrariness and unloveliness associated with difference both in the Classical and Elizabethan worlds, a fact that Shakespeare makes clear.

Without doubt *Titus Andronicus* is a chronicle of Renaissance beliefs and ideas. One of the most popular plays of its time,[14] it gave dramatic and cogent expression to the concerns of the playwright's world. Although a novice, Shakespeare wisely chose to experiment with a dramatic form that had paid rich dividends for Thomas Kyd and others. However, in employing the revenge theme, he was doing more than delighting playhouse audiences. In truth, he was also using the genre to excoriate a society that held up classical virtues as ideals, while indulging in typical human vices such as envy, malice, self-interest, deception and corruption. That theatergoers could identify with the Roman world of *Titus,* where rape, racism, cannibalism, dismemberment, and murder took place, is not surprising, considering the fact that both the playworld and the dramatist's milieu mirrored the collective psychoses of societies in varying states of flux. As is so often the case, when such national and social dilemmas occur, violence results. In his definitive study, *Violence and the Sacred,* René Girard discusses how corrosive violence is, labeling it a force that gnaws away at the human psyche until it is finally unleashed. He declares that "Violence too long held in check will overflow its bounds—and woe to those who happen to be nearby."[15] *Titus* proves the truth of this statement in that once Aaron realizes that there are familial and political hostilities brewing, he sets the mischief afoot that will usher in the cycle of violence that follows.

Violence is the Moor's instrument of empowerment. Rather than surrender to his racial legacy, Aaron defies the forces ranged against him by setting the wheels of violence in motion as a means to gain his ends. Ethical and moral constraints do not weigh heavily upon him, in great part because he feels no bond of kinship with the inhabitants of a society that forces dehumanization upon him. In the absence of the usual symbols of stability—family, beliefs, religion, traditions—he finds himself summarily cast adrift, rendered morally bankrupt by those who deride his difference. With no communal and familial ties to bind him, he is free to be a law unto himself, and in so doing, find his creative outlet through the plotting of violence. Estranged and isolated from those around him, Aaron must, of necessity, find ways to turn the tables on his oppressors. Moreover, in him, Shakespeare creates a character with no biography; in fact, any history he has is tied solely to his racial heritage. His societal dislocation thus is made even more startlingly total. So often defamed, the Moor, in accordance with his pariah status, decides to take vengeance on a race that holds him in contempt. Undoubtedly, he is avenging himself on white society for the many inequities it has visited upon him, foremost among these its refusal to grant him dignity and stature as a human being. What first seems like "motiveless malignity," then, is, conceivably, retaliation for ancient ills and past wrongs. Such a view is supported by Gordon Ross Smith in *Literature and Psychology:*

> The text of the play does not oblige us to accept Aaron's evil-doing as motiveless. To a medieval or Elizabethan audience the devil had commonly been represented as black, and by backward association we may suppose a black man a devil. . . . Along with his blackness supposedly went ill-doing, and he accepted that, too, . . . thereby at once conforming to what was thought of him and revenging himself from social acceptance just as surely as Shylock had been excluded.[16]

Simply put, this vilest of transgressors sins because he feels he is sinned against. When Shylock poses his famous questions in *The Merchant of Venice,* "If you prick us, do

Richard Mansfield as Shylock. 1897 photograph.

"Vengeance is in my heart, death in my hand, / Blood and revenge are hammering in my head" (II.iii.38-39), he exults. With violence as a touchstone, he can now map his heady course toward chaos and confrontation. His reign of terror just beginning, he studiedly dedicates himself to plunging Rome and the Andronici further into nightmare. That he succeeds in the fullest measure can be attributed to the fact that he is always one step ahead, carefully crafting his plans for attack. By keeping his eyes and ears open, the Moor strikes when the moment is propitious for him. In essence, this is his "time to murder and create."[17]

As Tamora's longtime lover, Aaron is in the position to help the new empress settle her score with Titus; indeed, he becomes the teacher to his paramour and her offspring and instructs them in the art of revenge. This is not to suggest that Aaron is Tamora's Mephistopheles, for, in point of fact, she is already well-versed in perfidy; indeed, she commits herself to vengeance as soon as the Andronici kill her oldest son. When as the new empress she promises to find a way to "massacre them [the Andronici] all" (I.i.450), we suspect that this is no idle threat. In Aaron, she finds a worthy accomplice for this goal. Possessed of the appetite for revenge, an imagination that can wax venomous, a vehement scorn for others, and an inborn boldness and daring, Aaron is eminently qualified to make Tamora's task a good deal easier. Given the plot to write his drama of blood, he sets about translating his schemes into action with stunning swiftness. Eldred Jones argues in *Othello's Countrymen* that the Moor truly is in his element as he pens the script for vicious reprisal. In reveling in the carnage and devastation he causes, Aaron, in Jones' opinion, is very much the creative artist who finds his muse in the revenge motif:

> Aaron [is] an artist in villainy. . . . He is the confident artist delighting in his own sense of timing, and in his ability to manipulate his material. He takes a ghoulish pride in his work, is very conscious of his own wit, and despises those who are witless enough to be taken in by him.[18]

we not bleed? / If you tickle us, do we not laugh? / If you poison us, do we not die? / And if you wrong us, shall we not revenge?" (III.i.57-59), he speaks not only for himself as a Jew, but also for Aaron and other outsiders. In all likelihood the racial bigotry that the other characters so blatantly display spurs Aaron to vengeful action; however, the rage of centuries spilling across the ages also evidently dwells in him. For such a man, there can be no painful confrontation with sin, no self-tormenting struggle with conscience. An opportunist, he knows most assuredly that he must be vigilant in looking for chances to wreak havoc on those who have ill-used him, past and present. If such openings are presented to him, he will employ them to his advantage, without misgivings. As he bides his time holding his long-suppressed anger in check, Aaron displays no red-hot fury; rather, he remains calm, detached and controlled, icy cold almost, as he waits to put into effect his deviously conceived machinations. Fortuitously, the Andronicus family conflict provides him with a forum to give form to his heretofore fanciful imaginings. Here, offered a stage to effect revenge and in so doing forge an existence in antagonistic surroundings, his ire turns fiery and lethal.

Certainly, Aaron's love of plotting and manipulating is evident throughout most of the play. But by all indications, it is not alone the working out of the performance that so enraptures him as Jones infers, but more importantly watching his pale-complexioned victims squirm. Toward this end, he plays on the other characters as if they were puppets, whose strings he relentlessly pulls at will, all the while enjoying the tumult which he sets astir. As a master schemer, he apprehends the importance of careful preparation. From laying the trap for Martius and Quintus in the forest to planning the rape of Lavinia, Aaron leaves nothing to chance. But although he directs, stages, and often acts in this blood-filled drama, he is never truly the divinity that shapes his own ends, much as he wishes to think so. Always Shakespeare reminds us that Aaron's personal script is pre-penned by a tense society that rationalizes and makes comprehensible his supposed inbred penchant for evil, a point which Emily Bartels underscores:

> For while Shakespeare brings Aaron near the center of the staged court, accords him a voice of eloquence and

knowledge, and allows his schemes to shape the plot, he concomitantly keeps the Moor on the outside, literally and figuratively, and both answers and promotes the darkest vision of the stereotype. Ironically, although the play creates a chaos in which distinctions between right and wrong, insider and outsider, self and other are problematically obscured, it does not challenge the racial stereotype. To the contrary, *Titus Andronicus* presents the stereotype as the one realistic measure of difference, the one stable and unambiguous sign of otherness. (442)

Significantly, though, much as others denigrate Aaron, the man himself is never ill at ease with his pigmentation. As he views the situation, dark is vastly superior to pale. In Act IV, Scene II, in which he upbraids Chiron and Demetrius for wishing their newborn half-brother dead, he holds white versus black up to the looking glass and triumphantly finds the latter color the stronger and more self-sufficient: "Ye white-lim'd walls! Ye alehouse painted signs!" he taunts Tamora's simpering sons. "Coal-black is better than another hue, / In that it scorns to bear another hue; / For all the water in the ocean / Can never turn the swan's black legs to white" (IV.ii.98-103). For him, blackness serves, moreover, as an impenetrable mask, a protective armor through which neither verbal nor physical abuse can pierce. In essence, no one can divine the mystery of this alien of dark mien; no soul is privy to his thoughts; none can view his mind's construction by simply looking at his face. Knowing that realistically there can be no erasure of difference, Aaron, in effect, validates his own existence by aggressively rejecting the prescribed negative notions of color. He does so by ridiculing whiteness, which he sees as the weak and "treacherous hue" that betrays by blushing. By way of contrast, as a Moor, he can take refuge symbolically behind his opaque color, while appearing to be the perfect servant. He can, in the words of Hamlet, "smile, and smile, and be a villain" (I.v.108), and no one is the wiser until it is too late. Seen from this perspective, blackness preserves the outward seeming while shielding the inner man. Aaron's color, in this instance, stands him in good stead, for he can use it as a means of self-concealment. Interestingly, African-American writers would later make much of the ability of blacks to hide their feelings from others in order to exist in an American society scarred by racism. As explained by Ralph Ellison,

> the Negro's masking is motivated not so much by fear as by profound rejection of the image created to usurp his identity. Sometimes it is for the sheer joy of the joke; sometimes to challenge those who presume, across the psychological distance created by race matters, to know his identity. . . . [He] wear[s] the mask for purposes of aggression as well as for defense. . . . In short, the motives hidden behind the mask are as numerous as the ambiguities the mask conceals.[19]

In a very real sense, Ellison's characterization holds true for Shakespeare's Moor despite the great interval between the fifteenth and the twentieth centuries. To a very large extent, Aaron, so much reviled because of his race, has mastered the art of inscrutability. Through this means, he is able to screen himself effectively from the eyes of the world. With his psychological mask always in place, Aaron, Janus-faced, looks askance at those around him in jovial derision, knowing that they view him as their racial inferior. His perennial amusement thus is always at the expense of those who feel themselves better than he. Oftentimes in *Titus Andronicus,* he might seem to be laughing hilariously with the Romans and the Goths, but in actuality he is always snickering scornfully at them.

That Aaron also loves the feelings of superiority and power that villainy gives him must also he factored into the complex equation that is the Moor. In his quest for vengeance, such a man as this must of necessity boast of his skill and gloat over the misfortune of his unfortunate, less clever victims. And he does so with gleeful and malicious vitality. After he cuts off Titus' hands, for example, he gives malevolent expression to his delight: "O, how this villainy / Doth fat me with the very thoughts of it!" (III.i.202-03). Indeed, his ominous laughter, heard so often in the play, is that of a self-satisfied rascal who chooses to wield the only authority that his blackness gives him—the power of villainy. Aaron's crimes are of course no cause for mirth, but at times he seems much like a comic villain whose humor entraps the reader. Even while casting his menacing shadow over the play, he still manages to exude his disarming wit, neither evincing any shred of conscience nor offering any apologies for his misdeeds. Notwithstanding his evident short-comings, thus he captures and holds our attention as no other character in the play does.

Writing in *Laughter, Pain and Wonder,* David Richman compares Aaron to two other noteworthy villains of towering stature: Shakespeare's Richard III and Marlowe's Barabas. Labeling them "creatures of splendid melodrama," he finds that "spectators are never allowed to forget the suffering they cause, but the audience's sense of that suffering is mitigated by a sense of their pleasure in causing it." In short, he continues, "the audience roots for the villains, carried along by sheer glee in evil."[20] Frequently in *Titus,* there is strong temptation to pass judgment on Aaron, because his spiritual and moral bankruptcy is so absolutely complete, but more often than not, we are forestalled by the power of his engaging and mesmerizing wit. As Richard T. Brucher finds, "It is not the love of violence that distinguishes Aaron from the Romans, but the witty conception of it."[21] In his introductory essay to his 1984 edition of the play, Eugene Waith comments along the same lines, pointing out that despite his depravity, Aaron still manages to emerge as an engaging character in the manner of Jonson's Volpone, a smoothly accomplished trickster, who is unfettered by scruples and unencumbered by conscience:

> The ingenuity of Aaron's schemes and his sheer vitality in carrying them out give him the ambiguous appeal of a Richard III, whose cleverness can be seen as admirable even though his downfall is desired. When such characters are presented from a comic perspective, there is an even greater temptation to suspend moral judgment and join in their cruel laughter at the expense of

their victims. Shakespeare offers precisely this temptation in the first scene of the fifth act, where Aaron tells of his trickery with . . . relish. In so doing he becomes no less villainous but, for the moment, undeniably more attractive.[22]

At once fiendish and captivating, Aaron is self-assured, haughty, witty, bold, intelligent, and fearless. Not surprisingly, despite his alien status, he is not the type of villain who slithers along the fringes of Roman society afraid to look with contempt upon those who view him as an anomaly. Rather, he bestrides the play, confident and unafraid, unsusceptible to threat or intimidation. Looming largely as a figure shrouded in darkness, Aaron seems at times to be both villian and hero. Not unlike Seneca's Atreus, he dominates the action, often overshadowing Titus, the play's protagonist. He does so almost from the minute he utters his first words in Act II and never truly relinquishes this central role.

Scoundrel though he is, Aaron, unlike both Tamora and Titus, puts child welfare before all other considerations. Tellingly, he refuses to lift his hand against his son, in marked contrast to the Andronici patriarch, who slays two of his children; moreover, he never contemplates infanticide as the empress does. Unlike these two, he never disowns his own flesh and blood. Whatever his profoundly moral failings, Aaron is, ironically, the one character in the play who comes closest to displaying the solicitous qualities that one normally associates with parents. Manifesting immediate paternal tenderness, he contemptuously disobeys Tamora's decree that the baby, the fruit of their illicit love affair, be killed. Doubtless she views her newborn as a threat to her reputation and position as consort to Saturninus; certainly, his color will proclaim to the world that she had "so preposterously . . . err[ed]."[23] Not without irony is the fact that as the play opens, the captive queen piteously pleads with Titus to spare the life of Alarbus, her oldest son, as a distressed and loving mother. No such importunings for her youngest; instead, for him she ordains death, displaying none of the maternal instincts that she exhibits for her first-born. Rather, in this case, she selfishly seeks to protect herself, caring little that she is authorizing that most unpalatable of crimes, child-murder. In remarkable contrast, Aaron takes pride in the baby, feeling instant kinship. For this unlikeliest of doting fathers, there is an immediate and inextricable bond with his son. No longer "himself alone," Aaron views the boy as his only link in an alien world. In short, the child is the one person whose life touches his in so special and personal a way. Not surprisingly, when the Nurse derisively refers to the infant as a "devil" (IV.ii.64), "a joyless, dismal, black, and sorrowful issue" (IV.ii.66), Aaron takes umbrage, immediately going on the offensive. "Is black so base a hue?" he asks (IV.ii.71). Once more, it is a question of racial perception. Where the white woman sees before her a creature "as loathsome as a toad / Amongst the fair-faced breeders of our clime" (IV.ii.67-68), the proud black father gazes fondly at the child, beholding "a beauteous blossom" (IV.ii.72). Loveliness and ugliness here are clearly in the eyes of the beholder.

For Aaron, his "first-born son and heir" (IV.ii.92) is a tiny being made in his sire's very own image, the triumphant embodiment of blackness. That the child means a great deal to him is evident when he informs the Nurse in no uncertain terms that Tamora's wishes are of no consequence to him at this point:

> My mistress is my mistress; this my self;
> The vigour and the picture of my youth:
> This before all the world do I prefer;
> This maugre all the world will I keep safe,
> Or some of you shall smoke for it in Rome.
>
> (IV.ii.107-11)

Without doubt, Aaron's narcissistic male ego is brought to bear on his feelings. Undeniably, he sees the infant as an extension of himself. But more than pride in his male potency or even his obvious celebration of blackness is his affirmation of his humanity, the capacity to care for someone other than himself. Aaron's concern for another person, albeit his own child, is the play's greatest surprise. This cynical man, for whom nothing prior to his son's birth is sacrosanct, in actuality, awakens to love. He might be brother to none, but he wishes desperately to be father to his son. This parental gentleness, so totally unexpected in Aaron, shows itself from the moment he first sees the baby. He will protect his child at all costs, notwithstanding Lucius'[24] desire to kill both erring father and blameless son. When Rome's next leader commands the soldiers to hang the infant along with his father, he is, in a very real sense, sanctioning infanticide, blinded by his inability to see beyond what he perceives to be the baby's sullying pigmentation. But Aaron will not be thwarted, intent as he is on shielding the boy from harm. Instead, once more he exerts his tremendous will, astutely negotiating with Lucius to save his son's life, uncaring of his own fate:

> Lucius, save the child;
> And bear it from me to the empress.
> If thou do this, I'll show thee wondrous things
> That highly may advantage thee to hear:
> If thou wilt not, befall what may befall,
> I'll speak no more but "Vengeance rot you all!"
>
> (V.i.53-58)

His bargain sealed, Aaron enumerates a list of all the cruelties he supposedly has done in his lifetime, expressing the wish that he could live to do many more. Whether or not he really commits these vicious deeds can only be a matter of conjecture. With the exception of his severing of Titus' hand and his killing of the Nurse, we do not actually see him perpetrating any other crimes. Indeed, more than anything else, the tales of unspeakable horrors that he tells appear to be nothing more than the hubristic boasts of a man who refuses to let anyone triumph over him, especially so as he faces what is most surely his day of doom. He will go out no cowardly sinner, but rather as an ignoble and defiant reprobate, blithely verbalizing his questionable misdeeds:

> But I have done a thousand dreadful things
> As willingly as one would kill a fly,

And nothing grieves me heartily indeed
But that I cannot do ten thousand more.

(V.i.141-44)

Of more import than the confessions themselves is the fact that Aaron's account of his intrigues saves the life of the child. Perhaps his fantastic repertoire of past criminal activity is his ingenious way of getting Lucius' ear. Once more, assuming the role of the archetypal virulent and vicious Moor, Aaron trades upon the stereotype to achieve his goal, which, in this instance, is to prevent his son's death.

As is so much the pattern in whatever he does, Aaron takes control of the situation, and once more he looms larger than he should at this, his moment of reckoning. Thus, where Lucius appears as a vengeful, mean-spirited, and unforgiving leader, Aaron appropriates the more positive role of concerned father. That he shows no fear of the hell that Shakespeare's audience would have assumed most definitely awaited him is in itself noteworthy, in large measure because this stance diminishes the punishment of hanging that Lucius first decrees for him. Adroitly, he upstages Rome's new head. Effectively setting up an arresting tableau, Shakespeare situates Aaron atop the scaffold from which he is scheduled to be hanged. Spewing venom as he scornfully looks down from his elevated perch, Aaron quite literally towers above Lucius in Scene I of Act V, shrinking the other man's stature at this most crucial time. Unlike Iago, to whom he has been likened, Aaron refuses to keep his silence after his crimes come to light. If, indeed, speaking is the means whereby he will be able to prevent his offspring's death, he will utilize this method to get his way. In truth, his hectoring rhetoric serves another purpose, since it communicates the idea that gods do not exist in Aaron's world. Once more, in fact, Shakespeare is showing his villain's difference by using the conventional image of the godless Moor. Needless to say, Aaron's impious disregard for religion constitutes yet another source of alienation, but as expected, the opprobrium of the Romans matters nothing to him. He knows he is thought of as an enemy of religion, an infidel. As such he wields his godlessness as a weapon to prove his independence and self-sufficiency in contrast to Lucius, who, according to Aaron, is "an idiot [who] holds his bauble for a god" (V.i.79). If deities are not of great moment to Aaron, devils do not figure largely in his universe either. But he does concede that if perchance fiends do exist, he would not mind casting his lot with them. Evidently, he feels that these infernal beings would give him demonic voice, and thus the pleasure of orally slaying his enemies in the hereafter:

If there be devils, would I were a devil,
To live and burn in everlasting fire,
So I might have your company in hell,
But to torment you with my bitter tongue.

(V.i.147-50)

Realizing that nothing he can say can counter Aaron's blistering verbal onslaught, Lucius remains mostly quiet in Act V, Scene I. In the face of such vituperative articulation of the villain's seething hatred, Lucius appears somewhat intimidated, unable to assert himself. However, Shakespeare is, in reality, setting Aaron up for his promised fall. As the wheel comes full circle for him, it becomes apparent that his seeming domination of Lucius is nothing more than a ploy by the playwright to make his villain/hero's fall all the greater. Always he reminds us that in this conflict between the black Moor and the white Roman, the former cannot win. Conceivably, the Elizabethans would see Aaron's furious rage as the splendidly rendered death-defying cry of a doomed man moving inexorably toward his fate. Once he is made to descend the platform, Aaron's control dwindles, and by the end of the play he is a mere pawn at the mercy of Lucius. Accordingly, rather than have Lucius stand up to Aaron, Shakespeare engages him more profitably in hatching the grotesque punishment that he feels befits this basest of criminals—burial from the chest down and eventual starvation. But characteristically, Aaron refuses to make his captor's job easy; rather, he sets the stage yet again, this time for his final performance. Once more, he disdainfully attempts to wrest Lucius' power from him, deftly manipulating his terrible sentence into another display of resistance. True to form, he enacts this, his last role, exceedingly well—with the bravura and energy that we have come to expect from him, this despite the fact that he is about to be planted firmly in the earth as if he were no more than a tree. When Aaron finally is reduced to less than a beast of the field, Lucius will have inflicted a lethal blow from which he will not be able to recover. But strangely enough, although Lucius, surnamed Pius,[25] is clearly the victor in this most decisive round, he is neither an imposing presence nor a dominant and gracious figure. He emerges, instead, as just another vindictive character in the grisly parade of the play's retaliation-seeking avengers, bent more on devising inhuman punishments to settle old scores than on healing Rome's wounds.

Aaron, the stranger who has never been allowed to feel at home on Roman soil, is forced into an ignominious exit, his denouement, reduction to a torso and existence in a limbo world tethering precariously between death and life, little more than a leaf blown about by the wind. Ironically, he finds no resting place at his journey's end, since he will be denied not only a normal death but also the return to dust to which all human beings tend. But Aaron, his insolence intact, refuses to go either silently or gently to his doom. Instead, displaying the towering rage that now fuels his every utterance, he takes his unrepentant farewell, still impudent, still unbowed:

Ah, why should wrath be mute, and fury dumb?
I am no baby, I, that with base prayers
I should repent the evils I have done;
Ten thousand worse than ever yet I did
Would I perform, if I might have my will.
If one good deed in all my life I did,
I do repent it from my very soul.

(V.iii.184-190)

Irreligious Aaron, having dropped his smiling mask, snarls his way to his end neither believing that, nor caring if, he has a soul. What he most wants to do is retain his selfhood. As such, he will remain doggedly a man, spitting in the face of a society that has tried to emasculate him psychologically and socially. Still isolated in this his final inglorious moment upon the stage, Aaron attempts to prove one last time that his skin color may set him apart, but his spirit cannot be broken. Hence, no remorse, no apology, no regrets—a rebel with a cause to the end.

Shakespeare evidently was very much interested in presenting Aaron as a character endowed with humanity, despite the racial categorizations that the play trades upon. Understanding that Aaron is not without human worth, Eldred Jones makes the point that in having his villain/hero respond so positively to his son, Shakespeare invests his hero with human qualities:

> Aaron emerges as a human being after all. His character . . . as a monster would have been all of a piece had he decided to regard the child . . . as an embarrassment. But Shakespeare veers away from this easier creation of a bogeyman, and makes Aaron, in spite of his villainy, into a human being. (59)

However, this very quality with which his creator invests Aaron, some critics take away. In fact, no less than for the Elizabethans, for most of the play's commentators Aaron is evil incarnate, a consummate and despicable villain devoid of any redeeming qualities. Put bluntly, for them Aaron is paradoxically less than, yet more than, a man; he is at once a black beast and a veritable demon. Representative of this viewpoint is James Calderwood, who finds no shred of humanity in Aaron; indeed, he goes so far as to make the Dracula connection in his book *Shakespeare and the Denial of Death*. In it he wonders "if there are enough crosses and sharpened stakes in Transylvania to harry this monster to his grave."[26] From his purview, Aaron deserves far worse than he gets. To him, the Moor is an animal in human guise, an absolutely hideous monster who is far too malevolent to die, leaving behind as he does his accursed heir. Indeed, he sees Aaron's offspring as the living representation of his father's evil. As if inheriting paternal sins were not heavy enough a load to be placed on his tiny shoulders, the boy, according to Calderwood, is also the embodiment of a damned racial heritage:

> [T]he villain is symbolically immortal. . . . More than that, however, the very viciousness of his punishment implies the kind of despairing overkill that comes from an attempt to destroy something more or less, or at any rate other than human, something that does not die like us. And to be sure whatever it is that pulses in Aaron pulses so strongly that his end is by no means certain. (199)

That the child is guilty of no sin other than being born black enters not at all into this critic's consciousness. Like the play's characters and its Elizabethan audience, Calderwood grounds his vision in the thinking of Shakespeare's era, and as a result arbitrarily links Aaron's offspring to his hereditary curse. In so doing, he brands the baby a thing of evil, the devil's spawn, whose presence will cast its blighting shadow over newly sanctified Rome. His color a mark of alienation, the boy will have no choice but to take his father's place as the intruding serpent in the soon to be restored Roman Garden of Eden. Curiously, former sworn enemies, Romans and Goths unite at the play's conclusion to bring an end to the civil war, but the little Moor remains on the outside, Rome's doors shut against his dark face. In a very telling sense, Aaron's son may well have been better off dead, for he will have to bear the yoke of lineage from the cradle to the grave. Without doubt, the sins of his father most certainly will be visited upon him. No matter what his leanings, the decks will be stacked heavily against him in much the same way as they had been against Aaron. Fated to be a lost soul and destined to be forever lodged outside the realm of grace, the infant will find no safe haven in the new Rome where Goths and Romans, the strangest of bedfellows, are now dubious allies.

Whatever designation is applied to Aaron, the fact remains that he has few options available to him as a Moor. Interestingly, Eldred Jones asserts that if nothing else, Aaron certainly had free will and therefore could have embraced good instead of evil had he so desired:

> [Aaron's]. . . choice of evil is deliberate. There is implied in his behaviour a conscious turning away from grace, which is presumed to be open to him. . . . There is thus, even in the presentation of a stereotype, an element of personal responsibility and deliberate choice. (54)

As a realist he knows full well that no matter what he does, his color renders him an outcast, unworthy of divine guidance; thus, he will follow his predestined course, the path to evil. That he apprehends this concept is glaringly apparent after he lops off Titus' hand. Joyfully applauding himself, he gives jubilant expression to his belief that since he is damned by hue anyhow, he might as well enjoy himself. "Let fools do good, and fair men call for grace, / Aaron will have his soul black like his face" (III.i.204-05), he chuckles. If in fact he deliberately makes of evil a virtue as Jones argues, this puts him in the company of Satan, no great surprise here! Whatever his connection to Lucifer, however, Aaron is clever enough to have figured out that wickedness can empower him as goodness and decency never can. Eliot Tokson reasons that "if [Elizabethans accepted the idea that] blackness is the color indigenous to hell, it was not likely that the black man could escape the consequences of inevitable association. . . . [H]e was made to play the role of hell's agent."[27] For his part, Aaron peforms the part remarkably well, never once deluding himself into believing that striving for redemption or divine sanction would render him attractive and thus acceptable to those who view him as malevolent and abominable. Doubtless he feels that to have done otherwise would have been to give in to the tenets of a world governed by racial prejudice.

In his fascinating essay "Twentieth-Century Fiction and the Black Mask of Humanity," Ralph Ellison observes that even in twentieth-century fiction, an African-American character is not allowed to be a well-rounded human being:

> Too often what is presented as the American Negro emerges an oversimplified clown, a beast, or an angel. Seldom is he drawn as that sensitively focused process of opposites, of good and evil, of instinct and intellect, of passion and spirituality, which great literary art has projected as the image of man. (43)

So it had been for Shakespeare's Moors; so it was for Aaron; so it will be for his son. In a very real sense, aside from the literary aspect of character portrayal, Ellison's comments underscore an unsettling truth: the fact that the passage of time has not wrought great changes in society's conceptions of the color black and those endowed with this hue. Indeed, the associations of *black* as emblematic of evil in eras past have survived to the fullest measure in our own distressing times. Seemingly, ancient fictions die hard. But Aaron rejects sitting idly by, miserably fettered by his so-called inherited sins. Rather, when the opportunity arises to rid himself of the shackles that restrain him because of his ethnicity, he boldly confronts his situation within Roman society, refusing to bear humbly the yoke of race. Instead, he strikes back at a world that reviles him because of his color. If his refusal to accept the reality of powers beyond his own depends upon trickery to alter events, this is probably due to the fact that this is the only avenue open to him. Very much his own justice system, Aaron is a lone adversary attempting to reshape the power wielded by the Romans and the Goths. That he succeeds only in propagating his ethnic stereotype in the eyes of the other characters attests to how much Shakespeare understood his audience's conception of the Moor as a racially inferior Other. As Joyce Green MacDonald points out,

> Shakespeare fully voices the fundamental Otherness of his Moorish villain. . . . The play understands his blackness as the sign of absolute resistance to incorporation in any system of social or moral order originating outside himself.[28]

In this early play, at least, good and evil could not coalesce in a character with black skin. Aaron, however, makes his presence felt and gives triumphant expression to his own personal conviction that black is not, in fact, the base hue that his detractors assume it to be. Shakespeare evidently concurs when he shows that his villain/hero is not a mere one-dimensional errant knave, but a splendidly witty and defective character who manages to assert the human worth everyone denies him. Although his son, the traditional "seed of time," will not grow in grace on Roman soil, Aaron's offspring will reappear in Venice, full-grown, bearing the name Othello. In this case, good and evil will be able to coexist in a person of dark complexion. The Moor, though still condemned to bear the crushing weight of race, will emerge as a tragic hero, experiencing in some measure many of the rights and privileges that such stalwart protagonists enjoy. Sinning and suffering, laughing and despairing, winning and losing, loving and hating will serve, by turn, to showcase this Moor's human qualities as they never could for the less civilized Aaron. Oftentimes, Othello is a flawed hero, not unlike a Hamlet, a Lear, a Macbeth, but he is still unable to traverse the ethnic divide successfully. Always like Aaron, he is a fated character whose pigmentation matters greatly. In short, his identity is shaped by his blackness in much the same sense as Aaron's. As Othello's literary ancestor, Aaron, Shakespeare's trailblazing Moor, leaps boldly into the consciousness of the Elizabethans, daring to assert that black is a hue like any other, no more base than white.

Notes

1. William Shakespeare, *The Merchant of Venice*, ed. Louis B. Wright and Virginia A. Lamar, The Folger Library General Reader's Shakespeare (New York: Simon and Schuster, 1957) II.i.1. Further references to this text will be cited parenthetically.

2. In his fascinating study *Black Face, Maligned Race: The Representation of Blacks in English Drama from Shakespeare to Southerne*, Anthony Barthelemy traces the literary usage back to the antique world. He quotes the following line (in translation) from Horace's *Satires, Epistles, Ars Poetic* to make his point: "This is a black, Roman; beware this" (2). He cites, too, a poem from the sixth century A.D. from the Codex Salmasianus that offers powerful evidence of the scorn with which the ancients looked upon blackness. As quoted in translation from Barthelemy's text, the verse reads:

   > The son of Dawn, foster son of rising Phoebus,Produced black thousands of his race.
   > Running to aid the Trojans with inauspicious omen,
   > He produceeded at once to die by the sword of the descendant of Pelius.
   > Already then it is shown how Troy awaits her fall,
   > When Priam accepts black help. (2)

3. Christopher Miller, *Blank Darkness: Africanist Discourse in French* (Chicago: U of Chicago P, 1985) 29.

4. Barthelemy discusses, too, the fact that the early Christians continued the tradition of linking sin with blackness and whiteness with purity (2-3).

5. Winthrop Jordan, *White Over Black* (New York: Norton, 1968) 7. Hereafter cited parenthetically in the text.

6. Although the term "Moor" could mean anyone other than white in the Renaissance, Aaron is described by everyone in the play as a character with distinctive Negroid features. Thus, I take Moor to mean black here, since all the descriptions of Aaron point to someone with very dark skin.

7. Ham was the son of Noah who, according to Genesis 9 and 10, saw his father lying naked in a drunken stupor, and unlike his brothers did not cover him or look away. Upon awakening, Noah reportedly cursed Ham, informing him that his

destiny would be to serve his brothers forever. Winthrop Jordan finds that tracing the origin of the notion that Africans were the descendents of Ham is a somewhat difficult task. However, he theorizes that some Jewish "Talmudic and Midrashic" writings may have been the source, since these suggested that God darkened Ham's descendents, rendering them ugly. He finds rather curious the fact that such luminaries as Sts. Jerome and Augustine "casually accepted the assumption that Africans were descended from one of several of Ham's four sons, an assumption which became universal despite the obscurity of its origin" (18). In analyzing the Biblical story, Jordan discovers no reference to skin color in Noah's curse. More logically, he argues, the phrase implies that Noah's erring son and his descendents would be slaves (18).

8. Gordon Ross Smith, "The Credibility of Shakespeare's Aaron," *Literature and Psychology* 10 (Winter 1960): 12.

9. Henry James, "Daisy Miller," *Great Short Stories* (New York: Harper, 1966) 54.

10. William Shakespeare, *Titus Andronicus*, ed. J. C. Maxwell, The Arden Shakespeare (London: Methuen, 1987) III.i.54. All future quotations will come from this edition.

11. Jack D'Amico, *The Moor in English Renaissance Drama* (Tampa: U of South Florida P, 1991) 2.

12. With the exception of Tamora, who always calls Aaron her "lovely Moor" or her "lovely Aaron," all the other major players refer to Aaron's color with disdain. In Act II, Scene III, Bassianus calls him a "swart Cimmerian" (72) who is "spotted, detested, and abominable" (74). A few lines later, Lavinia berates Tamora by calling Aaron the empress' "raven-colored love" (83). For Marcus, Aaron is so like a "black ill-favour'd fly" that he kills the insect. When Titus, too, strikes at the creature, he comments that the fly "comes in likeness of a coal-black Moor" (III.ii.66, 78). Demetrius labels his mother's lover a "hellish dog," a "foul fiend," after learning that Tamora has given birth to Aaron's child. Not to be outdone, Lucius, in Act V, characterizes Aaron as an "incarnate devil," with "a fiend-like face" (i. 40, 45), "a barbarous beastly villain" (i.96) "a ravenous tiger," an "accursed devil," an "inhuman dog" (ii.4, 5, 14).

13. Emily Bartels, "Making More of the Moor: Aaron, Othello and Renaissance Refashionings of Race," *Shakespeare Quarterly* 41:4 (Winter 1990): 444. Hereafter cited parenthetically in the text.

14. Along with *The Spanish Tragedy,* Thomas Kyd's blood-drenched revenge dramas, *Titus Andronicus* shared the distinction of being one of the sixteenth century's most popular plays.

15. René Girard, *Violence and the Sacred,* trans. Patrick Gregory (Baltimore: Johns Hopkins UP, 1991) 30.

16. Gordon Ross Smith, "The Credibility of Shakespeare's Aaron," *Literature and Psychology* 10 (Winter 1960): 12.

17. Quoted from T. S. Eliot, "The Love Song of J. Alfred Prufrock," line 28, *The Norton Introduction to Poetry,* ed. M. H. Abrams, 3rd ed. (New York: Norton, 1981).

18. Eldred Jones, *Othello's Countrymen* (London: Oxford UP, 1965) 55. Hereafter cited parenthetically in the text.

19. Ralph Ellison, *Shadow and Act* (New York: New American Library, 1966) 69-70. Hereafter cited parenthetically in the text.

20. David Richman, *Laughter, Pain, and Wonder* (Newark: U of Delaware P, 1990) 64.

21. Richard T. Brucher. "Tragedy, Laugh On": Comic Violence in *Titus Andronicus," Renaissance Drama* ns 10 (1979): 82.

22. Eugene Waith's introd. to *Titus Andronicus,* The Oxford Shakespeare (Oxford: Clarendon, 1984) 64.

23. William Shakespeare, *Othello,* ed. Norman Sanders, The New Cambridge Shakespeare (New York: Simon and Schuster, 1957) I.iii.62.

24. According to A. C. Hamilton, who quotes Holinshed in *The Early Shakespeare,* "Lucius was the first king of the Britains that received the faith of Jesus Christ" (84); thus Shakespeare's usage of this figure to lead Rome is not arbitrary. Coming from the Latin *lucius*—"born during the day"—the name "Lucius" means light, an appropriate choice for the character who ultimately restores order and rules Rome at the end of the play. That Lucius' son bears the same name suggests the continuation of the line. In addition, the figure of Lucius appears in Spenser's *The Faerie Queene,* Book II. Characters named Lucius also appear as emissaries of light in *Julius Caesar* and *Cymbeline.*

25. Notwithstanding the fact that Lucius is destined to lead his nation back to greatness, his character is somewhat troubling to critics. He is the one who demands Alarbus' sacrifice at the beginning of the play and who describes in grim detail the dismemberment of Tamora's first-born son by the Andronici. There is no marked change in his appetite for gruesome revenge when he devises the penalties for Aaron and Tamora at the end of the play. In fact, these do not differ greatly from the types of punishments that Aaron may have concocted for his enemies.

26. James L. Calderwood, *Shakespeare and the Denial of Death* (Amherst: U of Massachusetts P, 1987) 199. Hereafter cited in the text.

27. Eliot Tokson, *The Popular Image of the Black Man is English Drama, 1550-1688* (Boston: G. K. Hall, 1982) 43.

28. Joyce Green McDonald, "'The Force of the Imagination': The Subject of Blackness in

Shakespeare, Jonson, and Ravenscroft," *Renaissance Papers,* ed. George Walton Williams and Barbara J. Bain (Raleigh: Southeastern Renaissance Conference, 1991) 64.

FURTHER READING

Criticism

Callaghan, Dympna. "What's at Stake in Representing Race?" *Shakespeare Studies* XXVI (1998): 21–26.

    Examines the representation of non-white characters in modern productions of Shakespeare's plays.

Erickson, Peter. "The Moment of Race in Renaissance Studies." *Shakespeare Studies* XXVI (1998): 27-36.

    Considers the pitfalls of scholarly investigation into race in Renaissance studies. Erickson uses *Othello* among his examples, arguing that while "the drama begins by disrupting and temporarily suspending racially based stereotypes, it ends by reimposing them."

Hamlin, William M. "Men of Inde: Renaissance Ethnography and *The Tempest*." *Shakespeare Studies* XXII (1994): 15-44.

    Views *The Tempest* in the contexts of Renaissance colonial discourse, regarding Caliban as a culturally distinct and ambivalent figure.

López, Judith A. "'Black and White and "Read" All Over.'" *Shakespeare Studies* XXVI (1998): 49-58.

    Disputes the critical tendency to reduce racial and religious conflict to binary opposition when evaluating such texts as *The Merchant of Venice*.

Smith, Ian. "Barbarian Errors: Performing Race in Early Modern England." *Shakespeare Quarterly* 49, No. 2 (Summer 1998): 168-86.

    Explores the racializing function of language—which seeks to define through speech the cultural outsider—in relation to Shakespeare's *Othello*.

The Merchant of Venice

For further information on the critical and stage history of *The Merchant of Venice*, see *SC,* Volumes 4, 12, and 40.

INTRODUCTION

Sometimes listed among Shakespeare's "problem plays" because of its ambiguous treatment of issues such as religion, economics, and the role of women, *The Merchant of Venice* has also been a source of heated critical disagreement with regard to race. In this light, scholars have discussed not only Shakespeare's ambivalent depiction of the Jewish moneylender, Shylock, but also his derogatory presentation of minor, non-European characters such as the Prince of Morocco. Critics have debated whether this racial tension is evidence of Shakespeare's own opinions. Alternatively, some scholars have suggested that Shakespeare might have relied on his racially charged scenes to create an allegorical drama or to satirize and thereby condemn his own culture's prejudices.

Although Thomas Moisan (1987) and Stephen A. Cohen (1994) do not deal specifically with the issue of race, both critics see the character Shylock as a social outsider. Both also credit Shakespeare with using Shylock to subtly criticize his era and his fellow Europeans in their treatment of non-Europeans. Moisan, for example, argues that the play pokes fun at a European, Christian society that condemns the economics of usury even while it depends on its practice. Cohen, on the other hand, identifies Shylock as a lone and unsuccessful defender of equity and social freedoms against "royal authority"—an issue that would become increasingly important in England as the days of monarchical rule came to a close and the period of Cromwell's Commonwealth approached.

Marion D. Perret (1988) touches upon racial questions in *The Merchant of Venice* when he remarks that Shylock's race would have been irrelevant to Shakespeare's audience, who, he contends, would have been more concerned with the moneylender's business and religious practices. By contrast, John Picker (1994), Avraham Oz (1995), and James Shapiro (1995) all see race as a crucial issue in the play. Each stresses Europe's (and more specifically England's) fear of the outsider or non-European as a factor in the way in which Shylock is treated—first by Antonio, and later by Portia and the Duke of Venice in the trial scene. Oz observes that the treatment of Jews by European cities was, in fact, a means of enforcing power over all outsiders as well as over all Europeans who were subordinate to the local authority. Oz asserts that Shylock's bargain with Antonio represents an attempt to reverse the relationship between those who have power and those who do not. Shapiro looks at the play from a slightly different point of view: in his examination of British performances of *The Merchant of Venice* over the centuries, he observes that audiences and directors have struggled to accommodate Jews, whom they regard as a threatening, non-English race which is nevertheless of great economic importance. Mary Janell Metzger (1998) refers to color as a distinguishing factor for race in the play. Metzger notes the frequency with which Jessica is described as white-skinned and therefore noble in contrast to her father, Shylock, who is dark-skinned and untrustworthy. Jessica, Metzger argues, is white enough to be regarded by some of the characters as a "latent Christian"—thus "racializing" the conception of what it is to be Jewish. Kim F. Hall (1992) and B. J. Sokol (1998) discuss the treatment of other races in the play. Hall examines a brief reference in Act III to a "Moor," or black, woman whom Lorenzo claims has been impregnated by Launcelot. These few lines, Hall asserts, highlight the English nation's preoccupation with preserving its identity and power as a race—an issue that was of much concern to Elizabethan England, deeply involved as it was at the time in colonization and commerce overseas. Sokol acknowledges the fact that such prejudice against other races and colors was legally condoned in England, but he also argues that Shakespeare employs language and characterization to reveal the Elizabethan public's actual contempt for the discriminatory laws of the land. Sokol contends, for example, that Launcelot's crude jokes about the Moorish woman and Portia's vocal relief at not having to marry the Moroccan prince are meant to reflect badly on the speakers rather than on the victims of their remarks.

The discussion of *The Merchant of Venice* as an allegorical statement focuses more on Shylock's religion than his race. Some early critics argued, for example, that the trial scene during which Shylock is out-maneuvered by Portia and is punished for his cruelty stands for the triumph of Christianity over Judaism. Recently, however, scholars have taken a more specific and measured view of the allegorical elements in the play. While both Susan McLean (1996) and Judith Rosenheim (1996) note that the play intentionally echoes the parable of the Prodigal Son, neither concludes that this allusion to the New Testament functions unequivocally as a condemnation of one religion over another. Instead, McLean asserts that the complex and sometimes ironic "enactments" of different parts of the parable between various characters—Launcelot and Old Gobbo, Antonio and Shylock, Jessica and Shylock, Bassanio and Antonio—indicate that there is no easy way to forgive nor any one particular road to salvation. Similarly, Rosenheim argues that the genuine father/son relationship between Old Gobbo and the prodigal Launcelot reflects a symbolic one between Shylock and Antonio, and that the power struggle that occurs between each pairing represents both the flaws and virtues of the moral values of our own time as well as of Shakespeare's. Finally, Matthew A. Fike (1994) suggests an allegorical reading of the play when he observes that unlike other comedies by Shakespeare, *The Merchant of Venice* is filled with a sense of disappointment, be it in business dealings (Shylock and Antonio), friendship (Bassanio and Antonio), or love (the participants in the ring scene) and that in this highly complicated play, disappointment represents humanity's earthly condition as one in which flawed happiness is the only type possible.

OVERVIEWS AND GENERAL STUDIES

John Lyon (essay date 1988)

SOURCE: "Responses, Sources, Contexts," in *Harvester New Critical Introductions to Shakespeare: 'The Merchant of Venice,'* Harvester/Wheatsheaf, 1988, pp. 9-28.

[*In the essay below, Lyon describes* The Merchant of Venice *as a "controversial play." He demonstrates that literary critics have been widely divided concerning Shakespeare's views on anti-Semitism, and concludes that the play needs to be examined not only from the point of view of Shakespeare's era, but also within the context of his other plays.*]

The safest place to begin with so controversial a play as *The Merchant of Venice* is with effects rather than causes. In a brilliantly economical survey of the play's criticism, Norman Rabkin recently identified the essential quality of *The Merchant of Venice* to be its capacity to provoke a welter of diverging and opposing responses. Consequently Rabkin lamented the play's critical history as a series of strategies of evasion, determined either to dismiss the play, or through partiality and evasion, to coerce it into a thematic and tonal unity. Rabkin's crisp diagnosis of this critical tradition merits quotation at length:

> Such radical disagreements between obviously simplistic critics testify to a fact about their subject that ought to be the point of departure for criticism. Instead, critics both bad and good have constructed strategies to evade the problem posed by divergent responses. Some blame Shakespeare, suggesting that his confusion accounts for tension in the work and its audience. Others appeal to a narrow concept of cultural history which writes off our responses as anachronistic, unavailable to Shakespeare's contemporaries because of their attitudes towards usury or Jews or comedy. Still others suggest that, since the plays are fragile confections designed to display engaging if implausible characters, exegetical criticism is misplaced. Though all of these strategies attract modern practitioners, they have lost ground before the dominant evasion, the reduction of the play to a theme which, when we understand it, tells us which of our responses we must suppress. The ingenious thematic critic . . . is licensed to stipulate that 'in terms of the structure of the play Shylock is a minor character' and can be ignored, or that the action is only metaphorical and does not need to be examined as if its events literally happened, or that Shylock is only a Jew, or a banker, or a usurer, or a man spiritually dead, or a commentary on London life, never a combination of these; or that *The Merchant of Venice* is built on 'four levels of existence' corresponding to Dante's divisions—'Hell (Shylock), Purgatory proper (Antonio) and the Garden of Eden (Portia-Bassanio), and Paradise'; or that the play is exclusively about love, or whatever, and, insofar as it doesn't fit the critic's formulation, it is flawed.

(Rabkin 1981, pp. 7-8)

Only very recently have critics (Leggatt 1974; Rabkin himself; Nuttall 1983; Berry 1985) been prepared to display at length a perplexity which may perhaps account for the reticence of so many of our great Shakespearean critics on the subject of *The Merchant of Venice*. The critical response to the play proves less than directly rewarding. This can be ascribed in part, as Rabkin implies, to critics' obtuseness and interpretative aggression. But it also says something more interesting about the tenacity of the play's hold on the minds of its audiences and readers. *The Merchant of Venice* proves an extraordinarily difficult play from which to free oneself into an adequate degree of objectivity, and criticism tends to be symptomatic of the play rather than illuminating of it. Indeed, such criticism can often seem a reactive prolongation of that unfolding of postures, positions and habits of mind which both characters and audience assume, reject and reassume in the course of the play's performance. The oddities and embarrassments which surface in the course of these critical arguments are co-extensive with those occurring in the play and amount, in themselves, to something of a comedy.

There are two predominating and opposed ways of reading *The Merchant of Venice*. The basic division of opinion manifests itself in a variety of ways. Thus critics divide over Shylock. Some see in him the consistent villain of the piece, and consequently celebrate the Christian lovers' triumph over him. Against this, some see in Shylock victimised humanity and, accordingly, view the play's lovers with varying degrees of scepticism which, in extreme cases, can amount to hostility. More particularly, there are two focal points in such disagreements, two rich and complex scenes where, in Act 1 Scene 3, Shylock and Antonio first agree the terms of the bond, and, in Act 3 Scene 1, Shylock declares his intention to claim his rights in respect of it. Critical debate, though lively, is circumscribed, limited to discussion of character, and Shylock's character in particular. Prior to this century, the body of criticism of *The Merchant of Venice* has shown this emphasis on Shylock, but has proved less rich or rewarding than that which has accrued to many of Shakespeare's other plays; it has often been occasional, prompted by particular productions of the play and reveals, as the stage history does, the predictable shift, as we move from the eighteenth to the nineteenth century, in the characterisation of Shylock—from clown and villain to the figure of wronged humanity who merits our compassion. (See John Russell Brown, 'The Realization of Shylock', in Brown and Harris 1961, pp. 187-210.)

When we turn from critics who discuss character to those who discuss theme, we find the critical accounts broader, accommodating more of the play, but the critics remain similarly divided in their opinions and attitudes. Thus, for some critics the play secures and celebrates valued distinctions—between material and spiritual wealth; between venturing and usury; between generosity and possessiveness; between love and the law; between mercy and justice. For others the play works to quite the opposite effect, undermining such distinctions through dark and troubling ironies. And some such critics pursue what they see as the play's ironic mode to discover covert correspondences underlying the play's ostensible oppositions; hence, for example, the play's principal antagonists, Shylock and Antonio, are revealed to share the painful kinship of isolation and exclusion. These are larger discussions, not limited to a few of the play's great scenes, and exercised by questions of the relationship between the worlds of Belmont and Venice, and between the casket plot and the bond plot. As with considerations of character, however, the fundamental disagreement remains whether to regard the *The Merchant of Venice* as characterised by celebration or irony.

Frank Kermode is representative of those who emphasise celebration, and reveals incidentally the kind of oddity which typically accompanies the expression of such views:

> *The Merchant of Venice*, then, is 'about' judgment, redemption and mercy; the supersession in human history of the grim four thousand years of unalleviated justice by the era of love and mercy. It begins with usury and corrupt love; it ends with harmony and perfect love. And all the time it tells its audience that this is its subject; only by a determined effort to avoid the obvious can one mistake the theme of *The Merchant of Venice*.
>
> (Kermode, in Brown and Harris 1961, p.224)

The tone of this is reminiscent of that adopted by the overly brusque Antonio in his dealings with Shylock early in the play. With Kermode's earlier insistence on 'the correct interpretation' (ibid., p. 222), it is all the more surprising from a critic who is later to emerge as a champion of critical pluralism, and who has always emphasised the patience of Shakespeare before his interpreters. The tension between the claimed themes of harmony and love, and the impatience and intolerance with which they are urged is odd indeed. Kermode's method of argument is also interestingly representative in the way he appeals to analogies from *nondramatic* literary modes to 'resolve' the play's difficulties and thus stabilise, and perhaps falsify, the drama; in his case the appeals are to Spenser, Milton and the Bible. Barbara K. Lewalski pursues a similar interpretation of the play, with similar no-nonsense tone and similar appeals to nondramatic modes, here biblical allusion and allegory:

> comprehension of the play's allegorical meanings leads to a recognition of its fundamental unity, discrediting the common critical view that is a hotch-potch which developed contrary to Shakespeare's conscious intention.
>
> (Lewalski 1962, p.328)

But when the importing of an allegorical framework threatens to displace rather than illuminate the particularities of incident and character, might we not wonder whether drama should be subordinated to allegory in this way? We are getting remote from the experience of *The Merchant of Venice*.

Harley Granville-Barker has proved even more brusquely untroubled by the play in his insistence that the casket plot and the bond plot have all the unreality of fairy tales, unaware in that appeal that fairy tales and folklore rarely enjoy the psychological and sociological innocence he imputes to them (Granville-Barker 1958, Vol. 1, p.335). Concerned to assimilate *The Merchant of Venice* to the pattern of festivity and merriment which he discerns in Shakespearean comedy generally, C. L. Barber finds various embarrassments in pursuing this line of interpretation; Barber openly confesses his unease, but finds himself drawn into weak argument nevertheless:

> The whole play dramatizes the conflict between the mechanisms of wealth and the masterful, social use of it. The happy ending, which abstractly considered as an event is hard to credit, and the treatment of Shylock, which abstractly considered as justice is hard to justify, *work* as we actually watch or read the play because these events express relief and triumph in the achievement of a distinction.
>
> (Barber 1972, p. 170)

But a distinction which works only if we don't think about it, is more likely to be a distinction undermined than a distinction made.

John Russell Brown also sees *The Merchant of Venice* as a play which secures distinctions—between material wealth and love's wealth. He finds the play's own sententiousness catching, but proves less than fully responsive to the drama's dynamic testing of such static aphorisms and can be led into such contortedly protective logic as the suggestion that 'it is Shylock's fate to bring out the worst in those he tries to harm' (Brown 1962, p. 74).

Of course, all of these critics, and many others who share the same interpretative emphasis on celebration, have valuable and substantial things to say about the play, but the oddities here suggest that their readings bear a tangential relation to *The Merchant of Venice*'s essential nature.

Those critics who see *The Merchant of Venice* as an ironic play are also useful. Moreover, perhaps because they don't pursue extraneous authorities to verify their interpretations, their readings often have the advantage that they focus more attentively and sustainedly on the drama before us. Even when overingenious or wrong-headed, the particularity of their arguments seems closer to the particularities of the play itself. But is also true that these critics are often no less biased nor odd than their opponents. Both A. D. Moody and Harold C. Goddard are aware that they are not offering interpretations from first principles, as it were, but their corrective readings often prove less surefooted than these critics might intend. Moody sees *The Merchant of Venice* as a play which 'does not celebrate the Christian virtues so much as expose their absence' (Moody 1964, p. 10), but comes repeatedly close, in his emphasising of the covert above the overt, to seeing the transparent evil of Shylock as no evil at all; Shylock's 'villainy is almost naïve and innocent' by comparison with the Christians' (ibid., p.29). At times Goddard loses his footing entirely and sinks into rhetoric and implausible metaphor:

> Even Shylock, as we have seen, had in him at least a grain of spiritual gold, of genuine Christian spirit. Only a bit of it perhaps. Seeds do not need to be big. Suppose that Portia and Antonio, following the lead of the seemingly willing Duke, had watered this tiny seed with that quality that blesses him who gives as well as him who takes, had overwhelmed Shylock with the grace of forgiveness! What then? The miracle, it is true, might not have taken place. Yet it might have.
>
> (Goddard 1960, p. 111)

If Professor Kermode sounded uncomfortably like Antonio, then Professor Goddard's pleading out-Shylocks Shylock, but without the villain's vengeance.

The Merchant of Venice's capacity to prompt these contradictory reactions has led critics to speculate about the circumstances of the play's composition and its creator's intentions. Initially, the focus of attention is the portrayal of Shylock. In H. B. Charlton's influential view, the anti-Semitic Shakespeare sets out to pander to prejudices common to himself and his audience but finds, in spite of himself, that his characteristic powers and intuitions lead to a humanised Shylock; 'His Shylock is a composite production of Shakespeare the Jew-hater, and of Shakespeare the dramatist' (Charlton 1949, p. 132). It is a powerful thesis, reiterated as recently as 1980 by D. M. Cohen, with but one alteration in its argument:

> It is as though *The Merchant Venice* is an anti-Semitic play written by an author who is not an anti-Semite—but an author who has been willing to use the cruel stereotypes of that ideology for mercenary and artistic purposes.
>
> (Cohen 1980, p. 63)

The limitation in such arguments lies in their often unintentionally diminishing image of Shakespeare as naïve and inspirational, a great artist almost in spite of himself. Shakespeare does not *stumble* on the fact of Shylock's humanity; a writer who habitually confers inner life on the characters he finds in his sources and who, as we shall see, characteristically compounds the complexities of these sources, is *cultivating* difficulty in a spirit of exploration. The openness which allows him to make such discoveries is matched by a resourcefulness in subduing the arising discrepancies into some degree and some appearance, at least, of artistic coherence.

Most recently some critics have emphasised, in *The Merchant of Venice*, not a failure of artistic unity but the dynamism of drama, and have therefore shown themselves more thoroughly admiring of the play. Ralph Berry finds it to have 'the self-adjusting elasticity of the great play' (Berry 1985, p. 46), and finds design in the play in its temporal shaping of the sequence of its audience's diverse responses: the play is so organised as to *provoke* the audience's discomfort. The boldest and most ambitious of recent critics writing on the play locate discrepancy and incoherence, not in Shakespeare's play, but in his, and our, world beyond the drama, and they thus transform talk of incoherence into praise of the play's inclusiveness. A. D. Nuttall finds *The Merchant of Venice* characteristic of Shakespeare's tendency 'to take an archetype or a stereotype and then work, so to speak, against it, without ever overthrowing it' (Nuttall 1983, p.124). But 'Shakespeare will not let us rest even here. The subversive counterthesis is itself too easy. We may now begin to see that he is perhaps the least sentimental dramatist who ever lived. We begin to understand what is meant by holding the mirror up to nature' (ibid., p. 131). For Norman Rabkin, too, *The Merchant of Venice* in its inclusiveness, contradictions and complications, reflects the larger reality of a world itself unyielding of simple and single meanings. The 'artistic multivalence . . . is the mirror of an unfathomable reality which is the source of the trouble . . . a reality that cannot be cut down to a single understanding' (Rabkin 1981, p. 139-40). It misrepresents both Nuttall and Rabkin, each engaged in large considerations of Shakespeare and the nature of creativity and criticism, to adumbrate their arguments in this way and to narrow their speculations to apply only to *The Merchant of Venice*. Nevertheless, *tout comprendre c'est tout pardonner*, and we might worry that their emphasis on Shakespeare's reality and nature is at the cost of criticism *and* appreciation of his art, and that the play continues to trouble despite the grandeur of such exonerations: *The Merchant of Venice* perhaps represents a moment of integrity too questioning and insufficiently artful to contain multifarious truths within the coherence and consolation of art. Some, at least, of the irreconcilable elements in *The Merchant of Venice* are not shaped into telling insight, but remain unrewarding flaws, symptomatic of lines of thought discarded in the course of the exploratory process. Indeed, Nuttall's and Rabkin's arguments are not too far removed from the greater stringency of Dr Johnson who celebrates Shakespeare as the poet of nature whose incoherences and discrepancies, though natural, are incoherences and discrepancies none the less.

Like *King Lear*, *The Merchant of Venice*'s provocativeness goes beyond critical response to creative redaction. Famously, *King Lear* spawned Nahum Tate's corrective Restoration work, *The History of King Lear*, and more recently, Edward Bond's *Lear*. *The Merchant of Venice* follows a very similar pattern, giving rise to George Granville's *The Jew of Venice*, first performed in 1701 and dominating the stage until Macklin's return to the Shakespearean text in 1741; and, more recently, to *The Merchant*, by Arnold Wesker, himself Jewish. What is interesting in the case of both works, given my argument for the inherently problematic *and* dramatic nature of Shakespeare's play, is how both redactions, though in opposing ways, simplify and clarify the issues of the original by means which also substantially reduce the *dramatic* power of the results. Granville's play secures Shylock as comic villain and celebrates love and friendship in the figures of Antonio, Bassanio and Portia. The most relevant omission is that of the critically contentious Act 3 Scene 1 of Shakespeare's play, where we had seen Shylock's reaction both to the loss of his daughter and to Antonio's losses; Shylock's villainy becomes much less ambiguous as a result of that omission. The now clear contrast between Shylock and the Christians is repeatedly and crudely pointed up in such moments as Shylock's aside in the scene, merely reported in Shakespeare but now dramatised by Granville, of Bassanio's and Antonio's pained parting:

> *Bassanio*
> . . . Oh my Antonio! 'tis hard, tho' for a Moment,
> To lose the Sight of what we Love.
> *Shylock (aside)*
> These two Christian Fools put me in mind
> Of my Money: just so loath am I to part with that.
>
> (Spencer edn, 1965, p.372)

In Granville's version, the original play's sententiousness is heavily augmented, playing, as it does, into the Restoration's shrivelled sense of dramatic action as merely subservient to, and illustrative of moral statement. Granville reverses the characteristic Shakespearean process of creation to the extent that the drama is now contained by its moral *sententiae*, its 'good Morals and just Thought' as the play's Epilogue puts it (ibid., p. 401). Action once exploratory is now ornamental, and the resulting play is both stable and static. The dramatic urgency of the early scenes in Shakespeare's play is supplanted by an interpolated scene of stylised moralising in which Antonio, Bassanio and Shylock drink to Friendship, Love and Money, respectively, and this moralised tableau-like quality is further enhanced by the addition of a masque reiterating the values of Love and Friendship.

As a creative response to what he sees as Shakespeare's anti-Semitic play, Arnold Wesker's *The Merchant*, first performed in Stockholm in 1976, is altogether more extreme—and understandably so, given the racial identity of the playwright and the holocaust after which he writes. But the integrity of his intention is destructive of the dramatic qualities of his play, and it is unsurprising that *The Merchant* failed in New York and has never been performed in London.

Bassanio and Portia in Act III, scene ii of The Merchant of Venice.

In Wesker's version, the casket plot is but the foolish philosophical whim of Portia's father, and the love of Portia and Bassanio is marked, not by any romantic idealism, but by pragmatism and realism. Jessica runs off with the 'sort of' poet, Lorenzo, in similarly mundane fashion, although she later proves stouter and more articulate in Shylock's defence than Shakespeare's Jessica did. The shallowness of the young Venetians is much emphasised. Wesker's Shylock and Antonio are old friends in their mid-sixties. This Shylock dominates his play: he is tyrannically hospitable; he is a miser only in so far as he hides Hebrew books to prevent the Christians burning them, and only his daughter is treasured above these books; a committed feminist, Shylock is out to demonstrate in the education of Jessica that daughters can be the intellectual rivals of sons. Money-lending is never Shylock's full-time occupation, and he uses his wealth to function as a one-man Arts Council in the Venetian ghetto, financing art, music, literature, philosophy and architecture. His wealth is further used in helping the poor and the Jewish refugees fleeing the Inquisition. Moreover, the Jews, through taxes and forced 'loans', are shown to be one of Venice's principal sources of finance.

Wesker's Shylock and Antonio agree their bond reluctantly, only because the law demands it. And it is a merry nonsensical bond indeed, in mockery of the law and agreed over much mutual tickling. Later Shylock's sole reason for not abandoning the legal claims he has in respect of the lapsed bond is that others in the Jewish ghetto fear—and have cause to fear—that the Christians will use such a precedent against them in future dealings. Shylock must stick to the law to ensure the law's future protection of his people, and his reaction when Portia deploys her legal tricks is thus a relieved 'Thank God'. Shylock pays the price of seeming to threaten the life of a Christian, and now contemplates a departure for the Holy Land.

But Wesker's corrective urge is repeatedly of a vehemence and urgency in excess of what the immediate dramatic contexts he creates will sustain, and the emphatic extremity of his message is thus intelligibile only if we look beyond the particular moments in which it is delivered to the Shakespearean play against which it is a reaction. Wesker's *The Merchant* has a problematic status as a work of art and is not the autonomous drama it ostensibly appears but is parasitic on the play it reviles. The characters' voices are subordinated to the single, wilful voice of the playwright pursuing his argument with Shakespeare.

For us here, Wesker's redaction illuminates the Shakespearean original in two ways. In transforming his sources, Shakespeare had rendered Shylock a more complex and sympathetic character than the villain in the various tales he used, and clearly Wesker is moving very much further in the same direction. But in one important way Wesker is reversing the effect which Shakespeare had on his source materials. Wesker returns the story to its earlier simplicity, and unravels the teasings and testings which Shakespeare's creative amalgamation of a variety of sources had produced. The result is stridently univocal and undramatic. The three centres of narrative interest—Shylock and Antonio, Portia and Bassanio, Lorenzo and Jessica—are now securely and hierarchically ordered with the Shylockian tale almost eclipsing the other two. And the questions and challenges arising from the Shakespearean interplay of narratives are thus suppressed. Wesker renders the casket test cynical so that the Portia we see there is no longer at odds with the quick-witted character we see in the trial scene. Bassanio becomes once again the godson of the Antonio figure of Shakespeare's primary source, Ser Giovanni's *Il Pecorone,* and Antonio ages accordingly; the further amatory tension which the love of Antonio for Bassanio had introduced into Shakespeare's play is again excised in Wesker's version. The story, now so favourable to the Venetian Jews, has in other respects come full circle and Wesker is at odds with Shakespeare not merely in attitude but in method and art. While more obviously liberal, Wesker is also less exploratory.

Wesker's play vindicates his Jew. But it is a neat irony that Wesker's play is more akin to the flatter simplicities of Shakespeare's sources than to *The Merchant of Venice* itself; the story can become comforting for the prejudiced and the enlightened alike only if its Shakespearean truths are simplified.

The possible sources of *The Merchant of Venice* are multiple and various, admit of varying degrees of probability and influence, and extend both very far back to longstanding traditions of folklore, and to near-contemporary plays, some of which are now lost. (The full facts are discussed by Geoffrey Bullough [1957], Kenneth Muir [1977], and John Russell Brown in the Arden edition of the play [1961].) What is salient is the audacity implicit in Shakespeare's combining of such diverse material, his cultivation of the problematic and the probing. Shakespeare is going out of his way to make things difficult for himself and his audiences. In Ser Giovanni's *Il Pecorone,* the impecunious Giannetto is dependent on his Venetian godfather, Ansaldo, to finance the amatory pursuit of a widowed lady of Belmonte, whose devised test is altogether more basically sexual and mercenary. To win her, the suitor must bed her—not an easy task, since she habitually knocks him out, prior to bedtime, with some doped wine. If the suitor fails, he forfeits all his wealth. Effectively, the lady of Belmonte is running an enterprising business. Giannetto's third attempt on the lady is again financed by Ansaldo, despite the godfather's having been bankrupted by Giannetto's two previous ventures. Ansaldo now borrows from a Jew and is dependent on a bond which, if he fails to keep it, demands the payment of a pound of his flesh. The lady's maid warns Giannetto off the wine, Giannetto successfully performs the required test—the narrative spares us any details of the lady's initial surprise but reassures us that finally she is highly delighted by his performance—and Giannetto takes charge of Belmonte. Eventually, he recalls Ansaldo's bond and realises that his godfather's life must be in danger. Giannetto returns to Venice to be followed there by his lady in disguise, and she successfully performs her tricks in the Venetian courtroom. The ring intrigue follows but is quickly cleared up in Belmonte, where godfather Ansaldo is cheerfully married off to the lady's maid.

Borrowing from other sources, Shakespeare multiplies both his cast-list and the story's complications. Thus the Jessica story is the synthesis of elements and hints from a wide range of narratives: she owes something to Abigail, the daughter of Barabas, Marlowe's *Jew of Malta;* she echoes the daughter of the usurer in Munday's *Zelauto,* a story which, with its financial borrowings and cruel bonds, influences *The Merchant of Venice* in multiple ways; and Jessica derives, too, from *Il Novellino* of Masuccio, where a young girl plunders her miser father to run off with the youth who is his debtor. The important point here is that in *The Merchant of Venice* Shakespeare seems to be multiplying his young couples and to be producing a number of triangular relationships which mingle obligations and loyalties of love and money (father—daughter—lover, friend—suitor—lady). By such means he sets up testing analogies among the various centres of dramatic interest. In what ways are the relationships between, first, Jessica and Shylock and, second, Portia and her father, similar? How does Bassanio differ from Lorenzo? Do Portia's and Bassanio's attitudes to money differ substantially from those of Lorenzo and Jessica? To this end, too, Shakespeare alters the relationship in *Il Pecorone* between Ansaldo the godfather and Giannetto the godson, to the loving friendship of Bassanio and Antonio. And Shakespeare rejuvenates the Ansaldo figure to further that emphasis. The neatness of Ser Giovanni's original is intentionally disrupted as Gratiano now marries the lady's maid, Nerissa, and in Shakespeare's asymmetrical ending, Antonio is left in disquieting isolation. A new complicating relationship comes into play in Shakespeare's drama. In contrast, Wesker, as we have seen, firmly subordinates the various love stories to the story of Shylock, and restores Antonio to his former dignified and disinterested age.

The Jew and/or usurer who is to become Shylock in *The Merchant of Venice* is frustrated in courtrooms as diverse as those of *Il Pecorone, The Ballad of Gernutus* and Munday's *Zelauto,* but Shylock's antecedents are not further punished. The new emphasis on the trial of Shylock and its painful consequences for him is Shakespearean; it deepens the seriousness of the threatening villain and invites speculation about the inner condition of Shylock's future life and about the society that preserves itself by such harsh means. Characteristically, Wesker again mitigates the isolated silence of Shylock's exit from the Shakespearean play in the new image of his projected pilgrimage to Jerusalem.

But perhaps the largest change which Shakespeare makes is in the borrowing of material from the Christian allegory of *Gesta Romanorum,* which allows Ser Giovanni's test of virility and seduction to be displaced by the decorous formality of the casket test. The trickery of the trial scene and the sexual trickery in Belmonte in *Il Pecorone* are all of a piece. They belong to a coarser and simpler comic world, fabliau-like in its ribaldry. When Shakespeare imports the casket plot into his play, this bawdry gets pushed to the side of the drama and is expressed through the figures of Gratiano and Nerissa. Bassanio's wooing of Portia is conducted by way of the caskets and involves the elevated and stylised presentation of rich depths of human feeling. Fabliau-like tales concentrate on the entertaining intrigues of action, while what we might describe as the romantic elements in the narrative of *The Merchant of Venice* invite its audiences and readers to look beyond events to matters of morality, feeling and human worth. It is this curious mixture of kinds of story which produces the greatest interpretative puzzles of *The Merchant of Venice* and may afford some explanation of the play's capacity to prompt opposing responses.

Shakespeare's fusion of this variety of sources is not without flaw; Bassanio, for example, is introduced as Antonio's 'most noble kinsman', a residual detail left over from *Il Pecorone,* but this relationship is never again mentioned in the play. But Shakespeare's bringing together of the realism of *Il Pecorone* and the romantic qualities from *Gesta Romanorum* produces the distinctive challenge of *The Merchant of Venice:* the shifting nature of the literary worlds in which the various stories are played out; the uncertainties over the kinds of response appropriate to the play's various characters; and the typical tensions between the play's characters and the situations in which they find themselves. Is Bassanio out of place in the elevated world of Belmont's moral testings? Is Portia more suited to being the dignified lady of Belmont or the quick-thinking manoeuvrer in Venice? In which scene and in which world are Portia and Bassanio most truly themselves?

Again in contrast, Wesker in his version refuses to enter imaginatively into the expressive life of the casket plot convention and views it externally, as it were, as merely the mad whim of a foolish philosopher, a whim to be circumvented by some devious thought in order that a shallower and more tawdry love between Wesker's Portia and Bassanio can come to fruition.

Wesker's *The Merchant* illuminates the controversies which surround *The Merchant of Venice* in a second way. Throughout his play, Wesker is much exercised by the problem of interpretation and repeatedly off-loads undigested and undramatic lectures on Jewish history on the slender and insufficient pretext that Shylock, who gives voice to them, is a garrulous hoarder of books, much interested in his racial past. In attempting to locate some stability of attitude among the ambiguities of *The Merchant of Venice,* and to constrain the play's troublesome meanings, literary critics often appeal beyond literature to history and historical contexts. Although few literary historians would defend the assumption in the abstract, they often argue, in their considerations of *The Merchant of Venice, as if,* unlike literature, history were straightforwardly factual, unambiguous and not itself in need of interpretation. But *within* Wesker's play, historical information is extensively used as an honourable, if dramatically clogging, means to further Wesker's polemical argument and vindicate the Venetian Jews. Wesker's example usefully reminds us that historical argument, like art, is never merely factual and is rarely disinterested.

Arguing that Shylock is a villain, that Shakespeare and his audiences were, to a man, prejudiced against Jews, and that the practice of usury was universally reviled, though practised none the less, E. E. Stoll is representative in his naïve confidence in Shakespeare's 'thoroughly Elizabethan taste', 'the popular imagination', 'the established traditions' and so on. Stoll exhibits, too, a tendency to argue from origins, and in doing so, to argue *The Merchant of Venice* back to the cruder simplicities of its antecedents. Thus Shylock is dragged back to the Jews of medieval iconography and the Mystery plays, and to the Barabas of Marlowe's cruder, more farcical *Jew of Malta*—though, as Stoll doesn't note, the Christians in that play are not shown much more favourably than Barabas himself. But, even allowing that Stoll's characterisation of the times is predominantly accurate, *The Merchant of Venice* may be a response to, as well as a reflection of, popular beliefs and prejudices (Stoll 1927, pp. 255-336).

One particularly neat example of history's untidiness, its tendency to complicate rather than clarify, lies in Renaissance England's attitudes to usury, an issue central to our play. But even that is not strictly true. Rather oddly, critical interpretation of *The Merchant of Venice* so often circles around the issue of usury when, in fact, no transaction involving usury occurs in the dramatic action of the play. (See, for example, E. C. Pettet, 'The Merchant of Venice and the Problem of Usury', in Wilders 1969, pp. 100-13.) Shylock is by profession an usurer, although we never see him behaving as one on stage, and none of the numerous financial dealings and misdealings in the play involve usury. Yet characters within the play judge, or prejudge, Shylock by his profession rather than by his immediate actions, and critics beyond the play—especially those who see Shylock as the villain of the piece but wish to defend the play from accusations of anti-Semitism—maintain that emphasis. This phenomenon is but one of the play's examples of the workings of prejudice and its infectiousness: judgements are formed on the evidence of, or hearsay about, the past, and such judgemental habits preclude the possibility of innocence in the present and particular. Yet it remains true that Shylock is an usurer and that usury is important to the play, even if that importance has been exaggerated. History proves less helpful than it might, and, like the play, displays an ambiguous and equivocal attitude to usury.

In 1571 English law legalised usury, despite the evidence that it was ruining the more profligate among the landed gentry caught out by the inflation attendant on the rise of commerce. In 1572 Thomas Wilson published his *Discourse Upon Usury* which reiterates, energetically and at length, medieval and religious hostility to the practice of usury. And this is a text much favoured by purveyors of Elizabethan World Pictures, despite, it seems, Elizabethan practice. But in the third edition of his *Essays*, published in 1625, Francis Bacon, writing 'Of Usury', takes a more sanguine and balanced view. He argues that, given human frailty, usury is a necessity and discovers not merely the disadvantages but the benefits of the practice. Between Wilson and Bacon comes *The Merchant of Venice*, written at some time between 1596 and 1598. It would seem that in their actions, in their discursive writings, and, indeed, in their plays, these Elizabethans do not take an unequivocally black view of usury.

In this example I am gesturing briefly at the intellectual and social history of Renaissance England. But *which* history are we to appeal to? If we are seeking the security of a context for *The Merchant of Venice* then geography conspires with history to augment our difficulties. Do we look to Shakespeare's England? Or to the history of Venice? Or, more problematically still, to the history of Belmont? Are we not rather dealing with a coalescing of various kinds of history and fiction which occurs within the dramatist's mind and which we are more likely to recover from an examination of the play, than from history books? And if we look beyond Shakespeare to the history of his audience, we might wonder whether Shakespeare plays *to* his audience's assumptions, or plays *against* them or, most likely, does both in his usual complex way.

Nevertheless, *The Merchant of Venice* is not ahistorical. Indeed, it is itself an historical document which *contains* history's complexities and ambiguities—although the play is not *merely* that. But *The Merchant of Venice* isn't autonomous either, and if we need a context for the play, then what follows here suggests that Shakespeare's larger *oeuvre* answers most fully to that need. Of the same historical period, created by the same mind, and in the same literary mode, Shakespeare's other plays illuminate *The Merchant of Venice* but do violence neither to its individuality nor its complexity.

RACE

Marion D. Perret (essay date 1988)

SOURCE: "Shakespeare's Jew: Preconception and Performance," in *Shakespeare Studies,* Vol. XX, 1988, pp. 261-68.

[*In the essay below, Perret asserts that modern directors of* The Merchant of Venice *are wrong in worrying about Shakespeare's anti-Semitism, and claims that the playwright might in fact have been parodying his audience's views rather than pandering to them.*]

Because Bernard Beckerman was so interested in the theater, for this panel on "*The Merchant of Venice:* Problems of Influence" I have chosen to consider some ways in which preconceptions about Jews in Shakespeare's time and ours have influenced performance. My hope is that approaching the play through the preconceptions of its audience can reveal something about how the play, if not the playwright, works and shed some light on the problem of Shakespeare's supposed anti-Semitism.

Underlying my consideration are two assumptions. The first is that Shakespeare, consciously or unconsciously, would have taken his audience's preconceptions into account in shaping both text and performance of *The Merchant of Venice*. The second is that most Elizabethan playgoers and many modern ones would equate the performance they see with Shakespeare's text. In the theater the play is, effectively, what the audience sees played; what they see played depends partly upon what they notice, and what they notice depends upon their preconceptions.

As a practical man of the theater, Shakespeare must have recognized that the audience of *The Merchant of Venice* would bring to the playhouse certain assumptions about Jews, whom the Elizabethans would have encountered only as Marranos, apparent converts to Christianity who practiced their old faith secretly (Roth 139-43). Shakespeare would have known that most in his audience thought Jews cold-hearted usurers and crucifiers of Christ. That anti-Semitism in Shakespeare's day was not based on race

(Echeruo 5-8) is important because it explains why the Elizabethans could respond to some actions, such as Shylock's conversion under pressure, differently than we do. As Jonathan Miller notes, "if the Jew's fault stems from his failure to acknowledge Jesus as the Messiah," that fault disappears when he consents to becoming a Christian (821). The Elizabethan playgoers would have paid attention not to Shylock's race but to his occupation and his religion; to both their immediate response would have been negative.

Although Shakespeare may have written the play to capitalize on excitement stirred up by Marlowe's *The Jew of Malta* and the trial of Dr. Lopez, this does not necessarily mean that Shakespeare intended to present his Jew as stereotypically villainous—he may instead have felt a need to show that Jews are men rather than monsters. Nor does it necessarily mean that Shakespeare intended to focus on the nature of the Jew rather than on the nature of the Christian. Marrano or Puritan, usurers in Elizabethan England were Christian, allowed by the law of 1571 to charge ten percent interest (Pettet 21); in *The Description of England* (1587) William Harrison speaks of usury as "a trade brought in by the Jews, now perfectly practiced almost by every Christian and so commonly that he is accounted but for a fool that doth lend this money for nothing" (as quoted in Danson 146). Theatergoers stimulated by the play into thinking about the abuse of usury would be likely to reflect as much upon the cruelty of English Christians as upon the cruelty of a Venetian Jew.

The stir caused by *The Jew of Malta* and the trial of Dr. Lopez does mean, however, that Shakespeare's audience had strong preconceptions of the Jew for the playwright to work with or against. Playgoers would take for granted ways in which the presentation of the Jew fit their preconceived image. Playgoers attentive enough to note ways in which the Jew did not fit their stereotype—such as Shylock's sentimental attachment to the ring given him by Leah before their marriage—would be struck by these deviations. Paradoxically, thinking in terms of stereotypes could lead the playgoer away from thinking in terms of stereotypes.

The text does not prepare playgoers to see a moneylender in Jewish gaberdine; Shylock's entrance in I.iii in exotic garb and makeup would have startled the first audience into attention. Their preconceptions about Jews, confirmed by Shylock's aside explaining his hatred of Antonio, would lead them to hear more sinister undertones to Shylock's offer than Antonio does. Shakespeare has carefully set up the sequence of what the moneylender tells us to stress certain preconceptions more than others. Shylock's first words emphasize money, and his first aside announces that he hates the merchant more for business reasons than for religious ones. Shylock's long tale about how Jacob made ewes breed, "inserted to make interest good," irritates Antonio into insisting that the Jew get to the point; this should make the audience listen carefully for that point and consider not only how unconvincing the analogy is but also how convincing "Hath a dog money?" is. Shylock's point, "Is it possible / A cur can lend three thousand ducats?" is that self-interest should teach us to be humane to others, regardless of religion. Antonio's "The devil can cite Scripture for his purpose" warns the playgoers not to judge characters only by what they say, especially by what they say about religion. The way Shakespeare in I.iii plays with preconceptions about Jews and usurers works against our seeing religion as the central issue here. Because Shylock's first scene gives the moneylender as well as the merchant an opportunity to declare his feelings about the Jew's occupation and religion, Shylock, as Danson observes, "can be judged on the basis of what he will do in the course of the play, rather than on preconceived notions" (150).

Though *The Merchant of Venice* pleased King James so much that he ordered it played a second time during Shrovetide 1605 (Chambers 2: 332), we know almost nothing about how the play was originally presented and very little about how the audience perceived it. This is particularly frustrating because, as Styan points out, Shakespeare may have functioned like a modern director in shaping the performance (53), which would thus give us a clue as to his auctorial intentions. What contemporary evidence we have suggests that Shylock had theatrical impact out of proportion to the number of scenes in which he appears, but that this impact was not enough to change the play from comedy to tragicomedy or to give the bond plot predominance over the love plot.

There is no Elizabethan evidence that Shylock was perceived as a strong tragic element; the head- and running-titles of the first quarto (1600) call the play a "comicall Historie" (Chambers 1: 368), and Mere's list in *Palladis Tamia* (1598) includes it among the comedies. That the play was regarded as a comedy does not, however, mean that Shylock was originally presented as a comic villain, as Doggett played him in 1701, although the sight of Shylock with false nose and red wig and beard would work against serious or sympathetic consideration. Stage tradition cannot be indiscriminately relied upon in reconstructing the original performance. The tradition "that Shylock was intended as a comic figure," Grebanier points out, "dates from Granville's perversion of the play" (313). The tradition that Richard Burbage was the first Shylock is questionable because the sole authority for it is some lines, presumably forged, added by Collier to the *Elegy on the Death of Richard Burbadge* (Furness 370). Baldwin, in working out the roles acted by each member of Shakespeare's company, assigns Shylock not to Burbage but to Thomas Pope, the "high comedian and gruff villain" of the company (246).

We might know more about Shakespeare's intent if we knew who played Shylock. If Burbage, the leading actor, played Shylock rather than Bassanio, the audience would give more, and more careful, attention to the Jew. Regardless of who played Shylock, the plot guarantees dramatic importance to the moneylender, although he appears in only five of the twenty scenes, and Shakespeare develops the moneylender's character more fully than did his source *Il Pecorone*.

Whatever the playwright's intention, that the Elizabethans found Shylock a powerful presence onstage is sugested by the title page of the first quarto, which announces "The most excellent Historie of the Merchant of Venice. With the extreame crueltie of Shylocke the Jewe towards the sayd Merchant, in cutting a just pound of his flesh: and the obtayning of Portia by the choyse of three chests." Shylock is immediately individualized, pointed out by name, while Antonio, who gives the play its title, is referred to simply by his occupation.

Even so, the title page in no way indicates either that the play is focused on Shylock or that Shylock is seen as an opposite to Portia, the only other character accorded a name. The description calls attention to the casket scene rather than to Portia herself or to the intensely dramatic courtroom scene, although this must have appealed greatly in that litigious age. Instead of balancing Shylock's cruelty against Portia's charity or cleverness, the subtitles refer to Shylock's "crueltie" and Bassanio's "obtayning" of Portia—the polarity of values we have learned to see the characters as representing (Old Law/New Law, Justice/Mercy, getting/giving) appears not to have struck the Elizabethans as forcefully as it strikes us. Only in relation to Shylock does the title page draw on stereotypes: Shylock is referred to not as moneylender but as Jew, which for an Elizabethan effectively identifies his occupation, and the dominant impression of "extreame crueltie," a popular preconception about money lenders, Jewish or Gentile, has eclipsed the fact that Shylock does not actually cut any flesh.

We naturally know more about modern preconceptions and performances than about those of the Elizabethans. Preconceptions about how Shylock should be treated come from several sources: our own experience and belief; our reading about the play; our culture's acceptance of religious pluralism and rejection of the horrors of the Holocaust. Most of what we know invites us to extend sympathy to Shylock, so that as Hunter observes, we tend to "push modern reactions to modern anti-Semitism into a past where they do not belong" (66). When reading Shakespeare, we make an effort to subordinate our preconceptions to Elizabethan ones, but while watching Shakespeare, we instinctively react as though "what Shakespeare intended does not matter—what matters is what he did"—whether or not we go on to assert, as Stoll does, that "we have as good a right as Shakespeare to our opinion of Shylock" (331). Because current preconceptions are different from the Elizabethan ones, productions of *The Merchant of Venice* today are often shaped defensively. Directors have to deal with our assumption or fear that the play is anti-Semitic; accusations of prejudice dog the play because our consciousness, scarred by modern persecution of the Jews, encourages a stubborn tendency to see this Jew as symbolic of all Jews.

A major reason playgoers persist in seeing *The Merchant of Venice* primarily in terms of Jew against Christian, or, more precisely, of Christians against the Jew, is that Shylock encourages others to regard him as the victim of religious persecution (Grebanier 179). Our sense of his being persecuted because of his faith comes partly from historical fact, partly from the way he manipulates our perception of the cause of mistreatment, and partly from our preconceptions, which lead us to undervalue the second of the two reasons, religious and economic, he gives for his seeking revenge. To the Elizabethans it mattered little whether Shakespeare presents the Jew as villainous because he is a usurer or villainous because he is a Jew. To us it matters a great deal. Since we assume that interest will be asked when money is lent and we take commercial competitiveness (but not ethical values) for granted, we pay more attention to the religious motive Shylock stresses to the Christians than to the economic motive he stresses to his fellow Jews—which the text actually emphasizes, both in number of lines and in number of characters recognizing this motivation.

This tendency to separate economic motivation, that does not catch our attention or disturb us, from religious motivation, that does, leads many playgoers to hear in Shylock's "Hath not a Jew eyes?" a plea by one man on behalf of his race, without recognizing how the moneylender shifts the ground of offense to justify his personal desire for revenge. Willy-nilly, the modern audience throws on Shylock the burden of epitomizing a long-suffering people. Shylock invites us to respond this way by adopting in the presence of Christians the attitude of Persecuted Jew. That he has been mistreated by the Christians is made clear early in the play—Antonio, who has spat upon Shylock's Jewish gaberdine, declares he may do so again—yet it is also made clear that Antonio scorns Shylock not because Shylock is an enemy of Christ but because Shylock is a usurer. Our preconceptions keep us from noting that when no Christian is around, Shylock acts like a human being who just happens to be a Jew; he no longer acts the victim of anti-Semitism.

This inability to see Shylock simply as an individual causes a disquieting clash between our preconceptions about Shakespeare and our preconceptions about Jews. None of us likes to think that our Shakespeare, Shakespeare of the comprehensive humanity, could be prejudiced. Yet Shylock's inviting us to regard him as scorned simply because he is a Jew strikes a sensitive spot in playgoers haunted by memories of the Holocaust. Understandably supersensitive, playgoers may perceive an unflattering presentation of this particular Jew as an unflattering representation of all Jews and mistreatment of the Jew by other characters as mistreatment by the playwright. To view IV.i as primarily the destroying of Shylock and only incidentally the rescuing of Antonio is to see what happens through Shylock's eyes. We need to remember that Shakespeare is neither Gratiano nor Shylock. Shakespeare, innocent of modern history and not responsible for our preconceptions, gives us a Jew who is persecutor as well as

Colm Feore as Salerio, Stephen Russell as Gratiano, Shaun Austin-Olsen as Solanio, and John Neville as Shylock in the 1984 Stratford Festival production of The Merchant of Venice.

persecuted and who under pressure chooses to give up his religion rather than his money. If the audience could see Shylock as a human being who is also a Jew, rather than as *the* Jew, those who put on the play would be freer to find Shylock's rightful place in the delicate balance of the drama.

Long before the Holocaust, in 1911, Stoll declared that "on the popular stage . . . Shylock must be played pretty much as Irving played him," that is, as a tragic figure, "though this is not Shakespeare's Shylock" (334). Only five years ago the *New York Times* reported that "many Shakespearean scholars and Jewish critics agree that it is not so much the play itself as how it is played that really matters" (Kakutani 30), presumably because performance can vindicate their preconception of Shakespeare as too large of soul and sympathy to have written an anti-Semitic play. What keeps *The Merchant of Venice* onstage today seems to be less its greatness than the challenge of presenting it in ways that diminish in performance what can be perceived as bias in the text.

There are a number of strategies for making our sympathy for Shylock seem evoked by Shakespeare. Interpretive cutting can refocus the play. In the nineteenth century the last act was frequently omitted, so the play in effect ended with the exit of Shylock, broken. Jonathan Miller's 1970 production at the National Theatre, which starred Laurence Olivier as Shylock, made the Jew almost a tragic hero by changing the primary motive for his vengefulness. This was accomplished by eliminating the explanations Shakespeare gives him in I.iii.39-42,

> I hate him for he is a Christian,
> But more, for that in low simplicity
> He lends out money gratis, and brings down
> The rate of usance here with us in Venice,

and in III.i.119-21: "I will have the heart of him, if he forfeit; for, were he out of Venice, I can make what merchandise I will." Without these lines Shylock becomes more sympathetic; it appears that he seeks Antonio's heart not because the merchant has undercut his business but because his own heart, his daughter Jessica, has been stolen from him by one of Antonio's set. For those who saw the National Theatre production without a fresh memory of the play, the loving Shylock created by interpretive cutting was Shakespeare's Shylock.

Playing against the text as well as playing with the text reshapes our sense of Shakespeare's Shylock. For example, in the version of this production televised in 1974, III.i is carefully shaped to create sympathy through sentimental vignettes of a Jew more sinned against than sinning. Shylock, hearing of the ring traded for a monkey, stoops over his wife's picture and kisses it, sobbing. Opening a desk drawer, he takes out a prayer shawl, kisses it and puts it on, covers his eyes, then lifts them to heaven. The words that accompany these actions, "I will have the heart of him," are overpowered by the striking visual images insisting that Shylock is a devout man driven to hate by the loss of a loved one. We are invited to pity the prayer-shawled figure rocking back and forth in speechless grief without reflecting upon the words just uttered. We easily forget what we hear, that Shylock meets Tubal at the synagogue not to worship but to plan the legal butchering of a human being. We recall instead what we see, Shylock the loving father, the devoted husband, the devout man (Perret 150). Shylock is unquestionably the focus of sympathy in this production.

Yet another strategy for avoiding any appearance of modern anti-Semitism, blackening the Christians rather than whitewashing the Jew, is used by Miller in his 1981 BBC production. As he points out in his introduction for television, "The Christians are shown to be just as merciless and heartless as the unjust Shylock." The audience is forced to recognize that the inclination to torture knows no religious boundaries by the presentation of III.i, where the Christians cruelly make sport of a Jew whom they accuse of cruelty, and IV.i, where a Jew torments a Christian by insisting on the letter of the law, then is tormented by another Christian in the same way. To see Solanio lunge mockingly at Shylock's genitals when the Jew complains of the "rebellion" of his "flesh," then Salerio lock his arm around Shylock's neck, choking off protest, is to be shocked into feeling for the Jew's vulnerable humanity. To see Portia standing behind Shylock, her hand holding his on the knife, insisting as he had insisted that he take his pound of flesh, is to be shocked into thinking about the Christian's inhumanity.

The approach of favoring neither Christian nor Jew calls attention to rather than mutilates what is in the text. While the insistent emphasis on flaws can make the characters and their world so unattractive that the comedy loses any sense of joy and light, as did the 1973 Rabb production (Novick 1, 5), the 1981 BBC production shows that such heaviness is not necessary. That we have, in general, come but a little distance from the Elizabethan expectation that performance should indulge preconceptions is suggested by the kind of objections I have heard made to the BBC production. Some felt the Jew should have been presented more positively, given more dignity; none felt the Christians should have been presented less negatively. The time is yet to come when performances of *The Merchant of Venice,* shaped without reference to the audience's preconceptions about Jews, can fully realize the text's painful richness.

Works Consulted

Baldwin, Thomas Whitfield. *The Organization and Personnel of the Shakespearean Company.* Princeton: Princeton Univ. Press, 1927.

Chambers, E. K. *William Shakespeare: A Study of Facts and Problems.* 2 vols. Oxford: Clarendon, 1930.

Danson, Laurence. *The Harmonies or "The Merchant of Venice."* New Haven: Yale Univ. Press, 1978.

Echeruo, Michael J. C. "Shylock and the 'Conditioned Imagination': A Reinterpretation." *Shakespeare Quarterly* 22 (1971): 3-15.

Furness, Horace Howard, ed. *The Merchant of Venice. A New Variorum Edition of Shakespeare.* 13th. ed. Philadelphia: Lippincott, 1888.

Hunter, G. K. *Dramatic Identities and Cultural Tradition: Studies in Shakespeare and His Contemporaries.* New York: Barnes & Noble, 1978.

Grebanier, Bernard. *The Truth about Shylock.* New York: Random House, 1962.

Kakutani, Michiko. "Debate Over Shylock Simmers Once Again." *New York Times,* 22 Feb. 1981, pt. 2: 1, 30.

Lelyveld, Toby B. *Shylock on the Stage.* Cleveland: Western Reserve Press, 1960.

Miller, Jonathan. "Shakespeare and the Modern Director." In *William Shakespeare: His World, His Work, His Influence.* Ed. John F. Andrews. 3 vols. New York: Scribners, 1985. 815-22.

Novick, Julius. *New York Times,* 11 March 1973, pt. 2: 1, 5.

Perret, Marion D. "Shakespeare and Anti-Semitism: Two Television Versions of *The Merchant of Venice." Mosaic* 16 (1983): 146-63.

Pettet, E. C. "*The Merchant of Venice* and the Problem of Usury." *Essays and Studies* 31 (1946): 19-33.

Roth, Cecil. *A History of the Jews in England.* 3rd ed. Oxford: Clarendon Press, 1964.

Shakespeare, William. *The Merchant of Venice. The Complete Works of Shakespeare.* Ed. David Bevington. 3rd ed. Glenview: Scott, 1980. 260-91.

Stoll, Elmer Edgar. *Shakespeare Studies.* New York: Ungar, 1942.

Styan, J. L. *Shakespeare's Stagecraft.* Cambridge, Eng.: Cambridge Univ. Press, 1967.

Kim F. Hall (essay date 1992)

SOURCE: "Guess Who's Coming to Dinner? Colonization and Miscegenation in *The Merchant of Venice*," in *Renaissance Drama,* Vol. XXIII, n.s., 1992, pp. 87-111.

[*In the essay below, Hall focuses on lines in Act Three of* The Merchant of Venice *which describe Launcelot's impregnation of a black woman. Hall argues that this brief passage underscores a major theme of the play: the fear of racial intermingling that occurs when a country such as Elizabethan England makes imperialistic inroads into other countries.*]

Samuel Purchas introduces his popular collection of travel narratives, *Purchas His Pilgrimes* (the 1625 sequel to Richard Hakluyt's *Principal Voyages),* by recounting the virtues of trade. He equates the benefits of navigation with Christian charity and leads his reader into the collection proper by envisioning a world converted to Protestantism:

> . . . and the chiefest charitie is that which is most common; nor is there any more common then this of Navigation, where one man is not good to another man, but so many Nations as so many persons hold commerce and intercourse of amity withall; . . . the West with the East, and the remotest parts of the world are joyned in one band of humanitie; and why not also of Christianitie? Sidon and Sion, Jew and Gentile, Christian and Ethnike, as in this typicall storie? that as there is one Lord, one Faith, one Baptisme, one Body, one Spirit, one Inheritance, one God and Father, so there may be thus one Church truly Catholike, One Pastor and one Sheepfold?
>
> (1: 56)

Charity may not begin at home, but it certainly ends up there, as the charitable cause of conversion redounds to the economic benefit of the English world. The initial ideal of "commerce and intercourse of amity" among many types of men is replaced by a vision of global unity that denies difference just as Purchas's own language does. (The singular construction ["one Lord, one Faith"] subsumes difference when it replaces the "and" that allows differences to exist simultaneously ["Jew and Gentile"].) English trade, rather than fostering a mixing of cultures, will eradicate religious differences, as well as cultural and gender differences, under one patriarchal God.

Purchas's glorified version of the end of English colonization similarly serves to efface the multivalent anxieties over cross-cultural interaction that permeate English fictions of international trade. In uniting economics and Christian values, Purchas highlights the fact that colonial trade involves not only economic transactions, but cultural and political exchange as well. The anthropologist Gayle Rubin notes in her influential feminist critique of Lévi-Strauss, "Kinship and marriage are always parts of total social systems, and are always tied into economic and political arrangements" (207). Likewise, the exchange of goods (or even the circulation of money) across cultural borders always contains the possibility of other forms of exchange between different cultures. Associations between marriage, kinship, property, and economics become increasingly anxiety-ridden as traditional social structures (such as marriage) are extended when England develops commercial ties across the globe. Extolling the homogenizing influence of trade suggests that English trade will turn a world of difference into a world of Protestant similitude. However, it leaves unspoken the more threatening possibility—that English identity will be subsumed under foreign difference.

It is this problem of "commerce and intercourse," of commercial interaction inevitably fostering social and sexual contact, that underlies representations of miscegenation in the early modern period.[1] In addition to addressing domestic anxieties about the proper organization of male and female (particularly about the uncontrolled desires of women), the appearance of miscegenation in plays responds to growing concerns over English national identity and culture as England develops political and economic ties with foreign (and "racially" different) nations. This essay will draw on Purchas's dual sense of the all-encompassing nature of trade encounters and colonialism's alleged homogenizing power to suggest the significance of a brief instance of miscegenation in Shakespeare that has been insistently ignored by critics.

Although the most central—and most commented on—problem of difference and trade in *The Merchant of Venice* is between Jew and Christian, more general anxieties about the problem of difference within economic exchange are encapsulated in an instance of miscegenation never staged. In act 3, the audience witnesses a joking interchange between Shylock's servant, Launcelot, and Lorenzo and Jessica about their mixed marriage:

> JES.
> Nay, you need not fear us Lorenzo, Launcelot and I are out,—he tells me flatly that there's no mercy for me in heaven, because I am a Jew's daughter: and he says that you are no good member of the commonwealth, for in converting Jews to Christians, you raise the price of pork.
> LOR.
> I shall answer that better to the commonwealth than you can the getting up of the negro's belly: the Moor is with child by you Launcelot!
> LAUN.
> It is much that the Moor should be more than reason: but if she be less than an honest woman, she is indeed more than I took her for.
>
> (3.5.28-39)

The Arden edition of *Merchant* helpfully notes that "this passage has not been explained" and suggests, "Perhaps it was introduced simply for the sake of the elaborate pun on Moor/more" (99n35). Their joking conversation no doubt parodically reflects the investment of the commonwealth in sexual practices. Nonetheless, it also begs the question of the difference between Lorenzo's liaison with a Jew and Launcelot's with a Moor. The Renaissance stage abounds with jokes about bastards: if Launcelot's fault was merely the getting of another, there would be no reason to emphasize that this invisible woman is a Moor. In his *Black Face, Maligned Race,* Anthony Barthelemy notes that this exchange reflects ideas of the licentiousness of the black woman typical of the time (124).[2] However, it may be that this pregnant, unheard, unnamed, and unseen (at least by critics) black woman is a silent symbol for the economic and racial politics of *The Merchant of Venice*. She exposes an intricately wrought nexus of anxieties over gender, race, religion, and economics (fueled by the push of imperial/mercantile expansion) which surrounds the various possibilities of miscegenation raised in the play.

II

Before moving into the play itself, I would like to sketch out some of these anxieties over miscegenation by examining one of the play's possible "sub-texts" (Jameson 81). In 1596, despite her earlier support of English piracy in the slave trade, Queen Elizabeth expressed concern over the presence of blacks in the realm. She issued a proclamation to the Lord Mayor of London which states her "understanding that there are of late divers blackmoores brought into this realme, of which kinde of people there are allready here to manie" (qtd. in Fryer 10) and demands that blacks recently brought to the realm be rounded up and returned. This effort was evidently not very successful, as she followed up that proclamation with another order of expulsion:

> . . . whereas the Queen's Majesty, tendering the good and welfare of her own natural subjects greatly distressed in these hard times of dearth, is highly discontented to understand the great numbers of Negars and Blackamoors which (as she is informed) are crept into this realm since the troubles between Her Highness and the King of Spain, who are fostered and relieved here to the great annoyance of her own liege people that want the relief which those people consume; as also for that the most of them are infidels, having no understanding of Christ or his Gospel, hath given especial commandment that the said kind of people should be with all speed avoided and discharged out of this Her Majesty's dominions. . . . And if there shall be any person or persons which are possessed of any such Blackamoors that refuse to deliver them in sort as aforesaid, then we require you to call them before you and to advise and persuade them by all good means to satisfy Her Majesty's pleasure therein; which if they shall eftsoons willfully and obstinately refuse, we pray you then to certify their names unto us, to the end Her Majesty may take such further course therein as it shall seem best in her princely wisdom.
>
> (Qtd. in Jones, *Elizabethan Image* 20-21)[3]

While such critical attention as has been paid to this document concentrates on the attempt to discharge Moors from the realm and uses the attempt itself to prove the existence of a viable black presence in England (Newman, "And wash the Ethiop white" 148), the terms of the proclamation demand special attention. The image of large numbers of Moors having "crept into this realm" suggests that they suddenly appeared of their own volition (despite having been "fostered and relieved" here by unnamed residents).[4] The proclamation then lays the fault of this invasion at the foot of Spain, a country already suspect for its past history of interracial alliance.[5] The rest of the document is concerned to prevent contact between these "creeping" invaders and "her own liege" people despite its contradictory contention that Elizabeth's own subjects are the ones "possessed" of blackamoors to the detriment of the state.

Although chronic food shortages occurred throughout Elizabeth's reign and certainly seemed to be a goad to plantation and exploration, her naming of "these hard times of dearth" suggests that both of the expulsions occurred in the context of very immediate state concerns. England from 1594 to 1597 saw dramatic declines in grain harvests (the staple of the lower-class diet), culminating in the famine of 1597. Indeed, much of northern Europe (although, interestingly, not Italy) suffered from famine and starvation from 1595 to 1597. Although the famine in England hit hardest in the northwestern parishes, its effects were felt throughout the realm, as Andrew Appleby notes, "It is abundantly clear, however, that the grain harvest was the heart of the English economy . . . and that its malfunctions were felt, with disastrous results, throughout the kingdom" (137). Private citizens, the Privy Council, and the general public showed concern over the unavailability of bread even in the earliest of those years. These "dear years" carried with them a range of other social dislocations: a reduction in baptismal and marriage rates, a rise in mortality and civil unrest, and, significantly, the unemployment of servant classes. Key government measures were issued in proximity to both expulsions and indicate that the famine generated a degree of class conflict. Elizabeth's order to make starch from bran rather than grain needed for food was issued in the same month as the first order of expulsion. Another proclamation, ending price-fixing and compelling the landed classes to remain in the counties because "her majesty had thus determined for relief of her people to stay all good householders in their countries, there in charitable sort to keep hospitality" (Hughes and Larkin 172), was issued a few months later.

Equally important in the expulsion order is the reference to the religion (or lack of religion) of the Moors, which is based on the supposition that they are a logical group to cut off from state resources because they have "no understanding of Christ or his Gospel." In this time of crisis Christianity becomes the prerequisite for access to limited resources. Certainly, Elizabeth's evocation of the religious difference of the Moor would seem to support the common view that religion, not race, is the defining mark of difference in early modern England.[6] I would argue, however, that even though religion is given as a compelling reason for excluding Moors, emphasizing religious difference only clouds the political reality that the Moors' visibility in the culture made them a viable target for exclusion. In other words, it is their physical difference *in association with cultural differences* (a combination that is the primary basis for the category "race") that provokes their exclusion—not just their religion.

In Elizabeth's proclamation we see what may be a source of the threat posed by Launcelot's Moor. In times of economic stress, visible minorities very often become the scapegoat for national problems. The proclamation shares with *Merchant* an alarm over unregulated consumption. Launcelot's evocation of the scarcity of food through his jesting over the rising price of pork reveals a similar unease over limited resources. Thus, famine, one of the more specific rationales for English colonial plantation and expansion, becomes here associated with the black woman. Ultimately both texts draw on and reproduce the same racial stereotype. Just as the image of the black female as consumer of state resources in the twentieth-century United States is statistically inaccurate but politically powerful, so may the black presence have been a threat (albeit small) to white European labor, which is magnified by its very visibility.[7] This sense of privation produces an economic imperative in the play, which insists on the exclusion of racial, religious, and cultural difference. With the finite resources of a Venetian (or Elizabethan) society reserved for the wealthy elite, the offspring of Launcelot and the Moor presents a triple threat that in this world is perceived as a crime against the state. Their alliance is perhaps even more suspect than the ominous possibility of a marriage between Portia and the prince of Morocco, since it would produce a half-black, half-Christian child from the already starving lower classes who threatens to upset the desired balance of consumption. The pun on "Moor/more" further supports this image of the black woman as both consuming and expanding and is particularly striking in a play where the central image is the literal taking of flesh and where Christian males worry throughout about having "less."

The acute sense of privation amid plenty is signaled through *Merchant*'s ubiquitous images of starvation that are interwoven with the incessant eating in the play. Walter Cohen sees Launcelot as integral to the play and notes in particular the way he "systematically and wittily misconstrues Lorenzo's apparently straightforward order that the kitchen staff 'prepare for dinner!'" (210). Launcelot's first move is to remind Lorenzo of the servants' hunger: "they all have stomachs" (3.5.44). Earlier, he claims that he is starving in Shylock's employ: "I am famish'd in his service. You may tell every finger I have with my ribs" (2.2.101-03). Shylock's version, "The patch is kind enough, but a huge feeder" (2.5.45), may reinforce the idea that these outsiders literally starve rightful citizens, yet it also suggests a Christian appetite out of control. Bassanio, describing his poor finances, suggests bulk without sustenance in saying that he lost wealth, "By something showing a more swelling port / Than my faint means would grant continuance" (1.1.124-25). Finally, Antonio, in reminding Solanio of Venice's strict commercial laws, laments, "These griefs and losses have so bated me / That I shall hardly spare a pound of flesh / Tomorrow, to my bloody creditor" (3.3.32-34).

The associations with eating and starvation link outsiders, particularly Shylock, with one of the most compelling tropes of colonialist discourse: the cannibal.[8] Cannibalism was a source of as much anxiety as fascination for the traveler; it seemed to be one of the final lines drawn between the savage Other and the civilized self (Cheyfitz 42; Hulme 81-83; Kilgour 5-7). The reasons given for imperial plunder by Bertoldo in Philip Massinger's *The Maid of Honour* suggest that much of this obsession springs from a sense that the dividing line is not as clear as one might like:

> Nature did
> Designe us to be warriours, and to breake through
> Our ring the sea, by which we are inviron'd;
> And we by force must fetch in what is wanting,
> Or precious to us. Adde to this, wee are
> A populous nation, and increase so fast,
> That if we by our providence, are not sent
> Abroad in colonies, or fall by the sword,
> Not *Sicilie* (though now, it were more fruitfull,
> Then when 'twas stil'd the granary of great *Rome*)
> Can yeeld our numerous frie bread, we must starve,
> Or eat up one another.
>
> (1.1.202-13)

In specifically ascribing to the English an aggression and ferocity that are the essence of European definitions of the cannibal (Hulme 83), Bertoldo hints at the tentativeness of that division. The movement of the passage also suggests a blurring of boundaries: the opening image of the breach of England's geographic insularity which releases the energies of a warlike nation rapidly moves into an evocation of violent, desperate want which could easily turn in upon itself. Massinger skates a fine line between identity and difference in allowing his character to suggest that imperial expansion is the only thing separating the civilized Englishman from the cannibal and that the dangers of cannibalism lie on either side of England's borders. His metaphor is similar to an earlier and more specific reference to English want in Richard Hakluyt's *Discourse of Western Planting*. In this attempt to persuade Elizabeth to adopt a plantation policy, Hakluyt associates cannibalism with another marginalized group—the unemployed. He warns Elizabeth:

> But wee for all the Statutes that hitherto can be devised, and the sharpe execution of the same in poonishinge idle and lazye persons for wante of sufficient occasion of honest employment cannot deliver our common wealthe from multitudes of loyterers and idle vagabondes. . . . [W]e are growen more populous than ever heretofore: So that nowe there are of every arte and science so many, that they can hardly lyve one by another, nay rather they are readie to eate upp one another.
>
> (234)

The troping of cannibalism links actual shortages of food with the need to promote colonial trade in a way that also provides a compelling metaphor for the loss of communal identity in such trade. The desire to make contact with and to exploit Others always carries with it the possibility of engulfment. Such fears of erasure are embedded in metaphors of eating, but the figure of the cannibal specifically locates such fears within a framework of colonial trade and religious difference.

The language of eating in *The Merchant of Venice* situates Shylock within this framework by merging images of cannibalism with older accusations of blood libel. He claims, "But yet I'll go in hate, to feed upon / The prodigal Christian," and Gratiano describes him, "thy currish spirit / Govern'd a wolf, who hang'd for human slaughter—" (4.1.133-35).[9] According to Maggie Kilgour, feeding from (or eating with) the Other is a perilous involvement which carries the risk of being eaten by the Other:[10]

> To eat in a country is potentially to be eaten by it, to enter into a false identification by being absorbed by a foreign culture—what we call "going native"—and so be prevented from returning to a place of origin in which one is truly at home. The opposite of returning to one's own hearth is ultimately to be subsumed totally by a hostile host.
>
> (23)

Shylock's reluctance to eat with the Christians displays the fear of "be[ing] subsumed . . . by a hostile host," but in terms that ratify the reciprocal Christian fear of being consumed by a guest/alien who has been allowed into the home/country. Economic exchanges with an outsider like Shylock open up Venice to sexual and commercial intercourse with strangers; this breach brings with it the threat of economic upheaval and foreign invasion. Social activities such as eating and marriage resonate because of the already permeable borders of the Venetian economy. In defending his insistence on the completion of a legal bond, Shylock comments on the assumed rights of the Venetians to "bond" and to preserve their racial purity in a speech laden with references to problematic communal activities:

> You have among you many a purchas'd slave,
> Which (like your asses, and your dogs and mules)
> You use in abject and in slavish parts,
> Because you bought them,—shall I say to you,
> Let them be free, *marry them to your heirs?*
> Why sweat they under burthens? let their beds
> Be made as soft as yours, and let their palates
> Be season'd with such viands?
>
> (4.1.90-97; emphasis added)

Rhetorically, Shylock exposes the fears of a chauvinist culture by revealing the Venetians' problematic economic position, suggesting that, in such an open system, the slaves among them may just as well become sons-in-law.[11] The passage may also tie the problem of eating with colonial trade in the reminder ("let their palates / Be season'd with such viands") that the search for spices for aristocratic palates provided much of the momentum for foreign trade. His questions allow for a provocative glance at Queen Elizabeth's dilemma. Producers of labor are also consumers, and the blacks that she wants to exile are a presence precisely because of the increased economic expansion she supported.

As critics have often noted, the language of commerce and trade permeates the Venetian world. This mercantile vocabulary is tied to an erotic vocabulary in much the same way as Titania's description of her Indian votress in *A Midsummer Night's Dream* links the pregnant maid and Indian trade. Like his companion, Bassanio, Antonio begins the play in a melancholy mood; Solanio attributes his sadness not to love, but to the possibility of economic disaster: "Believe me sir, had I such a venture forth, / The better part of my affections would / Be with my hopes abroad" (1.1.15-17). Echoing the eroticized discourse of actual merchant adventure, Solanio's discussion of Antonio's afflictions as "affections" locates the erotic in the economic, particularly as he makes Antonio's fear of losing his ships sound much like the fear of losing a lover:[12]

> should I go to church
> And see the holy edifice of stone
> And not bethink me straight of dangerous rocks,
> Which touching my gentle vessel's side
> Would scatter all her spices on the stream,
> Enrobe the roaring waters with my silks. . . .
>
> (1.1.29-34)

Solanio's displacement is all the more resonant in its religious overtones and its hints at a loss of Christian belief. Foreign adventure proves a dangerous distraction as the stones of the Christian church provoke reminders of the beguiling hazards of trade.

The potential dangers of Antonio's mercantile involvement with foreign Others, read as seductive sexual union, are offset by the rejection of difference in the golden world of Belmont. Bassanio's discussion of his intent to woo Portia suggests an interesting inversion of Antonio's economic adventures. The narrative of his romantic quest is filled with economic metaphors, and his description of Portia makes it obvious that there is an unfavorable balance of trade on the marriage market. Rather than bringing wealth into the country, suitors are coming to Belmont to win away Portia's wealth, as Bassanio notes:

> Nor is the wide world ignorant of her worth,
> For the four winds blow in from every coast
> Renowned suitors, and her sunny locks
> Hang on her temples like a golden fleece,
> Which makes her seat of Belmont Colchos' strond,
> And many Jasons come in quest of her.
>
> (1.1.167-72)

While Antonio participates in the expansion of Venice's economic influence, Bassanio insulates the sexual economy of Venice from foreign "invasion." In language closely approximating Bassanio's, his competitor, the prince of Morocco, "a tawny moor" (and, we presume, a Muslim), frames his own courtship as colonial enterprise and religious pilgrimage when he chooses caskets:

> Why that's the lady, all the world desires her.
> From the four corners of the earth they come
> To kiss this shrine, this mortal breathing saint.
> The Hyrcanian deserts, and the vasty wilds
> Of wide Arabia are as throughfares now
> For princes to come view fair Portia.
> The watery kingdom, whose ambitious head
> Spets in the face of heaven, is no bar
> To stop the foreign spirits, but they come
> As o'er a brook to see fair Portia.
>
> (2.7.38-47)

Morocco reveals the peril of such international competition for wealth (and beauty). The test demanded by Portia's father expands the sex/gender system by opening up the romantic quest to foreign competition, as it were, inviting both the possibility of miscegenation and of another race absconding with the country's money and its native beauty. Morocco explicitly raises this idea and associates it with England:

> They have in England
> A coin that bears the figure of an angel
> Stamp'd in gold, but that's insculp'd upon:
> But here an angel in a golden bed
> Lies all within.
>
> (2.7.55-59)

At the very moment in which he loses the game by making the wrong choice, Morocco raises the specter of a monetary and sexual exchange in England with the image of Portia as an angel in a golden bed. Although the metaphor would seem to deny the comparison ("but that's insculp'd upon: / But here . . ."), Portia is imaged here as the literalized coin of the realm. She, as object of an expanded sex/gender system, can like a coin be circulated among strangers.

The boundaries of Portia's island are hardly impregnable: the surrounding water "is no bar" and no more than a "brook" to outsiders; Portia herself is the open "portal" to Venetian wealth. The sexual and the monetary anxieties of a Venetian state that is open to alien trade are displayed and dispelled in the casket plot, which allows Portia to avoid the threat of contact with others. The prince of Morocco is thus able to attempt to woo but ultimately to lose her. He also loses his right to reproduce his own bloodline, a right not explicitly denied the other suitors (Shell 72). The momentary threat posed by the prince's wooing is dispelled, as is the larger cultural threat posed by the sexuality of the black male. The denial of his fertility should perhaps be looked at in juxtaposition with the fertility of Launcelot's Moor: the prince's sexuality denied, Launcelot then has license to replace him as the Moor's "cultural partner" and to appropriate her body.

The Morocco scene is only the most obvious example of the exclusionary values of Belmont. Portia derides all other suitors for their national shortcomings, reserving her praise for her countryman, Bassanio (a man who at first glance seems to have little to recommend him). Interestingly, the joking about the effects of intermarriage is preceded by the prince of Morocco's attempt to win Portia and Portia's deliverance as he chooses the wrong casket. Portia's response to her narrow escape, "A gentle riddance,—draw the curtains, go,—/ Let all of his complexion choose me so" (2.7.78-79), is typical of the generally negative attitudes toward blacks prevalent at the time, but, in true Belmont fashion, in no way reveals the political and economic implications of her aversion.[13]

The economic issues which underlie the romantic world of Belmont rise to the surface in Venice, where there appears to be a real cash-flow problem. Most of the Christian men, it seems, are on the verge of bankruptcy. Bassanio reveals his monetary woes in the opening of the play, "'Tis not unknown to you Antonio / How much I have disabled mine estate" (1.1.122-23). Despite Antonio's denial, his funds are stretched and the possibility of his financial ruin is evoked from the very beginning. Tellingly, Antonio has no hope for a legal remedy from his bargain because strangers in Venice have certain economic privileges:

> The duke cannot deny the course of law:
> For the commodity that strangers have
> With us in Venice, if it be denied,
> Will much impeach the justice of the state,
> Since that the trade and profit of the city
> Consisteth of all nations.
>
> (3.3.26-31)

In Antonio's case, the very openness of Venetian trade has negative effects for the city's males. The protection Venetian law should afford its "own natural subjects" is weakened by the economic imperatives of mercantile trade.

In contrast to the males, the women are associated with an abundance of wealth. As we have seen, Portia comes with a large fortune and Lorenzo "steals" two thousand ducats along with a jewel-laden Jessica. The comic resolution of the play is not merely the proper pairing of male and female, but the redistribution of wealth from women and other strangers to Venice's Christian males. Portia's wealth goes to Bassanio, Antonio's is magically restored through her agency, and, most importantly, Shylock's is given over to the state through a law unearthed by Portia/Balthazar:

> It is enacted in the laws of Venice,
> If it be proved against an alien,
> That by direct, or indirect attempts
> He seek the life of any citizen,
> The party 'gainst the which he doth contrive,
> Shall seize one half his goods, the other half
> Comes to the privy coffer of the state.
>
> (4.1.344-50)

The law that allegedly gave advantage to aliens is counteracted by a law that repeals that advantage. More than providing an object lesson for Shylock, "hitting him where it hurts," as it were, the punishment makes sure that the uneven balance of wealth in the economy is righted along racial and gender lines. Antonio's modification of the sentence only highlights this impulse, as he insists that his portion of Shylock's money be passed down "unto the gentleman / That lately stole his daughter" (4.1.380-81). Lorenzo's final expression of gratitude to Portia, "Fair ladies, you drop manna in the way / Of starved people" (5.1.294-95), typifies the tonality of the play. Portia does indeed drop manna (which she redistributes from the city's aliens) upon the males of Venice: she is the bearer of fortunes for Bassanio, Antonio, and Lorenzo.

Economic alliances in the play are made with expectations of one-way exchange, which is often troped through conversion. Thus Bassanio and Antonio stress Shylock's "kindness" when making the deal in order to give Shylock the illusion of a communal interest and identity rooted in Christian values. Antonio takes his leave, claiming, "The Hebrew will turn Christian, he grows kind" (1.3.174), a phrase which only serves to remind Shylock and the audience that his "kindness" is still contingent. The pun on "kind" used throughout this scene reminds us that the courtesy and "kindness" shown in the play's world is only extended to those who are alike and judged of human "kin" by Christians. Shakespeare also demonstrates how selective such inclusion can be when the duke, in an attempt to make Shylock forgo his bond, invites him into the community, not by imagining a shared humanity, but by creating a cultural hierarchy which stresses Shylock's difference: "From stubborn Turks, and Tartars never train'd / To offices of tender courtesy" (4.1.32-33). Such rhetorical moves only emphasize that the power of exclusion and inclusion rests with what Frank Whigham calls the "elite circle of community strength" and that the outsider is powerless to determine his status within that group (106-07).

The imagery associated with Shylock in the play reveals an ongoing link between perceptions of the racial difference of the black, the religious difference of the Jew, and the possible ramifications of sexual and economic contact with both. We can see clearly how the discourses of Otherness coalesce in the language of the play.[14] In claiming that Chus is one of his countrymen, Shylock gives himself a dual genealogy that associates him with blackness, forbidden sexuality, and the unlawful appropriation of property.[15] Obviously, Shylock's recounting of the Jacob parable has its own cultural overtones and serves to highlight his religious difference.[16] However, his incomplete genealogy is further complicated by the fact that Jacob, the progenitor of the Jews, robbed his brother, Esau, of his birthright as eldest brother.[17] Both Jews and blacks become signs for filial disobedience and disinheritance in Renaissance culture. In the two biblical accounts of blackness, Chus (or Cush), the son of Ham, is born black as a sign of the father's sin. A popular explanation of blackness recounted by George Best in his description of the Frobisher voyages shows the problem of disinheritance:

> and [Ham] being persuaded that the first childe borne after the flood (by right and Lawe of nature) should inherite and possesse all the dominions of the earth, hee contrary to his fathers commandement [to abstain from sex] while they were yet in the Arke, used company with his wife, and craftily went about thereby to disinherite the off-spring of his other two brethren: for the which wicked and detestable fact as an example for contempt of Almightie God, and disobedience of parents, God would a sonne should be borne whose name was Chus, who not onely it selfe, but all his posteritie after him should bee so blacke and lothsome, that it might remaine a spectacle of disobedience to all the worlde.
>
> (Hakluyt, *Principal Navigations* 3: 52)[18]

Like Shylock's genealogy, Best's narrative gives disobedience and disinheritance a crucial role in the formation of difference. In reading Jews and blacks as signs for theft from rightful heirs, such genealogies may have supported the notion for the English reader that these "aliens" usurp the rightful prerogatives of innocent (pre-Christian) victims. (In other words, forcible seizure of their property is excusable because their ownership is suspect.) The Ham story is a bit more problematic because Ham, the originator of the sin, was himself white. Only his offspring, Chus, bears the burden of the original sin, and the blackness thus becomes a reflection of the nether side of a white self. These biblical "sub-texts" help support the play's central action: a circulation of wealth to an aristocratic, male elite that is predicated on the control of difference. Aliens must be either assimilated into the dominant culture (Shylock's and Jessica's conversions) and/or completely disempowered (Shylock's sentence). Their use as explanations for racial difference allows for the organization of property, kinship, and religion within an emerging national—and imperial—identity.

III

Since the Venetian sex/gender system is constructed along the axis of foreign trade, it is not surprising that female characters play key (if little noted) roles in the circulation of wealth. The successful end of courtship (endogamous marriage) is achieved through the balancing of the problems of conversion, inheritance, and difference. The proper pairing of male and female thus comes to represent the realignment of wealth and the reassertion of control over difference. In their active desire, these outspoken women are often the more conservative agents of the play. Associated with conversion, they assure that wealth is redistributed into the hands of the male elite.

Merchant offers the Jessica-Lorenzo courtship as a successful type of cross-cultural interaction: one like our original model in Purchas, where cultural difference—and property—are controlled under the aegis of a Christian God. Unlike another disobedient daughter, *Othello's* Desdemona, Jessica's filial disloyalty is lauded by the community largely because her actions constitute submission to the larger, racially motivated values of Belmont and Venice. Ironically, her very disobedience proves her "faith" to her husband just as it shows her "fairness." Lorenzo declares, "And fair she is, if that mine eyes be true, / And true she is, as she hath prov'd herself" (2.6.54-55). In cut-

Jessica and Lorenzo sit on the bank of the river near Portia's house in Act V, scene i of The Merchant of Venice.

ting herself off from her father, Jessica also divorces herself from her Jewish ancestry. When she leaves her father's house, Gratiano declaims, "Now (by my hood) a gentle, and no Jew" (2.6.51), punningly connecting her conversion with the race and the class privileges of Belmont.

In fact, the very desire to marry a Christian separates Jessica from her father's alienness. Shylock's claim of consanguinity is resolutely denied throughout the play. Salerio declares, "There is more difference between thy flesh and hers, than between jet and ivory, more between your bloods, than there is between red wine and Rhenish" (3.1.34-36). The terms of Salerio's insistence on absolute difference go as far to exclude Shylock from the realm of humanity (so defined by Christian Venetians) as they do to include Jessica. Jessica herself, in a rehearsal of her own conversion, parodically stages herself as the bride of the Song of Songs, saying, "I am glad 'tis night—you do not look on me" (2.6.34), and covering herself with gold, "I will make fast the doors and gild myself / With some moe ducats" (2.6.49-50), as she begins the "conversion" of money from Shylock to Lorenzo. Jessica's disobedience is acted out as a gender transgression: she escapes from her father's house dressed as a page and is playfully aware of her transgressive behavior, "For I am much asham'd of my exchange" (2.6.35). Of the "exchanges" Jessica makes (husband for father, male dress for female, Christian identity for Jewish), the change in dress is the one she marks as potentially subversive. However, Jessica's cross-dressing is seemingly less complicated than Portia's, since her transgression, taking place as it does during a carnival and facilitating her assimilation into the community of Belmont, is validated by the rest of the play.

Like Jessica's cross-dressing, which is not only excused but lauded in the play, Portia's actions work mainly to fulfill the larger economic needs of the commonwealth. Portia is the focal point of the Venetian economy and its marriage practices: it is through her that money is recirculated to the Christian males and difference is excluded or disempowered. She describes her betrothal as a conversion, "Myself, and what is mine, to you and yours / Is now converted" (3.2.166-67). Bassanio's "pilgrimage" results in the "conversion" of Portia and her possessions as she too fills the coffers of the male Christians. As Balthazar and as

Portia she performs a valuable service to the state. Her disguise allows her to become the agent of conversion and, as Frank Whigham notes, compulsory conversion is associated historically with confiscation of goods by the state. It is she (as Balthazar) who silences the alien. She is the enabling factor that "converts" cash to its "rightful owners," not only hers to Bassanio, but Shylock's to the state and to his Christian heirs.

With their cross-dressing and their active pursuit of female desire, both Portia and Jessica break the constraints of gender; nevertheless, in a text dense with cultural, economic, and gender conflict, glorifying these women as the transgressive disrupters of social order may serve only to obscure the very complex nature of difference for a changing society in which racial categories developed along with changing organizations of gender.[19] To look solely at hierarchies of gender defines the issue too narrowly and valorizes gender as the primary category of difference. Reading Portia as the heroic, subversive female proves particularly problematic when we place her actions in relation to other categories of difference. While her "witty" remarks about her suitors display a verbal acumen and forwardness typical of the unruly woman, her subversiveness is severely limited, for her strongest verbal abilities are only bent toward supporting a status quo which mandates the repulsion of aliens and outsiders. To valorize such cross-dressed figures as liberating Others is to ignore the way their freedom functions to oppress the racial/cultural Others in the play. Portia's originally transgressive act is disarmed and validated by the play's resolution when these "disorderly" women become pliable wives.

Although I have argued that these women serve in some ways as successful comic and economic agents, the play itself does not allow for the same neat elimination of difference offered by Purchas in the opening of this essay. Unlike other Shakespearean comedies, *The Merchant of Venice* ends not with a wedding or the blessing of the bridal bed, but with the exchange of rings and the evocation of adultery. The only immediately fertile couple presented in the play, Launcelot and the Moor, are excluded from the final scene. Her fecundity exists in threatening contrast to the other Venetians' seeming sterility, particularly as it is created with Launcelot Gobbo, the "gobbling," prodigal servant whose appetites cannot be controlled. Like Shylock's absence, their exclusion qualifies the expected resolution of the text and reminds us of the ultimate failure to contain difference completely even as the play's aliens are silenced. The Moor, whose presence may be a visible sign for the conflation of economic and erotic union with the Other in the rhetoric of travel, provides a pregnant reminder of the problematic underpinnings of the Venetian economy.

In her *Literary Fat Ladies,* Patricia Parker charts the appearance of dilated female bodies in Renaissance texts. While they are specifically located within the rhetorical technique of dilation, these "fat ladies" are figures for the delay and deferral that is a central topos of many important Renaissance subtexts such as the *Odyssey,* the *Aeneid,* and the Bible (texts that are also key in the troping of imperial desires). The chief purpose of dilation (amplification or the production of *copia*) is mired in an anxiety over uncontrolled excess; hence the texts become as preoccupied with mastery and control over expansion as with the expansion itself. Parker argues, "Dilation, then, is always something to be kept within the horizon of ending, mastery, and control" (14). Certainly the problem of controlled expansion reverberates within colonial discourses of the Renaissance as travel writers and editors struggle to produce texts which allow expansion but always within the confines of conversion and colonial mastery. In some ways, the figure of the fat lady serves the same purpose as Purchas's introduction: the promise of profitable conversion within the space allowed by deferral of the judgment of the Second Coming.

These fat ladies resonate within a varied field of meanings associated with the judicial, the temporal, the genealogical, and the erotic. Although Parker does not specifically name Launcelot's Moor in her catalogue of fat ladies, she too operates within a similar web of meaning. She appears in the dilated space of the play that postpones both the resolution of Antonio's dilemma and the consummation of Bassanio's and Portia's betrothal. Like Parker's first example (Nell from *The Comedy of Errors*), she is a large presence that is only described. Not permitted to speak, the Moor still encapsulates ideas of copious fertility and threatening female sexuality.[20] However, unlike the other Shakespearean fat ladies, Launcelot's Moor cannot be regarded as "a dilative means to a patriarchal end" (19), that is, as a momentary disruption of the text or a deferral that contains the promise of an ordered conclusion. Her pregnancy is a reminder of the dangerous result of uncontrolled crossing of borders, of trade that holds the dual (and irreconcilable) promises of the production of new wealth and of an insupportable excess. The end she promises is a mixed child, whose blackness may not be "converted" or absorbed within the endogamous, exclusionary values of Belmont.[21] This dusky dark lady is perhaps more like the women of the *Aeneid,* perpetrators "of delay and even of obstructionism in relation to the master or imperial project of the completion of the text" (Parker 13). She interferes with the "master/imperial" project of *The Merchant of Venice*—the eradication or assimilation of difference. Unlike other fat ladies, her "promised end" signals not resolution, but the potential disruption of Europe's imperial text, because in *Merchant*'s Venice—and Elizabeth's England—the possibility of wealth only exists within the dangers of cultural exchange.

Notes

1. Even though the word *intercourse* did not come to have its current sexual connotation until the eighteenth century, Purchas's use of "commerce and intercourse of amity" resonates powerfully in this way for a modern reader, and I would like to retain this anachronistic sense for the purposes of this paper. Indeed, this paper will read anachronistically

throughout. *Miscegenation,* too, is an eighteenth-century term which has particular resonances for the modern American reader. Like "race," the word *miscegenation* is particularly enabled by later scientific discourses; however, the concepts certainly predated the scientific sense. Although there certainly were Renaissance words, such as *mulatto,* for the offspring of certain interracial couples, I prefer to use the term *miscegenation,* just as I play on *intercourse,* to locate an emerging modern dynamic for which there was no adequate language.

2. Eldred Jones sees this moment as the first glimmer of an emerging stereotype of black women (*Othello's Countrymen* 119). He also seems to agree with the Arden editor. He argues that the Launcelot/Moor liaison is an "earthy basic relationship" which completes a structural pattern of romantic relationships in *Merchant,* yet he downplays the relationship's significance: "This cold douche of earthy realism is not unlike the Jacques/Audrey contrast to the Orlando/Rosalind, Silvius/Phebe love types in *As You Like It.* The fact that Launcelot's partner is a Moor only lends emphasis to the contrast" (*Othello's Countrymen* 71).

3. For a more complete discussion, see Peter Fryer's *Staying Power* (10-12). Fryer provocatively contends that the second order of expulsion was to make up the payment for the return of eighty-nine English prisoners from Spain and Portugal.

4. The reprintings of this document indicate some confusion. I have used Eldred Jones's transcription of the 1601 draft proclamation in the Cecil papers, which reads "are crept." In contrast, James Walvin's version of this same proclamation (65) reads "are carried," as does the version in Hughes and Larkin (220-21). The facsimile included in Jones (plate 5) appears to me to read "are crept" and I have thus accepted his transcription.

5. English travel writers, not surprisingly, frequently compared their visions of colonial rule with the Spanish model. England saw itself as in part "correcting" the vexed model of colonial rule in Spain. In his *View of the Present State of Ireland,* Spenser outlines one of the sources of this sense of Spain's mixed heritage, as he suggests that Spain's current riches are the inheritance of a long history of invasion, particularly by Africans: "ffor the Spaniarde that now is, is come from as rude and salvage nacions, as theare beinge As it maye be gathered by Course of ages and view of theire owne historye (thoughe they thearein labour muche to ennoble themselues) scarse anye dropp of the oulde Spannishe blodd lefte in them: . . . And yeat after all these the mores and Barbarians breakings over out of Africa did finallye possesse all spaine or the moste parte thereof And treade downe vnder theire foule heathenishe fete what euer litle they founde theare yeat standinge the which thoughe afterwardes they weare beaten out by *fferdinando* of *Arraggon* and Elizabeth his wiffe yeat they weare not so clensed but that thorogh the mariages which they had made and mixture with the people of the lande duringe theire longe Continvance theare they had lefte no pure dropp of Spanishe blodd no nor of Romayne nor Scithian So that of all nacions vnder heaven I suppose the Spaniarde is the most mingled moste vncertaine and most bastardlie . . . " (90-91).

6. Kwame Anthony Appiah is the most recent purveyor of this view. In the entry "Race," in *Critical Terms for Literary Study,* he argues, ". . . in Shakespearean England both Jews and Moors were barely an empirical reality. And even though there were small numbers of Jews and black people in England in Shakespeare's day, attitudes to 'the Moor' and 'the Jew' do not seem to have been based on experience of these people. Furthermore, despite the fact that there was an increasing amount of information available about dark-skinned foreigners in this, the first great period of modern Western exploration, actual reports of black or Jewish foreigners did not play an important part in forming these images. Rather, it seems that the stereotypes were based on an essentially theological conception of the status of both Moors and Jews as non-Christians; the former distinguished by their black skin, whose color was associated in Christian iconography with sin and the devil . . . " (277-78). It seems apparent in Elizabeth's document that there was a black presence that had its own reality for Elizabeth and that religion appears as rationale after the fact.

7. Patricia Hill Collins lucidly outlines the connections between the welfare mother and mammy stereotypes, arguing, "Each image transmits clear messages about the proper limits among female sexuality, fertility and Black women's roles in the political economy" (78). See also Angela Davis's description of specific political manipulations of the welfare mother image (23-27).

8. My brief discussion of cannibalism owes a great deal to Peter Hulme's materialist critique of the term "cannibal" (78-87) as well as to Maggie Kilgour's exploration of metaphors of incorporation. For an anthropologist's critique of the charge of cannibalism, see Arens.

9. On blood libel, see Poliakov 58 and Kilgour 5. Hulme also suggests a connection in his sense that the rise in accusations of anthropophagy involved the "ritual purging of the body of European Christendom just prior to, and in the first steps of, the domination of the rest of the world: the forging of a European identity" (85-86). Ben Jonson's *Every Man out of His Humour* contains similar links between economics, cannibalism, and anti-Semitism when Carlo Buffone exclaims, "Marry, I say, nothing resembling man more than a swine, it

follows nothing can be more nourishing: for indeed, but that it abhors from our nice nature, if we fed upon one another, we should shoot up a great deal faster, and thrive much better: I refer me to your usurous cannibals, or such like: but since it is so contrary, pork, pork is your only feed" (5.5.61-66).

10. Eric Cheyfitz briefly outlines the relationship of cannibalism to kinship structures in his discussion of Montaigne's "Of Cannibals": "Cannibalism expresses, or figures forth, a radical idea of kinship that cuts across the frontiers of hostile groups. To eat the other is to eat the self, for the other is quite literally composed of the selves of one's kin, who compose oneself, just as the self, it follows, is composed of the others one has eaten. Cannibalism, like kinship, expresses forthrightly the essentially equivocal relationship that obtains between self and other" (149). As I have suggested, it is precisely this aspect of cannibalism that appears so upsetting to European notions of social order and control. In *A Report of the Kingdome of Congo* (1597), Abraham Hartwell expresses horror at the idea of cannibals who eat their own kin: "True it is that many nations there are, that feede upon mans flesh as in the east *Indies*, and in *Bresill*, and in other places: but that is only the flesh of their adversaries and enemies, but to eat the flesh of their own friends and subjects and kinefolkes, it is without all example in any place of the worlde, saving onely in this nation of the Anzichi" (36).

11. I borrow this multivalent use of "chauvinist" from Susan Griffin (298-305).

12. For more on the gendering of the discourses of travel and trade, see Parker 142.

13. In his liberally sympathetic discussion of Morocco's rejection, Frank Whigham acknowledges the racism of courtly ideology by nothing that "[t]hroughout the scenes with Morocco the element of complexion provides a measure of the exclusive implications of courtesy in Portia's society" (98). However, Whigham then blames the Moroccan prince for his own loss because of "his statement of defiant insecurity regarding his skin color" (98), which is rhetorically out of sync with courtesy theory. His reading remystifies the color problem by blaming it on the prince. Portia never mentions his "imagery of martial exploit and confrontation" (98), only his complexion; so too the tradition of failed suitors indicates to the audience that his unsuitability is not so much a question of rhetorical decorum as racial "propriety." In Morocco's case, "defiant insecurity" may simply be a sensible response to the racism implicit in Portia's courtly ethic.

14. Shakespeare draws upon a system of associations between the Jew and the black which is as old as Christianity itself. For a brief outline of the association of blackness with the Jew, see Gilman 30-35.

15. For an excellent discussion of the racial and economic ramifications of the Jacob and Esau parable, see Shell.

16. In his *Pseudodoxia Epidemica,* Sir Thomas Browne uses this same parable to explain one theory of the causes of blackness, replacing the biblical injunctions against disobedience with a lesson about the powers of the imagination: "[I]t may be perpended whether it might not fall out the same way that Jacobs cattell became speckled, spotted and ring-straked, that is, by the power and efficacy of Imagination; which produceth effects in the conception correspondent unto the phancy of the Agents in generation" (513).

17. Lars Engle argues that this story is purposely incomplete: "It is this relation between Jacob and Laban, then, that Shylock is attempting to adduce as an explanation of his own place in the Venetian economy, and, more immediately, as a model for his relation to Antonio" (31).

18. It is in this same narrative that Best includes one of the earliest recorded instances of miscegenation in early modern England, which he uses to refute the climatic theory of the cause of blackness: "I my selfe have seene an Ethiopian as blacke as a cole brought into England, who taking a faire Englishwoman to wife, begat a sonne in all respects as blacke as the father was, although England was his native countrey, and an English woman his mother: whereby it seemeth this blacknes proceedeth rather of some natural infection of that man, which was so strong, that neither the nature of the Clime, neither the good complexion of the mother concurring, could any thing alter, and therefore wee cannot impute it to the nature of the Clime" (Hakluyt, *Principal Navigations* 3: 50-51).

19. Among critics of *The Merchant of Venice,* particularly feminists, there is a great deal of debate over the possible feminist implications of Portia's transvestite disguise. Is Portia truly the disorderly, unruly female preached against in tracts against cross-dressing or are such disguises diversions which ultimately serve to restore patriarchal order? Catherine Belsey finds the play less radical than its earlier counterparts: "*The Merchant of Venice* is none the less rather less radical in its treatment of women as subjects. . . . [The play] . . . reproduces some of the theoretical hesitation within which it is situated" (195-96). Lisa Jardine locates Portia within a tradition of "confused cultural response[s] to the learned woman" ("Cultural Confusion" 17) and notes that although Portia possesses many threatening advantages over the males in the play, the play still ends with the sexual subordination of women (17). In contrast, Karen Newman finds in Portia a necessary threat to social order: "Portia evokes the ideal of a proper Renaissance lady and then transgresses it; she becomes an unruly woman" ("Portia's Ring" 29). Lars Engle also notes a split

between conservative and radical elements in the play; however, he sees Portia as part of the latter precisely because she is the agent of exchange: "On the other hand, more than any other Shakespearean play, *The Merchant of Venice* shows a woman triumphing over men and male systems of exchange: the 'male homosocial desire' of Antonio is almost as thoroughly thwarted in the play as is Shylock's vengefulness" (37). Nonetheless, male homosocial desire (which can be a conservative force) is also a force which threatens the sex/gender system.

20. Parker draws on Jardine's connection of the figure of the pregnant woman and her "grossesse" with fertility and threatening sexuality (Jardine, *Still Harping* 131; Parker 18).

21. Black Africans become in the Renaissance signs for the impossible, which often comes to include the impossibility of their being subdued to European order. The emblem for the impossible, "washing the Ethiop white," suggests a sense of submission to a European order. Richard Crashaw's poem "On the Baptized Ethiopian" specifically adapts this as a figure for conversion and the Second Coming. For more see Newman, "And wash the Ethiop white," and ch. 2 of my dissertation, "Acknowledging Things of Darkness: Race, Gender and Power in Early Modern England."

Works Cited

Appiah, Kwame Anthony. "Race." *Critical Terms for Literary Study*. Ed. Frank Lentricchia and Thomas McLaughlin. Chicago: U of Chicago P, 1990. 274-87.

Appleby, Andrew B. *Famine in Tudor and Stuart England*. Stanford: Stanford UP, 1978.

Arens, W. *The Man-eating Myth: Anthropology and Anthropophagy*. Oxford: Oxford UP, 1979.

Barthelemy, Anthony Gerard. *Black Face, Maligned Race: The Representation of Blacks in English Drama from Shakespeare to Southerne*. Baton Rouge: Louisiana State UP, 1987.

Belsey, Catherine. *The Subject of Tragedy: Identity and Difference in Renaissance Drama*. London: Methuen, 1985.

Browne, Sir Thomas. *Pseudodoxia Epidemica*. Ed. Robin Robbins. Vol. 1. Oxford: Clarendon, 1981. 2 vols.

Cheyfitz, Eric. *The Poetics of Imperialism: Translation and Colonization from* The Tempest *to* Tarzan. Oxford: Oxford UP, 1991.

Cohen, Walter. *Drama of a Nation: Public Theater in Renaissance England and Spain*. Ithaca: Cornell UP, 1985.

Collins, Patricia Hill. *Black Feminist Thought: Knowledge, Consciousness, and the Politics of Empowerment*. Boston: Unwin Hyman, 1990.

Davis, Angela. *Women, Culture, and Politics*. New York: Random House, 1990.

Engle, Lars. "'Thrift is Blessing': Exchange and Explanation in *The Merchant of Venice*." *Shakespeare Quarterly* 37 (1986): 20-37.

Fryer, Peter. *Staying Power: The History of Black People in Britain*. Sydney: Pluto, 1984.

Gilman, Sander L. *Difference and Pathology: Stereotypes of Sexuality, Race, and Madness*. New York: Cornell UP, 1985.

Griffin, Susan. "The Sacrificial Lamb." *Racism and Sexism: An Integrated Study*. Ed. Paula S. Rothenberg. New York: St. Martin's, 1988. 296-305.

Hakluyt, Richard. *Discourse of Western Planting*. The Original Writings & Correspondence of the Two Richard Hakluyts. Vol. 2. 211-326. Hakluyt Soc. no. 77. London: Cambridge UP for the Hakluyt Soc., 1935. 2 vols.

———, ed. *The Principal Navigations, Voyages, Traffiques, & Discoveries of the English Nation*. Vol. 3. London, 1598-1600. 3 vols.

Hall, Kim F. "Acknowledging Things of Darkness: Race, Gender and Power in Early Modern England." Diss. U of Pennsylvania, 1990.

Hartwell, Abraham, trans. *A Report of the Kingdome of Congo, a Region of Africa. And of the Countries that border rounde about the same*. 1597. STC 16805.

Hughes, Paul F., and James F. Larkin, eds. *Tudor Royal Proclamations*. Vol. 3. New Haven: Yale UP, 1969.

Hulme, Peter. *Colonial Encounters: Europe and the Native Caribbean, 1492-1797*. London: Methuen, 1986.

Jameson, Fredric. *The Political Unconscious: Narrative as a Socially Symbolic Act*. Ithaca: Cornell UP, 1981.

Jardine, Lisa. "Cultural Confusion and Shakespeare's Learned Heroines: These Are Old Paradoxes." *Shakespeare Quarterly* 38 (1987): 1-18.

———. *Still Harping on Daughters: Women and Drama in the Age of Shakespeare*. New York: Harvester, 1983.

Jones, Eldred D. *The Elizabethan Image of Africa*. Charlottesville: UP of Virginia, 1971.

———. *Othello's Countrymen: The African in English Renaissance Drama*. London: Oxford UP, 1965.

Jonson, Ben. *Every Man out of His Humour*. The Complete Plays of Ben Jonson. Ed. G. A. Wilkes. Vol. 1. 275-411. Oxford: Clarendon, 1981. 4 vols.

Kilgour, Maggie. *From Communion to Cannibalism: An Anatomy of Metaphors of Incorporation*. Princeton: Princeton UP, 1990.

Massinger, Philip. *The Maid of Honour*. The Plays and Poems of Philip Massinger. Ed. Philip Edwards and Colin Gibson. Vol. 1. 117-97. Oxford: Clarendon, 1976. 5 vols.

Newman, Karen. "'And wash the Ethiop white': Femininity and the Monstrous in *Othello*." *Shakespeare Reproduced: The Text in History and Ideology.* Ed. Jean E. Howard and Marion F. O'Connor. New York: Methuen, 1987. 143-62.

———. "Portia's Ring: Unruly Women and Structures of Exchange in *The Merchant of Venice*." *Shakespeare Quarterly* 38 (1987): 18-33.

Parker, Patricia. *Literary Fat Ladies: Rhetoric, Gender, Property.* New York: Methuen, 1987.

Poliakov, Leon. *The History of Anti-Semitism.* Trans. Richard Howard. Vol. 1. New York: Vanguard, 1974-75. 3 vols.

Purchas, Samuel. *Hakluytus Posthumus, or Purchas His Pilgrimes: Contayning a History of the World in Sea Voyages and Lande Travells by Englishmen and others.* London, 1625.

Rubin, Gayle. "The Traffic in Women: Notes on the 'Political Economy' of Sex." *Toward an Anthropology of Women.* Ed. Rayna Reiter. New York: Monthly Review, 1975. 157-210.

Shakespeare, William. *The Merchant of Venice.* Ed. John Russell Brown. The Arden Shakespeare. Cambridge: Harvard UP, 1959.

Shell, Marc. "The Wether and the Ewe: Verbal Usury in *The Merchant of Venice*." *Kenyon Review* ns 1.4 (Fall 1979): 65-92.

Spenser, Edmund. *A View of the Present State of Ireland.* Ed. Rudolf Gottfried. *The Complete Works of Edmund Spenser: A Variorum Edition.* Ed. Edwin Greenlaw et al. Vol 9. Baltimore: Johns Hopkins P, 1949. 10 vols.

Walvin, James. *The Black Presence: A Documentary History of the Negro in England, 1555-1860.* New York: Schocken, 1971.

Whigham, Frank. "Ideology and Class Conduct in *The Merchant of Venice*." *Renaissance Drama* ns 10 (1979): 93-115.

John Picker (essay date 1994)

SOURCE: "Shylock and the Struggle for Closure," in *Judaism: A Quarterly Journal,* Vol. 43, No. 2, 1994, pp. 173-89.

[*In the essay below, Picker describes Elizabethan England's creation of and discrimination against the "other," or outsider, in order to preserve its own sense of a closed society. Picker observes that this "ghettoizing" is reflected in* The Merchant of Venice, *where Shylock is consistently excluded from communal life simply because he is a Jew.*]

1. "Go presently inquire, and so will I / Where money is": Theoretical and Historical Considerations

In his seminal work on Shakespearean festive comedy, C. L. Barber introduces a theory of comic form which attempts to account for the role of figures such as Shylock in the early plays. Emphasizing the connection between theatrical practices and social customs such as May Day and the Winter Revels, Barber argues that the early comedies celebrate natural vitality and social identity. He considers the underlying movement of Shakespearean comedy to be the passage "through release to clarification," that is, from revel and celebration to the formation of a durable communal bond. According to Barber, Shakespearean comedy requires integration and closure such that any marginal figures, or "butts," as Barber refers to them, must be restrained and expelled by society. By defeating such challenges, the society gains strength and, finally, reestablishes itself.[1] The presence of a threatening figure thus enables disparate groups to come together as a community, and overpower a common scapegoat. Yet, as Barber writes, "behind the laughter at the butts, there is always a sense of solidarity about pleasure, a communion embracing the merrymakers to the play and the audience."[2] Barber's theory of festive comedy, then, contains the underlying paradox that a welcoming community can be established only through ridicule and ostracism.

This essay examines how characters in *The Merchant of Venice* attempt to silence, ignore, interrupt, and otherwise stifle Shylock; at the same time, it demonstrates how Shylock's voice and personality undercut their attempts, to the extent that his presence informs a reading of the play. In what follows, I will argue that Shylock thwarts society's attempts to contain him. I would like to suggest that in *Merchant,* Shakespeare poses two similar questions, one focusing on historical circumstances, and the other dealing with issues of genre: just how can Venice's and Belmont's citizens reconcile the need for Shylock's money with the fact that they shun him socially? And secondly, how can the play reconcile its need for Shylock's threatening presence with the fact that it ultimately expels him from comic closure? By allowing Shylock to undermine closure, Shakespeare unites these historical and generic concerns, and exposes the paradoxical principle upon which his comedy and his society operate: the formation of communal identity through exclusionary practices.

Although Edward I expelled the majority of Jews from his kingdom in 1290, Jewish stereotypes continued to flourish in England throughout the Middle Ages and Renaissance. Elizabethans encountered few Jews in the city and countryside, yet Church sermons nevertheless proclaimed Jews to be "hard-hearted blasphemers who were also vain, ostentatious, and deceitful," and encouraged the association of the "devil Jew" with avarice.[3] The tradition of connecting Jews with cupidity had originated virtually as they arrived on European soil, and with good reason: moneylending was one of the few professions that European Jews were permitted to practice. As Cecil Roth writes, the "practice of usury was considered to be a sin for any man, but seemed in Gentile eyes to be less so for Jews, who had so many [sins] on their infidel consciences that one more or less hardly mattered."[4] While Christians considered usury sacrilegious, they did not hesitate to request extensive loans from Jews in order to conduct trading ventures and appease belligerent enemies. And, lacking the relatively modern invention of state-sponsored welfare programs, many Italian city governments depended upon Jewish usurers to support the poor by opening "loan banks." Jewish money thus represented a powerful force governing the sustenance, expansion, and protection of Christian societies.[5]

Yet, Renaissance Europe denied Jews the freedom to inhabit the same communities as Christians. In the words of Bernard Glassman, "there was the need for the Jew's services on the one hand, and the contempt for his person, on the other."[6] Christians welcomed Jewish money, and often *required* it, so long as accepting it did not necessitate welcoming the Jewish moneylender. Venice, the most important trading city in Italy, established the first ghetto in Western history for its substantial Jewish population. Because Venetian merchants relied heavily on usurers to finance business ventures, Jews who sought business flocked to the city. In 1516, however, the threat of a burgeoning Jewish population drove the Venetian government to legislate the confinement of Jews to a specified district. This was the New Foundry, or *geto nuovo,* from which the word "ghetto" originated.[7] Within the *geto nuovo,* Jewish heterodoxy was kept safely away from Christian homes, while, in the marketplace or *piazza,* those same Christians coveted loans from Jewish usurers. Hence, the very layout of Venice reproduced the Christians' paradoxical desire to embrace desperately needed Jewish money and simultaneously shun the Jews who possessed it.

There is a striking parallel between the bind in which Jewish usurers were placed by their Christian debtors, and the place of marginal figures in the model of Shakespearean comedy as expressed by C. L. Barber. As Jewish usurers were required to finance the growth of Renaissance European communities, so threatening figures must be present for communal growth to occur in Shakespeare's comedies. And, paradoxically, just as those Jews were socially ostracized by the societies that they financed, so the community that the outsider helped to construct had to expel him or her in order to reach closure. Throughout *Merchant,* Shakespeare dramatizes this paradox by allowing Shylock consistently to challenge the restraints of the Venetian community and, finally, by permitting him to undermine comic closure.

2. "I AM NOT BOUND TO PLEASE THEE WITH MY ANSWERS": SHYLOCK'S CONTAINMENT CHALLENGED

We are introduced to Shylock through a series of abrupt, grating conversations which feature his refusal to be manipulated and ostracized. In his first scene, Bassanio makes him acutely aware of his marginal status by approaching him solely to take out a loan of three thousand ducats. Shylock shows his resentment toward this treatment by manipulating their dialogue in fascinating ways:

SHYLOCK:
Three thousand ducats—well.
BASSANIO:
Ay, sir, for three months.
SHYLOCK:
For three months—well.
BASSANIO:
For the which, as I told you, Antonio shall be bound.
SHYLOCK:
Antonio shall become bound—well.
BASSANIO:
May you stead me? Will you pleasure me? Shall I know your answer?
SHYLOCK:
Three thousand ducats for three months, and Antonio bound.
BASSANIO:
Your answer to that.
SHYLOCK:
Antonio is a good man.

(I.iii. 1-11)[8]

Here, Shylock uses repetition and carefully-placed interjections to masterful effect. He entices Bassanio by echoing "for three months" and "Antonio shall become bound," but forces anxious pauses upon the dialogue with each irritating "well." His refusal to answer Bassanio with a simple yes or no is not simply a sign of verbal teasing or "dangling," as Lawrence Danson has suggested.[9] Rather, by withholding an answer, Shylock subtly resists conducting economic as well as linguistic transactions with Bassanio. In this way, Shylock establishes a connection between conversational and monetary exchange. Through pauses, repetition, and a final pun on the moral and economic connotations of "good," Shylock defies Bassanio's repeated attempts to impose limits on his response to the bond. Rather than reply in terms that readily satisfy Bassanio, Shylock disturbs and challenges him by remaining linguistically and economically unengageable.

If Shylock is subtly obdurate with Bassanio, he is ardently defiant toward Antonio's wishes. When Antonio enters the scene, he has little desire to speak directly to Shylock, from whom he only wants money; Antonio asks Bassanio, "Is he yet possessed / How much ye would?" (I.iii. 61-2). The odd wording of this question reveals contempt for Shylock in two ways. First, it suggests a low pun on the Jew's supposed "possession" by the devil. This gibe is consistent with Antonio's caustic remark about Shylock later in the scene, that the "devil can cite Scripture for his purpose" (95). Second, in his question, Antonio marginalizes Shylock by speaking about him in the third person despite his presence onstage. Shylock, however, refuses to be slighted or ignored, and he interrupts with, "Ay, ay, three thousand ducats" (62). This interjection enables him to disrupt Antonio's conversation with Bassanio and protest his relegation to a third-person presence.

In the Jacob and Laban story which follows this exchange, Shylock further challenges both his relegation to marginal status and the evil connotation implied in Antonio's use of "possession." Lars Engle, one of the few critics to grapple with the exegesis, provides an insightful analysis based on the premise that "the Jacob story . . . is full of danger for Shylock."[10] Indeed, notions of threat and discontinuity pervade Shylock's speech from the moment he starts to deliver it:

> SHYLOCK:
> When Jacob grazed his uncle Laban's sheep—
> This Jacob from our holy Abram was,
> As his wise mother wrought in his behalf,
> The third possessor; ay, he was the third—
> ANTONIO:
> And what of him? Did he take interest?
>
> (68-72)

The reference to the patriarchs is a calculated *non sequitur*, and to make its impact even more disturbing to Antonio, Shylock breaks off his narrative to supply apparently irrelevant background information. Thus, his words here seem carefully crafted to serve a double purpose: to defend the practice of usury while offending Antonio. The significance of Shylock's digression is revealed through his skillful mockery of Antonio's initial pun on possession. While the merchant had implied only ten lines earlier that the Jew was "possessed" with deviant spirits, Shylock subtly twists this double meaning to remove the negative connotation from "possession" and align himself with the patriarchs. Thus he ingeniously suggests that each patriarch was not "possessed" by evil because of his Judaism, but, quite the opposite, a "possessor" of God's promise.[11]

Such wordplay and digression annoy Antonio and prompt the merchant to ask impatiently, "And what of him? Did he take interest?" Shylock responds with a detailed description of Jacob's cunning actions, a speech which taunts both Antonio's argument for the abnormality of usury as well as the merchant's lack of children:

> SHYLOCK:
> . . . the ewes being rank,
> In the end of autumn turned to the rams;
> And when the work of generation was
> Between these woolly breeders in the act,
> The skillful shepherd pilled me certain wands,
> And in the doing of the deed of kind
> He stuck them up before the fulsome ewes,
> Who then conceiving, did in eaning time
> Fall parti-colored lambs, and those were Jacob's.
>
> (77-85)

This speech is part of Shylock's attempt to draw a parallel between Jacob's manipulative tactic and his own usury in order to suggest that usury is as natural as sexual propagation. Using alternatingly rolling and terse alliteration, Shylock makes the sheep's sexual activities uncomfortably visual: "rank" ewes "turned to the rams" "in the end of autumn" for "the work of generation" and "the doing of the deed of kind." He supplements this with the bizarre image of "woolly breeders," a coarse description of mating sheep. According to Shylock, Jacob himself takes an active role as the one who "stuck ["certain wands"] up before the fulsome ewes" in order to carry out his plan. Thus, through the use of a phallic object, Jacob makes the ewes conceive a specific type of lamb.

Shylock uses this tale of overt sexuality to disturb Antonio's containing presence. With references to the reproductive behavior of sheep, Shylock's exegesis of the Jacob story seems "full of danger," not so much for the Jew, as Lars Engle suggests, as for Antonio, who is confronted in this speech with a subtle criticism of both his opinion of usury and his own lack of offspring. Shylock, by craftily arguing that usury gives him the power to control acts of reproduction, directly challenges Antonio's belief that usury involves the use of "barren metal" (131). When Antonio expresses impatience once more with "Was this inserted to make interest good? / Or is your gold and silver ewes and rams?," Shylock retorts with a pun which aligns usury and reproduction: "I cannot tell; I make it breed a fast" (91-3). Shylock defends usury as natural and regenerative rather than abnormal and impotent. Furthermore, Shylock argues that interest, like sexual reproduction, is a creative, productive catalyst; he suggests that interest is necessary to produce new wealth, just as sex is essential to create new people. In this way, his words belie the definition of usury to which Antonio subscribes.

By emphasizing sexual regeneration in the Jacob story, Shylock further discomforts Antonio, the play's only bachelor and childless adult.[12] Although E. Pearlman considers Shylock "hungry for money but basically unsexual or antisexual," it seems that Shylock equates sexual regeneration with the interest he gains through usury.[13] In fact, Shylock blurs distinctions between the two, so that he would have his "gold and silver" "breed as fast" as "ewes and rams." Using this analogy to argue that usury is as natural as sexual reproduction, Shylock can only further disturb Antonio, who lacks offspring as well as the hope of marrying and producing them. Hence, Shylock's exegesis, as an argument for the legitimacy of usury and a statement of sexual fecundity, challenges and discomforts the very man who most detests him.

Antonio and Bassanio are not alone in failing to contain Shylock's presence. In the second act, after Jessica has absconded with a portion of her father's savings, Solanio presents a narrative of Shylock's reaction to Jessica's flight which attempts to satirize the Jew:

> SOLANIO:
> I never heard a passion so confused,
> So strange, outrageous, and so variable,
> As the dog Jew did utter in the streets:
> "My daughter! O my ducats! O my daughter!
> Fled with a Christian! O my Christian ducats!
> Justice! The law! My ducats and my daughter!
> A sealed bag, two sealed bags of ducats,
> Of double ducats, stol'n from me by my daughter!
> And jewels—two stones, two rich and precious stones,
> Stol'n by my daughter! Justice! Find the girl!
> She hath the stones upon her, and the ducats!"
>
> (II.viii.12-22)

We should be wary to take this passage at face value, for, as Paul Cantor correctly observes, Solanio's paraphrase of Shylock is not simply a quotation of Shylock's words verbatim, but a caricature.[14] As a caricature in the guise of a paraphrase, the speech becomes a complex form of containment. Solanio purports to repeat Shylock's words, but he actually exaggerates and manipulates them to construct a warped picture of how, as we later discover, Shylock reacted.[15] Although he delivers this report in order to make Shylock's personality seem, like a "dog Jew," inhuman and obsessive, Solanio ironically implicates not so much Shylock here as his own bad judgment. We might find it difficult to discover what in the speech seems "so strange . . . and so variable," for Solanio's rendition is nothing if not predictable in its reliance on the Jewish stereotype and in its redundant use of "daughter," "ducats," "justice," "stol'n," and so forth.

As we later see firsthand, Shylock's response to Jessica's departure uses much of the same language as Solanio's paraphrase, but exhibits anger and pain that the crude parody simply does not convey. When Tubal tells Shylock of Jessica's whereabouts, there is an almost chilling bitterness in the abandoned father's words: "I would my daughter were dead at my feet, and the jewels in her ear! Would she were hearsed at my foot, and the ducats in her coffin!" (III.i.83-5). With its funerary pall, this passage is anything but comic. Furthermore, there is mournful remorse in Shylock's tone as he realizes he will have "no satisfaction, no revenge, nor no ill luck stirring but what lights o' my shoulders, no sighs but o' my breathing, no tears but o' my shedding" (III.i.89-91). These lines convey a genuine sense of loss and tragedy, not the humorous obsessiveness of Solanio's shallow parody, which deprived Shylock's reaction of its emotional core and left only the empty shell of similar words ("daughter," "ducats," and "jewels"). It seems that Shakespeare allows Solanio to deliver his satiric paraphrase first, so that when Shylock finally speaks, his own deeper feelings undermine the limited portrayal that Solanio had previously constructed for him.

As we have seen thus far in *Merchant*, Shylock's physical presence is at once required by the Venetians—enabling Bassanio to finance travel to Belmont—and despised by them, as revealed by Solanio's demeaning paraphrase. However, rather than placidly acquiesce to the paradoxical constraints set on his shoulders, Shylock adamantly defies them. The play's famous "I am a Jew" speech represents the culmination of Shylock's rebellious attitude:

> SHYLOCK: Hath not a Jew eyes? Hath not a Jew hands, organs, dimensions, senses, affections, passions?—fed with the same food, hurt with the same weapons, subject to the same diseases, healed by the same means, warmed and cooled by the same winter and summer as a Christian is? If you prick us, do we not bleed? If you tickle us, do we not laugh? If you poison us, do we not die? And if you wrong us, shall we not revenge? If we are like you in the rest, we will resemble you in that. If a Jew wrong a Christian, what is his humility? Revenge! If a Christian wrong a Jew, what should his sufferance be by Christian example? Why revenge! The villainy you teach me I will execute, and it shall go hard but I will better the instruction.
>
> (II.i 55-69)

The cohesiveness of this speech pivots upon a series of intricate counterbalances. Nourishing feeding is juxtaposed against poisoning, the latter of which, with the wounds, the diseases, and pricking, is counteracted by healing. In the middle of the passage, warming and cooling conveniently neutralize each other. Shylock neatly places his tickling question next to his pricking one, thereby suggesting a metaphorical relationship between creeping fingers' and a puncturing point's contact with skin (in addition to the rhyming of the two verbs). This complex series of counterbalances gives the speech a symmetry which allows it to stand on its own, similar to a soliloquy.[16] Ironically, Shylock chooses an unpredictable moment—when he is in the company of two of the play's least significant characters—to deliver one of the play's most extraordinary pieces of rhetoric.

Embracing a plethora of corporal perceptions, from an animated tickle to cold-blooded murder, Shylock's lines emphasize a sensuality which transcends the social hierarchy imposed by the Christian community. While Shylock's previous earthiness relied on brash statements of sexual activity in order to rile Antonio, now the focus is on basic mortal characteristics and sensations: at first, eyes, hands, and organs; then, illness and health, life and death, and laughter. His images work to challenge and eradicate notions of difference which the Christians want desperately to maintain. For, Shylock speaks not only of Jewish experience, but of human experience. In doing so, he confronts Salerio and Solanio with what, for them, must seem a frightening prospect: that, despite his religious and cultural identity, he shares with them a fundamental humanity.

With his final query—"if you wrong us, shall we not revenge?"—Shylock consciously vocalizes his challenge to containment for the first time. No longer will he taunt and be taunted. His vow for vengeance is as eloquent a statement of defiance as it is a call for Antonio's pound of flesh. Kiernan Ryan artfully writes that this speech introduces "the full, protesting force of an irresistible egalitarian vision, whose basis in the shared faculties and needs of our common physical nature implicitly indicts all forms of inhuman discrimination."[17] Shylock's forcefulness leaves Salerio and Solanio stunned and speechless; the climactic affirmation of vengeance is only disturbed by the entrance of "a Man from Antonio" (s.d.). In the moment right before this, Solanio, Salerio, and perhaps the audience realize the shocking implications of Shylock's words. However irrational his response seems, it nevertheless represents a combative stance against the restraining power of the Christian community, particularly the stifling voice of Antonio and the deceptive actions of Lorenzo.

Following this decisive argument for equality, Shylock's more intimate conversation with Tubal aids in further humanizing him by providing details of his present condition as a forsaken father and of his previous role as a husband. We watch Shylock reveal anger and despair, with his emotional state at the mercy of Tubal's words.[18] In just forty lines, Shylock confesses his anguish over Jessica, his hatred towards Antonio, his attachment to his savings, and, perhaps most interestingly, his devotion to Leah, his wife:

> TUBAL:
> One of them showed me a ring that he had of your daughter for a monkey.
> SHYLOCK:
> Out upon her! Thou torturest me, Tubal. It was my turquoise; I had it of Leah when I was a bachelor. I would not have given it for a wilderness of monkeys.
>
> (III.i.111-16)

While this exchange contains an element of absurdity by juxtaposing a cherished ring against "a wilderness of monkeys," within the trade-off there is also, undeniably, a sense of poignancy. Clearly, Shylock values the "turquoise" that Leah gave him before their marriage, for the loss of the ring represents Jessica's paramount crime, the news of which actually goes so far as to "torture" him. Judging by the worth that Shylock places upon the ring, it quite possibly represents the only memento of Leah left to him. This passage, then, takes Shylock's "Hath not a Jew eyes?" argument one step further by establishing his humanity on an emotional level. He perceives his possessions as much more than simply a means to acquire more money and ensure prosperity in days to come. The turquoise ring represents for him not a method to build for his economic future, but a connection to his emotional past.

In the talk with Tubal, Shylock's character undergoes myriad developments which convey a multifaceted portrait. His urgent concerns of the present bring to the surface memorable past experiences. These, in turn, enable Shylock to appear as more of an individual human being and less a stereotypical menacing villain to us. As Norman Rabkin rightly argues, during this scene, we "respond to signals of Shylock's injured fatherhood, of his role as heavy father, of his light hearted mistreatment at the hands of the negligible Salerio and Solanio, of his motiveless malignity, and we try hopelessly to reduce to a single attitude our response.[19] At once, then, Shylock strikes us as more fully humanized than his oppressors, and his characterization seems more complex than theirs. Shylock thus maintains a significant humanity which succesfully undermines the other figures' attempts to belittle him.

In Shylock's first scene with Bassanio and Antonio, his resentment seems somewhat restrained and playful. But with Antonio behind bars, his tone suddenly shifts to an intractable extreme, beyond reason, humaneness, and even the ability to listen:

> ANTONIO:
> I pray thee hear me speak.
> SHYLOCK:
> I'll have my bond. I will not hear thee speak.
> I'll have my bond, and therefore speak no more.
> I'll not be made a soft and dull-eyed fool,
> To shake the head, relent, and sigh, and yield
> To Christian intercessors. Follow not.
> I'll have no speaking; I will have my bond.
>
> (III.iii.11-17)

Earlier, Antonio attempted to silence Shylock while attaining a monetary bond. Here, though, the power dynamics have been reversed, so that Shylock now plays the role of stifler and bond seeker to the imprisoned merchant. Furthermore, Shylock reverses the roles with a diabolical twist; while Antonio's original desire for a loan of money was innocuous, Shylock's bond is deadly.

With "I will not hear thee speak," Shylock openly admits to what he had only hinted at with his repetitive "well" to Bassanio in their first scene together. That is, he now refuses outright to participate in conversational exchange, nor will he listen to Antonio. Shylock's "I'll have my bond, and therefore speak no more" expresses precisely Antonio and Bassanio's original demand upon him: a binding economic agreement but not a conversation, the latter of which implies a linguistic communion formed between speakers and listeners. Shylock seems to hint at the paradox of his own position as a member of an economic but not a social community in Venice. Through demands for both silence and fulfillment of a bond, Shylock forces Antonio into the very position in which the merchant had previously placed him.

Thus, the play constructs Shylock as a man acutely aware of his subservient role in Venice and preoccupied with how to thwart those who have relegated him to that position. As we have seen, he accomplishes this through coarse references to the corporeal, through stylish rhetoric, or by bluntly refusing to listen. Uniting all of these responses, the climactic trial scene sets Shylock against *Merchant*'s community as it frantically tries to impose closure upon him by swaying him from his violent plan. Conflict in the scene does not occur solely between Christian mercy and Jewish hardheartedness, as has often been argued.[20] Rather, what gets played out during the trial is, in part, the battle between expectation, in the guise of comic closure, and defiance of what is expected, as represented by Shylock's determination to perform the directive of his bond.

Early on, the scene establishes the expectation that the Christian community will triumph over the outsider. The Duke hints at this when he tells Shylock, "We all expect a gentle answer, Jew" (IV.i.34). Indeed, the Duke does not simply want "a gentle answer," he *expects* it, as if he knows he is a player in a comedy, and that comedy requires overcoming obstacles to secure comic integration and closure. And if the title character succumbs to Shylock's knife, hope for such closure is, of course, doomed. The court scene, then, captures characters in *Merchant* as they struggle to save their own comedy from imminent collapse.

Portia, dressed as the judge Balthazar, functions both to interpret the law and to ensure that the comedy achieves closure. After Antonio confesses to Shylock's bond, Portia commands: "Then must the Jew be merciful" (181). Disguised as a representative of the law, Portia gains the authority to make such absolute decrees in Venice. Yet, her command serves a structural purpose as well. Portia does not say solely that Shylock should show mercy, but that he *must*. As with the Duke's desire for a "gentle answer," Portia's words suggest an underlying expectation for behavior which will guarantee proper comic closure. Indeed, by saving Antonio's life while defeating Shylock, Portia effectively removes the obstacle to the comic denouement. Shakespeare accomplishes a fascinating unity of plot and structure through her, since she serves a dual purpose as both judge *within* the intrigue of *Merchant,* decreeing what is correct behavior in Venice, and judge *without,* determining how best to overcome the obstacle to community and close the comic framework of the play.

Like Portia, the Duke attempts to overpower and ultimately expel Shylock. Rather than put Shylock to death, however, he forces the Jew to give up all of his savings:

> DUKE:
> Thou shalt see the difference of our spirit,
> I pardon thee thy life before thy ask it.
> For half thy wealth, it is Antonio's;
> The other half comes to the general state,
> Which humbleness may drive into a fine.
>
> (367-71)

Jean Howard has written that a "pardon so self-righteously granted seems more a gesture of pride than of spontaneous mercy," and she is right to see in the Duke's pronouncement a thinly veiled ego trip.[21] Also present, however, is the urge to deprive Shylock of his only source of power—his money. But, as Shylock says, such an action would do more than simply bankrupt him:

> SHYLOCK:
> Nay, take my life and all! Pardon not that!
> You take my house, when you do take the prop
> That doth sustain my house. You take my life
> When you do take the means whereby I live.
>
> (373-6)

Shylock makes a valid point here, since usury, as we have seen, was one of the only means by which Jews could earn a living.[22] In these lines, Shylock continues to drive home his paradoxical relationship with Venice's Christians, by imploring them to understand that their "pardon" promises not forgiveness but annihilation. Ironically, the Duke spares Shylock's life by "tak[ing]" the very things which enable Shylock to live. Thus, the "pardon" which seemed motivated by mercy reveals itself to be mercilessly sadistic. Had the Duke ordered Shylock's death, at least this would have been a terminal punishment, but the Duke's so-called pardon instead promises to be interminably torturous and humiliating. Stripped of his possessions—the very things which define his identity in Venetian society—Shylock retains his life, but no possible way to live it.

Together with the Duke's pardon, Antonio's final demand for Shylock's conversion constitutes a self-defeating and excessive punishment. Rather than let Shylock remain a Jew, albeit a poor one, Antonio suggests a different penalty:

> ANTONIO:
> So please the Duke and all the court
> To quit the fine for half his goods,
> I am content; so he will let me have
> The other half in use, to render it
> Upon his death to the gentleman
> That lately stole his daughter.
> Two things provided more: that for this favor
> He presently become a Christian;
> The other, that he do record a gift
> Here in the court of all he dies possessed
> Unto his son Lorenzo and his daughter.
>
> (379-89)

Not only does Antonio's supposed "favor" maintain, in the long run, total control over Shylock's possessions, but it further stipulates that Shylock "become a Christian." Hence, Antonio's punishment does not fully restore Shylock's independent economic status, and it completely obliterates Shylock's cultural and religious connections. The punishment comes to represent not so much a response to a misdeed as it does a personal attack on an outsider. By maintaining economic and religious control over Shylock, Antonio attempts to eradicate the Jew's identity on every level. Paul Cantor notes that, as we watch Antonio pronounce his punishment, we "sense that Venice is forcibly imposing conformity, responding to a challenge to its beliefs by simply trying to eliminate that challenge."[23] Ironically, rather than teach Shylock a lesson in compassion and display evidence of the mercy which just moments ago Portia had urged Shylock to use, Antonio goes too far.

The conversion's harshness reveals a fundamental anxiety among the Christians to reach closure. The conversion is so excessive that it does not elevate Shylock to the level of a gratified, merciful Christian, but reduces him to a broken, weary man. When Portia asks him, "art thou contented, Jew?," he merely echoes her resignedly with, "I am content" (392-3). There is no evidence of the conversion bringing Shylock any solace, newfound understanding, or acceptance into the Christian community. Rather, it humiliates him, and he exits anticlimactically:

> SHYLOCK:
> I pray you, give me leave to go from hence.
> I am not well. Send the deed after me,
> And I will sign it.
>
> (394-6)

The incomplete act of signing the deed seems to symbolize Shylock's relationship with the Christian community as he leaves the stage. The conversion, far from enlightening Shylock in the glories of Christianity, sickens him into silence. In their anxious rush to reach closure, the Venetians and Belmontians have attempted to overcome an obstacle to community at a terrible price. Denying Shylock his dignity, the Christians have mercilessly victimized him.

3. "And yet I am sure you are not satisfied / Of these events at full": Shylock's Containment Defied and Closure Denied

The cruel punishment of Shylock casts an ominous cloud over the final act's attempts at blissful closure. When E. C. Pettet writes that "the play dissolves, appropriately, in the exquisite love scene under the moon in Belmont," he disregards the very inappropriateness of the Christians' behavior toward Shylock and the way in which this flaws the play's comic ending.[24] As the Christians celebrate their own marriages and good tidings, their joy is undercut by an audience's acute awareness of Shylock's absence. The words of Portia and Jessica reveal that the Christians' improper treatment of Shylock overpowers the festive attempts of the final act.

Rather than revel in the triumph of community, the characters in Belmont struggle gloomily to honor their newly-formed bonds. Their conversations are overshadowed, literally and figuratively, by Shylock's mistreatment. Portia makes this clear when she compares Belmont's nighttime to a day plagued by dark clouds:

> PORTIA:
> This night methinks is but the daylight sick;
> It looks a little paler. 'Tis a day
> Such as the day when the sun is hid.
>
> (V.i. 124-6)

Portia's image of a sick, paling night undermines the attempts to create a lively scene in Belmont. While glorious sunshine would have portrayed the confident couples in brilliant light, the inclement weather seems to reflect discomfort below the play's surface. According to Portia, the clouds hide the sun from view, and this has the effect of infecting the day with disease. But Portia's metaphor also seems to give voice to a deeper message within the play. Just as the clouds cover the sun, the characters of *Merchant* have hidden Shylock away by refusing to acknowledge his cruel punishment and by attempting to forget him. As the sickness which Portia refers to darkens an otherwise sunny day, *Merchant*'s Christians have inflicted their comedy with an illness, the inability to deal satisfyingly with Shylock, which darkens what should be a radiant closure to the play.

Throughout the final act, pessimism, discomfort, and doubt emanate from Jessica. Her few lines and mysterious silences reveal a subtle alignment with her father's personality. During the act's opening exchange between herself and Lorenzo, she puts a damper on the romantic mood with a suggestion of dishonest love:

> JESSICA:
> In such a night
> Did young Lorenzo swear he loved her well,
> Stealing her soul with many vows of faith,
> And ne'er a true one.
>
> (V.i. 17-20)

Just as her father mocked Antonio's sexuality earlier, so Jessica now mocks Lorenzo's status as a faithful husband.[25] However, while Shylock disturbed the single Antonio by discussing the natural reproductive activity of "woolly breeders," Jessica teases the married Lorenzo with the dour insinuation that his "vows of faith" to her are suspect and that he is a liar, perhaps even an adulterer. Jessica, then, ridicules the sexual attitudes of the Christian community as her father had before her, and, by doing so, her personality is partially aligned with Shylock's. Thus, the Jew's presence, although banished, resurfaces through his daughter's attitudes and effectively challenges the supposed fidelity of the very thing which enables communal continuity—marriage—in the final act.

Furthermore, like Shylock, Jessica stubbornly refuses to conform to the wishes of the Christian community. As Lorenzo tries in vain to entertain her by speaking of celestial music as the "harmony . . . in immortal souls" and finally ordering music to be played, Jessica's discomfort becomes most acute:

> LORENZO:
> Come ho, and wake Diana with a hymn!
> With sweetest touches pierce your mistress' ear
> And draw her home with music.
> *Play music*
> JESSICA:
> I am never merry when I hear sweet music.
> LORENZO:
> The reason is, your spirits are attentive.
>
> (V.i. 70)

By calling for music, Lorenzo desires to envelop himself and Jessica in an illusion of blissful harmony, where only his notion of celestial notes played by "young-eyed cherubins" can be heard (62). Yet, with her remark, Jessica refuses to participate in this illusion. Her words betray deep feelings of anxiety and detract from the joyous atmosphere that Lorenzo struggles to attain. Jessica cannot easily make her "spirits" less "attentive" and simply disregard her sadness for the sake of a comic resolution. Rather than pretend, as Lorenzo does, that music has the power to resolve problematic situations, she acknowledges her discomfort and draws an audience's attention to the artificial nature of Lorenzo's request in light of what has happened to Shylock.

Both Jessica and Shylock represent what Ralph Berry describes as "the unmentionable" in the play, that is, threatening forces which the central community tries vainly to sweep aside and cover up.[26] In court, the Duke told Shylock that he "*expect[ed]* a gentle answer," and Portia announced that Shylock "must . . . be merciful," as if they knew that obstacles to comedy have to be defeated if comic closure is to be attained. Lorenzo seems to share this attitude when he elaborates on the beneficial effects of harmonious sounds and then concludes with an imperative for Jessica to "mark the music" (88). In effect, Lorenzo forces Jessica to endure the music, despite the fact that she seems unwilling to partake in his musical illusion of happiness.

Jessica's pessimistic remark about "sweet music" is also her last speaking moment in the play. Rather than permit the existence of challenges to comic progression, Lorenzo stifles Jessica's voice, just as Portia and the Duke do to Shylock's in the courtroom. Thus, the Christian community effectively marginalizes both the Jewish father and his converted daughter. Whereas Shylock leaves the stage, however, Jessica remains onstage in spite of her silent misgivings, watching but not conversing with the other characters. The audience never hears her respond to Lorenzo's silencing mechanism, and the text does not indicate how she reacts. This leads an audience to wonder whether or not Jessica remains internally torn between Jewish and Christian worlds and between her father's and her husband's households.[27] By stifling Jessica's voice, the Christians fail to resolve, and prevent Jessica from resolving, her religious, cultural, and social allegiances. Anxiously attempting to reach closure, the characters of *Merchant* have only compounded their difficulties by failing to deal satisfactorily not just with Shylock, but with Jessica as well.

Many of Shakespeare's festive comedies, including *Love's Labors Lost, A Midsummer Night's Dream,* and *Much Ado About Nothing,* end with song and dance celebrating the integration of community. But *The Merchant of Venice* ends quietly and anticlimactically, with Gratiano's crass quibble on "Nerissa's ring" and the Christians' hasty exit. In marked contrast to endings of other Shakespearean comedies, I envision a performance in which the stage remains absolutely silent and still, similar to Jack Gold's 1980 BBC production. Jessica has been left alone on the set; her solitude expresses her own hesitancy to participate in the revelry, just as it also parallels Shylock's own solitude offstage. She reads his "special deed of gift," the document that Nerissa has given to her and to Lorenzo, which states that they will inherit Shylock's property upon his death (291-2). This deed represents the only connection remaining between the Jewish father and his converted daughter, and I believe that it jars Jessica's memory to recall stealing Shylock's jewels and learning of his subsequent punishment. In this sudden moment of realization for her as well as for the audience, her expression slowly shifts from happy anticipation of married life as a Christian, to guilty regret for what she has tacitly allowed to be done to her father. Jessica's performance thus involves the skillful act of opening the play up to the audience and encouraging us along with her, to feel sorrow for Shylock's treatment.

4. Conclusion

In *The Merchant of Venice,* Shylock fulfills a necessary role in the Christians' economic community as a usurer, but he is simultaneously shunned because of his Judaism, while, within the play, he represents a threatening presence which a welcoming community must paradoxically ostracize in order to reach comic closure. Similarly, Jessica, as a wife with a large dowry, is required for the Christians' economic community, but, like her father, she, too, is alienated for voicing a challenge to closure. Hence, both Shylock and Jessica are necessary to the play's central community for their economic importance and their role as obstacles which must be overcome. Yet, in the community's efforts to reach closure, it fails to deal appropriately with these opposing voices. Rather than negotiate with its outsiders, the Christian community silences them, but with so much force that its attempts are undermined. In the process of restraining Shylock, the society ironically draws attention to the unrestrained cruelty that it uses in its own punishment of difference.

By allowing Shylock and Jessica to undermine closure, Shakespeare unites the historical and literary concerns outlined above. He seems to recognize the inherent similarity between Renaissance Venice's need for the Jew in order to define itself economically, and the need of his play's Venetians to ostracize Shylock in order to define themselves as a community. Indeed, Shakespeare creates a fascinating tension between the exclusionary practices of Venetian Christians and the demands of the comic genre.

Leaving this tension unresolved, Shakespeare makes a statement about the tendency of both comic form and historical circumstance to require an "other" for self-definition. He problematizes the fact that comic characters, like sixteenth-century Venetians, manipulate and finally ostracize those outside of their central community. By allowing Shylock to upset the play's closure, then, Shakespeare places in the foreground the position of the "other."[28] He suggests that, rather than operating under principles of egalitarianism and mercy, the Christians of the comedy and of Venice take what they want from Jews, only to hide them away in an attempt to silence their frustrated voices. Defying containment and overshadowing *The Merchant of Venice*'s closure, Shylock protests the fact that the comedy has established community at the paradoxical price of ghettoizing its outsider.

Notes

1. C. L. Barber, *Shakespeare's Festive Comedy* (Princeton: Princeton University Press, 1959), pp. 4, 6-8. Barber defines the "butts" as scapegoats who obstruct the actions of the play's central community in Shakespeare's comedies. Thus, characters such as Falstaff are not "butt" figures, according to Barber's use of the term.

2. *Ibid.,* pp. 8-9.

3. Bernard Glassman, "The New Jewish Villain," *Anti-Semitic Stereotypes without Jews* (Detroit: Wayne State University Press, 1975), p. 62. This chapter provides background information on the development of Jewish stereotypes during the Renaissance.

4. Cecil Roth, *The Jews in the Renaissance* (Philadelphia: The Jewish Publication Society of America, 1959), p. 6.

5. For a dramatic treatment of the ways in which city governments required and extracted Jewish funds for self-protection, see Christopher Marlowe's *The Jew of Malta*, one of Shakespeare's most important sources for *The Merchant*. For more on English Christian perceptions of, and relations with, Jews, see the introduction in James Bulman, *The Merchant of Venice* [Shakespeare in Performance Series] (Manchester: Manchester University Press, 1991).

6. Glassman, p. 68.

7. Roth, p. 13. John Gross's recent book *Shylock: A Legend and Its Legacy* (New York: Simon & Schuster, 1993), contains information and insights on the ghetto of Venice, pp. 23-28, as well as a marvelously detailed summary of the play's sources, Shylock's performance history, and critical and popular responses to him.

8. All references to *The Merchant of Venice* are taken from *The Merchant of Venice,* edited by Kenneth Myrick (New York: Signet Classic, 1987).

9. Lawrence Danson, *The Harmonies of The Merchant of Venice* (New Haven: Yale University Press, 1978), p. 139.

10. Lars Engle, "'Thrift is Blessing': Exchange and Explanation in *The Merchant of Venice,*" *Shakespeare Studies* 37 (1986), p. 29. See also, Gross, pp. 30-33.

11. I find Engle's word choice particularly suggestive when he writes that "Shylock claims to possess the, patriarchs . . . and to interpret their example with authority" (p. 29). Here, Engle uses a meaning of "possess" which, knowingly or unknowingly, plays on Antonio's possession pun by twisting it just as Shylock does. Instead of the Devil possessing Shylock, we now have Shylock possessing Abraham, Isaac, and Jacob.

12. Coppelia Kahn has argued convincingly for Antonio's homosexuality in "The Cuckoo's Note: Male Friendship and Cuckoldry in *The Merchant of Venice,*" *Shakespeare's "Rough Magic": Renaissance Essays in Honor of C. L. Barber,* ed. by Peter Erikson and Coppelia Kahn (Newark: University of Delaware Press, 1985), pp. 104-110.

13. E. Pearlman, "Shakespeare, Freud, and the Two Usuries, or, Money's a Meddlar," *English Literary Renaissance* 2 (1972): 222.

14. Paul A. Cantor, "Religion and the Limits of Community in *The Merchant of Venice,*" *Soundings: An Interdisciplinary Journal* 70 (1987): 249.

15. Shakespeare uses these notions of caricature and paraphrase similarly in *Othello,* when Iago relays what seem to be Cassio's sleepy outbursts to Othello:

IAGO: In sleep I heard him say, "Sweet Desdemona,Let us be wary, let us hide our loves!"
And then, sir, he would gripe and wring my hand,
Cry "O sweet creature!" Then kiss me hard,
As if he plucked up kisses by the roots
That grew upon my lips; laid his leg o'er my thigh,
And sigh, and kiss, and then cry, "Cursed fate
That gave thee to the Moor!"

(III.iii.416-23)

Just as Solanio slandered Shylock with the message equating daughters and ducats, so Iago condemns, and, even more extremely than Solanio, nearly dooms, Cassio by portraying him as a lusty, jealous suitor. Paraphrasing, then, represents for both Solanio and Iago a means to ridicule and manipulate their enemies.

16. This point gains even more credence if we accept James Bulman's suggestion that Shylock's speech may have originally been delivered directly to the audience as a soliloquy; see Bulman, p. 8.

17. Kieman Ryan, *Harvester New Readings: Shakespeare* (Atlantic Highlands, NJ: Humanities Press International, 1989), p. 17.

18. Ralph Berry, "Discomfort in *The Merchant of Venice,*" *Shakespeare and the Awareness of the Audience* (London: Macmillan Press, 1985), p. 57.

19. Norman Rabkin, "Meaning and *The Merchant of Venice,*" *Shakespeare and the Problem of Meaning* (Chicago: University of Chicago Press, 1980), p. 6.

20. See, for example, Barber, p. 185; Danson, p. 164; E. C. Pettet, "*The Merchant of Venice* and the Problem of Usury," *English Association Essays and Studies* 31 (1945), p. 29.

21. Jean Howard, "The Difficulties of Closure: An Approach to The Problematic in Shakespearean Comedy," in *Comedy from Shakespeare to Sheridan,* ed. by A. R. Braunmiuller and J. C. Bulman (Newark: University of Delaware Press, 1986), p. 124.

22. Bulman, p. 21.

23. Cantor, p. 253.

24. Pettet, p. 29.

25. Importantly, the act begins with Jessica and Lorenzo exchanging a series of remarks about various tragically doomed couples (Ryan, p. 22). The tragic subjects of the opening conversation ironically undermine the comic harmony that Lorenzo hopes to foster.

26. Berry, p. 57.

27. Lawrence Danson claims with hesitation that, in "I am never merry when I hear sweet music," Jessica expresses herself "with (I take it) a newcomer's insecurity" (Danson, p. 187). Rather than insecurity, it seems that Jessica reveals the reluctance that she, as well as the audience, feel toward rejoicing in

comic closure so soon after her father has been humiliatingly banished. I do not agree with John Gross's opinion that Jessica's "emotional bond with [Shylock] is broken" in this act, and that her silence suggests her acquiescence to the others (Gross, p. 62). Ralph Berry is perhaps correct when he writes that "Jessica becomes a focus of stillness and darkness" in the final act and that she "has a long way to go in Christian society" (Berry, pp. 61, 59).

28. I would not go so far as to claim that the ambiguous ending does enough to balance the oppression of Shylock. Rather, it avoids providing a simplistic comic resolution and thus calls into question the appropriateness of his treatment.

Avraham Oz (essay date 1995)

SOURCE: "'Which is the merchant here? and which the Jew?': Riddles of Identity," in *The Yoke of Love: Prophetic Riddles in The Merchant of Venice*, University of Delaware Press, 1995, pp. 93-133.

[*In the excerpt below, Oz remarks that the outsider status that Renaissance European cities imposed upon non-European inhabitants (and on Jews in particular) was an attempt to exert power over various members of society. Thus, in* The Merchant of Venice, *Shylock does his best to reverse this "master-slave" relationship through his pound of flesh arrangement with the European Antonio.*]

The question whereby Portia, clad as a young male judge, launches the process of justice at the court of Venice has intrigued many readers of the play. "She can't be serious," we tend to ask, shifting our eyes from the figure of Venice's prince of merchants, who retains his posture of gloomy dignity even at court, to that of "old Shylock," clad in his Jewish gaberdine. Thomas Moisan, who used the same question of Portia in the title of his illuminating discussion of *The Merchant of Venice,* concludes that seriousness is not at all what we must expect of this play; indeed it is the playfulness with which it treats the prevailing socioeconomic ideologies of the time, playfulness that produces something like Macherey's famous parodic distance toward them (Macherey 1978, esp. 61ff), which illuminates the dramatic tension in which the play holds "the competing impulses of recuperation and subversion" (Moisan 1987, 203). The idea that the play holds recuperation and subversion in dramatic tension seems, indeed, to be the only valid refutation of the age-old rivalry between the so-called "romantic" and "ironic," or "apologetic," interpretations of *The Merchant of Venice.* It is a way to recognize "the necessity that determines the work" without imposing a constraining "meaning" on the unresolved riddle of the play (Macherey 1978, 77-78). And yet Portia's question, raising one of the major issues of the play, the question of identity, should be taken more seriously into consideration. Coming from a character who but of late had openly yielded her identity to become the wife of he who won her in conforming his own identity to a heavily ideological construct, it is perhaps the very question that any judicious reading of the play must seriously attempt to leave open—not, however, without first scrutinizing its implications. It is, in other words, one of the most spontaneous and genuine expressions in *The Merchant of Venice* of that "process of riddle-work before its final completion," a necessary stage in the "confrontation with otherness," much upon which runs the wisdom of the play. Read against the background of the varied cluster of issues raised, addressed, suggested, and represented in the play by the plots of the merchant and the Jew, ranging from the politics of love and identity to the structure and meaning of cannibalism, slavery, private possession, money, and terrorism, Portia's "Which is the Merchant Here? and Which the Jew?" is not less crucial to *The Merchant of Venice* than Barnardo's no less riddilng "Who's there" that sets the course for the probing into the mysteries of "the world" in *Hamlet*. Some facets of that "process of riddle-work" informing the play will be addressed in the present chapter.

It has already been argued in the introduction that the character of Shylock could be transformed from one minority affiliation, that of the Jew, to another, be it an alien in general, a moneylender, or an early modern version of the terrorist. My project here is to examine what makes Shylock's conspicuous ethno-religious identity lend itself to any transformation at all. A provocative artistic formulation of this project was offered, a few years ago, in an Israeli film, Rafi Bokai's *Avanti Popolo* (1986). The film depicts the escape of two Egyptian soldiers through the Israeli lines in Sinai in an attempt to reach the Egyptian border. When captured by a group of Israeli soldiers, one of the Egyptians starts to recite Shylock's "hath not a Jew eyes" speech. An Israeli soldier comments: "He has changed the parts!" Has he, indeed? It seems that Shylock is carefully provided in the play with more solid distinctions than any other character in terms of ethno-religious identity, class, family hierarchy, or even gender (which is more than can be said of Portia at the time she poses her question). Can we separate the validity of his Jewishness from all the rest and ask to what extent is it to be taken literally as a token of ethnic identity?

The question of identity looms constantly through the major tensions, conflicts, and crises informing *The Merchant of Venice*. On the surface level, the ancient narrative picked up by Shakespeare is populated by effective, well-defined dramatic subjects. Yet on a deeper level all the seemingly stable intersubject boundaries are deliberately effaced, all the safe codes of individuality transgressed by language devices and ceremonial acts, to finally transform what was initially conceived as a lifelike, well-defined character into a "crystallized monad" of entirely different order. The riddles propounded by the late Master of Belmont to the living suitors who have come to appropriate the identity of his daughter concern (and devour, like an ancient monster) their own identities. The moral riddle propounded by Shylock to Venice not only transforms Venice's prince of merchants to a helpless victim, but robs also Bassanio of his newly acquired identity as the new master of Belmont and causes Portia to adopt a male identity in order to secure her recent "yoke of love." What we get here is a play about human subjects tampering with identities, attempting incessantly to contemplate, define, and fashion themselves and the others. This kind of mobility is barely surprising: "The Renaissance delighted in stories of the transformation of individuals out of all recognition—the king confused with the beggar, the great prince reduced to the condition of a wild man, the pauper changed into a rich lord" (Greenblatt 1988, 76). The interchangeability of characters as a major proclivity in Renaissance drama has been often marked by critics, but in many cases "recognition of change is resisted by the characters" (Loomba 1989, 100). Here, however, it is all premeditated and openly done. If Adam Smith is right to spot in human nature a basic "propensity to truck, barter and exchange one thing for another" (Smith 1950, 1:15), the characters of *The Merchant of Venice* constantly probe his point in dealing not only in merchandise, property and money, but also with their pliable identities. Subjects are yielding themselves to be restructured by socioeconomic circumstances; identities exchanged and bartered; and riddling formulations inscribed on caskets, informing bonds of credit, marriage and amity or consecrating rings disrupt any trace of the homogeneity of the subject. It is a play designed to dismay all essentialists: the moment we seem to have captured the properties qualifying a given dramatic subject, it leaps into another transformation, which explains the degree of personal offense taken by critics who painfully watch that slick prodigal, "self-loving parasite" (Eagleton 1986, 45), Bassanio, winning the top prize at the Belmont contest of wit.[1]

In most cases, however, one feels the identities resulting of those transformations were hardly worth the effort. *The Merchant of Venice* has often been proclaimed a flawed vessel, unworthy of the serious themes it contains. Those who find fault with its dramatic merits, holding the plot incredible and the characters flat, tend to blame the deficient skills of an immature author. For those, as John Lyon puts it, "it seems appropriate to talk of the defects of Shakespeare's creative virtues" (Lyon 1988, 64). Indeed, judging *The Merchant of Venice* from the stance of Shakespeare's later psychological achievements, the world surrounding Shylock and Antonio seems shallow, its complexities mechanical, and the discourse out of which the characters stem hardly sufficient to pierce the code of even those shallow complexities. But this impression of a less substantial pageant is not exclusively produced by the shortcomings of a lesser authorial skill (in spite of many attempts to present it as such)[2] for in *The Merchant of Venice* most characters turn out to be imaginary constructs forged either by themselves or by others. Disguises, deceptions, mistaken identities, and other forms of transformation are common in Shakespeare, especially in the comedies; but nowhere do they seem more obsessively practiced than here. The play opens with Antonio, having much ado to know himself, presenting his perplexion in turns to the entire guild of Venetian merchants, each of whom volunteers to tell him who he really is, what are his concerns, and what role he should play on the world's stage. Having adopted the role assigned to him by Bassanio, devoting to him not only his purse but his person, Antonio proceeds to let Shylock have a claim on his body. In the meantime Portia is having fun constructing before Nerissa each of her present suitors. Since Nerissa must have seen them all, what we have here is yet another instance of the common practice by which the characters of our play seem to pass their time: the forging of identities. Launcelot Gobbo comes on stage to entertain us by multiplying himself, in the vein of medieval moralities, into the triad of Launcelot, conscience, and the Fiend. Then he dons a different identity to "try confusions" (2.2.35) with his blind father, just to go on adopting a new identity as Bassanio's servant, a transformation that involves the immediate provision of "a livery more guarded than his fellows" (147-48). And then follows Jessica, eloping with Lorenzo to receive her new identity as a Christian amidst the turmoil of the masque, in which everybody around adopts borrowed identities.

All these, however, are but an introduction to the feast of transformations and riddles of identity the play still has in store for us. Antonio may believe naïvely that there is "no masque to-night" (2.6.64), once his friends have taken off their masks to set sail for Belmont. But we know better. Not only Gratiano, who describes in great detail the sober habit and the observance of civility he vows to put on in Belmont, but Bassanio himself, who implored him to transform himself, prepares to do the same. The Master of Belmont, we learn, has devised a special quiz for his daughter's suitors, who are asked to define her by subscribing to a chosen model of moral identity. One of the offered models corresponds to the official ideology held by the Christian society of the play, and the penalty exerted on those who fail to find it or to comply by it is, not fortuitously, to remain forever solitary, namely to be devoid of marital affiliation, which in the world of romantic comedy is the basic form of solidarity. Whereas Bassanio wins sexual and economic gratification by endorsing a ready-made identity, his rivals, cut off from the fulfillment of love and procreation, are doomed to total insularity, which precludes identity, as the gloomy tokens of death and folly that will qualify them from now on will attest. Thus, Morocco and Arragon, those two potential alter-egos of Bassanio, are convicted to eternal otherness, a lot not incompatible with that awaiting both Shylock and Antonio by the end of the play even though Shylock, who lost his marital status by death and his patriarchal status by folly, will be graciously offered a refuge from his spiritual seclusion by drowning his otherness in the font of the official Christian ideology.

While all this is taking place, Shylock seems to be the only one to withstand the sea of transformations and, by opposing, remain himself. Stephen Greenblatt would even applaud him for accumulating identity in the course of the play (Greenblatt 1980, 208), namely, establishing it even further: accumulating is a crucial word to describe him who defends interest by using the fable of Jacob's hire

(1.3.71-85). A closer look, however, will reveal the character of Shylock to be the most intricate construct among the play's *dramatis personae*. For whereas all the other characters are what we may call, for the sake of generality, regular dramatic constructs, the products of the dramatist's common skill of representing reality and his attentiveness to dramatic heritage, the representation of Shylock is doubly removed, namely a dramatic construct built on a cultural construct. It is a practice Shakespeare was scarcely to repeat in his work until the creation of Caliban in *The Tempest,* another dramatic construct built on the same principle (Aaron, Morocco, or Othello may not fall exactly into the same category, since their "alien" quality seems to immerse in their color symbolism rather than in a particular socioeconomic classification). For the sake of understanding the dramatic function of such a cultural construct in a play which otherwise seems to follow faithfully the narrative patterns of romantic comedy, we shall have to summarize some historical evidence. Thus we may learn, for instance, how Shylock's struggle to secure a complex identity by force of possession may be explained by its bearing on the history of Jewish economy in Renaissance Italy and Europe in general.

Since Jews were expelled from England by King Edward I in 1290, exactly three centuries before Shakespeare embarked on his playwriting career, he had no immediate model for Shylock. For whatever way we may read the play, we must acknowledge that Shylock baldly insists on his Jewish identity. Whether or not did the memory of self-confessed Jews remain sufficiently vivid to nourish Shakespeare's imagination three centuries after their expulsion (see, e.g., Poliakov 1966, 78), such a model was scarce in Elizabethan England. Indeed, both Shakespeare and Richard Burbage (who must have portrayed Shylock first) may have had an opportunity to meet in London the famous Doctor Roderigo Lopez, who, as Sidney Lee puts it, "shared with actors an intimacy with those noblemen who were the warmest patrons of the drama" (Lee 1880). Burbage could even have met him earlier, at Kenilworth, where his father's troupe was patronized by the Earl of Leicester, who then employed Lopez as his personal physician. And yet the small community of Marranos, to whom Lopez belonged, had officially to conceal their religious affiliation. Contemporary, London-born Amis, the possible relative of the Añes family (Lopez's in-laws), whom Thomas Coryat met in Constantinople, could hardly hope to observe the ceremony of circumcision as openly in England as in Turkey.[3] Lopez's own Jewishness, emphasized in his trial by both his prosecutor ("worse than Judas himself") and judge ("vile Jew") (Sinsheimer 1964, 66), served but to underline the main charge brought against him of conspiring to poison the Queen in the service of Spain. "That he was a Jew," says Lytton Strachey, not without justice, "was merely an incidental iniquity, making a shade darker the central abomination of Spanish intrigue." Unlike Shylock, Strachey adds, "Dr Lopez was europeanized and christianized—a meagre, pathetic creature who came to his ruin by no means owing to his opposition to his gentile surroundings, but because he had allowed himself to be fatally entangled in them" (Strachey 1971, 61). When the rope was put on his neck, Bishop Goodman tells us sympathetically, Lopez cried out that his love for the Queen was greater than his love for Jesus Christ to which the crowd responded: "He is a Jew! He is a Jew!" (Goodman 1839, 155). Shylock paraphrases Antonio in citing that same phrase: "I am a Jew" (3.1.52) in a way that combines self-dignity with defiant complaint.

Jews were not allowed back officially into England before the successful negotiations between Menassheh Ben Israel, the leader of Amsterdam Jewish community, and Cromwell in December 1655 (see Katz 1982). We have already noted how in 1607, a decade after Shylock was created, Sir Thomas Sherley was still trying to intercede with King James on behalf of a group of Levantine Jews, who wished to settle in England, be granted freedom of religion and allowed to build synagogues (for the payment of a considerable annual tribute), but to no avail. King James declined granting them similar rights also in Ireland, for a tribute of two ducats per head (see Davies 1967, 181-82; and see introduction, n.18. . .). There were converts, such as Nathaniel Menda, brought into Christianity in 1577 by John Foxe (Foxe 1578). However, the one case we know of in contemporary England in which a Jew, arrested following a religious dispute, openly asserted his Jewishness in court, that of mining technician Joachim Gaunz (a native of Bohemia who found his way to England as a foreign laborer), was exceptional, local, and scarcely known.[4] The Jewish gabardine was, at least in England, a visual metaphor; the antipathy between the population of London's Old Jewry and hogsflesh (as Jonson's Well-Bred testifies in *Every Man in His Humour*), was a thing of the past; and no usurer in usury-riddled London was a self-confessed Jew. To that extent was the reality of Jew hatred effaced from actual experience after three centuries of absence, that at the beginning of the seventeenth century, several Puritans dared convert themselves to Judaism, circumcision and all, while others demanded the recall of the Jews to England (Roth 1941, 149-54).

Even in contemporary Venice former Jewish moneylenders had to abandon their trade and revert to pawnbroking and the selling of second-hand merchandise (*veteramentarii*).[5] The civil emancipation through money, which Greenblatt is borrowing from Marx's *On the Jewish Question,* in his essay on Marlowe,[6] is but partly accurate: Marx's somewhat mystified figure of the "real Jew" is far from being methodologically scrupulous, drawing, as Julius Carlebach is showing, on descriptions of his intellectual predecessors from Kant and Hegel to Feuerbach and Bauer rather than on empirical experience.[7] In any case any such concept belongs to a later age: only from the later part of the seventeenth century onward do we find among Jews the common practice of monetary investments in industry, agriculture, and commerce on a large scale (see Katz 1961, 44). There is only scant historical evidence in the early modern period of Jews actually initiating the monetary process rather than joining it at less advantageous, hence less competitive, junctures. The exclusivity of the institutional framework made it difficult, if not impossible, for the Jews to launch any mainstream enterprise.[8] Credit is far from being a Jewish invention, but a basic element of capitalist economy, for which Jews, whose money was not often invested in immovable property (a point to the consequence of which I shall come back later) had normally more available assets (see Katz 1961, 47-48). Most European countries utilized Jewish material and human resources to enrich economic processes that were developing within the frameworks of their own established institutions, which were as a rule impenetrable by the Jews and thus uninfluenced by any allegedly emancipated Jewish economy. England, which has vigorously embarked on its capitalist era especially under the Tudors without a single Jewish catalyst of significance, is obviously a case in point.

The dramatic construct called Shylock (unlike the historical "Barabas," a name of obscure origin and without analogues)[9] had no representational bearing on contemporary reality in the sense that other characters did. Thus what distinguishes Shylock from the other characters of the play is a representational void, or an absence. It is, of course, a roaring absence, full of stage presence. We do not know whence, if at all, he came from, or how he came by his present occupation or wealth. The play does not tell us much about past events in the lives of its characters[10] and yet we know a good deal about Bassanio's prodigal career; about his former association with the Marquis of Montferrat, which has brought him to meet Portia before; we know about Portia's life as a rich heiress desired by suitors from all over the place; about Antonio's mercantile enterprises; and we even get a feeling of Launcelot Gobbo's childhood. The case of Shylock is entirely different. The only biographical detail we know about him is one which is revealed in a functional context: his having had a wife (or that, at least, is whom we assume she was) named Leah, who gave him a turquoise ring when he was a bachelor (3.1.111). But the absence of a personal biography suggests that Shylock partakes in the general, fairy-tale biography offered by the popular imagination for the cultural construct of the Jew. Such an exemplary biography is provided by Marlowe for his Barabas, involving all the clichéd activities and occupations traditionally attributed to, or associated with the Jew, from well poisoning and killing sick Christians, through practicing "physic" to the detriment of his Christian patients, to usury (*The Jew of Malta* 2.3.176-202). In terms of that nonbiography, the Jew is indeed very close to Marx's definition, cited by Greenblatt: "a universal *antisocial* element of the *present time*" (Greenblatt 1980, 204). Shylock's wish to see his daughter "dead at [his] foot, and the jewels in her ear . . . and the ducats in her coffin" (3.1.80-82) belongs to the same order of transgressive acts as Barabas's murdering Abigail: both are simultaneously deeds and non-deeds, devoid of the necessity of representation. For in the case of that cultural construct turned dramatic character, we cannot easily separate the positive limits, the finitude of the subject, which in Foucault's hostile description "is marked by the spatiality of the body, the yawning of desire, and the time of language" (Foucault 1970, 315), from the transgression of the subject, which suggests an absence of knowledge, or a knowledge of absence. Barabas has done a lot of mischief, as he himself admits and as we get a chance to see for ourselves; and yet, regardless of what he has actually done, there is a permanent stock of evil, inherent in the cultural construct of the Jew and ever ready to be assigned to him in people's minds with no need for factual evidence:

> *Barnardine.*
> . . . go with me
> And help me to exclaim against the Jew.
> *Jacomo.*
> Why, what has he done?
> *Barnardine.*
> A thing that makes me tremble to unfold.
> *Jacomo.*
> What, has he crucified a child?
>
> (*The Jew of Malta*, 3.6.45-49)

Marlowe even provides us with a lively illustration of the common process in which such a fictional identity, or "biography," is forged, when drunken Ithamore is gratuitously constructing the clichéd image of the mean Jew before the courtesan and her bully, with Barabas in disguise providing the truth for us, as he always does in his asides:

> *Ithamore.*
> 'Tis a strange thing of that Jew: he lives upon pickled grasshoppers and sauc'd mushrumps.
> *Barabas [aside].*
> What a slave's this! The governor feeds not as I do.
> *Ithamore.*
> He never put on a clean shirt since he was circumcis'd.
> *Barabas [aside].*
> O rascal! I change myself twice a day.
> *Ithamore.*
> The hat he wears, Judas left under the elder when he hang'd himself.
> *Barabas [aside].*
> 'Twas sent me for a present from the Great Cham.
>
> (4.4.65-74)

Such an imaginary biography awaits, potentially, Shylock as well; but since, unlike in the case of Barabas, which Marlowe took the pains to draw carefully to the last detail, it is not complemented in Shakespeare's play with actual, reliable details, Shylock lives in the public domain of common fictionality. Technically, of course, Shylock is a dramatic subject as any other character in the play. But even in his asides, even when citing his dreams, he seems to be nothing more than an abstract measure, qualifying and defining the immanent constitution of the others. Shylock is the zero point of all the other identities in the play: signifying all, representing none. Unlike an individual case of transgression, such as an evil eye cast by a local witch, the Jew is not counted as a particlar threat on a personal level. His effect is of a different, universal order.[11] He is the archetypal Other whose desire structures the subject. For on the one hand he is the great menace, penetrating the dream of love and humanity offered by the play with his blunt discourse of vulgar rationality, his seemingly soluble riddles, to reduce a mystery of enchanting volume into an impoverished pageant of disenchantment; but paradoxically he also represents at the same time the secret, unconscious desire of all the rest for a momentary (or maybe eternal?) liberation from the fetters of "legitimate" discourse and official ideology. Shylock may not be the only one in Venice who dreams of money-bags (2.5.18), but he is certainly the only one to admit it freely in public. Money-bags investing a dream, Jacob's staff informing a fable or a swear (2.5.36), and even a vision of jewels in one's dead daughter's ear (3.1.81) acquire a different symbolic meaning than "some more ducats" (2.6.50) gilding a romantic elopement in plain reality. The plain monetary transaction that threatens to reduce the narrative of the play to the level of a fortuitous, if curious, court proceeding suddenly acquires an aura of poetic acuteness and necessity.

The use of a cultural construct of great popular currency as a model for a dramatic character makes both for greater freedom and constraint: while immuned to factual refutation, it may prove qualified by the more unified image planted in the popular imagination than the variety of human subjects evoked by the other characters. The strategy adopted to avoid such a constraint was deliberate eclecticism. Shylock is a composite construct: the raw foundation of his character involves typically Jewish constituents such as Herod in the Nativity plays (especially in his wrathful appearances in 3.1 and 3.3), the vice in the moralities (be it Avaritia in Catholic *Respublica* or Infidelitio in Wager's Protestant *Maria Magdalena*), Judas, Gernutus, the Jews who burst in a grotesque, ecstatic dance round the foot of the cross at the moment of the crucifixion in the Coventry Cycle,[12] Sir Jonathas and his fellow Jews in the *Sacrament Play of Croxton*,[13] and the ritual killers of the boy Hugh of Lincoln. It also involves metaphorically Jewish constituents such as the usurer and non-Jewish constituents such as the pantaloon, the puritan, or the devil as the prosecutor in the medieval Processus Belial (see Rea 1929). Some of those constituents were interchangeable already on the level of ground material: Avaritia in *Respublica*, for instance, was often dressed as a Jew, but since the play was Catholic in its ideology this may have been intended as an insult to the Protestants rather than a direct representation of an ethnic or religious identity. And the tenets of "Moysaical Justice" as stereotypically represented in the popular imagination are expressed in *The Merchant of Venice*, as we shall see, in the argumentation of the Prince of Arragon no less than by Shylock himself. Shylock, however, evoked something larger and more complex than the common image of the Jew. As Stephen Greenblatt rightly notes, "the figure of the Jew is useful as a powerful rhetorical device, an embodiment for a Christian audience of all they loath and fear" but also "a true representative of his society," a qualification Greenblatt reserves for Barabas, but one that could equally be applied to Shylock, though in a different manner. Lacking an accurately corresponding identity, that bigger-than-life stereotype may represent at once no one and everyone, a threat and a form of desire, a mirror of fantasy, and the black hole of the play. There is no possible reconciliation which contains Shylock, yet no reconciliation is possible outside the discourse initiated by Shylock.

Thus *The Merchant of Venice*, a play whose poetry is curbed by a constant look to the rise and fall of shares in the Rialto, needs Shylock's fairy-tale cruelty to redeem its hidden depths of love and harmony. The dry words of Shylock's bond provide for Bassanio's encounter with the prophetic words which the Lord of Belmont had inscribed on the caskets, elicit Portia's poetic lecture on the quality of mercy, and make Lorenzo praise the harmony of the spheres. The legitimate discourse of Venice and Belmont, which has fallen prey to Antonio's sadness, Bassanio's prodigality, and Portia's weariness can only be recovered when Shylock's subversive discourse intervenes. But Shylock exacts his price. By the end of the trial scene both Venice and Belmont are buying their freedom from Shylock's constraint by the sole device of subscribing to his own discourse.

For Shylock is planted in a discourse within which human desire and happiness are almost totally subordinated to economic needs and gratification; where human sympathy and solidarity, redefined in a newly formed cosmoplitan world, is divorced from the all-embracing image of Christ (a divorce for which the obvious cases of Shylock or Morocco serve but radical symbolic signifiers) and becomes a function of a fragile, compromising alliance between interdependent classes, genders and races; where the notion of "good men" equals financially "sufficient" ones. In such a world of growing individualism any representation of harmony is but a token of coming to terms with the ever-multiplying, necessarily heterogeneous modes of one's own identity. In a world in which credit has become a precondition of commerce (see Cohen 1985, 199); where risk and hazard inform the very core of survival; where personal identities, so much dependent on power structures generated by economic status, are constantly prone to get diffused or totally lost in the procedures of mercantile ventures containing the calculated, though barely insured, risks of storms and pirates, one gets obsessed with fashioning and redefining one's identity by means of symbolic language games with ideological backing. The word, it seems, will hold even when everything else, including one's own identity, will fail, that is, of course, if you are at the right end of the political vocabulary, as Shylock is painfully to learn. Which is why Antonio, who at the outset is sufficiently provided with material wealth, craves for having his sadness and identity put in appropriate words; and why Portia's suitors have to know their way with words rather than with bed-pillows, as is the case with the earlier, medieval versions of the story, in the *Dolopathos* or the *Gesta Romanorum*.[14] A world reduced to moral riddles and legal phrasings will not be recuperated by psychological subtleties or accented realism but by symbolic acts, involving the breaking of a code of mystery, which at the same time negotiate their validity with the imaginary patterns of unconscious *jouissance*. And indeed, as Granville Barker rightly diagnosed, "There is no more reality in Shylock's bond and the Lord of Belmont's will than in Jack and the Beanstalk" (Barker 1963, 99). It is a telling phrase, since, whether or not we agree with its other implications, we cannot escape the notion that *The Merchant of Venice* is indeed a play governed by symbolic signifiers, by words and phrasings qualified by unconscious semiotic patterns, rather than by lifelike characters representing full-fledged human subjects motivated by rational considerations.

Without taking too seriously the extent of "reality" Granville-Barker's implied reader is supposed to expect, it is obvious that the provocative assertion with which he opens his discussion of *The Merchant of Venice* implicates the host of critics who for ages had attempted to endow the play with solid aura of reality, presenting the religious conflict as contributing to a "problem play" such as *Measure for Measure* is reputed to be, "pièce à thèse" attacking a topical political or moral problem in terms of a didactic theatrical event. As such, Granville-Barker's assertion is not entirely out of place: the prominent symbols investing the narrative of the play—the bond, the caskets, the pound of flesh, and the ring—are all assembled here from the popular repository of folklore and mythology, the powerhouse of human fantasy, the vocabulary of the imaginary order and the immediate constituents of the collective unconsciousness. As many nineteenth-century source hunters have assiduously shown, one may trace all the moral and ideological issues and narrative-units of *The Merchant of Venice* back to the realm of folktales and parables, *exemplum* and fairy tales.[15] A major property of the fairy tale, before it has been loaded by modern authors (especially from the eighteenth century onward) with heavy ideological burden (Zipes 1988, 3), is its potential indifference to moral criteria and psychological responses. The function of those, to the extent they exist at all in the world of fairy tales, is hardly more than to serve or decorate the narrative. Human subjects (and their interrelationships) are to be grasped more in terms of textual strategies, such as hermeneutical analysis (see, e.g., Ricoeur 1973), rather than conceived of as fully rounded, holistic human beings equipped with a distinct and definite psychological apparatus. If Shakespeare's fairy-tale characters haunt our deepest feelings long after the play has ended, it is because Shakespeare "could not help giving life to a character . . . no more . . . than the sun can help shining" (Barker 1963, 99); and the major function of those fairy-tale symbols in the world of the play may not be incompatible with providing for "the Utopian vocation of the newly reified sense, the mission . . . to restore at least a symbolic experience of libidinal gratification to a world drained of it, a world of extension, gray and merely quantifiable" (Jameson 1981, 63). For without that symbolic level, negotiating and appropriating imaginary patterns of uncounscious *jouissance*, both the language investing Shylock's bond and Portia's caskets, and the experience of love and harmony investing the play, cannot be reconciled with the world of the Real (or the Rialto, for that matter) but in terms of measure and calculation. And these are better expressed by signs and ratios rather than by full-fledged dramatic representations of human subjects.

A surprising feature (for some) of the early folk versions of the Pound of Flesh narrative is the absence of the Jew from the story.[16] But this should come as no surprise for anyone who will note that *The Merchant of Venice* has nothing to do with a narrow concept of Jewishness but rather with the general theme of power relations and their critical exposure and demystification. It is not just the power the Venetian state exerts on its citizens (among them Shylock), but also the power that the latters exert on the world and their fellow citizens. For power, which (as Foucault tells us) is always inseparably entangled with knowledge, has no constant, definite source but is revealed in an open, dialectical "cluster of relations" between the political and social factors (Foucault 1980, 199). Therefore, power is not solely the property of the political establishment, but is circulated by chain reaction from society to the individual. The very effect of power constitutes the individual, which is parallelly transformed into becoming a vehicle of power.[17] The same political establishment that gave privilege to the worldview (hence, to the system of knowledge or ideology) of the society of Christian merchants surrounding Antonio has simultaneously generated Shylock's power to exert moral and physical terror on that society by his knowledge of its constitution. Shylock is far from owning an essential dramatic identity: a function of the others' fears and desires, he is rather a dramatic process or a "flow," which can be construed either in terms of the signifying flow, whose discovery is assigned by Lacan to Freud and "the mystery of which lies in the fact that the subject does not even know where to pretend to be its organizer" (Lacan 1977, 259), or, alternatively, in Deleuze and Guattari's antioedipal terminology (Deleuze and Guattari 1977). Rather than becoming a unified subject, endowed with particular psychological or ethnic properties, Shylock embodies the nonsubjective, anarchic power contained in the subversive exploitation of judicial rationality by the other or the alien, and he is thus empowered by the very liberal-humanist discourse held by the society he turns against. The dramatic situation emanating from this cluster of relations is ambiguous and dialectical: on the one hand, Venetian society allows Shylock a seemingly protected legal standing, yet on the other hand this legal protection is precarious, owing to Shylock's alienation from that liberal-humanistic discourse, founded in the play on the magic unity of gentle and gentile, which is to *The Merchant of Venice* what kin and kind is to *Hamlet*.

Yet the signifying pattern gentle-gentile does not necessarily depend, as it would appear, solely on Shylock's ethno-religious identity. Rather, it may allude to every aspect of the Christian discourse of the play, which embraces such diverse themes as commerce, usury, music, love and amity, in all of which Shylock's otherness plays a crucial role. Instances of all these fields of dramatic tension will be touched upon in our reading of the play in chapter 3 of this book. It will suffice for our purpose in the present chapter to demonstrate how the "cluster" of power relations is activated in a socioeconomic context in which Shylock's Jewishness plays an important, yet not indispensable, part.

"'TIS MINE, AND I WILL HAVE IT": POSSESSION IN *THE MERCHANT OF VENICE*

An experienced merchant and capital owner, Antonio somewhat condescendingly rejects the suggestion, made by Salerio and Solanio, that his melancholy, which drives him to "have much ado to know [him]self" (*The Merchant of Venice*, 1.1.7), is caused by a worry for his scattered property. In business, as in mental economy, there are obvious advantages for diversification:

> Believe me no, I thank my fortune for it—
> My ventures are not in one bottom trusted,
> Nor to one place; nor is my whole estate
> Upon the fortune of this present year.
>
> (41-44)

There is, however, a point in their suggestion (if that is what they imply) that parts of his identity are imprinted in his material possessions. The latter, which range from his merchandise to his very body, are the symbolic battleground upon which much of the dramatic conflict of *The Merchant of Venice* is acted out.

Rising capitalism, which dominated English socioeconomic discourse in the early modern period, had a slower impact on legitimate ideology than on daily practice. This resulted in ideological controversies on the intellectual scene between conservatives and conformists, both lagging behind, and attempting to come to terms with social and economic realities. Under the influence of the Reformation, new theories of property were preached and advanced throughout the sixteenth and seventeenth centuries. In 1549, Sir John Cheke "warns the poor that an equal distribution of wealth would not be in their interest, as it would take from them the opportunity of becoming rich" (Schlatter 1951, 105). The changing perspectives on economy distinguish the obsolete attitude of fifteenth-century moralities toward material wealth from that of a sixteenth-century morality such as Skelton's *Magnyfycence*, in which material prosperity is not any more solely a function of faith and good deeds but of economic discretion and husbandry, and where Prince Magnyfycence (an updated Everyman, significantly endowed with an absolute hegemonic power, rather than a representation of the communal average like his fifteenth-century prototype) is not expected to renounce wealth altogether but use it conscientiously. Antonio, the prince of Venice's merchants, rehabilitates the contemptuous view of the merchant by the early authorities, for whom "A merchant shall hardly keep himself from doing wrong, and a huckster shall not be freed from sin."[18] The moral ambiguity regarding commerce investing the economic discourse since the revival of mercantile enterprise around the eleventh century still moderately haunts the conscience of Venice's Christian merchants in Shakespeare's play, and the economic aspects of the "good inspirations" informing the will of Portia's dead father curbing "the will of [his] living daughter" (1.2.24-25, 28) reflect, at least in theory, the sentiment informing the wills of many bankers and merchants in the late Middle Ages, who left a good deal of their worldly goods to the poor or the clergy as a token of repentance (see Pirenne 1969, 17ff). This ambiguity may account for the fact that Antonio will never be caught throughout the play in the actual process of dealing with any of his commercial enterprises (as opposed to Shylock, who considers Bassanio's offer, initially at least, as a regular, daily transaction and partakes with Salerio and Solanio in being constantly attentive to news from the Rialto).

A similar change of attitude affects the contemporary controversy over usury. As against the more orthodox views of ecclesiastical conservatives, reiterating Scriptural and patristic prohibitions, one may find contemporary voices defending the lending at interset as an act of Christian charity.[19] In his exegesis of the Deuteronomic passage concerning usury, Benjamin Nelson argues, Calvin himself "charted the path to the world of universal Otherhood, where all become 'brothers' in being equally 'others'. . . . prov[ing] that it was permissible to take usury from one's brother" (Nelson 1969, 73). Calvin's argumentation was adopted by many exponents of usury in Tudor and Stuart England, "a society of small property owners . . . borrowing and lending were common" (R.H. Tawney in Wilson 1925, 19). When a major seventeenth-century figure like Sir Robert Filmer enters that ideological battle, he supports a similar position, namely denying a godly warrant for the denouncement of usury and reducing it to a matter of personal conscience.[20] Nelson believes that Shakespeare may have joined the debate in *The Merchant of Venice*, in the special connotation given in this context to "Christians' and 'Jews', 'friends' and 'enemies'" (Nelson 1969, 86-87). In spite of Antonio's harsh words against Shylock's practice of usury, which seem to reflect the ideological position of the church's orthodoxy, the play follows the more pragmatic position in presenting many of its characters with the task of taking decisions on material wealth by using personal conscience: such is the case of Portia's suitors, Antonio and his Venetian merchant-companions, or the party concerned in deciding the fine on Shylock at the end of the trial.

Another field of ideological controversy was the realm of private possession. With the rise of capitalism, we are told, "property is equated with private property—the right of a natural or artificial person to exclude others from some use or benefit of something" (Macpherson 1975, 105). But though on the whole English society in the Renaissance was organized accordingly as a private property system,[21] the official ideology of the age was still committed to the orthodox idea that original communism was a state of purity from which the present system has diverted. Whether that diversion was sinful, tolerable, or justified under the circumstances was a matter of opinion. The world was promised to Adam to dominate, but was it allocated to any private individual? And how exactly was that domination qualified or compared to the domination of God? The orthodox monastic ideal, derived from the monks' traditional reading of the Bible and Patristic authorities, regarded private property as a major impediment to salvation, and thus considered its abolition part of the desirable return to the primary condition (see Reeve 1986, 53-55). More's *Utopia* could be taken to express implicitly a similar sentiment. Filmer, however, taking part in this controversy as well, defended private property in denying that there had ever been a stage in which it was absent.

Those two conflicting conceptions of private property are lying at the core of *The Merchant of Venice*. It is, in more than one way, a play about ownership. Antonio, the merchant of Venice, is faced in the play with at least three challenges to his identity as a possessor. In the first outer circle of ownership, he is challenged by natural and human powers as an owner of material possessions. In this struggle he is prone to lose his goods, ships, and money—all of which serve him as tokens or carriers of some other, imagined, yet undefined wealth. In the second circle of ownership he is challenged by human powers as an "owner" of a friend who is first to proclaim himself contracted to Antonio, owing him "the most in money and in love" (1.1.131). On the third, more personal level of ownership, Antonio is challenged by individual and corporate human powers as the owner of his own body. On all three levels his position of ownership is temporarily shaken, to be only partially recuperated. His material goods are partly returned to him at the very end, but the fact that he will never "know by what strange incident" three out of his five argosies have fortuitously "come to harbour" (5.1.277, 78) will forever undermine his sense of absolute domination of his property. His "ownership" of Bassanio as a friend is both reasserted and qualified at the end by the latter's marriage bond. And, finally, Antonio's domination of his body is returned to him, but its partial recuperation does not signify an absolute reassertion of Antonio's ownership rights as it does the fallibility of human reason in securing possession through language. In spite of Shylock's defeat in court, his terms, indicating the limits of Antonio's possession of his own body, are ultimately reasserted rather than challenged in principle. A similar crisis of ownership affects other characters in the play, from Portia, through Bassanio and Shylock down to Portia's bunch of suitors.

The solution of the Master of Belmont's ideological riddle contest, behind which the subject of possession is constantly and notably lurking, suggests (at least in theory) a restrained approach to private possession: one is rewarded for not aspiring (let alone proclaiming an aspiration) for lucrative wealth. This is the common compromise of the official Christian ideology in early capitalist Europe between orthodox humility before a guiding providence and pragmatic recognition of the power of wealth. The binary opposition to that dogmatic prescription is provided by Shylock, who would identify himself with Jacob in his capacity as "third possessor" and insist on his deserts. Confident in his autonomous ability to assess and formulate the latters, he phrases them eloquently in what seems at the time to be a carefully drawn bond. On the surface level, according to which the narrative appears to follow the pattern of romantic comedy, Shylock's project is doomed to failure. This position corresponds to the message of the silver casket, echoing Antonio's reproaching Shylock for making no distinction between his gold and silver and Jacob's ewes and rams. It is Antonio, who but now sought a judicious definition of his own identity, who introduces to the play Shylock's identification with the devil. On the face of it, there is no leap of imagination here, since the association of the Jew with the devil is a commonplace on the plane of symbolic order. Barabas, for instance, is described by Ithamore as the devil's instrument to perform sheer evil:

> the devil invented a challenge, my master writ it,
> and I carried it.
>
> *(The Jew of Malta,* 3.3.20-21)

But whereas Barabas serves the devil because he is "set upon extreme revenge" (3.3.47) on the Christians he hates, the association of Shylock with the devil is made in different terms. Though Shylock is presented by Antonio as "the devil [who] can cite Scripture for his purpose" (1.3.93), his identification with the devil is made in an economic, rather than religious, context. Like the devil who should be denied any right of possession in the human world, Shylock should be denied any such right for living of the breeding of a barren metal. Whereas the metaphor of procreation may be applied to substantial possessions of representational value, such as Portia's lands or Antonio's goods, Shylock's money is denied the right of breeding. In his delegitimation of Shylock as possessor, Antonio is joined by a surprising ally. It is Jessica who reiterates his identification of her father with the devil in describing her father's house as "hell," a clear indication of an illegitimate property. In fourteenth-century Venice, Jews were not allowed to possess even houses or land which were given them as a gift. They were only allowed to live temporarily in rented apartments (Shipper 1935, 425). The move of Launcelot Gobbo from the household of the Jew to that of the Christian, accompanied by the same identification of the Jew with the devil, belongs to the same pattern.

More complex in this context, however, are the implications of Jessica's obscure reference to Tubal and Chus as Shylock's "countrymen" (3.2.284). As opposed to Marx's aforementioned reference to the "*chimerical* nationality" of judaism as "the nationality of the merchant, of man of money in general," which may be read as a sociological or theological one (Marx 1975, 239), the reference to a Jew as a "countryman" is purely symbolic, implying absence rather than identity. Since Jews reached Europe through expulsion and a process of gradual dispersion rather than conquest, colonization, or mass migration, they could possess no economic positions which depended on hegemonic power or expropriation of lands:

> I must confess we come not to be kings:

That's not our fault: alas, our number's few,
And crowns come either by succession,
Or urg'd by force.

(*The Jew of Malta*, 1.1.127-30)

Even where the Jews could be in possession of lands, such as in Barabas's island, whose circumstances Marlowe appears to have studied carefully:

Barabas.
and I have bought a house
As great and fair as is the Governor's;
And there in spite of Malta will I dwell,
Having Ferneze's hand.

(2.3.13-16)

—they often preferred to deal in landed property not so much as "a form of family investment, as it was for the Christians in Malta as elsewhere, so much as a method of making money," since that tricky "mortgage" system served "to avoid the odium which the taint of usury brought with it" (Wettinger 1985, 40). With the continuing practice of expulsion of Jews, which became widespread especially in Western Europe throughout the fifteenth century, such a prospect becomes a considerable factor in the Jewish own investment policy (see Katz 1961, 47). The lack of lasting property, in Feudal and early modern Europe, meant a temporary status of citizenship and a perpetual state of alienation. Othello the Moor, another alien in Venice, is theoretically free to join his fellow countrymen in the realm of the Prince of Morocco. In *The Merchant of Venice,* all the characters are identified by local habitation: Portia's suitors are identified by their countries; there is a clear division, at the outset, between the Venetians and the residents of Belmont; Launcelot Gobbo defines himself as an Italian (2.2.150), and his father, who owns a horse and brings a dish of doves as a present, must own a plot of land in the country. Even "a poor Turk of tenpence" such as Ithamore would season his fantasy of marrying the courtesan with the vision of settling in "a country:"

Content: but we will leave this paltry land,
And sail from hence to Greece, to lovely Greece.
I'll be thy Jason, thou my golden fleece.

(*The Jew of Malta*, 4.2.92-94)

Whereas all the others may be referred to by their local habitation or country of origin, the Jew may cite a list of places where he visited for a purpose (Shylock's Frankfort, Barabas's Italy, France, etc.) or at best be related to his latest country of temporary residence, where, like here, he was residing in "hell." Not even the ancient, spiritual locus of Jewish desire will do: "creep[ing] to Jerusalem" (*The Jew of Malta,* 4.1.62) is brought up by Barabas as a mode of penance only when he shams a wish to become a Christian. Calling their fellow Jews "countrymen," as do Jessica (who, whether she reports faithfully or lies about Shylock's particular talk with Tubal or Chus, probably quotes her father's regular terminology) and Barabas, betrays aliens' conspiracy rather than citizens' local pride or patriotism:

Barabas.
. . . let 'em combat, conquer, and kill all,
So they spare me, my daughter, and my wealth.

(150-51)

The identification of Shylock with the devil is associated, both in principle and in the play's *praxis,* with the latter's unlawful possession of human souls and bodies. Again, it appertains to a breach of a socioeconomic restriction no less than to religion. The exchange of identities, as we have seen, is a common practice among the characters of the play. Portia, for instance, whose identity is first defined in the play as "a lady richly left" (1.1.161), yields herself to Bassanio in terms of identity and possession simultaneously:

Myself, and what is mine, to you and yours
Is now converted.

(*The Merchant of Venice,* 3.2.166-67)

By way of a specially designed system of restrictions, which proved to have defined the ethno-religious identity of Shylock and his "fellow countrymen" in terms of a separate socioeconomic class, Shylock is barred from possessing anything but faceless, "barren metal," which, on the one hand, is devoid of any representationable identity but for the "breeding use" of which, on the other hand, he is sharply reproached. Denied his rights to substantial possession, Shylock's subversion of power in striving for autonomous identity is diverted against the body of Antonio. The exertion of bodily punishment is one of the age-old emblems of absolute power: the right to dismember, fracture, or confine the human body to a forced asylum, as Essex, for instance, took the liberty to do to Doctor Lopez (a liberty that significantly will be qualified by a law of "habeas corpus") is a prerogative of kings and masters. Here it is appropriated for the private use of an individual who is himself coerced by the official system: the physical expropriation of Antonio's body will defeat the rival "legitimate discourse," which threatens Shylock's autonomy of otherness. The body, that "most quotidian part of our landscape and the most potent signifier known to us" (Gent & Llewellyn 1990, 9), is hardly confined in the context of the play to its physiological ontology. It indicates the boundaries of individual identity as recognized by the world (which Antonio emphatically interrogates at the opening scene of the play): "The subject originally locates and recognises desire through the intermediary, not only of his own image, but of the body of his fellow being" (Lacan 1988a, 147). Shylock, for whom a body is a rich metaphorical "habitation" (*The Merchant of Venice* 1.3.29), will regard his habitation as a body, with casements for ears (2.5.34). He would catch his rival "upon the hip" (1.3.41), feed upon him (2.5.14-15) and bait fish with his flesh (3.1.47). James Shapiro's suggestion that Shylock's design against Antonio's body has to do with castration places Shylock's otherness within a specific context through its implication of circumcision (Shapiro 1992). It would seem, however, that Shylock aspires to a more ambitious and universal project. By mutilating Antonio, Shylock will inscribe his own otherness on the body that stands nearest the heart of Venice's wholesome, dominant discourse. The wholeness of the human body is a vital condition for man's position in the world:

> Man is all symmetrie,
> Full of proportions, one limbe to another,
> And all to all ther world besides.
>
> (George Herbert, "Man," 13-15)

The complexity of human body is revealed in its symmetry and proportions, and "the first step in unraveling this complexity is to postulate that the system of man's body is both exhaustive and all-inclusive, that it has everything it needs and nothing superfluous." This complexity of the body serves also "as a figure for the world's complexity whether cosmic, political, or architectural" (Barkan 1975, 3-4, 6). By inscribing his will on Antonio's body in threatening to strike off a material pound of flesh and proclaiming his right to redesign its natural shape, not only does Shylock disrupt the inherent symmetry of Antonio's body, but he also offends the ideological values that symmetry stand for within the official Christian discourse (of which the harmony of the spheres, eulogized by Lorenzo in act 5 is a typical macrocosmic metaphor). For if Shylock's scheme prevails, it may subversively subordinate "objective" history to his own, rival discourse of divisiveness, quantifiable individuality, and reified personal deserts. Shylock's project of dismembering Antonio is thus one of self-assertion, an act of self-recognition on his own part:

> The body as fragmented desire seeking itself out, and the body as ideal self, are projected on the side of the subject as fragmented body, while it sees the other as perfect body. For the subject, a fragmented body is an image essentially dismemberably from its body.
>
> (Lacan 1988a, 148)

Shylock's design to cut off Antonio's body constitutes the peak of his imagery of feeding and devouring throughout the play, to serve as the diametrical opposition of the "barren metal" and the utmost stage of acquiring a substantial identity. The myth of eating a rival's body is widespread and influential in folk literature, and Shakespeare himself did not shy from using it literally in *Titus Andronicus*. Speculations regarding its relevance for *The Merchant of Venice* have ranged from ritual killing to therapeutic drinking of the heart's blood. In Declamation 95 of *The Orator* (1596), which has been suggested as a possible source for Shakespeare's play, the Jew says: "I might also say that I haue need of this flesh to cure a friend of mine of a certaine maladie, which is otherwise incurable."[22] The image of Shylock standing over Antonio with his pointed knife could also bring to mind Abraham, prevented at the last moment by the Angel of mercy from sacrificing Isaac. And yet the essential meaning of Shylock's act of transgression is verbal rather than physical. As he himself initially suggests (whether genuinely or cunningly one does not know), there is no material gain for him in exacting the forfeiture:

> A pound of man's flesh taken from a man,
> Is not so estimable, profitable neither
> As flesh of muttons, beefs, or goats.
>
> (1.3.161-63)

Hence the execution of Shylock's threat must be public and ceremonial, since it is not necessarily the actual pound of flesh he is after, but what it stands for, through the ritual proclamation of his possessing it. Cutting a person's body can be conceived as a statement, a speech act, as the case of the biblical Levite and his raped and murdered "concubine" tells us:

> And when he was come into his house, he took a knife, and laid hold on his concubine, and divided her, together with her bones, into twelve pieces, and sent her into all the coasts of Israel. And it was so, that all that saw it said, There was no such deed done nor seen from the day that the children of Israel came up out of the land of Egypt unto this day: consider of it, take advice, and speak your minds.
>
> (Judges 19:29-30)

Just as the severed body of the biblical girl speaks,[23] so is Shylock's bodily threat not surprisingly secured by language: its meaning is discursive rather than physical. Shylock's project, in other words, is not bodily punishing the Antonio who spat on him on Wednesday last (1.3.121) but to transform his identity into a human quantity, subject to possession by others. Nor is it surprising that only within the discourse generated by Shylock's phrasing of his bond, offered in "merry sport" (1.3.141), will Portia be able to defeat him at court, in adopting similar terms of *jouissance*. It is a battle of words that uncovers the two rival concepts of possession which, as we have seen, lie at the core of the play's ideological clash. On the one hand there is Shylock, who attempts to appropriate the constituted validity assigned to feudal property into the realm of mobile property where he reigns, and then in turn tries to convert his money, which in the domain of property is basically a signifier, into substantial property in the shape of human flesh (materializing the image of the body as "habitation"). Using the two signifying modes at his disposal, the money in his coffers and the language of his bond, Shylock would inscribe his power on Antonio's body, playing creator and destroyer in dominating the course of his victim's life and death. Shylock considers his proclaimed act of ceremonial mutilation as serving him to enact his symbolic richness in terms of the material world. Unlike Portia who claims the rights for her possessions by birth, Shylock uses his economic power and knowledge of Venetian law to carve for himself (literally) the identity of one "richly left" whose claim on material property is clearly evident. He is bound to find out, however, that it is much easier to handle an abstract quantitative possession such as money than any kind of substantial possession, let alone human flesh.

The standing of human body within the realm of property theory is far from decisive. Some would regard the body as a substance *sui generis* among the world's entities, and therefore deny any subordination of it to property laws. "What?" says St. Paul, "know ye not that your body is the temple of the Holy Ghost which is in you, which ye have of God, and ye are not your own? For ye are bought with a price: therefore glorify God in your body, and in your spirit, which are God's" (I Cor. 6:19-20). Hobbes, who "reduces the human essence to freedom from others' wills and proprietorship of one's own capacities" (Macpherson 1962, 264), observes accordingly that it is the law of nature (*lex naturalis*) that implies that "every man has a right to every thing, even to another's body," a liberty that endangers the security of everyone, and therefore it is a general rule of reason to seek peace (Hobbes 1929, 99). According to Common Law (which for Shakespeare's audience may be the normative representation of the law), the human body is "incapable in law of being [subject] of property" (Pollock and Wright 1888, 232). Others, however, "hold that the body should be thought of as property, and emphasize that each person owns or has title to himself or herself" (Munzer 1990, 37). For the Levellers, and especially Richard Overtone, the fundamental postulate of natural property right "was that every man is naturally the proprietor of his own person" (Macpherson 1962, 139-42), a position which will be readily endorsed by modern liberal theory (see, e.g., Nozick 1974). Shylock, no doubt, claims Antonio's pound of flesh by strength of property law:

> The pound of flesh which I demand of him
> Is dearly bought, 'tis mine and I will have it:
> If you deny me, fie upon your law!
>
> (4.1.99-101)

How would the original audience of the play conceive of the moral basis of Shylock's claim? The legal analogy Shylock uses in that same speech to support his claim is that of slavery: a more familiar demand which, he might hope, not improbably may help to render his original claim less striking. In this he follows a long conceptual tradition, which can be traced back to Aristotle's contention that "the slave is not only the slave of his master but wholly belongs to him" (*Politics* 1254a 12; Aristotle 1905). Christianity amplifies this, and St. Thomas Aquinas reminds one that for maiming one's servant "the penalty was forfeiture of the servant, who was ordered to be given his liberty" (*Summa Theologica*, 21, q. 105 art. 4). Rejecting James's claim on the English throne, Robert Parsons, in 1594, would appeal to property owners in reminding them that "the upholders of divine right . . . also maintain that the king reduces all subjects to slaves, for as Aristotle defined him, a slave is a man whose property belongs to his master" (Schlatter 1951, 113). Parsons does not address the issue of the body as property, but the persistence of the phenomenon of mutilating slaves (see, e.g., Patterson 1982, 59) betrays such a notion. For Shakespeare's audience, the slave is a less abstract cultural construct than is the Jew. Both the presence and impact of slavery, consisting in the radical legal claim of master on slave in terms of property, persisted uninterruptedly within the ideological framework of the Middle Ages, side by side with its common substitution in feudalism by the less radical relation of serfdom.[24] "As a commodity, the slave is property" (Finley 1983, 73), and for some writers his/her powerlessness is comparable with death, since "it always originated (or was conceived of as having originated) as a substitute for death" (Patterson 1982, 5; see also Phillips 1985, 5-6). Shylock's tricky formulation of his claim over Antonio's pound of flesh never mentions death explicitly, even though everyone knows with Portia that following the implementation of Shylock's bond Antonio is in danger to "bleed to death" (4.1.254). Shylock's reified conception of his "owned" part in Antonio's body precludes any notion of death, for there is no life in quantifiable property. In an ironic Foucauldian overturn of power relations, he who is not allowed to make "a barren metal" breed turns a living body into a lifeless property.

But not only the actual presence of slavery has affected medieval Europe and contributed to the cultural construct of the slave:

> The persistent and growing influence of Roman law, which contained a sophisticated set of regulations for slavery, helped shape the legal systems of the European West and provided a ready-made set of rules that could be put into force easily when slavery again became economically significant.
>
> (Phillips 1985, 3-4)

English law, we are told, "has never furnished a case in which a person claimed a pound of flesh as penalty, but it has been called upon to consider the case of a usurer who reduced his debtor by contract to virtual slavery, and has refused to enforce it" (Keeton 1967, 132-33). However, some earlier investigators of the legal implications of Shylock's claim did attempt to relate the latter to the persistent influence of the Roman law on contemporary legal practice. In the profused nineteenth-century practice of source hunting for the Pound of Flesh motif, no clear connection has ever been established between the early oriental, religious versions of the story and its medieval Western, secular ones. In the former versions, such as the one in the Indian *Mahabharata*, the human hero is tested by the gods in making him shelter a dove (Agni in disguise) from a pursuing Indra, disguised as a hawk: when the latter claims his right of feeding according to the law of nature, the hero finally yields to him a piece of his own flesh which equals the weight of the dove.[25] In the Western medieval versions, the secular bond substitutes the religious vow, the creditor or usurer substitutes the bird of prey (which may explain why the farfetched etymological association of the name Shylock and Shallach, the archaic Hebrew for cormorant, has fascinated some scholars), the legal penalty substitutes the religious sacrifice, and the secular law replaces moral tenets. As a consequence, several attempts have been made to trace the origins of the Pound of Flesh story back to the Roman laws of the Twelve Tables. The third Table accords the creditor with almost unrestricted rights over the debtor's freedom and body: after three days in which the debtor was exposed in the marketplace and the debt was still due, the several creditors were allowed by the law to divide his/her body between them, "and he who takes more or less than he legally deserves will not be held guilty."[26] Scholars who believed that the last clause is a direct reference to the Pound of Flesh story conjectured that the story itself preceded the Law of the Twelve Tables, or that the clause is a later interpolation (the fact that we do not have the original Table gives ground to such speculations).[27] Jacob Grimm (the elder of the two famous brothers) associated the story with the fifth-century Sallic Wergild law, which he argues is a relic of an ancient Teutonic law that decreed the death or mutilation penalty against a debtor failing to pay his debt (see Grimm 1828, 611-21). Grimm compares this law with a Norwegian law allowing the creditor of a debtor who would not be baled by his friends "to cut from the debtor's body as he pleases, from above or below."[28] English law followed the German in allowing the mutilation of the debtor's or offender's body.[29] Under the influence of the ancient slavery law, the amputation of a hand or a leg became a fashion during the rule of Henry II (Pollock and Maitland 1898, 461); and in Shakespeare's time (3 November 1579), John Stubbs and William Page, the author and distributor, respectively, of *The Discovery of the Gaping Gulf,* a "lewd and seditious" pamphlet against the queen, were punished by striking off their right hands with three blows.[30] But there was another, more direct yet unnoticed bearing of the Pound of Flesh narrative on the master-slave property relation. There is no evidence that Shakespeare might have read the earliest European version of the folk motif, the *Creditor* of the *Dolopathos;* but it is interesting to note that in it, the vengeful creditor is a former slave of the young hero, who bears a grude toward his former master who, at a burst of choler, once struck off his leg. The *Creditor* of the *Dolopathos* is not a Jew. If there is any connection in the common imagination between the Jew and slavery, it has to do with the major involvement of Jews in the slave trade since the early Middle Ages (see, e.g., Bloch 1975, 3). With the decline of feudalism and the rise of colonialism as an outcome of mercantile and early industrial capitalism, the master-slave relation was vigorously revived as a socioeconomic paradigm, especially in regard to Christians—non-Christian, European—non-European binary relations. We have Hakluyt's description of the first English slaving voyage under Hawkins's command, which left the coast of England in October 1562, and after having received "friendly intertainment" at Teneriffe,

> passed to Sierra Leona . . . where he stayed some good time, and got into his possession, partly by the sworde, and partly by other meanes, to the number of 300 Negros at the least, besides other merchandises which that countrey yeeldeth.
>
> (Craton, Walvin, and Wright 1976, 12)

The ethno-religious otherness of the enslaved party from the point of view of the official ideology helped suppress the moral problem potentially involved in the revived practice, establishing it as a legitimate institution rather than a moral category (See Finley 1983, 126). We may only speculate about the exact reaction of the original audience of Marlowe's play to Barabas's malicious hope "to see the Governor a slave, / And, rowing in a galley, whipp'd to death" (5.1.66-67), a wish granted him in the following scene, but if he wanted to let his illustrious heroic villain retain his dramatic stature and command of the audience's subversive sympathies until the very moment of his overthrow, Marlowe had to make Barabas relinquish white, Catholic Ferneze's slavery for strategic reasons. Similarly, Shylock would not bring up the issue of slavery in relation to Antonio but as an analogical case in terms of property relations. It is this property relation that is represented in Prospero's reference to Caliban: "this thing of darkness I / Acknowledge mine" (*The Tempest* 5.1.275-76) in which "mine" represents an identical claim to Shylock's reference to Antonio's pound of flesh, or Catholic Vice-Admiral del Bosco's account of his

> fraught [of] Grecians, Turks, and Afric Moors;
> . . . our slaves,
> Of whom we would make sale.
>
> (*The Jew of Malta,* 2.2.9, 17-18)

While Launcelot Gobbo is hired by Shylock for a wage, and by agreement may change his master at his own request, Barabas purchases Ithamore ("a poor Turk of tenpence . . . born in Thrace; brought up in Arabia" [4.2.42, 2.3.129-30]), at the marketplace and promptly marks him, as he would do with any piece of property. Such precedents enable Shylock to regard his bodily claim on Antonio in terms of a legitimate legal relation. The analogy between body rights and property rights is not contested by the Venetian court. In fact, Keeton argues,

> Portia was adopting precisely the attitude of the Court of Chancery of the period. Substitute "estate" for "pound of flesh," and you have a typical Elizabethan suit in Chancery. The creditor is about to take possession of the debtor's estate. Very well, says the Court, you may take possession, but you must use the profits you acquire by taking possession in satisfaction of the debt, and you must account strictly for everything you receive. . . . The estate must not suffer in the slightest degree from the entry into possession of the creditor. In both cases the creditor prefers the safer course, and refrains from entering into possession.
>
> (Keeton 1967, 145)

By introducing the second defense against the implementation of Shylock's bond (as she did earlier in "The quality of mercy" speech), Portia does contest, indeed, the total reification of Antonio's body implied by Shylock's argument. But this is but an added victory (which is therefore absent from the narrative, more basic, sources of the Pound of Flesh story). For all practical reasons, she won her legal battle in the first round, and that she did on Shylock's terms. Even her potentially spiritual arguments are subject to the logic of property law: the human body is not that well dissociated from spirit; and thus had even Shylock remembered to specify blood in his bond, Portia could get him on account of Antonio's spirit which is not to be separated by him from Antonio's body, whether by way of death or dementia. Like the devil's, Shylock's claim on anybody's soul (which lies beyond the controversial domain in which the body may be reified and conceived as subject to property law) is *a priori* unfounded, which is why Shylock himself would never have brought it up. Even here, however, the victory of the official Christian ideology over Shylock's transgression would have been granted on Shylock's terms.

Against Shylock's reifying argument the play had posited the public quiz proclaimed by the Master of Belmont for a lucrative prize: the contesters are required to fashion their own identity, assisted by the guidelines inscribed on the caskets, in order to gain possession of the late master's daughter, the Belmont heir. The ideological position represented by the clever charade devised by the Master of Belmont, as we have seen, is designed to reassert the ideological patterns shaping the official discourse of Christian Europe in the Renaissance. Those patterns consists in two basic tenets: one is to adopt a meek and humble position, relinquishing all claim to material possession, in order to gain such fortune as an answer to this obedient gesture. It is a typical post-medieval, early capitalist translation of the Christian-feudal idea of humbleness into the realm of mercantile venture. Antonio's conception of his commercial ventures is founded on the same ideological grounds. So do all the merchants of Venice accept some providential authority when they venture and hazard with their transitory "fortunes," that mobile property which can change hands in no time in the same way the goddess Fortune is tampering with human lots. It is the official knowledge, immersed in the "conscientious" solution of the identity riddles inscribed on Portia's caskets; conscientious, since it stands the test of the official, legitimate ideology: one is expected to yield one's material possessions in order to regain "conscientious" property.

The other basic tenet of early capitalist Christianity suggests a similar move regarding one's identity. It is clearly symbolized by the "egall yoke of love" (3.4.13), shared by those carrying that legitimate discourse in the play: Bassanio, Portia, and Antonio. Only they are capable of generating the word which, by countering Shylock's claim over Antonio's body, will physically bar Shylock from any threatening power position. Paradoxically, they will do so by coercing Shylock to baptize, namely accept the yoke of the legitimate discourse in an act in which love is enforced rather than willingly subscribed to. Thus this spiritual union, as indeed the play will later remind us, contains dialectically bodily and spiritual bondage that also counters the illusion of freedom and autonomy:

> *Ant.*
> I once did lend my body for his wealth,
> Which but for him that had your husband's ring
> Had quite miscarried. I dare be bound again,
> My soul upon the forfeit, that your lord
> Will never more break faith advisedly.
> *Por.*
> Then you shall be his surety.
>
> (*The Merchant of Venice*, 5.1.249-54)

The illusory autonomy of the legitimate discourse contains the submission of its major proponents in the play to the restrictive formations of that very discourse. Thus it is accustomed to blame Shylock for overobserving the written word rather than the spirit of the law. But Terry Eagleton, not less convincingly, argues that

> it is Shylock who has respect for the spirit of the law and Portia who does not. Shylock's bond does not actually state in writing that he is allowed to take some of Antonio's blood along with a pound of flesh, but this is a reasonable inference from the text, as any real court would recognize. . . . Portia's reading of the bond, by contrast, is "true to the text" but therefore lamentably false to its meaning.
>
> (Eagleton 1986, 36-37)

This is certainly true; as it may be true that "what is at stake in the courtroom . . . is less Shylock's personal desire to carve up Antonio than the law of Venice itself" (Eagleton 1986, 38). Yet Eagleton's excited defense of Shylock and just account of his dramatic position as some Brechtian alienating character does not make Shylock an Azdakian alienated (if biased) umpire. Although he is, as I have argued above, a function of the others' fears and desires, a dramatic process or a "flow," still he functions as a party in a dialectical move. As such he is not just a victim (as Eagleton would have him) but also a terrorist. What we have here, then (at least on one significant level), is a Foucauldian process of power, in which rivaling speech-acts are clashing rather than psychological human beings. Shylock's very knowledge of the official "truth" serves him as a subversive instrument for gaining power and control which contradict his otherness, which is why the legitimacy of his economic activity is rejected by the official society. When Shylock, armed with his knowledge of the Venetian legal and political discourse, exploits the power granted him by the Venetian book of laws to materialize his barbaric fantasies to the point of cannibalistic fit, he simultaneously asserts and challenges the power of the political system. In that mimetic procedure whereby power and knowledge combine to subvert hegemonic power, rather than in a subjective alignment of individual properties, lies the dramatic effectiveness of Shylock in the play.

Notes

1. See, e.g., Lloyd 1875, 100; Moody 1964, 23-24; Nuttall 1983, 122.
2. Of which Shakespeare was accused, ranging from alleged inability to master properly characters and situations (see Fergusson 1971, Goddard 1951, among others), to occasional slips such as the discrepancy, marked by Dr. Johnson, between the terms of the caskets ordeal (never to "woo a maid") and the schedule's addressing Arragon: "Take what wife you will to bed" (2.9.70), or the incredible testimony (timewise) by Jessica concerning her overhearing her father's talk with Tubal and Chus (see, however, Bradshaw 1986, who considers the latter slip as enriching the argument of the play).

3. See Coryat 1625, 1823-25. For an extensive analysis of the evidence concerning the absence of Jews from England between 1290 and their return in 1655, see Cardozo 1925, 85-140.

4. Gaunz was arrested in Bristol in 1598, about two years after the writing of *The Merchant of Venice.* See Roth 1941, 142.

5. See Shipper 1935, 420.

6. Greenblatt 1980, 204. And see Marx 1975, 239.

7. See Carlebach 1978, 152-53. For Kant's conjectures see chapter 1, n. 13.

8. "Each outsider, including the Jews as individuals, had to fit into the pre-existing economic structure and social fabric, upon neither of which he could expect to make any significant impact" (Arcadius Kahan, "The Early Modern Period," in Gross 1975, 58). See also Grebanier 1962, 82-83.

9. None of the the suggested etymologies and analogues is convincing. Biblical *Shèlah* or *Shiloh,* awkwardly glossed as "dissolving . . . mocked or deceiving" by a contemporary source, sound farfetched, whereas *Shallach,* an archaic Hebrew word for cormorant, was hardly used at all, let alone as a personal name.

10. See, however, the discussion about the relation between past and present in the play in Lyon 1988, "Beginning in the Middle," 29-52.

11. For this distinction, see Thomas 1973, 668.

12. See "The Crucifixion of Christ," in *Ludus Coventriae* 1841, 319.

13. See Manly 1897, 1:239-76.

14. See Johannis de Alta Silva 1913; *Gesta Romanorum* 1879.

15. These are discussed at large in the third chapter of Oz 1990. For the Pound of Flesh motif in folk literature, see also, e.g., Toulmin-Smith 1875-76; Conway 1880 and 1881; Manzi 1896; Vámbéri 1901; Friedlander 1921; Wenger 1929; Landa 1942; Sinsheimer 1964.

16. Such a later insertion of the Jew is not an uncommon practice. See, e.g., the discussion of pseudo-Jewish characters in folk literature in Bin-Gurion 1950, 205-12. In addition to the Pound of Flesh motif, Bin-Gurion counts among the legends in which the figure of the Jew was a later interpolation also "The Jew among the Thorns" (Grimm K-HM no. 110, type 592 in Aarne-Thompson [FFC 184]), where in the original version a Christian priest appears instead of the Jew; "The Revenge for a Murdered Jew" in its various versions (Grimm no. 115, Bechstein, DM 1845, 60, "Das Rebhuhn"; Aarne-Thompson 960), which reminds the Classical story of "The Murdered Ibicus"; Judas Iscariot; "The Wandering Jew"; and the story of the three rings, which Bocaccio borrowed from the "Novelino" and Lessing used in his *Nathan the Wise.*

17. Ibid., 98. And see chapter 1,n.54; Foucault 1979, 92-97; Foucault 1977, 213.

18. Ecclesiasticus 26, 29; and cf. also 27, 2: "As a nail sticketh fast between the joinings of the stones, so doth sin stick close between buying and selling." Demosthenes says it is a marvel to see a man practicing commerce remaining honest.

19. For an extensive summary of that controversy, see Jones 1989. See also Nelson 1969, 82ff.

20. See Filmer 1653, where in the preface Filmer summarizes his entire argument. And see Jones 1989, 158ff, and the whole chapter titled "The Evolution of the Concept of Usury."

21. Namely, in which "in principle, each resource belongs to some individual" (Waldron 1988, 38).

22. Silvayn 1596, 402 and see J. R. Brown's "New Arden" edition, Brown 1959, 169. For an extensive discussion of the use of the heart's blood for therapeutic needs, see Cassel 1882; see also Pouchelle 1990, 74-75. The Grimm Brothers speculated about some analogies between the Pound of Flesh theme and the German epic poem Poor Heinrich, where the doctor "whets his knife" like Gernutus or Shylock (94.1.121). A similar scene is found also in the Bluebeard story, which, the Grimm brothers argue, is also related to the therapeutic theme: Bluebeard is trying to cure himself from the rare disease that turns his beard blue by drinking his wives' blood. They relate theme to medieval allegations of Jews as seeking the blood of Christian children, possibly for therapeutic needs. This connection is unconvincing, and it should be remembered that in the first Western versions of the Pound of Flesh story the creditor is not a Jew.

23. The speech act implications of the Judges incident is illuminatingly discussed by Mieke Bal; see Bal 1988, 129-68. And cf. Felman 1980, who makes a similar case for Molière's *Don Juan,* reading it in the light of the speech act theories of Austin, Searle, etc.

24. Bloch's once neglected theory (Bloch 1975) is now borne out by new historical writing, dating the decline of slavery as a major socioeconomic system in Europe much later than was accepted before. See, e.g., Phillips 1985, especially part II; Bonnassie 1991.

25. For a detailed discussion of the oriental versions, see Oz 1990, 36-44; Wenger 1929; and see also, e.g., Foucaux 1862, 241-50; Benfey 1859, 1, 388-407; Conway 1880, 830-31.

26. "Si pluribus addictus sit, partes secanto, si plus minusve secuerint se [= sine fraude esto." The law is cited in Aulus Gellius, *Noctes Atticae,* 20, 1. See also Kohler 1919. Cardozo eagerly supports the

theory connecting the Pound of Flesh story with the Roman law, as well as similar Germanic and Nordic laws; see Cardozo 1932. Radin, however, stresses the fact that Gellius himself comments that the very severity of the law manifests that it was not designed to be actually executed, and that he, Gellius, himself did not know of any case in which the radical clause of the law was implemented. See Gellius, *loc. cit.*; Radin 1922. Radin denies the alleged connection between *The Merchant of Venice* and the "third Table," arguing that the whole motif is based on a private contract agreed upon by the parties concerned and not dependent on state law.

27. See Cardozo 1925, 242. Griston 1924 places the action of *The Merchant of Venice* in the second decade of the fourth century A.D., under the Law of the Twelve Tables.

28. See Kohler 1919, 91, where the Norwegian law is cited in the original.

29. See, e.g., Pollock and Maitland 1898, 453; Friedlander 1921, 27; Niemeyer 1912, 22.

30. See Stubbs 1968, introduction, xxxv-xvi; Landa 1942, 25. Mutilation was used, though rarely, as accompanying punishment on the pillory: "a Kent labourer convicted in 1599 for declaring that 'the Queen's Majestie was Antichrist and therefore she is throwne down into hell' was sentenced to be pilloried and to have his ears cut off, while a Colchester yeoman convicted in 1579 for calling the Earls of warwick and leicester traitors was sentenced to stand on the pillory in the town's market place and have his ear nailed to the pillory" (Sharpe 1990, 21).

Select Bibliography

Adorno, Theodor W. 1973. *The Jargon of Authenticity.* Translated by Knut Tarnowski and Frederic Will. London: Routledge & Kegan Paul.

Aeschylus. 1970. *The Seven against Thebes.* Translated by Christoper M. Dawson. Englewood Cliffs, N.J.: Prentice-Hall.

Alexander, Peter. 1951. *A Shakespeare's Primer.* London: James Nisbet.

Allen, Don Cameron. 1941. *The Star-Crossed Renaissance.* Durham, N.C.: Duke University Press.

Anderson, Ruth Leila. 1927. *Elizabethan Psychology and Shakespeare's Plays,* University of Iowa Humanistic Studies, 3:4. Iowa City: University of Iowa Press.

Appleby, Joyce. 1978. *Economic Thought and Ideology in Seventeenth Century England* Princeton: Princeton University Press.

Aquinas. 1922. *The "Summa Theologica" of St. Thomas Aquinas.* Translated by Fathers of the English Dominican Province. London.

Arendt, Hannah. 1968. *Between Past and Future.* New York: The Viking Press.

Aristotle. 1924. *Rhetoric.* Translated by W. Rhys Roberts. In *Aristotle: Works,* edited by David Ross. Oxford: Oxford University Press.

———. 1968. *Aristotle's Poetics.* Translated by Leon Golden. Englewood Cliffs, N.J.: Prentice-Hall.

Auden, W. H. 1963. *The Dyer's Hand.* London: Faber & Faber.

Auerbach, Erich. 1959. "Figura." In *Scenes from the Drama of European Literature.* New York: Meridian Books.

Aune, David E. 1983. *Prophecy in Early Christianity and the Ancient Mediterranean World.* Grand Rapids, Mich.: Eerdmans.

Bacon, Francis. 1857-1874 a. *Descriptio Globi Intellectualis.* In *The Works of Francis Bacon,* vol. 5. Collected and edited by James Spedding, Robert Leslie Ellis, and Douglas Denon Heath. London: Longmans & Co.

———. 1857-1874 b. *An Advertisement Touching the Controversies of the Church of England.* In *Works,* vol. 8.

———. 1857-74 c. *De Augmentis Scientiarum.* In *Works,* vol. 5.

———. 1857-74 d. *The Advancement of Learning.* In *Works,* vol. 3.

———. 1857-74 e. *The Wisdom of the Ancients.* In *Works,* vol. 6.

Bakhtin, Mikhail. 1968. *Rabelais and His World.* Translated by Hélène Iswolsky. Cambridge, Mass.: Harvard University Press.

Bal, Mieke. 1988. *Death & Dissymmetry: The Politics of Coherence in the Book of Judges.* Chicago and London: University of Chicago Press.

Bale, John. 1547. *A Tragedie Manyfesting the Chiefe Promises of God Unto Man in the Old Law.* Wesel.

Barber, C. L. 1959. *Shakespeare's Festive Comedy.* Princeton: Princeton University Press.

Barkan, Leonard. 1975. *Nature's Work of Art: The Human Body as Image of the World.* New Haven and London: Yale University Press.

Barker, Harley Granville. 1963. *Prefaces to Shakespeare,* 4. London: Batsford.

Barthes, Roland. 1970. *S/Z.* Paris: Seuil.

———. 1971. "Style and Its Image." In *Literary Style: A Symposium,* edited by Seymour Chatman. New York: Oxford University Press.

———. 1972. *Critical Essays.* Translated by Richard Howard. Evanston, Ill.: Northwestern University Press.

Belsey, Catherine. 1985. *The Subject of Tragedy: Identity & Difference in Renaissance Drama*. London and New York: Methuen.

Benfey, Theodor. 1859. *Pantschatantra*. Leipzig: F.A. Brockhaus.

Benjamin, Walter. 1973. "Theses on the Philosophy of History." In *Illuminations,* edited by Hannah Arendt, translated by Harry Zohn. London: Fontana.

———. 1977. *The Origin of German Tragic Drama*. Translated by John Osborne. London: NLB.

Bin-Gurion, Immanuel. 1950. *Shviley Ha'agada* (The Paths of Legend). Jerusalem: Mossad Bialik.

Blackburn, Ruth H. 1971. *Biblical Drama under the Tudors*. The Hague and Paris: Mouton.

Blackmur, R. P. 1964. *Eleven Essays in the European Novel*. New York and Burlingame: Harcourt, Brace and World.

Bloch, Marc. 1975. *Slavery and Serfdom in the Middle Ages*. Berkeley, Los Angeles, and London: University of California Press.

Boissonade, Jean Fr. 1829-33. *Anecdota Graeca e codicibus regiis*. Paris, n.p.

Bonnassie, Pierre. 1991. *From Slavery to Feudalism in South-Western Europe*. Cambridge: Cambridge University Press.

Bonus, Arthur. 1907. *Zur Biologie des Rätsels*. München: G. D. W. Callwey.

Bouillier, Francisque. 1872. *De la conscience en psychologie et en morale*. Paris: G. Baillière.

Bradshaw, Graham. 1986. "*The Merchant of Venice:* Does Jessica Lie?" *Meridian* 5:99-108.

Breton, André. 1954. "L'Un dans l'autre." *Médium,* N.S., 2 (February): 17-20; 3 (May): 59-61.

Brown, John Russell. 1959. *Shakespeare: The Merchant of Venice*. "New Arden" edition. London: Methuen.

———. 1962. *Shakespeare and His Comedies*. London: Methuen.

Browne, John. 1877. *History of Congregationalism, and Memorials of the Churches in Norfolk and Suffolk*. London: Jerrold and Sons.

Buck-Morss, Susan. 1989. *The Dialectics of Seeing: Walter Benjamin and the Arcades Project*. Cambridge, Mass., and London: MIT Press.

Bulman, James C. 1991. *The Merchant of Venice*. Manchester and New York: Manchester University Press.

Bundy, Murray Wright. 1924. "Shakespeare and Elizabethan Psychology." *Journal of English and Germanic Philology,* 23.

———. 1927. *The Theory of Imagination in Classical and Mediaval Thought*. University of Illinois Studies in Language and Literature, XII, 2-3. Urbana: University of Illinois Press.

Burton, Robert. 1938. *The Anatomy of Melancholy*. Edited by Floyd Dell and Paul Jordan-Smith. New York: Tudor.

Busby, Olive Mary. 1923. *Studies in the Development of the Fool in the Elizabethan Drama*. London: Oxford University Press.

Caillois, Roger. 1968. "Riddles and Images." Translated by Jeffrey Mehlman. *Yale French Studies,* 41. New Haven: Yale University Press; reprinted in Jacques Ehrmann, ed. 1971. *Game, Play, Literature*. Boston: Beacon Books.

Camden, Carroll. 1933. "Astrology in Shakespeare's Day." *Isis* 19:26-73.

Cardozo, Jacob Lopes. 1925. *The Contemporary Jew in the Elizabethan Drama*. Amsterdam: H. J. Paris.

———. 1977. "The Background of Shakespeare's *Merchant of Venice*." *English Studies* (Amsterdam) 14:177-86.

Carlebach, Julius. 1978. *Karl Marx and the Radical Critique of Judaism*. London, Henley, and Boston: Routledge & Kegan Paul.

Carpenter, Nan Cooke. 1972. "Music in the Secunda Pastorum." In *Medieval English Drama: Essays Critical and Contextual,* edited by Jerome Taylor and Alan H. Nelson. Chicago and London: University of Chicago Press.

Carson, Neil. 1972. "Hazarding and Cozening in The Merchant of Venice," *English Language Notes* 9: 168-77.

Cassel, Paulus. 1882. *Die Symbolik des Blutes und "Der arme Heinrich" von Hartmann von Ane*. Berlin: A. Hofmann.

Chadwick, Nora Kershaw. 1942. *Poetry and Prophecy*. Cambridge: Cambridge University Press.

Chambers, E. K. 1925. *Shakespeare: A Survey*. London: Sidgwick & Jackson.

Chandos, John, ed. 1971. *In God's Name: Examples of Preaching in England from the Act of Supremacy to the Act of Uniformity*. London: Hutchinson.

Chapman, George. 1941. *The Poems of George Chapman*. Edited by Phyllis Brooks Bartlett. New York: The Modern Language Association of America; and London: Oxford University Press.

Charney, Maurice. 1978. *Comedy High and Low*. New York: Oxford University Press.

Chaucer. 1957. *Works*. Edited by F.N. Robinson. 2d ed.; Oxford: Oxford University Press.

Child, Francis James. 1882. *The English and Scottish Popular Ballads*. Vol. 1. Boston: Houghton, Mifflin & Co.

Cirlot, J. E. 1962. *A Dictionary of Symbols*. Translated by Jack Sage. New York: Philosophical Library.

Coghill, Nevill. 1964. *Shakespeare's Professional Skills*. Cambridge: Cambridge University Press.

Cohen, Walter. 1985. *Drama of a Nation: Public Theater in Renaissance England and Spain.* Ithaca and London: Cornell University Press.

Cohn, Norman. 1967. *Warrant for Genocide: The Myth of the Jewish World-Conspiracy and the Protocols of the Elders of Zion.* London: Eyre & Spottiswoode.

———. 1970. *The Pursuit of the Millenium.* London: Paladin.

Cole, Douglas. 1970. Introduction. *Romeo and Juliet: A Collection of Critical Essays* Englewood Cliffs, N.J.: Prentice-Hall.

Cole, Howard C. 1981. *The "All's Well" Story from Boccaccio to Shakespeare.* Urbana, Chicago, and London: University of Illinois Press.

Collinson, Patrick. 1967. *The Elizabethan Puritan Movement.* London: Jonathan Cape.

———. 1980. "A Comment: Concerning the Name Puritan." *Journal of Ecclesiastical History* 31:483-88.

———. 1983. *Godly People: Essays on English Protestantism and Puritanism.* London: Hambledon Press.

———. 1988. *The Birthpangs of Protestant England: Religious and Cultural Change in the Sixteenth and Seventeenth Centuries.* Houndmills, Basingstoke, and London: Macmillan.

———. 1989. *The Puritan Character: Polemics and Polarities in Early Seventeenth-Century English Culture.* Los Angeles: The William Andrews Clark Memorial Library.

The Complaynt of Scotlande. 1872. Edited by James A. H. Murray, E. E. T. S. Extra Series, 17. London: Trübner.

Conway, Moncure D. 1880. "The Pound of Flesh." *The Nineteenth Century* 7:830-34.

———. 1881. *The Wandering Jew.* London: Chatto & Windus.

Cooke, G. A. 1936. *A Critical and Exegetical Commentary on the Book of Ezekiel.* Edinburgh: T. & T. Clark.

Coryat, Thomas. 1625. "Maturities." In *Purchas his Pilgrims.* London, vol. 2.

Craton, Michael, James Walvin, and David Wright, eds. 1976. *Slavery, Abolition and Emancipation: Black Slaves and the British Empire.* London and New York: Longman.

Crump, Thomas. 1981. *The Phenomenon of Money.* London, Boston, and Henley: Routledge and Kegan Paul.

Curry, Patrick. 1989. *Prophecy and Power: Astrology in Early Modern England.* Cambridge: Polity Press.

Daiches, David. 1972. "Literature and Social Mobility." In *Aspects of History and Class Consciousness,* edited by István Mészaros. New York: Herder & Herder.

Daniélou, Jean. 1950. *Sacramentum futuri: Etudes sur les origines de la typologie biblique.* Paris: Beaucheshe et ses Fils.

Danks, K. B. 1954. "The Case of Antonio's Melancholy." *Notes & Queries,* NS 1: 111.

Danson, Lawrence. 1978. *The Harmonies of "The Merchant of Venice."* New Haven and London: Yale University Press.

Davies, D. W. 1967. *Elizabethans Errant: The Strange Fortunes of Sir Thomas Sherley and His Three Sons.* Ithaca and New York: Cornell University Press.

Davies, Sir John. 1975. *Nosce Teipsum: The Poems of Sir John Davies.* Edited by Robert Krueger. London: Oxford University Press.

de Beauvoir, Simone. 1972. *The Second Sex.* Translated by H. M. Parshley. Harmondsworth: Penguin.

Dekker, Thomas. 1953-61. *Dramatic Works.* Edited by Fredson Bowers. Cambridge: Cambridge University Press.

Deleuze, Gilles. 1971. *Sacher-Masoch.* Translated by Jean McNeil. London: Faber and Faber.

———, and Félix Guattari. 1977. *Anti-Oedipus.* Translated by Robert Hurley, Mark Seem, and Helen R. Lane. Minneapolis: University of Minnesota Press.

Derrida, Jacques. 1978. "Structure, Sign and Play in the Discourse of the Human Sciences." *Writing and Difference.* Translated by Alan Bass. London and Henley: Routledge & Kegan Paul.

———. 1980. "The Law of Genre." Translated by Avital Ronnell. *Glyph* 7:202-32.

Dimock, Arthur. 1894. "The Conspiracy of Dr. Lopez." *English Historical Review* 9:440-72.

Dobin, Howard. 1990. *Merlin's Disciplines: Prophecy, Poetry, and Power in Renaissance England.* Stanford, Calif.: Stanford University Press.

Dodd, C. H. 1928. *The Authority of the Bible.* London: Nisbet.

Dodds, E. R. 1957. *The Greeks and the Irrational.* Boston: Beacon Press.

Dollimore, Jonathan. 1984. *Radical Tragedy: Religion, Ideology and Power in the Drama of Shakespeare and His Contemporaries.* Brighton: The Harvester Press.

———, and Alan Sinfield, eds. 1985. *Political Shakespeare: New Essays in Cultural Materialism.* Manchester: Manchester University Press.

Donne, John. 1640. *80 Sermons Preached by Iohn Donne.* Folio ed. London.

Douglas, Mary. 1966. *Purity and Danger: An Analysis of the Concepts of Pollution and Taboo.* London: Routledge & Kegan Paul.

Drakakis, John, ed. 1985. *Alternative Shakespeares.* London and New York: Methuen.

Draper, John W. 1935. "Usury in *The Merchant of Venice.*" *Modern Philology* 33:37-47.

Dubrow, Heather. 1982. *Genre.* London and New York: Methuen.

Eagleton, Terry. 1981. *Walter Benjamin, or Towards a Revolutionary Criticism.* London: Verso.

———. 1986. *William Shakespeare.* Oxford: Basil Blackwell.

Edwards, Francis. 1964. *The Dangerous Queen.* London: G. Chapman.

Edwards, John. 1988. *The Jews in Christian Europe 1400-1700.* London and New York: Routledge.

Edwards, Philip. 1978. "Shakespeare and the Healing Power of Deceit." *Shakespeare Survey* 31.

Eisenzweig, Uri. 1988. "Terrorism in Life and in Real Literature." *Diacritics* (Fall), 32-42.

Elias, Norbert. 1982. *Power and Civility.* Translated by Edmund Jephcott. New York: Panthon Books.

Ellul, Jacques. 1965. *Propaganda: The Formation of Men's Attitudes.* Translated by Konrad Kellen and Jean Lerner. New York: Alfred Knopf.

Empson, William. 1951. *The Structure of Complex Words.* London: Chatto & Windus.

Engelberg, Edward. 1972. *The Unknown Distance: From Consciousness to Conscience; Goethe to Camus.* Cambridge, Mass.: Harvard University Press.

Felman, Shoshana. 1980. *Le Scandale du corps parlant: Don Juan ave Austin ou La séduction en deux Langues.* Paris: Seuil.

———. 1987. *Jacques Lacan and the Adventure of Insight: Psychoanalysis in Contemporary Culture.* Cambridge, Mass., and London: Harvard University Press.

Fergusson, Francis. 1971. *Shakespeare: The Pattern in His Carpet.* New York: Delta Books.

Filmer, Robert. 1653. *Quaestio Quodlibetica, or Whether it May be Lawfull to Take Use of Money.* Edited by Roger Twisden. London.

Finley, Moses I. 1983. *Ancient Slavery and Modern Ideology.* Harmondsworth: Penguin.

Fizer, Irene. 1989. "The Name of the Daughter: Identity and Incest in *Evalina.*" In *Refiguring the Father: New Feminist Readings of Patriarchy,* edited by Patricia Yaeger and Beth Kowaleski-Wallace. Carbondale and Edwardsville: Southern Illinois University Press.

Fletcher, Angus. 1971. *The Prophetic Moment: An Essay on Spenser.* Chicago and London: University of Chicago Press.

Florio, John. 1611. *Queen Anna's New World of Words, or Dictionarie of the Italian and English.* London.

Forster E. M. 1927. *Aspects of the Novel.* New York: Harcourt, Brace and World.

Foucault, Michel. 1970. *The Order of Things: An Archaeology of the Human Sciences.* London: Tavistock.

———. 1977. *Language, Counter-Memory, and Practice: Selected Essays and Interviews.* Edited by Donald Bouchard. Ithaca: Cornell University Press.

———. 1979. *The History of Sexuality: An Introduction.* Translated by Robert Hurley. London: Allen Lane.

———. 1980. *Power/Knowledge: Selected Interviews and Other Writings 1972-1977.* Edited by Colin Gordon. Translated by Colin Gordon, Leo Marshall, and Kate Soper. New York: Pantheon.

Foucaux, Philippe E. 1862. *Le Mahabhrata.* Paris: B. Duprat.

Foxe, John. 1578. *Sermon Preached at the Christening of a Certain Jew, at London.* London.

Frank, Grace. 1960. *The Medieval French Drama.* Oxford: Oxford University Press.

Frazer, Sir James George. 1913. *The Golden Bough.* 3d ed. London: Macmillan.

Friedlander, Gerald. 1921. *Shakespeare and the Jews.* London and New York: Routledge & Son.

Freud, Sigmund. 1953-74a. "The theme of the three caskets." *The Standard Edition of the Complete Psychological Work of Sigmund Freud* [SE], edited by James Strachey. London: Hogarth Press and the Institute of Psycho-Analysis. 12:289-302.

———. 1953-74b. "Femininity." *New Lectures on Psycho-Analysis,* SE, 22:112-35.

Frye, Northrope. 1957. *Anatomy of Criticism.* Princeton: Princeton University Press.

Furness, Horace Howard. 1888. *Shakespeare: The Merchant of Venice.* "New Variorum" ed. Philadelphia: Lippincott.

Gadamer, Hans-Georg. 1975. *Truth and Method.* London: Sheed & Ward.

Gaer, Joseph. 1961. *The Legend of the Wandering Jew.* New York: Mentor Books.

Gallop, Jane. 1982. *The Daughter's Seduction: Feminism and Psychoanalysis.* Ithaca: Cornell University Press.

Garber, Marjorie. 1987. *Shakespeare's Ghost Writer Literature as Uncanny Causality.* New York: Methuen.

Geertz, Clifford. 1973. *The Interpretation of Cultures.* New York: Basic Books.

Genette, Gérard. 1987. *Seuils.* Paris: Seuil.

Gent, Lucy, and Nigel Llewellyn, eds. 1990. *Renaissance Bodies: The Human Figure in English Culture c. 1540-1660*. London: Reaktion Books.

Georges, Robert A., and Alan Dundes. 1963. "Toward a Structural Definition of the Riddles." *Journal of American Folklore* 76:111-18.

Gesta Romanorum. 1879. *The Early Versions of the "Gesta Romanorum."* Edited by Sidney J. H. Herrtage, E. E. T. S. Extra Series, 33. London: Early English Texts Society.

Glasser, Richard. 1972. *Time in French Life and Thought*. Translated by C. G. Pearson. Manchester: Manchester University Press.

Goddard, Harold C. 1951. *The Meaning of Shakespeare*. Chicago and London: University of Chicago Press.

Golancz, Sir Israel. 1931. *Allegory and Mysticism in Shakespeare*. London: G. W. Jones.

Goodman, Godfrey. 1839. *The Court of King James*. London: R. Bentley.

Gordon-Grube, Karen. 1988. "Antropophagy in Post-Renaissance Europe: The Tradition of Medieval Cannibalism." *American Anthropologist* 90:405-9.

Gosson, Stephen. 1868. *The School of Abuse*. Edited by Edward Arber. London: Alex. Murray.

Grätz, Henrich. 1880. *Shylock in der Sage, der Geschichte und in Drama*. Krotoschin.

Grebanier, Bernard. 1962. *The Truth about Shylock*. New York: Random House.

Greenblatt, Stephen. 1980. *Renaissance Self-Fashioning from More to Shakespeare*. Chicago and London: University of Chicago Press.

———. 1988. *Shakespearean Negotiations: The Circulation of Social Energy in Renaissance England*. Oxford: Clarendon Press.

Greville, Fulke. 1939. *A Treatie of Humane Learning*, in *Poems and Dramas of Fulke Greville, First Lord Brooke*. Edited by Geoffrey Bullough. Edinburgh and London: Oliver and Boyd.

Grimm, Jacob. 1828. *Deutsche Rechts-Altertümer*. Göttingen.

Grindal. 1710. *Memorials of Archbishop Grindal*. London.

Griston, Harris Jay. 1924. *Shaking the Dust from Shakespeare*. New York: Cosmopolis Press.

Gross, John. 1992. *Shylock: Four Hundred Years in the Life of a Legend*. London: Chatter and Windus.

Gross, Nahum, ed. 1975. *Economic History of the Jews*. Jerusalem: Keter.

Grudem, Wayne A. 1982. *The Gift of Prophecy*. Lanham and London: University Press of America.

Guillaume, Alfred. 1938. *Prophecy and Divination among the Hebrews and other Semites*. London: Hodder & Stoughton.

Guthke, Karl S. 1966. *Modern Tragicomedy*. New York: Random House.

Guthrie, Tyrone. 1965. *In Various Directions: A View of the Theatre*. London: Michael Joseph.

Hamnett, Ian. 1967. "Ambiguity, Classification and Change: The Function of Riddles." *Man* 2:379-92.

Harrison, William. 1877. *Harrison's Description of England in Shakespeare's Youth*. Edited by Frederick J. Furnivall. London: Trübner.

Hathorn, Richmond Y. 1962. *Tragedy, Myth and Mystery*. Bloomington: Indiana University Press.

Hawkes, Terence F. 1964. *Shakespeare and the Reason*. London: Routledge & Kegan Paul.

———. 1972. *Metaphor*. London: Methuen.

Haydn, Hyram. 1950. *The Counter-Renaissance*. New York: Charles Scribner's Sons.

Heller, Agnes. 1981. *Renaissance Man*. Translated by Richard E. Allen. New York: Schocken Books.

Herrick, Marvin T. 1962. *Tragicomedy: Its Origin and Development in Italy, France, and England*. Urbana: University of Illinois Press.

Hobbes, Thomas. 1929. *Leviathan*. Edited by W. G. Pogson Smith. Oxford: Clarendon Press.

Hollander, Robert. 1969. *Allegory in Dante's "Commedia."* Princeton: Princeton University Press.

Hopkins, Keith. 1980. "Brother-Sister Marriage in Ancient Egypt." *Comparative Studies in Society and History* 22:303-54.

Horwich, Richard. 1977. "Riddles and Dilemma in *The Merchant of Venice*," *Studies in English Literature* 17:191-200.

Hoy, Cyrus. 1964. *The Hyacinth Room: An Investigation into the Nature of Comedy, Tragedy and Tragicomedy*. London: Chatto & Windus.

Huizinga, Johan. 1970. *Homo Ludens: A Study of the Play Element in Culture*. Translated by R. F. C. Hull. London: Routledge & Kegan Paul.

Hume, Martin. 1908-10. "The So-Called Conspiracy of Dr. Lopez." *Transactions of the Jewish Historical Society* 6:32-55.

Hunter, G. K. 1959. Introduction. In Shakespeare, *All's Well That Ends Well*, New Arden Edition. London: Methuen.

Hurrell, John D. 1961. "Love and Friendship in *The Merchant of Venice*." *Texas Studies in Literature and Language* 3:328-41.

Ihering, Herbert. 1929. *Reinhardt, Jessner, Piscator oder Klassikertod?* Berlin: Ernst Rohwolt.

Irigaray, Luce. 1985. *Speculum of the Other Woman.* Translated by Gillian C. Gill. Ithaca: Cornell University Press.

Jameson, Fredric. 1981. *The Political Unconscious: Narrative as a Socially Symbolic Act.* London: Methuen.

Jardine, David. 1832. *Criminal Trials.* London: Charles Knight.

Jenkins, Priscilla. 1969. "Conscience: The Frustration of Allegory." In *"Piers Plowman": Critical Approaches*, edited by S. S. Hussey. London: Methuen.

Johannis de Alta Silva. 1913. *Dolopathos, sive De rege et septem sapientibus.* Edited by Alfons Hilka. Heidelberg: C. Winter.

Johnson, Ralph Henry. 1972. *The Concept of Existence in the "Concluding Unscientific Postscript."* The Hague: Martinus Nijhoff.

Jolles, André. 1930. *Einfache Formen.* Halle [Saale]: Max Niemeyer Verlag.

Jones, Norman. 1989. *God and the Moneylenders: Usury and Law in Early Modern England.* Oxford: Basil Blackwell.

Kaiser, Gerhard. 1974. *Benjamin. Adorno. Zwei Studien.* Frankfurt am Main: Athenäum.

Kant, Immanuel. 1974. *Anthropology from a Pragmatic Point of View.* Translated by Mary J. Gregor. The Hague: Martinus Nijhoff.

Kantorowicz, Ernst. 1957. *The King's Two Bodies.* Princeton: Princeton University Press.

Katz, David S. 1982. *Philo-Semetism and the Readmission of the Jews to England, 1603-1655.* Oxford: Clarendon Press.

———. forthcoming. *The Jews in the History of England, 1485-1850.* Oxford: Oxford University Press.

Katz, Jacob. 1961. *Tradition and Crisis: Jewish Society at the End of the Middle Ages).* New York: The Free Press of Glencoe.

———. 1989. *The "Shabbles Goy": A Steady in Halakhic Flexibility.* Translated by Yoel Lerner. Philadephia: Jewish Publication Society.

Keeton, George W. 1967. *Shakespeare's Legal and Political Background.* London: Pitman.

Kelso, James A. 1918. "Riddle." In *Encyclopaedia of Religion and Ethics*, edited by James Hastings, 10:765-70. Edinburgh: T. & T. Clark: New York: Scribner.

Kermode, Frank. 1967. *The Sense of an Ending: Studies in the Theory of Fiction.* New York: Oxford University Press.

———. 1971. "The Mature Comedies." In *Shakespeare, Spenser, Donne: Renaissance Essays.* London: Routledge & Kegan Paul.

———. 1973. "The Use of the Codes." in *Approaches to Poetics*, edited by Seymour Chatman. New York and London: Columbia University Press.

Kierkegaard, S. 1941. *Concluding Unscientific Postscript to the Philosophical Fragments.* Translated by David F. Swenson and Walter Lowrie. Princeton: Princeton University Press.

King, Henry C. 1957. *The Background of Astronomy.* London: Watts.

Kleinberg, Seymour. 1983. "*The Merchant of Venice:* The Homosexual as Anti-Semite in Nascent Capitalism" in *Literary Visions of Homosexuality*, edited by Stuart Kellogg. New York: The Haworth Press.

Knights, L. C. 1946. "How Many Children Had Lady Macbeth?" Reprinted in *Explorations.* London: Chatto and Windus.

Kohler, Joseph. 1919. *Shakespeare vor dem Forum der Jurisprudenz.* 2d ed. Berlin & Leipzig.

Kristeller, Paul Oskar. 1943. *The Philosophy of Marsilio Ficino.* Translated by Virginia Conant. New York: Columbia University Press.

Kristeva, Julia. 1969. *Séméiotiké: Recherches pour une sémanalyse.* Paris: Seuil.

———. 1980. *Desire in Language: A Semiotic Approach to Literature and Art.* Edited and translated by Leon S. Roudiez. Oxford: Blackwell.

———. 1982. *Powers of Horror: An Essay on Abjection.* Translated by Leon S. Roudiez. New York: Columbia University Press.

———. 1984. *Revolution in the Poetic Language.* Translated by Margaret Waller. New York: Columbia University Press.

Kugel, James L., ed. 1990. *Poetry and Prophecy: The Beginnings of a Literary Tradition.* Ithaca and London: Cornell University Press.

Kuhns, David F. 1991. "Expressionism, Monumentalism, Politics: Emblematic Acting in Jessner's *Wilhelm Tell* and *Richard III.*" *New Theatre Quarterly* 25:35-48.

Moody, Anthony David. 1964. *Shakespeare: "The Merchant of Venice."* London: Edward Arnold.

Muir, Kenneth. 1979. *Shakespeare's Comic Sequence.* New York: Barnes & Noble.

Mullaney, Steven. 1980. "Lying Like Truth: Riddle, Representation and Treason in Renaissance England." *ELH* 47:32-47

———. 1987. "Brothers and Others, or the Art of Alienation." In *Cannibals, Witches and Divorce:*

Estranging the Renaissance, edited by Marjorie Garber. Baltimore and London: The Johns Hopkins University Press.

Munzer, Stephen R. 1990. *A Theory of Property.* Cambridge: Cambridge University Press.

Murrin, Michael. 1969. *The Veil of Allegory.* Chicago and London: University of Chicago Press.

Neely, Carol Thomas. 1980. "Women and Men in *Othello:* "What should such a fool / Do with so good a woman?" In Lenz, Green, and Neely, eds. 1980.

Nelson, Benjamin N. 1947. "The Usurer and the Merchant Prince: Italian Businessmen and the Ecclesiastical Law of Restitution. 1100-1550." *Journal of Economic History,* Supplement 7:104-22.

———. 1969. *The Idea of Usury: From Tribal Brotherhood to Universal Otherhood.* 2nd ed. Chicago and London: University of Chicago Press.

———, and J. Starr. 1944. "The Legend of the Divine Surety and the Jewish Moneylender." *Annuaire de l'Institut de Philologie et d'Histoire Orientales et Slaves,* 7 (1939-44): 289-338.

Niemeyer, Theodor. 1912. *Der Rechtsspruch gegen Shylock.* München & Leipzig.

Nozick, Robert. 1974. *Anarchy, State, and Utopia.* New York: Basic Books.

Nuttall, A. D. 1983. *A New Mimesis: Shakespeare and the Representation of Reality.* London: Methuen.

Orgel, Stephen. 1987. "Shakespeare and the Cannibals." In *Cannibals, Witches and Divorce: Estranging the Renaissance,* edited by Marjorie Garber. Baltimore and London: The Johns Hopkins University Press.

Overton, Bill. 1987. *The Merchant of Venice.* Houndmills, Basingstoke, and London: Macmillan.

Oz, Avraham. 1980. "The Doubling of Parts in Shakespearean Comedy: Some Questions of Theory and Practice." In *Shakespearean Comedy,* edited by Maurice Charney. New York: *New York Literary Forum.*

———. 1988. "What's in a Good Name? The Case of Romeo and Juliet as a "Bad" Tragedy." In *Bad Shakespeare,* edited by Maruice Charney. Rutherford, N.J.: Fairleigh Dickinson University Press; London and Toronto: Associated University Presses.

———. 1990. *Shtar Hakhidah* (The riddle bond). Tel Aviv: Hakibbutz Hameuhad.

Packard, Maurice. 1919. *Shylock Not a Jew.* Boston: Stratford.

Pagis, Dan. 1986. *Al Sod Hatum* (A secret sealed): *Hebrew Baroque Emblem-Riddles from Italy and Holland.* Jerusalem: Magnes Press.

Panofsky, Dora, and Erwin Panofsky. 1965. *Pandora's Box.* 2d rev. ed. New York: Harper & Row.

Park, Clara Claiborne. 1980. "As We Like It: How a Girl Can Be Smart and Still Popular." In Lenz, Green, and Neely, eds. 1980.

Pascal. *Pensées.* 1962. Texte établi par Louis Lafuma. Paris: Librairies Associés.

Patterson, Orlando. 1982. *Slavery and Social Death: A Comparative Study.* Cambridge, Mass., and London: Harvard University Press.

Pepicello, W. J., and Thomas A. Green. 1984. *The Language of Riddles: New Perspectives.* Columbus: Ohio State University Press.

Perkins, William. 1607. *Prophetica, sive de sacra et vnica ratione Concionandi,* tractatus Cambridge. 1592. Translated by Thomas Tuke, The Arte of Prophecying. London.

Petch, Robert. 1899. *Neue Beiträge zur Kenntnis des Volkrätsels.* Palaestra 4. Berlin: Mayer and Müller.

Phillips William D. 1985. *Slavery from Roman Times to the Early Transatlantic Trade.* Manchester: Manchester University Press.

Pirenne, Henri. 1969. *Histoire économique et sociale du Moyen-Age.* Paris: Presses universitaires de France.

Plowman, Max. 1931. "Money and The Merchant." *Adelphi,* NS, 2: 508-13.

Poliakov, Léon. 1966. *The History of Anti-Semitism.* Vol. 1: *Time of Christ to the Court Jews.* Translated by Richard Howard. London: Elek.

———. 1974. *The History of Anti-Semitism.* Vol. 2: *From Mohammed to the Marranos.* Translated by Natalie Gerardi. London: Routledge & Kegan Paul.

———. 1975. *The History of Anti-Semitism.* Vol. 3: *From Voltaire to Wagner.* Translated by Miriam Kochan. London: Routledge & Kegan Paul.

Pollock, Frederick, and Robert Samuel Wright. 1888. *An Essay on Possession in the Common Law.* Oxford: Oxford University Press.

Popper, Karl Raimund. 1957. *The Poverty of Historicism.* Boston: Beacon Press.

———. 1969. "Prediction and Prophecy in the Social Sciences." In *Conjectures and Refutations.* 3d ed. London: Routledge & Kegan Paul.

Potter, Charles Francis. 1950. "Riddles." in *Funk and Wagnalls Standard Dictionary of Folklore, Mythology and Legend,* edited by Maria Leach and Jerome Fried. New York: Funk & Wagnalls.

Pouchelle, Marie-Christine. 1990. *The Body and Surgery in the Middle Ages.* Translated by Rosemary Morris. New Brunswick, N.J.: Rutgers University Press.

Price, Joseph. 1968. *The Unfortunate Comedy.* Toronto: University of Toronto Press.

Prothero, Sir George W. 1913. *Select Statutes and Other Constitutional Documents Illustrative of the Reign of Elizabeth and James I.* 4th ed. Oxford: Oxford University Press.

Pullan, Brian. 1971. *Rich and Poor in Renaissance Venice, The Social Institutions of a Catholic State to 1620.* Oxford: Blackwell.

———. 1983. *The Jews of Europe and the Inquisition of Venice, 1550-1670.* Oxford: Blackwell.

Quinones, Ricardo J. 1972. *The Renaissance Discovery of Time.* Cambridge, Mass.: Harvard University Press.

Radin, M. 1922. "Secare Partis: The Early Roman Law against a Debtor." *American Journal of Philology* 43:32-48.

Rank, Otto. 1979. *The Double.* Translated and edited by Harry Tucker, Jr. New York, London, and Scarborough: Meridian Books.

Rawlings, Carl Donn. 1973. "Prophecy in the Novel." Unpublished diss., University of Washington.

Rea, John D. 1929. "Shylock and the *Processus Belial.*" *Philological Quarterly* 8:311-13.

Reeve, Andrew. 1986. *Property.* Houndmills, Basingstoke, and London: Macmillan.

Reeves, Marjorie. 1969. *The Influence of Prophecy in the Later Middle Ages: A Study in Joachimism.* Oxford: Oxford University Press.

Reiss, Timothy J. 1982. *The Discourse of Modernism.* Ithaca: Cornell University Press.

Reynolds, Edward. 1640. *A Treatise of the Passions and Faculties of the Soule of Man.* London.

Rhu, Lawrence F. 1990. "After the Middle Ages: Prophetic Authority and Human Fallibility in Renaissance Epic." In Kugel 1990.

Ricoeur, Paul. 1973. "The Model of the Text: Social Action Considered as a Text." *New Literary History* 5:91-117.

Róheim, Géza. 1934. *The Riddle of the Sphinx, or Human Origins.* Translated by R. Money-Kyrle. London: Leonard and Virginia Woolf at the Hogarth Press, and the Institute of Psychoanalysis.

Rose, Mary Beth, ed. 1986. *Women in the Middle Ages and the Renaissance: Literary and Historical Perspectives.* Syracuse, N.Y.: Syracuse University Press.

Roth, Cecil. 1941. *A History of the Jews in England.* Oxford: Clarendon Press.

———. 1959. *A History of the Marranos.* New York: Meridian Books.

Rozik, Eli. 1988. "Apartheid in Venice." *Bamah* 111:74-86.

Saga Heidreks Konnungs ins Vitra [The Saga of King Heidrek the Wise]. 1960. Translated by Christopher Tolkien. London: Thomas Nelson & Sons.

Said, Edward W. 1975. *Beginnings: Intention and Method.* New York: Basic Books.

———. 1983. *The World, the Text and the Critic.* Cambridge, Mass.: Harvard University Press.

———, and Christopher Hitchens, eds. 1988. *Blaming the Victims: Spurious Scholarship and the Palestinian Question.* London and New York: Verso.

Salingar, Leo. 1974. *Shakespeare and the Traditions of Comedy.* Cambridge: Cambridge University Press.

Schatz, Thomas. 1981. *Hollywood Genres: Formulas, Fimmaking and the Studio System.* New York: Random House.

Schlatter, Richard. 1951. *Private Property: The History of an Idea.* London: George Allen and Unwin.

Sebillet, Thomas. 1932. *Art Poetique Françoys.* Edited by Félix Gaiffe. Paris: Droz.

Segaller, Stephen. 1986. *Invisible Armies: Terrorism into the 1990s.* London: Michael Joseph.

Seng, Peter J. 1958. "The Riddle Song in *Merchant of Venice.*" *Notes & Queries,* NS 5. 191-93.

Sepet, Marius. 1867-77. *Les Prophètes du Christ: Etude sur les origines du théâtre au moyen age.* Bibliotheque de l'Ecole des Chartes, sér. 6, tom. 3,4,13. Paris.

———. 1878. *Les Prophètes du Christ.* Paris: Didier.

Shapiro, James. 1992. "Shakespeare and the Jews." The Parkes Lectures at the University of Southampton.

Shepherd, Geoffrey. 1966. "Scriptural Poetry." In *Continuations and Beginnings.* London: Thomas Nelson.

Sharpe, J. A. 1990. *Judicial Punishment in England.* London and Boston: Faber and Faber.

Shipley, Joseph T., ed. 1955. *Dictionary of World Literary Terms.* London: George Allen & Unwin.

Shipper, Itzhak. 1935. *Toldot Hakalkala Hayehudit* (History of Jewish economy). Tel Aviv: Stiebel.

Shumaker, Wayne. 1972. *The Occult Sciences in the Renaissance.* Berkeley and Los Angeles: University of California Press.

Siegel, Paul N. 1968. *Shakespeare in his Time and Ours.* Notre Dame, Ind.: University of Notre Dame Press.

Silvayn, Alexander. 1596. *The Orator.* Translated by L. P[iot]. London.

Sinsheimer, Herman. 1964. *Shylock: The History of a Character.* New York: The Citadel Press.

Small, Samuel Asa. 1927. *Shakespearean Character Interpretation: "The Merchant of Venice."* Göttingen & Baltimore: Hesperia.

Smith, Adam. 1950. *The Wealth of Nations.* Edited by Edwin Canaan. London: Methuen.

Soellner, Rolf. 1972. *Shakespeare's Patterns of Self-Knowledge.* Columbus: Ohio University Press.

Sondheim, Moriz. 1938-39. "Shakespeare and the Astrology of His Time." *Journal of the Warburg Institute* 2.

Sophocles. 1954. *Oedipus the King.* Translated by David Grene. In *Sophocles: Three Tragedies,* edited by David Grene and Richmond Lattimore. Chicago and London: University of Chicago Press.

Spenser, Edmund. 1912. *Poetical Works.* Edited by J. C. Smith and E. De Selincourt. London: Oxford University Press.

Spinoza, Benedict. 1862. *Tractatus Theologico-Politicus.* Translated by Robert Willis. London.

Stahl, Ernst Leopold. 1947. *Shakespeare und das deutsche Theater.* Stuttgart: W. Kohlhammer.

Sternberg, Meir. 1985. *The Poetics of Biblical Narrative: Ideological Literature and the Drama of Reading.* Bloomington: Indiana University Press.

Strachey, Lytton. 1971. *Elizabeth and Essex.* Harmondsworth: Penguin.

Stype, John. 1710. *The history of the life and acts of the most reverend . . . Edmund Grindal . . . Archbishop of Canterbury.* London: J. Hartley,

———. 1718. *The life and acts of the most Reverend . . . John Whitgift . . . Archbishop of Canterbury.* London.

Stubb, John. 1968. *"Gaping Gulf," with Letters and Other Relevant Documents.* Edited Lloyd E. Berry. Charlottesville: University Press of Virginia.

Styan, J. L. 1984. *All's Well That Ends Well.* Manchester: Manchester University Press.

Szanto, George H. 1978. *Theater & Propaganda.* Austin and London: University of Texas Press.

Taeusch, Carl F. 1942. "The Concept of 'Usury': The History of an Idea." *Journal of the History of Ideas* 3:291-318.

Tawney, Richard Henry. 1969. *Religion and the Rise of Capitalism.* Harmondsworth: Penguin.

Taylor, Archer. 1948. *The Literary Riddle before 1600.* Berkeley and Los Angeles: University of California Press.

———. 1951. *English Riddles from Oral Tradition.* Berkeley and Los Angeles: University of California Press.

Taylor, Jeremy. 1647. *A Discourse of the Liberty of Prophesying.* London.

Taylor, Rupert. 1911. *The Political Prophecy in England.* New York: Columbia University Press.

Tennenhouse, Leonard. 1986. *Power on Display: The Politics of Shakespeare's Genres.* New York and London: Methuen.

Thomas, Keith. 1973. *Religion and the Decline of Magic.* 2d ed. Harmondsworth: Penguin.

———. 1983. *Man and the Natural World: Changing Attitudes in England, 1500-1800.* London: Allen Lane.

Thompson, Stith, ed. 1955-58. *Motif-Index of Folk Literature.* Rev. and enlarged ed. Copenhagen: Rosenkilde and Bagger.

Tomkis, Thomas. 1944. *Albumazar.* Edited by Hugh G. Dick. Berkeley and Los Angeles: University of California Press.

Toulmin-Smith, L. 1875-76. "On the Bond-Story in *The Merchant of Venice* and a Version of it in *Cursor Mundi.*" *New Shakespearean Society Transactions,* 181-89.

Torrell, Jean-Pierre. 1992. *Recherches sur la théorie de la prophétic au moyen âge.* Fribourg: Editions Universitaires Fribourg Suisse.

Trachtenberg, Joshua. 1943. *The Devil and the Jews: The Medieval Conception of the Jew and Its Relation to Modern Antisemitism.* New Haven: Yale University Press.

Tully, James. 1980. *A Discourse on Property: John Locke and His Adversaries.* Cambridge: Cambridge University Press.

Turner, Victor. 1982. *From Ritual to Theatre: The Human Seriousness of Play.* New York: Performing Arts Journal Publications.

Tuve, Rosemond. 1947. *Elizabethan and Metaphysical Imagery.* Chicago: University of Chicago Press.

———. 1966. *Allegorical Imagery.* Princeton: Princeton University Press.

Vámbéry, A. 1901. "Der Orientalische Ursprung von Shylock." *Kelety Szemle* 2:18-29.

Wagner-Pacifici, Robin Erica. 1986. *The Moro Morality Play: Terrorism as Social Drama.* Chicago and London: University of Chicago Press.

Waldron, Jeremy. 1988. *The Right to Private Property.* Oxford: Oxford University Press.

Walker, Roy. 1949. *The Time Is Free.* London: Andrew Dakers.

Wallace, Karl R. 1943. *Francis Bacon on Communication and Rhetoric.* Chapel Hill: University of North Carolina Press.

———. 1967. *Francis Bacon on the Nature of Man.* Urbana, Chicago, and London: University of Illinois Press.

Wardlaw, Grant. 1982. *Political Terrorism.* Cambridge: Cambridge University Press.

Weber, Max. 1958. *The Protestant Ethic and the Spirit of Capitalism.* Translated by Talcott Parsons. New York: Charles Scribner's Sons.

Webster, John. 1927. *The Complete Works of John Webster.* Edited by F. L. Lucas. London: Chatto and Windus.

Wenger, Berta Viktoria. 1929. "Shylocks Pfund Fleisch." *Shakespeare Jahrbuch* 65: 174-92.

Wesker, Arnold. 1993. "A Nasty Piece of Work." *The Sunday Times* 6.6:9.2-3.

Wettinger, Godfrey. 1985. *The Jews of Malta in the Late Middle Ages.* Valletta, Malta: Midsea Books.

Whitman, F. H. 1970. Medieval Riddling: Factors Underlying Its Development. *Neuphilologische Mitteilungen,* 71.

Widdowson, Peter. 1988. "Terrorism and Literary Studies." *Textual Practice* 2:1 (Spring 1988): 1-21.

Wikse, John R. 1977. *About Possession: The Self as Private Property.* University Park and London: The Pennsylvania State University Press.

Wilkinson, Paul. 1977. *Terrorism and the Liberal State.* London and Basingstoke: Macmillan.

Williamson, Marilyn L. 1986. *The Patriarchy of Shakespeare's Comedies.* Detroit: Wayne State University Press.

Wilson, Thomas. 1925. *A Discourse Upon Usury.* Introduction by R. H. Tawney. London: G. Bell and Sons.

Wittgenstein, Ludwig. 1961. *Tractatus Logico-Philosophicus.* Translation by D. F. Pears and B. F. McGuinness. London: Routledge & Kegan Paul; New York: The Humanities Press.

Wittreich, Joseph. 1984. *Image of that Horror": History, Prophecy, and Apocalypse in "King Lear."* San Marino, Calif.: The Huntington Library.

Wojcik, Jan, and Raymond-Jean Frontain. 1984. *Poetic Prophecy in Western Literature* Rutherford, Madison, and Teaneck, N.J.: Fairleigh Dickinson University Press.

Wolf, Lucien. 1924-27. "Jews in Elizabethan England." In *Transactions of the Jewish Historical Society in England* 11: 1-92.

———. 1934. *Essays in Jewish History.* Edited by Cecil Roth. London: The Jewish Historical Society in England.

Wolfson, Harry Austryn. 1968. *Philo.,* 4th rev. printing. Cambridge, Mass.: Harvard University Press.

Woodbridge, Linda. 1986. *Women and the English Renaissance: Literature and the Nature of Womankind, 1540-1620.* Urbana and Chicago: University of Illinois Press.

Ziegler, Leopold. 1922. *Gastaltwandel der Götter.* 3d ed. Darmstadt: O. Reichl

Zipes, Jack. 1988. *Fairy Tales and the Art of Subversion.* New York: Methuen.

Žižek, Slavoj. 1991. *For They Know Not What They Do: Enjoyment as a Political Factor.* London and New York: Verso.

Mary Janell Metzger (essay date 1998)

SOURCE: "'Now by My Hood, a Gentle and No Jew': Jessica, *The Merchant of Venice,* and the Discourse of Early Modern English Identity," in *PMLA,* Vol. 113, No. 1, 1998, pp. 52-63.

[*In the essay below, Metzger examines Elizabethan England's anxieties about racial and religious differences as symbolized by Shylock's daughter, Jessica, in* The Merchant of Venice. *Metzger contrasts the white-skinned, Christian-looking Jessica, who willingly and easily converts, with her dark-skinned father, who is forced by society to convert without ever, in fact, being accepted by society.*]

Jessica, the other Jew in *The Merchant of Venice,* is doubly distinguished.[1] Unlike her father, Shylock, she is said to be "gentle": at once noble and gentile. Yet as the "now" quoted in my title signifies and as Jessica readily admits, she remains "a daughter to [Shylock's] blood" despite her conversion (2.6.51, 2.3.18). Distinguished from Portia and Nerissa, whose marriages work to secure the social standing of the men they love, she is more saved than saving in her marriage to Lorenzo. Indeed, representations of Jessica, unlike those of other characters in the play, turn on alternating characterizations of her as a latent Christian and as a racialized and thus unintegrable Jew.[2]

Until recently, discussions of race or Jewishness in *The Merchant* tended to focus on Shylock alone. These readings suggested that critics could deal with religion, gender, or class but not with all three. There were no attempts to understand how such categories are, as Carol Neely puts it, "inseparable, unstable, disunified, and mutually constitutive" (303).[3] Critics like Neely, however, imply that reading Jessica both as a wealthy white woman who is thus coded as gentile and as "issue to a faithless Jew" (2.4.37) should highlight the interconnectedness of discourses of difference in Shakespeare's time.[4] This critical project has been considerably advanced by James Shapiro's *Shakespeare and the Jews,* which challenges assumptions about the significance of real and imagined Jews for early modern English audiences. By documenting both the actual lives and fictive representations of Jews in Shakespeare's England, Shapiro eliminates the distinction between theology and race implicit in G. K. Hunter's argument that Shakespeare and Marlowe did not depict "real" or "racial" Jews but, rather, portrayed a "moral condition" rooted in a "theological rather than ethnological framework" (215). Similarly, Kim Hall's studies of early modern representations of race and gender show how, in an age of soaring population and foreign immigration, English fears of uncontained female sexuality found expression in a "narrative of alien culture" that fused notions of blacks, Jews, and women (*Things* 39).

Yet like critics before them, Hall and Shapiro do not see Jessica as a central figure in *The Merchant* or in the play's discourse of racial difference. Although Shapiro grants that "the battle over *The Merchant of Venice* is a battle over the nature of Englishness itself and who has the right to stake a claim to it," he dedicates but a few pages of his book to Jessica (4). She does not appear in his index. More sensitive than many new-historicist critics to issues of gender, Shapiro nevertheless explains the focus on Jewish men in the texts he examines (and thus in his text) by noting "that Jewish men were represented as endowed with male and female traits" (38). Unfortunately, representations of men subsume those of women once again. Like Shapiro, Hall acknowledges the significance of Jessica as a figure of conversion. Yet while she skillfully traces the ambivalence present in the travel narratives she reads and in the imagery associated with Shylock, she finds Jessica's conversion an unambiguous portrayal of "a successful type of cross-cultural interaction" ("Guess" 102). Hall registers her uneasiness with this position, admitting that "glorifying" the transgressions of women like Jessica and Portia, as feminist critics often have, "may serve only to obscure the very complex nature of difference for a changing society in which racial categories developed along with changing organizations of gender" (103-04).

Hall's discomfort with readings that fail to acknowledge Jessica's ambivalent status in the play echoes my own. Indeed, I have long thought that Jessica's multiplicitous nature—as Jew and Christian and as "fair" beloved descended from blackened Chus, her father's "countrym[a]n" (2.4.39, 3.2.285)—constitutes an emblematic figure for the play's renowed discontinuities. The ambiguous mix of comedy and tragedy, humanism and racialism, patriarchal imperialism and festive rebellion in *The Merchant* corresponds to the inherent incompatibility of the identities Shakespeare attempts to unite in Jessica. Indeed, the nature and effects of Jessica's difference can illuminate how Shakespeare may have struggled with competing notions of Jewishness circulating in early modern England and how he worked to resolve them by creating not one Jew but two. In what follows I argue that only attention to the shifting emphases on discourses of gender, class, and religion in Shakespeare's representation of Jessica can elucidate *The Merchant*'s relation to early modern England's emerging ideology of race and to the bitter effects of that ideology that persist even today.[5]

Any discussion of conversion in Shakespeare must involve the Jew, just as any discussion of the Jew in Shakespeare inevitably involves the meaning of conversion in early modern England. As Hunter rightly observes, theology is central to the analysis of the early modern theatricalization of Jews because of the "long and torturous tradition" of interpreting Christianity *adversus Judeos*—that is, in opposition to Judaism (213). More simply, early modern Christian notions of what it means to be subject to God inevitably entail an account of the Jewish refusal to receive Christ as the Messiah. The English Reformation complicated Christians' response to Jews by offering an unqualified promise of conversion within a discourse shaped by the oppositional rhetoric of anti-Semitism. Further, as historical documents attest, the problem of the Jew in Christian England intersected with an emerging ideology of race to affirm a notion of English identity in which color, religion, and class converged.

In succeeding editions of *Actes and Monuments,* perhaps the most prevalent religious text in Elizabethan England excepting the Bible, the Protestant John Foxe offers "a complete history of the lives, sufferings and deaths of the Christian Martyrs from the commencement of Christianity to the present period" (1563 ed., title p.)—that is, the stories of men and women who met death rather than assert as true what they believed false. Foxe emphasizes the role of reason in the practice of the "true" Christian faith. Describing his text as an "[e]cclesiastical history" from which "the people may learn the rules and precepts of doctrine," Foxe takes a pedagogical tone: "They that be in error, let them not disdain to learn" (1570 ed., 4r). Or as he puts it in the 1563 edition, "Ignorance is the mother of all errors" (EE3v). Yet for Jews, the original recusants, choosing the truth was a matter not simply of learning but of a prior belonging that was denied them: "For like as the nature of truth so is the proper condition of the true church, that commonly none seeth it, but such only as be members and partakers thereof" (3r). Foxe argues even more ambivalently in the 1570 edition that Jews are to blame for their failure to choose wisely—"who should rather have known and received him than the Pharisees and Scribes of that people who had his law"? (E1r). He also repeatedly characterizes them as inherently unable to make such a choice. Foxe presents Jews both as "more tolerable than Papists" (1563 ed., K1v), who abandon their poor and worship idols and bread, and as "enemies to Christians" (1570 ed., index), as child murderers whose historical and bloody destruction confirms their rejection by God (1563 ed., E1r).[6] This ambivalence finds an analogue in *The Merchant,* where Jews are characterized as unwilling and unable to see the truth of the Messiah in Jesus, driven by their base natures, as Gratiano says with characteristic hyperbole, to pursue their "wolvish, bloody, starv'd, and ravenous" desires (4.1.138).

Foxe's apparent need to account for Jewish belief may be as old as Christianity itself, but the sixteenth century constitutes a specific and particularly significant moment in that history (see, e.g., Gerber; Netanyahu; Friedman; Shapiro). For the first time Jewishness was legally defined through Spain's pure-blood laws "not [as] a statement of faith or even a series of ethnic practices but a biological consideration" (Friedman 16). In England, as Foxe's text illustrates, the question of the Jews took on new importance in the light of Reformation struggles among Christians over the proper path to God's truth. How could one discern, as Foxe puts it, between "antiquitie and novelty" (1570 ed., iiv), between false worship and true faith? The Protestant emphasis on the inability of the individual to effect his or her own salvation, which Foxe's text elaborates, challenges the promise of Christianity made explicit in baptism. Called to "learn" and to "choose" rightly, one nevertheless could not "see" unless elected a "member or partaker thereof" by God's grace.

Readers like Hunter have been inclined to dismiss the import of such questions by asserting the relative scarcity of Jews in England in Shakespeare's time.[7] But the presence of crypto-Jews (converts to Christianity who secretly practiced Judaism) in Elizabethan England has been acknowledged since Lucien Wolf's discovery in the early twentieth century of a mostly Portuguese community of Jews. In fact, *The Merchant* followed fairly closely on the trial and execution of the most connected member of that community, Elizabeth's chief physician, Roderigo Lopez,[8] and Shylock's principal antagonist takes the name of the man whose political aspirations provided the context for Lopez's alleged treason: Don Antonio, pretender to the throne of Portugal following the death of the cardinal-king Henry. Such allusions would have been easily recognized by Shakespeare's audience.

According to Wolf, this Portuguese community "could not have remained altogether unknown to the general public, while to the Government, with its vigilant watch of all strangers hailing from Spain and Portugal, it must have been in every sense an open secret" (21); indeed, Wolf documents the government's knowledge in the correspondence of Lord Burghley, the queen's secretary of state, and his son Robert Cecil. But more important, Wolf argues that the Portuguese community of Jews was tolerated because they served the state without causing a stir—that is, because of economic interest: "they appear to have been, on the whole, quite decent folk, who worked honestly and unobtrusively at professions, trades and handicrafts which added appreciably to the well-being of the country" (22). Living and working "honestly and unobtrusively" meant becoming invisible as "former" Jews and convincingly performing the prerequisites for integration into English society. The cases of Joachim Gaunse on the one hand and of Bernard Leavis and Pedro Frere on the other illustrate this. Gaunse, a German Jewish mining chemist who worked in England for eight years, was expelled in 1598 on the grounds that he had challenged Christian doctrine in debating the status of Jesus with a Protestant minister from Bristol.[9] Portuguese agents pursuing prohibited Spanish goods on behalf of English traders, Frere and Leavis were accused by Mary May, a Christian investor, who claimed that their Jewishness was a principal cause of her losses. Though much evidence of their "secret practices" was procured from servants and acquaintances, the court did not expel them; rather, it was "moved with the losses and trobles which the poore straungers indured" as a consequence of doing English business (Sisson 51).[10] As long as Jews did not publicly insist on their Jewishness, economic interests prevailed.

As other deportations suggest, notions of religious and racial conformity may have contributed to the emerging concepts of the English subject and of its requisite other, the alien. In 1596, the year *The Merchant* was probably written, Elizabeth I wrote to the Privy Council to request the aid of the mayor of London, his aldermen, and "all the other Maiours, Sheryfes, etc." in deporting eighty-nine blacks, to be given to a Lubeck merchant in exchange for his return of an equal number of English prisoners of war held by Spain and Portugal (*Acts* 16). Elizabeth distinguished "people of our owne nation," "the subjectes of the land and Christian people, that perishe for want of service, whereby through labor they might be mayntained," from "those kinde of people," meaning blacks, brought to live and work in England (16, 20-21). As Elizabeth's equations among color, faith, wealth, and nationality confirm, to be black was to be a common laborer, non-Christian, and consequently not English.

While European Jews may appear to have had the advantage over blacks in their ability to pass, as it were, as white and Christian and hence English, analogies between blackness and Jewishness were long-standing. As Anthony Barthelemy has shown, the association of blackness with sin and evil, which dates from the ancient world, was adopted by Christianity and overlaid with a narrative of salvation and damnation: white became the color of the saved, black the color of the damned. First among the damned would, of course, have been the Jews, as a 1604 biography of Spain's Charles V demonstrates:

> Who can deny that in the descendent of the Jews there persists and endures the evil inclination of their ancient ingratitude and lack of understanding, just as in Negroes [there persists] the inseparability of their blackness? For if the latter should unite themselves a thousand times with white women, the children are born with the dark color of the father. Similarly, it is not enough for a Jew to be three parts aristocrat or Old Christian for one family-line [i.e., one Jewish ancestor] alone defiles and corrupts him.
>
> (Friedman 16-17)

Shakespeare's Jessica anticipates this equation when she describes her father as a countryman "[t]o Tubal and to Chus" (3.2.285), for the first is a Jew and the second the mythical originary black African.[11]

The connection between blacks and Jews as alien others helped construct the racialized notion of Englishness. Because of color privilege, however, the converted Jews of London were not always perceived as threats to emerging notions of English identity, as Roger Prior's discovery of an integrationist Italian Jewish community in Tudor London indicates. Like the Portuguese Jews, the Italian Jews owed their presence in England to royal patronage, engaged in trade, and had connections to Jews in Antwerp. They lived in the same places in and outside London as their Portuguese counterparts did, but they integrated into English society far more thoroughly through marriage to Christians (see Prior 138). According to Prior, Shakespeare draws distinctions between converted Italian Jews, like Emilia Bassano—better known now as the poet Emilia Lanier—the woman alleged to be the dark lady of his sonnets, and Portuguese converts like Lopez whose resistant Jewishness was seen as a threat to English identity.[12] Whether or not Prior's claims about Emilia Bassano are true, the history of the Italian Jewish community suggests that competing notions of Jewishness existed at the time Shakespeare wrote and staged *The Merchant*. The construction of Jews as "deserving" (as they would later be labeled in the state documents calling for their readmission to England) or alien may have functioned to authorize the social and political agendas of British imperialism and the racialism it depended on.[13] Foxe's concerns may be seen, then, as representative of larger political questions: How would the English distinguish resistant and finally unintegrable Jews like Lopez or Gaunse from more cooperative and thus "truly" convertible Jews like Bassano? How could they affirm this distinction without denying the meaning and promise of conversion to Christianity? And how could English Christians define the Jew's difference both as a difference of nature and as a difference of faith involving the act of will faith requires? These issues constitute Shakespeare's challenge in *The Merchant of Venice*—a challenge he meets by presenting Jessica as a "fair" Jewish alternative to Shylock.

Initially Launcelot describes Jessica as a "[m]ost beautiful pagan, [a] most sweet Jew," and her embodiment of such conjunctions is an obvious source of comic tension in the play. Significantly, however, Launcelot's oxymorons depend on anti-Semitic assumptions that are impressed on the audience when Shylock first appears onstage as the incarnation of the inherently evil Jew of medieval and early modern Christian legend: he is scheming ("If I can catch him once upon the hip . . ." [1.3.46]), greedy ("He lends out money gratis, and brings down / The rate of usuance" [1.3.44-45]), satanic ("The devil can cite Scripture for his purpose. . . . O, what a goodly outside falsehood hath!" [1.3.98, 102]), and eager for Christian blood ("[the] fair flesh, to be cut off and taken / In what part of your body pleaseth me" [1.3.150-51][14]).

Jessica must overcome these images if she is to be integrated into the world of the play, which is largely defined in opposition to the malevolent Jewish otherness of Shylock. The difficulties of doing so, however, become quickly apparent. Alone onstage at the end of her first scene, Jessica presents the audience with the first of several arguments for her convertibility.

> Alack, what heinous sin is it in me
> To be ashamed to be my father's child!
> But though I am a daughter to his blood,
> I am not to his manners. O Lorenzo,
> If thou keep promise, I shall end this strife,
> Become a Christian and thy loving wife!
>
> (2.3.16-21)

That Jessica distances herself from sin by blatantly disregarding her father's authority may be necessary, but it is also problematic. For Shakespeare's audience, patriarchal authority was divinely ordained, and it secured the right of princes as well as that of fathers.[15] Jessica's disregard for that authority thus creates the first obstacle to a Christian audience's acceptance of her as a Christian.

The late-sixteenth-century debate over the role of parental authority in choosing a spouse would have been equally familiar to Shakespeare's audience.[16] Moreover, texts such as Andrewe Kyngesmill's "Godly Advise Touchyng Mariage" (1580) and Charles Gibbon's *How to Bestow Children in Marriage* (1591) reveal that the contest between individual will and patriarchal authority in the choice of spouses was often most intense when marriages were proposed between "believers and nonbelievers" (Kyngesmill Jiv). Gibbon lays out the competing views about such marriages in a fictional debate between Philogus and Tychias. Philogus argues that a Christian should not "be unequally yoked with infidels for what fellowship hath righteousness & what communion hath light with darkness?" Tychias counters that "the unbelieving husband is sanctified by the believing wife" and vice versa (C2r-v).[17]

In this context, acceptance of Jessica's marriage to Lorenzo would require a Christian audience to conclude either that she is a believer before her marriage or that she is, as she insists, "sanctified" through her marriage. In fact, Jessica lays claim to both arguments. Distinguishing between her own and her father's manners to resolve the "sin" and "strife" implicit in her rebellion, she underscores her preconversion difference. She nullifies the claims of filial attachment by insisting that she is a different kind of Jew, one whose manners take precedence over blood and who thus can see the truth of Christianity. Conversely, she equates Shylock's blood and manners, asserting a racial notion of Jewishness that she claims not to share. To extend an argument Frank Whigham makes, material and aesthetic distinctions between the powerful and the powerless take on both moral and bodily force and thus reveal to the audience a "natural" social hierarchy in which men subordinate women and Christians subordinate Jews (95, 103). Indeed, though Jessica clearly prefers a Christian life, she is saved not so much by her own choice as by Lorenzo's choice to marry her. By uniting her willingness with the willingness of others to find her integrable, she combines the blessings of Christian grace with individual will.

The need to guarantee Jessica's willingness is demonstrated in the scene following her soliloquy, in which Lorenzo, Gratiano, Solanio, and Solerio plan how Jessica, along with "what gold and jewels she [shall be] furnished with," will be taken "from her father's house" (2.4.31, 2.4.30). Jessica's wealth and her willingness to spend it constitute the first of several distinctions that guarantee her integration into Christian society. The next is articulated by Lorenzo when he receives her letter setting the time of their elopement:

> I know the hand; in faith, 'tis a fair hand,

And whiter than the paper it writ on
Is the fair hand that writ.

(2.4.12-14)

The stress Lorenzo places on "fair" is echoed by Gratiano and again by Lorenzo before the scene concludes (2.4.28, 2.4.39). Early modern uses of *fair* combine the senses of color and beauty, and Lorenzo's direct reference to whiteness suggests color is related to his assertion of Jessica's worth.[18] Thus, while the scene establishes the means for Jessica's liberation from Shylock's house, it creates a color difference between father and daughter that justifies her removal, and it casts that difference as a source of comedy instead of tragedy: consider, for example, Desdemona's fate after eloping. Why color might be a prerequisite to differentiation from the Jewish stereotype is suggested later, in the seemingly comic debate between Launcelot and Jessica about the effectiveness of Jewish integration through marriage. In an awkward quotation of Exodus 20.5, Launcelot warns Jessica that "the sins of the father are to be laid upon the children" (3.5.1-2). She answers by repeating her earlier argument: "I shall be saved by my husband. He hath made me a Christian" (3.5.19-20). The power of her response is manifest not only in its simplicity, which contrasts with Launcelot's comic misprisions, but also in the representation of marriage as a force for order. But Lorenzo clarifies the bodily requirements for marriage as a means for the "making of Christians," as Launcelot puts it, when Jessica relays Launcelot's claims (3.5.23). "I shall answer that better to the commonwealth," Lorenzo warns Launcelot, "than you can the getting up of the Negro's belly; the Moor is with child by you, Launcelot" (3.5.37-39).

Jessica's defense and Lorenzo's rebuttal show how her whiteness and femaleness make possible her reproduction as a Christian in the eyes of the "commonwealth." As Hall notes, the scene reflects that institution's investment in "sexual practices" ("Guess" 89). Moreover, Jessica's marriage reconstitutes her as a body, for according to Christian ecclesiastical and legal authorities, a woman was incorporated into the body of her husband in marriage, becoming both one with and subject to him. As Portia says after Bassanio has successfully negotiated the prenuptial test devised by her father, "Myself, and what was mine, to you and yours / Is now converted" (3.2.166-67). In a play concerned with the conversion of Jews, Portia's terms make explicit the analogy between the transfer of her person and property to Bassanio and the incorporation of Jessica's person and property into Lorenzo. Like Portia's conversion from "lord," "master," and "[q]ueen" to "an unlessoned girl" ready "to be directed / As from her lord, her governor, her king" (3.2.167, 3.2.168, 3.2.169, 3.2.159, 3.2.164-65), Jessica's conversion from dark infidel to fair Christian is required by the play's ideology of order through marriage. As Jessica argues early in the play, becoming one with the body of Christ requires not only her marriage to a Christian but also the conversion of her body in distinctly racial and gendered terms (2.3.16-21).

It is in this context that Lorenzo's celebration of Jessica as "whiter" than the paper she writes on becomes significant. For unlike the offspring of Launcelot and his absent black lover, those of Jessica and Lorenzo will not differ bodily from the normative white Christian subject. Drawing on the work of Kim Hall and Janet Adelman, Lynda Boose explains the significance of this distinction:

> In terms of the ideological assumptions of a culture such as that of early modern England, the black male-white female union is not the narrative that requires suppression. What challenges the ideology substantially enough to require erasure is that of the black female-white male, for it is in the person of the black woman that the culture's preexisting fears both about the female sex and about gender dominance are realized. Through her, all free-floating anxieties about "the mother's dark place" contaminating the father's designs for perfect self-replication become vividly literal.

("Getting" 45-46)

Like Lorenzo, Hall and Boose consider Jessica visually white and therefore integrable within the racial and religious ideologies of early modern English patriarchy. But this view obscures the process of racialization in the play and thus the intersection of religion and gender in the production of racial ideology. In an inversion of the hierarchy of flesh and blood that Portia uses to incriminate Shylock, Jessica's "Jewish blood" is subordinated in the course of the play to her "fair" and hence convertible flesh (see 3.1.37-42). After her marriage, she will "appear," to quote Wolf, to be one of the "decent folk" who constitute Christian society.

In this context, Shylock's attempts in act 3 to defend himself against the attacks of Solanio and Solario take on new significance. Shylock appears to fail when he asserts, as Normand Lawrence writes, "that his daughter partakes of the same physical substance as himself, and so shares the same racial identity" (58): "I say my daughter is my flesh and blood," he declares (3.1.37). Solanio returns:

> There is more difference between thy flesh and hers than between jet and ivory, more between your bloods than there is between red wine and Rhenish.

(3.1.39-42)

Whereas Shylock merely cites the relation between his body and his daughter's, Solanio emphasizes a transformation in Jessica whereby color and gender combine to overcome less discernible differences of blood.

Shylock, like Launcelot's black child, cannot undergo such a transformation. The reasons for his inability to do so help explain the unsettling effect of the final order for his conversion.[19] For Shylock's body, like the body of any Jewish man, would "convert" a Christian bride. Further, unlike Jessica, Shylock bears the mark of Judaism on his body—circumcision—and the Jewish body lies at the center of early modern anti-Semitic discourse. Though this bodily difference is never explicitly referred to in the play,

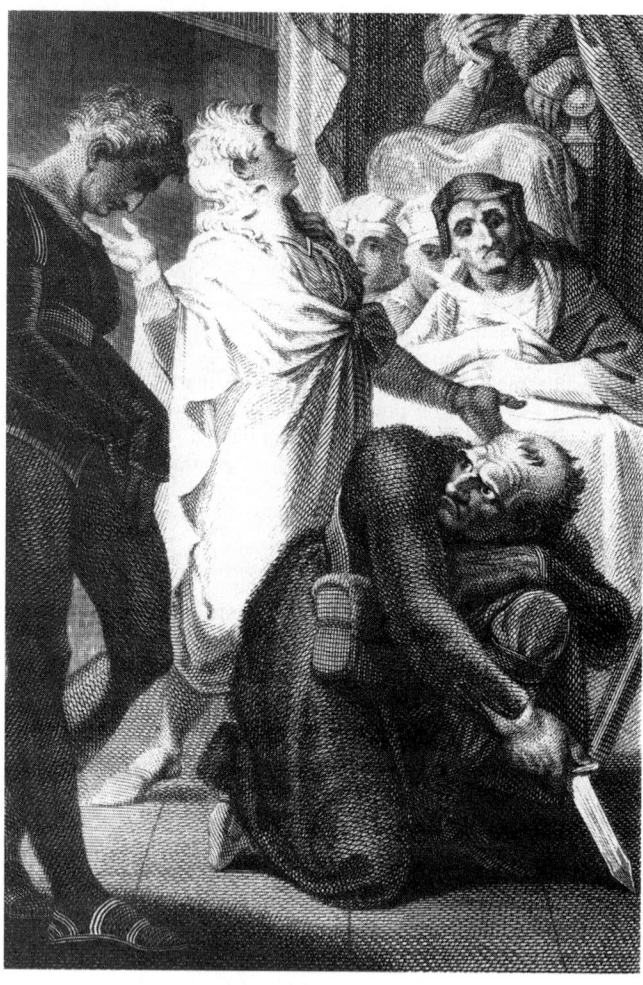

Shylock sharpens his knife as Bassanio looks on in Act IV, scene i of The Merchant of Venice.

the representation of Shylock as a devil intent on the apportionment of a Christian body is part of a tradition of anti-Semitic discourse in which Jews were said to be horned, tailed, and bearded like goats, to emit a distinct smell, and to be the source of leprosy and syphilis. According to this discourse, Jewish men, unlike Christian men, shared the mark of women's sexual difference: menstruation,[20] a feminizing trait that would effectively erase the patriarchal authority inscribed literally and figuratively on Jewish men. The male Jew incarnated the power of naming attributed to all men: this power became particularly threatening in a Jewish man because in placing his name on a Christian woman, and thus on future generations, he embodied the danger of the annihilating, consuming other.

For Shapiro, Christian obsession with circumcision and with the sacred covenant it symbolizes "shapes the final confrontation between Shylock and Antonio": thus Antonio's demand that Shylock "presently become a Christian" "metaphorically uncircumcise[s] him" (130).[21] The new covenant, represented by symbolic circumcision of the heart, supersedes the old, thus resolving the troubled relation between physical attributes and social identity through baptism.[22] As critics have noted, Shylock's conversion occurs only after the play ends, and it is cast as an act of submission on his part—"I pray you give me leave to go from hence, / I am not well. Send the deed after me, / And I will sign it" (4.1.395-97)—a portrayal that weakens the representative power of the transformation. In contrast, Jessica is to be incorporated into Venetian society because she has been excluded from the practice of circumcision. According to Shapiro, this exclusion "helps explain why Jewish daughters like Jessica in *The Merchant of Venice* and Abigail in *The Jew of Malta* can so easily cross the religious boundaries that divide their stigmatized fathers from the dominant Christian communities. The religious difference of women is not usually imagined as physically inscribed in their flesh" (120). But as I have argued, female difference was inscribed in the flesh not only by religious discourse but also by ideologies and emerging notions of race and nationality, which converged to define the "proper" English person.

From this perspective, the unsettling effect of Shylock's forced conversion can also be traced to the tension in Foxe's writing between the notion of free will implicit in baptism and the drive to delimit and thus control the oppositional other implicit in Christian imperialism. Like Othello, Shylock inspires feeling about his fate only insofar as he is capable of choosing Christian "goodness." Moreover, Shylock's malevolence depends on the shifting inscription of Jessica as racial Jew and freely choosing Christian. Jessica's incorporation into Christian society is essential to defining her father's alien status. Indeed, her nature in act 5 may be said to offer something of a reverse image of her father's in his final scenes: represented initially as her father's daughter, ruing her rebellion but longing for salvation through subordination in Christian marriage, she becomes the cool wit who seeks to "out-night" Lorenzo, trades the tokens of her mother's love for a monkey, and gains the trust of Portia in her plot against Bassanio (5.1.23). Shylock, by contrast, evolves from the resistant other to the raging and then nearly silent Jew of the fourth act and finally to a converted but unwilling, powerful yet alien figure, the image of the other against which English identity could be inscribed as white and Christian.

Still, such distinctions between Shylock and Jessica are perhaps too easy. As Lorenzo's attempt to claim the perceptual difference of Jessica's fairness makes clear, the logical incompatibility of the play's representations of Jews is impossible to sustain and requires endless permutations. Consequently, the Jessica of act 5 *may* be read not as an alternative and fully integrated Jew but as a homeless figure that suggests the dangers of consummating a relationship across such differences. In this reading she becomes an emblem of postcoital regret, ruing not her rebellion against patriarchal authority but the terms of her new commitment to it and the meager possibilities for unalienated pleasure they provide. In act 5, both Jessica and Lorenzo look to the past to make sense of their relationship. Further, the relationships with which they allegorize and thus make sense of their own all end tragically because of confusion and conflicting aims: Troilus and Cressida, Pyramus and Thisbe, Aeneas and Dido, Jason and Medea. Then, as if to illustrate and thus anticipate the potential for tragedy in their own union, Jessica and Lorenzo offer individual memories of the fateful night of their elopement. "In such a night / Did Jessica steal from a wealthy Jew, / And with an unthrift love did run from Venice, / As far as Belmont" (5.1.14-17), says Lorenzo, using metaphors of wealth, poverty, and thievery to underscore Jessica's betrayal of her father and the loss of security their mutual commitments guaranteed her. Playful or bitter, Jessica's version of the night hints at the difficulty of establishing trust between persons of different religions, colors, classes, and especially genders that is played up in the rest of act 5: "In such a night / Did young Lorenzo swear he lov'd her well, / Stealing her soul with many vows of faith, / And n'er a true one" (5.1.17-20).

These two distinct readings of the final act of *The Merchant* are both predicated on the idea that Jessica's difference—from her father and from the Christian characters—is crucial to the play's meaning. As the excluded other whose resistance to the truth of Jesus serves to delineate the essential, impermeable nature of the Christian story, the converted Jew could function to guarantee simultaneously both the promise of freedom implicit in baptism and the incontrovertible difference of white, Christian, and, by analogy turned equation, English forms of being. Indeed, only by taking Shylock's measure in the light of his daughter's difference—a difference that combines shifting representations of gender, color, class, and religion—is it possible to account for the play's inscription of contradictory notions of Jews. If *The Merchant*'s representation of Jews continues to haunt us—as the numbers of productions and critical responses to the play suggest it will and the survival of its racial discourse in contemporary politics suggests it should—we may get closer to the meaning of such ghosts by examining more closely the nature of their differences.

Notes

I am grateful to Janet Adelman, Michael Galchinsky, and Bruce Goebel, who read this essay at significant stages in its development and offered that combination of enthusiasm and critical insight we value in the best of colleagues and teachers.

1. Tubal is the only character other than Shylock described as "a Jew" in the dramatis personae. He is also Shylock's only friend and the source of the funds that guarantee Shylock's bond. Although Tubal is certainly worthy of study, I focus here on the play's major characters.

2. I use the term *integration* to refer to the acceptance of (forcibly or willingly) converted Jews by English Christians rather than *assimilation*, which in modern usage implies the freedom to continue practicing Judaism, an option unavailable to Jews in Shakespeare's England.

3. Compare, for example, the work of McKewin; Boose, "Comic Contract"; Leventen; and Newman, "Portia's Ring" with that of Whigham; S. Cohen; Moisan; W. Cohen; Oz; and Ferber. Though there are differences in the ways each group of critics sidesteps the issues raised by the intersection of gender, race, and class, Newman and Ferber both illustrate the problems such critical choices raise. Each addresses the issue in a footnote. Newman states that she has "chosen deliberately to leave Shylock out of [her] reading . . . to disturb readings of the play that center their interpretive gestures on the Jew." She "recognize[s] the suggestive possibilities, however, of readings . . . which link Shylock and Portia as outsiders by virtue respectively of their race and sex" ("Portia's Ring" 19). Ferber declares, "A fuller treatment of ideology than is possible here would take up 'male ideology' from a feminist standpoint. I omit it here because I think the issue of the status or rights of women is not foregrounded in the play, and the peculiarly male way of doing things is only passingly and obliquely indicated" (460). Both comments appear to acknowledge the importance of the critical claims they choose to ignore, then contradict their initial claims. Newman leaves Shylock out because he has somehow enabled readings that fail to account for the play's women, but her reference to other "possibilities" suggests that elision of Shylock's "race" in favor of his gender, which is implicit in her reasoning, is problematic. Jessica, who is a woman and a Jew, is not mentioned at all. Ferber's claims are manifestly absurd given the importance the play assigns to marriage and gender roles, such as father, daughter, brother, husband, and wife. When considered at all, Jessica is often presented solely as a contrast to Portia's image of filial feminine duty: "where Portia gives, Jessica takes; where Portia accepts constraints, Jessica rebels" (Leventen 62).

4. See, e.g., Boose ("Getting") and Callaghan, who argue for "the inherent interrelatedness" of categories of difference and its importance for any interpretation of Jews in *The Merchant* (Callaghan 170). Still, neither explains what a reconsideration of the terms *race* and *Jew* might mean for reading Shakespeare.

5. There is an important distinction between racism as an identifiable mode of twentieth-century thought and the racialist roots of this ideology in early modern culture. Others have made the same distinction (see Neill; Bartels; Boose, "Getting"; Erickson).

6. Foxe's attitude toward Jews seems to take a turn for the worse after the 1563 edition. While in that edition Jews frequently serve to point up the errors of Catholics (see, e.g., "Jewe's Reasoning with Master Wysehart" [NNiir]), in the 1570 edition Jews appear most often as ridiculous and deserving

targets of violence, willing victims like the "Jewe fallen into a privey [who] would not be taken out for kyping hys Sabboth day" (Nir).

7. See, e.g., Greenblatt, "Marlowe," and Ferber. On the historical presence of Jews in England, see Katz, *History* and *Philosemitism;* Rabb; Gwyer; Wolf; Roth; Samuel; Hyamson; Prior; Shapiro. Others who attempt to account for the representation of human difference in early modern Europe include Bartels; Mullaney; Pratt; Hulme; Brown; Said; Greenblatt, *Marvelous Possessions;* Erickson.

8. Hotine cites the publication in 1594 and possibly early 1595 of the popular account of Lopez's trial, *A True Report of Sundry Horrible Conspiracies to Have Taken Away the Life of the Queenes Majestie*, which along with Marlowe's *Jew of Malta* documents the popular taste for anti-Semitic representations that preceded Shakespeare's *Merchant*. See Hotine for a useful chronology of the revival of Marlowe's *Malta* that preceded and followed Lopez's trial in 1594; the play was revived yet again in early 1596, the year in which it is generally agreed Shakespeare wrote *The Merchant*. More recently, David Katz, the foremost historian of English Jews, has argued that "Lopez, the model for Shylock, had far greater influence in the long run on moulding public views and prejudices about the Jews than the worthy efforts of all the English Rabbis put together" (*History* ix). Katz argues for Lopez's guilt. For a competing interpretation of the case against Lopez, see Gwyer.

9. For more on Gaunse, see Feuer; Abrahams; Shapiro.

10. For the story of Frere and Leavis, see Sisson.

11. A 1578 adaptation of the biblical narrative of Ham and his sons by George Best, an English traveler, is a possible source for Jessica's reference to Chus. See Hakluyt for Best's complete text. For useful discussions of Best's representations of race, see Newman, "Ethiop" 78-82; Boose, "Getting" 43-48; Hall, *Things* 11-15.

12. For more on the influence of Lopez, see Katz, *History*.

13. The term *deserving* is used in a 1656 document in which a committee of the Council of State argues for the readmission of Jews to England. For a copy of the document, see Samuel.

14. For studies of the representation of the Jew in medieval and early modern European culture, see Trachtenberg; Poliakov; Edwards; Baron; Yardeni; Felsenstein; Shapiro. Tractenberg suggests that the equation of Jews with devils was the product of Christian legends in which "the inexorable enemies of Jesus . . . were the devil and the Jew." "It was inevitable," he argues, "that the legend should establish a causal relation between them" (20). Shapiro claims that "by the late sixteenth century the widespread medieval identification of Jews and the devil had virtually disappeared in England" (33), yet he locates the medieval myth of abduction and ritual murder in Shylock's desire to feast on his Christian enemies (110).

15. On patriarchalism in early modern England, see Schochet; Ezell.

16. On marriage without parental consent during the sixteenth century, see Ingram.

17. Kyngesmill's text takes up the topic under the heading "Certain places of Scripture touchyng ungodly matchyng in Mariage" and focuses on marriage to "women of a wicked kinred and Religion." Such marriages are inadvisable, he argues, because unbelieving wives don't properly fear and submit to their husbands and thus "overruleth the beleevyng husbande and causeth hym to make a plaine shipwracke of faith . . . " (4iiv).

18. On early modern constructions of the term *fair*, see Hall, *Things* and "Black-Moor."

19. Shylock's distaste for Christians is based on the historical practice of ritual separateness. As Johnson explains in his history of the Jews, "Circumcision set [Jews] apart and was regarded by the Greco-Roman world as barbarous and distasteful. But at least circumcision did not prevent social intercourse. The ancient Jewish laws of diet and cleanliness did" (133-34). Thus, Shylock's declaration "I will buy with you, sell with you, talk with you, walk with you, and so following; but I will not eat with you, drink with you nor pray with you" (1.3.33-35) can be read as evidence that Shakespeare's knowledge of Jewish practice and perspective went beyond stereotypes.

20. Poliakov claims that Christians believed in Jewish male menses; he cites late-fifteenth-century documents concerned with Jewish ritual murder (143). Foa discusses how sixteenth- and seventeenth-century beliefs in a Jewish cause of syphilis were related to the discourse of sexual difference long applied to women. In a study of the nineteenth-century British equation of usury and prostitution, Gilman documents the continuity of the practice of feminizing male Jews (cf. Gallagher).

21. Shapiro argues for a relation between circumcision—the ritual reenactment of God's convenant with Abraham—and Christian fears of castration and death in early modern England.

22. As Shapiro explains, Paul's letter to the Romans attempts to promote symbolic circumcision of the heart without condemning the trimming of the foreskin. Shapiro argues convincingly that the shift in *The Merchant*'s representation of the terms of Shylock's bond, from "fair flesh, to be cut off and taken / In what part of your body pleaseth me" (1.3.150-51) to "A pound of flesh, to be by him cut off / Nearest the merchant's heart" (4.1.232-33)

involves a "double displacement" of Paul's text: "For circumcision verily profiteth, if thou keep the law: but if thou be a breaker of the law, thy circumcision is made uncircumcision" (Rom. 2.25). Thus, Shapiro continues, "Shylock will cut his Christian adversary in that part of the body where the Christians believe themselves to be truly circumcised: the heart" (127). The heart takes the place of the penis, the spirit the place of the letter. However, as Shapiro notes, such a displacement depends on a distinction between the symbolic and the literal, between the spirit and the flesh, that Paul's text does not sustain. Paul's terms conflate the categories by begging the question of interpreting God's law. Instead of solving the problem of Jewish and Christian identity, Paul's concern with circumcision becomes a touchstone for obsessions about the relation between physical attributes and social identity.

Works Cited

Abrahams, Israel. "Joachim Gaunse: A Mining Incident in the Reign of Queen Elizabeth." *Transactions of the Jewish Historical Society of England* 4 (1899-1901): 83-101.

Acts of the Privy Council. Vol. 26 (1596-97). Ed. John Roche Dasent. London: HMSO, 1902.

Adelman, Janet. *Suffocating Mothers: Fantasies of Maternal Origin in Shakespeare's Plays,* Hamlet *to* The Tempest. New York: Routledge, 1992.

Baron, Salo Wittmayer, ed. *A Social and Religious History of the Jews*. 2nd ed. Vol. 4. New York: Columbia UP, 1957.

Bartels, Emily C. *Spectacles of Strangeness: Imperialism, Alienation, and Marlowe*. Philadelphia: U of Pennsylvania P, 1993.

Barthelemy, Anthony. *Black Face, Maligned Race: The Representation of Blacks in English Drama from Shakespeare to Southerne*. Baton Rouge: U of Louisiana P, 1987.

Boose, Lynda E. "The Comic Contract and Portia's Golden Ring." *Shakespeare Studies* 20 (1987): 241-54.

———. "'The Getting of a Lawful Race': Racial Discourse in Early Modern England and the Unrepresentable Black Woman." Hendricks and Parker 35-54.

Brown, Paul. "'This Thing of Darkness I Acknowledge Mine': *The Tempest* and the Discourse of Colonialism." *Political Shakespeare: New Essays in Cultural Materialism*. Ed. Jonathan Dollimore and Alan Sinfield. Ithaca: Cornell UP, 1985. 48-71.

Callaghan, Dympna. "Re-reading Elizabeth Cary's *The Tragedy of Miriam, Faire Queene of Jewry*." Hendricks and Parker 163-77.

Cohen, Stephen. "'Is This the Law?': Legal Ambiguity and Its Effects in *The Merchant of Venice* and *Measure for Measure*." *The Language of Power, the Power of Language: The Effects of Ambiguity on Sociopolitical Structures As Illustrated in Shakespeare's Plays*. Cambridge: Harvard UP, 1987. 80-118.

Cohen, Walter. "*The Merchant of Venice* and the Possibilities of Historical Criticism." *ELH* 49 (1982): 765-89.

Edwards, John, ed. *The Jews in Christian Europe, 1400-1700*. New York: Routledge, 1988.

Erickson, Peter. "Representations of Blacks and Blackness in the Renaissance." *Criticism* 35 (1993): 499-527.

Ezell, Margaret. *The Patriarch's Wife*. Chapel Hill: U of North Carolina P, 1987.

Felsenstein, Frank. "Jews and Devils: Anti-Semitic Stereotypes of Late Medieval and Renaissance England." *Journal of Literature and Theology* 4.1 (1990): 15-28.

Ferber, Michael. "The Ideology of *The Merchant of Venice*." *English Literary Renaissance* 20.3 (1990): 431-64.

Feuer, Lewis S. "Francis Bacon and the Jews: Who Was the Jew in the *New Atlantis*?" *Transactions of the Jewish Historical Society of England* 29 (1988): 1-25.

Foa, Anna. "The New and the Old: The Spread of Syphilis (1494-1530)." *Sex and Gender in Historical Perspective*. Ed. Edward Muir and Guido Ruggiero. Trans. Margaret A. Galluci with Mary M. Galluci and Carole C. Galluci. Baltimore: Johns Hopkins UP, 1990. 26-45.

Foxe, John. *Actes and Monuments*. London, 1563. Rev. ed. 1570.

Friedman, Jerome. "Jewish Conversion, the Spanish Pure Blood Laws and Reformation: A Revisionist View of Racial and Religious Antisemitism." *Sixteenth Century Journal* 18 (1987): 3-29.

Gallagher, Catherine. "George Eliot and Daniel Deronda: The Prostitute and the Jewish Question." *Sex, Politics, and Science in the Nineteenth-Century Novel*. Ed. Ruth Bernard Yeazell. Baltimore: Johns Hopkins UP, 1986. 39-62.

Gerber, Jane S. *The Jews of Spain: A History of the Sephardic Experience*. New York: Free, 1992.

Gibbon, Charles. *How to Bestow Children in Marriage*. London, 1591.

Gilman, Sander. *The Jew's Body*. New York: Routledge, 1991.

Greenblatt, Stephen. "Marlowe, Marx, and Anti-Semitism." *Learning to Curse: Essays in Early Modern Culture*. New York: Routledge, 1990. 40-58.

———. *Marvelous Possessions: The Wonder of the New World*. Chicago: U of Chicago P, 1991.

Gwyer, John. "The Case of Dr. Lopez." *Transactions of the Jewish Historical Society of England* 16 (1952): 163-84.

Hakluyt, R. *The Principal Navigations, Voyages Traffiques, and Discoveries of the English Nation.* Ed. Walter Raleigh. London, 1600.

Hall, Kim F. "Guess Who's Coming to Dinner? Colonization and Miscegenation in *The Merchant of Venice*." *Renaisance Drama* 23 (1992): 87-111.

———. "I Rather Would Wish to Be a Black-Moor: Beauty, Race and Rank in Lady Mary Wroth's *Urania*." Hendricks and Parker 178-94.

———. *Things of Darkness: Economies of Race and Gender in Early Modern England.* Ithaca: Cornell UP, 1995.

Hendricks, Margo, and Patricia Parker, eds. *Women, "Race," and Writing in the Early Modern Period.* New York: Routledge, 1994.

Hotine, Margaret. "The Politics of Anti-Semitism: *The Jew of Malta* and *The Merchant of Venice*." *Notes and Queries* 38.1 (1991): 35-38.

Hulme, Peter. *Colonial Encounters: Europe and the Native Caribbean, 1492-1797.* London, Methuen, 1986.

Hunter, G. K. "The Theology of Marlowe's *The Jew of Malta*." *Journal of the Warburg and Courtauld Institutes* 27 (1964): 211-40.

Hyamson, Albert. *The Sephardim of England.* London: Methuen, 1951.

Ingram, Martin. *Church Courts, Sex, and Marriage in England, 1570-1640.* London: Cambridge UP, 1997.

Johnson, Paul. *A History of the Jews.* New York: Harper, 1987.

Katz, David S. *Jews in the History of England.* Oxford: Oxford UP, 1994.

———. *Philosemitism and the Readmission of the Jews to England.* Oxford: Oxford UP, 1982.

Kyngesmill, Andrewe. "Godly Advise Touchyng Mariage." *A View of Man's Estate.* London, 1580. Jiv-L8v.

Lawrence, Normand. "Reading the Body in *The Merchant of Venice*." *Textual Practice* 5 (1991): 55-73.

Leventen, Carol. "Patrimony and Patriarchy in *The Merchant of Venice*." *The Matter of Difference: Materialist Feminist Criticism of Shakespeare.* Ed. Valerie Wayne. Ithaca: Cornell UP, 1991. 59-79.

McKewin, Carole. "Counsels of Gall and Grace: Intimate Conversations between Women in Shakespeare's Plays." *The Woman's Part: Feminist Criticism of Shakespeare.* Ed. Carol Ruth Swift Lenz, Gayle Greene, and Carol Thomas Neely. Chicago: U of Illinois P, 1980. 117-32.

Moisan, Thomas. "'Which Is the Merchant Here? And Which the Jew?': Subversion and Recuperation in *The Merchant of Venice*." *Shakespeare Reproduced: The Text in History and Ideology.* Ed. Jean E. Howard, Marion F. O'Connor, and Margaret Ferguson. New York: Methuen, 1987. 188-206.

Mullaney, Steven. *The Place of the Stage: License, Play, and Power in Renaissance England.* Chicago: U of Chicago P, 1988.

Neely, Carol Thomas. "Circumscriptions and Unhousedness: *Othello* in the Borderlands." *Shakespeare and Gender: A History.* Ed. Deborah Barker and Ivo Kamp. New York: Verso, 1995. 302-15.

Neill, Michael. "Unproper Beds: Race, Adultery, and the Hideous in *Othello*." *Shakespeare Quarterly* 40 (1989): 383-412.

Netanyahu, B. *The Origins of the Inquisition in Fifteenth Century Spain.* New York: Random, 1995.

Newman, Karen. "'And Wash the Ethiop White': Femininity and the Monstrous in *Othello*." *Fashioning Femininity and Renaissance Drama.* Chicago: U of Chicago P, 1991. 79-93.

———. "Portia's Ring: Unruly Women and Structures of Exchange in *The Merchant of Venice*." *Shakespeare Quarterly* 38 (1987): 19-33.

Oz, Avraham. "'Which Is the Merchant Here? And Which the Jew?': Riddles of Identity in *The Merchant of Venice*." *Shakespeare and Cultural Traditions: Selected Proceedings of the International Shakespeare Association World Congress, Tokyo, 1991.* Ed. K. Tetsuo, R. Pringle, and S. Wells. Newark: U of Delaware P, 1994. 155-73.

Poliakov, Leon. *The History of Anti-Semitism.* Vol. 1. Trans. Richard Howard. New York: Vanguard, 1965.

Pratt, Mary Louise. "Scratches on the Face of the Country; or, What Mr. Barrow Saw in the Land of the Bushmen." *Critical Inquiry* 12 (1985): 119-43.

Prior, Roger. "A Second Jewish Community in Tudor London." *Transactions of the Jewish Historical Society of England* 31 (1990): 137-52.

Rabb, Theodore K. "The Stirrings of the 1590s and the Return of the Jews to England." *Transactions of the Jewish Historical Society of England* 26 (1979): 26-33.

Roth, Cecil. *A History of the Jews in England.* Oxford: Oxford UP, 1964.

Said, Edward. *Orientalism.* London: Routledge, 1978.

Samuel, Edgar. "The Readmission of the Jews to England in 1656, in the Context of English Economic Policy." *Transactions of the Jewish Historical Society of England* 31 (1990): 153-70.

Schochet, Gordon. *The Authoritarian Family and Political Attitudes in Seventeenth-Century England: Patriarchalism in Political Thought.* New Brunswick: Transaction, 1988.

Shakespeare, William. *The Merchant of Venice. The Riverside Shakespeare.* Ed. G. Blakemore Evans. New York: Houghton, 1974. 254-85.

Shapiro, James. *Shakespeare and the Jews.* New York: Columbia UP, 1996.

Sisson, C. J. "A Colony of Jews in Shakespeare's London." *Essays and Studies* 23 (1938): 38-51.

Trachtenberg, Joshua. *The Devil and Jews: The Medieval Conception of the Jew and Its Relation to Modern Antisemitism.* New Haven: Yale UP, 1943.

Whigham, Frank. "Ideology and Class Conduct in *The Merchant of Venice*." *Renaissance Drama* 10 (1979): 93-115.

Wolf, Lucien. "Jews in Elizabethan England." *Transactions of the Jewish Historical Society of England* 11 (1924-27): 1-91.

Yardeni, Myriam. *Anti-Jewish Mentalities in Early Modern Europe.* New York: UP of America, 1990.

B. J. Sokol (essay date 1998)

SOURCE: "Prejudice and Law in *The Merchant of Venice*," in *Shakespeare Survey: An Annual Survey of Shakespeare Studies and Production*, Vol. 51, 1998, pp. 159-73.

[*In the essay below, Sokol discusses the legally sanctioned forms of racial prejudice in Elizabethan England—against Jews and people of color, for example—but argues that through characterization, language, and imagery in* The Merchant of Venice, *Shakespeare intimates that Renaissance public opinion condemned these prejudicial laws.*]

I

The legally institutionalized prejudice seen in *The Merchant of Venice* is repulsive from a modern perspective. I will argue that this play portrays deeply ironic images of social prejudice that offended Elizabethan standards of decency and fairness as well as ours. Paradoxically, these contemporary Elizabethan standards come into focus when the play is viewed from a perspective involving legal history, for they in fact trumped the prejudicial laws of Shakespeare's time.

In the updated approach to Shakespeare of his provocative book *Kill All the Lawyers?*, a practising American lawyer Daniel J. Kornstein advises Shylock to appeal against Portia's judgement.[1] And he makes frequent reference to modern legal doctrines, often specifically American, to show how these have evolved or advanced since Shakespeare's time. Yet Kornstein sometimes discusses issues and principles which have persisted in the Anglo-American legal tradition since Shakespeare's time, which may guide us to the shared social and moral vocabulary of Shakespeare and his age.

I share Kornstein's view that Shylock is presented by Shakespeare as distinctly ill-intentioned, yet still a man wronged and unjustly treated. I also agree that this 'minority view' in literary criticism negates certain *prima facie* appearances of the play, but it is a valid and necessary one because in the play's fictionally constructed world, as in the real world, 'appearances deceive'.[2] But I will base my position more historically than Kornstein's; to launch my own discussion I will note what is illuminating in his advice to Shylock, and how inaccuracies and anachronisms detract from it.

A first error is that this advice ignores Elizabethan jurisdictional and legal peculiarities relevant to *The Merchant of Venice*. The question of what jurisdiction, if any, Shakespeare had in mind for the play's fictional lawcase has been much debated. I have argued for the special appropriateness of a jurisdiction which was originally derived from Italy, but well known to Elizabethans. This was the jurisdiction of the pan-European traditional International Law Merchant. Uniquely in England, some Law Merchant tribunals allowed a combination of summary civil and criminal judgement (as is seen in the 'pie-Powders' court of Ben Jonson's *Bartholomew Fair*).[3] This very combination of judgements in the trial scene of *the Merchant of Venice* therefore need not have provided, *pace* Kornstein,[4] any grounds for an appeal.

Others of Kornstein's law points are less ahistorical. He discusses at length a social need for appropriate limitations on the freedom to make contracts,[5] and there were parallel (if subtly different) sixteenth-century discussions of enforcement or relief from the provisions of 'sealed bonds' like Shylock's.[6]

Even more interesting, in spite of partial anachronism, is Kornstein's citation of a modern principle of 'equal protection of the laws', under which he condemns the 'vile Alien Statute' invoked by Portia against Shylock.[7] Despite his revulsion at the *un*equally protective 'Alien Statute' of Venice cited by Portia, at first glance such a statute would seem hardly remarkable from an Elizabethan perspective. In 1601 Elizabeth arranged to expel from England all 'Negars and blackamoors'.[8] In 1594 she seemed hesitant to punish the unfortunate Doctor Lopez,[9] but Jews were so *un*equally protected in her realm as to be officially outlawed.[10] Although they were not enacted, other Elizabethan anti-Alien laws were repeatedly proposed, and economic surveys were undertaken to investigate their applicability. Roman Catholics also suffered legal disabilities in Shakespeare's time, and possibly Shakespeare's family suffered under these.[11] Yet, despite these circumstances, I will argue that legal and social inequality based on prejudice *is* intended to be seen as unjust within the context of *The Merchant of Venice*.

II

To bring this into focus, I will first trace allusions in the play to legalistic biblical materials. In the course of his dramatic handling of a litigious and mercantile Jew, Shakespeare drew so heavily upon biblical stories concerning especially property relations and legal vindication that *The Merchant of Venice* contains the most extensive biblical references in all his work. Current legal topics were also apparently meditated upon by Shakespeare for *The Merchant of Venice*. I believe that the play reflects a contemporary crisis about justice. Historically, this resulted from no simple matter of 'law before equity' or any converse formula, but rather from the philosophic casualties of a battleground between conflicting and combative jurisdictions.[12]

Certainly the riddle of where true justice lies was made more complex both in *The Merchant of Venice* and in Shakespeare's London by the presence of economically important alien subcommunities. Those were generally tolerated, although their rights, for instance to trade and to employ English men and women, suffered periodic verbal attack and occasional outbursts of unofficial anti-foreigner rioting. So Shakespeare's allusions to social and ethical questions concerning aliens, as in Gobbo's ruminations on employment by Shylock, touched live issues. Yet not entirely live, for it is most likely that Elizabethan London did not provide Shakespeare or his audience with visible prototypes for the legal treatment and actual behaviour of Jews.[13] There were, however, many refugee households, and foreign merchants or visitors whom Shakespeare could have asked about continental Jews; with certainty, by early Jacobean times, Shakespeare had contacts with artisans who numbered among London's alien communities.[14]

The balance of evidence indicates that Shakespeare's personal associations were unlikely to have produced close observation of any Jews.[15] One of the surprises of *The Merchant of Venice*, therefore, is that he imagined a Shylock exhibiting a propensity often seen in tolerated Jewish minorities, which is his enthusiastic voluntary turning to Christian courts and lawyers.[16] Shylock's doomed pursuit of a Venetian legal underpinning for his revenge against Venice embodies some of the most complex human motives portrayed in the play.

III

In his pursuit of revenge Shylock repeatedly makes references to Old Testament stories of the legal vindication of the oppressed and of the restoration of their denied freedom or rights. One such reference is made in a moment of anticipated triumph, when all seems to be going Shylock's way in his lawcase against the Christian merchant Antonio. Highly gratified by the apparent progress of the case, Shylock exclaims of the seemingly unbiased Christian justicer Portia/Balthazar: 'A Daniel come to judgment: yea, a Daniel!' (4.1.219). Significantly, the name 'Daniel' means in Hebrew 'God has judged'.

Shylock does not refer directly to the biblical book of Daniel in which the exiled Jewish hero is first valued for skill in interpreting dreams and visions, but then, for his piety, is thrown into a lions' den. Yet there is a parallel between various demands for the rigid application of Venetian laws in Shakespeare's play and the legalistic basis for Daniel's ordeal; Daniel is punished through the application of an inflexible law of the Medes and Persians obtained by his enemies solely in order to catch Daniel out.[17]

Let us delay discussion of such stories of jurisprudential chicanery to note first that Shylock explicitly refers to Daniel as a shrewd lawyer, rather than as an unfairly treated Jewish alien. Shylock's reference must then be to the story in the book of Susanna in which Daniel appears as a resourceful detective/advocate. In this apocryphal book of Shakespeare's frequently employed Geneva Bible, Daniel wins a court case for the innocent but vulnerable Susanna, and thereby defends justice itself. He astutely represents her, saving her person and her reputation despite the apparent hopelessness of confronting the perjured testimony of two salacious Elders. These lying old men are not only establishment figures, but also possess the crushing moral authority of actually being judges. What is crucial in Shylock's allusion is that Daniel's advocacy for Susanna before the court of the people defends the friendless weak against the socially powerful. It is also important that Daniel's defence of Susanna relies on a cunning legal stratagem; he separates the two false witnesses and traps them into contradictory statements. The risky legal adventures of Susanna lead to a biblical conclusion that God 'saves those who hope in him', even if they are in desperate straits.

As his own hopes rise, Shylock begins to identify himself with a socially weaker party avenged and vindicated by law, and so remembers Susanna's legal rescue by Daniel. His joy in seeming to win his law case with Portia's aid shows Shylock's complex motives, which include not only revenge against powerful Antonio, but also a desire for public acknowledgement of his rights, and thus for social recognition.

Shylock's intended foul revenge is only ambiguously legal, and is necessarily incapable of rendering the good he desires. Nevertheless, in the complexity of his motivation Shylock is unique among fictional Jews of the age. These were typically stereotyped as monsters of furtive, gloating, mass-murdering perfidy. Correspondingly, Shylock's broken-hearted ending is unlike the merely physical dismemberment through torture that demolishes other Elizabethan literary Jew-monsters.

IV

Shylock's excitement when he lauds Portia's Daniel-like astuteness is not only villainous gloating. The peculiarly urgent significance he attaches to his anticipated legal victory is clarified by a consideration of Shylock's lengthier allusions early in the play to the legal manoeuvres recorded in the Book of Genesis of the patriarch Jacob. These are manoeuvres that Shylock finds wholly good. Shylock first mentions Jacob's wrested inheritance, 'wrought' by his 'wise mother' (1.3.68), thus making the only approving comment on mothers in *The Merchant of Venice* (all others are bawdy, cynical or both).[18] This allusion introduces an explicitly approving account by Shylock of the trickery Jacob used to gain an advantage over the revenge upon Laban. Both biblical stories, purportedly told to justify lending money for interest, are oblique to this purpose, but both have other compelling resonances in *The Merchant of Venice*.

An important factor common to both of these stories is that they involve peculiar dealings with animals. This fact, if not its significance, is obvious in Shylock's account from Genesis 30-1 of how 'Jacob graz'd his uncle Laban's sheep' (1.3.66), but it arises also in connection with his allusion to how Jacob became holy Abraham's 'third possessor' (1.3.68-9), that is, the third Hebrew patriarch. Genesis 27 tells how Jacob's 'wise mother' Rebekah helped him to trick the second patriarch, Isaac, into giving to him a deathbed blessing intended for the first-born son Esau. To this end Rebekah covered Jacob with the 'skins of the kids' so that he appeared to blind Isaac's touch to be a 'hairy man' like Esau, and she dressed him in animal skins smelling of the hunter Esau. This looks like a direct application of a technique of benevolent deception still practised by shepherds today; to save an orphaned lamb they place the skin of a stillborn lamb over it to trick the stillborn's mother into accepting it as her own. Shakespeare, raised near the Cotswolds, knew of such techniques of husbandry, as many in his audiences may have done. For them Shylock's allusion to the biblical pastoralist's ruse was a first hint in *The Merchant of Venice* of an inspired use of trickery.

The story of Jacob and blind Isaac re-echoes in the play in the ludicrous episode of the 'confusions', or practical jokes, perpetrated by Launcelot Gobbo on his 'more than sand-blind' father, who refuses him blessings, finding him *too* hairy (2.2.30-95). This burlesque emphasizes how in the Bible divinely controlled fate, acting through means that may even seem unjust, selects a destined heir through deception.

After alluding to Jacob's inheritance, Shylock gives Antonio a rendition of the story of Jacob's revenge on Laban which, in the context of their ongoing financial negotiations, has sinister implications.[19] Involving a crafty contract, in effect a 'merry bond', which yields redress for a legitimate grievance, this story again describes Jacob's trickery. After Laban has repeatedly cheated Jacob of the rewards due for decades of labour, Jacob negotiates for a final wage all the (normally rare) black or parti-coloured offspring of his flocks. Jacob then employs specialized animal breeding techniques, to his great advantage.[20] By inducing all the best animals of Laban's flocks to conceive 'streak'd and pied' offspring, he gains all the profits of the herds.[21]

This biblical story, like the tale of Jacob acquiring Esau's blessing and birthright, might seem to us only an account of crafty cheating. But the Renaissance responded differently to Jacob's tactics.[22] The episode of the coloured sheep is followed in Genesis by Jacob's explanation to his two wives (Laban's daughters) that God Himself ordained his success (31:4-10). In the Geneva or 'Breeches' translation of the Bible often used by Shakespeare the passage is glossed marginally: 'This declareth that the thing which Iacob did before, was by Gods commandement, and not through deceite.'[23] Next Jacob tells his wives that in a dream God's angel showed him the way to his safe vindication, and the Geneva Bible glosses: 'This Angell was Christ.' Thus Shakespeare's audience may well have held Jacob's cunning legal moves to be an unorthodox but no less justified means of attaining an outcome ordained divinely, an outcome vindicating the oppressed.

Just like Jacob, whom he describes making a seemingly foolish but wily contract with oppressive Laban, Shylock obtains a silly-seeming 'merry bond' from Antonio. His aim is also to obtain compensation. Analogously with Jacob wearing animal skins, Shylock later mimics animality in his insistence on taking Antonio's flesh (justifying accusations he is a 'cut-throat dog' or 'wolf'). Antonio, for his part, notices merely that Shylock's story of Jacob's practice against Laban does not excuse the taking of monetary interest (nor does Shylock take any from Antonio on this occasion). There is deep irony in how the Christian merchant impatiently understands Shylock's stories in a mercantile light only, and cannot hear how much the Jew admires the third biblical patriarch's skill in obtaining a 'merry' legal redress for injustices.[24]

The picture unseen by Antonio in Shylock's story, of the powerless foreigner Jacob besting the established local patriarch Laban, explains why Shylock does not retire in defeat after the egregious theft of his wealth and his daughter. He seeks rather for vindication *on the terms of Venetian justice,* and yearns to present such an excellent legal case against Antonio that it is sure to succeed.[25] Just as Othello must show himself the most superb of Venetian soldiers to overcome the racial prejudices that he has internalized, so Shylock must show himself to be the most adroit Venetian litigant and businessman.

There are things in Shakespeare that cannot be appreciated without imagining that some of his characters have mental interiors. Why did Antonio fail to comprehend the point of Shylock's story about Jacob's divinely inspired revenge, and also why isn't he made suspicious by Shylock's willingness to lend him money without taking interest? Is he distracted even more than his unworldly 'want-wit' sadness described at the play's start might account for, or deaf to the ominous drift of Shylock's question: 'Hath a dog money? Is it possible / A cur can lend thee three thousand ducats?' (1.3.116-17)? In twenty lines Shylock five times repeats that Antonio has abused him as a 'dog' or 'cur'. Antonio's response is, 'I am as like to call thee so again, / To spet on thee again' (1.3.126). Thus Antonio flaunts his hatred of the Jew while he puts his life in hands that must be clenched at hearing his hate.

This may seem suicidal. Indeed by the time of his law trial Antonio's melancholy has deepened to the point where he craves only death. Using animal imagery in ways new to the play, he speaks of himself as a sacrificial lamb. Correspondingly, he and Gratiano relabel the former 'dog' Shylock as a 'wolf', perhaps recalling the name of the infamous Doctor Lopez. But unlike the historical Lopez,[26] Shylock makes an excellent legal case for himself, which despite prejudice seems to give him ascendancy.

At this point Shylock gleefully seizes the dramatic and linguistic initiative, transforming the Christians' animal images by saying that he intends to use Antonio in no other way than they use 'many a purchas'd slave, / Which (like your asses, and your dogs and mules) / You use in abject and in slavish parts, / Because you bought them' (4.1.90-3). In other words, Shylock spitefully reviles the Christians by claiming to imitate their low moral stature. Despite sentimentalists' readings, Shylock similarly concludes the famous 'Hath not a Jew eyes?' speech not with a noble plea for equality, but by spitefully justifying a Jew's desire for Bacon's 'wild justice' of illegal revenge on the basis of ferocious 'Christian example' (3.1.60-6). However, in his argument about asses and slaves Shylock may extend his sarcasm into an even more bitter and unexpected area than such levelling ethical nihilism. In the First Folio punctuation (more clearly than in the Arden), his ambiguous retort may even propose that the Christians might support bestiality:

> You haue among you many a purchast slaue,
> Which like your Asses, and your Dogs and Mules,
> You vse in abiect and in slauish parts,
> Because you bought them. Shall I say to you,
> Let them be free, marrie them to your heires?
>
> (TLN 1996-2000)

We will find the legal and ideological aspects of such a suggestion crucial. Before addressing them, we may note that Shylock, in taxing the Christians on keeping slaves, may recall with bitterness the Scholastic doctrine that 'all Jews collectively inherited servile status to Christians'.[27] It may also reflect the legal status of Jews as the king's property in England between the Conquest and their expulsion.[28]

But usually (or in practice) such semi-feudal ownership was more constrained by decency than Shylock's mercantile 'asses/slaves' equation,[29] which obliterates distinctions of human life, animal life and material goods. Indeed the very making of such an equation might seem to condemn Shylock's morality, compared with the Christians'. But the play quite promptly upsets this distinction, by showing two Venetian men blithely regarding their wives as their absolute property, as disposable as so much livestock:

> BASSANIO
> Antonio I am married to a wife
> Which is as dear to me as life itself,
> But life itself, my wife, and all the world,
> Are not with me esteem'd above thy life.
> I would lose all, ay sacrifice them all
> Here to this devil, to deliver you.
> [. . .]
> GRATIANO
> I have a wife who I protest I love,—
> I would she were in heaven, so she could
> Entreat some power to change this currish Jew.
>
> (4.1.278-88)

On hearing these edifying offers, Shylock remarks with wholly justified sarcasm, and also in dismay for his apostate daughter, 'These be the Christian husbands!'

V

Often without explicit censure, *The Merchant of Venice* repeatedly presents characters confusing human with animal life, thereby suggesting ethical equations of life with property. Thus Shylock dismisses his lazy servant Gobbo with comparisons to unprofitable livestock (2.5.45-50).

Later Shylock seems to equate his paternal relationship with cash when he polishes Marlowe's Barabas's 'O girl! O gold! O beauty! O my bliss!' to: 'My daughter, O my ducats! O my daughter!' (2.8.15). But Shakespeare, as opposed to Marlowe, tempers his Jew's mercenariness in relation to his daughter when the human/animal *distinction* becomes crucial in Shylock's shocked response to learning of Jessica's bartering of Leah's love-token turquoise ring for a monkey.

Shylock's hatred of Antonio is also not limited by a cash nexus; no amount of 'moneys' can buy off his revenge on his reviler and tormentor. Yet he explains this with bitter animal/human sarcasm, pretending that his hatred is as inexplicable as an animal phobia: 'men there are love not a gaping pig! / Some that are mad if they behold a cat!'

There are many other strange concatenations of hatred with animal imagery in the play, as when Shylock sarcastically mocks his own supposed mercenariness by asserting that a financial option on Antonio's human flesh is 'not so estimable, profitable neither / As flesh of muttons, beefs, or goats' (1.3.162-3). These concatenations are focused and elucidated by an oddity of legal history. To find the appropriate connection we must take a close look into some little regarded elements of the play.

VI

Seemingly minor excrescences of Shakespearian texts may hold clues to deep themes and meanings. One such excrescence produces a conundrum and tonal crux of *The Merchant of Venice* when, in supposedly idyllic Belmont, the newly married Lorenzo accuses Launcelot Gobbo of the 'getting up of the negro's belly' (3.5.35). This accusation is framed in a scene containing much quibbling, and might seem to disclose no more than the insignificant tastelessness of a bawdy mini-subplot. But the complex wording of Gobbo's reply to Lorenzo's accusation serves rather as a key, or the second half of a key, to unlock the cupboard of prevalent social attitudes as portrayed in Belmont. Evaluation of these attitudes is crucial for a proper understanding of the play.

The first half of the key provided by Gobbo's overtly crude excuse for his fornication is found in the concept behind a repulsive legality noted by Sir Edward Coke. Coke discusses a law symptomatic of fear and hatred which made a marriage between a Christian and Jew equivalent to the *clamantia peccata* of sodomy and bestiality. According to his *Institutes,* 'the party so offending should be burnt alive'.[30] Indeed an unusual case of such a burning in 1222 is discussed in Pollock and Maitland's monumental *History of English Law,*[31] which also ponders an alternative view that burial alive was more appropriate than burning for Christians married to Jews.[32]

However, for our discussion, not rare punishments but the legal equivalencing of Jewish miscegenation with bestiality is most significant. For, even beyond biblical injunctions, Shakespeare's age viewed the *damantia peccata* of bestiality with an anxiety fuelled by ideological terror.[33] Although actual indictments in Elizabethan England for bestiality were rare, and convictions still rarer,[34] the offence was violently condemned. According to the analysis of Keith Thomas, this was because it violated an insecure yet crucial division of humans from animals.[35] So nudity, long hair, night work, nocturnal burglary (for, said Coke's *Institutes,* night was 'the time [. . .] wherein beasts run about seeking their prey'), the play-acting of animal roles and even swimming caused great anxiety.[36] No wonder then, wrote Thomas:

> Bestiality, accordingly, was the worst of sexual crimes because, as one Stuart moralist put it, 'it turns man into a very beast, makes a man a member of a brute creature.' The sin was the sin of confusion; it was immoral to mix the categories. Injunctions against 'buggery with beasts' were standard in seventeenth-century moral literature, though occasionally the topic was passed over, 'the fact being more filthy than to be spoken of.' Bestiality became a capital offence in 1543 and, with one brief interval [1553-62], remained so until 1861. Incest, by contrast, was not a secular crime at all until the twentieth century.

In accord with what Keith Thomas identifies as persistent early-modern 'discourses on the animal nature of negroes',[37] the doctrine equating Jewish-Christian miscegenation with bestiality is extended to Moorish-European miscegenation also when envious Iago repeatedly describes newly married Othello and Desdemona as beasts coupling.[38] In the light of such equivalencing, suggesting ideological damnation beyond any aesthetic repugnance, we may understand why Portia so strongly abhors the prospect of marriage with a Prince having 'the complexion of a devil', even if 'he have the condition of a saint' (1.2.123-4).

The legal equivalencing of miscegenated human marriages with the terrible *clamantia peccata* of bestiality may also help explain why *The Merchant of Venice* contains nearly eighty references to animals, and why the most striking of these are to animals breeding.[39] In fact, Jewish Law prescribes a more humane standard of care for animals than Christian interpreters of Shakespeare's time recognized when they overlooked or anthropocentrically allegorized Old Testament demands for kind treatment.[40] Nonetheless, of all the characters in the play Shylock uses negative animal imagery most often (thirty-three times), and most vehemently. In Shakespeare's creation of Shylock it seems Jewish dietary restrictions were taken as characteristic of revulsion for all beasts, despite the many Old Testament laws protecting them.[41]

So, as mentioned earlier, Shylock describes an irrational detestation of animals or of certain music when asked to explain his hatred of Antonio:

> What if my house be troubled with a rat [. . .]
> Some men there are love not a gaping pig!
> Some that are mad if they behold a cat!
> And others when the bagpipe sings i' th' nose
> Cannot contain their urine.
>
> (4.1.44-50)

But Shylock's allusions to animal or music-phobia are a disingenuous opposite of what they claim to be: rather than describing an unfounded aversion, they recall how Antonio persistently called him a dog, and how the music of a Venetian festival covered the theft of his wealth and daughter.[42] Again, he images unpleasant animal/human interactions to represent more ugly human/human ill-will.

A mock denial of ill motives where these are crucial, a sly or spiteful self-denigration, and deliberate confusion of the animal with the human, characterize also the covert message of Lancelot Gobbo's dismissal of responsibility for his fornication. Like Shylock's jest about hating Antonio for 'no reason', Gobbo's self-exoneration for having illicitly impregnated an unseen and nameless female 'negro' or 'Moor' is ostensibly humorous. It caps a scene of quibbling, perhaps not really merry, in Belmont. This begins with Jessica cornered by her erstwhile servant/ally Gobbo, now elevated in rank, who over-familiarly, uncomfortably and blasphemously (by denying grace) wrangles that she must be 'damn'd' either with Jewish ancestry or else (if she is not Jewish) with bastardy. Next, in a parody recalling Shylock's commercial grievance against Antonio's interest-free lending which 'brings down / The rate of usance here with us in Venice' (1.3.39-40), Gobbo laments Jessica's religious conversion because:

> this making of Christians will raise the price of hogs,—if we grow all to be pork-eaters, we shall not shortly have a rasher on the coals for money.
>
> (3.5.21-3)

Although he is now a licensed clown, Gobbo's use of commercial/animal imagery in connection with Christian conversion may make the auditor begin to wonder if there is something untoward in his raillery.

At this moment Jessica's new husband Lorenzo enters, and she reports to him how Launcelot:

> tells me flatly there's no mercy for me in heaven because I am a Jew's daughter: and he says you are no good member of the commonwealth, for in converting Jews to Christians, you raise the price of pork.
>
> (3.5.29-33)

To this gibe against his wife and his marriage, Lorenzo retorts with a counter-accusation of miscegenation against Gobbo: 'I shall answer better to the commonwealth than you can the getting up of the negro's belly: the Moor is with child by you Launcelot!' To this Gobbo makes his riddling reply:

> It is much that the Moor should be more than reason: but if she be less than an honest woman, she is indeed more than I took her for.
>
> (3.5.37-9)

Lorenzo comments on this, 'How every fool can play upon the world!', presumably pointing towards quibbles including the multiple puns: 'more'/'Moor'; 'more' = greater vs. more = pregnant; and take = understand vs. take = sexually use.

Yet there is more going on in Gobbo's complexly phrased rationalization than simply his skill with what Lorenzo later calls the 'tricksy word'. Gobbo says that if the pregnant Moor is 'less than an honest woman' (and therefore *is* a woman) she is 'indeed more' than he took her for. This amounts to a confession or boast that Launcelot took her for less than a woman of any kind, for he 'took' her as an animal. With the greatest effrontery he frankly admits that racial miscegenation was, for him, just bestiality.

VII

Gobbo's 'humorous' crudeness about the pregnant Moor creates a unique and valuable episode of the play, yielding a context in which racial prejudice is stripped of its more usual disguise of politeness and social grace. The Clown's indecent racialism is not wholly different from the casual bigotry of the higher-born Belmontese visitors and natives, and it serves to point up what may tend to be confused or overridden by their charm.

Due appreciation of our distance from Shakespeare's age does not obscure his depiction of the 'better' classes of Belmont as comfortable and indeed satisfied with their offhanded disdain for aliens and minorities. Possibly the reason that their collective attitudes of scorn and unthinking bias have rarely been explicitly commented upon is that the racialist attitudes of the socially 'superior' characters of *The Merchant of Venice* need not affront us unless we choose to be painfully responsive to them. If we choose to enjoy a comedy with clear winners and losers, or to identify with a 'winning side', we may easily accept the self-estimation of the play's blithely overweening characters and evade whatever may taint their charismatic gloss, fashionable charm and eventual triumph.

Moreover Shakespeare makes the taking of an ethical stance which can question the dominant group's position very difficult for both Elizabethan and modern audiences. *The Merchant of Venice* is deliberately designed to evoke a specific anxiety inhibiting any disapproval of its luxury-loving Belmontese. Those who attack their leisured 'good life' may appear boorishly Malvolio-like or untutored in pleasure. Some of the finest poetry of the play specifically warns off resistance to Belmont's softer charms, disparaging that dangerous curmudgeon 'The man that hath no music in himself' (5.1.83). Many critics even go farther, identifying in wealthy Belmont a kind of utopia, a place of giving without stint and a community of unlimited selfless love. I would argue, rather, that a lesson is dearly bought in the play's last Act: that adult love distinctly requires both a clear sense of the self and an understanding of the need for limitations in giving.[43]

Despite the warnings and temptations of Belmont's elite, I believe that their mixture of bigotry and cruelty with social privilege and charm is a product of Shakespeare's deeply intentional irony. Such irony adds a clanging impact to the unruffled expression, at a moment of joy, of a racialist metaphor for mistaken or misled perception:

> Thus ornament is but the guiled shore
> To a most dangerous sea: the beauteous scarf
> Veiling an Indian beauty; in a word,
> The seeming truth which times put on
> To entrap the wisest.
>
> (3.2.97-101)

Bassanio's aberrant association of an in-reality ugly 'Indian beauty' with a trap and a sea of danger passes without any comment in the scene, as it does in most explicit criticism.[44] Yet corresponding unnoted particulars problematizing value are unquestionably manifest elsewhere in the play.

For example, the word 'good' is used in a particularly cynical way by Shylock when he carefully explains that by calling Antonio a 'good man' he means merely good for the ducats owed (1.3.11-15). The same word appears sixty-three times in the play, mainly used by the Venetian men to mean profitably effective or in conventional epithets (as in 'good signors' or 'good Leonardo'). But ethical 'good' is also discussed by Nerissa and Portia (1.2.10-28, 3.4.10, 4.1.257, 5.1.91); on varied uses of a single word hinge differences between material concerns, empty social conventions, and moral concerns.

If varied uses of a single word in *The Merchant of Venice* require irony-detecting discrimination, harder problems of interpretation arise in regard to the chauvinism of its Belmont. Veiled distinctions must be sifted without the aid of Shylock's very helpful key to his own comment on Antonio being only financially 'good':

> Ho, no, no, no, no: my meaning in saying he is a good man, is to have you understand me that he is sufficient.
>
> (1.3.13-15)

The only sure external test for literary irony requires a certainty about assumed values unavailable in *The Merchant of Venice,* where virtually all values presented are problematized. There may be clues, however, to an intended literary irony in the stylistic or structural quirks of overemphatic expression or repetition (as there are in the hyperaltruistic zeal of the cannibalistic letter-writer of Swift's *A Modest Proposal*). Accordingly, in basically monocultural Belmont one hears excessively many casual slurs against foreigners, some like Bassanio's aspersion quite violent, which may imply an habitual trend of prejudice there.

Discrimination on this point is perplexing. Are we being tested when we are invited to join the clear lead of Nerissa in approving Portia's repetitively jeering characterizations of her foreign suitors? Are Portia's remarks really witty, or are they desperate antidotes to her initially depressed weariness with 'this great world' (1.2.1-9)? Arguably, Portia's anti-foreigner invective may be an extra-dramatic 'stand-up comic' bid for the pit's vulgar laughter.[45] But in most instances her comments are not mere banter, for they purport to represent her offstage experiences of the Neapolitan, Palatine, French, English, Scottish, and German suitors' odd behaviours. Yet the culminating instance of Portia's anti-suitor gibes cannot be excused as wry reportage. In this she gratuitously dismisses the courtship of the Prince of Morocco *before she has seen or met him;* she denigrates his 'complexion of a devil' after seeing only his (presumably black) 'forerunner [. . .] who brings word the prince his master will be here to-night' (1.2.118-25). So Shakespeare presents us with the image of absolute racial *pre*judice.

We are placed at risk of being seduced by elements in the play asking for our tacit allowance of Portia's stark prejudice against Morocco. For one thing, the Belmontese world of genteel privilege, luxury and wit discourages all punctilious distinctions or unsuave scruples. In such a world, the harshness of racial discrimination may seem attenuated, as are the later cruelties of the sexual ring tricks, by being attuned to near-musical conventions of teasing and charm. A great majority of modern critics greatly favour what they hear as the social harmonies of Belmont,[46] which drown out for them Portia's prejudgement of the not-yet-seen, soon stunningly seen, *'tawnie Moore all in white'* (Folio stage direction, TLN 514).

But by making this one clear instance of Portia's wholly unsupported prejudice resemble her former wryly 'observant' nationality quips, the play tempts us to lose our own ethical bearings. Here, as often, *The Merchant of Venice* seems deliberately to make difficult its demands on audiences; here these are demands of the sort Peter Davison believes implicitly made with regard to racism: 'often in Elizabethan and Jacobean drama, and especially in [*Othello*] the audience is called upon to exercise judgement, to distinguish facts from its prejudices'.[47] But the misleading parallel of Portia's remarks on Morocco with her earlier ones on other suitors, rather than confusing us, may challenge us to identify a tonal difference. Such a difference does arise, because Portia cannot describe Morocco or his behaviour. Her barb must therefore be purely verbal. Although in Shakespeare's age punning could present true wit or even profundity, it could also portray moral shallowness.[48] Portia's equivocation between Morocco's 'complexion' meaning skin colour and his 'complexion' in the sense of humoural make-up or character does mark an unamiable decline in the quality of her repartee. It displays none of the fashionable skill in Theophrastian character sketching she has shown before—we may even feel vicarious embarrassment on account of her descent from high-spirited wryness into desperately brittle hilarity.[49]

But Shakespeare makes it impossible for audiences to dwell long on Portia's racial prejudice, although for some its acrid taste may linger. For when the Prince of Morocco arrives he indeed at first displays an unbalanced personality, or unfortunate 'complexion'. In a seeming anticipation of racial prejudice he shows himself vainglorious and magniloquent, over-vaunting his heroic valour and sexual 'blood'. So he begins, 'Mislike me not for my complexion', boasts of virility, and claims that he can 'Pluck the young suckling cubs from the she-bear / Yea mock the lion when a roars for prey' (2.1.1-38). Again, as with Shylock, animality is actually asserted by an individual who is subject to social prejudice. This is of course in accord with the prejudicial English marriage law.

Morocco's embattled vanity leads him to mis-choose the golden casket, which occasions Portia's gruesomely dismissive couplet:

> A gentle riddance,—draw the curtains, go,—
> Let all of his complexion choose me so.
>
> (2.7.78-9)

Her racialist relief is expressed with perhaps a telling displacement of idiom, wherein 'gentle riddance' substitutes for a more usual locution such as 'fair' or 'good riddance' (*OED*, 'riddance', 4). This may suggest that for Portia 'gentle' behaviour, good breeding, prevails over any other good.

On another plane, Portia's elation with being safe from marriage with Morocco may imply more than racial aversion. The defeat of any unwanted suitor may give her some relief from the feelings of oppression and powerlessness under the mortmain of her father's will: 'I may neither choose who I would, nor refuse who I dislike, so is the will of a living daughter curb'd by the will of a dead father' (1.2.23-5). Antipatriarchal motives may well inspire Portia's anti-foreigner gibes, all of which are made against sexually acquisitive men.[50] Yet, if Portia's sense of oppression is lightened by Morocco's defeat, she lacks compassion for a fellow-sufferer under the will that oppresses her. Shakespeare pointedly shows Portia administering to Morocco (and only to him) the oath required under the will, 'if you choose wrong / Never to speak to lady afterward / In way of marriage' (2.1.40-2). In accepting this stipulation, hazarding his sexual and dynastic future, Morocco is fully as brave as he claims to be. Because he risks a heavy loss for her, it is difficult to hear the pat, sententious couplet above, in which Portia welcomes his destruction.

Characteristically, the play complicates the issue. The Prince of Arragon soon after finds a mocking fool's head in his chosen silver casket, which seemingly releases him from his vow of permanent celibacy: 'take what wife you will to bed, / I will always be your head: / So be gone, you are sped' (2.9.70-2). Arragon's only punishment for his mistaken choice is humiliation. His choice of silver, although showing insincerity, may also reflect that he is white, not 'tawnie' or golden like Morocco. I would not insist on this contrast of Arragon's and Morocco's fate, but will note that it aligns with the variation in Portia's remarks about these suitors. Her sneers about Morocco's 'complexion of a devil' far exceed her brief gibe on Arragon's folly, suggesting that racial prejudice in Belmont is so virulent as to make miscegenation with bold Morocco more unacceptable than marriage with vain and foolish Arragon.

VIII

If all laws are enacted only to support the interests of powerful élites, or if law typically only strait-jackets human desires (these are the alternatives often proposed by recent commentaries on Literature and Law), then law can have little to do with literature's longstanding fascination with justice. But, conversely, part of the strong theatrical appeal of *The Merchant of Venice* may derive from what it shares with many other literary and folkloric portrayals of justice enacted. This is the satisfaction of a desire that may even be a human instinct, the desire to see redress of grievances and the orderly advancement of social good. Even a troubling critique of society, exposing the deficiencies of law, may hinge on a hope for such 'good'.

To carry a bit farther our prior discussion of the varied uses of the epithet 'good' in *The Merchant of Venice,* let us note that its application in an often-repeated and insincerely conventional form of address is once applied even to 'good Shylock' (3.3.3). This is Antonio's phrase when he is about to be arrested for debt, when his vital interests are at stake. The hollowness of this form of address could not be more poignantly indicated than by its use in imploring a reviled enemy.[51] But its typical hollowness in use is once made even more explicit, by means of an inversion. This occurs in another highly charged context, when Solanio, regretting his former cynical banter about Antonio's depression (1.1.47-56), brings the news of Antonio's merchant losses. Solanio here eschews what he calls his former 'slips of prolixity', and consciously if brokenly tries to rehabilitate the worn-out phrase 'good Antonio', and recover its meaning:

> it is true [. . .] that the good Antonio, the honest Antonio;—O that I had a title good enough to keep his name company!—
>
> (3.1.10-14)

That the very word 'good' can be used so feelingly in *The Merchant of Venice,* as well as in self-interested, sarcastic, and unthinkingly conventional ways, surely indicates that we must confront this play with very alert attention.

With such attention we have noted that the play's pervasive animal imagery, bearing both legal and ideological ramifications, rears up in a 'witty' exchange between a Clown and a newly married Jew and Christian to disgrace its often critically vaunted world of Belmont. Although Jessica identifies Portia as a near-goddess in the same short scene, Launcelot's guilt-dismissing 'confession' still exposes the submerged racialist values of Portia's realm. Well in advance of Gratiano's frighteningly obscene (not bawdy, nor erotic) castration jests, which cap Belmont's gender struggles while ending the play, Gobbo's ugly sexual gloating demonstrates how all the resolving finalities of the comedy are undercut by chronic confusions. These are confusions between seeking wealth or pleasure, fitting societal moulds, and possessing full humanity.

Notes

1. Daniel J. Kornstein, *Kill All the Lawyers?: Shakespeare's Legal Appeal* (Princeton University Press, 1994), 'Fie upon Your Law: *The Merchant of Venice*', pp. 63-89; the 'imaginary appeal' is outlined pp. 83-5.

2. Kornstein, *Kill All the Lawyers,* pp. 77-9. A similar theme is given a very sophisticated basis in René Girard, ' "To Entrap the Wisest" ', in *Shylock,* ed. Harold Bloom (New York: Chelsea House, 1991), pp. 291-304, esp. pp. 297-300.

3. My *'The Merchant of Venice* and the Law Merchant', *Renaissance Studies,* 6 (1992), 60-7, hereafter referred to as 'Law Merchant', argues that English *pie poudre* courts of the Law Merchant provided a model uniquely appropriate to the play, partly because they were able to combine civil and criminal judgements. Fascinatingly, Jewish Law tribunals in pre-expulsion England also attended to both criminal and civil matters—see Sir Frederick Pollock and F. W. Maitland, *The History of English Law Before the Reign of Edward I,* 2 vols. (Cambridge University Press, 1898, 2nd edn repr. 1968), vol. 1, p. 474.

4. Kornstein, *Kill All the Lawyers,* p. 84.

5. *Ibid.,* pp. 68-79.

6. See 'Law Merchant', pp. 64-5.

7. Kornstein, *Kill All the Lawyers,* pp. 79-81.

8. Eldred Jones, *Othello's Countrymen: the African in English Renaissance Drama* (London: Oxford University Press, 1965), pp. 12-13.

9. See David S. Katz, *The Jews in the History of England 1485-1850* (Oxford: Clarendon Press, 1994), pp. 49-101. The execution for treason of Lopez in 1594 occasioned a wave of Elizabethan anti-Semitism which was engineered 'in Essex's interest' according to J. R. Brown, ed. the Arden Edition *The Merchant of Venice* (1955; London: Methuen, 1977), p. xxiii. (Except where otherwise noted, all references to the play will be from this edition.) But *Merchant* was unlikely to have been occasioned or influenced by the Earl of Essex's manipulation of the Lopez affair, since Shakespeare was allied with an anti-Essex faction; see my 'Holofernes in Rabelais and Shakespeare and some manuscript verses of Thomas Harriot', *Etudes Rabelaisiennes* 25 (1992), pp. 131-5.

10. In 1148 an English court upheld the first prosecution based on the infamous Jewish 'blood libel' (the case of William of Norwich)—see R. Po-chia Hsia, *The Myth of Ritual Murder* (New Haven: Yale University Press, 1988), p. 2, and Frank Felsenstein, 'Jews and Devils: Semitic Stereotypes of Late Medieval and Renaissance England', *Journal of Literature and Theology,* 4 (1990), p. 17. Following this, increasing restrictions and agitation led to the first European expulsion of Jews, from England in 1290.

11. E. A. J. Honigmann, *Shakespeare: the 'Lost Years',* (Manchester University Press, 1985), pp. 115-25.

12. I argue in 'Law Merchant' that *The Merchant of Venice* is set in the context of profound jurisprudential problems arising from the competition for profitable business of King's Bench with Common Pleas, the intellectual jostling of common law with equity, and the common lawyers' attack on the powers of the special jurisdictions of Borough Courts, Merchant Law, Admiralty, Staple Courts, etc. (not officially over until 1977!).

13. A community of Sephardi Jews was present in Shakespeare's London: see Lucien Wolf, 'Jews in Elizabethan England', *Transactions of the Jewish Historical Society,* 11 (1928), 1-91, which states, pp. 21-2, that the Marranos were tolerated 'so long as they did not break the law or outrage public sentiment', although once, in 1592, they departed from secrecy to 'assemble for Divine worship in London' under diplomatic protection. According to Katz, *The Jews,* p. 108, these Marranos were generally so secretive that 'The only Jews of most people's acquaintance were biblical figures, literary characters, and entirely imaginary.' On contrary speculations see below.

14. As seen from the 1612 lawsuit *Bellot vs. Mountjoy,* discussed in S. Schoenbaum, *William Shakespeare: A Compact Documentary Life* (New York: New American Library, 1986), pp. 260-4 and E. K. Chambers, *William Shakespeare: A Study of Facts and Problems,* 2 vols. (Oxford: Clarendon Press, 1930), vol. 2, pp. 90-5. On Shakespeare and the mainly foreign Southwark sculptors see my 'Painted Statues, Ben Jonson and Shakespeare', *Journal of the Warburg and Courtauld Institutes,* 52 (1989), 250-3.

15. On whether Shakespeare knew any of the 'hundred or more' Jews in his London see James Shapiro, *Shakespeare and the Jews* (The Parkes Lecture: University of Southampton, 1992), pp. 1-7. This is generally sceptical, but notes, p. 17, that Thomas Coryate 'expresses no surprise [. . .] that Amis [a Jew Coryate met in Constantinople] had spent thirty years in a London that many scholars assume was free of Jews'.

Shakespeare's acquaintance with converted Italian Jews could be argued if he knew of John Florio's partial Jewishness, or else through the highly unlikely actuality that: (1) Emilia Bassano Lanier was intimate with Shakespeare, as alleged by A. L. Rowse, ed., Emilia Lanier, *The Poems of Shakespeare's Dark Lady* (London, 1978), pp. 6-37; (2) all of the musical Bassano family in England were Jews, as is well argued by Roger Prior, 'Jewish Musicians in the Tudor Court', *Musical Quarterly,* 49 (1983), 253-95, p. 253; (3) the staunchly Christian Emilia Bassano even knew of her ancestral faith; (5) she confided about this to Shakespeare. Only if these concur is it possible that Emilia's Jewishness might have influenced *The Merchant of Venice,* as alleged in A. L. Rowse, *What Shakespeare Read—and Thought* (New York: Coward, McCann and Geoghegan, 1981), p. 172.

16. As detailed by Robert Kirsner in 'Rabbi Sem Tob the Poetic "Melamed" of Fourteenth Century Spain', the *Sepharad 1492-1992* conference (7-10 May 1992) at San Francisco State University. To illustrate typicality Professor Kirsner told me a parallel anecdote from his own life: the congregation of the Feinberg synagogue of Cincinnati Ohio, divided in the 1950s over whether to seat women with men during religious services or to preserve traditional segregation, asked an eminent Christian judge to decide the issue (he chose integration).

17. Daniel 6:4. The conspiratorial legal moves of the envious rivals against Daniel are emphasized in the twelfth-century text of *The Play of Daniel* (Egerton Ms. 2615) and in W. H. Auden's poem 'Daniel [. . .] a sermon' written to accompany the play's 1958 performance: these texts are printed in the album booklet of the performance, Decca DL 9402.

18. Aside from Shylock's perceptions of Rebekah and Leah, the play excludes images of powerful women and of women valued as other than possessions. So, all of Portia's shrewd actions require denial of gender while her rival Antonio loses all his vigour when offering a breast in false-feminine nurturance. My 'Constitutive Signifiers or Fetishes in *The Merchant of Venice*?', *The International Journal of Psycho-Analysis,* 76 (1995), 373-87, finds these issues central.

19. These implications are not analysed in John Scott Colley, 'Launcelot, Jacob, and Esau: Old and New Law in *The Merchant of Venice*', *Yearbook of English Studies,* 10 (1980), 181-9, which sees Shylock's reference to the biblical story of Jacob and Laban only in relation to the story of Jacob and Esau. Colley references only the Bishops' Bible.

20. Vexed questions of just what Jacob's special methods of cattle breeding were, and particularly whether they were natural or miraculous in operation, are discussed in an essay on the tradition that maternal imagination may affect embryos: M. D. Reeve, 'Conceptions', *Proceedings of the Cambridge Philological Society,* 215 (1989), 81-112. Reeve's discussion of exegetical and textual problems relevant to Jacob and Laban, pp. 85-92, does not consider Shakespeare or the Bible translations that he used.

21. That Laban's coloured animals have especially high value is richly ironic in the racial contexts of *The Merchant of Venice,* as we shall see.

22. On divine validation of the trickery of Esau see Colley, 'Launcelot, Jacob and Esau', p. 186. Condoned trickery constitutes a huge theme reflected in Solomonic justice, Jesuit teachings on equivocation, the trick statue in Tirso de Molina's *Don Juan,* Duke Vincentio's 'craft' in *Measure for Measure,* etc.

23. *The Bible,* trans. L. Tomson (London: Christopher Barker, 1597).

24. Barbara K. Lewalski, 'Biblical Allusion and Allegory in *The Merchant of Venice*', in *Shylock,* ed. Harold Bloom (New York: Chelsea House, 1991), pp. 236-51, suggests in a note, p. 250, that Antonio may allude to the biblical justification of Jacob's action. But Antonio's impatient remark that Jacob's 'venture [. . .] sway'd and fashion'd by the hand of heaven' cannot 'make interest good? / Or is our gold and silver ewes and rams?' (1.3.86-90) shows that he has not understood how, for Shylock, trickery of the unjust may provide a divinely ordained recompense.

25. See 'Law Merchant', pp. 64-5.

26. See Katz, *The Jews,* pp. 49-101.

27. Hsia, *The Myth of Ritual Murder,* p. 114, discusses Aquinas' and Duns Scotus' views.

28. See Pollock and Maitland, *The History of English Law,* vol. 1, 468-75, and William Holdsworth, *A History of English Law,* 16 vols. (London: Methuen, 1903-), vol. 1, pp. 45-6.

29. Pollock and Maitland, *The History of English Law,* vol. 1, 471, explains: 'the Jew, though he is the king's serf, is a freeman in relation to all other persons'. See R. A. Routledge, 'The Legal Status of the Jews in England, 1190-1790', *The Journal of Legal History,* 3 (1982), 91-124.

30. Sir Edward Coke, *Third Part of the Institutes of the Laws of England* (London, 1644), p. 89. A note in a contemporary hand in the British Library copy 508.g.5(2.) adds, 'But if converted he shall not be burnt'.

31. Pollock and Maitland, *The History of English Law,* vol. 2, p. 584: 'Stephen Langton [. . .] degraded and handed over to lay power a deacon who had turned Jew for the love of a Jewess. The apostate was delivered to the sheriff of Oxfordshire, who forthwith burnt him [. . . This] prompt action seems to have surprised his contemporaries, but was approved by Bracton'. Archbishop Langton's proceedings became quite famous for legal and political reasons discussed in F. W. Maitland, 'The Deacon and the Jewess; or, Apostacy at Common Law', *Collected Papers,* ed. H. A. L. Fisher, 3 vols. (Cambridge University Press, 1911), vol. 1, pp. 385-406. Pollock and Maitland, vol. 2, p. 394 cites a converse case where one partner in a Jewish marriage converts to Christianity, a rare instance where a full divorce allowing remarriage was allowed, and another case in which 'a Jewish widow was refused her dower on the ground that her husband had been converted'.

32. *Ibid.,* vol. 2, p. 549.

33. For a lawyer's view of this *clamantia peccata* see Coke, *Institutes of the Laws of England,* pp. 58-9.

34. See statistics in 'Bestiality and Law in Renaissance England' pp. 147-50, an appendix to Bruce Thomas Boehrer, 'Bestial Buggery in *A Midsummer Night's Dream*', *The Production of English Renaissance Culture,* ed. David Lee Miller, Sharon O'Dair, and Harold Weber (Ithaca: Cornell University Press, 1994), 123-50.

35. Keith Thomas, *Man and the Natural World: Changing Attitudes in England 1500-1800* (Allen Lane: London, 1983), pp. 38-9, 94-117, 118-19, 134-5.

36. *Ibid.,* pp. 38-9. Slightly later human transfusion of animal blood, and still later vaccination, were opposed on the same basis.

37. *Ibid.,* p. 42; on later-emerging racialist theories of human polygenism see *ibid.,* p. 136.

38. Caroline Spurgeon, *Shakespeare's Imagery and What It Tells Us* (Cambridge: Cambridge University Press, 1935), p. 335, reveals that 'contemptuous or repellent' animal images dominate *Othello*. Othello at last compares himself to a 'base Indian' or in the Folio text a 'base Judean' (TLN 3658), and then stabs himself imaged as a 'circumcised dog'.

39. This search was done using the University of Toronto's *TACT* text analysis program applied to William Shakespeare, *The Complete Works,* ed. Stanley Wells and Gary Taylor, Electronic Ed. (Oxford: Oxford University Press, 1989).

40. Thomas, *Man and the Natural World,* pp. 22-4 and 151; but p. 137 claims that some common people

ignored this and regarded animals 'in the way that Jews had before them, as essentially within the covenant'.

41. Exodus 23:5 and 12; Deuteronomy 22:4; Proverbs 12:10; Hosea 2:18 even speaks of a holy covenant with beasts.

42. Jessica says at 3.2.6 that Shylock's murderous intention predated her elopement, but Ruth Nevo, *Comic Transformation in Shakespeare* (London: Methuen, 1980), argues persuasively, pp. 130-1, that by emotional logic it must develop afterwards.

43. I argue in 'Constitutive Signifiers' that Antonio's selfless code is necessarily defeated by Portia and the marriage contract.

44. What Bassanio has in mind is made explicit in Montaigne's sceptical 'An Apology', *Essays* (New York: Modern Library, 1933), p. 429: 'The Indians describe [beauty as] blacke and swarthy, with blabbered-thick lips, with a broad and flat nose, the inward gristle whereof they loade with great gold-rings, hanging downe to their mouth'. The Oxford text places Bassanio's lines in an aside, exonerating the others present from sharing his vision. Other editors emend, not seeing the implied contrast of Indian with the beauteous. Yet, as the Arden editor tersely notes, p. 82, 'the Elizabethan aversion to dark skins gives sufficient meaning to the passage'.

45. René Girard, *A Theatre of Envy* (Oxford University Press, 1991), p. 249 suggests *The Merchant of Venice* speaks to two simultaneous audiences, a 'refined' one on an ironic plane and a 'vulgar' one in accord with their bigotry. I propose that Shakespeare had a more complexly constituted audience in mind in my *Art and Illusion in 'The Winter's Tale'* (Manchester University Press, 1994), pp. 65-6.

46. Many seem influenced by the lauding of idyllic Belmont in C. L. Barber, *Shakespeare's Festive Comedy* (1959; rpt. Cleveland, OH: Meridian, 1963), pp. 163-91. Barber's chapter title, 'The Merchants and the Jew of Venice: Love's Communion and an Intruder', epitomizes a view that 'Shylock and the accounting mechanism which he embodies are crudely baffled in Venice and rhapsodically transcended in Belmont' (p. 173). This classic pro-Belmont argument is more temperate than many of its descendants: for instance, Colley, 'Launcelot, Jacob and Esau'; J. S. Coolidge, 'Law and Love in *The Merchant of Venice*', *Shakespeare Quarterly*, 27 (1976), 243-63; M. J. Hamill, 'Poetry, Law and the Pursuit of Perfection: Portia's role in *The Merchant of Venice*', *SEL*, 18 (1978), 229-43. Stephen J. Greenblatt, 'Marlowe, Marx, and Anti-Semitism', *Critical Inquiry*, 5 (1978), 291-307 (rpt. in Greenblatt, *Learning to Curse: Essays in Early Modern Culture*, NY: Routledge, 1990, pp. 40-58), contrasts Shylock's Venetian 'economic nexus' with Portia's world, 'not a field in which she operates for profit but a living web of noble values and moral orderliness' (p. 295), and seemingly excuses Marx's notion of the loathsome 'Jewishness' of capitalism.

47. Peter Davison, *Othello* (Basingstoke: Macmillan, 1988), p. 65.

48. On wordplay central to a Shakespeare play see my 'A Spenserian Idea in *The Taming of the Shrew*', *English Studies*, 66 (1985), 310-16; for an ignoble pun see *King Lear*, 1.1.11-12.

49. Production may highlight Portia's decline from witty discernment, may elide this, or may make it ambiguous and confusing. The last may be best, as it leaves uneasy responses unguided.

50. Lynda E. Boose, 'The Comic Contract and Portia's Golden Ring', *Shakespeare Studies*, 20 (1988), 241-54, p. 247, finds Portia's 'covertly manipulative subversions of passive aggression' used against 'the male system of female suppression'.

51. The locution 'good sir[s]', listed only four times by Bartlett, is actually very commonly used in Shakespeare's plays (62 times). In *Hamlet*, 2.1.47, Polonius explains its insincerity to his spy Reynoldo.

ALLEGORY

Susan McLean (essay date 1996)

SOURCE: "Prodigal Sons and Daughters: Transgression and Forgiveness in *The Merchant of Venice*," in *Papers on Language & Literature*, Vol. 32, No. 1, 1996, pp. 45-62.

[*In the essay below, McLean identifies allegorical elements in* The Merchant of Venice, *arguing that the parable of the rebellious but repentant Prodigal Son is reenacted numerous times between different character pairings. Consequently, by the end of the play the audience is left to contemplate the virtue of forgiveness.*]

The word "prodigal" appears more often in *The Merchant of Venice* than in any other play of Shakespeare's, yet the relevance to the play of the parable of the Prodigal Son has excited little critical attention.[1] Not only is Bassanio called "prodigal" by himself and Shylock, but Shylock also calls Antonio "a prodigal," and Gratiano alludes to the parable of the Prodigal Son just before Lorenzo elopes with Jessica. Bassanio and Antonio enact elements of the story of the Prodigal Son at a serious level, while Launcelot Gobbo and his father parody the same story. Jessica also rebels against paternal control, and Portia expresses her desire to do so, though she insists that she will never violate the conditions of her father's will.² Instead, she uses the ring plot to create a scenario of disobedience, sin, repentance, and forgiveness that exorcizes the threat of her previous independent behavior and embodies the New Testament ideal of love, in contrast to the unforgiving attitude of Shylock toward his daughter.

"Prodigal" has three key meanings in the context of *The Merchant of Venice*. It can refer to extravagant expenditure, lavish generosity, or the parable of the Prodigal Son (Luke 15:11-32), whose reckless defiance of paternal control led to sin, ruin, repentance, and ultimate forgiveness. In the parable, the younger of two sons asks his father for his inheritance, leaves home, spends all of his money on harlots and riotous living, and is reduced to becoming a famished swineherd. He then returns home in repentance to ask to become one of his father's servants, but is received gladly by his father, who gives him the best robe, a ring, and shoes, and feasts him on a fat calf. The elder brother begrudges his father's celebration, pointing out that he has never been similarly rewarded for being virtuous and obedient, but his father tells him that it is appropriate to rejoice, "for this thy brother was dead, and is alive againe: and he was lost, but he is found" (Luke 15: 32, Geneva Bible).

The paradox of the Prodigal Son—that the sin is a necessary prelude to the forgiveness—echoes the theme of the "fortunate fall."³ The parable presents generosity and mercy as the central attributes of Christianity, and it rejects the elder brother's narrow focus on desert and obedience to his father's commandments. Allegorically, in the parable the elder brother is identified with the Jews and the laws of the Old Testament, the younger brother with the Christians, and the father with the merciful God of the New Testament. The parable thus brings together several themes that are important in *The Merchant of Venice*: the triumph of mercy over justice, as portrayed in the trial scene; the rewarding of humility over presumed desert, as exemplified in the casket scene; and the forgiveness of penitents, as seen in the ring plot and in the subplots concerning Launcelot and his father, and Lorenzo and Jessica.

The popularity of the Prodigal Son story in Renaissance literature has been attributed to several sources. Richard Helgerson suggests that stories of prodigals embodied the ongoing conflict between the two Renaissance traditions of "civic humanism and courtly romance," in which "Humanism represented paternal expectation, and romance, rebellious desire" (41). Alan R. Young attributes the popularity of the theme in sixteenth- and seventeenth-century drama to its flexibility for exploring theological issues and "such special contemporary concerns as education, the proper use of wealth, and the responsibilities of a prince" (52-3). Young includes Shakespeare's *Henry IV, parts 1 and 2* (which were written around the same time as *The Merchant of Venice*) among the plays that use the Prodigal Son motif.

Marilyn Williamson connects the popularity in the 1590's of romantic comedies about penniless young men who marry heiresses (such as Bassanio and Orlando) to the death of opportunities for social advancement among educated but impoverished young men, which encouraged fantasies of upward mobility through marriage to a wealthy woman (14). Williamson notes that in Shakespeare's romantic comedies the prodigal males often "put the powerful lady in the parent's place by asking her forgiveness" (33). This pattern also appears in Shakespeare's problem comedies, in which errant males, such as Bertram and Angelo, are redeemed by the forgiveness of virtuous women (58, 101).

Shakespeare's treatment of the Prodigal Son story is a radical departure from the didactic, admonitory treatment that the story usually received in early Tudor drama and fiction, in which "The prodigality of a son who defies his father's counsel is ruinous, not momentarily, in the third act of a play that will surely end happily, but forever" (Helgerson 35). Shakespeare restores the forgiveness that is central to the biblical parable and extends its scope to include romantic as well as filial relationships. The story of the Prodigal Son may have appealed to Shakespeare not only because forgiveness had a powerful claim on his imagination, but also because it is crucial to the contrast that he wished to show in *The Merchant of Venice* between the values of the Old and the New Testaments.⁴

For men, "prodigality" has overtones of sexual as well as financial impropriety, because the Prodigal Son of the parable wasted his patrimony on harlots. When Bassanio confesses to Antonio that he has lived beyond his means, he does not specify what he has spent his money on, but says

> my chief care
> Is to come fairly off from the great debts
> Wherein my time something too prodigal
> Hath left me gag'd.
>
> (*Merchant* 1.1.127-30)⁵

In this context, the word "prodigal" could allude to sexual expenditures, but—if so—Bassanio's stated intention of seeking a wife suggests that he means to reform his behavior. When Shylock uses "prodigal" to describe Bassanio ("I'll go in hate, to feed upon / The prodigal Christian" 2.5.15-16) or Antonio ("A bankrupt, a prodigal, who dare scarce show his head on the Rialto" 3.1.41-42) his meaning is primarily financial, but with suggestions of shameful behavior. However, the word tends to take on *exclusively* sexual connotations when applied to a woman, as is clear in *Hamlet* in Laertes's advice to Ophelia: "The chariest maid is prodigal enough / If she unmask her beauty to the moon" (1.3.36). Because sexual misbehavior was considered venial in a man, but unforgivable in a woman, the "prodigality" of Portia or Jessica has necessary limitations.

Bassanio is the most obvious parallel to the Prodigal Son. He wastes both his patrimony and the money that he had previously borrowed from Antonio, who then acts the part of the forgiving father and lends him more money. Later,

Bassanio gives away Portia's ring and she accuses him of giving it to a woman, but once again he is forgiven.[6] Bassanio's inherent generosity is visible when he hires the scapegrace Launcelot and tells a servant, "Give him a livery / More guarded [i.e., ornamented] than his fellows'" (2.2.146-7). Marilyn Williamson argues that Bassanio's extravagance both clears him of suspicions of mercenary motives, and prepares the viewer for his ungreedy choice of the lead casket and his generosity in giving his wedding ring to the disguised Portia (33). Launcelot is more accurate than he knows when he tells Bassanio, "The old proverb is very well parted between my master Shylock and you, sir: you have the grace of God, sir, and he hath enough" (2.2.141-3). In the context of the play, Bassanio's open-handedness—like Antonio's and Portia's—is the human reflection of divine mercy.

Antonio resembles the Prodigal Son in the lavishness of his generosity, in its nearly disastrous consequences, and in his eventual redemption, but there is no hint of selfishness in his behavior, so there is nothing for him to repent in order to gain salvation. He is identified more closely with the father of the parable and with Jesus himself than with the repentant sinner. Not only does he forgive Bassanio for putting him into a life-threatening situation, but also he intercedes with the court to reduce Shylock's penalty and convert him to Christianity (thereby giving Shylock a chance at salvation as well).

The character of Launcelot Gobbo has often been considered irrelevant to the main action. Leo Rockas, however, argues that Launcelot participates in the theme of father-child relationships (347-48), and René E. Fortin draws a further connection to the incident in Genesis 27 in which the younger son Jacob tricks his blind father Isaac into giving him the blessing that should have gone to his elder brother Esau, an incident that Christians interpreted as prefiguring the transfer of divine favor from the Jews to the Christians (266-68). The Launcelot-Old Gobbo plot also functions as a comic parody of the Prodigal Son story. Like the Prodigal Son, Launcelot is famished in the service of a bad master, Shylock, and he turns to his father to get a better post as the servant of Bassanio, who rewards him with a fancy livery (just as the Prodigal Son is given the best robe on his return). Launcelot initially leads his blind father to believe that he is dead, which then increases the father's rejoicing upon learning that his son is actually alive. Old Gobbo does not kill a fat calf, but he does bring "a dish of doves" (2.2.127) as a present for Launcelot's master, and Launcelot persuades him to give them to Bassanio instead. As René E. Fortin has noted,

> The doves also recall the doves or pigeons offered as sacrifice in the Presentation of Jesus (Luke 2:22-24); the passage lays stress upon this ritual as being according to the Law of Moses and highlights the fact that Jesus was himself observant of the Law.
>
> (266n.)

The doves, which were prominently featured in pictorial representations of the Presentation in the Temple and were thus identified with paternal love, also recall the doves that Noah sent forth from the Ark (Genesis 8:8-12). They therefore are both a reminder of God's original covenant with the Jews and a symbol of the transfer of that covenant to the Christians, when the gift intended for Shylock is given to Bassanio instead.

The scene between the two Gobbos is funny because Launcelot's treatment of his father is distinctly unfilial, yet the father is no less happy to recover his son. Launcelot's behavior serves as a comic parallel to Jessica's treatment of Shylock (whose own attitude is so unfatherly that he wishes his daughter dead, if he could thus get his money back). Launcelot's effrontery also contrasts with the filial devotion of Portia to her father's will and of Bassanio to the fatherly Antonio. Launcelot's later concern that the conversion of Jews will raise the price of hogs (3.5.21-22) and his getting the Moor pregnant (3.5.37) may recall the Prodigal's working as a swineherd and consorting with harlots. Just as Launcelot's treatment of his father is the opposite of the Prodigal's humility, so his behavior after receiving his father's blessing is cheerfully unregenerate. Perhaps because his disrespect is neither malicious nor harmful, Launcelot participates in the general amnesty typical at the end of comedy, from which Shylock is excluded.

While waiting for Lorenzo to arrive and elope with Jessica, Gratiano alludes to the story of the Prodigal Son in a way that seems ominous for the eloping couple:

> All things that are,
> Are with more spirit chased than enjoy'd.
> How like a younger[7] or a prodigal
> The scarfed bark puts from her native bay,
> Hugg'd and embraced by the strumpet wind!
> How like the prodigal doth she return,
> With over-weather'd ribs and ragged sails,
> Lean, rent, and beggar'd by the strumpet wind!
>
> (2.6.13-20)

From the context, one might assume that Gratiano is identifying Lorenzo with the prodigal and Jessica with a strumpet who will ruin him. Lorenzo is certainly, like Bassanio, a penniless young man, but Jessica more nearly fits the pattern of the prodigal. She disobeys her father's orders; steals some of his money; runs off, disguised as a boy, with her lover Lorenzo, who is a Christian and therefore an inappropriate suitor in her father's eyes; and spends her father's money in an extravagant manner. Yet all of these "sins" have mitigating circumstances in the eyes of the audience. Because her father is wicked and a Jew, her disobeying and leaving him to become a Christian is presented as a change for the better. Because she is his only heir, she is seen as having some just claim to the money that she steals from him to be her dowry. Her running off with a lover would be sinful, except that she marries him. Her choice of Lorenzo, who has no money of his own, is a sign of the unselfishness of her love (Partee 18). Her subsequent wastefulness with money is both a suitable punishment on Shylock for his miserliness and, paradoxically, a sign of her own lack of mercenary attitudes.

Like the Prodigal Son, Jessica leaves her father's control and wastes part of her patrimony, but unlike him, she does not undergo ruin or repentance. Instead, Shylock himself undergoes ruin, (forced) repentance, and Christian forgiveness, at the cost of his own unwilling conversion to Christianity. Jessica reaps the Prodigal's reward of a generous welcome (though from Portia, not Shylock) and the rest of her patrimony upon Shylock's death (granted by Shylock at Antonio's insistence). This inversion of the parable, in which the child proves wiser than the father, depends on the fact that the child is Christian and the father Jewish. Shylock, indeed, resembles the narrow, rigid, calculating, and prohibitive Pharisees to whom the parable of the Prodigal Son was originally addressed. In rejecting her father, Jessica is rejecting Old Testament law for New Testament mercy, which is one reason that Shylock gets the full force of the law, while his daughter gets mercy.

Jessica leaves a patriarchal household, in which the man is a domineering autocrat, in favor of the loving mutuality of the Protestant ideal of companionate marriage.[8] Lorenzo is, of course, still the head of the household, and it is into his hands that Portia commits the running of her house while she is away. Yet Jessica's teasing, bantering tone in her conversations with Lorenzo shows that she is neither a submissive nor a silent wife, and has led some critics to question the happiness of her marriage.[9] When Jessica praises Portia, Lorenzo tries to turn her praise toward him:

> Jessica:
> Why, if two gods should play some heavenly match
> And on the wager lay two earthly women,
> And Portia one, there must be something else
> Pawn'd with the other, for the poor rude world
> Hath not her fellow.
> Lorenzo:
> Even such a husband
> Hast thou of me as she is for a wife.
> Jessica:
> Nay, but ask my opinion too of that!
> Lorenzo:
> I will anon. First let us go to dinner.
> Jessica:
> Nay, let me praise you while I have a stomach.
> Lorenzo:
> No, pray thee, let it serve for table-talk;
> Then, howsome'er thou speak'st, 'mong other things
> I shall digest it.
> Jessica:
> Well, I'll set you forth.
>
> (3.5.76-87)

Her teasing refusal to endorse his playfully exalted opinion of himself both asserts the independence of her mind and reveals his willingness to allow her to say whatever she pleases. Similarly, when the two exchange stories of unhappy lovers at the beginning of Act 5, Jessica refuses to let Lorenzo have the last word:

> Lorenzo:
> In such a night
> Did Jessica steal from the wealthy Jew,
> And with an unthrift love did run from Venice
> As far as Belmont.
> Jessica:
> In such a night
> Did young Lorenzo swear he lov'd her well,
> Stealing her soul with many vows of faith,
> And ne'er a true one.
> Lorenzo:
> In such a night
> Did pretty Jessica, like a little shrew,
> Slander her love, and he forgave it her.
> Jessica:
> I would out-night you, did nobody come; . . .
>
> (5.1.14-23)

Lorenzo refers to himself as being "unthrift"—a synonym for "prodigal," but also a word that recalls Shylock's statement that "thrift is blessing, if men steal it not" (1.3.87). Lorenzo and Jessica accuse each other of stealing, yet in a play in which Shylock's "thrift" is exposed as damnable, Jessica's theft of herself and her father's money and Lorenzo's theft of her soul are paradoxically virtuous because the lovers obey the rules of "love's wealth," stealing only in order to give (Brown 70-71).[10] The underlying generosity of their love is visible in Lorenzo's instant forgiveness of Jessica's "slander."

Lorenzo's jesting reference to Jessica as "a little shrew" does raise the issue of the threat to masculine authority that a wealthy wife traditionally represented to an impoverished husband. This threat is even more obvious in the case of Portia, who brings to Bassanio not only much greater wealth than Jessica's, but also extraordinary intelligence and even competence in the exclusively male field of law.[11] Because she has so much, it is essential that she give it all away if she is not to seem a threat to Bassanio's control. No sooner does he solve the riddle of the caskets than, in a speech that resembles Kate's speech of submission at the end of *The Taming of the Shrew*,[12] she compares herself to

> an unlesson'd girl, unschool'd, unpracticed;
> Happy in this, she is not yet so old
> But she may learn; happier than this,
> She is not bred so dull but she can learn;
> Happiest of all is that her gentle spirit
> Commits itself to yours to be directed,
> As from her lord, her governor, her king.
> Myself and what is mine to you and yours
> Is now converted. But now I was the lord
> Of this fair mansion, master of my servants,
> Queen o'er myself; and even now, but now
> This house, these servants, and this same myself
> Are yours, my lord's. I give them with this ring,
> Which when you part from, lose, or give away,
> Let it presage the ruin of your love
> And be my vantage to exclaim on you.
>
> (3.2.159-174)

The exaggerated humility of this speech (which contrasts strikingly with her witty, condescending comments on her previous suitors) is all the more necessary because it is so patently false. Neither before nor after the speech does Portia act at all like an "unlesson'd girl," yet it is essential that she acknowledge the legal reality that all of her possessions and her own independence now belong to her husband and that she accept the transfer of power ungrudgingly. She reserves to herself only woman's traditional weapon—speech—and promises to use it against Bassanio only if he breaks his marriage vow by relinquishing the ring.

Portia's subsequent behavior hardly seems consonant with her proclaimed submissiveness. She often thereafter refers to her house as "my house" or "my hall," and to her servants as "my people" or "my servants."[13] Moreover, she continues to direct the action, both openly and covertly, urging her husband to pay off Antonio's debt, no matter what it costs, and to leave for Venice as soon as the wedding vows are made. She then delegates the care of her house to Lorenzo, and follows her husband to Venice in disguise and without his knowledge. In Venice, she tricks Bassanio into relinquishing the ring and then uses her possession of it to lord it over her husband and to threaten him with the ultimate indignity of cuckoldry.

Yet Portia's behavior is not as insubordinate as it appears. Her references to the house and servants as hers are made mainly when Bassanio is not present, and could be less a statement of ownership than a sign of her continuing residence and authority in her husband's absence (when he is present, she welcomes his friends to "our house," 5.1.139, though she later reverts to saying "my house" twice, 5.1.223, 273). Bassanio seems bashful at first about assuming the authority that is his by marriage. When he chooses the correct casket, he says to Portia that he is "doubtful whether what I see be true / Until confirm'd, sign'd, ratified by you" (3.2.147-48). Later, in welcoming his friends to Belmont, he says,

> Lorenzo and Salerio, welcome hither,
> If that the youth of my new int'rest here
> Have power to bid you welcome. By your leave,
> I bid my very friends and countrymen,
> Sweet Portia, welcome.
>
> (3.2.220-24)

His hesitancy to assume command is something that Portia must help him to overcome. When she sees that he is moved by the contents of the letter he has received from Antonio, she urges him to share his trouble with her:

> With leave, Bassanio; I am half yourself,
> And I must freely have the half of anything
> That this same paper brings you.
>
> (3.2.248-50)

When she tells him to pay off Antonio's debt and to join his friend immediately, Portia knows that she is telling him to do what he really wants to do, but would hesitate to do for fear of seeming ungracious or spendthrift to her. Even her insistence on an immediate wedding is a generous action because it gives him the legal right to all of her property, but without any benefit to her, even of the physical satisfaction of the wedding night. Her statement to Bassanio—"Since you are dear bought, I will love you dear" (3.2.313)—is not a declaration of ownership, but, as John Russell Brown suggests, a sign of her "willingness to continue to give joyfully in love" (68). Lorenzo later commends Portia's "god-like amity, which appears most strongly / In bearing thus the absence of your lord" (3.4.3-4). It is Portia's own generosity that later makes her a suitable advocate for mercy.

Bassanio proves no match for Portia in generosity, so she is forced to give him a lesson in it. To do so, she turns herself into a "prodigal" to see whether he has the will to forgive her.[14] The trouble starts at the trial, when he exclaims

> Antonio, I am married to a wife
> Which is as dear to me as life itself;
> But life itself, my wife, and all the world,
> Are not with me esteem'd above thy life.
> I would lose all, ay, sacrifice them all
> Here to this devil to deliver you.
>
> (4.1.280-85)

Portia dryly responds, "Your wife would give you little thanks for that, / If she were by, to hear you make the offer" (4.1.286-7). She recognizes both that Bassanio would not say such a thing in front of his wife and that he does not have the right to make the offer. He would be justified in offering his own life, but not that of another. Her subsequent request of his ring is a test that he is predisposed to fail, because he has already established that he sets his obligations to his friend above those to his wife. His failure, however, is only partial. He demonstrates great reluctance to part with the ring; his sense of obligation to the friend who had risked his life for him is his sole reason for giving it up; and he is honest to Portia later about his reasons for losing it.

Because Bassanio defends his parting with the ring on grounds of honor, Portia tests him on those same grounds. He tells her,

> I was enforc'd to send it after him.
> I was beset with shame and courtesy.
> My honor would not let ingratitude
> So much besmear it.
>
> (5.1.216-19)

In upholding his obligations to his friend and his reputation among men, Bassanio ignores the equally binding obligation to keep his word to his wife. She picks up the theme of honor:

> Let not that doctor e'er come near my house.
> Since he hath got the jewel that I lov'd,
> And that which you did swear to keep for me,
> I will become as liberal as you:
> I'll not deny him any thing I have,

> No, not my body nor my husband's bed.
> Know him I shall, I am well sure of it.
> Lie not a night from home. Watch me like Argus;
> If you do not, if I be left alone,
> Now, by mine honor, which is yet mine own,
> I'll have that doctor for my bedfellow.
>
> (5.1.223-33)

She threatens to be as "liberal" (i.e., "generous") as Bassanio, and to give the doctor any thing she has—but, of course, the only thing that she still has any control over is her own body (even the bed is her husband's). A woman's honor is her chastity, and Portia can say that that still belongs to her because she has not yet given it to Bassanio. She reminds him that she has the power to ruin his honor—i.e., his reputation among men—by making him a cuckold. After he has begged her forgiveness for breaking his word and has sworn not to do so again, she asks his forgiveness and implies that she has already slept with the doctor.[15]

This is Bassanio's ultimate test—can he be as forgiving as she is?—and, interestingly, Portia does not wait for the answer because however he replied, he would look bad. The conscious cuckold was a figure of ridicule in the Renaissance, yet a refusal of forgiveness would be a failure of Christian charity. Portia saves Bassanio's face by revealing her imposture. Bassanio can then forgive her—not for adultery, but merely for playing a trick on him. Portia also gets one more chance to be generous, giving Antonio the news that his ships have come in safely and giving Lorenzo news of the bequest from Shylock. As a married woman, Portia can no longer give away money or property, but she can still use her energies and abilities to benefit others. Lorenzo's response—"Fair ladies, you drop manna in the way / Of starved people" (5.1.294-95)—again identifies Portia with divine generosity, and Antonio tells her, "Sweet lady, you have given me life and living" (5.1.286). As in the parable, he that was dead is alive, and that which was lost (the ships, the rings) is found.

The motif of the Prodigal Son not only links several plots and subplots of the play, but also should serve to moderate the current critical tendency to sympathize with Shylock and to judge the Christians harshly for not living up to the merciful ideals that they profess. The basic premise of Christianity—that the sinner who believes and begs forgiveness will find mercy, while the self-righteous and the nonbeliever will not—may seem unfair, as the parable of the Prodigal Son presumably did to the Pharisees to whom Jesus told it when they objected to his eating with sinners. Yet according to that premise, even such feckless or unfilial prodigals as Launcelot, Jessica, Gratiano,[16] and Bassanio must be forgiven, along with the more virtuous Portia and Antonio, while Shylock the Jew, the arrogant pagan Prince of Morocco, and the self-regarding Prince of Arragon may not.

Portia says of mercy, "It blesseth him that gives and him that takes" (4.1.185). Those who give forgiveness (Portia, Antonio, Lorenzo, Old Gobbo) and those who receive it gratefully (Bassanio, Gratiano, Launcelot, and Jessica, through her conversion to Christianity) are granted both mercy and good fortune. Those who are convinced of their own desert (Morocco, Arragon) or righteousness (Shylock asks "What judgment shall I dread, doing no wrong?" 4.1.89, and exclaims "My deeds upon my head!" 4.1.204) are subjected to the full rigors of the law. Shylock does not beg for mercy when Portia urges him to do so, and he objects to the terms of mercy when he is offered his life, saying

> Nay, take my life and all! Pardon not that!
> You take my house when you do take the prop
> That doth sustain my house. You take my life
> When you do take the means whereby I live.
>
> (4.1.372-75)

His inability to accept mercy gratefully when it is offered bodes ill for his future forced conversion.

To argue that Shakespeare uses the Prodigal Son motif to reinforce the sympathies of the audience with his Christian characters and to condemn the self-righteousness of Shylock does not minimize the ironies and moral ambiguities of the play. On the contrary, the variety of moral shadings in the different prodigals and self-righteous characters brings into sharp focus the paradoxes of salvation that are inherent in the parable itself. The combination in *The Merchant of Venice* of "optimistic faith in man's spiritual possibilities with an ironic sense of human fallibility" (Lucking 374) links it to Shakespeare's other "comedies of forgiveness." As Robert Grams Hunter suggests, the success of a comedy of forgiveness depends on the audience's identification with the sinner:

> Medieval men and their Elizabethan descendants were taught to be charitable out of a sense of common humanity, which meant a sense of common evil. . . . Modern charity . . . is more likely to be associated with making allowances, with pity and tolerance. We tend to forgive the man who does evil not because we recognize ourselves in him, but because we see him as a poor unfortunate, a victim of heredity and environment, the creature of an unhappy past—one who, through no fault of his own, is our inferior. We are likely, therefore, . . . to react rather as the pharisee reacted to the publican. This is not the reaction which the sinning mortals of Shakespeare's comedies . . . were intended to provoke. Such dramas invite us to forgive the sins of others not because we (unlike them) are good, but because we (like them) are not good.
>
> (243-44)

This difference between Renaissance ideals of charity and modern ideals of tolerance interferes with our ability to see Shylock as Renaissance viewers probably would have seen him—not as a scapegoat, but as a man whose lack of charity sets off, by contrast, that virtue in others.

Notes

1. The parable is not mentioned, for instance, by Barbara Lewalski in "Biblical Allusion and Allegory

Eric Donkin as Arragon, Jane Casson as Merissa, Maureen O'Brien as Portia, and Attendants in the 1970 Stratford Festival production of The Merchant of Venice.

in *The Merchant of Venice*." René E. Fortin does note that Bassanio functions as a "prodigal" son to Antonio (263), but he does not elaborate. Sylvan Barnet points out that Bassanio, Antonio, and Portia are all "prodigal" in the sense of being generous (and that Shylock is their antithesis). He denies that the honorable Bassanio should be identified with "the wretch who appears in school dramas concerning the Prodigal Son" (26), yet he concludes that "Shakespeare's use of the motif is in accord with Christ's parable: the prodigal is ultimately acceptable, and the 'virtue' of the self-satisfied uncharitable elder brother—a figure who, like Shylock, holds to the law, fulfills the bond—is not enough" (26). John S. Coolidge says that the parable of the prodigal son "supplies a minor leitmotif to the play" (245), but he does not develop the idea except to say that the parable embodies "the New Testament idea of love" (246) and to point out the hint of hope that the parable lends to the otherwise ominous overtones of Gratiano's allusion to it just before Jessica's elopement (260).

2. Whether Portia hints at the correct answer to the casket riddle through the song or her line "I stand for sacrifice" (3.2.57) is impossible to determine, though I side with Harry Berger, Jr., in thinking that the cues are more likely unconscious than deliberate (160). One does not offer one riddle as the solution to another, and Portia tells Bassanio directly that she will never be forsworn by telling him the answer (3.2.10-12).

3. See Gary Grund, "The Fortunate Fall and Shakespeare's *Merchant of Venice*," which discusses the motif of the Fortunate Fall, but does not connect it to the parable of the Prodigal Son.

4. Surprisingly, Robert Grams Hunter does not include *The Merchant of Venice* among Shakespeare's "comedies of forgiveness"—among which he includes *Much Ado About Nothing, All's Well That Ends Well, Cymbeline, The Winter's Tale, Measure*

for Measure, and *The Tempest*—because, despite its denouement of forgiveness, "Shylock is the serio-comic scapegoat of the drama" (87). Yet to ignore the entire fifth act, in which forgiveness and reconciliation figure prominently, seriously misrepresents the play.

5. All quotations from Shakespeare's plays are taken from *The Complete Works of Shakespeare,* ed. David Bevington, 3rd. ed., New York: HarperCollins, 1980.

6. Because Bassanio swears "when this ring / Parts from this finger, then parts life from hence" (3.2.183-84), his loss of the ring parallels the Prodigal Son's presumed death. As Ronald A. Sharp has noted, Bassanio's gift of the ring is his opportunity to "hazard all for love" and thus prove himself worthy of both Antonio and Portia (256-57).

7. "Younger," which appears in the Quarto and Folio texts of the play, is often emended to "younker," meaning "a young nobleman or fashionable young man," in order to remove a perceived redundancy in the allusion to the Prodigal Son. It is possible, however, that Shakespeare wished to evoke the situation of younger sons in general, as well as that of the biblical Prodigal, through his use of overlapping but not synonymous terms.

8. See Catherine Belsey (48-52) for a discussion of this new model of marriage in relation to Portia.

9. See Ralph Berry (59-61) and John Lyon (71) for a negative view of Jessica's relationship with Lorenzo.

10. For the opposite view, that Jessica's theft foreshadows an unhappy marriage, see Lynda E. Boose (336-37).

11. See Anne Parten (146-54) for a discussion of this threat in relation to Portia. She does not mention its relevance to Jessica.

12. The similarity of Portia's speech to Kate's has been noted by Lisa Jardine (60-61) and by Leonard Tennenhouse (55-56).

13. I am indebted for this observation to Joseph Wagner's paper, "From Obedience to Sovereignty in *The Merchant of Venice,*" which he delivered at the 1994 Midwest Modern Language Association conference in Chicago.

14. Shakespeare's later cross-dressed heroines, Rosalind and Viola, have the opportunity to educate their future husbands about the nature of love before they marry, but we do not see Bassanio and Portia together until the casket scene, so Portia is forced to be her husband's teacher after the wedding, a role that he may allude to when he tells her "Sweet doctor, you shall be my bedfellow" (5.1.284), "doctor" having its Latin meaning of "teacher."

15. It is crucial that the audience knows all along that Portia has *not* been unfaithful to Bassanio. The audience can thus enjoy Portia's clever equivocations and Bassanio's discomfiture without thinking that Portia is a monster. According to the double standard in operation at the time, sexual prodigality in a woman was not forgivable.

16. Gratiano, whose name means "grace," is a particularly ironic embodiment of the paradoxes of divine grace because he is vindictive toward Shylock and defensive rather than contrite to Nerissa about the loss of his ring. He tells Shylock

> Thou almost mak'st me waver in my faithTo hold opinion with Pythagoras,
> That souls of animals infuse themselves
> Into the trunks of men.
>
> (4.1.130-3)

He does not waver in his faith, however, and he does accept Nerissa's forgiveness with gratitude. Like Launcelot, another largely comic figure, Gratiano is allowed the latitude to misbehave without being condemned for it.

Works Cited

Barnet, Sylvan. "Prodigality and Time in *The Merchant of Venice.*" *PMLA* 87 (1972): 26-30.

Belsey, Catherine. "Love in Venice." *Shakespeare Survey: An Annual Survey of Shakespeare Studies and Production.* 44. Ed. Stanley Wells. Cambridge: Cambridge UP, 1992: 41-53.

Berger, Harry, Jr. "Marriage and Mercifixion in *The Merchant of Venice:* The Casket Scene Revisited." *Shakespeare Quarterly* 32 (1981): 155-62.

Berry, Ralph. *Shakespeare and the Awareness of the Audience.* London: Macmillan, 1985.

Boose, Lynda E. "The Father and the Bride in Shakespeare." *PMLA* 97 (1982): 325-47.

Brown, John Russell. *Shakespeare and His Comedies.* London: Methuen, 1957; rpt. 1964.

Coolidge, John S. "Law and Love in *The Merchant of Venice.*" *Shakespeare Quarterly* 27 (1976): 243-63.

Fortin, René E. "Launcelot and the Uses of Allegory in *The Merchant of Venice.*" *Studies in Literature, 1500-1900* 14 (1974): 259-70.

Grund, Gary. "The Fortunate Fall and Shakespeare's *Merchant of Venice.*" *Studia Neophilologica* 55 (1983): 153-65.

Helgerson, Richard. *The Elizabethan Prodigals.* Berkeley: U of California P, 1976.

Hunter, Robert Grams. *Shakespeare and the Comedy of Forgiveness.* New York: Columbia UP, 1965.

Jardine, Lisa. *Still Harping on Daughters: Women and Drama in the Age of Shakespeare.* Brighton: Harvester, 1983.

Lewalski, Barbara. "Biblical Allusion and Allegory in *The Merchant of Venice*," *Shakespeare Quarterly* 13 (1962): 327-43.

Lucking, David. "Standing for Sacrifice: The Casket and Trial Scenes in *The Merchant of Venice*." *University of Toronto Quarterly* 58 (1989): 355-75.

Lyon, John. *The Merchant of Venice*. Boston: Twayne, 1988.

Partee, Morriss Henry. "Love and Responsibility in *The Merchant of Venice*." *Greyfriar: Siena Studies in Literature* 29 (1988): 15-23.

Parten, Anne. "Re-establishing Sexual Order: The Ring Episode in *The Merchant of Venice*." *Women's Studies* 9 (1982): 145-55.

Rockas, Leo. "'A Dish of Doves': *The Merchant of Venice*." *ELH* 40 (1973): 339-51.

Shakespeare, William. *The Complete Works of Shakespeare*. Ed. David Bevington. 3rd. ed. New York: HarperCollins, 1980.

Sharp, Ronald A. "Gift Exchange and the Economies of Spirit in *The Merchant of Venice*." *Modern Philology* 83 (1986): 250-65.

Tennenhouse, Leonard. *Power on Display: The Politics of Shakespeare's Genres*. New York: Methuen, 1986.

Williamson, Marilyn. *The Patriarchy of Shakespeare's Comedies*. Detroit: Wayne State UP, 1986.

Young, Alan R. *The English Prodigal Son Plays: A Theatrical Fashion of the Sixteenth and Seventeenth Centuries*. Salzburg: Institut für Anglistik und Amerikanistik, 1979.

Judith Rosenheim (essay date 1996)

SOURCE: "Allegorical Commentary in *The Merchant of Venice*," in *Shakespeare Studies*, Vol. XXIV, 1996, pp. 156-210.

[*In the essay below, Rosenheim argues that the themes of power, fatherhood, and blindness are developed through allegory in* The Merchant of Venice. *These themes are principally presented through the parable of the Prodigal Son as it applies to Launcelot versus his father, Old Gobbo, and, by extension, to the "father" Shylock versus the "son" Antonio.*]

In Asserting the prevalence of "symmetry" or moral equivalence between Shylock and Antonio, René Girard is adding his voice to an enduring current in the criticism of *The Merchant of Venice*. It is much the same opinion that Hazlitt advances in suggesting that Shylock's "Jewish revenge is at least as good as Christian injuries;" that A. D. Moody holds in finding that *Merchant* is "about the essential likeness of Shylock and his judges"; or Harold Goddard in remarking that Antonio "catches his own reflection in [Shylock's] face"; or Kiernan Ryan in defining Shylock's "bloodthirsty cruelty" as the "mirror-image of [the Christians'] concealed real nature."[1] A factual basis for this parity can be identified in the observation of Walter Cohen and Michael Ferber that sixteenth century merchants like Antonio were themselves usurers like Shylock.[2] Yet those who draw these parallels are usually prompted by the consideration that Shylock's villainy should be weighed against his suffering. Indeed, Shylock has recently become the beneficiary of a critical tendency to censure the play's Christian society by showing him as its victim. Thus for Frank Whigham, Shylock is "a dehumanized tool and disposable slave of order," who falls prey to the Christians' hegemonic use of law; for Ryan, he is the victim of a "money-centred world" "projecting upon him its displaced hatred of itself"; for Lars Engle, he is the provident custodian of the money-supply whose forced conversion makes him "a final victim of the cruelty of typology"; for Thomas Moisan he is the "scapegoat" absorbing "the blame for whatever is 'wrong' with the [economic] system."[3] Still, hostility toward Christian society would probably not generate sympathy for Shylock were it not for an accompanying perception of something attractive in his characterization, as Engle seems to suggest in representing him, a bit dubiously, as civic-minded. This perception may derive at least partly from the recognition that Shylock is drawn as a character of exceptional power. Thus John Russell Brown observes that

> in performance Shylock is the dominating character of the play; none other has such emotional range, such continual development, such stature, force, subtlety, vitality; above all, none other has his intensity, isolation, and apparent depth of motivation.[4]

Brown's words attest the impact of what Moody and H. B. Charlton express as Shylock's humanity;[5] but this term also seems to imply a positive element in his makeup, an element boldly asserted in Goddard's declaration that "what is deep down in Shylock is precisely his goodness."[6]

I believe that, in their various ways, these perceptions of Shylock are valid. Yet the arguments supporting them are not entirely convincing. Those who would exculpate Shylock by likening him to the bad Christians encourage the skeptic to object that making the Christians bad cannot make Shylock good; as Girard admits in cautioning that "Shylock is rehabilitated only to the extent that the Christians are even worse than he is."[7] Even as he notes the power of Shylock's characterization, Brown fails to comprehend the function of that power in the drama, and thus is led to complain that Shylock's "dominance often does ill service to the play as a whole."[8] And while sensing a profound level of goodness in Shylock, Goddard identifies that goodness only as a yearning for acceptance,[9] a yearning not likely to impress those who see Shylock as evil and thus as deserving the contempt he endures. Rather than a villain because a victim, Shylock becomes for such critics as C. L. Barber, Frank Kermode, and Sylvan Barnet a victim of his own villainy.[10] And this view of Shylock, itself more or less explicitly informed by the negative attitude toward Jews prevailing in the sixteenth century, is reinforced by critics who emphasize the virulence of this attitude. To E. E. Stoll, Shylock's Jewishness is itself a "badge of opprobrium" associating him with Judas; add to this his identity as moneylender, and Shylock comes to embody "two of the deepest and most widely prevalent social antipathies of two thousand years."[11] G. K. Hunter similarly insists that Jewishness be historically understood as a morally corrupt condition "which rejected Christ and chose Barabbas, rejected the Saviour and chose the robber, rejected the spirit and chose the flesh, rejected the treasure that is in heaven and chose the treasure that is on earth."[12] And applying this view of Jewishness to Shylock, Alan Dessen sees him to exemplify the bad choice that Christians likewise make but should not.[13]

We cannot doubt that Stoll and Hunter accurately describe the accepted perception of Jews in Shakespeare's day. Nor can we doubt that this perception, including its darkest representation of Jews as deicides and cannibals, influences Shylock's characterization. What remains unclear is how this historically oriented perception can comport with the modern sense that, somehow, Shylock is good. To be sure, Girard would impugn the stereotypical aspects of Shylock's character by arguing that Shakespeare has put them into the play with the full intention of making them "an object of indignation and satire" comprehensible to "those who can be reached."[14] Girard thus sees Shakespeare as introducing an opposing current into his play, which he locates in the speeches of Shylock.[15] Yet rather than accounting for Shylock's perceived power and goodness, this satire merely relieves the badness of his historical traits by once again applying them to everyone. The insufficiency of Girard's analysis thus prompts us to consider that we will not succeed in justifying the sympathy that Shylock so often inspires until we can stop opposing his historical meaning to his modern meaning. And we will be able to end this opposition only by endowing Shylock with an original meaning that is positive, a meaning that gives strong evidence of being authorially intended and that redefines the basis for his perceived likeness to the Christians. In sum, we need to recover from the originally intended conception of Shylock a value that resonates with—and even refines—our own perception of him, thus bringing coherence to what Robert Weimann would call his "past significance" and his "present meaning."[16]

It is such a meaning, together with the meanings supporting it, that I will attempt to describe in the following pages. By complementing, adjusting, and extending the insights of previous interpreters, I propose to reveal the presence of a current in *Merchant* that contests Shylock's conventional badness in the very terms that have been seen to support it: the terms of Shakespeare's religious culture, which remains, if less authoritatively, our culture as well. From this religious culture Shakespeare will be shown to derive a positive meaning for Shylock's Jewishness and a similarly positive modification in the meaning of Antonio's Christianity. In deriving these meanings from the religious aspect of Shakespeare's culture, moreover, I depart from the recent critical tendency to define Shylock and Antonio with reference to their economic identities as usurer and merchant.[17] Rather, it seems to me that the economic identities of these antagonists subserve their more important identities as Jew and Christian. And this view of their identities leads me to address their conflict through the teachings of St. Paul rather than those of Karl Marx. Yet, as I shall argue, the ancillary character of economics in this play will be grasped only in the recognition that Shakespeare's use of it is not literal but symbolic, a possibility overlooked by those who focus their historical investigations of this play on its economics. Cohen, for example, may admit that approaching the play as a critique of British capitalism "fails even to account for all of the purely economic issues in the work; his purpose in this admission is to justify an investigation of the play's Venetian setting as the venue more nearly reflecting its opposition of Jewish fiscal capitalism to native mercantile capitalism.[18] Yet might we not alternatively refer to lack of precise realism in the play's economics to its function as the vehicle of a theological tenor? And would not such a function have the merit of integrating the play's economic and theological realms of meaning? My purpose in attempting this integration, however, is not to suggest that *Merchant* simply reflects received principles of religious orthodoxy; rather, it is to show how the distinctions that Shakespeare expresses through money present a formidable if highly constructive challenge to theological tenets engaged by the play.

The meanings I want to develop present Shylock not as a symbol of what Christianity negates, but rather as the symbolic source of its most treasured gift of salvation. But thus to redefine Shylock is by no means to regard him as free of defect or even as the play's main enunciator of this meaning. No doubt, he has morally compelling moments. Yet Shylock will be seen as contending with Antonio in a quarrel that is itself subject to censure, this censure tainting both antagonists. This censure has been partly discerned in the marginal dialogue between Launcelot and Old Gobbo in II.ii, which I shall further explore as an allegorical representation of the religious conflict represented in Antonio and Shylock. I suggest that this seemingly unimportant dialogue presents us with an instance of a literary device that André Gide in 1893 called *mise en abyme,* a term originally pertaining to heraldry, where it denotes a small figure placed at the heart of an escutcheon and replicating in miniature the escutcheon itself. *Mise en abyme* has been defined as "any enclave entertaining a relation of similarity with the work which contains it."[19] In *Merchant,* it appears as an encoded dialogue wherein two minor characters repeat on a smaller scale the play's major conflict, and in so doing, give new definition to this conflict. Not only repeating and redefining this conflict, however, they also exhibit a way of resolving it that seems to challenge the validity of its actual outcome. If the II.ii dialogue can be convincingly shown to perform these reflexive and critical functions in the play, it will emerge as a powerful key to its interpretation.

Yet assuming that the Launcelot/Old Gobbo dialogue harbors symbolic meaning, why should we assume that this meaning can be identified? Partly, perhaps, because it is expressed in terms that are arguably objective in comprising well-known elements of Shakespeare's religious culture. For, as we shall see, Launcelot and Old Gobbo are invested with two biblical allusions, and these allusions accord them typological identities that they then, as I think, transfer to Antonio and Shylock. These typological identities will be shown to have two functions. They refer the antagonism between these major characters to hegemonic impulses in both their traditions, Christianity attempting to dominate and assimilate Judaism, while Judaism would comparably dominate the gentile world by withholding its spiritual riches from that world. But these same allusions also identify a basis for the interaction of these characters that is not hegemonic but relational, and this relational basis turns out to be allegorically familial: Shylock and Antonio assume the relationship of father and son. It is this relationship that can support the pervasive but inadequately argued approbations of Shylock cited above. The biblical character of his paternity accounts for Shylock's power and goodness, and his fatherhood to Antonio places his perceived likeness to Antonio in a positive light that validates both these characters equally. For while the play certainly invests paternity with a connotation of authority, it also balances the father's authority over the son with the father's dependence on the son. This balance enables the relationship of father and son to imply not the "either/or" logic of domination but rather the "both/and" logic of mutual affirmation. And this "both/and" logic effectively destroys the legitimacy of a Christian or Jewish identity based on hegemony.

It is the evolution of power relations into family relations that the II.ii dialogue will be shown to achieve. And it is by contrast with this achieved evolution that the settlement between Antonio and Shylock in IV.i will be recognized as minimal and abortive. Thus the meanings generated by the II.ii dialogue tend to support the opinion of those who, in defiance of its historical justification, have found this settlement disturbing and unsatisfactory. Most importantly, these meanings shed light on the disputed significance of Shylock's forced conversion by suggesting that the play itself condemns it. The effect of the moral reference secreted in this dialogue is thus to endow *Merchant* with a refreshing, even startling, air of modernity. Yet what authenticates this modernity is its historic derivation. For since this dialogue can originate only in Shakespeare himself, its opposing voice will be regarded as his own allegorical commentary on the religious quarrel he depicts in Shylock and Antonio. Indeed, the force of this commentary emerges in the observation that Shakespeare compounds its new and relevant meanings out of wholly traditional components, and thus demonstrates how a poet of high and principled imagination validates his culture by causing it to transcend itself. In being grasped through its mimetic origin, the moral relevance of this dialogue reveals the play as both mirror and lamp: "a product of the past," but also "a 'producer' of the future."[20]

I

Given what Mikhail Bakhtin has said about the carnivalesque in its various manifestations—the tendency of its crude and abusive laughter to annihilate the "epic image of the absolute past" by bringing it close for free and fearless investigation; its exploitation for this purpose of "an accidental and insignificant pretext"; its capacity to combine "an intense spirit of inquiry" with "a utopian fantasy"; and especially its use of the clown as the author's vehicle (though in this case not his own mask) for exposing "all that is vulgar and falsely stereotyped in human relationships"[21]—it is hardly surprising that Shakespeare locates his own critical and visionary engagement of ancient texts in the dialogue of Launcelot with Old Gobbo in II.ii. For here is a marginal dialogue that shows a young man, identified as clown, toying with his blind father in a manner both crude and cruel.[22] Mistakenly supposing that this dialogue has an entertaining rather than a testing function, interpreters have often been baffled by its degraded humor. Accordingly, they have repeatedly dismissed Launcelot as, for example, "the slenderest and most pointlessly fatuous of Shakespeare's clowns."[23] Yet the mere gratuitousness of Launcelot's jesting has also prompted the suspicion that his antics somehow inform the action of the play. Leo Rockas and Jan Lawson Hinely have aptly noticed that Launcelot's conflicted decision to flee Shylock in II.ii, taken immediately before this dialogue, anticipates Jessica's similarly conflicted decision to flee Shylock in II.iii.[24] And with daring insight, René Fortin has found this dialogue to constitute an allegorical comment on the play's religious conflict, this comment providing a "counterstatement to the major allegorical statement of the play" that offers to correct "the one-sidedness and reductiveness of interpretation that the naive allegory invites."[25] In his view of this dialogue, Fortin uncovers important meanings; yet he only begins to mine them, his thesis thus begging the clarification and extension that this study will attempt to supply. To do this, however, requires that we first appreciate the importance of Fortin's thesis in light of the studies that inform it, particularly those of Dorothy Hockey and Barbara Lewalski.[26]

Like Henley before her,[27] Hockey discerns a biblical persona lurking within this dialogue, a persona referring not to Launcelot but rather to Old Gobbo. This old father is seen to embody the Old Testament figure of Isaac: more precisely, the Isaac of Genesis xxvii, where the patriarch is similarly old and blind, and where his son Jacob, guided by the instructions of his mother, deceives his father into granting him his blessing.[28] Hockey's observation suggests that Old Gobbo is conceived as an allegorical representation, or type, of Isaac. And because this representation is presumably intended and therefore serious, Hockey attempts to interpret it by suggesting that it refers to the characterization of Shylock. For, as she notices, Shylock likewise invokes Genesis xxvii.[29]

This Jacob from our holy Abram was
(As his wise mother wrought in his behalf)
The third possessor; ay, he was the third

—(I.iii.72-74)[30]

Hockey's guess assigns a meaning to the otherwise vacuous character of Old Gobbo. But what gives that meaning dramatic significance is its ability to suggest that Old Gobbo typifies Isaac in order to project this biblical identity onto Shylock: that is, in order to make Shylock himself a type of Isaac. And a further parallel between Old Gobbo and Shylock emerges in the suffering of derisive cruelty by them both, this parallel suggesting that Old Gobbo's suffering may likewise be meant to inform the suffering of Shylock. If this is so, it means that the disturbing effect of this dialogue is entirely deliberate, its lucid cruelty ultimately referring to Shylock in his typological identity as Isaac and somehow linking that identity with his suffering.

Yet if Shakespeare is really using Old Gobbo to project the identity of Isaac onto Shylock, he is proceeding in a manner conspicuously oblique, especially when we observe that Isaac is named neither by Old Gobbo who represents him nor by Shylock who alludes to him. And why Shakespeare should find it desirable to mediate the connection between these characters through an allusion itself veiled will emerge in the tendency of Old Gobbo's Isaac to draw in a further typological identity anchored in Launcelot, an identity whose still more obscured lineaments may well answer to the subversive nature of the meanings it will be shown to suggest. Before addressing this identity, however, we ought first to consider what the presence of Isaac in Shylock can mean; and doing this entails acknowledging Lewalski's understanding of Shylock. In a view shared by a number of interpreters but best developed by herself, Lewalski regards *Merchant* as informed by the dichotomies of Pauline theology, in which Judaism affirms the works and justice of law in opposition to the unearned mercy or grace of Christian faith.[31] This Pauline view of Judaism is what Lewalski finds Shylock to express, his individuality being subordinated to his symbolic representation of Judaism itself.[32] Moreover, as Lewalski reposes the justice of Jewish law in Shylock, she likewise reposes the grace of Christian faith in Antonio, by allegorizing him as "the very embodiment of Christian love," whose readiness to pay Bassanio's debt assigns him "the role of Christ satisfying the claim of Divine Justice by assuming the sins of mankind."[33] And reinforcing the play's involvement of Pauline theology is Lewalski's observation that the dénouement of the conflict between Shylock and Antonio enacts Paul's critique of Jewish law. Paul insists that, like a schoolmaster whose lessons are designed to render him superfluous, law obviates itself by instructing its followers that it does not save, but rather condemns them. Shylock similarly finds that the law he has adduced for his vindication in fact confutes him, as his astonished "Is that the law?" (IV.i.314) suggests[34]; and by identifying him as alien, law ends by condemning him. Thus Shylock's conflict with Antonio is found to dramatize "the confrontation of Judaism and Christianity as theological systems," with Shylock's eventual subjection to Antonio and forced conversion to Christianity expressing the supersession of Judaism as the religion of law by Christianity as the religion of faith.[35]

The pertinence of the biblical Isaac to this view of Shylock emerges in the ability of this figure to reflect Paul's explanation of why Judaism should of right be superseded. For the age and blindness that Isaac exhibits in Genesis xxvii are the very defects that Paul imputes to Judaism in presenting it as outworn. As "the ministration of death" which "is done away" (II Corinthian iii.7)[36] the dispensation of Moses is old, its law of works contrasting with the "Law of faith" (Romans iii.27), as "the oldenes of the letter" with the "newnes of Spirit" (Romans vii.6) and "newnes of life" (Romans vi.4). Paul also teaches that the old and outwardly literal meaning of Scripture is carnal, whereas its inwardly symbolic essence is spiritual; and that adherents to the Old Law of Judaism apprehend only the carnally literal meaning of Scripture and so are blind to its spiritual essence: God has given them "eyes that they shulde not se" (Romans xi.8); "The vaile is layed over their hearts" (II Corinthians iii.15). Thus Paul imputes a carnal unwisdom to Judaism, which he represents as blindness, this carnal unwisdom being what Isaac's blindness enables him to express. And the credibility of these Pauline meanings in Isaac is enhanced by their availability to Shakespeare in Calvin's *Commentary on Genesis*. Calvin here sees Isaac's physical blindness as a trope for the unwisdom or psychic blindness that causes him to prefer his elder son Esau above his younger and more deserving son Jacob: "With a blind, or, at least, a most inconsiderate love to his first-born, he [Isaac] undervalued the younger."[37] And further attesting his Pauline understanding of Isaac's blindness, Calvin notes its connection with his carnality: Isaac was "so enslaved to the indulgence of the palate" that he was "induced to give his preference to Esau, by the taste of his venison."[38] But most significantly, Calvin makes Isaac symbolic of the Jews: "Let the Jews now go and glory in the flesh; since Isaac, preferring food to the inheritance destined for his son, would pervert . . . the gratuitous covenant of God!"[39] Possibly instructed by Calvin, Shakespeare seems to be giving Isaac the same meaning that Calvin gives him.

Thus a typological perception of Old Gobbo seems to ramify into further allegorical associations that intensify the theological suggestiveness of Shylock. Old Gobbo transfers his identity as Isaac to Shylock. But to the extent that Shylock himself can be viewed as symbolic of Judaism, the Isaac in Shylock allegorizes his Judaism as old, carnal, and blind. Yet the allegorical significance of Isaac becomes still more specific when we pause to observe that Genesis xxvii presents a father-son drama. If the Isaac in this text allegorizes Judaism, he also expresses fatherhood, a theme of *Merchant* that is primarily exhibited in both Old Gobbo and Shylock. And though the non-Jewish Old Gobbo cannot himself relate Isaac's paternity to his Jewishness, these qualities are subtly linked in Shylock, whom

Lorenzo calls "father Jew" (II.vi.25),[40] thereby expressing Shylock's paternity as a function of his Jewishness. Thus in addition to being old, carnal, and blind, Judaism in Isaac emerges as paternal. And not adventitiously. For the carnal unwisdom of Isaac's blindness pertains to his paternity in preventing him from recognizing his son, Jacob. It is likewise a father-son drama that Old Gobbo and Launcelot present. And this same carnal unwisdom of father Isaac in failing to recognize his son Jacob is what blind Old Gobbo will be seen to exhibit in his own inability to recognize his son Launcelot. Yet if Old Gobbo's function is to apply the paternity of Isaac to Shylock, the carnal blindness of that paternity may plausibly pertain to him as well: Shylock too may have a son he cannot recognize; that is to say, a child other than Jessica, whom Shylock recognizes perfectly well. Carnal like Isaac, Shylock can be seen to recognize Jessica, because she is his carnal or biological daughter—Shylock calls her "My own flesh and blood" (III.i.34). But if Jessica's daughterhood is recognized because it is biological or carnal, this sonhood may well remain unrecognized because it is not carnal but rather spiritual: the same spiritual sonhood that Paul accords those whose faith in the redemption promised by God to Abraham makes them children of that promise and Abraham's true seed: "Nether are thei all children, because thei are the sede of Abraham: . . . That is, they which are the children of the flesh, are not the children of God: but the children of the promes are counted for the sede" (Romans ix.7-8). Paul thus identifies a spiritual as well as a carnal mode of sonhood; indeed, preferring the sonhood of the spiritual promise to the sonhood of the flesh. And since the play incorporates other cardinal tenets of Pauline theology, it is plausible to suspect that it incorporates this tenet as well, its involvement enabling Shakespeare to make Shylock father to an unrecognizably spiritual son. Yet not only hidden from Shylock, this son is also hidden from us, his hiddenness impelling us to ask if he really exists and thus obliging us to test for his existence. How might we do this? Perhaps by pursuing the suspicion that the identification of this son ought to parallel the recognition of Old Gobbo's association with Shylock. Just as Old Gobbo refers to Shylock, so Launcelot may be expected to refer to this son. And as Old Gobbo's reference to Shylock is veiled, emerging only through the mediating figure of Isaac that he typifies, so we can expect that the character to which Launcelot hypothetically refers will similarly resist identification until we discover a biblical figure that Launcelot likewise typifies. Does the play provide such a figure?

It would appear to in the biblical character of Jacob. For just as Launcelot is son to Old Gobbo, Jacob is son to Isaac. And Launcelot clearly invokes the Jacob of Genesis xxvii by twice asking Old Gobbo for his blessing: "Give me your blessing" (II.ii.78, 84). Moreover, by noting that Paul's Epistle to the Romans ix.6-13 represents Jacob's achievement of his elder brother Esau's blessing as symbolic of Christianity's supersession of Judaism, Fortin suggests that, even as an Old Testament figure, Jacob invokes sonhood as Christian;[41] just as Isaac represents paternity as Jewish. Thus in causing Old Gobbo and Launcelot to typify Isaac and Jacob, Shakespeare is said by Fortin to be placing Judaism and Christianity in the relation of father and son, an idea that Lewalski likewise entertains in finding the converted Jessica's relation to her Jewish father to express the filial relation of Christianity to Judaism.[42] It is, however, the failure of this father-son relationship that Fortin sees the II.ii dialogue to express, since he finds this relationship so represented as to require the paternal recognition that is lacking in Old Gobbo and the filial piety that is lacking in Launcelot.[43]

I think that Fortin has discerned the broad meaning of this dialogue. Yet a problem remains. For while Launcelot's pursuit of his father's blessing can be seen to invoke Jacob, his Jacob seems, in the absence of a fraternal rival, to lack the specifically Pauline connotation that the carnal unwisdom of Old Gobbo, by contrast, imparts to his Isaac. Though the Isaac in Old Gobbo bears a suggestion of Judaism, the Jacob in Launcelot need not, in the absence of further evidence, bear a corresponding suggestion of Christianity. Thus, as it is, Fortin's thesis cannot be sustained. Still, the insufficiency of its defense need not suggest that Fortin's insight is invalid but only that it requires better substantiation. And this possibility prompts me to suspect that if Jacob does not sustain Fortin's thesis, it may be because the identity we are looking for is not primarily Jacob but rather some other figure that is likewise provided by the play. This hunch is reinforced, moreover, by the recognition that Launcelot's cruelty to his father is unaccounted for by the Isaac story, where Jacob deceives his father at his mother's command but certainly does not torment him. While imitating the behavior of Jacob, Launcelot also exhibits behavior unlike that of Jacob. And just as the figure of Jacob cannot account for all that Launcelot does, so Isaac cannot entirely account for the behaviors of Old Gobbo, especially his suffering and eventual recognition of his son. These unaccounted for details suggest that in addition to the Isaac story, which is certainly present, a second model may be involved in the Launcelot/Old Gobbo dialogue, a model that theologizes Launcelot in his cruelty just as the Genesis xxvii model theologizes Old Gobbo in his blindness. If an Old Testament model defines blindness as both paternal and Jewish, we may expect this second model to be likewise biblical but drawn from the New Testament and defining cruelty as both filial and Christian.

Suggestively, the play appears to contain a filial model of New Testament provenance in its allusions to prodigality. In I.i we hear Bassanio describe his habit of living past his "faint means" as making his time "something too prodigal" (I.i.125, 129); and Shylock likewise calls Bassanio "The prodigal Christian" (II.v.15). Not limited to Bassanio, however, this trait is also ascribed to Antonio: once obliquely in I.iii.21, where Shylock refers to his ventures as "squand'red abroad," and again, more directly in III.i.45, where Shylock calls him "a prodigal" in the course of comparing him to the daughter who has fled with his wealth and squandered it. These allusions appear to invoke the story of the Prodigal Son in Luke xv. And these invocations are reinforced by the play's extended reference to this story in II.vi, a reference apparently directed at Jessica in immediately preceding the elopement that makes her a Christian. Might the Prodigal Son be the identity we are seeking? It seems probable. For, as we shall see, there is evidence to suggest that the sixteenth century understood this son to symbolize the Gentiles or Christians, it being this understanding that Shylock reflects in his reference to Bassanio as "The prodigal Christian." And notwithstanding David N. Beauregard's view of prodigality as expressing extreme liberality,[44] much as Barnet earlier takes it to express Christian generosity,[45] we may recall that the original Prodigal's way with money has nothing to do with generosity, extreme or otherwise, and everything to do with the profligacy sequent to his rebellion against his father. Moisan, indeed, recognizes that the play invokes this term in its biblical sense of profligacy, while also considering that this meaning commands the recognition of Shakespeare's audience.[46] And supporting Moisan's opinion is Bassanio's characterization of his "something too prodigal" time as making him "a willful youth" who wastes and loses another's money; "and like a willful youth, / That which I owe is lost" (I.i.146-47). In this confession, Bassanio becomes one of those high-born prodigals that Moisan finds repeatedly censured in anti-usury tracts of the period such as *The Death of Usury* (1594): those idle borrowers who sought loans in order "to consume in prodigall maner, in bravery, banketting, voluptuous living, & such like."[47] Yet in thus referring the censure of prodigality to the wasteful use of money not one's own, Moisan neglects other implications of this biblical term that the play may also be adducing: those nuances of rebellious flight and cruelty that are preeminent in Launcelot. For just as the Prodigal runs away from his father in an act of rebellion, so we meet Launcelot in the rebellious act of running away from Shylock. And just as the Prodigal's running away becomes an act of cruelty in making his father think him dead, so Launcelot exhibits cruelty in making *his* father think him dead. It thus becomes plausible to regard the rebellious flight and cruelty of Launcelot as enabling him to typify Luke's Prodigal Son,[48] just as Old Gobbo's blind nonrecognition of his son enables him to typify Isaac.

But if Old Gobbo projects his Isaac onto Shylock, who is the character upon whom Launcelot projects the identity of the Prodigal Son? As Launcelot is cruel, we can expect that the character he refers to will likewise be cruel. Suggestively, two of the characters verbally associated with prodigality demonstrate cruelty to Shylock in a manner evocative of Luke's Prodigal. The first is Jessica, who, like the Prodigal, takes her father's money, runs away from him, beggars herself, and causes her father, if not to think her dead, to wish her dead, in effect declaring her dead to him. Yet though fascinating and complex in her prodigality, and strongly associated with Launcelot, Jessica cannot be the character we are seeking, because she is both a biological and a recognized child. Besides Jessica, however, there is Antonio, who treats Shylock with contempt, this contempt resonating with the contempt that Launcelot likewise directs toward Shylock. And linked with Antonio's contempt is his demand to borrow Shylock's money, which enables him to invoke the Prodigal's demand for his father's money. Moreover, as the money demanded by the Prodigal facilitates the flight that repudiates and, in that sense, kills his own sonhood, so in the money he borrows from Shylock, Antonio actively abets Shylock's desire to kill him. These resemblances permit us to suspect that Antonio is the ultimate and hidden referent of Launcelot's prodigal sonhood. Just as the Gentiles are not the literal, biological children of the Jewish patriarch Abraham, and yet remain his symbolically spiritual children; so the gentile Antonio, while certainly not a literal, biological child of Shylock, may remain, in a realm of dramatic meaning restrictedly allegorical, the symbolically spiritual child of Shylock, the play's Jewish father, who invokes "holy Abram" and "father Abram" (I.iii.72, 160). And just as Shylock's psychic blindness comments on the Judaism he represents, so Antonio's prodigality can be seen to comment on the Christianity he represents. It may be the Christian cruelty of Antonio to Shylock in I.iii that Launcelot glosses as prodigal in II.ii, the prodigal representation of this cruelty turning its carnivalesque ridicule into an object of our ridicule. As exhibited in Launcelot, Antonio's contempt for Shylock can have no suggestion of revolutionary glamour; for, like Jack Cade of *2 Henry VI* as well as Stephano and Trinculo of *The Tempest*, Launcelot rebels not against the system so much as against his place in it, his desire being to supplant his father's authority with his own,[49] as we shall see.

Against such a thesis one could, of course, object that, in being motivated by Shylock's usury, Antonio's cruelty should be able to resist the charge of prodigality. For as a monitory practice denounced by the Church, usury can be honorably detested by Antonio for transgressing his Christian ethic. Yet such an exoneration is complicated by the curious tendency of money to supplant religion itself as a motive for hatred between Shylock and Antonio. While hating Antonio as Christian, Shylock hates him even more for the losses he sustains in Antonio's refusal to practice usury:

> I hate him for he is a Christian;
> But more, for that in low simplicity
> He lends out money gratis, and brings down
> The rate of usance here with us in Venice.
>
> (I.iii.41-45)

And with suggestive equivalence, Antonio "hates" Shylock's "sacred nation" but more vigorously "rails" against his usury:

> He hates our sacred nation, and he rails
> Even there where merchants most do congregate
> On me, my bargains, and my well-won thrift,
> Which he calls interest.
>
> (I.iii.48-51)

These emphases might well be taken to suggest that the religious conflict Shylock describes functions merely as the false consciousness of a conflict that is really economic.[50] Yet it also seems appropriate to observe that money can itself bear a spiritual meaning, as in Paul's references to divine grace as "the riches of [God's] bountifulnes" (Romans ii.4) and "the riches of his glorie" (Romans ix.23).[51] Thus while money can express a negative worldliness, as it certainly does in Marlowe's *Jew of Malta*,[52] Paul's words suggest that money can also be made to symbolize divine grace.[53] And the pertinence of this meaning to *Merchant* is suggested by the observation that Paul constitutes the riches of God's bountifulness in the blessing given by God to Abraham: the same blessing that Shylock in his I.iii defense of usury invokes as the possession lineally descending to Jacob from "our holy Abram" (I.iii.72). The association of money with blessing by both Paul and Shakespeare's character suggests to me that money in *Merchant* symbolizes this very blessing, the blessing of Abraham. Yet my intention in making this equivalence is hardly to ignore the play's negative portrayal of the money gained through usury, it is to explore the negative portrayal of usury for its own symbolic meaning. And this meaning will emerge in the interpretation of usury as symbolic of the Jews' claim to Abraham's blessing through a biological mode of inheritance that reserves that blessing exclusively to themselves. It is usury in its representation of this restrictedly Jewish blessing that can account for Antonio's detestation of it as well as his abuse of Shylock for practicing it, because the Christian Antonio claims this same blessing. Thus a theological competitiveness can be seen to inform the issue of money in this play. And by appreciating the theological resonance of this money, we can see that its Jewish grasping and Christian giving are not ultimate values but rather subserve the protagonists' differing needs. Shylock, the "rich Jew" (V.i.292), has the blessing and wants to keep it, so he favors grasping; the gentile Antonio needs this blessing and wants Shylock to give it to him, so he favors giving. Yet the one-sidedness of these values also distorts then, their distortion accounting for the representation of their exponents as blind and prodigal. Blind to the identity of Antonio as his spiritual son, Shylock, like father Isaac, would graspingly deny him the blessing of his wealth; while as Prodigal Son, Antonio demands the giving of Shylock's wealth in contemptuous repudiation of his carnal paternity.

To be sure, a still more problematical aspect of this thesis lies in its assertion of a relationship between Shylock and Antonio that lacks a literal basis in the text. Yet by invoking a theology that provides for a spiritual concept of sonhood, this thesis may mitigate if not solve the problem it raises. And further atoning for the allegorical character of this thesis is its usefulness in clarifying a number of critical perceptions about the play. By providing the play with typological identities that are relatively stable, it reinforces the conviction of Lewalski as well as Nevill Coghill, Kermode, John Cooper, Albert Wertheim, Norman Holland, Leslie Fiedler, Lawrence Danson, and to a lesser extent, Barber[54] that the conflict between Shylock and Antonio is religious. In postulating a symbolic view of money, this thesis dissolves the tension that Moody and Norman Rabkin see to trouble the play's ultimate enrichment of the Christians with the pelf that they have hated Shylock for possessing.[55] And in making money symbolic of Abraham's blessing, it reinforces John Coolidge's understanding of the conflict in *Merchant* as a struggle for possession of the Hebrew Scriptures that contain this blessing, a struggle that the Church conducted through the hermeneutics of its *adversos Judaeos* tradition.[56] This is the tradition that both Calvin and Shakespeare engage in their treatment of Isaac's blindness; and that Shakespeare appears, however surprisingly, to be adapting to his treatment of prodigality as well.

These typological references may also help to dispel some theoretical doubts regarding the play's interpretability by resolving discrepancies that Rabkin has observed between the meanings that the play tempts us to formulate and the nuanced responses that its experience demands. Identifying meaning as the product of intellection, Rabkin argues that an adequate definition of the play's meaning is not attainable because "all intellection is reductive": "the closer an intellectual system comes to full internal consistency and universality of application . . . the more obvious become the exclusiveness of its value," its "summary thematic statements" suppressing our "aesthetic experience."[57] To support this view, Rabkin observes in part that critical formulations of the play's meaning are beset with disagreement.[58] Yet in extending to the question of whether Shylock or Antonio is the more deserving of blame, this disagreement may be obviated by the tendency of their typological identities to validate detractors of them both. Because their blindness and prodigality make them both wrong, the censure of them both can be right. Beyond showing us how both these characters are wrong, however, these biblical allusions also show how they are also both right, as Coghill perceives in finding that the Old Law and the New Law lodged in these antagonists are "both inherently right."[59] For in also defining them as father and son, these typological identities refer the self-identity of each to the other, the father being father by virtue of the son and the son being son in having a father. Their relationship thus emerges as one of mutual dependency, which requires each to validate the other. And this shared validity can be seen to sustain the critical praise they have both received. The paternal and filial essences of these antagonists prevent their respective defenders from contradicting one another.

Moreover, by seeing that their defects of blindness and prodigality make them both wrong while their relationship as father and son makes them both right, we can see why the judgments they elicit from critics often exhibit the tentativeness, the backing and filling, the saying and unsaying that Rabkin has appropriately noticed.[60] Thus Barnet can declare Shylock to be "a hardhearted, self-regarding diabolical figure," while also admitting that "we powerfully feel his claim."[61] Similarly attesting that *Merchant* is not an "easy" play by the apparent design of its author, Brown observes that he so presents Shylock's "devilish motivation" and "inhuman demands" as to encourage his audience to sympathize with them.[62] And just as the play mitigates the evil of Shylock, so it impugns the goodness of Antonio, as Joan Ozark Holmer and Danson suggest in faulting his Christian failure to love his enemy Shylock.[63] Most importantly, however, the representation of these antagonists as both wrong and right prompts us to see what is wrong with them as vitiating what is right in them and thus as thwarting what should be a relationship of mutuality. As the source of their discord, then, the blindness and prodigality evinced by these characters become the objects of Shakespeare's censure and not the characters themselves. In Launcelot and Old Gobbo, moreover, these defects are largely surmounted, when Launcelot repents his cruelty to his father and Old Gobbo recognizes and blesses his son. Thus, as before suggested, Launcelot and Old Gobbo in II.ii seem to assume a paradigmatic function that renders their reconciliation prescriptive of a proper reconciliation between Antonio and Shylock. Yet while laying down this prescription, Shakespeare does not defy the realities of his world by having his antagonists fulfill it. Shylock's blindness is not lifted; rather, he is forced to bless Antonio with his symbolic money while remaining blind to his identity; and Antonio's prodigality seems to be reduced in one way, only to be maintained in another; specifically in his demand for Shylock's conversion, as we shall see.

Finally, recognizing the biblical character of Shylock's paternity can give us a surer sense of the play's tonality. For to the extent that this identity is derived from the Bible, it is not derived from New Comedy, and this means that Shylock is not a properly abandoned *senex* with whom we unaccountably sympathize, but rather a father whose dignity justly indicts the discontent and ensuing elopement of his daughter. Thus Shylock's biblical paternity lends support to those who deny that the tone of this play is romantic.[64] And since a romantic conception of the play is what impels critics to complain that Shylock's prominence impairs "the play as a whole" or raises "an interest beyond its resign,"[65] dispelling that conception also obviates the need for these complaints.

II

Yet before attempting to demonstrate how these meanings flow from the typological identities of Isaac and the Prodigal Son, I need to assure the reader by textual evidence that these identities exist in II.ii; and that they are there imposed on Launcelot and Old Gobbo in order to be transferred to Shylock and Antonio. Fortunately, a number of parallels suggesting the presence of blind Isaac in Old Gobbo have already been adduced by Hockey,[66] and need only to be restated and reinforced. Just as Genesis xxvii begins by telling us that Isaac "was olde," so Shakespeare calls Launcelot's father Old Gobbo. In Isaac, blindness is a defect of age: Isaac "was olde, & his eies were dimme so that he colde not se" (Genesis xxvii.1); similarly, Old Gobbo is "more than sand-blind, high gravel-blind" (II.ii.36-37) which means that his eyes are not only dim but that he cannot see. Isaac's blindness makes him unable to recognize his son Jacob: "For he knewe him not" (Genesis xxvii.23). Correspondingly, Launcelot associates his father's blindness with nonrecognition of his filial self: "O heavens, this is my true-begotten father, who being more than sand-blind, high gravel-blind, knows me not" (II.ii.35-37). And just as Isaac's blindness is symbolic of his unwisdom, so Launcelot imputes unwisdom to Old Gobbo's blindness by saucily reversing the proverb regarding the wise child's ability to know his own father: "Nay, indeed if you had your eyes you might fail of the knowing me; it is a wise father that knows his own child" (II.ii.75-77).[67] Isaac's blind unwisdom is characterized as carnal in being focused on food, as he shows in telling his favored son, Esau, to "make me savourie meat, such as I love, and bring it to me that I maie eat, and . . . my soule maie blesse thee, before I dye" (Genesis xxvii.4); Launcelot ascribes a lecherous carnality to his father, which he describes in terms of cooking and eating: "For indeed my father did something smack, something grow to, he had a kind of taste" (II.ii.16-18). Genesis xxvii focuses on the blessing of Abraham, Jacob asking his father to "eat of my venison, that thy soule maie blesse me" (Genesis xxvii.19); Launcelot twice asks Old Gobbo, "Give me your blessing" (II.ii.78, 84). Even as it accounts for his unwillingness to bless Jacob, Isaac's carnal blindness enables Jacob's mother to coerce him into blessing Jacob by disguising him as the hairy Esau: "And she covered his hands and the smothe of his necke with the skinnes of the kyds of the goates" (Genesis xxvii.16). Thus deceived by his blindness, Isaac mistakenly but properly blesses Jacob: "For he knewe him not, because his handes were rough as his brother Esaus handes; wherefore he blessed him" (Genesis xxvii.23). Insolently presenting the back of his head to his father,[68] Launcelot causes the old man's blessing hands to mistake his head for his face and thus to think his face much hairier than it is: "Lord worshipp'd might he be, what a beard hast thou got! Thou hast got more hair on thy chin that Dobbin my fill-horse has on his tail" (II.ii.93-95). And if Jacob's "wise mother" plays a part in securing his blessing, Launcelot's identification of his mother helps induce Old Gobbo to bless him: "I am sure Margery your wife is my mother" (II.ii.89-90); to which the old father replies: "Her name is Margery indeed. I'll be sworn, if thou be Launcelot, thou art mine own flesh and blood" (II.ii.91-93).

But while invoked by Old Gobbo who is not Jewish, Isaac seems to describe Shylock who is. By his own admission, Shylock too is "old" (II.v.2). In offering Antonio a bond of flesh, he shows his law to exhibit the carnality appropriate to its Jewishness. And to the extent that blindness symbolizes unwisdom Shylock's psychic blindness to Antonio as his spiritual son may be the unwisdom that Launcelot adduces, when he observes of his father, "Nay, indeed if you had your eyes you might fail of the knowing me; it is a wise father that knows his own child." Just as Isaac's carnal blindness requires Jacob's "wise mother" to deceive Isaac into blessing him, so Shylock's blindness to his son

Antonio requires another wise woman, Portia, to trick Shylock into endowing him with his blessing-symbolizing wealth.

Yet if Launcelot's pursuit of his father's blessing identifies him as Jacob, his running away from Shylock bears a different emphasis:

> Certainly my conscience will serve me to run from this Jew my master. The fiend is at mine elbow and tempts me, saying to me, "[Gobbo], Launcelot [Gobbo], good Launcelot," or "good [Gobbo], or "good Launcelot [Gobbo], use your legs, take the start, run away." My conscience says, "No; take heed, honest Launcelot, take heed, honest [Gobbo]," or as aforesaid, "honest Launcelot [Gobbo], do not run, scorn running with thy heels." Well, the most courageous fiend bids me pack. "Fia!" says the fiend; "away!" says the fiend; "for the heavens, rouse up a brave mind," says the fiend, "and run." Well, my conscience, hanging about the neck of my heart, says very wisely to me, "My honest friend Launcelot, . . . bouge not." "Bouge," says the fiend. "Bouge not," says my conscience. . . . To be rul'd by my conscience, I should stay with the Jew my master, who (God bless the mark) is a kind of devil; and to run away from the Jew, I should be rul'd by the fiend, who, saving your reverence, is the devil himself. Certainly the Jew is the very devil incarnation. . . . The fiend gives the more friendly counsel: I will run, fiend; my heels are at your commandment, I will run.
>
> (II.ii.1-32)

This speech depicts a psychic battle within Launcelot, a battle whose seriousness his flippant tone tries unsuccessfully to conceal. The fiend is prompting him to act on an impulse that his conscience is struggling to restrain. And the impulse that Launcelot's conscience would restrain is his desire to run away from Shylock, running away being variously alluded to seventeen times. Given the play's previous glances at prodigality, these insistent references to running away may well be inviting us to recall that Luke's Prodigal Son similarly "toke his journey into a farre countrey" where "he wasted his goods with riotous living" (Luke xv.13). So when Launcelot decides to run away from Shylock his master at the behest of the fiend, his action can plausibly acquire a prodigal connotation, especially in light of the association that II.ii will establish between master and father. But it also appears significant that, while decided, Launcelot's struggle is not resolved on the merits. By identifying his flight as prompted by the fiend, Launcelot recognizes that it is wrong. But Launcelot attempts to evade the wrongness of following the fiend's commandment by charging that Shylock too is "a kind of devil" and "the very devil incarnation."[69] In the absence of a valid reason for his defection. Launcelot demonizes Shylock, this demonization spuriously licensing his running away.

Despite its light tone, Launcelot's demonizing of Shylock seems loaded with a serious meaning that emerges in its connotation of contempt. In demonizing Shylock, Launcelot is obviously expressing contempt for him. And once recognized to express contempt, Launcelot's demonizing can be linked to the flight it licenses. For flight and contempt both express alienation, albeit in significantly different ways. Flight is an action and thus can be said to express alienation psychically or spiritually. Thus if the alienation of flight expresses prodigality, so too the alienation of contempt may express prodigality, the one expression being carnal while the other is spiritual. In their carnality and spirituality, moreover, Launcelot's two expressions of prodigal expressions of prodigal alienation assume an obviously Pauline connotation, the connotation of Pauline spirituality in Launcelot's contempt being enhanced by its verbal character. For it is by defining the blessing as a verbal promise that Paul makes it spiritual; just as he declares "faith preached" to be the way of receiving the "Spirit": "Received ye the Spirit by the workes of the Law, or by the hearing of faith preached?" (Galatians iii.2). But what makes these Pauline modes of prodigality significant is the observation that they are respectively displayed with great prominence by Jessica and Antonio. Like Launcelot, Jessica runs away from Shylock; and like Launcelot, Antonio treats him with contempt, in part, by calling him devil: "The devil can cite Scripture for his purpose" (I.iii.98). It thus becomes possible to suspect that the flight and contempt united in Launcelot associate him with both Jessica and Antonio in their respectively carnal and spiritual expressions of a common prodigality.

Further reinforcing Launcelot's association with Jessica and Antonio is his placement in the drama between these characters, Launcelot's prodigality in II.ii standing between Antonio's prodigality in I.iii and Jessica's prodigality in II.iii. This placement seems to enhance the ability of Launcelot to clarify the prodigality of Antonio. For it is by following and thus repeating the prodigality of Antonio that Launcelot can gloss that prodigality. But if Launcelot's prodigality follows that of Antonio, Jessica's prodigality follows that of Launcelot. And this suggests that just as Launcelot's situation enables him to comment on Antonio, Jessica's situation enables her to comment on Launcelot. Indeed, it would appear that if Launcelot's purpose is to comment on Antonio, it is Jessica that facilitates this purpose by clarifying prodigality in Launcelot. For Jessica expresses her prodigality in the physical action of flight, which is easily identified as prodigal, in contrast to contempt, which is relatively subtle. Thus an appreciation of how Launcelot's contempt identifies Antonio's contempt as prodigal should emerge from an appreciation of how Jessica's fight identifies Launcelot's flight as prodigal, it being Launcelot's flight that lends the connotation of prodigality to his contempt.

Jessica clarifies the prodigality of Launcelot's flight by repeating, and thus emphasizing, it in the next scene. But besides repeating Launcelot's flight, Jessica also repeats the thoughts and purposes attending it. In recognizing that shame for her lineage is a "heinous sin" (II.iii.16), Jessica exhibits the inner struggle that precedes Launcelot's flight. Like Launcelot, Jessica flees in order to "end [the] strife"

(II.iii.20) that cannot be resolved. And albeit subtly, Jessica preserves Launcelot's association of flight with demonizing contempt by referring to her father's house as "hell" (II.iii.2). As Launcelot's demonizing of Shylock reflects badly on himself, so in locating the hellishness of Shylock's house in its "tediousness" (II.iii.3), Jessica has been seen to betray the frivolity of her own nature.[70] Launcelot and Jessica also flee for the same prodigal purpose. Launcelot anticipates and gets the license of a fool in being given "a livery / More guarded than his fellows" (II.ii.154-55), and he expresses that license in "getting up of the Negro's belly" (III.v.38-39); Jessica leads a life of riot with Lorenzo. And besides repeating Launcelot's flight in its various aspects, Jessica further clarifies the prodigality of that flight by recasting it as a child's flight from a father.

In II.vi, moreover, Shakespeare all but explicitly identifies Jessica's flight as prodigal through Gratiano's extended allusion to the Prodigal Son. For in being delivered just before Jessica executes her flight, this allusion seems to point toward her:

> How like a younger or a prodigal
> The scarfed bark puts from her native bay,
> Hugg'd and embraced by the strumpet wind!
> How like the prodigal doth she return,
> With over-weather'd ribs and ragged sails,
> Lean, rent, and beggar'd by the strumpet wind!
>
> (II.vi.14-19)

Like Jessica, the "scarfed bark" is female. But this bark also seems to mediate between the behavior of the original Prodigal and Jessica. Like the Prodigal who takes his journey into a far country, the bark "puts from her native bay"; and like the bark, Jessica abandons her father's house, to journey abroad with Lorenzo. Like the lascivious Prodigal who "devoured [his father's] goods with harlots" (Luke xv.30), the bark is "Hugg'd and embraced by the strumpet wind"; and, like the embraced bark, Jessica is embraced by Lorenzo, who plays the harlot or "strumpet wind"; and like the bark, Jessica is beggared by her riot with Lorenzo.

Thus in II.vi, Shakespeare reinforces the prodigal character of the flight that Jessica clarifies in Launcelot, and Launcelot's flight, spiritualized into contempt, is what he clarifies in Antonio. Yet in mediating Jessica's prodigality to Antonio, Launcelot also orients these characters to each other; thus enabling us to regard them as the carnal and spiritual reflections of one another. As Jessica's flight acts out her contempt, Antonio's contempt emerges as a psychic flight from Shylock's strong claims against his conscience. As Jessica's flight becomes the recourse of an unresolved inner struggle, so the breakdown of Antonio's strained civility under the pressure of Shylock's arguments can likewise reflect an impasse in his own inner struggle.

Flight, however, is not the Prodigal's only behavior. For not only fleeing from his father, the Prodigal also demands his money: "And the yonger of them said to his father, Father, give me the portion of the goods that falleth to me. So he devided unto them his substance" (Luke xv.12). If the physicality of the Prodigal's flight suggests its carnality, the verbal character of his demand suggests its spirituality. And these distinctions become pertinent when we recall that both these prodigal behaviors are expressed in the play. If Jessica expresses the Prodigal carnally in her flight from Shylock, Antonio seems to express the Prodigal spiritually in his I.iii demand to borrow, or "have" (I.iii.116) Shylock's money. But one more complication obtains. For if, apart from the inherent spirituality of his demand, Antonio spiritualizes Jessica's flight into contempt, Jessica, apart from the carnality of her flight, may also be seen to carnalize Antonio's demand for Shylock's money by running away with Shylock's money. If Antonio spiritualizes what is carnal, Jessica carnalizes what is spiritual, these transformations enabling Jessica and Antonio to participate in both behaviors of the Prodigal, in both the taking of money and the flight that also appears as contempt. And this participation lends a moral significance to the observation that, even as he demands Shylock's money, Antonio treats him with contempt. His contemptuous demand for Shylock's money thus becomes a complex act of prodigality demonstrating his unworthiness to receive that money, as Shylock trenchantly observes:

> Signior Antonio, many a time and oft
> In the Rialto you have rated me
> About my moneys and my usances.
> Still have I borne it with a patient shrug
> (For suff'rance is the badge of all our tribe).
> You call me misbeliever, cut-throat dog,
> And spet upon my Jewish gaberdine,
> And all for use of that which is mine own.
> Well then, it now appears you need my help.
> Go to then, you come to me, and you say,
> "Shylock, we would have moneys," you say so—
> You, that did void your rheum upon my beard,
> And foot me as you spurn a stranger cur
> Over your threshold; moneys is your suit.
>
> (I.iii.106-19)

Once grasping a symbolic dimension in Shylock's "moneys," we begin to recognize a meaning in his indignant words that transcends the realm of economics. Rather than the usually cited speeches of III.i and IV.i, these words of Shylock address the theological core of his claim against Antonio, a claim whose merit, while not perfect, is reinforced by Antonio's defiant retort:

> I am as like to call thee so again,
> To spet on thee again, to spurn thee too.
> If thou wilt lend this money, lend it not
> As to thy friends, for when did friendship take
> A breed for barren metal of his friend?
>
> (I.iii.130-34)

Not only churlish, however, Antonio's prodigal demand for Shylock's money assumes a further and darker implication emerging from its suggestive parallel with Jessica's absconding from Shylock. For in running away with her father's money, Jessica commits physical, literal theft. Thus to the extent that Jessica's flight expresses physically what Antonio's contempt expresses spiritually, it may effectively accuse Antonio of an alternatively spiritual form of theft. In short, Shakespeare may be ascribing theft to prodigality in both Jessica and Antonio, thus giving point to Shylock's monitory observation to Antonio that "thrift is blessing, if men steal it not" (I.iii.90). And Shakespeare seems to be establishing this guilty equality between Jessica and Antonio with the view to establishing a further equality in guilt between Antonio and Shylock. For in being understood as theft from Shylock, Antonio's contemptuous demand assumes a likeness to Shylock's usury, which was understood as a legal form of theft,[71] a theft that Shylock at first intends to practice against Antonio. Further evidence for the view of Antonio's demand as theft will emerge in the discussion of how the text provides for a symbolic understanding of money as Abraham's blessing. What we need to notice now is that both the money stolen by Jessica and demanded by Antonio is lost, its loss in both cases invoking the Prodigal's loss of his father's money. If Jessica squanders Shylock's ducats in riot with Lorenzo, the ventures out of which Antonio is to repay Shylock's loan are analogously and therefore prodigally "squand'red abroad." As with Bassanio's self-referred observation that "like a willful youth, / That which I owe is lost," Antonio loses what he owes Shylock. But it is Shylock himself who most clearly and overtly identifies the bankrupt Antonio as prodigal by comparing him to his own profligate daughter: "There I have another bad match. A bankrout, a prodigal, who dare scarce show his head on the Rialto; a beggar, . . . " (III.i.44-46). Just as Jessica's riot reduces her to beggary, so Antonio's losses reduce him in III.iii to begging Shylock for his life. And the lost gains of Jessica and Antonio are what Launcelot will likewise be seen to anticipate in II.ii by seeking the paternal blessing that money symbolizes in a manner conducting to its loss.

III

The obviously subversive implication of thus defining the play's representatively Christian character as prodigal may go far toward explaining why Shakespeare presents this definition in so veiled and oblique a manner. He could not prudently express such a meaning in any other way. Yet prudence may not be the only cause of its obscurity. Further impeding a recognition of Antonio's prodigality is the presence in Launcelot and Old Gobbo of more than one biblical persona. For the allusions to Isaac and the Prodigal Son draw in their own stories, both of which are told simultaneously. And each of these stories contains a father and a son. So by telling both of them at once, Shakespeare endows his dialogue with two fathers and two sons, Old Gobbo primarily representing the blind Isaac but also the suffering father of the Prodigal; while Launcelot primarily represents the Prodigal Son but also Jacob, the fusing of the Prodigal Son with Jacob supporting Fortin's sense of Jacob in this play as a Pauline expression of Christianity. The conflation can account for the puzzling linkage of Old Gobbo's Isaac with his suffering, that suffering pertaining to his identity as father of the Prodigal. It can also account for Launcelot's ability to associate his prodigal flight from Shylock with a request for his father's blessing that, besides resonating with the Prodigal's request, is Jacob-like in its deceitful withholding of his identity; just as Jacob hides his identity from *his* father. Yet while doubtlessly troublesome, this doubling is probably not capricious. For attention to the characteristics of the dialogue's two fathers can reveal them as supplying one another's deficiencies, just as the two sons seem similarly to supply one another's deficiencies. If Isaac is blind, the father of the Prodigal can see and recognize his son; if the Prodigal's father suffers under the impiety of his son, Isaac does not so suffer. If the Prodigal is rebellious, Jacob is pious; but Jacob is also devious in his piety, whereas the Prodigal is honest and forthright in his rebellion, just as Antonio is forthright in his hostility to Shylock. These mutually amending identities seem to anticipate a composite father who sees with joy and a composite son who candidly expresses piety, these composites being achieved by a purging away of the paternal defects of blindness and suffering and the filial defects of rebellion and deceit. But this is not all. For it is also important to notice that, in their rectification, these composites seem to coalesce into new typological identities, these identities being the father and son of the Prodigal's return. For that is the father who sees with joy: "And when he was yet a great way of, his father sawe him, and had compassion, and ran & fel on his necke, and kissed him" (Luke xv.20). And that is the son who candidly expresses repentant piety: "Father, I have sinned against heaven, and before thee, And am no more worthie to be called thy sone: make me as one of thy hired servants" (Luke xv.18-19). It is in these transformations that father and son express the redemptiveness of their mutual dependency, the father being blessed in the reclamation of his son and the son being blessed in his return to his father. And these typological transformations are what Launcelot and Old Gobbo achieve in their II.ii reconciliation.

It would thus appear that the powerfully moving scene of the Prodigal's return to his father is what Old Gobbo and Launcelot set forth as the, albeit unachieved, ideal of reconciliation between Shylock and Antonio as Jewish father and Christian son. Yet this scenario requires that the two fathers and two sons culminating in these redeemed identities pertain not only to Old Gobbo and Launcelot but also to Shylock and Antonio. In Shylock these fathers are relatively easy to spot. His blindness to his spiritual son and his suffering enable Shylock, like Old Gobbo, to represent both blind Isaac and the father of the Prodigal. Likewise, Antonio can be seen to reflect Launcelot's prodigal contempt, to which he adds a similarly prodigal demand to "have" Shylock's money. And as Launcelot is like Jacob in deceitfully hiding his filial identity from Old Gobbo, so Antonio refuses to acknowledge his filial relation to Shylock. But there is a deeper sense in which Antonio may express the deceit of Jacob. For Antonio demands Shylock's money not for himself but on behalf of his friend

Shylock, Antonio, Solanio, and the jailer in Act III, scene iii of The Merchant of Venice.

and also, as I shall suggest, by demanding his wealth not for another but, more honestly and knowingly, for himself.

Yet Shakespeare's ability to meld the fathers and sons invoked by these two texts is also enhanced by similarities in the texts themselves. For in dealing alike with a father and son as well as with a father's gift to his son, these texts can almost be seen as Old and New Testament versions of the same story. And further suggesting their similarity is the observation that the original form of both these stories includes a third character in an elder brother who vies with the younger for paternal favor and loses out, or sees himself as losing out, to the younger. But what seems the most important similarity in these fraternal conflicts is their susceptibility to analogously allegorical interpretations that are pertinent to Shakespeare's play. As earlier observed in Romans ix.6-13, Paul takes the conflict of Jacob with Esau to symbolize the conflict between Christianity and Judaism, the elder Esau representing Judaism, while the younger Jacob who displaces him represents Christianity. In the Prodigal story, an elder brother interprets the father's celebration of the Prodigal's return as evidence that he loves this offending younger better than himself (Luke xv.29-30). Yet in this story the father assures the elder that his love for the returned Prodigal does not prejudice his love for him:

> Sonne, thou art ever with me, and all that I have, is thine. It was mete that we shoulde make mery, & be glad: for this thy brother was dead, and is alive againe: and he was lost, but he is founde.
>
> (Luke xv.31).

As with Paul's understanding of Esau and Jacob, the Geneva Bible glosses this verse in a manner that likewise makes the elder and younger brothers of Luke xv symbolic of the Jews and the Gentiles: "Thy parte, [who] art a Jewe, is nothing diminished by that ye Christ was also killed for the Gentiles."[73] This gloss attests the sixteenth-century understanding of the Prodigal Son as symbolic of the Gentiles or Christians. But the further importance of this gloss emerges in its ability to suggest that, not only derogating the Jews, sixteenth-century Christianity could also recognize a mutuality between Jews and Christians, this mutuality being what Shakespeare affirms, even as he gives it an alternative definition. For in both these stories Shakespeare deletes the elder brother, the only trace of him in *Merchant* residing in Gratiano's reference to "a younger or a prodigal" in II.vi.14, which implies an elder as well. In effect, Shakespeare no longer needs the elder brother because he has transferred the Judaism he represents to the father. But in thus making these stories express a conflict between the father and a remaining younger, Shakespeare also puts moral pressure on this younger. For a younger brother may justly refuse submission to an elder brother inherently inferior to himself, as Paul finds a symbolically Christian Jacob to do regarding a symbolically Jewish Esau. But it is problematical for a son to rebel against a father, however old and infirm, because, unlike an elder brother, the father is author of the

Bassanio. And by demanding this money in another's name, Antonio may subtly invoke Jacob as the son who asks for the blessing in the disguise of another's name. To be sure, this association may seem dubious in ignoring the sharp difference between Jacob's grasping and Antonio's generosity. Yet this difference seems curiously to fade in the observation that Antonio's generosity has in fact been challenged by a number of critics, who see it as his means of fast-binding Bassanio to himself.[72] And in confessing his inability "to know myself" (i.i.7), which suggests an ignorance of his own motivation, Antonio may well prompt us to regard him as self-deceived. It is the self-deceivedly self-serving character of his demand that seems most profoundly to associate Antonio with the deceitful selfishness of Jacob; just as the contemptuous character of that demand can reflect the rebellion of the Prodigal. And these associations gain plausibility in the contrasting observation that, while not expunging rebellion and deceit from the terms of his IV.i settlement with Shylock, Antonio mitigates these defects by muting his contempt for Shylock son; as Fortin likewise suggests in finding the II.ii dialogue to define Judaism as "the older tradition from which [Christianity] derives its richness."[74] And beyond the father's authority, there is his dependence. While II.ii will show paternal infirmity as tempting the son to abrogate his loyalty to his father, it will also show this infirmity as making the son essential to the father, as Old Gobbo suggests in calling Launcelot "the very staff of my age, my very prop" (II.ii.66-67).

The description of filial defection as prodigal becomes still more suggestive, moreover, if we consider that this biblical term tends to resonate with doctrines central to the Christian theology of supersession. For the Prodigal's behavior toward his father seems to resemble the behavior of the Church toward its own parental source. We have observed that the Prodigal both demands his father's wealth and rebels against him. But as Rosemary Ruether observes in her influential book, *Faith and Fratricide,* this curious combination of demand and rejection is what Christianity has historically exhibited toward Judaism. Ruether explains that the Church needed "to legitimate its revelation in Jewish terms," that is, to show that revelation as representing "the true meaning of the Jewish Scriptures and . . . the divinely intended fulfillment of Moses, the Psalms, and the Prophets."[75] Thus the Church claimed the texts of Judaism for itself. But its need to legitimate its own interpretation of Jewish Scripture also prompted the Church to reject the Jews' reading of these texts. And the pertinence of this hostile appropriation of Jewish Scripture to *Merchant* is what Antonio appears to evince in his I.iii response to Genesis xxx, the text relating Jacob's breeding of Laban's sheep, which Shylock takes for his discourse on usury. For while accepting the authority of Shylock's text, Antonio rejects Shylock's interpretation of it. While Shylock takes this text to show the blessing as gained by "what Jacob did" as "skillful shepherd" (I.iii.77, 84), Antonio contradictingly refers to Jacob's blessing as "A thing not in his power to bring to pass / But sway'd and fashion'd by the hand of heaven" (I.iii.92-93). Yet what confirms the theological suggestiveness of this dispute is the recognition that Shylock's approbation of Jacob's skillful deeds adumbrates Paul's characterization of works as a method of active self-reliance by which the Jews are said to earn Abraham's blessing; while Antonio's reliance on "the hand of heaven" adumbrates Paul's identification of grace as the passively unearned way of Christianity, the way that supplants Jewish works. Thus Antonio's negation of Shylock's interpretation can be seen to epitomize the larger claim of the Church to a superior understanding of the Jewish Scriptures that validates its superseding appropriation of these Scriptures. And while it is certainly plausible to assume that Antonio's opposing interpretation should enjoy the presumption of approval, we should also note that this presumption is subtly undermined by the continuity of his argument with his contemptuous, which is to say prodigal, demand for Shylock's money.

But not only demanding his father's wealth and rebelling against him, the Prodigal also turns the wealth he takes from his father into the means of his rebellion, that wealth being what enables him to run away. And in this behavior, the Prodigal seems to reflect the tendency of the Church not only to claim Jewish texts and interpret them differently, but also to search these very texts for passages that might be seen to delegitimate the claim of the Jews to be their rightful inheritors, passages that formed the hermeneutical tradition known as *adversos Judaeos.*[76] In effect, this tradition adduced Scriptural texts purporting to show Judaism as delegitimating itself,[77] texts that Paul calls to witness in declaring Judaism abrogated by the coming of Christ: "Now is the righteousness of God made manifest without the Law, having witnes of the Law and of the Prophetes" (Romans iii.21). Ruether, moreover, explains that one of the ways in which the Church turned the Jews' texts against them was by distorting the dual character of Hebrew prophecy: its dialectic of judgments and promises, denunciations and consolations. Whereas the prophets directed both the judgments and the promises to the Jews, the Church claimed the promises for itself while relegating the judgments to the Jews. Thus Jewish texts were used to define the Jews as a rejected and reprobate people,[78] and this charge of reprobation attained its culmination in Christian writings demonizing the Jews and the law. In John viii.44, Jesus tells the Jews that "Ye are of your father the devil." Associating law with the quasi-Gnostic realm of condemned nature, Paul defines it as "the traditions of men, according to the rudiments of the worlde" and as "ordinances of the worlde" (Colossians ii.8, 20); rudiments and ordinances, which in Galatians iv.3 and iv.8-10 assume the character of bondage: "Even so, we when we were children, were in bondage under the rudiments of the worlde." And as the most notorious demonizer of Judaism and Jews, St. Chrysostom charges in one typical passage that "demons inhabit the very souls of the Jews, as well as the places where they gather."[79]

It is thus to the *adversos Judaeos* tactic of turning the Jews' prophecies against them that the Christians' demonizing of Shylock can be traced. And this tactic also seems to be symbolically acted out by Jessica and Antonio in their prodigal rejection of Shylock through his own wealth. For as her letter to Lorenzo suggests in crudely detailing the items of her stolen dowry, "What gold and jewels she is furnish'd with" (II.iv.31), Jessica uses her father's money to purchase the marriage that effects her escape from him. But is the behavior of Antonio any different? He demeans Shylock for lacking the "friendship" he would triumphantly display toward Bassanio by lending him money free of interest: "for when did friendship take / A breed for barren metal of his friend?". Yet Antonio would express his superior generosity by means of money that belongs to Shylock. Just as Jessica uses her father's own wealth to flee from him, so Antonio uses Shylock's own wealth to insult him, the prodigality of their actions being reinforced by the financial ruin that overtakes them both. But the supersessionary implications of Antonio's prodigality also seem to invest the ruin it provokes with a specifically theological if unorthodox suggestion: which is that Christianity can void the validity of Judaism to Judaism only by voiding the validity of Judaism to itself as well, which is to say, by beggaring itself. We should note, moreover, that a comparably theological censure is applied to Shylock's Jewish blindness. As earlier observed, Shylock compares Antonio's financial losses to those of the prodigal Jessica in terms that finally include the overt identification of Antonio too as prodigal: "There I have another bad match. A bankrout, a prodigal, who dare scarce show his head on the Rialto; a beggar . . . " Since prodigality implicitly includes the notion of son or child, a notion explicit in the case of Jessica, Shylock's comparison of Antonio to Jessica while calling him prodigal can be read as all but divulging to us that Antonio too is his child. Yet subtly invoking Paul's view of the Jews as blind to the meaning of their own texts, Shylock speaks words that he himself fails to understand.

It thus appears that Shakespeare's use of the *adversos Judaeos* tradition is most startling in the impartiality of its application. Not only using a Jewish text "against the Jews," he also uses a Christian text "against the Christians," thus turning the hermeneutic of self-invalidation against its own practitioners. Eschewing, moreover, the tendency of this tradition to distort Hebrew prophecy by disjoining its condemnations from its promises, Shakespeare's biblical texts exhibit a prophetic balance in their conjoined implications of censure and approbation. Yet here a problem arises. For the *adversos Judaeos* claim that Judaism confutes itself is precisely what Shylock's Jewish law appears to illustrate in IV.i. Shylock is defeated by his own bond or law in failing to fulfill its stipulation that he exact a just pound of Antonio's flesh while spilling no drop of his blood. How then can the play censure the use of Judaism to confute Judaism as prodigal without contradicting its own plot? Serious as this objection is, I think that we can answer it by observing that this plot evinces a suggestive parallel between the fates of Shylock and Antonio. If the play defeats Shylock's law in IV.i, it defeats Antonio's love in V.i by alienating him from Bassanio. If Shylock's own bond or law is implicated in his defeat, Antonio's love seems likewise involved in his defeat. And if law expresses Judaism, love assumes a comparably Christian connotation by invoking the concept of the promise. For Gratiano subtly bases love, like Abraham's blessing, on the word of promise: "I got a promise of this fair one here / To have her love" (III.ii.206-7). And by granting her love in a manner that evokes God's promise to Abraham, Nerissa makes it an expression of her generosity, or charity, thus endowing that love with a dominant spirituality that warrants Gratiano's theologically nuanced response to it with a pledge of "faith." When Bassanio asks, "And do you, Gratiano, mean good faith?", he responds, "Yes, faith, my lord" (III.ii.210-11). It is, moreover, the spiritual character of his love for Bassanio that Antonio attests in offering to immolate his flesh for him.

Yet, as earlier observed, a number of critics have recognized that Antonio's love is tainted by possessiveness, and this possessiveness introduces contradiction into Antonio's character by challenging the spirituality of his love. For if love expresses its spirituality in charity, which defines it as generous, its possessiveness bespeaks not spirituality but carnality. This observation tallies, moreover, with the widespread critical awareness of a carnal element, whether implicit or explicit, in Antonio's love for Bassanio.[80] I myself tend to view this carnality as latent and becoming overt when Portia thwarts Antonio's martyrdom for Bassanio in IV.i. For to the extent that Antonio's martyrdom expresses his love's spirituality, it does this by containing the possessiveness of that love within a dominant generosity. Though his martyrdom for Bassanio would give Antonio a powerful hold on him, yet that hold would be achieved through the greatest of all gifts: life itself. Thus when Portia thwarts Antonio's martyrdom by defeating Shylock's bond, she destroys the greater mechanism of generosity that had subsumed the carnal possessiveness of Antonio's love, which forthwith emerges in the interaction of Bassanio, Antonio, and Portia concerning Bassanio's ring. In her disguise as the young doctor Balthazar, Portia asks Bassanio to give her his ring in payment for saving Antonio's life. And since this is the ring that Portia has commanded him to keep and that he himself has promised to keep, Bassanio denies her the ring. But Antonio now intervenes to insist that he surrender the ring: "Let his deservings and my love withal / Be valued 'gainst your wive's commandement" (Iv.i.450-51), the term "commandement" bearing the obvious connotation of law. By dismissing Portia's prohibition as a "commandement," Antonio seems to be urging Bassanio to disvalue his marriage with Portia as a merely legal arrangement. So when Bassanio reverses his refusal and sends the disguised Portia the ring, he can be seen to transgress the legal character of his marriage for the sake of Antonio. But this transgression also seems to convey a sense of sexual rejection. For with the carnality appropriate to the legality of the contract it betokens, Portia's ring has been seen to symbolize the sexual essence of the female body,[81] as Portia herself suggests in her ensuing threat to entitle the possessor of the ring to the sexual possession of her body:

> Since he hath got the jewel that I loved,
> And that which you did swear to keep for me,
> I will become as liberal as you,
> I'll not deny him any thing I have,
> No, not my body nor my husband's bed"
>
> (V.i.224-28)

It is important to notice, moreover, that Bassanio follows his surrender of the ring with a decision to accompany Antonio to his house, thus consenting to spend his wedding night not with his wife but with his friend. In a moment of special intimacy,[82] Bassanio tells Antonio,

> Come, you and I will thither presently,
> And in the morning early will we both
> Fly toward Belmont. Come, Antonio.
>
> (IV.i.455-57)

This decision suggests that, rather than merely expressing his choice of a spiritual love for Antonio above his carnal love for Portia, Bassanio's surrender of the ring effectively transfers his erotic allegiance from his wife to his friend. And further negating a spiritual value in Bassanio's decision to surrender the ring and go home with Antonio is the recognition that in both these actions, Bassanio breaks promises. Bassanio had promised Portia to keep her ring and had likewise promised her that, while he was in Venice, "No bed shal e'er be guilty of my stay, / Nor rest be interposer 'twixt us twain" (III.ii. 326-27). As the object of Portia's faith in Bassanio's love, these promises constitute the spiritual basis of their marriage, the basis that Bassanio destroys in breaking them. In acceding to Antonio's demand and going home with him, Bassanio would appear to be violating both the carnal and the spiritual integrity of his marriage to Portia.

Yet the implications of Bassanio's moral failure extend beyond himself to Antonio as the instigator of that failure. For in prompting Bassanio to surrender Portia's ring, Antonio subtly demands, and I think, attains, a carnal payment from him not entirely different from that which Shylock had tried to achieve through his bond. In making this demand, Antonio degrades his love from charity to lust, thereby contradicting the spirituality of his love that is fundamental to his Christian faith. But what gives a further significance to the sense of degraded self-contradiction in Antonio's love is the ability of that love to assume a parallel with Shylock's law, which has similarly degraded itself to an unfulfillable and therefore self-contradicting warrant for murder. Just as the contradiction in his degraded law, together with its identification of him as alien, betrays Shylock into guilt; so the contradiction of his faith by his carnally degraded love betrays Antonio into guilt. And as Shylock is then forced to surrender the law that incriminates him, so Antonio is, albeit more subtly, forced to surrender the love that incriminates him by handing Bassanio over to Portia.[83] It is this parallel that Brown decries in observing that Antonio's eventual loss of his friend has "a potential dramatic interest comparable to Shylock's isolation at the end of the trial."[84]

Are we then to view the play as rejecting faith in love or the greater faith in God defined as Love? It does not seem likely. But if faith can be defeated and yet not rejected, are we compelled to view Shylock's defeated law as rejected? Instead, might we not surmise that what has been rejected in Shylock and Antonio are not the principles of law and faith but rather these principles in the blindness and prodigality that cause them to deny the mutual dependency of their relation as father and son?

I shall interpret the cold accommodation between Shylock and Antonio in IV.i as beginning and then aborting the restoration of their relation as father and son. Yet since the terms of this aborted reconciliation are partly monetary, they will attain the theological meanings I am trying to impart to them only if we perceive money as a symbolic representation of Abraham's blessing. This symbolic view of money is what the play supports in its subtle association of the physical "goods" that the Prodigal's father gives his son with the spiritual blessing that Isaac gives Jacob. And a comparably symbolic meaning in money is what Shylock suggests, with the tacit concurrence of Antonio, by representing Jacob's wealth as making him "blest" (I.iii.89). But more extensive evidence for such a view seems to emerge from the play's focus on Shylock's usury. For in defending this practice, Shylock articulates three pairs of terms, two of these pairs pertaining to the monetary practice of usury, while the third pair not only mediates between the realms of money and blessing but also discriminates two separate ways of having this blessing. While Shylock adduces the terms of this third pair to express his exclusively Jewish claim to Abraham's blessing, his effect, contrary to his intent, is to disclose a way in which Jew and Christian can both share in this blessing. What, then, are the terms that Shylock invokes, and how do they enable his usury to both symbolize Abraham's blessing and provide for its sharing?

IV

In I.iii, Shylock analyzes his usury into "moneys" and "usances" (I.iii.108), components which are analogously rendered as principal and interest. Shylock repeatedly makes mention of "interest" (I.iii.51) in I.iii, while twice referring to "principal" in IV.i: "Give me my principal, and let me go" (IV.i.336); "Shall I not have barely my principal?" (IV.i.342). But in addition to "moneys" and "usances" with their apparent equivalence to principal and interest, Shylock's I.iii defense of usury introduces a third pair of terms: possession and thrift, thrift meaning profit. In calling Jacob "the third possessor," Shylock adverts obliquely to Abraham's blessing as the thing Jacob is possessor of; yet the possession he adduces also identifies a mode of having that blessing: the having of it as something owned, like Shylock's "moneys" or principal. Shylock also refers to Jacob as breeding thrift from his uncle's sheep. And Shylock likewise identifies thrift as blessing in observing that

> This was a way to thrive, and he was blest;
> And thrift is blessing, if men steal it not.
>
> (I.iii.89-90)

Yet if thrift, like possession, is thus identified as blessing, thrift is also differentiated from possession. For whereas possession pertains to the blessing owned as principal, thrift pertains to the blessing derived as profit from a principal that is not owned. Jacob breeds this thrift out of sheep owned, rather, by his uncle Laban, as Shylock observes in beginning, "When Jacob graz'd his uncle Laban's sheep" (I.iii.71). Thus possession and thrift emerge as terms denoting distinct ways of having Abraham's blessing. And as possession corresponds to "moneys" held as principal, thrift corresponds to the "usances" or interest on that principal, interest being the concept that thrift is introduced to defend.

But while Shylock shows Jacob to breed the thrift that is blessing from a principal not his, he also shows Jacob, as "third possessor," to possess the blessing as principal. Jacob is thus accorded a double having of Abraham's blessing. And it is Jacob's double having of Abraham's blessing that Shylock appears to adduce in justification of his own usury, since in usury Shylock similarly lays claim to both possession and thrift, as he emphasizes in referring to "my moneys and my usances." This double having, however, is subtly reproved by Antonio's reference to the interest added to principal as "excess" (I.iii.62). For to the extent that Shylock's money and usances represent a double having of Abraham's blessing, they suggest an excess of having for Shylock that results in a defect of having for Antonio. In contrast to Shylock's usurious possessing with a thrift that is "assur'd" (I.iii.29), Antonio is a merchant, which means that his wealth is given out at hazard and, like the Prodigal's goods, may be "squand'red abroad" and lost, the profit with the principal.

Not only represented as something owned like principal, however, possession is also associated with paternity, and paternity as carnally defined. For in calling Jacob "the third possessor," Shylock is obliquely referring possession to the three patriarchs of Israel, of whom Abraham and Isaac are first and second. And by referring to the first patriarchal possessor as "our holy Abram" and "father Abram," Shylock is further defining the first of the great fathers biologically. For Abram is the name by which Genesis applies the patriarch's fatherhood to the Jews as his sole children through biological descent; as opposed to the name, Abraham, by which God makes him "a father of manie nacions," a father defined by the Geneva Bible, citing Romans 4.17, "not only according to ye fleshe, but of a farre greater multitude by faith":

> Beholde, I make my covenant with thee, & thou shalt be a father of manie nacions, Nether shal thy name anie more be called Abram, but thy name shalbe Abraham: for a father of manie nacions have I made thee.
>
> (Genesis xvii.4-5)

Since the children of a father are his heirs, it follows that Shylock's restriction of the patriarch's paternity to the Jews likewise makes them the sole inheritors of his blessing. And it is as one of these exclusively biological heirs that Shylock claims possession of Abraham's blessing. Moreover, to the extent that Shylock shows the blessing to comprise not only possession but also thrift, his restriction of its possession to himself can be seen as just. For even if Antonio's gentile identification as spiritual son makes him ineligible for possession of Abraham's blessing, he remains entitled to the thrift or profit of this blessing. Yet not only justly claiming possession, Shylock unjustly claims thrift as well, the injustice of this claim being what Antonio registers in railing against Shylock's "thrift, / Which he calls interest."

It is Shylock's desire to claim thrift, moreover, that can explain his representation of its production as blatantly sexual: his conjuring up of "wooly breeders in the act" and "work of generation" (I.iii.83, 82). For these images establish the carnality and hence the Jewishness of Jacob's thrift that makes it rightfully his. And by comparing the thrift that Jacob breeds from sheep with the interest that he himself breeds from money, Shylock hopes to define his interest as likewise carnal, thereby rendering it Jewish and rightfully his.[85] It is thus appropriate that Antonio should challenge the legitimacy of Shylock's interest by challenging the carnality of its generation:

> Was this inserted to make interest good?
> Or is your gold and silver ewes and rams?
>
> (I.iii.94-95)

Yet it is not Shylock's thrift only that Antonio challenges. For when Shylock refuses to concede the inorganic character of his "gold and silver"—"I cannot tell, I make it breed as fast" (I.iii.96)—Antonio turns to Bassanio with the insulting observation that "The devil can cite Scripture for his purpose" (I.iii.98). Antonio all but calls Shylock devil to his face. And just as the *adversus Judaeos* tradition called the Jews devils in order to define them as blessed in no manner whatever but rather as cursed, Antonio's demonizing of Shylock can be seen to alienate him from Abraham's blessing not only in its thrift but also in its possession, as he further attests in railing not only against Shylock's thrift but also against "me" and "my bargains." Just as Shylock would deny the blessing to Antonio, Antonio would deny it to Shylock. Yet, it may be asked, how do we square such an argument with the eventual truth of Antonio's insult: the fact that Shylock indeed proves himself a "cruel devil" (IV.i.217) in Act IV. Perhaps by noting that, while showing Shylock to commit evil, the play also shows him to suffer evil, and may subtly be underlining that suffering through a positive meaning reposed in the name of Old Gobbo. In observing that "suff'rance is the badge of all our tribe," Shylock emphasizes his habitual patience under contempt, thereby anticipating the similar patience of Old Gobbo. And heightening the suggestiveness of this anticipation is Brown's observation that Old Gobbo's name appears in the quarto as "Iobbe," which is "the Italianized form of Job,"[86] the archetype of patience in suffering. Like Old Gobbo, Shylock is a kind of Job: a Job at the end of his patience.

If our sense of mutual wrong between Shylock and Antonio is clarified by the distinctions of possession and thrift, that sense is also informed by what has earlier been described as their common involvement in theft. Usury is, at first, to be Shylock's legal form of theft from Antonio. But Antonio too is associated with theft in being the object of Shylock's warning that "thrift is blessing, if men steal it not." And supporting the reference of Shylock's words to Antonio is the tendency of Jessica, in exhibiting literal theft, to define Antonio's contemptuous demand for Shylock's money as a correspondingly psychic version of that theft. But likewise suggesting theft in both Jessica and Antonio is the recognition that the conditionality Shakespeare applies to Antonio's thrift is likewise applied to Jessica's possession. As Antonio is spiritual heir to Shylock's thrift, Jessica is carnal heir to his possession; what she takes is, after all, destined to be her own. But Jessica is heir to Shylock's possession only so long as she acknowledges her biological daughterhood to him, the very relationship she repudiates by fleeing from him: "Farewell, and if my fortune be not cross'd / I have a father, you a daughter, lost" (II.v.56-57). Jessica's repudiation of her biological daughterhood is what her absconding expresses and what defines the possession she absconds with as stolen. But if Jessica repudiates her biological daughterhood to Shylock, Antonio repudiates his spiritual sonhood to Shylock. Thus if Jessica's repudiation constitutes her possession as stolen, may not Antonio's repudiation constitute his thrift as stolen? Viewed in this way, Antonio's theft resides not in his demand for thrift, which is just, but rather in a spiritual contempt for Shylock that denies him possession as the prerogative of his carnal paternity. Just as Shylock's initial refusal of the thrift of profit of his symbolic money to Antonio bespeaks a blind refusal to acknowledge his spiritual sonhood, so Antonio's denial of Shylock's possession bespeaks a prodigal refusal to acknowledge the carnal character of his paternity, a refusal that Antonio attests in desiring to convert him.

Moreover, since "thrift is blessing" only "if men steal it not," the loss of its efficacy as blessing would tend to suggest that it has indeed been stolen. And to the extent that the ability to bless is the ability to redeem or save, it is interesting to observe that thrift eventually proves unable to buy back or redeem Antonio from the condemnation of Shylock's law. Shylock eventually grants Antonio an interest-free loan, thus giving him the thrift of his money, but on the condition that he return its principal or possession within three months. And the terms Shylock establishes for his loan are such that no amount of interest or thrift will be allowed to compensate for the failure of Antonio to repay its possession by that time; rather, possession, inherently carnal to begin with because carnally claimed, will be claimed in the very flesh of Antonio. This is just what happens. Having failed to return the possession of Shylock's loan by the appointed time, Antonio finds that a ransom of thrift "ten times" (IV.i.211) the amount of that possession can be refused. Yet the spiritual meaning of this thrift is what reveals the true significance of its vitiation by suggesting that Christianity steals and thus vitiates its thrift or profit in Abraham's blessing by withholding its possession from the Jews. If this meaning is valid, it implies that the blessing of Abraham can be secured to neither Jew nor Christian unless secured to both together, by the allotment of possession to the Jews and thrift to the Christians. And that it may, despite its heterodoxy, be valid is supported by the observation that his dual allotment is what Antonio can be seen to propose in his IV.i disposition of Shylock's wealth.

Addressing the court, Antonio says,

> To quit the fine for one half of his goods,
> I am content; so he will let me have
> The other half in use . . .
>
> (IV.i.381-83)

Antonio divides Shylock's wealth between himself and Shylock, thus sharing that wealth with Shylock. But Antonio also stipulates that Shylock is to die "possess'd" (IV.i.389) of his half, whereas for the duration of Shylock's life, Antonio is to have the other half "in use," which is to say, in a trust. The significance of Antonio's proposal of a trust emerges in the recognition that this legal instrument can enable its trustee to eschew possession of the principal while claiming its profit, or thrift, which is what I think Antonio intends to do. To be sure, a trust need not by definition grant the trustee its profit, and critics unable to cope with Antonio's eventual consent to get as well as give balk at the idea of his profiting from his trust. Yet when we consider that Antonio has at this point no other means of living and has just declared his preference for death over "An age of poverty" (IV.i.271); and when we further consider the symbolic meaning of the profit in question, it becomes highly unlikely that Antonio means to refuse it.[87] Not validated, moreover, as the result of Christian hazard, since it entails no hazard, Antonio's profit is rather validated in accruing to him without his possession of the principal, which he yields to Shylock's heirs. It thus appears that Antonio claims the thrift of Abraham's blessing for his Christian self while restoring its possession to the Jewish Shylock. In light of the meanings associated with possession, this restoration can suggest Antonio's attempt to recognize, however incipiently and obliquely, that the blessing he would have is Shylock's abiding possession, the prerogative of his carnal paternity. By claiming Shylock's thrift in a manner that restores his possession, Antonio claims his thrift but steals it not. Thus he begins to make it an authentic blessing, as he further suggests in claiming that thrift both without the conspicuous contempt that had marked his demand for Shylock's money in I.iii, and also more honestly, which is to say, for himself. Did Antonio do no more than this, he would have begun to purge away the defects of his identities as Prodigal Son and Jacob, thus initiating the process that redefines him as the returned Prodigal.

V

Yet Antonio appears to take this course only to abandon it and revert to the contempt and deceit of the unreconstructed Prodigal Son and Jacob. This abandonment suggests that Antonio ends his conflict with Shylock still mired in the internal struggle that Launcelot exhibits at the outset of II.ii but eventually overcomes. Yet if Launcelot's II.ii dialogue with his father shows how the conflict of Antonio with Shylock should end and does not, that dialogue also epitomizes major elements in the dynamics of this larger quarrel. For Launcelot's interaction with Old Gobbo shows how the defects of paternal blindness and filial prodigality exacerbate each other; how the mutual exacerbation of their defects would propel father and son, albeit figuratively, toward mutual murder but for the supervening realization that mutual murder is also mutually suicidal; and how this recognition prompts father and son to abate the blindness and prodigality that estrange them. Turning now to a close reading of this dialogue, I shall try to show

how it conveys these meanings and invites their reference to Shylock and Antonio.

As Launcelot's flight from Shylock bespeaks his prodigality, his designation of Shylock as "this Jew my master" refers this prodigality to a resentment of authority. And appropriately leveling that resentment at the father he proceeds to meet, Launcelot determines to "try confusions" (II.ii.37) with him, just as Jacob tries confusions with old Isaac. By recalling, moreover, that Jacob's purpose in his confusions was to compass his father's blessing, we may surmise that Launcelot's purpose in these "confusions" is similarly to compass *his* father's blessing, presumably because he associates this blessing with authority. But if Jacob would seek this blessing by confusing himself with his brother Esau, Launcelot's reference to Old Gobbo as "my true-begotten father" (II.ii.35-36) suggests that he would seek this blessing by confusing the roles of father and son by making himself his father's father. And in forthwith demanding that his father address him as "Master Launcelot" (II.ii.48), Launcelot further suggests that his aim in this role reversal is to assume the mastery belonging to a father. Yet what enables Launcelot to act out his desire to dominate his father is his father's blindness. His blindness is what prevents Old Gobbo from recognizing that the stranger he stops to inquire the way to Shylock's house is his son. And this lack of recognition causes the old father to call him "Master young man" and "Master young gentleman" (II.ii.33, 39), as well as addressing him with the deferential "you" rather than the familiar "thou." Not merely basking in the pleasure of his father's error, however, Launcelot is prompted to affect the persona of authority and erudition that will encourage its continuance. Launcelot would reinforce his father's belief that he is addressing his social better, so that the old man will continue according him the honorific titles of "sir," "your worship," "your mastership," and "young gentleman" (II.ii.51, 56, 59, 70-71).

This deception becomes seriously mischievous, however, when Launcelot decides to tell his unrecognizing father that he is dead, much as Luke's Prodigal causes his father to think him dead: "For this my sonne was dead . . ." (Luke xv.24). Addressing Old Gobbo as "father," yet meaning him to perceive that address merely as a term appropriate to his age,[88] Launcelot says,

> Talk not of Master Launcelot, father, for the young gentleman, according to Fates and Destinies, and such odd sayings, the Sisters Three, and such branches of learning, is indeed deceas'd, or as you would say in plain terms, gone to heaven."
>
> (II.ii.60-65)

This statement is deliberately cruel, as Launcelot himself acknowledges in telling the audience with Vice-like candor that it is intended to bring his father to tears: "Mark me now, now will I raise the waters" (II.ii.49). But not only cruel, this false news impairs still further his father's ability to recognize him. And to the extent that nonrecognition of a child is what constitutes paternal blindness, Launcelot's prodigality can be seen to deepen that blindness, just as that blindness incites his prodigality.

Yet the cruelty of Launcelot's communication is not without purpose. For in anticipating that it will reduce his father to tears, Launcelot invites us to regard his false report as intended to break his father's spirit, thus making him submissive to himself. Launcelot appears to be using the report of his own death as a way of achieving authority over his father, a way that, indeed, succeeds, as the old man attests in begging his unknown son to deny the death that his authority has already convinced him is true: "I know you not, young gentleman, but I pray you tell me, is my boy, God rest his soul, alive or dead?" (II.ii.70-72).

Not only subjugating his father, however, this news also threatens to kill him, as Old Gobbo's self-centered reaction demonstrates: "Marry, God forbid, the boy was the very staff of my age, my very prop" (II.ii.66-67). Trying to evade the force of his father's distress, Launcelot attempts to treat it as matter for mirth and, turning to the audience, asks, "Do I look like a cudgel or a hovel-post [that is, a little hovel or house[89]], a staff, or a prop?" (II.ii.68-69). Yet the flatness of the joke seems to suggest that Launcelot's cruel heart is being disquieted by his conscience. And though, by contrast, there is no sense of deliberate cruelty in Old Gobbo's blindness, that blindness retains its own lethal potential. For Launcelot glancingly observes that "murder cannot be hid long; a man's son may" (II.ii.79-80), and the tendency of these words to associate murder with the hiddenness of "a man's son" enables them to suggest that a father's failure to recognize his son effectively, if subtly, murders him.

In the tendency of their blindness and prodigality to push them toward mutual murder, however, Old Gobbo and Launcelot seem to adumbrate a dangerously deepening bitterness in the settled antagonism between Shylock and Antonio. Because his habitual blindness makes him unable to see that Antonio is his spiritual son and, as such, entitled to the thrift of his possession, Shylock provokes him to the habitual insolence that parallels the Prodigal's flight from his father. But in I.iii, blindness and prodigality take a particularly nasty turn. Shylock's defense of his usury is dismissed by Antonio, and when Shylock in his turn scorns this dismissal, he incurs the ultimate contempt of demonization, which, confirmed and unrepented, prompts Shylock to propose the bond of flesh. It thus appears that Launcelot's reference to a son's murder by an unknowing father, which Old Gobbo displays only figuratively, really pertains to Shylock in his literal attempt to murder Antonio through the flesh bond. To be sure, it may be objected that the spectacle of Shylock similarly wishing his biological and acknowledged daughter Jessica "dead at my foot" (III.i.88) challenges this association of murder with nonrecognition or blindness. Yet Shylock's rejection of Jessica may have another point to make. It may be that just as Shakespeare shows antagonism between carnal law and spiritual faith to destroy both these principles, so he may also be working out that destruction in Jessica and Antonio as carnal and spiritual children of Shylock. In representing Shylock as a father who rejects the spiritual son he does not know only to eventually reject the carnal daughter he does know, Shakespeare may well be suggesting that Jewish paternity cannot choose between its children: that it will have both or neither. But setting aside Shylock's rejection of Jessica, what seems important to observe here is that, in his own way, Antonio shares the homicidal impulse of Shylock. For if the flesh bond serves Shylock's desire to murder Antonio physically, it also whets Antonio's desire to obliterate Shylock's Jewish identity through the spiritual means of conversion: "The Hebrew will turn Christian, he grows kind" (I.iii.178).

As Shakespeare cleverly demonstrates through Old Gobbo and Launcelot, however, these lethal impulses are self-defeating. For the true effect of Old Gobbo's paternal blindness toward his son is to enable that son to manipulate the father into denying his own authority. Seeking to assume his father's authority, Launcelot urges Old Gobbo to relinquish that authority by referring to his son as "Master Launcelot." And recognizing the self-demeaning implication of this request, Old Gobbo refuses to comply. Thus when Launcelot twice asks his father, "Talk you of young Master Launcelot?" (II.ii.48, 50), the old man responds, "No master sir, but a poor man's son" (II.ii.51). Yet Old Gobbo's blindness has the ironic effect of turning his denials into affirmations. Failing to perceive that the Launcelot whose mastership he denies is the very person he is addressing as "sir" and "Master," Old Gobbo in fact grants Launcelot the mastership he professes to refuse him, as Launcelot invites us to recognize. For when Launcelot proceeds to insist that "we talk of young Master Launcelot" (II.ii.54-55) and her father again objects, "Your worship's friend and Launcelot, sir" (II.ii.56), Launcelot rejoins with an emphatic and repeated "*ergo*," signifying that the father has proved his son's point: "But I pray you, *ergo*, old man, *ergo*, I beseech you, talk you of young Master Launcelot" (II.ii.57-58). And to Old Gobbo's uncomprehendingly stubborn "Of Launcelot, an't please your mastership" (II.ii.59), Launcelot triumphantly concludes, "*Ergo*, Master Launcelot" (II.ii.60). Just as Old Gobbo's blind inability to recognize his son effectively grants Launcelot the prodigal mastery so prejudicial to his paternal self, Shylock's carnal inability to call Antonio son may inform his own deferential address to him as "Signoir Antonio," that address more broadly referring the historical domination of Judaism by Christianity to Judaism itself in its failure to recognize its paternal relation to Christianity.

Launcelot's prodigality can likewise be seen to recoil against him by thwarting the very aim it pursues. His aim in dominating an unrecognizing father is to secure that father's blessing. But having attained this dominance through the report of his own death, Launcelot now finds himself unable to induce his father to bless a son he thinks dead. To the contrary, the more credit his authority has with Old Gobbo, the more remote his blessing becomes.

Not only self-defeating, however, the homicidal impulses of blindness and prodigality are eventually revealed as suicidal. For Launcelot achieves authority over his father by verbally killing himself. Seeking to usurp his father's paternity, he kills his own sonhood. And Launcelot's self-killing quest for authority invokes a similarly self-destructive recoil in Antonio's desire to dominate Shylock. Antonio is prompted to accept Shylock's bond partly by his determination to interpret it as signaling Shylock's impending conversion from carnal Jew to spiritual Christian. And prompting Antonio to this interpretation is his wish to void the paternity constituted in Shylock's Jewish identity in order to claim the authority of that paternity for himself. Yet his eagerness to supplant Shylock's Jewish paternity makes Antonio, like Shylock, blind by preventing him from discerning the bond's ability to reduce him to the flesh claimable on terms of Shylock's carnality. In attempting to spiritualize Shylock out of existence, Antonio incurs the risk of carnalizing himself out of existence, this consequence of his bargain once again impugning the larger Christian theology of supersession. And just as the murder and suicide associated in Launcelot seem evinced in Antonio, so the same association of murder and suicide can be discerned in both Old Gobbo and Shylock. As he admits, Old Gobbo cannot survive without the support of the son his own nonrecognition murders. And his tendency to destroy the basis of his own existence may well inform the condemnation that Shylock incurs in attempting to murder Antonio. Just as Old Gobbo needs Launcelot to be the prop of his age, Shakespeare seems to be suggesting that Judaism in Shylock needs Christianity in Antonio to become the prop of its age.

It is thus appropriate that the suicidal implications of blindness and prodigality should force the surrender of these defects. Launcelot reveals himself submissively to his father, thus enabling Old Gobbo to recognize and bless him. But while imperative, this surrender and recognition also require a capacity for self-transcendence that is difficult to achieve. And this difficulty, the tough struggle it entails for both father and son, is what the II.ii dialogue is at pains to exhibit. Recognizing that the announcement of his death has alienated him from the blessing he wants, Launcelot finally decides to reveal himself to his father. Yet blind from the first and made more so by the authority of his son, Old Gobbo resists Launcelot's pleas for recognition. And just as Old Gobbo's blindness is so firmly planted as hardly to be uprooted, so Launcelot revokes his prodigal death by reluctant stages. Suing for recognition, Launcelot first asks, "Do you know me, father?" (II.ii.69). But plausibly mistaking his nomination as father merely for an address to his age (since Launcelot has so used it), Old Gobbo poignantly replies, "Alack the day, I know you not, young gentleman" (II.ii.70-71). Again Launcelot asks for recognition: "Do you not know me, father?" (II.ii.73.) But helplessly lamenting his blindness, Old Gobbo again replies, "Alack, sir, I am sand-blind, I know not" (II.ii.74). Unyielding paternal blindness now prompts Launcelot to revive himself even to the prejudice of his authority, as he shows by kneeling down to ask his father's blessing: "Well, old man, I will tell you news of your son. Give me your blessing" (II.ii.77-78). Yet his own stubborn prodigality prevents Launcelot from identifying himself plainly and also causes him to kneel with his back to his father. And just as Launcelot's tergiversation comprises his filial submission, so Old Gobbo's inability to recognize him attests the old father's continuing blindness: "Pray you, sir, stand up. I am sure you are not Launcelot, my boy" (II.ii.81-82). The need to penetrate his father's blindness now drives Launcelot to concede that he can never be father to Old Gobbo. Dropping the title of master, he pleads, "I am Launcelot, your boy that was, your son that is, your child that shall be" (II.ii.84-86). But again, to no avail: "I cannot think you are my son" (II.ii.87). To overcome this blindness and secure his blessing, Launcelot must not only surrender his mastership; he must also, like the Prodigal asking to be as one of his father's hired servants, resume the rank of servant; which he does by styling himself "Launcelot, the Jew's man" (II.ii.89). This confession works. Now recognizing his son, Old Gobbo reclaims him with an exclamation of joy that drops the respectful "you" for the familiar "thou": "I'll be sworn, if thou be Launcelot, thou art mine own flesh and blood" (II.ii.91-93).[90] It is Antonio's similarly difficult—and unachieved—surrender of his Christian impulse to dominate the Jewish Shylock that seems prescribed as the condition of his filial recognition.

Yet we should also notice that Launcelot's confession not only vanquishes his own prodigality; it also accommodates the carnality of his father's blindness by adducing the identifiably carnal link between himself and his father, which is his mother: "I am Launcelot, the Jew's man, and I am sure Margery your wife is my mother" (II.ii.89-90). Significantly, Old Gobbo expresses his recognition of Launcelot in restrictedly carnal terms, terms that anticipate Shylock's later description of his biological daughter as "My own flesh and blood" (III.i.34). Yet while a maternal link allows Old Gobbo an at least carnal recognition of his son, no such carnal link can help Shylock recognize his wholly spiritual relationship to Antonio. He must either see spiritually or, as it proves, not at all. Thus if this dialogue posits the prodigality that Antonio does not vanquish as one condition of his recognition by Shylock, it also posits the carnality, which is to say, the blindness, that Shylock does not vanquish as another condition of that recognition.

By contrast, Old Gobbo so far sheds the psychic limitation of Isaac's blindness and the woe of the Prodigal's father as to liberate what is positive in these blessing fathers: their recognition and joy, which now coalesce to transform Old Gobbo into the father of the restored Prodigal, who blesses his son both knowingly and willingly. Old Gobbo places his hands on Launcelot's head in sign of blessing. And in the ability of his confession to purge away the rebellion of the Prodigal and the deceit of Jacob, Launcelot integrates the respective honesty and piety of these identities in evocation of the returned Prodigal. Validating these transformations, moreover, is their enabling of life to conquer death. By recognizing his son, Old Gobbo reclaims the staff and prop of his age; and in being restored to his father Launcelot evokes the Prodigal's return from death to life: "For this my sonne was dead, and is alive againe: and he was lost, but he is founde" (Luke xv.24).

Clearly, this satisfying reconciliation is not attained by Shylock and Antonio. Yet in supplying the pattern of a true reconciliation, Launcelot and old Gobbo enable us to recognize the movement, however tentative and aborted, that Antonio and Shylock make toward its achievement. As before observed, Antonio's request for Shylock's money in IV.i is devoid of the blatantly prodigal contempt he had exhibited in I.iii. Similarly, he drops his formerly Jacob-like pursuit of Shylock's blessing wealth in another's name. And in thus ameliorating his identities as the Prodigal and Jacob, Antonio offers to exchange them for the identity of the returned Prodigal. For just as Launcelot's self-revival as returned Prodigal also restores life to his father, Antonio restores life to himself and Shylock together by dividing between them both the wealth without which neither he nor Shylock could live, as Shylock, speaking for himself, attests:

> Nay, take my life and all, pardon not that:
> You take my house when you do take the prop
> That doth sustain my house; you take my life
> When you do take the means whereby I live.
>
> (IV.i.374-77)

In returning the wealth that supports his house, Antonio becomes to Shylock what Launcelot becomes to Old Gobbo: the "staff" and "prop" of his age.

Yet this amelioration does not progress. For while Launcelot eventually vanquishes his Jacob-like reluctance to identify himself as Old Gobbo's son, Antonio remains like Jacob in asking Shylock for his money without confessing his filial identity. And not only failing to progress, this amelioration seems to collapse in a reversion to prodigality. For in an act that reassociates the transmission of Shylock's wealth with theft, Antonio forces Shylock to bequeath his possession to "the gentleman / That lately stole his daughter" (IV.i.384-85). And whereas Launcelot surrenders his Prodigal desire to be his father's master and father, Antonio fulfills that prodigal desire for filial dominance. As master to Shylock, Antonio demands that he "presently become a Christian" (IV.i.387). And as one of two "god-fathers" to bring Shylock "to the font" (IV.i.398, 400) of baptism, Antonio likewise becomes his father, albeit a father from whom Shylock now evinces a prodigal desire to flee: "I pray you give me leave to go from hence, / I am not well" (IV.i.395-96). This evidence suggests that the moral status of Shylock's forced conversion, long disputed,[91] should be decided in the negative. Rather than prescriptive or remedial, this conversion can be seen as symptomatic of what remains wrong with both Antonio and Shylock. For not only attesting prodigality in Antonio, it also results from the self-defeating tendency of Shylock's blindness to incite that prodigality. Thus Shylock's conversion is congruent with his abidingly flawed identities as Isaac and father of the reprobate Prodigal. Like Isaac with Jacob, Shylock is made to bless Antonio in ignorance of his filial identity. And like the Prodigal's father, he endows Jessica in pained awareness of her unreformed prodigality. As a measure of what is wrong with both antagonists, moreover, this conversion appropriately informs the self-defeating events that Antonio's prodigality now prompts him to initiate. For the contempt of law that emboldens him to demand Shylock's conversion is what Antonio likewise exhibits in demanding that Bassanio break Portia's commandment, that demand culminating in the forfeiture of his friend. Had Antonio achieved a properly filial respect for Shylock's carnal law, and hence for his Jewishness, he would have observed Portia's analogously carnal law and kept his friend.

The play thus offers a sharp contrast between the failed reconciliation of Shylock with Antonio and the successful reconciliation of Old Gobbo with Launcelot. Yet even this paradigmatic reunion remains imperfect. For Old Gobbo remains blind. And in restricting his blessing hands to a carnally tactile knowing that mistakes his son's head for his beard, Old Gobbo's blindness suggests his enduring limitation. Comparably, Launcelot's atonement to his father does not expunge the appetitive aspect of his prodigality, which prompts him to continue hankering for a life of sexual license: "Here's a small trifle of wives! Alas, fifteen wives is nothing! Aleven widows and nine maids is a simple coming-in for one man" (II.ii.161-63). Yet while suggesting the partial persistence of paternal blindness and filial prodigality, the II.ii dialogue also tantalizes us with the fleeting vision of a time when these defects will be entirely dispelled. For to the request for his father's blessing, Launcelot appends a reflection of seemingly choric significance: "Give me your blessing; truth will come to light; murder cannot be hid long; a man's son may, but in the end truth will out" (II.ii.78-80). What can this truth be if it is not "a man's son" finally recognized by a father no longer blind? And if Shakespeare has designed this whole dialogue to point beyond itself to Shylock and Antonio, and especially to the religious traditions they embody, might not the truth here adduced refer to the eventually dispelled blindness of Shylock's paternal Judaism? But just as Launcelot's brief reference to the truth that must ultimately "come to light" may extend beyond Old Gobbo to Shylock's Jewishness, so Launcelot seems still more briefly and obliquely to reflect on Old Gobbo in a manner that likewise reflects on himself and, by extension, on the Christian Antonio. For in describing Old Gobbo as "this honest old man, and though I say it, though old man, yet poor man, my father" (II.ii.138-40), Launcelot is defining him as old, honest, and—poor man—father to a prodigal son! And if these words indeed imply a rueful self-awareness, might they not anticipate the remorse of the Prodigal that makes him no longer prodigal; just as Launcelot anticipates a time when the father will recognize his son? While such scent evidence cannot sustain so large an argument, its presence in this dialogue demands at least tentative recognition.

What seems more certain is that this dialogue is a highly articulated and profound allegory, which Shakespeare fashions out of received cultural elements that he molds into the vehicle of his own meaning. These elements are the two objectively biblical identities that he imposes on Launcelot and Old Gobbo, the resulting disproportion between the meaning of these characters and their marginal status prompting the justified suspicion that their function in this allegory is to mediate these typological meanings to the play's Venetian principals, Shylock and Antonio. These meanings allegorize their respectively Jewish and Christian identities as blind father Isaac and Prodigal Son. But it is in the II.ii dialogue that the complex interactions of these allegorized principals are epitomized. In their blindness and prodigality, Old Gobbo and Launcelot identify hegemonic impulses in the respective traditions of Shylock and Antonio that bring them into conflict; as father and son, Old Gobbo and Launcelot exhibit the properly familial relationship of these principal characters, with its reciprocal requirements of paternal duty and filial loyalty. In expressing an evolution of power relations into family relations, the II.ii dialogue shows how the quarrel between Shylock and Antonio should end, thus becoming an interpretive norm that Shakespeare inserts into his play. And by contrasting with the minimal and aborted settlement that Shylock and Antonio do in fact attain, this norm assumes an oppositional force censuring that settlement while also attesting Shakespeare's awareness of the difficulties involved in getting beyond it. Shakespeare thus makes old texts speak new meanings, meanings that show our religious culture as both flawed and instinct with the capacity for its own renewal; in their intellectual and moral refinement, these meanings secure the modern value of this play by making it a force for such renewal.

Notes

1. René Girard, "'To Entrap the Wisest': A Reading of *The Merchant of Venice*," in *Literature and Society: Selected Papers from the English Institute, 1978*, ed. Edward W. Said (Baltimore: Johns Hopkins University Press, 1980), 105. William Hazlitt, *Characters of Shakespeare's Plays* (New York: Wiley and Putnam, 1846), 174. A. D. Moody, *Shakespeare: The Merchant of Venice* (London: Edward Arnold, 1964), 10. Harold C. Goddard, *The Meaning of Shakespeare* (Chicago: University of Chicago Press, 1951), 88. Kiernan Ryan, "*The Merchant of Venice:* Past Significance and Present Meaning," *Shakespeare Jahrbuch,* 117 (1981): 51.

2. Walter Cohen, "*The Merchant of Venice* and the Possibilities of Historical Criticism," *ELH,* 49 (1982): 768-69; and Michael Ferber, "The Ideology of *The Merchant of Venice,*" *English Literary Renaissance,* 20 (1990): 437-38.

3. Frank Whigham, "Ideology and Class Conduct in *The Merchant of Venice,*" *Renaissance Drama,* NS 10 (1979): 108, 107; Ryan, 51; Lars Engle, "'Thrift is Blessing': Exchange and Explanation in *The Merchant of Venice,*" *Shakespeare Quarterly,* 37

(1986): 31, 36; Thomas Moisan, "'Which is the merchant here? and which the Jew?': subversion and recuperation in *The Merchant of Venice,*" in *Shakespeare Reproduced: The text in history and ideology,* ed. Jean E. Howard and Marion F. O'Connor (New York: Methuen, 1987), 197.

4. John Russell Brown, "The Realization of Shylock," in *Early Shakespeare,* ed. John Russell Brown and Bernard Harris (New York: St. Martin's Press, 1961), 205.

5. Moody, 14; H. B. Charlton, *Shakespearean Comedy* (New York: Macmillan, 1938), 133.

6. Goddard, 97.

7. Girard, 107.

8. Brown, 206.

9. Goddard, 97.

10. C. L. Barber, *Shakespeare's Festive Comedy* (1959; rpt. Cleveland: World Publishing Co., 1963), 169; Frank Kermode, *Early Shakespeare,* 223-24; Sylvan Barnet, *Twentieth Century Interpretations of "The Merchant of Venice,"* ed. Sylvan Barnet (Englewood Cliffs, New Jersey: Prentice-Hall, 1970, 3-8).

11. Elmer Edgar Stoll, *Shakespeare Studies: Historical and Comparative in Method* (1917; rpt. New York: Frederick Ungar, 1960), 271, 294-95. For concurring views, see Hazelton Spencer, *The Art and Life of William Shakespeare* (New York: Harcourt, Brace, 1940), 239-40; and Norman Holland, *The Shakespearean Imagination* (New York: Macmillan, 1964), 92.

12. G. K. Hunter, "The Theology of Marlowe's *The Jew of Malta,*" 1964, republished in his *Dramatic Identities and Cultural Tradition* (New York: Barnes & Noble, 1978), 64-65.

13. Alan C. Dessen, "The Elizabethan Stage Jew and Christian Example," *Modern Language Quarterly,* 35 (1974): 232-33, 239-41.

14. Girard, 108-09.

15. Girard, 100.

16. Robert Weimann, *Structure and Society in Literary History,* expanded edition (1976; rpt. Baltimore: The Johns Hopkins University Press, 1984), 1-56.

17. Cohen, 771; Ferber, 446.

18. Cohen, 767-71.

19. The quotation is from Lucien Dällenbach, *La Récit spéculaire* (Paris: Seuil, 1977), p. 17, as translated by Moshe Ron, "The Restricted Abyss: Nine Problems in the Theory of *Mise en Abyme,*" *Poetics Today,* 8 (1987), 421. Gide's diary entry appropriating this term is cited by Ron, p. 418, from pp. 30-31 of André Gide, *Journals 1889-1949,* trans. Justin O'Brien (Harmondsworth: Penguin, 1967). See also Lucien Dällenbach, "Reflexivity and Reading," *New Literary History,* 11 (1980), 435-449; and Ann Jefferson, "*Mise en abyme* and the Prophetic in Narrative," *Style,* 17 (1983), 196-208.

20. Weimann, 49.

21. M. M. Bakhtin, *The Dialogic Imagination,* ed. Michael Holquist, trans. Caryl Emerson and Michael Holquist (Austin: University of Texas Press, 1981), 23-26, 161-63.

22. In "Bond Priorities in *The Merchant of Venice,*" *Studies in English Literature,* 20 (1980): 220, Jan Lawson Hinely finds Launcelot's antics instinct with an "undercurrent of real cruelty."

23. Charlton, 128. See also Spenser, 244; Oscar Campbell, *Shakespeare's Satire* (London, Oxford University Press, 1943), 7; Leslie Fiedler, *The Stranger in Shakespeare* (New York: Stein and Day, 1972), 108; Bill Overton, *The Merchant of Venice: Text and Performance* (London: Macmillan, 1987), 39.

24. In "'A Dish of Doves': *The Merchant of Venice,*" *ELH,* 40 (1973): 347, Leo Rockas observes that Launcelot's moral dilemma in II.ii "is the same one that Jessica expresses in the following scene." Hinely, 220, observes that "Launcelot's initial struggle between his conscience and the fiend . . . is a farcical version of Jessica's situation, presented in the scene immediately following."

25. René Fortin, "Launcelot and the Uses of Allegory in *The Merchant of Venice,*" *Studies in English Literature,* 14 (1974): 259.

26. Dorothy C. Hockey, "The Patch is Kind Enough," *Shakespeare Quarterly,* 10 (1959), 448-50; Barbara K. Lewalski, "Biblical Allusion and Allegory in *The Merchant of Venice,*" *Shakespeare Quarterly,* 13 (1962): 327-43.

27. John Russell Brown, ed. the new Arden *Merchant of Venice* (London: Methuen, 1959), 39, note to line 75, citing Henley as seeing "allusions to the deception practiced on the blindness of Isaac; cf. the recognition by feeling Launcelot's hair."

28. Hockey, 448-49.

29. Hockey, 449.

30. All Shakespeare quotations are cited in *The Riverside Shakespeare,* ed. G. Blakemore Evans et al. (Boston: Houghton Mifflin, 1974).

31. Lewalski, 340-41. Barber, 185, had earlier identified St. Paul as providing the terms of law and grace in the trial sequence of IV.i. For subsequent arguments based on the operation of Pauline theology in the play, see John R. Cooper, "Shylock's Humanity," *Shakespeare Quarterly,* 21 (1970): 121; and Sylvan Barnet, "Prodigality and Time in *The Merchant of Venice,*" *Publications of the Modern Language Association,* 87 (1972): 26.

32. Lewalski, 342.

33. Lewalski, 329, 334, 339. For other associations of Antonio with Christ, see Kermode, 224; and Joan Ozark Holmer, "The Education of the Merchant of Venice," *Studies in English Literature,* 25 (1985): 310.

34. Lewalski, 341-42.

35. Lewalski, 331, 338.

36. All biblical citations are from *The Geneva Bible: A facsimile of the 1560 edition,* introd. Lloyd E. Berry (Madison: University of Wisconsin Press, 1969). Spelling has been minimally modernized.

37. John Calvin, *A Commentary on Genesis* (1554, Latin), (1578, English), Two Volumes in One, trans. and ed. John King (1847) (rpt. London: Calvin Translation Society, 1965) II, 50.

38. Calvin, 50.

39. Calvin, 50.

40. Fortin, 267.

41. Fortin, 266-67.

42. Lewalski, 334.

43. Fortin, 267-68.

44. David N. Beauregard, "Sidney, Aristotle, and *The Merchant of Venice:* Shakespeare's Triadic Images of Liberality and Justice," *Shakespeare Studies,* 20 (1988): 33.

45. Barnet, "Prodigality and Time in *The Merchant of Venice,*" 26. Like Barnet, Brown in the Arden *Merchant,* lviii, uses prodigality to describe the giving that he sees as the play's most important value: "Giving is the most important part—giving prodigality, without thought for the taking." And in "*The Merchant of Venice* and the Pattern of Romantic Comedy," *Shakespeare Survey,* 28 (1975): 82, R. F. Hill similarly views Jessica's squandering as "a free outgoing of that which was not given us to hoard."

46. Moisan, 198.

47. Moisan, 195.

48. At the 1985 meeting of the Shakespeare Association of America in Nashville, Tennessee, in seminar XIII entitled *The Merchant of Venice* Controversies: Past and Present, I presented the idea of Launcelot as a type of the Prodigal Son in a paper entitled "*The Merchant of Venice* and the Blessing of Abraham." The same sense of Launcelot's meaning as well as its extension to Jessica appears in Beuregard's 1988 essay, 39-40.

49. Manfred Pfister, "Comic Subversion: A Bakhtinian View of the Comic in Shakespeare," *Deutsche Shakespeare-Gesellschaft West,* 1987, 33-34, 35-36, 42.

50. For an example of this view, see Moisan, 191.

51. To appreciate Paul's insistent representation of grace as wealth, see Ephesians, where he calls God "riche in mercie" (ii.4) and refers to "his riche grace" (i.7), "the exceeding riches of his grace" (ii.7), and "the unsearcheable riches of Christ" (iii.8).

52. See Hunter, 64-65, for the conventionally negative representation of money in *The Jew of Malta* as worldly and anti-Christian.

53. For views of money in *Merchant* as symbolic, though not theological, see G. Wilson Knight, *The Shakespearean Tempest* (London: Oxford University Press, 1932), 129, 131; G. Wilson Knight, *Principles of Shakespearean Production* (London: Faber and Faber, 1936), 187; and John Russell Brown, "Love's Wealth and the Judgment of *The Merchant of Venice,*" in his *Shakespeare and His Comedies* (London: Methuen, 1957), 61.

54. Nevill Coghill, "The Basis of Shakespearean Comedy," *Essays and Studies,* N.S. 1-3 (1948-1950), 21; Kermode, 224; Cooper, 121; Albert Wertheim, "The Treatment of Shylock and Thematic Integrity in *The Merchant of Venice,*" *Shakespeare Studies,* 6 (1970): 79, 86; Holland, 93; Fiedler, 86-87; Lawrence Danson, *The Harmonies of "The Merchant of Venice"* (New Haven: Yale Univ. Press, 1978), 13; Barber, 185.

55. Moody, 50; Norman Rabkin, *Shakespeare and the Problem of Meaning* (Chicago: University of Chicago Press, 1981), 16.

56. John S. Coolidge, "Law and Love in *The Merchant of Venice,*" *Shakespeare Quarterly,* 27 (1976): 243 and note 15 on 249.

57. Rabkin, 20-21. For a full statement of Rabkin's argument, see 19-32.

58. Rabkin, 7.

59. Coghill, 21.

60. Rabkin, 10-12.

61. Barnet, *Twentieth Century Interpretations,* 6, 7.

62. Brown, *Shakespeare and His Comedies,* 71, 72-73.

63. Holmer, 309; Danson, 31-32.

64. Arthur Quiller-Couch, ed., *The Merchant of Venice* (1926; rpt. Cambridge: At the University Press, 1953), xxii; Charlton, 125; Moody, 17; Brown in the Arden Merchant, xxxiv, records the 1709 opinion of Nicholas Rowe that the play "was design'd Tragically by the Author." In "Brothers and Others," in *The Dyer's Hand and other Essays* (New York: Random House, 1948), 223, 221, W. H. Auden renders a common judgment in calling *Merchant* a "problem" play to be "classed among Shakespeare's 'Unpleasant Plays.'" And Ryan, 49, likewise repudiates "the traditional romantic idealist reading of the play."

65. Brown, "The Realization of Shylock," 206; Barber, 190. See also Ferber, 459, for the description of Shylock as "character not fully digested and assimilated into the structure of themes."

66. Hockey, 448-449.

67. Brown, the Arden *Merchant,* 39, note to 11. 73-74.

68. In the new Variorium edition of *The Merchant of Venice,* ed. Horace Howard Furness, 12fth ed. (Philadelphia: J. B. Lippincott Co., 1888), 69, the note to line 89 records Staunton's opinion that "stage tradition, not improbably from the time of Shakespeare himself, makes Launcelot, at this point, kneel with his back to the sand-blind old Father, who, of course, mistakes his long back hair for a beard, of which his face is perfectly innocent."

69. In *Love and Society in Shakespearean Comedy* (London: Univ. of Delaware Press, 1985), 33, Richard A. Levin these allegations as "Launcelot's rationalizations, offered . . . to ease his conscience . . ."

70. Charlton, 156, observes that Jessica's phrase "says more of [her] frivolous nature than of the repulsiveness of her father's house."

71. See Thomas Wilson, *A Discourse upon Usury* (1572), with an historical introduction by R. H. Tawney (New York: Augustus M. Kelley, 1965), 219, 275-76, 285.

72. The possessive taint in Antonio's love for Bassanio has frequently been noted. In "Portia and *The Merchant of Venice:* the Gentle Bond," *Modern Language Quarterly,* 28 (1967): 26, Robert Hapgood observes that "Antonio is at once too generous and too possessive." In "The Rival Lovers in *The Merchant of Venice,*" *Shakespeare Quarterly,* 21 (1970): 110, Lawrence W. Hyman observes that "Antonio's wealth which he puts at his friend's disposal is a means of holding on to Bassanio's love." Hinely, 234, likewise describes Antonio's love of Bassanio as "possessiveness expressed through generosity."

73. This reading of the Prodigal story is accepted by modern interpreters, as exemplified by Rosemary Radford Ruether, *Faith and Fratricide: The Theological Roots of Anti-Semitism* (New York: Seabury Press, 1974), 254.

74. Fortin, 267.

75. Ruether, 94.

76. Ruether, 65, 139-40. On 117-21 Ruether lists the various expressions of this tradition, including Tertullian's *Adversos Judaeos,* Augustine's *Tractatus adversus Judaeos,* the eight sermons against the Jews preached by John Chrysostom, and Justin Martyr's *Dialogue with Trypho.*

77. Ruether, 137-40.

78. Ruether, 230. While observing *Merchant* to evoke the patristic negation of the Jews' claim to the prophetic promises, Coolidge does not recognize this negation as censured by the prodigal identities of Launcelot, Jessica, and Antonio.

79. Ruether, 101-2, 176-79.

80. For the sexual character of Antonio's love, whether conscious, or initially suppressed and only gradually emerging to consciousness, see Auden, 231; Graham Midgley, "The Merchant of Venice: A Reconsideration," *Essays in Criticism,* 10 (1960): 125-26; John D. Hurrell, "Love and Friendship in *The Merchant of Venice,*" *Texas Studies in Literature and Language,*" 3 (1961): 340; Ralph Berry, *Shakespeare's Comedies* (Princeton: Princeton University Press, 1972), 125; Rockas, 346; Keith Geary, "The Nature of Portia's Victory: Turning to Men in *The Merchant of Venice,*" *Shakespeare Survey* 37 (1984): 58-59; and more tentatively, Levin, 31.

81. Fiedler, 136. See also Coppélia Kahn, "The Cuckoo's Note: Male Friendship and Cuckoldry in *The Merchant of Venice,*" in *Shakespeare's Rough Magic,* ed. Peter Erickson and Coppélia Kahn (Newark: University of Delaware Press, 1985), 109.

82. Hinely, 235, observes that following the forfeiture of the ring, the friends are "closer than at any other time in the play."

83. Fiedler, 135, observes that in returning her ring to Bassanio's finger, Antonio gives "the bridegroom away." And Geary, 67, similarly perceives that Antonio's return of Portia's ring to Bassanio means that "Portia has defeated him and displaced him in Bassanio's heart." See also Kahn, 107.

84. Brown, "The Realization of Shylock," 206.

85. Engle, 28-31, finds the Jacob/Laban story to express Shylock's just complaint that, like Jacob working for Laban, he serves the economy without being allowed full participation in it. By contrast, Joan Ozark Holmer takes a negative and, I think, more accurate view of Shylock's biblical defense of his usury. By finding this story mentioned in an anti-usury tract that excoriates those who adduce Scripture in defense of usury, she aptly suggests that this tract provides both the text for Shylock's defense of usury and the opinion that censures it. See "Miles Mosse's *The Arraignment and Conviction of Usurie* (1595): A New Source for *The Merchant of Venice,*" *Shakespeare Studies,* 21 (1993): 15-17, 21, 34.

86. See Brown, the Arden *Merchant,* xxii: "The quarto's repeated 'Iobbe' (II.ii.3 ff.) suggests that Shakespeare intended to use the Italianized form of Job."

87. The *OED* gives "Use 4" as "the act or fact of using, holding, or possessing land or other property so as to derive revenue, profit, or other benefit from such." "Use 4" has an alternate meaning b that defines it as "a trust or confidence reposed in a person for the holding of property, etc., of which another receives or is entitled to the profits or benefits." But it is meaning c that cites the phrase

"in use," not only showing that phrase to denote a trust but also referring the terms of that trust as readily to the primary definition that gives the profit to the trustee, as to the alternate meaning of b that gives the profit to another. It is the uncertainty thus introduced into "in use" that has prompted critics to disagree on the question of who gets the profit of Antonio's trust. Brown in the Arden *Merchant,* 119, note to line 379, suggests that it will go to Shylock. Holmer, "The Education of the Merchant of Venice," 317, agrees. Danson, 125, thinks that both principal and profit will go to Jessica and Lorenzo at Shylock's death. Yet Brown also recognizes Antonio's poverty, which suggests that he himself keeps it, as Johnson, I think correctly, concludes: "Antonio declares that, as the Duke quits one-half of the forfeiture, he is likewise content to abate his claim, and desires not the property but the use or produce only of the half, and that only for the Jew's life . . . " See Furness, the Variorum *Merchant,* 227, note to lines 398-402.

88. Furness, the Variorum *Merchant,* 68, note to line 65.

89. Furness, the Variorum *Merchant,* 68, note to line 64.

90. In the Variorum *Merchant,* 69, note to line 83, Furness asks us to "note Gobbo's respectful 'you,' until he recognizes Launcelot, and then his change to 'thou.'"

91. Among those offended by Shylock's forced conversion are Quiller-Couch, xix-xx; Charlton, 128; Goddard, 89; and Sigurd Burckhardt, "*The Merchant of Venice:* The Gentle Bond," *ELH,* 29 (1962): 253. Among those who defend it as saving Shylock's soul or bringing him social benefits are Coghill, 23; Lewalski, 341; Cooper, 121; Wertheim, 85; Barnet, *Twentieth Century Interpretations,* 7; and Holmer, "The Education of the Merchant of Venice," 321.

DISAPPOINTMENT

Matthew A. Fike (essay date 1994)

SOURCE: "Disappointment in *The Merchant of Venice,*" in *ANQ: A Quarterly Journal of Short Articles, Notes, and Reviews,* Vol. 7, No. 1, n.s., 1994, pp. 13-18.

[*In the essay below, Fike analyzes disappointment as a central theme in* The Merchant of Venice, *concluding that the disappointment found in love, friendship, and aspirations in the play mirrors Shakespeare's belief that perfect harmony is to be found solely in the afterlife.*]

While Jessica and Lorenzo's banter at the beginning of Act V of *The Merchant of Venice* has been viewed as out of character with the harmony one expects at this point in a comedy, it has not yet been analyzed in light of the theme of disappointment.[1] As Gratiano expresses it, "All things that are / Are with more spirit chasèd than enjoyed," a direct commentary on Lorenzo's tardiness for his liaison with Jessica (II.vi.12-13). Lorenzo, in other words, may derive more pleasure from striving for Jessica than he does from her permanent presence in his life. What may be true for him is definitely true for other characters: since it is more enjoyable to anticipate than to attain, disappointment is ascendant in the universe of the play. Thus the classical allusions in the "love duet" not only reflect disappointing circumstances earlier in the play but also contrast with what, ultimately, does satisfy.

Gratiano's comment introduces a simile that suggests a paradigm of disappointing experience: "How like a younger or a prodigal / The scarfèd bark puts from her native bay, / Hugg'd and embracèd by the strumpet wind! / How like the prodigal doth she return, / With over-weather'd ribs and ragged sails, / Lean, rent, and beggar'd by the strumpet wind!" (II.vi.14-19). Here is a nautical rendering of the prodigal son story, but with disappointment as a variation. There is a return, but it is not restorative. To illustrate his sense that all things are more heartily pursued than savored, Gratiano omits the part of the allusion that would qualify his assertion, stressing instead the negative effects on the ship of wind and water, which correspond to the prodigal son's debasement and destitution. That is, Gratiano stresses the flight from the stormy sea, and by implication from the sty, rather than the safe harbor or the positive life in the father's house. In reality, the return from sea or sty would presumably transcend expectations and be enjoyed with more spirit that it is pursued. But for Gratiano, if there even is a homecoming for son or ship, it is not the happy occasion that the parable depicts. What makes his allusion problematic is not only the omission of the welcome but also the implication that the homecoming, if it were achieved, would be a disappointment.

The fiscal ventures in the play bear out the prodigal's experience of pursuing what does not yield the hoped-for enjoyment. Bassanio, like the prodigal son, asks father-figure Antonio for an additional loan. His earlier use of borrowed money has not met his needs or fulfilled his expectations. Shylock pursues his bond with Antonio with great gusto, but his attempt to enforce it results in personal and financial ruin rather than satisfaction—the greatest disappointment suffered by any character in the play. Antonio himself suffers fiscal disappointment. While it is fortunate that three of his ships return, Shylock's earlier statement conveys the more significant fact that many more have been lost: "Yet [Antonio's] means are in supposition: he hath an argosy bound to Tripolis, another to the Indies; I understand moreover upon the Rialto, he hath a third at Mexico, a fourth for England, and other ventures he hath, squand'red abroad" (I.iii.17-21). The return by the three ships ironically implies the grim spectre of loss: the disappointing truth that most of Antonio's ships, in fact, have been wrecked or are still missing, much as the prodigal's return underscores his great financial losses. But Antonio, who denies in Act I that the anxiety of ownership causes his sadness, also subtly contrasts with the prodigal: he has achieved fiscal success. If Gratiano's insight holds, the hollowness of ownership causes Antonio's melancholy. His material wealth at the opening is enjoyed with less delight than presumably it was anticipated. If Antonio's prosperity has not lived up to his expectations and does not supply the happiness for which he yearns, disappointment results and sadness is its symptom.

Human relationships are fertile ground for disappointment as well. Antonio's sadness stems partly from his awareness that Bassanio's marriage to Portia diminishes Antonio's role in his friend's life. Solanio makes it clear how much Antonio loves Bassanio: "I think he only loves the world for him" (II.viii.50). The second loan affirms their friendship but ultimately results in diminished closeness. The suitors provide a more dramatic illustration of relational disappointment. Gratiano's image of a ship setting forth to encounter a natural force personified as a woman parallels their failure: they return home as romantic beggars, not having won Portia's hand but having sworn never to marry. They have chased marriage with great spirit but have forfeited married life along with the enjoyment it might have brought. Even apart from marriage, relationships cause disappointment in *The Merchant of Venice*. Shylock is devastated by Jessica's greed and insensitivity, and Launcelot's liaison with a black serving girl has resulted in a pregnancy. There is no evidence that this fazes the clown, but the pregnancy is clearly an unwanted inconvenience.

While Jessica and Lorenzo's banter in V.i is good-natured, their allusions suggest that the passage may participate in the disappointment that shadows the earlier action. They celebrate their love by allusion to mythical lovers—Troilus and Cressida, Pyramus and Thisbe, Aeneas and Dido, Jason and Medea—who come to grief because of misunderstanding or betrayal.[2]

A first possibility is that the allusions convey doubts about the stability of their marriage. Perhaps Jessica will betray Lorenzo as she has already betrayed Shylock—Lorenzo's reference to Cressida suggests that he is not unaware of that possibility. He may one day be to Jessica as Troilus is to Cressida, or as Gratiano's prodigal ship is to the "strumpet wind"—not just a disappointed husband but also the victim of betrayal. As for Lorenzo, Gratiano's insight may apply: perhaps he was more eager to pursue Jessica than to enjoy her in marriage. Shakespeare's own Cressida, in the later play bearing her name, offers words that sound very much like Gratiano's comment on his friend's tardiness, a connection furthering his suspicion about Lorenzo's attitude: "Women are angels, wooing: / Things won are done, joy's soul lies in the doing. / That she belov'd knows nought that knows not this: / Men prize the thing ungain'd more than it is. / That she was never yet that ever knew / Love got so sweet as when desire did sue"

(*Troilus and Cressida* I.ii.286-91). For men, as Gratiano would agree, the chase is more enjoyable than the achievement of a romantic goal. Perhaps Lorenzo, not having heard Gratiano's wry comment of Act II, fears that he will not enjoy his marriage to Jessica as much as he has anticipated because all things that are, including marriage, are enjoyed more in prospect than in attainment. Jessica playfully implies an awareness of Lorenzo's potential for infidelity in her reference to Medea and Aeson, for the story of Aeson's rejuvenation includes Jason's betrayal of Medea after years of marriage. In their banter, Jessica and Lorenzo thus hint at each other's potential for betrayal. Despite the loveliness of the setting and their good humor, the potential for marital disappointment is the faint undertone of their love duet—the extent of implications for Jessica and Lorenzo's attitudes toward each other. If doubts exist at this point, they are merely playful, as though they were a kind of inoculation against future infidelity or "a comic exorcism of the tragic side of love" (Leggatt 143).

Indicting unfaithful lovers of both sexes suggests a criticism of couples in general. In Lorenzo's statements the betrayers, Aeneas and Cressida, are both male and female—the myths he alludes to distribute blame for pain in relationships to both genders. It is tempting, however, to view Jessica's references in a different light, since her allusion to Pyramus and Thisbe evokes tragic misunderstanding, rather than betrayal. Moreover, her reference to Aeson's rejuvenation, a kind of rebirth, is appropriate to new life in Belmont. Yet the Medea-Aeson allusion undercuts itself because of the duet's parallelism. The earlier allusions to mythical women *and their lovers* call Jason to mind, despite specific reference only to his father. Shakespeare knew that, following the rejuvenation, Jason abandoned Medea who then burned "hir husbands bride by witchcraft" and "in hir owne deare childrens bloud had bathde hir wicked knife" (Ovid 146; VII.501, 503). Whereas Lorenzo refers to Cressida and Aeneas, unfaithful lovers, Jessica invokes Jason and Medea who are hateful to each other. The point of the four allusions, then, is not merely the fact that women like Cressida betray men like Troilus, or that men like Aeneas desert women like Dido, or that the mutual misunderstanding of a couple like Pyramus and Thisbe can lead to tragedy for both. More important than that, the recollection of Jason and Medea suggests mutual disappointment in marriage. The sad conclusion is that the sexes, in their shared humanity, are potentially hateful to each other, or more specifically that Jessica and Lorenzo will encounter their share of problems in married life.

Just as the love duet participates in the disappointment developed earlier in the play, it also signals disappointment in the future, as further parallelism reveals. The situation in each allusion is once removed from tragedy. Troilus mounts the Trojan walls and sighs for Cressida; he later achieves full understanding of her betrayal. Thisbe sees the lion and runs away . . . later Pyramus's discovery of her bloody veil leads to double suicide. Dido, having loved Aeneas and been deserted, longs for his return; she has not yet killed herself in despair. Medea gathers herbs that renew her husband's father; abandonment and murder happen years in the future. The allusions, therefore, create the sense of a coming storm. For Thisbe and Dido, a present problem (the presumed death of Pyramus, abandonment by Aeneas) leads to future suicide. Troilus and Medea, though they perform positive actions in the present, are betrayed in the future. Thus the play invites seeing Jessica and Lorenzo in a similar way. Underneath their banter lies the sense that their happiness may one day yield to disappointment and discord. That is in harmony with the pattern of disappointment established in Acts I through IV: anticipation transcends outcome.

The love duet also casts doubt on the future of other marriages in the play. The invocation of Jason and Medea colors Gratiano's earlier statement about the successful trip to Belmont: "I know that [Antonio] will be glad of our success; / We are the Jasons, we have won the fleece" (III.ii.240-41). He and Bassanio have achieved their goals, but the recollection of Jason and Medea in Act V ironically undercuts Gratiano's delight: he celebrates his marriage in terms of a classical figure who is famous for infidelity. Moreover, whereas Gratiano's own prophecy in Act II qualifies his fiscal and marital success, he is now blind to the violation of expectations and the potential for disappointment in his own marriage and in Bassanio's. He has forgotten that, in the problematic universe of *The Merchant of Venice,* it is simply impossible to attain with the same savor as one anticipates. Marital happiness is not an exception to the rule.

But marriage is merely synechdoche: as marriage carries the potential for disappointment, so does all of life, as Shakespeare's treatment of Belmont reveals. For Jessica, Belmont "figures forth the heavenly city" (Lewalski 343): "It is very meet / The Lord Bassanio live an upright life, / For having such a blessing in his lady, / He finds the joys of heaven here on earth" (III.v.73-76). It turns out, however, that Belmont is to the heavenly city as human life is to immortality. One "figures forth" the other in Jessica's imagination, but conflating the two—burdening an earthly state with expectations of heavenly bliss—can cause disappointment. The actual nature of Belmont is implied by Lorenzo's statement: "There's not the smallest orb which thou behold'st / But in his motion like an angel sings, / Still quiring to the young-ey'd cherubins; / Such harmony is in immortal souls, / But whilst this muddy vesture of decay / Doth grossly close it in, we cannot hear it" (V.i.60-65). Lorenzo refers to both the music of the spheres and the corresponding music within the human soul. As longing for heavenly music is frustrated in this life, so Belmont falls short of the heavenly city. If full spiritual enjoyment is not possible, then Jessica's prediction is unlikely to be realized. Lorenzo's message is simply that the afterlife transcends expectations; nothing earthly can satisfy. The happy banter of Jessica and Lorenzo, itself problematic, is fleeting, for marriage, Belmont, and all of life are subject to the same potential for disappointment.

Surprisingly Launcelot expresses the proper qualification in his statement to Bassanio, though he may not realize it. "The old proverb is very well parted between my master Shylock and you, sir: you have the grace of God, sir, and he hath enough" (II.ii.149-51). Whatever jokes Launcelot may be making, the important point is what the original proverb conveys: "He that hath the grace of God hath enough." Disappointment results from an earthly outcome's ultimate insufficiency, its inability to live up to expectations. Even rejuvenation like Aeson's cannot change the inner man, alter the fact of eventual death or ensure eternal life. Everything earthly is doomed to death, which is why Morocco finds a skull in the golden casket. God's grace, however, is sufficient in itself and does not disappoint us: "They called vpon thee, and were deliuered: they trusted in thee, and were not confounded" (Psalm 22:5). Ultimately, the play points toward the need for the salvation Portia alludes to—"mercy . . . above this sceptered sway" (IV.i.193). The problem with the love duet, then, is that, despite Jessica's conversion, the allusions are based not on Christian mercy but on thinking that predates the old law: revenge is justifiable (Medea), and suicide is an adequate response to loss (Pyramus, Thisbe, Dido, and perhaps Troilus). However humorous their banter may be and however hopeful their future may seem, Jessica and Lorenzo are still operating in a universe of disappointment and indirectly imply the need for grace and charity.

So instead of offering marriage as an end in itself, the playwright implies that no ending, however comedic, can be totally unproblematic, since harmony in this life and of the earth forever falls one step short of celestial harmony. It is true that the lovers have avoided tragedy, though they voice subtle reminders of its everpresent possibility. But no one can enjoy the goal with as much spirit as one pursues it because full enjoyment, Shakespeare suggest, abides only in the next life and in the realization of divine love. Otherwise, disappointment is the burden of mortality.

Notes

1. For commentary on V.i.1-24 see Auden 113-15, Baxter 74-77, Cosgrove 57ff., Gnerro 19-21, Hassel 69, Hill 85, and Leggatt 143.

2. Jessica actually refers not to Jason but to his father: "In such a night / Medea gathered the enchanted herbs / That did renew old Aeson" (V.i.13-15). The reference to Aeson and the argument for invoking Jason are examined below.

Works Cited

Auden, W. H. "Belmont and Venice." *Twentieth Century Interpretations of* The Merchant of Venice. Ed. Sylvan Barnet. Englewood Cliffs: Prentice-Hall, 1970. 113-15.

Baxter, John S. "Present Mirth: Shakespeare's Romantic Comedies." *Queen's Quarterly* 72 (1965): 52-77.

Cosgrove, Mark F. "Biblical, Liturgical, and Classical Allusions in *The Merchant of Venice.*" Diss. Univ. of Florida, 1970.

Gnerro, Mark L. "Easter Liturgy and the Love Duet in *MV* V, I," *American Notes & Queries* 18 (1979): 19-21.

The Geneva Bible. A facsimile of the 1560 edition. Madison: The Univ. of Wisconsin Press, 1969.

Hassel, Chris R., Jr. "Antonio and the Ironic Festivity of *The Merchant of Venice*." *Shakespeare Studies* 6 (1970): 67-74.

Hill, R. F. "*The Merchant of Venice* and the Pattern of Romantic Comedy." *Shakespeare Survey* 28 (1975): 75-87.

Leggatt, Alexander. *Shakespeare's Comedy of Love.* London: Methuen, 1974.

Lewalski, Barbara K. "Biblical Allusion and Allegory in *The Merchant of Venice*." *Shakespeare Quarterly* 13 (1962): 327-43.

Ovid. *The Metamorphoses.* Trans. Arthur Golding. Ed. J.M. Cohen. London: Centaur Press, 1961.

Shakespeare, William. *The Merchant of Venice* and *Troilus and Cressida. The Riverside Shakespeare.* Ed. G. Blakemore Evans. Boston: Houghton Mifflin, 1974: 250-85; 443-98.

ELIZABETHAN CULTURE AND VALUES

Thomas Moisan (essay date 1987)

SOURCE: "'Which is the merchant here? and which the Jew?': Subversion and Recuperation in *The Merchant of Venice*," in *Shakespeare Reproduced: The Text in History and Ideology,* edited by Jean E. Howard and Marion F. O'Connor, Methuen, Inc., 1987, pp. 188-206.

[*In the essay below, Moisan argues that while* The Merchant of Venice *appears to celebrate the Elizabethan values of Christian ethics and good business, the play instead subtly exposes a contradiction between the apparent belief in these values and whether or not they are actually practiced.*]

As a *locus* in which to ponder the ideological function of the Shakespearean text, *The Merchant of Venice* is an obvious, and obviously problematic, choice. At a glance, the *Merchant* seems to inscribe and affirm an ideological calculus that fused the interests of the state and the assertions of a providentialist Christianity with the prerogatives of an increasingly capitalist marketplace. We can perceive this calculus allegorized in the central action of the play and ratified in the ultimate thwarting of the Jewish usurer Shylock, the redemption of the Christian merchant Antonio, and the triumphs—forensic and domestic—of the bountiful aristocrat Portia, and we can see it reflected and legitimated in the sundry polarities the play has often been said to be—to use Frank Kermode's rather equivocal quotation marks—"'about'": the Old Law versus the New Law, Justice versus Mercy, Vengeance versus Love (1961, 224).[1] At the same time, however, the considerable residue of qualification that attends even the most compelling efforts to schematize the play in this way has made it no easy matter to say what the *Merchant* is "about;"[2] and in the degree to which the play leaves us, for example, feeling troubled over the treatment of Shylock, or appears to blur the distinctions on which the polarities above depend, leading us, in effect, to ask with Portia, "Which is the merchant here? and which the Jew?" (IV. i. 170), we may wonder whether the *Merchant* invokes the ideologically sanctioned mythologies of the time only to question and subvert them.

In part, of course, it can be argued that the contradictions we experience in the *Merchant* are evidence, not of its subversive design, but of its mimetic fidelity, and that the dissonances we detect in it are but echoes of the tensions and stresses of the society it reflects, a society in transition, confronting—or being confronted by—what Louis Adrian Montrose calls "the ideologically anomalous realities of change" (1980, 64). "Taken on its own terms," Jonathan Dollimore reminds us, "an ideology may appear internally coherent. When, however, its deep structure is examined it is often discovered to be a synthesis of contradictory elements" (1984, 20). Thus, in the inclination we feel to ask "Which is the merchant here? and which the Jew?" we may merely be responding to the traces in the play of a debate within the times over whether Old Religion and New Business were fully compatible, and whether the "thrifty" pursuit of trade and the "prodigal" indulgence of greed were fully distinct. On the other hand, to the extent to which we see in the *Merchant* a movement toward reconciliation and harmony—a thesis argued most fully by Lawrence Danson some years ago (1978, esp. 1-21, 170-95)—the play can be said to ritualize the ideological synthesis being wrought from the contrarieties of its society.

We find the *Merchant* scanned in these terms quite cogently in an essay published several years ago by Walter Cohen (1982). For Cohen the *Merchant* enacts a largely successful, and deeply comic, mediation between two differing conceptions of socioeconomic relations: the one rooted in English history and reflective of contemporary anxiety over the emerging economic order, the other derived from Shakespeare's Italian sources and reflecting both a less troubled view of the capitalist system and a more confident differentiation between the figure of the usurer, who incarnates, Cohen would suggest, "a quasifeudal fiscalism" in decline, and that of the merchant, who embodies, in Cohen's words, "an indigenous bourgeois mercantilism" on the ascent (1982, 771). In Cohen's reading the workings of dramatic form and ideological synthesis are persuasively integrated. Even as the central action of the play, Cohen argues, upholds a "formally dominant Christian, aristocratic ideology," we see in "the subversive side of the play" evidence of "an internal distancing," a distancing, however, which may complicate but does not annul that harmonic "movement" Cohen sees in the play "towards resolution and reconciliation" (pp. 779-81). In this way *The Merchant of Venice* can be seen to negotiate among the heterogeneous impulses and interests that characterized the "public" of the public theater. At the same time, the *Merchant* can also be taken to exemplify what might be called the emerging "containment" theory of Renaissance drama, to wit, that the Shakespearean stage offered a platform on which cultural heterodoxy could be at once expressed, engaged, and contained, a forum, Cohen observes, for "communal affirmation and social ratification, [and] a means of confronting fear and anger in a manner that promoted reassurance about the existence and legitimacy of a new order" (p. 783; see also Montrose, 1980, 62-4; Greenblatt, 1981, 40-61).

Still, that there is a "movement" in *The Merchant of Venice* "towards resolution and reconciliation" has not been, the annals of criticism would show, a truth universally acknowledged. To be sure, a play which has as much conflict in it and yet ends as happily as the *Merchant* does would seem to have something to do with resolution and reconciliation, and, certainly, the subject of harmony is much in the night air of Belmont in act V. Yet whether the play actually produces a harmonious resolution and reconciliation or merely invokes harmony by the power of dramatic *fiat* and in the interest of ideological conformity or capitulation is not an easy matter to settle, though it is an important one to consider if we are to assess the nature of the accommodation the *Merchant* reaches with its society.

At this point it might be useful to think of what it is we experience in, to use Cohen's words, that "internal distancing" at work in the play. For Cohen this distancing is evident in the articulation the *Merchant* accords sentiments that would qualify or subvert the ideological prescriptions the action, or fable, of the play would appear to embrace. Ultimately, though, I would suggest that in the "internal distancing" we perceive in it, the *Merchant* asserts its "play-ful" alterity, distancing itself simultaneously, on the one hand, from the ideological implications of its fable, and on the other, from the very questionings and subversive sentiments to which it gives notice. We get a hint of this distancing in the tendency of the play to leave unresolved dialogic exchanges in which it permits the mythologies it inscribes to be interrogated. We sense it more pointedly, though, in the, literally, "anti-literal" skepticism we hear displayed in it toward "words" and "texts," a skepticism through which the play pretends to dissociate itself from the very textuality that nourishes and complicates it. In this way the play implicitly underscores its theatricality and resolves, and "recuperates," the "confusions" in its text by posing—or imposing—a comic, a comically dramatic, solution.

What follows, then, is an attempt to read *The Merchant of Venice* in and, in a sense, out of the discourse of its times. First, and at the risk of viewing the play from the kind of distortingly narrow, overly economic, overly Anglicized, perspective that Cohen warns against—and avoids (pp. 768-70)—I will look at some of the ways in which the play participates in and interrogates the economic mythologies of its times by affiliating itself with the texts in which these mythologies are shaped, rehearsed, and questioned. From there, however, I would like to speculate on how the play strives to extricate itself from the complexities and contradictions of the times which its text, and textuality, have "uncovered."

1

In what sense, though, would *The Merchant of Venice*, with its eponymous setting and Italian literary pedigree, have held up a mirror to its English audience? Quite apart from the topicality commentators have detected in it,[3] of interest to us here is our awareness that the *Merchant* evokes the growing "trafficking" of the English nation in trade, or, rather, the growing identification of England and its institutions *with* trade and capitalist enterprise. We hear this prominence of trade and investment recorded not a little sardonically in the impecunious Thomas Dekker's observation in "The Guls Horn-Booke" (1609) that the theater "is your Poets Royal Exchange," and that the poets' muses "are now turned to Merchants" (pp. 246-7). We find it noted more positively in contemporary *sententiae* fusing the pursuit of trade and the interests of the state. Thus, for Bacon ("Of Vsurie," 1625 [1966]) the "Customs of Kings or States . . . Ebbe or flow with Merchandizing" (p. 170), an opinion seconded and elaborated upon by John Stow in *The Survey of London* (1603 [1912]), when he pauses in his account of London's past to recount the benisons produced by London's mercantile present, remarking that

> truly merchants and retailers do not altogether *intus canere*, and profit themselves only, for the prince and realm both are enriched by their riches: the realm winneth treasure, if their trade be so moderated by authority that it break not proportion, and they besides bear a good fleece, which the prince may shear when he seeth good.
>
> (p. 495)

In sum, the business of Britain is business, and what's good for business is good for Britain.

At the same time, as we know, such assertions do not infrequently bear the refrain that what is good for business and Britain is probably not displeasing to God either. It is in God's name that profit often gets pursued, and it is as a providential sign of God's favor that the attainment of profit often gets justified. Certainly we find this providentialist and Calvinist-based mucilage spread quite profusely and adhesively in contemporary accounts of exploration of the New World, in which the propagation of God's word and the true faith is invoked both as a necessary and sufficient condition for the successful pursuit of commercial gain and national enhancement, and, at times, as a happy consequence of that pursuit. "Godlinesse is great riches," Hakluyt declares at the outset of his *Divers Voyages* (1582 [1850, 8]), his implicit confusion of riches spiritual and material a characteristic illustration of the idiom in which the desire for gain and a concern for salvation could without the slightest betrayal of cynicism be reconciled as part of the same ideological "project."

Nor is this coupling of the propagation of faith and trade any less pronounced—though it sounds less ingenuous—in the accounts of the English Merchant Adventurers' dealings with the Old World, a recurrent theme of which, understandably, is the abundance of blessings that will accrue to all parties concerned through an expansion of English trading rights on the continent. Hence, in a letter from one such Adventurer (c. 1565) we find the Earls of East Friesland being advised that with a strong English trading presence in their realm, "God shall be known, praised and feared, and his whole Gospel and commandments taught and preached, to the comfort of all Christian nations" (Ramsay, 1979, 113), and, it should be added, to the intended discomfort of the Pope, the Turks, and any other infidels who might have political or religious, or, of course, commercial, designs on that part of Europe.

To an audience inured to such texts, *The Merchant of Venice* might well have seemed a transparent allegory of its times. It establishes the merchant in the figure of Antonio as a friend of the state (IV. i. 1-34), it trots out a biblical precedent for the association of profit by "venture" with the blessings of divine providence (I. iii. 86-8), and, in the rather "providential" restoration of Antonio's fortunes after his deliverance from the merciless Jew (V. i. 273-9), it might well appear to subscribe to the notion that "Godlinesse is great riches." Indeed, Cohen has alluded to act V in particular as an "aristocratic fantasy" in which the "concluding tripartite unity of Antonio, Bassanio, and Portia enacts precisely [an] interclass harmony between landed wealth and mercantile capital, with the former dominant" (1982, 772, 777). If, for the moment, we accept Sidney's contention in his *Defence of Poesie* (1595 [1968]) that the mimetic role of poetry is to show not "what is, or is not, but what should, or should not be" (p. 29), then we might say that the *Merchant* realizes its mimetic function by dramatizing a vision of how the established social order and religious values *could* be reconciled with the new economics.

Central to this vision, however, and deepening the involvement of the *Merchant* in the economic discourse of its time is the triumph the play enacts over usury in the figure of the usurer Shylock. That usury was at once a widespread practice and significant concern in Shakespeare's society, and that the resources of usurers were sought, not only by profligate young gentlemen and capital-hungry merchants, but by Parliament and the Queen herself, are facts well-established and oft remarked.[4] The purpose of underscoring them here is to recall the degree to which a work like the *Merchant*, "indebted" as it is to its Italian sources, could still integrate these sources with more localized and contemporary materials both to create a fulcrum for the expression of communal concerns and frustrations, and also, and more interestingly, to create the illusion that whatever the socially and economically diverse elements of Shakespeare's audience did *not* have in common, they at least shared a common enemy in the form of usury and its personification.

In no small part, of course, the domestic appeal of the *Merchant* would have lain in the domestication of its villain, Shylock, who—whatever kinship he may share with his thinly drawn counterpart in the putative source story, *Il Pecorone*, or with Marlowe's exotically evil and extravagant Machiavel, Barabas—should have been quite recognizable to any in Shakespeare's audience who had read or heard their share of the myriad of anti-usury harangues in circulation at the time. To those so fortunate the penalty ultimately imposed upon Shylock—harsher than that suffered by Fiorentino's usurer in *Il Pecorone*, and harsh enough to have occasioned a good deal of critical rationalization[5]—may well have seemed just what they had come to believe a usurer conventionally deserved, including the obligation to be converted and saved in spite of himself.[6] Certainly those in the audience who were versed in the anti-usury tracts of the times, and had heard interest taking excoriated by Henry Smith in *The Examination of Usury* (1591) as "biting usury" (p. 8), or had read in Thomas Lodge's *Alarum Against Usurers* (1584) that usurers possessed "the voracitie of wolves" with which to devour men's bodies and souls (p. 77), should have read the string of daimonic and "currish," wolverine epithets liberally bestowed upon Shylock in the play (I. iii. 106; II. ii. 22-6; II. viii. 14; III. i. 19-20; III. iii. 7; IV. i. 128; IV. i. 283) as merely a standard part of his job description.[7] Those, meanwhile, familiar with the tract wishfully entitled *The Death of Usury, or, The Disgrace of Usurers* (1594) would have read that when in days of yore "an usurer came to be knowne, his houses were called the devils houses, his fields the devils croppe" (p. 34), and may well have heard a familiar resonance in Jessica's preelopement complaint that "Our house is hell" (II. iii. 2).

Stephen Greenblatt has suggested that Jessica's description of her father's house as hell is an apt metonym for the peculiar social isolation of the Jew in the modern European society from which, and for which, he earned capital (1978, 295). We find this conception of the usurer's social alienation no less evident in the diatribes against the Jewish moneylender's Christian counterpart in Shakespeare's England. Cut off from the society his profession would undermine, the usurer—Henry Smith maintains (1591, 35)—will be cut off from posterity as well, a fate, we will recall, Shylock is spared only when, in the spirit of Christian forgiveness, Antonio compels Shylock to "re-inherit" his daughter and make her and her Christian husband his heirs (IV. i. 384-6). In his moral isolation the usurer is prone, Smith contends, to vices such as revenge, vices which may eventually work against the usurer's economic self-interest (pp. 6-7).[8] We are reminded of this especial, and ultimately self-destructive, perversity, of course, in Shylock's unwillingness to accept any compensation for the forfeiture of Antonio's bond except the penalty of flesh stipulated in the contract. "You'll ask me why I rather choose to have / A weight of carrion flesh, than to receive / Three thousand ducats," Shylock tauntingly declares. "I'll not answer that! / But say it is my humour,—is it answer'd?" (IV. i. 40-3).[9]

Nor, we might surmise, would Shakespeare's audience have had Shylock answer in any other way. For there must have been a certain rhetorical convenience and moral self-assurance in being able to cast the argument against usury in the terms of polar oppositions of good and evil that transcend purely economic considerations. Indeed, the pressure of ideology may manifest itself most strongly in the attempt evident in the rhetorical structure of the play to universalize its central conflict and suppress its more parochial economic antecedents. In the exchange with which the play opens, after all, Antonio is permitted to reject the insinuations of Salerio/Solanio that he is the total *homo economicus*, whose mind is "tossing on the ocean" with his investments (I. i. 8-45), and he implies both by his words here and by his actions shortly hereafter that, for him at least, it is not money that makes the world go round. For his part, Shylock may be sincere in attributing at least a part of his hatred of Antonio to the abuse he has suffered from Antonio on the Rialto (I. iii. 101-24), to the resentment he justifiably feels on behalf of his race (I. iii. 43-7), and to his perception of the hand Antonio's friends may have had in the elopement of Jessica and Lorenzo (III. i. 22-3), and we may well see in his enmity the traces of the economic rivalry in Venice between the Jewish moneylender and the up-and-coming Christian entrepreneur and banker (Cohen, 1982, 770-1). Yet as he proceeds in his bloodlust, Shylock acts in a way that would have confirmed the anti-usury polemicists of Shakespeare's audience in their darkest beliefs about usurers: he becomes that most reassuring of villains, the villain who pursues his villainy because "it is my humour," because he would "choose" it over, not only a more virtuous, but even a more lucrative alternative.

That Shylock should "choose" to do wrong reminds us, though, of the simultaneously most damning and yet socially and ideologically most reassuring charge to be leveled at usurers in Shakespeare's time, namely that usurers are heretics, willful choosers of the wrong course and, therefore, most deserving of unqualified reproach. "[O]ne saith well," Henry Smith observes, "that our Vsurers are Hereticks, because after manie admonitions yet they maintaine their errours, & persist in it obstinately as Papists do in Poperie" (1591, 2). In fact, we find this association of usury and heresy made quasi-official by that great collector of commonplaces and regurgitator of Elizabethan orthodoxy, Francis Meres, whose entries for "Vsurie" in his *Palladis Tamia* (1598) are followed immediately by those for "Heresie, Heretickes," which, doubtless by no accidental coincidence, are immediately followed by "Death" (pp. 322-7).

This association of usury with heresy and with choosing the wrong course is of "interest" on several counts. On the one hand, the connection between usury and heresy might suggest that the rhetoric was in place by which the usurer could be singled out, not simply as an economic scoundrel and renegade, but as an enemy of God and, therefore, a threat to the state, and our recognition of this possibility deepens our perception of the audience's perception of Shylock. On the other hand, the connection of usury with choosing enables us to see a link between Shylock and the unhappy "choosers" of the casket scenes, and suggests a sense in which both elements of the rather exotic source tradition behind the *Merchant,* both the flesh-bond and the caskets stories, could be said to respond to the domestic experience and economic concerns of Shakespeare's audience.

Here we might recall that oft cited passage from *The Schoole of Abuse* (1579) in which Stephen Gosson pauses in his drama-bashing long enough to bestow unwonted praise upon a play called *The Jew,* which Gosson describes as "representing the greedinesse of worldly chusers, and bloody mindes of usurers" (p. 30). Now, how indebted Shakespeare is to this play, if he is indebted at all, and whether Gosson's "worldly chusers" and "bloody minded usurers" refer to different characters or are merely different tags for the same character, are matters quite unsettled (Brown, 1955, xxix-xxxi; Bullough, 1964, 445-6). Still, we might observe that in the anti-usury parables to which Shakespeare's audience was likely to have been exposed two character types recur, the "bloody minded usurer" and the "wordly chuser," the figure, that is, whose craving for the riches and vain delights of the world creates the conditions in which the usurer thrives. We find evocations and validations of this antimaterialist sentiment in the unlucky choices of Morocco, who assays his choice of caskets by reckoning the things of this world he desires, and Aragon, who chooses by considering the things of this world he deserves. "*All that glisters is not gold,*" reads the not very consoling scroll Morocco finds in the death's head "awarded" him for choosing the golden casket (II. vii. 65), a truism Thomas Lodge invokes in his *Alarum Against Usurers* when he recounts how "a young Gentleman," smitten with promises of easy credit and easier living, listens to the blandishments of a wicked usurer, a "subtill underminer," and, "counting all golde that glysters," succumbs (p. 45).

Indeed, the wisdom of such antimaterialist apothegms is most volubly articulated, and heeded, by the one happy casket chooser, Bassanio, whose casket-selection musings resonate with the kind of *sententiae* one finds in Lodge or other anti-usury writers. Not for Bassanio is it to assume "all golde that glysters." Rather, "The world is still deceiv'd with ornament" (III. ii. 73). Obviously knowing something that eluded Morocco, Bassanio immediately rejects the allure of riches and beauty metonymized in the "crisped snaky golden locks" beneath which lurks "[t]he skull that bred them in the sepulchre" (92-6). Ornament "is but the guiled shore / To a most dangerous sea" (97-8), with "gaudy gold, / Hard food for Midas" (101-2), and silver but a "pale and common drudge / 'Tween man and man" (103-4).

Surely, though, there is at least a hint of incongruity in hearing this vein of rhetoric from Bassanio, whose tendency toward materialism and consumption has been deemed conspicuous enough to trouble a number of critics,[10] and whose reasons for seeking funds might well have reminded Shakespeare's audience of the idle borrowers condemned by the anti-usury authors, who seek loans, not to survive, but, as the author of *The Death of Usury* insists, "to consume in prodigall maner, in bravery, banketting, voluptuous living, & such like" (1594, 32). Bassanio may well love Portia for her "wondrous virtues," but, as we know, in limning her praises to Antonio, he notes first that she is "a lady richly left, / And she is fair" (I. i. 161-2). And, skeptical as Bassanio may later show himself to be toward "damned show," we recall that, by his own admission, it was precisely for the sake of "showing a more swelling port / Than my faint means" would permit that Bassanio "disabled mine estate" (I. i. 123-5)—even as his continued pursuit of financing will come close to disabling Antonio's estate and Antonio himself!

Surely there is an incongruity here, and it is an incongruity which reflects, not simply the hybrid traces of Shakespeare's sources,[11] but an ambivalence we find in Shakespeare's culture toward wealth and the "venturing" for it in trade. As we noted before, to those engaged in exploration for profit, there may have been something at once instructive and reassuring in Hakluyt's dictum that "Godlinesse is great riches." Yet for every suggestion that God and Plutus may not be incompatible, we hear the dissonant reminder that they are not identical either. "[S]hall we conclude," Lodge asks, not unrhetorically, "because the usurer is rich, he is righteous? because wealthie, wise? because full of gold, therefore godly?" (1584, 71). Indeed, we overlook the full rhetorical agenda of texts celebrating the benefits of trade if we fail to hear in them an attempt to calm the fears and quiet the antimaterialist objections the "prodigal" pursuit of profit had engendered. Thus, Stow (1603), we will recall, trumpets the blessings trade has brought to the many, even as he acknowledges the great riches that have accrued through trade to the few, and even as he adds the rather anti-laissez-faire proviso that merchants' business "be so moderated by authority that it break not proportion" (p. 495).

In a sense, contemporary attacks upon usurers are a reflection of the success of such utilitarian rationalizations as Stow's. For if it is granted that the fruits of trade enhance the "commonweal," then it only follows that the ills attendant upon the increases in trade and venture capitalism should be treated, not as inherent in the system, but as excesses or abuses, or even subversions of the system. Thus, it is quite consistent with the times that Bassanio, who so incarnates the entrepreneurial spirit of the age,[12] and whose very choice of the lead casket is encoded as an act of "hazard," should dissociate himself from the ornamental riches with which "the world is still deceiv'd," and the obsession which usurers and other breakers of economic proportion exploit.

As we know, however, usury and trade existed in a relationship that was far more ambiguous than anti-usury tracts might imply, indeed, a relationship that might be said to have been more symbiotic than inimical. Bacon puts the complexity of the relationship squarely when he observes (in "Of Vsurie," 1625) that, while the first "Discommoditie" of usury is that "it makes fewer Merchants" since, obviously, it diverts money from trading to trading in money, the first "Commoditie" of usury is, paradoxically, that it makes more merchants and "aduanceth" trade, since "it is certain, that the Greatest Part of Trade is driuen by Young Merchants, upon Borrowing at Interest" (pp. 170-1).

This embarrassing interrelationship is a fact that not even avowedly anti-usury discourses can fully suppress. So it is that we hear the author of *The Death of Usury* labor to give the most moral, anti-usury, reading to the law enacted by Elizabeth which voided the ban imposed by Edward VI upon the practice of usury, and which formally reinstated 10 per cent as the maximum interest rate.[13] The law, the author maintains, could not be construed as condoning usury, but, instead, "leaves it after a sort to the curtesie and conscience of the borrower"—rather as if interest payments were to be regarded as something no more coercive than tipping! Why did Elizabeth enact this statute if it was not the intent of her government to encourage the practice of usury? Our author notes that when, under Edward VI, usury was prohibited "this inconvenience came, fewe or none would lend because they might have no allowance, whereupon her Maiestie to avoyde this euill, made this remissiue clause" (1594; see also Smith, 1591, 30). Having rationalized the government's unapprovingly permissive policy on usury, the same author wonders why the usurer does not simply follow the example of a number of merchants and invest his money in trade where, with the likelihood of fewer risks and greater profits, "it will be lesse noted, and himself better esteemed" (p. 27). Which is the merchant here, and which the usurer?

Indeed, to keep the distinction straight, and to cope with the disquieting realities of the economic system, we find polemicists engaging in the sorts of polarization evident in the surface of the *Merchant*. Merchants follow a career, Lodge hastens to affirm, "both aunckient and lawdable, the professors honest and vertuous, their actions full of daunger, and therefore worthy gaine; and so necessary this sorte of men be, as no well governed state may be without them" (1584, 43). The blame for whatever is "wrong" with the system, then, is left for the usurer to absorb, whose function is rather that of the scapegoat: he embodies the enemy within that must be exorcised by being externalized and, literally, alienated.[14] What better figure to fill this role than, of course, the Jew, whose vices can be, as we suggested before, familiarized, but whose identity by type is comfortably different and distanced. Shakespeare's Shylock, rooted as he is in older and foreign literary and dramatic forms, is an appropriate focus for the domestic anxieties of Shakespeare's audience, not in spite of his difference, but, rather as Stephen Greenblatt has argued, because of it (1978, 295-6).

2

To enumerate ways in which a play "reflects" the discourse of its times is not the same, unfortunately, as saying how the play responds to that discourse, a truth one feels embarrassingly keenly in the case of *The Merchant of Venice*. It may be fair to suggest that what we encounter in the play is "merely" a mirroring both of the myths by which the age read itself and of the anxieties those myths could not entirely dispel. Yet in holding up the mirror to its age *so* faithfully, does the play affirm the myths it enacts, or does it subvert them by mirroring their qualifications as well? Or, rather, does it affirm the myths it dramatizes *by* mirroring their qualifications, by admitting them as qualifications which ultimately can be contained and "lived with"?

Recently, Greenblatt has explored this *tertium quid* in texts where the play of ideology much more clearly assumes the form of a conflict between authority and forces threatening to undermine that authority (1981, 40-2). In the *Merchant* what is questioned is not authority as such, but whether the accommodation of Christian orthodoxy and economic reality the play inscribes is entitled to the moral authority to which it appears to lay claim. The play allows this questioning to be voiced, and voiced forcibly, only to contextualize it in such a way that its implications are deflected or muted, or, as Cohen has observed, repressed.

Certainly, for example, we feel the justice of Shylock's enraged defense of his humanity (III. i. 47-66), and we recognize as valid both in that speech and in others by Shylock the doubt being cast upon the Venetian Christian' presumptions of moral superiority. Yet, as Cohen remarks, though Christians may well be abusive slaveholders, we encounter no Christian slaveholders within the fiction of the play (1982, 774), and, a point so often noted, when push comes to shove, we know who cannot be dissuaded from killing whom, and who is capable of mercy—at least on some terms. And even though, as could be rightly objected, Gratiano shows himself (IV. i. 360-3, 375, 394-6) to be one Christian in whom the quality of mercy appears quite strained—perhaps, even, drained—still, it could also be urged that Gratiano is interestingly differentiated from his fellow Christians, who, it would seem, find him not worth listening to (I. i. 114-18).

Again, what is worth noticing is not that the *Merchant* should mute or repress contradictions and qualifications, but that it should call them into play at all only to repress them, illuminating them only to cover them, or, perhaps, "re-cover" them. For an example we might consider the curious resonances in the play of the idea of "prodigality." The word "prodigal" occurs several times, twice on the tongue of Shylock (II. v. 15; III. i. 39-40), who employs it as a term of derision for Christians whose "prodigality" clearly differentiates them from the "thrift" Shylock tends to associate with his own endeavors (I. iii. 45, 85, 172; II. v. 54). Like "thrift," "prodigal" is a word prodigally used in anti-usury tracts, and is employed to castigate, or warn, those "worldly choosers" whose wasteful ways and love of material things make them the prey of the likes of Shylock (*The Death of Usury*, 1594, 32; Lodge, 1584, 50, 51, 53, 56, 62, 75). On the one hand, there is, doubtless, a purposeful irony in having Shylock condemn the Christians for the sort of fiscal irresponsibility off which he "thrives;" to paraphrase Antonio, not only can the devil cite Scripture, but he seems to have done his share of reading in anti-usury tracts as well. Moreover, that Shylock should find prodigality contemptible obviously gives prodigality something to commend it, and we feel invited to associate the word with those antipenurious, anti-Shylockean virtues that schematic interpretations of the play generally place on the Christian side of the ledger: love, mercy, liberality. On the other hand, however, in the degree to which Shylock's words recall the antimaterialist rhetoric of the age, they remind us that in some sense Shylock's charges against the Christians are true, that Bassanio in particular is conspicuously, perhaps, culpably, "consumptive," and we may hear in his words an evocation, rather muffled, of that anxiety over wealth which is a part of the cultural context of the play.

At the same time, it is difficlt for us, and was likely to have been even more difficult for Shakespeare's audience, to hear the recurrent references to "prodigal" without thinking of the parable from Luke 15 with which "prodigal" has become synonymous. An allusion to the parable occurs in the chattering Gratiano's description of the once finely fretted merchant ship returning from its voyage "like the prodigal . . . / With over-weather'd ribs and ragged sails—/ Lean, rent, and beggar'd by the strumpet wind!" (II. vi. 17-19). Dangling here in the idle Grantiano's idle simile, the parable of the prodigal son looms over much of the play, though it is a reference Shakespeare seems quite pointedly to have kept in the background. It informs the story in *Il Pecorone*, in which the surrogate Antonio is the adoptive father of the Bassanio figure and plays the part of the all-forgiving, self-sacrificing father when the son twice "hazards"—and loses—all he has (Bullough, 1964, 466-7, 469). It informs the *Alarum Against Usurers*, in which Lodge offers a variation on the parable, having the father at first forgive the son, only to disown him later when the prodigal proves unregenerate (1584, 56-7). In the *Merchant*, traces of the parable suggest themselves in the opening exchange between Antonio and Bassanio, only to remain submerged within the notoriously elliptical and elusive relationship between these characters. For Shakespeare to have made those traces more distinct would have strengthened the connection between Bassanio and the wastrel youths pilloried in the anti-usury tracts of the day, and, implicitly, would have given a sharper resonance to the antimaterialist evocations in Shylock's invective.[15] As it is, however, the parable of the prodigal son presents itself in the play as an analogy left teasingly inchoate, with our sense of its nonpresence keen enough for us to notice its suppression.

Still, is such suppression evidence that the *Merchant* participates in the religioeconomic mythology of its times, or that it parodies it? In reifying in its own text the rationalizations and contradictions we encountered in other texts of the times, is the *Merchant* exorcising these qualifications, or, rather, is it underscoring their persistence? As Norman Rabkin demonstrated several years ago, critical commentary on the *Merchant* documents nothing more clearly than the resistance we encounter if we seek answers to these questions in the text of the play (1981, 28-9). In fact, what the text of the play may lead us to infer is that "texts" themselves are not to be trusted. "Texts," the play insists, can mislead and can be misread. Scripture we may think is authoritative, but, as Antonio warns Bassanio, it can be cited by the devil "for his purpose" (I. iii. 93); *sententiae*, "Good sentences," no matter how "well pronunc'd," Portia reminds Nerissa, are far easier to pronounce than to follow (I. ii. 10-20); words are "tricksy," Lorenzo declares, and can be summoned to "Defy the matter" by any number of fools like Launcelot Gobbo, "who hath planted in his memory / An army of good words" for the purpose (III. v. 59-64); while "deliberate fools" can, like Morocco and Aragon, display their foolishness in the very deliberateness with which they puzzle over texts, showing that they "have the wisdom by their wit to lose" (II. ix. 81). Indeed, if we read E.F.J. Tucker's reading of the play aright, what Portia's climactic judgement against Shylock enshrines most of all is the principle that for the law to be properly applied it must be understood in its spirit or intent, rather than read for the "letter" of its text (1976, 100-1).

How do these expressions within the play of skepticism toward texts affect our reading of *The Merchant of Venice?* Collectively, they would appear to support the argument that the play allegorizes the triumph of love, mercy, divine justice, and other *desiderata* over the various mean-spirited and short-sighted impulses emblematized in a narrow, close-reading legalism. Bassanio, for example, does not have to ponder closely the wordings on caskets, since he has higher, intuitive impulses to guide him—not to mention, of course, the subliminally helpful hints and "mood music" provided by Portia! On the other hand, the antiliteralism we come upon in the play at times serves the ideologically salutary purpose of upholding orthodoxy against the subversive, and subversively unanswerable, "misuse" of the texts and authorities by which orthodoxy is normally enforced: Scripture, the law, formulations of the "best interests" of the "commonweal." Antonio issues his admonition about Scripture, after all, when Shylock proves uncomfortably adept at biblical exegesis, with Antonio's words, as A. D. Nuttall has put it, suggestive of "a man who is holding fast to a conviction that his opponent must be wrong but cannot quite see how" (1983, 128). Analogously, Lorenzo lodges his complaint against "tricksy" words and fools just after Launcelot has appealed to the laws of supply and demand to argue that Jessica's conversion to Christianity will raise the price of pork (III. v. 19-23). The "word" must be suspect if it allows a Jew to use Scripture to justify usury and a fool to use the economic calculus of the times to suggest that, at least in one respect, the interests of Christianity and the economic interests of the commonwealth are not identical!

Yet in underscoring the equivocality and ambiguity of texts and "the word," *The Merchant of Venice* distances itself from the very textuality which nourishes it and the texts which it evokes and by which its discourse is enriched and complicated: the Italian *novelle* that are the immediate source of its fable, anti-usury diatribes, accounts of commercial exploration and exploitation, parliamentary decrees and edicts of law, and, the most authoritative and yet misreadable text of all, Scripture. In calling attention to the ways in which texts can be misused to yield subversive generalizations, the *Merchant* would have its audience believe that it is something other than, more than, another text, and would persuade us that the way to true harmony and resolution lies in the playful particularity of its dramatic action. In this way the *Merchant* as a piece of *theater* distances itself from the subversive resonances it yields as a *text*. At the same time, however, by its very ludic nature the *Merchant* can pretend merely to "play" with the religioeconomic mythology its fable inscribes. In the degree to which the *Merchant* asserts its independence of the very textuality it evokes, its playwright can invoke the indemnity of Sidney's poet, who, Sidney glibly reminds us, cannot ever be said to lie, because he "nothing affirmeth" (1595, 29).

We find this curious negotiation between text and play epitomized at the outset of act V, in the exchange in which Jessica and Lorenzo lyrically recount some of the assorted amorous misadventures that occurred on just "such a night" as the moonlit one they are enjoying at Belmont (V. i. 1-24). It is a passage which can be cited to confirm the darkest misgivings that can be, and have been, entertained about the "prodigal" and "unthrift" manner in which Lorenzo and Jessica contrived to "steal from the wealthy Jew" (Moody, 1964, 46-7; Burckhardt, 1968, 224). It is a passage which, if read darkly, provides an ironic prelude to that "aristocratic fantasy" played out in the rest of this the concluding scene of the play. How we interpret this exchange depends very much on the degree of proximity we posit between Jessica and Lorenzo and the roster of literary amatory "unthrifts" whom they invoke and with whom they "playfully" associate themselves, or, rather, each other: Troilus and Cressida, Thisbe and Pyramus, Dido and Aeneas, Jason and Medea. To measure Jessica and Lorenzo by the texts in which they would inscribe themselves is not only to deepen our suspicion that Jessica and Lorenzo themselves either are not or will not be or do not deserve to continue to be happy, but also to bring the world of the play closer to the ambiguous light shed upon its proceedings by literary allusion and analogy. In the immediate context the intrusion of the dramatic action, in the person of Stephano arriving to announce the imminent return of Portia (V. i. 25), prevents Lorenzo and Jessica from fully shaping their own history to the specifications of the doleful texts they have been reciting. In this way they are permitted to maintain their theatrical "otherness" from the textual patterning by which they make it very tempting to read them. Hence, with no little tension, the world of texts is kept playfully separate from the world of the theatrical fiction.

Here, to be sure, it could be argued that the playfulness we have been claiming for the *Merchant* is but the rhetorical signature of its own textuality, with the distancing effect this playfulness produces nothing other than that parodic distance which Pierre Macherey contends must ever mark the relationship of "literary language" to the ideological discourses it evokes, that inherent distantiation through which "literary discourse merely mimics theoretical discourse, rehearsing but never actually performing its script" (1978, 59). At the same time, though—even as we must question whether "literary language" can in fact be so essentially distinguishable from other discourses as Macherey would maintain[16]—we are no less likely to recognize in the *Merchant* the symptoms of the curious dualism with which the public stage of Shakespeare's day "represented" the world of, and to, its public, and with which it negotiated—and accommodated—the ideological currents and cross-currents of the time. As Louis Montrose has demonstrated, Shakespearean drama in particular calls upon the affiliative power inherent in theater to "re-present" to the audience a "paradigm" of its culture even while calling attention, self-reflexively, to the devices, conventions, and forms that inscribe the experience of theater as but illusion, and its business but "play" (1980, 66; also 1981, 33). This dualism entails, of course, a certain artistic—and political—convenience, for even as it proclaims the mimetic power of drama to suggest and portray resemblances to "real life," it insists upon the figurative character of those resemblances and, thus, enables the playwright to claim limitations upon his responsibility, his accountability, for literal truth. "What childe is there," asks Sidney in his response to Gosson's attack, "that coming to a play, and seeing *Thebes* written in great letters upon an old doore, doth beleeve that it is Thebes?" (p. 29). Sidney's "question" is, in fact, an assertion of an artistic license which the more wary upholders of orthodoxy should have found disquieting: the license to be taken seriously but not literally, and, therefore, not *too* seriously!

In no form are this reflexivity and playing at representation so overt as in comedy, and in no Shakespearean comedy is the tension that this playing embodies—and the convenience it affords—more evident than in the *Merchant*, where, I have tried to suggest, we are treated to an exposition and interrogation of the prevailing religioeconomic mythologies of the day, even as we feel a pull toward the reassuring particularity only a dramatic solution and resolution can provide. Indeed, nothing better attests to the will and power of dramatic art to divert attention from the ideological contradictions it reflects to its own playful alterity than the sense that has permeated a good deal of criticism on the *Merchant* that "somehow," through some combination of conventions comic, festive, and carnivalesque, the play manages to transcend the issues its text problematizes to render a dramatically, theatrically, satisfying experience. "The happy ending," C. L. Barber observes, with a keen and generous appreciation for this festive *difference,* "which abstractly considered as an event is hard to credit, and treatment of Shylock, which abstractly considered as justice is hard to justify, *work* as we actually watch or read the play because these events express relief and triumph in the achievement of a distinction" (1959, 170). The *Merchant* "works"—and worked—and achieves its "triumph," of course, precisely in the degree to which it works upon its audience, and critics, to relax their discriminations and equate the illusion of a "distinction" with its "achievement."

Now, as Robert Weimann has shown, no figure in Shakespearean drama so well incarnates in action and speech the playfully representative force of Shakespearean drama as does the fool (1978, 30-48, 133-51), and so, to italicize the peculiarly playful relationship of the *Merchant* to the religioeconomic vision its fable enacts, we might conclude by looking once again at that exchange in act III (v. 19 ff.) in which the fool, Launcelot Gobbo, opines on the economic ramifications of Jessica's conversion. Cohen has observed how in general Launcelot's penchant for the verbal malapropos gives voice to "an alternative perspective on the related matters of Christian orthodoxy and social hierarchy" (1982, 780), and the truth of that observation is in no way belied by Launcelot's performance here. Yet what is most exemplary in what Lawrence Danson calls Launcelot's "wonderful confusion of carnal matters and spiritual" (1978, 97) is the complexity of response it elicits from us. Practiced as we have become in making sense of what we take to be the ostensible non-sense and inversions of sense that dot Launcelot's "normal" discourse, we have no difficulty in grasping an ulterior pertinence in the apparent impertinence of Launcelot's juxtaposition of things spiritual and porcine. After all, Launcelot is not the first character in the play, we are likely to recall, who has shown himself to be a *homo economicus* in matters related to Jessica; and whatever incongruity we may feel in hearing Jessica's conversion turn Launcelot's thoughts to pork is only a comic reprise of the incongruity we may have felt in hearing from Solanio that Jessica's elopement turned her father's thoughts to ducats (II. viii. 12-22). Still, even as Launcelot's reasoning reassuringly parodies the materialism we associate with and hear burlesqued in Solanio's burlesque of Shylock, it reminds us that it is not only the Jew and usurer who brings an economic algorithm to his reading of experience, and that the line in the play distinguishing the "thrift" of the usurer from the values of the Christian community is not so very reassuringly or consistently sharp.

At the same time, however, the associations called into play by Launcelot's words are kept at a playful distance by the comic theatricality of his character. Yet this distancing is double-edged. On the one hand, Launcelot's generic "foolishness" permits the play to articulate elements of social criticism without appearing to engage or take them seriously. Indeed, Launcelot's comicality enables the *Merchant* to glance yet glance but teasingly at assumptions left unquestioned by its fable: that godliness and riches are

Seana McKenna as Jessica, Keith Dinicol as Launcelot Gobbo, and Attendants in the 1984 Stratford Festival production of The Merchant of Venice.

linked, that Christianity and the economic interests of the commonwealth are in harmony. On the other hand, though it may distance itself from the kinds of question and questioning Launcelot's words may suggest, the *Merchant* leaves these same assumptions ultimately unaffirmed. Lorenzo deals with Launcelot's provocative—and provoking—thesis, we will recall, not by refuting it, but by changing the subject and grumbling about "tricksy words" in the mouths of fools. Like the exchange between Jessica and Lorenzo, the dialogue here is significantly disengaged. Above all, in having economic theory uttered from the mouth of a fool, the *Merchant* glances reflexively and parodically at the very sort of discourse in which it has involved itself and immersed us. In the playfulness of Launcelot the *Merchant* asserts its own playfulness and illuminates the dramatic tension in which it holds the competing impulses of recuperation and subversion.

Notes

1. For another synopsis of the polarities through which the play is often schematized, see Greenblatt (1978), 293-4. All references to the *Merchant* are to the Arden edition, edited by Brown (1955).

2. Consider the note of qualification obtruding in Barbara Lewalski's contention that the conversion imposed upon Shylock at the end of the play is a prefiguration of the final conversion of the Jews: "because Antonio is able to rise at last to the demands of Christian love, Shylock is not destroyed, but, albeit rather harshly, converted" (Lewalski, 1962, 334).

3. For a summary and discussion of a number of the topical possibilities, see Brown (1955), xxi-xxvii.

4. See Draper (1935), 39-45; Brown (1955), xliii; also, *Acts of the Privy Council,* December 5 and 24, 1598, cited in Harrison (1931), 324-6.

5. In the source story from *Il Pecorone,* "[t]he Jew, seeing that he could not do what he had wished, took his bond and tore it in pieces in a rage." See Bullough (1964), 474.

6. Thus, in the concluding remarks in Thomas Lodge's *Alarum Against Usurers* (1584), the moneylenders are exhorted to "harden not your hearts, but be you converted . . . and turne, turne, turne unto the Lord,

(I beseech you) least you perish in your own abhominations" (1584 [1853] 79). See also the penitence of the usurer at the conclusion of Lodge's *A Looking Glasse, for London and England* (1598 [1963, 69]).

7. See Lodge (1584 [1853], 77; Smith (1591), 8; also Brown (1955), xxiv.

8. Smith goes so far as to maintain that were there no usury, there would be no "revenging," and that "they which brought in Vsurie, brought in a law against themselves" (pp. 6-7).

9. In his insistence upon the letter of the bond, Shylock follows the example of the usurer in *Il Pecorone* (Bullough, 1964, 471), but in the defiance with which he teasingly defends his right to the pound of flesh, he seems akin to the moneylender in Alexander Silvayn's *The Orator* (trans. L.P., 1596), who, having speculated on various reasons why "I would not rather take silver of this man, then his flesh," shrugs them off, and "will onelie say, that by his obligation he oweth it me" (Bullough, 1964, 484).

10. In, perhaps, the most virulent expression of anti-Bassanian sentiment among critics, A. D. Moody observes of Bassanio that "[i]t would not be inappropriate if his name came to be suggestive of baseness, in the sense of 'opposed to high-minded'; and perhaps also to suggest the bass, 'the common perch', which catches the shallow and callow aspect, and also 'a voracious European marine fish', which catches the more serious underside" (1964, 23-4). A. D. Nuttall puts the case of Bassanio's apparent materialism in more silken accents when he notes, "There is a certain repellent ingenuousness about Bassanio. He can trust his own well-constituted nature. It would never allow him to fall in love with a poor woman; for, after all, poor women are not attractive" (1983, 122).

11. In *Il Pecorone,* after all, we also find an interesting admixture of *Eros* and commerce, though it could be argued that the *Merchant* is an inversion of the fable of its source. For in *Il Pecorone* what begins as a commercial venture turns into an erotic adventure; in the *Merchant* what we would presume to be an amatory quest seems persistently mixed with material considerations.

12. To take but one example, Bassanio's very appeal to Antonio for a renewal of his loan appropriates the vocabulary of investment. Were Antonio to give Bassanio the funds with which to replace the money Bassanio has already wasted, Bassanio promises either "to find both, / Or bring your latter hazard back again," while the thought of his courtship of Portia "presages me such thrift / That I should questionless be fortunate" (I. i. 150-1, 175-6).

13. For a brief discussion of this statute, see Draper (1935), 41.

14. For two quite complementary discussions of Shylock as the figure of the scapegoat, see Girard (1978), 108-14; and Barber (1959), 177-84.

15. Indeed, has Shakespeare given greater definition to the analogy between Bassanio and the prodigal son, he might have affiliated the fable of the play with a concern evident in the anti-usury complaints of the day, namely, that the profits of usurers were a threat to familial legacies and, thus, to nothing less than social continuity. Lodge, who may have been especially sensitive to the overthrows familial fortunes could suffer, exclaims that "Purchased arms now possess the place of ancient progenitors, and men made rich by young youth's misspendings doe feast in the halls of our riotous young spend thrifts" (1584, 48).

16. At the heart of Macherey's position on the nonideological nature of "literary language" is the assumption that "literary language" is essentially nonrepresentational. Indeed, to Sidney's self-exculpatory claim that the poet never lies because he "nothing affirmeth," Macherey might well add that the poet—or playwright—can *only* lie whenever he seems to affirm. "Literature is deceptive," Macherey argues, "in so far as it is evocative and apparently expressive. . . . Making us take the word for the thing, or vice-versa, it would be a fabric of lies, all the more radical for being unconscious" (1978, 61).

Works Cited

Bacon, Francis (1625) "Of Vsurie," in Bacon, Francis, *Essays,* Oxford, Oxford University Press, 1966.

Barber, C. L. (1959) *Shakespeare's Festive Comedy,* Princeton, Princeton University Press.

Brown, John Russell (ed.) (1955) *The Merchant of Venice* by William Shakespeare, Arden edn, London, Methuen.

Bullough, Geoffrey (1964) *Narrative and Dramatic Sources of Shakespeare,* London, Routledge & Kegan Paul.

Burckhardt, Sigurd (1968) *Shakespearean Meanings,* Princeton, Princeton University Press.

Cohen, Walter (1982) "*The Merchant of Venice* and the Possibilities of Historical Criticism," *English Literary History,* 49, 765-89.

Danson, Lawrence (1978) *The Harmonies of The Merchant of Venice,* New Haven, Yale University Press.

The Death of Usury, or, The Disgrace of Usurers, London, 1594, STC 6443.

Dollimore, Jonathan (1984) *Radical Tragedy: Religion, Ideology and Power in the Drama of Shakespeare and his Contemporaries,* Chicago, University of Chicago Press; Brighton, Harvester.

Draper, John W. (1935) "Usury in *The Merchant of Venice*," *Modern Philology*, 33, 37-47.

Girard, René (1978) "'To Entrap the Wisest': A Reading of *The Merchant of Venice*," in Said, Edward W. (ed.) (1980) *Literature and Society: Selected Papers from the English Institute*, Baltimore, Johns Hopkins University Press, 100-19.

Gosson, Stephen (1579) *The Schoole of Abuse, Containing a Pleasant invective against Poets, Pipers, Players, Jesters, and such like Caterpillers of a Commonwealth*, repr. 1841, London, The Shakespeare Society.

Greenblatt, Stephen (1978) "Marlowe, Marx, and Anti-Semitism," *Critical Inquiry*, 5, 291-307.

——— (1981) "Invisible Bullets: Renaissance Authority and its Subversion," *Glyph 8: Johns Hopkins Textual Studies*, Baltimore, Johns Hopkins University Press, 40-61.

Hakluyt, John (1582) *Divers voyages touching the Discouerie of America and the Ilands Adiacent*, ed. Jones, John Winter (1850), London, Hakluyt Society.

Harrison, G. B. (ed.) (1931) *A Second Elizabethan Journal: Being a Record of Those Things Most Talked of During the Years 1595-8*, London, Constable.

Kermode, Frank (1961) "The Mature Comedies," in Brown, John Russell and Harris, Bernard (eds), *Early Shakespeare*, Stratford-upon-Avon Studies, 3, London, Edward Arnold, 211-17.

Lewalski, Barbara (1962) "Biblical Allusion and Allegory in *The Merchant of Venice*," *Shakespeare Quarterly*, 13, 327-43.

Lodge, Thomas, (1584) *An Alarum Against Usurers*, repr. 1853, London, The Shakespeare Society.

——— (1598) *A Looking Glasse, for London and England*, vol. IV of *The Complete Works of Thomas Lodge*, 1883; repr. 1963, New York, Russell & Russell.

Macherey, Pierre (1978) *A Theory of Literary Production*, trans. Geoffrey Wall, London, Routledge & Kegan Paul.

Meres, Francis (1598) *Palladis Tamia*, London, facsimile repr. 1938, New York, Scholars' Facsimiles & Reprints.

Montrose, Louis Adrian (1980) "The Purpose of Playing: Reflections on a Shakespearean Anthropology," *Helios*, n.s. 7, 51-74.

——— (1981) "'The Place of a Brother' in *As You Like It*: Social Process and Comic Form," *Shakespeare Quarterly*, 32, 28-54.

Moody, A. D. (1964) *Shakespeare: The Merchant of Venice*, Woodbury, New York, Barron's Educational Series.

Nuttall, A. D. (1983) *A New Mimesis: Shakespeare and the Representation of Reality*, London, Methuen.

Rabkin, Norman (1981) *Shakespeare and the Problem of Meaning*, Chicago, University of Chicago Press.

Ramsay, G. D. (ed.) (1979) *The Politics of a Tudor Merchant Adventurer: A Letter to the Earls of East Friesland*, Manchester, Manchester University Press.

Sidney, Sir Philip (1595) *The Defence of Poesie*, London, vol. III of *The Prose Works of Sir Philip Sidney*, ed. Albert Feuillerat, 4 vols, 1912, repr. 1968, Cambridge, Cambridge University Press.

Smith, Henry (1591) *The Examination of Usury*, London, STC 22660.

Stow, John (1603) *The Survey of London*, introd. H.B. Wheatley (1912), London, J.M. Dent.

Tucker, E. F. J. (1976) "The Letter of the Law in *The Merchant of Venice*," *Shakespeare Survey*, 29, 93-101.

Weimann, Robert (1978) *Shakespeare and the Popular Tradition in the Theater: Studies in the Social Dimension of Dramatic Form and Function*, ed. Robert Schwartz, Baltimore, Johns Hopkins University Press.

Stephen A. Cohen (1994)

SOURCE: "'The Quality of Mercy': Law, Equity and Ideology in *The Merchant of Venice*," in *Mosaic*, Vol. 27, No. 4, 1994, pp. 35-54.

[*In the essay below, Cohen argues that* The Merchant of Venice *should be examined from a legal point of view in order to better understand the cultural changes that began to occur in Elizabethan England—specifically, the increasing use of common law by the "rising classes" to thwart the "ruling classes."*]

The interdisciplinary study of literature has received considerable impetus over the last two decades from the rise of New Historicism. Particularly in Renaissance studies, the work of Stephen Greenblatt, Louis Adrian Montrose and others has illuminated the relation of such diverse matters as exorcism, colonialism, architectural design and primogeniture to the cultural work performed by literary texts. One subject largely neglected by the New Historicists, however, is the law. This neglect may in part be attributable to the prominence of the law in older, positivist historical readings of Renaissance literature, and in turn to the New Historicists' desire both to distance themselves from this reflectionist model and to investigate unexplored areas of Renaissance culture. In any case, by conjoining the considerable work done by Renaissance legal scholars with New Historicism's characteristic questions—what are the sociopolitical functions of the cultural phenomenon in question, and how are those functions employed or adapted through the literary text—we may shed considerable light on both the law and the literature of the Renaissance.

Not surprisingly, given its explicitly economic central conflict and its intricately detailed legal climax, *The Merchant* of Venice has had considerable appeal for interdisciplinary critics. As O. Hood Phillips's investigations have shown, for over a century legal scholars and historians have studied the trial scene's relation to contemporary jurisprudence, debating its verisimilitude and its position in the period's jurisdictional and philosophical disputes, especially the conflict between the common law and equity (91-118). More recently, historical critics like Walter Cohen, Leonard Tennenhouse and Thomas Moisan have explored the play's relation to Renaissance social and economic history and ideology, and particularly its role in the period's transition from the cultural and financial structures of late feudalism to those of early capitalism. These two lines of inquiry have, however, remained almost entirely separate: legal readings of the trial scene tend to treat its legal significance in both cultural and textual isolation, failing to link it to the social and economic issues prominent in both text and cultural context; and socioeconomic readings of the play as a whole give little or no attention to the role of the trial's legal background in that framework.

A contemporary audience, however, would have made no such separation. The late 16th and early 17th centuries in England were notable both for unprecedented economic and social change and for a marked increase in legal activity; the connection between the two developments was sufficiently clear at the time that Francis Bacon could note almost as a commonplace that "times of peace, for the most part drawing with them abundance of wealth, and finenesse of cunning, doe draw also in further consequence multitudes of suits, and controversies . . . [which] do more instantly sollicite for the amendment of lawes, to restraine and repress them" ("Epistle Dedicatorie," n.p.).

Nor were such associations beyond the bounds of the theater. In the case of The Merchant of Venice, the susceptibility of the play's legal content to sociopolitical interpretation is attested to by no less a legal and political authority than Lord Chancellor Ellesmere, who in a 1615 judicial dispute over the power of King James to legislate economic policy without the concurrence of Parliament advised his fellow judges "to maintain the power and prerogative of the King; and in cases in which there is no authority and precedent, to leave it to the King to order it according to his wisdom and the good of his subjects, for otherwise the King would be no more than the Duke of Venice" (qtd. in Andrews 41). The significance of the reference—to the Duke's legal inability to act on his sympathy for Antonio—would not have been lost on James and his court, for whom The Merchant of Venice was performed twice in 1605 (Knight 108n8).

For its contemporary audience, then, the trial scene's legal conflict was firmly connected to the economic and political issues in which the period was increasingly embroiled. By bringing together the historical particularity of the play's legal critics and the ideological sensitivity of its newer historical readers, I hope to recapture the significance of this connection; and in shedding new light on the meaning of the trial scene's common law-versus-equity debate I will attempt to illuminate the role that The Merchant of Venice played in the culture of which it was a part.

The case that Shylock makes for the enforcement of his bond rests on three claims: 1) the self-evidence of the law's application to the case at hand; 2) the supremacy of that law over any other power, personal or governmental; and 3) the importance of that supremacy to the foundations of the state itself. "I [have] sworn / To have the due and forfeit of my bond," he tells the Duke as the trial opens; "If you deny it, let the danger light / Upon your charter and your city's freedom!" (4.1.36-39).[1] These three claims were the foundation of the case presented by the champions of the common law in their jurisdictional and philosophical conflict with the courts of equity. In supporting the inviolability of the common law's authority they argued that the order and security of the nation rested upon the adjudication of its increasingly complex web of rights and obligations by—as Sir Edward Coke phrased it—"the golden and straight mete-wand of the law, and not the incertain and crooked cord of discretion" (qtd. in Ives 125).

While acknowledging the technical legality of Shylock's suit—"Of a strange nature is the suit you follow, / Yet in such rule that the Venetian law / Cannot impugn you as you do proceed" (177-79)—Portia counters his claims by decrying the cruelty of the bond and the severity of the law that enforces it and insisting on the need for mercy "to mitigate the justice of thy plea" (203). The necessity of such mitigation was the basis of the argument presented by the advocates of equity's appellate superiority to the common law, in order, in the words of Lord Keeper John Williams, "to mix & temper mercie and equitie with the black and rigorous L[ette]re of the Law" (qtd. in Thomas 526). Consequently, Portia's victory has been read by legal critics like Mark Edwin Andrews, Maxine McKay and W. Nicholas Knight as Shakespeare's endorsement of the ethical importance of equity to mitigate the impartial but at times overly-strict justice of the common law.

As Lord Chancellor Ellesmere recognized, however, behind the ideological trappings of blind-but-strict law and corrective equity, the issue at stake in the trial plot is political power—specifically, the power of the Crown to further its social and economic agenda in the face of the legal challenge presented by the common law. As the complex, large-scale financial operations of early capitalism began to emerge in the middle years of the 16th century, its practitioners became acutely aware of the value of a comprehensive and predictable legal system that offered protection from arbitrary interference. As Max Weber notes:

> The modern capitalist concern . . . requires for its survival a system of justice and an administration whose workings can be *rationally calculated*, at least in principle, according to fixed general laws. . . . It is as little able to tolerate the dispensing of justice according to the judge's sense of fair play *in individual cases* or any

other irrational means of principles of administering the law . . . as it is able to endure a patriarchal administration that obeys the dictates of its own caprice, or sense of mercy. . . .

(qtd. in Whigham 107-08n14)

The common law, particularly after it began to recognize and incorporate the jurisprudence of the increasingly important international mercantile legal system (Hill 238), was clearly the law that best offered this protection, given its fundamental concern with *meum et tuum* property rights: "The person, goods and possessions of a man (as yow know) are the things which the Common lawes of England doe protect," wrote Edward Hake in the late years of Elizabeth's reign (69).

The Crown's difficulty with this conception of the common law was that the very same principles which facilitated the new economic activity could also be—and increasingly were—employed to protect the profits of that activity from royal exploitation. The value to the nation of this new commerce and industry provided the Crown with a strong disincentive to violate or abrogate the common law; yet with the steadily growing financial pressure on the royal treasury in the late 16th century, the maintenance of state power came increasingly to require the diversion of the profits of English capitalism into the government's coffers. The means by which the Elizabethan state attempted this diversion—ad hoc financial and commercial regulation, extra-parliamentary taxation and forced loans that were never repaid—brought it into direct conflict with the necessary predictability and inviolability of the common law, and those profiting from the new economy were quick to invoke those principles in their own interest. Even Hake, who was by no means a wholehearted ally of the new capitalists (his revised *Epieikeia* was presented to King James), held that "concerning the subiect's goods, neither subsidyes, taxes, contributions nor loans are by the lawe to take hold thereof or to be imposed upon any Englishe subiect without his free consent"; thus "any seisures to be made of an Englishe subiect's goods to the King's use withowt iust and lawfull tytle" were not to be considered (83-84).

Coupled with the ideological prestige of the common law's status as England's unique and indigenous legal heritage (insightfully described by J. G. A. Pocock), the Crown's reliance on the new economy made a royal attack on the common law in general both undesirable and impracticable. Instead, the Crown for the most part restricted its response to the particular instances in which the common law was used to oppose the Crown's will: thus while common-law tacticians cast their legal resistance to the state's unpopular financial devices as the defense of property rights against royal tyranny, the Crown countered by depicting that resistance as the economically self-interested *mis*use of the law contrary to the unity, order and security of the state. Equity, as the theoretical remedy for injustice produced by the misuse of the law, was consequently an essential component of the Crown's legal arsenal. While other legal weapons like the royally-dominated ecclesiastical courts, Star Chamber and the considerable direct prerogative power of the ruler himself would provide the Crown with greater practical power in the increasingly contentious years leading up to the Civil War, equity's established jurisprudential credentials allowed it to become one of the Crown's earliest and most powerful ideological tools in its efforts to stave off the political implications of capitalism's use of the common law.

Seen in this light, the broader social conflict behind the common-law/equity dispute is not the primarily economic battle between capitalism and feudalism, but the primarily political battle between two socioeconomic factions for the spoils of the nascent capitalist economy. These two factions were defined less by social status (aristocracy versus gentry or nascent bourgeoisie) than by a combination of economic interest and ideological affiliation. On one side were the merchants, financiers, landed gentry and even aristocrats who profited directly from the new economy and who perceived their interests—financial and otherwise—to be at least on occasion different from the Crown's (Stone, *Causes* 114-15). This group may be designated the "rising class," provided that we understand "rising" primarily in the economic rather than social sense and "class" as a taxonomy based on neither birth nor wealth but on economic activity.

Their opponents were the large landowners—Crown and older aristocracy—that for reasons both economic and social had been unable to adapt their financial practice to the new economy and who were consequently forced into an increasingly parasitical relationship to that economy—the Crown in the ways discussed above and the aristocracy as royal clients competing for monopolies and state offices (Tawney 9-13; Stone, *Crisis* 199-207). Despite the growing challenge posed by the rising class, this second group may still be referred to as the period's ruling class, for since Henry VII and Henry VIII subjugated the great noble families to the Crown, this royal-aristocratic bloc had wielded a nigh-hegemonic political and social power which in the late 16th century continued to hold most of the nation under its official or ideological sway.

Thus, while the immediate stakes in the conflict between the two groups were financial, the ultimate prize was much greater: the ability of the independent rising class to use the common law to thwart the sociopolitical will of the ruling class. Not simply a clash of legal principles or jurisdictions, the contest between common law and equity was one of the first and most important sites of the conflict between the rising and ruling classes that would climax (but not conclude) with the Civil War. As one of the earliest articulations—literary or otherwise—of this ideological struggle, the victory of Portia in the trial scene of *The Merchant of Venice* is not a simple reflection of a jurisprudential dispute or an all-but-complete economic shift but rather a highly partisan intervention in a growing cultural crisis.

As in the contemporary legal dispute, the trial's battle lines are drawn not between capitalism (Venice) and feudalism (Belmont), but between the socially and politically independent rising class (Shylock the Jew) and the ruling class and its ideological allies (the Christian aristocrats and Antonio). Even before the trial scene itself, the play makes clear that its target is neither capitalism nor common law *per se*. In response to Solanio's certainty that the Duke will void Shylock's bond, Antonio pointedly establishes not only the close connection between common law and nascent capitalism but also the importance of both to the economic survival of the state:

> The Duke cannot deny the course of law;
> For the commodity that strangers have
> With us in Venice, if it be denied,
> Will much impeach the justice of the state,
> Since that the trade and profit of the city
> Consisteth of all nations.
>
> (3.3.26-31)

During the trial, the legality of the contract itself, exemplar of both capitalist economics and common law, is never challenged: Antonio "confesses" the bond (181-82) and Portia declares, "Why, this bond is forfeit" (230)—that is, forfeited by Antonio upon his nonpayment. Instead, Shylock is vilified for the particular use to which he puts the law of contract: the enforcement of the bond's horrific stipulations at the expense of the Christian "royal merchant" Antonio.

The trial scene opens with a reassertion of its central sociopolitical division. Referring to Antonio by name, the Duke says: "I am sorry for thee" (3); the merchant responds by acknowledging the pains the Duke and the other "magnificoes" have already taken on his behalf (7-9; see also 3.2.279-83). Shylock, in contrast, is first referred to simply as "the Jew" (14), an epithet used throughout the trial to underline his social alienation. Despite (or more precisely because of) its prominence in the play's definition of his character, Shylock's religion is not to be taken at face value, but rather as an exemplary illustration of the play's mediation of Elizabethan sociopolitical reality for presentation on the stage. Without dismissing the importance of the considerable literature debating *The Merchant of Venice*'s anti-Semitism, I would argue that it is difficult to see Shylock primarily as a representative of Judaism. Shylock's Jewishness throughout the play is less theological than cultural: he is not identified by (and reviled for) his failure to accept Christ or the New Testament, but by his "Jewish gaberdine," his unwillingness to dine with his Christian business associates and especially his usury—in short, his social, economic and ideological alienation from Venice's dominant sociopolitical group.

Rather than a transparent religious designation, Judaism (certainly a flexible signifier in an England virtually devoid of professed Jews) functions in the play as a derogatory marker for a group extant but not fully delineated in the cultural consciousness of the late 16th century, a group characterized by its economic self-interest and its willingness to further that interest by opposing itself to the dominant social ideology: the rising class. If the play partakes in contemporary anti-Semitic stereotypes (greed, social separatism), it does so not in the service of their own furtherance, but in order to transfer those negative associations from the religious to the socio-economic sphere.

The Duke's first speech to Shylock (17-34) employs this transference in linking the trial's economic foundations to its larger social significance. Lacking the prerogative power to pardon Antonio—a power that belonged to the ruler only in criminal cases—the Duke resorts to the considerable extra-legal social power wielded by the ruling class. Antonio's financial straits, he says, should elicit pity and mercy not only from Christian hearts, but "from stubborn Turks, and Tartars never train'd / To offices of tender courtesy" (32-33). The Duke offers Shylock the following choice: either to remain more alien than even the Turks and Tartars in pursuing his suit, or to enter—as has Antonio—the hegemonic penumbra of the aristocracy by changing his pagan "malice" for Christian "courtesy" and economic cooperation. The full weight of the social pressure that the ruling class could bring to bear upon a recalcitrant individual is focused in the speech's final line (particularly in light of the recurring pun on gentle/gentile): "We all expect a gentle answer, Jew!"

In the not-too-distant Tudor past such a threat might well have proven the trump card that the Duke intends it to be. By the 1590s, however, the inviolability of the common law was providing the rising class with an increasingly effective shield with which to resist the Crown's efforts to assert its will over the law. Shylock's response to the Duke links the common law's economic domain, its class affiliation and its ideological status as foundation of the state:

> by our holy Sabaoth have I sworn
> To have the due and forfeit of my bond.
> If you deny it, let the danger light
> Upon your charter and your city's freedom!
>
> (36-39)

Throughout the trial scene, Shylock invokes the shield of the common law in the face of Christian attempts to coerce or cajole him by emphasizing his social exclusion or offering him inclusion at the price of his bond. "Till thou canst rail the seal from off my bond," he admonishes Gratiano, "Thou but offend'st thy lungs to speak so loud. / . . . I stand here for law" (139-42).

The lack of formal social submissiveness and regard for hierarchical distinctions implicit in both the substance and the tone of Shylock's response to his aristocratic opponents suggests the ultimate consequence of his common-law defense: the weakening of the sociopolitical hegemony that preserved royalist-aristocratic privilege. In keeping with the play's ideological agenda, this use of the law is presented as a threat to the safety and stability of a Venetian society whose social and juridical similarities to late 16th-century England would not be overlooked by a contemporary audience. This threat is clearest in Shylock's famous "Hath not a Jew eyes" speech (3.1.53-73).

Read in context—as a response to Salerio's suggestion that Shylock has nothing to gain by enforcing the bond—the speech is not the appeal to universal brotherhood it is often taken to be. Antonio's hostility towards Shylock is rooted in the latter's social alterity—"You call me misbeliever, cut-throat dog, / And spet upon my Jewish gaberdine" (1.3.111-12)—and it is this distinction between Jew and Christian that the speech rhetorically effaces. The result of this effacement, however, is not a pledge of mutual forbearance but a promise of retaliatory violence: "And if you wrong us, shall we not revenge? If we are like you in the rest, we will resemble you in that" (3.1.66-68). For Shylock, the bond's utility is not economic—"A pound of man's flesh," he tells Antonio and Bassanio, "Is not so estimable, profitable neither, / As flesh of muttons, beefs, or goats" (1.3.165-67)—but sociopolitical, through its power as an instrument of the common law to nullify the class privilege that protects Antonio from Shylock's vengeance. This association between the common law and violent social disruption is a crucial element of the play's ideological work.

The ruling class's response to Shylock's threat is presented by Portia. She begins by acknowledging both the validity of the bond (177-79) and the ideological power of the common law's promised consistency that underpins Shylock's confident intransigence. In reply to Bassanio's appeal to the Duke to "Wrest once the law to your authority" (215) she insists:

> It must not be, there is no power in Venice
> Can alter a decree established.
> 'Twill be recorded for a precedent,
> And many an error by the same example
> Will rush into the state. It cannot be.
>
> (218-22)

Consequently, her solution to Shylock's legal challenge—"Then must the Jew be merciful" (182)—at first seems identical to the Duke's. The mercy Portia seeks, however, is not the Duke's unconditional Christian mercy. While the Duke demands that Shylock forgive Antonio not only the interest owed but "a moi'ty of the principal" as well (26), Portia seeks not the abandonment of the bond but its payment, with justifiable interest, in place of the legal but abhorrent penalty Shylock demands. "Be merciful," she tells Shylock, "Take thrice thy money, bid me tear the bond" (233-34). It was precisely this type of mercy—that which does not mitigate justice for the sake of pity but mitigates (common) law for the sake of true justice—that the courts of equity claimed to dispense. Knight notes the distinction: "The 'mercy' of the High Court of Chancery's equitable decisions by the Lord Chancellor is not to be confused with . . . simple clemency or empathetic pity . . . for William West says: 'there is a difference between Equitie and Clemency: for Equitie is alwaies most firmly knit to the evil of the Law which way soever it bends, whether to clemency, or to severity'" ("Equity" 95-96). Many in the play's contemporary audience would have recognized Portia's suggested compromise—the payment of appropriate interest rather than the contractually stipulated forfeiture—as a solution typical of the equity courts of the day (Keeton 137).

Like Shylock's use of common law, Portia's invocation of equity has social as well as legal significance. According to the theory of equity which emerged during Elizabeth's reign, while equitable mercy assured the justness of the law, equity's own justness was in turn guaranteed by its origin in the royal conscience (Thorne viii). The monarch's conscience itself was validated by his role as the earthly conduit for divine justice, which by virtue of its source was necessarily superior to, and thus the ultimate venue of appeal from, the merely human common law. William Lambarde, in his *Archeion,* writes:

> And considering that the Prince of this Realme is the immediate minister of Iustice under God, and is sworn at his Coronation, to deliver to his subjects *aequam & rectam Iustitiam;* I cannot see how it may otherwise be, but that besides his Court of meere Law, he must either reserve to himselfe, or referre to others a certaine soveraigne and preheminent Power, by which he may both supply the want, and correct the rigour of that Positive or written Law. . . . if onely streight Law should bee administred, the helpe of GOD which speaketh in that Oracle of Equitie, should be denyed unto men that neede it.
>
> (42-44)

Accordingly, the court of Chancery was considered the "court of the King's conscience," its Chancellor deputized by the monarch to implement the justice of the royal will, correcting when necessary the injustices perpetrated by the common law by overruling the decisions of its courts. Contrary to the levelling effect of the common law that placed even the sovereign under the law, this construction of legal authority offered a hierarchical ideology which situated the monarch at the terrestrial pinnacle of the legal system.

Portia's response to Shylock's use of the common law is thus the jurisprudential reassertion of the fundamental value and necessity of social hierarchy, replacing his vision of inter-class violence with one of royally-regulated harmony. It is in this light that we must understand Portia's famous "quality of mercy" speech:

> The quality of mercy is not strain'd,
> It droppeth as the gentle rain from heaven
> Upon the place beneath. It is twice blest:
> It blesseth him that gives and him that takes.
> 'Tis mightiest in the mightiest, it becomes
> The throned monarch better than his crown.
> His sceptre shows the force of temporal power,
> The attribute to awe and majesty,
> Wherein doth sit the dread and fear of kings;
> But mercy is above this sceptred way,
> It is enthroned in the hearts of kings,

It is an attribute to God himself;
And earthly power doth then show likest God's
When mercy seasons justice.

(184-97)

Mercy, in short, descends from heaven into the heart of the monarch, allowing him to fulfill his role as the terrestrial conduit of God's justice, with which he "seasons" flawed human justice. In addition to justifying ideologically the supremacy of royal equity, however, Portia's speech also makes clear its practical implications. Her juxtaposition of the monarch's divine equitable authority with his "temporal power" sets up the speech's concluding union of Christian piety and *realpolitik* intimidation: "We do pray for mercy, / And that same prayer doth teach us all to render / The deeds of mercy" (200-02). The power that equity gives to the Crown by reinstating royal will as the ultimate legal authority assures that one can no more hope to prosper without the king's mercy than without God's, and that one who hopes for such mercy should be prepared to make concessions of his own. Some seven years after the play's composition, King James would make this same point less subtly in his July 1604 rebuke to a recalcitrant Parliament: "Justice I will give to all, and favour to such as deserve it . . . in cases of equity, if I should show favour, except there be obedience, I were no wise man" (qtd. in Kenyon 60).

While Portia replaces the social coercion of the Duke's Christian mercy with an equitable mercy which responds to Shylock's legal defense in kind, the ramifications of both threats are the same for him. To accept Portia's equitable resolution is to surrender his equal legal standing and accede to the existence of a higher legal and social authority. Not surprisingly, then, Shylock spurns Portia's veiled threat, preferring to rely on the power of his position under the common law to indemnify him from the need for royal mercy: "By my soul I swear / There is no power in the tongue of man / To alter me: I stay here on my bond" (240-42). What follows is one of the most dramatic—and ideologically potent—scenes in Shakespearean comedy, in which judgment is pronounced not once but twice, juxtaposing for the audience the results of the competing legal philosophies presented in the first half of the scene.

Portia's deliberations proceed first in accordance with the common law. When she declares the bond forfeit, Shylock esteems her for her knowledge of the law, suggesting the common law's justification of its judges' authority not by their own discretion but by their preeminent ability to administer consistently a time-tested body of law: "It doth appear you are a worthy judge; / You know the law, your exposition / Hath been most sound" (236-38). As the impartiality of the common law requires, Portia's ruling is pointedly faithful to the law of contract, despite her personal desire to offer mercy:

Por:
. . . lay bare your bosom.
Shy:
Ay, his breast,
So says the bond, doth it not, noble judge?
"Nearest his heart," those are the very words.
Por:
It is so. Are there balance here to weigh
The flesh?
Shy:
I have them ready.
Por:
Have by some surgeon, Shylock, on your charge,
To stop his wounds, lest he do bleed to death.
Shy:
Is it so nominated in the bond?
Por:
It is not so express'd, but what of that?
'Twere good you do so much for charity.
Shy:
I cannot find it, 'tis not in the bond.

(252-62)

Alongside this emphasis on the strict legality of the procedure, however, is the no less insistent emphasis on the materiality of its outcome: the mutilation and almost certain death of Antonio. Present throughout the trial scene, this linking of common-law principle to its horrific results is unmistakable as the scene reaches its climax. As Shylock approaches Antonio with whetted knife, Portia again reminds us that what we see is the result of the court's obligation to proceed according to the law: "The law allows it, and the court awards it" (303). The result is a vivid and ideologically charged illustration of the irrelevance of the common law's human consequences to its inflexible requirements.

The clear injustice of this strictly legal proceeding is, of course, precisely what the flexible, case-specific judgments of the courts of equity claimed to remedy. Before Shylock can strike, Portia halts him—"Tarry a little, there is something else" (305)—and the trial shifts from the procedures of a common-law court to those of equity. Portia's famous "quibble"—Shylock may have his pound of flesh according to the bond, but on the condition that "if thou dost shed / One drop of Christian blood, thy lands and goods / Are by the laws of Venice confiscate / Unto the state of Venice" (309-12)—is a stratagem typical of the equity courts. While the common law traditionally held that if the law granted an individual a right (including the right to take possession of property) it also granted him the means to exercise that right (Andrews 77nA), the courts of equity would often thwart a common-law award by placing such stringent restrictions and protections on the property to be seized as frequently to make the path of least resistance that taken by Shylock, the "voluntary" non-collection of the award (Andrews 66; Keeton 145). The relief and amazement, both on stage and off, at Portia's dramatic aversion of the travesty of justice almost perpetrated by the common law underscores the contrasting results of the two legal systems.

The audience's pleasure in Portia's victory is heightened by the irony of her use of Shylock's insistence on strict interpretation against him: "For as thou urgest justice, be assur'd / Thou shalt have justice more than thou desir'st" (315-16). In doing so, however, Portia has vexed legal scholars by belying the equitable principle most often associated with the trial scene, the mitigation of the strict letter of the law through recourse to its gentler spirit. The reason for this seeming contradiction lies in the political significance of Portia's legal device. While the mitigation of the letter of the law by its spirit or intent was indeed a central tenet of traditional equitable jurisprudence, in Shakespeare's time it was chiefly associated not with royally-controlled equity but with the judges of the common-law courts. Throughout the 16th century, as the limitations placed upon the common law by its codification into written rules became apparent, its judges began to revivify a procedure utilized by their predecessors in the 13th and 14th centuries: the interpretation of a law based on its intent rather than its precise wording (Thomas 515-16). Such an approach was entirely congruent with common-law ideology, basing the authority of the common-law judges to interpret rather than simply apply the law on their unmatched knowledge of its history and principles.

The practice of common-law equity was, of course, opposed by the equity courts, whose authority was based on the inadequacy of the common law to the requirements of justice and the necessity of an alternate source of justice—royal conscience—to remedy that inadequacy. To correct the letter of the law with its spirit was merely to affirm the ultimate wisdom of the common law. For this reason the principle of intent is emphatically not the basis of Portia's equitable decision. Portia herself discounts intent as a means of correcting the defects of the letter of the law when she pointedly acknowledges that the spirit as well as the letter of the law supports Shylock's claim: "the intent and purpose of the law / Hath full relation to the penalty, / Which here appeareth due upon the bond" (247-49). As the play takes pains to indicate, the intent of the law of contract is to protect the sanctity of contracts from external interference in order to ensure the rights of those who do business in Venice, regardless of the specific contents of those contracts.

The principle that Portia applies in reaching her verdict is not the mitigation of the letter of the law by its spirit, but the equally venerable equitable doctrine which holds that equity may mitigate the unjust results of the law's necessary generality by taking into account the aspects of a specific case of which the law takes no notice. This conception of equity is traceable to Aristotle's *Ethics,* in which he argues that "all law is universal but about some things it is not possible to make a universal statement which shall be correct. . . . this is the nature of the equitable, a correction of law where it is defective owing to its universality" (133; bk. 5, ch. 10). Elizabethan advocates of the courts of equity argued that the common law, in its quest for comprehensiveness and consistency, must operate on a general level and thus could never be made to take account of the "collaterall circumstances" of individual cases (Hake 123). As a result, equity was both necessary and necessarily superior to the common law, overruling the latter when the application of its general rules to a specific case produced evident injustice.

It was this theory of equity that was at the heart of the Crown's claims to legal authority: for even if superior knowledge of both the letter and the spirit of the common law must be conceded to the common-law judges, the individualized requirements of justice were the province of conscience: "the examination of the case by circumstances . . . doth necessarily appertayne to the high courte of Chauncery . . . by an Equity that is drawne from the only conscience of the Lord Chaunccllor" (Hake 123). The stipulations in Portia's ruling concerning the spilling of blood and the removal of an exact weight of flesh underline the gruesome specifics excluded from the common law's generality even as they correct the injustice produced by that exclusion. Neither the letter nor the spirit of the law make allowances for contracts like Shylock's; it is left to Portia and equity to mitigate the effects of the law's generality by considering the circumstances of the case at hand, overruling the requirements of the law in order to satisfy those of justice.

The sociopolitical consequences of equity's victory over the common law are immediately and decisively registered in the treatment of Shylock by a legal system once again under the control of the ruling class. During the first half of the interpretational contest, Portia in her role as common-law judge sets aside the scene's emphasis on Shylock's cultural difference, addressing him not as "Jew" but by name. The shift to equity, however, returns social difference and discrimination to the law, indicated by Portia's invocation of the statute specifically criminalizing the shedding of "Christian blood." For the remainder of the trial Shylock goes unnamed, referred to only as "Jew" not merely by his avowed Christian enemies but also by Portia, the representative of justice. This connection between equity and social differentiation casts the freeing of Antonio as a reassertion of the distinctions between classes that Shylock's use of the law attempted to erase.

As Shylock tries to leave the court—"Why then the devil give him good of it! / I'll stay no longer question"—he learns that "The law hath yet another hold on [him]" (345-47). Because Portia's equitable reading of the bond has disallowed the shedding of Christian blood as a contractually protected act, Shylock is guilty of attempted murder and thus subject under the criminal law to the forfeiture of life and property. The social basis of Shylock's predicament is suggested by the statute to which he falls prey, the law "against an alien, / That by direct or indirect attempts / [Seeks] the life of any citizen" (349-51).

Such a law is present in none of the sources of the pound-of-flesh plot; moreover, in the 16th-century England all felonies, including attempted murder, were punishable by death and loss of property no matter who the perpetrator (Auden 228; Keeton 146). There is thus no dramatic or historical justification for a law specifically targeting aliens except to emphasize the link between Shylock's social status and his fate forged by the power of the law to discriminate between—and against—social groups or classes: having resolutely maintained his status as cultural outsider, he now finds himself trapped by it. The pleasure we take in Shylock's resultant comeuppance reinforces the play's implicit rebuttal to the common law's central justification, the economic necessity of a law predictable and impartial even to the "strangers" whose "commodity" is so important to the nation. Punishing Shylock's abuse of the common law with a statute that explicitly discriminates against such "strangers" answers the economic arguments of the rising class by implying that despite its potentially deleterious effect on commerce a certain amount of regulation is necessary for the security and moral order of the state.

The reestablishment of the legal authority of the ruling class is complete when the statute places discretionary judicial power directly in the hands of the monarch: "the offender's life lies in the mercy / Of the Duke only" (355-56). Stripped of the common law's protection, Shylock is subject to Portia's earlier threat: his failure to grant mercy to Antonio puts him at the mercy of the Duke. That this mercy is not Portia's equitable mercy but instead the clemency which was the Crown's prerogative in criminal cases (as indicated by the Duke's use of the word "pardon" [369]) merely confirms the sociopolitical complicity of the two juristic principles.

Their legal power over him established, Shylock's antagonists immediately use it to nullify his socioeconomic threat: the loss of half of his wealth now to Antonio and the other half upon his death to Lorenzo places his economic power in the hands of the aristocracy and its allies, and his forced conversion symbolically completes his absorption by the dominant Christian-aristocratic culture. Notably, despite his earlier denunciation of Shylock's usury, Antonio makes no provision at this point to prevent its continuance; it would seem that the eventual appropriation of any profit made therein by the ruling class does much to mitigate usury's sinfulness. The Christians' true target is not Shylock's economic practice but the social and political ends to which it is employed.

Finally, the trial concludes with a further demonstration of the coercive power granted the Crown by the supremacy of equity that Portia intimates in the "quality of mercy" speech, as the Duke requires Shylock's acquiescence to Antonio's terms, "or else I do recent / The pardon that I late pronounced here" (391-92). Legally at the mercy of his enemies, Shylock can only accede to Portia's ironic query, "Art thou contented, Jew?" (393). Thoroughly humbled, he leaves the court not with the unregenerate curse of his attempted exit prior to the invocation of the law against aliens but with the entreaties of a broken man: "I pray you give me leave to go from hence, / I am not well" (395-96). The trial's last word, however, is given to Gratiano: "In christ'ning shalt thou have two godfathers: / Had I been judge, thou shouldst have had ten more, / To bring thee to the gallows, not to the font" (398-400). This taunting valediction, while reemphasizing the "mercy" granted Shylock in sparing his life, at the same time underlines the contingency of that mercy, suggesting how easily his fate could have been that which Gratiano prefers. That it was not is due less to the principles of equity than to the dramatic and ideological appropriateness of a punishment befitting Shylock's social and economic crime.

Seen from the dual perspective of legal and political history, the threat posed by Shylock to the Venetian social order is fundamentally the same threat that Lord Chancellor Ellesmere recognized nearly twenty years later in what was by then one in a growing number of legal challenges to the Crown's sociopolitical hegemony. Shylock's use of the common law represented to a contemporary audience a question not simply of jurisprudential principle, nor even of economic practice, but ultimately of "the power and prerogative of the King." And despite the efficacy of his defeat at Portia's hands in defining and resolving the conflict for the theater-going public in the interests of royal authority, the ideological battle fought in *Shylock v. Antonio* would prove to be but an early skirmish in the war between the rising and the ruling classes that was to dominate the next century of English politics.

Notes

1. All quotations from *The Merchant of Venice* are from *The Riverside Shakespeare*, ed. G. Blakemore Evans. References to the trial scene (Act 4, scene 1) will be cited by line number only.

Works Cited

Andrews, Mark Edwin. *Law versus Equity in "The Merchant of Venice."* Boulder: U of Colorado P, 1965.

Aristotle. *The Nicomachean Ethics.* Trans. David Ross. London: Oxford UP, 1961.

Auden, W. H. "Brothers and Others." *The Dyer's Hand and Other Essays.* New York: Random, 1948. 218-37.

Bacon, Francis. *The Elements of the Common Lawes of England.* 1630. Amsterdam: Da Capo, 1969.

Cohen, Walter. "*The Merchant of Venice* and the Possibilities of Historical Criticism." *ELH* 49 (1982): 765-89.

Hake, Edward. *Epieikeia: A Dialogue on Equity in Three Parts.* Ed. D. E. C. Yale. New Haven: Yale UP, 1953.

Hill, Christopher. *Intellectual Origins of the English Revolution.* Oxford: Clarendon, 1965.

Ives, E. W. "Social Change and the Law." *The English Revolution 1600-1660.* Ed. E. W. Ives. London: Arnold, 1968. 115-30.

Keeton, George W. *Shakespeare's Legal and Political Background.* New York: Barnes, 1967.

Kenyon, J. P. *Stuart England.* Vol. 6 of *The Pelican History of England.* Harmondsworth: Penguin, 1978.

Knight, W. Nicholas. "Equity, *The Merchant of Venice,* and William Lambarde." *Shakespeare Survey* 27 (1974): 93-104.

———. "Shakespeare's Court Case." *Law and Critique* 2 (1991): 103-12.

Lambarde, William. *Archeion or, a Discourse upon the High Courts of Justice in England.* 1635 (written c. 1591). Ed. Charles H. McIlwain and Paul L. Ward. Cambridge: Harvard UP, 1957.

McKay, Maxine. "*The Merchant of Venice:* A Reflection of the Early Conflict between Courts of Law and Courts of Equity." *Shakespeare Quarterly* 15 (1964): 371-75.

Moisan, Thomas. "'Which is the Merchant here? and which the Jew?': Subversion and Recuperation in *The Merchant of Venice.*" *Shakespeare Reproduced: The Text in History and Ideology.* Ed. Jean E. Howard and Marion F. O'Connor. New York: Methuen, 1987. 188-206.

Phillips, O. Hood. *Shakespeare and the Lawyers.* London: Methuen, 1972.

Pocock, J. G. A. *The Ancient Constitution and the Feudal Law: A Reissue with a Retrospect.* Cambridge: Cambridge UP, 1987.

Shakespeare, William. *The Merchant of Venice. The Riverside Shakespeare.* Ed. G. Blakemore Evans. Boston: Houghton, 1974. 254-85.

Stone, Lawrence. *The Causes of the English Revolution 1529-1642.* New York: Harper, 1972.

———. *The Crisis of the Aristocracy 1558-1641.* Abridged edition. London: Oxford UP, 1967.

Tawney, R. H. "The Rise of the Gentry, 1558-1640." *Economic History Review* 11 (1941). Rpt. in *Social Change and Revolution in England 1540-1640.* Ed. Lawrence Stone. London: Longman's, 1965. 6-18.

Tennenhouse, Leonard. *Power on Display: The Politics of Shakespeare's Genres.* New York: Methuen, 1986.

Thomas, G. W. "James I, Equity and Lord Keeper John Williams." *The English Historical Review* 91 (1976): 506-28.

Thorne, Samuel E. Preface to Hake. v-xii.

West, William. *Symboleography.* London, 1594.

Whigham, Frank. "Ideology and Class Conduct in *The Merchant of Venice.*" *Renaissance Drama* n.s. 10 (1979): 93-115.

FURTHER READING

Criticism

Cohen, Stephen. "Is This the Law?: Legal Ambiguity and Its Effects in *The Merchant of Venice* and *Measure for Measure.*" In *The Language of Power, the Power of Language: The Effects of Ambiguity on Sociopolitical Structures as Illustrated in Shakespeare's Plays,* pp. 80-118. Cambridge: Harvard University Press, 1987.

> Discusses the fact that while these two "problem plays" end with marriage—the classic solution to Renaissance comedies—neither ends with complete social harmony.

Gross, John. *Shylock: A Legend and Its Legacy.* New York: Simon & Schuster, 1992, 386 p.

> Examines the treatment of the character Shylock in Shakespeare's play, in performances throughout the history of the play, and in popular culture.

Holmer, Joan Ozark. "'Pardon this fault': Antonio and Shylock." In *The Merchant of Venice: Choice, Hazard and Consequence,* pp. 142-82. London: Macmillan Press Ltd., 1995.

> Looks at the complex relationship between Antonio and Shylock, noting their similarities and differences as well as their struggle for power over one another.

———. "'Joy be the consequence': Union and Reunion." In *The Merchant of Venice: Choice, Hazard and Consequence,* pp. 246-84. London: Macmillan Press Ltd., 1995.

> Analyzes the rings episode in the play as the second and final "trial" necessary to make all the characters repentant.

Legatt, Alexander. "*The Merchant of Venice.*" In *Shakespeare's Comedy of Love,* pp. 117-50. London: Methuen & Co. Ltd., 1974.

> Demonstrates how Shakespeare experiments in this play with more complex characters whose natures change during the course of the action.

Lerner, Laurence. "Wilhelm S and Shylock." *Shakespeare Survey* 48 (1995): 61-68.

> Argues that the interpretation of the play as either anti-Semitic or critical of those who are anti-Semitic depends upon the audience.

Newman, Karen. "Portia's Ring: Unruly Women and Structures of Exchange in *The Merchant of Venice.*" *Shakespeare Quarterly* 38, No. 1 (Spring 1987): 19-33.

> Observes that even in the love scenes, the play emphasizes economics, material exchange, and power.

Shapiro, James. "Shakespur and the Jewbill." *Shakespeare Survey* 48 (1995): 51–60.

> Surveys the influence of *The Merchant of Venice* on the public debate of England's Jewish Naturalization Act of 1753.

Othello

For further information on the critical and stage history of *Othello,* see *SC,* Volumes 4, 11, and 35.

INTRODUCTION

Critics have not formed any sort of consensus about the role of race in *Othello*, despite the fact that the topic of racism continues to be one of the most predominant issues in modern scholarship about the play. Some commentators have held that *Othello* is not about racism, that Othello is essentially white, or that his race is irrelevant. This position, rather popular among nineteenth- and early twentieth-century critics, including Charles Lamb and A. C. Bradley, has sparked numerous responses among modern critics who maintain emphatically that race is the essential element of the play. Scholars who assign primacy to race in *Othello* can be divided roughly into three categories. Critics such as John Gillies, for instance, argue that Shakespeare was upholding the racist views of the Renaissance, and that the play advocates racism. Conversely, other critics, among them Martin Orkin and Emily C. Bartels, state that Shakespeare, through his sympathetic portrayal of Othello, was critiquing racism, and taking his society to task for its racist behavior. Finally, Michael Neill (1998) and other scholars argue that it is anachronistic to apply modern ideas of racism to an earlier period. These scholars maintain that Shakespeare and his audience would have understood race, a cultural construct, in a wholly different way than we do today.

Other theorists offer additional nuances to the analysis of race in *Othello*. Several feminist scholars, among them Karen Newman and Marianne Novy (1984), explore the relationship of gender and race. Newman's argument that Desdemona and Othello are scorned equally by Venetian society, and that Othello's race and Desdemona's freely expressed sexuality represent the same threat to the dominant white male society, has sparked a heated debate. In a second significant development of theory, such scholars as Paul A. Cantor and Emily C. Bartels, apply anthropologists' concepts of "Self" and "Other" to *Othello*. They argue that Shakespeare wanted to distinguish Othello from the rest of the play's cast, to set him apart, in order to make a point about society's propensity to vilify those who are not like the "Self." Cantor maintains that the issue of race is a means unto an end for Shakespeare, allowing the playwright to create an opportunity for the dominant society to isolate, ridicule, even destroy Othello, and through the telling of the story Shakespeare warns the audience against such behavior. Many of these critiques liken the role of Othello with that of Shylock in *The Merchant of Venice.*

A third trend in modern studies of the play is the examination of the ramifications of *Othello* across time and among different ethnicities. Critics explore the history of the play's production from the Renaissance (when people of color were relatively unknown to the audience), through the seventeenth and eighteenth centuries (the height of the slave trade and institutionalized racism), and into the twentieth century with its move toward greater racial tolerance. Ferial J. Ghazoul studies *Othello*'s influence on Arab culture and literature; Jyotsna Singh's work focuses on the impact of *Othello* on African and Asian writers. James R. Andreas (1992) compares the work of three twentieth-century writers who have manipulated the plot of *Othello* to highlight personal concerns about race in their society. Andreas concludes that "the play itself seems to incriminate Western society at large for its predisposition to the periodic, ritual slaughter of marginal and aboriginal groups and all whites—especially women—who consort with them."

RACE

Ruth Cowhig (essay date 1977)

SOURCE: "The Importance of Othello's Race," in *The Journal of Commonwealth Literature,* Vol. XII, No. 2, December, 1977, pp. 153-61.

[*In the following essay, Cowhig argues that race is essential to the meaning of* Othello.]

There has recently been general agreement amongst critics that Shakespeare conceived of Othello as a Negro, and not as the tawny Arab on whom Coleridge insisted with such vehemence. But there is a considerable gap between critical opinion and the ideas and assumptions that linger on, even when people have some degree of specialized interest. It is more than usually so where Othello's colour is concerned. To speak of a conspiracy of silence might be to use too strong a phrase; but there is a reluctance to disturb accepted ideas, and a Negro Othello has a greater novelty than the study either of critical writing or of stage history would lead one to expect—as I found when reading *Othello* with a group of adult students. The edition we were using included a series of critical essays, but none even mentioned Othello's colour; that it was an American publication had an obvious significance.

Eldred Jones's *Othello's Countrymen* has clearly established the familiarity of the Elizabethans with Negroes, especially in London.[1] Traders with West Africa used them as interpreters and often brought a few home as gifts, or for the family household. Thus Shakespeare must have had opportunities for contact with Negroes, although there is no direct evidence of any. There was also a strong stage tradition which made use of Negroes in the role of villain or of villain-hero. As Shakespeare had himself followed this tradition with Aaron in *Titus Andronicus,* first performed between 1590 and 1592, it follows that his choice of a Negro as the hero of his tragedy of *Othello,* thus completely breaking the tradition, must have been deliberate. It is true that the plot was taken from Cinthio's *Hecatommithi;* but hardly any of Shakespeare's plots were original, and there was evidently something about this tale that led him to select it out of many. The story as it stands is crude and lacking in subtlety: the only thing that distinguishes it is that it is concerned with the love between a Moor and a young Venetian girl of high birth.

The reasons for Shakespeare's choice remain obscure, and we can only speculate about them; perhaps Shakespeare felt sympathy for aliens in an intolerant society, as is suggested by his treatment of Shylock in *The Merchant of Venice,* though here he was hampered by an inflexible story, with the result that Shylock's moving speeches burst out of the framework of the play. In *Othello* there is no suggestion of deliberate social injustice; but one wonders whether, as he watched the humiliation of Negro slaves and servants, Shakespeare found himself imagining the feelings of proud men, perhaps of royal descent like Othello, whose black skins betrayed no blushes. 'Haply for I am black', cries Othello, as the first doubts begin to torment him: it is the first of the alternative reasons that he considers in trying to account for her betrayal, so that we cannot ignore his awareness of the colour barrier. Shakespeare has moved far from his acceptance of the traditional Negro in *Titus Andronicus,* whose colour reflects his evil motives:

> Let fools do good and fair men call for grace,
> Aaron will have his soul black like his face.
>
> (III, i, 202-5)

Whatever Shakespeare's intentions may have been, we have to take seriously the importance of Othello's race in our interpretation of the play.

The first effect of Othello's blackness is immediately grasped by the audience, but not always by the reader of the play. It is that he is, from the beginning, placed in a position of isolation from the other characters. In the same way, Hamlet's black clothes isolate him visually from the rest of the Danish court. This isolation is such an integral part of Othello's experience that it is constantly operative, even if not necessarily at a conscious level. Anyone who is black would appreciate its importance in understanding the character of Othello. Before he appears, our attention is forcibly focussed on Othello's race. The speeches of Iago and Roderigo in the first scene are full of racial antipathy. Othello is 'the thick-lips', 'an old black ram', 'a lascivious Moor' and 'a Barbary horse', and he 'is making the beast with two backs' with Desdemona. The language is purposely offensive and sexually coarse, and the animal images convey, as such images always do, the idea of someone who is less than human. Coriolanus expresses his contempt for the plebeians similarly, through a series of animal comparisons. Iago calculates on arousing in Brabantio all the latent prejudice of Venetian society, and he succeeds. The union is, to Brabantio, 'a treason of the blood', and he feels that its acceptance will reduce Venetian statesmen to 'bondslaves and pagans'. We, the audience, are not at first given any opportunity of forming our own opinion of Othello, although Iago's personal grievances over his lack of promotion may put us on our guard against his claims to impartiality.

Brabantio occupies a strong position in society. He is 'much beloved', and 'hath in his effect a voice potential / As double as the Duke's', if we can believe Iago. His attitude to Othello's race is as prejudiced as Iago's, though it is important to realize that he represents a more liberal outlook, at least on the surface. Willing to entertain Othello in his own home, it is he who makes Othello's meetings with Desdemona possible. His reaction to the news of the elopement is predictable. He is outraged that this Negro should presume so far, and at once concludes that charms and witchcraft must have been used, since otherwise his daughter could never 'fall in love with what she feared to look on'. To him the match is 'against all rules of nature'; only spells and medicines could make it possible 'for nature so prepost'rously to err'. When he confronts Othello his abuse is no less bitter than Iago's.

Before this confrontation Othello makes his first appearance, and two characteristics impress us. First his pride:

> I fetch my life and being
> From men of royal siege
>
> (I, ii, 21-2)

Secondly, his confidence in his own achievements:

> My services which I have done the Signiory
> Shall out-tongue his complaints.
>
> (I, ii, 95-7)

It is difficult to estimate the reactions of an Elizabethan audience to this Negro, so obviously in control of the situation and so noble in his bearing. No black man remotely like him had ever appeared on the English stage before, nor has one since. However great his confidence, however, his colour makes his vulnerability plain to all. Brabantio is sure of the Duke's support, since he and the other senators 'cannot but feel this wrong as 'twere their own'. He is disappointed, but he would probably have been right if the state had not been in danger and Othello essential for its defence. As it is, Brabantio gets cold comfort; he is to 'take up this mangled matter at the best'. The Duke treats Othello as befits his position as Commander-in-Chief, addressing him as 'valiant Othello', whereas Brabantio never uses his name, calling him scornfully just 'Moor!'. The First Senator gives Othello some support, but his parting words, 'Adieu, brave Moor. Use Desdemona well', while not unfriendly, reveal an attitude of superiority. Would a senator have made such an injunction to a newly-married general if he had been white, and an equal?

It is Desdemona's stand before the Senate that first breaks Othello's isolation. Her stature is immensely increased by the fact that he is black. Her passivity in later scenes cannot be seen as a natural docility after the spirited independence which she shows in her defence of the marriage. Beneath a quiet exterior lay the strength to resist the pressures of society; she was

> So opposite to marriage that she shunned
> The wealthy, curled darlings of our nation
>
> (I, ii, 67-8)

The choice of words makes clear to us the kind of suitors who were unable to attract Desdemona, but there is no suggestion that Brabantio wished, like Capulet, to force his daughter against her inclination. The marriage is something that he could not anticipate, and Othello and Desdemona are trapped by their predicament, just as Romeo and Juliet were, but with the great difference that theirs is a mature match in which the couple are well aware of the seriousness of the step they have taken: 'My downright violence and storm of fortunes', Desdemona calls it. It is made very clear, in Othello's account of the wooing, that she had to take the initiative:

> She thanked me
> And bade me, if I had a friend that loved her
> I should but teach him how to tell my story,
> And that would woo her. Upon this hint I spake.
>
> (I, iii, 163-6)

It is, of course, because of Othello's race; there would be no need for Desdemona to break with the long and absolute custom, that the man must speak first, in any but the rarest circumstances. Before the Senate she remains level-headed. In her speech about 'divided duty' she softens the blow, but does not try to avoid the issue. Finally, when she says that she 'saw Othello's visage in his mind', the audience has to make the effort to overcome, with her, the tendency to connect Othello's black face with evil. Brabantio's insistence that she is going against nature is repudiated. 'Nature' has a variety of meanings in Shakespeare's plays; in this one it is linked with Iago's cynical and materialistic outlook, whereas the love between Othello and Desdemona belongs to another plane.

The ease with which Othello succumbs to Iago's insinuations has puzzled many critics. Some have been led to a grudging admiration of Iago's 'diabolic intellect', while others have belittled Othello for being such easy prey. Dr. Leavis's analysis reduces Othello to a pitiable figure; he is 'beyond any question, the nobly massive man of action', but 'his habit of self-approving self-dramatization' is evidence of his egotism. Nevertheless, most playgoers have been deeply moved by Othello's suffering. Perhaps the explanation lies in Othello's colour, which Dr. Leavis does not think important: 'his colour, whether or not "colour feeling" existed among the Elizabethans, we are certain to take as emphasizing the disparity of the match.'[2] I do not think that Othello's colour can be relegated to a parenthesis in this way. It is the basic cause of his insecurity, which, when the part is played by a Negro, needs no explanation. Its origin is there for us to see. If we do need words to make it clear, they are there too. Iago harps mercilessly on the unnaturalness of the match:

> Not to affect many proposed matches,
> Of her own clime, complexion and degree,
> Whereto we see in all things nature tends—
> Foh! one may smell in such a will most rank,
> Foul disproportions, thoughts unnatural.
>
> (III, iii, 233-7)

The exclamation of disgust and the words 'smell' and 'foul' reveal a phobia so obvious that it is strange it is so often passed over. The attack demolishes Othello's defences simply because there is no defence against this kind of racial contempt. 'For she had eyes, and chose me', changes to:

> Haply for I am black
> And have not those soft parts of conversation
> That chamberers have, or for I am declined
> Into the vale of years . . .
>
> (III, iii 267-70)

It is one of the most moving moments in the play. Othello's vulnerability is no surprise to himself, for he has had to marry in secret, and his confidence is based on his knowledge that his expertise is valuable to the state, not on the expectation of being valued for himself. Given Iago's hatred and astuteness in exploiting other people's weaknesses, which we see in the trap he sets for Cassio, the black Othello is easy game. We are not watching the collapse of a self-deceiving fool, but the baiting of an alien who cannot fight back on equal terms.

Othello's stature as a tragic hero is built up mainly through his prowess as a soldier. He is unique amongst Shakespeare's soldier heroes because he has achieved his position as general on merit, after hard and bitter experience. The early history described in the account of his wooing is typical of the experience of an African of his times who has been 'taken by the insolent foe / And sold to slavery'. His whole life, since the age of seven, has been the precarious life of the soldier, and against this background his blackness is evidence of his outstanding ability. As a Negro, employed by the state of Venice, he receives tributes from all: he is 'the warlike Moor Othello', 'brave Othello', and 'our noble and valiant general'. The war with the Turks is presented in a businesslike way as a national emergency, and the ironic undertones that we find in the presentation of war in the history plays (even *Henry V* gives us Williams's speech about the legs and arms and heads joining together at the latter day to confront the warrior king) seem to be excluded from *Othello*. The hero is marked by his self-control and refusal to be roused to anger, as in 'Put up your bright swords for the dew will rust them' and 'Were it my cue to fight I should have known it / Without a prompter'. After Othello's disintegration we are sadly reminded of this moral strength by Lodovico's words: 'Is this the nature / Whom passion could not shake?' (IV, i, 261-2). The portrait is of a kind of soldier who does not exist elsewhere in the plays, except in minor characters. Othello tries to control emotion, unlike Henry V, who before battle has to:

> Imitate the action of the tiger;
> Stiffen the sinews, summon up the blood,
> Disguise fair nature with hard-favoured rage

This emphasis gives his breakdown of control in Act III a more intense effect, and is also in direct contradiction to the conception of the Negro as a man swayed by passion which was current in Shakespeare's time.

The famous 'farewell' speech also becomes more meaningful when spoken by a black Othello. 'The big wars / That make ambition virtue', a phrase which one tends to accept as a piece of rhetoric, gains a literal truth, because the sin of ambition (and ambition was still reckoned as a sin) has been purified, in Othello, by courage and endurance, and by the fact that only ambition could enable him to escape the hardships and humiliations of his early life. The speech is not merely the longing for military action of the incurable romantic. The pride, pomp and circumstance, the spirit-stirring drum, and the rest must be seen in relation to the harshly realistic conclusion, 'Othello's occupation's gone'. This moment reduced Kean's audiences to tears; it was a part of Othello's experience which Kean, with his precarious and uneven career, was well able to understand and convey. The realization that his career is irrevocably over throws an aura of nostalgia over Othello's war experience, so that he looks back at the trappings of war as a dying man looks back at life.

As we approach the tragic climax, when jealousy has taken possession, Othello behaves very like the Moor of ancient tradition; his irrational acceptance of the flimsiest evidence, his return to superstitious beliefs, his uncontrollable anger, and his resort to violence and revenge—all these are consistent with mediaeval tradition. Nevertheless, it seems to me unlikely that Shakespeare intended to go back to an acceptance of the popular preconceptions which he had flouted in the early scenes. *Othello* was very closely followed by *King Lear*, and in both plays Shakespeare seems to be exploring the basic nature of man, and especially the effect on that nature of the subservience of reason to the passions. In *Lear* reason is literally overthrown when Lear becomes mad, while in *Othello* jealousy and rage take control. By portraying the disintegration of a black hero whose nobility had been effectively established, Shakespeare was able to show man as the prey of his uncontrollable emotions with extra dramatic effect, and it suggests another reason for the choice of a black hero. No more extreme example of jealousy could be imagined than that of a man who kills the wife he deeply loves, but there would have been difficulty in making such a theme acceptable to the audience. If, however, the jealous husband who must commit the murder is black, it removes the crime of sexual violence from everyday surroundings and experience and makes the audience more prepared to accept it. By taking an alien from a strange cultural background the dramatist would feel liberated. True, it is made quite explicit that Othello is a baptized Christian, which brings him closer to the audience and separates him from the Turkish enemy. But once subservient to Iago, and having taken his terrible vow of revenge, Othello reverts to superstitious belief. Here, I think, lies the significance of the much-discussed speech about the handkerchief, although there are other possible interpretations. The Christian veneer is thin, and Othello is left exposed to unknown forces of evil. In the same way, Macbeth succumbs to the destructive influence of the witches once he has embarked on the series of murders; the first one involves the betrayal of the most sacred laws of kinship. Shakespeare's tragedies are much concerned with the precariousness of civilized behaviour in man.

The Russian actor, Alexander Ostumov, who set himself to study the part of Othello throughout his career, identifying with him as if he were a real man, saw the problem of the final scene to be that of acting the part so as to make people love Othello and forget he is a murderer. 'Forget' may seem an over-statement, but Shakespeare comes near to making it possible when Othello answers Lodovico's question, 'What shall be said of thee?' (a question which hardly expects a reply) with the words, 'An honourable murderer, if you will'. Rather than being outraged by such a statement, we see in it a terrible pathos. Our sympathy for Othello is never completely destroyed. Here again Othello's colour plays some part. Throughout the scene he is a lonely but dominating figure. Emilia's horror at what has happened brings her racial prejudice to the fore: 'O my good lord', as she enters, becomes 'you the blacker devil!', 'her most filthy bargain', and 'O thou dull Moor'. By this time the audience is expecting the event for which they have long been waiting, the unmasking of Iago. When it comes, Othello looks down at Iago's feet for the mythical cloven hoofs, and demands an explanation from 'that demi-devil', and we are once more reminded that blackness of soul belongs to the white villain rather than to his black victim. The term 'slave' is used several times: Montano pursues Iago, 'for 'tis a damnèd slave'; Lodovico reproaches Othello for having 'fall'n in the practice of a cursèd slave', and later refers to Iago as 'this slave'. Slavery here represents degraded behaviour, and it is the deed, the 'practice' of Othello (who was once redeemed from slavery) that is slavish, whereas in Iago's case it is the man himself.

There is no record of any controversy over the type of Moor intended by Shakespeare until late in the eighteenth

Kenneth Branagh as Iago, Laurence Fishburne as Othello, and Irene Jacob as Desdemona in the 1995 Castle Rock production of Othello.

century. Before that the principal actor blacked himself as far as he could. Edmund Kean was the first to play Othello as a 'tawny' Moor and he was so successful in the part that he dominated the stage for many years. The Romantic critics, especially Lamb and Coleridge, reacted so violently against the idea of a Negro Othello that their views became firmly established. The great Negro actor, Ira Aldridge, played in London just as Kean's career was ending. In 1833 the critics wrote scathing reviews of his performance, although the audiences received him well. He did not play again in London for many years, but he did return in 1865, after playing in *Othello* all over Europe and winning many awards and medals. By that time he had more favourable notices; but although no other actor had much success as Othello during the rest of the nineteenth century, the question of colour remained unresolved. In 1876 Henry Irving played him 'slightly tinged with walnut brown, according to the Edmund Kean precedent, so much applauded by Coleridge'.[3] In 1881 he acted the part again, this time as black as possible, so that Ellen Terry records: 'Before he had done with me, I was nearly as black as he.' Neither production was successful.

The other outstanding Negro actor to play Othello was Paul Robeson. When he first came to London he studied voice and diction with Amanda Aldridge, Ira Aldridge's youngest daughter, who was only an infant when her father died in 1867. It is thus more than likely that some of the tradition of the first great Negro actor was passed on to the next, since Amanda would know many people who had seen her father's performances. Robeson first played in London in 1930, and his last performance in England was in Stratford in 1959: Aldridge's appearances in *Othello* covered thirty-nine years. It is an interesting example of the potential time-span of theatrical tradition.

These Negro actors did much to change the accepted ideas about Othello's colour, as contemporary tributes show. Two examples provide enough evidence that the importance of this question is not merely hypothetical. Theophile Gautier wrote of Ira Aldridge's Othello in St. Petersburg:

> L'origine d'Ira Aldrigge le dispensait de toute teinture au jus de réglisse et au marc de café; il n'avait pas besoin de mettre ses bras dans les manches d'un tricot

chocolat. La peau du rôle était la sienne, et il ne lui fallait nul effort pour y entrer. Aussi son entrée en scène fut-elle magnifique: c'était Othello lui-meme comme l'a créé Shakespeare, avec ses yeux à demi-fermés comme éblouis du soleil d'Afrique, sa nonchalante attitude orientale et cette désinvolture de nègre qu'aucun Européen ne peut imiter.[4]

When John Dover Wilson wrote his introduction to the New Cambridge edition of *Othello* in 1943, he recorded the lasting impression which Robeson made on him. His first heading is 'The Moor', indicating that he felt that the question of Othello's race should be considered before everything else. He writes:

> I felt I was seeing the tragedy for the first time, not merely because of Robeson's acting, which despite a few petty faults of technique was magnificent, but because the fact that he was a true Negro seemed to floodlight the whole drama. Everything was slightly different from what I had previously imagined; new points, fresh nuances, were constantly emerging; and all had, I felt, been clearly intended by the author. The performance convinced me, in short, that a Negro Othello is essential to the full understanding of the play.

It is exciting to think that the truth of this view may be demonstrated by an infinite set of variations in the interpretations of the part of Othello, as more Negro actors undertake it.

Notes

1. Eldred Jones, *Othello's Countrymen,* 1965.
2. F. R. Leavis, 'Diabolic Intellect and the Noble Hero', *The Common Pursuit,* Chatto & Windus, 1952, pp. 136-59.
3. Clement Scott, *From 'The Bells' to 'King Arthur',* 1897, pp. 83-8.
4. Theophile Gautier, *Voyage en Russie,* 1895, pp. 254-6.

Phyllis Natalie Braxton (essay date 1990)

SOURCE: "Othello: The Moor and the Metaphor," in *South Atlantic Review,* Vol. 55, No. 4, November, 1990, pp. 1-17.

[*In the essay below, Braxton contends that* Othello *is not a play about race, and suggests "a dramaturgical purpose for the character's blackness. . . ."*]

Although the circumstance of Othello's blackness is often assumed to embody a racial problem, as in K. W. Evans's assertion in "The Racial Factor in *Othello*" that "no analysis of the play can be adequate if it ignores the factor of race" (125), Shakespeare's play itself demonstrates that Othello's color outweighs in significance the element of race.[1] Physical characteristics, of course, help define race, and Othello's black skin and thick lips identify him as a member of the Negroid race, as distinguished from either the Caucasoid or Mongoloid races. The difficulty of determining Othello's specific ethnic background on the basis of textual evidence suggests that those details that relate to race are included for the purpose of lending verisimilitude to the character's black skin color and not for the purpose of describing an ethnic black of any fixed derivation. In this article, I will try, first, to demonstrate the manner in which race is used in the play primarily to support the fact of Othello's black skin color and, second, to suggest a dramaturgical purpose for the character's blackness in light of the ambiguity of his race.

I

The attempt of critics to discover Othello's specific ethnic background has generally resulted in identifying the character as a native of the African continent. A. W. Schlegel, for example, who seems to have initiated the subject of Othello's ethnicity in his *Lectures on Dramatic Art and Literature,* comments that Shakespeare transformed Cinthio's Moor—"a baptized Saracen of the Northern coast of Africa"—into a Negro, whom Schlegel located in the southern regions of Africa (401). A. C. Bradley, in *Shakespearean Tragedy,* similarly accepted Othello as a native of the African continent, even though he considered it of little consequence "whether Shakespeare imagined Othello as a Negro or as a Moor" (166). In his study of *Othello's Countrymen,* Eldred Jones considers Othello, together with all stage Moors, as natives of the African continent, without specifying the particular location (87).

In an essay entitled "Did Shakespeare Know *Leo Africanus?*" Lois Whitney proposes that Shakespeare drew the salient features of Othello's portrayal from the work of this early historian, adding that "Shakespeare was describing neither a Moor nor a negro in our modern conception of the terms but a confusion of the two types" (477). M. R. Ridley, in his edition of *Othello,* judges that the evidence about Othello's origins is "indecisive" (liii). He accepts the description of the black-skinned, thick-lipped Othello as that of an African, but observes that, while the character may look like a "negro," two words used in connection with Othello—"'Barbary' and 'Mauritania'"—suggest that he may be an Arab from North Africa (liii).

While such criticism tends to assume that Negroes occupy sub-Saharan Africa, whereas Arabs live in North Africa, the suggestion of ambiguity about Othello's geographical background is not addressed in terms of the significance this feature may have for dramaturgical necessity.

Those sociological and historical discussions of race that include Shakespeare's *Othello* as a document illustrating Elizabethan racism seem to assume that Othello is an African, but do not concern themselves about the particular region in Africa from which he may derive. In *White Over Black,* his influential study of racial attitudes in the United States of America, Winthrop Jordan simply accepts the character as an example of the average Elizabethan Englishman's idea of a black African or Moor—Jordan, like

Jones, uses the terms interchangeably (37-38). Jordan then ascribes to Shakespeare and his contemporary audiences the pernicious notions about blacks that the playwright had been careful to assign to Iago as an element in Iago's plot to destroy Othello (37). Like Jordan, Joseph Washington, in *Anti-Blackness in English Religion, 1500-1800,* uses Othello as an example of what he considers the English nation's antipathy towards blacks (71). In his view, Othello is "deliberately caricatured as an African" (71).

Such views to the contrary, criticism has also taken the position that Othello is white. Mary Preston of Maryland, for example, in her 1869 *Studies in Shakespeare,* declared that "Othello was a white man" (qtd. in Furness 395). Washington judges that Shakespeare created Othello to be "in reality black but in character white" (71). Jonathan Miller, in *Subsequent Performances,* claims dramaturgical necessity for having presented the white actor Anthony Hopkins as a white Othello in the BBC-TV version of the play so as to minimize the differences between Othello and Desdemona (159).[2]

Textual evidence, of course, is conclusive that the character is black in color. Othello calls himself "black" (3.3.263) and describes his face as "begrim'd and black" (3.3.387); Iago likens him to "an old black ram" (1.1.88) and refers to him as "black Othello" (2.3.32); Brabantio notes his "sooty bosom" (1.2.70); the Duke, praising Othello's character, tells Brabantio that "your son-in-law is far more fair than black" (1.3.290); and Roderigo initially sets Iago to thinking in terms of race when he characterizes Othello to Iago, by a feature common to native Africans and their descendants, as "the thick lips" (1.1.66).

The unequivocal manner in which Othello's blackness is described in the text suggests that the playwright wanted the character understood as literally black in color, as he seems to be in twentieth-century criticism, just as Aaron in *Titus Andronicus* is literally black in color (*Titus Andronicus* 3.1.205). He is not a light-skinned or "tawny Moor," as is the Prince of Morocco in *The Merchant of Venice* (2.1.1.s.d.), although, according to Bradley, nineteenth-century criticism tended to describe Othello in this way (168).

While insisting that the character is black in color, the text does not point to any one ethnic background for Othello. Features in his portrayal seem to have been drawn from all of the blacks who may have been in England during Shakespeare's lifetime. This would have included Spanish Moors, as well as Africans from a variety of locations on the African continent. Indeed, the playwright seems to have avoided assigning to Othello a specific geographical origin or ethnic background.

Eldred Jones, in *The Elizabethan Image of Africa,* notes that blacks from Africa had been present in England since 1554, chiefly in the capacity of slaves, although he points out that, until the initiation of the triangular slaving voyages in the following decade, Africans also traveled freely between Africa and England (*Elizabethan Image* 15-16).

Africans in Elizabethan England—either slave or free—might have come from a variety of backgrounds, and their skin colors might have varied in shade (Jones, *Elizabethan Image* 16). Whatever the Africans may have called themselves, literature on the subject seems to designate as Negroes those Africans of native African ancestry who predominated in the lands south of the Sahara, although they lived in North Africa as well; they were generally dark-skinned. West Africans might be almost any shade from black to cream. Africans of Arabian ancestry seemed to predominate in North Africa, but dwelt south of the Sahara also. The prevailing religion in North Africa was Islam; native African religions predominated in the sub-Saharan regions (Bennett 17-25). Jones, in an evident reference to Africans of any background, comments that "not only is it certain that Shakespeare, living as he did in London and being so much a part of his times, would have had the opportunity to see Negroes, it seems impossible that he could have escaped seeing them" (*Elizabethan Image* 16-17). Jones probably did not exclude Arabs of African birth from his observation. He comments on the presence of the Moslem nobleman who had been "sent by the king of Morocco on an embassy" to Elizabeth's court in 1600 (*Elizabethan Image* 35); it does not seem unreasonable to assume that this North African was also seen by Shakespeare. This visit occurred too late to influence the portrayal of Shakespeare's Prince of Morocco in *The Merchant of Venice* but the ambassador's exotic presence could have affected his creation of *Othello,* presented in 1604.

In addition to Africans, Spanish Moors seem also to have been present in England in Shakespeare's lifetime. The Spanish Moors were descendants of those Moslems who rode out of the Arabian peninsula in the seventh century (Abercrombie 87), "carr[ying] Islam across North Africa and into Spain" (Bennett 12). Many African Negroes, converts to Islam, accompanied the Moslem armies into Spain (Bennett 12). As Thomas J. Abercrombie notes, in his article "When the Moors Ruled Spain," these Moorish conquerors, who were not ousted from power until 1492, "brought no women with them. From this heady mix of race and culture sprang the Moorish civilization" of Spain (88). These Spanish Moors seem to be the subject of the decrees which Queen Elizabeth issued in 1599 and 1601 concerning the numbers of blacks in England. In the 1601 decree, the Queen complains that

> whereas the Queen's majesty . . . is highly discontented to understand the great numbers of Negars and Blackamoors which (as she is informed) are crept into this realm since the troubles between Her Highness and the King of Spain, who are fostered and relieved here to the great annoyance of her own liege people that want the relief which those people consume; as also for that most of them are infidels, having no understanding of Christ or his Gospel, hath given especial commandment that the said kind of people should be with all speed avoided and discharged out of this Her Majesty's dominions.

> (qtd. in Jones, *Elizabethan Image* 20)[3]

In his history of *The Moriscos of Spain*, Henry Charles Lea points out that those Islamic Moors in Spain who had refused, despite the threat of reprisals, to convert to Catholicism had sought assistance from Spain's enemies—France and, later, England (Lea 281-82, 287; see also 292-365). Officially, England denied assistance to the Islamic Moors from Spain (287), but Elizabeth's order seems to indicate that they were in the kingdom, albeit unofficially, where Shakespeare may well have had an opportunity to observe them.

Accustomed to seeing these various dark-skinned people in England, and probably having developed no special attitudes towards them, either disparaging or complimentary, a playwright might have exploited their characteristics in a portrayal of a fictional character who was black in color. Nothing in the text of *Othello* suggests that Shakespeare was concerned with depicting Othello exclusively as an African. The character is not identified in the play as an African. Instead, throughout the play, he is called either by the name "Othello," or, following Cinthio's practice, is designated "The Moor" (Kermode 1198). One might, of course, ask whether the term "African" is simply missing from Shakespeare's customary vocabulary, but in *The Tempest*, he demonstrates that he has no hesitation in describing someone as an African. In that play, on the occasion of the supposed drowning of Alonso's son, during the storm that occurs as the royal family are returning from the wedding of Alonso's daughter, the playwright causes Sebastian to declare to Alonso:

> Sir, you may thank yourself for this great loss,
> That would not bless our Europe with your daughter,
> But rather loose her to an African.
>
> (*The Tempest* 2.1.124-26)

Even though the playwright is not specific about Othello's background, critics generally consider that Shakespeare developed the character as an African, and many details in his portrayal can be traced to African sources. Whitney conjectures that Othello is composed of features drawn from both North Africans and sub-Saharan Africans (see above, p. 2). Jones considers that the character is a "blend of characteristics popularly attributed to North African Moors with the color known to be more common in West Africa, and called no more erroneously then than now, black" (*Elizabethan Image* 37). The character's black skin, of course, could have derived from any of the blacks observed in England. The insistence upon "sooty" black skin and upon thick lips suggests that the playwright selected these details from among those Africans who would have provided what Jones terms the greatest "dramatic contrast" with Europeans (*Elizabethan Image* 41). The character's claim of descent from "men of royal siege" indicates a background resembling that of that Moroccan nobleman who visited the court in 1600, and, as Whitney demonstrates in her speculative article, Othello's nobility also seems to parallel the status of the historian Leo Africanus (477),[4] who converted to Christianity as an adult, after his Moslem parents had taken him to Africa during his childhood when the Moors were finally defeated at Granada (Washington 64-65). Whether or not Shakespeare knew the English translation of Leo's *History of Africa* (1600), his probable knowledge of the blacks in England would have no doubt provided him with ample information for his portrayal of Othello.

Cultural details in Shakespeare's portrait of Othello are as ambiguous as are details about the character's background. Othello's language, for example, may have been influenced by his conception of Arabic as much as by the playwright's acquaintance with native African tongues. The copiousness of Othello's speech has been commented upon in criticism at least since the observation by Thomas Rymer in *A Short View of Tragedy* that "our Noble Venetian['s] . . . words flow in abundance; no Butter-Quean can be more lavish" (Rymer 139). At least one critic, G. B. Harrison, in *Shakespeare: The Complete Works*, considers that Othello "has some characteristics of the savage [including] a hyperbolic utterance when aroused" (1057), suggesting with his unfortunate locution that Othello's speech is influenced by native African languages. While it is possible, of course, that Shakespeare was influenced by what he may have known of native African tongues, it is also possible that he found a model for Othello's language among the Moors, either from North Africa or Spain, and their Arabic, with its "wealth of vocabulary [and] its sonorous sounds" (Abercrombie 107). Othello's melodious speech seems to imitate these features of the Arabic.[5]

While the depiction of Othello's background and his language both could have been influenced by knowledge of Africans from any location on that continent, or of Moors from Africa or Spain, some of the details in his portrayal seem to have a uniquely Spanish source. In religion Othello is a Christian. He exhorts Cassio and the other brawling soldiers "for Christian shame" (2.3.172) to cease fighting, and Iago, speaking in a soliloquy, muses about Othello's wanting Desdemona, even if it means that the Moor has to "renounce his baptism" (2.3.343). This feature in Shakespeare's portrayal of Othello seems to refer specifically to the Spanish Moors. The conversion of many of the Moors in Spain to Christianity is well-documented in history (Lea 82-177). Whether great numbers of native Africans became converts to Christianity is doubtful. There seems to have been no exigency in Africa that urged conversion to any religion other than Islam similar to the impetus in Spain for Moors to become Christians.

Similarly, when Othello describes himself as a slave who has been redeemed (1.3.137-38), the detail seems to allude to a situation prevailing among the Spanish Moors. The Moors in Spain were repeatedly enslaved for reasons of war or religion, and often their chief reason for converting to Christianity was to regain their freedom (Lea 27). Africans, on the other hand, seem usually to have been held as bond slaves (Craton xii-xiii), and bond slaves did not seem to have the option of redemption open to them. It appears, therefore, that Shakespeare had in mind the type of slavery common in Spain when he included this feature in his portrayal of Othello. Brabantio's sneering reference to "bond slaves and pagans" (1.2.99) seems to be an oblique attempt to sully the reputation of the redeemed slave and baptized Christian, Othello.

As with his ancestry and his language, details of Othello's military career and his travels may have been influenced by either African or Spanish sources, or both. The bravery of the Africans is noted by Basil Davidson, who points out in his *The African Slave Trade* that African armies successfully resisted invasion from outside the continent for centuries (27). Leo Africanus praises the Moors in Africa as "brave and noble soldiers" (Whitney 480). The Moors in Spain were also great warriors, as their conquest and long occupation of that land attests. The threat of a Moorish reconquest of Spain remained so real that, in 1570 (Lea 230-65) and again in 1609, the monarchy ordered the expulsion of all non-Catholic Moors from Spanish soil (Livermore 289). This demonstrated military prowess of the Spanish Moors may, therefore, have influenced Shakespeare in describing Othello's military ability as much as any knowledge of African warriors he may have had.

Those details concerning Othello's travels that could have been drawn from African sources suggest that he may have traveled widely, but they do not give any indication of the particular countries to which he traveled or from which he came. The sights that he reports seeing are strange to him; he tells

> of antres vast and deserts idle
> Rough quarries, rocks [and] hills whose [heads] touch
> heaven,
> . . . . .
> And of the Cannibals that each [other] eat,
> The Anthropophagi, and men whose heads
> [Do grow] beneath their shoulders.
>
> (1.3.140-45)

Othello does not identify these sights as belonging to any particular country. Geographically speaking, the description could refer to Africa (Jones, *Elizabethan Image* 5) or India (French 808); in the text of the play, these features seem to belong to some vague, unidentified (perhaps, to Othello, unidentifiable) lands. The source for the description is unclear. Ridley suggests that it "seems as idle as the deserts to try to determine whether Shakespeare was primarily indebted to Mandeville or Raleigh [*sic*] or Holland's Pliny" as a source for such "travellers' tales" (Ridley 29). Othello, of course, states that he had come to know these places as a traveler (1.3.139). Shakespeare had it within his power to name the lands to which his Moor traveled, as easily as he named, in *The Merchant of Venice*, the Goodwins, where one of Antonio's ships had been wrecked (3.1.2-4). Dramaturgically, he must have found it necessary to be unspecific about Othello's travels, just as he was about the Moor's origins.

The details of Shakespeare's portrayal of Othello seem to indicate that the character was not meant to be limited to either an African, from whatever locale, or a Moor, either Spanish or African. Unlike Leo Africanus, the historian, who came from a particular place, Granada, and went specifically to Africa and, later, to Italy, Othello is represented as traveling constantly, but to vague, unspecified places, while his homeland is not named. Even the designation of Othello as a Moor is ambiguous. Anthony Gerard Barthelemy's etymology of Moor, in *Black Face, Maligned Race*, while probably exaggerating the Elizabethans' total identification of this term with "black African" (1), at least makes it clear that to the Elizabethans "Moor" described "at the simplest level . . . the Other, the non-English, the non-Christian" (17). Although a Christian, the non-Venetian Othello is indeed the Other. But the term "Moor" is vague. According to Abercrombie, Moors never called themselves Moors: "they were Arabs from Damascus and Medina, leading armies of North African Berber converts" (Abercrombie 88). To Elliot H. Tokson in *The Popular Image of the Black Man in English Drama, 1550-1688,* the only definite feature about a Moor was that he was black in color (3). Unlike the terms used to describe characters such as Portia's suitors—"the Neapolitan prince," "the French lord," "the County Palentine" (*The Merchant of Venice* 1.2.39-54), or the Princes of Morocco (1.2.125) and Arragon (2.9.2), all of which indicate the characters' origins—Othello's origin is not named. The details in his characterization confirm that Othello is black in color without making the blackness that of a black of any one particular background.

II

Why does Othello have to be black? When I heard this question at a scholarly meeting, it was raised by a person who probably just wanted an answer. Long accustomed to having black heroes belittled by the dominant culture, I reacted with a barely restrained hostility, demonstrating my susceptibility to the modern tendency to foreground race. On reflection, I realized that the questioner seemed to be trying to place the problem within the context of the fictional world of the play.

Within the context of the fictional worlds of Venice and Cyprus, "why," as Washington phrases the question, "did Shakespeare choose to develop Othello in the character and action of a black Moor?" (70). Washington's answer was that Shakespeare wanted "to show the particular problems of a black in white society" (72). Yet the playwright seems to have made no effort to create a black of any specific ethnicity. He simply insists upon the character's black skin color.

Shakespeare could be demonstrating, in the nonspecific nature of Othello's background and the ambiguity of the cultural details in his portrayal, that the Other is always mysterious and without clear definition. Once defined, he is no longer the Other. Immediately contradicting this theory is *The Merchant of Venice,* in which Shylock may be defined as the Other. Shylock's background as a Jew is never in doubt. A Jew supposed to be living in Venice in the Renaissance could be assumed to be a resident of the ghetto (Sachar 251). Although he may be the Other in his relationship to the majority of Venetians, he is located securely within a tradition, a culture, and a history. However, Shylock's role does not seem to be designed for the purpose of exploring the character of a Jew but rather of exploiting the characteristics of a usurer.[6] The dramatic structure called for a character who takes no chances. Shakespeare found such a feature in the character of a money lender, and money lenders at that time were Jewish. Consequently, the playwright wove into his plot the Jewish money lender, apologizing in advance for any implied anti-Semitism by placing in Shylock's mouth a moving plea for understanding (3.1.53-73).

In the same way that Shylock fills a specific need in the dramatic structure by virtue of the usurer's characteristic of absolute caution (while he remains the Other in terms of societal relationships), Othello's color seems to derive from a specific dramaturgical requirement. As with Shylock, the playwright does not seem to be exploring the character; he is exploiting one feature—in Othello's case, he is exploiting the black skin color. Other features are included only insofar as they are required to complete a believable portrayal of a black. These other details are drawn from the many blacks who were presumably present in England in Shakespeare's lifetime. From the great variety in the appearance of these strangers, the playwright seems to have selected those physical features which would most clearly distinguish Othello from the native inhabitants of Venice (which was, of course, a way of making the character most alien to an audience of native Englishmen). Othello, therefore, was given black skin and thick lips.

As I have attempted to show, the character is not a black of a particular ethnicity; furthermore, the play does not focus upon his problems as a black in the community. His problems do not seem to be with the community at large: he has the respect of the Duke and the government; he has a sensitive and trusted position as general; he marries a girl who has previously been the object of many suitors of her own race. His problems seem to be confined to Iago's personal animosity toward him. Thus, the thesis that Othello's tragedy derives from his status as the Other is not dramaturgically defensible. Despite his physical identification as the Other, his interaction with the native Venetians (other than Iago) would discourage an interpretation of him as the Other in the sense of an outsider who is totally alienated from the community. In this respect, then, the plot does not require that he be black. He is not white—although, to some critics in the nineteenth century, his personal characteristics may have seemed at variance with certain widely-held notions of the proper traits for a stage black.[7] The motive of jealousy in the play does not require that he be black. Yet the playwright seems to have gone to extraordinary pains to develop this character so that his black skin color would be clearly understood.

The reason for the character's black skin color should be inherent in the dramatic elements of character and plot.

Thus, the need for the Jewish money lender in *The Merchant of Venice* grows out of the demands of character and plot, and Aaron's black skin color in *Titus Andronicus* is dramaturgically necessary and probable because black is usually accepted as the color of the evil that Aaron personifies (3.1.205). The seeming failure of character and plot in *Othello* to yield a dramaturgical purpose for the character's black skin color is perhaps what has led to the critical assumption that the purpose is extradramatic, residing in the audience's response to the relationship between blacks and whites. When examined, however, even this reason has less validity for Shakespeare's Elizabethan audiences than it has for later audiences viewing the play against the background of bond slavery.

Additionally, the visual and emblematic contrasts provided by Othello's color are insufficient to explain why he is black. Visually, the blackness contrasts with Desdemona's "whiter skin . . . than snow" (5.2.4). But there seems to be little point in providing a visual contrast that does not appear to illuminate the text. Emblematically, the traditional associations with black and white are reversed, as Doris Adler demonstrates in her article on "The Rhetoric of Black and White in *Othello*," so that in the play, as G. K. Hunter observes in "Othello and Colour Prejudice," Iago is represented as "the white man with the black soul while Othello is the black man with the white soul" (151). Moreover, as Adler points out (255), Bianca, whose name translates as "white," with its resonances of "good" and "pure," is so far from being pure that she is characterized as a courtesan, or in Iago's words, Cassio's "whore" (4.1.177). In *Romeo and Juliet*, verbal contrasts, including black-versus-white imagery, support the tragic conflict between the two feuding families; along similar lines, one might assume that the black-and-white contrasts in *Othello* are employed for the purpose of supporting the major theme, but the major theme of the play seems to contradict this notion. Iago and Othello are not equal antagonists as are the families in *Romeo and Juliet*, and as the diametric opposition in a black-versus-white contrast suggests should be the case. Othello is a passive victim who does not recognize Iago as his antagonist until Desdemona is dead and Iago's plot to destroy Othello is irreversible. The seeming divergence between traditional color symbolism and the use of color in *Othello* suggests that color in the play is not used primarily to underscore a conflict between evenly matched contestants.

Othello is destroyed as the result of the machinations of Iago, who is nevertheless not punished within the confines of the dramatic action. Such an absence of predetermined poetic justice demonstrates an arbitrary working of fate. While this theme of the arbitrariness of fate seems to be reflected in the unexpected reversal of the color symbolism, the skin color, as a detail of the characterization of the protagonist, calls for an explanation arising out of both character and plot. Within the great chain of being that the Elizabethans assumed gave order to the universe (Tillyard 25-36), one could find illustrations of the arbitrariness of fate among the meanest creatures of the earth. E. M. W.

Tillyard explains in *The Elizabethan World Picture* how the Elizabethans drew lessons about their own lives by observing these humble creatures:

> [T]he Elizabethans looked on the lower end of the chain of being mainly in the light of themselves. Its great variety and ingenuity were indeed testimonies of the creator's wonderful power, but its main function was to provide symbols or to point morals for the benefit of man. The ant was a wonderful creation, but the chief thing was that he was there for the sluggard to go to.
>
> (80)

Ben Jonson's *Volpone* demonstrates the manner in which Elizabethans gave dramatic form to such lessons drawn from observation of the lower orders. The behavior of the fictional Volpone, who pretends to be dying in order to expose the rapaciousness of his friends, parallels the *modus operandi* in the legends that Jonson's sources gave him about the fox, who "feigned death in order to catch birds, especially 'ravens, crows, and other birds,' which light near the supposed carcass and are seized" (Nethercot 131).

An easily observable natural phenomenon, which demonstrates the arbitrariness of fate and which requires no confirmation except the evidence of one's eyes, occurs in the action of a spider capturing a fly in its web. The events of *Othello* parallel the actions of the spider in his destruction of the fly. Iago is the spider who, with true "motiveless malignity," seeks the destruction of Othello for a variety of invented reasons, but chiefly for the unspoken reason that Othello, the fly, is his natural enemy. The metaphor, which can be traced throughout the language as well as the action of the play, has been noted by Caroline Spurgeon. In her seminal study, *Shakespeare's Imagery,* she includes a description of the preponderance of animal imagery in *Othello* (336); Spurgeon comments that, in this play,

> we see a low type of life, insects and reptiles, swarming and preying on each other, not out of special ferocity, but just in accordance with their natural instincts. . . . This reflects and repeats the spectacle of the wanton torture of one human being by another, which we witness in the tragedy, the human spider and his fly.
>
> (336)

Iago's language reflects this metaphor of the "human spider and his fly," while, at the same time, it reveals his method of trapping his intended victims. At one moment, when Iago, Cassio, Emilia, and Desdemona are engaged in conversation, Iago observes Cassio touch Desdemona's hand, and the ensign murmurs to himself, "With as little a web as this will I ensnare as great a fly as Cassio" (2.1.168-69). Later, in a soliloquy, he declares of Desdemona that "out of her own goodness [will I] make the net / That shall enmesh them all" (2.3.361-62). Iago turns the circumstances of the victim's own life into the material to destroy the victim: Othello's blackness; Cassio's casual action of respect for Desdemona; Desdemona's goodness. Although he is eventually unsuccessful in his plot against Cassio, Iago has included him in his widening plot, as the destruction of everyone seems to have become, for him, an end in itself. As with spiders, his "web" will snare any creature that falls into it.

Iago is portrayed throughout with features peculiar to the spider; details in Othello's portrait conform to the characteristics of the fly. The resemblances between both of these fictional inventions and their counterparts in the insect world are too consistent to be considered coincidental. From his childhood to his death, Othello corresponds in development to a fly. He has been a warrior since the age of seven; in other words, upon his transformation from infancy and early childhood, he has assumed the responsibilities of an adult. In the same way, the fly assumes adult status immediately upon emerging from the larval stage. Othello's residence on islands—areas surrounded by seas—parallels the fly's tendency to inhabit almost exclusively damp places. Othello travels constantly, just as flies are always on the wing; Othello's sonorous and repetitive speech has the droning quality associated with insects such as flies and mosquitoes. Maturity is accompanied, in humans and animals alike, by courtship rituals—Desdemona is attracted by Othello's stories of his wondrous exploits—and the sudden elopement of the sheltered Desdemona with Othello is perhaps not dissimilar to the abrupt mating of the creatures of the wild, which select mates independently of any authority, and depart suddenly from the nurturing habitation without plan or warning. Most significantly, the Moor is helpless to save himself when in the throes of his enemy, Iago, just as the fly is a helpless victim when it is caught in the web of its natural enemy, the spider.[8]

Through this metaphor, Othello's blackness is revealed as a function of both character and plot. The spider's victim is typically some kind of wandering insect who blunders into the spider's web. The spider does not seek out its victim, but when it sees one in its web, it sets out immediately to destroy that victim. The play, therefore, required first of all a character who would be recognized by the audience as someone out of his native element—a wanderer. Persons with black skin in Elizabethan England could generally be classified as wanderers; Othello is thus depicted with the black skin common to these wanderers, the color of his skin conforming to the color of the spider's most frequent victim, the fly. The spider, who remains in its web awaiting a victim, need only be characterized as a creature on its home grounds, prepared to destroy any unwitting trespasser. In the dramatic structure, therefore, the spider is depicted with the protective coloring of one who is native to the environment; consequently, Iago (a Florentine [3.1.40]), has the white skin of a native of the Italian peninsula. The action of the play dramatizes the manner in which the fly wanders into the spider's web and is destroyed by the spider.

Just as the Holocaust has altered our reaction to Shylock, so that, in recoiling from the horror of recent historical events, we now foreground the humanity of the Jew in the fictive tragedy of *The Merchant of Venice* rather than the caution of the usurer, so the legacy of chattel slavery has affected modern responses to *Othello*. Audiences and critics now try to come to terms with what they perceive as a racial emphasis in the play and, in the process, fail to realize that Othello, as a fictional construct, is an element in the controlling metaphor. In his thoughtful essay on "Othello and the 'plain face' of Racism," Martin Orkin asserts that the play stands against racism. While Shakespeare's play is perhaps less consciously didactic than Orkin claims, the playwright does demonstrate the virulence of racism by having Iago introduce it into the plot as a fatal "poison" (1.1.68), just as the spider injects venom into its victim. Iago gloats as he lets his "medicine" work (4.1.45), just as the spider lets its victim writhe under the effect of the poison.

The playwright lets the punishment of the poisoner remain uncertain, reflecting the manner in which the spider in nature is not necessarily punished for killing the fly. Iago's punishment, if any, which is urged by Lodovico, but left to the discretion of Cassio (5.2.367-69), does not take place within the confines of the dramatic action. Those in the audience who demand retribution are therefore free to conjecture that Iago suffers proper punishment for his evil. The playwright, meanwhile, remains true to the natural order that is demonstrated in the mimetic action when he refrains from actively punishing this "human spider," for nature does not judge as evil a natural force, or treat as evil the natural enmity of one species towards another. If the spider should also be killed as a result of this struggle, it is not in the nature of retribution, punishment, or revenge, but simply another incident in the bitter fight for survival. If the spider is not killed, that also is in the natural order of things. The destruction of Othello as a result of the machinations of Iago reflects this cosmic struggle, with the absence of predetermined poetic justice in the drama suggesting both the amoral aspects of the natural forces at work and the arbitrariness of an indifferent fate.[9]

Notes

1. Norman Verrle McCullough, in contrast to the actor Paul Robeson and director Margaret Webster, both of whom, he asserts, tried to prove that *Othello* is a "play about race," is sure that "*Othello* is not a play of race, and only by following a raceless approach to the play will the reader or viewer discover the true tragic thrill of Shakespeare's play" (*The Negro in English Literature* 47).

2. According to James C. Bulman in an article in the *Shakespeare Quarterly,* the original producer of the BBC-TV series, Cedric Messina, had "tried to cast James Earl Jones as Othello but was forbidden to do so by British Equity" (580).

3. Jones cites this order to support his theory that the Queen thought the number of African natives in England so great as to create a problem (*Elizabethan Image* 20). That the Queen included not only Spanish Moors but also African slaves in her order, seems evident from her special statement that people who were "possessed of any such Blackamoors" should surrender them (10).

4. According to John Pory, who, in 1600 had translated Leo's *History of Africa* into English, prefacing it with a biography of the author, Leo's "[p]arentage seemeth not to have bin ignoble" (qtd. in Whitney 477).

5. Othello's speech before the Senate, in which he relates how his marriage came about, occupies forty-three lines (1.3.127-70). His language frequently includes repetition, in phrases such as the following: "She swore, in faith 'twas strange, 'twas passing strange: / 'Twas pitiful, 'twas wondrous pitiful" (1.3.160-61), and "Put out the light, and then put out the light" (5.2.7), as he utters a thought and returns to utter it again.

6. Warren D. Smith, who also suggests this idea in an essay entitled "Shakespeare's Shylock," does not follow the notion up for its dramaturgical possibilities (195).

7. Barthelemy notes that the "overwhelming majority" of black characters presented on the stage in England "between 1589 and 1695 endorsed, represented, or were evil" (72). Characters such as the Moor Muly Mahamet in George Peele's *Battle of Alcazar* were strong, self-confident characters, but as blacks, they stood for evil. The strength and confidence of the evil black characters were perhaps mistaken by Preston in the nineteenth century (see above, page 2) for traits more appropriate for white characters. During the nineteenth century, audiences were probably more accustomed to the representation on stage of the type of subservient, menial blacks that appeared in such popular plays as Dion Boucicault's *The Octoroon* (1859). This new stereotype of the stage black was a result of the crystallization of attitudes developed in an attempt to justify chattel slavery (Jordan 27). This social conditioning is perhaps what caused Preston, "Coleridge, and . . . the American writers" who professed to believe that Othello was a white or tawny Moor (Bradley 168) to allow their critical judgment to falter.

8. The allegory of spiders and flies was familiar to Shakespeare's audiences from John Heywood's poem, *The Spider and the Flie,* which had appeared a generation previously in 1556. In the introduction to this long, allegorical work, A. W. Ward reports that, in one reading of the poem, anthropomorphic spiders and flies, representing respectively Protestants and Catholics, fight a war about idolatry, until the head spider—who represents the Duke of Northumberland, the leader of the Protestant plot against the Catholic Queen Mary—is crushed underfoot by the Maid, signifying the beheading of the Duke (Heywood vii-ix). The poem demonstrates how the Renaissance imagination could seriously entertain an insect metaphor that modern audiences tend to deem trivial.

9. The lesson of an arbitrary fate was probably not lost upon the audience at court for whom the play seems to have had its first performance on 1 November 1604, during the second year of the reign of James I. The description of James's life by Maurice Ashley in *England in the Seventeenth Century* suggests that James was at the mercy of a particularly arbitrary fate. Before he was a year old, the man who was presumably his father, Lord Darnley, was murdered, if not with the actual connivance of James's mother, Mary, Queen of Scots, at least with her approval. James inherited the throne of Scotland as James VI when his mother abdicated and fled to England, where she was eventually executed by Parliament with the consent of her cousin, Queen Elizabeth. Elizabeth provided no heirs to the throne and, on her deathbed, is supposed to have named "our cousin of Scotland" to succeed her, a prize that James secured for himself when he "contented himself with restrained protests" to his mother's execution (9).

Works Cited

Abercrombie, Thomas J. "When the Moors Ruled Spain." *National Geographic* 174 (1988): 86-119.

Adler, Doris. "The Rhetoric of *Black* and *White* in *Othello*." *Shakespeare Quarterly* 25 (1974): 248-57.

Ashley, Maurice. *England in the Seventeenth Century.* Rev. ed. The Pelican History of England 6. Baltimore: Penguin, 1967.

Barthelemy, Anthony Gerard. *Black Face, Maligned Race: The Representation of Blacks in English Drama from Shakespeare to Southerne.* Baton Rouge: Louisiana State UP, 1987.

Bennett, Lerone, Jr. *Before the Mayflower: A History of the Negro in America, 1619-1964.* Rev. ed. Baltimore: Penguin, 1966.

Boucicault, Dion. *The Octoroon. The Signet Classic Book of 18th- and 19th-Century British Drama.* Ed. Katharine Rogers. New York: Signet-NAL, 1979. 404-57.

Bradley, A. C. *Shakespearean Tragedy: Hamlet, Othello, King Lear, Macbeth.* Gen. ed. Irving Howe. Literature and Ideas Series. Greenwich, CT: Fawcett Premier, n.d.

Bulman, James C. "The BBC Shakespeare and 'House Style.'" *Shakespeare Quarterly* 35 (1984): 571-81.

Craton, Michael. *Sinews of Empire: A Short History of British Slavery.* Garden City, NY: Doubleday-Anchor, 1974.

Davidson, Basil. *The African Slave Trade.* Rev. and exp. ed. Boston: Little, Brown, 1961.

Evans, K. W. "The Racial Factor in *Othello*." *Shakespeare Studies* 5 (1969): 124-40.

French, J. Milton. "Othello Among the Anthropophagi." *PMLA* 49 (1934): 807-09.

Furness, Horace Howard, ed. *A New Variorum Edition of Shakespeare: Othello.* 8th ed. Philadelphia: Lippincott, 1886.

Harrison, G. B., ed., "Introduction to *Othello*," *Shakespeare: The Complete Works.* New York: Harcourt, 1968. 1056-58.

Heywood, John. *The Spider and the Flie.* 1556. Introd. A. W. Ward. 1894. New York: Franklin, 1967.

Hunter, G. K. "Othello and Colour Prejudice." *Proceedings of the British Academy* 53 (1967). London: Oxford UP, 1968.

Jones, Eldred D. *The Elizabethan Image of Africa.* Charlottesville: UP of Virginia, 1971.

———. *Othello's Countrymen: The African in English Renaissance Drama.* London: Oxford UP, 1965.

Jonson, Ben. *Volpone. Stuart Plays.* Ed. Arthur H. Nethercot. Rev. ed. New York: Holt, 1971. 129-93.

Jordan, Winthrop D. *White Over Black: American Attitudes Toward the Negro, 1550-1812.* Chapel Hill: U of North Carolina P, 1968.

Kermode, Frank. Introduction to *Othello.* Shakespeare, *The Riverside Shakespeare* 1198-1202.

Lea, Henry Charles. *The Moriscos of Spain: Their Conversion and Expulsion.* 1901. New York: Haskell, 1968.

Livermore, Harold. *A History of Spain.* London: Allen, 1958.

McCullough, Norman Verrle. *The Negro in English Literature: A Critical Introduction.* Devon: Stockwell, 1962.

Miller, Jonathan. *Subsequent Performances.* New York: Viking-Elizabeth Sifton, 1986.

Nethercot, Arthur H., ed. *Stuart Plays.* Rev. ed. New York: Holt: 1971.

Orkin, Martin. "Othello and the 'plain face' of Racism." *Shakespeare Quarterly* 38 (1987): 166-88.

Peele, George. "The Battle of Alcazar." *The Dramatic Works of George Peele.* Ed. John Yoklavich. New Haven, CT: Yale UP, 1961. 293-347.

Ridley, M. R., ed. *Othello.* The Arden Shakespeare. London: Methuen, 1958.

Rymer, Thomas. *The Critical Works of Thomas Rymer.* Ed. Curt A. Zimansky. New Haven, CT: Yale UP, 1956.

Sachar, Abram Leon. *A History of the Jews.* New York: Knopf, 1967.

Schlegel, August Wilhelm [von]. *Lectures on Dramatic Art and Literature.* Trans. John Black. 2nd ed. rev. Ed. A. J. W. Morrison. London: Bell, 1909.

Shakespeare, William. *The Tragedy of Othello, the Moor of Venice. The Riverside Shakespeare.* Ed. G. Blakemore

Evans. Boston: Houghton, 1974. References to the texts of this and other plays by Shakespeare are to this edition.

Smith, Warren D. "Shakespeare's Shylock." *Shakespeare Quarterly* 15 (1964): 193-99.

Spurgeon, Caroline F. E. *Shakespeare's Imagery and What It Tells Us.* 1935. Cambridge, England: Cambridge UP, 1971.

Tillyard, E. M. W. *The Elizabethan World Picture.* New York: Vintage-Random, n.d.

Tokson, Elliot H. *The Popular Image of the Black Man in English Drama, 1550-1688.* Boston: Hall, 1982.

Washington, Joseph R., Jr. *Anti-Blackness in English Religion, 1500-1800.* Texts and Studies in Religion 19. New York: Mellen, 1984.

Whitney, Lois. "Did Shakespeare Know *Leo Africanus*?" *PMLA* 37 (1922): 470-83.

James R. Andreas (essay date 1992)

SOURCE: "Othello's African American Progeny," in *South Atlantic Review*, Vol. 57, No. 4, November, 1992, pp. 39-57.

[*In the essay below, Andreas compares* Othello, *Richard Wright's* Native Son, *Ralph Ellison's* Invisible Man, *and Amiri Baraka's* Dutchman *in order to discuss myths and cultural conceptions of race.*]

Derrida writes; "There's no racism without a language."[1] I take this to mean that racism—and all the violence historically associated with it—is generated by language. Racial difference is not genetically "real," nor is it grounded in real experience but is a product of verbal conditioning.[2] Racism cannot long survive without the verbal and symbolic apparatus that generates and sustains it: the names, the jokes, the plays, the speeches, the casual exchanges, the novels. In short, racism is a cultural virus that is verbally transmitted and its antidote must therefore be verbally administered as well. *Othello*—along with the many African American texts it has inspired—provides a running record of Western civilization's attempt to confront what Paul Robeson called "the problem of my own people." *Othello*, he said, "is a tragedy of racial conflict, a tragedy of honor, rather than jealousy."[3]

As such, the play has traumatized African American literature, and indeed Western culture at large, for most of its existence. The racist's nightmare of biracial sexual relationships between white women and black males, which Gunnar Myrdal claimed suffered "the full fury of anti-amalgamation sanctions,"[4] is the paradigm for three great revisions—"three rewritings"—of the myth: *Native Son* by Richard Wright, *Invisible Man* by Ralph Ellison, and *Dutchman*, by Amiri Baraka.[5] Briefly, Wright restages and reinterprets the problematic relationship of Othello and Desdemona; Ellison represents it comically; and Baraka reverses or inverts it. We might note in passing that many literary works have been written that deal with unwanted sexual attentions of white males sometimes violently imposed on African American females; among these works are many slave narratives, including *Incidents in the Life of a Slave Girl*, as well as a number of celebrated novels such as *Uncle Tom's Cabin, Puddn'head Wilson, Quicksand, Oxherding Tale, Beloved,* and *Absalom, Absalom!*[6] James Kinney claims that interracial sexual relations flourished in colonial and antebellum America and that the violent response to miscegenation began only in the 1830s, "when the economics of slavery led to [the] systematic justification [of slavery] based on innate irreconcilable 'racial differences'" (xii).[7] In any case, the vast number of nineteenth- and twentieth-century works that feature the fate of mulattoes in American culture provides graphic evidence that miscegenation has long been on the minds of African and European American authors alike. What we get in Shakespeare's play and the African American works under investigation here is, of course, the typical patriarchal perspective on the cultural trauma of miscegenation in the West. Another article representing women's perspectives on this trauma needs to be written.

Robeson's statement that *Othello* "is a tragedy of racial conflict," would probably have seemed self-evident to Shakespeare and his contemporaries, both in terms of the social background and the performance and interpretation of the play.[8] A score of historical studies in the last thirty years has unearthed evidence proving that the response to Africans and Moors in the seventeenth century, before the advent of institutional slavery, was complicated and problematic.[9] Sylvan Barnet has shown in a masterful new essay on the performance history of the play that "the Elizabethans thought of Moors as black" (274). Barnet and Errol Hill, in his *Shakespeare in Sable,* have demonstrated conclusively that Othello's part was played in blackface, corkface actually, well into the nineteenth century, because blacks were thought of as inappropriate for or incapable of playing the role.[10] A single quotation from Coleridge indicates what the problem was by the time of the romantics:

> Can we suppose [Shakespeare] so utterly ignorant as to make a barbarous *negro* plead royal birth? . . .[N]egroes [were] then known but as slaves. . . . No doubt Desdemona saw Othello's visage in his [Othello's] mind; yet, as we are constituted, and most surely as an English audience was disposed in the beginning of the seventeenth century, it would be something monstrous to conceive this beautiful Venetian girl falling in love with a veritable negro. It would argue a disproportionateness, a want of balance in Desdemona, which Shakespeare does not appear to have in the least contemplated.
>
> (qtd. in Barnet 273-74)

Thus, by the nineteenth century, when the barbarities of "the peculiar institution" of slavery had peaked in the Western world, audiences could no longer tolerate nor would directors depict the "monstrous" sexual relationship of black males and white females on stage.[11] To get the picture, audiences no longer needed Iago lashing up racist sentiments in the credulous Roderigo and Brabantio with incendiary remarks such as "Even now, . . . an old black ram / Is tupping your white ewe"; "[Y]ou'll have your daughter cover'd with a Barbary horse"; and "Your daughter and the Moor are now . . . making the beast with two backs" (1.1.88-89, 110-11, 115-17).[12] Such explosive preconceptions were ingrained in the psyches of playgoers well before arriving at the theater. Accordingly, Othello paled and such lines were often cut in production; the Moor was played "in tawny" throughout the nineteenth and well into the twentieth century, as evidenced by the films of Olivier and Jonathan Miller. In regard to the relatively recent BBC version of the play, Jonathan Miller defended his choice of Anthony Hopkins in blackface for the Moor because, he said, "I do not see the play as being about color but as being about jealousy. . . . When a black actor does the part, it offsets the play, puts it out of balance. It makes it a play about blackness, which it is not."[13] Now that we are recovering the black *Othello,* such sentiments seem a bit awkward, if not downright ludicrous. Anyone who has seen Miller's *Othello* or a live production in which the hero is played in blackface knows the murder scene may well evoke laughter in the audience.

From the earliest moments in *Othello,* the language is imbued with traditional racist sentiment and prejudice that erupt into predictable violence by the play's end, when "Chaos is come again" (3.3.92). Collective violence—read riot—is, in fact, the outcome of all the literary vehicles of the myth under investigation here, even the comic *Invisible Man.* The catalyst for and efficient cause of such violence in the play is Iago, perhaps the most important of all Shakespeare's notorious stage directors, with the possible exception of Hamlet. Both Iago and Hamlet are tricksters, variations, as has often been noted, on the role of the traditional fool. Iago's humor takes a *peculiar* turn, however. He is the racist trickster; his is the scenario that eventually defines and corners Othello exclusively in his color, a scenario like the "blueprints" for behavior the hero of *Invisible Man* must live with. Is Iago without motive, as he is traditionally conceived to be? In terms of the racial themes in the play, hardly! He tells us repeatedly that Othello has slept with his wife, Emilia, and whether this is the case or not is irrelevant; as a racist, he believes what he imagines and brilliantly formulates his preconceptions verbally to himself and to others under his influence.

Iago fuels his nefarious plots to undermine the relationship between Othello and Desdemona by playing the bigot's game; he preys upon the vulnerability of all the players to sneaking suspicions about the behavior of the racial alien, in the long run convincing even Othello himself that he is inferior. "Rude . . . in speech, and little blessed with the soft phrase of peace," Othello declares himself while suing for Brabantio's daughter in marriage, although he woos and wins Desdemona with his spellbinding stories (1.3.81-82). As an alien, Othello doubts his capacities for speech and for peace. "Haply, for I am black, / And have not those soft parts of conversation / That chamberers have" (3.3.264-65), he says. Brabantio, for one, is simply aghast that Desdemona has chosen "to marry one." Would his daughter "t'incur a general mock, / Run from her guardage to the sooty bosom / Of such a thing as thou—to fear, not to delight" (1.2.69-71)? The disturbed father feels certain that Othello has influenced his daughter's foul choice with powerful drugs (1.2.73-75). Centuries later, the police will assume Bigger Thomas has plied Mary Dalton with liquor before murdering her in *Native Son,* and Sybil is depicted as drunk when she is "raped by Santa Claus" in *Invisible Man* (511). Iago can even use blatant racist arguments on Othello, who does not seem to blink an eye:

> Ay, there's the point; as (to be bold with you)
> Not to affect many proposéd matches
> Of her own clime, complexion, and degree,
> Whereto we see in all things nature tends—
> Foh, one may smell in such, a will most rank,
> Foul disproportions, thoughts unnatural.
>
> (3.3.228-33)

Does not Iago suggest throughout—even directly to Othello—that Desdemona is not to be trusted because she has already committed the unpardonable sin against her "kind": the sexual choice of an alien? Even Othello accepts the argument, as is indicated by his admission that Desdemona's name and virtue have been blackened and fouled by her relationship with him: "Her name, that was as fresh / As Dian's visage, is now begrim'd and black / As mine own face" (3.3.386-87). This is a play about reputation, real and attributed, and the jealousy and passion that such "reputation" can evoke. Racism is predicated on "repute," that is, on "evil" imputed to a cultural group so conditioned by the dominant culture that the "evil" often materializes in real behavior. Shakespeare, in fact, cleverly interweaves the themes of the destructive effects exerted by the emotions of sexual jealousy and racial bigotry in the play, both of which inflame the imagination with illusions about the "other," alienate the parties involved artificially, and lead to violent ends based on often unfounded presuppositions or prejudices about the behavior of the "other."

A number of motifs in the murder scene of the play will be echoed and revised in the African American scenarios to follow. When sexual consummation between the black male and white female is to occur in this "master trope" of white racism, we get murder instead. The murder is always *witnessed* in the works investigated, often, significantly, by a white woman who is presumably forewarned of the consequences of her actions—Emilia in the play and Mrs. Dalton in *Native Son.* Also, the murdered victims are portrayed as human beings of flesh-and-blood, not passive victims. During the scene just prior to the murder, when Desdemona asks Emilia about fidelity and admits an attraction for Lodovico, we question the credibility of the fragile purity that is usually attributed to Desdemona.[14] Like the white women who follow in the African American novel, for example, Mary Dalton and the anonymous "sister" in the brotherhood, Desdemona is a woman with real desires and considerable courage. The murderers in these works often remark that they feel like actors in a play or figures in a dream. Othello carries a candle into the bedroom and comments that he feels like a character in a dream. In *Dutchman*, Lula, as we shall see, repeatedly calls the conversation she is having with Clay, her future victim, a "script."

No matter how hard critics since Bradley have tried to saddle Othello with the full burden of the guilt for his passionate crime and to view Iago as "motiveless," the play itself seems to incriminate Western society at large for its predisposition to the periodic, ritual slaughter of marginal and aboriginal groups and all whites—especially women—who consort with them. Trevor Nunn's recent controversial production at the Young Vic in London (fall 1989) unleashed the social and political possibilities of this play that have lain dormant in the text for centuries, with the exception of the powerful portrayals of Othello by Paul Robeson in the thirties and forties. Nunn's production featured American Civil War decor and uniforms to underscore the racial implications of the text, and Willard White, a black operatic baritone debuted as a huge, barrel-chested Othello. Iago, played brilliantly by Ian McKellan, entertained as he conspired with an audience of white males—Roderigo, Cassio, and Brabantio—as willing partners in his plot to murder lovers soiled in the blood feud between races. McKellan as Iago assumed he had many willing collaborators in the audience, because Iago projects and exacerbates the deepest Western fears of the "other," of the alien free to prowl and pollute the streets of Venice. During his many soliloquies—for Iago is the most perniciously private character in all the canon—McKellan closed the shutters on the set, pulled up a chair, leaned toward the audience and told them what they had been conditioned to know and fear implicitly all their lives: a "liver lips" has been given professional preferment over him and has desired and taken his wife right from under his very nose. What's more, this "black ram," this "Barbary horse" is about to "tup" the most eligible maid in Venice and produce the "monstrous offspring" of miscegenation. Ian McKellan's Iago, like the Native American mischief maker *Iagoo*, was played as the sprite of malice, in this case, of racial hatred. McKellan's purpose was to arrange and realize our basest fears on stage: the ritual slaughter of a couple transgressing racial and sexual codes. The invisible theme of racism and the murder it provokes were rendered visible for all to see in this gruesome production. The scenario of European colonial history with its periodic racial assassination, rape, and riot was here dramatized; this was a history that was beginning to peak during Shakespeare's time.

In *Exorcising Blackness: Historical and Literary Lynching and Burning Rituals*, Trudier Harris has given us a book on the subject of this gruesome scenario in its most virulent form, which developed after the American Civil War during Reconstruction. The "primal crime" in a racist society, the coupling of black male and white female—either real or, most often, imagined and impugned—justifies and drives the ritual retaliation of the mutilation, castration, and lynching of black male victims in the presence of white women and children, often on Sunday afternoons and accompanied by "carnival." Harris writes:

> I have defined ritual initially as a ceremony, one which by countless repetitions has made it traditional among a given group of people or within a given community. Such repetitions are homage to certain beliefs that are vital to the community. . . . To violate the inviolable, as any Black would who touched a white woman . . . is taboo. It upsets the white world view or conception of the universe. Therefore, in order to exorcise the evil and restore the topsyturvy world to its rightful position, the violator must be symbolically punished
>
> (11-12).[15]

The horror of these events is graphically documented in the newspapers and monthlies of the times—*Harper's, The Atlantic Monthly*—and only then becomes the material fictionalized in the novels. Charles Herbert Stember calls "intimacy between a Negro male and a white female" the "master taboo" of white racism dating back for centuries (10).

The "primal scene" of the white racist, the "black ram . . . tupping your white ewe," is recreated and revised by African American writers some 350 years after *Othello* in *Native Son, Invisible Man*, and *Dutchman*. Bigger Thomas is America's black "native son," raised in the sordid conditions of ghetto life on Chicago's southside. Bigger, his name screaming the rhyme with "nigger," is the all-but-inevitable product of the racist nightmare he will be made to play out in the novel. Perhaps drawing on the ultimate recognition and understanding of the racist process Othello experiences just before his suicide, Richard Wright takes Bigger through a long educational ordeal under the tutelage of Max, his lawyer. However, the primal scene and crime—the sexual relationship between black male and white female and its reputedly inevitable consequence, the brutal murder of the white female—is reenacted with gruesome precision as the pivotal moment in the novel. Othello is momentarily accepted by Venetian society as an equal and, through the machinations of Iago, is reduced to acting the part of the alien "Turk" or "African" by the play's end. Bigger, however, is destined to act the "young Turk" immediately, replicating the violent image of the "African" he watches on the silver screen in films like *Trader Horn* every Saturday afternoon. As Wright explains in his introduction to the novel, "How Bigger was Born," his hero "is a product of a dislocated society; he is a dispossessed and disinherited man," and his violence is predictable and inevitable (xx). However, risking "premature closure," Wright proceeds beyond the murder early in the novel to show that this violence, however misguided on Bigger's part, has spawned in his hero a new understanding of his life and destiny by the novel's end. After his conviction and reconciliation with Jan, the fiancé of the woman he has murdered, Bigger becomes what every Venetian wants to believe Othello is at the beginning of the play: aware, self-reflective, and bold.

> Having been thrown by an accidental murder into a position where he had sensed a possible order and mean-

ing in his relations with the people about him; having accepted the moral guilt and responsibility for that murder because it had made him feel free for the first time in his life, [Bigger realizes] . . . a new pride and a new humility would have to be born in him, a humility springing from a new identification with some part of the world in which he lived.

(255-56)

Bigger is from the modern "Cyprus"—the slums of south Chicago; the Daltons, of course, are "Venetians"—from the suburbs. The ideological rivalry between the Turk and the Christian has been displaced by the confrontation between the Communists and capitalists in the novel. Moreover, Mary's father, Mr. Dalton, as a wealthy slum landlord, is, like Brabantio, a true "Senator," that is, Iago quips, "a villain" (1.1.18-19). Mary Dalton, like Desdemona, is thrilled by what she imagines to be the primitive power of Bigger's race. To be sure, Mary is more aggressive in her pursuit of Bigger as an exotic than Desdemona is in her relationship with Othello, ostensibly because she, under the influence of Jan, is sympathetic with his political plight: "[T]his rich girl walked over everything, put herself in the way, and, what was strange beyond understanding, talked and acted so simply and directly she confounded him" (56). Mary asks her boyfriend, "Say, Jan, do you know many Negroes? I want to meet some. . . . They have so much *emo*tion! What a people! If we could ever get them going. . . . And their songs—the spirituals! Aren't they marvelous?" (76). The white heroine in each of our "stories" becomes increasingly aggressive in pursuing her black lover, violently so, as we shall see, in *Dutchman*.

The sexuality of Desdemona has always been a moot question. As I suggested earlier, critics have debated just how aggressive and even promiscuous she is in her obvious interest in and pursuit of Othello.[16] There is no doubt that Mary Dalton, stimulated perhaps by all her drinking that evening, has sex on her mind just prior to the death scene in the novel, although Wright makes it clear that very little sexual contact occurs and that there certainly is no rape, no sexual consummation whatsoever, in spite of the lurid "reports" in the Chicago newspapers. Mary sidles up to Bigger in the car drunk, garters showing, her scent arousing him, her breath, like Desdemona's in the death scene, on his face:

> She was resting on the small of her back and her dress was pulled up so far that he could see where her stockings ended on her thighs. . . . He helped her and his hands felt the softness of her body as she stepped to the ground. Her dark eyes looked at him feverishly from deep sockets. Her hair was in his face, filling him with its scent.

(80-81)

Most significantly, in all versions of the primal scene of biracial contact and murder, witnesses to the murder are involved, either directly, as in the case of *Othello,* or implied, as in the case of *Invisible Man*. Emilia in the former

Paul Robeson as Othello in the 1943 Theater Guild production of Othello *at the Shubert Theater, New York.*

and Mrs. Dalton in the latter both intrude on the ritual murder, which in each of the works begins as a sexual encounter. In both cases white females who are blind to their own husband's evil witness the murder. My point here, and perhaps this is the point of the biracial myth I am trying to identify, is that sexual encounters between the races are not private moments as they would be in normal relationships. They represent a public shattering of the racist taboo and as such demand an audience whose predisposition toward the event alters its outcome in violent, ritualistic ways. Once that audience appears, the deed can run its gruesome course.

In both *Othello* and *Native Son,* the females are passive when they are murdered, in every sense sacrificial victims to what might be interpreted psychologically as the demands of the *mythos*—the script being enacted through their characters and witnessed by the onstage audience. It is significant that Iago is always played as an eavesdropper, whose access to private moments allows him to reinterpret events in a manner that will inevitably precipitate the racial violence at the play's climax. In the Nunn production, McKellan's Iago returns just before curtain to glare at the lovers finally united in bed—dead. Both Mary in *Native Son* and, as we shall see, Sybil in *Invisible Man,* are drugged in a sense and are thus not cognizant of their participation in this ritual event. Desdemona is nearly asleep when Othello strangles her. There are other similarities in the structures of *Othello* and *Native Son* that we might mention in passing. The novel has a Cassio figure in Jan and a Bianca in Bessie, and both works conclude with a judgment scene and the final appearance of the heroes, Othello and Bigger, who are given speeches underscoring the dignity and pathos of their respective characters.

Ralph Ellison sums up the problem under investigation here succinctly and comically in *Invisible Man:*

> Why did they have to mix their women into everything? Between us and everything we wanted to change in the world they placed a woman: socially, politically, economically. Why, goodamit, why did they insist upon confusing the class struggle with the ass struggle, debasing both us and them—all human motives?
>
> (408)

The hero confronts a series of white women in *Invisible Man,* beginning with the stripper who is brought in by the elders to teach little black boys a lesson in attraction and repulsion; they are encouraged to desire sexually what they cannot have—a white woman. The stripper is as frightened as the boys, and when she performs, both parties are watched by the elders who represent the omnipresent audience cuing and skewing the interpretation of these illicit, public sexual events. There are other brief encounters between the hero and white women, one on the subway where he is pressed by the crowd up against a blond in a scene that may have sparked the imagination of Baraka, who stages his fatal biracial ritual on the subway in *Dutchman.* White women represent one of the perpetual challenges the hero faces throughout the novel along with his speeches, the accumulation of the bric-a-brac of his "heritage" in the briefcase he is perpetually trying to discard, and his run-ins with various political parties.

Ellison is perfectly aware that his hero is acting in a performance scripted with racist assumptions, and the result in the novel is usually farcical. Before his affair with the appropriately anonymous white wife of a "brother," the hero wishes he were Paul Robeson:

> If only I were a foot taller and a hundred pounds heavier, I could simply stand before them with a sign across my chest, stating I KNOW ALL ABOUT THEM, and they'd be as awed as though I were the original boogey man—somehow reformed and domesticated. I'd no more have to speak than Paul Robeson had to act; they'd simply thrill at the sight of me.
>
> (399)

"They," of course, are the audience intruding on the couple in each of the instances examined here. When the hero first meets this woman, she "glowed as though acting a symbolic role of life and feminine fertility" (399). The white woman here has become more solicitous than Mary Dalton and conspicuously more aggressive than Desdemona. She is almost a willing pawn in the white racist's game. She appears by "the uncoiled fire hose" (400), and the phallic jokes abound in this chapter, just as they do in *Othello,* where Cassio quips to Iago "That he [Othello] may bless this bay with his tall ship, / Make love's quick pants in Desdemona's arms" (2.1.79-80) and Othello himself remarks, after he has killed his own wife on the night he is to have consummated his marriage, "Behold, I have a weapon; / A better never did itself sustain / Upon a soldier's thigh" (5.2.259-61).

The woman's conversation is full of erotic overtones of which she, as opposed to her predecessors, seems perfectly aware. She is attracted to the hero by the same attributes Desdemona discovers in Othello: both are drawn to the primitive "vitality," exoticism, and strength of the African. Of the hero's ideology, she wishes to embrace "[a]ll of it, . . . to embrace the whole of it" (402). Like Desdemona, she thrills to hear the hero speak: "[S]omehow you convey the great throbbing vitality of the movement" (402). His speech is so "primitive, . . . *forceful,* powerful. . . .[It] has so much naked power that it goes straight through me" (403).

The hero sees the "ivory" arms of the woman in her huge "white bed" (407), just as Othello had characterized Desdemona's skin as "whiter . . . than snow, / And smooth as monumental alabaster" (5.2.4-5). But the hero, unlike Othello, watches himself and his sexual actions replicated infinitely in the bedroom's multiple mirrors, "caught in a guilty stance, my face taut, tie dangling; and behind the bed another mirror which now like a surge of the sea tossed our images back and forth, back and forth, furiously multiplying the time and the place and the circumstance" (406). Moreover, the hero thinks he might have seen the husband of the woman at the door momentarily. He also conjectures that he might just be dreaming. Here we have the omnipresent witness to the act again as well as the suggestion that the terrible ritual of sexual contact between the races is a collective dream or nightmare. As ritual scenario, biracial sexual contact can be infinitely duplicated, reflected in the repetition of the infamous act. What has changed in Ellison's novel for the most part is the genre; Ellison replays the mating ritual of blacks and whites comically. The hero is a little man, a clown in a farce that Robeson would not dignify, and like all clowns, he is self-reflective. He sees what the audience demands even before he performs his role.

Farce gives way to high comedy in the hero's escapade with Sybil at the end of the novel. By this time the hero is perfectly aware that he is playing a role, although Sybil, his white victim, is still in the dark. She, like Mary Dalton, is intoxicated throughout the encounter, but she wants to be "raped." However, the hero has learned to manipulate the illusions of racism to his own advantage from one Rinehart, a hustler-turned-preacher on the streets of Harlem. In short, he has become his own Iago and continues to monitor himself in the mirror of others' expectations for him. Sybil, consistent with the preconceptions she has about her race and sex in the biracial context, claims to be a "nymphomaniac" (508). What other motive could she have in seeking out the sexual favors of a "black buck"? "'Threaten to kill me, if I don't give in. You know, talk rough to me, beautiful,'" she pleads (508). "What would Rinehart do about *this*," the hero ponders, "and knowing," he is "determined not to let her provoke [him] to violence" (506).

Unlike Othello, his literary progenitor, Ellison's hero will not be manipulated sexually and racially. He speculates on the motives behind the ridiculous spectacle that he and Sybil are cornered into performing to corroborate preconceptions about sexual relationships between the races: "Who's taking revenge on whom? But why be surprised, when that's what they [white women] hear all their lives. . . . With all the warnings against it, some are bound to want to try it out for themselves. The conquerors conquered" (509). The hero's reaction is pity for Sybil: "She had me on the ropes; I felt punch drunk, I couldn't deliver and I couldn't be angry either. I thought of lecturing her on the respect due one's bedmate in our society" (509). He realizes she thinks he is an "entertainer," and he accepts the role temporarily. The hero, however, assumes control of the script, the blueprint, as Ellison calls it, for the spectacle. There will be no sex, no rape, no violence, no murder. He gets Sybil drunk, promising her that he "rapes real good" when he's drunk, and scribbles across her belly with lipstick, "Sybil, you were raped by Santa Claus. Surprise!" (511). The hero has anticipated the outcome of the tragedy he is expected to play out; he recontextualizes the encounter as comedy, and hearts and lives are spared in the process. Like the other roles the hero attempts, manipulates, and sets aside for further refinement, the "part" of Othello is played only momentarily, and its "erasure" allows the hero the opportunity to spare Sybil the mutual humiliation and injury of "raping" her. But of course, the function of comedy is to repeat in a finer tone, to recontextualize tragic situations, and to reverse tragic outcomes through reconciliation and clarification. The variation Ellison achieves in his representation of the racist *mythos* is a function of generic—read verbal—manipulation.

Dutchman may well represent the ultimate African American revision of *Othello*. Amiri Baraka alludes to Shakespeare frequently in his works, particularly in *The Slave*, the companion piece to *Dutchman*. The myth of the ritual murder of innocent white virgins is, in *Dutchman*, fully deconstructed or inverted to reflect more accurately the relationship between the races that has existed throughout Western history. Lula—the white woman—has become the aggressor in a war overtly declared and waged between the races, and Clay is her black victim. Baraka is suggesting that the true victim in the biracial sexual struggle is the black *male*, and he is the partner who is ritually sacrificed in *Dutchman*. The setting of the play is the subway, which is "heaped in modern myth" (3). Clay, a poet who would be "the black Baudelaire," watches Lula enter the car and take the seat next to him in an ironic recreation of the very action that launched the civil rights movement just ten years before the first production of the play—integration of the city transit system.

Clay, "without a trace of self-consciousness," naively "hopes that his memory of this brief encounter will be pleasant" (4). The young black man, putty or "clay" in the hands of the white vamp, will be made to react to a taunting series of white stereotypes about black male behavior, and Lula will cue the "lines" (16) he is "supposed" (10) to say. Clay does realize early on that the "struggle" here is indeed over "abstract asses" (7) and that nothing sexual will come of this relationship. As we have seen in previous versions of the biracial sexual encounter, the act is rarely consummated. Nevertheless, Lula immediately accuses Clay, saying, "You think I want to pick you up, get you to take me somewhere and screw me, huh?" (8).

Unlike any of her predecessors, Lula knows what she is doing throughout the play—lying. "I lie a lot. It helps me control the world" (9). She tells Clay she is an actress, and he nicknames her Tallulah Bankhead. Both "players" agree they know what is "supposed to happen" between them (10). Only Lula really does, however. Lula thinks Clay is a "well-known type" (12) and proceeds to "dictate" the script, the "chronicle" as Clay calls it, of their predictable melodrama (24). Lula cues Clay throughout the play with taunts such as, "It's your turn, and let those be your lines." (16). She warns him, "Don't get smart with me, Buster, I know you like the palm of my hand" (17). Lula suggests a series of stereotypes for Clay to emulate. She notices he is wearing a three-button suit, even though his grandfather had been a slave. Lula claims he does not know who he is, taunting him by saying, "I bet you never once thought you were a black nigger" (19). Clay hopes the two of them can pretend to be "free of [their] own history," but Lula knows better (21). She has another more predictable and more violent outcome in mind. They are about to "groove," as she announces at the end of scene 1—and they are indeed in the "groove" of the biracial ritual (21).

At the beginning of scene 2, the players are rehearsing their "codes of lust" (23). Lula will "make a map" of Clay's "manhood" (26). She tries to pretend they are in *Romeo and Juliet* (26). He will call her room "black," when they arrive there later, "like Juliet's tomb." But the play is not *Romeo and Juliet*, it is *Othello* revised. Lula will be no victim of jealously and racial misunderstanding, much less a suicide-for-love at the end of the play. She is the murderer this time. The black male is the victim as he so often is in the very real historical lynching of the nineteenth and early twentieth century.

Clay wants "the whole story," and he will get it; Lula will keep "turning pages" to arrive at the ritual climax of the story (28). As the scenario unfolds, Lula realizes there is a problem here: Clay, like Othello, Bigger, and Ellison's hero, is "an escaped nigger" (29). As such, he must be exposed; she threatens him in front of an audience of middle-class businessmen that assembles in the car between scenes. These businessmen represent the ever-important witnesses to the biracial murder who will, in Baraka's version, become accomplices, and the jury judging the deed as well. Lula continues her verbal abuse: she calls Clay a "black son of a bitch," an "Uncle Thomas Woolly-Head," and an "Uncle Tom Big Lip" because he will not do the belly-rub with her (32-33). "You're afraid of white people. And your father was," she taunts (33). What follows is Clay's impassioned plea to let him live, to let him be, to let him make choices about his life, even the choice to be middle class if that is what he wants (33).

Finally angered, Clay explains why blacks should kill, but usually show restraint. Like his predecessors, Clay is ready to strangle the symbolic white female. "Such a tiny ugly throat. I could squeeze it flat, and watch you turn blue, on a humble. For dull kicks. And all these weak-faced ofays squatting around here, staring over their papers at me. Murder them too. Even if they expected it" (33). The moment of truth has arrived; the audience has been primed; but, Clay, just as Ellison's hero, refuses to play the role. Othello and Bigger have wised up in *Invisible Man* and *Dutchman*. Ellison and Baraka have revised, actually inverted, the paradigm of the biracial sexual encounter. Clay then proceeds to tell us what he and black artists do instead of killing hateful whites—they create music and poetry: "And the only thing that would cure the neurosis would be your murder. Simple as that. I mean if I murdered you, then other white people would begin to understand me. You understand? . . . If Bessie Smith had killed some white people she wouldn't have needed that music. She could have talked very straight and plain about the world. No metaphors" (35). In short, the "[c]razy niggers [are] turning their backs on sanity. When all it needs is that simple act. Murder. Just murder! Would make us all sane" (35). But he "wearies" and counters his own argument. "Ahhh. Shit. But who needs it? I'd rather be a fool. Insane. Safe with my words, and no deaths, and clean, hard thoughts, urging me to new conquests. My people's madness" (35).

At this point, Baraka tells us that Lula's "voice takes on a different, more businesslike quality." She concludes, "I've heard enough" (36) and stabs Clay with an impunity that might well have anticipated that of Bernard Goetz. The businessmen on the car then "come and drag Clay's body down the aisle" (34). In *Othello* and *Native Son,* the citizens of Venice and Chicago are violently outraged about the murders of Desdemona and Mary Dalton, but the murder of Clay in *Dutchman* is virtually ignored. Lula's next young victim then enters the car and the ritual begins again, but not before an old black conductor tips his hat to Lula and shuffles down the aisle exiting the train, a survivor in the struggle, like Ellison's "moon-mad" war veterans in *Invisible Man* (132).

Baraka knows precisely what he is up to here, and in *The Slave,* a companion play usually reprinted with *Dutchman,* he tells us all about it. In this play, Easely, a white professor, argues politics with Walker Vessels, a former black theater student, and Grace, Easely's wife, listens in. Grace announces that "Mr. Vessels is playing the mad scene from *Native Son,*" when Walker mentions having played a "second-rate Othello" in college: "Grace there was Desdemona . . . and you [Easely] were Iago . . . [*Laughs*] or at least between classes, you were Iago. . . . If a white man is Iago when you see him . . . uhh . . . chances are he's eviler when you don't." Grace, like Lula, tells Vessels to shut up, but, like Clay in *Dutchman,* Vessels refuses (57-58).

Black writers have revised the biracial sexual myth that represents the primal impediment to the freedom and equal treatment of black people as human beings. Sexual parity is the ultimate expression of racial equality. If language inscribes racial difference and dissension, and then ascribes or even prescribes behavior based on that inscription, perhaps it may also *de-scribe* such behavior, or at least rewrite the story as it exists in the Western mind. Obviously such a hope informs the rereading and representation of the crucial myth of biracial relationship discussed here.

The philologist Leo Spitzer offers us some help. The problem of "race," the great problem of our century according to W. E. B. DuBois, might indeed hinge on the misunderstanding of a single word: the word "race" itself. In his inimitable fashion Spitzer, as linguistic sleuth, traces the word "race" through its German, French, Italian, and English uses and abuses to the Latin root *ratio*. The concept of race, and perhaps the attitudes associated with racism, are all locked up in this term *ratio,* perhaps most artfully wielded by Thomas Aquinas in his *Summa:* "God, in willing himself, wills all the things which are in himself; but all things in a certain manner preexist in him by their types (*rationes*)" (qtd. in Spitzer 147). Spitzer explains, "Thus *rationes* is a rendering of *ideai* and can shift to the meaning 'types' [which becomes 'races'] precisely because all the different *rationes* of things are integrated in the creator of things" (148). *Rationes* or "races" may be conceived, then, as figments of the collective mind derived from what are presumed to be God's categories of human existence. Spitzer concludes, "What a significant comment this affords on the modern 'racial' beliefs!" (152).

If "race" is a platonic concept, existing in genres and not in genes, existing in subjective human judgments rather than in the "nature of things" and if it is historically conditioned instead of "predetermined," then this notion, this "idea," can be changed, can be modified, can be adapted to new circumstances and experience. Through language, which gave us the notion of "race" in the first place, we can model a new reality, a reality that reverses outcomes posited as necessities in the racist mentality. Through the clever manipulation of the language of traditional character and circumstance, the writers under investigation here, Shakespeare included, have helped us perceive new solutions to a problem that remains catastrophically troublesome in the modern world, the problem of racial violence.

Notes

1. Derrida continues, "The point is not that acts of racial violence are only words, but rather that they have to have a word. [Racism] institutes, declares, writes, inscribes, prescribes" (Derrida 331).

2. Tzvetan Todorov writes, "[W]hereas racism is a well-attested social phenomenon, 'race' itself does not exist! Or, to put it more clearly: there are a great number of physical differences among human groups, but these differences cannot be superimposed; we obtain completely divergent subdivisions of the human species according to whether we base our description of the 'races' on an analysis of their epidermis or their blood types, their genetic heritages or their bone structures. For contemporary biology, the concept of 'race' is therefore useless" (370-71).

3. Quoted in Barnet 280. For an honest history of Robeson's reactions to his roles in the two great productions of *Othello* in which he starred (London, 1930, and New York, 1943) and the pronounced racial implications of and reactions to these productions, see Martin Duberman's biography of Robeson (134, 263). Some items of interest: Peggy Ashcroft, who played Desdemona in the London production, found her entire experience in *Othello* (1930) "an education in racism," particularly the public reaction to the kissing scenes between Desdemona and Othello (134-35); significant passages from the play were cut by the director, Nellie Van Volkenburg, who Aschroft decided was a "racist" because of her treatment of Robeson. The murder scene was staged with the bed tucked inconspicuously away in a corner of the room, and the light was so dimmed to the point of "inscrutability" that Ralph Richardson, who played Iago, kept a flashlight up his sleeve to negotiate the stage after his departure (136). The attempt to take the production to the United States was virtually sabotaged, and when it was produced here in 1943, it provoked broad racial protest, especially in the southern states (265).

4. Gunnar Myrdal writes, "The illicit relations freely allowed or only frowned upon are, however, restricted to those between white men and Negro women. A white woman's relation with a Negro man is met by the full fury of anti-amalgamation sanctions" (56).

5. Baraka's play is given in the list of works cited under his original name, Leroi Jones, as it is in the original edition of the play used for this article.

6. I am in debt here to an anonymous reader for *SAR* who provided this list of novels dealing with our theme and who suggested especially that Charles Johnson's *Oxherding Tale* offers "first a kind of mock acknowledgement of the myth of the supersexual black male, and then [completely dismantles] the tradition . . . of its original fears, prejudices, and taboos."

7. Kinney goes on to discuss some sixty novels of the nineteenth and early twentieth centuries with the theme of miscegenation, novels by luminaries in the canon including James Fenimore Cooper, William Gilmore Simms, George Washington Cable, and W. E. B. DuBois.

8. The reevaluation of *Othello* in its historical context is well underway at this point. I am much indebted to Emily Bartels's "Making More of the Moor: Aaron, Othello, and Renaissance Refashionings of Race." Bartels's article as well as my own are products of a seminar on "Shakespeare's Aliens" convened at the 1988 meeting of the Shakespeare Association of America by Edward Berry. On the matter of race, see Phyllis Braxton's recent article, "Othello: The Moor and the Metaphor," which argues "that Othello's color outweighs in significance the element of race" (1). According to Braxton, Shakespeare leaves the matter of Othello's ethnic identification deliberately ambiguous but ominous, because "the Other is always mysterious and without clear definition. Once defined, he is no longer the Other" (9).

9. See, for instance, the studies of Barthelemy, Braxton, Brown, Dabydeen, D'Amico, Hulme, Hunter, Eldred D. Jones, Jordan, Loomba, Miller, Pratt, Said, and Tokson.

10. Black actors, too, have been strongly attracted to the role because, as Hill suggests, the play offers "an opportunity vividly to convey to audiences the message that racism is the green-eyed monster that destroys not just its victim but also its perpetrator and innocent bystanders who fall into its clutches" (41).

11. For other indignant, clearly racist reviews of nineteenth-century performances of the play, see Ruth Cowhig's essay (14-20).

12. All quotations from the plays are taken from *The Riverside Shakespeare*.

13. Quoted in Barnet 284. Miller's sentiment typifies critical comment about all of Shakespeare's plays dealing with the problem of "complexion"—*Titus Andronicus, The Merchant of Venice,* and *Othello.* For instance, both Frank Kermode and Alvin Kernan ignore racial themes altogether in their respective introductions to *Othello* in *The Riverside Shakespeare* and the 1987 Signet edition of the play. Kermode does use interesting language to discuss other issues arising in the text, however: "The whiteness of Desdemona blackened, we see the white and tranquil mind of Othello darkened by atavistic shock and disgust. . . . He has behaved like a Turk (used throughout the play as an enemy of civility and grace, a type of cunning and disorder). He has become that person of different 'clime, complexion, and degree' whom it was wanton of Desdemona to marry" (*The Riverside Shakespeare* 1201). Braxton claims Miller was trying "to minimize the differences between Othello and Desdemona" by using Anthony Hopkins in the role (2-3 and 14).

14. See, however, Wayne Holmes's article. Holmes goes so far as to suggest "that Desdemona and Cassio, some time prior to Desdemona and Othello's marriage, had an affair" (1).

15. Harris speculates, "Almost all of the deaths [by ritual lynchings] have as their causes the improper interactions of black males and white females. But what happened in depictions after 1968? Are black writers now beginning to suggest that black males and white females can interact with each other without some fatal violence occurring?" (xii). In another passage she writes, "Historically, in their ritualistic lynchings of black people, white Americans were carrying out rites of exorcism in which they seemed determined to eradicate the black 'beast' from their midst, except when he existed in the most servile, accommodationist, and helpful of positions" (xiii).

16. Howard Felperin, for one, is so incensed by Holmes's suggestion (cited in note 14 above) that Desdemona might be more "experienced" than we usually suppose her, that he charitably leaves the author of the article "unnamed for reasons by now apparent" (3).

Works Cited

Baraka, Amiri. See Leroi Jones.

Barnet, Sylvan. "Othello on Stage and Screen." *Othello*. Ed. Alvin Kernan. New York: Signet, 1986. 270-86.

Bartels, Emily. "Making More of the Moor: Aaron, Othello, and Renaissance Refashionings of Race." *Shakespeare Quarterly* 41 (1990): 433-54.

Barthelemy, Anthony. *Black Face, Maligned Race: The Representation of Blacks in English Drama from Shakespeare to Southerne*. Baton Rouge: Louisiana State UP, 1987.

Braxton, Phyllis Natalie. "Othello: The Moor and the Metaphor." *South Atlantic Review* 55.3 (1990): 1-17.

Brown, Paul. "'This thing of darkness I acknowledge mine': *The Tempest* and the Discourse of Colonialism." *Political Shakespeare: New Essays in Cultural Materialism*. Ed. Jonathan Dollimore and Alan Sinfield. Ithaca, NY: Cornell UP, 1985. 48-71.

Cowhig, Ruth. "Blacks in English Renaissance Drama." Dabydeen 1-26.

Dabydeen, David, ed. *The Black Presence in English Literature*. Manchester, UK: Manchester UP, 1985.

D'Amico, Jack. *The Moor in English Renaissance Drama*. Tampa: UP of South Florida, 1991.

Derrida, Jacques. "Racism's Last Word." Gates 329-38.

Duberman, Martin Bauml. *Paul Robeson*. New York: Knopf, 1989.

Ellison, Ralph. *Invisible Man*. New York: Vintage-Random House, 1972.

Felperin, Howard. "The Deconstruction of Presence in *The Winter's Tale*." *Shakespeare and the Question of Theory*. Ed. Patricia Parker and Geoffrey Hartman. New York: Methuen, 1985. 3-18.

Gates, Henry Louis, Jr., ed. *"Race," Writing, and Difference*. Chicago: U of Chicago P, 1985.

Harris, Trudier. *Exorcising Blackness: Historical and Literary Lynching and Burning Rituals*. Bloomington: Indiana UP, 1984.

Hill, Errol. *Shakespeare in Sable: A History of Black Shakespearean Actors*. Amherst: UP of Massachusetts, 1984.

Holmes, Wayne. "Othello: Is't Possible?" *Upstart Crow* 1 (1978): 1-23.

Hulme, Peter. *Colonial Encounters: Europe and the Native Caribbean, 1492-1797*. London: Methuen, 1986.

Hunter, G. K. "Othello and Colour Prejudice." *Dramatic Identities and Cultural Tradition: Studies in Shakespeare and his Contemporaries*. Ed. G. K. Hunter. New York: Barnes, 1978. 31-59.

Jones, Eldred D. *The Elizabethan Image of Africa*. Charlottesville: UP of Virginia, 1971.

———. *Othello's Countrymen: The African in English Renaissance Drama*. London: Oxford UP, 1965.

Jones, Leroi [now Amiri Baraka]. *Dutchman* and *The Slave*. New York: Morrow, 1964.

Jordan, Winthrop D. *White Over Black: American Attitudes Toward the Negro, 1550-1812*. New York: Norton, 1968.

Kermode, Frank. Introduction. Shakespeare 1198-202.

Kernan, Alvin. Introduction. *Othello*. By William Shakespeare. New York: Signet, 1987. xxiii-xxxv.

Kinney, James. *Amalgamation! Race, Sex, and Rhetoric in the Nineteenth-Century American Novel*. Westport, CT: Greenwood, 1985.

Loomba, Ania. *Gender, Race, Renaissance Drama*. Manchester, UK: Manchester UP, 1989.

Myrdal, Gunnar. *An American Dilemma*. New York: Harper, 1944.

Miller, Christopher. *Blank Darkness: Africanist Discourse in French*. Chicago: U of Chicago P, 1985.

Pratt, Mary Louise. "Scratches on the Face of the Country: Or, What Mr. Barrow Saw in the Land of the Bushmen." *Critical Inquiry* 12 (1985): 119-43.

Said, Edward W. *Orientalism*. London: Routledge, 1978.

Shakespeare, William. *Othello*. *The Riverside Shakespeare*. Ed. G. Blakemore Evans. Boston: Houghton, 1974.

Spitzer, Leo. "Ratio Race." *Essays in Historical Semantics.* New York: Russell, 1948. 147-70.

Stember, Charles Herbert. *Sexual Racism: The Emotional Barrier to an Integrated Society.* New York: Elsevier, 1976.

Todorov, Tzvetan "'Race,' Writing, and Culture." Gates 370-80.

Tokson, Elliot H. *The Popular Image of the Black Man in English Drama, 1550-1688.* Boston: Hall, 1982.

Wright, Richard. *Native Son.* New York: Harper, 1940.

Kim Hall (essay date 1993)

SOURCE: "Reading What Isn't There: 'Black' Studies in Early Modern England," in *Stanford Humanities Review,* Vol. 3, No. 1, Winter, 1993, pp. 23-33.

[*In the following essay, Hall examines the figure of the black woman in order to show the "problematics of the historical study of race and gender."*]

It is particularly difficult to "attend" to racial difference in early modern England.[1] Given the lessening but still widely held assumption, that "race" is not a viable category of analysis not only in the early modern period, but for literature in general, added to the distressing lack of data on people of color in England before the codification of the slave trade, it is not surprising that women of color constitute a largely "invisible" presence in the English Renaissance. In its very title, Elliot Tokson's *The Popular Image of the Black Man in English Drama, 1550-1688,* a standard work on the subject, announces the absence of black women.[2] Another influential text, Winthrop Jordan's *White Over Black,* devotes very little space to the problem of gender in racial discourse, even in his discussion of the English obsession with fairness.[3]

In this article, I will use the figure of the black woman as an example for the problematics of the historical study of race and gender. My concerns spring from my own investment in a politicized historical study of Europe that dialogues with the work being done by women of color which has been at the forefront of critiquing both assumptions about race and gender and the role of "race" in identity formation. Rather than making a specific argument about the linkages of race and gender, my goals for the essay are twofold: (1) to question the underlying assumptions of two contemporary constructions of the black presence in early modern England and to suggest ways in which both the standard tools of analysis and the materials subject to analysis work to elide black women from discussions of race; (2) to question the somewhat arbitrary boundaries between "history" and "literature" by juxtaposing an historical document with a literary representation of a black woman and to thereby suggest some possible relationships between representation and history in studies of race in the early modern period.[4]

The historical study of black women poses interesting problems for critical practice. As Audre Lorde has argued, "Within this country where racial difference creates a constant, if unspoken, distortion of vision black women have on one hand always been highly visible, and so, on the other hand, have always been rendered invisible through the depersonalization of racism."[5] Certainly discourses of race did not begin in America and the combination of distortion and high visibility that Lorde notes may operate in early modern culture as well. The distortion Lorde notes suggests that black women are in a sense unretrievable in such a past since they are objects "named only in ways that define [their] relationship to those who are subject."[6] Yet we disregard their infrequent appearances with peril, since their very visibility and the purposes it serves in a white supremacist culture means that representations of black women have a significance that the actual number of appearances would belie.

In the recent anthology *Critical Terms for Literary Study,* African-American critic Kwame Anthony Appiah begins his entry on "race" by recognizing a continuing bias against the inclusion of race in literary studies: "the idea that the concept of *race* should have any place, let alone an important one—in literary studies has been attacked from a good many directions."[7] Working against such a notion, Appiah then goes on to outline a history of racial "conceptions," and contends that earlier conceptions of race, particularly in the Renaissance, are rooted in theological distinctions rather than "racial" ones. He begins what is to be a discussion of *Othello, The Merchant of Venice,* and *The Jew of Malta* with the assertion:

> In each of these plays a central figure—Othello, Shylock, Barabas—plays out a role we can understand only in terms of a stereotype of a people, Moors or Jews; a stereotype we are likely, if we are hasty, to conceive of as simply racialist. So it is important to go carefully. *We should begin by recognizing that in Shakespearean England both Jews and Moors were barely an empirical reality. And even though there were small numbers of Jews and black people in England in Shakespeare's day, attitudes toward 'the Moor' and 'The Jew' do not seem to have been based on experience of these people. Furthermore, despite the fact that there was an increasing amount of information available about dark-skinned foreigners in this, the first great period of modern Western exploration,* actual reports of black or Jewish foreigners did not play an important part in forming these images (Appiah 277 emphasis added).[8]

His notions of Elizabethan England are a clear articulation of a largely unstated bias against the study of "pre-slavery" Europe by scholars centrally concerned with race: that studies of race and blackness should primarily be concerned with the construction of black subjectivity (the corollary being that the early modern period cannot be the subject of black studies because there were no blacks to study). In Women's Studies, this problem can best be summed up by the now famous words of Audre Lorde, "The Master's Tools Will Never Dismantle the Master's House." Her formulation proposes that a study of the master himself with scholarship defined by the academy can never lead to scholarship with a significant political impact. Too often, it can be used to erase the study of the formation of dominant culture altogether.

Appiah's admonitions for care in discussing "race" in early modern England simultaneously authorizes and de-authorizes race as a "critical" term for study in the Renaissance. His sense that race is an unexplored category in literature empowers the critic who wants to examine the category. However, his insistence on empirical evidence is particularly oppressive from a text that purports to enable new reading strategies[9] as is his curious declaration of the irrelevence of "actual reports" in discussion of early modern formations of difference. This sense that the "experience of" actual blacks or Jews did not inform literary representation excludes one of the more enabling strategies of the "new historicism"—"describing culture in action" (Veeser xiii)—as well as ignores the possibility that both the reports and "actual experience were inflected by the assumptions about the character" of certain peoples.

While Appiah is rightly concerned with our making broad generalizations about a category, "race," that has an historical specificity, at the same time he falls into the trap of accepting the post-Enlightenment science that created "racialism" on its own terms. Specifically, this entry seems backed by a narrative of modern science and a myth of empiricism that relies on a clear break from the historical past. Rather, I would argue that the "inherited characteristics" (Appiah 26) that are an elemental part of modern scientific discourses on race are in large part the result of lingering notions of "difference" that resided at the intersections of English travel and trade, plantation, empire, and science in the early modern period. Science merely takes up already pre-existing terms of difference, such as skin color and features, that have been combined with physical and mental characteristics. It is no accident that Sir Thomas Browne, one of the forerunners of modern science, devotes three chapters of his *Pseudodoxia Epidemica* (1672) to dispelling myths on "the blackness of Negroes."[10] Despite these laudable intentions, his investigation is heavily weighted with value judgements concerning color, such as "they of Europe in Candy, Sicily, and some parts of Spaine deserve not properly so low a name as Tawny" (512). The bias that appears in Appiah, even as he deconstructs the terms of nineteenth-century science and biological determinism, can be located specifically in his insistence on "empirical evidence" of a black presence. This delimits the permitted reading strategies of Renaissance critics because we are not allowed to read "backwards," to draw from the insights of current theorists on race and racism to investigate the birth pangs of these modern attitudes in the early modern period.[11]

Appiah's vision of an England populated with mere images of non-white, non-Christians contrasts sharply with that of white feminist critic Karen Newman who, in her influential essay, "And wash the Ethiop white': femininity and the Monstrous in *Othello*," argues that "In England itself, by 1596, blacks were numerous enough to generate alarm."[12] With apologies for making too broad generalizations, I would like to suggest that these critics are fairly typical of the assumptions made about race in the Renaissance. Both confront the problem of the evidence of a viable black presence (albeit with differing conclusions) and both base their work on an equation of race with blackness. "White" as a racial category is left unexamined.[13] While there is no way of establishing how many blacks there were in England, there were numerous Englishmen and women fashioning their cultural identity with discourses of race. Without ignoring the problem of evidence, I do want to suggest that an uncritical (or overly critical) emphasis on proof may impede historical studies before they have even begun.

What is the evidence for the black presence? Most of the data from Europe on Africans in particular emerge from travel narratives and historical/bureaucratic accounts of Transatlantic trade. The English were late, but eager arrivals in the European slave trade. In 1562, John Hawkins crashed the Portuguese market and organized the first transatlantic slave trading venture, thereby demonstrating the potential value of the market to England and thus encouraging England's future encroachments in the slave trade.[14] With Elizabeth I's consent, other traders attempted to make inroads into the Portuguese monopoly, and slaves were bought surreptitiously or kidnapped and sold along with stolen gold and ivory. As merchants made inroads into the African trade, they brought to England slaves who served as personal attendants. In 1618, James I gave the charter of monopoly to 30 London merchants, the Company of Adventurers of London Trading into parts of Africa. It was not until 1663 that the English incorporated a company, The Royal Adventurers into Africa, which had as its primary goal the acquisition of slaves. Even at this point its primary objective was to provide labor for English plantations in America. The demand for sugar made the trade grow at a furious pace; however, until that point, evidence for a black population in England remained fairly small. Until the codification of slavery, we only get elusive hints of the Africans brought to England as the slaves, servants, linguists, and curiosities who constituted England's black population.

Not surprisingly, most documentary evidence concerning blacks in the period before the signing of the Asiento in the 1660's is extremely limited. Consequently the few documents available have assumed monumental importance in discussions of the black presence. I would like to look at one such document in juxtaposition with a representation of a black woman fairly invisible to modern criticism. Despite her support of English piracy in the slave trade, in 1596 Queen Elizabeth sent an open letter to the Lord Mayor of London and to the mayors of other towns, stating, "Her majesties understanding that there are of late divers blackmoores brought into this realme, of which kind of people there are allready here too manie"[15] and demanding the confiscation of Africans brought to England in a recent voyage by Thomas Baskerville. In 1601 Elizabeth again expressed concern over the presence of blacks in the realm and sent this proclamation to the Lord Mayor of London:

> whereas the Queen's Majesty, tendering the good and welfare of her own natural subjects greatly distressed in these hard times of dearth, is highly discontented to understand the great numbers of Negars and Blackamoors which (as she is informed) are crept into this realm since the troubles between Her highness and the King of Spain, who are fostered and relieved here to the annoyance of her own liege people that which co[vet?] the relief which these people consume; as also for that the most of them are infidels having no understanding of Christ or his Gospel, hath given a special commandment that the said kind of people should be with all speed avoided and discharged out of this her majesty's realms; *and to that end and purpose hath appointed Casper van Denden, merchant of Lucbeck, for their speedy transportation, a man that hath somewhat deserved of this realm in respect that by his own labor and charge he hath relieved and brought from Spain divers of our English nation who otherwise would have perished ther . . . and . . .* if there be any person or persons which be possessed of any such Blackamoors that refuse to deliver them in sort aforesaid, then we require you to call them before you and to advice and persuade them by all good means to satisfy her Majesty's pleasure therein *which if they shall eftsoons willfully and obstinately refuse, we preay you then to certify their names unto us, to the end her majesty may take such futher course therein as it shall seem best in her princely wisdom* (emphasis added).[16]

This document and the image of Elizabeth, that white and red icon of English racial purity and superiority, casting out her polar opposites, "Moors and Negars" gives startling materiality to Winthrop Jordan's assertion that discourses on blackness occured in tandem with ideals of female beauty as represented by Elizabeth (8). While such critical attention as has been paid to this document concentrates on the attempt to discharge Moors out of the realm and uses the attempt to prove the existence of a viable black presence in England (Newman 148), the terms of the proclamation demand special attention. The image of large numbers of Moors having "crept into this island" suggests that they suddenly "appeared" on their own volition (despite having been "fostered and relieved" here by unnamed residents). The rest of the document is concerned to prevent contact between these invaders and "her own liege" people despite its contradictory contention that her own subjects are the ones "possessed" of "Blackamoors" to the detriment of the state.

Equally important is the reference to the religion (or lack of religion) of the Moors which supposes that they are a logical group to cut off from state resources because they have "no understanding of Christ or his Gospel." In this time of perceived crisis Christianity becomes the prerequisite for access to limited resources. Certainly, Elizabeth's evocation of the religious difference of the Moor would seem to support Appiah's contention that religious difference is the crucial part of the construction of black "difference." I would argue, however, that even though religion is given as a compelling reason for excluding Moors, merely emphasizing religious difference only clouds the political reality that the Moors' visibility in the culture made them a viable target for exclusion. In other words, it is their physical difference and the moral/spiritual qualities associated with it that provokes their exclusion, not simply their religion.

This is the document Newman uses to support her contention that blacks were "numerous enough to generate alarm." The tone of the document does imply a state of national emergency, since Elizabeth opens with a reminder of "these hard times of dearth." If we take the proclamation at face value, the "great numbers of Negars or Blackamoors . . . of which kind there is allready here too manie" suggests a large number, but the furor caused by the presence of Moroccan ambassadors at Elizabeth's court in 1601 suggests that blacks, particularly royal blacks, were still a novelty. There is no evidence that this had to constitute a large number, particularly if we remember that the threat of the black to the state is continually magnified in a racist culture. Given such contradictory evidence and Basil Davidson's early warning in *The African Slave Trade* that "A great deal of historical writing is propaganda" (26), a more fruitful and significant question might be not how many black Africans were in early modern England, but "How many Moors does it take to generate alarm in England"?

In his *Staying Power: The History of Black People in Britain,* commenting on this passage, Peter Fryer suggests that the first expulsion of these "Negars" was payment for the release of English hostages. The merchant involved asked for the right to confiscate black slaves in exchange for his arrangement for the release of 89 English hostages in Spain and Portugal. Fryer's evidence convincingly demonstrates the real political and economic factors underlying the expulsions and forces us to question the rhetoric of the second expulsion as well. Nevertheless, his explanation only heightens our curiosity about the specificity of the terms of the expulsion. Certainly the political/religious rationale mystifies the wholesale confiscation of "property" from her citizens. However, the reliance on the good of the commonwealth suggests that Queen Elizabeth draws on a series of associations about Moors as a group that seem to persist in contemporary Anglo-American racial discourse: in times of economic stress, visible minorities very often become the scapegoat for a national problem.

Elizabeth's proclamation may open up another text which reveals the economic and racial fears of Elizabethan England, *The Merchant of Venice.* At the end of Act III of Shakespeare's *The Merchant of Venice,* the audience witnesses a joking interchange between Shylock's servant, Launcelot Gobbo, and Lorenzo and Jessica about their mixed marriage:

> JESSICA:
> Nay you need not fear us, Lorenzo, Launcelot and I are out. He tells me flatly that there's no mercy for me in heaven because I am a Jew's daughter; and he says that you are no good member of the commonwealth, for in converting Jews to Christians, you raise the price of pork.
> LORENZO:
> I shall answer that better to the commonwealth than you can the getting up of the Negro's belly; the Moor is with child by you Launcelot.
> LAUNCELOT:
> It is much that the Moor should be more than reason; but if she be less than an honest woman, she is indeed more than I took her for.
>
> (III.v.31-42).[17]

This passage proves to be a very problematic re-presentation (with the double distancing that this implies) for Shakespearean criticism. The female Moor is not a character presented to the audience by an actor, but one only spoken about by other characters; she literally does not exist on stage. So too, she barely exists in the area of textual analysis. The Arden edition of *Merchant* helpfully notes that "this passage has not been explained" and suggests "Perhaps it was introduced simply for the sake of the elaborate pun on Moor/more" (99, n.35). The annotations in the Variorum Shakespeare suggest that this emphasis on the purely linguistic aspects of the scene is typical, giving several such reading, including, "A change of 'less' into '*more*' makes the jingle fuller." Even editions that acknowledge the racial charge in this scene still elide the black woman as a part of the play. The notes to the 1926 Cambridge edition attribute this scene to an adapter rather than to Shakespeare and then asks:

> *Who was the black woman referred to in this passage? Clearly she has nothing to do with the play as it stands. Was she a character in an earlier version, e.g. a member of Morocco's train? Or was she a real figure, a London notoriety familiar to the audience for whom the dialogue was written? Holding the opinion we do on the authorship of this scene, we are inclined to interpret this reference as a topical one* (emphasis added).[18]

Interestingly, even an edition that confronts the startling reference to a black woman and posits the existence of an actual black woman completely detaches her from the Shakespearean text by asserting that the dialogue is not Shakespeare's and that the figure "has nothing to do with the play." Both readings, the linguistic and the topical, insist on the obscurity of the scene and of the black woman.[19] For one, she exists only as a text; for the other, she may exist in history, but not in the text.

This joking conversation no doubt parodically reflects the investment of the commonwealth in marriage practices. Nevertheless, the audience is left to question the difference between Lorenzo's liaison with a Jew and Launcelot's with a Moor. The Renaissance stage abounds with jokes about bastards. Certainly, if Launcelot's fault was merely the getting of another bastard, there would be no reason to emphasize that this invisible woman is a Moor. Anthony Barthelemy, in his *Black Face, Maligned Race*, notes that this exchange reflects ideas of the licentiousness of the black woman typical of the time. However, the pregnant, unheard (and by critics unseen) black woman becomes in some ways the silent symbol for the economic and racial politics of *The Merchant of Venice*. Like the pregnant Indian maid in *A Midsummer Night's Dream*, she works within the desire for the riches that come from cultural interaction; however, she also exemplifies the necessity for controlling such interactions. She is, perhaps, an example of what Peter Stallybrass has called "the female grotesque" which "interrogate[s] class and gender hierarchies alike, subverting the enclosed body in the name of a body that is 'unfinished, outgrows itself, transgresses its own limits'."[20]

The pressures of race, religion, and economics in Elizabeth's proclamation help contextualize the threat posed by a Launcelot Gobbo and his Moor. A similar sense of a critical scarcity of resources pervades *The Merchant of Venice*. This sense of privation felt by the citizens of Venice produces an economic imperative in the play which insists on the exclusion of racial, religious, and cultural difference. In Gobbo's jesting evocation of the scarcity of food we see the same unease over limited resources and possibly, famine. Famine, one of the particular rationales for colonial plantation and expansion, becomes here associated with the black woman. With the finite resources of a Venetian (or Elizabethan) society reserved for the wealthy elite, the offspring of Gobbo and the Moor present a triple threat that in this world is perceived as a crime against the state. This miscegenation is perhaps more suspect than the possibility of that between a Portia and a Morocco; it raises the possibility of a half Black, half Christian child from the lower classes threatens to upset the desired balance of consumption.

Ultimately both sources draw on/create the same racial stereotype. Just as the image of the black female as consumer of state resources in twentieth-century United States is statistically inaccurate but politically powerful, so may the black presence have been a threat to white European labor, a threat magnified by its very visibility. I borrow here from Patricia Hill Collins' discussion of the image of the welfare mother in the United States:

> *Controlling Black women's fertility in such a political economy becomes important. The image of the welfare mother fulfills this function by labeling as unnecessary and even dangerous to the values of the country the fertility of women who are not white and middle class . . . The image of the welfare mother thus provides ideological justification for the dominant group's interest in limiting the fertility of black mothers who are seen as producing too many unproductive children.*[21]

Similarly, the alignment of class, race, and religious difference in the jesting over the female Moor in *Merchant* serves to label her fertility as dangerous and ultimately disruptive of the desired homology between Christianity and economic vitality.

The unnoticed black woman in *The Merchant of Venice* suggests a great deal about the racial and sexual politics of reading and consequently "writing" the Renaissance. Much attention is paid to Portia's gender-bending and the Prince of Morocco's role in the sex/gender system of Venice. However, modern critical attention to the play in some ways replicates a dynamic typical of modern Europe. The current historical work on the black presence in England, not surprisingly, ignores gender difference as well. Then, as now, black women fall into the margins of difference. As Gloria Hull, Patricia Bell Scott, and Barbara Smith propose in their provocatively titled anthology, *All of the Men are Black, All the Women are White, But Some of Us are Brave*, the elision of the female from the category of race only contributes to the invisibility of black women.[22]

This tendency in modern works is only exacerbated by early discourses of race. A travel narrative printed in Richard Hakluyt's influential *Principal Voyages*, "The Prosperous Voyage of Master James Lancaster to the towne of Fernambruck in Brasil," graphically illustrates this point. The English, in the midst of a battle with the Portuguese and the Native Americans in Brazil, block off a harbor and commandeer all enemy ships:

> *And this farther good chance or blessing of God we had to helpe us, that assoone as we had taken our cartes, the next morning came in a ship with some 60 Negros, 10 Portugall woman, and 40 Portugals: the women and the Negros we turned out of the towne, but the Portugals our Admirall kept us to draw the carts when they were laden, which to us was a very great ease. For the country is very hote and ill for our nation to take any great travell in.*[23]

At this point in Lancaster's narrative, issues of numbering and cataloguing seem to take precedence over narrative detail. While we are given the illusion of numerical specificity in the numbering of the Portuguese by nationality and gender, the "Negroes" are made genderless (or all male): "the women and the Negroes we turned out of the towne."

Similarly, we find in Peter Fryer's account of the use of blacks as symbols of status in seventeenth-century England, the revelation of a 100 year tradition of the Sackville family who kept a page who was always to be known as John Morocco. A look at the diary of Lady Anne Clifford shows that, in addition to John Morocco, the Sackvilles acquired a black laundrymaid, named Grace Robinson around 1613.[24] Even with this seemingly innocent piece of evidence, we need to question (without valorizing) why it is that the black male's name and identity is subsumed under his racial status. The Sackville family literally name him "Morocco" and make him the focus of necessary racial distinctions that shaped family status. Grace Robinson and her labor (like most women's work) disappears from the narrative of the Sackville family only to appear in a list of family retainers at the end of the text. If nothing else, her appearance suggests that although most slaves were men, black women were not absent. Such narrative fragments hint at the possibilities for the study of race in early modern England; however, they should also represent a cautionary tale about the ways in which the terms of representation dictate the terms of critical analysis. The master's tools cannot dismantle the master's house: the insistence on traditional standards of evidence, on "ocular proof" of a black female presence before any discussion of the gendering of race, merely maintains the traditional silence that surrounded black women from their earliest experiences in England and America.

Newman ends her essay on *Othello* urging that Shakespeare be read from a position of opposition:

> *We need to read Shakespeare in ways which produce resistant readings, ways which contest the hegemonic forces the plays at the same time affirm. Our critical task is not merely to describe the formal parameters of a play, not is it to make claims about Shakespeare's politics, conservative or subversive, but to reveal the discursive and dramatic evidence for such representations, and their counterparts in criticism and representations* (158).

I want to suggest here that Newman's contention needs expansion: Not only do we need to read Shakespeare in ways that produce resistant readings, we need to read "other" documents with the same care. The documents that would seem to provide empirical evidence are as deeply imbricated by the same cultural assumptions as Shakespeare's plays. Thus, we need to interpret Elizabeth's "creation" as carefully and with as the same critical consciousness as we read Shakespeare's. The reticence Appiah states in speaking of Renaissance notions of race may be rooted in the apprehension that one might take a European representation of difference as an "accurate" sense of difference. This does not mean that representations of blackness are not in the proper purview of critical theories of race. It does, however, mean that we need to read with the constant recognition that the evidence of that presence is still the product of a European—and Eurocentric—mind.

Notes

1. I adopt the term "Black" as a more inclusive term that takes into account the study early descriptions of blackness as well as the presence of Africans in Europe and the Americas.

2. Although his title might seem to acknowledge the difficulty of analyzing a black female presence, the text itself suggests that the work is based on the assumption that the category "black" means "black male." His text is full of sentences such as the following which equate African difference with masculinity: "Put briefly, English dramatists were trying to respond imaginatively to a *black African* who was a stranger to their land and their consciousness at exactly the same time that English commercial interests were beginning to exploit *that same Black man* as the most suitable material for

slave labor." Elliot Tokson, *The Image of the Black Man in English Drama* (Boston: G.K. Hall, 1982), ix (emphasis added). A more recent work that substantially revises Tokson, Anthony Barthelemy's *Black Face/Maligned Race: The Representation of Blacks in English Drama from Shakespeare to Southerne* (Baton Rouge: Louisiana State University Press, 1987), while not feminist in its approach, pays much more attention to representations of black women.

3. Winthrop Jordan, *White Over Black: American Attitudes Toward the Negro: 1550-1812* (Chapel Hill: North Carolina UP Press, 1968), 8.

4. This latter question may in fact seem wellworn to those who have been in immersed in the arguments over the "New Historicism." I bring up this specific question again, because this issue of "evidence" is of pressing concern to historical studies of race, as one faces from students and from peers the need to "prove" a significant black presence in the Renaissance. Elizabeth Fox-Genovese's essay "Literary Criticism and The New Historicism" charges that the reading strategies of the more prominent "new historicists" ignore the unique qualities of history: "In most cases they have implicitly preferred to absorb history into the text or discourse without (re)considering the specific characteristics of history herself. Such a blanket charge may appear churlish, especially since so much of the work in new historicism has attempted to restore women, working people, and other marginal groups (although rarely, so far, black people) to the discussion of literary texts." in *The New Historicism*, H.Aram Veeser ed., (New York and London: Routledge, 1989), 217. Interestingly, even as she foregrounds the absence of blacks from analysis, she proposes a reading of history which may perpetuate that absence, "Both in the past and in the interpretation of the past history follows a pattern or structure, according to which some systems of relations and some events possess greater significance than others" (218). Such an emphasis on patterns and degrees of significance, this essay should demonstrate, still works to preclude the restoration of marginalized figures to literature and history.

5. Audre Lorde, "The Transformation of Silence into Language and Action" in *SisterOutsider: Essays and Speeches by Audre Lorde* (Trumansburg, N.Y.: The Crossing Press, 1984), 42.

6. bell hooks, "feminist scholarship: some ethical issues" in *Talking Back: Thinking Feminist *Thinking Black* (Boston: South End Press, 1989), 43.

7. Kwame Anthony Appiah, "Race" in *Critical Terms for Literary Study*, Frank Lentricchia and Thomas McLaughlin eds., (Chicago and London: U of Chicago Press, 1990), 276.

8. I use Appiah here because, as the author of an entry presumably designed to enable further discussions on this category, he shows some recalcitrance in his thinking on the Renaissance which is, in effect, not unlike the objections made by more conservative scholars against race as a focus of inquiry in earlier periods.

9. In the introduction to the volume, editor Thomas McLaughlin outlines the project of the individual entries: "Each theorist considered a different term prevelant in literary discourse, examining its history, the controversies it generates, the questions it raises, *the reading strategies it permits*" (emphasis added).

10. Sir Thomas Browne, *Pseudodoxia Epidemica; or, Enquiries into very many received tenets and commonly presumed truths,* ed. Bruce Robbins (New York: Oxford UP, 1981).

11. I am thinking here specifically of such writers on feminism and identity politics such as Gloria Anzaldúa, Angela Davis and bell hooks and post-colonial critics such as Gayatri Spivak. One tantalizing moment that suggests what such an intersection might look like occurs in a conversation between bell hooks and Barbara Bowen on sixteenth century misogynist literature and Shaharazad Ali's *Black Man's Guide to Understanding the Black Woman*, recounted by bell hooks in *Breaking Bread: Insurgent Black Intellectual Life,* eds. bell hooks and Cornel West (Boston: South Bend Press, 1991), 88.

12. in Jean E. Howard et al., eds., *Shakespeare Reproduced: The Text in History and Ideology* (New York: Methuen, 1987), 148.

13. I make these claims with some qualifications. Newman's study is very much concerned with the way black and white work against each other in miscegenative pairings. However, the effect is to locate "race" in Othello and "gender" in Desdemona.

14. See Basil Davidson, *The African Slave Trade* (Boston: Little Brown Company, 1980), 70-71 (originally entitled, *The Black Mother*).

15. Peter Fryer, *Staying Power: The History of the Black People in Britain* (London and Sydney: Pluto Press, 1984), 10.

16. James Walvin, *The Black Presence: A Documentary History of the Negro in England: 1550-1860* (New York: Schocken Books, 1972), 65.

17. William Shakespeare, *The Merchant of Venice,* ed. Horace Howard Furness (New York: Dover Publications, 1964); originally published 1888.

18. William Shakespeare, *The Merchant of Venice,* eds. Arthur Quiller-Couch and John Dover Wilson (Cambridge: Cambridge UP, 1926), 158.

19. I do not rule out a topical allusion. One could consider it a reference to the infamous case of the black woman, Maria, impregnated and abandoned

by Drake and his crew on his third circumnavigation: "Drake left behind him upon this island two negroes . . . and likewise the negro wench Maria. She being gotten with child in the ship and now being very great was left here on the island, which Drake named the isle Francisco after one of the negroes" (196). There is no way of knowing how long such an incident would remain in the public memory. William Camden's 1625 *Annales* records castigations of Drake for this and other actions on that voyage. See John Hampden, ed. *Francis Drake: Privateer: Contemporary Narratives and Documents.* (Alabama: The U of Alabama P, 1972).

20. Peter Stallybrass, "Patriarchal Territories: The Body Enclosed" in *Rewriting the Renaissance: The Discourses of Sexuality in Early Modern Europe,* eds. Margaret W. Ferguson, Maureen Quilligan, and Nancy J. Vickers (Chicago and London: U of Chicago P, 1986), 142.

21. Patricia Hill Collins, *Black Feminist Thought: Knowledge, Consciousness and the Politics of Empowerment* (Boston: Unwyn Hyman, 1990), 76-77. See also Angela Davis, "Racism, Birth Control and Reproductive Rights" in *Women, Race and Class* (New York: Vintage, 1981).

22. Gloria T. Hull, Patricia Bell Scott, and Barbara Smith, *All the Women are White, All the Men are Black, But Some of us are Brave* (New York: The Feminist Press at CUNY, 1982).

23. Richard Hakluyt, *The Principle Voyages, Traffiques and Discoveries of the English Nation,* 12 Vols (Glasgow: James MacLehose and Sons, 1903-05), 57.

24. Vita Sackville-West, ed., *The Diary of Lady Anne Clifford* (London: William Heinemann, 1923), n. p.

James R. Aubrey (essay date 1993)

SOURCE: "Race and the Spectacle of the Monstrous in *Othello,*" in *CLIO,* Vol. 22, No. 3, Spring, 1993, pp. 221-38.

[*In the essay below, Aubrey attempts to show that Shakespeare's construction of Othello's character would have "engaged such popular associations of blacks with monsters and thereby would have intensified audience responses to early performances."*]

Whoever believed in the Ethiopians before actually seeing them?

Pliny

Near the end of *The Tempest,* Antonio jests that the monster Caliban "is a plain fish, and no doubt marketable." As an earlier remark in the play makes clear, however, Caliban would be valuable not only in a fishmarket but also as an exotic creature for display at court, "a present for any emperor that ever trod on neat's leather."[1] When Shakespeare was writing *Othello,* his attraction to Cinthio's narrative about a black Moor in Venice may likewise have been a playwright's recognition that Othello's skin color would give him a "marketable," spectacular charge on the stage, as a character whose appearance marked him as Other, as having originated somewhere beyond the boundaries of the familiar. Although blacks had appeared on stage in earlier English plays, such roles were still extraordinary in 1604, when *Othello* was probably first performed.[2] The opening scene of the play further exoticizes Othello with its references to him not by name but as "the Moor," and as an "extravagant and wheeling stranger" (1.1.58 and 1.1.37). Blacks were outsiders in a more profound sense as well, at this time, for they were associated in the popular imagination with monsters, so that the play's numerous references to monstrosity would have resonated with Othello's racial characteristics to establish his extreme difference from typical Europeans. Whether some biographical Shakespeare actually considered such ideas "marketable" is not a question I can answer, but I will show that Othello's character is constructed in a way that would have engaged such popular associations of blacks with monsters and thereby would have intensified audience responses to early performances.

From the thirteenth century, monstrous races were increasingly reported to be living in Africa rather than in Asia, as Rudolf Wittkower notes.[3] Other critics have suggested that the English in the early 1600s still thought of blacks much as they thought of monsters, as strange creatures from outside the boundaries of the known world. Michael Neill touches the issue when he discusses linkage between blackness and moral monstrosity.[4] Emily C. Bartels locates Othello's power as a character partly in the audience's perception of his racial difference, on the basis of which people "demonize an Other as a means of securing the self."[5] Karen Newman asserts that there is a cultural association of blacks with monsters: by virtue of his color, "Othello is a monster in the Renaissance sense of the word."[6] Although precise attitudes in the early seventeenth century are not recoverable, documents from that time can enable us to understand more about what constituted this "Renaissance sense" of Othello's monstrousness.

The most useful evidence is, of course, contemporaneous with *Othello.* An example is the pamphlet translated in 1605 by Edward Gresham, who summarizes the contents in an arresting title:

> *Strange fearful & true news, which happened at Carlstadt, in the kingdom of Croatia. Declaring how the sun did shine like blood nine days together, and how two armies were seen in the Air, the one encountering the other. And how also a Woman was delivered of three prodigious sons, which Prophesied many strange & fearful things, which should shortly come to pass.*

Whether or not Gresham's London bookseller believed the report to be true, he evidently believed that there was a paying readership for such "news" and sold it with a cover illustration just as sensational as the contents (Figure 1). The cover visually represents the battle in the air and the three "prodigious sons," described inside as follows: "The first of these Prodigious Children had four heads, which spoke and uttered strange things. The second Child was black like a Moor, and the third Child like unto Death." Depicted as fully grown and articulate, these newly-born "children" prophesy eventual defeat of the Turks and a time of dearth "both here and in other places." Devout buyers no doubt took the pamphlet seriously; others probably bought it for the kind of textual pleasures available today from supermarket tabloids. The predicted conflict in Croatia may seem ironic to historians of the late twentieth century, but of more historical interest is the cover's use of black skin as a sign of monstrosity, indeed, as the child's only monstrous characteristic.

Social anthropologists would say that this idea, that blacks and monsters are related, if not equated, on some level of the popular imagination, constituted part of early modern London's "habitus," what Pierre Bourdieu defines as "a system of lasting, transposable dispositions which, integrating past experiences, functions at every moment as a *matrix of perceptions, appreciations, and actions,*" or more simply, "a socially constituted system of cognitive and motivating structures."[7] If there was a social disposition in 1604-5 to regard blacks and monsters as similar manifestations of the Other, as *Strange News* implies that there was, such a disposition would have affected both the generation and the reception of *Othello* at that historical moment. Indeed, as parts of the same habitus, each text simultaneously reflected and reinforced that very mental linkage.

Strange News and *Othello* are by no means the only documents of the late-sixteenth or early-seventeenth century to connect blacks and monsters. In 1569 *Histoires Prodigeuses* was translated as *Certain Secret Wonders of Nature,* in which Pierre Boiastuau rehearsed various explanations for "monstrous childbearing" including "the influence of the stars," the "superabundance or default and corruption of the seed and womb," or "an ardent and obstinate imagination, which the Woman hath, whilst she conceives the child." Boiastuau illustrates this last cause both verbally and visually, first with two anecdotes:

> Damascenus a grave author doth assure this to be true, that being present with Charles, the iiv. Emperor and king of *Bohemia,* there was brought to him a maid, rough and covered with hair like a bear, the which the mother had brought forth in so hideous and deformed a shape, by having too much regard to the picture of S[aint] John clothed with a beast's skin, the which was tied or made fast continually during her conception at her bed's feet. By the like means Hippocrates saved a princess accused of adultery, for that she was delivered of a child black like an *Ethiopian,* her husband being of a fair and white complexion, which by the persuasion of Hippocrates, was absolved and pardoned, for that the child was like unto a [picture of a] *Moor,* accustomably tied at her bed.[8]

If the first child had been the offspring of hirsute parents, or if the second child had been the offspring of an adulterous, interracial union, they would not have been considered monsters. Boiastuau considers them to be monstrous because of the "unnatural" intervention by the female imagination during the process of conception. Whether or not Shakespeare read Boiastuau, he would have recognized in this folk-theory of teratogenesis a consistency with the Biblical story he cites in *The Merchant of Venice,* the story of Jacob's intervention to produce parti-colored lambs by placing striped wands in front of ewes while they mate (1.3.75-85).

Boiastuau's contemporary Ambroise Paré, in his treatise *Of Monsters and Prodigies,* recounts a story that is similar to Boiastuau's but which reverses the colors, as a white child is born to black parents:

> We have read in *Heliodorus* that *Persiana,* Queen of *Ethiopia,* by her husband *Hidustes,* being also an Ethiope, had a daughter of a white complexion, because in the embraces of her husband, by which she proved with child, she earnestly fixed her eye and mind upon the picture of the fair *Andromeda* standing opposite to her.[9]

Here, too, it is not the color but the extraordinary process by which the child's skin color is determined that gives this child the status of monster, the fact that its "formation is contrary to the general rule and to what is usual"—as Aristotle once defined monstrosities.[10]

The illustrations in both Paré and Boiastuau, however, unlike the verbal texts, suggest that black skin alone could constitute a sign of monstrosity (Figures 2 and 3). Regardless of who the illustrators may have been, or whether the second copied the first, both chose to depict as a monster—along with the hairy girl—the black child born to white parents rather than the white one born to black parents. The illustrators must on some level have recognized that for a white audience of readers, the representation of a white child-monster would appear "normal" rather than "monstrous" until one had read the accompanying narratives. The illustrators' artistic decision to show only the black child points to the existence of a deep cultural centrism, linked with what would come to be known as racial identity, centrism of a kind which is likely also to have shaped audience responses to the still extraordinary sight of a black person seen on the street—or represented on the stage of a predominantly white culture such as France or England.

It is hard to imagine that Shakespeare is not deliberately exploiting such Anglo-centrism in the way he prepares an audience for Othello's entrance. In the first scene, Iago awakens Brabantio with the cry that "an old black ram / Is tupping your white ewe" (1.1.89-90)—an image of Othello and Desdemona intended to horrify her father. Iago next represents their sexual union as "your daughter cover'd with a Barbary horse" (1.1.112). Desdemona's imagined mating with an African animal is the kind of act which

Paré describes among the causes of monsters, a "copulation with beasts" that leads to "the confusion of seed of diverse kinds" (25.982). Reminding her father that Othello and Desdemona may be generating monsters, Iago further baits Brabantio, "you'll have your nephews neigh to you," then reinforces the idea with a final image of Othello and Desdemona during sexual intercourse with the conventional figure of "the beast with two backs" (1.1.112-18). The first scene of the play thus prepares an audience verbally for the entrance of some "thing" that is not-human; that this "Barbary horse" will turn out to be more human than Iago—who initially seems to be the audience's kinsman—is an irony that can prove as unsettling as Gulliver's discovery that Houyhnhnms behave like people and the creatures that look like himself behave like animals.

In scene two, the metaphors applied to Othello take on more social and political overtones. Brabantio addresses Othello as a "foul thief" whose enchantment of his daughter has led her to flee from "the wealthy curled darling of our nation" to "the sooty bosom / Of such a thing as thou" (1.2.62-72). Although the word "thing" is in accord with Iago's earlier beauty-and-beast metaphors, Brabantio seems to see Othello's offense as more political than personal, a transgression of the boundaries of acceptable behavior in Venetian culture because Othello's "sooty" color marks him as ineligible to compete legitimately for Desdemona with the white males of "our nation." Anthropologist Robin Fox has observed that "[g]roups speaking the same language and being alike in other ways might well exchange wives among themselves—but the connubium stopped at the boundaries of the language, territory, or colour, or whatever marked 'us' off from 'them.'"[11] A marriage between an African black and a Venetian white would have seemed clearly beyond the bounds of acceptable exogamy to Shakespeare's audience—especially to the white, aristocratic males, whose marital options in England Lawrence Stone has described as "very limited" in social and geographical range and reflecting "a very high degree of social and economic endogamy."[12] Even without the language depicting Othello as less than human, then, Desdemona's unauthorized choice of husband would itself have seemed socially and politically "monstrous."

Persons watching the play would not yet appreciate Othello's virtues when he appears at court in Scene Three, so his self-justification must persuade a theater audience as well as the Duke of Venice. To indicate how he captivated Desdemona, Othello mentions two exotic races he has told her about: "The Anthropophagi, and men whose heads / Do grow beneath their shoulders" (1.3.146-47). Desdemona evidently has responded to his exotic stories with awe:

> She swore in faith 'twas strange, 'twas passing strange,
> 'Twas pitiful, 'twas wondrous pitiful.
> She wish'd she had not heard it, yet she wish'd
> That heaven had made her such a man.
>
> (1.3.161-64)

Desdemona's response to the "wondrous" and "strange" narratives is confused with her response to the wonderful stranger who narrates them; as she puts it, the tales themselves "woo her" (1.3.168). Shakespeare gives Othello's wooing additional credibility by including exotic but recognizable travel lore such as the anthropophagi, which Montaigne had recently written about in his essay "Of Cannibals." The headless monsters were formerly described by Pliny as "some people without necks, having their eyes in their shoulders," in ancient India; but they also had been described in the more recent, 1582 edition of Mandeville's *Travels,* where they were illustrated (Figure 4), and in Hakluyt's expanded *Voyages* published between 1598 and 1600, where Sir Walter Raleigh was said to have been assured that headless monsters could be found just two rivers away from the place he was visiting in Guiana.[13] If the existence of this monstrous race was commonly thought to have been validated by recent travelers to remote places, then surely theatergoers—the auditors of Othello's auditors—would, like Desdemona, have found the teller as exotic as his tales.

Of course, Othello's most obvious difference is his skin color, a sign of his African origin. Pliny once remarked, "Whoever believed in the Ethiopians before actually seeing them?" (511), and black Africans seem not to have lost their associations with such marvels by 1581, when Stephen Bateman in his *Doom Warning All Men to the Judgment* turned first to Africa in his catalogue of monsters whose existence testifies to God's continuing punishment of man. Bateman's catalogue includes *Negritae,* with lips that hang down to their breasts, who are labeled in the margin as "Black Monsters," and what seems to be something of a catch-all:

> *Ethiopes* a people in the west part of Ethiopia: also there are of those black men, that have four eyes: and it is said that in Eripia be found very comely bodied men, notwithstanding they are long necked, and mouthed as a crane, the other part of the head like a man: also sundry strange and deformed men and women there are, which we omit. . . .[14]

However suspect such reports may have become by the late sixteenth century, they still were being published and read. Even if Othello was not considered to be a Batemanesque "black monster" himself, as an African he might have been assumed to know first hand about monstrous races.

There seems to have been further confusion over, or failure to distinguish between, traditional races of monsters in far-off lands and the occasional birth closer to home of a monstrous, individual child. Readers could find discussion of both kinds of monster in James Rueff's treatise *The Expert Midwife,* translated into English in 1637, whose chapter "Of Unperfect Children, Also of Monstrous Births" contains both a description of a terribly deformed, yet human child born in Oxford in 1551, and a description of a beast with a man's head, a beast's tail, and dogs' heads at its elbows and knees, followed by a description of a mythical creature with two wings and one foot. Rueff notes that such misshapen offspring must be manifestations of God's will but that "through the insight of our reason, we may perceive also the detestable sin of Sodomy." Rueff's assumption that particular births of monsters indicate breeding between humans and animals suggests that he considers even animal-like monsters to be individual cases rather the offspring of monstrous races, but he goes on to mention Pliny's "reports of living creatures in Africa that have such various forms and shapes."[15] Even Rueff seems unwilling to let go completely of the older explanations of monsters that associates them, like Blacks, with Africa.

Anthropologists have noticed a relation between attitudes toward such outsiders and stories of monsters. Claude Lévi-Strauss refers to the Gobineau hypothesis as a way of accounting for the proliferation of fantastic beings in a culture as less the result of rich imagination than of "the inability of fellow-citizens to conceive of strangers in the same way as themselves."[16] Othello as "blackamoor" is visibly marked as a member of a culture different from that of everyone else on the stage or in the audience; he may have seemed as fantastic as the monsters associated with him.

There is another kind of historical evidence on which to base an inference that theatergoers would have felt a thrill of disturbed awe at the sight of Othello: the fact that a black person would still have been an unusual sight to most English theatergoers. The exact size of the black population in England at the turn of the seventeenth century is uncertain, and historians are reluctant even to guess, but there is no doubt that their numbers had been growing over the forty years since the first West Africans had been introduced to London in 1563.[17] Ruth Cowhig has written that "there were several hundreds of black people living in the households of the aristocracy and landed gentry, or working in London taverns," so she imagines that "the sight of black people must have been familiar to Londoners."[18] Even if most Londoners had seen blacks, however, the appearance on stage of a black person who spoke and felt must still have seemed remarkable. And even if blacks were visible on the streets, they may not have been accepted as "familiar." Parish records from Barking for 1 October 1599 show two blacks living in the parish of All Hallows: "'Clare a Negra at Widdow S[tokes?]" and "M[a]ry a Negra at Richard Wood.'" W. E. Miller used this in 1961 as evidence that there were Blacks in London in 1599, a point no longer in doubt; what is more interesting is that the two blacks are further described not as inhabitants but as "'Straungers' in the parish."[19] This word may be merely an expression of parochialism, a reference to the fact that they were not locally born, but the term also suggests that they were thought of in terms of their "otherness."

The 1601 draft of a royal proclamation further indicates the extent to which blacks in England were thought of as "strangers" at the turn of the seventeenth century. Endorsed by Queen Elizabeth, the document authorizes the transportation to Spain or Portugal of any "Negroes and blackamoors . . . within the realm of England." She justifies this action partly in terms of the precedent of prisoner exchanges, the tradition that a captive may be enslaved by the victor in warfare. A second justification is a perception of social unrest. Both these arguments are based on an assumption of cultural centrism and racial difference:

> Whereas the Queen's majesty, tendering the good and welfare of her own natural subjects, greatly distressed in these hard times of dearth, is highly discontented to understand the great number of Negroes and blackamoors which (as she is informed) are carried into this realm since the troubles between her highness and the King of Spain; who are fostered and powered here, to the great annoyance of her own liege people that which co[vet?] the relief which these people consume, as also for that the most of them are infidels having no understanding of Christ or his Gospel: hath given a special commandment that the said kind of people shall be with all speed avoided and discharged out of this her majesty's realms.[20]

The proclamation goes on to license Casper van Senden, a merchant who had rescued eighty-nine English subjects detained by Spain and Portugal, to take "such Negroes and blackamoors to be transported as aforesaid as he shall find within the realm of England." Van Senden is not authorized to use force, but if any persons "possessed of any such blackamoors . . . refuse to deliver them," the proclamation authorizes him to "advise and persuade them by all good means to satisfy her majesty's pleasure therein" and to report the names of anyone who refuses to cooperate.

The proclamation indicates that a black person can only be a servant, "possessed" by a master who should hand over the possession. Blacks are a "kind of people," different not only in color but also by virtue of their religion—rather, their lack of Christian religion—which makes them "infidels." The concern expressed in the proclamation is perhaps over their probable lack of political as well as religious fidelity, for the comment about infidels follows close upon a description of the English people as Elizabeth's "liege," or loyal subjects. And political concerns seem to be what have led at least some people to feel annoyed that blacks are "powered" as well as "fostered" at the expense of the English. The black population is said to be "great," but the document includes a parenthetical "as she is informed," perhaps indicating some doubt in Elizabeth's mind over the claimed growth in size of the black population. Or, the absence of a numerical estimate could be a deliberate omission, if the approximate number was small enough to have reduced the force of the argument that deportation of blacks would significantly ease the shortages of food.

The proclamation perhaps exaggerates the problems in order to further the financial interests of van Senden, who had been petitioning for this kind of support for more than four years.[21] Nevertheless, the arguments were evidently thought plausible enough by the court that the power of the monarchy was invoked to formally delineate a social boundary based on skin color and even to bring the power of the state to bear on racially-marked strangers in what amounted to a kind of cultural exorcism. Given the presence of such an attitude among the English toward blacks as unwelcome intruders, the character of Othello as both different from Venetians but powerful within that culture must have contained a particularly powerful social charge for those who originally watched *Othello*.

A perception of African blacks as "not English" would further have reinforced the idea that Africa is an exotic, mysterious world. In 1600 that world was of sufficient interest that John Leo's *A Geographical History of Africa* was translated into English and published in London. Leo was a Moor from Morocco who had converted to Christianity, according to John Pory's introduction.[22] His book had first been published in Italian around 1526.[23] Leo did not offer just one more traveler's rehearsal of sights mixed with legends but an ethnographer's report, sometimes describing particular details from particular kingdoms in a given geographical area, sometimes drawing inferences from the observations, and sometimes making moral judgments. Leo's "General Description" notes that there are five "principal nations" in that part of the world, the Cafri, the Abyssins, the Egyptians, the Arabians, and "the Africans or Moors, properly so called; which last are of two kinds, namely white or tawny Moors, and Negroes or black Moors."[24] Members of these groups can be found in various regions, he goes on to point out, but later, in Book Seven, he states that "the fifteen kingdoms of the land of the Negroes known to us, are all situated upon the river of Niger, and upon other rivers which fall thereunto" (285). In his description of these kingdoms, Leo is not inclined to offer sweeping judgments, but in his General Description he offers some statements about the vices of the people of Africa which would have reinforced English fears and stereotypes of blacks, attitudes implicit in phrases such as Ben Jonson's "quick Negro"[25] or Shakespeare's "lascivious moor" (1.1.126):

> The Negroes [compared to the "lewd" and "brutish" inhabitants of Libya] likewise lead a beastly kind of life, being utterly destitute of the use of reason, of dexterity of wit, and of all arts. Yea they so behave themselves, as if they had continually lived in a forest among wild beasts. They have great swarms of harlots among them; whereupon a man may easily conjecture their manner of living.
>
> (42)

Perhaps John Leo's tone of abhorrence is a sop to European readers, or perhaps the Western-educated Leo was feeling an urge to scrawl in the margin, "Exterminate all the brutes!" as Conrad's Kurtz would do in his report on dark Africa. In any case Leo's *History of Africa* tended to reinforce the European view of black moors as "beasts," and it was probably known to Shakespeare, as it certainly was to Jonson.[26] The book's London publication at the turn of the seventeenth century is one more event that helped to constitute the London habitus from which *Othello* emerged and into which it was received.

Much as associations of monsters and Blacks would have affected how a playgoer regarded Othello in the first act of the play, ideas about how monsters were conceived, carried, and delivered inform many other passages in the play and would further have shaped responses to characters on stage.

The language of monstrous childbearing appears frequently in the play, often in the tradition of prodigious births hinting at some ominous event to come. At the end of the first act of *Othello,* Iago appeals to Roderigo to plot with him against the Moor:

> [L]et us be conjunctive in our revenge against him; if thou canst cuckold him, thou does thyself a pleasure, and me a sport. There are many events in the womb of time, which will be deliver'd.
>
> (1.3.369-72)

Iago's description of time as a womb from which events will issue gives him a role something like that of Edward Gresham, the doomsday pamphleteer who warned that the monstrous births in *Strange News* portended future calamities. Iago is a more cheerful prophet, perhaps because he sees himself less as human victim than as divine ordinator of the supernatural events: "I have 't. It is engender'd. Hell and night / Must bring this monstrous birth to the world's light" (1.3.404-05). The emphasis is on the "I have 't." Iago, not God or the devil, is engendering, or conceiving the offspring. "Hell and night" are cast in the lesser role of midwives, as enabling rather than causative agents.

Iago's metaphor is noteworthy for its implied equivalence between an idea and a birth, a concept and a conception—a metaphor that will recur. The idea that the brain gives birth to thoughts as the body gives birth to children—or monsters—was well-embedded in the culture of early modern England. Other examples of the metaphor include the dedication of Shakespeare's sonnets to "their only begetter" and the complaint of Sidney's Astrophil that he feels "great with child to speake," as well as Thomas Underdowne's compliment to Edward DeVere: "in your Honour is, I think, expressed the right pattern of a Noble Gentleman, which in my head I have conceived."[27] In *Othello* the metaphor is used deliberately, almost literally, so that the comparison becomes explicit between mental conception and physical birth. Iago plays with the metaphor in Act Two, when Desdemona asks him to compose some lines of praise; he describes how his invention is taxing his brain, then announces: "But my Muse labours, / And thus she is deliver'd" (2.1.127-28). As the comparison is extended with reference to Iago's plot, however, playgoers are reminded of the metaphor's basis in ideas about biological generation, and they may also recall Iago's reference at the end of Act One to the impending "birth" as "monstrous"; as the metaphor becomes conscious, it helps to convey the morally monstrous nature of Iago's "conception."

In Act Three, Iago transfers the monstrous conception, which includes the idea of Desdemona's infidelity, from his own mind to Othello's. Othello comments in an aside that Iago seems to echo Othello's own doubts about Cassio, "[a]s if there were some monster in his thought, / Too hideous to be shown" (3.3.111-12). He then says to Iago that there must be some reason Iago has looked concerned as they were discussing Cassio:

> [Thou] didst contract and purse thy brow together,
> As if thou then hadst shut up in thy brain
> Some horrible conceit. . . .
> [Thou] weigh'st thy words, before thou giv'st them breath,
> Therefore these stops of thine fright me the more;
> For such things in a false disloyal knave
> Are tricks of custom, but in a man that's just
> They're close dilations, working from the heart
> That passion cannot rule.
>
> (1.3.118-29)

The first lines, about a "horrible conceit," seem an obvious continuation of the metaphorical language of generation that has previously represented Iago's thoughts as some hideous progeny awaiting birth, confined in the womb of his brain. The contracting and pursing of Iago's brow are symptoms of metaphorical labor to bring forth the offspring, to present the idea to Othello—who is afraid to see it. The description of Iago's pausing before giving breath to his words may also be a continuation of the birth imagery, as well as a literal declaration that Iago thinks before he speaks; although the "stops" Othello refers to are what he senses to be Iago's hesitations, that is, stoppages of the breath that gives voice to his thoughts, they also resemble the breathing of a prospective mother in labor. Indeed, this pattern of references to childbirth provides a justification for the Folio reading of "dilations" instead of the First Quarto's "denotements," since dilations (of the cervix) could be one more reference to the birth process, whose ineluctability "passion cannot rule." All these images of childbirth help to constitute an understanding that Iago is carrying a monstrous idea as a mother might carry a deformed child in her womb.

In subsequent lines of the play, however, Iago does not give birth to his monstrous thoughts but, somehow, transfers the metaphorical pregnancy to Othello. Perhaps the metaphor breaks down, here, since pregnancy could not (until the late twentieth century) be moved from one womb to another. Elizabeth Sacks has tried to explain the process of transfer as metaphorical "theft," first by showing that wombs were sometimes compared to purses in the seventeenth century, then by suggesting that Othello somehow, "psychosexually," has stolen Iago's "purse" of "trashy thoughts."[28] The pregnancy is not necessarily shifted from Iago to Othello, however, if one thinks of this mental conception, like physical conception, as a process requiring two partners. The idea that Desdemona has been unfaithful is generated by verbal intercourse between partners, analogous to sexual intercourse with Iago as male and Othello as female, impregnated through his ear. The conception process can be understood in terms of Aristotle's theories about the *Generation of Animals*, current well into the eighteenth century, according to which male seed is not simply deposited in the female, nor does it join with female seed in the womb, but it shapes the female seed. Aristotle describes the process with a comparison to carpentry, where the artisan forms wood into a shape but does not join himself with the material; "the active partner is not situated within the thing which is being formed" (113). As Thomas Laquer has summarized this way of understanding generation, "conception is for the male to have an idea, an artistic or artisanal conception, in the brain-uterus of the female."[29] Aristotle's theory would also allow the play's metaphorical impregnation of one male by another male to seem less strained, for in this traditional view of human generation, neither mind and body nor gender and sex were so clearly distinguished as they have since come to be. In *Othello,* then, the possibility that Desdemona has been unfaithful is the idea actively imparted by Iago, like a formative male seed, into the brain-uterus of Othello, whose tractable character provides the passive material to be shaped. Then, like a pregnant woman with a seemingly irrational desire for something, Othello insists that Desdemona show him the misplaced handkerchief decorated with strawberries—the fruit commonly associated with maternal cravings, the frustration of which could supposedly result in "strawberry marks" on children.[30] Othello's "maternal" imagination thus deforms the gestating conception of possible infidelity into the "green-eyed monster" of jealousy he had been warned to beware (3.3.170-72).

Although the metaphorical language is not perfectly consistent, this underlying idea that a monstrous birth is impending continues to inform the play. Later in Act Three, Othello refers to cuckoldry as a matter of destiny: "Even then this forked plague is fated to us / When we do quicken" (3.3.282-83). The audience hears a statement capable of another construction than Othello's intended fatalism, however, for he will be plagued when he suspects that he is a cuckold, when the green-eyed monster will "quicken" in the womb of his own brain. A few lines later Othello says, "I have a pain upon my forehead here" (3.3.290)—as the monstrous thought kicks in its mental womb, perhaps, or as Othello feels a mental contraction that anticipates the birth of the idea. In the next scene, Emilia repeats the comparison of jealousy to "a monster / Begot upon itself, born on itself," to which Desdemona replies "Heaven keep that monster from Othello's mind!" (3.4.161-63). Anyone attending to the play has heard enough auditory images to know that Othello already is bearing that very monster of a conception, as he announces to Desdemona in Act Five:

> . . . confess thee freely of thy sin;
> For to deny each article with oath
> Cannot remove, nor choke the strong conception,
> That I do groan withal. Thou art to die.
>
> (5.2.56-59)

For Othello to contemplate the murder is for his mental womb to labor painfully to give birth to its deformed "child"; his monstrous conception will issue forth as horrifying action.

Othello has always been one of Shakespeare's moving dramas, but it moves its audiences in different ways as their mentalities differ. A part of its effect when first performed in the early seventeenth-century England would have resided in the confused mixture of powerful ideas about monsters and about blacks circulating in the culture that was producing Shakespeare and *Othello,* as that culture was in turn being reproduced by them.

Notes

1. *The Complete Works of Shakespeare,* ed. David Bevington, 3d edition (Glenview, IL: Scott, Foresman, 1980), 5.1.269 (act 5, scene 1, line 269), and 2.2.70-71. Subsequent citations to Shakespeare's work are from this edition.

2. See Eldred Jones, *Othello's Countrymen: The African in English Renaissance Drama* (London: Oxford UP, 1965), 40-50, and M. R. Ridley, Introduction, *Othello,* Arden Shakespeare (London: Methuen, 1958), xv.

3. Rudolf Wittkower, "Marvels of the East: A Study in the History of Monsters," *Journal of the Warburg and Courtauld Institute* 5 (1942): 197.

4. Michael Neill, "Unproper Beds: Race, Adultery, and the Hideous in *Othello,*" *Shakespeare Quarterly* 40 (1989): 409.

5. Emily C. Bartels, "Making More of the Moor: Aaron, Othello, and Renaissance Refashionings of Race," *Shakespeare Quarterly* 41 (1990):454.

6. Karen Newman, "'And wash the Ethiop white': Femininity and the Monstrous in *Othello*" in *Shakespeare Reproduced: The Text in History and Ideology,* ed. Jean E. Howard and Marion F. O'Connor (New York: Methuen, 1987), 153.

7. Pierre Bourdieu, *Outline of a Theory of Practice,* trans. Richard Nice, *Cambridge Studies in Social Anthropology* 16 (1972; Cambridge: Cambridge UP, 1977), 76, 82-83.

8. Pierre Boiastuau, *Certain Secret Wonders of Nature,* trans. Edward Fenton (London, 1589), 13-14.

9. Ambroise Paré, in *Works,* trans. Thomas Johnson (London, 1634), 25.

10. Aristotle, *Generation of Animals,* trans. A. L. Peck (Cambridge, MA: Harvard UP, 1979), 439.

11. Robin Fox, *Kinship and Marriage: An Anthropological Perspective* (1967; Cambridge: Cambridge UP, 1983), 178.

12. Lawrence Stone, *The Family, Sex and Marriage in England: 1500-1800* (New York: Harper and Row, 1979), 60.

13. Pliny, *Natural History,* trans. H. Rackham (Cambridge, MA: Harvard UP), 2:521; John Mandeville, *The Travels of Sir John Mandeville,* trans. C. W. R. D. Moseley (1582; New York: Penguin, 1983), 137; Richard Hakluyt, *Voyages and Discoveries: The Principal Navigations Voyages, Traffiques and Discoveries of the English Nation,* ed. Jack Beeching (1598-1600; New York: Penguin, 1972), 402.

14. Stephen Bateman, *The Doom Warning All Men to the Judgment* (London, 1581), 6-7.

15. James Rueff, *The Expert Midwife, or an Excellent and most Necessary Treatise of the Generation and Birth of Man,* trans. E. Griffin (London, 1637), 157-58.

16. Claude Lévi Strauss, *The Elementary Structures of Kinship* (Boston: Beacon, 1969), 46.

17. James Walvin, *The Black Presence: A Documentary History of the Negro in England, 1555-1860* (London: Orbach and Chambers, 1971), 8, 12.

18. Ruth Cowhig, "Blacks in English Drama and the Role of Shakespeare's *Othello,*" in *The Black Presence in English Literature,* ed. David Dabydeen (Manchester, UK: Manchester UP, 1985), 5, 7.

19. W. E. Miller, "Negroes in Elizabethan London," *Notes and Queries* 206 (1961):138.

20. "Licensing Casper van Senden to Deport Negroes [draft]," Proclamation 804.5 (1601), in *Tudor Royal Proclamations,* ed. Paul L. Hughes and James F. Larkin (New Haven: Yale UP, 1969), 3:221.

21. See Cowhig, "Blacks in English Drama and the Role of Shakespeare's *Othello,*" 1-25.

22. *A Geographical History of Africa, Written in Arabic and Italian by John Leo a Moor, Born in Granada and Brought Up in Barbary,* trans. John Pory (London, 1600), not paginated.

23. See Winthrop D. Jordan, *The White Man's Burden: Historical Origins of Racism in the United States* (New York: Oxford UP, 1974), 18.

24. *A Geographical History of Africa,* 6.

25. Ben Jonson, *Volpone,* ed. Alvin Kernan (New Haven: Yale UP), 3.7.232.

26. Jones, *Othello's Countrymen: The African in English Renaissance Drama,* 21.

27. For a discussion of Shakespeare as the begetter of the sonnets, see Donald W. Foster, "Master W. H., R. I. P.," *PMLA* 102 (1987): 42-54; Philip Sidney, *The Poems of Sir Philip Sidney,* ed. William A. Ringler, Jr. (Oxford: Clarendon, 1962), 165; Thomas Underdowne, "Epistle Dedicatory, to the Right Honorable Edward Devere," *An Ethiopian Historie* (London, no date [1569]), no pagination.

28. Elizabeth Sacks, *Shakespeare's Images of Pregnancy* (London: MacMillan, 1980), 71.

29. Thomas Laquer, *Making Sex: Body and Gender from the Greeks to Freud* (Cambridge, MA: Harvard UP, 1990), 42.

30. *Othello* 3.3.439; see Henry Fielding, *Joseph Andrews,* ed. Homer Goldberg (New York: Norton, 1987), 176.

Margo Hendricks (essay date 1996)

SOURCE: "'The Moor of Venice,' or The Italian on the Renaissance English Stage," in *Shakespearean Tragedy and Gender*, edited by Shirley Nelson Garner and Madelon Sprengnether, Indiana University Press, 1996, pp. 193-209.

[*In the following essay, Hendricks explores the importance of Venice as the play's setting, and proposes that Venice is "a crucial yet often critically neglected racial persona in Othello."*]

A number of critics have read *Othello* principally with an eye toward illuminating the moral sense of the problematic racial and sexual politics engendered not only by the play's depiction of what is viewed as an interracial marriage but also by Othello's sensationalized murder of his wife, Desdemona.[1] The obstacle facing all such critical readings, as Michael Neill astutely points out, is that the play itself conspicuously denies us (even as it denies Othello) an opportunity to enact "the funeral dignities that usually serve to put a form of [moral] order upon such spectacles of ruins," creating an "ending [that is] perhaps the most shocking in Shakespearean tragedy" (383-412). Neill concludes that it is the final tragic scene, where "white" Desdemona is murdered and her husband/murderer, "black" Othello, violently avenges her murder—"I took by th'throat the circumcised dog / And smote him thus" (5.2.351-52)[2]—which most "articulate[s] the [racial] anxiety evident almost everywhere in the play's history—a sense of scandal that informs the textual strategies of editors and theatrical productions as much as it does the disturbed reactions of audiences and critics" (384).

Feminist scholars have made clear that this "scandal" actually begins long before this most "unnatural" ending to the marriage of Othello and Desdemona. For example, Patricia Parker sees the "simultaneously eroticized and epistemological impulse to open up to show" the "'fantasies' of race and gender" in *Othello* as an anxiety-ridden linkage of female sexuality and the exotic narratives of "African or New World discovery" (92), while Janet Adelman argues that the "whole of his exchange with Desdemona demonstrates Othello's terrible conflict between his intense desire for fusion with the woman he idealizes as the nurturant source of his being and his equally intense conviction that her participation in sexuality has contaminated her and thus contaminated the perfection that he has vested in her" (66-67). What has become obvious in these recent studies of *Othello*, as Valerie Traub contends, is that "Othello's anxiety is culturally and psychosexually overdetermined by erotic, gender, and racial anxieties, including . . . the fear of chaos [usually] associate[d] with sexual activity."[3] In what follows, I wish to reconsider the possibilities of reading the racial and sexual anxieties latent in Shakespeare's *Othello*. The focus of my discussion is not so much the personal relationships represented in the play as it is the cultural assumptions which may be coincident with the notion of race in *Othello*; in particular, I want to argue the possibility that the social site of Shakespeare's tragedy, Venice, is a much more significant *player* in the construction of early modern English racialist ideology than critics have hitherto illuminated. Simply stated, my purpose is to show that Venice is a crucial yet often critically neglected racial persona in *Othello*.[4]

My reading builds upon and diverges from studies that examine Shakespeare's use of Italian city-states, in particular Venice, in his dramatic works—a usage which, according to these critics, highlights an Elizabethan "fascination" with Italian culture.[5] In the case of Venice, this fascination is rooted in, as David C. McPherson terms it, the "myth of Venice," wherein the city is perceived as a state whose wealth, political stability, justice, and civility set it above all others (27). This image, of course, has its origins in early modern Italian political theories whose principal goal was to conceptualize a model civil society that "was to be paradigmatic for [Italian] civic humanism" (Pocock 271). In these theories Venice is represented as an uncorrupted, tranquil, and stable state, in fact, "Venice appears, both physically and politically, 'rather framed by the hands of the immortal Gods, than any way by the arte, industry or inuention of men.'"[6] Ultimately, as J. G. A. Pocock has shown, this "myth of Venice (at its most mythical) was to lie in the assertion that the Venetian commonwealth was an immortally serene, because perfectly balanced, combination of the three elements of monarchy, aristocracy, and democracy" (102).

It is my contention that this myth inheres in Shakespeare's *Othello* and exercises a "compulsive force on the imagination," of both the characters within the play and the audience watching events unfold. But, because it is a mythology, "framed by the hands, . . . arte, industry, [and] invention of men," the ideal of Venice is also a paradox which ultimately subverts its illusion of perfection by drawing attention not only to the dichotomies (pure/impure, black/white) it constructs but also to the interiority that the myth and its dichotomies seek to conceal (Pocock 102). In other words, while the myth extols an image of Venice as the idealized feminine body, beautiful, desirable, and virginal, it also vicariously projects an image of Venice as the imperfect body—corruptive, desiring, and easily violated. If, as Patricia Parker argues, "the gaze is a vicarious gaze, a substitution of narrative" (89), then our attempt to discern how this paradox works racially must make use of this vicarious perspective.

"The Cunning Whore of Venice"

Lewes Lewkenor's 1599 translation of Gasparo Contarini's *De Magistratibus et Republica Venetorum* (along with Thomas Coryat's *Crudities*) did much to circulate this particular variant of the "myth of Venice" in Elizabethan and Jacobean England. In his dedication to the reader, Lewkenor writes that visitors to Venice, at least those "of a grauer humor,"

> would dilate of the greatnes of their Empire, the grauitie of their prince, the maiesty of their Senate, the vnuiola-

Powys Thomas as the Duke of Venice, William Needles as Brabantio, Douglas Campbell as Othello, and Douglas Rain as Iago in the 1959 Stratford Festival production of Othello.

blenes of their lawes, their zeale in religion, and lastly their moderation, and equitie, wherewith they gouerne such subiected prouinces as are vnder their dominion, binding them therby in a faster bond of obedience then all the cytadels, garrisons, or whatsoeuer other tyrannicall inuentions could euer haue brought them vnto. (A2)

Lewkenor uses the dedication to set the context for his dilation of the greatness of Venice and to encourage his readers to gaze upon the book as if it were the city itself. Characterized as a "pure and vntouched virgine, free from the taste or violence of any forraine enforcement," Venice is laid open for the "admiration" and entertainment of the book's English readers. Though not often viewed as a narrative of discovery, Lewkenor's text might well be included in that genre, as it has in common with other narratives of discovery what Patricia Parker calls "the language of opening, uncovering or bringing to light . . . what had been secret, closed or hid" from the majority of the English reading public whose travels were limited to environs of London (87).

Of course, Venice is neither Africa nor the "New World," and Lewkenor's dedication to the reader of *The Commonwealth and Gouernment of Venice* is intended merely to set the stage for his translation of a work of political philosophy. Even so, the edition circulates conflicting images of the republic known as *La Serenissima*. In contrast to Lewkenor's praise of Venice's "unblemished" status, the commendatory poems written in praise of Lewkenor's endeavor convey a somewhat different vision of Venice. For example, one poem compares Venice to the "antique" cities of Babel, "fallen" "with the weight of their own furquedry." In another poem, though her "virgins state ambition nere could blot," the "swarmes" from "forrein nation[s]" prompt the writer to proclaim Venice's "ruinous case" which, of course, is reflected in the city's "painted face." Ironically, what is intended to honor the celebrated myth of Venetian stability and invulnerability, Lewkenor's dedication and the commendatory poems, actually draws attention to what stands behind the myth—Venice's notoriety as a site of illicit sexuality, dangerous passions, violence, and extraordinary cunning.

Thomas Coryat's *Crudities* exhibits a similar ambivalence toward Venice. In the account of his travel to Italy in 1608, Coryat begins with a description of Venice as "the fairest Lady," a "noble citie" (311). After a rather detailed description of the magnificence of Venice's architecture, Coryat interrupts his narrative to warn his readers to be wary of the city's gondoliers, who are "the most vicious and licentious varlets about all the City" (311). Coryat's warning is typical of his tendency to juxtapose an image of Venice as "this thrice worthie city . . . yea the richest Paragon" with an image of Venice as a city whose blatant acceptance of sexuality (the seeming valorization of the courtesans and the touted infidelity of Venetian wives) and violence denotes the "Virgin's" corruptibility. Coryat's maneuver serves strategically, as Ann Rosalind Jones suggests, as both a lure and an admonition: "Coryat writes with a double agenda: to thrill his readers and to protect their morals, to sell his book with the promise of titillation and to dignify it by setting his ethical seriousness as an Englishman against the variety of 'Ethnicke' types he encounters" (104). Jones rightly observes that the Venice "of English [writers such as Coryat] from the 1580s on was not a geographer's record but a fantasy setting for dramas of passion, Machiavellian politics, and revenge—a landscape of the mind" (110). For Coryat and others, within this "landscape of the mind" it is the "interplay of pleasure and danger" (Jones 102) posed by Venice's gendered and Janus-like status within European culture that must be castigated and the city reclaimed as the paradigm of cultural perfection.[7] And it is this gendered "interplay" that Shakespeare distills in *Othello*, coupling the metaphoric blackness of Venice's reputation as a site of feminine sexual corruption and the literalness of Moorish Othello's black skin with the unstained honor of the Venetian military commander Othello and the symbolic whiteness of an uncorrupted Venice. Shakespeare's *Othello* joins these other early modern English texts in presenting a perspective of Venice that satisfies the desire to see encompassed in one racialized body, even if vicariously, both the virgin and the whore. And that body belongs, of course, to a woman.

"Desdemona's Choice"

From the play's inception, when Brabantio reprimands Iago for his indecent language and both Roderigo and Iago for their disruption of Brabantio's peace—"What, tell'st thou me of robbing? this is Venice, my house is not a grange" (1.1.105-106)—the paradoxical "myth of Venice" is instantiated as a paradigm for reading the play's presumed sexual and racial deviances. Brabantio's words obviously are intended to correct what he perceives to be a misperception on the part of Iago, namely that there are no farm animals in his house. Significantly, Brabantio's rebuke conjures images of the Venice, *La Serenissima*, extolled in Lewkenor's translation, as the tone of Brabantio's declaration suggests that such a crime could never take place in Venice, and, more important, that Roderigo's and Iago's accusations of a barnyard theft would not have been brought surreptitiously to the victim's door in the middle of the night. Brabantio's reprimand indicates that he is a man possessed of the judicious gravity praised in Lewkenor's preface: a man whose "moderation and equitie" will lead him to behave rationally when confronted by what appears to be the irrational pranks of a spurned suitor.

Once he understands the implication of Iago's salacious words, however, Brabantio begins to exhibit the stereotypical irrationality which came to be a metaphoric staple of Jacobean dramatic depictions of Italians. Governed by his fury, Brabantio accuses Othello of sorcery or witchcraft even before the marriage is confirmed by the couple: "is there not charms, / By which the property of youth and maidhood, / May be abused? Have you not read, Roderigo, / Of such a thing?" (1.1.171-74) When we consider Brabantio's grave "This is Venice," the sight of the rational "senator's" descent into illogic is somewhat surprising as he attempts to explain what he perceives to be unexplainable:

> My daughter, O my daughter, . . .
> She is abus'd, stol'n from me and corrupted,
> By spells and medicines, bought of mountebanks,
> For nature so preposterously to err,
> (Being not deficient, blind, or lame of sense,)
> Sans witchcraft could not.
>
> (1.3.60-64)

Brabantio's "My daughter, O my daughter" poignantly recalls Solanio's account of Shylock's pained cry at Jessica's elopement with Lorenzo—"My daughter! O my ducats! O my daughter!—" and Shylock's own descent into irrationality (*MV* 2.8.15). Given Desdemona's position as only child and heir to Brabantio's estate, a situation analogous to Jessica's in *The Merchant of Venice*, it is not without significance that Shakespeare alludes to this earlier work in depicting a father's reaction to the news that his daughter has married without his approval and apparently to someone outside her ethnic community.

Shakespeare draws one other parallel between Brabantio and Shylock, in that both men seek to exploit the strict terms of Venetian law to extract justice from their perceived enemies. When he finally confronts Othello, Brabantio tells the general, "I therefore apprehend and do attach thee" (1.2.77).[8] In this moment, the rational Venetian has displaced the irrational father who has roused his "kindred" to pursue the couple. Once he has Othello in custody, Brabantio is confident that he will be able to prove Othello guilty of witchcraft and that the Venetian legal institution will prove "pure and uncorrupted" as it evaluates the truth of his accusation. And, not unexpectedly, when Venetian law appears, in the persona of the Duke, it reaffirms Brabantio's faith in its exactitude:

> Whoe'er he be, that in this foul proceeding
> Hath thus beguil'd your daughter of herself,
> And you of her, the bloody book of law
> You shall yourself read, in the bitter letter,
> After its own sense, though our proper son
> Stood in your action
>
> (1.3.65-69)

No matter the cost, Brabantio is being guaranteed that the "penal Lawes [will be] most unpardonably executed" (Pocock 325).

Whatever Brabantio's cause, when Othello is named the guilty party, the senators who have accompanied the Duke respond to Brabantio's accusation in a rather cryptic fashion: "We are very sorry for't" (1.3.73). This comment can, of course, be interpreted in one of two ways. First, it can be seen as an expression of regret that Othello's service will be lost to Venice, given the political tensions that exist between Venetians and Turks. Or it can be read as an expression of compassion for Brabantio and the loss of his daughter in the manner he has described. I would propose that the former reading (regret at the loss of Othello's service to Venice) is the more likely intent behind the senators' words. When Othello and Brabantio first come into the presence of the Duke and senators, one senator refers to Othello as "the valiant Moor." More telling of the esteem Othello has in Venice is the Duke's reaction after hearing Othello's narrative, when the Duke exhorts Brabantio to "Take up this mangled matter at the best; / Men do their broken weapons rather use, / Than their bare hands" (1.3.172-74). Brabantio's refusal to comply with the Duke's admonition is, as Lynda Boose argues, a refusal to "act out," to ritualize the symbolic transfer of his daughter to her husband not because Othello is necessarily unworthy but because the selection of Desdemona's husband was not Brabantio's: that right had been usurped by his daughter ("Father and Daughter" 327).

Desdemona's choice of a husband has been the object of critical gaze ever since Thomas Rymer first questioned Shakespeare's use of a "Blackamoor" as the tragic protagonist in *Othello:* whether in M. R. Ridley's introduction to the Arden edition of *Othello,* where Ridley writes, "It is the very essence of the play that Desdemona in marrying Othello—a man to whom her 'natural' reaction should (her father holds) have been fear, not delight—has done something peculiarly startling" (liii), or in Stanley Cavell's careful explanation that, in choosing Othello, Desdemona has "overlooked his blackness in favor of his inner brilliance": in effect, "that she saw his visage as he sees it, that she understands his blackness as he understands it, as the expression (or in his word, his manifestation) of his mind" (129).

Complicating these, and other, critical attempts to explain Desdemona's choice is the fact that Shakespeare's play presents a world whose very social codes are frequently contradictory and conflicting, thus enabling Desdemona to act as she does. On one level, Venice is a place where the contagious rhetoric of racialism can easily destroy lives and careers, as Iago's manipulation so aptly illustrates. Yet it seems that early modern Venice is also a society where a man such as Othello can achieve success and fame to such a degree that a duke is moved to declare, "I think this tale would win my daughter too" (1.3.171). Othello's status and position, that is, his "honours and valiant parts" (1.3.253), prove as desirable to Desdemona as the narratives for which "She gave . . . a world of sighs" (1.3.159) and . . ." lov'd [Othello] for the dangers [he] had pass'd" (1.3.167).

Though a Moor, Othello is perceived as a valuable member of Venetian society and his action as nothing more than "a *mischief* that is past and gone" [emphasis mine] (1.3.204). Emily Bartels rightfully argues that Othello's acceptance includes Iago, who "even as he attempts to prove Othello the outsider, . . . represents him as an authorizing insider."[9] As Lewkenor's translation of Contarini work documents and J. G. A. Pocock's study substantiates, Venice was often cited by early modern political theorists as a state to be commended for its successful handling of its imperial aims through the hiring of foreign nationals to provide its military force and to police the city. This long-standing practice, plus the city's mercantile zeal, created a cosmopolitan environment where "one sees in this city an infinite number of men from different parts of the world" (McPherson 30). Furthermore, according to Lewkenor, it was apparently not unusual for "forreyn mercenarie souldiers" to be "enabled, with the title of citizens & gentlemen of Venice" (S2).

Brabantio's cultivation and acceptance of Othello, therefore, may very well reflect this custom, so that when Othello explains that Desdemona's "father lov'd me, oft invited me" (1.3.128), we are reminded that it was Brabantio himself, as a senator, who first acknowledged Othello an "insider."[10] It is the senator Brabantio, and thus by extension Venice, who sets up contradictory notions about racial identity and social place within Venetian society. Desdemona's marital choice, therefore, may very well enact not only adherence to assumptions about appropriate spouses (Othello is, by birth, a prince, by merit a general, and through patronage wealthy) but, in addition, the transference of the daughter's love for her father to another Venetian father figure and not an "outsider." Thus we may want to ask not why Othello drew her love but what is it in the *man that her father loved* that moves a woman "So opposite to marriage, that she shunn'd / The wealthy curled darlings of our nation . . ." (1.2.67-68) to set aside her reluctance to marriage and elope? And, whether Brabantio's reaction to the marriage, and Othello, is linked not to Othello's physical appearance but to that "thing . . . to fear, not to delight" in (1.2.71)—an incestuous desire for his daughter? If we view Desdemona's choice as being consistent with Shakespeare's characterization of her, of Othello, of Desdemona's willingness to perform her symbolic role in the ritual expression of marriage, and the myth of Venice, then perhaps it is Brabantio who continually refuses to participate in the ritual by subverting the activities which would require that he allow himself to be dispossessed of his daughter, that he permit another Venetian to sexually claim the one female body that he himself cannot sexually possess.[11]

Thus Brabantio's earlier rebuke of Iago becomes an ironic echo when Brabantio employs not only the language of theft to accuse Othello, "O thou foul thief," but also the language often associated with witchcraft, "chains of magic" and "foul charms," in an effort to destabilize the ritualized exchange of the female body that marks the institution of marriage. And Brabantio's charges, like his censure of Iago, allude to the complex and often contradictory social attitudes in Venice which allow for an Othello and a Desdemona but which also demand that they adhere to the customs and laws which govern that society.

Jacques Lacan has argued that "In our relation to things, in so far as this relation is constituted by the way of vision, and ordered in the figures of representation, something slips, passes, is transmitted from stage, to stage, and is always to some degree eluded in it—that is what we call the gaze" (73). I have been arguing that throughout *Othello*, this "something" is Venice, and I wish to conclude by looking briefly at the paradox that Shakespeare's play reveals Venice to be.

THE VENETIAN MOOR, OR THE ITALIAN ON THE ENGLISH STATE

One of the disturbing things about *Othello*, despite centuries of ideological intervention, is the play's ability to disrupt any attempt to make uneven the level playing field Shakespeare has created in his tragedy. This dilemma is further exacerbated by the crudely psychosexual dimensions engendered by Iago's rhetoric in the very first scene of the play:

> Zounds, sir, you are robb'd, for shame put on your gown,
> Your heart is burst, you have lost half your soul;
> Even now, very now, an old black ram
> Is tupping your white ewe. . . .
>
> (1.1.86-89)

Iago's words neatly transform what is an act of elopement into an imagined cuckoldry; that is, in the double reference to Brabantio's nakedness (he lacks both property and his "gown"), Iago sets the stage for a further shaming of Brabantio by subtly naming what is lost as if it were a wife ("half your soul") and luridly localizing this *pseudowife* in a pornographic fantasy. And though this fantasy is momentarily displaced by the intrusion (in the person of Othello) of Lewkenor's Venice, its affective power to create and sustain its image of perversion is not altered one whit.

Ironically, Iago's thematization of an imagined (and bestial) cuckoldry insinuates itself not only in Brabantio's imagination but in his later replacement of that anxiety onto Othello: "Look to her, Moor, have a quick eye to see: / She has deceiv'd her father, may do thee" (1.3.292-93). Predictably, Othello reenacts the violent passions that drove Brabantio to repudiate Desdemona, once again bringing to the surface the male anxiety about female sexuality (despite Desdemona's married state), considered the hallmark of "corrupt" Venice, that initiates the "tragedy of Othello." However, Othello's complete displacement of Brabantio can occur only when, I would argue, he takes to its ultimate, punitive conclusion (by killing Desdemona) Brabantio's disowning of his daughter.[12] In effect, it is the Venetian Othello who must see to it that Venice's "penal Lawes [are] most unpardonably executed" when the virgin is shown to be a whore.[13]

Representations of early modern Venice were always gendered feminine: it was a city "so beautiful, so renowned, so glorious a Virgin" and, at the same time, a "'Circe's court,' teeming with 'wanton and dallying' Calypsos and Sirens."[14] This allusion to the seductive women who delayed Ulysses' return to Ithaca finds its parallel in Desdemona's "supersubtle" seduction of the warrior Othello: "she thank'd me, / And bade me, if I had a friend that lov'd her, / I should but teach him how to tell my story, / And that would woo her" (1.3.163-66). Like Venice, Desdemona has the appearance of purity (and discretion) even as she boldly lays herself open to Othello's suit. Even so, when Iago calls into question Desdemona's virtue, Othello iterates his faith in his wife—"For she had eyes, and chose me" (3.3.193)—even as he leaves open the possibility of her infidelity: "No Iago, / I'll see before I doubt, when I doubt, prove, / And on the proof, there is no more but this: / Away at once with love or jealousy" (3.3.194-96).

Othello's insistence on "proof," of course, becomes the opening that Iago needs to "abuse Othello's ear" (1.3.393). It is not insignificant that both Othello and Desdemona initially are swayed by what is heard rather than what is seen. From its inception, the play luridly juxtaposes rumor and storytelling, on the one hand, and an emphasis on seeing, on the other. Brabantio must see for himself the truth of Roderigo's and Iago's report of Desdemona's elopement. Othello will not question Desdemona's virtue until he sees proof; but once rumor "abuses" his ear, Othello, as did Brabantio, begins the process of "bringing to light" the blackness of his Venetian wife.[15] If the first act of the play serves to displace Othello's blackness into his Venetian identity, then the remaining acts serve to dilate Desdemona's.

Iago is the first to constitute Desdemona black when, in response to her question "what wouldst thou write of me, if thou shouldst / praise me" (2.1.118), he reiterates a familiar trope of femininity:

> If she be fair and wise, fairness and wit;
> The one's for use, the other using it. . . .
> If she be black, and thereto have a wit,
> She'll find a white, that shall her blackness hit.
>
> (2.1.129-33)

Lines 132-33, not surprisingly, find their close interpretive echo in the adage "wash the Ethiop white." If Desdemona is "black" and possesses a "wit," Iago's advice to her is to seek that which will transform her, her opposite. Iago ends his "praise" of Desdemona by railing against even fair women, terming them "wight[s]" who "suckle fools, and chronicle small beer" (2.1.160).

This exchange, for all its seeming irreverence, finds its dramatic replay in act 4, scene 2. After a mournful lament for his "affliction," Othello turns his fury to Desdemona: "Turn thy complexion there; / Patience, thy young and rose-lipp'd cherubin, / I here look grim as hell" (4.2.63-65). Othello then goes on to say,

> O thou black weed, why art so lovely fair?
> Thou smel'st so sweet, that the sense aches at thee,
> Would thou hads't ne'er been born!
>
> (4.2.69-71)

Othello's language enacts the familiar Petrarchan opposition of fair/dark, yet it also perverts that rhetoric with its reluctance to further denigrate the object which it initially constitutes as undesirable (see Hall, esp. 178-79). More important, this semantic instantiation of Desdemona's desirability registers the allure traditionally associated with Venice, and which prompts Othello later to name Desdemona that which no Englishman who has read Coryat would have failed to understand, "that cunning whore of Venice."

Once again, despite the domesticity of this bedroom scene, it is Venice which becomes the object of our gaze as both the symbolic virgin that the warrior Othello defends and the corrupted bride he has wed.[16] In an emotionally charged accusation to Desdemona, Othello declares, "I took you for that cunning whore of Venice / That married with Othello" (4.2.91). Othello's words become a distorted projection of Brabantio's caution that the mask of virginity hid a corruption. It is Venice itself which suffers the "dilation" of its exterior to reveal the blackness inside. Othello's search for "proof" must begin "in" Venice, and thus with himself. What is revealed is the sameness of the interior and exterior: the Moor without is the Venetian within, and the Venetian within is the Moor without. And, in a remarkable mimicry of Brabantio's incredulity over Desdemona's willing participation in the marriage, Othello stages himself as the innocent seduced by the wiles of the Venetian whore—aided and abetted by the plot's initial and careful delineation of Othello as a Venetian. We see mirrored in Othello's rage that of Brabantio. Though born a Moor, in his irrationality Othello is very much a Venetian. And in an ironic though not surprising twist of fact, both the father and the husband, whose violations of the rites of marriage set into motion the tragic events of Shakespeare's tragedy, die as a result of their attempts to defend the illusion of perfection that is the myth of Venice.

"I TOOK BY TH' THROAT THE CIRCUMCISED DOG"

At the conclusion of *Othello,* Shakespeare leaves us with a disturbing dramatic tableau: the corpses of Othello, Desdemona, and Emilia upon the bed which has occupied (most likely) center stage for much of the final act; a (for once) silent Iago; and the Venetian lords as witnesses to this final tragic event. Just before he commits suicide, Othello says,

> And say besides, that in Aleppo once,
> where a malignant and a turban'd Turk
> Beat a Venetian, and traduc'd the state,
> I took by the throat the circumcised dog,
> And smote him thus.
>
> (5.2.353-57)

This speech has often been read as, symbolically, a racialized confirmation of Othello's awareness of himself as an outsider—a Moor. But if my argument is valid, then such a reading is highly questionable and may point to the deployment of the "racial anxiety" that Michael Neill suggests is "everywhere" in the play's critical and cultural history rather than in Shakespeare's representation of Othello's self-consciousness.

I would argue that what Othello does is to draw upon the myth of Venice to re-create not just a racial image but also a political one where Venetian law is exact, swift, and inviolate—whether one is a Turk or, in the case of Othello, a Venetian. More important, as the symbol of Venetian law on Cyprus, it is Othello who must stand in for the Duke and affirm the "bloody book of law" against those who have violated that very law. It is Venetian Othello who judges and executes the Turk who assaulted a Venetian, and it's this same Othello who must judge and execute the murderer of another Venetian, Desdemona. The race of this judge cannot, therefore, be viewed in terms of his color but as identical to that of the Duke in whose stead Othello carries out Venetian law.

It seems imperative, therefore, not to overlook the complex history that the concept and the word *race* may project in early modern English discourses and its implications for interpretations of *Othello.* In a world where women were often described as a "race," where the word *race* signified aristocratic or noble lineage, where *race* was often used as synonymous with *nation,* to argue that issues of race in *Othello* are easily reducible to one matrix—color—is a problematic misreading of an emerging taxonomic shift in the process of classifying human beings. In early modern Venice and England, where racial and social identities are formulated as much in genealogy as in ethnicity or geography, in gender as in color, the "illusion of perfection" cannot sustain itself as its own discourse points to the almost yet not quite invisible fractures that inevitably occur in the process of mythologizing "race." And it is this paradox which must be recognized in *Othello* rather than, as Jack D'Amico suggests, the idea that "Shakespeare revealed how a man could be destroyed when he accepts a perspective that deprives him of his humanity, . . . Othello is debased by a role that he adopts and acts out on the *Venetian-Elizabethan* stage" (177). Ignoring, for the moment, the problematic collapsing of Venice and England, I want to call into question the implicit assumption that there is English identification with the Venetians as a homogeneous racial group. As I have suggested elsewhere, "the contours of race may not be as fixed, as transcendental, as universal as critical practices and postmodern social discourses seem to infer" ("Managing the Barbarian" 183). English writers, Shakespeare included, pointedly distinguished within the European community just as they did without (perhaps even more so given their more extensive knowledge of nations within Europe). One has only to recall Portia's mockery of her French, German, Scottish, and English suitors, or Shakespeare's depiction of the Welsh and French in *Merry Wives of Windsor* to know that D'Amico's "Venetian-Elizabethan" elides the powerful sense of national consciousness that encodes itself in the dramatic representation of other cultures (see Howard).

It seems to me that we might derive a better understanding of Shakespeare's tragedy if we recognize that the "lustful" Moor is the "whorish" Venetian. Behind Desdemona stands the duplicitous Venice, behind Iago the cunning "Machiavel," and behind Othello the irrationality of Italian masculinity. What sets into motion the tragic events in Shakespeare's tragedy, and what makes *Othello* an ideological quagmire, is the Venetian ambivalence that accepts Othello as a well-born, honorable, successful military commander and courtier even as it insists that he remain an outsider, an alien who must resort to sorcery or witchcraft to become a part of the world he inhabits already. In the end, our interpretive and critical imperative, in addition to tracing the overdetermined markings formalized by the racialist rhetoric figured by the references to the color of Othello, should be one of exploring the multifaceted and often subtly nuanced discourse of race that aligns color, gender, geography as it sees fit. In this vein, we might also want to pose another query that Shakespeare's tragedy seems to invoke and which has bearing for our understanding of racial discourse in early modern English contexts. Who, symbolically, comes to be racialized as the "cunning whore" of Venice capable of causing nature to err from itself? The answer, not surprisingly, is all in how one defines the concept of race.

Notes

1. See Newman; Boose, "Othello's Handkerchief"; and Little. For a useful summary of critical responses to the play, see Neill, "Unproper Beds," particularly 391-95.

2. All *Othello* quotations are from the Arden edition, ed. M. R. Ridley.

3. Traub 36. See also Boose, "Othello's Handkerchief"; and Neill, "Changing Places."

4. Most references to Venice note either the city's significance in the Mediterranean political economy, its idealization as a model republic, or its exoticization as an international cultural site. See, for example, McPherson, esp. 27-50; Parker 95-96; Bartels; D'Amico 177; Cantor 296-319; and Braxton. In most other discussions of Shakespeare's tragedy, as I will argue, Venice appears to implicitly "stand in" for England.

5. See, for example, Levith, Partridge, McWilliam, Lievsay, Hale, and McPherson.

6. This panegyric appears in Lewes Lewkenor's 1599 translation of the Italian version of Gasparo Contarini's *De Magistratibus et Republica Venetorum*. Qtd. in Pocock 320.

7. Here I am referring to Stephanie Jed's brilliant argument in *Chaste Thinking*.

8. See Ruggerio, who argues that "in the Renaissance, ideally, the honor dynamic, with its threat of vendetta, was supposed to limit the level of violence in society. One did not cross the honor of another, one did not do violence to another, because that would require vendetta, that is violence and dishonor in return. Thus ideally, violence was avoided without formal institutions or additional violence within a community or group simply by maintaining a balance of honor." However, as Ruggerio further adds, if an individual "did not have the power to pursue vendetta, the support of threatened violence fell away, one's honor became problematic, and violent passions became easier to indulge, especially for the powerful."

9. Bartels 450. While Bartels's argument makes less of Othello's color than other critical essays, her reading succeeds in "making more" of the Moor-Venetian dichotomy than it makes of the racial ideology the play fashions. For similar discussions see Berry; D'Amico 177-96; Cantor; and Braxton.

10. Bartels cogently makes this argument in "Making More of the Moor" 435.

11. Garner argues that Shakespeare "keeps Desdemona off a pedestal and shows her to have a full range of human feelings and capacities. Yet he is careful not to allow her to fail in feeling or propriety" (238).

12. Snow notes that when Iago manipulates Othello's husbandly anxiety about Desdemona's chastity, Othello "comes to see Cassio in his place" as Brabantio came to see Othello in his (Brabantio's). What also needs to be explored is the continual replay of the incestuous undertones created by Iago's words to Brabantio. See esp. 395.

13. It is not my intent to prove or disprove Desdemona's guilt or innocence, but to "dilate" her significance to Shakespeare's handling of the myth of Venice.

14. Roger Ascham, *The Schoolmaster*, quoted in Jones 102.

15. I am indebted to Parker's "Fantasies of 'Race' and 'Gender': Africa, *Othello* and Bringing to Light" for this analysis. What I would add to Parker's cogent discussion on the "visual" necessity of "bringing to light" that which is secret is the way aurality serves as a prefiguration to such dilation.

16. I am indebted to Adelman's excellent discussion in *Suffocating Mothers* for this idea.

Works Cited

Adelman, Janet. *Suffocating Mothers: Fantasies of Maternal Origin in Shakespeare's Plays, "Hamlet" to "The Tempest."* New York and London: Routledge, 1992.

Bartels, Emily C. "Making More of the Moor: Aaron, Othello and Renaissance Refashionings of Race." *Shakespeare Quarterly* 41 (1990): 433-54.

Berry, Edward. "Othello's Alienation." *Studies in English Literature* 30 (1990): 315-33.

Boose, Lynda E. "The Father and Daughter in Shakespeare." *PMLA* 97 (1982): 327.

———. "Othello's Handkerchief: 'The Recognizance and Pledge of Love.'" *English Literary Renaissance* 5 (1975): 360-74.

Braxton, Phyllis Natalie. "Othello: The Moor and the Metaphor." *South Atlantic Review* 55 (1990): 1-17.

Cantor, Paul A. "*Othello:* The Erring Barbarian among the Supersubtle Venetians." *Southwest Review* 75 (1990): 296-345.

Cavell, Stanley. *Disowning Knowledge in Six Plays of Shakespeare.* Cambridge: Cambridge UP, 1987.

Coryat, Thomas. *Crudities.* Glasgow: J. Maclehose and Sons, 1905.

D'Amico, Jack. *The Moor in English Renaissance Drama.* Tampa: U of South Florida P, 1993.

Garner, Shirley Nelson. "Shakespeare's Desdemona." *Shakespeare Studies* (1976): 235-39.

Hale, John R. *England and the Italian Renaissance.* London: Faber and Faber, 1954.

Hall, Kim F. "'I rather would wish to be a Black-Moor': Beauty, Race, and Rank in Lady Mary Wroth's *Urania.*" *Women, "Race," and Writing in the Early Modern Period.* Ed. Margo Hendricks and Patricia Parker. London and New York: Routledge, 1994. 178-94.

Hendricks, Margo. "Managing the Barbarian: *The Tragedy of Dido Queen of Carthage.*" *Renaissance Drama* n.s. (1992): 165-88.

Howard, Jean E. "An English Lass amid the Moors: Gender, Race, Sexuality, and National Identity in Heywood's *The Fair Maid of the West.*" *Women, "Race," and Writing in the Early Modern Period.* Ed. Margo Hendricks and Patricia Parker. London: Routledge, 1994. 101-17.

Jed, Stephanie. *Chaste Thinking.* Bloomington: Indiana UP, 1989.

Jones, Ann Rosalind. "Italians and Others: Venice and the Irish in Coryat's Crudities and *The White Devil.*" *Renaissance Drama* n.s. (1987): 101-19.

Lacan, Jacques. *The Four Fundamental Concepts of Psycho-Analysis.* Ed. Jacques-Alain Miller. Trans. Alan Sheridan. New York: W. W. Norton and Co., 1978.

Levith, Murray J. *Shakespeare's Italian Settings and Plays.* New York: St. Martin Press, 1989.

Lewkenor, Lewes. *The Commonwealth and Gouernment of Venice. Written by the Cardinall Gasper Contareno, and translated out of Italian into English.* 1599. Facsimile copy, Amsterdam and New York: Da Capo Press, 1966.

Lievsay, John. *The Elizabethan Image of Italy.* Published for the Folger Shakespeare Library. Ithaca: Cornell UP, 1964.

Little, Arthur, L. Jr. "'An essence that's not seen': The Primal Scene of Racism in *Othello.*" *Shakespeare Quarterly* 44 (1993): 304-24.

McPherson, David C. *Shakespeare, Jonson, and the Myth of Venice.* Newark: U of Delaware P, 1990.

McWilliam, George W. *Shakespeare's Italy Revisited.* Leicester: Leicester UP, 1974.

Neill, Michael. "Changing Places in *Othello.*" *Shakespeare Survey* 37 (1984): 115-31.

———. "Unproper Beds: Race, Adultery, and the Hideous in *Othello.*" *Shakespeare Quarterly* 40 (1989): 383-412.

Newman, Karen. "'And wash the Ethiop white': Femininity and the Monstrous in *Othello.*" *Shakespeare Reproduced: The Text in History and Ideology.* Ed. Jean E. Howard and Marion F. O'Connor. New York and London: Methuen, 1987. 141-62.

Parker, Patricia. "Fantasies of 'Race' and 'Gender': Africa, *Othello* and Bringing to Light." *Women, "Race," and Writing in the Early Modern Period.* Ed. Margo Hendricks and Patricia Parker. London and New York: Routledge, 1994. 84-100.

Partridge, A. C. "Shakespeare and Italy." *English Studies in Africa* 4 (1961): 117-27.

Pocock, J. G. A. *The Machiavellian Moment: Florentine Political Thought and the Atlantic Republican Tradition.* Princeton: Princeton UP, 1975.

Ruggerio, Guido. *Binding Passions.* Oxford and New York: Oxford UP, 1993.

Shakespeare, William. *The Merchant of Venice.* New York: Viking, 1969.

———. *Othello.* Ed. M. R. Ridley. London and New York: Routledge, 1958.

Snow, Edward A. "Sexual Anxiety and the Male Order of Things in *Othello.*" *English Literary Renaissance* 10 (1980): 384-412.

Traub, Valerie. *Desire and Anxiety: Circulations of Sexuality in Shakespearean Drama.* London and New York: Routledge, 1992.

Janet Adelman (essay date 1997)

SOURCE: "Iago's Alter Ego: Race as Projection in *Othello*," in *Shakespeare Quarterly*, Vol. 48, No. 2, Summer, 1997, pp. 125-44.

[*In the following essay, Adelman discusses Iago's role in corrupting Othello's views on race and sexuality.*]

Othello famously begins not with Othello but with Iago. Other tragedies begin with ancillary figures commenting on the character who will turn out to be at the center of the tragedy—one thinks of *Lear, Macbeth, Antony and Cleopatra*—but no other play subjects its ostensibly tragic hero to so long and intensive a debunking before he even sets foot onstage. And the audience is inevitably complicit in this debunking: before we meet Othello, we are utterly dependent on Iago's and Roderigo's descriptions of him. For the first long minutes of the play, we know only that the Moor, "the thicklips" (1.1.66),[1] has done something that Roderigo (like the audience) feels he should have been told about beforehand; we find out what it is for the first time only through Iago's violently eroticizing and racializing report to Brabantio: "Even now, very now, an old black ram / Is tupping your white ewe" (ll. 88-89).[2]

At this point in my teaching of the play, I normally point to all the ways in which Othello belies Iago's description as soon as he appears; in the classroom my reading of race in *Othello* turns on this contrast as Shakespeare's way of denaturalizing the tropes of race, so that we are made to understand Othello not as the "natural" embodiment of Iago's "old black ram" gone insanely jealous but as the victim of the racist ideology everywhere visible in Venice, an ideology to which he is relentlessly subjected and which increasingly comes to define him as he internalizes it—internalizes it so fully that, searching for a metaphor to convey his sense of the soil attaching both to his name and to Desdemona's body, Othello can come up with no term of comparison other than his own face ("My name, that was as fresh / As Dian's visage, is now begrim'd, and black / As mine own face" [3.3.392-94]).[3] Othello's "discovering" that his blackness is a stain—a stain specifically associated with his sexuality—and "discovering" that stain on Desdemona are virtually simultaneous for him; hence the metaphoric transformation of Dian's visage into his own begrimed face. If Desdemona becomes a "black weed" (4.2.69)[4] for Othello, her "blackening" is a kind of shorthand for his sense that his blackness has in fact contaminated her; as many have argued, his quickness to believe her always-already contaminated is in part a function of his horrified recoil from his suspicion that he is the contaminating agent.[5]

In other words, in the classroom I usually read race in *Othello* through what I take to be the play's representation of Othello's experience of race as it comes to dominate his sense of himself as polluted and polluting, undeserving of Desdemona and hence quick to believe her unfaithful. But although the play locates Othello in a deeply racist society, the sense of pollution attaching to blackness comes first of all (for the audience if not for Othello) from Iago; though Iago needed Brabantio to convince Othello of Desdemona's tendency to deception and the "disproportion" of Othello as her marriage choice, Iago legitimizes and intensifies Brabantio's racism through his initial sexualizing and racializing invocation of Othello. And if the play offers us a rich representation of the effects of racism on Othello, it offers us an equally rich—and in some ways more disturbing—representation of the function of Othello's race *for Iago*. I offer the following reading of that representation as a thought-experiment with two aims: first, to test out the applicability of psychoanalytic theory—especially Kleinian theory—to problems of race, an arena in which its applicability is often questioned; and, second, to identify some of the ways in which racism is the psychic property (and rightly the concern) of the racist, not simply of his victim.

Iago erupts out of the night (this play, like *Hamlet*, begins in palpable darkness), as though he were a condensation of its properties. Marking himself as opposite to light through his demonic "I am not what I am," Iago calls forth a world, I will argue, in which he can see his own darkness localized and reflected in Othello's blackness, or rather in what he makes—and teaches Othello to make—of Othello's blackness.

Iago's voice inducts us into the play: long before Othello has a name, much less a voice, of his own, Iago has a distinctive "I." The matter of Othello, and satisfaction of the audience's urgent curiosity about what exactly Roderigo has just learned, are deferred until after we have heard Iago's catalogue of injuries to that "I" ("I know my price, I am worth no worse a place" [1.1.11]; "And I, of whom his eyes had seen the proof, . . . must be lee'd, and calm'd" [ll. 28-30]; "And I, God bless the mark, his worship's ancient" [l. 33]). Iago's "I" beats through the dialogue with obsessive insistence, claiming both self-sufficiency ("I follow but myself" [l. 58]) and self-division, defining itself by what it is not ("Were I the Moor, I would not be Iago" [l. 57]), in fact simultaneously proclaiming its existence and nonexistence: "I am not what I am" (l. 65). I, I, I: Iago's name unfolds from the Italian *io*, Latin *ego*; and the injured "I" is his signature, the ground of his being and the ground, I will argue, of the play. For Iago calls up the action of the play as though in response to this sense of injury: "Call up her father, . . . poison his delight" (ll. 67-68), he says, like a stage manager, or like a magician calling forth spirits to perform his will; and with his words, the action begins.

The structure of the first scene models Iago's relation to the world that he calls up, for the play proper seems to arise out of Iago's injured "I": it is not only set in motion by Iago's "I" but becomes in effect a projection of it, as Iago successfully attempts to rid himself of interior pain by replicating it in Othello. Othello—and particularly in relation to Desdemona—becomes Iago's primary target in part because Othello has the presence, the fullness of being, that Iago lacks.[6] Othello is everywhere associated with the kind of interior solidity and wholeness that stands as a reproach to Iago's interior emptiness and fragmentation: if Iago takes Janus as his patron saint (1.2.33) and repeatedly announces his affiliation with nothingness ("I am not what I am"; "I am nothing, if not critical" [2.1.119]), Othello is initially "all in all sufficient" (4.1.261), a "full soldier" (2.1.36), whose "solid virtue" (4.1.262) and "perfect soul" (1.2.31) allow him to achieve the "full fortune" (1.1.66) of possessing Desdemona. "Tell me what you need to spoil and I will tell you what you want," says Adam Phillips:[7] the extent to which Othello's fullness and solidity are the object of Iago's envy can be gauged by the extent to which he works to replicate his own self-division in Othello. Split himself, Iago is a master at splitting others: his seduction of Othello works by inscribing in Othello the sense of dangerous interior spaces—thoughts that cannot be known, monsters in the mind—which Othello seems to lack, introducing him to the world of self-alienation that Iago inhabits;[8] by the end, Othello is so self-divided that he can take arms against himself, Christian against Turk, literalizing self-division by splitting himself graphically down the middle.[9] Though Iago is not there to see his victory, we might imagine him as invisible commentator, saying in effect, "Look, he is not all-in-all sufficient, self-sustaining and full; he is as self-divided as I am."[10]

To shatter the illusion of Othello's fullness and presence is also to shatter the illusion of his erotic power; his division from himself is first of all his division from Desdemona and from the fair portion of himself invested in her. If Cassio is any indication, that erotic power is heavily idealized by the Italians:

> Great Jove, Othello guard,
> And swell his sail with thine own powerful breath,
> That he may bless this bay with his tall ship,
> Make love's quick pants in Desdemona's arms
> Give renew'd fire to our extinct spirits. . . .
>
> (2.1.77-81)[11]

But for Iago it is intolerable: what begins as a means to an end (Iago creates Othello's suspicions about Desdemona to discredit Cassio in order to replace him as lieutenant) increasingly becomes an end in itself, as Iago drives Othello toward a murderous reenactment of sexual union on the marriage bed, even though that reenactment will make Othello incapable of bestowing the position Iago initially seeks. The thrust of his plot toward the marriage bed, even at the cost of his own ambition, suggests that what Iago needs to spoil is on that bed: the fullness and presence signified by Othello's possession of Desdemona, the sexual union that reminds him of his own extinct spirits. For Iago's own erotic life takes place only in his head; though he seems to imagine a series of erotic objects—Desdemona (ll. 286-89), Cassio (3.3.419-32), and Othello himself (in the coded language—"the lustful Moor / Hath leap'd into my seat" [2.1.290-91]—that makes cuckoldry an anal invasion of Iago's own body)—he imagines them less as realizable erotic objects than as mental counters in his revenge plot, and he imagines them only in sexual unions (Othello with Desdemona, Othello with Emilia, Cassio with Desdemona, Cassio with Emilia) that everywhere exclude and diminish him. And in response, he effectively neutralizes the erotic potency that mocks his own lack.

His primary tool in this neutralization is the creation of Othello as "black": and in fact it is Othello as progenitor that first excites Iago's racializing rage. His first use of the language of black and white is in his call to Brabantio: "An old black ram / Is tupping your white ewe." If Cassio needs to make Othello into an exotic super-phallus, capable of restoring Italian potency, Iago needs to make him into a black monster, invading the citadel of whiteness. (The idealization and the debasement are of course two sides of the same coin, and they are equally damaging to Othello: both use him only as the container for white fantasies, whether of desire or fear.) *Your white ewe/you:* Iago's half-pun invokes the whiteness of his auditors via the image of Othello's contaminating miscegenation;[12] true to form in racist discourse, "whiteness" emerges as a category only when it is imagined as threatened by its opposite. Iago's language here works through separation, works by placing "blackness" outside of "whiteness" even as it provokes terror at the thought of their mixture. But the play has already affiliated Iago himself with darkness and the demonic; the threat of a contaminating blackness is already there, already present inside the "whiteness" he would invoke. Iago creates Othello as "black"—and therefore himself as "white"—when he constructs him as monstrous progenitor; and he uses that racialized blackness to destroy what he cannot tolerate. But the trope through which Iago imagines that destruction makes Iago himself into the monstrous progenitor, filled with a dark conception that only darkness can bring forth: "I ha't, it is engender'd," he tells us; "Hell and night / Must bring this monstrous birth to the world's light" (1.3.401-2). This trope makes the blackness Iago would attribute to Othello—like his monstrous generativity—something already inside Iago himself, something that he must project out into the world: as though Iago were pregnant with the monster he makes of Othello.[13]

If the structure of the first scene predicts the process through which Iago becomes the progenitor of Othello's racialized blackness, the trope of the monstrous birth in the first act's final lines perfectly anticipates the mechanism of projection through which Iago will come to use Othello's black skin as the container for his own interior blackness. Cassio uses Othello as the locus for fantasies of inseminating sexual renewal; Iago uses him as the repository for his own bodily insufficiency and his self-disgust. For Iago needs the blackness of others: even the "white ewe" Desdemona is blackened in his imagination as he turns "her virtue into pitch" (2.3.351). How are we to understand Iago's impulse to blacken, the impulse for which Othello becomes the perfect vehicle? What does it mean to take another person's body as the receptacle for one's own contents? The text gives us, I think, a very exact account of what I've come to call the psycho-physiology of Iago's projection: that is, not simply an account of the psychological processes themselves but also an account of the fantasized bodily processes that underlie them. "Projection" is in its own way comfortingly abstract; by invoking the body behind the abstraction, *Othello* in effect rubs our noses in it.[14]

Let me begin, then, by thinking about the way Iago thinks about bodies, especially about the insides of bodies. For Iago is the play's spokesman for the idea of the *inside,* the hidden away. At the beginning of his seduction of Othello, he defends the privacy of his thought by asking "where's that palace, whereinto foul things / Sometimes intrude not?" (3.3.141-42); no palace is impregnable, no inside uncontaminated. Characteristically, Othello takes this image and makes it his own, reinscribing it in his later anatomy of Desdemona as "a cistern, for foul toads / To knot and gender in" (4.2.62-63). But merely by insisting on the hidden inwardness of thought, Iago has already succeeded in causing Othello to conflate the *hidden* with the *hideous,* as though that which is inside, invisible, must inevitably be monstrous ("he echoes me, / As if there were some monster in his thought, / Too hideous to be shown" [3.3.110-12]).[15] According to this logic, the case against Desdemona is complete as soon as Iago can insinuate that she, too, has—psychically and anatomically—an inside, unknowable and monstrous because it *is* inside, unseen.

If Iago succeeds in transferring his own sense of hidden contamination to Desdemona, localizing it in her body, the sense of the hideous thing within—monstrous birth or foul intruder—begins with him. Seen from this vantage point, his initial alarum to Brabantio ("Look to your house, your daughter, and your bags. . . . Are all doors lock'd?" [1.1.80, 85]) looks less like a description of danger to Brabantio or Desdemona than like a description of danger to Iago himself. For Iago finds—or creates—in Brabantio's house the perfect analogue for his own sense of vulnerability to intrusion, and he can make of Othello the perfect analogue for the intrusive "foul thing," the old black ram who is tupping your white ewe/you—or, as we later find out, tupping Iago himself in Iago's fantasy, and leaving behind a poisonous residue ("I do suspect the lustful Moor / Hath leap'd into my seat, the thought whereof / Doth like a poisonous mineral gnaw my inwards" [2.1.290-92]).

But even the image of the body as a breached and contaminated "palace" suggests rather more interior structure than most of Iago's other images for the body. Again and again Iago imagines the body filled with liquid putrefaction, with contents that can and should be vomited out or excreted. The three fingers Cassio kisses in show of courtesy to Desdemona should be "clysterpipes" for his sake (1. 176), Iago says; through the bizarre reworking of Iago's fantasy, Cassio's fingers are transformed into enema tubes, an imagistic transformation that violently brings together not only lips and faeces, mouth, vagina, and anus, but also digital, phallic, and emetic penetration of a body—Desdemona's? Cassio's?—imagined only as a container for faeces. Early in the play, poor Roderigo is a "sick fool . . . Whom love has turn'd almost the wrong side outward" (2.3.47-48); by the end, he is a "quat" rubbed almost to the sense (5.1.11), that is, a pus-filled pimple about to break. The congruence of these images suggests that Roderigo becomes a "quat" for Iago because he can't keep his insides from running out: the love that has almost turned him inside out is here refigured as pus that threatens to break through the surface of his body. In Iago's fantasy of the body, what is inside does not need to be contaminated by a foul intruder because it is already pus or faeces; in fact, anything brought into this interior will be contaminated by it. Iago cannot imagine ordinary eating, in which matter is taken in for the body's nourishment; any good object taken in will be violently transformed and violently expelled. When he is done with her, Iago tells us, Othello will excrete Desdemona ("The food that to him now is as luscious as locusts, shall be to him shortly as acerb as the coloquintida," an emetic or purgative [1.3.349-50]); when Desdemona is "sated" with Othello's body (1.351), she will "heave the gorge" (2.1.231-32). (Poor Emilia has obviously learned from her husband: in her view men "are all but stomachs, and we all but food; / They eat us hungerly, and when they are full, / They belch us" [3.4.101-3].)

Given this image of the body's interior as a mass of undifferentiated and contaminated matter, it's no wonder that Iago propounds the ideal of self-control to Roderigo in the garden metaphor that insists both on the rigid demarcation and differentiation of the body's interior and on its malleability to the exercise of will:

> . . . 'tis in ourselves, that we are thus, or thus: our bodies are gardens, to the which our wills are gardeners, so that if we will plant nettles, or sow lettuce, set hyssop, and weed up thyme; supply it with one gender of herbs, or distract it with many; either to have it sterile with idleness, or manur'd with industry, why, the power, and corrigible authority of this, lies in our wills.
>
> (1.3.319-26)

This is not, presumably, his experience of his own body's interior or of his management of it; it seems rather a defensive fantasy of an orderly pseudo-Eden, in which man is wholly in control both of the inner processes of his body/garden and of the troublesome business of gender, and woman is wholly absent.[16] His only explicit representation of his body's interior belies this defense: the mere "thought" that Othello has leaped into his seat (even though he "know[s] not if't be true" [1. 386]) "Doth like a poisonous mineral gnaw [his] inwards." No reassuring gardener with his tidy—or even his untidy—rows here: Iago's "inwards" are hideously vulnerable, subject to a poisonous penetration. Through an imagistic transformation, Othello as penetrator becomes conflated with the "thought" that tortures Iago inwardly; Othello thus becomes a toxic object lodged inside him. (The garden passage simultaneously expresses and defends against the homoerotic desire that here makes Othello a poisonous inner object, insofar as it voices a fantasy of "supply[ing]" the body with one gender rather than "distract[ing]" it with many.[17])

What I have earlier called Iago's injured "I"—his sense that he is chronically slighted and betrayed, his sense of self-division—produces (or perhaps is produced by) fantasies of his body as penetrated and contaminated, especially by Othello. In fact, any traffic between inner and outer is dangerous for Iago, who needs to keep an absolute barrier between them by making his outside opaque, a false "sign" (1.1.156 and 157) of his inside; to do less would be to risk being (Roderigo-like) turned almost the wrong side outward, to "wear [his] heart upon [his] sleeve, / For dawes to peack at" (ll. 64-65).[18] To allow himself to be seen or known is tantamount to being stabbed, eaten alive: pecked at from the outside unless he manages to keep the barrier between inner and outer perfectly intact, gnawed from the inside if he lets anyone in. Iago's need for sadistic control of others ("Pleasure, and action, make the hours seem short" [2.3.369], he says, after managing Cassio's cashiering) goes in tandem with his extraordinarily vivid sense of vulnerability: unable to be gardener to himself, he will sadistically manage everyone else, simultaneously demonstrating his superiority to those quats whose insides are so sloppily prone to bursting out, and hiding the contamination and chaos of his own insides.

Roderigo plays a pivotal role in this process. As the embodiment of what Iago would avoid, Roderigo exists largely to give Iago repeated occasions on which to display his mastery over both self and other: in effect, Iago can load his contaminated insides into Roderigo and then rub him to the sense in order to demonstrate the difference between them and, hence, the impermeability of Iago's own insides. Moreover, in managing Roderigo, Iago can continually replenish himself with the fantasy of new objects to be taken into the self: objects over which—unlike the thought of Othello, which gnaws at his inwards—he can exert full control. Obsessively—six times in fourteen lines—Iago tells Roderigo to "Put money in thy purse . . . fill thy purse with money" (1.3.340, 348). We know that Iago has received enough jewels and gold from Roderigo to have half-corrupted a votarist (4.2.189), but we never see Iago taking the miser's or even the spendthrift's ordinary delight in this treasure; detached from any ordinary human motivation, the money accrues almost purely psychic meaning, becoming the sign not of any palpable economic advantage but of Iago's pleasure in being able to empty Roderigo out, to fill himself at will. "Put money in thy purse," he repeats insistently, and then adds, "Thus do I ever make my fool my purse" (1.3.381), as though the emptied-out Roderigo becomes the container that holds the illusion of Iago's fullness. For his repetition signals a compulsive need to fill himself with objects in order to compensate for the contamination and chaos inside: hard shiny objects that might be kept safe and might keep the self safe, objects that could magically repair the sense of what the self is made of and filled with.

Iago's hoarding, his sadism, his references to purgatives and clyster-pipes can be read through the language of classical psychoanalysis as evidence of an anal fixation; in that language the equation of money with faeces is familiar enough, as is the association of sadistic control with the anal phase.[19] Iago's obsessive suspicion that Othello has leaped into his seat, along with his heavily eroticized account of Cassio's dream, similarly lend themselves to a classically psychoanalytic reading of Iago as repressed homosexual.[20] While these readings are not "wrong" within their own terms, they nonetheless seem to me limited, and not only insofar as they can be said to assume a historically inaccurate concept of the subject or of "the homosexual":[21] limited even within the terms of psychoanalysis insofar as they do not get at either the quality of Iago's emotional relationships (his inability to form *any* kind of libidinal bond, his tendency to treat others as poisonous inner objects) or the terrifying theatrical seductiveness of the processes of projection that we witness through him. I want consequently to move from the consideration of libidinal zones and conflicted object choices characteristic of classical psychoanalysis to the areas opened up by the work of Melanie Klein; a Kleinian reading of Iago will, I think, help us to understand the ways in which Iago's imagination of his own interior shapes his object relations as he projects this interior onto the landscape of the play.

In Klein's account the primitive self is composed in part of remnants of internalized objects (people, or bits and pieces of people, taken into the self as part of the self's continual negotiation with what an outside observer would call the world) and the world is composed in part of projected bits and pieces of the self. Ideally, "the good breast is taken in and becomes part of the ego, and the infant who was first inside the mother now has the mother inside himself."[22] Internalization of the good object "is the basis for trust in one's own goodness";[23] "full identification with a good object goes with a feeling of the self possessing goodness of its own" and hence enables the return of goodness to the world: "Through processes of projection and introjection, through inner wealth given out and reintrojected, an enrichment and deepening of the ego comes about. . . . Inner wealth derives from having assimilated the good object so that the individual becomes able to share its gifts with others."[24] And the corollary is clear: if the infant cannot take in the experience of the good breast (either because of his/her own constitutional conditions or because the experience is not there to be had in a consistent way), the bad breast may be introjected, with accompanying feelings of one's own internal badness, poverty, poisonousness, one's own inability to give back anything good to the world.

But, in the words of Harold Boris, a contemporary post-Kleinian analyst of envy, "the infant who cannot, sooner or later, feed the hand from which it feeds . . . is the child who will then attempt to bite it."[25] The infant stuck with a depleted or contaminated inner world will, Klein suggests, exist in a peculiar relation to the good breast: even if it is there and apparently available, the infant may not be able to use it. For if the infant cannot tolerate either the discrepancy between its own badness and the goodness outside itself or the sense of dependency on this external source of goodness, the good breast will not be available for the infant's use: its goodness will in effect be spoiled by the infant's own envious rage. The prototype for Kleinian envy is the hungry baby, experiencing itself as helplessly dependent, empty, or filled only with badness, confronted with the imagined fullness of a source of goodness outside itself: "the first object to be envied is the feeding breast, for the infant feels that it possesses everything he desires and that it has an unlimited flow of milk, and love which the breast keeps for its own gratification."[26] Klein's insistence on the priority of the breast as the first object of envy effectively reverses Freud's concept of penis envy; in Klein's account even penis envy becomes secondary, derivative from this earlier prototype.[27] But Klein's concept of envy turns on an even more startling innovation: for most analysts of infantile destructiveness and rage, the source and target is the frustrating "bad" object—a maternal object that doesn't provide enough, is not at the infant's beck and call, provides milk that in some way is felt to be spoiled; but in Klein's reading of envy, the source and target of rage is not the frustrating or poisonous bad breast but the good breast, and it is exactly its goodness that provokes the rage. Hence the peculiar sensitivity of the envious to the good—and the consequent need not to possess but to destroy it, or, in Klein's terms, "to put badness, primarily bad excrement and bad parts of the self, into the mother, and first of all into her breast, in order to spoil and destroy her."[28] But the breast so destroyed is of course no longer available to the child as a source of good: "The breast attacked in this way has lost its value, it has become bad by being bitten up and poisoned by urine and faeces."[29] Insofar as the infant has succeeded in destroying the good object, he has confirmed its destruction as a source of goodness within himself; hence the peculiarly vicious circle of envy, which destroys all good both in the world and in the self, and hence also its peculiar despair.

We do not, of course, need the help of a Kleinian perspective to identify Iago as envious. His willingness to kill Cassio simply because "He has a daily beauty in his life, / That makes me ugly" (5.1.19-20) marks the extent to which he is driven by envy; in an older theatrical tradition he might well have been named Envy. Here, for example, is Envy from *Impatient Poverty*:

> A syr is not thys a ioly game . . .
> Enuy in fayth I am the same . . .
> I hate conscience, peace loue and reste
> Debate and stryfe that loue I beste
> Accordynge to my properte
> When a man louethe well hys wyfe
> I brynge theym at debate and stryfe.[30]

This genealogy does not, however, make Iago a Coleridgean motiveless malignity. For in Iago, Shakespeare gives motiveless malignity a body: incorporating this element of the morality tradition, he releases through Iago the range of bodily fantasies associated with a specifically Kleinian envy.

Klein describes an envy so primal—and so despairing—that it cannot tolerate the existence of goodness in the world: its whole delight lies not in possessing what is good but in spoiling it. And that spoiling takes place in fantasy through a special form of object-relating: through the violent projection of bits of the self and its contaminated objects—often localized as contaminated bodily products—into the good object. By means of this projection, the self succeeds in replicating its own inner world "out there" and thus in destroying the goodness it cannot tolerate; at the end of the process, in the words of one Kleinian analyst, "There is nothing left to envy."[31] Through the lens of a Kleinian perspective, we can see traces of this process as Iago fills Othello with the poison that fills him.

In Iago's fantasy, as I have suggested, there is no uncontaminated interior space: he can allow no one access to his interior and has to keep it hidden away because it is more a cesspool than a palace or a garden. And there are no uncontaminated inner objects: every intruder is foul; everything taken in turns to pus or faeces or poison; everything swallowed must be vomited out. This sense of inner contamination leaves him—as Klein would predict—particularly subject to the sense of goodness in others and particularly ambivalent toward that goodness. His goal is to make those around him as ugly as he is; but that goal depends on his unusual sensitivity to their beauty. Even after he has managed to bring out the quarrelsome drunkard and class-conscious snob in Cassio, transforming him into a man who clearly enjoys sneaking around to see his general's wife, Iago remains struck by the daily beauty in Cassio's life—at a point when that beauty has become largely invisible to the audience. To Roderigo, Iago always contemptuously denies the goodness of Othello and Desdemona (he is an erring barbarian and she a supersubtle Venetian); but in soliloquy he specifically affirms their goodness—and affirms it in order to imagine spoiling it. Othello's "free and open nature" he will remake as the stupidity of an ass who can be led by the nose (1.3.397-400). He will not only use Desdemona's virtue; he will turn it into pitch, in a near-perfect replication of the projection of faeces into the good breast that Klein posits.

For Iago the desire to spoil always takes precedence over the desire to possess; one need only contrast him with Othello to see the difference in their relation to good objects.[32] Othello's anguish over the loss of the good object gives the play much of its emotional resonance. He imagines himself as safely enclosed in its garnery, nourished and protected by it, and then cast out: "But there, where I have garner'd up my heart, / Where either I must live, or bear no life, / The fountain, from the which my current runs, / Or else dries up, to be discarded thence" (4.2.58-61). When he is made to imagine that object as spoiled—"a cistern, for foul toads / To knot and gender in"—its loss is wholly intolerable to him; even at the end, as he kills Desdemona, he is working very hard to restore some remnant of the good object in her. Although he approaches Desdemona's bed planning to bloody it ("Thy bed, lust-stain'd, shall with lust's blood be spotted" [5.1.36]), his deepest desire is not to stain but to restore the purity of the good object, rescuing it from contamination, even the contamination he himself has visited upon it. By the time he reaches her bed, he has decided not to shed her blood (5.2.3). Instead he attempts to recreate her unviolated wholeness ("that whiter skin of hers than snow, / And smooth, as monumental alabaster" [ll. 4-5]) in a death that he imagines as a revirgination;[33] in fantasy he cleanses "the slime / That sticks on filthy deeds," remaking her unmarred and unpenetrated, "one entire and perfect chrysolite" (ll. 149-50, 146).

But Iago's only joy comes in spoiling good objects: Othello mourns being cast out from the garnery/fountain that has nourished him; Iago mocks the meat he feeds on (3.3.170-71). His description of the green-eyed monster he cautions Othello against marks the workings of a very Kleinian envy in him:[34] like the empty infant who cannot tolerate the fullness of the breast, he will mock the objects that might nourish and sustain him, spoiling them by means of his corrosive wit.[35] (Or perhaps—in good Kleinian fashion—by tearing at them with his teeth: especially in conjunction with the image of feeding on meat, "mock" may carry traces of *mammock*,[36] to tear into pieces, suggesting the oral aggression behind Iago's biting mockery and hence the talion logic in his fantasy of being pecked at.) Mockery—especially of the meat he might feed on—is Iago's signature: different as they are, Othello, Cassio, and Roderigo share an almost religious awe toward Desdemona; Iago insists that "the wine she drinks is made of grapes" (2.1.249-50), that even the best woman is only good enough "To suckle fools, and chronicle small beer" (l. 160). If "the first object to be envied is the feeding breast," Iago's devaluation of maternal nurturance here is just what we might expect.

But envy does not stop there. As Klein suggests, "Excessive envy of the breast is likely to extend to all feminine attributes, in particular to the woman's capacity to bear children. . . . The capacity to give and to preserve life is felt as the greatest gift and therefore creativeness becomes the deepest cause for envy."[37] If Othello's potency and fullness make him the immediate target of Iago's envious rage, the destruction of Desdemona's generativity has been Iago's ultimate goal from the beginning: "poison his delight," he says; "And though he in a fertile climate dwell, / Plague him with flies" (1.1.70-71). The image half-echoes Hamlet's linking of conception and breeding with the stirring of maggots in dead flesh,[38] for the "fertile climate" that Iago will transform into a breeding ground for plague is Desdemona's generative body. Hence, I think, the urgency with which Iago propels the plot toward the marriage bed ("Do it not with poison, strangle her in her bed, even the bed she hath contaminated" [4.1.203-4]): the ultimate game is to make father destroy mother on that bed in a parody of the life-giving insemination that might have taken place there.[39]

And hence the subterranean logic of Iago's favorite metaphor for that destruction, his monstrous birth. For if Iago enviously devalues Desdemona's generativity (she can only suckle, and only suckle fools; her body will breed only flies), he also appropriates it, and appropriates it specifically through imitation. Here both senses of *mock*—as devaluation and derisive imitation—come together, as Boris's work on envy predicts: "The urge to take charge of the envied object has several components to it. First, of course, is the denuding (an idea) and disparagement (an emotion) of the inherent value of the original. This makes possible what follows, namely the idea that the 'knockoff' (the 'as-if') is in every way the equal of the real thing."[40] In conceiving of his monstrous birth, that is, Iago not only mocks but also displaces Desdemona's generativity by taking on its powers for himself, denying the difference—between her fruitfulness and his barrenness, between her fullness and his emptiness—that he cannot tolerate. Iago's substitution in fact proceeds by stages. When he first invokes the metaphor of pregnancy, he is merely the midwife/observer: "There are many events in the womb of time, which will be delivered" (1.3.369-70). But his triumphant "I ha't" only thirty lines later—"I ha't, it is engender'd; Hell and night / Must bring this monstrous birth to the world's light"—replaces time's womb with his own: as I have already argued, his is the body in which the monstrous birth is engendered, and hell and night have become the midwives.

Through this metaphor, Iago's mental production becomes his substitute birth, in which he replaces the world outside himself[41]—the world of time's womb, or of Desdemona's—with the projection of his own interior monstrosity; thus conceived, his plot manages simultaneously to destroy the generativity that he cannot tolerate and to proclaim the superior efficacy of his own product. Emilia's description of the jealousy Iago creates in Othello—it is "a monster, / Begot upon itself, born on itself" (3.4.159-60)—is not accurate about Othello, but it suggestively tracks Iago's own envy to its psychic sources. If Iago imagines himself enacting a substitute birth, making the world conform to the shape of his envy by undoing the contours of the already-existing generative world, Emilia expresses the wish behind his metaphor: the wish to *be* begot upon oneself, born on oneself, no longer subject to—dependent on, vulnerable to—the generative fullness outside the self and the unendurable envy it provokes.[42] Unable to achieve that end, he will empty himself out on the wedding bed, substituting his own monstrous conception for the generative fullness that torments him, and destroying in the process the envied good object in Desdemona.

And it is just here, in this fantasy, that Othello's blackness becomes such a powerful vehicle for Iago. I have already suggested that Iago's capacity to spoil good objects rests on his capacity to blacken them, and to blacken them through a bodily process of projection. His monstrous birth is from the first associated with the darkness of hell and night; and when, in his conversation with Desdemona, he imagines his invention as his baby, that baby is associated specifically with the extrusion of a dark and sticky substance:

> my invention
> Comes from my pate as birdlime does from frieze,
> It plucks out brain and all: but my Muse labours,
> And thus she is deliver'd. . . .
>
> (2.1.125-28)[43]

Presumably Iago means that his invention is as slow—as laborious—as the process of removing birdlime from rough cloth (frieze), in which the nap of the cloth is removed along with the soiling agent (hence "plucks out brain and all"). But the route to this relatively rational meaning is treacherous: the syntax first presents us with birdlime oozing from his head ("invention / Comes from my pate as birdlime does"), takes us on an apparent detour through the soiling of cloth (the birdlime stuck to the frieze), and ends with the image of his head emptied out altogether ("plucks out brain and all"), as though in a dangerous evacuation. Then, through a buried pun on *conception*, the concealed intermediary term, the evacuation becomes a pregnancy and delivery, displaced from his own body to that of the Muse, who labors and is delivered.

Invention, in other words, becomes the male equivalent of pregnancy, the production of a sticky dark baby. What we have here, I suggest, is the vindicative fantasy of a faecal pregnancy and delivery that can project Iago's inner monstrosity and darkness into the world:[44] initially displaced upward to the evacuated pate, this faecal baby is then returned to its source as his monstrous birth, the baby he has conceived in response to Desdemona's request for praise (2.1.124) and the easy generativity (his own is a difficult labor) that he envies in her. This baby's emergence here marks, I think, both the source of his envy and the exchange that envy will demand: he will attempt in effect to replicate his dark sticky baby in her, soiling her generative body by turning her virtue into pitch,[45] spoiling the object whose fullness and goodness he cannot tolerate by making it the receptacle for his own bodily contents. And he counts on the contagion of this contaminated object: he will turn Desdemona into pitch not only because pitch is black and sticky—hence entrapping—but because it is notoriously defiling;[46] his scheme depends on using Desdemona as a kind of tar baby, counting on her defilement—her blackening—to make Othello "black." In fantasy, that is, Iago uses Desdemona and Othello to contaminate each other; they become for him one defiled object as he imagines them on that wedding bed. But at the same time, Othello plays a special role for Iago: in Othello's black skin Iago can find a fortuitous external sign for the entire process, or, more accurately, a container for the internal blackness that he would project outward, the dark baby that hell and night must bring to the world's light; emptying himself out, Iago can project his faecal baby into Othello, blackening him with his own inner waste.

Iago plainly needs an Othello who can carry the burden of his own contamination; and to some extent the play makes us complicit in the process, as it makes Othello in effect into Iago's monstrous creation, carrying out Iago's "conception" as he murders Desdemona on her wedding bed, enacting a perverse version of the childbirth that might have taken place there. Othello himself seems to recognize that a birth of sorts is taking place, though he does not recognize it as Iago's: preparing to kill Desdemona on that bed, he says that her denials "Cannot remove, nor choke the strong conception, / That I do groan withal" (5.2.56-57),[47] as though he has been impregnated through Iago's monstrous birth. And in fact he has: part of the peculiar horror of this play is that Othello becomes so effective a receptacle for—and enactor of—Iago's fantasies. If Iago imagines himself filled with a gnawing poisonous mineral through what amounts to Othello's anal insemination of him (2.1.290-92), he turns that poison back on Othello: "I'll pour this pestilence into his ear" (2.3.347). This retaliatory aural/anal insemination fills Othello with Iago's own contents, allowing Iago to serve his turn on Othello by doing to Othello what he imagines Othello has done to him. ("I follow him to serve my turn upon him" is sexualized in ways not likely to be audible to a modern audience [1.1.42]. For *turn*, see Othello's later "she can turn, and turn, and yet go on, / And turn again" [4.1.249-50];[48] characteristically, Othello replicates in Desdemona the "turn" Iago has replicated in him.) And "The Moor already changes with my poison," Iago says, adding for our benefit—in case we have not noticed the links between his poisonous conceit and Othello's—"Dangerous conceits are in their natures poisons, / Which . . . Burn like the mines of sulphur" (3.3.330-34).

"The Moor already changes with my poison": the line marks what is distinctive about projection in this play—and distinctively Kleinian. Before Klein, projection was usually understood as a relatively uncomplicated process in which disowned ideas and emotions were displaced onto an external figure. Klein insisted both on the fantasies of bodily function accompanying this process and on the extent to which it is specifically pieces of the self and its inner objects that are thus relocated, with the consequence that pieces of the self are now felt to be "out there," both controlling the object into which they have been projected and subject to dangers from it; Klein renamed this process "projective identification." And her followers have expanded on the concept, stressing the effects of these projected contents on the recipient of the projection, the ways in which the projector can in fact control the recipient. In this version of projective identification, the recipient will not only experience the bits of self projected into him but also enact the projector's fantasy scenarios, hence relieving the projector of all responsibility for them.[49] When Iago imagines Roderigo turned inside out, his body filled with pus, he seems to me to be engaging in something close to garden-variety projection: he is attributing to Roderigo portions of himself, or ideas about himself, that he would like to disown; and, as far as we know, Roderigo does not come to experience himself as pus-filled or inside out. But when Iago imagines filling Othello with his poison, when he imagines (in Klein's formulation) "the forceful entry into the object and control of the object by parts of the self,"[50] he is much closer to a specifically Kleinian projective identification; and, as Klein's followers would predict, Othello really does change with Iago's poison, as he begins to experience himself as contaminated and hence to act out Iago's scenarios.

And the play depends on precisely this specialized kind of projective identification, in which Iago's fantasies are rep-

Desdemona as "foul" (5.2.201), as a "begrim'd" Diana or a "black weed," and will evacuate his good object as Iago had predicted (1.3.350); by the end of the play, Emilia can call Othello "the blacker devil," Desdemona's "most filthy bargain," "As ignorant as dirt" (5.2.132, 158, 165) because he has so perfectly introjected Iago's sense of inner filth.

Insofar as Iago can make Othello experience his own blackness as a contamination that contaminates Desdemona, he succeeds in emptying himself out into Othello; and insofar as Othello becomes in effect Iago's faecal baby, Othello—rather than Iago—becomes the bearer of the fantasy of inner filth. Through projective identification, that is, Iago invents blackness as a contaminated category before our eyes, enacting his monstrous birth through Othello, and then allowing the Venetians (and most members of the audience) to congratulate themselves—as he does—on their distance from the now-racialized Othello. Through this process, Othello becomes assimilated to, and motivated by, his racial "type"—becomes the monstrous Moor easily made jealous—and Iago escapes our human categories altogether, becoming unknowable, a motiveless malignity.

But this emptying out of Iago is no more than Iago has already performed on himself: if the projection of his own inner contamination into Othello is Iago's relief, it is also his undoing, and in a way that corroborates both the bodiliness of the fantasy of projection and its dangers to the projector as well as the recipient. Klein notes that excessive use of projective identification results in the "weakening and impoverishment of the ego"; in the words of Betty Joseph, "at times the mind can be . . . so evacuated by projective identification that the individual appears empty."[53] If at the end of the play there is nothing left to envy, there is also no one left to experience envy: Iago's projection of himself into the racial other he constructs as the container for his contamination ends not only by destroying his (and our) good objects but also by leaving him entirely evacuated. Having poured the pestilence of himself into Othello, Iago has nothing left inside him: his antigenerative birth hollows him out, leaving him empty. The closer he is to his goal, the flatter his language becomes; by the end, there is no inside left, no place to speak from. The play that begins with his insistent "I" ends with his silence: from this time forth he never will speak word.

Edwin Booth as Iago, 1870.

licated in Othello's actions. When we first meet Othello, he is confident enough about his status and his color that he wishes to be found; he can confidently wish "the goodness of the night" (1.2.35) on Cassio and the duke's servants because blackness has not yet been poisoned for him. But as Iago projects his faecal baby into him, Othello comes more and more to imagine himself as the foul thing—the old black ram—intruding into the palace of Venetian civilization or the palace of Desdemona's body; as Iago succeeds in making Othello the container for his own interior waste, Othello himself increasingly affiliates his blackness with soiling (he becomes "collied" or blackened by passion [2.3.197];[51] his name is "begrim'd, and black" as his face) and with bad interior objects. (In "Arise, black vengeance, from thy hollow cell" [3.3.454], he calls on "black vengeance" to arise as though from within the hollow of himself.)[52] His experience of himself, that is, comes increasingly to resemble what Iago has projected into him; and he begins to act in accordance with that projection, replicating in Desdemona the contagion of projection itself. The Othello who feels himself begrimed because he has internalized Iago's foul intruder will necessarily see

Notes

1. Quotations follow the Arden edition of *Othello*, edited by M. R. Ridley (London: Methuen, 1958). Ridley follows the 1622 quarto, which often differs from the Folio *Othello;* I have noted the differences where they seem significant to my argument. Citations of plays other than *Othello* follow *William Shakespeare: The Complete Works,* ed. Alfred Harbage (Baltimore: Penguin, 1969).

2. *Race* is of course a vexed term; many have pointed out that the word *race* gained its current meaning

only as it was biologized in support of the economic institution of slavery and that the link between race and skin color is a peculiarly contemporary obsession, that (for example) Irish and Jews might in 1604 have been thought of as racially separate from the English. For a particularly lucid account of the questions surrounding the invocation of race as a category in early modern England, see Lynda E. Boose, "'The Getting of a Lawful Race': Racial discourse in early modern England and the unrepresentable black woman" in *Women, "Race," and Writing in the Early Modern Period,* Margo Hendricks and Patricia Parker, eds. (London and New York: Routledge, 1994), 35-54, esp. 35-40; see also John Gillies, *Shakespeare and the geography of difference* (Cambridge: Cambridge UP, 1994), for the claim that early modern otherness was based on geography rather than on the anachronistic category of race (25). Nonetheless, in Iago's capacity to make Othello's blackness the primary signifier of his otherness—as Boose observes, "once his Ensign has raised the flag inscribing Othello within the difference of skin color, all the presumably meaningful differences Othello has constructed between himself and the infidel collapse" (38)—the text insists on the visible difference of skin color that will increasingly come to define race, perhaps because, unlike religion, it (proverbially) cannot be changed. For a discussion of the significance of visible difference in early modern England, see Kim Hall, "Reading What Isn't There: 'Black' Studies in Early Modern England," *Stanford Humanities Review* 3 (1993): 23-33, esp. 25-27; in her account "science merely takes up already pre-existing terms of difference, such as skin color and features, that have [previously] been combined with physical and mental characteristics" (25).

3. Ridley follows the Folio reading of line 392, since this line occurs in a passage not found in Q1; Q2 (1630) famously reads "Her name" in place of F's "My name," perhaps to rationalize Othello's peculiar association of his name with the fairness of a figure for female virginity. I prefer "My name," partly because it suggests the identificatory dynamics that underlie Othello's love for Desdemona; but either reading points toward Othello's association of the stain on Desdemona's virgin body with the blackness of his own face.

4. Desdemona becomes a *"black"* weed" only in the quartos; F omits the adjective.

5. This position was powerfully—and variously—articulated in three classic essays published in 1979-80: Edward A. Snow's "Sexual Anxiety and the Male Order of Things in *Othello,*" *English Literary Renaissance* 10 (1980): 384-412; Stanley Cavell's "Othello and the Stake of the Other" in *Disowning Knowledge in Six Plays of Shakespeare* (Cambridge: Cambridge UP, 1987), 125-42 (originally published in 1979 in *The Claim of Reason* [Oxford: Oxford UP]); and Stephen Greenblatt's "The Improvisation of Power" in *Renaissance Self-Fashioning: From More to Shakespeare* (Chicago and London: U of Chicago P, 1980), 222-54, esp. 232-52. For the association of Othello's blackness specifically with sexual contamination, and Othello's internalization of this association, see especially Snow, 400-402; and Cavell, 136-37. For a fuller reading of the association between blackness and monstrous sexuality in early modern English culture and in *Othello,* see especially Karen Newman, "'And wash the Ethiop white': femininity and the monstrous in *Othello*" in *Shakespeare Reproduced: The text in history and ideology,* Jean E. Howard and Marion F. O'Connor, eds. (New York and London: Methuen, 1987), 143-62, esp. 148-53; for a fuller reading of the ways in which Othello internalizes the Venetian construction of his blackness, see Edward Berry, "Othello's Alienation," *Studies in English Literature 1500-1900* 30 (1990): 315-33. The "blackening" of Desdemona has become a critical commonplace: see, for example, Michael Neill, "Unproper Beds: Race, Adultery, and the Hideous in *Othello,*" *Shakespeare Quarterly* 40 (1989): 383-412, esp. 410; Berry, 328; Ania Loomba, *Gender, race, Renaissance drama* (Manchester and New York: Manchester UP, 1989), 59; Parker, "Fantasies of 'Race' and 'Gender': Africa, *Othello* and bringing to light" in Hendricks and Parker, eds., 84-100, esp. 95; and especially Newman, 151-52, for whom the blackening of Desdemona indicates the convergence of woman and black in the category of monstrous sexuality.

6. See W. H. Auden's related account of Iago as practical joker: "The practical joker despises his victims, but at the same time he envies them because their desires, however childish and mistaken, are real to them, whereas he has no desire which he can call his own. . . . If the word motive is given its normal meaning of a positive purpose of the self like sex, money, glory, etc., then the practical joker is without motive. Yet the professional practical joker is certainly driven, . . . but the drive is negative, a fear of lacking a concrete self, of being nobody. In any practical joker to whom playing such jokes is a passion, there is always an element of malice, a projection of his self-hatred onto others, and in the ultimate case of the absolute practical joker, this is projected onto all created things" (*The Dyer's Hand and other essays* [New York: Random House, 1962], 256-57). The emptiness of Auden's practical joker is sometimes associated by later critics with Iago's facility in role-playing; see, e.g., Shelley Orgel, whose Iago gains a temporary sense of self by playing the roles that others project onto him ("Iago," *American Imago* 25 [1968]: 258-73, esp. 272). Greenblatt's Iago "has the role-player's ability to imagine his nonexistence so that he can exist for a moment in

another and as another"; but for Greenblatt, Iago's imagined emptiness is less an ontological state than a cover for his emptying out of his victim (235 and 236). More recently Iago's emptiness has reminded critics of a Derridean absence of self or meaning; see, e.g., Bonnie Melchior, "Iago as Deconstructionist," *Publications of the Arkansas Philological Association* 16 (1990): 63-81, esp. 79; or Karl F. Zender, "The Humiliation of Iago," *SEL* 34 (1994): 323-39, esp. 327-28. In Alessandro Serpieri's brilliant semiotic reading, Iago suffers from an "envy of being" that is the deconstructionist's equivalent of the state Auden describes: "Iago cannot identify with any situation or sign or *énoncé,* and is thus condemned to deconstruct through his own *énonciations* the *énoncés* of others, transforming them into simulacra. Othello is precisely the lord of the *énoncé*" (Serpieri, "Reading the signs: towards a semiotics of Shakespearean drama," trans. Keir Elam, in *Alternative Shakespeares,* John Drakakis, ed. [London and New York: Methuen, 1985], 119-43, esp. 139). In its emphasis on envy and projection, Auden's and Serpieri's work is closest to my own; but see also David Pollard's powerful Baudelairian reading of Iago's emptiness and the sadistic projections through which he attempts to fill it ("Iago's Wound" in *Othello: New Perspectives,* Virginia Mason Vaughan and Kent Cartwright, eds. [Rutherford, Madison, and Teaneck, NJ: Fairleigh Dickinson UP; London and Toronto: Associated University Presses, 1991], 89-96).

7. Adam Phillips, "Foreword" in Harold N. Boris, *Envy* (Northvale, NJ, and London: Jason Aronson, 1994), vii-xi, esp. ix.

8. For some, Othello is split long before Iago begins his work. In Berry's account, for example, Othello is divided from the beginning by the two contradictory self-images he absorbs from Venice; his failure to escape this limiting framework and hence to "achieve a true sense of personal identity" is a powerful source of tragic feeling in the play (323 and 330). But for critics who read Othello as an early instance of a colonized subject, this "failure" is not personal but systemic: both Loomba (32, 48, and 54) and Jyotsna Singh ("Othello's Identity, Postcolonial Theory, and Contemporary African Rewritings of *Othello*" in Hendricks and Parker, eds., 287-99, esp. 288) position Othello specifically in opposition to what Singh calls "the dominant, Western fantasy of a singular, unified identity" (288). But Iago at least insists that he is the divided one, and Othello initially claims that his soul is "perfect" or undivided; whatever the state to which Othello is reduced, *Othello*—like *The Tempest*—seems to me to encode the fantasy that the exotic other possesses a primitive unitary identity before his induction into a Western-style split self.

9. I first read this paper to a very helpful and responsive audience at Notre Dame in November 1994, on which occasion Richard Dutton called my attention to the way in which Othello's self-division is literally played out on the stage.

10. As Iago's self-alienation passes to Othello, so does his habit of soliloquizing. Soliloquies are usually in Shakespearean tragedy the discourse of self-division: only those whose selves are in pieces need to explain themselves to themselves and have distinct-enough interior voices to carry out the job for our benefit. Initially Iago's soliloquies formally mark him as fractured in comparison with Othello's wholeness; by the end, Othello is the soliloquizer.

11. I here depart from Ridley in following F's version of line 80; Ridley and Q1 (1622) give "And swiftly come to Desdemona's arms." Ridley himself finds Q1's version of line 80 "pallid" and thinks Shakespeare probably revised it for F; that he nonetheless rejects the Folio version on the grounds that it is inconsistent with Cassio's character suggests his resistance to seeing just how eroticized Cassio's idealizing of Othello is (xxix-xxx and 52n). In the context of lovemaking, *spirits* is not a neutral term; for its specifically sexual senses, see Stephen Booth, *Shakespeare's Sonnets* (New Haven, CT, and London: Yale UP, 1977), 441-43.

12. See Neill's powerful account of the ways in which the audience is implicated in Iago's invocation of the horrors of miscegenation, the improper sexual mixture that medieval theologians called adultery (395-99 and 407-9). For Arthur L. Little Jr. the whole of the play constitutes "the primal scene of racism," a forbidden sexual sight/site from which the audience "constructs the significance of race" ("'An essence that's not seen': The Primal Scene of Racism in *Othello,*" *SQ* 44 [1993]: 304-24, esp. 305-6).

13. The familiar associations of blackness with monstrosity (see, e.g., Newman, 148; and James R. Aubrey, "Race and the Spectacle of the Monstrous in *Othello,*" *Clio* 22 [1993]: 221-38) and specifically with monstrous births (see Neill, 409-10; and Aubrey, 222-27) would probably have made the subterranean connection between Othello and Iago's monstrous birth more available to Shakespeare's audiences than it is to a modern audience.

14. Projection has classically been invoked as a mechanism in *Othello,* but usually in the other direction, from Othello to Iago; see, e.g., J. I. M. Stewart, *Character and Motive in Shakespeare: Some Recent Appraisals Examined* ([London, New York, and Toronto: Longmans, Green and Company, 1949], 102-5), though Stewart ultimately abandons a naturalistic reading of the play through projection for a symbolic reading of Iago and Othello as parts of a single whole. For somewhat later versions of Iago as Othello's projection, see, e.g., Henry L.

Warnken, "Iago as a Projection of Othello" in *Shakespeare Encomium 1564-1964,* Anne Paolucci, ed. (New York: The City College, 1964), 1-15; and Orgel, 258-73. In these accounts projection is loosely used to indicate that Iago expresses unacknowledged doubts or desires in Othello's mind (or, in Orgel's reading, Othello's unacknowledged need for a punitive superego); they generally do not explore the mechanism of projection or consider the degree to which the structure of the play posits Iago—not Othello—as its psychic starting point. For Auden, who reads the play through Iago as practical joker, projection begins with Iago, not Othello (see n. 6, above); see also Leslie Y. Rabkin and Jeffrey Brown, who read Iago as a Horneyan sadist, assuaging his pain by projecting his self-contempt and hopelessness onto others ("Some Monster in His Thought: Sadism and Tragedy in *Othello*," *Literature and Psychology* 23 [1973]: 59-67, esp. 59-60); and Pollard, who reads Iago as Baudelairian sadist, filling the world with sadistic projections with which he then identifies to fill his inner emptiness (92-95). Serpieri sees Iago as the "artificer of a *destructive projection*"; in his semiotic analysis, litotes—Iago's characteristic nay-saying figure—becomes the linguistic equivalent of projection, "a figure of persuasion which, by denying, affirms in the 'other' all that—the diabolical, the lustful, the alien—which it refutes or censures in the 'self'" (134 and 142). Attention to the status of "others" has made contemporary criticism particularly sensitive to Othello as the site of Iago's projections rather than as the originator of projection; see, e.g., Parker on "the violence of projection" (100). My account differs from those cited here largely in giving projection a body and in specifying the mechanisms of projective identification at work in the play.

15. Although Neill emphasizes the hidden/hideousness of the bed rather than of bodily interiors (394-95), my formulation here is very much indebted to his. In the course of her enormously suggestive account of the cultural resonances of the hidden/private in *Othello* and *Hamlet,* Parker comments extensively on the association of the hidden with the woman's private parts, partly via gynecological discourse; see Parker, "*Othello* and *Hamlet:* Dilation, Spying, and the 'Secret Place' of Woman," *Representations* 44 (1993): 60-95, esp. 64-69.

16. *Gender* can of course mean "kind"; but, as Ridley notes, "Shakespeare normally uses it of difference of sex" (40n).

17. Ridley notes that "*supply* = satisfy" (40n); for a specifically sexualized use, see *Measure for Measure,* 5.1.210.

18. "Doves" is the reading in Ridley and Q1; I here depart from it in giving F's and Q2's "dawes."

19. On the relationship between money and faeces, see Sigmund Freud, "Character and Anal Eroticism" in *The Standard Edition of the Complete Psychological Works of Sigmund Freud,* ed. James Strachey, 24 vols. (London: Hogarth Press and the Institute of Psycho-Analysis, 1953-74), 9:167-76, esp. 171 and 173-74; Ernest Jones, "Anal-Erotic Character Traits," *Journal of Abnormal Psychology* 13 (1918): 261-84, esp. 272-74 and 276-77; Karl Abraham, "Contributions to the Theory of the Anal Character" in *Selected Papers of Karl Abraham* (New York: Brunner/Mazel, 1927), 370-92, esp. 383; and Otto Fenichel, *The Psychoanalytic Theory of Neurosis* (New York: Norton, 1945), 281. On sadism and anality, see Abraham, "The Narcissistic Evaluation of Excretory Processes in Dreams and Neurosis" in *Selected Papers,* 318-22, esp. 319 and 321; Jones, 268; and Fenichel, 283.

20. The *loci classici* for this reading are Martin Wangh, "*Othello:* The Tragedy of Iago," *Psychoanalytic Quarterly* 19 (1950): 202-12; and Gordon Ross Smith, "Iago the Paranoiac," *American Imago* 16 (1959): 155-67. Both essays are based on Freud's account of delusional jealousy as a defense against homosexual desire in the Schreber case. For an extension and elaboration of this view, with particular focus on Iago's hatred of women, see also Stanley Edgar Hyman, *Iago: Some Approaches to the Illusion of His Motivation* (New York: Atheneum, 1970), 101-21. Contemporary critics who comment on the homoerotic dynamic between Iago and Othello tend to locate their readings not in this model but in the complex of metaphors that makes Iago's seduction of Othello into an aural penetration and insemination, with a resulting monstrous (and miscegenistic) conception; see, e.g., Coppélia Kahn, *Man's Estate: Masculine Identity in Shakespeare* (Berkeley, Los Angeles, and London: U of California P, 1981), 144-45; and Parker in Hendricks and Parker, eds., 99-100. Parker notes that the imagined penetration is anal as well as aural (99); see also, e.g., Graham Hammill's brief discussion of Iago's anal eroticism, "The Epistemology of Expurgation: Bacon and *The Masculine Birth of Time*" in *Queering the Renaissance,* Jonathan Goldberg, ed. (Durham, NC, and London: Duke UP, 1994), 236-52, esp. 251n.

21. For historically based arguments against Iago-as-repressed-homosexual, see Jonathan Dollimore, *Sexual Dissidence* (Oxford: Clarendon Press, 1991), 157-62; and Bruce R. Smith, *Homosexual Desire in Shakespeare's England: A Cultural Poetics* (Chicago and London: U of Chicago P, 1991), 61-63 and 75. Both Dollimore and Smith stress the social functions of the male homosocial bond rather than the dynamics of homoerotic feeling partly on the grounds that the homosexual subject is an anachronism in the early modern period. But Shakespeare does not need to have the category of the "homosexual subject" available to him in order to represent Iago as acting

out of desires inadmissible to him, including sodomitical desires; and critics who insist that we do away with "the homosexual" as a category sometimes throw out the baby with the bathwater. In "Homosexuality and the Signs of Male Friendship in Elizabethan England" (in Goldberg, ed., 40-61) Alan Bray demonstrates the cultural (nonsexual) uses to which the "bedfellow" could be put; but in order for Smith, for example, to invoke Iago's report of Cassio's "bedfellow" dream to make the argument that Iago is a self-conscious male-bonder rather than a repressed homosexual, he has to ignore the explicit sexiness of the dream (the hard kisses plucked up by the roots, the leg over the thigh). The dream clearly crosses the line—between male friendship and sodomy—that Bray delineates, more strikingly because Iago need not have included all that sexiness to convey his "information" to Othello; and whether or not the reported dream proclaims Iago a "repressed homosexual," its effect on Othello clearly depends as much on its crossing of that line as on the information that Cassio dreams about Desdemona. As for subjectivity: whether or not the Renaissance shared our sense of the bourgeois subject—in any case, emphatically not the subject as it is construed by psychoanalysis—*Othello* is obsessively about what is hidden away within the person, the inner, private, and unknowable self that might harbor inaccessible desires. For a good summary of these controversies—and a sensible middle position—see Alan Sinfield, *Cultural Politics—Queer Reading* (Philadelphia: U of Pennsylvania P, 1994), 12-14.

22. Melanie Klein, "Envy and Gratitude" (1957) in *Envy and Gratitude and Other Works 1946-1963* (London: Hogarth Press and the Institute of Psycho-Analysis, 1975), 176-235, esp. 179.

23. Klein, 188.

24. Klein, 192 and 189.

25. Boris, xvi.

26. Klein, 183.

27. For an early statement of this position, see Klein, "Early Stages of the Oedipus Conflict" (1928) in *Love, Guilt and Reparation and Other Works 1921-1945* (London: Hogarth Press and the Institute of Psycho-Analysis, 1975), 186-98, esp. 190-91 and 193-96.

28. Klein, *Envy and Gratitude,* 181.

29. Klein, *Envy and Gratitude,* 186.

30. Quoted here from Bernard Spivack's discussion of Iago and the morality tradition in *Shakespeare and the Allegory of Evil: The History of a Metaphor in Relation to His Major Villains* (New York: Columbia UP, 1958), 184.

31. Betty Joseph, "Envy in everyday life" in *Psychic Equilibrium and Psychic Change: Selected Papers of Betty Joseph,* ed. Michael Feldman and Elizabeth Bott Spillius (London and New York: Tavistock/Routledge, 1989), 181-91, esp. 185.

32. In Kleinian terms, Othello has reached the depressive position, characterized by the capacity to mourn for the damaged object and to make reparations to it (see especially Klein, "A Contribution to the Psychogenesis of Manic-Depressive States" [1935] and "Mourning and its Relation to Manic-Depressive States" [1940], both in *Love, Guilt and Reparation,* 262-89 and 344-69); Iago functions from within the more primitive paranoid-schizoid position, with its characteristic mechanisms of splitting and projection/introjection (see especially Klein, "Notes on Some Schizoid Mechanisms" in *Envy and Gratitude,* 1-24).

33. As many have argued: see especially Cavell, 134; and Snow, 392. See also my *Suffocating Mothers: Fantasies of Maternal Origin in Shakespeare,* Hamlet *to* The Tempest (New York and London: Routledge, 1992), 69-70.

34. Iago's words here, like Emilia's at 3.4.157-60, refer explicitly to *jealousy* but nonetheless define the self-referential qualities of *envy*. Although the two terms are sometimes popularly confused, they are distinct in psychoanalytic thought: jealousy occurs in a three-body relationship, derived from the oedipus complex, in which the loss of a good object to a rival is at stake; envy occurs in a pre-oedipal two-body relationship, in which the "good" qualities of the object are felt to be intolerable. Jealousy seeks to preserve the good object, if necessary by killing it; envy seeks to spoil the good object. (For these distinctions, see Klein, *Envy and Gratitude,* 196-99; and Joseph in Feldman and Spillius, eds., 182.) Jealousy is a derivative of envy but is more easily recognized and more socially acceptable (Klein, *Envy and Gratitude,* 198; Joseph in Feldman and Spillius, eds., 182); partly as a consequence, it can sometimes serve as "an important defence against envy" (Klein, *Envy and Gratitude,* 198). This defensive structure seems to me at work both in Iago and in the play at large: in Iago, who repeatedly comes up with narratives of jealousy as though to justify his intolerable envy to himself (tellingly, he uses the traditional language of envy—Spenser's Envy "inwardly . . . chawed his owne maw" in *The Faerie Queene* [I.iv.30]—to register the gnawing effects of jealousy on him); and in *Othello* itself, insofar as its own narratives of jealousy are far more legible and recognizably "human" than the envy represented through Iago and dismissed in him as unrecognizable, inhuman, or demonic.

35. "Mock" has puzzled commentators for years, occasioning five pages of commentary in the New Variorum edition of *Othello* (ed. Horace Howard Furness [Philadelphia: J. B. Lippincott, 1886]).

William Warburton (1747) glosses "mocke" (in terms strikingly close to my own) as "loaths that which nourishes and sustains it" (176). With very little plausibility but some interest for my argument, Andrew Becket (1815) transforms "mocke" to "*muck*," glossing it as to "*bedaub* or *make foul*"; two other commentators—Zachariah Jackson and Lord John Chedworth—approved of this emendation enough to come up with candidates for the monstrous animal that befouls its food, mouse and dragon-fly, respectively (179).

36. Zachary Grey suggested in 1754 that "mock" is a contraction for "mammock" (Furness, ed., 176); as far as I can tell, his suggestion has been entirely ignored.

37. Klein, *Envy and Gratitude,* 201-2.

38. See *Hamlet,* 2.2.181-82.

39. This destruction also has the effect of separating the two figures whose conjunction has haunted Iago's imagination. Klein hypothesizes the combined parent figure as a special target of envy ("the suspicion that the parents are always getting sexual gratification from one another reinforces the phantasy . . . that they are always combined" [*Envy and Gratitude,* 198]); Iago in fact evokes such a fantasy-figure in his initial description of Othello and Desdemona as fused, a "beast with two backs" (1.1.116), always in the process of achieving the "incorporate conclusion" (2.1.258-59) that is always denied him.

40. Boris, 36.

41. My formulation here is partly indebted to Janine Chausseguet-Smirgel's work on perversion, expecially anal perversion, which she sees as an attempt to dissolve generational and gender differences in order to defend against acknowledgment of the pervert's own puniness and vulnerability; though she does not draw specifically on Klein's concept of envy, her work sometimes intersects usefully with Klein's. In Chausseguet-Smirgel's reading, Sade's intention, for example, is "to reduce the universe to faeces, or rather to annihilate the universe of differences" ("Perversion and the Universal Law" in Chausseguet-Smirgel, *Creativity and Perversion* [New York: W. W. Norton, 1984], 4). Insofar as perversion attempts to replace God's differentiated universe with its own undifferentiation, it is "the equivalent of Devil religion (9); the undifferentiated and universe "constitutes an imitation or parody of the genital universe of the father" (11). While this formulation is suggestive for Iago, I think that Chausseguet-Smirgel is hampered by her Lacanian milieu, with its overvaluation of the phallus and the father's law; Iago is at least as intent on imitating and ultimately replacing the mother's generative function as the father's law.

42. With the kind of psychological intuition that everywhere animates his portrayal of Satan, Milton reworks Emilia's comment: unable to stand the "debt immense of endless gratitude" to the God who has created him (*Paradise Lost,* Bk. 4, l. 52), Satan proclaims himself "self-begot, self-rais'd / By our own quick'ning power" (Bk. 5, ll. 860-61). Klein cites Milton's Satan as an instance of "the spoiling of creativity implied in envy" (*Envy and Gratitude,* 202).

43. According to the *Oxford English Dictionary,* birdlime is a sticky substance made out of the bark of the holly tree and smeared on branches to entrap birds; "With the barkes of Holme they make Bird-lyme," cited from Henry Lyte's 1578 *Niewe herball or historie of plantes* (*Oxford English Dictionary,* prep. J. Simpson and E.S.C. Weiner, 2d ed., 20 vols. [Oxford: Clarendon Press, 1989], 2:216). *Holme* is confusing; it is cited as "blacke Holme" in Spenser's *Virgils Gnat* (l. 215), but there apparently refers to the oak, not the holly. In any case, despite the echo of lime, birdlime seems to have been dark, not white.

44. The equation of faeces with baby is familiar to psychoanalysis; see, e.g., Freud, "On the Sexual Theories of Children," on the cloacal theory of birth ("If babies are born through the anus, then a man can give birth just as well as a woman" [9:205-26, esp. 219-20]); Jones, 274-75; and Susan Isaacs, "Penis-Feces-Child," *International Journal of Psycho-analysis* 8 (1927): 74-76. For fantasies that overvalue the power of faecal creation "to create or destroy every object," see Abraham, "The Narcissistic Evaluation of Excretory Processes," 322; about one of his patients he reports, "That night he dreamed that he had to expel the universe out of his anus" (320).

45. Oddly, Ridley associates the pitch into which Iago will turn Desdemona's virtue with birdlime without noting its source in Iago's earlier metaphor (88n).

46. For Shakespeare's reworkings of the proverbially defiling properties of pitch, see, e.g., *Love's Labor's Lost,* 4.3.3; *1 Henry IV,* 2.4.394-96; and *Much Ado About Nothing,* 3.3.53.

47. I here depart from Ridley in following F and Q2; Q1, Ridley's copytext, gives "conceit." The half-buried metaphor of childbirth is, I think, present in either case, both through the association of "groan"—especially in proximity to a bed—with childbirth (see, e.g., *All's Well That Ends Well,* 1.3.140 and 4.5.10; and *Measure for Measure,* 2.2.15) and through the family relation between *conceit* and Latin *conceptus,* cited in the *OED;* the *OED* also gives "Conception of offspring" as an obsolete meaning for *conceit* with a 1589 instance, though it notes that this usage is "Perhaps only a pun" (3:647-48, esp. 648).

48. See also "the best turn i' th' bed" (*Antony and Cleopatra,* 2.5.59). For *serve,* see *Lear's* Oswald, "A serviceable villain, / As duteous to the vices of

thy mistress / As badness would desire" (4.6.248-50); for *serve my turn,* see Costard's exchange with the king (*Love's Labor's Lost,* 1.1.281-82). For *follow/fallow,* see Parker in Hendricks and Parker, eds., 99, citing Herbert A. Ellis, *Shakespeare's Lusty Punning in Love's Labour's Lost* (1973).

49. This is an oversimplified summary of a very complex development in psychoanalytic theory; for a fuller summary, see "Projective Identification" in R. D. Hinshelwood's *A Dictionary of Kleinian Thought* (London: Free Association Books, 1991), 179-208; or Elizabeth Bott Spillius's "Clinical experiences of projective identification" in *Clinical Lectures on Klein and Bion,* Robin Anderson, ed. (London and New York: Tavistock/Routledge, 1992), 59-73, esp. 59-64. For Klein's initial development of the concept of projective identification, see *Envy and Gratitude,* 8-11. The development of the concept by her followers has had broad ramifications for clinical work; for a particularly lucid account of some of these, see, in addition to Spillius, Joseph, "Projective identification—some clinical aspects" in *Melanie Klein Today: Developments in Theory and Practice,* Elizabeth Bott Spillius, ed., 2 vols. (London and New York: Routledge, 1988), 1:138-50.

50. Klein, *Envy and Gratitude,* 11.

51. *Collied* is conjecturally related to *coaly* by the *OED,* 3:390-91.

52. Folio gives "hell" for Q1's "cell." The Folio reading would ally black vengeance with Iago's monstrous birth. In either reading, the apparently superfluous hollowness suggests an inner space; as Ridley notes, it occurs, again redundantly, in the reference to a "hollow mine" (4.2.81). Shortly after he calls up black vengeance, and again in 5.2, Othello imagines his revenge swallowing up his victims (3.3.467 and 5.2.76), as though returning them to the interior source of his vengeance.

53. Klein, *Envy and Gratitude,* 11; Joseph in Spillius, ed., *Melanie Klein Today,* 140.

Michael Neill (essay date 1998)

SOURCE: "'Mulattos,' 'Blacks,' and 'Indian Moors': *Othello* and Early Modern Constructions of Human Difference," in *Shakespeare Quarterly,* Vol. 49, No. 4, Winter, 1998, pp. 361-74.

[*In the following essay, Neill discusses the contradictory significance of race in* Othello.]

"I think this play is racist, and I think it is not":[1] Virginia Vaughan's perplexed response to *Othello* is symptomatic of the problems faced by late-twentieth-century critics in approaching the racial dimensions of Shakespeare's play. For if the work of recent scholars has taught us anything about early modern constructions of human difference, it is that any attempt to read back into the early modern period an idea of "race" based on post-Enlightenment taxonomy is doomed to failure.[2] To talk about race in *Othello* is to fall into anachronism; yet not to talk about it is to ignore something fundamental about a play that has rightly come to be identified as a foundational text in the emergence of modern European racial consciousness—a play that trades in constructions of human difference at once misleadingly *like* and confusingly *unlike* those twentieth-century notions to which they are nevertheless recognizably ancestral. In the latter part of this paper, I hope to cast some light on Shakespeare's treatment of what came to be called "race" by exploring an experience of alterity in the East Indian archipelago, a theater of colonial encounter which may at first seem far away from the Mediterranean world of *Othello.* But I should like to frame that discussion by briefly considering some of the ways in which this tragedy perplexes the notions of ethnic and national identity that its subtitle so casually invokes.

In an essay that provides a useful corrective to anachronistically postcolonial understandings of race in *Othello,* Emily Bartels has stressed the ideological openness of the play's treatment of human difference, arguing that (except in the eyes of Iago and those he manipulates) "Othello *is,* as the subtitle announces, 'the Moor of Venice'. . . . neither an alienated nor an assimilated subject, but a figure defined by two worlds, a figure (like Marlowe's Jew of Malta) whose ethnicity occupies one slot, professional interests another, compatibly"—the fortunate possessor, then, of "a dual, rather than divided, identity."[3] But the invocation of Barabas as a parallel type of comfortably hyphenated hybridity seems something of a give-away here. One has only to think of the extreme anxieties surrounding the question of what it meant to belong to, say, the "Old English" of Ireland to recall how easily dual identity could be interpreted as sinister doubleness or self-contradiction: from the viewpoint of "New English" settlers like Spenser, the adoption of Irish customs and speech by the Old English descendants of Norman conquerors could signal only a treacherous repudiation of their birthright.[4] The unease of hybridity (whether elective or enforced), in a world where the hybrid was always liable to be construed as prodigious or monstrous, is apparent in the ambivalent ethnographic discourse of one of Shakespeare's principal sources for *Othello*—the *Geographical Historie of Africa,* written by the Granada-born Moor John Leo Africanus. In a somewhat poignant moment, this native informant and Christian *converso,* for whom African peoples are both "them" and "us," describes himself as an "amphibian,"[5] thereby acknowledging his contradictory position as a denizen of both Muslim and Christian worlds, as both African and European, humanist scholar and "barbarian." It is a position that can seem inscribed in an adopted Latin name equally suggestive of dedicated papal allegiance and an unreconstructed bestial ferocity.[6] In much the same way, Othello's Africa is at once the place that authenticates his birth "from men of royal siege" (1.2.22) and a wilderness of Plinian monstrosities, of "Anthropophagi, and men whose heads / Do grow beneath their shoulders" (1.3.145-46).[7] One way of describing the action of his tragedy is in terms of the process by which Iago progressively prises open the contradictions in an oxymoronic subtitle that marks the uneasy translation of "erring Barbarian" into "civil monster" (1.3.356; 4.1.64)—the process (to put it another way) by which he successfully essentializes or "racializes" Othello's difference.

When Roderigo, under Iago's tutelage, dismisses Othello as "an extravagant and wheeling stranger / Of here and everywhere" (1.1.134-35), he issues a fundamental challenge to the syntax of identity inscribed in the play's subtitle, "The Moor of Venice."[8] To be a Moor, he insists, is to be a fundamentally dislocated creature, a wandering denizen of that un-place known as wilderness, heath, or *moor*—"an erring Barbarian" in the punning phrase with which Iago assimilates Barbary to the notoriously vagrant condition of barbarism. From Roderigo's perspective, then, to be a "Moor of Venice" is to represent a principle of wild disorder lodged in the very heart of metropolitan civilization—to be, in another of Iago's violent oxymorons, a kind of "civil monster." The innocent-seeming preposition that yokes Moorish origin to Venetian identity is thus a site of violent contradiction.[9] Yet the *of* in "Moor of Venice" is easily passed over as a mere instrument of descriptive amplification, as unproblematic in its implications as the similarly deployed locatives in, say, Timon of Athens, The Two Gentleman of Verona—or, indeed, The Merchant of Venice, the play that is in some respects Othello's counterpart in Shakespeare's comic canon. To remember *The Merchant of Venice* in this context, however, is to recall the tellingly ambiguous description of the play in the Stationers' Register, "a booke of the Marchaunte of Venyce, or otherwise called the Jew of Venyce," and hence to be confronted with the troubling implications of Portia's question, "Which is the Merchant here, and which the Jew?" (4.1.171)—a question that directs us toward a reading of that play in which issues of place and identity, of the "native" and the "stranger," become so vexed as to seriously destabilize the innocent-seeming *of* that ties both Shylock and Antonio to their native city. The effect is to send us further back to Marlowe's satiric deconstruction of geographic identity in *The Jew of Malta*. As the alienated representative of "a scatter'd Nation" (1.1.121), Barabas is not so much *of* Malta as *in* it—just as his vaunted colleagues in international Jewry are located "in" Bairseth, Portugal, Italy, and France.[10] Scorning allegiance not only to "those of Malta" (l. 143) but even to his own professed "Countreymen" (l. 159), the fellow Jews who share his persecution, Barabas takes sardonic pleasure in representing himself as an archetypal cosmopolitan, whose politic schooling in Machiavelli's Florence has helped him to manipulate "the warres 'twixt *France* and *Germanie*" (2.3.187) as it now enables him to exploit the conflict between Turk and Christian. Yet the pseudo-cathartic action of his "tragedy," with its ludicrously repeated efforts to purge him from the costive body politic, suggests a more organic relationship between this outsider and "those of Malta" than either Barabas or his Christian persecutors would acknowledge.

Of course the particular fear that attaches to the demon-Jew in early modern European culture has to do with his insidious role as the hidden stranger, the alien whose otherness is the more threatening for its guise of semblance. This was a culture whose own expansionism, ironically enough, generated fears of a hungrily absorptive otherness which were expressed in complementary fantasies of dangerous miscegenation, degeneration, and cannibalistic desire; in its fictions the Jew represents the deepest threat of all—that of a *secret* difference masquerading as likeness, whose presence threatens the surreptitious erosion of identity from within.[11] One reason why Shylock remains such a deeply troubling figure at the end of *Merchant* is the unspoken possibility that his forcible conversion (like that of Jews in sixteenth-century Spain) will only institutionalize the very uncertainty it is designed to efface. Jessica's marriage to Lorenzo—albeit that marriage in some sense confers the husband's identity on the wife—contains the same latent threat; hence, perhaps, the uneasy silence that surrounds her in the concluding moments of the play.

The great advantage of Moors over Jews—or so it might seem to early modern Europeans—was that they could not so easily disguise their difference:[12] blackness (as Aaron boasts in *Titus Andronicus*) "scorns to bear another hue" (4.2.99); and the ultimately reassuring thing about George Best's famous story of the English mother who gave birth to a black baby is that the taint of alterity seems compelled by nature to discover itself—"the blacke More," as Scripture and proverb insisted, "[cannot] change his skin [any more than] the leopard his spottes," for it was impossible "to wash the Ethiop white."[13] Yet, of course, Aaron's boast is undercut by his own scheme to substitute the impeccably white offspring of his "countryman" Muliteus for Tamora's black infant, and—as the parallel campaigns of persecution against converted Jews (*marranos*) and converted Moors (*moriscos*) were calculated to demonstrate[14]—it turns out that Moorishness was almost as capable as Jewishness of concealing its aggressive Otherness within the body of the Same. This was the case partly because of the notorious indeterminacy of the term *Moor* itself: insofar as it was a term of racial description, it could refer quite specifically to the Berber-Arab people of the part of North Africa then rather vaguely denominated as "Morocco," "Mauritania," or "Barbary"; or it could be used to embrace the inhabitants of the whole North African littoral; or it might be extended to refer to Africans generally (whether "white," "black," or "tawny" Moors); or, by an even more promiscuous extension, it might be applied (like "Indian") to almost any darker-skinned peoples—even, on occasion, those of the New World.[15] Consequently when Marlowe's Valdes refers to the supine obedience of "Indian *Moores*" to "their Spanish Lords" (*Faustus*, 1.1.148),[16] it is usually assumed that the two terms are simply mutually intensifying synonyms, and that the magician means something like "dusky New World natives." But *Moor* could often be deployed (in a fashion perhaps inflected, even for the English, by memories of the Spanish *Reconquista*) as a religious category. Thus Muslims on the Indian subcontinent were habitually called "Moors," and the same term is used in East India Company literature to describe the Muslim inhabitants of Southeast Asia, whether they be Arab or Indian traders, or indigenous Malays. So Valdes's "Indian Moores" could equally well be Muslims from the Spanish-controlled Portuguese East Indies. In such contexts it is simply impossible to be sure whether *Moor* is a description of color or religion or some vague amalgam of the two, and in the intoxicated exoticism of Marlovian geography, such discriminations hardly matter.

But in less fantastical contexts they could matter a great deal—as, for example, when renegade Europeans in the East Indies were said to "turn Moor," just as in the Mediterranean they were more usually said to "turn Turk."[17] In travel literature of the period these two expressions are sometimes interchangeable, "Turk" being used even in descriptions of the East Indies as a loosely generic description of the people otherwise called "Islams" or "Mahomettans." The Dutch voyager William Cornelison Schouten, for example, describes an encounter with the men of Tidore, "some [of whom] . . . had Wreathes about their heads, which they say were Turkes or Moores in Religion."[18] Turkishness or Moorishness here is a matter of religious allegiance, rendered visible (like the malignancy of Othello's "turbanned Turk" [5.2.351]) in details of costume. Thus when Othello, the Moor turned Christian, accuses his brawling Venetian followers of "turn[ing] Turk . . ." (2.3.166), his hyperbole has a disturbing irony that (as critics now routinely observe) resonates with a suicide in Act 5 that takes the form of a re-enacted slaughter of the Turk. Moreover, because the religious and racial parameters of Moorishness were seldom entirely distinct, the exact implications of the metamorphoses whereby Christians "turned Moor" and Moors "turned Christian" were disturbingly blurred. If a Christian turned Moor, did he in some sense "blacken" himself? If a Moor "turned Christian," did he thereby cease in some important sense to be a Moor? If he did not, would residual Moorishness turn out to be a matter of blood, color, or faith?[19] It is true that the purely religious connotations of "Christian" produce a significant asymmetry between "turning Christian" and "turning Turk (or Moor)," making it seem as though the "racial" component of identity can be transformed in only one direction; yet these questions were difficult to answer with any assurance, so long as the language of difference remained as shifting and uncertain as it was before the emergence of the modern discourses of race and color. The history of the simultaneous (and largely inseparable) campaigns for purity of blood (*limpieza de sangre*) and purity of religion in Spain are only extreme symptoms of a larger European difficulty that threatened to turn a phrase such as "Moor of Venice" into a hopeless oxymoron.[20] That, indeed, is what Richard Brome clearly felt it to be when he dubbed his comedy of senile jealousy *The English Moore* (1637). Brome's plot turns on the performance of a "Masque of Blackamoors" (a self-conscious travesty of his old master Ben Jonson's *Masque of Blackness*), in the course of which it is prophesied that the princess of Ethiopia will be blanched by marriage to an Englishman. But in the play proper, metamorphosis never amounts to anything more than the shedding of the heroine's blackface disguise. And just as (in the words of the inset masque) "'tis no better then a Prodigee / To haue white children in a black Contree" (4.4.22-23),[21] so it appears that there can be no such thing in nature as an "English Moor."

Of course the English (like other Europeans) brought some important cultural baggage to their encounters with foreign peoples: ideas about genealogy, about the biblical separation of humankind, and about the moral symbolism of color, all of which pushed them toward an essentialist reading of phenotypic difference. Yet, as Karen Ordahl Kupperman has recently argued, because they were predisposed to think "in terms of socially or culturally created categories," treating most "differences between people . . . [as] 'accidental' . . .[consequences of] environment or experience," they had not yet learned to "divide humankind into broad fixed classifications demarcated by visible distinctions."[22] As with the disdainful attitudes of the English toward the Irish—a people whose physical similarities to the English were conveniently obscured by their cultural differences—categories such as "civil" and "barbarous," "naked" and "clothed" were often of far more significance in establishing the boundaries of otherness than the markers of mere biological diversity.[23] In the later sixteenth century, however, the rapid expansion of national horizons through exploration and trade increasingly faced the English with foreign cultures whose sophisticated ways of life resisted assimilation into the cultural categories by which the threat of alterity had traditionally been contained.

In the early part of the period, the English often approached these peoples with a certain ethnographic objectivity. Much of the travel literature collected by Hakluyt is quite assiduous in cataloguing the various "distinction[s] of color, Nation, language[,] . . . condition" that divide the peoples of the earth;[24] and variations of dress, weapons, manners, custom, social organization, and (above all) religion figure at least as prominently as differences of skin and feature. But as we move into the seventeenth century, the pressure of encounter with so many unfamiliar peoples begins to shift definitions of alterity away from the dominant paradigm of culture. In another telling asymmetry, it is possible to see color emerging as the most important criterion for defining otherness, even as *nation* becomes the key term of *self*-definition.[25] The gradations of color appear to cause significant difficulties for the Dutch traveler Van Linschoten, for example, in his influential *Voyages* (translated and published with Hakluyt's endorsement in 1598), as he struggles (in sometimes-contradictory language) to define the nature of the differences between the various Asian peoples he encountered. The people of Ormuz are "white like the Persians," those of Bengal "somewhat whiter then the Chingalas";"The people of Aracan, Pegu, and Sian are . . . much like those of China, onely one difference they haue, which is, that they are somewhat whiter then the Bengalon, and somewhat browner then the men of China"; in China itself, "Those that dwell on the Sea side . . . are a people of a *brownish* colour, like the *white* Moores in Africa and Barbaria, and part of the Spaniards, but those that dwell within the land, *are for color like Netherlanders & high Dutches*." Yet "[t]here are many among them that are *cleane blacke*," while "[i]n the lande lying westward from China, they say there are white people, and the land called Cathaia, where (as it is thought) are many Christians."[26]

The East Indian archipelago posed particular problems of definition since the islands were themselves undergoing a rapid cultural transformation, as a militant, expansionist Islam progressively displaced well-established Hindu and surviving Buddhist and animist practices. The proliferation of religious, cultural, and ethnic differences must have been baffling to the English newcomers, subjecting their available definitions to peculiar strains. The various indigenous peoples and the rival groups of traders who clustered in their towns could of course be classified according to the geographical or political entities to which they belonged as "Javans, Chineses, Men of Pegu, Bandaneses," and so forth; or they might be categorized according to religion as "ethnicks," "pagans," or "Moors"; or they might be grouped, together with the inhabitants of the Indian subcontinent, as "Indians" or "East Indians" (in a regional designation that the uncertainties of post-Columbian geography had permanently confused with differences of complexion). What precisely this meant in terms of color was a little confused: George Best's *A Trve Discovrse of the late voyages of discouerie* (1578), for example, had described East Indians, along with American "Indians," as being "not blacke, but white," though this was altered in Hakluyt's version of the *True Discovrse* to "tauney and white,"[27] a distinction that other observers typically aligned with gender, remarking (in the words of Thomas Cavendish) that "although the men bee tawnie of colour . . . yet their women be faire of complexion"—something they attributed to the effects of clothing and exposure to the sun.[28] In the familiar (and deeply ambiguous) trope routinely employed in both West and East Indian contexts, the hue of the natives is figured as "the sun's livery." So we are told of Princess Quisara in Fletcher's *The Island Princess* (1621) that "The very Sun I thinke, affects her sweetnesse, / And dares not as he does to all else, dye it / Into his tauny Livery" (1.1.60-62).[29] The princess's whiteness is the sign of inward "sweetnesse" that will be expressed in the conversion to Christianity that accompanies her betrothal to the Portuguese hero Armusia at the end of the play. The issue of color cannot be entirely erased, however; and the cynical Pyniero is allowed to suggest that there is something unnatural about the princess's "wear[ing] her complexion in a case," because if exposed to the sun's kisses, it would so readily convert to a dusky hue: "let him but like it / A week or two, or three, she would look like a Lion" (ll. 63-64). East Indian tawniness (whether actual or, like Quisara's, merely potential) may constitute an accident of culture and geography, but it is also a kind of servile "Livery," the badge of allegiance to the false religion to which the princess and her countrymen are in thrall.[30] And it resonates dangerously with those contemporary discourses that interpreted dark skin (in both African and West Indian contexts) as a sign of natural servitude.[31]

One way of dealing with the taxonomic complications exemplified in Van Linschoten and reflected in *The Island Princess* was to develop a notion of difference that would effectually obscure the confusing variations of hue that Van Linschoten acknowledges in both European and non-European populations by establishing a more absolute division between "them" and "us". During the first three decades of the seventeenth century, uncertainties about the nature of human difference are gradually flattened out in the literature of East Indian voyaging, as the peoples of the region begin to be categorized, according to the crudest distinction of color, as "black"—a designation that serves solely to distinguish them from "white" Europeans.[32]

This idea of Europeanness as a form of group identity delimited by color seems itself to have been something new. In a probing analysis, "'The Getting of a Lawful race,'" Lynda Boose has posed the question whether English notions of Moorishness, for example, were shaped by anything resembling "the modern sense of some definitively *racial* shared 'Europeanness'? Or was the difference between a 'Moor' and someone we would call a 'European' conceptually organized around the religio-political geography of Christian vs. Muslim more than around a geography of skin color?"[33] In this regard, it might seem significant that the *Oxford English Dictionary*'s earliest cited use of *European* to distinguish the inhabitants of Europe from "Indians" is in Massinger's *The City Madam* (1632)—"You are learn'd Europeans, and we worse / Than ignorant Americans" (3.3.127-28);[34] for in this case the grounds of distinction are clearly cultural and religious rather than racial. Moreover, the dictionary offers no example of the word as a generic term for "white" people before 1696. But in fact Samuel Purchas had used *European* to define a community of color as early as 1613, when, in describing the divided condition of postlapsarian humankind, he contrasted "the tawney Moore, black Negro, duskie Libyan, ash-colored Indian, oliue-colored American. . . . with the whiter European."[35] In Purchas's taxonomy Europeans are united by a common whiteness, while other peoples are divided by differing degrees of color, even as those colors taken together associate them in a common non-Europeanness.

It is important to recognize, I think, that this way of discriminating otherness—whatever its ultimate *effects* may have been—was not in itself motivated by an aggressive colonialism. On the contrary, as the section of Purchas's *Hakluytus Posthumus* devoted to East Indian voyaging suggests, it seems to have arisen from the profound sense of insecurity experienced by the increasingly embattled English trading community in the region, an insecurity felt as a disorienting challenge to their own identity. Included among Purchas's documents is Edmund Scott's *An Exact Discourse of the Subtilties, Fashions, Religion and Ceremonies of the East Indians,* a narrative that offers a particularly revealing glimpse of the processes by which an acute anxiety about the sustainability of their enterprise and community helped to shape an ideology of color.[36] In *An Exact Discourse,* a text almost exactly contemporary with *Othello,* the negotiation and demonstration of various kinds of difference—in rank, nation, and color—become crucial to the preservation of the identity of the vulnerable enclave that Scott calls "the English nation at Bantan."[37]

At the heart of Scott's narrative, as I have argued elsewhere, is an acute anxiety about the threat to English identity experienced by the mercantile representatives of "the English nation" in the newly established trading factory of the East India Company at Bantam in Java. This threat was triggered initially by the perplexing discovery (referred to elsewhere in Purchas's documents) that their Dutch rivals had been passing themselves off as English: "the common people knew us not from the Hollanders, for both they and wee were called by the name of Englishmen, by reason of their usurping our name at their first coming to trade."[38] The potential for violence in such a confusion of identities is registered in the quibbling chapter title that Purchas added to Scott's narrative: "*Differences* [i.e., quarrels] betwixt the Hollanders (stiling themselves English), the Javans, and other things remarkable." The problem was an especially vexing one because the English self-image was partially dependent on their sense of affinity with the Dutch, of whom Scott writes: "though wee were mortall enemies in our trade, in all other matters wee were friends, and would haue liued and dyed one for the other."[39] But the merchants were able to overcome this difficulty through a display of self-fashioning pageantry when they resolved to stage their difference from the Dutch through an improvised Accession Day triumph: marching in elaborately sinuous patterns up and down their compound, clad in their best finery, with scarves and hatbands of red-and-white taffeta, the tiny company ("being but fourteene in number") waved their banners of St. George, beat their drums, and discharged volumes of shot into the air. This swaggering (if undermanned) performance of Englishness so impressed the natives, according to Scott, that he and his companions felt empowered to deliver a brief disquisition on the linguistic and political distinctions between Dutch and English, thereby ensuring that this unhappy confusion would never be repeated.[40]

But even as Scott's band succeeded in shoring up their sense of national distinctiveness on one front, they found it threatened with dissolution on another: for this crisis of identity with the Dutch was quickly followed by a second in which the terms of difference were much less easy to define and whose menace the English could only disarm by appealing to a rhetoric of color. This "Tragedie" (as Scott calls it) concerned "a *Mullato* of *Pegu*" (i.e., a man of mixed race from Burma) who, as a result of his ambiguous role as a servant in the English trading factory, was taken for an Englishman. The story begins with what we might now read as an explosion of racial resentment on the part of its protagonist. Having been drinking with a second mulatto, "one of his countreymen" who belonged to a visiting Flemish vessel, the "English" mulatto became enraged when the Flemish provost attacked his fellow Peguan and beat him back onto the Flemish ship.[41] "Seeing his countryman misused, and being somewhat tickled in the heade with wine," the mulatto planned to "reuenge his countryman's quarrell."[42] A small orgy of killing ensued: the mulatto sought out and stabbed both the Fleming and the other mulatto (whom he allegedly feared as a potentially hostile witness); he then tried unsuccessfully to kill a Philippino slave who accompanied his victims; and finally, "being nuzled in blood," as Scott puts it, and "meeting with a poore *Iauan* . . . [he] stabde him likewise."[43] Unfortunately for the killer, however, the Fleming lived long enough to give some clues as to the identity of his assailant; and the mulatto, incriminated by inconsistencies in his own story as well as by the testimony of the slave, was at last brought to confess all three murders.

Scott, who was now the senior East India Company man in Bantam, found himself torn between a righteous desire to appease "the bloud of those Christians that were murthered"[44] and a proprietorial insistence on his exclusive claim to administer justice to members of his own community. He resisted both what he saw as extravagant Javan demands for compensation and an arrogant Dutch insistence that he hand over the killer for a lingering death: they "saying hee should haue the bones of his legs and armes broken, and so he should lye and dye, or else haue his feete and hands cut off, and so lye and starue to death."[45] Treating the issue as one of both personal pride ("I answered, that it lay not in them to put him to death, if I list to saue him") and national prestige ("for an Englishman scornes to giue place to Hollanders in any forraine countrie"), he roundly declared that the murderer "should dye the ordinary death of the country, & no other."[46] Hiring a local executioner, Scott made him promise to dispatch the mulatto as swiftly and humanely as possible, even lending the "hangman" his own well-sharpened *kris* (short sword), "which was very seruiceable for such a purpose."[47] The choice of this quintessentially Malay (though English-owned) weapon to be the proxy instrument of judicial Englishness seems fraught with ironies at least as complicated as those that attend Othello's flourishing of Spanish steel to reassert his hybrid identity as "Moor of Venice." But the choice had a certain appropriateness to a situation in which the contradictions of mixed identity became a source of significant unease—an unease strikingly illustrated, I think, in Purchas's brutal abridgment of this section of Scott's narrative. In Purchas all but the bare details of the killing and of the murderer's execution have been excised—reducing Scott's complex "Tragedie" to a simple monitory account of physical "*Dangers by a Molato.*"[48] There are numerous other cuts in Purchas's version of the pamphlet, but this is the only one for which he feels constrained to apologize, in a marginal note that disingenuously pleads the danger of prolixity.

No doubt Purchas's anxiety, like Scott's own, had everything to do with the ambiguous status given to the killer by the contradictory identity that the text ascribes to him—that of a man "*of* Pegu" who is, at the same time, "*our* mulatto." Scott's possessive pronoun mediates as uneasily between ownership, community, and kinship as the deeply equivocal "mine" that announces Prospero's final acknowledgment of Caliban. It is the same unstable pronoun that both defines and masks the relationship of Shakespeare's mercenary "stranger" to the Venetian state when "the Moor" is transformed into "*our* noble and valiant general" (2.2.1-2). In Scott the dangerous ambiguity of the connection that his "our" at once declares and mystifies becomes apparent at the point where the dying provost is said to have claimed that "an *Englishman* had slaine him." A deputation of Dutch went at once to the English house to inform Scott that "one of *our* men had slaine one of *theirs* . . . [and] they thought it was *our Mulatto*."[49] The Dutch rhetoric here is pointed: they contrive to taint the English by association with the mulatto killer, who is denounced as "one of *our* men," while holding themselves aloof from their own murdered mulatto, who is carefully excluded from the opposite category, "one of *theirs*." Subsequent events intensify this unhappy confusion but also provide Scott with an opportunity to purge it and to realign his own people with their fellow Europeans, the offended Hollanders.

When the mulatto denies the Dutch accusation, he is dispatched, along with Scott's deputy, Gabriel Towerson, to question the mortally wounded Fleming: "when they came, they asked him who had hurt him, hee said an English man. Maister *Towerson* asked him whether it was a white man, or a blacke, . . . because he named still an English man, wee were in some doubt: the Fleming being also in drinke said, a white man, then presently hee said againe, it was darke, hee knew not well, and so gaue up his life."[50] Resonating with the symbolism of Othello's "Put out the light" soliloquy, darkness temporarily effaces the markers of difference here; but what is really extraordinary about the passage is the almost casual way in which the English seem to acceded to the mulatto's inclusion in the category "English man"—almost as if there could be such a creature as a "Mulatto of England." This temporary recognition of kinship was perhaps partly enabled by the murderer's status as Christian—"though he was a *Pegu* borne, yet he was a Christian, & brought vp among the *Portingalls*"—so that Scott was at charitable pains to have the murderer brought to repentance before his death. The chosen agent of religious instruction, fittingly enough, was another hybrid figure—a renegade Muslim, "an *Arabian* borne [who] belonged to the *Dutch* ships, and spake the *Spanish* tongue maruellous well"; this go-between convinced the murderer of the power of God's son "to redeeme vs, and to wash away our sinnes were they neuer so bloudy."[51] The inclusive "us" here brings the reader momentarily close to the pieties of Purchas's climactic vision in the *Pilgrimage,* when he imagines a future redemption in which the divided branches of humanity will be reunited, "*their long robes made white in the bloud of the Lambe . . .* without any more distinction of color, Nation, language, sexe, condition."[52] But the efficacy of this emulsifying mystery belongs only to the extratemporal moment of penitence: it cannot affect the day-to-day management of difference in a situation where any loss of distinction threatens the elimination of "the English nation at Bantan." Hence the narrative now goes on to detach the condemned man from the English camp and to link him, through the indelible mark of color, with the proper denizens of Bantam, the East Indian and Chinese, whose vicious and guileful "subtilties" Scott finds so threatening to English interests.

By a convenient rhetorical sleight, the mulatto is first kinned with his own executioner. Scott records with some satisfaction the hangman's promise to serve this prisoner better than he had earlier served a counterfeiter whose punishment he grievously botched: "when he killed the coyner," the man protests, "he did not execute his own father." Scott explains this as a reference to the custom whereby "when a Iauan of any account is put to death[,] . . . their nearest of kin doth execute [the common executioner's] office, and it is held the greatest fauour they can do them."[53] The executioner, we can surmise, intends a compliment to Scott by identifying the humblest of the "Englishmen" as his own senior kinsman. But Scott's failure to spell out the meaning of the hyperbole has the effect of stressing the tie between the headsman and his victim, rhetorically severing the mulatto from the English camp and consigning him to the community of Others. But then, as the condemned man is led into the fields outside the town of Bantam to meet his death, a large crowd of townspeople, "both *Iauans* and *Chyneses,*" comes "flocking amaine," excited by the rumor "that there was an Englishman to be executed." They are disconcerted by their sight of the victim, however: "many were blanke, and wee might heare them tell one another it was a black man." Scott and his men immediately seize the opportunity to deliver a second lesson on difference which completes the alienation of "our Mulatto": "wee told them, he was iust of their own color and condition and that an Englishman or white man would not doe such a bloody deed."[54] At this moment a common blackness is announced as the defining condition of all who are not English or white, regardless of whether they are Chinese, Javan, men of mixed race, or men of Pegu (groups whose various gradations of color are elsewhere quite carefully catalogued). By the same token, the mulatto's crime becomes a proof of his racial difference, just as his color is the badge of his reprobate condition.

Something very similar, it seems to me, happens in *Othello* through the systematic blackening of the Moor and the symbolic detachment from Venice that it involves. To begin with, Othello's blackness seems to be an almost casual effect of Iago's improvisatory malice and of Roderigo's and Brabantio's gullibility. It is at best an accident whose superficial significance could even be underpinned (in ways to which Dympna Callaghan has alerted us[55]) by the audience's pleasurable consciousness that it is only a cosmetic illusion: "Othello" is, after all, a white man; so his appearance of blackness is something easily annulled by the duke's invocation of that essential whiteness that unites all Christians under the skin ("your son-in-law is far more fair than black" [1.3.291]). Yet by the end of the play, the Venetian world—and the audience, too, if they are not careful—will have come to see it as the sign not only of his reprobate condition but of the irreducible alterity that the language of racial abuse insists is inseparable from it: "blacker devil," "filthy bargain," "gull . . . / As ignorant as dirt," "dull Moor" (5.2.129, 153, 159-60, 223).[56] In the reading of the Moor's body so successfully propagated by Iago, none of Othello's efforts to reinstitute the sustaining paradoxes of his mixed condition, as an "honorable murderer" whose suicide triumphantly enacts and cancels out the contradictions that have been exposed in the designation "Moor of Venice," is sufficient to overcome the suggestion that such a creature can only constitute a kind of "civil monster." Othello's re-enacted killing of the "circumcised dog" is also a re-enactment of his original apostasy by one whose contradictory position forces him to "turn, and turn . . . / And turn again" (4.1.253-54). But such desperate iteration is as hopeless as it is compulsive. For, as the outcast condition of Scott's mulatto implies, while a Moor may turn Christian, he can never "turn" Venetian. Like the mulatto's thinly motivated stabbing of his own countryman, Othello's overdetermined killing of the "turbanned Turk" is on one level a demonstration of his own essential unkindness; on another, like the executioner's hyperbolic killing of "his own father," it enacts a violent re-absorption into the domain of the Other—confirming the rhetorical estrangement by which the Venetians return "he that was Othello" to the condition of anonymous "Moor" in which he was first brought into the play. It is in this sense that we can speak of the play's progressive racialization of the protagonist.

Yet Emily Bartels's insistence on *Othello*'s openness is not entirely misplaced, and Virginia Vaughan's perplexity ("I think this play is racist, and I think it is not") remains understandable. Even Edmund Scott, after all, is only partially successful in his attempt to purge "the English nation at Bantan" of the confusions created by the hybridizing presence of "our Mulatto." As the murderer's body lies "gasping on the ground," Scott cannot forbear offering it to the Dutch as a reproof to their own vices—"I openly told the Hollanders that, that was the fruite of drunkennesse, & byd them euer after beware of it"—thus carelessly blurring the boundary between colors and conditions which his lesson to the townspeople had established. And as he pauses to reflect on the fatal sickness of yet another of his fellow-merchants, the chief factor's anxiety at the fragile state of the English trading community seems to re-admit the ghostly presence of his scapegoat to membership of a "we" that is once again exposed as dangerously unstable: "*we* had lost in all, since the departure of our ships eight men *besides the Mulatto that was executed,* and we were now ten liuing and one boy."[57] The "Mulatto of Pegu" is once again one of "our" men, a "Mulatto of England," as it were. In *Othello* it is precisely the desperate haste with which the Venetians seek to efface the admonitory spectacle of slaughter ("The object poisons sight, / Let it be hid" [5.2.362-63]) that calls into question the sustainability of the racial scapegoating that Iago has brought about, forcing us to pay attention to a very different narrative—the one that ends not in the self-alienating and murderous expulsion of a Moor turned Turk again but in a kiss that self-consciously proclaims an act of union. The play, however—and this is why it continues to torment us—refuses to align itself with either narrative, retreating instead into the obliquity of the taunting pleonasm with which Iago at once challenges and disables judgment: "What you know, you know. / From this time forth I never will speak word" (ll. 300-301).

Notes

Earlier versions of this paper were presented at the 1997 South Atlantic Modern Language Association conference in Atlanta, at the Folger Shakespeare Library's Midday Colloquium, at Muhlenberg College, and to members of the Graduate Seminar at Trinity College, Cambridge. I am grateful to all four audiences for their constructive comments and suggestions.

1. Virginia Mason Vaughan, *Othello: a contextual history* (Cambridge: Cambridge UP, 1994), 70.

2. See, for example, Kim F. Hall, *Things of Darkness: Economies of Race and Gender in Early Modern England* (Ithaca, NY, and London: Cornell UP, 1995); Margo Hendricks, "Civility, Barbarism, and Aphra Behn's *The Widow Ranter*," and Lynda Boose, "'The Getting of a Lawful Race': Racial discourse in early modern England and the unrepresentable black woman," both in *Women, "Race," and Writing in the Early Modern Period*, Margo Hendricks and Patricia Parker, eds. (London and New York: Routledge, 1994), 225-39 and 35-54. The literature on the treatment of race in *Othello* has become so extensive as to make full citation impossible, but a convenient summary will be found in Vaughan, 51-70.

3. Emily C. Bartels, "*Othello* and Africa: Postcolonialism Reconsidered," *William and Mary Quarterly*, 3rd ser., 54 (1997): 45-64, esp. 61-62, emphasis added.

4. See, e.g., Patricia Coughlan, ed., *Spenser and Ireland: An Interdisciplinary Perspective* (Cork: Cork UP, 1989); Willy Maley, *Salvaging Spenser: Colonialism, Culture and Identity* (New York: St. Martin's Press, 1997); Christopher Highley, *Shakespeare, Spenser, and the crisis in Ireland* (Cambridge: Cambridge UP, 1997); and Michael Neill, "Broken English and Broken Irish: Nation, Language, and the Optic of Power in Shakespeare's Histories," *Shakespeare Quarterly* 45 (1994): 1-32.

5. John Leo, *A Geographical Historie of Africa,* trans. John Pory (London, 1600), 41-42, 41, and 43.

6. In his First Book, for example, Leo breaks off his description of the vices to which "they" are subject in order to acknowledge his own relationship to these Others as one whose life resembles that of the strange fish-bird he calls "Amphibia": "Neither am I ignorant, how much mine owne credit is impeached, when I my selfe write so homely of Africa, vnto which countrie I stand indebted both for my birth, and also for the best part of my education. . . . For mine owne part, when I heare the Africans euill spoken of, I will affirme my selfe to be one of Granada: and when I perceiue the nation of Granada to be discommended, then will I profess my selfe to be an African" (42-44). For a more extended treatment of Leo's ambivalence about his identity, see Emily C. Bartels, "Making More of the Moor: Aaron, Othello, and Renaissance Refashionings of Race," *SQ* 41 (1990): 433-54, esp. 436-38.

7. Citations follow the Arden Shakespeare *Othello*, ed. E.A.J. Honigmann (London: Thomas Nelson, 1997); citations of all other Shakespeare plays follow *William Shakespeare, The Complete Works*, ed. Stanley Wells and Gary Taylor (Oxford: Clarendon Press, 1986).

8. The significance of the subtitle is indicated by the remarkable consistency with which (in contrast to the generally fluid treatment of nomenclature in the period) it is repeated from the Stationers' Register entry to the Quarto and Folio and the other early texts deriving from them.

9. The same point is made by Peter Swaab in his program notes for the recent Royal National Theatre production of *Othello*: "Shakespeare's title has the force of a paradox. How far can 'the Moor' really be 'of' Venice? Like Marlowe's Jew of Malta, Othello is a resident who remains in important ways alien; like Shakespeare's Timon of Athens, his downfall involves too much trusting that a culture can give him an identity; and as with a historical figure such as Lawrence of Arabia, the word 'of' conceals a vulnerable fantasy of power in distant lands. 'The Moor of Venice' is a mixed marriage of a phrase" (quoted from the program for the run at the Brooklyn Academy of Music, 8-11 April 1998; this production was first staged at the Salzburg Festival on 22 August 1997 and subsequently at the Lyttelton Theatre in London).

10. "There's . . . Obed in *Bairseth*, Nones in *Portugall*, / My selfe in *Malta*, some in *Italy*, / Many in *France*, and wealthy every one" (1.1.125-27); citations of Marlowe follow *The Complete Works of Christopher Marlowe*, ed. Fredson Bowers, 2d ed., 2 vols. (Cambridge: Cambridge UP, 1981), 1:253-335, esp. 1:267-68.

11. For an outstanding account of the cultural fantasies surrounding Jews in early modern culture, see James S. Shapiro, *Shakespeare and the Jews* (New York: Columbia UP, 1996), esp. 167-94. See also Avraham Oz, *The Yoke of Love: Prophetic Riddles in* The Merchant of Venice (Newark: U of Delaware P, 1995), 93-133, esp. 100-103.

12. For the resemblances between Moor and Jew as figures of alterity, see Leslie A. Fielder, *The Stranger in Shakespeare* (New York: Stein and Day, 1972), 103-6 and 195-96. Cf. Shapiro, 171-72, on Jewish "blackness."

13. Jeremiah 13:23. This version, from the 1560 *Geneva Bible,* gives particular prominence to the figure by printing "The blacke More" as a title at the head of the column. On the history of this motif in literature and in the visual arts, see Jean Michel Massing, "From Greek Proverb to Soap Advert: Washing the Ethiopian," *Journal of the Warburg and Courtauld Institutes* 58 (1995): 180-201; and Karen Newman, "And wash the Ethiop white': femininity and the monstrous in *Othello*" in *Shakespeare Reproduced: The text in history and ideology,* Jean Howard and Marion O'Connor, eds. (London: Methuen, 1987), 143-62. For Best's story, see Richard Hakluyt, *The Principal Navigations Voyages Traffiques and Discoveries of the English Nation* (1589), 12 vols. (Glasgow: James MacLehose and Sons, 1903-05), 7:263-64.

14. On the forcible conversion of the Spanish Moors and the suspicion to which it paradoxically rendered them vulnerable, thereby exposing them to the malice of the Inquisition, see Henry Charles Lea, *The Moriscos of Spain: Their Conversion and Expulsion* (Westport, CT: Greenwood Press, 1968). The near paranoia that inspired the official campaign for *limpieza de sangre* (purity of blood) in Spain issued directly from this fear of the hidden stranger masquerading as one of the familiar.

15. See also Bartels, "Making More of the Moor," 434.

16. The phrase is common to both A and B texts; see Bowers, ed., 2:165.

17. For a useful account of the significance of "turning Turk" in this period, see Daniel J. Vitkus, "Turning Turk in *Othello*: The Conversion and Damnation of the Moor," *SQ* 48 (1997): 145-76.

18. William Cornelison Schouten of Horne, "Voyage of 1615-17" in Samuel Purchas, *Hakluytus Posthumus or Purchas His Pilgrimes* (1625), 20 vols. (Glasgow: James MacLehose and Sons, 1905-07), 2:232-84, esp. 280.

19. Cf. Shapiro on the ambiguities surrounding "what happened to racial otherness when [Jews] converted" (170).

20. For a useful account of the complex entanglement of color and religion in early Iberian racism, see James H. Sweet, "The Iberian Roots of American Racist Thought," *William and Mary Quarterly,* 3rd ser., 54 (1997): 143-66; in the same issue, see also Robin Blackburn, "The Old World Background to European Colonial Slavery," 65-102, esp. 77-78. On

the uncertain denotation of *Moor* in the play, see Vitkus: "Othello, the noble Moor of Venice, is . . . not to be identified with a specific, historically accurate racial category; rather he is a hybrid who might be associated, in the minds of Shakespeare's audience, with a whole set of related terms—*Moor, Turk, Ottomite, Saracen, Mahometan, Egyptian, Judean, Indian*—all constructed and positioned in opposition to Christian faith and virtue" (160). The opposition, however, is never *simply* religious or even cultural.

21. Quotations of Richard Brome's *The English Moore* are from *The English Moore; or The Mock-Marriage*, ed. Sara Jayne Steen (Columbia: U of Missouri P, 1983).

22. Karen Ordahl Kupperman, "Presentment of Civility: English Reading of American Self-Presentation in the Early Years of Colonization," *William and Mary Quarterly*, 3rd ser., 54 (1997): 193-228, esp. 193.

23. See Neill, "Broken English and Broken Irish," 6n.

24. Samuel Purchas, *Purchas His Pilgrimage or Relations of the World and the Religions Observed in All Ages* (London, 1613), 546.

25. In his richly informative "The Sons of Noah and the Construction of Ethnic and Geographical Identities in the Medieval and Early Modern Periods" (*William and Mary Quarterly*, 3rd ser., 54 [1997]: 103-42) Benjamin Braude discerns an analogous shift in the treatment of African peoples between 1589 and 1625, as the biblical Curse of Ham was increasingly interpreted as an explanation of both color and moral character: "slavery," he argues, "had started to make it credible" (138).

26. John Huighen Van Linschoten, *Iohn Hvighen Van Linschoten his Discours of Voyages into ye Easte & West Indies* (London, 1598), 14, 28, 29, 40, and 37.

27. George Best, *A Trve Discovrse of the late voyages of discouerie, for the finding of a passage to Cathaya, by the Northwest* (London, 1578), 28; cited in Alden T. Vaughan and Virginia Mason Vaughan, "Before *Othello*: Elizabethan Representations of Sub-Saharan Africans," *William and Mary Quarterly*, 3rd ser., 54 (1997): 19-44, esp. 27; cf. Kupperman, 207-8 and 226-27.

28. Thomas Cavendish in Purchas, *Hakluytus Posthumus*, 2:181.

29. John Fletcher, *The Island Princess* in *The Dramatic Works in the Beaumont and Fletcher Canon*, ed. Fredson Bowers, 10 vols. (Cambridge: Cambridge UP, 1966-96), 5:539-642. For American examples of descriptions featuring this trope, see Kupperman, 207.

30. In a deliberate confusion of reality, the Islamic allegiance of the actual Moluccans is assimilated in the play with idolatry through the disguise adopted by the villainous Governor of Ternata, who is at once a (presumably Mahometan) "Moore Priest" (4.1. s.d.) and the false prophet of "the Sun and Moon" (4.5.70). For more detailed discussion of this play as an instrument of mercantile colonialism, see Shanker Raman, "Imaginary Islands: Staging the East," *Renaissance Drama* n.s. 26 (1995): 131-61; and my essay "'Materiall flames': The Space of Mercantile Fantasy in John Fletcher's *The Island Princess*," forthcoming in *Renaissance Drama*.

31. See Sweet, 146-47, 149, 155-56, and 166.

32. See, e.g., "The Journall of Master Nathaniel Courthop" in Purchas, *Hakluytus Posthumus*, 5:86-125, esp. 109. Cf. the continuation of Courthop's journal by Robert Hayes in Purchas, *Hakluytus Posthumus*, 5:126-37, esp. 126 and 135; and "An Answere to the Hollanders Declaration . . ." in Purchas, *Hakluytus Posthumus*, 5:155-74, esp. 170.

33. Boose in Hendricks and Parker, eds., 306n.

34. Philip Massinger, *The City Madam*, ed. Cyrus Hoy (Lincoln: U of Nebraska P, 1964), 61. In this episode Luke Frugal salutes the supposed "Indians" of the play (in fact a group of disguised Londoners led by his own brother) for their worship of Plutus, God of Riches.

35. Purchas, *Purchas His Pilgrimage*, 546. On Purchas's shift toward an increasingly moralized construction of blackness in his later writing, see Braude, 135-37.

36. Published in London, the *Exact Discourse* survives in two significantly different texts—the original pamphlet of 1606 and the abbreviated and annotated version (apparently based on a separate manuscript) published in *Purchas His Pilgrimage*. The different manuscript origins of the two versions are suggested by numerous minor variants. Unless otherwise indicated, citations of Scott follow the 1606 edition.

37. Scott, $A1^r$. See also Michael Neill, "Putting History to the Question: An Episode of Torture at Bantam in Java, 1604," *English Literary Renaissance* 25 (1995): 45-75.

38. Scott, $C2^v$.

39. Scott, $H3^r$.

40. Scott, $C2^v$.

41. For Scott the word *mulatto* seems to describe any person of part-European ethnicity; although the term is nowadays considered offensive, I have felt bound to replicate Scott's usage, since the protagonist of his story is identified in no other way.

42. Scott, $D1^v$-$D2^r$.

43. Scott, $D2^r$.

44. Scott, $D3^v$.

45. Scott, $D4^r$.

46. Scott, $D3^v$, $D3^r$, and $D4^r$.

47. Scott, $D4^v$.

48. Purchas, *Hakluytus Posthumus,* 2:461, marginal note.
49. Scott, D2ʳ, emphasis added.
50. Scott, D2ᵛ.
51. Scott, D4ʳ.
52. Purchas, *Purchase His Pilgrimage,* 546.
53. Scott, D4ᵛ.
54. Scott, D4ᵛ
55. See Dympna Callaghan, "'Othello was a white man': properties of race on Shakespeare's stage" in *Alternative Shakespeares 2,* Terence Hawkes, ed. (London: Routledge, 1996), 192-215.
56. "[D]ull Moor"—involving as it does a complicated quibble that depends on the resemblances and etymological links (supposed or otherwise) between Medieval Latin *Morus* = Moor; Latin *morus* (from Greek γρίς) = dull, stupid; and *morum* = blackberry or mulberry (hence *morulus* = black, dark-colored)—can be construed as a contemptuous inversion of the oxymoronic "Moor of Venice."
57. Scott, E1ʳ, emphasis added.

Patrick C. Hogan (essay date 1998)

SOURCE: "*Othello*, Racism, and Despair," in *CLA Journal,* Vol. XLI, No. 4, June, 1998, pp. 431-51.

[*In the essay below, Hogan argues that race is a central issue in* Othello, *stating that Shakespeare opposed racism because it was not Christian.*]

In the middle of this century, in the context of the anticolonial struggles being waged throughout Africa and the Caribbean, writers such as Frantz Fanon explored the effects of racism on the minds and hearts of those black men and women who came to internalize the inhuman attitudes of their oppressors, conceiving of themselves in the same brutish terms.[1] More recently, Derek Walcott has spoken of having black skin but looking at the world through blue eyes—seeing oneself and others through the distorting lenses of white racism. One result of this, Walcott tells us, is "racial despair,"[2] despondency over the possibilities for accomplishment, for change, fulfillment, a good life—what the Greeks called *eudaimonia*. Racial despair is a secular descendent of spiritual despair. The latter results from a sense that one's sin is too great even for all-merciful God to forgive, that this sin blots out one's soul. The former results from a sense that one's skin is too black for anyone to accept—to forget or to "forgive"—that one's skin blots out one's soul.

This, I wish to argue, is the tragedy of Othello, the reason that he murders both Desdemona and himself. Like many tragic heroes, Othello is greater than those around him. He is, in Aristotle's term, *spoudaios:*[3] excellent in character, intense in thought, elevated in feeling. But the forces arrayed against him are immense—not superhuman forces, Greek gods or Satan in a usurped human form, but all of intimate society. Everywhere he turns, Othello confronts racism. Its different faces or masks—not only enmity, disdain, abuse, but friendship, admiration, love—serve to make it more insistent, compelling, inexorable. In the end, he succumbs to the racist vision of those around him. The consequent despair leads to murder and to suicide.

A number of critics have argued that *Othello* is, in effect, an antiracist play.[4] Others have seen the play as racist or at least as partially acquiescing in racist views about miscegenation.[5] Still others have argued that it is anachronistic to see the play in terms of racism at all. Thus Michael Neill maintains against Martin Orkin that it was not "possible for Shakespeare to 'oppose racism' in 1604 . . . the argument simply could not be constituted in those terms."[6]

As to the third ("historicist") position, it is a critical commonplace today that there is profound discontinuity and incommensurability between different historical periods, and between cultures. We cannot discuss this view at length here, but its status as dogma seems, at best, questionable. Orkin, Anthony Barthelemy,[7] and others offer considerable evidence that many Europeans of Shakespeare's time categorized people according to skin color, analogized nonwhites to animals, judged nonwhites inferior to whites and, more specifically, lascivious, "hypersexualized,"[8] etc., in keeping with standard stereotypes. Indeed, citing work done by Fanon only a few decades ago, Fintan O'Toole argues that in the seventeenth century blacks were demeaned in the very same terms as they are today.[9] It seems odd to deny that this is racism. Moreover, Orkin argues convincingly that there were many people of the time (most famously, Montaigne[10]) who deplored, and thus opposed, this tendency to denigrate non-Europeans. It seems odd to insist that this is not antiracism.

But our use of the word "racism" is, in any case, not the point. We can, after all, substitute another term if "racism" seems too burdened by modern biological pseudoscience. What is important is just that Shakespeare recognized when people were not conceived of nor treated as human beings. He sensed the emotional violence of this; he could see its sources—including its sources in beliefs relating to skin color and national origin—and its devastating effects. In *Othello,* Shakespeare has illustrated this human recognition. And sharing that recognition is crucial to our experience of the play's tragedy.

Indeed, my purpose in writing this essay is perhaps not so much to defend a particular interpretive thesis, as to facilitate a particular tragic experience. In doing this, I follow the great Arabic theorists—al-Farabi, Ibn Sina, Ibn Rushd—in seeking the ethical and political value of a literary work not in its "message," but in its *takhyil*, the imaginative experience which inspires and focusses our moral feelings.[11] In other words, following the views of these writers, my aim is not merely to analyze the play in a particular manner, but to foster a takhyil that is at once more fully tragic and more pointedly ethical.

The idea is worth elaborating briefly. The major medieval Arabic theorists saw the prime function of literature as ethical. However, they did not conceive of this ethical function as a matter of a work expressing or inculcating some moral precept. Rather, they saw it as the fostering of an imaginative experience which serves to excite moral feelings, particularly the Islamic feelings of *rahmah* and *taqwa*[12]—the former signifying mercy or *"tenderness requiring the exercise of beneficence"*;[13] the latter meaning piety or *"observance of duty."*[14] For these writers, the moral aim of literature is not the teaching of ideas, but rather what, many centuries later, European Romantic theorists came to call "the training of sensibility."

Keeping in mind recent work on reception and response, we may further develop this view in a way that links it productively with practical literary criticism. Many modern European theorists have emphasized the incompleteness of the literary work, stressing the role of the readers in completing the story, "filling in" the character as they read. Roman Ingarden speaks of "concretizing" the literary work;[15] Wolfgang Iser talks of filling gaps.[16] If we combine this insight with the Arabic view, we see directly that a single literary work may produce a number of very different imaginative experiences depending upon how it is completed by a reader. These different imaginative experiences may, in turn, have quite different ethical functions. Some may stifle rahmah and taqwa; others may foster them. A critical practice concerned primarily with the takhyil of a work, would, then, aim to develop, from these possible readings, an interpretation conducive toward a literary experience that would foster such moral feelings, not stifle them.

In the following pages, I wish to make the interpretive argument that *Othello* is a play focussed on the devastating effects of racism. But at the same time, and more importantly, I wish to encourage a particular "concretization" of the play, and thus a particular imaginative experience of it. In other words, while the focus of my analysis is on meaning, my underlying concern is with takhyil. In this way, my project is continuous with that set out by Kiernan Ryan, "to activate the revolutionary imaginative vision which invites discovery in [Shakespeare's] plays today," "to make his drama more disturbing in its impact on the institutions through which Shakespeare is reproduced, and more constructively alert to our most pressing problems and needs."[17] In short, the overarching goal, which I share with Ryan, is to integrate our imagination of Shakespeare with current concerns about political and social dilemmas—in this case, the persistent dilemmas of racism and racial despair. It is precisely this sort of integration that the Arabic theorists conceptualized many centuries ago as takhyil.

Is Othello a Furious Moor?

In Giraldi Cinthio's *Hecatommithi,* from which Shakespeare drew the story of Othello, Desdemona tells her husband outright, "You Moors are of so hot a nature that every little trifle moves you to anger and revenge."[18] A common stereotype was the hot-blooded Turk, the vengeful Arab, the passionate and impulsive African.[19] Shakespeare was, of course, free to create a character who fit this stereotype. And if he did, if Othello is indeed a furious Moor whose (more than human) passion overpowers his (less than human) reason, then there is nothing to be explained in the final murder and suicide. He kills Desdemona and himself because the divine faculty of reason is racially weak, and the animal impulses of passion are racially potent.

But it is easy to see that this is not the case. Shakespeare is at pains to portray Othello as more reasonable (more contemplative, calm, reflective, discerning) and less passionate (less impulsive, desirous, pugnacious) than any of the Venetians around him. Roderigo is a fool, his reason pathetically overwhelmed by lust for Desdemona. Cassio, deceived into inebriation, loses self-control and brawls on the slightest provocation. Brabantio storms into Othello's company crying havoc and flailing his sword hysterically. Most of all, Iago is crazed with the green-eyed monster, jealousy. It takes labor, and stage-craft, and practiced deceit to convince Othello that Desdemona has been unfaithful. It also takes *moira,* a tragic conspiracy of fate: Cassio bragging of his conquest, the compromising appearance of a handkerchief. But Iago requires no such evidence to accuse his wife of multiple adulteries. He speaks darkly of rumors: "[I]t is thought abroad that 'twixt my sheets / H'as done my office" (I.iii.378-79).[20] Later, he delivers a mad speech on female "Lechery . . . lust and foul thoughts" (II.i.257-59), culminating with a fantastical accusation:

> [T]he lusty Moor
> Hath leaped into my seat; the thought whereof
> Doth, like a poisonous mineral, gnaw my inwards;
> And nothing can or shall content my soul
> Till I am evened with him, wife for wife.
>
> (II.i.295-99)

He concludes by elaborating the delusion further still: "I fear Cassio with my nightcap too" (II.i.307). In sum, the Venetians of the play fit Desdemona's description well: almost to a man, they are "of so hot a nature that every little trifle moves [them] to anger and revenge."[21]

But Othello does not fit at all. When we first see Othello, Iago is trying to anger him. He gossips that a nobleman "spoke . . . scurvy and provoking terms" against Othello (I.ii.8). In the preceding scene, Iago's ploys had successfully inflamed Brabantio and duped Roderigo. But with Othello, he has no success: "Let him do his spite," Othello responds, unmoved (I.ii.16). When Brabantio, Roderigo, and the officers enter, and both sides draw their swords, in preparation for bloody combat, Othello merely says: "Keep up your bright swords, for the dew will rust them" (I.ii.58). Then, after Brabantio abuses him with gross racial invective, he continues, "Hold your hands, / Both you of my inclining and the rest" (I.ii.80-81). The scene and the phrase "Keep up your bright swords" are reminiscent of the garden at Gethsemane. When the armed men sent by the chief priests have come to arrest and imprison him, Jesus commands his followers not to fight, ordering Simon Peter (in the Geneva translation of 1560), "Put up thy sword"[22]—a famous phrase alluded to in Othello's first command.[23] Later, in a similar manner, Othello is calm, though forceful, in ending the brawl between Cassio and Montano. Here he makes the religious significance of the act explicit, calling out, "For Christian shame put by this barbarous brawl!" (II.iii.171).

Othello is not committed to peace, however, due to some flaw; he is not pusillanimous or lacking in military skill. Despite the great racism of Venetian society (to which we shall turn presently), he has risen to command the Venetian troops. All acknowledge him valiant (see, for example, I.iii.48), and his status indicates his strategic abilities. In opposing battle, he is reasonable, not timorous. Moreover, his rational skills go beyond those of strategy. For example, he is a physican also, capable in the art of healing (see II.iii.253), where he comforts Montano, saying, "Sir, for your hurts, myself will be your surgeon"). Even Iago, despite his vicious hatred, must acknowledge that Othello is "constant, loving, noble" (II.i.289). In short, he, almost alone among the major characters in the play, is guided by reason, not passion. He is as far from the stereotype of the passionate Moor as he could possibly be, and as far superior to his white associates.

Why, then, does he kill?

The Ubiquity of Racism

In almost every way, the attitude of the Venetians toward Othello is racialist, even when it is not derogatory. Othello is a great general in the Venetian army, a friend and colleague of many Venetians. And yet, they refer to him far less frequently as "Othello," as this particular man, than as "the Moor"—when counted up, the proportion is almost two to one in favor of the generic category over the name. In other words, they routinely discuss, and even address him, not as an individual person, but as an instance of his race.[24]

Of course, much of the address and discussion is indeed derogatory as well—and in all the standard ways. Iago is particularly adept at racial slander. After Roderigo has referred to Othello as "the thick-lips" (I.i.63), Iago goes on to characterize Othello as a brute beast. He shouts that Othello is "an old black ram" (I.i.85). He taunts Brabantio with the dreadful possibility that Brabantio's grandchildren will be of mixed race, saying, "[Y]our daughter [is] covered with a Barbary horse, [hence] you'll have nephews neigh to you, you'll have coursers for cousins, and gennets for germans" (I.i.108-11). Worse still, at times he sees Othello as demonic: "[T]he devil will make a grandsire of you" (I.i.88). Though, later, Shakespeare has Iago admit that it is he himself, not Othello, who is of Satan's party. Speaking of his plot against Othello, Iago says: "When devils will the blackest sins put on, / They do suggest at first with heavenly shows, / As I do now" (II.iii.351-53). And at the end of the play, Othello repeats the characterization, asking Cassio to inquire of "the demi-devil" Iago "Why he hath thus ensnared my soul and body?" (V.ii.297-98).

Despite his own degradation, however, Iago finds Desdemona degraded in loving Othello. It is a violation of nature—akin almost to the bestiality of Pasiphaë—for this woman who is so "fair" (both so beautiful and so white) to choose "the gross clasps of a lascivious Moor" (I.i.119,123). It is beyond reason: "[W]hat delight shall she have to look on the devil?" he asks Roderigo (II.i.224-25).

Brabantio takes up this theme most vehemently, accusing Othello of witchcraft. Only magic, "foul charms" and "drugs" could drive Desdemona "from her guardage to the sooty bosom / Of such a thing as thou—to fear, not to delight" (I.ii.72, 73, 69-70). Because he is black, he is hideous (another common stereotype of the period; see, for example, Barthelmy 27). His natural color is soot, filth—a physical degradation paralleling a spiritual degradation. No fair woman could love "such a thing." Later, he questions again how she could "fall in love with what she feared to look on" (I.iii.99). In the brief period of the play, Brabantio pines away and dies. He too is struck down by despair. What point is there to living, once his daughter has espoused the kin of Lucifer?

When I teach this play, I ask my students to imagine themselves in Othello's position, to make a self-conscious effort at developing a particular takhyil. It is, I think, a worthwhile exercise. To the society around Othello, it makes no sense that Desdemona would love him. His father-in-law vilifies him and demands that he be tried, for it is unimaginable that a white woman could genuinely love a black demonic thing. And this father-in-law's racial hatred is so immense and implacable that it drives him to his grave. It is important to try to imagine this: you are in a society which is almost entirely racially different. Everyone of your race is repulsive to the eye, socially and spiritually subhuman. The father of the person you love drags you to the law courts screeching these obscenities.

Now imagine that even this man or woman you love has not entirely escaped the racist view. Sometimes he/she refers to you by name, but sometimes simply invokes your racial category—your wife or husband calling you not "John" or "Jane," but "the caucasian," or "the oriental," or "the hispanic." And he/she implicitly agrees that you, and everyone like you, is repugnant to the eye. This is how Othello lives. Of the men in the play, the Duke is certainly the most enlightened. He can see the value in Othello's work, his skill, the character of his mind. Yet he too acknowledges the outer man blackly repulsive: "If virtue no delighted beauty lack, / Your son-in-law is far more fair than black" (I.ii.284-85). In complimenting Othello's virtue, he simultaneously characterizes all beauty—primarily physical beauty, but also spiritual beauty—as white, as "fair." Even for the Duke, Othello's appearance is grotesque. Indeed, in this, the most enlightened view of the play, Othello has achieved his inner virtue only insofar as he has become "fair" inside, insofar as he is not black within.

Desdemona is worse. In her first speech, discussing her recent marriage, she does not refer to her new husband as "Othello," but as "the Moor" (I.iii.187). In her next reference to him, she expresses deep affection, but still does not give him a name, and thus a personal identity. "I love the Moor," she says (I.iii.243). She then goes on to *account* for this love—for she too implicitly acknowledges that it is queer to love "such a thing" as Othello, that it requires an explanation. Indeed, she too implicitly acknowledges that he is unsightly. "My heart's subdued / Even to the very quality of my lord" (I.iii.245-46), she says. The phrase is ambiguous. It may mean, as it is sometimes glossed, that she has accepted his warlike profession. But this does not fit the general context. As Othello has already explained (I.iii.166), she fell in love with him *because* of his martial and other exploits. Thus it makes no sense to say that she accepts *even* these. It seems likely, then, that "quality" here refers to the nature or origin of Othello, or to a salient attribute of his person, thus to his being African and black. Desdemona's heart has, it seems, been subdued even to the dark foreignness—the frightful sooty bosom—of what Roderigo called "an extravagant and wheeling stranger" (I.i.133). This meaning is made fully clear in the following line, where Desdemona explains her intent to the curious auditors, who still baffle at this strange marriage of fair and foul. What does she mean when she says that her heart's subdued to the very quality of Othello? She means, "I saw Othello's visage in his mind" (I.iii.247). In the presence of her husband, on her first day of marriage, she announces publicly that, because of his valor, she could love him despite his color. Her comment is akin to that of the Duke: I see him as fair, because I see his virtue, not the dreadful blackness of his face. And, again like the Duke, in affirming Othello's transcendence of his race, she simultaneously affirms that, in Venice, or among Venetians, he will never be considered anything other than an instance of that race.

Othello's Crime

The apparent ease with which Othello is convinced by Iago's deceptions already becomes more comprehensible in this context: the almost universal judgment of Venetians is that Othello is a racial eyesore. Few of us would feel secure if our spouses casually acknowledged that they had to become reconciled to our disagreeable appearance. Moreover, Desdemona might seem to have manifest an impetuous character by eloping with Othello. And, then, she speaks gaily with other men, the fair men, pink-skinned and comely. She even pleads the case of Michael Cassio, a "curled darling of our nation," as Brabantio might put it (see I.ii.67). Certainly, these are no faults, yet to a husband whom she has publicly portrayed as unalluring, they might appear significant.

But Othello does not succumb this easily. Again, it takes ill-fortune and the evil genius of Iago. Despite her belief that black is ugly, despite her references to him as "the Moor," Desdemona is the one Venetian, the one white person by whom Othello feels—at least at times—acknowledged as a subject. She, almost alone, gives him love and respect. She alone will defy convention and self-interest for him. (Even the Duke's respect may be strategic, motivated by Othello's usefulness—for he has done the state some service.) That her heart and mind too should be warped by racism is, almost necessarily, Othello's deepest fear. If this were so, the one link connecting him with the Venetian community would be severed. He would in effect no longer have a place in human society.

And yet, she has already called him "the Moor," already affirmed that black is ugly. Her words have already sown uncertainty in Othello's mind. He tries to suppress the doubts and questions. But Iago will not let him. At first, Othello is unconvinced, affirming Desdemona's honesty (III.iii.225). He recognizes that even good natures can err (III.iii.227), but this is brief, Christian doubt, expressed in Christian terms. Iago intentionally twists Othello's point, perverting it into a statement about race—that Desdemona has erred from "nature" in not marrying a European: "Not to affect many proposed matches / Of her own clime, complexion, and degree, / Whereto we see in all things nature tends" (III.iii.229-31). Iago's point is that the mating of white and black is unnatural—all nature moves to unite like with like, thus not Desdemona and Othello, but (perhaps) Desdemona and Cassio. He continues, "I may fear / Her will, recoiling to her better judgment, / May fall to match you with her country forms, / And happily repent" (III.iii.235-38). He cautions Othello: Beware. If she is reasonable, and follows nature, she will at last compare you with the fair-complexioned men of Venice and repent her wedding vows—just as she might repent a sin, a temporary alliance with the devil.

This persuasion works deeply on Othello, and in his next long speech, he pathetically concludes that Iago is correct: "She's gone" (II.iii.266). He gives two possible reasons for her betrayal. One is age, that he is "declined / Into the vale of years," but this he dismisses, "yet that's not much" (III.iii.264-65). The remaining reason, then, is the reason he accepts, the compelling reason. It is very simple: "I am black" (III.iii.263).

From this point on, the language in which Othello speaks of Desdemona's infidelity is saturated with images of blackness and whiteness, and the beginnings of racial despair. In considering his reputation, he says, "My name, that was as fresh / As Dian's visage, is now begrimed and black / As mine own face" (III.iii.383-85). It does not take a psychoanalyst to see the incipient self-hate below the shallow surface of anger. The contrast between Diana's whiteness and Othello's blackness displaces only slightly his sense that Desdemona has betrayed him because of his black face. When he contemplates revenge, it is "black vengeance, from the hollow hell!" (III.iii.444), vengeance by a black man betrayed due to his blackness, but also vengeance by a man who is perhaps beginning to sink into despondency, believing that he is indeed not human, that he is instead some ill-formed demon, a wretched and diminished image of black Lucifer. (Later, accusing Desdemona of infidelity, he similarly contrasts the "complexion" of Desdemona with his own appearance, "grim as hell" [IV.ii.61-63].)

The misplaced handkerchief is, of course, the final datum edging Othello over the brink to complete despair, and murder. In part, it is an ordinary love token, similar to the love tokens in so many comedies of forbidden love. But it has further resonance as well, resonance amplified by Othello's sense that he has been betrayed due to his race. It was his mother's handkerchief, from Egypt (III.iv.56). She gave it to Othello for his wife. When he gave it to Desdemona, it was a token not only of his love, but of his family, his heritage, his home—Africa, from which he was "taken by the insolent foe / And sold to slavery" (I.iii.136-37). For Desdemona to give away this handkerchief to the curled darling Cassio, that he might pass it casually to a prostitute—this not only denigrates Othello's love, but dishonors his family, his past, his origins, his race. Again, the deepest hurt is not that he has lost sexual possession of his wife, but that he has lost the one point of contact with human community, that even Desdemona's love conceals mockery and disdain.

The murder too follows this pattern. But here the self-hatred, the racial despair, has progressed even further. The imagery of her death is all imagery of white and black: putting out the light (V.ii.7), or, more suggestively, "a huge eclipse / Of sun and moon" (V.ii.98-99). There are more literal connections as well. Indeed, putting out the light is an image of suffocation, and Othello chooses to suffocate Desdemona for a racial reason, for a reason which indicates that he has, at least in part, internalized the racism of Venetian society: "I'll not shed her blood, / Nor scar that whiter skin of hers than snow" (V.ii.3-4). Her whiteness has become sacred, just as his blackness has become demonic. Emilia makes this explicit when she summarizes the murder: "the more angel she, / And you the blacker devil!" (V.ii.129-30). Of course, Othello does at moments reverse this, asserting that Desdemona is a "fair devil" (III.iv.475), that her soul has "gone to burning hell" (V.ii.128). But, then, racial despair does not exclude ambivalence. Indeed, one despairs precisely because one has moments when one feels and sees oneself as human, and recognizes with horror the inhumanity of the oppressor.

Turks, Venetians, Christians

Shakespeare, it seems, was not only aware but deeply critical of racial hatred and related forms of exclusion and oppression. He was pained by the brutality of majority toward minority groups. But his empathy was not our multicultural empathy. It was, rather, thoroughly Christian. His plays indicate that he believed in the unity and equality of humankind, but that he believed in this unity and equality as meaningful only in and through Christian belief and practice. Indeed, that unity and equality would appear to have been, for Shakespeare, a doctrine of Christianity. The racism of the Venetians against Othello is thoroughly unchristian, as is their racism against Shylock in *The Merchant of Venice*. In both plays, Shakespeare sets out to represent a putatively Christian society violating the precepts of Christianity and, in consequence, driving men to acts of barbarism. In short, he shows "Christian" society turning people away from God, when it is their Christian duty to lead people towards God.

A unfortunate aspect of Shakespeare's Christian antiracism is his apparent willingness to condemn all religions other than Christianity. On the other hand, these condemnations were not directed against people but against beliefs and practices. Moreover, they were aimed not at extending colonial oppression but at achieving conversion, and they were paired with equally strong condemnations of hypocritical Christianity.

Put differently, there are two ways in which one may conceive of the opposition between Turk and Venetian. One is religious, the other racial. One identifies Othello with the Venetians as a Christian. The other identifies Othello with the Turks as a Moor. Shakespeare stacks the deck strongly in favor of the former opposition. Othello is the general in charge of defeating the Turks. A violent tempest destroys the Turkish fleet, giving victory to the Venetians before military engagement, thus without loss or suffering. The storm is not, however, a mere natural occurrence. It is too discerning to be random: destroying the Turkish fleet alone, sparing the Venetians, it is a classic literary act of divine providence. For a few moments, it is unclear whether God has chosen to spare Othello or to drown him with the Ottomites, whether God has identified Othello with the Venetians as a Christian or has identified him with the Turks as a Moor. Of course, Othello is spared. God has judged on religious, not racial grounds.

Later, Othello makes this opposition clear, referring to the providential nature of the storm. When restraining the inebriated Cassio, he asks, "Are we turned Turks, and to ourselves do that / Which heaven hath forbid the Ottomites? / For Christian shame put by this barbarous brawl!" (II.iii.169-71). In saying that heaven has forbidden the Ottomites to kill the Venetian soldiers, Othello is referring to the storm and explicitly characterizing it as a manifestation of divine will. In addition, he implicitly explains this providential intervention of God in religious terms. For Othello, "turning Turk" is opposed not to being Venetian, being white, but to being "Christian." Indeed, Othello refers to the entire group as "we," rightly including himself in the body opposed to the Turks—more rightly than those around him, for he alone remembers "Christian shame."

But not everyone sees the division in these terms. Early in the play, Brabantio draws an analogy between Othello's marriage to Desdemona and the Turks' conquest of Cyprus, at that point not yet prevented by the tempest (I.iii.207-08). For him, it is clear that the difference between Turks and Venetians is racial, not religious. The final and perhaps most devastating tragedy of Othello is that, in the end, Othello himself comes to believe Brabantio. He comes to accept that he is not an individual with a name and all the attributes of humanity, that he is not, even more importantly, a soul whose worth is defined by devotion to God rather than outward color. He comes to see himself as nothing but an instance of blackness. Through this distorting lens, he sees the horror of his crime, but he fails to see its nature. He has killed Desdemona because he fell prey to "Christian" inhumanity and became himself as "unchristian" as those around him. But this is not what he sees. When he looks at his crime, and when he looks into the heart of darkness deep in European society, he does not recognize the brutal racism of that society. Instead, he accepts it. Falling headlong into racial despair, he sees his crime as confirmation that he is a dog, a demon, a Turk, that he is all and only blackness, in body and in spirit. Indeed, this racial despair is not only similar to spiritual despair; it is, for Shakespeare, an instance of spiritual despair. Othello cannot dream of forgiveness, for his sin is his very being. It cannot be washed away from his soul by divine grace any more than the "soot" of his bosom or the "grime" of his face can be washed away. The only way to end the sin is to destroy the life which sustains it—and so he murders himself, perversely driven to spiritual despair by the "Christian" community which should have functioned precisely to prevent such feelings, to inspire faith in divine mercy.

There are hints of this self-hatred earlier, as we have already seen. But it is only in his final speech, leading to self-murder, that they are fully developed and fully articulated. *Spoudaios* even in disgrace, he asks his captors to "extenuate" nothing. His full acceptance of his crime, and the racial despair which follows from this, is, again, an aspect of his "constant, loving, noble" character. He will not blame others, only himself. But he blames himself racially, seeing himself through the blue eyes of a racist society. (O'Toole: "Racism isn't just the context in which Othello lives. It has entered his mind and his soul."[25]) In the final lines leading to the suicide, he stops speaking of himself in the first person, as a subject, and begins to speak of himself in the third person, as "one," as an object. He draws three comparisons. First, he is like a "Judean" (V.ii.343); second, he is like an "Arabian tree"; and, finally, he is a "Turk." All are variations on his racial difference from those around him. His final conception of himself is of a Moor only, a dark stranger, no longer this singular man, Othello.

In the first comparison, he is a Jew who "threw a pearl away / Richer than all his tribe" (V.ii.343-44). The pearl was, of course, Desdemona. She was a pearl because she was white, and in being white worth more than an entire Semitic "tribe," her fairness giving her greater value than all the dark men and women in combination. In the second analogy, he is like a tree from Arabia, his sorrow producing a curative balm. The balm is his tears of repentance—the cure, one must assume, is death.

The final comparison is the most painful. Othello has already announced that he will not speak of service he has done the state. But he ends with a story of this service:

> [I]n Aleppo once,
> Where a malignant and a turbaned Turk
> Beat a Venetian and traduced the state,
> I took by th' throat the circumcised dog
> And smote him—thus.
>
> (V.ii.348-52)

In speaking the final words, he stabs himself, as if he were that very Turk.[26] Othello is no longer capable of seeing either Desdemona or himself as individual people, even as husband and wife. She and he have become merely Venetian and Turk, white and black. Othello is now a "malignant" Turk who beat a Venetian, and who must, in consequence, be killed. Looking at himself, he sees an inhuman beast, a "circumcised dog." He has come around to the view of Iago and of Brabantio. He must be punished not because he, Othello, took the life of his beloved Desdemona, but because this black, subhuman Turk took the life of a fair Venetian. When Othello plunges the dagger into his chest, he is not killing himself, for he no longer recognizes himself as a self, a subject, a human body with a divine soul. He is, rather, slaying a dark beast.

This is what makes the ending of the play so devastating, especially for a Christian such as Shakespeare. Othello was a greater Christian than all the Christians of Venice, but he was driven to these final acts of desperation because of the evil of the "Christians" around him, and because of his own "constant, loving, noble nature" (II.i.289). Thus, by Christian doctrine, he is condemned to eternal torment, the death of the soul which he, in Christian conscience, did not wish to inflict on anyone, even Desdemona, even at the extremity of loathing and despair: "If you bethink yourself of any crime / Unreconciled as yet to heaven and grace, / Solicit for it straight. . . . I would not kill thy unprepared spirit. / No, heavens forfend! I would not kill thy soul" (V.ii.26-27, 31-32). It is worth contrasting this attitude with that of Hamlet, who once refrains from killing Claudius for fear that Claudius is at prayer and thus would rise to heaven. To kill someone at prayer, he reflects, "is hire and salary, not revenge!" (III.iii.82). For Shakespeare, the difference between this and the attitude of Othello is not trivial. And both remind a Christian reader of the eternal tragedy that follows inexorably from Othello's unsanctified death. Unlike Hamlet, who piled up corpses on the stage and would even have killed a man's soul—all based on evidence as flimsy as an apparition—unlike Hamlet, Othello will never have "flights of angels sing [him] to [his] rest" (*Hamlet* V.ii.386).

Indeed, even for those of us who do not accept the Christian attitudes behind the work, the dual culmination of events is devastating. In any moral system—religious or secular—it is all too brutally unnecessary and unjust. *Othello* is one of the most impassioned and moving studies of racism in English literature, one of the most powerful in *takhyil*. For Shakespeare makes painfully clear the quiet, pervasive cruelty of racism, and its terrible human consequences.

Notes

1. See Frantz Fanon, *Black Skin, White Masks*, trans. Charles Lam Markmann (New York: Grove, 1967).

2. Derek Walcott, "What the Twilight Says: An Overture," *Dream on Monkey Mountain and Other Plays* (New York: Noonday, 1970) 21.

3. Aristotle, *Peri Poietikes*, in *Aristotle's Theory of Poetry and Fine Art*, ed. and trans S. H. Butcher (New York: Dover, 1951) 10.

4. See especially Martin Orkin, *Shakespeare Against Apartheid* (Craighall: Ad. Donker, 1987) and citations; see also Emily C. Bartels, "Making More of the Moor: Aaron, Othello, and Renaissance Refashionings of Race," *Shakespeare Quarterly* 41.4 (Winter 1990): 433-54.

5. See, for example, John Gillies, *Shakespeare and the Geography of Difference* (New York: Cambridge UP, 1994) 25-27.

6. Michael Neill, "Unproper Beds: Race, Adultery, and the Hideouts in *Othello*," *Shakespeare Quarterly* 40.4 (Winter 1989): 393.

7. Anthony Gerard Barthelemy, *Black Face Maligned Race: The Representation of Blacks in English Drama from Shakespeare to Southerne* (Baton Rouge: Louisiana State UP, 1987).

8. See Jonathan Crewe, "Outside the Matrix: Shakespeare and Race-Writing," *Yale Journal of Criticism* 8.2 (Fall 1995): 28n25.

9. Fintan O'Toole, *No More Heroes: A Radical Guide to Shakespeare* (Dublin: Raven Arts, 1990) 63-64.

10. Michel de Montaigne, "Of the Cannibals," *Shakespeare's World: Background Readings in the English Renaissance*, ed. Gerald M. Pinciss and Roger Lockyer (New York: Continuum, 1989).

11. Al-Farabi, "Canons of the Art of Poetry," *Arabic Poetics in the Golden Age: Selection of Texts Accompanied by a Preliminary Study*, ed. and trans. Vicente Cantarino (Leiden: E. J. Brill, 1975); Ibn Sina, *Avicenna's Commentary on the Poetics of Aristotle*, ed. and trans. Ismail Dahiyat (Leiden: E. J. Brill, 1974); Ibn Rushd, *Averroes' Middle Commentary on Aristotle's Poetics*, ed. and trans., Charles Butterworth (Princeton: Princeton UP, 1986).

12. Dahiyat 89n4.

13. Maulana Muhammad Ali, ed. and trans., *The Holy Qur'an: Arabic Text, English Translation and Commentary* (Columbus, Ohio: Ahmadiyyah Anjuman Isha'at Islam Lahore, 1995) 3n2.

14. Ali 1180n2745.

15. Roman Ingarden, *The Cognition of the Literary Work of Art*, trans. Ruth Ann Crowley and Kenneth R. Olson (Evanston: Northwestern UP, 1973).

16. Wolfgang Iser, "The Reading Process: A Phenomenological Approach," *Reader-Response Criticism: From Formalism to Post-Structuralism*, ed. Jane Tompkins (Baltimore: Johns Hopkins UP, 1980).

17. Kiernan Ryan, *Shakespeare*, 2nd ed. (London: Harvester, Wheatsheaf, 1995) 1, 5.

18. Giraldi Cinthio, "Selection from Giraldi Cinthio Hecatommithi," *The Tragedy of Othello, the Moor of Venice*, ed. Alvan Kernan (New York: Signet, 1986) 175.

19. Cf. Peter Davison, *Othello* (Atlantic Highlands, NJ: Humanities Press International, 1988) 63. The contrast between Shakespeare's treatment of blacks and that of the source has been noted by several critics; see, for example, Edward Berry, "Othello's Alienation," *Studies in English Literature 1500-1900* 30.3 (Spring 1990) 316. For an historical overview of racist stereotyping in the Renaissance, see Barthelmy, note 7 above.

20. This and subsequent citations refer to William Shakespeare, *The Tragedy of Othello, the Moor of Venice*, ed. Alvin Kernan, rev. ed. (New York: New American Library, 1986).

21. Cinthio 175.

22. Matthew 26.52 and John 18.11, in *Geneva Bible: A Facsimile of the 1560 Edition* (Madison: U. of Wisconsin P, 1969).

23. This parallel seems to have gone unnoticed; indeed, despite the obviously Judas-like character of Iago and the occasional links between Othello and Jesus, critics have tended to associate Othello with Judas—bizarrely, in my view; for an overview, see Roy Battenhouse, ed., *Shakespeare's Christian Dimension: An Anthology of Commentary* (Bloomington: Indiana UP, 1994).

24. This point has been noted by several critics; see, for example, Derek Cohen, "Othello's Suicide," *University of Toronto Quarterly* 62.3 (Spring 1993): 324.

25. O'Toole 64.

26. Cf. Leslie A. Fiedler, *The Stranger in Shakespeare* (New York: Stein and Day, 1972) 195.

Virginia Mason Vaughan (essay date 1998)

SOURCE: "Race Mattered: *Othello* in Late Eighteenth-Century England," in *Shakespeare Survey*, Vol. 51, 1998, pp. 57-66.

[*In the following essay, Vaughan provides insight into the seemingly irreconcilable popularity of* Othello *among eighteenth-century audiences during a time of tense racial debates.*]

'When Paul Robeson stepped onto the stage for the very first time', Margaret Webster recalled, 'when he spoke his very first line, he immediately, by his very presence, brought an incalculable sense of reality to the entire play.'[1] That reality emanated from Robeson's status as the first actor of African descent to impersonate Shakespeare's Othello on Broadway. Because of his biological heritage, Robeson was perceived as being more 'real' as the Moor than a white actor in blackface. Robeson's performance in the longest-running Shakespeare production ever staged on Broadway thus revolutionized the way many people felt about its hero.

As public reaction to Webster's *Othello* demonstrated, a play in performance is both a maker and a transmitter of cultural codes; it is necessarily imbricated in the broader discourses that surround it. Shakespearians concerned with the history of performance must determine the nature of those discourses and how they shaped the text's reception and transmission. For the history of *Othello,* especially, the discourses inevitably include the messy matter of racial ideology.[2]

The received view of *Othello* in the late eighteenth century seems to deny this premise, however, and to isolate the play in performance from the broad context of English culture. At a time when the justice of British enslavement of black Africans in England and the West Indies was hotly debated,[3] Othello's race and his relation to a white woman seem, in the eyes of most theatre historians, not to have mattered. Thus two contradictory discourses circulated simultaneously and, at first glance, seem to have had little or no impact on each other: (1) the pro- and anti-slavery polemics in pamphlets and magazines, and (2) criticism of *Othello* on stage in memoirs, acting treatises, and reviews.

Perhaps because *Othello* boasts a continuous acting history from the Restoration to the present, or perhaps because of its privileged place in the canon as one of the Big Four, there is abundant perceptive commentary about its early performance history. Marvin Rosenberg began his long and fruitful career with *The Masks of Othello* in 1961. His chapter on the eighteenth century argues that 'a proper, neoclassic hero was aimed at' and demonstrates how cuts in the acting text were designed to display Othello at his best and to protect the audience from overt sexual references.[4] Rosenberg never mentions race *per se*. Carol Carlisle's thoughtful study of actor-critic responses to the Big Four, *Shakespeare from the Greenroom*, recognizes that colour had indeed created problems in the performance history of *Othello* but concludes that 'there is no interpretation of Othello advanced by an actor-critic of that period [the eighteenth century] that might not bear the stamp of nobility upon it'.[5] Julie Hankey's performance edition also offers a detailed survey of *Othello's* acting history; she characterizes the eighteenth-century Moor as 'the hero-and-the-lover' and suggests that theatre critics such as James Boaden saw little significance in Othello as an African; rather, in Hankey's words, 'Othello was in their minds a hot and fiery southern gentleman in whom the qualities of an Englishman were not so much abandoned as exaggerated.'[6] Gino Matteo is more emphatic, insisting that the issue of race 'simply never materialised in the eighteenth-century theatre'.[7] Even so astute a critic as James Siemon is reticent on the topic of race, asserting 'the age's nearly universal insistence on Othello's nobility'.[8]

This reticence about the racial dynamics of eighteenth-century *Othello* performances, which is admittedly exhibited in my recent book,[9] reflects the traditional sources. They are either silent about Othello's race or insist that it was not an issue. William Cooke, for example, anointed Spranger Barry as the best eighteenth-century Othello in his *Memoirs of Charles Macklin* because he was the perfect hero and lover. Cooke concludes: 'those who before doubted of the poet's consistency in forming a mutual passion between such characters as the *black* Othello, and the *fair* Desdemona, were now convinced of his propriety. They saw, from Barry's predominant and fascinating manner, that mere colour could not be a barrier to affection'.[10]

In somewhat the same vein, Francis Gentleman's 1777 edition of *Othello* emphasizes that the Moor should 'be amiably elegant and above the middle stature; his expression full and sententious, for the declamatory part; flowing and harmonious, for the love-scenes; rapid and powerful for each violent climax of jealous rage'.[11] In *The Dramatic Censor*, Gentleman describes Othello as 'open, generous, free, subject to violent feelings, not, as himself expresses it, *easily jealous*, yet rouzed by that pernicious passion above all violent restraint; weak in his confidence, partial in discernment, fatal in resolution'.[12] Despite his expansive concern with character, Gentleman never mentions colour or race. Nor is there any reference to Othello's make-up or colour in Kemble's promptbook.[13]

There are, to be sure, some hints in the standard sources that Othello's blackness was sometimes of passing interest. In a frequently cited anecdote, David Garrick is said to have answered the question, 'why Shakespeare made his hero black?' with this rejoinder:

> Shakespeare had shown us white men jealous in other pieces, but . . . their jealousy had limits, and was not so terrible; . . . in . . . Othello, he had wished to paint that passion in all its violence, and that is why he chose an African in whose veins circulated fire instead of blood, and whose true or imaginary character could excuse all boldnesses of expression and all exaggerations of passion.[14]

Garrick drew here upon the common assumption that people living in Africa, Ethiopia, and Egypt were violent by nature, whereas people from more northern climes were steadier in temperament.[15] But what had been a cultural bias during the late sixteenth century became a fixed ideology two hundred years later when London had acquired a substantial black population.

James Boaden's memoir of John Philip Kemble echoes this received wisdom when he describes the actor-manager's Moor as 'grand and awful and pathetic. But he was a European: there seemed to be philosophy in his bearing; there was reason in his rage'.[16] Because Kemble was too northern, or English, in his self-control, Boaden implies, the actor never fully realized the role's emotional dynamics. The 29 October 1787 *Public Advertiser* echoes Boaden's assessment in its evaluation of the first act: 'in his first scenes [Kemble] was judicious, but too studiously so; and though most critically correct in his address to the Senate, evidenced he was more anxious to do justice to the text of his author than the feelings of Othello'. The reviewer praises the actor's performance in the later scenes, but, in a curious aside, comments: 'We much approve his dressing Othello in the Moorish habit . . . [but] is it necessary the Moor should be as *black* as a native of Guiney?'[17]

That Kemble's Moor was too like an African from Guinea (most likely a slave to be exported to the West Indian sugar plantations) suggests that, to some viewers at least, the distinction between the white actor playing a black man and the real thing had to be maintained. This may be one explanation for David Garrick's failure in the role of Othello—not that he was too black, but that in his turban and feather, he looked too much like the black servants fashionable Londoners encountered every day. The historian Peter Fryer estimates that by the late eighteenth century approximately 10,000 black people resided in a nation whose total population was approaching nine million.[18] Despite the popular impression that there was no slavery in England during the eighteenth century, slaves were regularly bought and sold in London and the port cities of Bristol and Liverpool.[19] The majority of blacks in England had been imported by West Indian planters returning to the mother country. Slaves, many of them children, often decked in special livery, accompanied wealthy white women, their blackness highlighting by contrast the mistress's fair beauty. 'Given classical names like Pompey and Caesar', contends historian Gretchen Gerzina, 'they were dressed in brightly coloured silks and satins, silver padlocked collars, and feathered turbans'.[20] William Hogarth's 'The Harlot's Progress', Plate 2, satirized this social practice with a be-turbaned black child bearing the tea kettle to his mistress's table.[21] David Dabydeen observes in his study of Hogarth's blacks that the boy's

> sartorial elegance, his silver collar and his polite domestic duties (English ladies employed black boys to wait at the tea-table, to carry their fans and smelling-salts, to comb their lap dogs, and so on) belies the sordid reality of the servitude of naked and manacled blacks in the colonies.[22]

Hogarth's engraving thus illustrates the context for actor James Quin's famous quip about Garrick's representation of Shakespeare's Moor: 'There was a little black boy, like Pompey attending with a tea-kettle, fretting and fumbling about the stage; but I saw no Othello.'[23] As the hero of a major tragedy crafted by the National Poet, Othello could not look like a little black slave. Garrick's diminutive stature and exotic turban thus doomed his Othello. Eighteenth-century audiences sought a Moor, as I concluded in 1994, who appeared 'as a high ranking, noble, courageous general, an English gentleman, represented by a white actor in blackface'.[24]

But does this performance preference mean that, as I once thought, race was not an issue in the late eighteenth-century interpretation of *Othello*? How could it not be an issue when cultural anxiety about Britain's black population and the future of the slave trade was at its peak, when litigation such as the highly contested Somerset case of 1772 sparked a public debate about the merits of the slave system? In the 1770s, after the Somerset ruling set a precedent that escaped slaves could not be deported to the West Indies, allowing them to claim freedom on English soil, the pro-slavery lobby countered with loud assertions of Negro inferiority and bestiality, claims that blacks had a better life on the plantations than they would in London competing for scarce employment, and predictions of an English future polluted by miscegenation. By 1783, when a new influx of blacks who had served the Loyalist cause in America arrived to claim their promised freedom, public discussion of their status accelerated. A scheme to remove the black poor from London streets and resettle them in Sierra Leone won backing even from those in favour of abolition and was actually implemented in 1786, though to little success.

London's theatres may seem far removed from this political battlefield, but the same volumes that we comb for theatre reviews—journals like *The Public Advertiser* and *The Gentleman's Magazine*—published letters, reports, and reviews from both sides. The literate gentlemen who read such magazines probably knew *Othello* well, but perhaps it was to avoid making any connections between Shakespeare's moving tragedy and the reality of most black people's lives that they insisted on the Moor's nobility and exalted status.

Outside the magazines and other standard theatrical sources, there is admittedly slender but nonetheless suggestive evidence as to how Othello was constructed within the larger culture. His blackness, of course, was a given, so it is not surprising to find Othello as the name of a slave[25] or a member of an all-black military musical regiment.[26] That Othello married a white woman was also a given. Thus the white chambermaids who flirted with the Duchess of Queensberry's black servant, Julius Soubise (notorious for womanizing and other vices), called him 'the young Othello'.[27] Othello was jealous. So, when Hester Piozzi reported the jealous quarrel between Francis Barber, Samuel Johnson's black servant, and his white wife, she called the wife 'his Desdemona'.[28]

More surprising is that literate Africans also used Othello as a self-construction when writing to a white audience.

For example, when the West Indian pro-slavery lobby attacked the writings of the ex-slave Olaudah Equiano (who had gained a large and sympathetic white audience), claiming he was not African at all, he added this to the 1792 edition of his popular *Interesting Narrative:* 'An invidious falsehood having appeared . . . with a view to hurt my character, and to discredit and prevent the sale of my Narrative . . . it is necessary [to]

> Speak of me as I am,
> Nothing extenuate, nor set down aught
> In malice.'[29]

If Equiano, a passionate advocate for abolition, did not otherwise identify himself with Shakespeare's Moor, he probably assumed his white readers would make the connection and respond sympathetically, as they did in the theatre, to words from Othello's suicide speech.

Ignatius Sancho is another well-known exslave from the period. Hogarth's engraving 'Taste in High Life' (1746) depicts him as a child. Like Pompey with the tea kettle, Sancho is dressed in fancy livery with a feathered turban, serving—as does the monkey in the engraving's foreground—as a plaything to his fashionable white mistress.[30] But Sancho was lucky. Despite his first mistress's reservations, he learned to read and, in the service of the Duke of Montagu, he found greater opportunities to exercise his musical and literary talents.

In the 1770s, after Sancho became goutridden and incapable of further service, the Montagus helped to set him up in London as a grocer. From his shop, Sancho associated with many of London's artists and literati, including David Garrick. His letters, published after his death in 1782, quoted frequently from eighteenth-century writers such as Pope, Sterne, and Fielding, and less frequently from Shakespeare. In one letter, he adopts Othello's words and describes himself as 'unused to the melting mood'.[31] In another, more telling, letter, he jokingly speculates as to why gentlemen should 'make elections of wide different beings than Blackamoors for their friends'. The reason is obvious, he concludes, '—from Othello to Sancho the big—we are either foolish—or mulish—all—all without a single exception'.[32] Mocking the stereotyping of black people, Sancho chooses the black best known in the dominant white culture, Shakespeare's Othello.

Equiano and Sancho were powerful spokesmen for the abolitionist cause. After gaining their freedom, both constructed identities for themselves in the white world of eighteenth-century London, yet in their writings both display the double consciousness described by W. E. B. DuBois, 'the simultaneous and sometimes conflicting awareness of being both a part of the political and social organism as a citizen, and of being a descendant of Africa'.[33] When they presented themselves to the mainstream culture, whether seriously or playfully, they chose Othello, a black hero constructed by whites, to speak for them.

Eighteenth-century publishing was, of course, controlled by white men, and it was through the efforts of white abolitionists that Equiano and Sancho's writings circulated. Would the ex-slaves have been as successful at being heard in other venues? Sancho's earliest biographer, Joseph Jekyll, reports that the grocer had a passion for the theatre and that as a young man, 'He had been even induced to consider the stage as a resource . . . and his complexion suggested an offer to the manager [David Garrick] of attempting Othello and Oroonoko; but a defective and incorrigible articulation rendered it abortive.'[34] Perhaps Garrick would have arranged for Sancho's debut as the noble Moor had the plump grocer been endowed with Paul Robeson's voice and heroic figure, but it seems more likely that the performance would never have materialized.

I draw here on the distinction Dympna Callaghan makes in her recent essay, '"Othello was a white man"', between 'the display of black people themselves' (an exhibition) and 'the simulation of negritude' (an imitation or mimesis).[35] As she convincingly concludes, the actor who imitates can control the image and its signification; the person on display, in contrast, is passive, leaving the spectators in charge of determining her or his signification. White actors impersonating Othello could—and if we believe contemporary accounts, did—reinforce the stereotype of African passion. If Sancho had been able to portray Othello in the London theatres, his occupation of a speaking, subject position would have been too threatening. This may be a reason, among others, why London theatres would not accept Ira Aldridge as Othello fifty years later. Joyce Green MacDonald contends in a recent essay that by being black instead of acting black, in a 'self-authorization of blackness', Aldridge 'disrupted and complicated the economy of race in unforeseen ways'.[36] In any case, the distinction between exhibit—the thing itself—and imitation may explain why, as one historian puts it, Londoners in the eighteenth century could read about slave auctions at home and 'sensational stories of revolts on West Indian plantations quite coolly in the morning newspaper, and then shed tears that evening over similar situations presented on stage'.[37]

Although Francis Gentleman never mentions race in his comments on *Othello,* he repeatedly frets about indecorous sexual suggestions, something Rosenberg pointed out long ago. Decorum was certainly an eighteenth-century preoccupation, and most plays were emended or cut to satisfy current tastes. For example, Gentleman describe Mercutio's reference to the 'demesnes' that lie adjacent to Rosaline's (in Garrick's version, Juliet's) thigh as 'a very indecent line of ludicrous conjuration'.[38] Though Juliet's contemplation of the loss of her maidenhead is removed from her 'Gallop apace' soliloquy in Gentleman's edition, the cuts in *Romeo and Juliet* are nevertheless minor compared to those in Gentleman's *Othello.* Moreover, Gentleman's commentary on *Othello* has a touch of hysteria about it that clearly contrasts with his sentimental acceptance of Romeo and Juliet's passion. There are, to be sure, many differences between these two tragedies, but I suggest that the impulse to clean up and cut loomed larger when it came to *Othello* because black sexuality and the prospect of miscegenation caused far more anxiety than sexual relations between two white lovers.

As Michael Neill shows in his analysis of the early illustrations of the murder scene, the figures of the white Desdemona, prone and helpless in her bed, and the black Othello who hovers over her 'foreground not merely the perverse eroticism of the scene but its aspect of forbidden disclosure'.[39] Neill shows how fear and fascination at the idea of miscegenation lurked behind audience responses to the play's final scene. William Leney's engraving of J. Graham's painting of the same scene, commissioned for the Boydell Gallery, shows a diminutive, be-turbaned figure who recalls descriptions of Garrick's performance. The engraving also suggests quasi-pornographic eroticism encoded in black and white. Like the black page whose dark skin highlights by contrast his mistress's whiteness, the black Othello hovers in the shadows of the bed curtains while Desdemona's exposed neck and breast form the picture's erotic centre. As Othello holds the light in one hand and the dagger in the other, the viewer is implicitly invited to contemplate what will happen when the black man 'tops' the helpless white female figure and kills her in an erotic embrace. Leney's engraving encodes the spectre of racial intermarriage and 'contamination' incessantly invoked by the West Indian slavery lobby, a spectre that according to Fryer, haunted England from the 1770s well into the next century.[40] Though this fear was not articulated in contemporary theatrical discourse, Cooke's denial of its existence in his description of Spranger Barry suggests its power. Moreover, the spectre's widespread circulation in larger social discourses may well explain the repeated insistence that Othello had to bear himself like an English gentleman and wear makeup that everyone recognized as artificial. Reality would be too terrifying.

However contradictory this may seem on the surface, it is less a contradiction than it is a paradox of the times and of the history of *Othello* in performance. Returning to Francis Gentleman's description of Othello—

> he is open, generous, free, subject to violent feelings, not, as himself expresses it, *easily jealous,* yet rouzed by that pernicious passion above all violent restraint; weak in his confidence, partial in discernment, *fatal in resolution.* [my italics][41]

we find striking similarities with Hector McNeill's *Observations on the Treatment of the Negroes in the Island of Jamaica,* a pro-slavery treatise published in 1788:

> The Negro is possessed of passions not only strong but ungovernable; a mind dauntless, warlike, and unmerciful; a temper extremely irascible; a disposition indolent, selfish, and deceitful . . . He has certain portions of kindness for his friends, generosity and friendship for his favourites, and affection for his connections . . . Furious in his love as in his hate.[42]

Perhaps Gentleman's seeming silence about race is not silence at all; perhaps it is simply the product of shared cultural assumptions—that Othello's blackness and his jealous passion are integrally connected. This linking of race with character, temperament, and values is an incipient form of the racialism that flowered in England and America during the next century.

When theatre historians look outside the standard *theatrical* resources for the late eighteenth century and examine the personal and political discourses that circulated simultaneously, the evidence is impressive that Shakespeare's *Othello* was deeply imbricated in England's growing racialism. Race mattered to performances of *Othello* but in ways that were discussed only when an inviolable line was crossed; when stage representations moved uncomfortably close to verisimilitude—when Kemble was too black, like a native of Guinea, or Garrick too like Hogarth's depiction of the slave boy Pompey with his tea kettle—only then did Othello's biological heritage merit serious comment.

As theatre historians, we should be especially careful when dealing with texts that foreground volatile issues of race, class, gender, religion, or sexual identity. Eighteenth-century reviews and memoirs were written by educated white men whose prosperous standard of living often rested on traffic in human flesh; what they did not discuss may be as important as what they did. We need to ponder their silences and, as best we can, burrow in alternative discourses to understand fully Shakespeare's role within the cultural tradition.

Notes

My title is an allusion to Cornel West's recent analysis of race relations in the United States, *Race Matters* (New York: Vintage, 1994). Earlier versions of this essay were presented at the Shakespeare Association of America, the Higgins School of Humanities Lecture Series at Clark University, and the Shakespearian Studies Seminar at the Harvard Center for Literary and Cultural Studies; the essay has benefitted greatly from the ensuing discussions and I thank all who generously shared their ideas with me. I am also grateful to Alden T. Vaughan and R. A. Foakes for suggestions about sources and revisions.

1. Margaret Webster, *Shakespeare Without Tears* (New York: Capricorn Books, 1975; orig. pub. 1995), p. 179.

2. James C. Bulman proposes in his introduction to *Shakespeare, Theory, and Performance* that in contrast to the essentialistic approach to performance pioneered in the 1970s by John Styan, contemporary theatre historians and performance critics should examine how 'acts of representation are implicated in the dynamics of contemporary culture and in themselves acquire meaning' (London: Routledge, 1996), p. 1.

3. For historical accounts of blacks in England during this period, see Gretchen Gerzina, *Black London: Life Before Emancipation* (New Brunswick, NJ: Rutgers University Press, 1995); James Walvin, *Black and White: The Negro and English Society*

(London: Allen Lane the Penguin Press, 1973), esp. chaps. 4-8; and Peter Fryer, *Staying Power: The History of Black People in Britain* (London: Pluto Press, 1984), esp. chaps. 3-8.

4. Marvin Rosenberg, *The Masks of Othello* (Berkeley: University of California Press, 1961), pp. 29-53; quote from p. 34.

5. Carol Jones Carlisle, *Shakespeare from the Greenroom* (Chapel Hill: University of North Carolina Press, 1969), pp. 172-263; quote from p. 200.

6. Julie Hankey, ed. *Othello (Plays in Performance)* (Bristol: Bristol Classical Press, 1987), pp. 36-61; quotes from pp. 36 and 49.

7. Gino M. Matteo, *Shakespeare's Othello: The Study and the Stage, 1604-1904* (Salzburg: Institut für Englische Sprache und Literatur, 1974), pp. 85-200; quote from p. 123.

8. James R. Siemon, '"Nay, that's not next": *Othello*, v.ii. in Performance, 1700-1900', *Shakespeare Quarterly*, 37 (1986), 38-51; quote from p. 41.

9. Virginia Mason Vaughan, *Othello: A Contextual History* (Cambridge: Cambridge University Press, 1994), pp. 113-34.

10. William Cooke, *Memoirs of Charles Macklin* (London: James Asperne, 1804), p. 155.

11. Francis Gentleman, ed. *Othello* (London: John Bell, 1777), p. 10.

12. Francis Gentleman, *The Dramatic Censor*, vol. 1 (London: John Bell, 1770), p. 150.

13. See the reproduction of Kemble's promptbook in *John Philip Kemble Promptbooks*, vol. 7, ed. Charles H. Shattuck (Charlottesville: University Press of Virginia for the Folger Shakespeare Library, 1974).

14. From Frank A. Hedgcock, *David Garrick and his French Friends* (London: Stanley Paul, 1912), p. 341n.

15. J. B. Bamborough discusses this English Renaissance conception in *The Little World of Man* (London: Longmans, Green and Co., 1952), pp. 72-3.

16. James Boaden, *Memoirs of the Life of John Philip Kemble*, vol. 1 (London: Longman et al., 1825), p. 256. Earlier in his career, Kemble produced an adaptation of *The Comedy of Errors*, called *OH! 'tis Impossible;* Boaden attributes the staging of the twin Dromios as black slaves (so that the faces of Dromio of Syracuse and Dromio of Ephesus could not be distinguished by the audience) as the reason for the production's failure (p. 33).

17. Quoted from *The London Stage, 1660-1800, Part 5*, vol. 2, ed. Charles Beecher Hogan (Carbondale: Southern Illinois University Press, 1969), p. 1016.

18. Fryer, *Staying Power*, p. 68.

19. *Ibid.*, pp. 58-61.

20. Gerzina, *Black London*, p. 16.

21. See also *Hogarth: The Complete Engravings*, ed. Joseph Burke and Colin Caldwell (New York: Harry N. Abrams, 1960), plate 135.

22. David Dabydeen, *Hogarth's Blacks: Images of Blacks in Eighteenth-Century English Art* (Athens: University of Georgia Press, 1987), p. 114.

23. Cooke, *Memoirs*, p. 113.

24. Vaughan, *Othello: A Contextual History*, p. 121.

25. Gerzina, *Black London*, p. 31.

26. Fryer, *Staying Power*, p. 87.

27. Gerzina, *Black London*, p. 55.

28. Hesther Lynch Piozzi, *Anecdotes of Samuel Johnson*, ed. S. C. Roberts (Cambridge: Cambridge University Press, 1932), pp. 136-7.

29. The preface is reprinted as Appendix A in *The Life of Olaudah Equiano*, vol. I, ed. Paul Edwards (London: Dawsons, 1969).

30. The description of plate 200 in *Hogarth: The Complete Engravings* identifies the black boy as Ignatius Sancho. Dabydeen suggests that the lady's seductive gesture implies the sexual role sometimes played by the black male slave with aristocratic white ladies; see *Hogarth's Blacks*, p. 79.

31. Ignatius Sancho, *The Letters of Ignatius Sancho*, ed. Paul Edwards and Polly Rewt (Edinburgh: Edinburgh University Press, 1994), p. 40.

32. Sancho, *Letters*, p. 191.

33. Gerzina, *Black London*, p. 63.

34. Sancho, *Letters*, p. 23.

35. Dympna Callaghan, '"Othello was a white man"', in *Alternative Shakespeares 2* (London: Routledge, 1996), pp. 192-215; quotes from pp. 194-5.

36. Joyce Green MacDonald, 'Acting Black: *Othello*, *Othello* Burlesques, and the Performance of Blackness', *Theatre Journal*, 46 (1994), 231-49; quotes from p. 234.

37. Gerzina, *Black London*, p. 7.

38. *Romeo and Juliet* (London: John Bell, 1774), p. 100. Gentleman used Garrick's acting edition which, among other changes, cut Rosaline from the play's beginning and added an extended dialogue between Romeo and Juliet before they expire at the end.

39. Michael Neill, 'Unproper Beds: Race, Adultery, and the Hideous in *Othello*', *Shakespeare Quarterly*, 40 (1989), 383-412; quote from p. 385. Paul H. D. Kaplan concludes in his overview of early illustrations that the 'repeated selection of the murder scene at the end of the play reveals a taste for the melodramatic, and implies a reading of the

tragedy in which Othello's violence assumes the most important position'. See 'The Earliest Images of Othello', *Shakespeare Quarterly,* 39 (1988), 171-85; quote from p. 185.

40. Fryer, *Staying Power,* p. 161.
41. Gentleman, *Dramatic Censor,* vol. 1, p. 150.
42. *Gentleman's Magazine,* 1788, part 2, pp. 1093-4.

GENDER ISSUES

June Sturrock (essay date 1984)

SOURCE: "*Othello*: Women and 'Woman'," in *Atlantis,* Vol. 9, No. 2, Spring, 1984, pp. 1-8.

[*In the essay below, Sturrock examines Shakespeare's attack on anti-feminist propaganda, arguing that in* Othello *Shakespeare urges the audience to recognize the worth of the individual.*]

> It hath ever beene a common custome amongst Idle, and humerous Poets, Pamphleters, and Rimers, out of passionate discontents, or having little otherwise to imploy themselves about, to write some bitter Satire-Pamphlet, or Rime against women: in which argument he who could devise anything more bitterly, or spitefully, against our sexe hath never wanted the liking, allowance and applause of giddy-headed people.[1]

Women in Shakespeare's England, as in the England of the Wife of Bath and Janekin, were among the easiest and commonest targets of satire. According to Louis B. Wright in his *Middle Class Culture in Elizabethan England,* the increasingly active role of women during this period "aroused the ire of conservatives, who vented their displeasure in pulpit and pamphlet."[2] The mid-16th century publication of *The School-House of Women* (1542?)[3] renewed the arguments for and against women which continued throughout the rest of the century. In the early years of the next century, partly through the license given by King James's notorious dislike of women, anti-feminism gathered momentum, and these years produced such works as Barnabe Riche's *Faultes, Faultes, and Nothing Else but Faultes* (1606) and Joseph Swetnam's *The Arraignment of Lewde, Idle, Forward and Unconstant Women* (1615) which brought public responses from outraged women. Throughout Shakespeare's lifetime, for all the glorification of Elizabeth, there was a living tradition of anti-feminism.

In *Othello,* Shakespeare takes this English tradition of satire against women and uses it dramatically and ironically: the old libels on women are voiced repeatedly by the speeches of the principal male characters while their falsity, inadequacy, and destructive nature are demonstrated amply by the actions of the women in the play. The anti-feminist invective of the play is weighed against the action of the play, in which all three women are almost entirely motivated by love and loyalty, and in which indeed their major function is to demonstrate various kinds of love and loyalty. Here, as elsewhere, Shakespeare makes use of current and facile generalizations about groups of people; he also compels us in various ways to question such generalizations and to recognise that any person's individuality and humanity signifies more than his or her membership of a group.

Iago is obviously the chief mouthpiece for such attitudes in *Othello* and especially for the attack on women. Although he is notoriously chameleon-like, adapting his attitudes and his bearing to his company and to his own complex motives—"I am not what I am," he says of himself, (I.i.65)[4]—the one constant feature in his various guises, whether he is with Cassio, Roderigo, or Desdemona, is his contempt for women. When he is with Desdemona and Emilia, he makes this contempt appear like the jovial banter of a rough soldier. Cassio, indeed, half-apologizes to Desdemona for him in just these terms: "You may relish him more in the soldier than in the scholar" (II.i.165). When alone with his wife, Iago shows his contempt in dirty jokes and insults:

> Emilia:
> I have a thing for you.
> Iago:
> A thing for me? it is a common thing—
> Emilia:
> Ha!
> Iago:
> To have a foolish wife.
>
> (III.iii.301-04)

With Cassio, Iago is more circumspect—no doubt the "daily beauty" in Cassio's life warns him off—but his description of Desdemona ignores her finer qualities and stresses her sexuality and availability; it is an implicit testing of Cassio's attitude to Desdemona: "She is sport for Jove—And, I'll warrant her, full of game. . . . What an eye she has! methinks it sounds a parley of provocation . . . and when she speaks, is it not an alarum to love?" With Roderigo, who notably lacks daily beauty in his life, Iago is more openly cynical. Desdemona is a "guinea hen," a "supersubtle Venetian," and Roderigo's love for her is "merely a lust of the blood and the permission of the will" (I.iii.318, 364 & 339). With Othello, Iago plays on the comparative social ignorance of his General and calumniates Desdemona through a condemnation of Venetian women in general, thus making use of two traditions of prejudice:

> In Venice they do let heaven see the pranks
> They dare not let their husbands see. Their best conscience
> Is not to leave't undone but keep't unknown.
>
> (III.iii.202)

Whatever form this hostility takes, it is always present: one feature which Iago never quite discards or disguises in his contempt for women and indeed it is supremely useful to him.

His attack on women is inevitably the traditional attack; as Desdemona observes of his strictures on women, "These are old fond paradoxes to make fools laugh in th'alehouse" (II.i.140). Iago's misogyny is such that he apparently feels that the highest possible feat of the best of possible women is merely trivially domestic: "to suckle fools and chronicle small beer" (II.i.159). Women, according to Iago, are idle, shrewish, ignorant, wilful, avaricious, vain and above all lecherous and adulterous—Iago accuses every one of the women of the play of faithlessness to the man she loves. Every one of these faults is a commonplace of the Elizabethan satirists' case against women. Thomas Nashe for instance brings all his learning—or perhaps all his invention—to the cause:

> The olde Sages did admonish young men, if ever they matche wyth any wife, not to take a rich wife, because if she be rich, shee wyll not be content to be a wife, but will be a Master or Mistresse, in commaunding, chiding, correcting & controlling . . . *Socrates* deemed it the desperatest enterprise that one can take in hand, to governe a womans will . . . *Demosthenes* saide, that it was the greatest tormente, that a man could invent to his enemies vexation, to give him his daughter in marriage, as a domesticall Furie to disquiet him night and day. *Democritus* accounted a faire chaste woman a miracle of miracles, a degree of immortality, a crowne of tryumph because shee is so harde to be founde.[5]

The views ascribed to Democritus here remind one of Iago consoling Othello by referring to the normality, even universality, of female adultery. "Think every beared fellow that's but yoked may draw with you" (IV.i.65-67). On the common Elizabethan theme of the vanity of women Nashe writes:

> She had rather view her face a whole morning in a looking Glasse then worke by the howre Glasse, shee is more sparing of her Spanish needle than her Spanish gloves, occupies oftner her setting stick then sheeres, and joyes more in her Jewels then in her Jesus.[6]

The related sin of female pride—indeed when reading some satirists one might almost be tempted to say female sin of pride—is usually central in the satirists' version of the female character. For Iago, "she that was ever fair and never proud" (II.i.149) is a rare, perhaps nonexistent, woman. For Arthur Dent, writing in 1601, female pride was almost literally earth-shaking:

> And truly wee may thinke the very stones on the streete, and the beames in the house do quake, & wonder at their monstrous, intollerable, and excessive pride: for it seemeth that they are altogether a lumpe of pride, a mass of pride, even altogether made of pride, and nothing else but pride, pride.[7]

Rodney Poisson has written interestingly of the "Italianate antifeminism" of Iago, in an article which establishes the relevance of Renaissance anti-feminism to this play.[8] There is no need to place the anti-feminism as particularly Italian: there is abundant anti-feminist material written in English, published in England in Shakespeare's lifetime. Iago's point of view would be familiar enough to the average member of Shakespeare's audience.

Shakespeare uses this ancient though still lively tradition to place Iago and his hatred and fear of women and sexuality. Indeed, Iago is presented as a character who is prepared to accept and to voice group hatred in general, and clichés about groups. Robert Heilman comments on Iago's use of plurals, generic singulars and abstractions to "subtly imply universal experience."[9] It is Iago too who uses the well-known contemporary national slurs: "Your Dane, your German, and your swag-bellied Hollander . . . are nothing to your English [as drinkers, that is]" (II.iii.79-80). It is he who condemns Venetian women with the traditional insult; it is he who stresses Othello's blackness and strangeness: Iago describes Othello as "an old black ram," a "Barbary horse" (I.i.88,112) and "an erring Barbarian" and as a typical member of his race: "These Moors are changeable in their wills (I.iii.355). Because of this vision of people as grouped and labelled, he can speak of Desdemona's love for Othello as being, because it is exogamous, a sexual perversion, as displaying a "will most rank" (III.iii.232). And Othello tragically comes to accept this generalized view of his marriage and the generalized view of Desdemona.

For as Iago gradually takes possession of Othello, Othello loses sight of the actual Desdemona, his wife whom he trusts and admires and of whose love he has ample evidence; he sees instead only the sexual generalization, the woman, the Venetian, the stranger. Though his own senses assure him of her truth: "If she be false, then Heaven mocks itself," he prefers rather to trust Iago's words. Indeed, this play is very much concerned with the power of words as opposed to the lesser power of evidence. Othello comes to see Desdemona as a "lewd minx" (II.iii.476), "public commoner" (IV.ii.73), "impudent strumpet" (IV.ii.81) and "that cunning whore of Venice" (IV.ii.89). Othello is, as Rodney Poisson points out, all the more easily convinced by Iago because Iago's accusations would sound all too familiar to him, as to any man or woman of the period. The pattern is ready waiting for any calumniated woman to be fitted into it, as Imogen was fitted into it, and even the unaccused Hermione. And Othello knew little of women and of the ordinary world of social intercourse:

> Little of this great world can I speak
> More than pertains to feats of broil and battle
>
> (I.iii.86-87)

This is why Iago chooses to ruin Othello in the way that he does, realizing that Othello depends on his ancient's superior knowledge of the Venetian world and of women. Othello says of Iago:

> This fellow's of exceeding honesty,

> And knows all qualities, with a learned spirit
> Of human dealings
>
> (III.iii.258-60)

Othello, then, is a play which voices clearly a bitter hostility towards women and towards sex. Women are whores or madams, sheep and mares. But while voicing this attitude, *Othello* also demonstrates clearly, though with hardly any direct comment, a contrasting view, so that there is an ironic counterpoint between words and action. The actual women of the play compel our admiration partly for their command of the very virtues which Iago and the satirists believe them to lack. Desdemona has indeed been criticized as being excessively saintly. When Cassio greets her:

> Hail to thee, lady! and the grace of heaven,
> Before, behind thee, and on every hand
> Enwheel thee round
>
> (II.i.85-87)

his words sound more like a description of her present state than a wish for her future state. Her chastity is so instinctive that she cannot imagine considering adultery. Her charity is almost beyond comprehension: despite her natural terror of death, she entirely forgives Othello to the point of lying with her last breath to shield him. She even forgives and prays for her unknown defamer, when Emilia guesses that such a person must exist: "If any such there be, Heaven pardon him" (IV.ii.135). Every speech in its very structure and diction shows her frankness and her simplicity: even her two lies reveal her nature, one in its childlike anxiety to avert the anger of an authority, the other in its final nobility. Above all, Shakespeare stresses Desdemona's love for Othello. He presents her with superb economy so that she becomes a sort of embodiment of love in speech and action. She is prepared to court Othello, to defy her father for him, to go to war with him, to bear his blows and insults, and to lie with her last breath for his sake. Indeed, as Winifred Nowottny has shown, it is the very strength of the love for which she marries a stranger which leaves her particularly vulnerable to Iago's insinuations in the temptation scene.[10] For Othello too easily forgets that her bold actions are tokens of love, and in his lack of confidence in his own judgement of such matters, is made to think them rather signs of female depravity. He has been told that women are depraved: his knowledge that a woman can love is based merely on his own senses. Even by the end of the play, Othello has not fully grasped the completeness and depth of Desdemona's love, for if he had, he could never claim that he was "one that loved not wisely, but too well." The comparative poverty of his love would be too clear. His love is rich enough in its power to delight: even when he is convinced of her adultery, his sense of her graces and talents compel him to acknowledge "the pity of it" (IV.i.197); even as he is about to kill her, he is overcome with her beauty. His love is also strong enough in its power to shatter lives. Yet it is less than Desdemona's in that it lacks the power of forgiveness, and of perfect trust. As Philip Edwards says, "the fact that he can allow suspicion of Desdemona to enter his mind . . . argues his love as simply not on her level."[11]

Desdemona in her lovingness and virtue is obviously remarkable and exceptional. As such, she cannot really be seen as necessarily counteracting the views of the antifeminists, as most of the satirists after all would be prepared to concede some remarkable exceptions to their rule—perhaps the Virgin Mary, perhaps the Virgin Queen. But, of course, Desdemona is not the only female character of the play. And if her virtues seem rare and remote, then those of Emilia and Bianca are much more readily imaginable and accessible—more human in that they are more flawed.

Emilia, indeed, voices the one explicit defence of woman in the play by stressing the common, flawed humanity of men and women, in much the same way that Shylock expresses the common needy humanity of Jews in *The Merchant of Venice*—Shakespeare's earlier Venetian play of justice and forgiveness:

> Hath not a Jew eyes? hath not a Jew hands, organs, dimensions, senses, affections, passions? fed with the same food, hurt with the same weapons, subject to the same diseases, healed by the same means, warmed and cooled by the same winter and summer as a Christian is? If you prick us, do we not bleed? If you tickle us, do we not laugh? If you poison us, do we not die? and if you wrong us shall we not revenge?
>
> (III.i.62-70)

In a similar vein, with similar rhetorical questions, and similarly to defend a hypothetical or proposed wrong action, Emilia points out the ordinary human fallibility of women:

> Let husbands know
> Their wives have sense like them. They see, and smell,
> And have their palates both for sweet and sour,
> As husbands have. What is it that they do
> When they change us for others? Is it sport?
> I think it is. And doth affection breed it?
> I think it doth. Is't frailty that thus errs?
> It is so too. And have not we affections,
> Desires for sport, and frailty as men have?
>
> (IV.iii.94-102)

As E. A. M. Colman points out, "Emilia's apologia, even by its very pace and tone, establishes for *Othello* as a whole, the feeling that reasonableness still exists, that despite all the perversion and furies an ordinary recognisable world will somehow prevail."[12] Like her husband, Emilia is well aware of human weaknesses; but whereas he responds to such weakness with a kind of gloating contempt, her reaction is more humane and charitable. Emilia, in her basic humanity, has a most useful function in the play in that she provides a kind of release for the audience by voicing its ordinary spontaneous "low" reactions to the speech and actions of the major characters. For instance, after Desdemona's breath-taking prayer for her hypothetical accuser "Heav'n pardon him," Emilia retorts "A halter pardon him and hell gnaw his bones," (IV.ii.136), and in the final scene, she relieves the audience greatly by actually naming Othello a fool. She is not too scrupulous to pilfer the handkerchief, not too pure to use the word "whore" or to consider a suitably rewarded adultery; yet it should be noted that in these faults she is in a twisted way considering her husband's welfare. However, finally she rises above the moral level at which her marriage has established her: "Tis proper I obey him, but not now" (V.ii.195). In extremes, her instinct is for truth and for faithfulness to the best that she knows, which is Desdemona. She tells her husband in outraged love and truth:

> You told a lie; an odious, damned lie;
> Upon my soul, a lie, a wicked lie . . .
>
> (V.ii.180-82)
>
> I will speak liberal as the north.
> Let heaven and men and devils, let them all,
> All, all cry shame against me, yet I'll speak.
>
> (V.ii.220-22)

She shows an unquestioning courage in the face of the swords of both Iago and Othello:

> Thou hast not half the power to do me harm
> As I have to be hurt.
>
> (V.ii.257-61)

Like Desdemona, she dies at the hands of her husband; like Desdemona, she dies full of love, vindicating the person she loves best:

> Hark, canst thou hear me? I will play the swan
> And die in music. [singing] Willow, willow, willow.
> Moor, she was chaste; she loved thee, cruel Moor;
> So come my soul to bliss as I speak true;
> So speaking as I think, I die, I die.
>
> (V.ii.257-61)

Ultimately, her motive and her values are the same as Desdemona's: Emilia's essential role as the revealer of the truth in this last scene of the play is an expression of love.

Indeed, this is true of all the women in the play. The third of these, Bianca, is of course foolish, inarticulate and ridiculous, but again what is significant and remarkable about her is her love for Cassio, a love which, like Desdemona's for Othello and Emilia's for Desdemona, is uncommon, in excess of what is normally expected: "I never knew a women love man so" (IV.i.111). Shakespeare rapidly establishes through her speech habits two significant elements of Bianca's love, its absurdity and its jealous tendency. Her absurdity is established through her use of the standard lover's hyperbole, appropriate enough in the lips of a Juliet but not on those of a whore:

> What, keep a week away? Seven days and nights?
> Eight score eight hours? And lovers' absent hours
> More tedious than the dial eight score times
> O weary reck'ning.
>
> (III.iv.172-75)

Her jealousy appears through vigorous, vulgar (and totally realistic) scolding:

> This is some minx's token and I must take out the work? There! [*She throws down the handkerchief*].
> Give it to your hobbyhorse.
>
> (IV.i.151-55)

Both the jealousy and the absurdity are significant because Othello must see Cassio laugh at Bianca and think he is laughing at Desdemona, and because he must also see Bianca throw down the handerkerchief. These actions, which spring from her excessive passion, provide Bianca with a dramatic function. Her inordinate love gives her a role in the play, in the same way as Emilia's love gives her the role of revealer of the truth in the last scene, and Desdemona's love provides a basic tenet of the whole plot. And although like Othello Bianca is jealous, her love is not like his—ultimately destructive, but protective. Her love gives her courage, as it gave courage to Desdemona and Emilia; it gives her the courage to stay with the wounded Cassio, the courage to avow her actions to Iago, and to defy his condemnation of her.

Thus all the women in the play are lovers, are faithful and courageous. In contrast with most of the men of the play, with Roderigo, Cassio and of course, above all Othello, they are uncorrupted, unmoved from their avowed standards and acknowledged alliances. Under pressure from Iago's mastery of words and skill in manipulating established prejudices, Roderigo abandons his hazy sense of Desdemona's virtue and the special nature of his love for her, Cassio his abstinence, and Othello his trust in Desdemona; but Bianca, Emilia and Desdemona stay firm.

The intensity of this play, which is reinforced by its speed, the singleness of its plot, and its small cast, is made yet stronger by its constant references to heaven and hell, to the ultimate destination of the soul.[13] All the main characters refer, however thoughtlessly, to redemption and damnation: the bitterest part of Othello's final sufferings is his sense of his eternal severance from Desdemona.

> When we shall meet at compt,
> This look of thine will hurl my soul from heaven
> And fiends will snatch at it.
>
> (V.ii.276)

This stress on eternal justice has an ironic relation with Othello's insistence on temporal justice, for this is in clear contrast to Desdemona's instinctive forgiveness. Whatever Shakespeare's beliefs were, and this is not at issue here, this play obviously uses in its "evaluation of justice in its relation to love"[14] the Pauline contrast between the new covenant and the old, between grace and law, forgiveness and justice. It is, in this context, the women of the play who embody Christian values. They are motivated by love, not by justice, that is by the new covenant and not the old. Desdemona's love for Othello is larger than his for her because it includes *agape* as well as *eros*. Futhermore, their behaviour is Christian in that they are not transmitters of the pain they receive, as Iago is when he turns his large and general sense of being wronged into a brilliant campaign of destruction, or as Othello is when his agony of jealousy drives him to murder. Desdemona, in forgiving any wrong which has been done her, attempts to prevent that wrong from passing on, while Emilia, more effectively, finally insists on full publicity for the truth and thus prevents her husband's lies from doing any further damage.[15]

The issue between Iago and Emilia is honesty and dishonesty, as the issue between Othello and Desdemona is love and justice. Indeed, the complex interaction between the two marriages is illuminating. In this play, we see Iago deliberately lead Othello away from his trust in Desdemona, his wife, into corruption and folly. Desdemona, quite unconsciously, causes Emilia to be led from her trust in Iago, her husband, and thus from corruption and folly. Desdemona weighs against Iago not only with Othello but with Emilia. Man gravitates towards man destructively, woman towards woman redemptively. Emilia has an Othello-like role again in Act Five where, as Othello had before, she must face an accusation against her spouse. But in Othello's position, Emilia is direct, immediate: immediately and publicly she faces her husband with the charge against him and insists on verification. Othello had indeed also asked for verification:

> Villain be sure thou prove my love a whore!
> Be sure of it; give me the ocular proof;
> Or by the worth of my eternal soul,
> Thou hadst been better have been born a dog
> Than answer my waked wrath.
>
> (III.iii.359-63)

But this demand is satisfied more by its own dramatic force than by a proper answer and is in any case addressed to the wrong person. Othello is diverted by the extremity of his own emotion, and by the vehement expression of it, and yet it is sincere emotion. Emilia is not without feelings: indeed she's almost dumbstruck: "my husband" she repeats incredulously; yet unlike Othello, she does not allow the strength of her feelings to divert her from action and the quest for truth.

Of course, part of the tragedy springs from the inadequacy of the women of the play, from Bianca's amorousness, Emilia's willingness to pilfer and above all Desdemona's reluctance to oppose and question Othello. Yet on the whole, the women of the play are dramatic contradictions of Iago's generalized and distorted view of human nature because they are concerned with love, and because, as John Bayley says in his discussion of Othello, "the capacity to love—though it contains the desire of possession—is quite separate from the urge to dominate by knowing and placing,"[16] as Iago does.

The wide currency in Shakespeare's England of the traditional prejudice against women which Iago voices is demonstrated by the host of pamphlets with such titles as: *The Proude Wyves Pater Noster; The deceyte of women, to the instruction and example of all men, yonge and olde; A glass to view the Pride of Vainglorious women; My Ladies Looking Glasse; The Slights of Wanton Maids* and so on. This tradition clearly enables the jealous husbands of faithful wives in Shakespeare's later plays, Othello, Posthumus, and Leontes, to turn circumstantial evidence into an instant conviction of guilt and a hatred of woman—"there's no motion / That tends to vice in man, but I affirm / it is the woman's part" (*Cymbeline* II.v.20-22). In *Othello*, such prejudice is used to place evil: Iago is placed partly by his use of such destructive and demonstrably false generalizations and cynical stock attitudes. And these attitudes in turn are implicitly and strongly placed by the very fact that they are the stock-in-trade of such a man as Iago.

Notes

1. Esther Sowernam (pseud.) *Ester hath Hang'd Haman* . . . 1617 pp. 31-2, quoted by Juliet Dusinberre in *Shakespeare and the Nature of Women* (London: Macmillan, 1975) p. 180.
2. Louis B. Wright, *Middle Class Culture in Elizabethan England* (Chapel Hill: University of Carolina Press, 1935), p. 466.
3. *The School-House of Women* was probably written by Edward Gosynhill: the date of its first edition is probably 1542, though the earliest copy extant is dated (doubtfully) 1550 by the *Short Title Catalogue*. See Wright, p. 468.
4. All references to Shakespeare's works are to *The Complete Works of Shakespeare* ed. Hardin Craig (Glenview, Ill.: Scott, Foresman & Co., 1961).
5. *The Anatomie of Absurditie* (1588) in *Works* ed. Ronald B. McKerrow, Rev. F. P. Wilson (Oxford: Blackwell, 1958) I, 12-13.
6. Nashe, 18.
7. *The Plaine Mans Path-way to Heaven* (1601) quoted by Wright, p. 479.
8. "The 'Calumniator Credited' and the Code of Honour in Shakespeare's *Othello*," *English Studies in Canada* II (1976), 381-401.
9. *Magic in the Web: Action & Language in Othello* (Lexington: University of Kentucky Press, 1956), pp. 196-97.
10. "Justice and Love in *Othello*," *University of Toronto Quarterly*, 21 (1951), 330-344.
11. *Shakespeare and the Confines of Art* (London: Methuen, 1968), p. 126.
12. *The Dramatic Use of Bawdy in Shakespeare* (London: Longman's, 1974), p. 126.
13. See *Magic in the Web*, p. 251 for a descriptive catalogue.

14. Nowottny, 330.

15. Both the behaviour of these two women and its varying effectiveness is in keeping with their roles in the stories of detraction discussed by Joyce C. Sexton in *The Slandered Woman in Shakespeare* (Victoria, B.C.: ELS Monograph Series 12, 1978). She speaks of "the traditional sense that the victim of detraction is helpless" and goes on to discuss "the absolute necessity that the unjustly accused woman regain her good fame, that the truth be widely publicized" (p. 45). Such publicity for the truth is Emilia's achievement.

16. John Bayley, *The Characters of Love* (New York: Basic Books, 1961), p. 205.

Marianne Novy (essay date 1984)

SOURCE: "Marriage and Mutuality in *Othello*," in *Love's Argument: Gender Relations in Shakespeare*, University of North Carolina Press, 1984, pp. 125-49.

[*In the essay below, Novy considers patriarchy in the marriage of Othello and Desdemona.*]

In an article entitled "Marriage and the Construction of Reality," the sociologists Peter Berger and Hansfried Kellner say, "Unlike an earlier situation in which the establishment of the new marriage simply added to the differentiation and complexity of an already existing social world, the marriage partners are now embarked on the often difficult task of constructing for themselves the little world in which they will live."[1] By this definition, Othello and Desdemona seem to begin their marriage in a situation more modern than traditional. Othello is cut off from his ancestry; Desdemona is disowned by her father. They spend most of the play in Cyprus, a setting native to neither of them. Thus they have some of both the opportunities and the difficulties of constructing their own world that Berger and Kellner discuss. "The re-construction of the world in marriage," they continue, "occurs principally in the course of conversation. . . . The implicit problem of this conversation is how to match two individual definitions of reality."[2]

Marriage for Berger and Kellner, as, I have argued, for Shakespeare's comedies, involves a combination of ideals of mutuality and assumptions of patriarchy, though of course patriarchy takes a different form in twentieth-century America than in seventeenth-century England. Though the balance may tip in one direction or the other, the predominance of playfulness and of festive disguise helps to remove threatening elements. In Shakespeare's tragedies, however, the combination of patriarchy and mutuality breaks down. We never see Othello and Desdemona creating together a private game-like world of conversation onstage. All the early scenes where they both speak are public, and events in the outside world remain important to their relationship. Othello's public role as warrior is part of what Desdemona loves in him. Furthermore, Berger and Kellner assume a situation in which "the husband typically talks with his wife about his friend, but *not* with his friend about his wife"; in *Othello* the opposite is true.[3] One principal representative of the already existing social world stays with Othello and Desdemona—Iago. And accompanying his presence is the persistence of conventional attitudes from the outside world in Othello's mind. Othello cannot completely free himself from the conventional assumption that Desdemona's marriage to him is unnatural. He cannot keep distrust of women out of his marriage. Brabantio may not be physically present, but his message, "She has deceived her father, and may thee" (1.3.293), rings in Othello's memory. And after Othello has stopped believing anything Desdemona says, Iago's presence makes it impossible for Othello to keep out of his marriage a code of proving manhood by violent revenge. Between patriarchy and racism, the initial mutuality between Desdemona and Othello is destroyed. To restore it is the aim of Othello's suicide.

In Shakespeare's comedies we usually see mutuality being established; in *Othello* we hear the process described. Othello calls it, "How I did thrive in this fair lady's love / And she in mine" (1.3.125-26). While he told his life story to her father,

> This to hear
> Would Desdemona seriously incline;
> But still the house affairs would draw her thence;
> Which ever as she could with haste dispatch,
> She'd come again, and with a greedy ear
> Devour up my discourse. Which I observing,
> Took once a plaint hour, and found good means
> To draw from her a prayer of earnest heart
> That I would all my pilgrimage dilate,
> Whereof by parcels she had something heard,
> But not intentively. I did consent,
> And often did beguile her of her tears
> When I did speak of some distressful stroke
> That my youth suffered.
>
> (1.3.145-58)

Here Othello gives a description of a process of initiative and response leading to further response—Othello talks, Desdemona listens, Othello sees her listening and encourages it, hopes she will ask to hear more; she does, he agrees, and she responds with tears of sympathy. Othello is gratified by her initial interest in his performance and draws her out for more active participation.

While this scene fits some conventions of patriarchy—male activity and female response—the imagery by which Othello's words become food that Desdemona devours should signal that roles here are not altogether limited to conventional ones. As Brabantio says, Othello's story portrays Desdemona as "half the wooer" (1.3.176). She goes beyond the audience's responsiveness, as an earlier chapter noted, to initiate courtship by her hint. The content of their conversation in this story is Othello's experience, not Desdemona's, but we should notice how closely he has

Scott Wentworth as Roderigo, Colm Feore as Iago, Howard Rollins as Othello, Wenna Shaw as Desdemona, Goldie Semple as Emilia, and Derek Boyes as Cassio in the 1987 Stratford Festival production of Othello.

observed her, how carefully he has elicited her request. While Desdemona has been an audience to Othello's performance, he has also behaved like an audience in closely observing her. In the narrative Othello tells, he has judged Desdemona's feelings from her gestures, guessed at meaning beneath her words, and he has been right about her interest in him—beyond his dreams. Othello describes a powerful experience of emotional sharing—he has gone back to his youth and relived his sufferings and she has felt them along with him: "She loved me for the dangers I had passed, / And I loved her that she did pity them" (1.3.167-68).

Yet in spite of her active participation, Desdemona describes her loyalty to Othello as a matter of duty. Furthermore, Desdemona makes as many concessions as she can to her father in explaining her "divided duty" (1.3.181); she speaks first of her bonds as a daughter, and she compares her choice of Othello with her mother's choice of her father. One of few Shakespearean women who claim to imitate their mothers, she is trying to reassure Brabantio by putting her marriage into an orderly continuity of marriages, trying to remind him that his marriage too was won at the cost of separation from a father.

In these introductory statements by Othello and Desdemona, their marriage appears as a combination of patriarchy and mutuality. Othello makes the marriage proposal and keeps the title of lord, yet there is a genuine emotional sharing and companionship. Desdemona further emphasizes both these elements later on in this scene. "That I did love the Moor to live with him," she says,

> My downright violence, and storm of fortunes,
> May trumpet to the world.
>
> (1.3.248-50)

She joins him in his imagery as in his career. "My heart's subdued / Even to the very quality of my lord" (1.3.250-51). She identifies with him in a way that subordinates her.[4] He does not, for example, ask that she accompany him to Cyprus until after she does, and he makes a point of saying that he asks it only as a magnanimous gesture, "to be free and bounteous to her mind" (1.3.265). Although his description of their courtship revealed the importance to him of her emotional response—the mutual dependence that they have created—he wants to deny his need of her and, most emphatically, to deny any sexual appetite that would clamor for satisfaction—"Not to comply with heat—the young affects / In me defunct" (1.3.263-64). Furthermore, while she values his world, his words here suggest that he scorns the domestic world she comes from; his curse to be imposed on himself if he neglects his duty because of her ends:

> Let housewives make a skillet of my helm,
> And all indign and base adversities
> Make head against my estimation!
>
> (1.3.272-74)

In their meeting in Cyprus, it is Othello who uses imagery that describes their love as a fusion of Desdemona's essence into his: he calls her "My fair warrior . . . my soul's joy" (2.1.180-82). In this reunion, as in his scene of self-revelation to her described earlier, social structures and temperamental differences may drop away and two people can create the illusion of unity; such scenes are the end of love as quest and of the typical plot of romantic comedy.[5] But what can follow them? Othello's words of joy are filled with apprehension. It is as if the hardships of his life have led him always to expect disaster:

> If it were now to die,
> 'Twere now to be most happy; for I fear
> My soul hath her content so absolute
> That not another comfort like to this
> Succeeds in unknown fate.
>
> (2.1.187-91)

It is easier for Othello to imagine a *Liebestod* than a love enduring the test of daily life; yet he sees their love not as the passion usually identified with *Liebestod* but as calm, content, comfort. This suggests, perhaps, the element in their love that involves regression to a relationship like that of mother and infant.

Desdemona's response, however, is more active and creative:

> The heavens forbid
> But that our loves and comforts should increase
> Even as our days do grow.
>
> (2.1.191-93)

Othello quickly agrees, but the memory of his fear is there to mix with the ominous suggestions of Iago's asides.

Why is Iago so successful in his attempts to destroy the relationship between Othello and Desdemona? Many different approaches can work toward answers to this question; here I am interested in looking at what the play shows about the vulnerability of the combination of patriarchy and mutuality that we see in that relationship, and about how Iago manipulates Othello's persisting need for mutuality.

If mutuality and patriarchy are to be combined, as we have already suggested, the woman must make the gesture of subordinating herself to the man; in addition, in *Othello*, much more than in the comedies, the man believes he must subdue qualities in himself that he considers would make him woman-like or too dependent on a woman. Othello's need for control to assert his manliness often coalesces with the need for control to assert that he is civilized and not a barbarian slave to passion. It is important to note here the overlap between the stereotypes of the woman and of the Moor: conventional Renaissance European views would see both as excessively passionate.[6] Othello's first appearance, contrary to this stereotype, is an amazing show of self-possession under Brabantio's attacks. Even in his description of his life history, he recounts his adventures in a controlled tone. He is, however, moved when Desdemona cries over them; if he beguiles her of her tears, she can express his emotions for him. It further suggests his control, based on his sense of social distinctions, that *Desdemona* first speaks of love, and Othello can see himself as loving only in response, and therefore rationally. Indeed, he is, as we have seen, curiously emphatic about his lack of sexual passion.

Othello's stress on control of passion may add to the implications of his dismissal of Cassio. Just after the announcement that Othello has proclaimed a general festivity because of the coincidence of the victory over the Turks and the celebration of his nuptial, Othello says to Cassio:

> Good Michael, look you to the guard to-night.
> Let's teach ourselves that honorable stop,
> Not to outsport discretion.
>
> (2.3.1-3)

Here Othello seems to be identifying himself with Cassio, the potential drunkard, in a common need for control. A few lines later, Othello leaves with Desdemona, saying

> Come, my dear love.
> The purchase made, the fruits are to ensue;
> That profit's yet to come 'tween me and you.
>
> (2.3.8-10)

After the first line, this is a rather business-like description for the sexual initiation of a wedding night. Again it suggests a concern for sharing, but it is odd that he should turn pleasure into financial imagery. Iago's words a few lines later suggest one kind of language Othello has avoided using: "He hath not yet made wanton the night with her, and she is sport for Jove" (2.3.15-17).

Thus, while Cassio drinks too much and gets into a fight with Rodrigo and then with Montano, the characters and the audience are frequently reminded that Othello and Desdemona are meeting in bed for the first time. Iago, in fact, brings this juxtaposition shockingly into focus when he describes the fight to Othello, who has been called back by its clamor:

> Friends all, but now, even now,
> In quarter, and in terms like bride and groom

Devesting them for bed; and then but now—
As if some planet had unwitted men—
Swords out, and tilting one at other's breast
In opposition bloody.

(2.3.169-74)

What Iago has described is perilously close to the reality of the wedding night, when at least briefly rational control must be abandoned and blood must be shed.

I suggest that, partly under Iago's influence, partly because of his own emphasis on self-control, Othello feels guilty about the passion involved in his intercourse with Desdemona; he identifies with the offender who has also let passion run away with him, and in effect he makes Cassio a scapegoat for himself. When he dismisses Cassio, as later when he kills Desdemona, he insists that he is acting justly when he is really moved by his emotions. Here he returns to Desdemona saying "All's well now, sweeting" (2.3.242), because Cassio is dismissed, and so too, Othello thinks, is the disturbing image of sexuality becoming violent with which Iago has associated him. Like Stanley Cavell, I think that Othello's guilt about sexuality is an important subtext of the play;[7] but in addition to the guilt about hurting Desdemona, which Cavell stresses, I see him as feeling guilty for loss of control of his passions, such loss of control as many medieval theologians whose views were still reflected in some Elizabethan sermons thought made sex inevitably suspect even within marriage.[8]

Of course, *Othello* is a play about passionate love; but part of its impact comes from the tension between that passion and the restraints that Othello is constantly trying to place on it, as suggested by his words. Furthermore, Othello's very idealization of Desdemona has a passionate component. He is passionate in wishing her to be totally fused in identification with him, in a symbiosis possible only for the mother and infant before the infant's discovery of sex. In one of his final confrontations with Desdemona, he describes her, in language that brings to mind the dependence of the infant at the mother's breast, as the place

Where either I must love or bear no life,
The fountain from the which my current runs
Or else dries up.

(4.2.58-60)

C. L. Barber has suggested that many of Shakespeare's female characters have the resonance for the hero, and for the audience, of the Virgin Mary; Shakespeare's audience still had the fantasy of a total and pure relationship such as one could have only with a mother who was perpetually a virgin, and this fantasy could no longer be dealt with through religious symbolism and ritual because of the Reformation. Thus Othello projects the kind of religious need onto Desdemona that no merely human being could fulfill.[9]

In his description of the handkerchief and its provenance, there are more suggestions of Othello's fantasy of love as fusion with a woman both maternal and virginal. He describes a gypsy sorceress as telling his mother that the handkerchief,

while she kept it,
[would] make her amiable and subdue my father
Entirely to her love; but if she lost it
Or made a gift of it, my father's eye
Should hold her loathèd.

(3.4.58-62)

In sharp contrast with Desdemona's description of her parents as bound by duty, here are the precarious bonds of magic. The mere chance loss of the handkerchief can turn one side of the polarized image—Othello's father entirely subdued to her love—to the other—loathing. Furthermore, by concluding the description with a reference to dye made from maiden's hearts. Othello calls up the image of dead women and associates it with the blood lost in the loss of virginity, which Lynda Boose has shown might well be visually suggested by the handkerchief.[10] Othello's words imply that if Desdemona could keep the handkerchief, could keep her fidelity safe from any accusation, could define herself as the virgin who shed her blood for him, then she would be like his mother and would keep his love.

Othello's desire for a love that is total fusion is, in part, his attempt to escape from his underlying sense of separateness. His blackness is a visual sign of how his history differs from that of the other characters; his narrative tells of an early life far from ordinary family and domestic connections. His ties in Venice, except with Desdemona, are those made by military service, and as Brabantio's behavior shows, they are precarious. Thus it is particularly easy for Iago to play on Othello's sense of separateness with regard to Desdemona, who is not only Venetian but also a woman. Othello is defenseless against commonplaces of antifeminism when couched as the insider's sociological observation:

I know our country disposition well:
In Venice they do let God see the pranks
They dare not show their husbands.

(3.3.201-3)

It is at this key point that Iago's hints depend most on the structure of a patriarchal society; because of fathers' controls over their daughters, women can choose their husbands only through some deception—and that deception can forever after be held against them. "She did deceive her father, marrying you" (3.3.206). There is always a latent male alliance, which Iago brings to the surface here as a compensation for the sense of alienation he is arousing in Othello. By stressing Desdemona's youth, also, Iago makes her sound like a diabolically clever child:

She that, so young, could give out such a seeming
To seel her father's eyes up close as oak—
He thought 'twas witchcraft.

(3.3.209-11)

The witchcraft charges originally applied to Othello have been projected to Desdemona. Othello's sense of being an outsider is evident as he resigns himself:

> Haply, for I am black
> And have not those soft parts of conversation
> That chamberers have, or for I am declined
> Into the vale of years—yet that's not much—
> She's gone. I am abused, and my relief
> Must be to loathe her.
>
> (3.3.263-68)

One of the reasons that Iago can play so easily on Othello's sense of separateness to break up his relationship with Desdemona is that he himself can supply a pretense of the mutuality Othello so longs for. It is ironic that Iago is one of the few characters in Shakespeare to use in his dialogue a form of the word "mutuality"; to him it is a suggestive word that can make Cassio's gestures of courtesy to Desdemona sound like foreplay: "When these mutualities so marshal the way, hard at hand comes the master and main exercise, th' incorporate conclusion" (2.1.255-57). To Iago, sincere mutuality of feeling is impossible, and most of the time he assumes that other people are as shallow in their relationships. He reduces love to a precariously matched set of appetites that he can easily manipulate.

It is unsettling to see, with Stephen Greenblatt, how well Iago's attitude toward Othello fits some definitions of empathy.[11] As W. H. Auden has noted, "Iago treats Othello as an analyst treats a patient except that, of course, his intention is to kill, not to cure. Everything he says is designed to bring to Othello's consciousness what he has already guessed is there."[12] Iago cleverly postpones making direct charges against Desdemona and Cassio. Rather he drops hints and raises questions, leaving Othello to imagine the charges himself. His technique here is particularly poignant because it plays on the attempt to read gestures and see unspoken thoughts which worked for Othello in his recounted conversation with Desdemona. While earlier we heard about Desdemona and Othello creating a mutual trust together, here we see Iago and Othello creating a union based on suspicion of Desdemona, pretended by Iago and believed by Othello. Furthermore, Iago speaks openly of his own love for Othello—knowing that Othello will respond—and uses this technique especially when Othello sounds as if he is likely to doubt him: "From hence / I'll love no friend, sith love breeds such offence" (3.3.379-80). Othello's growing fascination with Iago's words is heightened as Iago calls up the image of Cassio and Desdemona in bed, "as prime as goats, as hot as monkeys" (3.3.403), and then the image of Cassio in bed with Iago, mistaking him for Desdemona; the dream-like image of sexual union between two men parallels and charges the emotional union that Iago is creating with Othello. The excitement of the image adds to the tension of the conversation.

The parody marriage ceremony enacted when they kneel and vow murder, and Iago says, "I am your own forever" (3.3.480), offers a return to a relationship in one respect like the one Othello earlier had with Desdemona. In the worldview Iago offers, Othello again has someone's total dedication:

> Witness that here Iago doth give up
> The execution of his wit, hands, heart
> To wronged Othello's service!
>
> (3.3.465-67)

Desdemona, by contrast, has given evidence that she extends her sympathy not only to Othello but also to Cassio.

In loving Desdemona, Othello has ventured outside of the man's world of war and made himself vulnerable to charges of being ruled by his emotions and therefore, in Renaissance terms, less than manly; remember his oath that if he neglects his duty because of Desdemona, "Let housewives make a skillet of my helm" (1.3.272). Iago plays on these fears as well by the way he acts the advocate of cold reason. His image of Cassio and Desdemona in bestial lust is introduced by "It is impossible you should see this" (3.3.402). The struggle between passion and control that initially was internal to Othello is now externalized; all of Iago's qualifications and admonitions to patience serve to enrage Othello further:

> *Iago:*
> And this may help to thicken other proofs
> That do demonstrate thinly.
> *Othello:*
> I'll tear her all to pieces!
>
> (3.3.430-31)

After Othello's emotions have surfaced so powerfully that he falls into a fit, Iago begins to harp on the issue of manhood.[13] "Would you would bear your fortune like a man. . . . Be a man . . . grief—a passion most unsuiting such a man" (4.1.61, 64, 76-77). By trying to emphasize the need for control, he is still promoting Othello's passion, but helping to channel it toward revenge:

> *Iago:*
> Marry, patience!
> Or I shall say y'are all in all in spleen,
> And nothing of a man.
> *Othello:*
> Dost thou hear, Iago?
> I will be found most cunning in my patience
> But—dost thou hear?—most bloody.
>
> (4.1.87-91)

Under Iago's influence, Othello starts to name Desdemona in ways that fit more into the harshest potential of the patriarchal structure of marriage than into a mutuality of love. The images that he uses for Desdemona put her into categories of objects to be controlled or possessed. His sense of her as different from him becomes more and more an image of her as strange, not quite human. He compares her to a hawk, using one of Petruchio's more patriarchal images:

If I do prove her haggard,
Though that her jesses were my dear heartstrings,
I'd whistle her off and let her down the wind
To prey at fortune.

(3.3.260-63)

He cannot bear to think that total control of her is impossible—the impossibility seems to threaten reducing him to an animal as well:

O curse of marriage,
That we can call these delicate creatures ours,
And not their appetites! I had rather be a toad,
And live upon the vapor of a dungeon
Than keep a corner in the thing I love
For others' uses.

(3.3.268-73)

"The thing I love"—that is now Othello's phrase for Desdemona. Emilia and Iago echo the word, with similar undertones of sexuality and a reductive approach to women, a few lines later, when they gain possession of the handkerchief:

Emilia:
I have a thing for you.
Iago:
A thing for me? It is a common thing—
Emilia:
Ha?
Iago:
To have a foolish wife.

(3.3.301-4)

The word suggests the reduction of woman to object and particularly to sexual object that has occurred in Othello's mind under Iago's influence.

When Othello starts to doubt Desdemona, he also uses more images of dirt, often associated with sexuality. Desdemona, instead of a clear fountain, becomes "a cistern for foul toads / To knot and gender in" (4.2.61-62). This dirt also becomes associated with blackness. Here too we see Othello showing more self-hatred in his imagery as his distrust of Desdemona grows. "Her name, that was as fresh / As Dian's visage, is now begrimed and black / As mine own face" (3.3.386-88).

This opposition between cleanness and dirt is another reason why the handkerchief becomes central to Othello's rejection of his love for Desdemona. "Such a handkerchief . . . ," says Iago, "did I today / See Cassio wipe his beard with" (3.3.437-39), and Othello explodes: "O, that the slave had forty thousand lives! / One is too poor, too weak for my revenge" (3.3.443-44). The handkerchief, something originally clean, is juxtaposed with dirt from Cassio's beard and for Othello it is as if that dirt soiled Desdemona herself.

When Othello becomes more distrusting of Desdemona, he also becomes more conscious of his passionate physical attraction to her, which earlier in the play he did not speak of, or denied.[14] While initially he called her "My soul's joy," now he speaks of "her sweet body" (3.3.346) and declares, "I'll not expostulate with her, lest her body and beauty unprovide my mind again" (4.1.200-202). The more he imagines her guilt, the more he feels his own attraction to her; he feels it more intensely, no doubt, because it appears split off from all her good qualities in which he no longer believes. He plans to kill her as a way to control his own unruly passion for her body as he punishes her passion.

In spite of this general tendency, Othello has moments even as he is planning the murder when he sees Desdemona not as an object to be controlled or punished but as an active, even civilizing woman. "So delicate with her needle! an admirable musician! O, she will sing the savageness out of a bear! of so high and plenteous wit and invention" (4.1.184-87). Struck by his admiration of her, Othello is moved to exclaim, "But yet the pity of it, Iago! O Iago, the pity of it, Iago" (4.1.192-93). But Iago can expel this mood in a moment by returning to the patriarchal imagery of possession: "If you are so fond over her iniquity, give her patent to offend; for if it touch not you, it comes near nobody" (4.1.194-95).

As Othello is torn by the conflict between his admiration and his disgust, Desdemona's synthesis of attitudes breaks up disastrously. After the marriage Desdemona's combination of initiative—which contributes to mutuality—and pretense—which accommodates to patriarchy—dissolves, and both forms of acting contribute to Othello's anger at her. Her commitment to Cassio is carried out with such vehemence that some critics have accused her of trying to take away Othello's military authority; on the other hand, her resort to the evasive technique of lying about the handkerchief causes his anger even more intensely.

Desdemona knows that in some ways she is transcending patriarchal categories in pleading for Cassio with Othello (although of course she would not have called it that); she uses images suggesting that she sees herself in roles held predominantly by men in Renaissance society: "His bed shall seem a school, his board a shrift. / . . . Thy solicitor shall rather die / Than give thy cause away" (3.2.24, 27-28). Furthermore, she asks that Othello pardon Cassio not as an obedient inferior asks for a favor from a condescending superior but with the suggestion that their marriage is one of mutual generosity: "I wonder in my soul / What you could ask me that I should deny / Or stand so mamm'ring on" (3.3.68-70). At the same time she goes on to suggest a different vision of their relationship: "Why, this is not a boon; / 'Tis as I should entreat you wear your gloves, / Or feed on nourishing dishes, or keep you warm" (3.3.76-78). This imagery suggests either that she is imagining total identification with him—she is asking for this because it is what he needs—or that she sees herself as taking care of him as a nurturing mother does a child. In the light of psychoanalytic theory it is easy to conflate these two suggestions and to see the lines as hints that she too participates in the fantasy of a union with Othello as close as that of mother and infant. It is at this point that she swears "By'r Lady [By Our Lady], I could do much" (3.3.74), and Othello dismisses her by saying, "Leave me but a little to myself" (3.3.85), words that suggest he feels his identity threatened by engulfment. He has wanted fusion, yes, but it is also threatening, especially for someone who values control as Othello does.

As Othello's jealousy becomes clearer, Desdemona's attitudes are a mixture of mature strength and evasion.[15] When openly accused she defends herself forcefully to Othello:

> *Othello:*
> Are not you a strumpet?
> *Desdemona:*
> No, as I am a Christian!
>
> (4.2.82)

But after this scene she emphasizes her innocence in language that makes her seem more weak and passive:

> Those that do teach young babes
> Do it with gentle means and easy tasks:
> He might have child me so; for, in good faith,
> I am a child to chiding.
> . . . . .
> Am I that name, Iago?
>
> (4.2.111-14, 118)

She has been slow to see that Othello is jealous and even slower to see that he is jealous of Cassio: she has intuitions that she is in danger in her last scene with Emilia, but she dismisses them:

> Good faith, how foolish are our minds!
> If I do die before thee, prithee shroud me
> In one of those same sheets.
>
> (4.3.22-24)

Early in the play she seems mature and aware of people's limitations ("I would not there reside, / To put my father in impatient thoughts / By being in his eye"—1.3.241-43) and worldly-wise enough to deal with Iago's antifeminist jokes with a cool "O heavy ignorance! Thou praisest the worst best" (2.1.143-44). She can be calm and tolerant about Othello's bad temper, although this tolerance sounds like evasion in the light of later events:

> Nay, we must think men are not gods,
> Nor of them look for such observancy
> As fits the bridal.
>
> (3.4.148-50)

Near the end, with Emilia, she retreats into a willful ignorance, as her disillusionment with Othello leads her to cling harder, perhaps, to a belief in women:

> *Desdemona:*
> O, these men, these men!
> Dost thou in conscience think—tell me, Emilia—
> That there be women do abuse their husbands
> In such gross kind?
> *Emilia:*
> There be some such, no question.
> . . . . .
> *Desdemona:*
> I do not think there is any such woman.
>
> (4.3.58-61, 82)

At this point it is Emilia who takes over the articulate awareness that Desdemona showed earlier. She makes a speech attacking the institution behind Othello's assumption of his right to kill Desdemona—the double standard. Elsewhere than in this speech, the play alludes to adultery by men only in Iago's fantasies—and there, of course, he sees it as an offense against one man by another. Here, suddenly, the whole perspective changes, and we see adultery not as a world-shaking crime committed by women, but as one of a whole group of men's possible behaviors annoying to wives—in the same category as jealousy, violence, and stinginess. How different it is to see adultery as a violation of "there where I have garnered up my heart" and to see it as analogous to cutting an allowance. Emilia rejects the patriarchal valuation of female adultery as worse than male adultery:

> Let husbands know,
> Their wives have sense like them. They see and smell,
> And have their palates both for sweet and sour,
> As husbands have. . . .
> . . . And have not we affections,
> Desires for sport, and frailty, as men have?
>
> (4.3.92-95, 99-100)

Othello's murder of Desdemona is the epitome of his failure to accept the fact that both of them have what Emilia calls frailties and affections. When he sees her sleeping, his words show appreciation of her beauty as a passive object, which he can describe in static, lifeless terms—sensuous conversions of passion to coldness and art—"That whiter skin of hers than snow, / And smooth as monumental alabaster" (5.2.3-4). As he becomes more aware of the irrevocability of her death, the imagery changes:

> I know not where is that Promethean heat
> That can thy light relume. When I have plucked the rose,
> I cannot give it vital growth again.
>
> (5.2.12-14)

Yet this awareness falters: "I will kill thee, / And love thee after" (5.2.18-19). When seeing her sleeping, he talks tenderly of her, even kisses her, in spite of his intent to kill, and wants to give her time to confess her sins, but on confronting the awakened woman, who struggles for life and denies his accusations, he becomes enraged.

Again Desdemona defends her innocence stoutly in a mix of assertiveness, generosity, and naiveté:

> I never did
> Offend you in my life; never loved Cassio

But with such general warranty of heaven
As I might love.

(5.2.58-61)

But her earlier resourcefulness and understanding of Othello have left her. She cannot believe that he will kill her. "Why I should fear I know not, / Since guiltiness I know not; but yet I feel I fear" (5.2.38-39), she says, after he has already begun to talk of killing. The best she can do for her survival, when she learns that Othello will not believe her and Cassio is dead, is to ask for a stay of execution.

In her last words, uttered after she is apparently dead and Emilia has returned, her first impulse is to proclaim her murder and thus to maintain her own innocence. But when Emilia asks her to name her murderer, Desdemona shows that she has forgiven Othello—"Commend me to my kind lord"—and for the last time uses a lie to try to cover up—this time Othello's guilt—"Nobody—I myself" (5.2.125-26).

Othello does not see her forgiveness but rather the lie that fits with his insistence on her dishonesty. But eventually he learns the truth, when Emilia tells the story of her own responsibility in the loss of the handkerchief—at the cost of her life. Yet Othello's words at the end show that he still fails to understand Desdemona. If she were true, he says, after Emilia has challenged his charges,

If heaven would make me such another world
Of one entire and perfect chrysolite,
I'd not have sold her for it.

(5.2.145-47)

And at the end he compares her to a foolishly discarded "pearl . . . / Richer than all his tribe" (5.2.347-48). Value is evident in these images, but it is lifeless, inanimate—a possession: "Cold, cold, my girl? / Even like thy chastity" (5.2.276-77). His identification of her chastity with the coldness of death shows his inability to connect it with the warmth of her love; it is in keeping with this that he does not understand the forgiveness that she has already granted him:

When we shall meet at compt,
This look of thine will hurl my soul from heaven,
And fiends will snatch at it.

(5.2.274-76)

At the end Othello seems again to regain control of himself and can finally admit his earlier lack of control, his passivity to "being wrought, / Perplexed in the extreme" (5.2.345-46). He maintains control of his own destiny by killing himself but also intends a return to mutuality. The final image of three people dead on a bed is on one level an image of the power of sexual passion to take life. Yet unlike the first two deaths, inflicted in passion, this one is calm. These deaths show not the simple destructiveness of passion but the more complicated destructiveness of passion combined with an attempt to control, closely related to social structures of sexual polarization.

Let us consider briefly three of the ways that Shakespeare's characters see sexual relations between man and woman. They can be seen as a sharing of passion and action in mutual responsiveness, as the man asserting his dominance over the woman, or as the man overcome by his passion for the woman. The second and third views come out of a mental structure of sexual polarization, in which either man = action and woman = passivity or man = control and woman = passion. In the comedies, the first view of sexuality (mutuality) balances the second (male dominance), as in *The Taming of the Shrew,* or the second and third (male submission to passion, represented by a woman), as in *As You Like It.* Comic game-playing helps keep this balance. Either male or female dominance can seem less threatening and less permanent if portrayed as a game, and the participation of the lovers in a game not understood by other characters adds to the sense of their existence in a shared world that dramatizes the strength of their relationship. This structure of play allows the lovers to try out the extremity of passion ("Then, in mine own person, I die"—*As You Like It,* 4.1.84) and to draw back from it ("No, faith, die by attorney"—*As You Like It,* 4.1.85). The fears of betrayal and rejection surface and are dealt with. Desdemona has something of the playful attitude, the ability to try out situations through imagining alternatives. But unlike the comedy heroes, Othello lacks any trace of such flexibility. "Disport" seems a bad word to him. Unlike them, also, he is matched with Iago, one of the most notable game-players in Shakespeare, who uses his abilities to create false mutuality and destroy true mutuality. Under his influence, Othello's wish to assert his dominance over Desdemona and control their passions becomes desperate and contaminated by the masculine code of revenge by murder. When he discovers his guilt, however, Desdemona becomes identified with control ("Cold, cold as thy chastity") and himself with passion. Then with his final act he turns his activity against himself and tells us that this gesture of control is intended as a union with her.

While in the first part of the speech, his guilt about his excess of passion is apparent—"one that loved not wisely, but too well" (5.2.344)—there is a section of it in which he speaks of a kind of passion in himself that by implication becomes healing:

One whose subdued eyes,
Albeit unusèd to the melting mood,
Drop tears as fast as the Arabian trees
Their med'cinable gum.

(5.2.348-51)

He is following Desdemona in weeping and in speaking of himself as subdued. Furthermore, his image momentarily suggests a reconciliation with nature and its fluids. Othello has often used similar images of biological viscosity with disgust—"The slime / That sticks on filthy deeds" (5.2.149-

50).¹⁶ Now for perhaps the first time he sees something in nature as healing. Furthermore, the gum is from Arabian trees—from an exotic, non-European land, one closer to Othello's heritage. It is a brief moment—only four lines—of relative peace—with the trees and the tears that recall Desdemona's willow song, where "Her salt tears fell from her, and soft'ned the stones" (4.2.45). Othello knows his heart is not the stone he once said it was. For these few moments he transcends the stereotype of masculine control to which he has elsewhere aspired. But he cannot accept as adequate the forgiveness that Desdemona has already granted him; he must return to the code of violence and control, and kill the passionate alien self that he earlier thought he was killing in Desdemona: "No way but this, / Killing myself, to die upon a kiss" (5.2.358-59).

The violent events of *Othello* dramatize, in hyperbolical form, many aspects of the predominant form of emotional symbiosis between men and women that remains in our society still. The references that I have occasionally made to echoes of the mother-child relationship in the imagery of the play are not intended as a prologue to comments about special pathologies in Othello's childhood, or Shakespeare's; rather, they are meant to underline the psychological influence that the restriction of child-rearing to women has had for centuries over the prevailing feelings of both sexes about women. Some of *Othello*'s resonance comes from the imagery by which Othello's words about Desdemona evoke, at one moment, the way she gives him such joy as the mother gives the infant, and, at another moment, the way that his disillusionment with her re-creates the total desolation of the infant in a temporary state of frustration. I am following here the analysis of Dorothy Dinnerstein in *The Mermaid and the Minotaur*.¹⁷ Dinnerstein believes that the boy raised by a woman feels "that the original, most primitive source of life will always lie outside himself, that to be sure of reliable access to it he must have exclusive access to a woman" (p. 43). Before the child has a defined self "a woman is the helpless child's main contact with the natural surround. . . . She is this global, inchoate, all-embracing presence before she is a person, a discrete, finite human individual with a subjectivity of her own" (p. 93). She is, perhaps, more a place than a person:

> There where I have garnered up my heart,
> Where either I must live or bear no life,
> The fountain from the which my current runs
> Or else dries up.
>
> (4.2.57-60)

Initially, in her warmth and sympathy for him Desdemona seems to fulfill Othello's dreams of how a woman ought to behave. Indeed, we in the audience know, though Othello does not, that she never loses that warmth and sympathy and that her only conflict with him arises because she also takes on the role of trying to help Cassio.

But that conflict does arise, and Othello's experience of it, magnified by Iago's hints, has echoes of the discovery, as Dinnerstein puts it, "that the infant does not own or control the mother's body. Because this body has needs and impulses of its own, its responsiveness to the infant's needs is never totally reliable" (p. 60). "We can call these delicate creatures ours / And not their appetites." We never completely learn to deal with this truth, says Dinnerstein: "That the other to whom we look for nurturance has, like any sentient other, needs and a viewpoint separate from and never wholly subject to our own" (p. 240). But conventional female behavior serves to hide this fact as much as possible; "woman traditionally agrees to listen to man's opinions and keep her own to herself, lets him hog the limelight and offers herself as audience, allows herself activity only as it nourishes his projects" (pp. 239-40). Desdemona does more than this, but like many such women she possesses what Dinnerstein calls "a monstrously overdeveloped talent for unreciprocated empathy, an adult talent that she must exercise in a situation in many ways as vulnerable as a child's" (p. 236).

Desdemona's "talent for empathy"—perhaps "sympathy" is more accurate in view of her misunderstandings of him—and her inability to fight back when her life is at stake are symmetrical to Othello's military prowess and inability to sympathize when he feels wronged. His role as a soldier makes the point about the contrast between his and Desdemona's skills according to typical sex roles in the most emphatic way. Yet Desdemona admires Othello's military abilities and identifies with them so much that Othello calls her "fair warrior," and she later calls herself "unhandsome warrior" (3.4.151). They are re-creating the traditional woman's "privilege of enjoying man's achievements and triumphs vicariously" (p. 211).

When Desdemona hears of Othello's earlier experiences, her tears serve, as Dinnerstein suggests that women's tears often do, to help a man go on—"for she is doing his weeping for him, and he is doing what she weeps about for her" (p. 226). The flashback to his earlier life in this speech is the only time in the play when we have a glimpse of Othello acting without regard to Desdemona, and even that is put in the context of their relationship by its position in the story of their courtship. Thus we see his identity as a soldier as connected with his confidence in Desdemona's admiration and sympathy from almost the beginning of the play. It is in keeping with this connection that when he loses faith in Desdemona he says farewell not only to the tranquil mind but also to "the big wars / That make ambition virtue" (3.3.349-50). After he has regained belief in Desdemona's faith, at the end, he speaks again of his service to the state and he stages his suicide as a re-creation of an earlier battle against a Turk.

Dinnerstein's analysis illuminates the connections between three attitudes that we have seen linked in Othello: emphasis on control, rejection of physicality, and rejection of women. Her analysis suggests that the kind of mutuality at the beginning of *Othello*, moving though it may be, contains some of the seeds of the disaster that follows. Erikson defines mutuality, we recall, as a relationship in which partners depend on one another for the development of their respective strengths: after Dinnerstein's analysis, we may be more critical of that word "respective," if it implies a traditional differentiation of roles. As she puts it, "what each sex knows best has been distorted by . . . sealing off from what the other knows best" (p. 272). Finally, Othello's and Desdemona's definitions of reality diverge so much that no conversation can match them. Othello's limited development of sympathy combines with Desdemona's limited development of self-defense, and with all the powers that both of them *have* developed, to destroy both of them. And this destruction is more poignant because neither of them is simply stereotypical, because Desdemona has shown initiative and courage, because Othello has felt more love for her than he can kill. But finally they act out ideals of their own culture, ideals that are still part of our own culture. It is Shakespeare's genius that the play can suggest both the limitations and infantile roots of these ideals and their magnetic power.

Notes

1. Peter L. Berger and Hansfried Kellner, "Marriage and the Construction of Reality," *Diogenes* 46 (Summer 1964): 9.
2. Ibid., p. 13.
3. Ibid., p. 12.
4. Cf. John Bayley, *The Characters of Love* (New York: Basic Books, 1960), p. 159.
5. See Susan Snyder, *The Comic Matrix of Shakespearean Tragedy* (Princeton: Princeton University Press, 1980), p. 74.
6. On the Moor, see, for example, Eldred Jones, *Othello's Countrymen* (London: Oxford University Press, 1945), especially pp. 8, 22, 71.
7. Stanley Cavell, *The Claims of Reason* (New York: Oxford University Press, 1979), pp. 490-91. Since writing this, I have discovered that this interpretation is also argued by Arthur Kirsch, "The Polarization of Erotic Love in *Othello*," *Modern Language Review* 73 (1978): 721-40; and Stephen Greenblatt, *Renaissance Self-Fashioning* (Chicago: University of Chicago Press, 1980), pp. 232-54.
8. John T. Noonan, Jr., *Contraception* (Cambridge, Mass.: Harvard University Press, 1966), pp. 252-53, 319; C. S. Lewis, *The Allegory of Love* (New York: Oxford University Press, 1958), pp. 15-17; cf. Derrick Sherwin Bailey, *Sexual Relation in Christian Thought* (New York: Harper and Row, 1959), pp. 206-7.
9. C. L. Barber, "The Family in Shakespeare's Development: Tragedy and Sacredness," in *Representing Shakespeare: New Psychoanalytic Essays*, ed. Murray Schwartz and Coppélia Kahn (Baltimore: Johns Hopkins University Press, 1980), pp. 95-201.
10. Lynda Boose, "Othello's Handkerchief: 'The Recognizance and Pledge of Love,'" *English Literary Renaissance* 5 (Autumn 1975): 363-67. See also David Kaula, "Othello Possessed: Notes on Shakespeare's Use of Magic and Witchcraft," *Shakespeare Studies* 2 (1966): 126.
11. Greenblatt, *Renaissance Self-Fashioning*, p. 225, refers to Daniel Lerner's definition of empathy as "the capacity to see oneself in the other fellow's situation" in *The Passing of Traditional Society* (1958; rev. ed., New York: Free Press, 1964), p. 49.
12. W. H. Auden, "The Joker in the Pack," in *The Dyer's Hand* (New York: Random House, 1963), reprinted in *Othello: A Casebook*, ed. John Wain (London: MacMillan, 1971), p. 217.
13. Cf. Terence Hawkes, *Shakespeare's Talking Animals* (New York: Rowman and Littlefield, 1974), p. 135.
14. Cf. Jones, *Othello's Countrymen*, p. 97; Kaula, "Othello Possessed," p. 121.
15. Her continued strength is emphasized by Carol Thomas Neely, "Women and Men in *Othello*: what should such a fool / Do with so good a woman?," *Shakespeare Studies* 10 (1977): 133-58. I am much indebted to this article for its redress of critical disparagement of Desdemona, and my emphasis on her limitations is meant to be juxtaposed with Neely's lengthier discussion of her strengths.
16. Cf. William Empson, "Honest in Othello," *The Structure of Complex Words* (New York: New Directions, 1951), reprinted in Wain, ed., *Othello: A Casebook*, pp. 109-10.
17. Dorothy Dinnerstein, *The Mermaid and the Minotaur* (New York: Harper and Row, 1977) (hereafter cited in the text by page number).

Mark Rose (essay date 1985)

SOURCE: "Othello's Occupation: Shakespeare and the Romance of Chivalry," in *English Literary Renaissance*, Vol. 15, No. 3, Autumn, 1985, pp. 293-311.

[*In the following essay, Rose discusses the role of chivalry in* Othello.]

> O now, for ever
> Farewell the tranquil mind! farewell content!
> Farewell the plumed troops, and the big wars
> That makes ambition virtue! O, farewell!
> Farewell the neighing steed and the shrill trump,
> The spirit-stirring drum, th' ear-piercing fife,
> The royal banner, and all quality,
> Pride, pomp, and circumstance of glorious war!
> And O you mortal engines, whose rude throats
> Th' immortal Jove's dread clamors counterfeit,
> Farewell! Othello's occupation's gone.[1]

Othello's adieus to tranquility and content at the start of this speech evoke something more like the pastoral than the military ideal. Even when the imagery becomes explicitly military in the evocation of the "plumed troops" and the "big wars" there is a subtle continuity with the opening pastoralism. Here the lines suggest a transformation in which "ambition," which is a vice in a world defined by pastoral content, becomes a "virtue" in a martial context—that is, both a positive good, and in the archaic sense of *virtu*, a source of strength. Moreover, the static quality of "plumed troops" and "big wars" is compatible with the feeling the lines convey that something like pastoral *otium* is being continued in a martial vein. Explicit activity enters the picture when Othello imagines the world he has lost as a parade of neighing horses and playing instruments—trumpet, drum, and fife—an ascending procession of sound that climaxes in the godlike roar of the cannon. "Farewell! Othello's occupation's gone." Six times in eleven lines Othello says farewell. The repetition articulates the speech, contributing to the sense of a procession passing with Othello bidding adieu to each of the squadrons in the parade of his life. It also unifies the speech, turning it into a nostalgic lament for a paradoxically apprehended martial pastoral.

What has Othello lost? The contradictions in this speech, at once static and active, pastoral and martial, convey the emotional urgency with which an image of the perfected world of absolute being is here fashioned. It is a world in which everything, including the neighing of horses and the booming of cannon, takes on the aspect of music; a world without stress, one in which even ambitious striving for glory has been reconceived as a form of tranquility. To participate in the harmonious clamor of this grand march in which mortal engines counterfeit the huge sounds of immortal Jove is to live at the farthest verge of human possibility. It is to be nearly as absolute as a god. Plainly such a state of being, one in which there is no gap between desire and satisfaction, between, as Macbeth puts it, the firstlings of the heart and the firstlings of the hand, is a condition radically incompatible with self-reflection, thought, or uncertainty of any kind. To banish Othello from such an Eden, proof of Desdemona's infidelity is unnecessary; mere suspicion will do as well as certainty.

Why should suspicion of Desdemona's infidelity end Othello's occupation as a soldier? It helps to observe that Othello conceives himself in this speech as a type of the knight validated by the absolute worthiness of the mistress he serves. Call the mistress into question and not only the knight's activity but his very identity collapses. Of course in this case the mistress, the necessarily unattainable lady of romance, has become the wife: sexual availability—as opposed to the intensity of mere fantasizing—has entered the picture. Even without Iago's machinations, then, the romantic image of the absolute worthiness of the lady is at best unstable. Others have developed this aspect of Othello's vulnerability to Iago.[2] Here let us note simply that this speech is a clue to Othello's romanticizing imagination. It is of a piece with his address to the Senate in which he retells the story of his adventures among cannibals and monsters, his speech to Desdemona about the magic in the web of the handkerchief in which he invokes witches and charms as a way of explaining its overwhelming significance, or his final speech in which he recalls the exotic turbaned Turk in order to explain why he is about to slay himself. One might interpret *Othello* as a kind of tragic *Don Quixote*, a play in which Shakespeare explores the ways in which a romanticizing imagination can lead to devastating error. Yet despite the appeal of such an approach—and certainly it would be illuminating up to a point—we should note that Othello's romanticism is neither so explicit as Don Quixote's nor so firmly demarcated from the general world of the narrative.

There are no giants or dragons in *Othello*. The play's military world consists of generals, lieutenants, and ancients rather than knights, squires, evil magicians, and faithless Saracens. It is a world in which career advancement can be presented as a plausible motive for action; it is a comparatively workaday place of fleets, intelligence reports, and expeditionary forces. But the proximate realism should not blind us to the play's romantic aspects. There are Christian soldiers and threatening infidels here. Othello, a black warrior of royal lineage who turns out to be capable of astonishing violence, has something of a Savage Knight about him, and Desdemona may well in the constancy of her affection recall a Princess of Love and Chastity. Iago is no magician—indeed, he explicitly denies that he works by witchcraft—and yet his ensnarement of Othello's soul together with his manipulation of his perceptions may recall Spenser's Archimago, who similarly provides Redcross with ocular proof of his lady's infidelity. Moreover, all these elements reminiscent of chivalric romance—Othello's royal blood and adventurous past, the somewhat miraculous quality of Desdemona's innocence, the air of diabolical mystery that clings to Iago, the background of war with the infidel—are Shakespeare's additions to the Othello story as he found it in Cinthio's novella. Not just Othello's imagination but, I would suggest, Shakespeare's own is informed by the patterns of chivalric romance.

II

A few words about the Elizabethan chivalric revival are in order here. As Roy Strong says, "It is one of the great paradoxes of the Elizabethan world, one of its touchstones, that an age of social, political and religious revolution should cling to and deliberately erect a façade of the trappings of feudalism"[3] Elizabethan culture was saturated with feudal idealism. In life and in art chivalric themes were pervasive. By the 1580s the spectacular Accession Day Tilts had reached their fully developed form. In this period, too, Robert Smythson was designing such fantasy castles as Wollaton Hall, Sidney was writing the *Arcadia*, Spenser was writing *The Faerie Queene*, and the London stages were populated by damsels in distress, knights in armor, and wicked enchanters in dozens of plays—most now lost—with names like *Herpetulus the Blue Knight and Perobia, The History of the Solitary Knight*, and *Sir Clyomon and Sir Clamydes*.[4] Chivalric fantasies of service to the Virgin Queen shaped Elizabethan court style and also affected foreign policy. One product of the chivalric revival was Sidney's *Arcadia,* another was his death in 1586 in a campaign in which romantic notions continually obscured for Eliza's knights the complex facts of a situation in which Dutch burghers were attempting to throw off Spanish rule.[5]

Northrop Frye's conception of romance as "the search of the libido or desiring self for a fulfillment that will deliver it from the anxieties of reality but will still contain that reality"[6] might well be a gloss on the Elizabethan effort to turn reality into a romance. The late sixteenth century was a time of dramatic social changes and probably also a period of considerable social anxiety. London was burgeoning, commerce was developing rapidly, old bonds of service and obligation were yielding to new relationships based on the marketplace, and the religious unity of Europe was gone forever. Chivalric games and ceremonies helped to obscure the relative newness of so many of the noble families as well as the fact that, despite the continuing prestige of war, the aristocracy had ceased to be a warrior class and was becoming an administrative elite. By this period, as Lawrence Stone has shown, there was little that was particularly feudal about the English nobility, who from an early time had been deeply engaged in entrepreneurial activity.[7] On the other hand, there was little that was clearly bourgeois—in the modern sense—about the sensibility of the Elizabethan middle class. Interestingly, the bourgeois hero tales of the 1590s and early 1600s—Deloney's *Jack of Newbury,* Dekker's *Shoemaker's Holiday* and other stories and plays celebrating the virtues of the new men of commerce—show middle-class figures in feudal postures, fighting and feasting like knights.[8] The usual aspiration of the successful businessman was not to oppose the interests of the landed aristocracy and gentry but to join them as soon as possible, one notable case in point being Shakespeare himself.

The chivalric revival assimilated the complexities of the present to a mythical world of the past, but at its center was the living Queen. In her own person Elizabeth held the contradictions of her culture together, and she did this in part by turning herself into a character, Gloriana, and her life and that of her country into a story. But the moment of magical balance was necessarily brief. By the late 1590s the fervor of the previous decade was gone. Corruption at court was more marked and commented on, and it had become increasingly more difficult for the Queen, who was now a full generation older than her principal courtiers, to play the role of the virginal beauty.[9] Nor should the traumatic effect of the Earl of Essex's rebellion and execution be underestimated. Essex, who is one of the very few contemporary figures to whom Shakespeare directly alludes, was the inheritor of Philip Sidney's sword and of his position in the national imagination as the embodiment of chivalry. According to his biographer, his rise and sudden fall in 1601 probably affected the nation more deeply than any event since the defeat of the Spanish Armada.[10] In any case, the time came when the Elizabethan romances—both the romance enacted by the Queen and those composed by her poets and dramatists—could no longer carry conviction. Despite a brief revival of some of its themes in 1610-1612 at the court of Prince Henry, nothing like the special quality of Elizabethan chivalry could occur again.

III

I know of no general study of Shakespeare's relation to the romance dramas of the 1570s and 1580s and to the Elizabethan chivalric revival.[11] Nevertheless, it is not hard to see how, for instance, *1 Henry VI* with its opposition between the heroic knight Talbot and the wicked enchantress Joan represents a continuation and transformation of chivalric romance materials, or how similar materials influence the romantic comedies with their disguised and wandering heroines. Moreover, the theme of both historical tetralogies is the disintegration of an absolute world of chivalry, and in this theme the histories might be said to look forward to Othello's farewell to arms. Thus the first tetralogy begins with Henry V's funeral, a symbolic procession that suggests the death of chivalry itself, after which the *Henry VI* plays trace the collapse of the heroic society into faction and civil war. There follows the emergence of Richard the Third, a monstrous antitype of the chivalric hero, and finally the return of chivalry in the person of the Earl of Richmond. The pattern of the second tetralogy is similar. Here the interrupted combat at the start of *Richard II* establishes the lost world of perfected chivalric kingship, after which the plays trace a decline into strife and rebellion and finally the emergence of a new chivalric figure, Prince Hal as Henry V. But this time, we note, the chivalric return is not simply a return. Hal's chivalry is political and contingent rather than mystical and absolute in the vein of Richmond at the end of *Richard III*. Like Elizabeth holding the contradictions of her culture together in her person, Hal holds the contradictions of his history-play world together, and, like her, he does it through self-conscious role-playing.

The tone of Shakespeare's treatment of chivalric themes, like so much else, changes in the early seventeenth century. *Troilus and Cressida,* probably written the year after the Essex rebellion, is biting in its exposure of the putrefied core that seems to hide within the goodly armor of chivalric pretentions, and in *King Lear* not even the spectacular romancelike triumph of the unknown knight Edgar over his evil brother Edmund can prevent the ugly hanging of Cordelia and the play's tragic end. Particularly relevant to *Othello,* however, is the tragedy that immediately precedes it chronologically. It would be hard, I think, to overemphasize the importance of chivalry to *Hamlet.* The play takes its point of departure, and finds its image of the lost chivalric world, in Horatio's evocation of King Hamlet and King Fortinbras locked in a valiant single combat ratified by law and chivalry. It is this evocation of heroic combat in a past time when things were absolutely what they seemed to be that gives meaning to the great falling off that constitutes the play's present world. In creeping into the garden to poison his brother, Claudius has in effect poisoned chivalry. His secret duel with Hamlet, fought with such human weapons as Polonius, Rosencrantz and Guildenstern, and the actors, represents a travesty of chivalric ideals, and the play moves not toward the heroic restorations of the histories but toward a grotesque and deadly recapitulation of the original combat between the kings in Hamlet and Laertes' duel with the poisoned foils, overseen by Osric as chivalric judge-at-arms.

IV

"I'll pour this pestilence into his ear" (2.3.356): the language with which Iago introduces his plan for undoing Othello strikingly recalls Claudius' poison poured into the porches of King Hamlet's ears. We can note, too, that Othello's farewell to arms figures in the play's structure in a manner analogous to the image of the kings in combat, providing in its martial pastoral a point of reference against which the present situation, Othello in the agonies of Iago's poison, is to be measured. But the fact that in Othello the nostalgic reference point comes in the middle rather than at the start of the tragedy is important; whereas in Hamlet chivalry is dead before the play begins, in Othello we observe the process of the poisonous transformation. In fact we do more than observe, we participate. In Hamlet the audience's representative, the figure who draws us into dramatic engagement with his purposes, is the prince, and Claudius, as his antagonist, becomes in consequence a relatively opaque figure. In Othello, as in Richard III and Macbeth, Shakespeare plays the dynamics of theatrical engagement against moral judgment, and this is one reason that Othello does not lapse into melodrama. From the opening in which Iago manipulates Roderigo and Brabantio the play is structured so that we enter the action from Iago's point of view, and his many strategically placed soliloquies and asides confirm our dramatic engagement with him through at least the first half of the play. Othello himself is magnificent, a commanding and dominating figure, but until the temptation scene and the start of his falling off he is also, like Claudius, apprehended at a certain distance, observed as one might observe a public figure and a stranger.

Othello, the exotic black man from Africa, is a stranger in another, more literal, sense as well. In Hamlet and in the history plays the representatives of chivalric perfection—King Hamlet, Henry V in the first tetralogy, Edward the Black Prince as he is evoked at the start of the second tetralogy—are generally ancestral figures. Even the Earl of Richmond and Henry V in the second tetralogy are ancestral figures to the audience if not to the characters in the plays. In Othello, however, the knightly defender of Christian civilization is projected as an alien. Othello's blackness is the index of a different orientation toward the chivalric figure. Moreover, as many critics since Bradley have remarked, Iago is a kind of playwright, an artist carefully maneuvering his characters into position to bring his tragedy to fulfillment.[12] Perhaps, then, we can think of Othello as a play in which Shakespeare is recapitulating his own earlier representations of an absolute world of chivalry, alienating them, and through Iago representing something like his own role in plotting the disintegration of the absolute world.

V

Put money in thy purse . . . I say put money in thy purse . . . put money in thy purse . . . put but money in thy purse . . . fill thy purse with money . . . put money in thy purse . . . Make all the money thou canst . . . therefore make money . . . go make money . . . go, provide thy money . . . put money enough in your purse.

(1.3.339-81)

It is more than a little tempting to think of Iago as an embodiment of the prodigious energies of the new commercialism of the Renaissance, and thus to turn Othello into an allegory in which bourgeois man destroys the representative of the older feudal values. Thus, whereas Othello speaks of the plumed troop and the royal banner in terms that evoke an activity of transcendent worth, Iago can talk casually of "the trade of war" (1.2.1). Iago's speech is shot through with the language of commerce. "I know my price," he says when he describes being passed over for promotion, "I am worth no worse a place" (1.1.11), and, contrasting himself with Cassio, he dismisses the lieutenant as a mere accountant, a "debitor and creditor," and a "counter-caster" (1.1.31). Yet even though he has money and purses on his mind, Iago's motive for bringing down Othello is certainly not profit. Moreover, Othello too can speak in commercial terms, as when he invites Desdemona to bed after their arrival in Cyprus: "Come, my dear love, / The purchase made, the fruits are to ensue; / The profit's yet to come 'tween me and you" (2.3.8-10).

To reduce Othello to historical allegory would plainly be to distort the play. Such a reduction would also be anachronistic. As Lawrence Stone and other social historians have taught us, we must beware of imagining anything like a clear-cut opposition in this period between a declining feudal class and a rising bourgeoisie.[13] The late sixteenth and early seventeenth centuries were a time of transition and contradiction, a period in which fundamentally incompatible social forms and structures of thought sat uneasily side by side in a manner that may make us think of those sixteenth-century account books kept partly in Arabic, partly in Roman numerals.[14] An old world of traditional forms and values was largely gone, but a new one had not yet clearly taken shape.

Particularly apparent were the tensions between the traditional feudal values of honor, loyalty, and service, and the less absolute imperatives of the marketplace. On the one hand honor might be regarded as a kind of religion, something worth dying for, as for instance when Cassio equates his good name with his soul: "Reputation, reputation, reputation! O, I have lost my reputation! I have lost the immortal part of myself, and what remains is bestial" (2.3.262-64). On the other, it was often treated as merchandise. "I would to God thou and I knew where a commodity of good names were to be bought," Falstaff says mockingly to Hal (1 Henry IV, 1.2.82-83), and a few years later in the Jacobean debasement of honors, good names were openly traded like stocks and bonds. Thus Stone reports that in 1606 Lionel Cranfield bought the making of six knights from his friend Arthur Ingram for £373.1s.8d.[15] In this transitional moment, no simple antithesis between the values of the marketplace and those of the field of honor is possible. Despite his skepticism about honor, Sir John Falstaff is not a bourgeois figure. Likewise, Antonio, the paragon of lordly generosity who is contrasted with Shylock in *The Merchant of Venice,* is not, as we might suppose given the values that he embodies, a feudal figure.[16] Perhaps, then, we should imagine the tension between feudal and commercial codes at this time as less like a modern class struggle than like a medieval psychomachia—that is, as a still internalized struggle in which members of the same group, or even at times a single individual, can be found operating inconsistently, now according to one set of values, now according to another.

The mediation of contradiction can be understood as one of the functions of drama or even of narrative generally. With this in mind let us briefly note that Shakespeare often plays romantic and absolute attitudes against contingent and commercial ones, building drama out of the tension. *The Merchant of Venice* is an obvious case in point, as is *As You Like It* where the absoluteness of Orlando's professions of love is measured against the more mundane view evoked in Rosalind's mockery of dying for love and her advice to Phoebe, "Sell when you can, you are not for all markets" (3.5.60). And yet for all her mockery, Rosalind is, we know, a very romantic young lady, many fathoms deep in love. Just so *1 Henry IV,* in which the romanticism is expressed in chivalric rather than erotic terms, measures Hotspur against Falstaff. Like Rosalind, Hal is able to play both mocker and romantic, or, to make the point at the level of diction where it may be easiest to observe, he is able to blend the language of commerce with that of chivalry, as when he predicts his triumph over Hotspur:

> Percy is but my factor, good my lord,
> To engross up glorious deeds on my behalf;
> And I will call him to so strict account
> That he shall render every glory up,
> Yea, even the slightest worship of his time,
> Or I will tear the reckoning from his heart.
>
> (3.2.147-52)

In this way the flexibility of language allows contrary systems of value to be expressed. At the same time, the conventions of narrative achieve forward thrust. No practical resolution of the cultural contradiction may be possible but at least there can be the satisfactions of the achievement of narrative closure. In any case, *Othello,* too, incorporates the tension between romantic absolutism and the antithetical values of the marketplace, but here instead of being held in triumphant balance in the style of the 1590s, the brutal power latent in the contradiction is used to drive a tragedy.

VI

Let us begin by observing a major change that Shakespeare makes in the structure of Cinthio's narrative. In the novella the wicked ensign's revenge is not directed at the Moor so much as at the lady. Cinthio's ensign is a rebuffed suitor whose passion for Desdemona turns to hate. Shakespeare, however, pits Iago directly against Othello. One effect of this change is to obscure the villain's motive. Another is to alter the lady's position in the narrative structure, demoting her from one of the two ultimate figures in the story to an intermediary. Like the handkerchief with which she is associated, Desdemona becomes a kind of object, an instrument of Iago's revenge against Othello. Passed first from Brabantio's hands into the Moor's and then ignorantly thrown away, Shakespeare's Desdemona figures in the narrative as property. Iago's revenge looks forward to the bourgeois style of a later age; he achieves satisfaction by depriving his enemy of his most valued possession.

At the same time that Shakespeare's narrative demotes Desdemona from a person to property, it also elevates her to an angel. Cinthio's lady is a rather matter of fact heroine, but Shakespeare's is a transcendent figure who refracts the long series of divine ladies that reaches back through the sonnet and romance heroines of the sixteenth century to, among others, Petrarch's Laura and Dante's Beatrice. Her conversation with Emilia about women who betray their husbands evokes the realm of the marketplace precisely in order to separate her from it absolutely. "Wouldst thou do such a deed for all the world?" she asks Emilia, who replies less romantically that while she would not do it for anything trivial such as a ring or a dress, she certainly would do it for the world: "The world's a huge thing; it is a great price / For a small vice" (4.3.67-69). Later, guiltlessly dying, Desdemona refuses to blame Othello for anything: "Commend me to my kind lord. O, farewell!" (5.2.125). At once property and an angel of selflessness, Desdemona, too, looks forward to the bourgeois age and to its conception of woman.

Behind the contradictions implicit in Shakespeare's Desdemona may be glimpsed the tensions of a moment of cultural transformation. In a penetrating observation, Kenneth Burke suggests that *Othello* incorporates an analogue in the realm of human affinity to the enclosure acts whereby common lands were made private. Shakespeare's play inscribes an act of spiritual enclosure, love transformed into private property. Whatever is owned may be seized. The fear of loss is integral to the principle of property and thus the threat that Iago represents comes as much from within Othello as from without; Shakespeare externalizes the already implicit fear in the figure of Iago, making the villain, in Burke's phrase, into a voice at Othello's ear. Othello and Iago, possessor and the threat of loss, are dialectically related parts of the one "fascination." Add Desdemona to the integral, Burke says, "and you have a tragic trinity of ownership in the profoundest sense of ownership, the property in human affections, as fetishistically localized in the object of possession."[17]

Property implies theft: therein lies the play's premise. Opening in Venice, the city of fabled commercial wealth,

Othello is structured as a series of thefts. The first is a variant of the stock comic action of the stolen daughter that Shakespeare uses also in his other play set in Venice when Jessica escapes from Shylock's house laden with ducats and jewels. Here, in an episode that foreshadows his later and more subtle arousing of Othello, Iago wakes Brabantio: "Awake! what ho, Brabantio! thieves, thieves! / Look to your house, your daughter, and your bags! / Thieves, thieves!" (1.1.79-81). And a moment after: "Zounds, sir, y'are robb'd! For shame, put on your gown; / Your heart is burst, you have lost half your soul" (1.1.86-87).

Let us note the fusion of spiritual and proprietary ideas: Desdemona is both half her father's soul and a possession equivalent to his money. Let us note, too, that so far as the play is concerned Desdemona might have no mother. She is represented as wholly her father's possession, and the principal question concerning her at the opening is whether the transfer from father to husband has been rightfully made, whether she has in fact been stolen from Brabantio or properly won. Again, the play fuses spiritual and proprietary themes when in the Senate scene the Duke decides the case on romantic principles. "I think this tale would win my daughter too" (1.3.171), he comments on Othello's speech, and when Desdemona acknowledges that she freely loves the Moor, Brabantio must yield.

The play's first movement is "The Abduction of Desdemona"; the second is "The Theft of Cassio's Name." Cassio supposes that he is wholly responsible for the loss of his reputation, but we know that Iago, plying his victim with wine, has robbed him. The presentation of Cassio as a decent man changed into a drunken madman foreshadows the action with Othello to come, specifically, the theme of diabolic possession: "O thou invisible spirit of wine, if thou hast no name to be known by, let us call thee devil! . . . To be now a sensible man, by and by a fool, and presently a beast! O strange! Every inordinate cup is unbless'd, and the ingredient is a devil" (2.3.281-308). To which Iago replies in language that plays upon the theme: "Come, come; good wine is a good familiar creature, if it be well us'd" (2.3.309-10).

In the transitional culture of the early modern period the concept of the soul is also affected by the hegemonic principle of property. Now a soul is something a person *has* as well as something a person *is*. We think, of course, of Marlowe's Faustus selling his soul by contract like an aristocrat turning his land into cash; and it may be, too, that the interest in cases of possession and exorcism at the end of the sixteenth century reveals the influence of proprietary modes of thought.[18] In *Othello,* at any rate, the theme of diabolic possession is related to the play's concern with property. Here the ideas of soul, property, and honor join together in a complex dance of equivalences and ironies, as when Iago tells Brabantio that he has been robbed of half his soul or when Cassio speaks of his reputation as his immortal part.

The play's main action, which begins in the temptation scene when Iago at last turns to work directly upon Othello, depends upon this system of unstable equivalences. Speaking to Cassio, Iago has dismissed the loss of reputation as insignificant, but now he echoes Cassio when he proclaims the opposite to Othello:

> Good name in man and woman, dear my lord,
> Is the immediate jewel of their souls.
> Who steals my purse steals trash; 'tis something, nothing;
> 'Twas mine, 'tis his, and has been slave to thousands;
> But he that filches from me my good name
> Robs me of that which not enriches him,
> And makes me poor indeed.
>
> (3.3.155-61)

With the idea of theft thus implanted in his thoughts, Othello himself is soon speaking of robbery—"What sense had I in her stol'n hours of lust?" (3.3.338)—accusing Desdemona of filching her honor, which as her husband belongs ultimately to him, and thus of stealing also his own good name.

"I am your own for ever" (3.3.480). When at the end of the temptation scene Iago says that he belongs to Othello forever we understand that he means the opposite of what he speaks: Othello is now his. Othello believes that Desdemona has been stolen from him but the truth is that he has been stolen from himself. The demi-devil Iago has taken possession of his soul. Soon, like a classic case of demonic possession, Othello will be thrashing on the ground, foaming and raving in a fit. Soon, too, diabolic powers will in effect speak through Othello's mouth as the smooth and authoritative cadences of what Wilson Knight calls the "Othello music" yield to the staccato fragments and ugly images associated with Iago. In this way the unitary world of absolute self-possession that is recapitulated in "Farewell the tranquil mind" is split open and Othello becomes estranged not only from Desdemona but from himself. Like Spenser's Redcross knight, who is also launched into a world of doubleness, Othello is propelled into a nightmare of duplicity in which his love and his doubt are at war with each other. This process of self-alienation climaxes in Othello's suicide, the one half of his divided self executing justice upon the other as once he administered justice to the Turk in Aleppo. Thus the narrative—although not of course the contradictions that drive the narrative—is resolved.

VII

Iago's diabolism is of course only metaphorical. Shakespeare is exploring a secular equivalent to demonic possession, showing how a terrible misapprehension can take control of a normally rational mind. *Othello,* in which there are neither ghosts, soothsayers, witches, nor supernatural prodigies, is one of the most secular of Shakespeare's tragedies. Nevertheless, it is significant that the world "devil" occurs in its various forms more often here than in any other Shakespeare play. The word "faith," too, is prominent whether it is used casually as in Iago and Cassio's discussion of Bianca where it occurs repeatedly as a mild expletive (4.1) or whether it is used portentously as in Othello's tremendous oath, "My life upon her faith" (1.3.294). What Shakespeare is doing in this play is appropriating spiritual conceptions, turning them into metaphors for secular experiences. But metaphors work two ways. If *Othello* incorporates a process of demystification, the assimilation of the supernatural to the natural world, it also incorporates the antithetical movement. The story may not literally be the temptation and fall of man from faith, but the play is not purely domestic tragedy either. An interpretation may legitimately stress either the process of naturalization or the way the domestic drama suggests events of cosmic significance. Like all of Shakespeare's work, *Othello* is implicated in the Renaissance system of analogical thought in which the realms of matter and spirit are not yet wholly divided and distinguished. Thus the play can be at once domestic and cosmic, secular and supernatural.

Othello is fascinating as a historical document because of the way it inscribes a transitional moment in Western culture. In it we can almost see the supernatural realm receding. The feudal world of honor, fidelity, and service is becoming the bourgeois world of property and contractual relations. Heroic tragedy is turning into domestic tragedy. It was Shakespeare's fortune to partake of two worlds without belonging completely to either. Shakespeare's myriad-mindedness—the quality that Norman Rabkin speaks of as complementarity—has much to do with this particular historical situation, as does his endless self-consciousness, the metadramatic aspect of his plays that has been emphasized by Sigurd Burckhardt and James Calderwood.

We can locate Shakespeare's historical situation with some precision by observing that his friend and colleague Ben Jonson, a man less than ten years younger than Shakespeare, belongs much more to the new era. Whereas Shakespeare fuses and blends the spiritual and the secular, the realms of honor and commerce, Jonson uses comic irony to create distinctions. The spectacularly blasphemous opening of *Volpone*—a play like *Othello* set in the commercial city of Venice—makes the point.

> Good morning to the day; and next, my gold!
> Open the shrine that I may see my saint.
> Hail the world's soul, and mine! More glad than is
> The teeming earth to see the longed-for sun
> Peep through the horns of the celestial Ram,
> Am I, to view thy splendor darkening his;
> That lying here, amongst my other hoards,
> Show'st like a flame by night, or like the day
> Struck out of chaos, when all darkness fled
> Unto the center.[19]

Here the Renaissance system of correspondence between matter and spirit, microcosm and macrocosm, is used against itself to expose the gap between traditional values and the realities of the marketplace and to suggest the emptying out of spiritual significance from the world.

Jonson typically pokes fun at magicians, monsters, and fairy queens Concerned with verisimilitude and poetic justice, his plays look forward in a way that Shakespeare's, with their marvels, anachronisms, and freedoms of time and place, do not. His attitude toward chivalric romanticism is also different from Shakespeare's. In *Prince Henry's Barriers*, the masque that Jonson wrote in connection with the Prince of Wales's first bearing arms in January 1610, Henry is cast as the reviver of chivalry. The masque begins with the Lady of the Lake praising James's court as greater than Arthur's but lamenting the decay of chivalry which is represented by the scene, the ruined House of Chivalry. Arthur appears and prophesies the advent of a knight who will restore chivalry, whereupon Merlin rises from his tomb to reveal Prince Henry, discovered with his companions in arms in a new scene representing St. George's Portico, where knighthood now lives. In a long speech Merlin lectures the Prince on English history, emphasizing industriousness, peaceability, and other values that are distinctly not chivalric.[20] Most interesting, Merlin says that Henry will not seek to emulate the deeds of "antique knights" by thinking to rescue ladies from giants or to do battle with a score of men at once.

> These were bold stories of our Arthur's age;
> But here are other acts; another stage
> And scene appears; it is not since as then:
> No giants, dwarfs or monsters here, but men.[21]

The arts of the modern hero must be to govern and give laws and to preserve the peace whenever possible.

The matter-of-factness incorporated in the apparently romantic and chivalric pageant of *Prince Henry's Barriers* may remind us of the similar quality in Francis Beaumont's *The Knight of the Burning Pestle*, probably performed three years earlier in 1607. Here too we are in a world of men, a world drained of the supernatural and marvelous. Like Jonson in the comedies, Beaumont uses comedy to make distinctions between realms that Shakespeare characteristically blends. Shakespeare's Hal fuses the language of the marketplace and that of the field of honor, speaking of Hotspur as his factor to purchase glorious deeds for him wholesale. Beaumont disjoins the two realms, gaining comic mileage by placing Hotspur's "bright honor" speech in Rafe the grocer's man's mouth and then by placing Rafe and his chivalric posturings in a world in which innkeepers expect to be paid and servants to be tipped. In this unromantic place things are simply what they are, and the comedy ridicules Rafe's attempt to transvalue them by renaming forests and heaths "deserts," horses "palfreys," and by referring to females as either "fair lady" or "distressed damsel" depending upon whether they have their desires or not.[22]

At this point *Don Quixote*, which may have influenced both Beaumont and Jonson, virtually demands to be mentioned. I referred to Cervantes earlier in order to distinguish between his novelistic exploration of the romanticizing imagination and Shakespeare's play in which the protagonist's romanticism is not perfectly demarcated from the general world of the narrative. Published in 1605, a year after *Othello* was performed, *Don Quixote* marks a cultural watershed, the emergence of what Michel Foucault calls the classical epistemé. In the Renaissance, Foucault suggests, the principle of resemblance plays a constitutive role in knowledge. The Renaissance conceives a universe of magical correspondences. From this point of view the cosmos is a single vast text and knowledge is a form of interpretation, a matter of reading the mystic signatures written in things. There is finally no difference between language and nature, authority and observation. In *Don Quixote,* however, the bond between words and things has been severed. The Don seeks to reestablish a world of magical resemblances; his entire journey is a quest for similitudes. But the world he inhabits is one in which things are simply what they are, one in which flocks and serving girls are not subject to the transmutation of language. The Renaissance cosmos has dissolved. In its place the empire of fact is emerging and language is retreating into a special domain, literature, with only an indirect relationship to the world in the neo-classical doctrines of representation and verisimilitude.[23]

It is indicative of the importance of chivalry as a locus for the contradictions of Renaissance culture that such a crucial text as *Don Quixote* should take the form of a negation of chivalric romance. While the chivalric revival of the sixteenth century helped to obscure some of the social and intellectual contradictions of the period, it also contributed to them, raising, as it were, the level of tension by a notch. We can note that in its nostalgia the chivalric revival was a way of possessing the past, of turning chivalry into property. To turn honor literally into property, as the sale of honors did, or to portray merchants and tradesmen in heroic postures, as the bourgeois hero tales did, was to approach the breaking point. In Jonson, Beaumont, and above all in Cervantes, the contradictions of the late Renaissance snap into laughter. *Don Quixote* in particular prefigures the bourgeois civilization of the later seventeenth and eighteenth centuries in which the romance becomes the novel and the emblematic theater of the world, Shakespeare's theater, becomes the illusionistic theater of scenes and stage properties, the theater of things.

VIII

But what of Shakespeare, whose sensibility is perhaps as close to that of Spenser as to Jonson? Shakespeare, who came to maturity in the 1580s at the height of the Elizabethan revival of chivalry, was not ready to write anti-romances like *Don Quixote* or *The Knight of the Burning Pestle*. He was, I think, still too deeply possessed by the absolute world of fidelity. He could write about the death of chivalry or the corruption of chivalry but he could not distance himself sufficiently from its imaginative claims to burlesque it. As a principal shareholder in London's most successful theatrical company and an energetic accumulator of wealth in Stratford and London, Shakespeare evidently participated in the new ethos of the marketplace. But he was also still something of a romantic, even if an unillusioned one.

I suggested earlier that we might think of *Othello* as a play in which Shakespeare recapitulates his own earlier representations of the absolute world of chivalry and that we might regard Iago, the cunning artist of tragedy, as at least in part a representation of Shakespeare himself. Iago is not bourgeois man—that creature had not, so to speak, been thought in 1604. Nevertheless, he is a figure in which the age could find something like the bourgeois cast of mind, together with the multitude of fears and desires that it aroused, made manifest. But Iago is not simply the pragmatist and materialist that he seems to take himself to be. Why should he want to destroy Othello? Iago and Othello are reciprocal figures, part of the same—to use Burke's word—fascination. Just as Othello is possessed by Iago, so Iago is from the beginning of the play possessed by Othello. But though Iago succeeds in destroying the Moor and Desdemona as well, he does not, we might say, succeed in exorcising the spirit they embody. Desdemona remains a miracle of fidelity to the end, and Othello, released from the demi-devil's snares, dies reasserting his allegiance to his heroic self.

True enough; yet to conclude our discussion on this romantic note of sustained fidelity and reasserted heroism misrepresents the tenor of Shakespeare's play. Othello may be an honorable murderer but he is a murderer nonetheless, and at the story's end both Desdemona and the Moor are dead. The world of *Othello* is not that of the novel, the characteristic genre of bourgeois civilization, but neither is it that of Elizabethan romance. *Othello* represents an intermediate moment in cultural development and an intermediate form, tragedy. Romance incorporates certainties, absolute opposites of good and evil. Tragedy subverts, deconstructs, certainties and absolutes, or, as Fredric Jameson puts it, tragedy rebukes romance.[24] What Shakespeare has done in *Othello* is to convert the material of Elizabethan romance into tragedy.

Tragedy involves *katharsis:* purging, cleansing, exorcising. The scapegoats of this particular tragic sacrifice are Desdemona and Othello, figures of an exquisite and dangerous romantic beauty. The high priest is Iago, who draws us as audience into dynamic engagement with his purposes, mobilizing destructive emotions that we may not wish to acknowledge. We participate with Iago in splitting open the absolutes of Othello's martial pastoral. We assist in his project of driving the romance hero and his lady out of the world, of torturing Othello and Desdemona to death. Like Othello, we too are in a sense possessed. But because this is theater we are simultaneously dispossessed. Iago engages our rapaciousness, jealousy, and fear, but he also allows us to alienate ourselves from those ungentle emotions, projecting them onto him. Thus he too becomes a scapegoat. Protagonist and antagonist cancel each other out.[25] We are left at the end with neither a reassertion of an old world nor a prefiguration of a new one, but a mere vacancy, or, rather, a tableau of corpses and a disconcerting promise that Iago too will be tortured.

Notes

1. 3.3.347-57. All citations of Shakespeare refer to *The Riverside Shakespeare,* ed. G. Blakemore Evans (Boston, Mass., 1974).

2. See in particular Stephen Greenblatt's exciting discussion in *Renaissance Self-Fashioning* (Chicago, Ill., 1980), pp. 222-57.

3. *The Cult of Elizabeth: Elizabethan Portraiture and Pageantry* (London, 1977), pp. 161-62. See also Frances A. Yates, "Elizabethan Chivalry: The Romance of the Accession Day Tilts," in *Astraea: The Imperial Theme in the Sixteenth Century* (London, 1975), pp. 88-111.

4. On chivalric themes in architecture see Mark Girouard, *Robert Smythson and the Elizabethan Country House* (New Haven, Conn., 1983), esp. pp. 205-32. Betty J. Littleton discusses the romance dramas of the 1570s and 1580s and provides a list of titles in her critical edition of *Clyomon and Clamydes* (The Hague, 1968).

5. See Jan Albert Dop, *Eliza's Knights: Soldiers, Poets, and Puritans in the Netherlands* (Leiden, 1981).

6. *The Anatomy of Criticism* (Princeton, NJ., 1957), p. 193.

7. See *The Crisis of the Aristocracy 1558-1641* (Oxford, 1965), esp. pp. 335-84. Diane Bornstein, *Mirrors of Courtesy* (Hamden, Conn., 1975), studies English chivalric manuals and makes a number of suggestive comments on the social functions of Renaissance chivalry.

8. See Laura Stevenson O'Connell's important "The Elizabethan Bourgeois Hero-Tale: Aspects of an Adolescent Social Consciousness," in *After the Reformation: Essays in Honor of J. H. Hexter*, ed. Barbara C. Malament (Philadephia, Pa., 1980), pp. 267-90.

9. See J. E. Neale, "The Elizabethan Political Scene," in *Essays in Elizabethan History* (London, 1958), pp. 59-84, on the tenor of late Elizabethan court life. Stephen Orgel, "Making Greatness Familiar," *Genre*, 15 (1982), 41-48, has suggestive comments about late Elizabethan chivalry.

10. G. B. Harrison, *The Life and Death of Robert Devereux Earl of Essex* (London, 1937), pp. 274-75.

11. There have been a number of interesting particular studies, among them Paul N. Siegel's "Shakespeare and the Neo-Chivalric Cult of Honor," *The Centennial Review of Arts and Sciences*, 8 (1964), 39-70, which focuses on the code of the duello; Sheldon Zitner's "Hamlet, Duellist," *University of Toronto Quarterly*, 34 (1969), 1-18, which discusses *Hamlet* and the duello; and Frances A. Yates' controversial *Shakespeare's Last Plays* (London, 1978), which discusses the late plays in the context of the chivalric revival at the court of Prince Henry.

12. A. C. Bradley, *Shakespearean Tragedy* (London, 1904), pp. 230-31.

13. The literature on this subject is vast, but besides Stone's *Crisis of the Aristocracy* see J. H. Hexter's seminal essays printed in revised versions in *Reappraisals in History* (London, 1961), esp. "The Myth of the Middle Class in Tudor England," pp. 71-116, and "Storm Over the Gentry," pp. 117-62.

14. I owe this apt image to O'Connell, "The Bourgeois Hero-Tale," p. 272.

15. *Crisis of the Aristocracy*, p. 77.

16. Giorgio Melchiori makes this point in his suggestive "Shakespeare and the New Economics of His Time," *Review of National Literatures*, 3 (1972), 123-37. Melchiori's general argument is that Shakespeare's ambiguity reveals his full awareness of the social changes taking place in his time, but his discussion is grounded in a misleading conception of clear class distinctions in the period.

17. "Othello: An Essay to Illustrate a Method," *The Hudson Review*, 4 (1951), 165-203. In a few brilliant pages (pp. 165-69) Burke anticipates many of the points made here in a different context.

18. On possession and dispossession in Elizabethan England see Keith Thomas, *Religion and the Decline of Magic* (London, 1971), pp. 477-92, and D. P. Walker, *Unclean Spirits: Possession and Exorcism in France and England in the Late Sixteenth and Early Seventeenth Centuries* (London, 1981). On *Othello* see David Kaula's excellent "Othello Possessed: Notes on Shakespeare's Use of Magic and Witchcraft," *Shakespeare Studies*, 2 (1966), 112-32. See also Stephen Greenblatt's extremely suggestive "*King Lear* and Harsnett's 'Devil-Fiction,'" *Genre*, 15 (1982), 239-42.

19. *Volpone*, ed. Alvin B. Kernan (New Haven, Conn., 1962), p. 38.

20. See Norman Council, "Ben Jonson, Inigo Jones, and the Transformation of Tudor Chivalry," *ELH*, 47 (1980), 259-75.

21. *Ben Jonson: The Complete Masques*, ed. Stephen Orgel (New Haven, Conn., 1969), p. 149.

22. *The Knight of the Burning Pestle*, 1.1.271-77; ed. John Doebler, Regents Renaissance Drama Series (London, 1967), p. 24. Doebler suggests 1607 as a likely date for the play.

23. See *The Order of Things: An Archaeology of the Human Sciences* (London, 1970), esp. pp. 17-50.

24. *The Political Unconscious: Narrative as a Socially Symbolic Art* (Ithaca, N.Y., 1981), pp. 115-16.

25. Cf. Franco Moretti: Shakespeare "may announce the dawn of bourgeois civilization, but not by prefiguring it. On the contrary, he demonstrates inexorably how, obeying the old rules, which are the only ones he knows, the world can only fall apart," *Signs Taken For Wonders: Essays in the Sociology of Literary Forms* (London, 1983), p. 68. Moretti's exciting discussion of Elizabethan and Jacobean tragedy also appears in abridged form as "'A Huge

Eclipse': Tragic Form and the Deconsecration of Sovereignty," *Genre,* 15 (1982), 7-40.

LANGUAGE AND IMAGERY

Graham Bradshaw (essay date 1992)

SOURCE: "Obeying the Time in *Othello*: A Myth and the Mess It Made," in *English Studies,* Vol. 73, No. 3, June, 1992, pp. 211-28.

[*In the following essay, Bradshaw explores whether Othello consummates his marriage to Desdemona, examining the element of timing in the play.*]

Although it is factitious and distracting, the theory or myth of 'double time' is still respectfully trundled out in every modern scholarly edition of *Othello,* even the most recent.[1] It has been as long-lived as Nahum Tate's adaptation of *King Lear,* which held the stage for a century and a half, and, like that adaptation, deserves to be firmly laid to rest. It betrays its bad nineteenth century provenance in three different (though related) ways. First, it expects Shakespearean poetic drama to repay an approach which (as C.P. Sanger's examination of the handling of time in *Wuthering Heights* famously showed) is more appropriate to mid-nineteenth century novels; this, as Jane Adamson crisply put it, leads 'our attention away from Othello's obsession, towards the kind of details that might obsess an Inspector from Scotland Yard'.[2] Secondly, it is bardolatrous, and offends against what Richard Levin has called the undiscussed principle of Knowing When to Give Up.[3] For although the theory describes and depends on what is unashamedly called a 'trick', which makes a few scrupulous critics like Bradley and Emrys Jones squeamish, this is usually seen as an occasion for bardolatrous rejoicing. Finally, the theory cannot be separated from that nineteenth century tendency which found its glorious apotheosis in Verdi's *Otello.* Othello is the 'Noble' Moor, Desdemona is beatified, Iago is demonised—and, in the opera, even gets a satanic 'Credo'. There is then no need for a drastically compressed time scheme, and indeed Verdi's lovers, like Giraldi Cinthio's in the Italian source story, have been married for some time: here Arrigo Boito, Verdi's brilliant librettist and collaborator in *Otello* and *Falstaff,* might just as well have claimed of *Otello* what he claimed of *Falstaff*—that he had returned the Shakespearean play to its native Italian source.[4] *Otello* is a work of genius, and the 'Double Time Scheme' a product of misguided bardolatrous ingenuity; but neither makes sense of (I want to say, more bluntly, the nineteenth century couldn't make sense of) the dramatic and psychological effect of Shakespeare's *purposefully* drastic compression of the loose, indefinite 'romance' time in the Italian novella.[5]

As Emrys Jones emphasises in *Scenic Form in Shakepeare,*[6] it is important not to confuse 'double time' with accelerated time, which is theatrically indispensable, commonplace, and usually untroubling. So, for example, nearly five hours of 'stage' time and less than a minute of 'real' time pass *between* that moment in 2.2 when we hear the Herald proclaim 'full libertie of Feasting from this present houre of five', and our hearing Iago observe in 2.3 that "tis not yet ten o'clocke'. What follows in 2.3 is more remarkable, since the first night in Cyprus passes *during* this scene; Jones pertinently compares this with *Richard III,* 5.3, which takes us through the night before the battle of Bosworth. So, by the time the scene ends, the triumphant Iago can tell Roderigo that

> Thou know'st we worke by Wit, and not by Witchcraft
> And Wit depends on dilatory time,

and exclaim, with self-congratulatory cheerfulness:

> Introth 'tis Morning;
> Pleasure, and Action, make the houres seeme short.
> (2.3.362-3, 368-9)

Indeed this is exuberantly and unnervingly witty: the surrogate dramatist who has produced chaos in this scene and whose reference to 'Witchcraft' gleefully recalls his earlier triumph over Brabantio seems here to be sharing a professional joke with the real dramatist, whose own skill in managing this scene's *accelerated* time has helped to 'make the houres seeme short'.

The third act follows in similarly precipitate fashion. When Iago encounters Cassio again in 3.1 he asks, 'You have not bin a-bed then?', and Cassio reminds him that 'the day had broke before we parted'; Emilia then enters, telling Cassio (and us) that the 'Generall and his wife are talking' of Cassio's disgrace—not were, but 'are', talking of it, now. Although Emilia has heard enough of this conversation to be able to assure Cassio that Desdemona 'speakes for you stoutly', while Othello 'protests' that he 'needs no other Suitor, but his likings' to reinstate Cassio after a prudent interval, Cassio determines to stay for 'some breefe Discourse' with Desdemona 'alone'. The brief glimpse of Othello in 3.2 shows him already busy with the day's work: the letters for the Senate have already been written, and he sets off to inspect the 'Fortification'. By now the play is half over, without its being at all obvious that this is a play—the play—about 'adultery' and jealousy'.

Throughout this first half of the play the only indeterminate period of time is that taken up by the voyage to Cyprus, when (it is emphasised) Othello and Desdemona are in different ships. To say there is nothing troubling about this carefully managed compression of the Italian story's time scheme would be heartless: to be sure, it maximises tension and the continuity between the scenes in a theatrically impressive way, but it also ensures—takes pains to ensure—that the newly married lovers have so little time together. When Othello leads Desdemona off to bed some hours after their arrival in Cyprus (and immediately after telling Cassio to report the next morning at *his* 'earliest' convenience) he confirms that the marriage still has not been consummated:

> Come my deere Love,
> The purchase made, the fruites are to ensue,
> That profit's yet to come 'tweene me, and you.
>
> (2.3.10-12)

The stage direction for Iago's entrance follows these lines, leaving open the possibility that he arrives on stage just in time to hear Othello's words and perhaps register some malignantly interested response. Be that as it may, his next words show that Iago is well aware that the marriage still hasn't been consummated, and he immediately insinuates, in his busy, tirelessly malicious way, that Othello is neglecting his official duties:

> 'tis not yet ten o'th'clocke. Our Generall cast us thus earely for the love of his
> Desdemona:
> Who, let us not therefor blame; he hath not yet made wanton the night with her . . .
>
> (2.3.13-16)

Learning that the marriage still hasn't been consummated is, for the audience, a confirmation rather than a surprise—precisely because Shakepeare's handling of time has been both careful and suggestive, constantly bringing home how little time these lovers are allowed together. In the second scene they were interrupted by Iago's warning that Brabantio's posse is on its way. Then, after Desdemona's bold affirmation in the Senate scene that she would not be 'bereft' of the 'Rites', it was determined that the newly-weds would leave that night, in different ships; as Othello tells Desdemona, he has

> but an houre
> Of Love, of wordly matter, and direction
> To spend with thee. We must obey the time.
>
> (1.3.329-331)

And of course in 2.3 they are disturbed once again, by that riot which Iago engineers; after quelling the riot Othello goes off to dress Montano's wounds while Desdemona goes back to bed. Indeed, the accelerated time in 2.3 makes it impossible to know how much time the lovers have together before they are disturbed; although critics assume that the marriage is consummated, it is not clear whether this happens before or after the riot, or not at all.

I shall return to this point later, but advocates of the double time theory are more concerned that Desdemona hasn't had time to sleep with Cassio. So, the 'difficulty' which—as the New Arden editor puts it—threatens to make 'nonsense' of the 'dramatic action' is that within the play's 'short time' there is no time in which 'adultery' could have ocurred. Nobody doubts that (as Frank Kermode assures us in the Riverside edition) Shakespeare 'is clearly aware' of this difficulty.[7] But we are to suppose that, having taken such pains to get into it, Shakespeare 'resolved' it not by a real extension, or loosening, of the stage time, like that in the second half of *The Merchant of Venice*,[8] but by what the New Arden editor, M. R. Ridley, describes as a craftily engineered 'trick': 'What Shakespeare is doing is to present, before our eyes, an unbroken series of events happening in "short time", but to present them against a background, of events not presented but implied, which gives the needed impression of "long time"' (p. lxx). Instead of feeling uneasy about a play that must resort to a trick 'to make the whole progress of the plot credible' (p. lxix), the excited Ridley affirms that this 'throws light on Shakespeare's astonishing skill and judgement as a practical craftsman': 'He knew to a fraction of an inch how far he could go in playing a trick upon his audience, and the measure of his success is precisely the unawareness of the audience in the theatre that any trick is being played' (p. lxx). Dover Wilson similarly invites us to discover and marvel over 'yet another piece of dramatic legerdemain, the most audacious in the whole canon, which has come to be known as Double Time'.[9]

2

One strange feature of this argument appears in that question-begging emphasis on a needful 'impression': since 'short time' is also, and no less, an 'impression' or dramatic illusion, it is hard to see what could prevent the one 'impression' jarring against the other. Moreover, although having an 'impression' of 'long time' is thought to be wonderfully helpful where Desdemona's (alleged) relationship with Cassio is concerned, it wouldn't be at all helpful to any spectator who then began wondering about Desdemona's (actual) relationship with her husband. What would they be talking about? Where would Othello sleep for however many nights are in question? I hasten to add that I don't for one moment think we do ask such questions, in reading or watching Shakespeare's play. But then *Othello* is constantly making us think, and dredging monsters in the mind—whereas the presumed point of creating the 'impression' of 'long time' is to prevent thought.

Another general difficulty is that the 'trick' can work only if we first *notice,* but then *don't* think about, the various alleged 'instances' and 'indications' of an illusory period of 'long time'.[10] Here the argument becomes alarmingly circular, and also depends on an elaborate but confidently predictive set of assumptions about what our old, dim friend—the Audience as Monolithic Entity: a fabulous beast with many bodies but a single, unimpressive mind—can be relied upon to notice or not to notice. Evidently, we *don't* reflect, when reading or watching *Othello,* that there has been no time for Desdemona to commit adultery. But then, it's assumed, we *would* notice this, or would have noticed it, were it not for all those craftly planted 'indications' of an illusory period of 'Long Time'; and this in turn assumes that we *will* notice, and be tricked by, the 'indications' of 'long time'. Finally, this magic circle closes with the further assurance, or assumption, that we *won't* also notice and reflect on the discrepancy between the 'short time' of the stage action and the illusory 'impression' of 'long time'. Noticing that discrepancy would of course expose the very 'difficulty' which the 'trick' is to prevent us from noticing—along with other new difficulties which, we shall see, the 'trick' introduces. But later, as a kind of reward, we are also being invited to notice, and marvel at, this 'legerdemain' as a supreme instance of Shakespearean art. Part of the theory's appeal is that of feeling superior—of being initiated into a bardolatrous inner circle that knows how the trick works and is (as Catherine Earnshaw might say, but all this is very nineteenth century) incomparably above and beyond that dumb uncomprehending creature, the Audience.

Something is evidently wrong, but how much is wrong in Shakespeare's play? To take one of the 'instances', it is apparent—on reflection, if not in the theatre—that Lodovico's arrival in Cyprus in Act IV is implausibly rapid, and involves the sort of discrepancy which diligent editors are quite properly expected to spot, and try to account for. As the very diligent New Arden editor observes, 'the government of Venice can hardly be supposed to recall Othello till there has been time for the report of the Turkish disaster to reach them and for them to send the order for recall' (p. lxx). Here is a case where we might readily agree that Shakespeare has nodded. Perhaps he failed to notice the lapse; perhaps he noticed it but saw that nothing was to be done, since he could hardly postpone the play's climax for however many days would suffice to forestall such a fribblingly literal-minded objection. We cannot know either way; more to the point, we have little reason to care. So long as we do regard it as an instance of nodding—of Shakespeare failing to notice what few members of his audience would notice—it is not difficult to account for as a loose end, or unwanted consequence of Shakespeare's drastic compression of the Italian story's loose and indeterminate time scheme. However, it is a quite different matter to suppose that this is, as the New Arden editor tells us, a 'very clear instance' of the conscious, deliberate and wonderfully crafty way in which the Bard tricks us by including various 'indications' of an illusory period of 'long time'. Nor could we suppose that the trick works in this 'very clear instance' unless we believe what seems inherently unlikely: that the dim but sturdily reliable Audience (which, if we gave it a shape and form, might resemble Orwell's Boxer) could be counted upon to take in the 'indication', though without thinking any more about it.

Let us try another, instructively different 'instance'. Beady-eyed sleuths have assumed that Bianca's complaint about Cassio's weeklong absence (3.4.173) must refer to a period of time spent in Cyprus:

> *Bianca:*
> 'Save you (Friend *Cassio*).
> *Cassio:*
> What make you from home?
> How is't with you, my most faire *Bianca*?
> Indeed (sweet Love) I was comming to your house.
> *Bianca:*
> And I was going to your Lodging, *Cassio*.
> What? keepe a weeke away? Seven dayes and Nights?
> Eight score eight houres? And Lovers absent howres
> More tedious then the Diall, eight score times?
> Oh weary reck'ning.
> *Cassio:*
> Pardon me, *Bianca:*
> I have this while with leaden thoughts beene prest,
> But I shall in a more continuate time
> Strike off this score of absence . . .
>
> (3.4.168-79)

I have quoted so much of this dreadfully undistinguished exchange because I don't want to be accused of special pleading: Cassio must live in army lodgings and Bianca clearly can't, but it's easy to see how the references to her 'house' and his 'Lodging' made double-time sleuths pounce—supposing that the week in question has passed in Cyprus, and that Cassio's fumbled excuse for his weeklong absence refers back to his catastrophe on the first night in Cyprus. Nonetheless, this must be wrong. If we do take Bianca's reference to a weeklong absence as another 'indication' of 'long time', then a moment's reflection is enough to suggest that the long time in question must be real not illusory, while the period of time spent in Cyprus must then be considerably longer than a week—since it is also being assumed that the liaison between Cassio and Bianca has run its whole course in Cyprus. We see the New Arden editor assuming this (without reflecting further) when he observes that, although there is 'no doubt' that Iago's reference to Bianca as a 'Huswife, that by selling her desires / Buyes her selfe Bread, and Cloath' (4.1.94-5) gives 'Huswife' its bawdy sense, meaning that Bianca is a courtesan, 'there is also little doubt that Bianca is also a housewife in the normal sense, a citizen of Cyprus, with her own house, and not a mere camp-follower' (p. 141). Norman Sanders hedges on this point in the recent New Cambridge edition, saying that 'there is no clear evidence in the play for or against the idea that Cassio knew Bianca before he landed in Cyprus' (p. 189); but again a moment's reflection suggests what more is 'clear'. For if the relationship was going on before the journey to Cyprus, there is no need to take Bianca's reference to a weeklong absence as an 'indication' of 'long time'; moreover, the alternative—supposing that they have been in Cyprus for more than a week—produces a quite horrendous difficulty, since the business with the handkerchief in 4.1 is so important within the main action. Nobody can suppose that 4.1 is taking place on the second day in Cyprus *and* more than a week after the arrival in Cyprus. Iago acquires the handkerchief in 3.3, and that scene clearly takes place on the first morning in Cyprus. In the latter part of 3.4 Cassio enters with Iago and gives Bianca the handkerchief he has found in his 'lodging'; in the next scene—4.1—she angrily returns it, having examined it 'even now' and found impossible to 'take out'. Time passes between and during these successive scenes, but how much time? Pressing Ridley's argument to its logical conclusion would mean having to suppose that in the handkerchief scene we have that impression of 'short time' which the stage action establishes, *and* a cunningly contrived 'impression' of an illusory period of 'long time', *and* a logically inescapable impression of non-illusory 'long time'.

The 'double time' theory cannot resolve this difficulty, since it is what has produced it. Nor can I believe that any spectator or reader who was not already distracted by the theory, and peering excitedly round every textual corner for 'evidence' to support it, could suppose that Bianca's complaint shows that a week has passed in Cyprus without also feeling some disturbance and dissatisfaction. Yet the difficulty dissolves if we forget the theory and stay with the 'short time'. If the meetings between Cassio and Bianca in Acts III and IV take place later on the second day in Cyprus, Bianca's complaint about a weeklong absence then confirms that she was already Cassio's mistress in Venice—where he was already avoiding her, since he likes sleeping with her but has no intention of marrying her. The doting, determined Bianca has followed him to Cyprus, provoking Cassio's complacent complaint to Iago that she 'haunts me in every place' (4.1.132): she is a camp-follower in this literal sense, while he, like Mann's Felix Krull, understands that since he is irresistible he should try to make some allowances.

3

In the Italian story the captain is married; it is Shakespeare who makes his captain a ladies' man, invents 'the faire Bianca', and so provides his play with three couples or two trios of men and women with very different attitudes towards the opposite sex, sexual relationships, and marriage. It is not easy to believe that in inventing the Cassio-Bianca liaison Shakespeare never considered when and where it starts. If we suppose that it starts in Cyprus this produces far more problems than the only alternative—which is to stay with the 'short time'. But then that also helps with two textual cruces, which have led editors who are loyal to the nonsense about double time to pronounce Shakespeare 'careless' in his handling of Cassio. They are another part of the mess the myth of double time has made.

We know from Othello's first speech to the Senators that he has spent the last nine months in Venice and found this first experience of civilian life enervating:

> since these Armes of mine, had seven years pith,
> Till now, some nine Moones wasted, they have us'd
> Their deerest action, in the Tented Field . . .
>
> (1.3.83-5)

We also know that during this period Cassio has been with Othello, who *prefers* him to Iago not only as his chosen lieutenant, but also as the close, trusted friend who frequently accompanied him in his secret wooing and knew of Othello's love 'from first to last' (3.3.97). The obvious need for discretion in that case explains Cassio's circumspection in the play's second scene when he pretends not even to know whom Othello might have married, and asks Iago, 'To who?' (1.2.53). Similarly, keeping to the 'short time' yields a consistent explanation of that other much debated 'crux' which is so often said to show that Shakespeare is careless or that the text needs emendation: Iago's apparently knowing but mysterious joke about Cassio being 'A Fellow almost damn'd in a fair Wife' (1.1.18) seems mysterious and is knowing because Iago already knows what we cannot yet know.[11] Cassio is 'almost damn'd in a faire Wife' because, although *he* wants nothing more than a sexually convenient liaison with the 'very faire *Bianca*', she is determined to marry him—and because, for Iago, to be almost married is to be almost married is to be almost damned.

Iago clearly knows about the Cassio-Bianca relationship and its difficulties in 4.1, when we hear him planning to make use of that knowledge:

> Now will I question *Cassio* of *Bianca*,
> A Huswife, that by selling her desires
> Buyes her selfe Bread, and Cloath. It is Creature
> That dotes on *Cassio,* (as 'tis the Strumpets plague
> To be-guile many, and be be-guil'd by one)
> He, when he heares of her, cannot restraine
> From the excesse of Laughter.
>
> (4.1.93-7)

Unless we have been distracted by the 'double time' theory, it is also clear that whatever Iago knows about this liaison in 4.1, on the second day in Cyprus, must also have been known to him in the play's first scene, which takes place only hours before Iago and Cassio set off (again in different ships) for Cyprus. But the New Arden and New Cambridge editors have been distracted by the theory. Ridley explains in his long note on 'A Fellow almost damn'd in a faire Wife' that this cannot allude to Cassio's liaison with Bianca, since at this 'moment he has not met her' (p. 4)—just as Barbara Everett refers to, and supposes that Iago's cynical joke cannot refer to, 'Cassio's future affair with the whore, Bianca' (p. 209). And in the recent New Cambridge edition Norman Sanders recycles the idea that both Iago's remark and the way in which Cassio 'appears to be completely ignorant of Othello's interest in Desdemona' in 1.2 are 'inconsistencies', and make the character of Cassio 'something of a puzzle' (pp. 189, 16).

I think this wrong, but it might be objected that the kind of explanation I am offering is embarrassingly *like* the argument for 'double time', which floats on an elaborate and implausible tapestry of assumptions about what an audience would or would not notice in performance. Yet there is an important difference.

Certainly, no spectator watching the play for the first time could know, when Cassio asks, 'To who?', that Cassio has reason to be discreet. Edwin Booth's recommendation that the actor playing Cassio should signal circumspection—letting on that there is something Cassio isn't letting on—is pedantically fussy and dramatically unhelpful: even if we noticed and stored the signal we couldn't make sense of it until the revelations in 3.3, while any such signalling would threaten to make Cassio seem the kind of friend who couldn't be trusted to keep a confidence. Similarly, nobody watching the play for the first time and hearing Iago describe Cassio as 'almost damn'd in a faire Wife' could know about the liaison with Bianca and its difficulties. Shakespeare is giving Iago and Cassio lines that are consistent with their characters and situation—but the first-time spectator or reader is in no position to see how.

In other words, this kind of explanation is peculiar because it addresses a peculiar kind of 'problem': the problem is as remote as its solution from theatrical experience. No spectator would see the 'inconsistency' in Cassio's question, or start trembling before a 'crux'. As for Iago's joke, since it is ambiguously phrased a spectator might feel uncertain how to take it, or might just mistake it, supposing that Cassio must be married and, for some reason, badly matched. The play has only just begun, Cassio has only just been mentioned, and we know nothing about Bianca. We are only beginning to put things together and make sense of what we are making out: in a significant sense we *expect* to understand, and have no reason to suspect that our information may be contradictory. In both cases the 'problem' or 'crux' appears only when we are studying the text closely and, as it were, reading and thinking forwards and backwards—or when we are reading the text in a modern scholarly edition and letting our eye be dragged down to the ballast of notes beneath the precious ribbon of Shakespearean matter. As that ribbon thins, we know that scrupulous editors have discovered a difficulty which we had better attend to, now, if we want to be sure we won't forget its existence; but unfortunately, because editors are usually more concerned with the play as text than with the text as play, they rarely point out (or notice) when a difficulty which the text throws out and which has exercised generations of editors isn't apparent in performance. The 'problem' is there in the text but, like its explanation, cannot be a part of our initial dramatic experience.

This peculiar kind of problem is best considered as a question about dramatic intention. Shakespeare clearly *was* in a unique situation to be thinking backwards and forwards, and wouldn't have given Cassio his question or Iago that joke unless he thought the lines meant something when he wrote them. Shakespeare wrote quickly, and on the whole rather well, but he could write badly, as in that slovenly verse exchange between Cassio and Bianca; he could fail to notice some problems which are there in the text *and* there in the play, like Lady Macbeth's giving suck or Jessica's account of conversations between Shylock and Tubal which could only have taken place after her elopement; he could be negligent about minor matters and characters, like Lodovico's implausibly rapid arrival in Cyprus. But such things aren't as surprising as it would be if, after taking pains to compress his time scheme and keep Othello and Desdemona apart, Shakespeare had carelessly given them an extra week or two in Cyprus without considering what they might do there, or talk about. As for Cassio and Bianca, Shakespeare *is* perfunctory about filling in the background of their relationship. Ibsen once remarked that he liked to work everything out 'down to the last button' before beginning to write; Shakespeare doesn't attend to buttons so closely, but there is an important difference between not working things out and not making them clear. That an explanation *is* available within the play's 'short time' suggests that in this case—as indeed with Iago's joke—the perfunctoriness is that of a dramatist who is writing rapidly and with a very sure sense of his characters and their situations, but hasn't paused to consider whether what is clear to him might seem less than clear to an audience. Once we comb through the *text,* putting together scattered references and weighing alternative possibilities, the text shows why the Cassio-Bianca relationship *must* have been going on during the same nine month period as Othello's secret wooing. To say this is not to suppose that Othello's specific reference to 'nine Moones' would be noticed and remembered by every attentive spectator: the theatre is not a court or classroom, and we might well pay more attention to the information that this was his first experience of civilian life than to his specification of the precise period of time in question. The point is rather that we could expect, and can confirm, that Shakespeare thought carefully about what important matters need to have taken place before his play starts.

4

But now we can observe what is most strange about that basic assumption on which the 'double time' theory rests. It is always taken for granted that there is a 'difficulty' which, as Dover Wilson proudly observes, 'might well have seemed insuperable to any ordinary dramatist': 'For, if Othello and Desdemona consummated their marriage during the first night in Cyprus, when could she have committed the adultery that Iago charges her with?' (p. xxxii). This is true only if we are using the word 'adultery' in a strict, legalistic sense—but what warrant does the play provide for supposing that Othello is concerned only with what might have happened *after* his marriage?

Early in 3.3, the ever vigilant Iago hears Desdemona protest to Othello that she could not have 'so much to do' in pleading on behalf of that very friend who

> came a wooing with you? and so many a time
> (When I have spoke of you disprasingly)
> Hath tane your part . . .
>
> (3.3.71-3)

Once Iago is alone with Othello, he can launch his first direct assault by concentrating on that very question to which Desdemona has just provided the answer:

> *Iago:*
> Did *Michael Cassio*
> When you woo'd my Lady, know of your love?
> *Othello:*
> He did, from the first to last: Why dost thou aske?
> *Iago:*
> But for a satisfaction on my Thought,

> No further harme.
> *Othello:*
> What of thy thought, *Iago?*
> *Iago:*
> I did not thinke he had bin acquinted with hir.
> *Othello:*
> O yes, and went betweene us very oft.
> *Iago:*
> Indeed?
> *Othello:*
> Indeed? I indeed. Discern'st thou ought in that?
> Is he not honest?
> *Iago:*
> Honest, my Lord?
> *Othello:*
> Honest? I, Honest.
> *Iago:*
> My Lord, for ought I know.
> *Othello:*
> What do'st thou thinke?
> *Iago:*
> Thinke, my Lord?
> *Othello:*
> Thinke, my Lord? Alas, thou ecchos't me;
> As if there were some Monster in thy thought
> Too hideous to be shewne . . .

In capitalising on his new knowledge Iago must tread very carefully: if the marriage was consummated hours before, Othello is likely to know whether his wife was a virgin. Throughout this first stage of the assault what is in question is *not* the absurd suggestion that Desdemona has committed adultery with Cassio since her wedding, in what would indeed be 'stolen hours'; Iago's insinuation, as he feels his way forward, is that something took place *before* the wedding, which can be expected to continue, and would explain Desdemona's passionate concern to have Cassio reinstated—and we see the 'Monster' emerging in Othello's own mind as he begins to make out what is in question. Similarly, when Iago later promises Othello that he will persuade Cassio to 'tell the Tale anew; / Where, how, how, how oft, how long ago, and when / He hath, and is againe to cope your wife' (4.1.85-6), this is not another 'indication' of 'long time', as editors tell us: Iago is once again conjuring up that nightmare of a promiscuous liaison which began when Cassio was the trusted friend who 'very oft' went between the lovers. This nightmare is familiar: the situation in the *Sonnets* is not as irrelevant as Dover Wilson supposes.

Yet this suggests that there is no 'difficulty' which requires a 'needful impression' of 'long time'. Not only does the theory of 'Double Time' not work, or work to ruinous effect: it is redundant. At this point, and with these various objections to the theory in mind, it is worth quickly running through those other alleged 'indications' of 'long time' which are conveniently (and confidently) set out in the New Arden introduction and notes. The first two 'instances', involving references to the handkerchief, are perhaps the most troubling, but suggest negligence rather than the carefully laid foundation for the edifice of Double Time. The others are no more compelling than the 'very clear instance' of Lodovico's premature arrival (really an instance of Shakespeare nodding) or of Cassio's weeklong absence from Bianca (which makes good sense in the play's 'short time', and produces nightmarish complications if taken as evidence of 'long time').

(1) 3.3.296 [Iago's asking Emilia to steal the handkerchief 'a hundred times']. There is no reason to suppose that Iago had not often seen it. in Othello's possession or in Desdemona's when, in her girlish way, she kisses and talks to it (3.3.295).

(2) 3.3.313 ['so often did you bid me steale'] Ditto; and, as Ridley himself observes, this 'might have been on voyage'.

(3) 3.3.344-8 [Othello on 'stolne houres of Lust' which 'harm'd not me']. Othello's speech is rapid and excited, but makes better sense in relation to the lengthy period before the marriage. His reference to 'the next night' need not refer to the first night in Cyprus, unless we refuse to suppose that Othello could have kissed Desdemona before marriage.

(4) 3.3.419 ['I lay with Cassio lately']. That is, in Venice, where (as Iago *now* knows) Cassio was 'very oft' alone with Desdemona; the 'foregone conclusion' Othello tormentedly imagines would have preceded the marriage.

(5) 3.4.97 ['I nev'r saw this before'] Desdemona (who has been pursued by other suitors) is simply saying that she has never before seen any sign that Othello is prone to jealousy.

(6) 4.1.50f [the 'second Fit' of 'Epilepsie']. Iago is lying about the earlier fit, in order to get rid of Cassio. Any direct confrontation between Othello and Cassio might be catastrophic, so he improvises cleverly, assuring Cassio that this has happened before and that he knows what to do.

(7) 4.1.85-6 [Iago's promise to make Cassio 'tell the Tale anew']. Iago is speaking of the whole period from the wooing to the present—and into the future.

(8) 4.1.132 ['I was the other day talking on the Seabanke with certaine Venetians']. The conversation was taking place in Venice; ironically, Ridley finds in 'Seabanke' a 'suggestion of something raised above sea-level'—which might in turn have suggested Venice if Ridley were not so sure that Bianca is a Cypriot householder.

(9) 4.1.274 [Iago's 'what I have seene and knowne']. It is quite arbitrary to take this as an indication of 'long time'.

(10) 4.2.23 ['she'le kneele, and pray: I have seene her do't']. Othello's remark makes perfectly good sense if he has only ever seen her kneel and pray once, on their first night in Cyprus.

(11) 4.2.1-10 [dialogue between Emilia and Othello]. This is compatible with 'short time'; Emilia *was* with Desdemona and Cassio, at the beginning of 3.3.

(12) 5.2.213 ['a thousand times committed']. Othello is speaking wildly, not attempting a sober calculation of what sexual feats a young hotblooded Florentine might

manage; still, the exaggeration is less grotesque if the period in question includes the months (up to nine) of the wooing.

To dismiss this horribly long-lived idea that the play depends upon a trick to make its action credible is a critical relief, but historically disquieting—unless we can also see why the theory has had so long a life. Here, rather than simply dismiss it as groundless, we should notice how it is grounded on that willingness to generalise about the audience as a monolithic entity which has resurfaced in the 'new' historiscism[12], and on a corresponding *interpretative* assumption which emerges very clearly in Dover Wilson's Cambridge edition: 'An accusation of premarital incontinence would not have served either [Iago's] purpose or Shakespeare's, since adultery was required to make Othello a cuckold, and it is the dishonourable stigma of cuckoldry that maddens Othello once his confidence has gone and, we may add, greatly increased the excitement for a Jacobean audience' (p. xxxii). This of course raises fundamental questions about what Shakespeare's play is 'about', but Dover Wilson tells us, and in terms which show that persisting nineteenth-century tendency to see Shakespeare's *Othello* in terms more appropriate to Verdi's *Otello:* in 'its simplest terms', 'the tragedy of *Othello* represents the destruction of a sublime love between two noble spirits through the intrigues of a villain devilish in his cunning and unscrupulousness' (p. xxx). These terms are indeed 'simple', or simplistic; they deliver a play very much less intelligent than Shakespeare's, not least by preserving the Romantic, Coleridgean assumption that murdering Desdemona would have been all right, or at least compatible with being very noble, if only she had committed adultery.

5

'We must obey the time', Othello tells his bride: the 'rites' she eagerly awaits must wait. But here too critics who are obedient to the myth of double time get into further difficulties. As I observed earlier, there is nothing in 2.3 to tell us—and the accelerated time makes it more than ever difficult to guess—whether the marriage is consummated before the riot, or after it, or not at all. The established assumption is that it is consummated, and some readings—like that in Stephen Greenblatt's immensely influential *Renaissance Self-Fashioning*—fall apart if we think that it isn't.

Here it seems worth recording how my own experience ran counter to what critics and editors assume we 'naturally' assume. Having seen the play twice as a schoolboy before I ever read it, then read it several times before I 'studied' it and consulted critics, I had always supposed that the marriage wasn't consummated. I still thought that in a 1979 article where I refered to the murder as this marriage's 'poetic consummation', giving that word 'poetic' the unfairly cruel sense it has in talk of 'poetic justice'.[13] That was unguarded, in assuming what is by no means an inevitable reading, and I found myself prompted to a more systematic consideration in 1983, when *Essays in Criticism* published an article called 'Othello's Unconsummated Marriage'.[14] The authors, T.G.A. Nelson and Charles Haines, carefully explored the whole question of whether we are to suppose that the marriage is consummated, and concluded that it isn't. Since they were also arguing that Othello's behaviour is the result of unbearable sexual frustration their reading was diametrically opposed to Greenblatt's, though similarly reductive. Setting that aside, their textual arguments for thinking that the marriage is not consummated were unprecedentedly thorough, but open to three objections.

The first may well seem the most important to readers who assume that consummation takes place in 2.3. Nelson and Haines are confusing 'stage' time with 'real' time when they say that 'Othello and Desdemona have hardly gone to bed when a brawl begins' (p. 4), and that when Othello does, 'in the end, get back to bed' (after going off with the seriously injured Montano to tend his wounds), 'there is, indeed, nothing left of the night' (p. 5). Later, Desdemona's touchingly innocent assumption that the 'pain' on Othello's forehead is caused by 'watching' (3.3.289) confirms that Othello has spent much of the night looking after Montano, but doesn't tell us how much. In other words, Nelson and Haines don't reckon with the complications caused by accelerated time—which is not to be confused with double time. The second objection is prompted by what these critics say of the scene between the clown and the musicians at the start of Act III. Most critics ignore this scene; Nelson and Haines argue, like Lawrence Ross[15], that its dramatic 'point' is to signal that the serenade is 'ill-timed, for the even it is intended to celebrate has not yet taken place' (p. 6). Unfortunately the persuasive argument that the incompetently executed serenade becomes a badly timed, inadvertently mocking *charivari* is shackled to a far from persuasive argument about Othello's 'impotence' and 'temporary failure of virility' (p. 17). The third objection seems to me the most important, and is that Nelson and Haines aren't sufficiently concerned with the wedding sheets. Because they are disposed—like Leavis and Greenblatt—to pluck out the mystery of *Othello* by offering a psychologically reductive account of Othello as a 'case', their textual argument is weakened by their interpretative assumptions. More precisely, because they are so sure *how* the failure to consummate the marriage matters, they aren't sufficiently concerned to specify *when* it most clearly matters, as the play unfolds. Here those sheets matter, quite crucially.

They evidently matter very much to Desdemona in 4.2—either because she has already lost her virginity on them or because she still hasn't and still wants to. 'Prythee', she carefully instructs Emilia, 'Lay on my bed my wedding sheetes, remember' (4.2.105). And when Emilia returns in the next scene to assure Desdemona that she has 'laid those Sheetes you bad me on the bed', she receives this unnerving reply:

> All's one: good Father, how foolish are our minds!
> If I do die before, prythee shrow'd me
> In one of these same Sheetes.
>
> (4.3.23-5)

Laurence Olivier as Othello, Maggie Smith as Desdemona, and Joyce Redman as Emilia in Act II, scene i of the 1965 Warner Brothers-Seven Arts production of Othello.

And in the penultimate scene the idea of bloodied sheets is inflaming Othello's mind, as he determines, 'Thy bed lust-stain'd, shall with Lusts blood bee spotted' (5.1.36).

Here, if anywhere, is a 'difficulty' which threatens to make 'nonsense' of the 'dramatic action'—or, since an interpretative choice is in question, of all those readings which depend upon the assumption that the marriage is consummated. To take an extreme but influential case, Greenblatt's reading altogether depends upon his assumption that Othello 'took' Desdemona's 'virginity', 'shed her blood', and then not only noticed but became violently obsessed by the condition of the wedding sheets. So, in the final scene the play's 'symbolic center' becomes 'increasingly visible' (not before time, since there isn't much left) as the raging Othello 'comes close to revealing his tormenting identification of marital sexuality—limited perhaps to the night he took Desdemona's virginity—and adultery'.[16] Yet this throws out a difficulty which Greenblatt doesn't recognise because his sampling of the text is so partial, and because in offering his curious explanation of why the sheets matter so much to Othello he never explains, or asks, why they also matter so much to Desdemona. Part of the difficulty, put bluntly and indelicately, is that of understanding why, if Desdemona is no longer a virgin, she should want lust-stained sheets relaid. I dare say there is someone, somewhere, who believes that she is wanting to confront her husband with visual proof of her chastity, so that it is a great pity when Othello decides to put out the light. But that only underlines the other part of the difficulty, which is that of understanding what kind of mental defective could first take his wife's virginity and then, the morning after, become convinced of her continued infidelity. Here Greenblatt's reading might well seem to need—or, if it is not to become risible, depend upon—the double time theory which his 'perhaps' discreetly acknowledges. But that theory cannot help here, since 3.3 clearly takes place the morning after the first night in Cyprus, and not even the most convinced advocates of 'long time' suppose that Othello and Desdemona are making love between 3.3 and the murder. If the marriage isn't consummated on that first night in Cyprus it isn't consummated at all; here the double time theory merely blurs the textual and dramatic issues.

I had better add, since Greenblatt's reading is so influential, that its 'historical' component doesn't help either. Where Leavis saw Othello as a deluded egotist Greenblatt sees him as a deluded Christian convert who is unhinged by the neurotic-making dynamics of 'orthodox' Christian (that is, Pauline) teaching on sexuality: so, the 'dark essence of Iago's whole enterprise' is to 'play upon Othello's buried perception of his own sexual relations with Desdemona as adulterous' (p. 233). Greenblatt's exposition of the 'centuries-old', 'orthodox doctrine that governs Othello's sexual attitudes' starts from Jerome's 'An adulterer is he who is too ardent a lover of his wife', and runs through Augustine and Calvin and other 'orthodox' warnings like that in the *King's Book*, 'attributed to Henry VIII', that a man may break the Seventh Commandment and 'live unchaste with his own wife, if he do unmeasurable or inordinately serve his or her fleshly appetite or lust'. In other words, Greenblatt provides an old historicist *cento* of highly selective quotations which briskly cuts through many complicated historical and theological issues and is most obviously selective where it matters most—at the Renaissance end. There is no doubt that the desert fathers took up the Pauline exaltation of celibacy with an anti-sexual vengeance, and that—despite some dissidents, like the fifth-century Synesius of Cyrene—this then dominated 'orthodox' Christian teaching from the fourth to the fourteenth centuries.[17] Nor can we soften the force of Jerome's fourth-century application of the stoic Xystus's ugly little maxim that 'He who loves his won wife too ardently is an adulterer' (*omnis ardentior amator propriae uxoris adulter est*) by supposing that Jerome means that pleasure in marital sex should be ardent but not *too* ardent: in Jerome's majestic view *any* sexual pleasure is excessive and sinful. But this was not quite the view taken by Peter Lombard and Aquinas a millenium later, when they discussed Jerome's recyclings of Xystus's maxim, as appears in this modern theologian's commentary: 'The man thus denounced is not, apparently, he who entertains too warm an affection for his wife, but he whose *amor* (that is, his desire for veneral pleasure—the word here does not mean 'love', as we understand it) is so vehement that it impels him to abandon the restraint which pays careful regard to the *bona matrimonii,* and incites him to treat her as if she were merely, like any other woman, a means of lustful gratifications'.[18] On this view sexual pleasure is not sinful *per se,* although it cannot be pursued for its own sake without sin—a venial sin when sought within marriage, and a mortal sin when sought outside it. Greenblatt doesn't make room for Lombard or Aquinas, and quotes Calvin's warning that 'the man who shows no modesty or comeliness in conjugal intercourse is committing adultery with his wife' as though Calvin thought on this matter like Jerome; yet Calvin specifically and very sternly repudiated Jerome's argument that 'If it is good not to touch a woman, it is bad to touch one'—affirming that sexual intercourse is a pure institution of God and that the idea that 'we are polluted by intercourse with our wives' emanates from Satan (not Paul).[19] Greenblatt quotes from the 'influential' Raymond and Jacobus Ungarelli, but what of Luther, of Thomas Becon's The *Book of Matrimony,* or Erasmus's colloquies on marriage—where there is a direct link, not only with the 'marriage group' of *Sonnets* but with the witty sexual frankness of women in Shakespeare's romantic comedies? After quoting Nicolaus of Ausimo's warning that the conjugal act may be without sin, but only if 'in the performance of this act there is no enjoyment of pleasure', Greenblatt solemnly concludes that 'Few *summas* and no marriage manuals take so extreme a position, but virtually all are in agreement that the active *pursuit* of pleasure in sexuality is damnable'—but are we then to conclude that Shakespeare's audiences would have thought that Desdemona's forthright declaration in the Senate of what Greenblatt himself describes as a 'frankly, though by no means exclusively sexual' passion was 'damnable'? And if not, why not?

To return to the textual and critical issue: were it not for those references to the sheets, the question of whether this marriage has been consummated—whether Othello and Desdemona had slept together once, like Romeo and Juliet, or not at all—wouldn't matter in the same way. It might still occur to us to wonder how Othello could entertain the idea of Desdemona's infidelity if, as Greenblatt supposes, he so recently 'took her virginity' and 'shed her blood'; but such a worry would still be, as it were, dispersed through the latter half of the play. The references to the sheets—not to mention a strawberry-spotted handkerchief—are what make this worry immediately pressing and alarmingly definite. And that throws out another difficulty, the moment we ask what on earth Shakespeare is up to. I take it that we should ask that, ignoring the protests of those who prefer to talk of plays 'emerging' from 'fields of discourse', like poppies: one reason we don't argue about how to interpret poppies is that poppies aren't *meant*.[20] And it seems inconceivable that, in so drastically compressing the Italian novella's time scheme, making Othello and Desdemona newly married lovers and then taking such pains to keep them physically apart, Shakespeare never considered whether this marriage was consummated. If we are to think that it is, Shakespeare should have been no less anxious than Iago that Othello shouldn't consider (and that the audience shouldn't notice Othello failing to consider) any physical evidence of Desdemona's virginity—especially in an age when it was not uncommon, after nuptials, to display the bloodied wedding sheets or a blood-spotted (strawberry-spotted!) napkin or handkerchief.

By now we might be relieved that the textual evidence of whether the marriage is or is not consummated in 2.3 is so uncertain. For if we think the received idea that it is consummated throws out too many problems, we are free to prefer the alternative reading. Desdemona wants the sheets to be relaid because she is still a virgin, and still poignantly longs for 'such observancie / As fits the Bridall' (3.4.147-8). When Othello determines that 'Thy Bed lust-stain'd, shall with Lusts blood bee spotted' he is tormenting himself with the deluded thought of what somebody else has done: as Montaigne might say, another bed, other sheets. Virginity, like a life, can only be taken once: in Othello's diseased, self-tormenting imagination all that remains for him to do—the only way in which *he* can 'shed her blood'—is to murder her.

In the final scene that horrible tragicomic irony is given a still more dreadful twist. Just as Desdemona could not bring herself to say the word 'whore' in 4.2, Othello tells the 'chaste Starres' that he cannot 'name' the 'Cause', but will *not* 'shed her blood' (5.2.2-3). 'Yet Ile not shed her blood . . . Yet she must dye . . .': what he is talking about—what he has now changed his mind about—is not whether to kill her, but how. This resolution is still insanely ensnarled with his obsessive sense of what *he* has never done and thinks he can never do—and what his still virginal bride still hopes he will do, as she lies waiting for him on those relaid, unspotted wedding sheets. The murder is indeed this marriage's only consummation, and the ghastly parody of an erotic 'death':

> Desdemona:
> And yet I feare you: for you're fatall then
> When your eyes rowle so. Why I should feare. I know not,
> Since guiltinesse I know not: But yet I feele I feare.
> Othello:
> Thinke on thy sinnes.
> Desdemona:
> They are Loves I beare to you.
> Othello:
> I, and for that thou dy'st.
> Desdemona:
> That death's unnaturall, that kils for loving.
> Alas, why gnaw you so your nether-lip?
> Some bloody passion shakes your very Frame . . .

Her 'Rose' is 'pluck'd' when the 'Light' is finally 'put out'. I find myself wanting to ask not only Greenblatt but every critic who thinks Othello took Desdemona's virginity not long before, on this bed and these relaid sheets, how they understand Othello's horrible, wrenching words when he realises what he has done and bends over what is now a corpse:

> Cold, cold, my Girle?
> Even like thy Chastity.

Indeed he has not 'shed her blood': that final sniffing and snuffing has been his only 'possession of this Heavenly sight'. The irony seems obvious, and 'as grim as hell'.

Notes

Quotations from *Othello* are from the First Folio; scene and line references are to *The Riverside Shakespeare*, ed. G. Blakemore Evans (Boston, 1974).

1. The double time theory was first outlined by John Wilson ('Christopher North') in *Blackwood's Magazine,* November 1849; April and May 1850. The lengthy discussion in the Variorum *Othello,* ed. H.H. Furness (Philadelphia, 1886), pp. 358-372, is rather more sceptical than the lengthy discussions in M.R. Ridley's New Arden edition (London, 1965), pp. lxvii-lxx, and Norman Sanders's recent New Cambridge edition (Cambridge, 1984), pp. 14-17.
2. Jane Adamson, *'Othello' as Tragedy: Some problems of judgement and feeling* (Cambridge, 1980), p. 7.
3. Richard Levin, 'Shakespearean Defects and Shakespeareans' Defenses', in Maurice Charney, ed., *'Bad' Shakespeare: Revaluations of the Shakespeare Canon* (London and Toronto, 1988), pp. 23-36.
4. See my essay 'Verdi and Boito as Translators', in James Hepokoski, *Giuseppe Verdi: Falstaff* (Cambridge, 1983), pp. 152-171. For an excellent discussion of what *Otello* owes to the nineteenth-century Continental understanding of Shakespeare see Hepokoski's 'Boito and F.-V. Hugo's "Magnificent Translation": A Study in the Genesis of the *Otello* Libretto', in Arthur Groos and Roger Parker's collection, *Reading Opera* (Princeton, 1988), pp. 34-59.
5. See the discussion of Shakespeare's treatment of Italian *novelle* in my *Shakespeare's Scepticism* (Brighton, 1987), pp. 22-4.
6. See the very searching chapter on 'Time and Continuity' in Emrys Jones, *Scenic Form in Shakespeare* (Oxford, 1971), especially pp. 41-3 and 54-63.
7. *The Riverside Shakespeare,* p. 1199.
8. I discuss this in *'The Merchant of Venice:* Does Jessica Lie?', *Meridian* (October 1986), pp. 99-108.
9. See John Dover Wilson's New Cambridge edition of *Othello* (Cambridge. 1957), p. xxxi.
10. The quotations in this paragraph are all from Ridley's discussion in the New Arden edition.
11. In *Young Hamlet* (Oxford, 1989) Barbara Everett discusses this at length, as 'one of the best-known and longest-unresolved cruces in the canon', and proposes that *damn'd* (Q: *dambd*) should read *limn'd:* pp. 208-225. The Furness Variorum footnotes cover five pages.
12. At the outset of *Shakespearean Negotiations* (Oxford, 1988) Greenblatt explains that the '"Shakespearean theater" is the product of collective intentions' and 'manifestly addresses its audience as collectivity'; it 'depends upon a felt community', and there is 'no attempt to isolate and awaken the sensibilities of each individual member of the audience, no sense of the disappearance of the crowd' (p. 5).
13. 'Another Sentimentalist's *Othello?*', *Dutch Quarterly Review,* vol. 4 (1979), pp. 49-61.
14. T.A.G. Nelson and Charles Haines, 'Othello's Unconsummated Marriage', *Essays in Critisism,* vol. 33 (1983). pp. 1-18.
15. See Lawrence J. Roses, 'The Meaning of Strawberries in Shakespeare', *Studies in the*

Renaissance 7 (1960) pp. 225-240, and 'Shakespeare's "Dull Clown" and Symbolic Music', *Shakespeare Quarterly* 17 (1966), pp. 107-28. Curiously, these very scholarly essays both approach the issue that concerns Nelson and Haines by different routes, without pressing to their conclusion. They must have felt Ross was mumbling the game he dared not, quite, bite.

16. Stephen Greenblatt, *Renaissance Self-Fashioning: From More to Shakespeare*, (Chicago, 1980). p. 251.

17. See Peter Brown's magnificent study, *The Body and Society: Men, Women and Sexual Renunciation in Early Christianity* (New York, 1988).

18. D.S. Bailey, *The Man-Woman Relation in Christian Thought* (London, 1959), p. 137.

19. See Bailey, pp. 171-2.

20. See the queer but representative passage in *Shakespeare: The Play of History* (London, 1987) where Graham Holderness explains why 'We have not . . . made the personal qualities of William Shakespeare our subject': 'with no disrespect to the writer's talents or powers, it seems safer to locate the drama's play of ideological contradictions in the heterogeneous and pluralistic fields of discourse from which it emerged, rather than to infer superhuman potencies in an "author" whose name may have been, for all we know, legion'. A work of art is worked.

David Lucking (essay date 1994)

SOURCE: "Putting Out the Light: Semantic Indeterminacy and the Deconstitution of Self in *Othello*," in *English Studies*, Vol. 75, No. 2, March, 1994, pp. 110-22.

[*In the essay below, Lucking explores Othello's attempts to assess and define his identity.*]

One of the cardinal tenets underpinning contemporary theory in the fields of linguistics, semiotics and literary criticism is that enunciated in Saussure's famous assertion that the relation between signifier and signified is an arbitrary one. Although this intuition is by now indelibly associated with the author of its most celebrated formulation, very clear anticipations of the notion can be detected in the literature of preceding centuries.[1] While the statements to which I am referring are predominantly philosophical in character, in the case of certain works the arbitrary nature of signification does not constitute a theoretical problem only, but is conceived instead as entailing potentially far-reaching consequences for all human beings. We are constrained to use signs in order to compose experience and render it intelligible but, because the signs we employ are only contingently related to the world we seek to impose them on, a radical incongruity between the sign and its referent can make itself felt at any moment. And because as culturally constituted beings we inhabit a world of signification, within the framework of which we formulate our own selves as well as the reality that surrounds us, this means that not only the codes we employ, but in the final analysis our very identities as well, are perpetually in jeopardy.

In this paper I propose to discuss the manner in which Shakespeare explores these ideas in *Othello,* a work that is vitally concerned with the nature of signification and the problematics involved in the interpretation of signs. My argument will be that *Othello* might instructively be analyzed as a dramatization of the existential consequences ensuing from the disruption of a single paradigmatic system of semiotic contrapositions, a system which Shakespeare himself habitually manipulated in the form of puns and other varieties of verbal play. Reduced to essentials, this system consists in the image clusters light/white/fair on the one hand, and dark/black/foul on the other, a structure of binary oppositions which embraces the sphere of values as well as that of physical properties, and which therefore establishes a parallel between otherwise discrete areas of experience.[2] Although in exploiting such a pattern Shakespeare was drawing on a consolidated iconographical tradition, he did so in ways that were very much peculiar to himself, ways which are symptomatic of the critical and profoundly dialectical cast of his thought.

In the European cultural tradition at least, the clusters of words and images I am examining have been more or less consistently employed to refer to concepts which, although heterogeneous in character and even type, are nonetheless considered to be related by some degree of affinity. Light, or its associated colour white, might variously symbolize goodness, virtue, life, reason, order, truth, purity, or faith; while darkness, or the colour black, serves as the emblem of the contrary of all these things. These two image-families thus comprise categories which are mutually exclusive and yet formally related to one another if only in an antithetical sense—which is to say that a term in one cluster might be definable only in inverse relation to a corresponding term in the other. A considerable degree of semantic uncertainty inevitably arises therefore whenever any incompatibility emerges between different associations of the same term, when connotations are invoked which seem to contradict the more customary meanings of the words and hence challenge the stability of the system of polarities these encode. In extreme instances, as in that of the albino whale in *Moby Dick* for example, the physical attribute can become the node or point of intersection between conceptual and emotive complexes which, because they comprehend mutually exclusive properties, are not reconcilable even in principle.[3] In such cases, the sign has become radically ambivalent, transforming itself from vehicle of meaning into mere cipher, designating little other than a semantic vacancy within which conflicting meanings collide.

Through the deft manipulation of the divergent meanings—or simply the denotative and connotative dimensions—of terms belonging to the same cluster, Shakespeare frequently generates an atmosphere of paradox analogous to that which occasions Melville's Ishmael such perplexity. This process can assume a relatively uncomplicated form in which figurative meaning is merely substituted for the literal, as when the Duchess of Gloucester, in the second part of *Henry VI,* responds to public disgrace and the prospect of exile with the lament that henceforth 'dark shall be my light, and night my day'.[4] A somewhat different order of semantic confusion is produced however when multiple connotation is exploited so as to invest words with qualities which are formally opposed to them, thereby making them appear self-contradictory at least on the strictly verbal level. An example of this occurs when Enobarbus in *Antony and Cleopatra,* speaking of the sumptuous banquets to which he has been witness while in Egypt, reports that 'we did sleep day out of countenance, and made the night light with drinking'.[5] In much the same way, the use of the word 'fair' in the sense of beautiful makes possible such elaborate transpositions of meaning as are to be found in Berowne's remark in *Love's Labour's Lost* that Roseline has been born 'to make black fair', which provokes in turn Dumain's sarcastic observation that 'Dark needs no candles now, for dark is light'.[6] These more or less frivolous quibbles on the various meanings of the words 'fair' and 'black', together with their respective cognates and synonyms, anticipate a number of very similar puns in *Othello,* where however they assume a rather less innocuous character. While it would certainly be a gross simplification to suggest that *Othello* is a single pun writ large, there is nonetheless a sense in which the manipulations to which the luminary imagery of the play is subjected enact on the verbal level the movement of the play as a whole, just as there is a sense in which the three witches are forecasting the entire course of events in *Macbeth,* and not merely indulging in idle wordplay, when they too announce that fair is foul and foul is fair.

In *Othello,* the symbolic pattern based on the opposition of light and darkness is of course invoked most vividly in the contrast between the Moor's notorious blackness and Desdemona's no less insistently proclaimed fairness. Initially at least, the clear suggestion is conveyed that the physical attributes of these personages might be emblematic of less manifest qualities of a moral or spiritual nature, that there is an essential continuity in other words between the denotative and connotative aspects of the terms involved. It has been argued indeed that Othello's colour would have assimilated him in the mind of the original spectator to what one critic refers to as the 'exo-cultural stereotype' of the Moor, and that the Elizabethan audience would have projected onto him certain stock expectations—of lustfulness, credulousness, jealousy, bravery, simplicity, etc.—in relation to which his dramatic identity would necessarily have to define itself.[7] Whether we in fact agree that this strictly racial stereotype figures as a significant factor in our response to the play or not, there seems little doubt that the emphatic contrast of black and white is calculated to appeal to a predisposition, conceptually Manichean in tendency, to construe characters and events in terms of radical dichotomies or antithetical principles.

One of the profounder ironies of this drama resides in the fact that Othello himself, whose colour defines one term in the symbolic polarity around which much of the imagery of the play is articulated, is called upon to fathom the significance of precisely that polarity, upon the understanding of which his sense of self ultimately depends. Othello's fundamental problem is how to construe signs, a difficulty compounded in his case by the circumstance that as a foreigner, comparatively unconversant with the complex customs of his adopted country, he is uncertain what readings to place on signs, and even what qualifies as a sign in the first place. It is this perplexity which puts him at the mercy of Iago, to whom he too ingenuously defers as an authority on the category of signs in question, those having to do with the conduct of a 'super-subtle Venetian' such as Desdemona (I.iii.357).[8] His faith in Iago's capacity to interpret such signs with frankness and accuracy is uncritical to the point of being almost culpably obtuse:

> This fellow's of exceeding honesty,
> And knows all qualities, with a learned spirit,
> Of human dealing . . .
>
> (III.iii.263-4)

As his own remarks indicate, however, Iago is not so much an exegete of signs as their accomplished manipulator, who recognizes that there is no inevitable correspondence between sign and referent, and who is therefore able to impose on events whatever constructions suit his evil fancy. It is symptomatic of the immense delight he takes in the ambiguity of signs that he should at one point lower his guard to the extent of swearing by Janus (I.ii.33), and symptomatic too of Othello's enormous naiveté that he should fail so egregiously to take the hint.

The essential character of Othello's dilemma announces itself in the opening scene of the play, when the Moor's trusted 'ancient' declares to Roderigo that

> I must show out a flag, and sign of love,
> Which is indeed but sign.
>
> (I.i.156-7)

In this remarkably candid statement of intent, Iago is punning among other things on the etymology of his own official title, his military rank being that of ensign—or standard-bearer—a term of which the word 'ancient' is a corruption.[9] In Shakespeare's time the term 'ensign' also meant 'sign' or' token', which suggests that Iago is not only a bearer of signs by nominal profession, but himself a 'sign' by titular designation as well.[10] As his own private remarks to Roderigo imply, however, there is no connection whatsoever between the signs he parades before the world and the reality to which they purportedly refer. He commends the shrewdness of those who are only 'trimm'd in forms, and visages of duty' (I.i.50), avows that his ostentatious displays of regard for his general are no more than 'shows of service' (I.i.52), and protests 'not I for love and duty, / But seeming so, for my peculiar end' (I.i.59-60). He habitually defines himself and his conduct in terms of negatives, assuring Roderigo that 'Were I the Moor, I would not be Iago' (I.i.57), and delivering himself of the portentously cryptic announcement that 'I am not what I am' (I.i.65). Othello's ensign thus incarnates what G. Wilson Knight aptly described as the 'spirit of denial',[11] a fact which has induced various critics to compare his role to that of Mephistopheles.[12] Another way of characterizing Iago's dramatic function is to say that he insinuates himself into the world of established values as an infinitely mutable sign whose want of fixed referent calls into question the authority of all other signs.[13] As he himself sardonically acknowledges at one point, 'I am nothing, if not critical' (II.i.119).

To a very large degree this disjunction between outward conduct and underlying intention extends also to the relation between Iago's *covert* activities and the personal motives ostensibly prompting them, which means that even the audience—privy to his soliloquies and confidential asides though it may be—is denied a satisfactory understanding of the nexus. As Coleridge was remarking when he alluded in a famous phrase to 'the motive-hunting of motiveless malignity',[14] although Iago perfunctorily cites several reasons for his animosity towards Othello, they are not really plausible and probably not meant even to appear so. It is to be noted that even at the end of the tragedy, after his villainy has been unmasked and he has nothing more either to gain or to lose, Iago obstinately persists in concealing his true motives: 'what you know, you know, / From this time forth I never will speak word' (V.ii.304-5). This elusiveness is essential to the function Iago performs within the play, for if Shakespeare had furnished him with a truly credible grievance he would have become less menacing at the same time that he became more human. There would have been a definable relation, though only an inverse one, between appearance and reality or, more specifically, sign and substance. As things stand, however, we are presented with signs in abundance, but nothing definite with which to correlate them. The trajectory of the play is essentially that of the process by which Othello himself, who is dependent to a more than average degree upon the stability of the semiotic order, inexorably falls victim to this indeterminateness.

It has already been remarked that the connotations of the colour images that Shakespeare makes use of in this play do not at first seem to deviate in any marked degree from those traditionally assigned to them. At least in appearance, in other words, the symbolic pattern based on the contrast of light and darkness is both coherent and stable, and consonant in all essential respects with the dictates of convention.[15] An instance of this initial orthodoxy may be found in the commonplace equation of blackness with hell invoked by Iago in the opening scene, when by means of a volley of obscene innuendoes he tries to goad Desdemona's father into taking violent action against the Moor:

Even now, very now, an old black ram

Is tupping your white ewe: arise, arise,
Awake the snorting citizens with the bell,
Or else the devil will make a grandsire of you

(I.i.88-91)

Although nobody is expected to take the imputation of diabolism seriously, Brabantio is sufficiently influenced by the infernal associations of blackness as to leap to the conclusion that Othello has resorted to 'practices of cunning hell' to work his will on Desdemona (I.iii.102). 'Damn'd as thou art, thou hast enchanted her' (I.ii.63), he accuses him, several times linking the Moor's dark complexion with the 'foulness' of his alleged tactics (I.ii.62, 73).

At the hastily improvised inquiry subsequently held in the presence of the Duke, however, Othello is exonerated from all suspicion of impropriety in his courtship of Desdemona, the girl having according to her own testimony been won not by 'foul' means but by what one senator describes as 'such fair question, / As soul to soul affordeth' (I.iii.113-14). From what we learn of his past history and personal disposition, such 'fairness' seems to characterize all of Othello's proceedings. If Iago can accurately sum up his own paradoxical identity in the enigmatic statement 'I am not what I am', Othello is quite palpably everything he professes to be—'all in all sufficient' (IV.i.261), as one member of the Senate later puts it. He is, moreover, vividly conscious of this coherence in his personality, confidently asserting even when his conduct falls under temporary suspicion that 'My parts, my title, and my perfect soul, / Shall manifest me rightly' (I.ii.31-2). In terms of the moral and spiritual connotations with which colours are conventionally invested, however, this apparently seamless continuity between what Othello is and what he appears to be, his proud and triumphant integrity as a human being, might seem somewhat at variance with his physical aspect as a black man among whites. If white Iago is not what he is, black Othello is only too emphatically what *he* is, yet it is blackness, not whiteness, that is traditionally associated with the principle of negation. The tribute which the Moor's notable accomplishments elicit from the Duke contains an implicit recognition of such a reversal, an acknowledgement that the conventional values attaching to colour have, in Othello's case, no application:

If virtue no delighted beauty lack,
Your son-in-law is far more fair than black.

(I.iii.289-90)

This is all very well, but the logical inference is that a sign can, through the multiplicity of its potential meanings, effectively contradict itself. It is precisely this possibility, subversive of the conventions which give codes their meanings, which invest experience itself with its shape and significance, that Iago contrives to exploit. If black Othello can, by identifying him exclusively with the 'delighted beauty' of his virtue,[16] be represented as essentially fair, then fair Desdemona can through an inversion of this process be made to look black. 'So will I turn her virtue into pitch' (II.iii.351), Iago proclaims as he prepares to transform fairness itself into its diametrical opposite. This radical transmutation of light into darkness has a precedent in Iago's earlier and less ambitious scheme, represented in this case as well as an attack on colour, to mar the tranquillity of Othello's wedding night, 'poison his delight', by inciting Brabantio against him:

> . . . though that his joy be joy,
> Yet throw such changes of vexation on 't,
> As it may lose some colour.
>
> (I.i.71-3)

Iago's project, consisting in the systematic inversion of a code, is implicitly an attack upon the possibility of signification at large, and to the degree that signs actually constitute the reality in which human beings live, may be seen as tending toward the destruction of the ordered universe itself.

Iago's sinister power derives from the circumstance that, consisting himself solely of empty signs, he is uniquely aware that there is no inevitability in signs or in their relation to what they purport to represent. Signs can be cast adrift from their conventional meanings, to the infinite confusion of those who inhabit—as all men do—a universe of signs. Such a process of semiotic dissociation is to be seen operating in the symbolic metamorphosis undergone by the handkerchief which Othello has bestowed upon his wife as a love-token, a 'flag, and sign of love' par excellence, but once again patently arbitrary in its character as signifier,[17] and ironically susceptible of being transformed into what seems to be an incontrovertible sign of Desdemona's infidelity. Iago's distinctive rhetoric frequently makes use of the discrepancies that can arise between a sign and its referent, or between the various possible meanings of the same sign. He relishes paradoxes that depend on multiple connotation: Cassio, he remarks for instance at the beginning of the play, is a man 'almost damn'd in a fair wife' (I.i.21). The sequence of mildly ribald epigrams with which he entertains Desdemona and Emilia as they are awaiting Othello's arrival in Cyprus reveals how adept he is at juggling with the various meanings of this crucial word 'fair' and its two possible antonyms 'black' and 'foul':

> If she be fair and wise, fairness and wit;
> The one's for use, the other using it.
>
> If she be black, and thereto have a wit,
> She'll find a white, that shall her blackness hit.
>
> She never yet was foolish, that was fair,
> For even her folly help'd her, to an heir.
>
> There's none so foul, and foolish thereunto,
> But does foul pranks, which fair and wise ones do.
>
> (II.i.129-42)

Part of the significance of this humorous interlude lies in the fact that while Iago is exercising his talent for verbal prestidigitation Desdemona is dissembling her anxiety for Othello's safety beneath a false display of levity: 'I am not merry, but I do beguile / The thing I am, by seeming otherwise' (II.i.122-3). However irreproachable her solicitude for her husband may be in itself, in other words, she reveals herself capable of exploiting precisely that distinction between 'appearance' and 'reality' that Iago's machinations pivot on. For a brief interval she too, like Iago himself, is 'not what she is', for she is simulating signs that bear no relation to her actual state of mind, using them to project a persona at variance with her true self. When Othello greets his wife with the words 'fair warrior' while Iago's set of variations on the theme of fairness is still vibrating in the air, therefore, the spectator might well register the epithet with a certain diffidence (II.i.182).

Before succumbing to Iago's malevolent influence Othello himself appears to be, as I have remarked, incapable of the least duplicity in his personal conduct. His outward action is always an unambiguous sign for what he 'really' is, and Iago is obviously mocking his general's own unexamined assumption when he sanctimoniously declares that 'men should be that they seem' (III.iii.130). The world inhabited by the Moor is essentially one of face values and, when he is confronted even by the mere possibility that Desdemona might be capable of being something other than what she seems, he is driven into a state of mental turmoil which threatens at every moment to erupt into outright insanity. The sensation induced in him as his certitudes begin to crumble is that 'Chaos is come again' (III.iii.93), and the inevitable consequence of this impression of general dissolution is that the stability even of his own identity is menaced. He resorts to forms of behaviour that would previously have been totally repugnant to him, presenting a false front to the world, concealing himself according to Iago's instructions, spying, eavesdropping, brooding obsessively over trivial or sordid details, echoing the cheap wordplay of the clown who is his own servant.[18] He absorbs not only Iago's repulsive conception of mankind, but also his distinctive idiom, his predilection for couching his observations in bestial and infernal imagery. It is clear that there is something more in this than sexual jealousy or the sense of outraged personal honour or the anxiety experienced by an unwitting representative of a threatened patriarchal order.[19] More profoundly disorientating than any of these is the intolerable *cognitive* challenge to which Othello's mental faculties are being subjected, and to which in his simplicity he does not know how to respond. Perceived now solely in the light of Iago's dark insinuations, Desdemona has become for him an incarnate paradox, a fair woman whose whiteness, once the manifest emblem of an immaculate virtue, is now the perverse symbol of its own opposite. 'O thou black weed, why art so lovely fair' (IV.ii.69), is the anguished question he addresses to his wife at one point, and his subsequent remarks continue to advert to the same apparent disparity: 'Was this fair paper, this most goodly book, / Made to write "whore" on?' (IV.ii.73-4). Desdemona's conspicuous fairness has thus been transformed into a radically ambiguous sign. She is now 'the fair devil' (III.iii.485), a living contradiction for

Othello's semiotically unsophisticated mind, an affront to the conventions that make experience intelligible.

Since it is in terms of these very conventions that Othello has defined his own identity, this subversion of meaning has fatal implications for his personal self-conception as well, compromising the integrity of the sign which is his name. Othello's own remarks make the association between his name—or the public self of which that name is the verbal token—and the polarity of light and darkness perfectly explicit:

> . . . my name, that was as fresh
> As Dian's visage, is now begrim'd, and black
> As mine own face . . .
>
> (III.iii.392-4)

Iago is diabolically aware of the critical role played by cultural codes in the constitution of selfhood, and his attack on meaning—in particular on the meaning of personal names—is an attack on identity as well.[20] 'He that filches from me my good name', he slyly remarks at one point, '. . . makes me poor indeed' (III.iii.163-5). Cassio is the first major character to be deprived of his good name through Iago's scheming, and when he expresses his humiliation in the exclamation 'Reputation, reputation, I ha' lost my reputation! I ha' lost the immortal part, sir, of myself, and what remains is bestial' (II.iii.254-6), he is anticipating Othello's still more critical loss of self. Even Desdemona, accused of harlotry by her husband, is finally driven to the extreme of asking 'Am I that name, Iago?'—to which the ensign replies with only barely concealed irony: 'What name, fair lady?' (IV.ii.120).

Almost for relief Othello, confronted with this growing uncertainty as to the real significance of names and signs, allows himself to be swallowed up in the oblivion of mindless passion, seeking certitudes of a different order in the absolute and uncomplicated darkness of revenge: 'Arise, black vengeance, from thy hollow cell' (III.iii.454). Interestingly enough, it is precisely at this juncture of the play, when triumphant darkness seems on the point of overwhelming everything, that a new personage is introduced—in time as it happens to be woven into Iago's ever more intricate web. This is Cassio's mistress, hitherto unmentioned, whose name *Bianca* might seem to collocate her instantly within a universe of self-contradicting signs. While fair Desdemona is represented as the blackest of harlots, the real harlot is dignified with a name that means white. It is perhaps arguable, however—though this is not the place to pursue the point—that Bianca's appearance, rather than complicating matters still further, in fact heralds the beginning of a restorative movement back towards the clarification of signs and their meanings. Despite her manifest defects she is not an unsympathetic character, and her unrequited devotion to Cassio seems unfeigned; she protests that her life is as honest as Emilia's, and perhaps, according to her 'lights' at least, she is right (V.i.121-2).

Such positive notes are sounded only later in the play, however, and in the meantime the momentum of the drama continues in the direction of ever greater perplexity. As I have suggested, perhaps the most ironic aspect of Othello's deterioration is that, plunged without warning into an alien world in which signs have become divorced from their meanings, he too has been severed from his own identity. He has been incorporated into a deeply problematic universe in which things do not even represent themselves, in which the Iago-principle prevails and nothing is what it is. 'My lord is not my lord' (III.iv.121), says Desdemona in explanation for her husband's aberrant behaviour, and Iago archly excites Lodovico's apprehensions regarding the Moor's psychological state with the characteristically circuitous observation:

> He's that he is; I may not breathe my censure,
> What he might be; if, as he might, he is not,
> I would to heaven he were!
>
> (IV.1.266-8)

The terrible resolution to exact vengeance seems to act as a stabilizing factor, however, presumably because it affords a precise, if only momentary, focus around which Othello's disintegrating personality can realign itself. In view of the confounding of colour values that has been taking place throughout the play, it is perhaps entirely to be expected that the invocation of 'black vengeance' should be paradoxically associated with light, Othello swearing 'by yond marble heaven' (III.iii.467) to punish the supposed malefactors, and Iago calling to witness 'you ever-burning lights above' (III.iii.470) when he pledges himself to the same dark purpose.

By the time the Moor actually addresses himself to what he has come to look upon as the 'sacrifice' of his wife, he has recovered a measure of self-control and achieved a genuine, though desperate, equilibrium. Among other things, this manifests itself in the restored stateliness of his diction, and in the elevated soliloquy commencing with the phrase 'It is the cause' we perceive the more traditional associations of light and darkness beginning to reaffirm themselves despite the symbolic confusion generated by the preceding scenes. Ironically, however, this rehabilitation of colour values is rendered possible only through what amounts to the annihilation of the positive term in that symbolic contraposition which has by now become hopelessly corrupt. If light and darkness can exchange places with one another with such facility that they lose their separate characters, then the readiest and most definitive remedy that an absolutist such as Othello can resort to is simply to eliminate the problematic element in the contrast, by both literally and figuratively 'putting out the light':

> . . . yet I'll not shed her blood,
> Nor scar that whiter skin of hers than snow,
> And smooth, as monumental alabaster;
> Yet she must die, else she'll betray more men.
> Put out the light, and then put out the light:
> If I quench thee, thou flaming minister,
> I can again thy former light restore,
> Should I repent me; but once put out thine,

> Thou cunning pattern of excelling nature,
> I know not where is that Promethean heat
> That can thy light relume . . .
>
> (V.ii.3-13)

In thus extinguishing light in the person of Desdemona—who has continued to invoke 'this light of heaven' (IV.ii.152) and 'this heavenly light' (IV.iii.64) in the final hours of her life—Othello does seem, in his own terms at least, to accomplish his purpose. A semiotic order in continual flux, that for the Moor has been a source only of perpetual confusion, has been stabilized through the simple expedient of giving the world over to a complete and absolute darkness that does not admit of potentially dangerous discriminations:

> O heavy hour!
> Methinks it should be now a huge eclipse
> Of sun and moon . . .
>
> (V.ii.99-101)

The irony latent in Othello's effort to impose perfect coherence upon what seems to be the incessantly mutating world of signs lies of course in the circumstance that the dilemma, or at least the assumption precipitating the dilemma, has been a false one, that there has been in fact no discrepancy between Desdemona's colour and her conduct. The process by which Othello is disabused of his enormous error implicates the final reconstitution of a cognitively familiar, though no less terrible world, a world in which the Moor has ironically justified the infernal associations evoked by his colour at the beginning of the play. Emilia refuses to admit that Desdemona's dying effort to exculpate Othello perjures her soul: on the contrary 'the more angel she, / And you the blacker devil!' (V.ii.131-2). Words like 'filth' and 'slime', denoting substances that make white things black, abound in the dialogue between the Moor and Emilia. Until Iago is unmasked by his wife Othello rather desperately persists in believing that Desdemona was 'foul' (V.ii.201), but in the end he sees the light, in every sense of the expression. Desdemona is once again unambiguously white ('Pale as thy smock'), even if her pallor is ironically now only that of death (V.ii.274), Iago is at last identified as the real fiend in the piece (V.ii.287-8), and Othello is restored to a world in which the distinction between light and darkness makes some sort of sense.

There is reason to suspect that, in consequence of the delirium of despair provoked in him by the discovery of his error, Othello briefly undergoes a final phase of dissociation from self, and that it is for this reason that he momentarily refers to himself not in the first but in the third person: 'Man but a rush against Othello's breast, / And he retires. Where should Othello go?' (V.ii.271-2). Even if this is so, however, it would appear that the Moor's belated recognition of the truth ultimately makes possible, if not the complete restoration of his lost identity, then at least the capacity to perceive himself in relation to that identity. When Lodovico demands to see 'this rash and most unfortunate man' the Moor recognizes himself instantly in the sombre epithet, replying 'That's he that was Othello; here I am' (V.ii.284-5). Instead of being 'not what he is' ('My lord is not my lord'), he now perceives himself to be not what he *was,* and this opens up the possibility at least of forging some kind of link between what he is now and what he has been previously. I would suggest that it is precisely this that Othello is attempting to accomplish in his final speech, which culminates in a suicide that he explicitly assimilates to one of the many colourful exploits in his past. Readers of the play have not always been entirely convinced by Othello's grandiloquent and enormously self-conscious eulogy for himself, which seems to betray, as T. S. Eliot and others have pointed out in disparagement of the Moor, an '*aesthetic* rather than a moral attitude' towards himself and what he has done, and thus raises doubts concerning his sincerity.[21] But since Othello seems always to have identified his personality with his public performances, to the extent that even his courtship of Desdemona has assumed the form of a detailed recitation of his autobiography, it is perhaps only to be expected that under the present circumstances he will try to recapture a sense of the continuity of that personality through the identical means.[22] The Moor is not, in other words, attempting to deliver judgement or render an account of himself in his concluding speech, and still less is he seeking to elicit anyone's compassion. What he is really trying to do is discover, in the final moments of his life, an adequate signification for that complex and fatally compromised sign which is the name Othello. While the question of whether he has fully succeeded in this endeavour doubtless remains an open one, the terse encomium pronounced by Cassio over the body of his dead commander that 'he was great of heart' (V.ii.362) perhaps suggests that his final effort at self-definition has not met with total defeat.

Notes

1. Cf. for instance Locke's account of the process by which 'a word is made arbitrarily the mark of . . . an idea', Berkeley's comparison of names with the abstract letters employed in algebra, and Coleridge's reference to 'words used as the arbitrary marks of thought, our smooth market-coin of intercourse'. John Locke, *An Essay Concerning Human Understanding,* edited by John W. Yolton (London, reprinted 1990), p. 207; George Berkeley, *Treatise concerning the Principles of Human Knowledge,* Introduction XIX, in *A New Theory of Vision and Other Writings* (London, reprinted 1969), p. 107; S. T. Coleridge, *Biographia Literaria,* Chap. XXII, in *Samuel Taylor Coleridge: Selected Poetry and Prose,* edited by Elisabeth Schneider (New York, reprinted 1966), pp. 340-1. Original emphasis deleted.

2. These oppositions have been examined in rhetorical terms by Doris Adler in her article 'The Rhetoric of *Black* and *White* in *Othello*', *Shakespeare Quarterly* 25 (1974), 248-57. Though very different in

viewpoint and emphasis, my own argument coincides with Adler's analysis at a number of points.

3. Melville's Ishmael makes this explicit. He refers to the 'elusive quality' which 'causes the thought of whiteness, when divorced from more kindly associations, and coupled with any object terrible in itself, to heighten that terror to the furthest bounds'. And specifically adducing the whiteness of the polar bear, he advances a hypothesis according to which 'that heightened hideousness . . . only arises from the circumstance, that the irresponsible ferociousness of the creature stands invested in the fleece of celestial innocence and love; and hence, by bringing together two such opposite emotions in our minds, the Polar bear frightens us with so unnatural a contrast'. Herman Melville, *Moby Dick* (London, reprinted 1975), pp. 164-5.

4. *Henry VI,* Part 2, II.iv.40. The edition cited here is W. J. Craig, *Shakespeare: Complete Works* (Oxford, reprinted 1965). All subsequent references to Shakespeare's plays other than *Othello* will be in this edition.

5. *Antony and Cleopatra,* II.ii.184-5.

6. *Love's Labour's Lost,* IV.iii.261, 269.

7. Michael Echeruo, *The Conditioned Imagination from Shakespeare to Conrad* (London, 1978), p. 57.

8. This and all subsequent references to *Othello* are in the New Arden Edition of the play, edited by M. R. Ridley (London, reprinted 1979), and conform to the lineation of that text.

9. Under the entry 'Ancient' the *Oxford English Dictionary* cites *2 Henry IV* (II.iv.120 [II.iv.118 in Craig]) and *Henry V* (III.vi.20 [III.vi.19 in Craig]) as early instances of this usage.

10. Cf. Romeo's lines: 'beauty's ensign yet / Is crimson in thy lips and in thy cheeks, / And death's pale flag is not advanced there.' *Romeo and Juliet,* V.iii.94-6.

11. G. Wilson Knight, *The Wheel of Fire* (London, reprinted 1968). p. 116.

12. See for instance Knight, op. cit., pp. 114-16, and Maud Bodkin, *Archetypal Patterns in Poetry* (Oxford, reprinted 1971), pp. 217-24.

13. For a more technical semiological analysis of this play, see Alessandro Serpieri, 'Reading the Signs: Towards a Semiotics of Shakespearean Drama', translated by Keir Elam, in *Alternative Shakespeares,* edited by John Drakakis (London, reprinted 1986), pp. 119-43.

14. Coleridge, Note on *Othello,* in *Samuel Taylor Coleridge: Shakespearean Criticism,* edited by Thomas Middleton Raysor (London, reprinted 1961), vol. I, p. 44.

15. The word 'light' recurs in a variety of senses throughout *Othello,* sustaining the verbal momentum if not always reinforcing the symbolic implications of the play. See for instance Brabantio's 'Destruction light on me, if my bad blame / Light on the man!' (I.iii.177-8); Othello's reference to 'light-wing'd toys' (I.iii.268); his warning to his quarrelling officers that whoever commits any further act of aggression 'Holds his soul light' (II.iii.165); Cassio's disparagement of himself as 'so light, so drunken, and indiscreet an officer' (II.iii.270-1); Iago's observation that 'trifles light as air / Are to the jealous, confirmations strong' (III.iii.327-8); Iago's reference to 'Poor Cassio's smiles, gestures, and light behaviour'(IV.i.102); and Lodovico's inquiry with regard to Othello: 'is he not light of brain?' (IV.1.265).

16. Although there is no etymological connection between the words 'delight' and 'light', it appears quite evident that in *Othello* Shakespeare is associating the two words in an imaginative sense at least. The reader might note for instance the contraposition of colours implicit in Brabantio's question to Othello as to whether it is credible that his daughter would have 'Run from her guardage to the sooty bosom / Of such a thing as thou? to fear, not to delight' (I.ii.70-71). In a similar vein, Iago later remarks of Desdemona that 'Her eye must be fed, and what delight shall she have to look on the devil?' (II.i.224-5).

17. The seeming inevitability of the symbolic associations with which the handkerchief is invested does not make its status as a sign any less arbitrary. Lynda E. Boose's ingenious analysis of the emblematic significance of this object, for instance, is not an effort to tease out intrinsic meanings but to recuperate the codes (embodied chiefly in European folk practices surrounding nuptials and in the Book of Deuteronomy) that might have enabled meaning in the minds of Shakespeare's audience. See Boose, 'Othello's Handerkchief: "The Recognizance and Pledge of Love"', *English Literary Renaissance* 5 (1975), 360-74.

18. 'We say lie on her, when they belie her' (IV.i.35-6). Cf. the clown's quip: 'I know not where he [Cassio] lodges, and for me to devise a lodging, and say he lies here, or he lies there, were to lie in mine own throat' (III.iv.9-11).

19. A thorough analysis of this latter aspect of Othello's plight is to be found in Edward A. Snow, 'Sexual Anxiety and the Male Order of Things in *Othello', English Literary Renaissance* 10 (1980), 384-412. To the degree that the patriarchal view of the world itself represents a codification of reality in which the individual's identity is vested, of course, the potential challenge posed to that order by the empowering of the woman as an active sexual being in her own right might be seen as correlative to the subversion of the luminary code that I am discussing here.

20. For a stimulating recent discussion of the more specifically 'linguistic' determinants of Othello's dilemma, see Kenneth Gross, 'Slander and Skepticism in *Othello*', *ELH* 56 (1989), 819-52.

21. T.S. Eliot, 'Shakespeare and the Stoicism of Seneca' in *Selected Essays* (London, reprinted 1986), p. 131. Emphasis in the original.

22. For an acute analysis of the interdependency of identity and narrative in *Othello* see Stephen Greenblatt, *Renaissance Self-Fashioning* (Chicago, 1980), pp. 232-52.

SOCIAL BACKGROUND

Mark Matheson (essay date 1995)

SOURCE: "Venetian Culture and the Politics of *Othello*," in *Shakespeare Survey*, Vol. 48, 1995, pp. 123-33.

[*In the following essay, Matheson explores Shakespeare's concept of life in Venice as portrayed in* Othello.]

In *Othello* Shakespeare represents a society in many ways fundamentally different from his own, and rather than minimizing or obscuring these differences he explores them in a politically creative way. The play is a powerful illustration of his ability to perceive and represent different forms of political organization, and to situate personal relationships and issues of individual subjectivity in a specific institutional context. Here and in much of his other work Shakespeare displays what might be described as a sociological imagination. He portrays in *Othello* not a feudal monarchy or Renaissance court but an enduring Italian city-state, a republic which continued to survive despite growing Habsburg domination in the rest of the peninsula. Taken in the context of his career as a whole the play is a fascinating example of Shakespeare's interest in republicanism, which is evident from 'The Rape of Lucrece' to *The Tempest*. It provides clear evidence that he was neither an uncritical advocate of conservative Tudor ideology, as an older critical tradition maintained, nor a writer materially unable to think and imagine beyond the monarchical paradigm, as a more recent historicist criticism has sometimes suggested. In the English context the act of representing a republican culture was itself a progressive gesture, since Venice offered an existing and stable alternative to the 'natural' and 'eternal' order of monarchy. In addition to this, and to a degree not usually recognized, Shakespeare represents the city's institutions exercising a shaping influence on personal relationships and individual experience. These institutions inform and complicate the ongoing process of cultural exchange at the heart of the play, which is Othello's attempt to thrive in the foreign cultural world of an aggressive European power, and they also influence the representation of women's experience, which the play suggests would be different in a patriarchal but non-monarchical culture. The play is itself the product of cultural exchange, and Shakespeare's imaginative sensitivity to the ways of a different society generates political energies in the text which carry it beyond the ideological boundaries of official English culture.

The extent of Shakespeare's interest in the institutional life of Venice can be suggested by a comparison with contemporary playwrights. John Marston's *Antonio's Revenge* (c. 1600) is set in the city but offers little sense of its specific social and political practices. Jonson's *Volpone* (1605) reveals a much greater interest in particular Venetian institutions, and Daniel C. Boughner has argued that Jonson's research for the play was stimulated in part by Shakespeare's recent portrayal of Venice in *Othello*.[1] Shakespeare had probably read Lewes Lewkenor's *The Common-Wealth and Government of Venice* (1599), a translation of Contarini's laudatory exposition of the Venetian state.[2] Those who wrote dedicatory poems for this volume include Edmund Spenser, who praises not only the beauty of Venice but its 'policie of right', and John Harington, who compares it 'For Freedome' with the Roman republic.[3] Jonson read Contarini for *Volpone*, in which Sir Politic Would-Be reveals that he has hastily studied 'Contarene' in order to pass himself off as a Venetian citizen (4.1.40). Boughner has argued that in this play Jonson deliberately undercuts the idealized portrait of Venice in Contarini's work and Lewkenor's introduction. This is a plausible view, since the Venice of *Volpone* is a greed-driven city where predatory relations are the norm, where the citizens take a Machiavellian attitude toward religion (4.1.22-7), and where the supposedly democratic law courts are venues in which 'multitude' and 'clamour' overcome justice (4.6.19).

Shakespeare's more favourable representation of Venice may suggest an imaginative willingness to explore the strengths of a republican culture, and may also reflect a sympathy with the political interests of the Sidney and Essex circles, with which of course he had some connection. Members of these aristocratic circles were interested in the mixed government of the Venetian republic, and as Protestants they approved of its steadfast opposition to the authoritarianism of the Counter-Reformation. Some took a specific interest in the work of Lewkenor, who in his address to the reader describes the Venetian state as comprising monarchical, aristocratic, and democratic elements. The prince has 'all exterior ornamentes of royall dignitie' but is nevertheless 'wholy subiected to the lawes'; the 'Councell of Pregati or Senators' is invested with great authority but has no 'power, mean, or possibility at all to tyranize'; and a 'Democrasie or popular estate' is evident in the existence of a 'great councell, consisting at least of 3000. Gentlemen, whereupon the highest strength and mightinesse of the estate absolutely relyeth.'[4] Lewkenor's adverb in this final clause demonstrates how terms usually associated with monarchy could slip from their ordinary usage in descriptions of a state with a mixed constitution, and his account is an example of how cultural exchange could destabilize and enrich conventional English political discourse. There is unquestionably a degree of idealization in Lewkenor's discussion of Venice, just as there is in the text of Contarini, but the enthusiasm he reveals is itself suggestive of the political interest the city was generating in England at the end of the sixteenth century.

The governmental structure of Venice may seem to be of only incidental importance to *Othello,* but in fact it is indispensable for generating the basic dramatic situation, and it influences every personal relationship in the play. In the first act Shakespeare offers a compelling representation of the city's political and cultural life, and his interest in its institutional structure is evident in a variety of ways. There is a notable shift, for instance, to a more explicitly republican discourse than he had used in *The Merchant of Venice.* In part this might be due to his intervening work with Roman republicanism in *Julius Caesar,* which seems to have influenced the later play. The councilmen who were simply 'magnificoes' (4.1.1 stage directions) in *The Merchant* have become 'Senators' in *Othello* (1.3.1 stage directions). Other traces of a discourse associated with republican Rome include Iago's early reference to 'togaed consuls' (1.1.24), with whom he compares Cassio for their common lack of military experience. Iago may be making a vague reference to classical culture, but he is probably referring instead to the current members of the Venetian council, as becomes clear in the next scene when Cassio uses the republican term 'consuls' for the senators who are meeting with the Duke (1.2.43). Iago's words may glance at Rome but can also be read as referring to a specifically Venetian practice. It was widely known that the members of the Venetian council had no military pretensions, and Lewkenor finds it extraordinary that these 'vnweaponed men in gownes' should give direction to 'many mightie and warlike armies'.[5] The practice of employing foreign mercenary officers and generals—by law no Venetian citizen could have more than twenty-five men in his command—was also based on republican principle. Contarini writes that Venetian leaders and armies involved in long wars on land would inevitably fall into 'a Kinde of faction' against the other 'peaceable citizens'. This could easily lead to civil war, and he notes in an analysis identical to Machiavelli's that this problem helped to undermine the Roman republic, since Caesar drew the loyalty of his men away from the state and to himself, and this permitted him 'to tyrannize ouer that commonwealth to which hee did owe all duty and obedience'.[6] The Venetian policy designed to prevent any conquering Caesar from turning against the republican state opened the way for men like Othello, and owing to its setting in this particular city the play has genuine plausibility.

Perhaps the character most clearly shaped by the institutional life of Venice is Desdemona. In part this influence is traditional, since Brabanzio's household functions on a typical patriarchal model. His rule seems to have been mostly benign, but a specifically political idiom emerges in his spontaneous laments over Desdemona's behaviour: 'O heaven, how got she out? O, treason of the blood!' (1.1.171) After he learns that she has willingly married Othello he employs the same political language:

> I am glad at soul I have no other child,
> For thy escape would teach me tyranny,
> To hang clogs on 'em.
>
> (1.3.195-7)

Throughout Act 1 Brabanzio speaks the language of fatherly ownership with a frightening intensity, and he has inculcated in Desdemona obedience to the father's word. But Brabanzio's absolutist regime at home exists in tension with the government of the state, which as the council scene attests is based on debate and consultation. His household is built on the older political model of a *corpus,* of which he is unquestionably the head, but it exists within a larger political order based on the more progressive model of a *res publica,* whose participants are citizens rather than subjects, and whose leaders conduct affairs of state on a generally equal footing.[7]

In the council scene Brabanzio uses a kind of absolutist discourse in his address to Desdemona, asking if she knows where most she owes 'obedience', and she replies by saying that what she owes her father is 'respect' (1.3.179, 183). Desdemona's response represents a cultural shift away from her father's conception of the family, with her carefully chosen term 'respect' indicating in part the degree to which she has been shaped by the relatively liberal institutions of Venice. It seems to be a word in some ways specific to the republican context, where it characterizes the tenor of relations among members of the council, and this government has certainly made Desdemona aware of alternatives to the royalist doctrine of unquestioning obedience. Desdemona herself introduces the concept of a broader cultural order in her reply to Brabanzio before the senators, in which she makes repeated mention of her 'education' (1.3.181)—the only time this word appears in Shakespearian tragedy. This education is partly responsible for her independence, and for the verbal agility with which she disengages herself from the identities constructed for her by her father. The most striking line by which she accomplishes this is 'I am hitherto your daughter' (1.3.184), in which she brings out an instability in the word 'daughter' itself, using it to designate not the natural bond she refers to earlier when she says she is 'bound' to Brabanzio for 'life', but rather a relationship of power in which the daughter is the father's possession as guaranteed by a specific set of cultural arrangements. By using the word in this second sense she implicitly asserts the role of culture in establishing such identities, and thus disturbs Brabanzio's simple distinction between a nature which cannot 'err' and the supernatural order of 'witchcraft' (1.3.62, 64).

The problem for Brabanzio is that the progressive political and economic life of Venice is at work beneath his conservative ideology of gender and paternal relations, and Shakespeare's broad representation of Venetian political life makes Desdemona's capacity for independent judgment and action more convincing. A comparison with the sexual politics of *The Merchant of Venice* can be instructive here. As Walter Cohen has pointed out Belmont functions in that play as a 'green' world inhabited by a traditional landed aristocracy, who in the course of events are brought into contact with the commercial and urban world of contemporary Venice.[8] The central figure of this green world is Portia, 'a living daughter curbed by the will of a dead father' (1.2.23-4), and one who completely accepts that her father's word has taken away her choice in marriage. As witty and resourceful as she is Portia never contemplates the transgression of the patriarchal decree, and even allowing for the difference in genre her behaviour makes a notable contrast with that of the city-dwelling Desdemona, who does something incomparably more daring. It also happens that Portia is visited by the Moorish Prince of Morocco, who comes in suit to her for marriage, and of whom she says 'If he have the condition of a saint and the complexion of a devil, I had rather he should shrive me than wive me' (1.2.126-8). The first thing Morocco says to her is 'Mislike me not for my complexion' (2.1.1), and when he has departed after failing to choose the correct casket Portia says 'Let all of his complexion choose me so' (2.7.79). Next to Desdemona's cosmopolitan open-mindedness Portia's response looks very provincial, a predictable reaction to cultural otherness from the daughter of a traditionalist aristocracy. Portia lives idly in her great house on inherited wealth, with perhaps the nearest neighbour a 'monastery two miles off' (3.4.31); by contrast Desdemona lives in the city which Contarini describes as 'a common and generall market to the whole world', its streets thronging with a 'wonderful concourse of strange and forraine people'.[9] In this setting the traditionalist gender and racial ideologies of Belmont are on rather more shaky ground, subjected as they are to the pressures of a society moved by the concerns of commercial exchange and with a practical-minded government ready to reward merit rather than birth.

Shakespeare thus represents Desdemona's self-confidence as partly a product of the progressive Venetian culture he portrays in the play. Othello comes to this culture as an outsider, and his association with the city is based on both the government's republican principles and its readiness to seek out those with merit and to pay for their services. Much of Othello's relationship with Venetian culture is determined by the racial prejudice (like Portia's) he encounters there, which Shakespeare makes a deliberate point of portraying in the opening scenes of the play. This prejudice surfaces repeatedly, as in Brabanzio's insistence that the case be heard that very night:

> For if such actions may have passage free,
> Bondslaves and pagans shall our statesmen be.
>
> (1.2.99-100)

This is one of the earliest recorded uses of 'statesmen', a noun which evokes the republican setting of the Italian city-state. (Jonson had used it a few years earlier to name a category of men typified by Machiavelli.)[10] The limits to popular participation in contemporary republican government are abundantly clear in Brabanzio's speech, in which he apparently alludes to the period when Othello was 'sold to slavery' (1.3.137). He also leaves little doubt about his view of Othello's conversion to Christianity, which he evidently regards as a flimsy overlay for an essentially pagan nature. It seems to be Shakespeare's imaginative sympathy for the experience of the cultural outsider, particularly in the hostile environment often created by natives like Brabanzio, which enables him to move beyond the stereotypical images of Moorish people retailed in plays and pageants in England throughout his lifetime.[11] He created this highly original character by imagining Othello in a concrete social situation, and by permitting him to bring to Venice an ideological orientation formed under a different set of cultural institutions.

If one judges this orientation in the context of the Venice Shakespeare represents, Othello emerges as arguably the most conservative character in the play. The rich portrayal of his conservative sensibility seems to be generated in part by Shakespeare's interest in liberal Venetian institutions, and in the contrasts which accordingly emerge as Othello's relationship with Venice unfolds. He finds a model for his personal and political relationships in the tradition of monarchy, and in his first appearance he offers an indication of the degree to which his sense of self has been shaped by this tradition: 'I fetch my life and being / From men of royal siege' (1.2.21-2). Among the things to which Othello will later bid farewell is 'the royal banner' (3.3.358), a detail suggesting once again his experience of a political order remote from the republican institutions of contemporary Venice. Othello's language before the council in Act 1 tends to obscure the economic basis of his relationship with the state, which is accurately described by Iago's reference to their employment in 'the trade of war' (1.2.1).[12] Othello has a more nearly feudal conception of this relationship, which he speaks of in terms of duty and religious devotion. He conveys this in his first address to the senators—'Most potent, grave, and reverend signors, / My very noble and approved good masters' (1.3.76-7)— where his devotional attitude contrasts with the practical tone of the council's deliberations. Othello positions himself here in the role of devoted servant, and interestingly to the men themselves rather than to the state as an institution. His sense of his relationship with Venice as a personal tie rather than a contractual agreement is also evident when he prefaces a request to the council with 'Most humbly therefore bending to your state' (1.3.234), where 'state' slips from its usual sense of designating the Venetian republic and refers instead to the personal status of the senators. At one point he likens their council to the judgement seat of the Christian God:

> as truly as to heaven
> I do confess the vices of my blood,
> So justly to your grave ears I'll present
> How I did thrive in this fair lady's love,
> And she in mine.
>
> (1.3.122-6)

Some have read this as an ominous passage, as perhaps revealing an unconscious identification in Othello's mind between sexual vice and his love for Desdemona,[13] but more plainly it indicates the hierarchical understanding he has of both political and religious institutions. The deep identification Othello makes in these lines would seem to be between Roman Catholicism and political absolutism, a conceptual integration roughly on the Habsburg model.

The council acts in a way which contrasts sharply with the political world as understood by Othello. Shakespeare represents them as a functioning participatory government, with a large measure of equality among aristocratic peers. Brabanzio makes reference to 'my brothers of the state' (1.2.97), an unusual locution which recalls the republican rhetoric of *Julius Caesar*, in which the anti-imperial faction employs the metaphor of fraternity in regarding themselves as the true sons of Rome. The members of the council make no sweeping ideological claims about what is at stake, but engage instead in a business-like attempt to calculate the number of ships in the Turkish fleet. In denying the accuracy of a certain report the First Senator says ''tis a pageant / To keep us in false gaze' (1.3.19-20), which suggests the deliberative nature of their government, and their ability to see through theatrical displays of power associated in contemporary culture (and in present-day criticism of Renaissance texts) with imperial and absolutist governments. The practical-mindedness of the council was objected to in the late seventeenth century by Thomas Rymer, who found that Shakespeare's presentation lacked sufficient nobility:

> By their Conduct and manner of talk, a body must strain hard to fancy the Scene at *Venice;* And not rather in some of our Cinq-ports, where the Baily and his Fisher-men are knocking their heads together on account of some Whale, or some terrible broil up the Coast.[14]

What Rymer sees as a fault (and exaggerates to make his point) can also be read in terms of Shakespeare's awareness of different political cultures. He may have thought it fitting that the senators of this commercial republic should be less concerned with shows of worldly greatness than with shrewd calculation and getting their figures right.

Certainly the religious character of Othello's devotion to the Venetian cause cannot be found among members of the council, who make no plea of any kind for Christendom. In fact in the context of Venetian culture Othello's religious sensibility seems rather antiquated. More than any other character he invests the Turkish-Christian conflict with spiritual significance, as his attribution of the Turkish defeat to God's will and his plea for 'Christian shame' among the victors makes clear (2.3.163-5). His piety seems to belong more to the era of the Crusades than to the increasingly secular world of sixteenth-century politics, when the powers of Europe were sometimes willing to ally themselves with the Ottoman empire to gain an advantage over other Christian states. Desdemona's sensitivity to this aspect of her husband's character may emerge when she tells Emilia that instead of losing the 'handkerchief' she would rather have lost her purse 'Full of crusadoes' (3.4.26). This is Shakespeare's only reference to this coin, which was stamped with a cross and current in contemporary England, and its name evokes the larger context of religious war in which Othello is involved, and perhaps also his tendency to regard the Christian-Turkish conflict in heroic and romantic terms. Desdemona's reference to 'crusadoes' might thus be read as an involuntary testimony to her sympathetic understanding of Othello's motives.

The character most aware of how Othello's traditionalist perspective makes him vulnerable to exploitation in Venice is Iago. Shakespeare makes a point of emphasizing Iago's role in the Venetian army, whose rigidly hierarchical relations contrast markedly with those within the state government, where the rule is consultation among equals rather than a structure of command and obedience. Like Brabanzio's household, the army and the martial law government in Cyprus have absolutist associations. Marguerite Waller has pointed out how Iago derives a sense of his own value from the military hierarchy—'I know my price, I am worth no worse a place' (1.1.11)—and that what he regards as the intrusion of Othello and the Florentine Cassio helps to create the 'obsessive energy' with which he plots their ruin.[15] Othello and Cassio are also incorporated into the structure of the army in a way which shapes their subjective experience, but their concept of this institution lacks the commercial connotations of Iago's view. Both tend to regard the army as an instance of the organic community envisioned by the ideology of contemporary monarchy, and the politicized language of love which typifies political discourse in absolutism comes easily to them both. Cassio reveals this in his fall from Othello's favour, particularly in his request to Desdemona to intercede on his behalf:

> I do beseech you
> That by your virtuous means I may again
> Exist and be a member of his love
> Whom I, with all the office of my heart,
> Entirely honour.
>
> (3.4.108-12)

Cassio's identity is dependent on his place within the institution, though he figures this not in practical political or economic terms but in the language of love, with the term 'member' recalling the traditional monarchical rhetoric of the 'body' politic and the organic community. Shakespeare may represent Cassio in this way partly because he is a product of the absolutist government of Florence, which had reverted from its earlier republicanism to the autocracy of the later Medici. In any case the crucial role played by the army in supporting Cassio's sense of self is evident in his use of the surprisingly strong verb 'Exist', and in its prominent placement. The play offers an analysis of male identity within the army as profoundly dependent on place and hierarchical relations, and as being distinct in this way from the system of relative equality among members of the Venetian governing class. In the speech quoted above Cassio's discourse of love and duty is suggestive of the personalized politics of absolute monarchy, and at odds with the legalism and practical business relationships of Venetian society as a whole. As a product of this society Desdemona is influenced by these more progressive conditions, and the legal or contractual basis for relationships in the city is evident in her language. She tells Cassio 'If I do vow a friendship I'll perform it / To the last article' (3.3.21-2).

Othello prefers to conduct his political relationships in the older language of loyalty and loving service, and Iago plays on this idealistic and somewhat dated vocabulary to exploit him. In the central scene of the play (3.3) he is attuned to Othello's habit of viewing power relations in terms of devotion and love. When Othello threatens to kill him he projects indignation at his general's ingratitude: 'I'll love no friend, sith love breeds such offence' (3.3.385). At this Othello retreats, and presently Iago swears himself to 'wronged Othello's service':

> Let him command,
> And to obey shall be in me remorse,
> What bloody business ever.
> OTHELLO
> I greet thy love,
> Not with vain thanks, but with acceptance bounteous.
>
> (3.3.470-3)

In the speech partly quoted Iago never mentions love, and that Othello interprets his promise of devoted obedience in this way reveals the politicized nature of 'love' in his discourse. The extent to which Othello's mind is imbued with the monarchical is evident in the despairing language he uses after falling to Iago's treachery. It emerges in his vow of revenge, 'Yield up, O love, thy crown and hearted throne / To tyrannous hate!' (3.3.452-3), in which Othello represents his own subjective world as an absolutist political order. The following image in which he compares his 'bloody thoughts' to the rushing Pontic Sea is a remarkable intensification of a conventional Renaissance metaphor for tyranny, in which the boundless ocean is used to figure engulfing despotism.

There is also a religious element in the political discourse Othello uses at this point in the play, as in his accusation that Desdemona's hand is 'moist':

> This argues fruitfulness, and liberal heart.
> Hot, hot and moist—this hand of yours requires
> A sequester from liberty; fasting, and prayer,
> Much castigation, exercise devout,
> For here's a young and sweating devil here
> That commonly rebels. 'Tis a good hand,
> A frank one.
> DESDEMONA
> You may indeed say so,
> For 'twas that hand that gave away my heart.
> OTHELLO
> A liberal hand. The hearts of old gave hands,
> But our new heraldry is hands, not hearts.

It is typical of Othello's deeply conservative notions of service and heroism that he praises the 'old' ways and speaks of infidelity in love in terms of the debasement of heraldic signs. His speeches here are an interesting mix of political and sexual discourse, in which he conflates the Venetian tradition of political liberty with sexual licence—another tradition for which the city was widely known.[16] Othello uses the term 'liberty' to imply sexual indulgence, and the remedy he prescribes is the very un-Venetian practice of authoritarian religious discipline, indicating once again the distance of his sensibility from the religion and politics of Venice.

One further aspect of Othello's ideological orientation needs to be mentioned: he has no conception of a world divided into public and private spheres. This is manifest when Iago impugns the fidelity of Desdemona, and Othello responds by bidding farewell to his career in war, uttering in a painful lament that his 'occupation's gone' (3.3.362). Michael Neill has noted Othello's tendency to make no distinction in his life between public and private roles, and that his reference to 'occupation' can be read at a variety of levels both political and sexual.[17] The play seems to suggest in fact that the domestic or private sphere is in the process of evolving as a practical and conceptual category within the broader institutional life of the Venetian state. Francis Barker has argued that a conception of the public and private as autonomous spheres developed mostly after Shakespeare's work in the theatre, and he cites the second scene of *Hamlet* to support his point.[18] He suggests that in that scene the looming war with Norway, Laertes' intention to return to France, and Hamlet's melancholy are all represented as continuous issues within a single conceptual and political order. The scene which invites comparison in *Othello* is the gathering of the council, in which the Duke responds tellingly to the question of whether Desdemona should be permitted to accompany Othello to Cyprus: 'Be it as you shall privately determine' (1.3.275). In *Hamlet* Claudius involves himself much more conspicuously in the familial debate over whether Laertes should return to France.[19] What Shakespeare seems to suggest in *Othello* is that the distinction between public and private is more developed in the context of a commercial and republican society. If it is less evident in *Hamlet* this is probably because in that play he represents a monarchy in which the traditions of feudalism continue to exert an influence. In royalist countries the corporate ideology which Barker finds in *Hamlet* may have inhibited any sharp distinction between the domestic and public spheres, but Shakespeare's treatment of the issue in his play about Venice suggests his ability to think beyond the social practices of monarchy, and perhaps also his awareness of how the conceptual order would be different in a commercial state based on citizenship rather than on the older notion of membership in a body politic.

As the play develops Shakespeare shows an increasing interest in the association of Venetian women with the private sphere, and in the different roles they play there. In part this seems to be because the domestic sphere is

Elizabeth's court such royal control over the travels of the nobility was the general rule, and Shakespeare was thus departing from the custom of his own society in imagining a different political practice for contemporary Venice. See 'William Herbert, third Earl of Pembroke', *Dictionary of National Biography,* vol. 9, p. 678.

20. Carol McKewin has noted that the women's friendship in this scene is an 'implied rebuke' to relationships between men in the play. See her 'Counsels of Gall and Grace: Intimate Conversations between Women in Shakespeare's Plays', in *The Woman's Part: Feminist Criticism of Shakespeare,* ed. by Carolyn Ruth Swift Lenz, Gayle Greene, and Carol Thomas Neely (Urbana: University of Illinois Press, 1980), p. 128.

FURTHER READING

Criticism

Bartels, Emily C. "Making More of the Moor: Aaron, Othello, and Renaissance Refashionings of Race." *Shakespeare Quarterly* 41, No. 4 (Winter 1990): 433-54.

    Compares Shakespeare's treatment of Moors in *Titus Andronicus* and *Othello,* arguing that dominant Renaissance racial views were contested in *Othello.*

Cantor, Paul A. "Othello: The Erring Barbarian among the Supersubtle Venetians." *Southwest Review* 75, No. 3 (Summer 1990): 296–319.

    Traces Othello's struggle between the domestic world of Venice and his past as a warrior and outsider.

Cohen, Derek. "Othello's Suicide." *University of Toronto Quarterly* 62, No. 3 (Spring 1993): 323-33.

    Links Othello's suicide to his ultimate capitulation to the dominant Venetian society.

Ghazoul, Ferial J. "The Arabization of Othello." *Comparative Literature* 50, No. 1 (Winter 1998): 1–31.

    Discusses Arab reactions to and interpretations of *Othello.*

Grennan, Eamon. "The Women's Voices in Othello: Speech, Song, Silence." *Shakespeare Quarterly* 38, No. 3 (Autumn 1997): 275-92.

    Argues the importance of the female voices in *Othello* and posits that their speeches play a pivotal role in creating the play's moral landscape.

Jones, Eldred. "*Othello*—An Interpretation." In *Critical Essays on Shakespeare's "Othello",* pp. 39-54. Edited by Anthony Gerard Barthelemy. New York: G. K. Hall & Co., 1994.

    Considers Shakespeare's depiction of Othello in relation to the traditional depiction of Moors in England. Jones argues that Shakespeare exploits the stereotype, but that Othello emerges as an individual whose weaknesses are attributable to human nature.

Little, Arthur L., Jr. "'An essence that's not seen': The Primal Scene of Racism in Othello." *Shakespeare Quarterly* 44, No. 3 (Fall 1993): 304-24.

    Explores the transformation of the meaning of Othello's race throughout the play.

Loomba, Ania. "Sexuality and Racial Difference." In *Critical Essays on Shakespeare's "Othello",* pp. 162-86. Edited by Anthony Gerard Barthelemy. New York: G. K. Hall & Co., 1994.

    Discusses race and feminist ideology in *Othello.*

Newman, Karen. "'And wash the Ethiop white': Femininity and the Monstrous in *Othello.*" In *Fashioning Femininity and English Renaissance Drama,* pp. 71-94. Chicago: The University of Chicago Press, 1991.

    Examines race and femininity in *Othello,* arguing that the play is centered around miscegenation.

Singh, Jyotsna. "Othello's Identity, Postcolonial Theory, and Contemporary African Rewritings of *Othello.*" In *Women, 'Race,' and Writing in the Early Modern Period,* pp. 287-99. Edited by Margo Hendricks and Patricia Parker. New York: Routledge, 1994.

    Reexamines the racial nature of *Othello* from the perspective of post-colonial African writers.

Slights, Camille Wells. "Slaves and Subjects in *Othello.*" *Shakespeare Quarterly* 48, No. 4 (1997): 377-90.

    Considers emerging ideas about self and their relationship to concepts of slavery and race in *Othello.*

Widmayer, Martha. "Brabantio and Othello." *English Studies* 77, No. 2 (March 1996): 113-26.

    Argues that both Desdemona's father and Othello are obsessed with the concept of absolute goodness, which they ascribe to the character of Desdemona.

Elizabeth's court such royal control over the travels of the nobility was the general rule, and Shakespeare was thus departing from the custom of his own society in imagining a different political practice for contemporary Venice. See 'William Herbert, third Earl of Pembroke', *Dictionary of National Biography,* vol. 9, p. 678.

20. Carol McKewin has noted that the women's friendship in this scene is an 'implied rebuke' to relationships between men in the play. See her 'Counsels of Gall and Grace: Intimate Conversations between Women in Shakespeare's Plays', in *The Woman's Part: Feminist Criticism of Shakespeare,* ed. by Carolyn Ruth Swift Lenz, Gayle Greene, and Carol Thomas Neely (Urbana: University of Illinois Press, 1980), p. 128.

FURTHER READING

Criticism

Bartels, Emily C. "Making More of the Moor: Aaron, Othello, and Renaissance Refashionings of Race." *Shakespeare Quarterly* 41, No. 4 (Winter 1990): 433-54.

  Compares Shakespeare's treatment of Moors in *Titus Andronicus* and *Othello*, arguing that dominant Renaissance racial views were contested in *Othello*.

Cantor, Paul A. "Othello: The Erring Barbarian among the Supersubtle Venetians." *Southwest Review* 75, No. 3 (Summer 1990): 296–319.

  Traces Othello's struggle between the domestic world of Venice and his past as a warrior and outsider.

Cohen, Derek. "Othello's Suicide." *University of Toronto Quarterly* 62, No. 3 (Spring 1993): 323-33.

  Links Othello's suicide to his ultimate capitulation to the dominant Venetian society.

Ghazoul, Ferial J. "The Arabization of Othello." *Comparative Literature* 50, No. 1 (Winter 1998): 1–31.

  Discusses Arab reactions to and interpretations of *Othello*.

Grennan, Eamon. "The Women's Voices in Othello: Speech, Song, Silence." *Shakespeare Quarterly* 38, No. 3 (Autumn 1997): 275-92.

  Argues the importance of the female voices in *Othello* and posits that their speeches play a pivotal role in creating the play's moral landscape.

Jones, Eldred. "*Othello*—An Interpretation." In *Critical Essays on Shakespeare's "Othello",* pp. 39-54. Edited by Anthony Gerard Barthelemy. New York: G. K. Hall & Co., 1994.

  Considers Shakespeare's depiction of Othello in relation to the traditional depiction of Moors in England. Jones argues that Shakespeare exploits the stereotype, but that Othello emerges as an individual whose weaknesses are attributable to human nature.

Little, Arthur L., Jr. "'An essence that's not seen': The Primal Scene of Racism in Othello." *Shakespeare Quarterly* 44, No. 3 (Fall 1993): 304-24.

  Explores the transformation of the meaning of Othello's race throughout the play.

Loomba, Ania. "Sexuality and Racial Difference." In *Critical Essays on Shakespeare's "Othello",* pp. 162-86. Edited by Anthony Gerard Barthelemy. New York: G. K. Hall & Co., 1994.

  Discusses race and feminist ideology in *Othello*.

Newman, Karen. "'And wash the Ethiop white': Femininity and the Monstrous in *Othello*." In *Fashioning Femininity and English Renaissance Drama,* pp. 71-94. Chicago: The University of Chicago Press, 1991.

  Examines race and femininity in *Othello,* arguing that the play is centered around miscegenation.

Singh, Jyotsna. "Othello's Identity, Postcolonial Theory, and Contemporary African Rewritings of *Othello*." In *Women, 'Race,' and Writing in the Early Modern Period,* pp. 287-99. Edited by Margo Hendricks and Patricia Parker. New York: Routledge, 1994.

  Reexamines the racial nature of *Othello* from the perspective of post-colonial African writers.

Slights, Camille Wells. "Slaves and Subjects in *Othello*." *Shakespeare Quarterly* 48, No. 4 (1997): 377-90.

  Considers emerging ideas about self and their relationship to concepts of slavery and race in *Othello*.

Widmayer, Martha. "Brabantio and Othello." *English Studies* 77, No. 2 (March 1996): 113-26.

  Argues that both Desdemona's father and Othello are obsessed with the concept of absolute goodness, which they ascribe to the character of Desdemona.

Cumulative Character Index

The Cumulative Character Index identifies the principal characters of discussion in the criticism of each play and non-dramatic poem. The characters are arranged alphabetically. Page references indicate the beginning page number of each essay containing substantial commentary on that character.

Aaron
  Titus Andronicus **4:** 632, 637, 650, 651, 653, 668, 672, 675; **27:** 255; **28:** 249, 330; **43:** 176; **53:** 86, 92

Adonis
  Venus and Adonis **10:** 411, 420, 424, 427, 429, 434, 439, 442, 451, 454, 459, 466, 473, 489; **25:** 305, 328; **28:** 355; **33:** 309, 321, 330, 347, 352, 357, 363, 370, 377; **51:** 345, 377

Adriana
  The Comedy of Errors **16:** 3; **34:** 211, 220, 238

Albany
  King Lear **32:** 308

Alcibiades
  Timon of Athens **25:** 198; **27:** 191

Angelo
  Measure for Measure
    anxiety **16:** 114
    authoritarian portrayal of **23:** 307; **49:** 274
    characterization **2:** 388, 390, 397, 402, 418, 427, 432, 434, 463, 484, 495, 503, 511; **13:** 84; **23:** 297; **32:** 81; **33:** 77; **49:** 274, 293, 379
    hypocrisy **2:** 396, 399, 402, 406, 414, 421; **23:** 345, 358, 362
    repentance or pardon **2:** 388, 390, 397, 402, 434, 463, 511, 524

Anne (Anne Boleyn)
  Henry VIII See **Boleyn**

Anne (Anne Page)
  The Merry Wives of Windsor See **Page**

Anne (Lady Anne)
  Richard III **52:** 223, 227, 239, 249, 280

Antigonus
  The Winter's Tale
    characterization **7:** 394, 451, 464
    death (Act III, scene iii) **7:** 377, 414, 464, 483; **15:** 518, 532; **19:** 366

Antonio
  The Merchant of Venice
    excessive or destructive love **4:** 279, 284, 336, 344; **12:** 54; **37:** 86
    love for Bassanio **40:** 156
    melancholy **4:** 221, 238, 279, 284, 300, 321, 328; **22:** 69; **25:** 22
    pitiless **4:** 254
    as pivotal figure **12:** 25, 129;
    versus Shylock **53:** 187
  Twelfth Night **22:** 69

Antonio and Sebastian
  The Tempest **8:** 295, 299, 304, 328, 370, 396, 429, 454; **13:** 440; **29:** 278, 297, 343, 362, 368, 377; **45:** 200

Antony
  Antony and Cleopatra
    characterization **6:** 22, 23, 24, 31, 38, 41, 172, 181, 211; **16:** 342; **19:** 270; **22:** 217; **27:** 117; **47:** 77, 124, 142
    Caesar, relationship with **48:** 206
    Cleopatra, relationship with **6:** 25, 27, 37, 39, 48, 52, 53, 62, 67, 71, 76, 85, 100, 125, 131, 133, 136, 142, 151, 161, 163, 165, 180, 192; **27:** 82; **47:** 107, 124, 165, 174
    death scene **25:** 245; **47:** 142
    dotage **6:** 22, 23, 38, 41, 48, 52, 62, 107, 136, 146, 175; **17:** 28
    nobility **6:** 22, 24, 33, 48, 94, 103, 136, 142, 159, 172, 202; **25:** 245
    political conduct **6:** 33, 38, 53, 107, 111, 146, 181
    public vs. private personae **6:** 165; **47:** 107
    self-knowledge **6:** 120, 131, 175, 181, 192; **47:** 77
    as superhuman figure **6:** 37, 51, 71, 92, 94, 178, 192; **27:** 110; **47:** 71
    as tragic hero **6:** 38, 39, 52, 53, 60, 104, 120, 151, 155, 165, 178, 192, 202, 211; **22:** 217; **27:** 90
  Julius Caesar
    characterization **7:** 160, 179, 189, 221, 233, 284, 320, 333; **17:** 269, 271, 272, 284, 298, 306, 313, 315, 358, 398; **25:** 272; **30:** 316
    funeral oration **7:** 148, 154, 159, 204, 210, 221, 238, 259, 350; **25:** 280; **30:** 316, 333, 362

Apemantus
  Timon of Athens **1:** 453, 467, 483; **20:** 476, 493; **25:** 198; **27:** 166, 223, 235

Arcite
  The Two Noble Kinsmen See **Palamon and Arcite**

Ariel
  The Tempest **8:** 289, 293, 294, 295, 297, 304, 307, 315, 320, 326, 328, 336, 340, 345, 356, 364, 420, 458; **22:** 302; **29:** 278, 297, 362, 368, 377

Armado
  Love's Labour's Lost **23:** 207

Arthur
King John **9**: 215, 216, 218, 219, 229, 240, 267, 275; **22**: 120; **25**: 98; **41**: 251, 277

Arviragus
Cymbeline See **Guiderius and Arviragus**

Audrey
As You Like It **46**: 122

Aufidius
Coriolanus **9**: 9, 12, 17, 19, 53, 121, 148, 153, 157, 169, 180, 193; **19**: 287; **25**: 263, 296; **30**: 58, 67, 89, 96, 133; **50**: 99

Autolycus
The Winter's Tale **7**: 375, 380, 382, 387, 389, 395, 396, 414; **15**: 524; **22**: 302; **37**: 31; **45**: 333; **46**: 14, 33; **50**: 45

Banquo
Macbeth **3**: 183, 199, 208, 213, 278, 289; **20**: 279, 283, 406, 413; **25**: 235; **28**: 339

Baptista
The Taming of the Shrew **9**: 325, 344, 345, 375, 386, 393, 413

Barnardine
Measure for Measure **13**: 112

Bassanio
The Merchant of Venice **25**: 257; **37**: 86; **40**: 156

the Bastard
King John See **Faulconbridge (Philip) the Bastard**

Beatrice and Benedick
Much Ado about Nothing
  Beatrice's femininity **8**: 14, 16, 17, 24, 29, 38, 41, 91; **31**: 222, 245
  Beatrice's request to "kill Claudio" (Act IV, scene i) **8**: 14, 17, 33, 41, 55, 63, 75, 79, 91, 108, 115; **18**: 119, 120, 136, 161, 245, 257
  Benedick's challenge of Claudio (Act V, scene i) **8**: 48, 63, 79, 91; **31**: 231
  Claudio and Hero, compared with **8**: 19, 28, 29, 75, 82, 115; **31**: 171, 216
  marriage and the opposite sex, attitudes toward **8**: 9, 13, 14, 16, 19, 29, 36, 48, 63, 77, 91, 95, 115, 121; **16**: 45; **31**: 216; **48**: 14
  mutual attraction **8**: 13, 14, 19, 24, 29, 33, 41, 75; **48**: 14
  nobility **8**: 13, 19, 24, 29, 36, 39, 41, 47, 82, 91, 108
  popularity **8**: 13, 38, 41, 53, 79
  transformed by love **8**: 19, 29, 36, 48, 75, 91, 95, 115; **31**: 209, 216
  unconventionality **8**: 48, 91, 95, 108, 115, 121
  vulgarity **8**: 11, 12, 33, 38, 41, 47
  wit and charm **8**: 9, 12, 13, 14, 19, 24, 27, 28, 29, 33, 36, 38, 41, 47, 55, 69, 95, 108, 115; **31**: 241

Belarius
Cymbeline **4**: 48, 89, 141

Benedick
Much Ado about Nothing See **Beatrice and Benedick**

Berowne
Love's Labour's Lost **2**: 308, 324, 327; **22**: 12; **23**: 184, 187; **38**: 194; **47**: 35

Bertram
All's Well That Ends Well
  characterization **7**: 15, 27, 29, 32, 39, 41, 43, 98, 113; **26**: 48; **26**: 117; **48**: 65
  conduct **7**: 9, 10, 12, 16, 19, 21, 51, 62, 104; **50**: 59
  physical desire **22**: 78
  transformation or redemption **7**: 10, 19, 21, 26, 29, 32, 54, 62, 81, 90, 93, 98, 109, 113, 116, 126; **13**: 84

Bianca
The Taming of the Shrew **9**: 325, 342, 344, 345, 360, 362, 370, 375
  Bianca-Lucentio subplot **9**: 365, 370, 375, 390, 393, 401, 407, 413, 430; **16**: 13; **31**: 339

the boar
Venus and Adonis **10**: 416, 451, 454, 466, 473; **33**: 339, 347, 370

Boleyn (Anne Boleyn)
Henry VIII **2**: 21, 24, 31; **41**: 180

Bolingbroke
Richard II See **Henry (King Henry IV, previously known as Bolingbroke)**

Borachio and Conrade
Much Ado about Nothing **8**: 24, 69, 82, 88, 111, 115

Bottom
A Midsummer Night's Dream
  awakening speech (Act IV, scene i) **3**: 406, 412, 450, 457, 486, 516; **16**: 34
  folly of **46**: 1, 14, 29, 60
  imagination **3**: 376, 393, 406, 432, 486; **29**: 175, 190; **45**: 147
  self-possession **3**: 365, 376, 395, 402, 406, 480; **45**: 158
  Titania, relationship with **3**: 377, 406, 441, 445, 450, 457, 491, 497; **16**: 34; **19**: 21; **22**: 93; **29**: 216; **45**: 160
  transformation **3**: 365, 377, 432; **13**: 27; **22**: 93; **29**: 216; **45**: 147, 160

Brabantio
Othello **25**: 189

Brutus
Coriolanus See **the tribunes**
Julius Caesar **50**: 194, 258
  arrogance **7**: 160, 169, 204, 207, 264, 277, 292, 350; **25**: 280; **30**: 351
  as chief protagonist or tragic hero **7**: 152, 159, 189, 191, 200, 204, 242, 250, 253, 264, 268, 279, 284, 298, 333; **17**: 272, 372, 387
  citizenship **25**: 272
  funeral oration **7**: 154, 155, 204, 210, 350
  motives **7**: 150, 156, 161, 179, 191, 200, 221, 227, 233, 245, 292, 303, 310, 320, 333, 350; **25**: 272; **30**: 321, 358
  nobility or idealism **7**: 150, 152, 156, 159, 161, 179, 189, 191, 200, 221, 242, 250, 253, 259, 264, 277, 303, 320; **17**: 269, 271, 273, 279, 280, 284, 306, 308, 321, 323, 324, 345, 358; **25**: 272, 280; **30**: 351, 362
  political ineptitude or lack of judgment **7**: 169, 188, 200, 205, 221, 245, 252, 264, 277, 282, 310, 316, 331, 333, 343; **17**: 323, 358, 375, 380; **50**: 13
  self-knowledge or self-deception **7**: 191, 200, 221, 242, 259, 264, 268, 279, 310, 333, 336, 350; **25**: 272; **30**: 316
  soliloquy (Act II, scene i) **7**: 156, 160, 161, 191, 221, 245, 250, 253, 264, 268, 279, 282, 292, 303, 343, 350; **25**: 280; **30**: 333
The Rape of Lucrece **10**: 96, 106, 109, 116, 121, 125, 128, 135

Buckingham
Henry VIII **22**: 182; **24**: 129, 140; **37**: 109

Cade (Jack Cade)
Henry VI, Parts 1, 2, and 3 **3**: 35, 67, 92, 97, 109; **16**: 183; **22**: 156; **25**: 102; **28**: 112; **37**: 97; **39**: 160, 196, 205

Caesar
Antony and Cleopatra
  Antony, relationship with as leader **48**: 206
Julius Caesar **50**: 189, 230, 234
  ambiguous nature **7**: 191, 233, 242, 250, 272, 298, 316, 320
  ambitious nature **50**: 234
  arrogance **7**: 160, 207, 218, 253, 272, 279, 298; **25**: 280
  idolatry **22**: 137
  leadership qualities **7**: 161, 179, 189, 191, 200, 207, 233, 245, 253, 257, 264, 272, 279, 284, 298, 310, 333; **17**: 317, 358; **22**: 280; **30**: 316, 326; **50**: 234
  as tragic hero **7**: 152, 200, 221, 279; **17**: 321, 377, 384
  weakness **7**: 161, 167, 169, 179, 187, 188, 191, 207, 218, 221, 233, 250, 253, 298; **17**: 358; **25**: 280

Caius, Doctor
The Merry Wives of Windsor **47**: 354

Caliban
The Tempest **8**: 286, 287, 289, 292, 294, 295, 297, 302, 304, 307, 309, 315, 326, 328, 336, 353, 364, 370, 380, 390, 396, 401, 414, 420, 423, 429, 435, 454; **13**: 424, 440; **15**: 189, 312, 322, 374, 379; **22**: 302; **25**: 382; **28**: 249; **29**: 278, 292, 297, 343, 368, 377, 396; **32**: 367; **45**: 211, 219, 226, 259; **53**: 45, 64

Calphurnia
Julius Caesar
Calphurnia's dream **45:** 10

Cambridge
Henry V See **traitors**

Canterbury and the churchmen
Henry V **5:** 193, 203, 205, 213, 219, 225, 252, 260; **22:** 137; **30:** 215, 262

Cardinal Wolsey
Henry VIII See **Wolsey**

Casca
Julius Caesar
as Cynic **50:** 249
as proto-Christian **50:** 249

Cassio
Othello **25:** 189

Cassius
Julius Caesar **7:** 156, 159, 160, 161, 169, 179, 189, 221, 233, 303, 310, 320, 333, 343; **17:** 272, 282, 284, 344, 345, 358; **25:** 272, 280; **30:** 351; **37:** 203

Celia
As You Like It **46:** 94

Chorus
Henry V
role of **5:** 186, 192, 226, 228, 230, 252, 264, 269, 281, 293; **14:** 301, 319, 336; **19:** 133; **25:** 116, 131; **30:** 163, 202, 220

the churchmen
Henry V See **Canterbury and the churchmen**

Cinna
Julius Caesar
as poet **48:** 240

Claudio
Much Ado about Nothing
boorish behavior **8:** 9, 24, 33, 36, 39, 44, 48, 63, 79, 82, 95, 100, 111, 115; **31:** 209
credulity **8:** 9, 17, 19, 24, 29, 36, 41, 47, 58, 63, 75, 77, 82, 95, 100, 104, 111, 115, 121; **31:** 241; **47:** 25
mercenary traits **8:** 24, 44, 58, 82, 91, 95
noble qualities **8:** 17, 19, 29, 41, 44, 58, 75
reconciliation with Hero **8:** 33, 36, 39, 44, 47, 82, 95, 100, 111, 115, 121
repentance **8:** 33, 63, 82, 95, 100, 111, 115, 121; **31:** 245
sexual insecurities **8:** 75, 100, 111, 115, 121

Claudius
Hamlet **13:** 502; **16** 246; **21:** 259, 347, 361, 371; **28:** 232, 290; **35:** 104, 182; **44:** 119, 241

Cleopatra
Antony and Cleopatra
Antony, relationship with **6:** 25, 27, 37, 39, 48, 52, 53, 62, 67, 71, 76, 85, 100, 125, 131, 133, 136, 142, 151, 161, 163, 165, 180, 192; **25:** 257; **27:** 82; **47:** 107, 124, 165, 174
characterization **47:** 77, 96, 113, 124
contradictory or inconsistent nature **6:** 23, 24, 27, 67, 76, 100, 104, 115, 136, 151, 159, 202; **17:** 94, 113; **27:** 135
costume **17:** 94
creativity **6:** 197; **47:** 96, 113
death **6:** 23, 25, 27, 41, 43, 52, 60, 64, 76, 94, 100, 103, 120, 131, 133, 136, 140, 146, 161, 165, 180, 181, 192, 197, 208; **13:** 383; **17:** 48, 94; **25:** 245; **27:** 135; **47:** 71
personal attraction of **6:** 24, 38, 40, 43, 48, 53, 76, 104, 115, 155; **17:** 113
self-knowledge **47:** 77, 96
staging issues **17:** 94, 113
as subverter of social order **6:** 146, 165; **47:** 113
as superhuman figure **6:** 37, 51, 71, 92, 94, 178, 192; **27:** 110; **47:** 71, 174, 192
as tragic heroine **6:** 53, 120, 151, 192, 208; **27:** 144
as voluptuary or courtesan **6:** 21, 22, 25, 41, 43, 52, 53, 62, 64, 67, 76, 146, 161; **47:** 107, 174

Cloten
Cymbeline **4:** 20, 116, 127, 155; **22:** 302, 365; **25:** 245; **36:** 99, 125, 142, 155; **47:** 228

Collatine
The Rape of Lucrece **10:** 98, 131; **43:** 102; **48:** 291

Cominius
Coriolanus **25:** 245

Conrade
Much Ado about Nothing See **Borachio and Conrade**

Constance
King John **9:** 208, 210, 211, 215, 219, 220, 224, 229, 240, 251, 254; **16:** 161; **24:** 177, 184, 196

Cordelia
King Lear
attack on Britain **25:** 202
characterization **2:** 110, 116, 125, 170; **16:** 311; **25:** 218; **28:** 223, 325; **31:** 117, 149, 155, 162; **46:** 218, 225, 231, 242
as Christ figure **2:** 116, 170, 179, 188, 222, 286
gender identity **48:** 222
rebelliousness **13:** 352; **25:** 202
on stage **11:** 158
transcendent power **2:** 137, 207, 218, 265, 269, 273
women, the Christian ideal of **48:** 222

Corin
As You Like It See **pastoral characters**

Coriolanus
Coriolanus
anger or passion **9:** 19, 26, 45, 80, 92, 157, 164, 177, 189; **30:** 79, 96
as complementary figure to Aufidius **19:** 287
death scene (Act V, scene vi) **9:** 12, 80, 100, 117, 125, 144, 164, 198; **25:** 245, 263; **50:** 110
as epic hero **9:** 130, 164, 177; **25:** 245; **50:** 119
immaturity **9:** 62, 80, 84, 110, 117, 142; **30:** 140
inhuman attributes **9:** 65, 73, 139, 157, 164, 169, 189, 198; **25:** 263
internal struggle **9:** 31, 43, 45, 53, 72, 117, 121, 130; **44:** 93
introspection or self-knowledge, lack of **9:** 53, 80, 84, 112, 117, 130; **25:** 296; **30:** 133
isolation or autonomy **9:** 53, 65, 142, 144, 153, 157, 164, 180, 183, 189, 198; **30:** 58, 89, 111;**50:** 128
manipulation by others **9:** 33, 45, 62, 80; **25:** 296
as military leader **48:** 230
modesty **9:** 8, 12, 19, 26, 53, 78, 92, 117, 121, 144, 183; **25:** 296; **30:** 79, 96, 129, 133, 149
narcissism **30:** 111
noble or aristocratic attributes **9:** 15, 18, 19, 26, 31, 33, 52, 53, 62, 65, 84, 92, 100, 121, 148, 157, 169; **25:** 263; **30:** 67, 74, 96; **50:** 13
pride or arrogance **9:** 8, 11, 12, 19, 26, 31, 33, 43, 45, 65, 78, 92, 121, 148, 153, 177; **30:** 58, 67, 74, 89, 96, 129
punishment of **48:** 230
reconciliation with society **9:** 33, 43, 45, 65, 139, 169; **25:** 296
as socially destructive force **9:** 62, 65, 73, 78, 110, 142, 144, 153; **25:** 296
soliloquy (Act IV, scene iv) **9:** 84, 112, 117, 130
as tragic figure **9:** 8, 12, 13, 18, 25, 45, 52, 53, 72, 80, 92, 106, 112, 117, 130, 148, 164, 169, 177; **25:** 296; **30:** 67, 74, 79, 96, 111, 129; **37:** 283; **50:** 99
traitorous actions **9:** 9, 12, 19, 45, 84, 92, 148; **25:** 296; **30:** 133
as unsympathetic character **9:** 12, 13, 62, 78, 80, 84, 112, 130, 157

the courser and the jennet
Venus and Adonis **10:** 418, 439, 466; **33:** 309, 339, 347, 352

Cranmer
Henry VIII
prophesy of **2:** 25, 31, 46, 56, 64, 68, 72; **24:** 146; **32:** 148; **41:** 120, 190

Cressida
Troilus and Cressida
as ambiguous figure **43:** 305
inconsistency **3:** 538; **13:** 53; **16:** 70; **22:** 339; **27:** 362
individual will vs. social values **3:** 549, 561, 571, 590, 604, 617, 626; **13:** 53; **27:** 396

infidelity **3:** 536, 537, 544, 554, 555; **18:** 277, 284, 286; **22:** 58, 339; **27:** 400; **43:** 298
lack of punishment **3:** 536, 537
as mother figure **22:** 339
objectification of **43:** 329
as sympathetic figure **3:** 557, 560, 604, 609; **18:** 284, 423; **22:** 58; **27:** 396, 400; **43:** 305

Dark Lady
Sonnets **10:** 161, 167, 176, 216, 217, 218, 226, 240, 302, 342, 377, 394; **25:** 374; **37:** 374; **40:** 273; **48:** 346; **51:** 284, 288, 292, 321

the Dauphin
Henry V See **French aristocrats and the Dauphin**

Desdemona
Othello
as Christ figure **4:** 506, 525, 573; **35:** 360
culpability **4:** 408, 415, 422, 427; **13:** 313; **19:** 253, 276; **35:** 265, 352, 380
innocence **35:** 360; **43:** 32; **47:** 25; **53:** 310, 333
as mother figure **22:** 339; **35:** 282; **53:** 324
passivity **4:** 402, 406, 421, 440, 457, 470, 582, 587; **25:** 189; **35:** 380
spiritual nature of her love **4:** 462, 530, 559
staging issues **11:** 350, 354, 359; **13:** 327; **32:** 201

Diana
Pericles
as symbol of nature **22:** 315; **36:** 233; **51:** 71

Dogberry and the Watch
Much Ado about Nothing **8:** 9, 12, 13, 17, 24, 28, 29, 33, 39, 48, 55, 69, 79, 82, 88, 95, 104, 108, 115; **18:** 138, 152, 205, 208, 210, 213, 231; **22:** 85; **31:** 171, 229; **46:** 60

Don John
Much Ado about Nothing See **John (Don John)**

Don Pedro
Much Ado about Nothing See **Pedro (Don Pedro)**

Dromio Brothers
Comedy of Errors **42:** 80

Duke
Measure for Measure
as authoritarian figure **23:** 314, 317, 347; **33:** 85; **49:** 274, 300, 358
characterization **2:** 388, 395, 402, 406, 411, 421, 429, 456, 466, 470, 498, 511; **13:** 84, 94, 104; **23:** 363, 416; **32:** 81; **42:** 1; **44:** 89; **49:** 274, 293, 300, 358
as dramatic failure **2:** 420, 429, 441, 479, 495, 505, 514, 522
godlike portrayal of **23:** 320

noble portrayal of **23:** 301
speech on death (Act III, scene i) **2:** 390, 391, 395
Othello **25:** 189

Edgar
King Lear **28:** 223; **32:** 212; **32:** 308; **37:** 295; **47:** 9; **50:** 24, 45
Edgar-Edmund duel **22:** 365

Edmund
King Lear **25:** 218; **28:** 223
Edmund's forged letter **16:** 372

Edmund of Langley, Duke of York
Richard II See **York**

Elbow
Measure for Measure **22:** 85; **25:** 12

Elbow (Mistress Elbow)
Measure for Measure **33:** 90

elder characters
All's Well That Ends Well **7:** 9, 37, 39, 43, 45, 54, 62, 104

Elizabeth I
Love's Labour's Lost **38:** 239

Emilia
Othello **4:** 386, 391, 392, 415, 587; **35:** 352, 380; **43:** 32
The Two Noble Kinsmen **9:** 460, 470, 471, 479, 481; **19:** 394; **41:** 372, 385; **42:** 361

Enobarbus
Antony and Cleopatra **6:** 22, 23, 27, 43, 94, 120, 142; **16:** 342; **17:** 36; **22:** 217; **27:** 135

Evans, Sir Hugh
The Merry Wives of Windsor **47:** 354

fairies
A Midsummer Night's Dream **3:** 361, 362, 372, 377, 395, 400, 423, 450, 459, 486; **12:** 287, 291, 294, 295; **19:** 21; **29:** 183, 190; **45:** 147

Falstaff
Henry IV, Parts 1 and 2
characterization **1:** 287, 298, 312, 333; **25:** 245; **28:** 203; **39:** 72, 134, 137, 143; **48:** 117, 151
as comic figure **1:** 287, 311, 327, 344, 351, 354, 357, 410, 434; **39:** 89; **46:** 1, 48, 52
as comic versus tragic figure **49:** 178
as coward or rogue **1:** 285, 290, 296, 298, 306, 307, 313, 317, 323, 336, 337, 338, 342, 354, 366, 374, 391, 396, 401, 433; **14:** 7, 111, 125, 130, 133; **32:** 166
as deceiver deceived **47:** 308
diminishing powers of **47:** 363
dual personality **1:** 397, 401, 406, 434; **49:** 162

female attributes **13:** 183; **44:** 44; **47:** 325
Iago, compared with **1:** 341, 351
as Jack-a-Lent **47:** 363
Marxist interpretation **1:** 358, 361
as outlaw **49:** 133
as parody of the historical plot **1:** 314, 354, 359; **39:** 143
as positive character **1:** 286, 287, 290, 296, 298, 311, 312, 321, 325, 333, 344, 355, 357, 389, 401, 408, 434
rejection by Hal **1:** 286, 287, 290, 312, 314, 317, 324, 333, 338, 344, 357, 366, 372, 374, 379, 380, 389, 414; **13:** 183; **25:** 109; **39:** 72, 89; **48:** 95
as satire of feudal society **1:** 314, 328, 361; **32:** 103
as scapegoat **1:** 389, 414; **47:** 358, 363, 375
stage interpretations **14:** 4, 6, 7, 9, 15, 116, 130, 146; **47:** 1
as subversive figure **16:** 183; **25:** 109
Henry V **5:** 185, 186, 187, 189, 192, 195, 198, 210, 226, 257, 269, 271, 276, 293, 299; **28:** 146; **46:** 48
The Merry Wives of Windsor
characterization in 1 and 2 *Henry IV*, compared with **5:** 333, 335, 336, 337, 339, 346, 347, 348, 350, 373, 400; **18:** 5, 7, 75, 86; **22:** 93
diminishing powers **5:** 337, 339, 343, 347, 350, 351, 392
as Herne the Hunter **38:** 256, 286; **47:** 358
incapability of love **5:** 335, 336, 339, 346, 348; **22:** 93
personification of comic principle or as Vice figure **1:** 342, 361, 366, 374; **5:** 332, 338, 369, 400; **38:** 273
recognition and repentance of follies **5:** 338, 341, 343, 348, 369, 374, 376, 397
sensuality **5:** 339, 343, 353, 369, 392
shrewdness **5:** 332, 336, 346, 355
threat to community **5:** 343, 369, 379, 392, 395, 400; **38:** 297
as unifying force **47:** 358
vanity **5:** 332, 339
victimization **5:** 336, 338, 341, 347, 348, 353, 355, 360, 369, 373, 374, 376, 392, 397, 400
as villain **47:** 358

Faulconbridge, (Philip) the Bastard
King John **41:** 205, 228, 251, 260, 277; **48:** 132
as chorus or commentator **9:** 212, 218, 229, 248, 251, 260, 271, 284, 297, 300; **22:** 120
as comic figure **9:** 219, 271, 297
development **9:** 216, 224, 229, 248, 263, 271, 275, 280, 297; **13:** 158, 163
as embodiment of England **9:** 222, 224, 240, 244, 248, 271
heroic qualities **9:** 208, 245, 248, 254, 263, 271, 275; **25:** 98
political conduct **9:** 224, 240, 250, 260, 280, 297; **13:** 147, 158; **22:** 120

Fenton
The Merry Wives of Windsor
Anne Page-Fenton plot **5:** 334, 336, 343, 353, 376, 390, 395, 402; **22:** 93

Ferdinand
The Tempest **8:** 328, 336, 359, 454; **19:** 357; **22:** 302; **29:** 362, 339, 377

Feste
Twelfth Night
characterization **1:** 558, 655, 658; **26:** 233, 364; **46:** 1, 14, 18, 33, 52, 60, 303, 310
role in play **1:** 546, 551, 553, 566, 570, 571, 579, 635, 658; **46:** 297, 303, 310
song **1:** 543, 548, 561, 563, 566, 570, 572, 603, 620, 642; **46:** 297
gender issues **19:** 78; **34:** 344; **37:** 59

Flavius and Murellus
Julius Caesar **50:** 64

Fluellen
Henry V **30:** 278; **37:** 105

Fool
King Lear **2:** 108, 112, 125, 156, 162, 245, 278, 284; **11:** 17, 158, 169; **22:** 227; **25:** 202; **28:** 223; **46:** 1, 14, 18, 24, 33, 52, 191, 205, 210, 218, 225

Ford, Francis
The Merry Wives of Windsor **5:** 332, 334, 343, 355, 363, 374, 379, 390; **38:** 273; **47:** 321

Ford, Mistress Alice
The Merry Wives of Windsor **47:** 321

Fortinbras
Hamlet **21:** 136, 347; **28:** 290

French aristocrats and the Dauphin
Henry V **5:** 188, 191, 199, 205, 213, 281; **22:** 137; **28:** 121

Friar
Much Ado about Nothing **8:** 24, 29, 41, 55, 63, 79, 111

Friar John
Romeo and Juliet See **John (Friar John)**

Friar Lawrence
Romeo and Juliet See **Lawrence (Friar Lawrence)**

the Friend
Sonnets **10:** 279, 302, 309, 379, 385, 391, 394; **51:** 284, 292, 300, 304, 316, 321

Ganymede
A Winter's Tale **48:** 309

Gardiner (Stephen Gardiner)
Henry VIII **24:** 129

Gaunt
Richard II **6:** 255, 287, 374, 388, 402, 414; **24:** 274, 322, 325, 414, 423; **37:** 222; **52:** 174, 183

Gertrude
Hamlet **21:** 259, 347, 392; **28:** 311; **32:** 238; **35:** 182, 204, 229; **43:** 12; **44:** 119, 160, 189, 195, 237, 247
death monologue **48:** 255

Ghost
Hamlet **1:** 75, 76, 84, 85, 128, 134, 138, 154, 171, 218, 231, 254; **16:** 246; **21:** 17, 44, 112, 151, 334, 371, 377, 392; **25:** 288; **35:** 152, 157, 174, 237; **44:** 119

Gloucester
King Lear **46:** 254

Gobbo, Launcelot
The Merchant of Venice **46:** 24, 60; **53:** 187, 214

Goneril
King Lear **31:** 151; **46:** 231, 242

Gonzalo
The Tempest **22:** 302; **29:** 278, 343, 362, 368; **45:** 280

Gower chorus
Pericles **2:** 548, 575; **15:** 134, 141, 143, 145, 149, 152, 177; **36:** 279; **42:** 352

Grey
Henry V See **traitors**

Guiderius and Arviragus
Cymbeline **4:** 21, 22, 89, 129, 141, 148; **25:** 319; **36:** 125, 158

Hal
See **Henry (King Henry V, formerly known as Prince Henry of Wales)**

Hamlet
Hamlet
as a fool **46:** 1, 29, 52, 74
delay **1:** 76, 83, 88, 90, 94, 98, 102, 103, 106, 114, 115, 116, 119, 120, 148, 151, 166, 171, 179, 188, 191, 194, 198, 221, 268; **13:** 296, 502; **21:** 81; **25:** 209, 288; **28:** 223; **35:** 82, 174, 212, 215, 237; **44:** 180, 209, 219, 229
divided nature **16:** 246; **28:** 223; **32:** 288; **35:** 182, 215; **37:** 241
elocution of the character's speeches **21:** 96, 104, 112, 127, 132, 172, 177, 179, 194, 245, 254, 257
madness **1:** 76, 81, 83, 95, 102, 106, 128, 144, 154, 160, 234; **21:** 35, 50, 72, 81, 99, 112, 311, 339, 355, 361, 371, 377, 384; **35:** 117, 132, 134, 140, 144, 212; **44:** 107, 119, 152, 209, 219, 229
melancholy **21:** 99, 112, 177, 194; **35:** 82, 95, 117; **44:** 209, 219
as negative character **1:** 86, 92, 111, 171, 218; **21:** 386; **25:** 209; **35:** 167
reaction to his father's death **22:** 339; **35:** 104, 174; **44:** 133, 160, 180, 189
reaction to Gertrude's marriage **1:** 74, 120, 154, 179; **16:** 259; **21:** 371; **22:** 339; **35:** 104, 117; **44:** 133, 160, 189, 195

religion **48:** 195
romantic aspects of the character **21:** 96; **44:** 198
as scourge or purifying figure **1:** 144, 209, 242; **25:** 288; **35:** 157
sentimentality vs. intellectuality **1:** 75, 83, 88, 91, 93, 94, 96, 102, 103, 115, 116, 120, 166, 191; **13:** 296; **21:** 35, 41, 44, 72, 81, 89, 99, 129, 132, 136, 172, 213, 225, 339, 355, 361, 371, 377, 379, 381, 386; **25:** 209; **44:** 198
soliloquies **1:** 76, 82, 83, 148, 166, 169, 176, 191; **21:** 17, 31, 44, 53, 89, 112, 268, 311, 334, 347, 361, 384, 392; **25:** 209; **28:** 223; **44:** 107, 119, 229
theatrical interpretations **21:** 11, 31, 78, 101, 104, 107, 160, 177, 179, 182, 183, 192, 194, 197, 202, 203, 208, 213, 225, 232, 237, 249, 253, 254, 257, 259, 274, 311, 339, 347, 355, 361, 371, 377, 380; **44:** 198
virility **21:** 213, 301, 355

Helena
All's Well That Ends Well
as agent of reconciliation, renewal, or grace **7:** 67, 76, 81, 90, 93, 98, 109, 116
as dualistic or enigmatic character **7:** 15, 27, 29, 39, 54, 58, 62, 67, 76, 81, 98, 113, 126; **13:** 66; **22:** 78; **26:** 117; **48:** 65
as "female achiever" **19:** 113; **38:** 89
desire **38:** 96; **44:** 35
pursuit of Bertram **7:** 9, 12, 15, 16, 19, 21, 26, 27, 29, 32, 43, 54, 76, 116; **13:** 77; **22:** 78; **49:** 46
virginity **38:** 65
virtue and nobility **7:** 9, 10, 12, 16, 19, 21, 27, 32, 41, 51, 58, 67, 76, 86, 126; **13:** 77; **50:** 59
A Midsummer Night's Dream **29:** 269

Henry (King Henry IV, previously known as Bolingbroke)
Henry IV, Parts 1 and 2 **39:** 123, 137
effectiveness as ruler **49:** 116
guilt **49:** 112
historical context **49:** 139
illegitimacy of rule **49:** 112, 133, 137
power **49:** 139
as tragic figure **49:** 186
as usurper **49:** 116, 137
Richard II
Bolingbroke and Richard as opposites **24:** 423
Bolingbroke-Mowbray dispute **22:** 137
comic elements **28:** 134
guilt **24:** 423; **39:** 279
language and imagery **6:** 310, 315, 331, 347, 374, 381, 397; **32:** 189
as Machiavellian figure **6:** 305, 307, 315, 331, 347, 388, 393, 397; **24:** 428
as politician **6:** 255, 263, 264, 272, 277, 294, 364, 368, 391; **24:** 330, 333, 405, 414, 423, 428; **39:** 256; **52:** 124
Richard, compared with **6:** 307, 315, 347, 374, 391, 393, 409; **24:** 346, 349, 351, 352, 356, 395, 419, 423, 428; **52:** 108, 124
seizure of Gaunt's estate **49:** 60
his silence **24:** 423
structure, compared with **39:** 235

usurpation of crown, nature of **6:** 255, 272, 289, 307, 310, 347, 354, 359, 381, 385, 393; **13:** 172; **24:** 322, 356, 383, 419; **28:** 178; **52:** 108, 124

Henry (King Henry V, formerly known as Prince Henry of Wales)
Henry IV, Parts 1 and 2
and betrayal 49: 123
as the central character **1:** 286, 290, 314, 317, 326, 338, 354, 366, 374, 396; **39:** 72, 100
dual personality **1:** 397, 406; **25:** 109, 151; **48:** 95; **49:** 112, 139, 153, 162
as Everyman **1:** 342, 366, 374
from audience's perspective 49: 153
from Henry's perspective 49: 153
fall from humanity **1:** 379, 380, 383
general assessment **1:** 286, 287, 289, 290, 314, 317, 326, 327, 332, 357, 397; **25:** 245; **32:** 212; **39:** 134; **48:** 151
as ideal ruler **1:** 289, 309, 317, 321, 326, 337, 342, 344, 374, 389, 391, 434; **25:** 109; **39:** 123; **47:** 60
as Machiavellian ruler 47: 60
as negative character **1:** 312, 332, 333, 357; **32:** 212
as outlaw 49: 112
preparation for rule 49: 112
as restorer of law 49: 133
Richard II, compared with **1:** 332, 337; **39:** 72
Henry V
brutality and cunning **5:** 193, 203, 209, 210, 213, 219, 233, 239, 252, 260, 271, 287, 293, 302, 304; **30:** 159; **43:** 24
characterization in 1 and 2 Henry IV contrasted **5:** 189, 190, 241, 304, 310; **19:** 133; **25:** 131; **32:** 157
chivalry **37:** 187
courage **5:** 191, 195, 210, 213, 228, 246, 257, 267
disguise **30:** 169, 259
education **5:** 246, 267, 271, 289; **14:** 297, 328, 342; **30:** 259
emotion, lack of **5:** 209, 212, 233, 244, 264, 267, 287, 293, 310
as heroic figure **5:** 192, 205, 209, 223, 244, 252, 257, 260, 269, 271, 299, 304; **28:** 121, 146; **30:** 237, 244, 252; **37:** 187; **49:** 194, 200, 236, 247
humor **5:** 189, 191, 212, 217, 239, 240, 276
intellectual and social limitations **5:** 189, 191, 203, 209, 210, 225, 226, 230, 293; **30:** 220
interpersonal relations **5:** 209, 233, 267, 269, 276, 287, 293, 302, 318; **19:** 133; **28:** 146
mercy **5:** 213, 267, 289, 293
mixture of good and bad qualities **5:** 199, 205, 209, 210, 213, 244, 260, 304, 314; **30:** 262, 273; **49:** 211
piety **5:** 191, 199, 209, 217, 223, 239, 257, 260, 271, 289, 310, 318; **30:** 244; **32:** 126
public vs. private selves **22:** 137; **30:** 169, 207
self-doubt **5:** 281, 310
slaughter of prisoners **5:** 189, 205, 246, 293, 318; **28:** 146
speech **5:** 212, 230, 233, 246, 264, 276, 287, 302; **28:** 146; **30:** 163, 227

Henry (King Henry VI)
Henry VI, Parts 1, 2, and 3
characterization **3:** 64, 77, 151; **39:** 160, 177; **47:** 32
source of social disorder **3:** 25, 31, 41, 115; **39:** 154, 187
as sympathetic figure **3:** 73, 143, 154; **24:** 32

Henry (King Henry VIII)
Henry VIII
as agent of divine retribution **2:** 49
characterization **2:** 23, 39, 51, 58, 60, 65, 66, 75; **28:** 184; **37:** 109
incomplete portrait **2:** 15, 16, 19, 35; **41:** 120
as realistic figure **2:** 21, 22, 23, 25, 32

Henry (Prince Henry)
King John **41:** 277

Hermia
A Midsummer Night's Dream **29:** 225, 269; **45:** 117

Hermione
The Winter's Tale
characterization **7:** 385, 395, 402, 412, 414, 506; **15:** 495, 532; **22:** 302, 324; **25:** 347; **32:** 388; **36:** 311; **47:** 25; **49:** 18
restoration (Act V, scene iii) **7:** 377, 379, 384, 385, 387, 389, 394, 396, 412, 425, 436, 451, 452, 456, 464, 483, 501; **15:** 411, 412, 413, 518, 528, 532; **49:** 18
sex as identity **48:** 309
supposed death **25:** 339; **47:** 25
trial of 49: 18

Hero
Much Ado about Nothing **8:** 13, 14, 16, 19, 28, 29, 44, 48, 53, 55, 82, 95, 104, 111, 115, 121; **31:** 231, 245; **47:** 25

Hippolyta
A Midsummer Night's Dream **48:** 23

Holofernes
Love's Labour's Lost **23:** 207

Horatio
Hamlet **44:** 189
stoic perfection, example of **48:** 195

Hotspur
Henry IV, Parts 1 and 2 **25:** 151; **28:** 101; **39:** 72, 134, 137; **42:** 99
and prisoners of war 49: 137
versus Henry 49: 137
Henry V **5:** 189, 199, 228, 271, 302

Humphrey
Henry VI, Parts 1, 2, and 3 **13:** 131

Iachimo
Cymbeline **25:** 245, 319; **36:** 166; **47:** 274

Iago
Othello
affinity with Othello **4:** 400, 427, 468, 470, 477, 500, 506; **25:** 189; **44:** 57
as conventional dramatic villain **4:** 440, 527, 545, 582; **53:** 238
as homosexual **4:** 503; **53:** 275
Machiavellian elements **4:** 440, 455, 457, 517, 545; **35:** 336, 347
motives **4:** 389, 390, 397, 399, 402, 409, 423, 424, 427, 434, 451, 462, 545, 564; **13:** 304; **25:** 189; **28:** 344; **32:** 201; **35:** 265, 276, 310, 336, 347; **42:** 273; **53:** 246, 275, 324
revenge scheme **4:** 392, 409, 424, 451
as scapegoat **4:** 506
as victim **4:** 402, 409, 434, 451, 457, 470

Imogen
Cymbeline **4:** 21, 22, 24, 29, 37, 45, 46, 52, 56, 78, 89, 108; **15:** 23, 32, 105, 121; **19:** 411; **25:** 245, 319; **28:** 398; **32:** 373; **36:** 129, 142, 148; **47:** 25, 205, 228, 245, 274, 277
reawakening of (Act IV, scene ii) **4:** 37, 56, 89, 103, 108, 116, 150; **15:** 23; **25:** 245; **47:** 252

Isabella
Measure for Measure **2:** 388, 390, 395, 396, 397, 401, 402, 406, 409, 410, 411, 418, 420, 421, 432, 437, 441, 466, 475, 491, 495, 524; **16:** 114; **23:** 278, 279, 280, 281, 282, 296, 344, 357, 363, 405; **28:** 102; **33:** 77, 85

Jack Cade
Henry VI, Parts 1, 2, and 3 See **Cade**

the jailer's daughter
The Two Noble Kinsmen **9:** 457, 460, 479, 481, 486, 502; **41:** 340; **50:** 295, 305, 310, 348, 361

Jaques
As You Like It
love-theme, relation to **5:** 103; **23:** 7, 37, 118, 128
as malcontent **5:** 59, 70, 84
melancholy **5:** 20, 28, 32, 36, 39, 43, 50, 59, 63, 68, 77, 82, 86, 135; **23:** 20, 26, 103, 104, 107, 109; **34:** 85; **46:** 88, 94
pastoral convention, relation to **5:** 61, 63, 65, 79, 93, 98, 114, 118
Seven Ages of Man speech (Act II, scene vii) **5:** 28, 52, 156; **23:** 48, 103, 105, 126, 138, 152; **46:** 88, 156, 164, 169
Shakespeare, relation to **5:** 35, 50, 154; **48:** 42
as superficial critic **5:** 28, 30, 43, 54, 55, 63, 65, 68, 75, 77, 82, 86, 88, 98, 138; **34:** 85

the jennet
Venus and Adonis See **the courser and the jennet**

Jessica
The Merchant of Venice **4:** 196, 200, 228, 293, 342; **48:** 54, 77; **53:** 159, 211

Joan of Arc
Henry VI, Parts 1, 2, and 3 **16:** 131; **32:** 212

John (Don John)
Much Ado about Nothing **8:** 9, 12, 16, 17, 19, 28, 29, 36, 39, 41, 47, 48, 55, 58, 63, 82, 104, 108, 111, 121

John (Friar John)
Romeo and Juliet
  detention of **5:** 448, 467, 470

John (King John)
King John **41:** 205, 260
  death **9:** 212, 215, 216, 240
  decline **9:** 224, 235, 240, 263, 275
  Hubert, scene with (Act III, scene iii) **9:** 210, 212, 216, 218, 219, 280
  moral insensibility **13:** 147, 163
  negative qualities **9:** 209, 212, 218, 219, 229, 234, 235, 244, 245, 246, 250, 254, 275, 280, 297
  positive qualities **9:** 209, 224, 235, 240, 244, 245, 263

John of Lancaster, Prince
Henry IV **49:** 123
  and betrayal **49:** 123

Julia
The Two Gentlemen of Verona **6:** 450, 453, 458, 476, 494, 499, 516, 519, 549, 564; **40:** 312, 327, 374

Juliet
Romeo and Juliet See **Romeo and Juliet**

Launcelot Gobbo
The Merchant of Venice See **Gobbo**

Kate
The Taming of the Shrew
  characterization **32:** 1; **43:** 61
  final speech (Act V, scene ii) **9:** 318, 319, 329, 330, 338, 340, 341, 345, 347, 353, 355, 360, 365, 381, 386, 401, 404, 413, 426, 430; **19:** 3; **22:** 48
  love for Petruchio **9:** 338, 340, 353, 430; **12:** 435
  portrayals of **31:** 282
  shrewishness **9:** 322, 323, 325, 332, 344, 345, 360, 365, 370, 375, 386, 393, 398, 404, 413
  transformation **9:** 323, 341, 355, 370, 386, 393, 401, 404, 407, 419, 424, 426, 430; **16:** 13; **19:** 34; **22:** 48; **31:** 288, 295, 339, 351

Katherine
Henry V **5:** 186, 188, 189, 190, 192, 260, 269, 299, 302; **13:** 183; **19:** 217; **30:** 278; **44:** 44
Henry VIII
  characterization **2:** 18, 19, 23, 24, 38; **24:** 129; **37:** 109; **41:** 180
  Hermione, compared with **2:** 24, 51, 58, 76
  politeness strategies **22:** 182
  religious discourse **22:** 182
  as tragic figure **2:** 16, 18

Kent
King Lear **25:** 202; **28:** 223; **32:** 212; **47:** 9

King
All's Well That Ends Well **38:** 150

King Richard II
Richard II See **Richard**

King Richard III, formerly Richard, Duke of Gloucester
Richard III See **Richard**

Lady Macbeth
Macbeth See **Macbeth (Lady Macbeth)**

Laertes
Hamlet **21:** 347, 386; **28:** 290; **35:** 182

Launce and Speed
The Two Gentlemen of Verona
  comic function of **6:** 438, 439, 442, 456, 458, 460, 462, 472, 476, 478, 484, 502, 504, 507, 509, 516, 519, 549; **40:** 312, 320

Lavatch
All's Well That Ends Well **26:** 64; **46:** 33, 52, 68

Lavinia
Titus Andronicus **27:** 266; **28:** 249; **32:** 212; **43:** 1, 170, 239, 247, 255, 262

Lawrence (Friar Lawrence)
Romeo and Juliet
  contribution to catastrophe **5:** 437, 444, 470; **33:** 300; **51:** 253
  philosophy of moderation **5:** 427, 431, 437, 438, 443, 444, 445, 458, 467, 479, 505, 538
  as Shakespeare's spokesman **5:** 427, 431, 437, 458, 467

Lear
King Lear
  curse on Goneril **11:** 5, 7, 12, 114, 116
  love-test and division of kingdom **2:** 100, 106, 111, 124, 131, 137, 147, 149, 151, 168, 186, 208, 216, 281; **16:** 351; **25:** 202; **31:** 84, 92, 107, 117, 149, 155; **46:** 231, 242
  madness **2:** 94, 95, 98, 99, 100, 101, 102, 103, 111, 116, 120, 124, 125, 149, 156, 191, 208, 216, 281; **46:** 264
  as scapegoat **2:** 241, 253
  self-knowledge **2:** 103, 151, 188, 191, 213, 218, 222, 241, 249, 262; **25:** 218; **37:** 213; **46:** 191, 205, 225, 254, 264

Leontes
The Winter's Tale
  characterization **19:** 431; **43:** 39; **45:** 366
  jealousy **7:** 377, 379, 382, 383, 384, 387, 389, 394, 395, 402, 407, 412, 414, 425, 429, 432, 436, 464, 480, 483, 497; **15:** 514, 518, 532; **22:** 324; **25:** 339; **36:** 334, 344, 349; **44:** 66; **45:** 295, 297, 344, 358; **47:** 25
  Othello, compared with **7:** 383, 390, 412; **15:** 514; **36:** 334; **44:** 66; **47:** 25
  repentance **7:** 381, 389, 394, 396, 402, 414, 497; **36:** 318, 362; **44:** 66

Lord Chief Justice
Henry IV
  as keeper of law and justice **49:** 133

Lucentio
The Taming of the Shrew **9:** 325, 342, 362, 375, 393

Lucio
Measure for Measure **13:** 104; **49:** 379

Lucrece
The Rape of Lucrece
  chastity **33:** 131, 138; **43:** 92
  as example of Renaissance virt[0097] **22:** 289; **43:** 148
  heroic **10:** 84, 93, 109, 121, 128
  patriarchal woman, model of **10:** 109, 131; **33:** 169, 200
  self-perception **48:** 291
  self-responsibility **10:** 89, 96, 98, 106, 125; **33:** 195; **43:** 85, 92, 158
  unrealistic **10:** 64, 65, 66, 121
  verbose **10:** 64, 81, 116; **25:** 305; **33:** 169
  as victim **22:** 294; **25:** 305; **32:** 321; **33:** 131, 195; **43:** 102, 158

Macbeth
Macbeth
  ambition **44:** 284, 324
  characterization **20:** 20, 42, 73, 107, 113, 130, 146, 151, 279, 283, 312, 338, 343, 379, 406, 413; **29:** 139, 152, 155, 165; **44:** 289
  courage **3:** 172, 177, 181, 182, 183, 186, 234, 312, 333; **20:** 107; **44:** 315
  disposition **3:** 173, 175, 177, 182, 186; **20:** 245, 376
  imagination **3:** 196, 208, 213, 250, 312, 345; **20:** 245, 376; **44:** 351
  as "inauthentic" king **3:** 245, 302, 321, 345
  inconsistencies **3:** 202
  as Machiavellian villain **3:** 280
  manliness **20:** 113; **29:** 127, 133; **44:** 315
  psychoanalytic interpretations **20:** 42, 73, 238, 376; **44:** 284, 289, 297, 324; **45:** 48, 58
  Richard III, compared with **3:** 177, 182, 186, 345; **20:** 86, 92; **22:** 365; **44:** 269
  as Satan figure **3:** 229, 269, 275, 289, 318
  self-awareness **3:** 312, 329, 338; **16:** 317; **44:** 361
  as sympathetic figure **3:** 229, 306, 314, 338; **29:** 139, 152; **44:** 269, 306, 337
  as tragic hero **44:** 269, 306, 315, 324, 337

Macbeth (Lady Macbeth)
Macbeth
  ambition **3:** 185, 219; **20:** 279, 345
  characterization **20:** 56, 60, 65, 73, 140, 148, 151, 241, 279, 283, 338, 350, 406, 413; **29:** 109, 146

childlessness **3:** 219, 223; **48:** 214
good and evil, combined traits of **3:** 173, 191, 213; **20:** 60, 107
inconsistencies **3:** 202; **20:** 54, 137
influence on Macbeth **3:** 171, 185, 191, 193, 199, 262, 289, 312, 318; **13:** 502; **20:** 345; **25:** 235; **29:** 133
psychoanalytic interpretations **20:** 345; **44:** 289, 297; **45:** 58
sleepwalking scene **44:** 261
as sympathetic figure **3:** 191, 193, 203

Macduff
    Macbeth **3:** 226, 231, 253, 262,; **25:** 235; **29:** 127, 133, 155

MacMorris
    Henry V **22:** 103; **28:** 159; **30:** 278

Malcolm
    Macbeth **25:** 235
    fatherhood **48:** 214

Malvolio
    Twelfth Night
        characterization **1:** 540, 544, 545, 548, 550, 554, 558, 567, 575, 577, 615; **26:** 207, 233, 273; **46:** 286
        forged letter **16:** 372; **28:** 1
        punishment **1:** 539, 544, 548, 549, 554, 555, 558, 563, 577, 590, 632, 645; **46:** 291, 297, 338
        as Puritan **1:** 549, 551, 555, 558, 561, 563; **25:** 47
        role in play **1:** 545, 548, 549, 553, 555, 563, 567, 575, 577, 588, 610, 615, 632, 645; **26:** 337, 374; **46:** 347

Mamillius
    The Winter's Tale **7:** 394, 396, 451; **22:** 324

Margaret
    Henry VI, Parts 1, 2, and 3
        characterization **3:** 18, 26, 35, 51, 103, 109, 140, 157; **24:** 48
        Suffolk, relationship with **3:** 18, 24, 26, 157; **39:** 213
    Richard III **8:** 153, 154, 159, 162, 163, 170, 193, 201, 206, 210, 218, 223, 228, 243, 248, 262; **39:** 345

Marina
    Pericles **37:** 361; **51:** 118

Menenius
    Coriolanus **9:** 8, 9, 11, 14, 19, 26, 78, 80, 106, 148, 157; **25:** 263, 296; **30:** 67, 79, 89, 96, 111, 133

Mercutio
    Romeo and Juliet
        bawdy **5:** 463, 525, 550, 575
        death **5:** 415, 418, 419, 547; **33:** 290
        as worldly counterpart to Romeo **5:** 425, 464, 542; **33:** 290; **51:** 195

minor characters
    Richard III **8:** 154, 159, 162, 163, 168, 170, 177, 184, 186, 201, 206, 210, 218, 223, 228, 232, 239, 248, 262, 267

Miranda
    The Tempest **8:** 289, 301, 304, 328, 336, 370, 454; **19:** 357; **22:** 302; **28:** 249; **29:** 278, 297, 362, 368, 377, 396; **53:** 64

Mistress Elbow
    Measure for Measure See **Elbow (Mistress Elbow)**

Mistress Quickly
    Henry V See **Quickly**

Mortimer
    Henry IV, Parts 1 and 2 **25:** 151

Norfolk
    Henry VIII **22:** 182

Northumberland
    Richard II **24:** 423

Nurse
    Romeo and Juliet **5:** 419, 425, 463, 464, 575; **33:** 294

Oberon
    A Midsummer Night's Dream
        as controlling force **3:** 434, 459, 477, 502; **29:** 175

Octavius
    Antony and Cleopatra **6:** 22, 24, 31, 38, 43, 53, 62, 107, 125, 146, 178, 181, 219; **25:** 257
    Julius Caesar **30:** 316

Olivia
    Twelfth Night **1:** 540, 543, 545; **46:** 286, 324, 369; **47:** 45

Ophelia
    Hamlet **1:** 73, 76, 81, 82, 91, 96, 97, 154, 166, 169, 171, 218, 270; **13:** 268; **16:** 246; **19:** 330; **21:** 17, 41, 44, 72, 81, 101, 104, 107, 112, 136, 203, 259, 347, 381, 386, 392, 416; **28:** 232, 325; **35:** 104, 126, 140, 144, 182, 238; **44:** 189, 195, 248
    in art **48:** 255
    death **48:** 255
    as icon **48:** 255
    influence on popular culture **48:** 255

Orlando
    As You Like It
        as ideal man **5:** 32, 36, 39, 162; **34:** 161; **46:** 94
        as younger brother **5:** 66, 158; **46:** 94

Orsino
    Twelfth Night **46:** 286, 333; **47:** 45

Othello
    Othello
        affinity with Iago **4:** 400, 427, 468, 470, 477, 500, 506; **25:** 189; **35:** 276, 320, 327
        as conventional "blameless hero" **4:** 445, 486, 500; **53:** 233, 238, 298, 304
        credulity **4:** 384, 385, 388, 390, 396, 402, 434, 440, 455; **13:** 327; **32:** 302; **47:** 25, 51
        Desdemona, relationship with **22:** 339; **35:** 301, 317; **37:** 269; **43:** 32; **53:** 315
        divided nature **4:** 400, 412, 462, 470, 477, 493, 500, 582, 592; **16:** 293; **19:** 276; **25:** 189; **35:** 320; **53:** 268, 289, 343
        egotism **4:** 427, 470, 477, 493, 522, 536, 541, 573, 597; **13:** 304; **35:** 247, 253
        self-destructive anger **16:** 283; **53:** 324
        self-dramatizing or self-deluding **4:** 454, 457, 477, 592; **13:** 313; **16:** 293; **35:** 317
        self-knowledge **4:** 462, 470, 477, 483, 508, 522, 530, 564, 580, 591, 596; **13:** 304, 313; **16:** 283; **28:** 243; **35:** 253, 317; **53:** 233, 343
        spiritual state **4:** 483, 488, 517, 525, 527, 544, 559, 564, 573; **28:** 243; **35:** 253

Page, Anne
    The Merry Wives of Windsor **47:** 321
    Anne Page-Fenton plot **5:** 334, 336, 343, 353, 376, 390, 395, 402; **22:** 93; **47:** 308

Page, Mistress Margaret
    The Merry Wives of Windsor **47:** 321

Painter
    Timon of Athens See **Poet and Painter**

Palamon and Arcite
    The Two Noble Kinsmen **9:** 474, 481, 490, 492, 502; **50:** 295, 305, 348, 361

Parolles
    All's Well That Ends Well
        characterization **7:** 8, 9, 43, 76, 81, 98, 109, 113, 116, 126; **22:** 78; **26:** 48, 73, 97; **26:** 117; **46:** 68
        exposure **7:** 9, 27, 81, 98, 109, 113, 116, 121, 126
        Falstaff, compared with **7:** 8, 9, 16

pastoral characters (Silvius, Phebe, and Corin)
    As You Like It **23:** 37, 97, 98, 99, 108, 110, 118, 122, 138; **34:** 147

Paulina
    The Winter's Tale **7:** 385, 412, 506; **15:** 528; **22:** 324; **25:** 339; **36:** 311

Pedro (Don Pedro)
    Much Ado about Nothing **8:** 17, 19, 48, 58, 63, 82, 111, 121

Perdita
    The Winter's Tale
        characterization **7:** 395, 412, 414, 419, 429, 432, 452, 506; **22:** 324; **25:** 339; **36:** 328; **43:** 39
        reunion with Leontes (Act V, scene ii) **7:** 377, 379, 381, 390, 432, 464, 480

Pericles
Pericles
characterization **36**: 251; **37**: 361
patience **2**: 572, 573, 578, 579
suit of Antiochus's daughter **2**: 547, 565, 578, 579; **51**: 126
Ulysses, compared with **2**: 551

Petruchio
The Taming of the Shrew
admirable qualities **9**: 320, 332, 341, 344, 345, 370, 375, 386
as lord of misrule 50: 64
audacity or vigor **9**: 325, 337, 355, 375, 386, 404
characterization **32**: 1
coarseness or brutality **9**: 325, 329, 365, 390, 393, 398, 407; **19**: 122; **43**: 61
as lord of misrule **9**: 393
love for Kate **9**: 338, 340, 343, 344, 386; **12**: 435
portrayals of **31**: 282
pragmatism **9**: 329, 334, 375, 398, 424; **13**: 3; **31**: 345, 351
taming method **9**: 320, 323, 329, 340, 341, 343, 345, 355, 369, 370, 375, 390, 398, 407, 413, 419, 424; **19**: 3, 12, 21 **31**: 269, 295, 326, 335, 339

Phebe
As You Like It See **pastoral characters**

Pistol
Henry V **28**: 146

plebeians
Coriolanus **9**: 8, 9, 11, 12, 15, 18, 19, 26, 33, 39, 53, 92, 125, 153, 183, 189; **25**: 296; **30**: 58, 79, 96, 111

Poet and Painter
Timon of Athens **25**: 198

the poets
Julius Caesar **7**: 179, 320, 350

Polixenes
The Winter's Tale
Leontes, relationship with **48**: 309

Polonius
Hamlet **21**: 259, 334, 347, 386, 416; **35**: 182

Porter
Henry VIII **24**: 155
Macbeth **3**: 173, 175, 184, 190, 196, 203, 205, 225, 260, 271, 297, 300; **20**: 283

Portia
The Merchant of Venice **4**: 194, 195, 196, 215, 254, 263, 336, 356; **12**: 104, 107, 114; **13**: 37; **22**: 3, 69; **25**: 22; **32**: 294; **37**: 86; **40**: 142, 156, 197, 208

Posthumus
Cymbeline **4**: 24, 30, 53, 78, 116, 127, 141, 155, 159, 167; **15**: 89; **19**: 411; **25**: 245, 319; **36**: 142; **44**: 28; **45**: 67, 75; **47**: 25, 205, 228

Prince Henry
King John See **Henry (Prince Henry)**

Prospero
The Tempest
characterization **8**: 312, 348, 370, 458; **16**: 442; **22**: 302; **45**: 188, 272
as God or Providence **8**: 311, 328, 364, 380, 429, 435
magic, nature of **8**: 301, 340, 356, 396, 414, 423, 458; **25**: 382; **28**: 391; **29**: 278, 292, 368, 377, 396; **32**: 338, 343
psychoanalytic interpretation **45**: 259
redemptive powers **8**: 302, 320, 353, 370, 390, 429, 439, 447; **29**: 297
as ruler **8**: 304, 308, 309, 420, 423; **13**: 424; **22**: 302; **29**: 278, 362, 377, 396
self-control **8**: 312, 414, 420; **22**: 302; **44**: 11
self-knowledge **16**: 442; **22**: 302; **29**: 278, 292, 362, 377, 396
as Shakespeare or creative artist **8**: 299, 302, 308, 312, 320, 324, 353, 364, 435, 447
as tragic hero **8**: 359, 370, 464; **29**: 292

Proteus
The Two Gentlemen of Verona **6**: 439, 450, 458, 480, 490, 511; **40**: 312, 327, 330, 335, 359; **42**: 18

Puck
A Midsummer Night's Dream **45**: 96, 158

Quickly (Mistress Quickly)
Henry V **5**: 186, 187, 210, 276, 293; **30**: 278

Regan
King Lear **31**: 151; **46**: 231, 242

Richard (King Richard II)
Richard II
artistic temperament **6**: 264, 267, 270, 272, 277, 292, 294, 298, 315, 331, 334, 347, 368, 374, 393, 409; **24**: 298, 301, 304, 315, 322, 390, 405, 408, 411, 414, 419; **39**: 289
Bolingbroke, compared with **24**: 346, 349, 351, 352, 356, 419; **39**: 256; **52**: 108, 124
characterization **6**: 250, 252, 253, 254, 255, 258, 262, 263, 267, 270, 272, 282, 283, 304, 343, 347, 364, 368; **24**: 262, 263, 267, 269, 270, 271, 272, 273, 274, 278, 280, 315, 322, 325, 330, 333, 390, 395, 402, 405, 423; **28**: 134; **39**: 279, 289; **52**: 169
dangerous aspects **24**: 405
delusion **6**: 267, 298, 334, 368, 409; **24**: 329, 336, 405
homosexuality **24**: 405
kingship **6**: 253, 254, 263, 272, 327, 331, 334, 338, 364, 402, 414; **24**: 278, 295, 336, 337, 339, 356, 419; **28**: 134, 178; **39**: 256, 263; **52**: 169
loss of identity **6**: 267, 338, 368, 374, 381, 388, 391, 409; **24**: 298, 414, 428
as martyr-king **6**: 289, 307, 321; **19**: 209; **24**: 289, 291; **28**: 134
nobility **6**: 255, 258, 259, 262, 263, 391; **24**: 260, 263, 274, 280, 289, 291, 402, 408, 411

political acumen **6**: 263, 264, 272, 292, 310, 327, 334, 364, 368, 374, 388, 391, 397, 402, 409; **24**: 405; **39**: 256
private vs. public persona **6**: 317, 327, 364, 368, 391, 409; **24**: 428
role in Gloucester's death **52**: 108, 124
role-playing **24**: 419, 423; **28**: 178
seizure of Gaunt's estate **6**: 250, 338, 388
self-dramatization **6**: 264, 267, 307, 310, 315, 317, 331, 334, 368, 393, 409; **24**: 339; **28**: 178
self-hatred **13**: 172; **24**: 383; **39**: 289
self-knowledge **6**: 255, 267, 331, 334, 338, 352, 354, 368, 388, 391; **24**: 273, 289, 411, 414; **39**: 263, 289
spiritual redemption **6**: 255, 267, 331, 334, 338, 352, 354, 368, 388, 391; **24**: 273, 289, 411, 414; **52**: 124

Richard (King Richard III, formerly Richard, Duke of Gloucester)
Henry VI, Parts 1, 2, and 3
characterization **3**: 35, 48, 57, 64, 77, 143, 151; **22**: 193; **39**: 160, 177
as revenger **22**: 193
soliloquy (3 Henry VI, Act III, scene ii) **3**: 17, 48
Richard III
ambition **8**: 148, 154, 165, 168, 170, 177, 182, 213, 218, 228, 232, 239, 252, 258, 267; **39**: 308, 341, 360, 370, 383; **52**: 201, 223
attractive qualities **8**: 145, 148, 152, 154, 159, 161, 162, 165, 168, 170, 181, 182, 184, 185, 197, 201, 206, 213, 228, 243, 252, 258; **16**: 150; **39**: 370, 383; **52**: 272, 280
credibility, question of **8**: 145, 147, 154, 159, 165, 193; **13**: 142
death **8**: 145, 148, 154, 159, 165, 168, 170, 177, 182, 197, 210, 223, 228, 232, 243, 248, 252, 258, 267
deformity as symbol **8**: 146, 147, 148, 152, 154, 159, 161, 165, 170, 177, 184, 185, 193, 218, 248, 252, 267; **19**: 164
inversion of moral order **8**: 159, 168, 177, 182, 184, 185, 197, 201, 213, 218, 223, 232, 239, 243, 248, 252, 258, 262, 267; **39**: 360; **52**: 205, 214
as Machiavellian villain **8**: 165, 182, 190, 201, 218, 232, 239, 243, 248; **39**: 308, 326, 360, 387; **52**: 201, 205, 257, 280, 285
as monster or symbol of diabolic **8**: 145, 147, 159, 162, 168, 170, 177, 182, 193, 197, 201, 228, 239, 248, 258; **13**: 142; **37**: 144; **39**: 326, 349; **52**: 227, 272
other literary villains, compared with **8**: 148, 161, 162, 165, 181, 182, 206, 213, 239, 267
role-playing, hypocrisy, and dissimulation **8**: 145, 148, 154, 159, 162, 165, 168, 170, 182, 190, 206, 213, 218, 228, 239, 243, 252, 258, 267; **25**: 141, 164, 245; **39**: 335, 341, 387 **52**: 257, 267
as scourge or instrument of God **8**: 163, 177, 193, 201, 218, 228, 248, 267; **39**: 308
as seducer **52**: 223, 227
as Vice figure **8**: 190, 201, 213, 228, 243, 248, 252; **16**: 150; **39**: 383, 387; **52**: 223, 267

Richard Plantagenet, Duke of York
Henry VI, Parts 1, 2, and 3 See **York**

Richmond
Richard III **8**: 154, 158, 163, 168, 177, 182, 193, 210, 218, 223, 228, 243, 248, 252; **13**: 142; **25**: 141; **39**: 349; **52**: 214, 257, 285

the Rival Poet
Sonnets **10**: 169, 233, 334, 337, 385; **48**: 352

Roman citizenry
Julius Caesar
portrayal of **7**: 169, 179, 210, 221, 245, 279, 282, 310, 320, 333; **17**: 271, 279, 288, 291, 292, 298, 323, 334, 351, 367, 374, 375, 378; **22**: 280; **30**: 285, 297, 316, 321, 374, 379; **37**: 229

Romeo and Juliet
Romeo and Juliet
death-wish **5**: 431, 489, 505, 528, 530, 538, 542, 550, 566, 571, 575; **32**: 212
first meeting (Act I scene v) **51**: 212
immortality **5**: 536
Juliet's epithalamium speech (Act III, scene ii) **5**: 431, 477, 492
Juliet's innocence **5**: 421, 423, 450, 454; **33**: 257
maturation **5**: 437, 454, 467, 493, 498, 509, 520, 565; **33**: 249, 257
rebellion **25**: 257
reckless passion **5**: 419, 427, 431, 438, 443, 444, 448, 467, 479, 485, 505, 533, 538, 542; **33**: 241
Romeo's dream (Act V, scene i) **5**: 513, 536, 556; **45**: 40; **51**: 203
Rosaline, Romeo's relationship with **5**: 419, 423, 425, 427, 438, 498, 542, 575

Rosalind
As You Like It **46**: 94, 122
Beatrice, compared with **5**: 26, 36, 50, 75
charm **5**: 55, 75; **23**: 17, 18, 20, 41, 89, 111
disguise, role of **5**: 75, 107, 118, 122, 128, 130, 133, 138, 141, 146, 148, 164, 168; **13**: 502; **23**: 35, 42, 106, 119, 123, 146; **34**: 130; **46**: 127, 134, 142
femininity **5**: 26, 36, 52, 75; **23**: 24, 29, 46, 54, 103, 108, 121, 146
love-theme, relation to **5**: 79, 88, 103, 116, 122, 138, 141; **23**: 114, 115; **34**: 85, 177

rustic characters
As You Like It **5**: 24, 60, 72, 84; **23**: 127; **34**: 78, 161
A Midsummer Night's Dream **3**: 376, 397, 432; **12**: 291, 293; **45**: 147, 160

Scroop
Henry V See **traitors**

Sebastian
The Tempest See **Antonio and Sebastian**

Shylock
The Merchant of Venice
alienation **4**: 279, 312; **40**: 175; **48**: 77; **49**: 23, 37
ambiguity **4**: 247, 254, 315, 319, 331; **12**: 31, 35, 36, 50, 51, 52, 56, 81, 124; **40**: 175; **53**: 111
ghettoization of **53**: 127
forced conversion **4**: 209, 252, 268, 282, 289, 321
Jewishness **4**: 193, 194, 195, 200, 201, 213, 214, 279; **22**: 69; **25**: 257; **40**: 142, 175, 181; **48**: 65, 77
master-slave relationship **53**: 136
motives in making the bond **4**: 252, 263, 266, 268; **22**: 69; **25**: 22
as outsider **53**: 127, 224
as Puritan **40**: 127, 166
as scapegoat figure **4**: 254, 300; **40**: 166; **49**: 27
as traditional comic villain **4**: 230, 243, 261, 263, 315; **12**: 40, 62, 124; **40**: 175
as tragic figure **12**: 6, 9, 10, 16, 21, 23, 25, 40, 44, 66, 67, 81, 97; **40**: 175

Sicinius
Coriolanus See **the tribunes**

Silvia
The Two Gentlemen of Verona **6**: 450, 453, 458, 476, 494, 499, 516, 519, 549, 564; **40**: 312, 327, 374

Silvius
As You Like It See **pastoral characters**

Sly
The Taming of the Shrew **9**: 320, 322, 350, 370, 381, 390, 398, 430; **12**: 316, 335, 416, 427, 441; **16**: 13; **19**: 34, 122; **22**: 48; **37**: 31; **50**: 74

soldiers
Henry V **5**: 203, 239, 267, 276, 281, 287, 293, 318; **28**: 146; **30**: 169,

Speed
The Two Gentlemen of Verona See **Launce and Speed**

Stephano and Trinculo
The Tempest
comic subplot of **8**: 292, 297, 299, 304, 309, 324, 328, 353, 370; **25**: 382; **29**: 377; **46**: 14, 33

Stephen Gardiner
Henry VIII See **Gardiner**

Talbot
Henry VI, Parts 1, 2, and 3 **39**: 160, 213, 222

Tamora
Titus Andronicus **4**: 632, 662, 672, 675; **27**: 266; **43**: 170

Tarquin
The Rape of Lucrece **10**: 80, 93, 98, 116, 125; **22**: 294; **25**: 305; **32**: 321; **33**: 190; **43**: 102
Petrarchan lover **48**: 291
platonic tyrant **48**: 291
Satan role **48**: 291

Thersites
Troilus and Cressida **13**: 53; **25**: 56; **27**: 381

Theseus
A Midsummer Night's Dream
characterization **3**: 363
Hippolyta, relationship with **3**: 381, 412, 421, 423, 450, 468, 520; **29**: 175, 216, 243, 256; **45**: 84
as ideal **3**: 379, 391
"lovers, lunatics, and poets" speech (Act V, scene i) **3**: 365, 371, 379, 381, 391, 402, 411, 412, 421, 423, 441, 498, 506; **29**: 175
as representative of institutional life **3**: 381, 403; **51**: 1

Time-Chorus
The Winter's Tale **7**: 377, 380, 412, 464, 476, 501; **15**: 518

Timon
Timon of Athens
comic traits **25**: 198
as flawed hero **1**: 456, 459, 462, 472, 495, 503, 507, 515; **16**: 351; **20**: 429, 433, 476; **25**: 198; **27**: 157, 161
misanthropy **13**: 392; **20**: 431, 464, 476, 481, 491, 492, 493; **27**: 161, 175, 184, 196; **37**: 222; **52**: 296, 301
as noble figure **1**: 467, 473, 483, 499; **20**: 493; **27**: 212

Titania
A Midsummer Night's Dream **29**: 243

Titus
Titus Andronicus **4**: 632, 637, 640, 644, 647, 653, 656, 662; **25**: 245; **27**: 255

Touchstone
As You Like It
callousness **5**: 88
comic and farcical elements **46**: 117
as philosopher-fool **5**: 24, 28, 30, 32, 36, 63, 75, 98; **23**: 152; **34**: 85; **46**: 1, 14, 18, 24, 33, 52, 60, 88, 105
relation to pastoral convention **5**: 54, 61, 63, 72, 75, 77, 79, 84, 86, 93, 98, 114, 118, 135, 138, 166; **34**: 72, 147, 161
satire or parody of pastoral conventions **46**: 122
selflessness **5**: 30, 36, 39, 76

traitors (Scroop, Grey, and Cambridge)
Henry V **16**: 202; **30**: 220, 278

the tribunes (Brutus and Sicinius)
Coriolanus **9**: 9, 11, 14, 19, 33, 169, 180

Trinculo
The Tempest See **Stephano and Trinculo**

Troilus
Troilus and Cressida
contradictory behavior **3**: 596, 602, 635; **27**: 362
Cressida, relationship with **3**: 594, 596, 606; **22**: 58
integrity **3**: 617
opposition to Ulysses **3**: 561, 584, 590
as unsympathetic figure **18**: 423; **22**: 58, 339; **43**: 317
as warrior **3**: 596; **22**: 339

Ulysses
Troilus and Cressida
speech on degree (Act I, scene iii) **3**: 549, 599, 609, 642; **27**: 396

Venetians
The Merchant of Venice **4**: 195, 200, 228, 254, 273, 300, 321, 331

Venus
Venus and Adonis **10**: 427, 429, 434, 439, 442, 448, 449, 451, 454, 466, 473, 480, 486, 489; **16**: 452; **25**: 305, 328; **28**: 355; **33**: 309, 321, 330, 347, 352, 357, 363, 370, 377; **51**: 335, 352, 377, 388

Viola
Twelfth Night **26**: 308; **46**: 286, 324, 347, 369

Virgilia
Coriolanus **9**: 11, 19, 26, 33, 58, 100, 121, 125; **25**: 263; **30**: 79, 96, 133; **50**: 99

Volumnia
Coriolanus
Coriolanus's subservience to **9**: 16, 26, 33, 53, 62, 80, 92, 100, 117, 125, 142, 177, 183; **30**: 140, 149; **44**: 79
influence on Coriolanus **9**: 45, 62, 65, 78, 92, 100, 110, 117, 121, 125, 130, 148, 157, 183, 189, 193; **25**: 263, 296; **30**: 79, 96, 125, 133, 140, 142, 149; **44**: 93
as noble Roman matron **9**: 16, 19, 26, 31, 33
personification of Rome **9**: 125, 183; **50**: 119

Wat the hare
Venus and Adonis **10**: 424, 451

the Watch
Much Ado about Nothing See **Dogberry and the Watch**

Williams
Henry V **13**: 502; **16**: 183; **28**: 146; **30**: 169, 259, 278

witches
Macbeth
and supernaturalism **3**: 171, 172, 173, 175, 177, 182, 183, 184, 185, 194, 196, 198, 202, 207, 208, 213, 219, 229, 239; **16**: 317; **19**: 245; **20**: 92, 175, 213, 279, 283, 374, 387, 406, 413; **25**: 235; **28**: 339; **29**: 91, 101, 109, 120

Wolsey (Cardinal Wolsey)
Henry VIII **2**: 15, 18, 19, 23, 24, 38; **22**: 182; **24**: 80, 91, 112, 113, 129, 140; **37**: 109; **41**: 129

York (Edmund of Langley, Duke of York)
Richard II **6**: 287, 364, 368, 388, 402, 414; **24**: 263, 320, 322, 364, 395, 414; **39**: 243, 279

York (Richard Plantagenet, Duke of York)
Henry VI, Parts 1, 2, and 3
death of **13**: 131

Cumulative Topic Index

The Cumulative Topic Index indentifies the principal topics of discussion in the criticism of each play and non-dramatic poem. The topics are arranged alphabetically. Page references indicate the beginning page number of each essay containing substantial commentary on that topic. A parenthetical reference after a topic indicates that the topic is extensively discussed in that volume.

absurdities, inconsistencies, and shortcomings
The Two Gentlemen of Verona **6**: 435, 436, 437, 439, 464, 507, 541, 560

accident or chance
Romeo and Juliet **5**: 418, 444, 448, 467, 470, 487, 573

acting and dissimulation
Richard II **6**: 264, 267, 307, 310, 315, 368, 393, 409; **24**: 339, 345, 346, 349, 352, 356

adolescence
Romeo and Juliet **33**: 249, 255, 257

adultery
The Comedy of Errors **34**: 215

aggression
Coriolanus **9**: 112, 142, 174, 183, 189, 198; **30**: 79, 111, 125, 142; **44**: 11, 79

alienation
Timon of Athens **1**: 523; **27**: 161

allegorical elements
Antony and Cleopatra **52**: 5
King Lear **16**: 311
Measure for Measure **52**: 69
The Merchant of Venice **4**: 224, 250, 261, 268, 270, 273, 282, 289, 324, 336, 344, 350
The Phoenix and Turtle **10**: 7, 8, 9, 16, 17, 48; **38**: 334, 378; **51**: 138, 188
The Rape of Lucrece **10**: 89, 93
Richard II **6**: 264, 283, 323, 385
Richard III **52**: 5

The Tempest **8**: 294, 295, 302, 307, 308, 312, 326, 328, 336, 345, 364; **42**: 320
Troilus and Cressida **52**: 5
Venus and Adonis **10**: 427, 434, 439, 449, 454, 462, 480; **28**: 355; **33**: 309, 330

ambiguity
Antony and Cleopatra **6**: 53, 111, 161, 163, 180, 189, 208, 211, 228; **13**: 368
Hamlet **1**: 92, 160, 198, 227, 230, 234, 247, 249; **21**: 72; **35**: 241
King John **13**: 152; **41**: 243
Measure for Measure **2**: 417, 420, 432, 446, 449, 452, 474, 479, 482, 486, 495, 505
A Midsummer Night's Dream **3**: 401, 459, 486; **45**: 169
Richard III **44**: 11; **47**: 15
10: 251, 256; **28**: 385; **40**: 221, 228, 268
Troilus and Cressida **3**: 544, 568, 583, 587, 589, 599, 611, 621; **27**: 400; **43**: 305
Twelfth Night **1**: 554, 639; **34**: 287, 316
Venus and Adonis **10**: 434, 454, 459, 462, 466, 473, 480, 486, 489; **33**: 352; **51**: 368, 377, 388

ambition or pride
Henry VIII **2**: 15, 38, 67
Macbeth **44**: 284, 324;
Richard III **52**: 201, 223

ambivalent or ironic elements
Henry VI, Parts 1, 2, and 3 **3**: 69, 151, 154; **39**: 160
Richard III **44**: 11
Troilus and Cressida **43**: 340

amorality, question of
The Two Noble Kinsmen **9**: 447, 460, 492

amour-passion or Liebestod myth
Romeo and Juliet **5**: 484, 489, 528, 530, 542, 550, 575; **32**: 256; **51**: 195, 219, 236

amputations, significance of
Titus Andronicus **48**: 264

anachronisms
Julius Caesar **7**: 331

androgyny
Antony and Cleopatra **13**: 530
As You Like It **23**: 98, 100, 122, 138, 143, 144; **34**: 172, 177; **46**: 134
Romeo and Juliet **13**: 530

anti-Catholic rhetoric
King John **22**: 120; **25**: 98

anti-romantic elements
As You Like It **34**: 72

antithetical or contradictory elements
Macbeth **3**: 185, 213, 271, 302; **25**: 235; **29**: 76, 127; **47**: 41

anxiety
Romeo and Juliet **13**: 235

appearance, perception, and illusion
A Midsummer Night's Dream **3**: 368, 411, 425, 427, 434, 447, 459, 466, 474, 477, 486, 497, 516; **19**: 21; **22**: 39; **28**: 15; **29**: 175,190; **45**: 136

Appearance versus Reality (Volume 34: 1, 5, 12, 23, 45, 54)
All's Well That Ends Well **7**: 37, 76, 93; **26**: 117

As You Like It **34:** 130, 131; **46:** 105
The Comedy of Errors **34:** 194, 201
Coriolanus **30:** 142
Cymbeline **4:** 87, 93, 103, 162; **36:** 99; **47:** 228, 286
Hamlet **1:** 95, 116, 166, 169, 198; **35:** 82, 126, 132, 144, 238; **44:** 248; **45:** 28
Macbeth **3:** 241, 248; **25:** 235
The Merchant of Venice **4:** 209, 261, 344; **12:** 65; **22:** 69
Much Ado about Nothing **8:** 17, 18, 48, 63, 69, 73, 75, 79, 88, 95, 115; **31:** 198, 209
The Taming of the Shrew **9:** 343, 350, 353, 365, 369, 370, 381, 390, 430; **12:** 416; **31:** 326
Timon of Athens **1:** 495, 500, 515, 523; **52:** 311, 329
The Two Gentlemen of Verona **6:** 494, 502, 511, 519, 529, 532, 549, 560
Twelfth Night **34:** 293, 301, 311, 316
The Winter's Tale **7:** 429, 446, 479

appetite
Twelfth Night **1:** 563, 596, 609, 615; **52:** 57

archetypal or mythic elements
Macbeth **16:** 317

archetypal structure
Pericles **2:** 570, 580, 582, 584, 588; **25:** 365; **51:** 71, 79

aristocracy and aristocratic values
As You Like It **34:** 120
Hamlet **42:** 212
Julius Caesar **16:** 231; **22:** 280; **30:** 379; **50:** 194, 196, 211

art and nature
See also **nature**
Pericles **22:** 315; **36:** 233
The Phoenix and Turtle **10:** 7, 42

art versus nature
See also **nature**
As You Like It **5:** 128, 130, 148; **34:** 147
The Tempest **8:** 396, 404; **29:** 278, 297, 362
The Winter's Tale **7:** 377, 381, 397, 419, 452; **36:** 289, 318; **45:** 329

artificial nature
Love's Labour's Lost **2:** 315, 317, 324, 330; **23:** 207, 233

Athens
Timon of Athens **27:** 223, 230

Athens and the forest, contrast between
A Midsummer Night's Dream **3:** 381, 427, 459, 466, 497, 502; **29:** 175

assassination
Julius Caesar **7:** 156, 161, 179, 191, 200, 221, 264, 272, 279, 284, 350; **25:** 272; **30:** 326

audience interpretation
Julius Caesar **48:** 240

audience perception
The Comedy of Errors **1:** 37, 50, 56; **19:** 54; **34:** 258
King Lear **19:** 295; **28:** 325
Richard II **24:** 414, 423; **39:** 295
Pericles **42:** 352; **48:** 364

audience perception, Shakespeare's manipulation of
The Winter's Tale **7:** 394, 429, 456, 483, 501; **13:** 417; **19:** 401, 431, 441; **25:** 339; **45:** 374

audience perspective
All's Well That Ends Well **7:** 81, 104, 109, 116, 121

audience response
Antony and Cleopatra **48:** 206
Hamlet **28:** 325; **32:** 238; **35:** 167; **44:** 107
Julius Caesar **7:** 179, 238, 253, 255, 272, 316, 320, 336, 350; **19:** 321; **48:** 240
Macbeth **20:** 17, 400, 406; **29:** 139, 146, 155, 165; **44:** 306
Measure for Measure **48:** 1

audience versus character perceptions
The Two Gentlemen of Verona **6:** 499, 519, 524

authenticity
The Phoenix and Turtle **10:** 7, 8, 16
Sonnets **10:** 153, 154, 230, 243; **48:** 325

Authorship Controversy (Volume 41: 2, 5, 18, 32, 42, 48, 57, 61, 63, 66, 76, 81, 85, 98, 110)
Cymbeline **4:** 17, 21, 35, 48, 56, 78
Henry VI, Parts 1, 2, and 3 **3:** 16, 18, 19, 20, 21, 26, 27, 29, 31, 35, 39, 41, 55, 66; **24:** 51
Henry VIII **2:** 16, 18, 19, 22, 23, 27, 28, 31, 35, 36, 42, 43, 44, 46, 48, 51, 58, 64, 68; **41:** 129, 146, 158, 171
Love's Labour's Lost **2:** 299, 300; **32:** 308
Pericles **2:** 538, 540, 543, 544, 545, 546, 548, 550, 551, 553, 556, 558, 564, 565, 568, 576, 586; **15:** 132, 141, 148, 152; **16:** 391, 399; **25:** 365; **36:** 198, 244
Timon of Athens **1:** 464, 466, 467, 469, 474, 477, 478, 480, 490, 499, 507, 518; **16:** 351; **20:** 433
Titus Andronicus **4:** 613, 614, 615, 616, 617, 619, 623, 624, 625, 626, 628, 631, 632, 635, 642
The Two Gentlemen of Verona **6:** 435, 436, 437, 438, 439, 449, 466, 476
The Two Noble Kinsmen
 Shakespeare not a co-author **9:** 445, 447, 455, 461
 Shakespearean portions of the text **9:** 446, 447, 448, 455, 456, 457, 460, 462, 463, 471, 479, 486; **41:** 308, 317, 355
 Shakespeare's part in the overall conception or design **9:** 444, 446, 448, 456, 457, 460, 480, 481, 486, 490; **37:** 313; **41:** 326; **50:** 326

autobiographical elements
As You Like It **5:** 25, 35, 43, 50, 55, 61
The Comedy of Errors **1:** 16, 18

Cymbeline **4:** 43, 46; **36:** 134
Hamlet **1:** 98, 115, 119; **13:** 487
Henry VI, Parts 1, 2, and 3 **3:** 41, 55
King John **9:** 209, 218, 245, 248, 260, 292
King Lear **2:** 131, 136, 149, 165
Measure for Measure **2:** 406, 410, 414, 431, 434, 437
A Midsummer Night's Dream **3:** 365, 371, 379, 381, 389, 391, 396, 402, 432
Othello **4:** 440, 444
Pericles **2:** 551, 554, 555, 563, 581
The Phoenix and Turtle **10:** 14, 18, 42, 48; **51:** 155
Sonnets **10:** 159, 160, 166, 167, 175, 176, 182, 196, 205, 213, 215, 226, 233, 238, 240, 251, 279, 283, 302, 309, 325, 337, 377; **13:** 487; **16:** 461; **28:** 363, 385; **42:** 296; **48:** 325
The Tempest **8:** 302, 308, 312, 324, 326, 345, 348, 353, 364, 380
Timon of Athens **1:** 462, 467, 470, 473, 474, 478, 480; **27:** 166, 175
Titus Andronicus **4:** 619, 624, 625, 664
Troilus and Cressida **3:** 548, 554, 557, 558, 574, 606, 630
Twelfth Night **1:** 557, 561, 599; **34:** 338
The Winter's Tale **7:** 395, 397, 410, 419

avarice
The Merry Wives of Windsor **5:** 335, 353, 369, 376, 390, 395, 402

battle of Agincourt
Henry V **5:** 197, 199, 213, 246, 257, 281, 287, 289, 293, 310, 318; **19:** 217; **30:** 181

battle of the sexes
Much Ado about Nothing **8:** 14, 16, 19, 48, 91, 95, 111, 121, 125; **31:** 231, 245

bawdy elements
As You Like It **46:** 122
Cymbeline **36:** 155

bear-baiting
Twelfth Night **19:** 42

beauty
Sonnets **10:** 247; **51:** 288
Venus and Adonis **10:** 420, 423, 427, 434, 454, 480; **33:** 330, 352

bed-trick
All's Well That Ends Well **7:** 8, 26, 27, 29, 32, 41, 86, 93, 98, 113, 116, 126; **13:** 84; **26:** 117; **28:** 38; **38:** 65, 118; **49:** 46
Measure for Measure **13:** 84; **49:** 313

bird imagery
The Phoenix and Turtle **10:** 21, 27; **38:** 329, 350, 367; **51:** 145, 181, 184

body, role of
Troilus and Cressida **42:** 66

body politic, metaphor of
Coriolanus **22:** 248; **30:** 67, 96, 105, 125; **50:** 105, 110, 119, 140, 145, 152

bonding
 The Merchant of Venice **4:** 293, 317, 336; **13:** 37

British nationalism
 See also **nationalism and patriotism**
 Cymbeline **4:** 19, 78, 89, 93, 129, 141, 159, 167; **32:** 373; **36:** 129; **45:** 6; **47:** 219, 265

brutal elements
 A Midsummer Night's Dream **3:** 445, 491, 497, 511; **12:** 259, 262, 298; **16:** 34; **19:** 21; **29:** 183, 225, 263, 269; **45:** 169

Cade scenes
 Henry VI, Parts 1, 2, and 3 **50:** 45, 51

Caesarism
 Julius Caesar **7:** 159, 160, 161, 167, 169, 174, 191, 205, 218, 253, 310; **30:** 316, 321; **50:** 196, 234

Calvinist implications
 Hamlet **48:** 195

capriciousness of the young lovers
 A Midsummer Night's Dream **3:** 372, 395, 402, 411, 423, 437, 441, 450, 497, 498; **29:** 175, 269; **45:** 107

caricature
 The Merry Wives of Windsor **5:** 343, 347, 348, 350, 385, 397

carnival elements
 Henry IV, Parts 1 and 2 **28:** 203; **32:** 103
 Henry VI, Parts 1, 2, and 3 **22:** 156
 Richard II **19:** 151; **39:** 273 casket scenes
 The Merchant of Venice **49:** 27

censorship
 Richard II **24:** 260, 261, 262, 263, 386; **42:** 118; **52:** 141, 144

ceremonies, rites, and rituals, importance of
 See also **pageantry**
 Coriolanus **9:** 139, 148, 169
 Hamlet **13:** 268; **28:** 232
 Julius Caesar **7:** 150, 210, 255, 259, 268, 284, 316, 331, 339, 356; **13:** 260; **22:** 137; **30:** 374; **50:** 258, 269;
 Richard II **6:** 270, 294, 315, 368, 381, 397, 409, 414; **24:** 274, 356, 411, 414, 419
 Titus Andronicus **27:** 261; **32:** 265; **48:** 264
 The Two Noble Kinsmen **9:** 492, 498

change
 Henry VIII **2:** 27, 65, 72, 81

characterization
 As You Like It **5:** 19, 24, 25, 36, 39, 54, 82, 86, 116, 148; **34:** 72; **48:** 42
 The Comedy of Errors **1:** 13, 21, 31, 34, 46, 49, 50, 55, 56; **19:** 54; **25:** 63; **34:** 194, 201, 208, 245
 Henry IV, Parts 1 and 2 **1:** 321, 328, 332, 333, 336, 344, 365, 383, 385, 389, 391,
397, 401; **19:** 195; **39:** 123, 137; **42:** 99, 162; **49:** 93
 Henry V **5:** 186, 189, 192, 193, 199, 219, 230, 233, 252, 276, 293; **30:** 227, 278; **42:** 162
 Henry VI, Parts 1, 2, and 3 **3:** 18, 20, 24, 25, 31, 57, 64, 73, 77, 109, 119, 151; **24:** 22, 28, 38, 42, 45, 47; **39:** 160; **47:** 32
 Henry VIII **2:** 17, 23, 25, 32, 35, 39; **24:** 106
 King John **9:** 222, 224, 229, 240, 250, 292; **41:** 205, 215
 King Lear **2:** 108, 125, 145, 162, 191; **16:** 311; **28:** 223; **46:** 177, 210
 Love's Labour's Lost **2:** 303, 310, 317, 322, 328, 342; **23:** 237, 250, 252; **38:** 232; **47:** 35
 Macbeth **20:** 12, 318, 324, 329, 353, 363, 367, 374, 387; **28:** 339; **29:** 101, 109, 146, 155, 165; **45:** 67; **47:** 41
 Measure for Measure **2:** 388, 390, 391, 396, 406, 420, 421, 446, 466, 475, 484, 505, 516, 524; **23:** 299, 405; **33:**
 The Merry Wives of Windsor **5:** 332, 334, 335, 337, 338, 351, 360, 363, 366, 374, 379, 392; **18:** 74, 75; **38:** 264, 273, 313, 319
 The Tempest **8:** 287, 289, 292, 294, 295, 308, 326, 334, 336; **28:** 415; **42:** 332; **45:** 219
 Titus Andronicus **4:** 613, 628, 632, 635, 640, 644, 647, 650, 675; **27:** 293; **43:** 170, 176,;
 Troilus and Cressida **3:** 538, 539, 540, 541, 548, 566, 571, 604, 611, 621; **27:** 381, 391
 Twelfth Night **1:** 539, 540, 543, 545, 550, 554, 581, 594; **26:** 257, 337, 342, 346, 364, 366, 371, 374; **34:** 281, 293, 311, 338; **46:** 286, 324
 The Two Gentlemen of Verona **6:** 438, 442, 445, 447, 449, 458, 462, 560; **12:** 458; **40:** 312, 327, 330, 365
 The Two Noble Kinsmen **9:** 457, 461, 471, 474; **41:** 340, 385; **50:** 305, 326
 The Winter's Tale **47:** 25

chastity
 A Midsummer Night's Dream **45:** 143

Chaucer's Criseyde, compared with
 Troilus and Cressida **43:** 305

chivalry
 Troilus and Cressida **16:** 84; **27:** 370, 374
 The Two Noble Kinsmen **50:** 305, 348

Christian elements
 See also **religious, mythic, or spiritual content**
 As You Like It **5:** 39, 98, 162
 Coriolanus **30:** 111
 King Lear **2:** 137, 170, 179, 188, 191, 197, 207, 218, 222, 226, 229, 238, 249, 265, 286; **22:** 233, 271; **25:** 218; **46:** 276; **52:** 95
 Macbeth **3:** 194, 239, 260, 269, 275, 286, 293, 297, 318; **20:** 203, 206, 210, 256, 262, 289, 291, 294; **44:** 341, 366; **47:** 41
 Measure for Measure **2:** 391, 394, 399, 421, 437, 449, 466, 479, 491, 511, 522; **48:** 1; **49:** 325
 The Merchant of Venice **52:** 89
 Much Ado about Nothing **8:** 17, 19, 29, 55, 95, 104, 111, 115; **31:** 209
 The Phoenix and Turtle **10:** 21, 24, 31; **38:** 326; **51:** 162, 171, 181
 The Rape of Lucrece **10:** 77, 80, 89, 96, 98, 109
 Sonnets **10:** 191, 256
 Titus Andronicus **4:** 656, 680
 Twelfth Night **46:** 338
 The Two Gentlemen of Verona **6:** 438, 494, 514, 532, 555, 564
 The Winter's Tale **7:** 381, 387, 402, 410, 417, 419, 425, 429, 436, 452, 460, 501; **36:** 318

as Christian play
 King Lear **48:** 222

Chorus, role of
 Henry V **49:** 194, 200, 211, 219, 260

church versus state
 King John **9:** 209, 212, 222, 235, 240; **22:** 120

civilization versus barbarism
 Titus Andronicus **4:** 653; **27:** 293; **28:** 249; **32:** 265

Clarissa, (Samuel Richardson), compared with
 King Lear **48:** 277
 Measure for Measure **48:** 277
 Othello **48:** 277
 Titus Andronicus **48:** 277

class distinctions, conflict, and relations
 General Commentary **50:** 1, 34
 Henry V **28:** 146
 Henry VI, Parts 1, 2, and 3 **37:** 97; **39:** 187; **50:** 45, 51
 The Merry Wives of Windsor **5:** 338, 343, 346, 347, 366, 390, 395, 400, 402; **22:** 93; **28:** 69
 A Midsummer Night's Dream **22:** 23; **25:** 36; **45:** 160; **50:** 74, 86
 The Taming of the Shrew **31:** 300, 351; **50:** 64, 74
 The Two Noble Kinsmen **50:** 295, 305, 310

classical influence and sources
 The Comedy of Errors **1:** 13, 14, 16, 31, 32, 43, 61
 The Tempest **29:** 278, 343, 362, 368

Clowns and Fools in Shakespeare's Works (Volume 46: 1, 14, 18, 24, 29, 33, 48, 52, 60)
 As You Like It **5:** 24, 28, 30, 32, 36, 39, 54, 61, 63, 72, 75, 76, 77, 79, 84, 86, 93, 98, 114, 118, 135, 138, 166; **23:;** **152;** **34:** 72, 85, 147, 161; **46:** 88, 105, 117, 122
 King Lear **2:** 108, 112, 125, 156, 162, 245, 278, 284; **11:** 17, 158, 169; **22:** 227; **25:** 202; **28:** 223; **46:** 191, 205, 210, 218, 225
 Twelfth Night **1:** 543, 548, 558, 561, 563, 566, 570, 572, 603, 620, 642, 655, 658; **26:** 233, 364; **46:** 297, 303, 310

colonialism
  Henry V **22:** 103
  A Midsummer Night's Dream **53:** 32
  The Tempest **13:** 424, 440; **15:** 228, 268, 269, 270, 271, 272, 273; **19:** 421; **25:** 357, 382; **28:** 249; **29:** 343, 368; **32:** 338, 367, 400; **42:** 320; **45:** 200, 280; **53:** 11, 21, 45, 67

combat
  King Lear **22:** 365
  Macbeth **22:** 365

comedy of affectation
  Love's Labour's Lost **2:** 302, 303, 304; **23:** 191, 224, 226, 228, 233

comic and tragic elements, combination of
  King Lear **2:** 108, 110, 112, 125, 156, 162, 245, 278, 284; **46:** 191
  Measure for Measure **16:** 102
  Romeo and Juliet **5:** 496, 524, 528, 547, 559; **46:** 78
  Troilus and Cressida **43:** 351

comic and farcical elements
  All's Well That Ends Well **26:** 97, 114; **48:** 65
  Antony and Cleopatra **6:** 52, 85, 104, 125, 131, 151, 192, 202, 219; **47:** 77, 124, 149, 165
  The Comedy of Errors **1:** 14, 16, 19, 23, 30, 34, 35, 43, 46, 50, 55, 56, 59, 61; **19:** 54; **26:** 183, 186, 188, 190; **34:** 190, 245
  Coriolanus **9:** 8, 9, 14, 53, 80, 106
  Cymbeline **4:** 35, 56, 113, 141; **15:** 111, 122; **47:** 296
  Henry IV, Parts 1 and 2 **1:** 286, 290, 314, 327, 328, 336, 353; **19:** 195; **25:** 109; **39:** 72
  Henry V **5:** 185, 188, 191, 192, 217, 230, 233, 241, 252, 260, 276; **19:** 217; **28:** 121; **30:** 193, 202
  The Merry Wives of Windsor **5:** 336, 338, 346, 350, 360, 369, 373; **18:** 74, 75, 84
  Richard II **24:** 262, 263, 395; **39:** 243
  Twelfth Night **26:** 233, 257, 337, 342, 371; **51:** 1; **52:** 57
  Venus and Adonis **10:** 429, 434, 439, 442, 459, 462, 489; **33:** 352; **51:** 377

comic form
  As You Like It **46:** 105; **51:** 1
  Measure for Measure **2:** 456, 460, 479, 482, 491, 514, 516; **13:** 94, 104; **23:** 309, 326, 327; **49:** 349

comic resolution
  As You Like It **52:** 63
  Love's Labour's Lost **2:** 335, 340; **16:** 17; **19:** 92; **38:** 209; **51:** 1

comic, tragic, and romantic elements, fusion of
  The Winter's Tale **7:** 390, 394, 396, 399, 410, 412, 414, 429, 436, 479, 483, 490, 501; **13:** 417; **15:** 514, 524, 532; **25:** 339; **36:** 295, 380

commodity
  King John **9:** 224, 229, 245, 260, 275, 280, 297; **19:** 182; **25:** 98; **41:** 228, 269

communication, failure of
  Troilus and Cressida **43:** 277

compassion, theme of
  The Tempest **42:** 339

complex or enigmatic nature
  The Phoenix and Turtle **10:** 7, 14, 35, 42; **38:** 326, 357; **51:** 145, 162

composition date
  The Comedy of Errors **1:** 18, 23, 34, 55
  Henry VIII **2:** 19, 22, 35; **24:** 129
  Pericles **2:** 537, 544
  Sonnets **10:** 153, 154, 161, 166, 196, 217, 226, 270, 277; **28:** 363, 385
  Twelfth Night **37:** 78

conclusion
  All's Well That Ends Well **38:** 123, 132, 142
  Love's Labour's Lost **38:** 172
  Troilus and Cressida **3:** 538, 549, 558, 566, 574, 583, 594
    comedy vs. tragedy **43:** 351

conflict between Christianity and Judaism
  The Merchant of Venice **4:** 224, 250, 268, 289, 324, 344; **12:** 67, 70, 72, 76; **22:** 69; **25:** 257; **40:** 117, 127, 166, 181; **48:** 54, 77; **53:** 105, 159, 214

conscience
  Macbeth **52:** 15
  Richard III **8:** 148, 152, 162, 165, 190, 197, 201, 206, 210, 228, 232, 239, 243, 252, 258; **39:** 341; **52:** 5, 196, 205

as consciously philosophical
  The Phoenix and Turtle **10:** 7, 21, 24, 31, 48; **38:** 342, 378

conspiracy or treason
  The Tempest **16:** 426; **19:** 357; **25:** 382; **29:** 377
  Henry V **49:** 223

constancy and faithfulness
  The Phoenix and Turtle **10:** 18, 20, 21, 48; **38:** 329

construing the truth
  Julius Caesar **7:** 320, 336, 343, 350; **37:** 229

consummation of marriage
  Othello **22:** 207

contemptus mundi
  Antony and Cleopatra **6:** 85, 133

contractual and economic relations
  Henry IV, Parts 1 and 2 **13:** 213
  Richard II **13:** 213; **49:** 602

contradiction, paradox, and opposition
  As You Like It **46:** 105
  Romeo and Juliet **5:** 421, 427, 431, 496, 509, 513, 516, 520, 525, 528, 538; **33:** 287; **44:** 11
  Troilus and Cressida **43:** 377

contrasting dramatic worlds
  Henry IV, Parts 1 and 2 **14:** 56, 60, 61, 84, 105; **48:** 95; **49:** 162
  The Merchant of Venice **44:** 11

contrasts and oppositions
  Othello **4:** 421, 455, 457, 462, 508; **25:** 189

corruption in society
  As You Like It **46:** 94
  King John **9:** 222, 234, 280, 297

costume
  As You Like It **46:** 117
  Hamlet **21:** 81
  Henry VIII **24:** 82, 87; **28:** 184
  Richard II **24:** 274, 278, 291, 304, 325, 356, 364, 423
  Romeo and Juliet **11:** 505, 509
  Troilus and Cressida **18:** 289, 371, 406, 419

counsel
  The Winter's Tale **19:** 401

Court of Love
  The Phoenix and Turtle **10:** 9, 24, 50

court society
  The Winter's Tale **16:** 410

courtly love
  Troilus and Cressida **22:** 58

courtly love tradition, influence of
  Romeo and Juliet **5:** 505, 542, 575; **33:** 233

courtship and marriage
  See also **marriage**
  As You Like It **34:** 109, 177; **48:** 32; **51:** 44
  Much Ado about Nothing **8:** 29, 44, 48, 95, 115, 121, 125; **31:** 191, 231; **51:** 33, 44

credibility
  Twelfth Night **1:** 540, 542, 543, 554, 562, 581, 587

critical history
  Henry IV, Parts 1 and 2 **42:** 185; **48:** 167

cynicism
  Troilus and Cressida **43:** 298

dance
  Henry VI, Parts 1, 2, and 3 **22:** 156

dance and patterned action
  Love's Labour's Lost **2:** 308, 342; **23:** 191, 237

dark elements
All's Well That Ends Well **7**: 27, 37, 39, 43, 54, 109, 113, 116; **26**: 85; **48**: 65; **50**: 59
Twelfth Night **46**: 310

death, decay, nature's destructiveness
Antony and Cleopatra **47**: 71
As You Like It **46**: 169
Hamlet **1**: 144, 153, 188, 198, 221, 242; **13**: 502; **28**: 280, 311; **35**: 241; **42**: 279
King Lear **2**: 93, 94, 101, 104, 106, 109, 112, 116, 129, 131, 137, 143, 147, 149, 156, 160, 170, 179, 188, 197, 207, 218, 222, 226, 231, 238, 241, 245, 249, 253, 265, 269, 273; **16**: 301; **25**: 202, 218; **31**: 77, 117, 137, 142; **46**: 264
Love's Labour's Lost **2**: 305, 331, 344, 348
Measure for Measure **2**: 394, 452, 516; **25**: 12; **49**: 370
Venus and Adonis **10**: 419, 427, 434, 451, 454, 462, 466, 473, 480, 489; **25**: 305; **33**: 309, 321, 347, 352, 363, 370

decay of heroic ideals
Henry VI, Parts 1, 2, and 3 **3**: 119, 126

deception, disguise, and duplicity
As You Like It **46**: 134
Henry IV, Parts 1 and 2 **1**: 397, 406, 425; **42**: 99; **47**: 1, 60; **48**: 95
The Merry Wives of Windsor **5**: 332, 334, 336, 354, 355, 379; **22**: 93; **47**: 308, 314, 321, 325, 344
Much Ado about Nothing **8**: 29, 55, 63, 69, 79, 82, 88, 108, 115; **31**: 191, 198
Sonnets **25**: 374; **40**: 221
The Taming of the Shrew **12**: 416

Deconstructionist interpretation of
Pericles **48**: 364

deposition scene
Richard II **42**: 118

Desire (Volume 38: 1, 19, 31, 40, 48, 56)
All's Well That Ends Well **38**: 96, 99, 109, 118
As You Like It **37**: 43; **52**: 63
Love's Labour's Lost **38**: 185, 194, 200, 209
The Merchant of Venice **22**: 3; **40**: 142; **45**: 17
The Merry Wives of Windsor **38**: 286, 297, 300
Romeo and Juliet **51**: 227, 236
Troilus and Cressida **43**: 317, 329, 340

disappointment, theme of
The Merchant of Venice **53**: 211

discrepancy between prophetic ending and preceding action
Henry VIII **2**: 22, 25, 31, 46, 49, 56, 60, 65, 68, 75, 81; **32**: 148; **41**: 190

disillusioned or cynical tone
Troilus and Cressida **3**: 544, 548, 554, 557, 558, 571, 574, 630, 642; **18**: 284, 332, 403, 406, 423; **27**: 376

disorder
Troilus and Cressida **3**: 578, 589, 599, 604, 609; **18**: 332, 406, 412, 423; **27**: 366

disorder and civil dissension
Henry VI, Parts 1, 2, and 3 **3**: 59, 67, 76, 92, 103, 126; **13**: 131; **16**: 183; **24**: 11, 17, 28, 31, 47; **25**: 102; **28**: 112; **39**: 154, 177, 187, 196, 205

displacement
All's Well That Ends Well **22**: 78
Measure for Measure **22**: 78

divine right versus justice
Henry IV **49**: 116

divine vs. worldly
King Lear **49**: 1

divine will, role of
Romeo and Juliet **5**: 485, 493, 505, 533, 573

domestic elements
As You Like It **46**: 142
Coriolanus **42**: 218; **50**: 145
Venus and Adonis **51**: 359

double-plot
King Lear **2**: 94, 95, 100, 101, 104, 112, 116, 124, 131, 133, 156, 253, 257; **46**: 254
Troilus and Cressida **3**: 569, 613

doubling of roles
Pericles **15**: 150, 152, 167, 173, 180

dramatic elements
Sonnets **10**: 155, 182, 240, 251, 283, 367
Venus and Adonis **10**: 459, 462, 486

dramatic shortcomings or failure
As You Like It **5**: 19, 42, 52, 61, 65
Love's Labour's Lost **2**: 299, 301, 303, 322
Romeo and Juliet **5**: 416, 418, 420, 426, 436, 437, 448, 464, 467, 469, 480, 487, 524, 562

dramatic structure
The Comedy of Errors **1**: 19, 27, 40, 43, 46, 50; **26**: 186, 190; **34**: 190, 229, 233; **37**: 12
Cymbeline **4**: 17, 18, 19, 20, 21, 22, 24, 38, 43, 48, 53, 64, 68, 89, 116, 129, 141; **22**: 302, 365; **25**: 319; **36**: 115, 125
Othello **4**: 370, 390, 399, 427, 488, 506, 517, 569; **22**: 207; **28**: 243; **53**: 261
The Winter's Tale **7**: 382, 390, 396, 399, 402, 407, 414, 429, 432, 473, 479, 493, 497, 501; **15**: 528; **25**: 339; **36**: 289, 295, 362, 380; **45**: 297, 344, 358, 366

as dream-play
A Midsummer Night's Dream **3**: 365, 370, 372, 377, 389, 391; **29**: 190; **45**: 117

Dreams in Shakespeare (Volume 45: 1, 10, 17, 28, 40, 48, 58, 67, 75)
Antony and Cleopatra **45**: 28
Cymbeline **4**: 162, 167; **44**: 28; **45**: 67, 75

Hamlet **45**: 28
Julius Caesar **45**: 10
A Midsummer Night's Dream **45**: 96, 107, 117
Romeo and Juliet **45**: 40
The Tempest **45**: 236, 247, 259

dualisms
Antony and Cleopatra **19**: 304; **27**: 82
Cymbeline **4**: 29, 64, 73

duration of time
As You Like It **5**: 44, 45
A Midsummer Night's Dream **3**: 362, 370, 380, 386, 494; **45**: 175

economic relations
Henry V **13**: 213

economics and exchange
Coriolanus **50**: 152
The Merchant of Venice **40**: 197, 208; **53**: 116

editorial and textual issues
Sonnets **28**: 363; **40**: 273; **42**: 296

education
All's Well That Ends Well **7**: 62, 86, 90, 93, 98, 104, 116, 126
The Two Gentlemen of Verona **6**: 490, 494, 504, 526, 532, 555, 568

education or nurturing
The Tempest **8**: 353, 370, 384, 396; **29**: 292, 368, 377

egotism or narcissism
Much Ado about Nothing **8**: 19, 24, 28, 29, 55, 69, 95, 115

Elizabeth, audience of
Sonnets **48**: 325

Elizabeth's influence
The Merry Wives of Windsor **5**: 333, 334, 335, 336, 339, 346, 355, 366, 402; **18**: 5, 86; **38**: 278; **47**: 344

Elizabethan and Jacobean politics, relation to
Hamlet **28**: 232; **28**: 290, 311; **35**: 140

Elizabethan attitudes, influence of
Richard II **6**: 287, 292, 294, 305, 321, 327, 364, 402, 414; **13**: 494; **24**: 325; **28**: 188; **39**: 273; **42**: 118; **52**: 141, 144

Elizabethan betrothal and marriage customs
Measure for Measure **2**: 429, 437, 443, 503; **49**: 286

Elizabethan culture, relation to
General Commentary **50**: 34; **53**: 169
Antony and Cleopatra **47**: 103
As You Like It **5**: 21, 59, 66, 68, 70, 158; **16**: 53; **28**: 46; **34**: 120; **37**: 1; **46**: 142
The Comedy of Errors **26**: 138, 142; **34**: 201, 215, 233, 238, 258; **42**: 80

Hamlet **1:** 76, 148, 151, 154, 160, 166, 169, 171, 176, 184, 202, 209, 254; **13:** 282, 494; **19:** 330; **21:** 407, 416; **22:** 258
Henry IV, Parts 1 and 2 **19:** 195; **48:** 117, 143, 151, 175
Henry V **5:** 210, 213, 217, 223, 257, 299, 310; **16:** 202; **19:** 133, 233; **28:** 121, 159; **30:** 215, 262; **37:** 187; **49:** 260
Julius Caesar **16:** 231; **30:** 342, 379; **50:** 13, 211, 269, 280
King Lear **2:** 168, 174, 177, 183, 226, 241; **19:** 330; **22:** 227, 233, 365; **25:** 218; **46:** 276; **47:** 9; **49:** 67
Measure for Measure **2:** 394, 418, 429, 432, 437, 460, 470, 482, 503
The Merchant of Venice **32:** 66; **40:** 117, 127, 142, 166, 181, 197, 208; **48:** 54, 77; **49:** 37; **53:** 105, 111, 116, 127, 159
A Midsummer Night's Dream **50:** 86
Much Ado about Nothing **8:** 23, 33, 44, 55, 58, 79, 88, 104, 111, 115; **51:** 15
The Rape of Lucrece **33:** 195; **43:** 77
The Taming of the Shrew **31:** 288, 295, 300, 315, 326, 345, 351
Timon of Athens **1:** 487, 489, 495, 500; **20:** 433; **27:** 203, 212, 230; **50:** 13; **52:** 320, 354
Titus Andronicus **27:** 282
Troilus and Cressida **3:** 560, 574, 606; **25:** 56
Twelfth Night **1:** 549, 553, 555, 563, 581, 587, 620; **16:** 53; **19:** 42, 78; **26:** 357; **28:** 1; **34:** 323, 330; **46:** 291; **51:** 15

Elizabethan dramatic conventions
Cymbeline **4:** 53, 124
Henry VIII **24:** 155

Elizabethan literary influences
Henry VI, Parts 1, 2, and 3 **3:** 75, 97, 100, 119, 143; **22:** 156; **28:** 112; **37:** 97

Elizabethan love poetry
Love's Labour's Lost **38:** 232

Elizabethan poetics, influence of
Romeo and Juliet **5:** 416, 520, 522, 528, 550, 559, 575

Elizabethan politics, relation to
Henry IV, Parts 1 and 2 **22:** 395; **28:** 203; **47:** 60; **48:** 117, 143, 167, 175
Henry VIII **22:** 395; **24:** 115, 129, 140; **32:** 148
King John **48:** 132
Richard III **22:** 395; **25:** 141; **37:** 144; **39:** 345, 349; **42:** 130; **52:** 201, 214, 257

Elizabethan setting
The Two Gentlemen of Verona **12:** 463, 485

Elizabethan society
The Merry Wives of Windsor **47:** 331

Epicureanism **50:** 249

emulation or rivalry
Julius Caesar **16:** 231; **50:** 211

England and Rome, parallels between
Coriolanus **9:** 39, 43, 106, 148, 180, 193; **25:** 296; **30:** 67, 105

English language and colonialism
Henry V **22:** 103; **28:** 159

English Reformation, influence of
Henry VIII **2:** 25, 35, 39, 51, 67; **24:** 89

epic elements
Henry V **5:** 192, 197, 246, 257, 314; **30:** 181, 220, 237, 252

erotic elements
A Midsummer Night's Dream **3:** 445, 491, 497, 511; **12:** 259, 262, 298; **16:** 34; **19:** 21; **29:** 183, 225, 269
Venus and Adonis **10:** 410, 411, 418, 419, 427, 428, 429, 442, 448, 454, 459, 466, 473; **25:** 305, 328; **28:** 355; **33:** 321, 339, 347, 352, 363, 370; **51:** 345, 352, 359, 368

as experimental play
Romeo and Juliet **5:** 464, 509, 528

Essex Rebellion, relation to
Richard II **6:** 249, 250; **24:** 356

ethical or moral issues
King John **9:** 212, 222, 224, 229, 235, 240, 263, 275, 280
King Lear **52:** 1, 95;
Measure for Measure **52:** 69
Twelfth Night **52:** 57

ethnicity
The Winter's Tale **37:** 306

Euripides, influence of
Titus Andronicus **27:** 285

evil
See also **good versus evil**
Macbeth **3:** 194, 208, 231, 234, 239, 241, 267, 289; **20:** 203, 206, 210, 374; **52:** 23
Othello **52:** 78
Richard III **52:** 78
Romeo and Juliet **5:** 485, 493, 505
Titus Andronicus **53:** 86, 92

excess
King John **9:** 251

fable of the belly
Coriolanus **50:** 13, 110, 140

fame
Coriolanus **30:** 58

family honor, structure, and inheritance
Richard II **6:** 338, 368, 388, 397, 414; **39:** 263, 279
Richard III **8:** 177, 248, 252, 263, 267; **25:** 141; **39:** 335, 341, 349, 370

family, theme of
Cymbeline **44:** 28

fancy
Twelfth Night **1:** 543, 546

as farce
The Taming of the Shrew **9:** 330, 337, 338, 341, 342, 365, 381, 386, 413, 426

farcical elements
See **comic and farcical elements**

fate
Richard II **6:** 289, 294, 304, 352, 354, 385
Romeo and Juliet **5:** 431, 444, 464, 469, 470, 479, 480, 485, 487, 493, 509, 530, 533, 562, 565, 571, 573; **33:** 249

Fathers and Daughters (Volume 36: 1, 12, 25, 32, 37, 45, 70, 78)
As You Like It **46:** 94
Cymbeline **34:** 134
King Lear **34:** 51, 54, 60
cruelty of daughters **2:** 101, 102, 106; **31:** 84, 123, 137, 142
Pericles **34:** 226, 233
The Winter's Tale **34:** 311, 318, 328

Feast of the Lupercal
Julius Caesar **50:** 269

feminist criticism
As You Like It **23:** 107, 108
Comedy of Errors **42:** 93
Love's Labour's Lost **42:** 93
Measure for Measure **23:** 320

feminist interpretation
A Midsummer Night's Dream **48:** 23

festive or folklore elements
Twelfth Night **46:** 338; **51:** 15

feud
Romeo and Juliet **5:** 415, 419, 425, 447, 458, 464, 469, 479, 480, 493, 509, 522, 556, 565, 566, 571, 575; **25:** 181; **51:** 245

fire and water
Coriolanus **25:** 263

flattery
Coriolanus **9:** 26, 45, 92, 100, 110, 121, 130, 144, 157, 183, 193; **25:** 296
Henry IV, Parts 1 and 2 **22:** 395
Henry VIII **22:** 395
Richard III **22:** 395

folk drama, relation to
The Winter's Tale **7:** 420, 451

folk elements
The Taming of the Shrew **9:** 381, 393, 404, 426

folk rituals, elements and influence of
Henry VI, Parts 1, 2, and 3 **39:** 205

The Merry Wives of Windsor **5**: 353, 369, 376, 392, 397, 400; **38**: 256, 300

food, meaning of
The Comedy of Errors **34**: 220
Troilus and Cressida **43**: 298

forest
The Two Gentlemen of Verona **6**: 450, 456, 492, 514, 547, 555, 564, 568

Forest of Arden
As You Like It
as "bitter" Arcadia **5**: 98, 118, 162; **23**: 97, 98, 99, 100, 122, 139
Duke Frederick's court, contrast with **5**: 46, 102, 103, 112, 130, 156; **16**: 53; **23**: 126, 128, 129, 131, 134; **34**: 78, 102, 131; **46**: 164
pastoral elements **5**: 18, 20, 24, 32, 35, 47, 50, 54, 55, 57, 60, 77, 128, 135, 156; **23**: 17, 20, 27, 46, 137; **34**: 78, 147; **46**: 88
as patriarchal society **5**: 168; **23**: 150; **34**: 177
as source of self-knowledge **5**: 98, 102, 103, 128, 130, 135, 148, 158, 162; **23**: 17; **34**: 102
as timeless, mythical world **5**: 112, 130, 141; **23**: 132; **34**: 78; **37**: 43; **46**: 88
theme of play **46**: 88

forgiveness or redemption
Venus and Adonis **51**: 377
The Winter's Tale **7**: 381, 389, 395, 402, 407, 436, 456, 460, 483; **36**: 318

free will versus fate
Macbeth **3**: 177, 183, 184, 190, 196, 198, 202, 207, 208, 213; **13**: 361; **44**: 351, 361, 366, 373
The Two Noble Kinsmen **9**: 474, 481, 486, 492, 498

freedom and servitude
The Tempest **8**: 304, 307, 312, 429; **22**: 302; **29**: 278, 368, 377; **37**: 336

French language, Shakespeare's use of
Henry V **5**: 186, 188, 190; **25**: 131

Freudian analysis
A Midsummer Night's Dream **44**: 1

friendship
See also **love and friendship** and **love versus friendship**
Coriolanus **30**: 125, 142
Sonnets **10**: 185, 279; **28**: 380; **51**: 284, 288
The Two Noble Kinsmen **9**: 448, 463, 470, 474, 479, 481, 486, 490; **19**: 394; **41**: 363, 372; **42**: 361

Gender Identity and Issues (Volume 40: 1, 9, 15, 27, 33, 51, 61, 65, 75, 90, 99**)**
All's Well That Ends Well **7**: 9, 10, 67, 126; **13**: 77, 84; **19**: 113; **26**: 128; **38**: 89, 99, 118; **44**: 35
Antony and Cleopatra **13**: 368; **25**: 257; **27**: 144; **47**: 174, 192; **53**: 67, 77

As You Like It **46**: 127, 134
The Comedy of Errors **34**: 215, 220
Coriolanus **30**: 79, 125, 142; **44**: 93; **50**: 128
Hamlet **35**: 144; **44**: 189, 195, 198
Henry IV, Parts 1 and 2 **13**: 183; **25**: 151; **44**: 44; **48**: 175
Henry V **13**: 183; **28**: 121, 146, 159; **44**: 44
Julius Caesar **13**: 260
The Merchant of Venice **40**: 142, 151, 156
Othello **32**: 294; **35**: 327
A Midsummer Night's Dream **53**: 1
Othello **53**: 255, 268, 310
The Rape of Lucrece **53**: 1
Richard II **25**: 89; **39**: 295
Richard III **25**: 141; **37**: 144; **39**: 345; **52**: 223, 239
Romeo and Juliet **32**: 256; **51**: 253
Sonnets **37**: 374; **40**: 238, 247, 254, 264, 268, 273; **53**: 1
The Taming of the Shrew **28**: 24; **31**: 261, 268, 276, 282, 288, 295, 300, 335, 351
The Tempest **53**: 64, 67
Twelfth Night **19**: 78; **34**: 344; **37**: 59; **42**: 32; **46**: 347, 362, 369
The Two Gentlemen of Verona **40**: 374
The Two Noble Kinsmen **42**: 361

genre
All's Well That Ends Well **48**: 65
As You Like It **5**: 46, 55, 79
The Comedy of Errors **34**: 251, 258
Coriolanus **9**: 42, 43, 53, 80, 106, 112, 117, 130, 164, 177; **30**: 67, 74, 79, 89, 111, 125; **50**: 99
Hamlet **1**: 176, 212, 237
Love's Labour's Lost **38**: 163
The Merchant of Venice **4**: 191, 200, 201, 209, 215, 221, 232, 238, 247; **12**: 48, 54, 62
Much Ado about Nothing **8**: 9, 18, 19, 28, 29, 39, 41, 44, 53, 63, 69, 73, 79, 82, 95, 100, 104; **48**: 14
Richard III **8**: 181, 182, 197, 206, 218, 228, 239, 243, 252, 258; **13**: 142; **39**: 383; **52**: 239
The Taming of the Shrew **9**: 329, 334, 362, 375; **22**: 48; **31**: 261, 269, 276
Timon of Athens **1**: 454, 456, 459, 460, 462, 483, 492, 499, 503, 509, 511, 512, 515, 518, 525, 531; **27**: 203
Troilus and Cressida **3**: 541, 542, 549, 558, 566, 571, 574, 587, 594, 604, 630, 642; **27**: 366
The Two Gentlemen of Verona **6**: 460, 468, 472, 516; **40**: 320

genres, mixture of
Timon of Athens **16**: 351; **25**: 198

gift exchange
Love's Labour's Lost **25**: 1

good versus evil
See also **evil**
Measure for Measure **2**: 432, 452, 524; **33**: 52, 61; **52**: 69
The Tempest **8**: 302, 311, 315, 370, 423, 439; **29**: 278; 297

grace
The Winter's Tale **7**: 420, 425, 460, 493; **36**: 328

grace and civility
Love's Labour's Lost **2**: 351

Greece
Troilus and Cressida **43**: 287

grotesque or absurd elements
Hamlet **42**: 279
King Lear **2**: 136, 156, 245; **13**: 343; **52**: 1

handkerchief, significance of
Othello **4**: 370, 384, 385, 396, 503, 530, 562; **35**: 265, 282, 380

Hercules Furens (Seneca) as source
Othello **16**: 283

heroism
Henry V **49**: 194, 200, 211, 236

Hippolytus, myth of
A Midsummer Night's Dream **29**: 216; **45**: 84

historical accuracy
Henry VI, Parts 1, 2, and 3 **3**: 18, 21, 35, 46, 51; **16**: 217; **24**: 16, 18, 25, 31, 45, 48
Richard III **8**: 144, 145, 153, 159, 163, 165, 168, 213, 223, 228, 232; **39**: 305, 308, 326, 383

historical allegory
The Winter's Tale **7**: 381; **15**: 528
The Merchant of Venice **53**: 179, 187

historical elements
Cymbeline **47**: 260

historical and dramatic elements
Henry IV **49**: 93

historical and romantic elements, combination of
Henry VIII **2**: 46, 49, 51, 75, 76, 78; **24**: 71, 80, 146; **41**: 129, 146, 180

historical content
Henry IV, Parts 1 and 2 **1**: 310, 328, 365, 366, 370, 374, 380, 387, 421, 424, 427, 431; **16**: 172; **19**: 157; **25**: 151; **32**: 136; **39**: 143; **48**: 143, 167
Henry V **5**: 185, 188, 190, 192, 193, 198, 246, 314; **13**: 201; **19**: 133; **25**: 131; **30**: 193, 202, 207, 215, 252
King John **9**: 216, 219, 220, 222, 235, 240, 254, 284, 290, 292, 297, 300, 303; **13**: 163; **32**: 93, 114; **41**: 234, 243
The Tempest **8**: 364, 408, 420; **16**: 426; **25**: 382; **29**: 278, 339, 343, 368; **45**: 226; **53**: 21, 53

historical determinism versus free will
Julius Caesar **7**: 160, 298, 316, 333, 346, 356; **13**: 252

historical epic, as epilogue to Shakespeare's
Henry VIII **2**: 22, 25, 27, 39, 51, 60, 65

historical epic, place in or relation to Shakespeare's
Henry IV, Parts 1 and 2 **1**: 309, 314, 328, 374, 379, 424, 427
Henry V **5**: 195, 198, 205, 212, 225, 241, 244, 287, 304, 310; **14**: 337, 342; **30**: 215
Henry VI, Parts 1, 2, and 3 **3**: 24, 59; **24**: 51; **48**: 167

historical principles
Richard III **39**: 308, 326, 387

historical relativity, theme of 41: 146

historical sources, compared with
Richard II **6**: 252, 279, 343; **28**: 134; **39**: 235; **49**: 60

historiography
Henry VIII **37**: 109

homoerotic elements
As You Like It **46**: 127, 142
Henry V **16**: 202
Sonnets **10**: 155, 156, 159, 161, 175, 213, 391; **16**: 461; **28**: 363, 380; **37**: 347; **40**: 254, 264, 273; **51**: 270, 284

homosexuality
As You Like It **46**: 127, 142
Measure for Measure **42**: 1
The Merchant of Venice **22**: 3, 69; **37**: 86; **40**: 142, 156, 197
Twelfth Night **22**: 69; **42**: 32; **46**: 362
The Winter's Tale **48**: 309

honor or integrity
Coriolanus **9**: 43, 65, 73, 92, 106, 110, 121, 144, 153, 157, 164, 177, 183, 189; **30**: 89, 96, 133

hospitality
The Winter's Tale **19**: 366

as humanistic play
Henry VI, Parts 1, 2, and 3 **3**: 83, 92, 109, 115, 119, 131, 136, 143

hunt motif
Venus and Adonis **10**: 434, 451, 466, 473; **33**: 357, 370

hypocrisy
Henry V **5**: 203, 213, 219, 223, 233, 260, 271, 302

ideal love
See also **love**
Romeo and Juliet **5**: 421, 427, 431, 436, 437, 450, 463, 469, 498, 505, 575; **25**: 257; **33**: 210, 225, 272; **51**: 25; **51**: 44, 195, 203, 219

idealism versus pragmatism
Hamlet **16**: 246; **28**: 325

idealism versus realism
See also **realism**
Love's Labour's Lost **38**: 163
Othello **4**: 457, 508, 517; **13**: 313; **25**: 189; **53**: 350

identities of persons
Sonnets **10**: 154, 155, 156, 161, 166, 167, 169, 173, 174, 175, 185, 190, 191, 196, 218, 226, 230, 233, 240; **40**: 238

identity
The Comedy of Errors **34**: 201, 208, 211
Coriolanus **42**: 243; **50**: 128
A Midsummer Night's Dream **29**: 269
The Two Gentlemen of Verona **6**: 494, 511, 529, 532, 547, 560, 564, 568; **19**: 34

illusion
The Comedy of Errors **1**: 13, 14, 27, 37, 40, 45, 59, 63; **26**: 188; **34**: 194, 211

illusion versus reality
Love's Labour's Lost **2**: 303, 308, 331, 340, 344, 348, 356, 359, 367, 371, 375; **23**: 230, 231

imagery
Venus and Adonis **10**: 414, 415, 416, 420, 429, 434, 449, 459, 466, 473, 480; **25**: 328; **28**: 355; **33**: 321, 339, 352, 363, 370, 377; **42**: 347; **51**: 335, 388

imagination and art
A Midsummer Night's Dream **3**: 365, 371, 381, 402, 412, 417, 421, 423, 441, 459, 468, 506, 516, 520; **22**: 39; **45**: 96, 126, 136, 147

immortality
Measure for Measure **16**: 102

imperialism
Antony and Cleopatra **53**: 67, 77
Henry V **22**: 103; **28**: 159
The Merchant of Venice **53**: 116

implausibility of plot, characters, or events
All's Well That Ends Well **7**: 8, 45
King Lear **2**: 100, 136, 145, 278; **13**: 343
The Merchant of Venice **4**: 191, 192, 193; **12**: 52, 56, 76, 119
Much Ado about Nothing **8**: 9, 12, 16, 19, 33, 36, 39, 44, 53, 100, 104
Othello **4**: 370, 380, 391, 442, 444; **47**: 51

inaction
Troilus and Cressida **3**: 587, 621; **27**: 347

incest, motif of
Pericles **2**: 582, 588; **22**: 315; **36**: 257, 264; **51**: 97, 110

inconsistencies
Henry VIII **2**: 16, 27, 28, 31, 60

inconsistency between first and second halves
Measure for Measure **2**: 474, 475, 505, 514, 524; **49**: 349, 358

induction
The Taming of the Shrew **9**: 320, 322, 332, 337, 345, 350, 362, 365, 369, 370, 381, 390, 393, 407, 419, 424, 430; **12**: 416, 427, 430, 431, 441; **19**: 34, 122; **22**: 48; **31**: 269, 315, 351

as inferior or flawed play
Henry VI, Parts 1, 2, and 3 **3**: 20, 21, 25, 26, 35
Pericles **2**: 537, 546, 553, 563, 564; **15**: 139, 143, 156, 167, 176; **36**: 198; **51**: 79
Timon of Athens **1**: 476, 481, 489, 499, 520; **20**: 433, 439, 491; **25**: 198; **27**: 157, 175; **52**: 338, 349

infidelity
Troilus and Cressida **43**: 298

innocence
Macbeth **3**: 234, 241, 327
Othello **47**: 25
Pericles **36**: 226, 274

innocence to experience
The Two Noble Kinsmen **9**: 481, 502; **19**: 394

Ireland, William Henry, forgeries of
Sonnets **48**: 325

Irish affairs
Henry V **22**: 103; **28**: 159

ironic or parodic elements
The Two Gentlemen of Verona **6**: 447, 472, 478, 484, 502, 504, 509, 516, 529, 549; **13**: 12
Henry VIII **41**: 129

irony
All's Well That Ends Well **7**: 27, 32, 58, 62, 67, 81, 86, 109, 116
Antony and Cleopatra **6**: 53, 136, 146, 151, 159, 161, 189, 192, 211, 224
As You Like It **5**: 30, 32, 154
Coriolanus **9**: 65, 73, 80, 92, 106, 153, 157, 164, 193; **30**: 67, 89, 133
Cymbeline **4**: 64, 77, 103
Henry V **5**: 192, 210, 213, 219, 223, 226, 233, 252, 260, 269, 281, 299, 304; **14**: 336; **30**: 159, 193
Julius Caesar **7**: 167, 257, 259, 262, 268, 282, 316, 320, 333, 336, 346, 350
The Merchant of Venice **4**: 254, 300, 321, 331, 350; **28**: 63
Much Ado about Nothing **8**: 14, 63, 79, 82; **28**: 63
The Rape of Lucrece **10**: 93, 98, 128
Richard II **6**: 270, 307, 364, 368, 391; **24**: 383; **28**: 188
Sonnets **10**: 256, 293, 334, 337, 346; **51**: 300
The Taming of the Shrew **9**: 340, 375, 398, 407, 413; **13**: 3; **19**: 122
The Two Noble Kinsmen **9**: 463, 481, 486; **41**: 301; **50**: 348
The Winter's Tale **7**: 419, 420

the island
The Tempest **8:** 308, 315, 447; **25:** 357, 382; **29:** 278, 343

Italian influences
Sonnets **28:** 407

Jacobean culture, relation to
Coriolanus **22:** 248
Macbeth **19:** 330; **22:** 365
Pericles **37:** 361; **51:** 86, 110
The Winter's Tale **19:** 366, 401, 431; **25:** 347; **32:** 388; **37:** 306

jealousy
The Merry Wives of Windsor **5:** 334, 339, 343, 353, 355, 363; **22:** 93; **38:** 273, 307
Othello **4:** 384, 488, 527; **35:** 253, 265, 282, 301, 310; **44:** 57, 66; **51:** 30
The Winter's Tale **44:** 66; **47:** 25

Jonsonian humors comedy, influence of
The Merry Wives of Windsor **38:** 319

judicial versus natural law
Measure for Measure **2:** 446, 507, 516, 519; **22:** 85; **33:** 58, 117; **49:** 1, 293

justice
As You Like It **46:** 94
Henry IV **49:** 112, 123
King Lear **49:** 1
Othello **35:** 247

justice and mercy
Measure for Measure **2:** 391, 395, 399, 402, 406, 409, 411, 416, 421, 437, 443, 463, 466, 470, 491, 495, 522, 524; **22:** 85; **33:** 52, 61, 101; **49:** 1, 274, 293, 300
The Merchant of Venice **4:** 213, 214, 224, 250, 261, 273, 282, 289, 336; **12:** 80, 129; **40:** 127; **49:** 1, 23, 27, 37
Much Ado about Nothing **22:** 85

justice, divine vs. worldly
King Lear **49:** 67, 73

juxtaposition of opposing perspectives
As You Like It **5:** 86, 93, 98, 141; **16:** 53; **23:** 119; **34:** 72, 78, 131

Kingship (Volume 39: 1, 16, 20, 34, 45, 62)
Henry IV, Parts 1 and 2 **1:** 314, 318, 337, 366, 370, 374, 379, 380, 383, 424; **16:** 172; **19:** 195; **28:** 101; **39:** 100, 116, 123, 130; **42:** 141; **48:** 143
Henry V **5:** 205, 223, 225, 233, 239, 244, 257, 264, 267, 271, 287, 289, 299, 302, 304, 314, 318; **16:** 202; **22:** 137; **30:** 169, 202, 259, 273; **42:** 141; **49:** 200
Henry VI, Parts 1, 2, and 3 **3:** 69, 73, 77, 109, 115, 136, 143; **24:** 32; **39:** 154, 177, 187; **47:** 32
Henry VIII **2:** 49, 58, 60, 65, 75, 78; **24:** 113; **41:** 129, 171
King John **9:** 235, 254, 263, 275, 297; **13:** 158; **19:** 182; **22:** 120
Richard II **6:** 263, 264, 272, 277, 289, 294, 327, 354, 364, 381, 388, 391, 402, 409, 414; **19:** 151, 209; **24:** 260, 289, 291, 322, 325, 333, 339, 345, 346, 349, 351, 352, 356, 395, 408, 419, 428; **28:** 134; **39:** 235, 243, 256, 263, 273, 279, 289; **42:** 173
Richard III **39:** 335, 341, 345, 349

knighthood
The Merry Wives of Windsor **5:** 338, 343, 390, 397, 402; **47:** 354

knowledge
Love's Labour's Lost **22:** 12; **47:** 35

language and imagery
All's Well That Ends Well **7:** 12, 29, 45, 104, 109, 121; **38:** 132, 65
Antony and Cleopatra **6:** 21, 25, 39, 64, 80, 85, 92, 94, 100, 104, 142, 146, 155, 159, 161, 165, 189, 192, 202, 211; **13:** 374, 383; **25:** 245, 257; **27:** 96, 105, 135
As You Like It **5:** 19, 21, 35, 52, 75, 82, 92, 138; **23:** 15, 21, 26; **28:** 9; **34:** 131; **37:** 43; **48:** 42
The Comedy of Errors **1:** 16, 25, 39, 40, 43, 57, 59; **34:** 233
Coriolanus **9:** 8, 9, 13, 53, 64, 65, 73, 78, 84, 100, 112, 121, 136, 139, 142, 144, 153, 157, 174, 183, 193, 198; **22:** 248; **25:** 245, 263; **30:** 111, 125, 142; **37:** 283; **44:** 79
Cymbeline **4:** 43, 48, 61, 64, 70, 73, 93, 108; **13:** 401; **25:** 245; **28:** 373, 398; **36:** 115, 158, 166, 186; **47:** 205, 286, 296
Hamlet **1:** 95, 144, 153, 154, 160, 188, 198, 221, 227, 249, 259, 270; **22:** 258, 378; **28:** 311; **35:** 144, 152, 238, 241; **42:** 212; **44:** 248; **52:** 35
Henry IV, Parts 1 and 2 **13:** 213; **16:** 172; **25:** 245; **28:** 101; **39:** 116, 130; **42:** 153; **47:** 1
Henry V **5:** 188, 230, 233, 241, 264, 276; **9:** 203; **19:** 203; **25:** 131; **30:** 159, 181, 207, 234; **30:** 159, 181, 207, 234
Henry VI, Parts 1, 2, and 3 **3:** 10, 50, 52, 55, 57, 66, 67, 71, 75, 76, 97, 105, 109, 119, 126, 131; **24:** 28; **37:** 157; **39:** 213, 222
Henry VIII **41:** 180, 190
Julius Caesar **7:** 148, 155, 159, 188, 204, 207, 227, 242, 250, 277, 296, 303, 324, 346, 350; **13:** 260; **17:** 347, 348, 350, 356, 358; **19:** 321; **22:** 280; **25:** 280; **30:** 333, 342; **50:** 196, 258
King Lear **2:** 129, 137, 161, 191, 199, 237, 257, 271; **16:** 301; **19:** 344; **22:** 233; **46:** 177
King John **9:** 212, 215, 220, 246, 251, 254, 267, 280, 284, 292, 297, 300; **13:** 147, 158; **22:** 120; **37:** 132; **48:** 132
Love's Labour's Lost **2:** 301, 302, 303, 306, 307, 308, 315, 319, 320, 330, 335, 344, 345, 348, 356, 359, 362, 365, 371, 374, 375; **19:** 92; **22:** 12, 378; **23:** 184, 187, 196, 197, 202, 207, 211, 221, 227, 231, 233, 237, 252; **28:** 9, 63; **38:** 219, 226
Macbeth **3:** 170, 193, 213, 231, 234, 241, 245, 250, 253, 256, 263, 271, 283, 300, 302, 306, 323, 327, 338, 340, 349; **13:** 476; **16:** 317; **20:** 241, 279, 283, 367, 379, 400; **25:** 235; **28:** 339; **29:** 76, 91; **42:** 258; **44:** 366; **45:** 58

Measure for Measure **2:** 394, 421, 431, 466, 486, 505; **13:** 112; **28:** 9; **33:** 69; **49:** 370
The Merry Wives of Windsor **5:** 335, 337, 343, 347, 351, 363, 374, 379; **19:** 101; **22:** 93, 378; **28:** 9, 69; **38:** 313, 319
The Merchant of Venice **4:** 241, 267, 293; **22:** 3; **25:** 257; **28:** 9, 63; **32:** 41; **40:** 106; **53:** 169
A Midsummer Night's Dream **3:** 397, 401, 410, 412, 415, 432, 453, 459, 468, 494; **22:** 23, 39, 93, 378; **28:** 9; **29:** 263; **45:** 143, 169, 175; **48:** 23, 32
Much Ado about Nothing **8:** 9, 38, 43, 46, 55, 69, 73, 88, 95, 100, 115, 125; **19:** 68; **25:** 77; **28:** 63; **31:** 178, 184, 222, 241, 245; **48:** 14
Othello **4:** 433, 442, 445, 462, 493, 508, 517, 552, 587, 596; **13:** 304; **16:** 272; **22:** 378; **25:** 189, 257; **28:** 243, 344; **42:** 273; **47:** 51; **53:** 261
Pericles **2:** 559, 560, 565, 583; **16:** 391; **19:** 387; **22:** 315; **36:** 198, 214, 233, 244, 251, 264; **51:** 86, 99
The Rape of Lucrece **10:** 64, 65, 66, 71, 78, 80, 89, 93, 116, 109, 125, 131; **22:** 289, 294; **25:** 305; **32:** 321; **33:** 144, 155, 179, 200; **43:** 102, 113, 141
Richard II **6:** 252, 282, 283, 294, 298, 315, 323, 331, 347, 368, 374, 381, 385, 397, 409; **13:** 213, 494; **24:** 269, 290, 298, 301, 304, 315, 325, 329, 333, 339, 356, 364, 395, 405, 408, 411, 414, 419; **28:** 134, 188; **39:** 243, 273, 289, 295; **42:** 173; **52:** 154, 157, 169, 174, 183
Richard III **8:** 159, 161, 165, 167, 168, 170, 177, 182, 184, 186, 193, 197, 201, 206, 218, 223, 243, 248, 252, 258, 262, 267; **16:** 150; **25:** 141, 245; **39:** 360, 370, 383; **47:** 15; **52:** 285, 290
Romeo and Juliet **5:** 420, 426, 431, 436, 437, 456, 477, 479, 489, 492, 496, 509, 520, 522, 528, 538, 542, 550, 559; **25:** 181, 245, 257; **32:** 276; **33:** 210, 272, 274, 287; **42:** 266; **51:** 203, 212, 227
Sonnets **10:** 247, 251, 255, 256, 290, 353, 372, 385; **13:** 445; **28:** 380, 385; **32:** 327, 352; **40:** 228, 247, 284, 292, 303; **51:** 270, 304
The Taming of the Shrew **9:** 336, 338, 393, 401, 404, 407, 413; **22:** 378; **28:** 9; **31:** 261, 288, 300, 326, 335, 339; **32:** 56
The Tempest **8:** 324, 348, 384, 390, 404, 454; **19:** 421; **29:** 278; **29:** 297, 343, 368, 377
Timon of Athens **1:** 488; **13:** 392; **25:** 198; **27:** 166, 184, 235; **52:** 329, 345, 354
Titus Andronicus **4:** 617, 624, 635, 642, 644, 646, 659, 664, 668, 672, 675; **13:** 225; **16:** 225; **25:** 245; **27:** 246, 293, 313, 318, 325; **43:** 186, 222, 227, 239, 247, 262
Troilus and Cressida **3:** 561, 569, 596, 599, 606, 624, 630, 635; **22:** 58, 339; **27:** 332; **366; **42:** 66
Twelfth Night **1:** 570, 650, 664; **22:** 12; **28:** 9; **34:** 293; **37:** 59
The Two Gentlemen of Verona **6:** 437, 438, 439, 445, 449, 490, 504, 519, 529, 541; **28:** 9; **40:** 343
The Two Noble Kinsmen **9:** 445, 446, 447, 448, 456, 461, 462, 463, 469, 471, 498, 502; **41:** 289, 301, 308, 317, 326; **50:** 310

The Winter's Tale **7**: 382, 384, 417, 418, 420, 425, 460, 506; **13**: 409; **19**: 431; **22**: 324; **25**: 347; **36**: 295; **42**: 301; **45**: 297, 344, 333; **50**: 45

language versus action
Titus Andronicus **4**: 642, 644, 647, 664, 668; **13**: 225; **27**: 293, 313, 325; **43**: 186

Law and Justice (Volume 49: 1, 18, 23, 27, 37, 46, 60, 67, 73)
Henry IV **49**: 112,116,123,133,137
Henry V **49**: 223, 236, 260
Measure for Measure **49**: 274, 286, 293
The Merchant of Venice **53**: 169
Othello **53**: 288, 350

law versus passion for freedom
Much Ado about Nothing **22**: 85

laws of nature, violation of
Macbeth **3**: 234, 241, 280, 323; **29**: 120

legal issues
King Lear **46**: 276

legitimacy
Henry VI, Parts 1, 2, and 3 **3**: 89, 157; **39**: 154,
Henry VIII **37**: 109

legitimacy or inheritance
King John **9**: 224, 235, 254, 303; **13**: 147; **19**: 182; **37**: 132; **41**: 215

liberty versus tyranny
Julius Caesar **7**: 158, 179, 189, 205, 221, 253; **25**: 272

love
See also **ideal love**
All's Well That Ends Well **7**: 12, 15, 16, 51, 58, 67, 90, 93, 116; **38**: 80; **51**: 33, 44
As You Like It **5**: 24, 44, 46, 57, 79, 88, 103, 116, 122, 138, 141, 162; **28**: 46, 82; **34**: 85
King Lear **2**: 109, 112, 131, 160, 162, 170, 179, 188, 197, 218, 222, 238, 265; **25**: 202; **31**: 77, 149, 151, 155, 162
Love's Labour's Lost **2**: 312, 315, 340, 344; **22**: 12; **23**: 252; **38**: 194; **51**: 44
The Merchant of Venice **4**: 221, 226, 270, 284, 312, 344; **22**: 3, 69; **25**: 257; **40**: 156; **51**: 1, 44
sacrificial love **13**: 43; **22**: 69; **40**: 142
A Midsummer Night's Dream
passionate or romantic love **3**: 372, 389, 395, 396, 402, 408, 411, 423, 441, 450, 480, 497, 498, 511; **29**: 175, 225, 263, 269; **45**: 126, 136; **51**: 44
Much Ado about Nothing **8**: 24, 55, 75, 95, 111, 115; **28**: 56; **51**: 30
Othello **4**: 412, 493, 506, 512, 530, 545, 552, 569, 570, 575, 580, 591; **19**: 253; **22**: 207; **25**: 257; **28**: 243, 344; **32**: 201; **35**: 261, 317; **51**: 25, 30
Othello **53**: 315
The Phoenix and Turtle **10**: 31, 37, 40, 50; **38**: 342, 345, 367; **51**: 145, 151, 155

Sonnets **10**: 173, 247, 287, 290, 293, 302, 309, 322, 325, 329, 394; **28**: 380; **37**: 347; **51**: 270, 284, 288, 292
The Tempest **8**: 435, 439; **29**: 297, 339, 377, 396
Twelfth Night **1**: 543, 546, 573, 580, 587, 595, 600, 603, 610, 660; **19**: 78; **26**: 257, 364; **34**: 270, 293, 323; **46**: 291, 333, 347, 362; **51**: 30; **52**: 57
The Two Gentlemen of Verona **6**: 442, 445, 456, 479, 488, 492, 494, 502, 509, 516, 519, 549; **13**: 12; **40**: 327, 335, 343, 354, 365; **51**: 30, 44
The Two Noble Kinsmen **9**: 479, 481, 490, 498; **41**: 289, 301, 355, 363, 372, 385; **50**: 295, 361
The Winter's Tale **7**: 417, 425, 469, 490; **51**: 30, 33, 44

love and friendship
See also **friendship**
Julius Caesar **7**: 233, 262, 268; **25**: 272

love and honor
Troilus and Cressida **3**: 555, 604; **27**: 370, 374

love and passion
Antony and Cleopatra **6**: 51, 64, 71, 80, 85, 100, 115, 159, 165, 180; **25**: 257; **27**: 126; **47**: 71, 124,, 174, 192; **51**: 25, 33, 44

love and reason
See also **reason**
Othello **4**: 512, 530, 580; **19**: 253

Love and Romance (Volume 51: 1, 15, 25, 30, 33, 44)
Pericles topic:locators
51: 71
The Phoenix and Turtle **51**: 145, 151, 155
Romeo and Juliet **51**: 195, 203, 212
Sonnets **51**: 284, 288, 292
Venus and Adonis
The Rhetoric of Desire **51**: 345, 352, 359, 368

love, lechery, or rape
Troilus and Cressida **43**: 357

love versus fate
Romeo and Juliet **5**: 421, 437, 438, 443, 445, 458; **33**: 249

love versus friendship
See also **friendship**
The Two Gentlemen of Verona **6**: 439, 449, 450, 458, 460, 465, 468, 471, 476, 480; **40**: 354, 365

love versus lust
Venus and Adonis **10**: 418, 420, 427, 434, 439, 448, 449, 454, 462, 466, 473, 480, 489; **25**: 305; **28**: 355; **33**: 309, 330, 339, 347, 357, 363, 370; **51**: 359

love versus reason
See also **reason**
Sonnets **10**: 329

love versus war
Troilus and Cressida **18**: 332, 371, 406, 423; **22**: 339; **27**: 376

Machiavellianism
Henry V **5**: 203, 225, 233, 252, 287, 304; **25**: 131; **30**: 273
Henry VI, Parts 1, 2, and 3 **22**: 193
Macbeth **52**: 29

Madness (Volume 35: 1, 7, 8, 24, 34, 49, 54, 62, 68)
Hamlet **19**: 330; **35**: 104, 117, 126, 132, 134, 140, 144
King Lear **19**: 330
Macbeth **19**: 330
Othello **35**: 265, 276, 282
Twelfth Night **1**: 554, 639, 656; **26**: 371

Magic and the Supernatural (Volume 29: 1, 12, 28, 46, 53, 65)
The Comedy of Errors **1**: 27, 30
Macbeth
supernatural grace versus evil or chaos **3**: 241, 286, 323
witchcraft and supernaturalism **3**: 171, 172, 173, 175, 177, 182, 183, 184, 185, 194, 196, 198, 202, 207, 208, 213, 219, 229, 239; **16**: 317; **19**: 245; **20**: 92, 175, 213, 279, 283, 374, 387, 406, 413; **25**: 235; **28**: 339; **29**: 91, 101, 109, 120; **44**: 351, 373
A Midsummer Night's Dream **29**: 190, 201, 210, 216
The Tempest **8**: 287, 293, 304, 315, 340, 356, 396, 401, 404, 408, 435, 458; **28**: 391, 415; **29**: 297, 343, 377; **45**: 272
Sonnets
occult **48**: 346
The Winter's Tale
witchcraft **22**: 324

male discontent
The Merry Wives of Windsor **5**: 392, 402

male domination
Love's Labour's Lost **22**: 12
A Midsummer Night's Dream **3**: 483, 520; **13**: 19; **25**: 36; **29**: 216, 225, 243, 256, 269; **42**: 46; **45**: 84

male/female relationships
As You Like It **46**: 134
The Comedy of Errors **16**: 3
The Rape of Lucrece **10**: 109, 121, 131; **22**: 289; **25**: 305; **43**: 113, 141,
Troilus and Cressida **16**: 70; **22**: 339; **27**: 362

male sexual anxiety
Love's Labour's Lost **16**: 17

manhood
Macbeth **3**: 262, 309, 333; **29**: 127, 133

Marlowe's works, compared with
Richard II **42**: 173

marriage
See also **courtship and marriage**
The Comedy of Errors **34:** 251
Hamlet **22:** 339; **51:** 44
Love's Labour's Lost **2:** 335, 340; **19:** 92; **38:** 209, 232; **51:** 1, 44
Measure for Measure **2:** 443, 507, 516, 519, 524, 528; **25:** 12; **33:** 61, 90; **49:** 286; **51:** 44
The Merry Wives of Windsor **5:** 343, 369, 376, 390, 392, 400; **22:** 93; **38:** 297; **51:** 44
A Midsummer Night's Dream **3:** 402, 423, 450, 483, 520; **29:** 243, 256; **45:** 136, 143; **48:** 32; **51:** 1, 30, 44
Othello **35:** 369; **51:** 44;
The Taming of the Shrew **9:** 322, 325, 329, 332, 329, 332, 334, 341, 342, 343, 344, 345, 347, 353, 360, 362, 375, 381, 390, 398, 401, 404, 413, 426, 430; **13:** 3; **19:** 3; **28:** 24; **31:** 288; **51:** 44
Titus Andronicus
marriage as political tyranny **48:** 264
Troilus and Cressida **22:** 339; **51:** 44
The Two Gentlemen of Verona **48:** 32

martial vs. civil law
Coriolanus **48:** 230

Marxist criticism
Hamlet **42:** 229
King Lear **42:** 229
Macbeth **42:** 229
Othello **42:** 229

masque elements
The Two Noble Kinsmen **9:** 490
The Tempest **42:** 332

master-slave relationship
Troilus and Cressida **22:** 58

mediation
The Merry Wives of Windsor **5:** 343, 392

as medieval allegory or morality play
Henry IV, Parts 1 and 2 **1:** 323, 324, 342, 361, 366, 373, 374; **32:** 166; **39:** 89; **47:** 60
Measure for Measure **2:** 409, 421, 443, 466, 475, 491, 505, 511, 522; **13:** 94
Timon of Athens **1:** 492, 511, 518; **27:** 155

medieval chivalry
Richard II **6:** 258, 277, 294, 327, 338, 388, 397, 414; **24:** 274, 278, 279, 280, 283; **39:** 256
Troilus and Cressida **3:** 539, 543, 544, 555, 606; **27:** 376

medieval dramatic influence
All's Well That Ends Well **7:** 29, 41, 51, 98, 113; **13:** 66
King Lear **2:** 177, 188, 201; **25:** 218
Othello **4:** 440, 527, 545, 559, 582

medieval homilies, influence of
The Merchant of Venice **4:** 224, 250, 289

medieval influence
Romeo and Juliet **5:** 480, 505, 509, 573

medieval literary influence
Henry VI, Parts 1, 2, and 3 **3:** 59, 67, 75, 100, 109, 136, 151; **13:** 131
Titus Andronicus **4:** 646, 650; **27:** 299

medieval mystery plays, relation to
Macbeth **44:** 341

medieval physiology
Julius Caesar **13:** 260

mercantilism and feudalism
Richard II **13:** 213

merit versus rank
All's Well That Ends Well **7:** 9, 10, 19, 37, 51, 76; **38:** 155; **50:** 59

Messina
Much Ado about Nothing **8:** 19, 29, 48, 69, 82, 91, 95, 108, 111, 121, 125; **31:** 191, 209, 229, 241, 245

metadramatic elements
As You Like It **5:** 128, 130, 146; **34:** 130
Henry V **13:** 194; **30:** 181; **49:** 200, 211
Love's Labour's Lost **2:** 356, 359, 362
Measure for Measure **13:** 104
A Midsummer Night's Dream **3:** 427, 468, 477, 516, 520; **29:** 190, 225, 243; **50:** 86
The Taming of the Shrew **9:** 350, 419, 424; **31:** 300, 315
The Winter's Tale **16:** 410

metamorphosis or transformation
The Merry Wives of Windsor **47:** 314
Much Ado about Nothing **8:** 88, 104, 111, 115
The Taming of the Shrew **9:** 370, 430

metaphysical poem
The Phoenix and Turtle **10:** 7, 8, 9, 20, 31, 35, 37, 40, 45, 50; **51:** 143, 171, 184

Midlands Revolt, influence of
Coriolanus **22:** 248; **30:** 79; **50:** 140, 172

military and sexual hierarchies
Othello **16:** 272

mimetic rivalry
The Two Gentlemen of Verona **13:** 12; **40:** 335

as "mingled yarn"
All's Well That Ends Well **7:** 62, 93, 109, 126; **38:** 65

Minotaur, myth of
A Midsummer Night's Dream **3:** 497, 498; **29:** 216

as miracle play
Pericles **2:** 569, 581; **36:** 205; **51:** 97

misgovernment
Measure for Measure **2:** 401, 432, 511; **22:** 85
Much Ado about Nothing **22:** 85

misogyny
King Lear **31:** 123
Measure for Measure **23:** 358

misperception
Cymbeline **19:** 411; **36:** 99, 115; **47:** 228, 237, 252, 277, 286, 296

mistaken identity
The Comedy of Errors **1:** 13, 14, 27, 37, 40, 45, 49, 55, 57, 61, 63; **19:** 34, 54; **25:** 63; **34:** 194

modernization
Richard III **14:** 523

Montaigne's Essais, relation to
Sonnets **42:** 375
The Tempest **42:** 339

moral choice
Hamlet **52:** 35
Julius Caesar **7:** 179, 264, 279, 343

moral corruption
Macbeth **52:** 15, 23, 78
Othello **52:** 78
Troilus and Cressida **3:** 578, 589, 599, 604, 609; **18:** 332, 406, 412, 423; **27:** 366

moral corruption of English society
Richard III **8:** 154, 163, 165, 177, 193, 201, 218, 228, 232, 243, 248, 252, 267; **39:** 308; **52:** 201

moral inheritance
Henry VI, Parts 1, 2, and 3 **3:** 89, 126

moral intent
Henry VIII **2:** 15, 19, 25; **24:** 140

moral lesson
Macbeth **20:** 23

moral relativism
Antony and Cleopatra **22:** 217; **27:** 121

moral seriousness, question of
Measure for Measure **2:** 387, 388, 396, 409, 417, 421, 452, 460, 495; **23:** 316, 321

Morality in Shakespeare's Works (Volume 52: 1, 5, 15, 23, 29, 35, 43, 57, 63, 69, 78, 89, 95)
Antony and Cleopatra **52:** 5
As You Like It **52:** 63
Henry V **5:** 195, 203, 213, 223, 225, 239, 246, 260, 271, 293
Macbeth **52:** 29
The Merchant of Venice **52:** 89
The Merry Wives of Windsor **5:** 335, 339, 347, 349, 353, 397
Richard III **52:** 5
The Tempest **52:** 43

Troilus and Cressida **52:** 5
The Two Gentlemen of Verona **6:** 438, 492, 494, 514, 532, 555, 564
Venus and Adonis **10:** 411, 412, 414, 416, 418, 419, 420, 423, 427, 428, 439, 442, 448, 449, 454, 459, 466; **33:** 330

multiple endings
Henry IV **49:** 102

multiple perspectives of characters
Henry VI, Parts 1, 2, and 3 **3:** 69, 154

music
The Tempest **8:** 390, 404; **29:** 292; **37:** 321; **42:** 332
Twelfth Night **1:** 543, 566, 596

music and dance
A Midsummer Night's Dream **3:** 397, 400, 418, 513; **12:** 287, 289; **25:** 36
Much Ado about Nothing **19:** 68; **31:** 222

mutability, theme of
Sonnets **42:** 375

mythic or mythological elements
See also **religious, mythic, or spiritual content**
Richard II **52:** 154, 157, 169

mythological allusions
As You Like It **46:** 142
Antony and Cleopatra **16:** 342; **19:** 304; **27:** 110, 117; **47:** 71, 192

naming, significance of
Coriolanus **30:** 58, 96, 111, 125

narrative strategies
The Rape of Lucrece **22:** 294

nationalism and patriotism
See also **British nationalism**
Henry V **5:** 198, 205, 209, 210, 213, 219, 223, 233, 246, 252, 257, 269, 299; **19:** 133, 217; **30:** 227, 262; **49:** 219, 247
Henry VI, Parts 1, 2, and 3 **24:** 25, 45, 47
King John **9:** 209, 218, 222, 224, 235, 240, 244, 275; **25:** 98; **37:** 132
The Merry Wives of Windsor **47:** 344
The Winter's Tale **32:** 388

nature
See also **art and nature** *and* **art versus nature**
As You Like It **46:** 94
The Tempest **8:** 315, 370, 390, 408, 414; **29:** 343, 362, 368, 377
The Winter's Tale **7:** 397, 418, 419, 420, 425, 432, 436, 451, 452, 473, 479; **19:** 366; **45:** 329

nature as book
Pericles **22:** 315; **36:** 233

nature, philosophy of
Coriolanus **30:** 74

negative appraisals
Cymbeline **4:** 20, 35, 43, 45, 48, 53, 56, 68; **15:** 32, 105, 121
Richard II **6:** 250, 252, 253, 255, 282, 307, 317, 343, 359
Venus and Adonis **10:** 410, 411, 415, 418, 419, 424, 429

Neoclassical rules
As You Like It **5:** 19, 20
Henry IV, Parts 1 and 2 **1:** 286, 287, 290, 293
Henry VI, Parts 1, 2, and 3 **3:** 17, 18
King John **9:** 208, 209, 210, 212
Love's Labour's Lost **2:** 299, 300
Macbeth **3:** 170, 171, 173, 175; **20:** 17
Measure for Measure **2:** 387, 388, 390, 394; **23:** 269
The Merry Wives of Windsor **5:** 332, 334
Romeo and Juliet **5:** 416, 418, 426
The Tempest **8:** 287, 292, 293, 334; **25:** 357; **29:** 292; **45:** 200
Troilus and Cressida **3:** 537, 538; **18:** 276, 278, 281
The Winter's Tale **7:** 376, 377, 379, 380, 383, 410; **15:** 397

Neoplatonism
The Phoenix and Turtle **10:** 7, 9, 21, 24, 40, 45, 50; **38:** 345, 350, 367; **51:** 184
Sonnets **10:** 191, 205

nightmarish quality
Macbeth **3:** 231, 309; **20:** 210, 242; **44:** 261

nihilistic elements
King Lear **2:** 130, 143, 149, 156, 165, 231, 238, 245, 253; **22:** 271; **25:** 218; **28:** 325
Timon of Athens **1:** 481, 513, 529; **13:** 392; **20:** 481
Troilus and Cressida **27:** 354

nihilistic or pessimistic vision
King Lear **49:** 67

"nothing," significance of
Much Ado about Nothing **8:** 17, 18, 23, 55, 73, 95; **19:** 68

nurturing or feeding
Coriolanus **9:** 65, 73, 136, 183, 189; **30:** 111; **44:** 79; **50:** 110

oaths, importance of
Pericles **19:** 387

obscenity
Henry V **5:** 188, 190, 260

Oldcastle, references to
Henry IV, Parts 1 and 2 **48:** 117

omens
Julius Caesar **22:** 137; **45:** 10; **50:** 265, 280

oppositions or dualisms
King John **9:** 224, 240, 263, 275, 284, 290, 300

order
Henry V **5:** 205, 257, 264, 310, 314; **30:** 193; *Twelfth Night* **1:** 563, 596; **34:** 330; **46:** 291, 347

order versus disintegration
Titus Andronicus **4:** 618, 647; **43:** 186, 195

other sonnet writers, Shakespeare compared with
Sonnets **42:** 296

Ovid, compared with
Venus and Adonis **51:** 335, 352

Ovid, influence of
A Midsummer Night's Dream **3:** 362, 427, 497, 498; **22:** 23; **29:** 175, 190, 216
Titus Andronicus **4:** 647, 659, 664, 668; **13:** 225; **27:** 246, 275, 285, 293, 299, 306; **28:** 249; **43:** 195, 203, 206

Ovid's Metamorphoses, relation to
The Winter's Tale **42:** 301
Venus and Adonis **42:** 347

pagan elements
King Lear **25:** 218

pageantry
See also **ceremonies, rites, and rituals, importance of**
Henry VIII **2:** 14, 15, 18, 51, 58; **24:** 77, 83, 84, 85, 89, 91, 106, 113, 118, 120, 126, 127, 140, 146, 150; **41:** 120, 129, 190

paradoxical elements
Coriolanus **9:** 73, 92, 106, 121, 153, 157, 164, 169, 193

parent-child relations
A Midsummer Night's Dream **13:** 19; **29:** 216, 225, 243

pastoral convention, parodies of
As You Like It **5:** 54, 57, 72

pastoral convention, relation to
As You Like It **5:** 72, 77, 122; **34:** 161; **37:** 1

pastoral tradition, compared with
A Lover's Complaint **48:** 336

patience
Henry VIII **2:** 58, 76, 78
Pericles **2:** 572, 573, 578, 579; **36:** 251

patriarchal claims
Henry VI, Parts 1, 2, and 3 **16:** 131; **25:** 102

patriarchal or monarchical order
King Lear **13:** 353, 457; **16:** 351; **22:** 227, 233; **25:** 218; **31:** 84, 92, 107, 117, 123, 137, 142; **46:** 269

patriarchy
Cymbeline **32:** 373; **36:** 134; **47:** 237; **51:** 25
Henry V **37:** 105; **44:** 44

Titus Andronicus **50:** 13
Troilus and Cressida **22:** 58

patriotism
See **nationalism and patriotism**

Pattern of Painful Adventures (Lawrence Twine), compared with
Pericles **48:** 364

Pauline doctrine
A Midsummer Night's Dream **3:** 457, 486, 506

pedagogy
Sonnets **37:** 374
The Taming of the Shrew **19:** 122

perception
Othello **19:** 276; **25:** 189, 257; **53:** 246, 289

performance history
The Taming of the Shrew **31:** 282

performance issues
See also **staging issues**
Julius Caesar **50:** 186
King Lear **2:** 106, 137, 154, 160; **11:** 10, 20, 27, 56, 57, 132, 136, 137, 145, 150, 154; **19:** 295, 344; **25:** 218
Much Ado about Nothing **18:** 173, 174, 183, 184, 185, 186, 187, 188, 189, 190, 191, 192, 193, 195, 197, 199, 201, 204, 206, 207, 208, 209, 210, 254
Sonnets **48:** 352
The Taming of the Shrew **12:** 313, 314, 316, 317, 337, 338; **31:** 315

pessimistic elements
Timon of Athens **1:** 462, 467, 470, 473, 478, 480; **20:** 433, 481; **27:** 155, 191

Petrarchan poetics, influence of
Romeo and Juliet **5:** 416, 520, 522, 528, 550, 559, 575; **32:** 276; **51:** 212, 236

philosophical elements
Julius Caesar **7:** 310, 324; **37:** 203
Twelfth Night **1:** 560, 563, 596; **34:** 301, 316; **46:** 297

physical versus intellectual world
Love's Labour's Lost **2:** 331, 348, 367

pictorial elements
Venus and Adonis **10:** 414, 415, 419, 420, 423, 480; **33:** 339

Platonic elements
A Midsummer Night's Dream **3:** 368, 437, 450, 497; **45:** 126

play-within-the-play, convention of
Henry VI, Parts 1, 2, and 3 **3:** 75, 149
The Merry Wives of Windsor **5:** 354, 355, 369, 402
The Taming of the Shrew **12:** 416; **22:** 48

plebians
Coriolanus **50:** 13, 105; **50:** 189, 196, 230

plot
The Winter's Tale **7:** 376, 377, 379, 382, 387, 390, 396, 452; **13:** 417; **15:** 518; **45:** 374

plot and incident
Richard III **8:** 146, 152, 159; **25:** 164

Plutarch and historical sources
Coriolanus **9:** 8, 9, 13, 14, 16, 26, 39, 92, 106, 130, 142, 164; **30:** 74, 79, 105; **50:** 99

poet-patron relationship
Sonnets **48:** 352

poetic justice, question of
King Lear **2:** 92, 93, 94, 101, 129, 137, 231, 245; **49:** 73
Othello **4:** 370, 412, 415, 427

poetic style
Sonnets **10:** 153, 155, 156, 158, 159, 160, 161, 173, 175, 182, 214, 247, 251, 255, 260, 265, 283, 287, 296, 302, 315, 322, 325, 337, 346, 349, 360, 367, 385; **16:** 472; **40:** 221, 228; **51:** 270

political and social disintegration
Antony and Cleopatra **6:** 31, 43, 53, 60, 71, 80, 100, 107, 111, 146; 180, 197, 219; **22:** 217; **25:** 257; **27:** 121

political content
Titus Andronicus **43:** 262

Politics (Volume 30: 1, 4, 11, 22, 29, 39, 42, 46, 49)
Coriolanus **9:** 15, 17, 18, 19, 26, 33, 43, 53, 62, 65, 73, 80, 92, 106, 110, 112, 121, 144, 153, 157, 164, 180; **22:** 248; **25:** 296; **30:** 58, 67, 79, 89, 96, 105, 111, 125; **37:** 283; **42:** 218; **48:** 230; **50:** 13, 140, 172
Hamlet **44:** 241
Henry V **49:** 219, 247, 260
Henry IV, Parts 1 and 2 **28:** 101; **39:** 130; **42:** 141; **48:** 143, 175
Henry VIII **2:** 39, 49, 51, 58, 60, 65, 67, 71, 72, 75, 78, 81; **24:** 74, 121, 124; **41:** 146
Julius Caesar **7:** 161, 169, 191, 205, 218, 221, 245, 262, 264, 279, 282, 310, 324, 333, 346; **17:** 317, 318, 321, 323, 334, 350, 351, 358, 378, 382, 394, 406; **22:** 137, 280; **25:** 272, 280; **30:** 285, 297, 316, 321, 342, 374, 379; **37:** 203; **50:** 13
King John **9:** 218, 224, 260, 280; **13:** 163; **22:** 120; **37:** 132; **41:** 221, 228
King Lear **46:** 269; **50:** 45
Macbeth **52:** 29
Measure for Measure **23:** 379; **49:** 274
A Midsummer Night's Dream **29:** 243
Pericles **37:** 361
The Tempest **8:** 304, 307, 315, 353, 359, 364, 401, 408; **16:** 426; **19:** 421; **29:** 339; **37:** 336; **42:** 320; **45:** 272, 280; **52:** 43

Timon of Athens **27:** 223, 230; **50:** 13
Titus Andronicus **27:** 282; **48:** 264
Troilus and Cressida **3:** 536, 560, 606; **16:** 84

popularity
Pericles **2:** 536, 538, 546; **37:** 361
Richard III **8:** 144, 146, 154, 158, 159, 162, 181, 228; **39:** 383
The Taming of the Shrew **9:** 318, 338, 404
Venus and Adonis **10:** 410, 412, 418, 427; **25:** 328 Portia
The Merchant of Venice **49:** 27

power
Henry V **37:** 175
Measure for Measure **13:** 112; **22:** 85; **23:** 327, 330, 339, 352; **33:** 85
The Merchant of Venice **53:** 136
A Midsummer Night's Dream **42:** 46; **45:** 84
Much Ado about Nothing **22:** 85; **25:** 77; **31:** 231, 245

pride and rightful self-esteem
Othello **4:** 522, 536, 541; **35:** 352

primitivism
Macbeth **20:** 206, 213; **45:** 48

primogeniture
As You Like It **5:** 66, 158; **34:** 109, 120
Titus Andronicus **50:** 13

as "problem" plays
The Comedy of Errors **34:** 251
Julius Caesar **7:** 272, 320
Measure for Measure **2:** 416, 429, 434, 474, 475, 503, 514, 519; **16:** 102; **23:** 313, 328, 351; **49:** 358, 370
Troilus and Cressida **3:** 555, 566
lack of resolution **43:** 277

procreation
Sonnets **10:** 379, 385; **16:** 461
Venus and Adonis **10:** 439, 449, 466; **33:** 321, 377

providential order
King Lear **2:** 112, 116, 137, 168, 170, 174, 177, 218, 226, 241, 253; **22:** 271; **49:** 1, 73
Macbeth **3:** 208, 289, 329, 336
Measure for Measure **48:** 1;
Tempest **52:** 43

Psychoanalytic Interpretations of Shakespeare's Works (Volume 44: 1, 11, 18, 28, 35, 44, 57, 66, 79, 89, 93)
As You Like It **5:** 146, 158; **23:** 141, 142; **34:** 109; **48:** 42
Coriolanus **44:** 93
Cymbeline **45:** 67, 75
Hamlet **1:** 119, 148, 154, 179, 202; **21:** 197, 213, 361; **25:** 209; **28:** 223; **35:** 95, 104, 134, 237; **37:** 241; **44:** 133, 152, 160, 180, 209, 219
Henry IV, Parts 1 and 2 **13:** 457; **28:** 101; **42:** 185; **44:** 44
Henry V **13:** 457; **44:** 44
Julius Caesar **45:** 10

Macbeth **3:** 219, 223, 226; **44:** 11, 284, 289, 297; **45:** 48, 58
Measure for Measure **23:** 331, 332, 333, 334, 335, 340, 355, 356, 359, 379, 395; **44:** 89
Merchant of Venice **45:** 17
A Midsummer Night's Dream **3:** 440, 483; **28:** 15; **29:** 225; **44:** 1; **45:** 107, 117
Othello **4:** 468, 503; **35:** 265, 276, 282, 301, 317, 320, 347; **42:** 198; **44:** 57
Romeo and Juliet **5:** 513, 556; **51:** 253
The Tempest **45:** 259
Troilus and Cressida **43:** 287
Twelfth Night **46:** 333

psychological elements
Cymbeline **36:** 134; **44:** 28

public versus private principles
Julius Caesar **7:** 161, 179, 252, 262, 268, 284, 298; **13:** 252

public versus private speech
Love's Labour's Lost **2:** 356, 362, 371

public versus private worlds
As You Like It **46:** 164
Coriolanus **37:** 283; **42:** 218
Romeo and Juliet **5:** 520, 550; **25:** 181; **33:** 274

as "pure" poetry
The Phoenix and Turtle **10:** 14, 31, 35; **38:** 329

Puritanism
Measure for Measure **2:** 414, 418, 434; **49:** 325
Twelfth Night **1:** 549, 553, 555, 632; **16:** 53; **25:** 47; **46:** 338

Pyramus and Thisbe interlude
A Midsummer Night's Dream **50:** 74

Race (Volume 53: 1, 11, 21, 32, 45, 53, 64, 67, 77, 86, 92**)**
Antony and Cleopatra **53:** 67, 77
The Merchant of Venice **53:** 111, 116, 127, 136, 159, 169
A Midsummer Night's Dream **53:** 1, 32
Othello **4:** 370, 380, 384, 385, 392, 399, 401, 402, 408, 427, 564; **13:** 327; **16:** 293; **25:** 189, 257; **28:** 249, 330; **35:** 369; **42:** 198; **53:** 1, 233, 238, 246, 255, 261, 268, 275, 289, 298, 304
The Rape of Lucrece **53:** 1
Sonnets **53:** 1
The Tempest **53:** 1, 21, 45, 64, 67
Titus Andronicus **53:** 86, 92

rape
Titus Andronicus **43:** 227, 255; **48:** 277

realism
See also **idealism versus realism**
The Merry Wives of Windsor **38:** 313
The Tempest **8:** 340, 359, 464
Troilus and Cressida **43:** 357

reality and illusion
The Tempest **8:** 287, 315, 359, 401, 435, 439, 447, 454; **22:** 302; **45:** 236, 247

reason
See also **love and reason** and **love versus reason**
Venus and Adonis **10:** 427, 439, 449, 459, 462, 466; **28:** 355; **33:** 309, 330

reason versus imagination
Antony and Cleopatra **6:** 107, 115, 142, 197, 228; **45:** 28
A Midsummer Night's Dream **3:** 381, 389, 423, 441, 466, 506; **22:** 23; **29:** 190; **45:** 96

rebellion
See also **usurpation**
Henry IV, Parts 1 and 2 **22:** 395; **28:** 101
Henry VIII **22:** 395
King John **9:** 218, 254, 263, 280, 297
Richard III **22:** 395

rebirth, regeneration, resurrection, or immortality
All's Well That Ends Well **7:** 90, 93, 98
Antony and Cleopatra **6:** 100, 103, 125, 131, 159, 181
Cymbeline **4:** 38, 64, 73, 93, 105, 113, 116, 129, 138, 141, 162, 170
Measure for Measure **13:** 84; **16:** 102, 114; **23:** 321, 327, 335, 340, 352; **25:** 12
Pericles **2:** 555, 564, 584, 586, 588; **36:** 205
The Tempest **8:** 302, 312, 320, 334, 348, 359, 370, 384, 401, 404, 414, 429, 439, 447, 454; **16:** 442; **22:** 302; **29:** 297; **37:** 336
The Winter's Tale **7:** 397, 414, 417, 419, 429, 436, 451, 452, 456, 480, 490, 497, 506; **25:** 339 452, 480, 490, 497, 506; **45:** 366

reconciliation
As You Like It **46:** 156
All's Well That Ends Well **7:** 90, 93, 98; **51:** 33
Antony and Cleopatra **6:** 100, 103, 125, 131, 159, 181
Cymbeline **4:** 38, 64, 73, 93, 105, 113, 116, 129, 138, 141, 162, 170
The Merry Wives of Windsor **5:** 343, 369, 374, 397, 402
A Midsummer Night's Dream **3:** 412, 418, 437, 459, 468, 491, 497, 502, 513; **13:** 27; **29:** 190
Romeo and Juliet **5:** 415, 419, 427, 439, 447, 480, 487, 493, 505, 533, 536, 562
The Tempest **8:** 302, 312, 320, 334, 348, 359, 370, 384, 401, 404, 414, 429, 439, 447, 454; **16:** 442; **22:** 302; **29:** 297; **37:** 336; **45:** 236

reconciliation of opposites
As You Like It **5:** 79, 88, 103, 116, 122, 138; **23:** 127, 143; **34:** 161, 172; **46:** 156

redemption
The Comedy of Errors **19:** 54; **26:** 188

regicide
Macbeth **3:** 248, 275, 312; **16:** 317, 328

relation to tetralogy
Henry V **49:** 223

relationship to other Shakespearean plays
Twelfth Night **46:** 303
Henry IV, Parts 1 and 2 **42:** 99, 153; **48:** 167; **49:** 93, 186

relationship between Parts 1 and 2
Henry IV, Parts 1 and 2 **32:** 136; **39:** 100; **49:** 178

religious and theological issues
Macbeth **44:** 324, 341, 351, 361, 366, 373
Measure for Measure **48:** 1

religious, mythic, or spiritual content
See also **Christian elements**
All's Well That Ends Well **7:** 15, 45, 54, 67, 76, 98, 109, 116
Antony and Cleopatra **6:** 53, 94, 111, 115, 178, 192, 224; **47:** 71
Cymbeline **4:** 22, 29, 78, 93, 105, 108, 115, 116, 127, 134, 138, 141, 159; **28:** 373; **36:** 142, 158, 186; **47:** 219, 260, 274
Hamlet **1:** 98, 102, 130, 184, 191, 209, 212, 231, 234, 254; **21:** 361; **22:** 258; **28:** 280; **32:** 238; **35:** 134
Henry IV, Parts 1 and 2 **1:** 314, 374, 414, 421, 429, 431, 434; **32:** 103; **48:** 151
Henry V **25:** 116; **32:** 126
King Lear **49:** 67
Macbeth **3:** 208, 269, 275, 318; **29:** 109
Measure for Measure **48:** 1
Othello **4:** 483, 517, 522, 525, 559, 573; **22:** 207; **28:** 330
Pericles **2:** 559, 561, 565, 570, 580, 584, 588; **22:** 315; **25:** 365; **51:** 97
The Tempest **8:** 328, 390, 423, 429, 435; **45:** 211, 247
Timon of Athens **1:** 505, 512, 513, 523; **20:** 493

repentance and forgiveness
Much Ado about Nothing **8:** 24, 29, 111
The Two Gentlemen of Verona **6:** 450, 514, 516, 555, 564
The Winter's Tale **44:** 66

resolution
Measure for Measure **2:** 449, 475, 495, 514, 516; **16:** 102, 114
The Merchant of Venice **4:** 263, 266, 300, 319, 321; **13:** 37; **51:** 1
The Two Gentlemen of Verona **6:** 435, 436, 439, 445, 449, 453, 458, 460, 462, 465, 466, 468, 471, 476, 480, 486, 494, 509, 514, 516, 519, 529, 532, 541, 549; **19:** 34

retribution
Henry VI, Parts 1, 2, and 3 **3:** 27, 42, 51, 59, 77, 83, 92, 100, 109, 115, 119, 131, 136, 151
Julius Caesar **7:** 160, 167, 200
Macbeth **3:** 194, 208, 318; **48:** 214
Richard III **8:** 163, 170, 177, 182, 184, 193, 197, 201, 206, 210, 218, 223, 228, 243, 248, 267

revenge
  Hamlet **1:** 74, 194, 209, 224, 234, 254; **16:** 246; **22:** 258; **25:** 288; **28:** 280; **35:** 152, 157, 167, 174, 212; **44:** 180, 209, 219, 229
  The Merry Wives of Windsor **5:** 349, 350, 392; **38:** 264, 307
  Othello **35:** 261

revenge tragedy elements
  Julius Caesar **7:** 316
  Titus Andronicus **4:** 618, 627, 628, 636, 639, 644, 646, 664, 672, 680; **16:** 225; **27:** 275, 318

reversal
  A Midsummer Night's Dream **29:** 225

rhetoric
  Venus and Adonis **33:** 377; **51:** 335, 345, 352
  Romeo and Juliet **42:** 266

rhetoric of consolation
  Sonnets **42:** 375

rhetoric of politeness
  Henry VIII **22:** 182

rhetorical style
  King Lear **16:** 301; **47:** 9

riddle motif
  Pericles **22:** 315; **36:** 205, 214

rightful succession
  Titus Andronicus **4:** 638

rings episode
  The Merchant of Venice **22:** 3; **40:** 106, 151, 156

role-playing
  Julius Caesar **7:** 356; **37:** 229
  The Taming of the Shrew **9:** 322, 353, 355, 360, 369, 370, 398, 401, 407, 413, 419, 424; **13:** 3; **31:** 288, 295, 315

as romance play
  As You Like It **5:** 55, 79; **23:** 27, 28, 40, 43

romance or chivalric tradition, influence of
  Much Ado about Nothing **8:** 53, 125; **51:** 15

romance or folktale elements
  All's Well That Ends Well **7:** 32, 41, 43, 45, 54, 76, 104, 116, 121; **26:** 117

romance or pastoral tradition, influence of
  The Tempest **8:** 336, 348, 396, 404; **37:** 336

Roman citizenry, portrayal of
  Julius Caesar **50:** 64, 230

romantic and courtly conventions
  The Two Gentlemen of Verona **6:** 438, 460, 472, 478, 484, 486, 488, 502, 507, 509, 529, 541, 549, 560, 568; **12:** 460, 462; **40:** 354, 374

romantic elements
  The Comedy of Errors **1:** 13, 16, 19, 23, 25, 30, 31, 36, 39, 53
  Cymbeline **4:** 17, 20, 46, 68, 77, 141, 148, 172; **15:** 111; **25:** 319; **28:** 373
  King Lear **31:** 77, 84
  The Taming of the Shrew **9:** 334, 342, 362, 375, 407

royalty
  Antony and Cleopatra **6:** 94

Salic Law
  Henry V **5:** 219, 252, 260; **28:** 121

as satire or parody
  Love's Labour's Lost **2:** 300, 302, 303, 307, 308, 315, 321, 324, 327; **23:** 237, 252
  The Merry Wives of Windsor **5:** 338, 350, 360, 385; **38:** 278, 319; **47:** 354, 363,

satire or parody of pastoral conventions
  As You Like It **5:** 46, 55, 60, 72, 77, 79, 84, 114, 118, 128, 130, 154

satirical elements
  The Phoenix and Turtle **10:** 8, 16, 17, 27, 35, 40, 45, 48
  Timon of Athens **27:** 155, 235
  Troilus and Cressida **3:** 539, 543, 544, 555, 558, 574; **27:** 341

Saturnalian elements
  Twelfth Night **1:** 554, 571, 603, 620, 642; **16:** 53

schemes and intrigues
  The Merry Wives of Windsor **5:** 334, 336, 339, 341, 343, 349, 355, 379

Scholasticism
  Macbeth **52:** 23
  The Phoenix and Turtle **10:** 21, 24, 31; **51:** 188

School of Night, allusions to
  Love's Labour's Lost **2:** 321, 327, 328

self-conscious or artificial nature of play
  Cymbeline **4:** 43, 52, 56, 68, 124, 134, 138; **36:** 99

self-deception
  Twelfth Night **1:** 554, 561, 591, 625; **47:** 45

self-indulgence
  Twelfth Night **1:** 563, 615, 635

self-interest or expediency
  Henry V **5:** 189, 193, 205, 213, 217, 233, 260, 287, 302, 304; **30:** 273; **49:** 223

self-knowledge
  As You Like It **5:** 32, 82, 102, 116, 122, 133, 164
  Much Ado about Nothing **8:** 69, 95, 100
  Timon of Athens **1:** 456, 459, 462, 495, 503, 507, 515, 518, 526; **20:** 493; **27:** 166

self-love
  Sonnets **10:** 372; **25:** 374; **51:** 270, 300, 304

Senecan or revenge tragedy elements
  Timon of Athens **27:** 235
  Titus Andronicus **4:** 618, 627, 628, 636, 639, 644, 646, 664, 672, 680; **16:** 225; **27:** 275, 318; **43:** 170, 206, 227

servitude
  See also **freedom and servitude**
  Comedy of Errors **42:** 80

setting
  The Merry Wives of Windsor **47:** 375
  Much Ado about Nothing **18:** 173, 174, 183, 184, 185, 186, 187, 188, 189, 190, 191, 192, 193, 195, 197, 199, 201, 204, 206, 207, 208, 209, 210, 254
  Richard III **14:** 516, 528; **52:** 263
  The Two Gentlemen of Verona **12:** 463, 465, 485

sexual ambiguity and sexual deception
  As You Like It **46:** 134, 142
  Twelfth Night **1:** 540, 562, 620, 621, 639, 645; **22:** 69; **34:** 311, 344; **37:** 59; **42:** 32
  Troilus and Cressida **43:** 365

sexual anxiety
  Macbeth **16:** 328; **20:** 283

sexual politics
  The Merchant of Venice **22:** 3; **51:** 44
  The Merry Wives of Windsor **19:** 101; **38:** 307

Sexuality in Shakespeare (Volume 33: 1, 12, 18, 28, 39)
  As You Like It **46:** 122, 127, 134, 142
  All's Well That Ends Well **7:** 67, 86, 90, 93, 98, 126; **13:** 84; **19:** 113; **22:** 78; **28:** 38; **44:** 35; **49:** 46; **51:** 44
  Coriolanus **9:** 112, 142, 174, 183, 189, 198; **30:** 79, 111, 125, 142
  Cymbeline **4:** 170, 172; **25:** 319; **32:** 373; **47:** 245
  King Lear **25:** 202; **31:** 133, 137, 142
  Love's Labour's Lost **22:** 12; **51:** 44
  Measure for Measure **13:** 84; **16:** 102, 114; **23:** 321, 327, 335, 340, 352; **25:** 12; **33:** 85, 90, 112; **49:** 286, 338; **51:** 44
  A Midsummer Night's Dream **22:** 23, 93; **29:** 225, 243, 256, 269; **42:** 46; **45:** 107; **53:** 45
  Othello **22:** 339; **28:** 330, 344; **35:** 352, 360; **37:** 269; **44:** 57, 66; **51:** 44; **53:** 275, 310, 315
  Romeo and Juliet **25:** 181; **33:** 225, 233, 241, 246, 274, 300; **51:** 227, 236
  Sonnets **25:** 374; **48:** 325
  The Tempest **53:** 45
  Troilus and Cressida **22:** 58, 339; **25:** 56; **27:** 362; **43:** 365

Shakespeare and Classical Civilization (Volume 27: 1, 9, 15, 21, 30, 35, 39, 46, 56, 60, 67)
  Antony and Cleopatra

Egyptian versus Roman values **6:** 31, 33, 43, 53, 104, 111, 115, 125, 142, 155, 159, 178, 181, 211, 219; **17:** 48; **19:** 270; **27:** 82, 121, 126; **28:** 249; **47:** 96, 103, 113, 149

The Rape of Lucrece
Roman history, relation to **10:** 84, 89, 93, 96, 98, 109, 116, 125, 135; **22:** 289; **25:** 305; **33:** 155, 190

Timon of Athens **27:** 223, 230, 325
Titus Andronicus **27:** 275, 282, 293, 299, 306
Roman elements **43:** 206, 222
Troilus and Cressida
Trojan versus Greek values **3:** 541, 561, 574, 584, 590, 596, 621, 638; **27:** 370

Shakespeare's artistic growth, Richard III's contribution to
Richard III **8:** 165, 167, 182, 193, 197, 206, 210, 228, 239, 267; **25:** 164; **39:** 305, 326, 370

Shakespeare's canon, place in
Titus Andronicus **4:** 614, 616, 618, 619, 637, 639, 646, 659, 664, 668; **43:** 195
Twelfth Night **1:** 543, 548, 557, 569, 575, 580, 621, 635, 638

Shakespeare's dramas, compared with
The Phoenix and Turtle **51:** 151, 155
The Rape of Lucrece **43:** 92

Shakespeare's moral judgment
Antony and Cleopatra **6:** 33, 37, 38, 41, 48, 51, 64, 76, 111, 125, 136, 140, 146, 163, 175, 189, 202, 211, 228; **13:** 368, 523; **25:** 257

Shakespeare's other plays, compared with
The Taming of the Shrew **50:** 74
The Merchant of Venice: **53:** 74

Shakespeare's political sympathies
Coriolanus **9:** 8, 11, 15, 17, 19, 26, 39, 52, 53, 62, 80, 92, 142; **25:** 296; **30:** 74, 79, 89, 96, 105, 133; **50:** 172
Richard II **6:** 277, 279, 287, 347, 359, 364, 391, 393, 402
Richard III **8:** 147, 163, 177, 193, 197, 201, 223, 228, 232, 243, 248, 267; **39:** 349; **42:** 130

Shakespeare's Representation of Women (Volume 31: 1, 3, 8, 12, 16, 21, 29, 34, 35, 41, 43, 48, 53, 60, 68)
Henry VI, Parts 1, 2, and 3 **3:** 103, 109, 126, 140, 157; **16:** 183; **39:** 196
King John **9:** 222, 303; **16:** 161; **19:** 182; **41:** 215, 221
King Lear **31:** 117, 123, 133
Love's Labour's Lost **19:** 92; **22:** 12; **23:** 215; **25:** 1
The Merry Wives of Windsor **5:** 335, 341, 343, 349, 369, 379, 390, 392, 402; **19:** 101; **38:** 307
Much Ado about Nothing **31:** 222, 231, 241, 245
Othello **19:** 253; **28:** 344
The Taming of the Shrew **31:** 288, 300, 307, 315

The Winter's Tale **22:** 324; **36:** 311; **42:** 301; **51:** 30

Shakespeare's romances, compared with
Henry VIII **41:** 171

shame
Coriolanus **42:** 243

sibling rivalry
As You Like It **34:** 109
Henry VI, Parts 1, 2, and 3 **22:** 193

slander or hearsay, importance of
Coriolanus **48:** 230
Much Ado about Nothing **8:** 58, 69, 82, 95, 104

social action
Sonnets **48:** 352

social and moral corruption
King Lear **2:** 116, 133, 174, 177, 241, 271; **22:** 227; **31:** 84, 92; **46:** 269

social and political context
All's Well That Ends Well **13:** 66; **22:** 78; **38:** 99, 109, 150, 155; **49:** 46

social aspects
Measure for Measure **23:** 316, 375, 379, 395
The Merchant of Venice **53:** 214

Social Class (Volume 50: 1, 13, 24, 34, 45, 51, 59, 64, 74, 86)
General Commentary **50:** 1, 34
Coriolanus **50:** 105, 110, 119
Julius Caesar **50:** 189, 194, 196, 211, 230
Timon of Athens **1:** 466, 487, 495; **25:** 198; **27:** 184, 196, 212
The Two Noble Kinsmen **50:** 295, 305, 310

social milieu
The Merry Wives of Windsor **18:** 75, 84; **38:** 297, 300

social order
As You Like It **37:** 1; **46:** 94
The Comedy of Errors **34:** 238

society
Coriolanus **9:** 15, 17, 18, 19, 26, 33, 43, 53, 62, 65, 73, 80, 92, 106, 110, 112, 121, 144, 153, 157, 164, 180; **22:** 248; **25:** 296; **30:** 58, 67, 79, 89, 96, 105, 111, 125; **50:** 13, 105, 119, 152
Troilus and Cressida **43:** 298

soldiers
Henry V **49:** 194

songs, role of
Love's Labour's Lost **2:** 303, 304, 316, 326, 335, 362, 367, 371, 375

sonnet arrangement
Sonnets **10:** 174, 176, 182, 205, 226, 230, 236, 315, 353; **28:** 363; **40:** 238

sonnet form
Sonnets **10:** 255, 325, 367; **37:** 347; **40:** 284, 303; **51:** 270

sonnets, compared with
A Lover's Complaint **48:** 336

source of tragic catastrophe
Romeo and Juliet **5:** 418, 427, 431, 448, 458, 469, 479, 480, 485, 487, 493, 509, 522, 528, 530, 533, 542, 565, 571, 573; **33:** 210; **51:** 245

sources
Antony and Cleopatra **6:** 20, 39; **19:** 304; **27:** 96, 126; **28:** 249
As You Like It **5:** 18, 32, 54, 59, 66, 84; **34:** 155; **46:** 117
The Comedy of Errors **1:** 13, 14, 16, 19, 31, 32, 39; **16:** 3; **34:** 190, 215, 258
Cymbeline **4:** 17, 18; **13:** 401; **28:** 373; **47:** 245, 265, 277
Hamlet **1:** 76, 81, 113, 125, 128, 130, 151, 191, 202, 224, 259
Henry VI, Parts 1, 2, and 3 **3:** 18, 21, 29, 31, 35, 39, 46, 51; **13:** 131; **16:** 217; **39:** 196
Henry VIII **2:** 16, 17; **24:** 71, 80
Julius Caesar **7:** 149, 150, 156, 187, 200, 264, 272, 282, 284, 320; **30:** 285, 297, 326, 358
King John **9:** 216, 222, 300; **32:** 93, 114; **41:** 234, 243, 251
King Lear **2:** 94, 100, 143, 145, 170, 186; **13:** 352; **16:** 351; **28:** 301
Love's Labour's Lost **16:** 17
Measure for Measure **2:** 388, 393, 427, 429, 437, 475; **13:** 94; **49:** 349
The Merry Wives of Windsor **5:** 332, 350, 360, 366, 385; **32:** 31; **52:** 69
A Midsummer Night's Dream **29:** 216
Much Ado about Nothing **8:** 9, 19, 53, 58, 104
Othello **28:** 330
Pericles **2:** 538, 568, 572, 575; **25:** 365; **36:** 198, 205; **51:** 118, 126,
The Phoenix and Turtle **10:** 7, 9, 18, 24, 45; **38:** 326, 334, 350, 367; **51:** 138
The Rape of Lucrece **10:** 63, 64, 65, 66, 68, 74, 77, 78, 89, 98, 109, 121, 125; **25:** 305; **33:** 155, 190; **43:** 77, 92, 148
Richard III **52:** 263, 290
chronicles **8:** 145, 165, 193, 197, 201, 206, 210, 213, 228, 232
Marlowe, Christopher **8:** 167, 168, 182, 201, 206, 218
morality plays **8:** 182, 190, 201, 213, 239
Seneca, other classical writers **8:** 165, 190, 201, 206, 228, 248
Romeo and Juliet **5:** 416, 419, 423, 450; **32:** 222; **33:** 210; **45:** 40
Sonnets **10:** 153, 154, 156, 158, 233, 251, 255, 293, 353; **16:** 472; **28:** 407; **42:** 375
The Taming of the Shrew
folk tales **9:** 332, 390, 393
Old and New Comedy **9:** 419
Ovid **9:** 318, 370, 430
Plautus **9:** 334, 341, 342
shrew tradition **9:** 355; **19:** 3; **32:** 1, 56
The Tempest **45:** 226
Timon of Athens **16:** 351; **27:** 191; **52:** 301

Troilus and Cressida **3:** 537, 539, 540, 541, 544, 549, 558, 566, 574, 587; **27:** 376, 381, 391, 400
Twelfth Night **1:** 539, 540, 603; **34:** 301, 323, 344; **46:** 291
The Two Gentlemen of Verona **6:** 436, 460, 462, 468, 476, 480, 490, 511, 547; **19:** 34; **40:** 320
The Two Noble Kinsmen **19:** 394; **41:** 289, 301, 363, 385; **50:** 326, 348
Venus and Adonis **10:** 410, 412, 420, 424, 429, 434, 439, 451, 454, 466, 473, 480, 486, 489; **16:** 452; **25:** 305; **28:** 355; **33:** 309, 321, 330, 339, 347, 352, 357, 370, 377; **42:** 347

spectacle
 Love's Labour's Lost **38:** 226
 Macbeth **42:** 258
 Pericles **42:** 352

spectacle versus simple staging
 The Tempest **15:** 206, 207, 208, 210, 217, 219, 222, 223, 224, 225, 227, 228, 305, 352; **28:** 415

stage history
 As You Like It **46:** 117
 Antony and Cleopatra **17:** 84, 94, 101
 The Merry Wives of Windsor **18:** 66, 67, 68, 70, 71

staging issues
 See also **performance issues**
 All's Well That Ends Well **19:** 113; **26:** 15, 19, 48, 52, 64, 73, 85, 92, 93, 94, 95, 97, 114, 117, 128
 Antony and Cleopatra **17:** 6, 12, 84, 94, 101, 104, 110; **27:** 90; **47:** 142
 As You Like It **13:** 502; **23:** 7, 17, 19, 22, 58, 96, 97, 98, 99, 101, 110, 137; **28:** 82; **32:** 212
 The Comedy of Errors **26:** 182, 183, 186, 188, 190
 Coriolanus **17:** 172, 242, 248
 Cymbeline **15:** 6, 23, 75, 105, 111, 121, 122; **22:** 365
 Hamlet **13:** 494, 502; **21:** 11, 17, 31, 35, 41, 44, 50, 53, 78, 81, 89, 101, 112, 127, 139, 142, 145, 148, 151, 157, 160, 172, 182, 183, 202, 203, 208, 225, 232, 237, 242, 245, 249, 251, 259, 268, 270, 274, 283, 284, 301, 311, 334, 347, 355, 361, 371, 377, 379, 380, 381, 384, 386, 392, 407, 410, 416; **44:** 198
 Henry IV, Parts 1 and 2 **32:** 212; **47:** 1; **49:** 102
 Henry V **5:** 186, 189, 192, 193, 198, 205, 226, 230, 241, 281, 314; **13:** 194, 502; **14:** 293, 295, 297, 301, 310, 319, 328, 334, 336, 342; **19:** 217; **32:** 185
 Henry VI, Parts 1, 2, and 3 **24:** 21, 22, 27, 31, 32, 36, 38, 41, 45, 48, 55; **32:** 212
 Henry VIII **24:** 67, 70, 71, 75, 77, 83, 84, 85, 87, 89, 91, 101, 106, 113, 120, 127, 129, 136, 140, 146, 150, 152, 155; **28:** 184
 Julius Caesar **48:** 240; **50:** 186
 King John **16:** 161; **19:** 182; **24:** 171, 187, 203, 206, 211, 225, 228, 241, 245, 249

King Lear **11:** 136, 137, 142, 145, 150, 151, 154, 158, 161, 165, 169; **32:** 212; **46:** 205, 218
Love's Labour's Lost **23:** 184, 187, 191, 196, 198, 200, 201, 202, 207, 212, 215, 216, 217, 229, 230, 232, 233, 237, 252
Macbeth **13:** 502; **20:** 12, 17, 32, 64, 65, 70, 73, 107, 113, 151, 175, 203, 206, 210, 213, 245, 279, 283, 312, 318, 324, 329, 343, 345, 350, 353, 363, 367, 374, 376, 379, 382, 387, 400, 406, 413; **22:** 365; **32:** 212
Measure for Measure **2:** 427, 429, 437, 441, 443, 456, 460, 482, 491, 519; **23:** 283, 284, 285, 286, 287, 291, 293, 294, 298, 299, 311, 315, 327, 338, 339, 340, 342, 344, 347, 363, 372, 375, 395, 400, 405, 406, 413; **32:** 16
The Merchant of Venice **12:** 111, 114, 115, 117, 119, 124, 129, 131
The Merry Wives of Windsor **18:** 74, 75, 84, 86, 90, 95
A Midsummer Night's Dream **3:** 364, 365, 371, 372, 377; **12:** 151, 152, 154, 158, 159, 280, 284, 291, 295; **16:** 34; **19:** 21; **29:** 183, 256; **48:** 23
Much Ado about Nothing **8:** 18, 33, 41, 75, 79, 82, 108; **16:** 45; **18:** 245, 247, 249, 252, 254, 257, 261, 264; **28:** 63
Othello **11:** 273, 334, 335, 339, 342, 350, 354, 359, 362
Pericles **16:** 399; **48:** 364; **51:** 99; **53:** 233, 304
Richard II **13:** 494; **24:** 273, 274, 278, 279, 280, 283, 291, 295, 296, 301, 303, 304, 310, 315, 317, 320, 325, 333, 338, 346, 351, 352, 356, 364, 383, 386, 395, 402, 405, 411, 414, 419, 423, 428; **25:** 89
Richard III **14:** 515, 527, 528, 537; **16:** 137; **52:** 263, 272
Romeo and Juliet **11:** 499, 505, 507, 514, 517; **13:** 243; **25:** 181; **32:** 212
The Tempest **15:** 343, 346, 352, 361, 364, 366, 368, 371, 385; **28:** 391, 415; **29:** 339; **32:** 338, 343; **42:** 332; **45:** 200
Timon of Athens **20:** 445, 446, 481, 491, 492, 493
Titus Andronicus **17:** 449, 452, 456, 487; **25:** 245; **32:** 212, 249
Troilus and Cressida **16:** 70; **18:** 289, 332, 371, 395, 403, 406, 412, 419, 423, 442, 447, 451
Twelfth Night **26:** 219, 233, 257, 337, 342, 346, 357, 359, 360, 364, 366, 371, 374; **46:** 310, 369
The Two Gentlemen of Verona **12:** 457, 464; **42:** 18
The Winter's Tale **7:** 414, 425, 429, 446, 464, 480, 483, 497; **13:** 409; **15:** 518; **48:** 309

Stoicism
 Hamlet **48:** 195
 Julius Caesar **50:** 249

strategic analysis
 Antony and Cleopatra **48:** 206

structure
 All's Well That Ends Well **7:** 21, 29, 32, 45, 51, 76, 81, 93, 98, 116; **22:** 78; **26:** 128; **38:** 72, 123, 142

As You Like It **5:** 19, 24, 25, 35, 44, 45, 46, 86, 93, 116, 138, 158; **23:** 7, 8, 9, 10, 11; **34:** 72, 78, 131, 147, 155
Coriolanus **9:** 8, 9, 11, 12, 13, 14, 16, 26, 33, 45, 53, 58, 72, 78, 80, 84, 92, 112, 139, 148; **25:** 263; **30:** 79, 96
Hamlet **22:** 378; **28:** 280, 325; **35:** 82, 104, 215; **44:** 152
Henry IV **49:** 93
Henry V **5:** 186, 189, 205, 213, 230, 241, 264, 289, 310, 314; **30:** 220, 227, 234, 244
Henry VI, Parts 1, 2, and 3 **3:** 31, 43, 46, 69, 83, 103, 109, 119, 136, 149, 154; **39:** 213
Henry VIII **2:** 16, 25, 27, 28, 31, 36, 44, 46, 51, 56, 68, 75; **24:** 106, 112, 113, 120
Julius Caesar **7:** 152, 155, 159, 160, 179, 200, 210, 238, 264, 284, 298, 316, 346; **13:** 252; **30:** 374
King John **9:** 208, 212, 222, 224, 229, 240, 244, 245, 254, 260, 263, 275, 284, 290, 292, 300; **24:** 228, 241; **41:** 260, 269, 277
King Lear **28:** 325; **32:** 308; **46:** 177
Love's Labour's Lost **22:** 378; **23:** 191, 237, 252; **38:** 163, 172
Macbeth **16:** 317; **20:** 12, 245
Measure for Measure **2:** 390, 411, 449, 456, 466, 474, 482, 490, 491; **33:** 69; **49:** 379
The Merchant of Venice **4:** 201, 215, 230, 232, 243, 247, 254, 261, 263, 308, 321; **12:** 115; **28:** 63
The Merry Wives of Windsor **5:** 332, 333, 334, 335, 343, 349, 355, 369, 374; **18:** 86; **22:** 378
A Midsummer Night's Dream **3:** 364, 368, 381, 402, 406, 427, 450, 513; **13:** 19; **22:** 378; **29:** 175; **45:** 126, 175
Much Ado about Nothing **8:** 9, 16, 17, 19, 28, 29, 33, 39, 48, 63, 69, 73, 75, 79, 82, 115; **31:** 178, 184, 198, 231
Othello **22:** 378; **28:** 325
The Phoenix and Turtle **10:** 27, 31, 37, 45, 50; **38:** 342, 345, 357; **51:** 138, 143
The Rape of Lucrece **10:** 84, 89, 93, 98, 135; **22:** 294; **25:** 305; **43:** 102, 141
Richard II **6:** 282, 304, 317, 343, 352, 359, 364, 39; **24:** 307, 322, 325, 356, 395
Richard III **8:** 154, 161, 163, 167, 168, 170, 177, 184, 193, 197, 201, 206, 210, 218, 223, 228, 232, 243, 252, 262, 267; **16:** 150
Romeo and Juliet **5:** 438, 448, 464, 469, 470, 477, 480, 496, 518, 524, 525, 528, 547, 559; **33:** 210, 246
Sonnets **10:** 175, 176, 182, 205, 230, 260, 296, 302, 309, 315, 337, 349, 353; **40:** 238
The Taming of the Shrew **9:** 318, 322, 325, 332, 334, 341, 362, 370, 390, 426; **22:** 48, 378; **31:** 269
The Tempest **8:** 294, 295, 299, 320, 384, 439; **28:** 391, 415; **29:** 292, 297; **45:** 188
Timon of Athens **27:** 157, 175, 235; **52:** 338, 345, 349 375
Titus Andronicus **4:** 618, 619, 624, 631, 635, 640, 644, 646, 647, 653, 656, 659, 662, 664, 668, 672; **27:** 246, 285
Troilus and Cressida **3:** 536, 538, 549, 568, 569, 578, 583, 589, 611, 613; **27:** 341, 347, 354, 391

Twelfth Night **1:** 539, 542, 543, 546, 551, 553, 563, 570, 571, 590, 600, 660; **26:** 374; **34:** 281, 287; **46:** 286
The Two Gentlemen of Verona **6:** 445, 450, 460, 462, 504, 526
The Two Noble Kinsmen **37:** 313; **50:** 326, 361
Venus and Adonis **10:** 434, 442, 480, 486, 489; **33:** 357, 377

style
Henry VIII **41:** 158
The Phoenix and Turtle **10:** 8, 20, 24, 27, 31, 35, 45, 50; **38:** 334, 345, 357; **51:** 171, 188
The Rape of Lucrece **10:** 64, 65, 66, 68, 69, 70, 71, 73, 74, 77, 78, 81, 84, 98, 116, 131, 135; **43:** 113, 158
Venus and Adonis **10:** 411, 412, 414, 415, 416, 418, 419, 420, 423, 424, 428, 429, 439, 442, 480, 486, 489; **16:** 452

subjectivity
Hamlet **45:** 28
Sonnets **37:** 374

substitution of identities
Measure for Measure **2:** 507, 511, 519; **13:** 112; **49:** 313, 325

subversiveness
Cymbeline **22:** 302
The Tempest **22:** 302
The Winter's Tale **22:** 302

supernatural grace versus evil or chaos
Measure for Measure **48:** 1

suffering
King Lear **2:** 137, 160, 188, 201, 218, 222, 226, 231, 238, 241, 249, 265; **13:** 343; **22:** 271; **25:** 218; **50:** 24
Pericles **2:** 546, 573, 578, 579; **25:** 365; **36:** 279

symbolism
The Winter's Tale **7:** 425, 429, 436, 452, 456, 469, 490, 493

textual arrangement
Henry VI, Parts 1, 2, and 3 **24:** 3, 4, 6, 12, 17, 18, 19, 20, 21, 24, 27, 42, 45; **37:** 165
Richard II **24:** 260, 261, 262, 263, 271, 273, 291, 296, 356, 390

textual issues
Henry IV, Parts 1 and 2 **22:** 114
King Lear **22:** 271; **37:** 295; **49:** 73
A Midsummer Night's Dream **16:** 34; **29:** 216
The Taming of the Shrew **22:** 48; **31:** 261, 276; **31:** 276
The Winter's Tale **19:** 441; **45:** 333

textual problems
Henry V **5:** 187, 189, 190; **13:** 201

textual revisions
Pericles **15:** 129, 130, 132, 134, 135, 136, 138, 152, 155, 167, 181; **16:** 399; **25:** 365; **51:** 99

textual variants
Hamlet **13:** 282; **16:** 259; **21:** 11, 23, 72, 101, 127, 129, 139, 140, 142, 145, 202, 208, 259, 270, 284, 347, 361, 384; **22:** 258; **32:** 238

theatrical viability
Henry VI, Parts 1, 2, and 3 **24:** 31, 32, 34

theatricality
Antony and Cleopatra **47:** 96, 103, 107, 113
Macbeth **16:** 328
Measure for Measure **23:** 285, 286, 294, 372, 406; **49:** 358
The Merry Wives of Windsor **47:** 325

thematic disparity
Henry VIII **2:** 25, 31, 56, 68, 75; **41:** 146

time
As You Like It **5:** 18, 82, 112, 141; **23:** 146, 150; **34:** 102; **46:** 88, 156, 164, 169
Macbeth **3:** 234, 246, 283, 293; **20:** 245
Richard II **22:** 137
Sonnets **10:** 265, 302, 309, 322, 329, 337, 360, 379; **13:** 445; **40:** 292
The Tempest **8:** 401, 439, 464; **25:** 357; **29:** 278, 292; **45:** 236
Troilus and Cressida **3:** 561, 571, 583, 584, 613, 621, 626, 634
Twelfth Night **37:** 78; **46:** 297
The Winter's Tale **7:** 397, 425, 436, 476, 490; **19:** 366; **36:** 301, 349; **45:** 297, 329, 366, 374

time and change, motif of
Henry IV, Parts 1 and 2 **1:** 372, 393, 411; **39:** 89; **48:** 143
As You Like It **46:** 156, 164, 169

time scheme
Othello **4:** 370, 384, 390, 488; **22:** 207; **35:** 310; **47:** 51

topical allusions or content
Hamlet **13:** 282
Henry V **5:** 185, 186; **13:** 201
Love's Labour's Lost **2:** 300, 303, 307, 315, 316, 317, 319, 321, 327, 328; **23:** 187, 191, 197, 203, 221, 233, 237, 252; **25:** 1
Macbeth **13:** 361; **20:** 17, 350; **29:** 101

traditional values
Richard III **39:** 335

tragedies of major characters
Henry VIII **2:** 16, 39, 46, 48, 49, 51, 56, 58, 68, 81; **41:** 120

tragic elements
The Comedy of Errors **1:** 16, 25, 27, 45, 50, 59; **34:** 229
Cymbeline **25:** 319; **28:** 373; **36:** 129; **47:** 296

Henry V **5:** 228, 233, 267, 269, 271
Julius Caesar **50:** 258, 265
King John **9:** 208, 209, 244
Macbeth **52:** 15
A Midsummer Night's Dream **3:** 393, 400, 401, 410, 445, 474, 480, 491, 498, 511; **29:** 175; **45:** 169
The Rape of Lucrece **10:** 78, 80, 81, 84, 98, 109; **43:** 85, 148
The Tempest **8:** 324, 348, 359, 370, 380, 408, 414, 439, 458, 464
Twelfth Night **1:** 557, 569, 572, 575, 580, 599, 621, 635, 638, 639, 645, 654, 656; **26:** 342

treachery
Coriolanus **30:** 89
King John **9:** 245

treason and punishment
Macbeth **13:** 361; **16:** 328

trial scene
The Merchant of Venice **49:** 1, 23, 37

trickster, motif of
Cymbeline **22:** 302
The Tempest **22:** 302; **29:** 297
The Winter's Tale **22:** 302; **45:** 333

triumph over death or fate
Romeo and Juliet **5:** 421, 423, 427, 505, 509, 520, 530, 536, 565, 566; **51:** 219

Trojan War
Troilus and Cressida as myth **43:** 293

The Troublesome Reign (anonymous), compared with
King John **41:** 205, 221, 260, 269; **48:** 132

Troy
Troilus and Cressida **43:** 287

Troy passage
The Rape of Lucrece **43:** 77, 85

Tudor doctrine
King John **9:** 254, 284, 297; **41:** 221

Tudor myth
Henry VI, Parts 1, 2, and 3 **3:** 51, 59, 77, 92, 100, 109, 115, 119, 131; **39:** 222
Richard III **8:** 163, 165, 177, 184, 193, 201, 218, 228, 232, 243, 248, 252, 267; **39:** 305, 308, 326, 387; **42:** 130

Turkish elements
Henry IV, Parts 1 and 2 **19:** 170
Henry V **19:** 170

two fathers
Henry IV, Parts 1 and 2 **14:** 86, 101, 105, 108; **39:** 89, 100; **49:** 102

tyranny
King John **9:** 218

unity
  Antony and Cleopatra **6:** 20, 21, 22, 24, 25, 32, 33, 39, 43, 53, 60, 67, 111, 125, 146, 151, 165, 208, 211, 219; **13:** 374; **27:** 82, 90, 135
  Hamlet **1:** 75, 76, 87, 103, 113, 125, 128, 142, 148, 160, 184, 188, 198, 264; **16:** 259; **35:** 82, 215
  Henry VI, Parts 1, 2, and 3 **39:** 177, 222
  A Midsummer Night's Dream **3:** 364, 368, 381, 402, 406, 427, 450, 513; **13:** 19; **22:** 378; **29:** 175, 263

unity of double plot
  The Merchant of Venice **4:** 193, 194, 201, 232; **12:** 16, 67, 80, 115; **40:** 151

unnatural ordering
  Hamlet **22:** 378
  Love's Labour's Lost **22:** 378
  The Merry Wives of Windsor **22:** 378
  A Midsummer Night's Dream **22:** 378
  Othello **22:** 378

as unsuccessful play
  Measure for Measure **2:** 397, 441, 474, 482; **23:** 287

usurpation
  See also **rebellion**
  Richard II **6:** 263, 264, 272, 287, 289, 315, 323, 331, 343, 354, 364, 381, 388, 393, 397; **24:** 383; **52:** 108, 141, 154
  The Tempest **8:** 304, 370, 408, 420; **25:** 357, 382; **29:** 278, 362, 377; **37:** 336

utopia
  The Tempest **45:** 280

value systems
  Troilus and Cressida **3:** 578, 583, 589, 602, 613, 617; **13:** 53; **27:** 370, 396, 400

Venetian politics
  Othello **32:** 294

Venice, Elizabethan perceptions of
  The Merchant of Venice **28:** 249; **32:** 294; **40:** 127

Venus and Adonis
  The Rape of Lucrece **43:** 148

Vergil, influence of
  Titus Andronicus **27:** 306; **28:** 249

verisimilitude
  As You Like It **5:** 18, 23, 28, 30, 32, 39, 125; **23:** 107

Verona society
  Romeo and Juliet **5:** 556, 566; **13:** 235; **33:** 255; **51:** 245

Violence in Shakespeare's Works (Volume 43: 1, 12, 24, 32, 39, 61)
  Henry IV, Parts 1 and 2 **25:** 109
  Henry VI, Parts 1, 2, and 3 **24:** 25, 31; **37:** 157
  Julius Caesar **48:** 240
  Love's Labour's Lost **22:** 12
  Macbeth **20:** 273, 279, 283; **45:** 58
  Othello **22:** 12
  The Rape of Lucrece **43:** 148, 158
  Titus Andronicus **13:** 225; **25:** 245; **27:** 255; **28:** 249; **32:** 249, 265; **43:** 186, 203, 227, 239, 247, 255, 262
  Troilus and Cressida **43:** 329, 340, 351, 357, 365, 377

virginity or chastity, importance of
  Much Ado about Nothing **8:** 44, 75, 95, 111, 121, 125; **31:** 222

Virgo vs. Virago
  King Lear **48:** 222

visual arts, relation to
  Sonnets **28:** 407

visual humor
  Love's Labour's Lost **23:** 207, 217

war
  Coriolanus **25:** 263; **30:** 79, 96, 125, 149
  Henry V **5:** 193, 195, 197, 198, 210, 213, 219, 230, 233, 246, 281, 293; **28:** 121, 146; **30:** 262; **32:** 126; **37:** 175, 187; **42:** 141; **49:** 194, 236, 247, 260

Wars of the Roses
  Richard III **8:** 163, 165, 177, 184, 193, 201, 218, 228, 232, 243, 248, 252, 267; **39:** 308

Watteau, influence on staging
  Love's Labour's Lost **23:** 184, 186

wealth
  The Merchant of Venice **4:** 209, 261, 270, 273, 317; **12:** 80, 117; **22:** 69; **25:** 22; **28:** 249; **40:** 117, 197, 208; **45:** 17; **49:** 1; **51:** 15

wealth and social class
  Timon of Athens **1:** 466, 487, 495; **25:** 198; **27:** 184, 196, 212; **50:** 13

wheel of fortune, motif of
  Antony and Cleopatra **6:** 25, 178; **19:** 304
  Hamlet **52:** 35
  Henry VIII **2:** 27, 65, 72, 81

widowhood and remarriage, themes of
  Hamlet **32:** 238

wisdom
  King Lear **37:** 213; **46:** 210

wit
  The Merry Wives of Windsor **5:** 335, 336, 337, 339, 343, 351
  Much Ado about Nothing **8:** 27, 29, 38, 69, 79, 91, 95; **31:** 178, 191

witchcraft
  See **Magic and the Supernatural**

women, role of
  See **Shakespeare's Representation of Women**

wonder, dynamic of
  The Comedy of Errors **37:** 12

wordplay
  As You Like It **46:** 105
  Romeo and Juliet **32:** 256

written versus oral communication
  Love's Labour's Lost **2:** 359, 365; **28:** 63

youth
  The Two Gentlemen of Verona **6:** 439, 450, 464, 514, 568

youth versus age
  All's Well That Ends Well **7:** 9, 45, 58, 62, 76, 81, 86, 93, 98, 104, 116, 126; **26:** 117; **38:** 109

Cumulative Topic Index, by Play

The Cumulative Topic Index, by Play identifies the principal topics of discussion in the criticism of each play and non-dramatic poem. The topics are arranged alphabetically by play. Page references indicate the beginning page number of each essay containing substantial commentary on that topic. A parenthetical reference after a play indicates which volumes discuss the play extensively.

All's Well That Ends Well (Volumes 7, 26, 38)

appearance versus reality **7**: 37, 76, 93; **26**: 117
audience perspective **7**: 81, 104, 109, 116, 121
bed-trick **7**: 8, 26, 27, 29, 32, 41, 86, 93, 98, 113, 116, 126; **13**: 84; **26**: 117; **28**: 38; **38**: 65, 118; **49**: 46
Bertram
 characterization **7**: 15, 27, 29, 32, 39, 41, 43, 98, 113; **26**: 48; **26**: 117
 conduct **7**: 9, 10, 12, 16, 19, 21, 51, 62, 104; **50**: 59
 desire **22**: 78
 transformation or redemption **7**: 10, 19, 21, 26, 29, 32, 54, 62, 81, 90, 93, 98, 109, 113, 116, 126; **13**: 84
comic elements **26**: 97, 114; **48**: 65
dark elements **7**: 27, 37, 39, 43, 54, 109, 113, 116; **26**: 85; **48**: 65; **50**: 59
Decameron (Boccaccio), compared with **7**: 29, 43
desire **38**: 99, 109, 118
displacement **22**: 78
education **7**: 62, 86, 90, 93, 98, 104, 116, 126
elder characters **7**: 9, 37, 39, 43, 45, 54, 62, 104
conclusion **38**: 123, 132, 142
gender issues **7**: 9, 10, 67, 126; **13**: 77, 84; **19**: 113; **26**: 128; **38**: 89, 99, 118; **44**: 35
genre **48**: 65
Helena
 as agent of reconciliation, renewal, or grace **7**: 67, 76, 81, 90, 93, 98, 109, 116
 as dualistic or enigmatic character **7**: 15, 27, 29, 39, 54, 58, 62, 67, 76, 81, 98, 113, 126; **13**: 66; **22**: 78; **26**: 117
 as "female achiever" **19**: 113; **38**: 89
 desire **38**: 96; **44**: 35

pursuit of Bertram **7**: 9, 12, 15, 16, 19, 21, 26, 27, 29, 32, 43, 54, 76, 116; **13**: 77; **22**: 78; **49**: 46
virginity **38**: 65
virtue and nobility **7**: 9, 10, 12, 16, 19, 21, 27, 32, 41, 51, 58, 67, 76, 86, 126; **13**: 77; **50**: 59
implausibility of plot, characters, or events **7**: 8, 45
irony, paradox, and ambiguity **7**: 27, 32, 58, 62, 67, 81, 86, 109, 116
King **38**: 150
language and imagery **7**: 12, 29, 45, 104, 109, 121; **38**: 132; **48**: 65
Lavatch **26**: 64; **46**: 33, 52, 68
love **7**: 12, 15, 16, 51, 58, 67, 90, 93, 116; **38**: 80; **51**: 33, 44
merit versus rank **7**: 9, 10, 19, 37, 51, 76; **38**: 155; **50**: 59
"mingled yarn" **7**: 62, 93, 109, 126; **38**: 65
morality plays, influence of **7**: 29, 41, 51, 98, 113; **13**: 66
Parolles
 characterization **7**: 8, 9, 43, 76, 81, 98, 109, 113, 116, 126; **22**: 78; **26**: 48, 73, 97; **26**: 117; **46**: 68
 exposure **7**: 9, 27, 81, 98, 109, 113, 116, 121, 126
 Falstaff, compared with **7**: 8, 9, 16
reconciliation **7**: 90, 93, 98; **51**: 33
religious, mythic, or spiritual content **7**: 15, 45, 54, 67, 76, 98, 109, 116
romance or folktale elements **7**: 32, 41, 43, 45, 54, 76, 104, 116, 121; **26**: 117
sexuality **7**: 67, 86, 90, 93, 98, 126; **13**: 84; **19**: 113; **22**: 78; **28**: 38; **44**: 35; **49**: 46; **51**: 44
social and political context **13**: 66; **22**: 78; **38**: 99, 109, 150, 155; **49**: 46

staging issues **19**: 113; **26**: 15, 19, 48, 52, 64, 73, 85, 92, 93, 94, 95, 97, 114, 117, 128
structure **7**: 21, 29, 32, 45, 51, 76, 81, 93, 98, 116; **22**: 78; **26**: 128; **38**: 72, 123, 142
youth versus age **7**: 9, 45, 58, 62, 76, 81, 86, 93, 98, 104, 116, 126; **26**: 117; **38**: 109

Antony and Cleopatra (Volumes 6, 17, 27, 47)

allegorical elements **52**: 5
All for Love (John Dryden), compared with **6**: 20, 21; **17**: 12, 94, 101
ambiguity **6**: 53, 111, 161, 163, 180, 189, 208, 211, 228; **13**: 368
androgyny **13**: 530
Antony
 characterization **6**: 22, 23, 24, 31, 38, 41, 172, 181, 211; **16**: 342; **19**: 270; **22**: 217; **27**: 117; **47**: 77, 124, 142
 Cleopatra, relationship with **6**: 25, 27, 37, 39, 48, 52, 53, 62, 67, 71, 76, 85, 100, 125, 131, 133, 136, 142, 151, 161, 163, 165, 180, 192; **27**: 82; **47**: 107, 124, 165, 174
 death scene **25**: 245; **47**: 142
 dotage **6**: 22, 23, 38, 41, 48, 52, 62, 107, 136, 146, 175; **17**: 28
 nobility **6**: 22, 24, 33, 48, 94, 103, 136, 142, 159, 172, 202; **25**: 245
 political conduct **6**: 33, 38, 53, 107, 111, 146, 181
 public versus private personae **6**: 165; **47**: 107
 self-knowledge **6**: 120, 131, 175, 181, 192; **47**: 77
 as superhuman figure **6**: 37, 51, 71, 92, 94, 178, 192; **27**: 110; **47**: 71
 as tragic hero **6**: 38, 39, 52, 53, 60, 104, 120, 151, 155, 165, 178, 192, 202, 211;

22: 217; **27:** 90
audience response **48:** 206
Cleopatra
    Antony, relationship with **6:** 25, 27, 37, 39, 48, 52, 53, 62, 67, 71, 76, 85, 100, 125, 131, 133, 136, 142, 151, 161, 163, 165, 180, 192; **25:** 257; **27:** 82; **47:** 107, 124, 165, 174
    characterization **47:** 77, 96, 113, 124
    contradictory or inconsistent nature **6:** 23, 24, 27, 67, 76, 100, 104, 115, 136, 151, 159, 202; **17:** 94, 113; **27:** 135
    costume **17:** 94
    creativity **6:** 197; **47:** 96, 113
    death, decay, and nature's destructiveness **6:** 23, 25, 27, 41, 43, 52, 60, 64, 76, 94, 100, 103, 120, 131, 133, 136, 140, 146, 161, 165, 180, 181, 192, 197, 208; **13:** 383; **17:** 48, 94; **25:** 245; **27:** 135; **47:** 71
    personal attraction of **6:** 24, 38, 40, 43, 48, 53, 76, 104, 115, 155; **17:** 113
    self-knowledge **47:** 77, 96
    staging issues **17:** 94, 113
    as subverter of social order **6:** 146, 165; **47:** 113
    as superhuman figure **6:** 37, 51, 71, 92, 94, 178, 192; **27:** 110; **47:** 71, 174, 192
    as tragic heroine **6:** 53, 120, 151, 192, 208; **27:** 144
    as voluptuary or courtesan **6:** 21, 22, 25, 41, 43, 52, 53, 62, 64, 67, 76, 146, 161; **47:** 107, 174
comic elements **6:** 52, 85, 104, 125, 131, 151, 192, 202, 219; **47:** 77, 124, 149, 165
contemptus mundi **6:** 85, 133
dreams **45:** 28
dualisms **19:** 304; **27:** 82
Egyptian versus Roman values **6:** 31, 33, 43, 53, 104, 111, 115, 125, 142, 155, 159, 178, 181, 211, 219; **17:** 48; **19:** 270; **27:** 82, 121, 126; **28:** 249; **47:** 96, 103, 113, 149
Elizabethan culture, relation to **47:** 103
Enobarbus **6:** 22, 23, 27, 43, 94, 120, 142; **16:** 342; **17:** 36; **22:** 217; **27:** 135
gender issues **13:** 368; **25:** 257; **27:** 144; **47:** 174, 192; **53:** 67, 77
imperialism **53:** 67, 77
irony or paradox **6:** 53, 136, 146, 151, 159, 161, 189, 192, 211, 224
language and imagery **6:** 21, 25, 39, 64, 80, 85, 92, 94, 100, 104, 142, 146, 155, 159, 161, 165, 189, 192, 202, 211; **13:** 374, 383; **25:** 245, 257; **27:** 96, 105, 135
love and passion **6:** 51, 64, 71, 80, 85, 100, 115, 159, 165, 180; **25:** 257; **27:** 126; **47:** 71, 124, 174, 192; **51:** 25, 33, 44
monument scene **13:** 374; **16:** 342; **17:** 104, 110; **22:** 217; **47:** 142, 165
morality **52:** 5
moral relativism **22:** 217; **27:** 121
mythological allusions **16:** 342; **19:** 304; **27:** 110, 117; **47:** 71, 192
Octavius **6:** 22, 24, 31, 38, 43, 53, 62, 107, 125, 136, 146, 178, 181, 219; **25:** 257
political and social disintegration **6:** 31, 43, 53, 60, 71, 80, 100, 107, 111, 146; 180, 197, 219; **22:** 217; **25:** 257; **27:** 121
race **53:** 67, 77
reason versus imagination **6:** 107, 115, 142, 197, 228; **45:** 28

reconciliation **6:** 100, 103, 125, 131, 159, 181
religious, mythic, or spiritual content **6:** 53, 94, 111, 115, 178, 192, 224; **47:** 71
royalty **6:** 94
Seleucus episode (Act V, scene ii) **6:** 39, 41, 62, 133, 140, 151; **27:** 135
Shakespeare's major tragedies, compared with **6:** 25, 53, 60, 71, 120, 181, 189, 202; **22:** 217; **47:** 77
Shakespeare's moral judgment **6:** 33, 37, 38, 41, 48, 51, 64, 76, 111, 125, 136, 140, 146, 163, 175, 189, 202, 211, 228; **13:** 368, 523; **25:** 257
sources **6:** 20, 39; **19:** 304; **27:** 96, 126; **28:** 249
stage history **17:** 84, 94, 101
staging issues **17:** 6, 12, 84, 94, 101, 104, 110; **27:** 90; **47:** 142
strategic analysis **48:** 206
theatricality and role-playing **47:** 96, 103, 107, 113
unity **6:** 20, 21, 22, 24, 25, 32, 33, 39, 43, 53, 60, 67, 111, 125, 146, 151, 165, 208, 211, 219; **13:** 374; **27:** 82, 90, 135
wheel of fortune, motif of **6:** 25, 178; **19:** 304

As You Like It (Volumes 5, 23, 34, 46)

Appearance versus Reality **46:** 105
androgyny **23:** 98, 100, 122, 138, 143, 144; **34:** 172, 177; **46:** 134
anti-romantic elements **34:** 72
aristocracy **34:** 120
art versus nature **5:** 128, 130, 148; **34:** 147
Audrey **46:** 122
autobiographical elements **5:** 25, 35, 43, 50, 55, 61
bawdy elements **46:** 122
Celia **46:** 94
characterization **5:** 19, 24, 25, 36, 39, 54, 82, 86, 116, 148; **34:** 72; **48:** 42
Christian elements **5:** 39, 98, 162
contradiction, paradox, and opposition **46:** 105
comic form **46:** 105; **51:** 1
comic resolution **52:** 63
corruption in society **46:** 94
costume **46:** 117
courtship and marriage **34:** 109, 177; **48:** 32; **51:** 44
death, decay, nature's destructiveness **46:** 169
deception, disguise, and duplicity **46:** 134
desire **37:** 43; **52:** 63
domestic elements **46:** 142
dramatic shortcomings or failure **5:** 19, 42, 52, 61, 65
duration of time **5:** 44, 45
Elizabethan culture, relation to **5:** 21, 59, 66, 68, 70, 158; **16:** 53; **28:** 46; **34:** 120; **37:** 1; **46:** 142
Fathers and Daughters **46:** 94
feminism **23:** 107, 108
Forest of Arden
    as "bitter" Arcadia **5:** 98, 118, 162; **23:** 97, 98, 99, 100, 122, 139
    Duke Frederick's court, contrast with **5:** 46, 102, 103, 118, 130, 156; **16:** 53; **23:** 126, 128, 129, 131, 134; **34:** 78, 102, 131; **46:** 164
    pastoral elements **5:** 18, 20, 24, 32, 35, 47, 50, 54, 55, 57, 60, 77, 128, 135, 156; **23:** 17, 20, 27, 46, 137; **34:** 78, 147; **46:** 88
    as patriarchal society **5:** 168; **23:** 150; **34:** 177
    as source of self-knowledge **5:** 98, 102, 103, 128, 130, 135, 148, 158, 162; **23:** 17; **34:** 102
    as timeless, mythical world **5:** 112, 130, 141; **23:** 132; **34:** 78; **37:** 43; **46:** 88
    theme of play **46:** 88
gender identity **46:** 127, 134,
genre **5:** 46, 55, 79
homoerotic elements **46:** 127, 142
homosexuality **46:** 127, 142
Hymen episode **5:** 61, 116, 130; **23:** 22, 48, 54, 109, 111, 112, 113, 115, 146, 147
irony **5:** 30, 32, 154
Jaques
    love-theme, relation to **5:** 103; **23:** 7, 37, 118, 128
    as malcontent **5:** 59, 70, 84
    melancholy **5:** 20, 28, 32, 36, 39, 43, 50, 59, 63, 68, 77, 82, 86, 135; **23:** 20, 26, 103, 104, 107, 109; **34:** 85; **46:** 88, 94
    pastoral convention, relation to **5:** 61, 63, 65, 79, 93, 98, 114, 118
    Seven Ages of Man speech (Act II, scene vii) **5:** 28, 52, 156; **23:** 48, 103, 105, 126, 138, 152; **46:** 88, 156, 164, 169
    Shakespeare, relation to **5:** 35, 50, 154
    as superficial critic **5:** 28, 30, 43, 54, 55, 63, 65, 68, 75, 77, 82, 86, 88, 98, 138; **34:** 85
justice **46:** 94
juxtaposition of opposing perspectives **5:** 86, 93, 98, 141; **16:** 53; **23:** 119; **34:** 72, 78, 131
language and imagery **5:** 19, 21, 35, 52, 75, 82, 92, 138; **23:** 15, 21, 26; **28:** 9; **34:** 131; **37:** 43; **48:** 42
love **5:** 24, 44, 46, 57, 79, 88, 103, 116, 122, 138, 141, 162; **28:** 46, 82; **34:** 85
Love in a Forest (Charles Johnson adaptation) **23:** 7
metadramatic elements **5:** 128, 130, 146; **34:** 130
morality **52:** 63
mythological allusions **46:** 142
nature **46:** 94
Neoclassical rules **5:** 19, 20
Orlando
    as ideal man **5:** 32, 36, 39, 162; **34:** 161; **46:** 94
    as younger brother **5:** 66, 158; **46:** 94
pastoral characters (Silvius, Phebe, and Corin) **23:** 37, 97, 98, 99, 108, 110, 118, 122, 138; **34:** 147
pastoral convention, parodies of **5:** 54, 57, 72
pastoral convention, relation to **5:** 72, 77, 122; **34:** 161; **37:** 1
primogeniture **5:** 66, 158; **34:** 109, 120
psychoanalytic interpretation **5:** 146, 158; **23:** 141, 142; **34:** 109; **48:** 42
public versus private worlds **46:** 164
reconciliation of opposites **5:** 79, 88, 103, 116, 122, 138; **23:** 127, 143; 34: 161, 172; **46:** 156
as romance **5:** 55, 79; **23:** 27, 28, 40, 43
Rosalind **46:** 94, 122,
    Beatrice, compared with **5:** 26, 36, 50, 75

charm **5:** 55, 75; **23:** 17, 18, 20, 41, 89, 111
disguise, role of **5:** 75, 107, 118, 122, 128, 130, 133, 138, 141, 146, 148, 164, 168; **13:** 502; **23:** 35, 42, 106, 119, 123, 146; **34:** 130; **46:** 134
femininity **5:** 26, 36, 52, 75; **23:** 24, 29, 46, 54, 103, 108, 121, 146
   as Ganymede **46:** 127, 142
love-theme, relation to **5:** 79, 88, 103, 116, 122, 138, 141; **23:** 114, 115; **34:** 85, 177
rustic characters **5:** 24, 60, 72, 84; **23:** 127; **34:** 78, 161
sexual ambiguity and sexual deception **46:** 134, 142
Sexuality in Shakespeare **46:** 122, 127, 134, 142
as satire or parody of pastoral conventions **5:** 46, 55, 60, 72, 77, 79, 84, 114, 118, 128, 130, 154
self-knowledge **5:** 32, 82, 102, 116, 122, 133, 164
sibling rivalry **34:** 109
social order **37:** 1; **46:** 94
sources **5:** 18, 32, 54, 59, 66, 84; **34:** 155; **46:** 117
stage history **46:** 117
staging issues **13:** 502; **23:** 7, 17, 19, 22, 58, 96, 97, 98, 99, 101, 110, 137; **28:** 82; **32:** 212
structure **5:** 19, 24, 25, 35, 44, 45, 46, 86, 93, 116, 138, 158; **23:** 7, 8, 9, 10, 11; **34:** 72, 78, 131, 147, 155
time **5:** 18, 82, 112, 141; **23:** 146, 150; **34:** 102; **46:** 88, 156, 164, 169
Touchstone
   callousness **5:** 88
   comic and farcical elements **46:** 117
   as philosopher-fool **5:** 24, 28, 30, 32, 36, 63, 75, 98; **23:** 152; **34:** 85; **46:** 1, 14, 18, 24, 33, 52, 60, 88, 105,
   relation to pastoral convention **5:** 54, 61, 63, 72, 75, 77, 79, 84, 86, 93, 98, 114, 118, 135, 138, 166; **34:** 72, 147, 161
   selflessness **5:** 30, 36, 39, 76
verisimilitude **5:** 18, 23, 28, 30, 32, 39, 125; **23:** 107
wordplay **46:** 105

The Comedy of Errors (Volumes 1, 26, 34)

Adriana **16:** 3; **34:** 211, 220, 238
adultery **34:** 215
audience perception **1:** 37, 50, 56; **19:** 54; **34:** 258
autobiographical elements **1:** 16, 18
characterization **1:** 13, 21, 31, 34, 46, 49, 50, 55, 56; **19:** 54; **25:** 63; **34:** 194, 201, 208, 245
classical influence and sources **1:** 13, 14, 16, 31, 32, 43, 61
comic elements **1:** 43, 46, 55, 56, 59; **26:** 183, 186, 188, 190; **34:** 190, 245
composition date **1:** 18, 23, 34, 55
dramatic structure **1:** 19, 27, 40, 43, 46, 50; **26:** 186, 190; **34:** 190, 229, 233; **37:** 12
Elizabethan culture, relation to **26:** 138, 142; **34:** 201, 215, 233, 238, 258; **42:** 80
Dromio brothers **42:** 80
farcical elements **1:** 14, 16, 19, 23, 30, 34, 35, 46, 50, 59, 61; **19:** 54; **26:** 188, 190; **34:** 245

feminist criticism **42:** 93
food, meaning of **34:** 220
gender issues **34:** 215, 220
genre **34:** 251, 258
identity **34:** 201, 208, 211
illusion **1:** 13, 14, 27, 37, 40, 45, 59, 63; **26:** 188; **34:** 194, 211
language and imagery **1:** 16, 25, 39, 40, 43, 57, 59; **34:** 233
male/female relationships **16:** 3
marriage **34:** 251
mistaken identity **1:** 13, 14, 27, 37, 40, 45, 49, 55, 57, 61, 63; **19:** 34, 54; **25:** 63; **34:** 194
Plautus's works, compared with **1:** 13, 14, 16, 53, 61; **16:** 3; **19:** 34
problem comedy **34:** 251
redemption **19:** 54; **26:** 188
romantic elements **1:** 13, 16, 19, 23, 25, 30, 31, 36, 39, 53
servitude **42:** 80
social order **34:** 238
sources **1:** 13, 14, 16, 19, 31, 32, 39; **16:** 3; **34:** 190, 215, 258
staging issues **26:** 182, 183, 186, 188, 190
supernatural, role of **1:** 27, 30
tragic elements **1:** 16, 25, 27, 45, 50, 59; **34:** 229
wonder, dynamic of **37:** 12

Coriolanus (9, 17, 30, 50)

aggression **9:** 112, 142, 174, 183, 189, 198; **30:** 79, 111, 125, 142; **44:** 11, 79
Anthony and Cleopatra, compared with **30:** 79, 96; **50:** 105
appearance versus reality **30:** 142
Aufidius **9:** 9, 12, 17, 19, 53, 121, 148, 153, 157, 169, 180, 193; **19:** 287; **25:** 263, 296; **30:** 58, 67, 89, 96, 133; **50:** 99
body politic, metaphor of **22:** 248; **30:** 67, 96, 105, 125; **50:** 105, 110, 119, 140, 145, 152
butterfly episode (Act I, scene iii) **9:** 19, 45, 62, 65, 73, 100, 125, 153, 157
capitulation scene (Act V, scene iii) **9:** 19, 26, 53, 65, 100, 117, 125, 130, 157, 164, 183
ceremonies, rites, and rituals, importance of **9:** 139, 148, 169
Christian elements **30:** 111
comic elements **9:** 8, 9, 14, 53, 80, 106
Cominius **25:** 245
Cominius's tribute (Act II, scene ii) **9:** 80, 100, 117, 125, 144, 164, 198; **25:** 296
Coriolanus
   anger or passion **9:** 19, 26, 45, 80, 92, 157, 164, 177, 189; **30:** 79, 96
   as complementary figure to Aufidius **19:** 287
   death scene (Act V, scene vi) **9:** 12, 80, 100, 117, 125, 144, 164, 198; **25:** 245, 263; **50:** 110
   as epic hero **9:** 130, 164, 177; **25:** 245; **50:** 119
   immaturity **9:** 62, 80, 84, 110, 117, 142; **30:** 140
   inhuman attributes **9:** 65, 73, 139, 157, 164, 169, 189, 198; **25:** 263
   internal struggle **9:** 31, 43, 45, 53, 72, 117, 121, 130; **44:** 93

   introspection or self-knowledge, lack of **9:** 53, 80, 84, 112, 117, 130; **25:** 296; **30:** 133
   isolation or autonomy **9:** 53, 65, 142, 144, 153, 157, 164, 180, 183, 189, 198; **30:** 58, 89, 111; **50:** 128
   manipulation by others **9:** 33, 45, 62, 80; **25:** 296
   modesty **9:** 8, 12, 19, 26, 53, 78, 92, 117, 121, 144, 183; **25:** 296; **30:** 79, 96, 129, 133, 149
   narcissism **30:** 111
   noble or aristocratic attributes **9:** 15, 18, 19, 26, 31, 33, 52, 53, 62, 65, 84, 92, 100, 121, 148, 157, 169; **25:** 263; **30:** 67, 74, 96; **50:** 13
   pride or arrogance **9:** 8, 11, 12, 19, 26, 31, 33, 43, 45, 65, 78, 92, 121, 148, 153, 177; **30:** 58, 67, 74, 89, 96, 129
   reconciliation with society **9:** 33, 43, 45, 65, 139, 169; **25:** 296
   as socially destructive force **9:** 62, 65, 73, 78, 110, 142, 144, 153; **25:** 296
   soliloquy (Act IV, scene iv) **9:** 84, 112, 117, 130
   as tragic figure **9:** 8, 12, 13, 18, 25, 45, 52, 53, 72, 80, 92, 106, 112, 117, 130, 148, 164, 169, 177; **25:** 296; **30:** 67, 74, 79, 96, 111, 129; **37:** 283; **50:** 99
   traitorous actions **9:** 9, 12, 19, 45, 84, 92, 148; **25:** 296; **30:** 133
   as unsympathetic character **9:** 12, 13, 62, 78, 80, 84, 112, 130, 157
domestic elements **42:** 223; **50:** 145
economics **50:** 152
England and Rome, parallels between **9:** 39, 43, 106, 148, 180, 193; **25:** 296; **30:** 67, 105; **50:** 172
fable of the belly (Act I, scene i) **9:** 8, 65, 73, 80, 136, 153, 157, 164, 180, 183, 189; **25:** 296; **30:** 79, 105, 111; **50:** 13, 110, 140
fame **30:** 58
fire and water **25:** 263
flattery or dissimulation **9:** 26, 45, 92, 100, 110, 121, 130, 144, 157, 183, 193; **25:** 296
friendship **30:** 125, 142
gender issues **30:** 79, 125, 142; **44:** 93; **50:** 128
genre **9:** 42, 43, 53, 80, 106, 112, 117, 130, 164, 177; **30:** 67, 74, 79, 89, 111, 125; **50:** 99
honor or integrity **9:** 43, 65, 73, 92, 106, 110, 121, 144, 153, 157, 164, 177, 183, 189; **30:** 89, 96, 133
identity **42:** 248; **50:** 128
irony or satire **9:** 65, 73, 80, 92, 106, 153, 157, 164, 193; **30:** 67, 89, 133
Jacobean culture, relation to **22:** 248
language and imagery **9:** 8, 9, 13, 53, 64, 65, 73, 78, 84, 100, 112, 121, 136, 139, 142, 144, 153, 157, 174, 183, 193, 198; **22:** 248; **25:** 245, 263; **30:** 111, 125, 142; **37:** 283; **44:** 79
Macbeth, compared with **30:** 79
martial vs. civil law **48:** 230
Menenius **9:** 8, 9, 11, 14, 19, 26, 78, 80, 106, 148, 157; **25:** 263, 296; **30:** 67, 79, 89, 96, 111, 133
Midlands Revolt, influence of **22:** 248; **30:** 79; **50:** 140, 172
naming, significance of **30:** 58, 96, 111, 125
nature, philosophy of **30:** 74

nurturing or feeding 9: 65, 73, 136, 183, 189; 30: 111; 44: 79; 50: 110
paradoxical elements 9: 73, 92, 106, 121, 153, 157, 164, 169, 193
plebeians 9: 8, 9, 11, 12, 15, 18, 19, 26, 33, 39, 53, 92, 125, 153, 183, 189; 25: 296; 30: 58, 79, 96, 111; 50: 13, 105
Plutarch and historical sources 9: 8, 9, 13, 14, 16, 26, 39, 92, 106, 130, 142, 164; 30: 74, 79, 105; 50: 99
politics 9: 15, 17, 18, 19, 26, 33, 43, 53, 62, 65, 73, 80, 92, 106, 110, 112, 121, 144, 153, 157, 164, 180; 22: 248; 25: 296; 30: 58, 67, 79, 89, 96, 105, 111, 125; 37: 283; 42: 223; 48: 230; 50: 13, 140, 172
psychoanalytic interpretations 44: 93
public versus private worlds 37: 283; 42: 223
sexuality 9: 112, 142, 174, 183, 189, 198; 30: 79, 111, 125, 142
shame 42: 248
Shakespeare's political sympathies 9: 8, 11, 15, 17, 19, 26, 39, 52, 53, 62, 80, 92, 142; 25: 296; 30: 74, 79, 89, 96, 105, 133; 50: 145, 172
slander 48: 230
society 9: 15, 17, 18, 19, 26, 33, 43, 53, 62, 65, 73, 80, 92, 106, 110, 112, 121, 144, 153, 157, 164, 180; 22: 248; 25: 296; 30: 58, 67, 79, 89, 96, 105, 111, 125; 50: 13, 105, 119, 152
staging issues 17: 172, 242, 248
structure 9: 8, 9, 11, 12, 13, 14, 16, 26, 33, 45, 53, 58, 72, 78, 80, 84, 92, 112, 139, 148; 25: 263; 30: 79, 96
treachery 30: 89
the tribunes (Brutus and Sicinius) 9: 9, 11, 14, 19, 33, 169, 180
Virgilia 9: 11, 19, 26, 33, 58, 100, 121, 125; 25: 263; 30: 79, 96, 133; 50: 99
Volumnia
  Coriolanus's subservience to 9: 16, 26, 33, 53, 62, 80, 92, 100, 117, 125, 142, 177, 183; 30: 140, 149; 44: 79
  influence on Coriolanus 9: 45, 62, 65, 78, 92, 100, 110, 117, 121, 125, 130, 148, 157, 183, 189, 193; 25: 263, 296; 30: 79, 96, 125, 133, 140, 142, 149; 44: 93
  as noble Roman matron 9: 16, 19, 26, 31, 33
  personification of Rome 9: 125, 183; 50: 119
war 25: 263; 30: 79, 96, 125, 149

Cymbeline (Volumes 4, 15, 36, 47)

appearance versus reality 4: 87, 93, 103, 162; 36: 99; 47: 228, 286
authorship controversy 4: 17, 21, 35, 48, 56, 78
autobiographical elements 4: 43, 46; 36: 134
bawdy elements 36: 155
Beaumont and Fletcher's romances, compared with 4: 46, 52, 138
Belarius 4: 48, 89, 141
British nationalism 4: 19, 78, 89, 93, 129, 141, 159, 167; 32: 373; 36: 129; 45: 67; 47: 219, 265
Cloten 4: 20, 116, 127, 155; 22: 302, 365; 25: 245; 36: 99, 125, 142, 155; 47: 228
combat scenes 22: 365
comic elements 4: 35, 56, 113, 141; 15: 111, 122; 47: 296
dramatic structure 4: 17, 18, 19, 20, 21, 22, 24, 38, 43, 48, 53, 64, 68, 89, 116, 129, 141; 22: 302, 365; 25: 319; 36: 115, 125
dreams 4: 162, 167; 44: 28; 45: 67, 75
dualisms 4: 29, 64, 73
Elizabethan dramatic conventions 4: 53, 124
family, theme of 44: 28
Guiderius and Arviragus 4: 21, 22, 89, 129, 141, 148; 25: 319; 36: 125, 158
historical elements 47: 260
Iachimo 25: 245, 319; 36: 166
Imogen 4: 21, 22, 24, 29, 37, 45, 46, 52, 56, 78, 89, 108; 15: 23, 32, 105, 121; 19: 411; 25: 245, 319; 28: 398; 32: 373; 36: 129, 142, 148; 47: 25, 205, 228, 245, 274, 277
Imogen's reawakening (Act IV, scene ii) 4: 37, 56, 89, 103, 108, 116, 150; 15: 23; 25: 245; 47: 252
irony 4: 64, 77, 103
language and imagery 4: 43, 48, 61, 64, 70, 73, 93, 108; 13: 401; 25: 245; 28: 373, 398; 36: 115, 158, 166, 186; 47: 205, 286, 296
Lucretia, analogies to 36: 148
misperception 19: 411; 36: 99, 115; 47: 228, 237, 252, 277, 286, 296,
negative appraisals 4: 20, 35, 43, 45, 48, 53, 56, 68; 15: 32, 105, 121
patriarchy 32: 373; 36: 134; 47: 237; 51: 30
Posthumus 4: 24, 30, 53, 78, 116, 127, 141, 155, 159, 167; 15: 89; 19: 411; 25: 245, 319; 36: 142; 44: 28; 45: 67, 75; 47: 25, 205, 228,
psychological elements 36: 134; 44: 28; 45: 67, 75
reconciliation 4: 38, 64, 73, 93, 105, 113, 116, 129, 138, 141, 162, 170
religious, mythical, or spiritual content 4: 22, 29, 78, 93, 105, 108, 115, 116, 127, 134, 138, 141, 159; 28: 373; 36: 142, 158, 186; 47: 219, 260, 274
romantic elements 4: 17, 20, 46, 68, 77, 141, 148, 172; 15: 111; 25: 319; 28: 373
self-conscious or artificial nature of play 4: 43, 52, 56, 68, 124, 134, 138; 36: 99
sexuality 4: 170, 172; 25: 319; 32: 373; 47: 245
Shakespeare's lyric poetry, compared with 13: 401
sources 4: 17, 18; 13: 401; 28: 373; 47: 245, 265, 277
staging issues 15: 6, 23, 75, 105, 111, 121, 122; 22: 365
subversiveness 22: 302
tragic elements 25: 319; 28: 373; 36: 129; 47: 296
trickster, motif of 22: 302
vision scene (Act V, scene iv) 4: 17, 21, 28, 29, 35, 38, 78, 105, 108, 134, 150, 167; 47: 205
wager plot 4: 18, 24, 29, 53, 78, 155; 22: 365; 25: 319; 47: 205, 277

Hamlet (1, 21, 35, 44)

ambiguity 1: 92, 160, 198, 227, 230, 234, 247, 249; 21: 72; 35: 241
appearance versus reality 1: 95, 116, 166, 169, 198; 35: 82, 126, 132, 144, 238; 44: 248; 45: 28
aristocracy 42: 217
audience response 28: 325; 32: 238; 35: 167; 44: 107
autobiographical elements 1: 98, 115, 119; 13: 487
Calvinist implications 48: 195
classical Greek tragedies, compared with 1: 74, 75, 130, 184, 212; 13: 296; 22: 339
Claudius 13: 502; 16: 246; 21: 259, 347, 361, 371; 28: 232, 290; 35: 104, 182; 44: 119, 241
closet scene (Act III, scene iv) 16: 259; 21: 151, 334, 392; 35: 204, 229; 44: 119, 237
costume 21: 81
death, decay, and nature's destructiveness 1: 144, 153, 188, 198, 221, 242; 13: 502; 28: 280, 311; 35: 241; 42: 284
dreams 45: 28
dumbshow and play scene (Act III, scene ii) 1: 76, 86, 134, 138, 154, 160, 207; 13: 502; 21: 392; 35: 82; 44: 241; 46: 74
Elizabethan culture, relation to 1: 76, 148, 151, 154, 160, 166, 169, 171, 176, 184, 202, 209, 254; 13: 282, 494; 19: 330; 21: 407, 416; 22: 258
Elizabethan and Jacobean politics, relation to 28: 232; 28: 290, 311; 35: 140
fencing scene (Act V, scene ii) 21: 392
Fortinbras 21: 136, 347; 28: 290
gender issues 35: 144; 44: 189, 195, 198,
genre 1: 176, 212, 237
Gertrude 21: 259, 347, 392; 28: 311; 32: 238; 35: 182, 204, 229; 44: 119, 160, 189, 195, 237, 248
Ghost 1: 75, 76, 84, 85, 128, 134, 138, 154, 171, 218, 231, 254; 16: 246; 21: 17, 44, 112, 151, 334, 371, 377, 392; 25: 288; 35: 152, 157, 174, 237; 44: 119
gravedigger scene (Act V, scene i) 21: 392; 28: 280; 46: 74
grotesque elements 42: 284
Hamlet
  delay 1: 76, 83, 88, 90, 94, 98, 102, 103, 106, 114, 115, 116, 119, 120, 148, 151, 166, 171, 179, 188, 191, 194, 198, 221, 268; 13: 296, 502; 21: 81; 25: 209, 288; 28: 223; 35: 82, 174, 212, 215, 237; 44: 180, 209, 219, 229
  divided nature 16: 246; 28: 223; 32: 288; 35: 182, 215; 37: 241
  elocution of the character's speeches 21: 96, 104, 112, 127, 132, 172, 177, 179, 194, 245, 254, 257
  as a fool 46: 1, 29, 52, 74
  madness 1: 76, 81, 83, 95, 102, 106, 128, 144, 154, 160, 234; 21: 35, 50, 72, 81, 99, 112, 311, 339, 355, 361, 371, 377, 384; 35: 117, 132, 134, 140, 144, 212; 44: 107, 119, 152, 209, 219, 229
  melancholy 21: 99, 112, 177, 194; 35: 82, 95, 117; 44: 209, 219
  as negative character 1: 86, 92, 111, 171, 218; 21: 386; 25: 209; 35: 167
  reaction to his father's death 22: 339; 35: 104, 174; 44: 133, 160, 180, 189
  reaction to Gertrude's marriage 1: 74, 120, 154, 179; 16: 259; 21: 371; 22: 339; 35: 104, 117; 44: 133, 160, 189, 195

romantic aspects of the character **21**: 96; **44**: 198
  as scourge or purifying figure **1**: 144, 209, 242; **25**: 288; **35**: 157
  sentimentality versus intellectuality **1**: 75, 83, 88, 91, 93, 94, 96, 102, 103, 115, 116, 120, 166, 191; **13**: 296; **21**: 35, 41, 44, 72, 81, 89, 99, 129, 132, 136, 172, 213, 225, 339, 355, 361, 371, 377, 379, 381, 386; **25**: 209; **44**: 198
  soliloquies **1**: 76, 82, 83, 148, 166, 169, 176, 191; **21**: 17, 31, 44, 53, 89, 112, 268, 311, 334, 347, 361, 384, 392; **25**: 209; **28**: 223; **44**: 107, 119, 229
  theatrical interpretations **21**: 11, 31, 78, 101, 104, 107, 160, 177, 179, 182, 183, 192, 194, 197, 202, 203, 208, 213, 225, 232, 237, 249, 253, 254, 257, 259, 274, 311, 339, 347, 355, 361, 371, 377, 380
  virility **21**: 213, 301, 355; **44**: 198
Hamlet with Alterations (David Garrick adaptation) **21**: 23, 334, 347
Horatio **44**: 189
idealism versus pragmatism **16** 246; **28**: 325
Laertes **21**: 347, 386; **28**: 290; **35**: 182
language and imagery **1**: 95, 144, 153, 154, 160, 188, 198, 221, 227, 249, 259, 270; **22**: 258, 378; **28**: 311; **35**: 144, 152, 238, 241; **42**: 217; **44**: 248; **52**: 35
madness **19**: 330; **35**: 104, 126, 134, 140, 144; **44**: 107, 119, 152, 209, 219, 229
marriage **22**: 339; **51**: 44
Marxist criticism **42**: 234
moral choice **52**: 35
nunnery scene (Act III, scene i) **21**: 157, 381, 410
Ophelia **1**: 73, 76, 81, 82, 91, 96, 97, 154, 166, 169, 171, 218, 270; **13**: 268; **16**: 246; **19**: 330; **21**: 17, 41, 44, 72, 81, 101, 104, 107, 112, 136, 203, 259, 347, 381, 386, 392, 416; **28**: 232, 325; **35**: 104, 126, 140, 144, 182, 238; **44**: 189, 195, 248
Polonius **21**: 259, 334, 347, 386, 416; **35**: 182
prayer scene (Act III, scene iii) **1**: 76, 106, 160, 212, 231; **44**: 119
psychoanalytic interpretations **1**: 119, 148, 154, 179, 202; **21**: 197, 213, 361; **25**: 209; **28**: 223; **35**: 95, 104, 134, 237; **37**: 241; **44**: 133, 152, 160, 180, 209, 219
religious, mythic, or spiritual content **1**: 98, 102, 130, 184, 191, 209, 212, 231, 234, 254; **21**: 361; **22**: 258; **28**: 280; **32**: 238; **35**: 134
revenge **1**: 74, 194, 209, 224, 234, 254; **16**: 246; **22**: 258; **25**: 288; **28**: 280; **35**: 152, 157, 167, 174, 212; **44**: 180, 209, 219, 229
Richard II, compared with **1**: 264
ceremonies, rites, and rituals, importance of **13**: 268; **28**: 232
sources **1**: 76, 81, 113, 125, 128, 130, 151, 191, 202, 224, 259
staging issues **13**: 494, 502; **21**: 11, 17, 31, 35, 41, 44, 50, 53, 78, 81, 89, 101, 112, 127, 139, 142, 145, 148, 151, 157, 160, 172, 182, 183, 202, 203, 208, 225, 232, 237, 242, 245, 249, 251, 259, 268, 270, 274, 283, 284, 301, 311, 334, 347, 355, 361, 371, 377, 379, 380, 381, 384, 386, 392, 407, 410, 416; **44**: 198
Stoicism **48**: 195

structure **22**: 378; **28**: 280, 325; **35**: 82, 104, 215; **44**: 152
subjectivity **45**: 28
textual variants **13**: 282; **16**: 259; **21**: 11, 23, 72, 101, 127, 129, 139, 140, 142, 145, 202, 208, 259, 270, 284, 347, 361, 384; **22**: 258; **32**: 238
topical allusions or content **13**: 282
unity **1**: 75, 76, 87, 103, 113, 125, 128, 142, 148, 160, 184, 188, 198, 264; **16**: 259; **35**: 82, 215
unnatural ordering **22**: 378
wheel of fortune, motif of **52**: 35
widowhood and remarriage, themes of **32**: 238

Henry IV, Parts 1 and 2 (Volumes 1, 14, 39, 49)

  carnival elements **28**: 203; **32**: 103
  characterization **1**: 321, 328, 332, 333, 336, 344, 365, 383, 385, 389, 391, 397, 401; **19**: 195; **39**: 123, 137; **42**: 101, 164; **49**: 93
  comic elements **1**: 286, 290, 314, 327, 328, 336, 353; **19**: 195; **25**: 109; **39**: 72
  contractual and economic relations **13**: 213
  contrasting dramatic worlds **14**: 56, 60, 61, 84, 105; **48**: 95; **49**: 162
  critical history **42**: 187; **48**: 167
  deception, disguise, and duplicity **1**: 397, 406, 425; **42**: 101; **47**: 1, 60; **48**: 95
  divine right versus justice **49**: 116
  Elizabethan culture, relation to **19**: 195; **48**: 117, 143, 151, 175
  Elizabethan politics, relation to **22**: 395; **28**: 203; **47**: 60; **48**: 117, 143, 167, 175
  Falstaff
    characterization **1**: 287, 298, 312, 333; **25**: 245; **28**: 203; **39**: 72, 134, 137, 143
    as comic figure **1**: 287, 311, 327, 344, 351, 354, 357, 410, 434; **39**: 89; **46**: 1, 48, 52; **49**: 178
    as coward or rogue **1**: 285, 290, 296, 298, 306, 307, 313, 317, 323, 336, 337, 338, 342, 354, 366, 374, 391, 396, 401, 433; **14**: 7, 111, 125, 130, 133; **32**: 166
    dual personality **1**: 397, 401, 406, 434; **49**: 162
    female attributes **13**: 183; **44**: 44
    Iago, compared with **1**: 341, 351
    Marxist interpretation **1**: 358, 361
    as outlaw **49**: 133
    as parody of the historical plot **1**: 314, 354, 359; **39**: 143
    as positive character **1**: 286, 287, 290, 296, 298, 311, 312, 321, 325, 333, 344, 355, 357, 389, 401, 408, 434
    rejection by Hal **1**: 286, 287, 290, 312, 314, 317, 324, 333, 338, 344, 357, 366, 372, 374, 379, 380, 389, 414; **13**: 183; **25**: 109; **39**: 72, 89
    as satire of feudal society **1**: 314, 328, 361; **32**: 103
    as scapegoat **1**: 389, 414
    stage interpretations **14**: 4, 6, 7, 9, 15, 116, 130, 146; **47**: 1
    as subversive figure **16**: 183; **25**: 109
    as Vice figure **1**: 342, 361, 366, 374
  flattery **22**: 395
  gender issues **13**: 183; **25**: 151; **44**: 44; **48**: 175
  Hal

audience's perspective of **49**: 153
  and betrayal **49**: 123
  as the central character **1**: 286, 290, 314, 317, 326, 338, 354, 366, 374, 396; **39**: 72, 100
  dual personality **1**: 397, 406; **25**: 109, 151; **49**: 112, 139, 153, 162
  as Everyman **1**: 342, 366, 374
  fall from humanity **1**: 379, 380, 383
  general assessment **1**: 286, 287, 289, 290, 314, 317, 326, 327, 332, 357, 397; **25**: 245; **32**: 212; **39**: 134
  Henry's perspective of **49**: 153
  as ideal ruler **1**: 289, 309, 317, 321, 326, 337, 342, 344, 374, 389, 391, 434; **25**: 109; **39**: 123; **47**: 60
  as Machiavellian ruler **47**: 60
  as negative character **1**: 312, 332, 333, 357; **32**: 212
  as outlaw **49**: 112
  preparation for rule **49**: 112
  Richard II, compared with **1**: 332, 337; **39**: 72
  as restorer of law **49**: 133
Henry **39**: 123, 137; **49**: 139
  effectiveness as ruler **49**: 116
  guilt **49**: 112
  illegitimacy of rule **49**: 112, 133, 137
  as tragic figure **49**: 186
  as usurper **49**: 116, 137
historical content **1**: 310, 328, 365, 366, 370, 374, 380, 387, 421, 424, 427, 431; **16**: 172; **19**: 157; **25**: 151; **32**: 136; **39**: 143; **48**: 143, 167; **49**: 139
historical and dramatic elements **49**: 93
historical epic, place in or relation to Shakespeare's **1**: 309, 314, 328, 374, 379, 424, 427; **48**: 167
Hotspur **25**: 151; **28**: 101; **39**: 72, 134, 137; **42**: 101; **49**: 137
  and prisoners of war **49**: 137
  versus Henry **49**: 137
John of Lancaster, Prince
  and betrayal **49**: 123
justice **49**: 112, 123
kingship **1**: 314, 318, 337, 366, 370, 374, 379, 380, 383, 424; **16**: 172; **19**: 195; **28**: 101; **39**: 100, 116, 123, 130; **42**: 143; **48**: 143
language and imagery **13**: 213; **16**: 172; **25**: 245; **28**: 101; **39**: 116, 130; **42**: 155; **47**: 1
Lord Chief Justice
  as keeper of law and justice **49**: 133
as medieval allegory or morality play **1**: 323, 324, 342, 361, 366, 373, 374; **32**: 166; **39**: 89; **47**: 60
Mortimer **25**: 151
multiple endings **49**: 102
Neoclassical rules **1**: 286, 287, 290, 29
politics **28**: 101; **39**: 130; **42**: 143; **48**: 143, 175
power **49**: 139
psychoanalytic interpretations **13**: 457; **28**: 101; **42**: 187; **44**: 44
rebellion **22**: 395; **28**: 101
references to **22**: 114; **32**: 166; **48**: 117
relationship to other Shakespearean plays **1**: 286, 290, 309, 329, 365, 396; **28**: 101; **42**: 101, 155; **48**: 167; **49**: 93, 186
relationship of Parts 1 and 2 **32**: 136; **39**: 100; **49**: 178

religious, mythic, or spiritual content **1:** 314, 374, 414, 421, 429, 431, 434; **32:** 103; **48:** 151
   as autonomous works **1:** 289, 337, 338, 347, 348, 373, 387, 393, 411, 418, 424
   comparison **1:** 290, 295, 329, 348, 358, 393, 411, 419, 429, 431, 441
   unity of both parts **1:** 286, 290, 309, 314, 317, 329, 365, 373, 374, 396, 402, 404, 419
staging issues **32:** 212; **47:** 1; **49:** 102
structure **49:** 93
textual issues **22:** 114
time and change, motif of **1:** 372, 393, 411; **39:** 89; **48:** 143
Turkish elements **19:** 170
two fathers **14:** 86, 101, 105, 108; **39:** 89, 100; **49:** 102
violence **25:** 109

Henry V (Volumes 5, 14, 30, 49)

   battle of Agincourt **5:** 197, 199, 213, 246, 257, 281, 287, 289, 293, 310, 318; **19:** 217; **30:** 181
   Canterbury and churchmen **5:** 193, 203, 205, 213, 219, 225, 252, 260; **22:** 137; **30:** 215, 262
   characterization **5:** 186, 189, 192, 193, 199, 219, 230, 233, 252, 276, 293; **30:** 227, 278
   Chorus, role of **5:** 186, 192, 226, 228, 230, 252, 264, 269, 281, 293; **14:** 301, 319, 336; **19:** 133; **25:** 116, 131; **30:** 163, 202, 220; **49:** 194, 200, 211, 219, 260
   class distinctions, conflict, and relations **28:** 146
   colonialism **22:** 103
   comic elements **5:** 185, 188, 191, 192, 217, 230, 233, 241, 252, 260, 276; **19:** 217; **28:** 121; **30:** 193, 202,
   economic relations **13:** 213
   Elizabethan culture, relation to **5:** 210, 213, 217, 223, 257, 299, 310; **16:** 202; **19:** 133, 233; **28:** 121, 159; **30:** 215, 262; **37:** 187; **49:** 260
   English language and colonialism **22:** 103; **28:** 159
   epic elements **5:** 192, 197, 246, 257, 314; **30:** 181, 220, 237, 252
   Falstaff **5:** 185, 186, 187, 189, 192, 195, 198, 210, 226, 257, 269, 271, 276, 293, 299; **28:** 146; **46:** 48
   Fluellen **30:** 278; **37:** 105
   French aristocrats and the Dauphin **5:** 188, 191, 199, 205, 213, 281; **22:** 137; **28:** 121
   French language, Shakespeare's use of **5:** 186, 188, 190; **25:** 131
   gender issues **13:** 183; **28:** 121, 146, 159; **44:** 44
   Henry
      brutality and cunning **5:** 193, 203, 209, 210, 213, 219, 233, 239, 252, 260, 271, 287, 293, 302, 304; **30:** 159,
      characterization in 1 and 2 Henry IV contrasted **5:** 189, 190, 241, 304, 310; **19:** 133; **25:** 131; **32:** 157
      chivalry **37:** 187
      courage **5:** 191, 195, 210, 213, 228, 246, 257, 267
      disguise **30:** 169, 259

      education **5:** 246, 267, 271, 289; **14:** 297, 328, 342; **30:** 259
      emotion, lack of **5:** 209, 212, 233, 244, 264, 267, 287, 293, 310
      as heroic figure **5:** 192, 205, 209, 223, 244, 252, 257, 260, 269, 271, 299, 304; **28:** 121, 146; **30:** 237, 244, 252; **37:** 187; **49:** 194, 200, 236, 247
      humor **5:** 189, 191, 212, 217, 239, 240, 276
      intellectual and social limitations **5:** 189, 191, 203, 209, 210, 225, 226, 230, 293; **30:** 220
      interpersonal relations **5:** 209, 233, 267, 269, 276, 287, 293, 302, 318; **19:** 133; **28:** 146
      mercy **5:** 213, 267, 289, 293
      mixture of good and bad qualities **5:** 199, 205, 209, 210, 213, 244, 260, 304, 314; **30:** 262, 273; **49:** 211
      piety **5:** 191, 199, 209, 217, 223, 239, 257, 260, 271, 289, 310, 318; **30:** 244; **32:** 126
      public versus private selves **22:** 137; **30:** 169, 207
      self-doubt **5:** 281, 310
      slaughter of prisoners **5:** 189, 205, 246, 293, 318; **28:** 146
      speech **5:** 212, 230, 233, 246, 264, 276, 287, 302; **28:** 146; **30:** 163, 227
   heroism **49:** 194, 200, 211, 236
   historical content **5:** 185, 188, 190, 192, 193, 198, 246, 314; **13:** 201; **19:** 133; **25:** 131; **30:** 193, 202, 207, 215, 252; **49:** 223
   historical epic, place in or relation to Shakespeare's **5:** 195, 198, 205, 212, 225, 241, 244, 287, 304, 310; **14:** 337, 342; **30:** 215
   homoerotic elements **16:** 202
   Hotspur **5:** 189, 199, 228, 271, 302
   hypocrisy **5:** 203, 213, 219, 223, 233, 260, 271, 302
   imperialism **22:** 103; **28:** 159
   Irish affairs **22:** 103; **28:** 159
   irony **5:** 192, 210, 213, 219, 223, 226, 233, 252, 260, 269, 281, 299, 304; **14:** 336; **30:** 159, 193,
   Katherine **5:** 186, 188, 189, 190, 192, 260, 269, 299, 302; **13:** 183; **19:** 217; **30:** 278; **44:** 44
   kingship **5:** 205, 223, 225, 233, 239, 244, 257, 264, 267, 271, 287, 289, 299, 302, 304, 314, 318; **16:** 202; **22:** 137; **30:** 169, 202, 259, 273; **49:** 200
   language and imagery **5:** 188, 230, 233, 241, 264, 276; **19:** 203; **25:** 131; **30:** 159, 181, 207, 234
   law and justice **49:** 223, 226, 260
   Machiavellianism **5:** 203, 225, 233, 252, 287, 304; **25:** 131; **30:** 273
   MacMorris **22:** 103; **28:** 159; **30:** 278
   Marlowe's works, compared with **19:** 233
   metadramatic elements **13:** 194; **30:** 181; **49:** 200, 211
   Mistress Quickly **5:** 186, 187, 210, 276, 293; **30:** 278
   morality **5:** 195, 203, 213, 223, 225, 239, 246, 260, 271, 293
   obscenity **5:** 188, 190, 260
   order **5:** 205, 257, 264, 310, 314; **30:** 193,
   patriarchy **37:** 105; **44:** 44
   politics and ideology **49:** 219, 247, 260
   nationalism and patriotism **5:** 198, 205, 209, 210, 213, 219, 223, 233, 246, 252, 257,

269, 299; **19:** 133, 217; **30:** 227, 262; **49:** 219, 247
   Pistol **28:** 146
   power **37:** 175
   psychoanalytic interpretations **13:** 457; **44:** 44
   religious, mythic, or religious content **25:** 116; **32:** 126
   Salic Law **5:** 219, 252, 260; **28:** 121
   self-interest or expediency **5:** 189, 193, 205, 213, 217, 233, 260, 287, 302, 304; **30:** 273; **49:** 223
   soldiers **5:** 203, 239, 267, 276, 281, 287, 293, 318; **28:** 146; **30:** 169; **49:** 194
   staging issues **5:** 186, 189, 192, 193, 198, 205, 226, 230, 241, 281, 314; **13:** 194, 502; **14:** 293, 295, 297, 301, 310, 319, 328, 334, 336, 342; **19:** 217; **32:** 185
   structure **5:** 186, 189, 205, 213, 230, 241, 264, 289, 310, 314; **30:** 220, 227, 234, 244
   tetralogy, relation to **49:** 223
   textual problems **5:** 187, 189, 190; **13:** 201
   topical allusions or content **5:** 185, 186; **13:** 201
   tragic elements **5:** 228, 233, 267, 269, 271
   traitors (Scroop, Grey, and Cambridge) **16:** 202; **30:** 220, 278
      Southampton conspiracy **49:** 223
   Turkish elements **19:** 170
   violence **43:** 24
   war **5:** 193, 195, 197, 198, 210, 213, 219, 230, 233, 246, 281, 293; **28:** 121, 146; **30:** 262; **32:** 126; **37:** 175, 187; **42:** 143; **49:** 194, 236, 247, 260
   Williams **13:** 502; **16:** 183; **28:** 146; **30:** 169, 259, 278
   wooing scene (Act V, scene ii) **5:** 186, 188, 189, 191, 193, 195, 260, 276, 299, 302; **14:** 297; **28:** 121, 159; **30:** 163, 207

Henry VI, Parts 1, 2, and 3 (Volumes 3, 24, 39)

   ambivalent or ironic elements **3:** 69, 151, 154; **39:** 160
   authorship controversy **3:** 16, 18, 19, 20, 21, 26, 27, 29, 31, 35, 39, 41, 55, 66; **24:** 51
   autobiographical elements **3:** 41, 55
   Bordeaux sequence **37:** 165
   Cade scenes **3:** 35, 67, 92, 97, 109; **16:** 183; **22:** 156; **25:** 102; **28:** 112; **37:** 97; **39:** 160, 196, 205; **50:** 45, 51
   carnival elements **22:** 156
   characterization **3:** 18, 20, 24, 25, 31, 57, 64, 73, 77, 109, 119, 151; **24:** 22, 28, 38, 42, 45, 47; **39:** 160
   class distinctions, conflict, and relations **37:** 97; **39:** 187; **50:** 45, 51
   dance **22:** 156
   decay of heroic ideals **3:** 119, 126
   disorder and civil dissension **3:** 59, 67, 76, 92, 103, 126; **13:** 131; **16:** 183; **24:** 11, 17, 28, 31, 47; **25:** 102; **28:** 112; **39:** 154, 177, 187, 196, 205
   Elizabethan literary and cultural influences **3:** 75, 97, 100, 119, 143; **22:** 156; **28:** 112; **37:** 97
   Folk rituals, elements and influence of **39:** 205
   Henry
      characterization **3:** 64, 77, 151; **39:** 160, 177; **47:** 32

source of social disorder **3:** 25, 31, 41, 115; **39:** 154, 187
  as sympathetic figure **3:** 73, 143, 154; **24:** 32
historical accuracy **3:** 18, 21, 35, 46, 51; **16:** 217; **24:** 16, 18, 25, 31, 45, 48
historical epic, place in or relation to Shakespeare's **3:** 24, 59; **24:** 51
as humanistic play **3:** 83, 92, 109, 115, 119, 131, 136, 143
Humphrey **13:** 131
as inferior or flawed plays **3:** 20, 21, 25, 26, 35
Joan of Arc **16:** 131; **32:** 212
kingship **3:** 69, 73, 77, 109, 115, 136, 143; **24:** 32; **39:** 154, 177, 187; **47:** 32
language and imagery **3:** 21, 50, 52, 55, 57, 66, 67, 71, 75, 76, 97, 105, 109, 119, 126, 131; **24:** 28; **37:** 157; **39:** 213, 222
legitimacy **3:** 89, 157; **39:** 154,
Machiavellianism **22:** 193
Margaret
  characterization **3:** 18, 26, 35, 51, 103, 109, 140, 157; **24:** 48
  Suffolk, relationship with **3:** 18, 24, 26, 157; **39:** 213
Marlowe's works, compared with **19:** 233
medieval literary influence **3:** 59, 67, 75, 100, 109, 136, 151; **13:** 131
molehill scene (3 Henry VI, Act III, scene ii) **3:** 75, 97, 126, 149
moral inheritance **3:** 89, 126
multiple perspectives of characters **3:** 69, 154
Neoclassical rules **3:** 17, 18
patriarchal claims **16:** 131 **25:** 102
nationalism and patriotism **24:** 25, 45, 47
play-within-the-play, convention of **3:** 75, 149
retribution **3:** 27, 42, 51, 59, 77, 83, 92, 100, 109, 115, 119, 131, 136, 151
Richard of Gloucester
  characterization **3:** 35, 48, 57, 64, 77, 143, 151; **22:** 193; **39:** 160, 177
  as revenger **22:** 193
  soliloquy (3 Henry VI, Act III, scene ii) **3:** 17, 48
sibling rivalry **22:** 193
sources **3:** 18, 21, 29, 31, 35, 39, 46, 51; **13:** 131; **16:** 217; **39:** 196
staging issues **24:** 21, 22, 27, 31, 32, 36, 38, 41, 45, 48, 55; **32:** 212
structure **3:** 31, 43, 46, 69, 83, 103, 109, 119, 136, 149, 154; **39:** 213
Talbot **39:** 160, 213, 222
textual arrangement **24:** 3, 4, 6, 12, 17, 18, 19, 20, 21, 24, 27, 42, 45; **37:** 165
theatrical viability **24:** 31, 32, 34
Tudor myth **3:** 51, 59, 77, 92, 100, 109, 115, 119, 131; **39:** 222
Unity **39:** 177, 222
violence **24:** 25, 31; **37:** 157
women, role of **3:** 103, 109, 126, 140, 157; **16:** 183; **39:** 196
York's death **13:** 131

Henry VIII (Volumes 2, 24, 41)

ambition or pride **2:** 15, 38, 67
authorship controversy **2:** 16, 18, 19, 22, 23, 27, 28, 31, 35, 36, 42, 43, 44, 46, 48, 51, 58, 64, 68; **41:** 129, 146, 158, 171,
Anne Boleyn **2:** 21, 24, 31; **41:** 180
Buckingham **22:** 182; **24:** 129, 140; **37:** 109
change **2:** 27, 65, 72, 81
characterization **2:** 17, 23, 25, 32, 35, 39; **24:** 106
composition date **2:** 19, 22, 35; **24:** 129
costumes **24:** 82, 87; **28:** 184
Cranmer's prophecy **2:** 25, 31, 46, 56, 64, 68, 72; **24:** 146; **32:** 148; **41:** 120, 190
Cymbeline, compared with **2:** 67, 71
discrepancy between prophetic ending and preceding action **2:** 22, 25, 31, 46, 49, 56, 60, 65, 68, 75, 81; **32:** 148; **41:** 190
Elizabethan politics, relation to **22:** 395; **24:** 115, 129, 140; **32:** 148
Elizabethan dramatic conventions **24:** 155
English Reformation, influence of **2:** 25, 35, 39, 51, 67; **24:** 89
flattery **22:** 395
historical and romantic elements, combination of **41:** 129, 146, 180
historical epic, as epilogue to Shakespeare's **2:** 22, 25, 27, 39, 51, 60, 65
historical relativity, theme of **41:** 146
King Henry
  as agent of divine retribution **2:** 49
  characterization **2:** 23, 39, 51, 58, 60, 65, 66, 75; **28:** 184; **37:** 109
  incomplete portrait **2:** 15, 16, 19, 35; **41:** 120
  as realistic figure **2:** 21, 22, 23, 25, 32
historical and romantic elements, combination of **2:** 46, 49, 51, 75, 76, 78; **24:** 71, 80, 146
historiography **37:** 109
inconsistencies **2:** 16, 27, 28, 31, 60
ironic aspects **41:** 129
Katherine
  characterization **2:** 18, 19, 23, 24, 38; **24:** 129; **37:** 109; **41:** 180
  Hermione, compared with **2:** 24, 51, 58, 76
  politeness strategies **22:** 182
  religious discourse **22:** 182
  as tragic figure **2:** 16, 18
kingship **2:** 49, 58, 60, 65, 75, 78; **24:** 113; **41:** 129, 171
language and imagery **41:** 180, 190
legitimacy **37:** 109
moral intent **2:** 15, 19, 25; **24:** 140
Norfolk **22:** 182
pageantry **2:** 14, 15, 18, 51, 58; **24:** 77, 83, 84, 85, 89, 91, 106, 113, 118, 120, 126, 127, 140, 146, 150; **41:** 120, 129, 190
patience **2:** 58, 76, 78
politics **2:** 39, 49, 51, 58, 60, 65, 67, 71, 72, 75, 78, 81; **24:** 74, 121, 124; **41:** 146
Porter **24:** 155
rebellion **22:** 395
rhetoric of politeness **22:** 182
Shakespeare's romances, compared with **2:** 46, 51, 58, 66, 67, 71, 76; **41:** 171
sources **2:** 16, 17; **24:** 71, 80
staging issues **24:** 67, 70, 71, 75, 77, 83, 84, 85, 87, 89, 91, 101, 106, 113, 120, 127, 129, 136, 140, 146, 150, 152, 155; **28:** 184
Stephen Gardiner **24:** 129
structure **2:** 16, 25, 27, 28, 31, 36, 44, 46, 51, 56, 68, 75; **24:** 106, 112, 113, 120
style **41:** 158
thematic disparity **2:** 25, 31, 56, 68, 75; **41:** 146
tragedies of major characters **2:** 16, 39, 46, 48, 49, 51, 56, 58, 68, 81; **41:** 120
wheel of fortune, motif of **2:** 27, 65, 72, 81
Cardinal Wolsey **2:** 15, 18, 19, 23, 24, 38; **22:** 182; **24:** 80, 91, 112, 113, 129, 140; **37:** 109; **41:** 129

Julius Caesar (Volumes 7, 17, 30, 50)

anachronisms **7:** 331
Antony
  characterization **7:** 160, 179, 189, 221, 233, 284, 320, 333; **17:** 269, 271, 272, 284, 298, 306, 313, 315, 358, 398; **25:** 272; **30:** 316
  funeral oration **7:** 148, 154, 159, 204, 210, 221, 238, 259, 350; **25:** 280; **30:** 316, 333, 362
aristocratic values **16:** 231; **22:** 280; **30:** 379; **50:** 194, 196, 211
the assassination **7:** 156, 161, 179, 191, 200, 221, 264, 272, 279, 284, 350; **25:** 272; **30:** 326
audience interpretation **48:** 240
audience response **7:** 179, 238, 253, 255, 272, 316, 320, 336, 350; **19:** 321; **48:** 240
Brutus **50:** 194, 258
  arrogance **7:** 160, 169, 204, 207, 264, 277, 292, 350; **25:** 280; **30:** 351
  as chief protagonist or tragic hero **7:** 152, 159, 189, 191, 200, 204, 242, 250, 253, 264, 268, 279, 284, 298, 333; **17:** 272, 372, 387
  citizenship **25:** 272
  funeral oration **7:** 154, 155, 204, 210, 350
  motives **7:** 150, 156, 161, 179, 191, 200, 221, 227, 233, 245, 292, 303, 310, 320, 333, 350; **25:** 272; **30:** 321, 358
  nobility or idealism **7:** 150, 152, 156, 159, 161, 179, 189, 191, 200, 221, 242, 250, 253, 259, 264, 277, 303, 320; **17:** 269, 271, 273, 279, 280, 284, 306, 308, 321, 323, 324, 345, 358; **25:** 272, 280; **30:** 351, 362; **50:** 194
  political ineptitude or lack of judgment **7:** 169, 188, 200, 205, 221, 245, 252, 264, 277, 282, 310, 316, 331, 333, 343; **17:** 323, 358, 375, 380; **50:** 13
  self-knowledge or self-deception **7:** 191, 200, 221, 242, 259, 264, 268, 279, 310, 333, 336, 350; **25:** 272; **30:** 316
  soliloquy (Act II, scene i) **7:** 156, 160, 161, 191, 221, 245, 250, 253, 264, 268, 279, 282, 292, 303, 343, 350; **25:** 280; **30:** 333
Caesar **50:** 189, 230, 234
  ambiguous nature **7:** 191, 233, 242, 250, 272, 298, 316, 320
  ambitious nature **50:** 234
  arrogance **7:** 160, 207, 218, 253, 272, 279, 298; **25:** 280
  idolatry **22:** 137
  leadership qualities **7:** 161, 179, 189, 191, 200, 207, 233, 245, 253, 257, 264, 272, 279, 284, 298, 310, 333; **17:** 317, 358; **22:** 280; **30:** 316, 326; **50:** 234
  as tragic hero **7:** 152, 200, 221, 279; **17:** 321, 377, 384
  weakness **7:** 161, 167, 169, 179, 187, 188, 191, 207, 218, 221, 233, 250, 253, 298; **17:** 358; **25:** 280
Caesarism **7:** 159, 160, 161, 167, 169, 174, 191, 205, 218, 253, 310; **30:** 316, 321; **50:** 196, 234

Calphurnia
  dream **45:** 10
Casca
  as Cynic **50:** 249
  as proto-Christian **50:** 249
Cassius **7:** 156, 159, 160, 161, 169, 179, 189, 221, 233, 303, 310, 320, 333, 343; **17:** 272, 282, 284, 344, 345, 358; **25:** 272, 280; **30:** 351; **37:** 203
ceremonies, rites, and rituals, importance of **7:** 150, 210, 255, 259, 268, 284, 316, 331, 339, 356; **13:** 260; **22:** 137; **30:** 374; **50:** 258, 269
construing the truth **7:** 320, 336, 343, 350; **37:** 229
Elizabethan culture, relation to **16:** 231; **30:** 342, 379; **50:** 13, 211, 269, 280
emulation or rivalry **16:** 231
Epicureanism **50:** 249
Flavius and Murellus **50:** 64
gender issues **13:** 260
historical determinism versus free will **7:** 160, 298, 316, 333, 346, 356; **13:** 252
irony or ambiguity **7:** 167, 257, 259, 262, 268, 282, 316, 320, 333, 336, 346, 350
language and imagery **7:** 148, 155, 159, 188, 204, 207, 227, 242, 250, 277, 296, 303, 324, 346, 350; **13:** 260; **17:** 347, 348, 350, 356, 358; **19:** 321; **22:** 280; **25:** 280; **30:** 333, 342; **50:** 196, 258
liberty versus tyranny **7:** 158, 179, 189, 205, 221, 253; **25:** 272
love and friendship **7:** 233, 262, 268; **25:** 272
medieval physiology **13:** 260
moral choice **7:** 179, 264, 279, 343
Octavius **30:** 316
omens **22:** 137; **45:** 10; **50:** 265, 280
patricians versus plebeians **50:** 189, 196
philosophical elements **7:** 310, 324; **37:** 203
plebeians versus tribunes **50:** 230
the poets **7:** 179, 320, 350
politics **7:** 161, 169, 191, 205, 218, 221, 245, 262, 264, 279, 282, 310, 324, 333, 346; **17:** 317, 318, 321, 323, 334, 350, 351, 358, 378, 382, 394, 406; **22:** 137, 280; **25:** 272, 280; **30:** 285, 297, 316, 321, 342, 374, 379; **37:** 203; **50:** 13
as "problem play" **7:** 272, 320
psychoanalytic interpretation **45:** 10
public versus private principles **7:** 161, 179, 252, 262, 268, 284, 298; **13:** 252
quarrel scene (Act IV, scene iii) **7:** 149, 150, 152, 153, 155, 160, 169, 188, 191, 204, 268, 296, 303, 310
retribution **7:** 160, 167, 200
revenge tragedy elements **7:** 316
role-playing **7:** 356; **37:** 229
Roman citizenry, portrayal of **7:** 169, 179, 210, 221, 245, 279, 282, 310, 320, 333; **17:** 271, 279, 288, 291, 292, 298, 323, 334, 351, 367, 374, 375, 378; **22:** 280; **30:** 285, 297, 316, 321, 374, 379; **37:** 229; **50:** 230
Senecan elements **37:** 229
Shakespeare's English history plays, compared with **7:** 161, 189, 218, 221, 252; **22:** 137; **30:** 369
Shakespeare's major tragedies, compared with **7:** 161, 188, 227, 242, 264, 268
sources **7:** 149, 150, 156, 187, 200, 264, 272, 282, 284, 320; **30:** 285, 297, 326, 358
staging **48:** 240; **50:** 186
Stoicism **50:** 249
structure **7:** 152, 155, 159, 160, 179, 200, 210, 238, 264, 284, 298, 316, 346; **13:** 252; **30:** 374
tragic elements **50:** 258, 265
violence **48:** 240

King John (Volumes 9, 24, 41)

ambiguity **13:** 152; **41:** 243
anti-catholic rhetoric **22:** 120; **25:** 98
Arthur **9:** 215, 216, 218, 219, 229, 240, 267, 275; **22:** 120; **25:** 98; **41:** 251, 277
autobiographical elements **9:** 209, 218, 245, 248, 260, 292
characterization **9:** 222, 224, 229, 240, 250, 292; **41:** 205, 215
church versus state **9:** 209, 212, 222, 235, 240; **22:** 120
commodity or self-interest **9:** 224, 229, 245, 260, 275, 280, 297; **19:** 182; **25:** 98; **41:** 228
commodity versus honor **41:** 269
Constance **9:** 208, 210, 211, 215, 219, 220, 224, 229, 240, 251, 254; **16:** 161; **24:** 177, 184, 196
corruption in society **9:** 222, 234, 280, 297
Elizabethan politics, relation to **48:** 132
ethical or moral issues **9:** 212, 222, 224, 229, 235, 240, 263, 275, 280
excess **9:** 251
Faulconbridge, the Bastard **41:** 205, 228, 251, 260, 277
  as chorus or commentator **9:** 212, 218, 229, 248, 251, 260, 271, 284, 297, 300; **22:** 120
  as comic figure **9:** 219, 271, 297
  development **9:** 216, 224, 229, 248, 263, 271, 275, 280, 297; **13:** 158, 163
  as embodiment of England **9:** 222, 224, 240, 244, 248, 271
  heroic qualities **9:** 208, 245, 248, 254, 263, 271, 275; **25:** 98
  political conduct **9:** 224, 240, 250, 260, 280, 297; **13:** 147, 158; **22:** 120
Henry **41:** 277
historical content **9:** 216, 219, 220, 222, 235, 240, 254, 284, 290, 292, 297, 300, 303; **13:** 163; **32:** 93, 114; **41:** 234, 243
John **41:** 205, 260
  death, decay, and nature's destructiveness **9:** 212, 215, 216, 240
  decline **9:** 224, 235, 240, 263, 275
  Hubert, scene with (Act III, scene iii) **9:** 210, 212, 216, 218, 219, 280
  moral insensibility **13:** 147, 163
  negative qualities **9:** 209, 212, 218, 219, 229, 234, 235, 244, 245, 246, 250, 254, 275, 280, 297
  positive qualities **9:** 209, 224, 235, 240, 244, 245, 263
kingship **9:** 235, 254, 263, 275, 297; **13:** 158; **19:** 182; **22:** 120
language and imagery **9:** 212, 215, 220, 246, 251, 254, 267, 280, 284, 292, 297, 300; **13:** 147, 158; **22:** 120; **37:** 132; **48:** 132
legitimacy or inheritance **9:** 224, 235, 254, 303; **13:** 147; **19:** 182; **37:** 132; **41:** 215
Neoclassical rules **9:** 208, 209, 210, 212
oppositions or dualisms **9:** 224, 240, 263, 275, 284, 290, 300
Papal Tyranny in the Reign of King John (Colley Cibber adaptation) **24:** 162, 163, 165

nationalism and patriotism **9:** 209, 218, 222, 224, 235, 240, 244, 275; **25:** 98; **37:** 132
politics **9:** 218, 224, 260, 280; **13:** 163; **22:** 120; **37:** 132; **41:** 221, 228
rebellion **9:** 218, 254, 263, 280, 297
Roman citizenry, portrayal of **50:** 64
Shakespeare's other history plays, compared with **9:** 218, 254; **13:** 152, 158; **25:** 98
sources **9:** 216, 222, 300; **32:** 93, 114; **41:** 234, 243, 251
staging issues **16:** 161; **19:** 182; **24:** 171, 187, 203, 206, 211, 225, 228, 241, 245, 249
structure **9:** 208, 212, 222, 224, 229, 240, 244, 245, 254, 260, 263, 275, 284, 290, 292, 300; **24:** 228, 241; **41:** 260, 269, 277
tragic elements **9:** 208, 209, 244
treachery **9:** 245
The Troublesome Reign (anonymous), compared with **9:** 216, 244, 260, 292; **22:** 120; **32:** 93; **41:** 205, 221, 260, 269; **48:** 132
Tudor doctrine **9:** 254, 284, 297; **41:** 221
tyranny **9:** 218
women, role of **9:** 222, 303; **16:** 161; **19:** 182; **41:** 205, 221

King Lear (Volumes 2, 11, 31, 46)

Albany **32:** 308
allegorical elements **16:** 311
audience perception **19:** 295; **28:** 325
autobiographical elements **2:** 131, 136, 149, 165
characterization **2:** 108, 125, 145, 162, 191; **16:** 311; **28:** 223; **46:** 177, 210
Christian elements **2:** 137, 170, 179, 188, 191, 197, 207, 218, 222, 226, 229, 238, 249, 265, 286; **22:** 233, 271; **25:** 218; **46:** 276; **49:** 67; **52:** 95
as Christian play **48:** 222
Clarissa (Samuel Richardson), compared with **48:** 277
combat scenes **22:** 365
comic and tragic elements, combination of **2:** 108, 110, 112, 125, 156, 162, 245, 278, 284; **46:** 191
Cordelia
  attack on Britain **25:** 202
  characterization **2:** 110, 116, 125, 170; **16:** 311; **25:** 218; **28:** 223, 325; **31:** 117, 149, 155, 162; **46:** 225, 231, 242
  as Christ figure **2:** 116, 170, 179, 188, 222, 286
  rebelliousness **13:** 352; **25:** 202
  self-knowledge **46:** 218
  on stage **11:** 158
  transcendent power **2:** 137, 207, 218, 265, 269, 273
cruelty of daughters **2:** 101, 102, 106; **31:** 84, 123, 137, 142
death, decay, and nature's destructiveness **2:** 93, 94, 101, 104, 106, 109, 112, 116, 129, 131, 137, 143, 147, 149, 156, 160, 170, 179, 188, 197, 207, 218, 222, 226, 231, 238, 241, 245, 249, 253, 265, 269, 273; **16:** 301; **25:** 202, 218; **31:** 77, 117, 137, 142; **46:** 264
double-plot **2:** 94, 95, 100, 101, 104, 112, 116, 124, 131, 133, 156, 253, 257; **46:** 254
Dover Cliff scene **2:** 156, 229, 255, 269; **11:** 8, 151

Edgar **28:** 223; **32:** 212; **32:** 308; **37:** 295; **47:** 9; **50:** 24, 45
Edgar-Edmund duel **22:** 365
Edmund **25:** 218; **28:** 223
Edmund's forged letter **16:** 372
Elizabethan culture, relation to **2:** 168, 174, 177, 183, 226, 241; **19:** 330; **22:** 227, 233, 365; **25:** 218; **46:** 276; **47:** 9; **49:** 67
ethical and moral issues **52:** 1
Fool **2:** 108, 112, 125, 156, 162, 245, 278, 284; **11:** 17, 158, 169; **22:** 227; **25:** 202; **28:** 223; **46:** 1, 14, 18, 24, 33, 52, 191, 205, 210, 218, 225
Gloucester **46:** 254
Goneril **31:** 151; **46:** 231, 242
grotesque or absurd elements **2:** 136, 156, 245; **13:** 343; **52:** 1
implausibility or plot, characters, or events **2:** 100, 136, 145, 278; **13:** 343
Job, compared with **2:** 226, 241, 245; **25:** 218
justice, divine vs. worldly **49:** 1, 67, 73
Kent **25:** 202; **28:** 223; **32:** 212; **47:** 9
language and imagery **2:** 129, 137, 161, 191, 199, 237, 257, 271; **16:** 301; **19:** 344; **22:** 233; **46:** 177
Lear
  curse on Goneril **11:** 5, 7, 12, 114, 116
  love-test and division of kingdom **2:** 100, 106, 111, 124, 131, 137, 147, 149, 151, 168, 186, 208, 216, 281; **16:** 351; **25:** 202; **31:** 84, 92, 107, 117, 149, 155; **46:** 231, 242
  madness **2:** 94, 95, 98, 99, 100, 101, 102, 103, 111, 116, 120, 124, 125, 149, 156, 191, 208, 216, 281; **46:** 264
  as scapegoat **2:** 241, 253
  self-knowledge **2:** 103, 151, 188, 191, 213, 218, 222, 241, 249, 262; **25:** 218; **37:** 213; **46:** 191, 205, 225, 254, 264,
legal issues **46:** 276
love **2:** 109, 112, 131, 160, 162, 170, 179, 188, 197, 218, 222, 238, 265; **25:** 202; **31:** 77, 149, 151, 155, 162
madness **19:** 330
Marxist criticism **42:** 234
medieval or morality drama, influence of **2:** 177, 188, 201; **25:** 218
misogyny **31:** 123
moral or ethical issues **52:** 95
nihilistic or pessimistic vision **2:** 130, 143, 149, 156, 165, 231, 238, 245, 253; **22:** 271; **25:** 218; **28:** 325; **49:** 67
pagan elements **25:** 218
patriarchal or monarchical order **13:** 353, 457; **16:** 351; **22:** 227, 233; **25:** 218; **31:** 84, 92, 107, 117, 123, 137, 142; **46:** 269
performance issues **2:** 106, 137, 154, 160; **11:** 10, 20, 27, 56, 57, 132, 136, 137, 145, **150, 154; 19:** 295, 344; **25:** 218
poetic justice, question of **2:** 92, 93, 94, 101, 129, 137, 231, 245; **49:** 73
politics **46:** 269; **50:** 45
providential order **2:** 112, 116, 137, 168, 170, 174, 177, 218, 226, 241, 253; **22:** 271; **49:** 1, 73
Regan **31:** 151; **46:** 231, 242
rhetorical style **16:** 301; **47:** 9
romantic elements **31:** 77, 84
sexuality **25:** 202; **31:** 133, 137, 142

social and moral corruption **2:** 116, 133, 174, 177, 241, 271; **22:** 227; **31:** 84, 92; **46:** 269
sources **2:** 94, 100, 143, 145, 170, 186; **13:** 352; **16:** 351; **28:** 301
staging issues **11:** 1-178; **32:** 212; **46:** 205, 218
structure **28:** 325; **32:** 308; **46:** 177
suffering **2:** 137, 160, 188, 201, 218, 222, 226, 231, 238, 241, 249, 265; **13:** 343; **22:** 271; **25:** 218; **50:** 24
Tate's adaptation **2:** 92, 93, 94, 101, 102, 104, 106, 110, 112, 116, 137; **11:** 10, 136; **25:** 218; **31:** 162
textual issues **22:** 271; **37:** 295; **49:** 73
Timon of Athens, relation to **16:** 351
Virgo vs. Virago **48:** 222
wisdom **37:** 213; **46:** 210

Love's Labour's Lost (Volumes 2, 23, 38)

Armado **23:** 207
artificial nature **2:** 315, 317, 324, 330; **23:** 207, 233
authorship controversy **2:** 299, 300; **32:** 308
Berowne **2:** 308, 324, 327; **22:** 12; **23:** 184, 187; **38:** 194; **47:** 35
characterization **2:** 303, 310, 317, 322, 328, 342; **23:** 237, 250, 252; **38:** 232; **47:** 35
as comedy of affectation **2:** 302, 303, 304; **23:** 191, 224, 226, 228, 233
comic resolution **2:** 335, 340; **16:** 17; **19:** 92; **38:** 209; **51:** 1
conclusion **38:** 172
dance and patterned action **2:** 308, 342; **23:** 191, 237
death, decay, and nature's destructiveness **2:** 305, 331, 344, 348
desire **38:** 185, 194, 200, 209
dramatic shortcomings or failure **2:** 299, 301, 303, 322
Elizabeth I **38:** 239
Elizabethan love poetry **38:** 232
feminist criticism **42:** 93
genre **38:** 163
gift exchange **25:** 1
grace and civility **2:** 351
Holofernes **23:** 207
illusion versus reality **2:** 303, 308, 331, 340, 344, 348, 356, 359, 367, 371, 375; **23:** 230, 231
knowledge **22:** 12; **47:** 35
language and imagery **2:** 301, 302, 303, 306, 307, 308, 315, 319, 320, 330, 335, 344, 345, 348, 356, 359, 362, 365, 371, 374, 375; **19:** 92; **22:** 12, 378; **23:** 184, 187, 196, 197, 202, 207, 211, 221, 227, 231, 233, 237, 252; **28:** 9, 63; **38:** 219, 226
love **2:** 312, 315, 340, 344; **22:** 12; **23:** 252; **38:** 194; **51:** 44
male domination **22:** 12
male sexual anxiety **16:** 17
marriage **2:** 335, 340; **19:** 92; **38:** 209, 232; **51:** 1, 44
metadramatic elements **2:** 356, 359, 362
Neoclassical rules **2:** 299, 300
as satire or parody **2:** 300, 302, 303, 307, 308, 315, 321, 324, 327; **23:** 237, 252
physical versus intellectual world **2:** 331, 348, 367
public versus private speech **2:** 356, 362, 371

School of Night, allusions to **2:** 321, 327, 328
sexuality **22:** 12; **51:** 44
songs, role of **2:** 303, 304, 316, 326, 335, 362, 367, 371, 375
sources **16:** 17
spectacle **38:** 226
staging issues **23:** 184, 187, 191, 196, 198, 200, 201, 202, 207, 212, 215, 216, 217, 229, 230, 232, 233, 237, 252
structure **22:** 378; **23:** 191, 237, 252; **38:** 163, 172
theme
  idealism versus realism **38:** 163
topical allusions or content **2:** 300, 303, 307, 315, 316, 317, 319, 321, 327, 328; **23:** 187, 191, 197, 203, 221, 233, 237, 252; **25:** 1
unnatural ordering **22:** 378
violence **22:** 12
visual humor **23:** 207, 217
Watteau, influence on staging **23:** 184, 186
women, role of **19:** 92; **22:** 12; **23:** 215; **25:** 1
written versus oral communication **2:** 359, 365; **28:** 63

Macbeth (Volumes 3, 20, 29, 44)

antithetical or contradictory elements **3:** 185, 213, 271, 302; **25:** 235; **29:** 76, 127; **47:** 41
appearance versus reality **3:** 241, 248; **25:** 235
archetypal or mythic elements **16:** 317
audience response **20:** 17, 400, 406; **29:** 139, 146, 155, 165; **44:** 306
banquet scene (Act III, scene iv) **20:** 22, 32, 175
Banquo **3:** 183, 199, 208, 213, 278, 289; **20:** 279, 283, 406, 413; **25:** 235; **28:** 339
characterization **20:** 12, 318, 324, 329, 353, 363, 367, 374, 387; **28:** 339; **29:** 101, 109, 146, 155, 165; **44:** 289; **47:** 41
Christian elements **3:** 194, 239, 260, 269, 275, 286, 293, 297, 318; **20:** 203, 206, 210, 256, 262, 289, 291, 294; **44:** 341, 366; **47:** 41
combat scenes **22:** 365
conscience **52:** 15
dagger scene (Act III, scene i), staging of **20:** 406
evil **3:** 194, 208, 231, 234, 239, 241, 267, 289; **20:** 203, 206, 210, 374; **52:** 23
free will versus fate **3:** 177, 183, 184, 190, 196, 198, 202, 207, 208, 213; **13:** 361; **44:** 351, 361, 366, 373
innocence **3:** 234, 241, 327
Jacobean culture, relation to **19:** 330; **22:** 365
Lady Macbeth
  ambition **3:** 185, 219; **20:** 279, 345
  characterization **20:** 56, 60, 65, 73, 140, 148, 151, 241, 279, 283, 338, 350, 406, 413; **29:** 109, 146
  childlessness **3:** 219, 223
  good and evil, combined traits of **3:** 173, 191, 213; **20:** 60, 107
  inconsistencies **3:** 202; **20:** 54, 137
  influence on Macbeth **3:** 171, 185, 191, 193, 199, 262, 289, 312, 318; **13:** 502; **20:** 345; **25:** 235; **29:** 133

psychoanalytic interpretations **20:** 345; **44:** 289, 297, 324; **45:** 58
as sympathetic figure **3:** 191, 193, 203
language and imagery **3:** 170, 193, 213, 231, 234, 241, 245, 250, 253, 256, 263, 271, 283, 300, 302, 306, 323, 327, 338, 340, 349; **13:** 476; **16:** 317; **20:** 241, 279, 283, 367, 379, 400; **25:** 235; **28:** 339; **29:** 76, 91; **42:** 263; **44:** 366; **45:** 58
laws of nature, violation of **3:** 234, 241, 280, 323; **29:** 120
letter to Lady Macbeth **16:** 372; **20:** 345; **25:** 235
Macbeth
   ambition **44:** 284, 324
   characterization **20:** 20, 42, 73, 107, 113, 130, 146, 151, 279, 283, 312, 338, 343, 379, 406, 413; **29:** 139, 152, 155, 165; **44:** 289
   courage **3:** 172, 177, 181, 182, 183, 186, 234, 312, 333; **20:** 107; **44:** 315
   disposition **3:** 173, 175, 177, 182, 186; **20:** 245, 376
   imagination **3:** 196, 208, 213, 250, 312, 345; **20:** 245, 376; **44:** 351
   as "inauthentic" king **3:** 245, 302, 321, 345
   inconsistencies **3:** 202
   as Machiavellian villain **3:** 280
   manliness **20:** 113; **29:** 127, 133; **44:** 315
   psychoanalytic interpretations **20:** 42, 73, 238, 376; **44:** 284, 289, 297, 324; **45:** 48, 58
   Richard III, compared with **3:** 177, 182, 186, 345; **20:** 86, 92; **22:** 365; **44:** 269
   as Satan figure **3:** 229, 269, 275, 289, 318
   self-awareness **3:** 312, 329, 338; **16:** 317; **44:** 361
   as sympathetic figure **3:** 229, 306, 314, 338; **29:** 139, 152; **44:** 269, 306, 337
   as tragic hero **44:** 269, 306, 315, 324, 337
Macduff **3:** 226, 231, 253, 262,; **25:** 235; **29:** 127, 133, 155
Machiavellianism **52:** 29
madness **19:** 330
major tragedies, relation to Shakespeare's other **3:** 171, 173, 213; **44:** 269
Malcolm **25:** 235
manhood **3:** 262, 309, 333; **29:** 127, 133
Marxist criticism **42:** 234
medieval mystery plays, relation to **44:** 341
morality **52:** 15, 23, 29
moral lesson **20:** 23
murder scene (Act II, scene ii) **20:** 175
Neoclassical rules **3:** 170, 171, 173, 175; **20:** 17
nightmarish quality **3:** 231, 309; **20:** 210, 242; **44:** 261
politics **52:** 29
Porter scene (Act II, scene iii) **3:** 173, 175, 184, 190, 196, 203, 205, 225, 260, 271, 297, 300; **20:** 283; **44:** 261; **46:** 29, 78
primitivism **20:** 206, 213; **45:** 48
providential order **3:** 208, 289, 329, 336
psychoanalytic interpretations **3:** 219, 223, 226; **44:** 11, 284, 289, 297
regicide **16:** 317, 328; **45:** 48 248, 275, 312
religious and theological issues **44:** 324, 341, 351, 361, 366, 373
religious, mythic, or spiritual content **3:** 208, 269, 275, 318; **29:** 109

retribution **3:** 194, 208, 318; **48:** 214
Scholasticism **52:** 23
sexual anxiety **16:** 328; **20:** 283
sleepwalking scene (Act V, scene i) **3:** 191, 203, 219; **20:** 175; **44:** 261
staging issues **13:** 502; **20:** 12, 17, 32, 64, 65, 70, 73, 107, 113, 151, 175, 203, 206, 210, 213, 245, 279, 283, 312, 318, 324, 329, 343, 345, 350, 353, 363, 367, 374, 376, 379, 382, 387, 400, 406, 413; **22:** 365; **32:** 212
structure **16:** 317; **20:** 12, 245
supernatural grace versus evil or chaos **3:** 241, 286, 323
theatricality **16:** 328
time **3:** 234, 246, 283, 293; **20:** 245
topical allusions or content **13:** 361; **20:** 17, 350; **29:** 101
tragic elements **52:** 15
treason and punishment **13:** 361; **16:** 328
violence **20:** 273, 279, 283; **45:** 58
witches and supernaturalism **3:** 171, 172, 173, 175, 177, 182, 183, 184, 185, 194, 196, 198, 202, 207, 208, 213, 219, 229, 239; **16:** 317; **19:** 245; **20:** 92, 175, 213, 279, 283, 374, 387, 406, 413; **25:** 235; **28:** 339; **29:** 91, 101, 109, 120; **44:** 351, 373

Measure for Measure (Volumes 2, 23, 33, 49)

allegorical elements **52:** 69
ambiguity **2:** 417, 420, 432, 446, 449, 452, 474, 479, 482, 486, 495, 505
Angelo
   anxiety **16:** 114
   authoritarian portrayal of **23:** 307; **49:** 274
   characterization **2:** 388, 390, 397, 402, 418, 427, 432, 434, 463, 484, 495, 503, 511; **13:** 84; **23:** 297; **32:** 81; **33:** 77; **49:** 274, 293, 379
   hypocrisy **2:** 396, 399, 402, 406, 414, 421; **23:** 345, 358, 362
   repentance or pardon **2:** 388, 390, 397, 402, 434, 463, 511, 524
audience response **48:** 1
autobiographical elements **2:** 406, 410, 414, 431, 434, 437
Barnardine **13:** 112
bed-trick **13:** 84; **49:** 313
characterization **2:** 388, 390, 391, 396, 406, 420, 421, 446, 466, 475, 484, 505, 516, 524; **23:** 299, 405; **33:** 77
Christian elements **2:** 391, 394, 399, 421, 437, 449, 466, 479, 491, 511, 522; **48:** 1; **49:** 325
Clarissa (Samuel Richardson), compared with **48:** 277
comic form **2:** 456, 460, 479, 482, 491, 514, 516; **13:** 94, 104; **23:** 309, 326, 327; **49:** 349
death, decay, and nature's destructiveness **2:** 394, 452, 516; **25:** 12; **49:** 370
displacement **22:** 78
Duke
   as authoritarian figure **23:** 314, 317, 347; **33:** 85; **49:** 274, 300, 358
   characterization **2:** 388, 395, 402, 406, 411, 421, 429, 456, 466, 470, 498, 511; **13:** 84, 94, 104; **23:** 363, 416; **32:** 81; **42:** 1; **44:** 89; **49:** 274, 293, 300, 358

   dramatic shortcomings or failure **2:** 420, 429, 441, 479, 495, 505, 514, 522
   godlike portrayal of **23:** 320
   noble portrayal of **23:** 301
   speech on death (Act III, scene i) **2:** 390, 391, 395
Elbow **22:** 85; **25:** 12
Elbow, Mistress **33:** 90
Elizabethan betrothal and marriage customs **2:** 429, 437, 443, 503; **49:** 286
Elizabethan culture, relation to **2:** 394, 418, 429, 432, 437, 460, 470, 482, 503
ethical or moral issues **52:** 69
feminist interpretation **23:** 320
good and evil **2:** 432, 452, 524; **33:** 52, 61; **52:** 69
homosexuality **42:** 1
immortality **16:** 102
inconsistency between first and second halves **2:** 474, 475, 505, 514, 524; **49:** 349, 358
Isabella **2:** 388, 390, 395, 396, 397, 401, 402, 406, 409, 410, 411, 418, 420, 421, 432, 437, 441, 466, 475, 491, 495, 524; **16:** 114; **23:** 278, 279, 280, 281, 282, 296, 344, 357, 363, 405; **28:** 92; **33:** 77, 85
judicial versus natural law **2:** 446, 507, 516, 519; **22:** 85; **33:** 58, 117; **49:** 293
justice and mercy **2:** 391, 395, 399, 402, 406, 409, 411, 416, 421, 437, 443, 463, 466, 470, 491, 495, 522, 524; **22:** 85; **33:** 52, 61, 101; **49:** 274, 293, 300
judicial vs. natural law **49:** 1
justice and mercy **49:** 1
language and imagery **2:** 394, 421, 431, 466, 486, 505; **13:** 112; **28:** 9; **33:** 69; **49:** 370
Lucio **13:** 104; **49:** 379
marriage **2:** 443, 507, 516, 519, 524, 528; **25:** 12; **33:** 61, 90; **49:** 286; **51:** 44
as medieval allegory or morality play **2:** 409, 421, 443, 466, 475, 491, 505, 511, 522; **13:** 94
metadramatic elements **13:** 104
misgovernment **2:** 401, 432, 511; **22:** 85
misogyny **23:** 358
moral seriousness, question of **2:** 387, 388, 396, 409, 417, 421, 452, 460, 495; **23:** 316, 321
Neoclassical rules **2:** 387, 388, 390, 394; **23:** 269
politics **23:** 379; **49:** 274
power **13:** 112; **22:** 85; **23:** 327, 330, 339, 352; **33:** 85
as "problem play" **2:** 416, 429, 434, 474, 475, 503, 514, 519; **16:** 102; **23:** 313, 328, 351; **49:** 358, 370
providential order **48:** 1
psychoanalytic interpretations **23:** 331, 332, 333, 334, 335, 340, 355, 356, 359, 379, 395; **44:** 79
Puritanism **2:** 414, 418, 434; **49:** 325
rebirth, regeneration, resurrection, or immortality **13:** 84; **16:** 102, 114; **23:** 321, 327, 335, 340, 352; **25:** 12
religious and theological issues **48:** 1
religious, mythic, or spiritual content **48:** 1
resolution **2:** 449, 475, 495, 514, 516; **16:** 102, 114
sexuality **13:** 84; **16:** 102, 114; **23:** 321, 327, 335, 340, 352; **25:** 12; **33:** 85, 90, 112; **49:** 286, 338; **51:** 44
social aspects **23:** 316, 375, 379, 395; **49:** 338

sources **2:** 388, 393, 427, 429, 437, 475; **13:** 94; **49:** 349; **52:** 69
staging issues **2:** 427, 429, 437, 441, 443, 456, 460, 482, 491, 519; **23:** 283, 284, 285, 286, 287, 291, 293, 294, 298, 299, 311, 315, 327, 338, 339, 340, 342, 344, 347, 363, 372, 375, 395, 400, 405, 406, 413; **32:** 16
structure **2:** 390, 411, 449, 456, 466, 474, 482, 490, 491; **33:** 69; **49:** 379
substitution of identities **2:** 507, 511, 519; **13:** 112; **49:** 313, 325
supernatural grace vs. evil or chaos **48:** 1
theatricality **23:** 285, 286, 294, 372, 406; **49:** 358
comic and tragic elements, combination of **16:** 102
as unsuccessful play **2:** 397, 441, 474, 482; **23:** 287

The Merchant of Venice (Volumes 4, 12, 40, 53)

Act V, relation to Acts I through IV **4:** 193, 194, 195, 196, 204, 232, 270, 273, 289, 300, 319, 321, 326, 336, 356
allegorical elements **4:** 224, 250, 261, 268, 270, 273, 282, 289, 324, 336, 344, 350; **53:** 179, 187
Antonio
  excessive or destructive love **4:** 279, 284, 336, 344; **12:** 54; **37:** 86
  love for Bassanio **40:** 156
  melancholy **4:** 221, 238, 279, 284, 300, 321, 328; **22:** 69; **25:** 22
  pitiless **4:** 254
  as pivotal figure **12:** 25, 129
  versus Shylock **53:** 187
appearance versus reality **4:** 209, 261, 344; **12:** 65; **22:** 69
Bassanio **25:** 257; **37:** 86; **40:** 156
bonding **4:** 293, 317, 336; **13:** 37
casket scenes **4:** 226, 241, 308, 344; **12:** 23, 46, 47, 65, 117; **13:** 43; **22:** 3; **40:** 106; **49:** 27
Christian elements **52:** 89
comparison to other works of Shakespeare **53:** 105
contrasting dramatic worlds **44:** 11
conflict between Christianity and Judaism **4:** 224, 250, 268, 289, 324, 344; **12:** 67, 70, 72, 76; **22:** 69; **25:** 257; **40:** 117, 127, 166, 181; **48:** 54, 77; **53:** 105, 159, 214
desire **22:** 3; **40:** 142; **45:** 17
disappointment, theme of **53:** 211
Economics and exchange **40:** 197, 208; **53:** 116
Elizabethan culture, relation to **32:** 66; **40:** 117, 127, 142, 166, 181, 197, 208; **48:** 54, 77; **49:** 37; **53:** 105, 111, 127, 159, 169, 214, 224
genre **4:** 191, 200, 201, 209, 215, 221, 232, 238, 247; **12:** 48, 54, 62
homosexuality **22:** 3, 69; **37:** 86; **40:** 142, 156, 197
imperialism **53:** 116
implausibility of plot, characters, or events **4:** 191, 192, 193; **12:** 52, 56, 76, 119
irony **4:** 254, 300, 321, 331, 350; **28:** 63
Jessica **4:** 196, 200, 228, 293, 342; **53:** 159, 211

justice and mercy **4:** 213, 214, 224, 250, 261, 273, 282, 289, 336; **12:** 80, 129; **40:** 127; **49:** 1, 23, 27, 37
language and imagery **4:** 241, 267, 293; **22:** 3; **25:** 257; **28:** 9, 63; **32:** 41; **40:** 106; **53:** 169
Launcelot Gobbo **46:** 24, 60; **50:** 64; **53:** 187, 214
law and justice **53:** 169
love **4:** 221, 226, 270, 284, 312, 344; **22:** 3, 69; **25:** 257; **40:** 156; **51:** 1, 44
medieval homilies, influence of **4:** 224, 250, 289
morality **52:** 89
Portia **4:** 194, 195, 196, 215, 254, 263, 336, 356; **12:** 104, 107, 114; **13:** 37; **22:** 3, 69; **25:** 22; **32:** 294; **37:** 86; **40:** 142, 156, 197, 208; **49:** 27
psychoanalytic interpretation **45:** 17
race **53:** 111, 116, 127, 136, 159, 169
resolution **4:** 263, 266, 300, 319, 321; **13:** 37; **51:** 1
rings episode **22:** 3; **40:** 106, 151, 156
sacrificial love **13:** 43; **22:** 69; **40:** 142
sexual politics **22:** 3; **51:** 44
Shylock
  alienation **4:** 279, 312; **40:** 175; **49:** 23, 37
  ambiguity **4:** 247, 254, 315, 319, 331; **12:** 31, 35, 36, 50, 51, 52, 56, 81, 124; **40:** 175; **53:** 111
  forced conversion **4:** 209, 252, 268, 282, 289, 321
  ghettoization of **53:** 127
  Jewishness **4:** 193, 194, 195, 200, 201, 213, 214, 279; **22:** 69; **25:** 257; **40:** 142, 175, 181
  master-slave relationship **53:** 136
  motives in making the bond **4:** 252, 263, 266, 268; **22:** 69; **25:** 22
  as outsider **53:** 127, 224
  as Puritan **40:** 127, 166
  as scapegoat figure **4:** 254, 300; **40:** 166 **49:** 27
  as traditional comic villain **4:** 230, 243, 261, 263, 315; **12:** 40, 62, 124; **40:** 175
  as tragic figure **12:** 6, 9, 10, 16, 21, 23, 25, 40, 44, 66, 67, 81, 97; **40:** 175
social criticism **53:** 214
staging issues **12:** 111, 114, 115, 117, 119, 124, 129, 131
structure **4:** 201, 215, 230, 232, 243, 247, 254, 261, 263, 308, 321; **12:** 115; **28:** 63
trial scene **13:** 43; **25:** 22; **40:** 106, 156; **49:** 1, 23, 27, 37
unity of double plot **4:** 193, 194, 201, 232; **12:** 16, 67, 80, 115, **40:** 151
Venetians **4:** 195, 200, 228, 254, 273, 300, 321, 331
Venice, Elizabethan perceptions of **28:** 249; **32:** 294; **40:** 127
wealth **4:** 209, 261, 270, 273, 317; **12:** 80, 117; **22:** 69; **25:** 22; **28:** 249; **40:** 117, 197, 208; **45:** 17; **49:** 1; **51:** 15

The Merry Wives of Windsor (Volumes 5, 18, 38, 47)

Anne Page-Fenton plot **5:** 334, 336, 343, 353, 376, 390, 395, 402; **22:** 93; **47:** 308
avarice **5:** 335, 353, 369, 376, 390, 395, 402

Caius, Doctor **47:** 354
caricature **5:** 343, 347, 348, 350, 385, 397
characterization **5:** 332, 334, 335, 337, 338, 351, 360, 363, 366, 374, 379, 392; **18:** 74, 75; **38:** 264, 273, 313, 319
class distinctions, conflict, and relations **5:** 338, 343, 346, 347, 366, 390, 395, 400, 402; **22:** 93; **28:** 69
comic and farcical elements **5:** 336, 338, 346, 350, 360, 369, 373; **18:** 74, 75, 84
The Comical Gallant (John Dennis adaptation) **18:** 5, 7, 8, 9, 10
deception, disguise, and duplicity **5:** 332, 334, 336, 354, 355, 379; **22:** 93; **47:** 308, 314, 321, 325, 344
desire **38:** 286, 297, 300
Elizabethan society **47:** 331
Elizabeth's influence **5:** 333, 334, 335, 336, 339, 346, 355, 366, 402; **18:** 5, 86; **38:** 278; **47:** 344
Evans, Sir Hugh **47:** 354
Falstaff
  characterization in 1 and 2 Henry IV, compared with **5:** 333, 335, 336, 337, 339, 346, 347, 348, 350, 373, 400, **18:** 5, 7, 75, 86; **22:** 93
  diminishing powers **5:** 337, 339, 343, 347, 350, 351, 392; **28:** 373; **47:** 363
  as Herne the Hunter **38:** 256, 286; **47:** 358
  incapability of love **5:** 335, 336, 339, 346, 348; **22:** 93
  as Jack-a-Lent **47:** 363
  personification of comic principle or Vice figure **5:** 332, 338, 369, 400; **38:** 273
  recognition and repentance of follies **5:** 338, 341, 343, 348, 369, 374, 376, 397
  as scapegoat **47:** 358, 363, 375
  sensuality **5:** 339, 343, 353, 369, 392
  shrewdness **5:** 332, 336, 346, 355
  threat to community **5:** 343, 369, 379, 392, 395, 400; **38:** 297
  as unifying force **47:** 358
  vanity **5:** 332, 339
  victimization **5:** 336, 338, 341, 347, 348, 353, 355, 360, 369, 373, 374, 376, 392, 397, 400
  as villain **47:** 358
  as a woman **47:** 325
folk rituals, elements and influence of **5:** 353, 369, 376, 392, 397, 400; **38:** 256, 300
Ford, Francis **5:** 332, 334, 343, 355, 363, 374, 379, 390; **38:** 273; **47:** 321
Ford, Mistress Alice **47:** 321
insults **47:** 331
jealousy **5:** 334, 339, 343, 353, 355, 363; **22:** 93; **38:** 273, 307
Jonsonian humors comedy, influence of **38:** 319
knighthood **5:** 338, 343, 390, 397, 402; **47:** 354
language and imagery **5:** 335, 337, 343, 347, 351, 363, 374, 379; **19:** 101; **22:** 93, 378; **28:** 9, 69; **38:** 313, 319
male discontent **5:** 392, 402
marriage **5:** 343, 369, 376, 390, 392, 400; **22:** 93; **38:** 297; **51:** 44
mediation **5:** 343, 392
morality **5:** 335, 339, 347, 349, 353, 397
Neoclassical rules **5:** 332, 334
Page, Anne **47:** 321
Page, Mistress Margaret **47:** 321
play and theatricality **47:** 325

play-within-the-play, convention of **5**: 354, 355, 369, 402
realism **38**: 313
reconciliation **5**: 343, 369, 374, 397, 402
revenge **5**: 349, 350, 392; **38**: 264, 307
as satire or parody **5**: 338, 350, 360, 385; **38**: 278, 319; **47**: 354, 363
schemes and intrigues **5**: 334, 336, 339, 341, 343, 349, 355, 379
setting **47**: 375
sexual politics **19**: 101; **38**: 307
social milieu **18**: 75, 84; **38**: 297, 300
sources **5**: 332, 350, 360, 366, 385; **32**: 31
stage history **18**: 66, 67, 68, 70, 71
staging issues **18**: 74, 75, 84, 86, 90, 95
structure **5**: 332, 333, 334, 335, 343, 349, 355, 369, 374; **18**: 86; **22**: 378
unnatural ordering **22**: 378
wit **5**: 335, 336, 337, 339, 343, 351
women, role of **5**: 335, 341, 343, 349, 369, 379, 390, 392, 402; **19**: 101; **38**: 307

A Midsummer Night's Dream (Volumes 3, 12, 29, 45)

adaptations **12**: 144, 146, 147, 153, 280, 282
ambiguity **3**: 401, 459, 486; **45**: 169
appearance, perception, and illusion **3**: 368, 411, 425, 427, 434, 447, 459, 466, 474, 477, 486, 497, 516; **19**: 21; **22**: 39; **28**: 15; **29**: 175,190; **45**: 136
Athens and the forest, contrast between **3**: 381, 427, 459, 466, 497, 502; **29**: 175
autobiographical elements **3**: 365, 371, 379, 381, 389, 391, 396, 402, 432
Bottom
  awakening speech (Act IV, scene i) **3**: 406, 412, 450, 457, 486, 516; **16**: 34
  folly of **46**: 1, 14, 29, 60
  imagination **3**: 376, 393, 406, 432, 486; **29**: 175, 190; **45**: 147
  self-possession **3**: 365, 376, 395, 402, 406, 480; **45**: 158
  Titania, relationship with **3**: 377, 406, 441, 445, 450, 457, 491, 497; **16**: 34; **19**: 21; **22**: 93; **29**: 216; **45**: 160
  transformation **3**: 365, 377, 432; **13**: 27; **22**: 93; **29**: 216; **45**: 147, 160
brutal elements **3**: 445, 491, 497, 511; **12**: 259, 262, 298; **16**: 34; **19**: 21; **29**: 183, 225, 263, 269; **45**: 169
capriciousness of the young lovers **3**: 372, 395, 402, 411, 423, 437, 441, 450, 497, 498; **29**: 175, 269; **45**: 107
chastity **45**: 143
class distinctions, conflict, and relations **22**: 23; **25**: 36; **45**: 160; **50**: 74, 86
colonialism **53**: 32
as dream-play **3**: 365, 370, 372, 377, 389, 391; **29**: 190; **45**: 117
dreams **45**: 96, 107, 117
duration of time **3**: 362, 370, 380, 386, 494; **45**: 175
Elizabethan culture, relation to **50**: 86
erotic elements **3**: 445, 491, 497, 511; **12**: 259, 262, 298; **16**: 34; **19**: 21; **29**: 183, 225, 269
fairies **3**: 361, 362, 372, 377, 395, 400, 423, 450, 459, 486; **12**: 287, 291, 294, 295; **19**: 21; **29**: 183, 190; **45**: 147
feminist interpretation **48**: 23
gender **53**: 1
Helena **29**: 269
Hermia **29**: 225, 269; **45**: 117
Hippolytus, myth of **29**: 216; **45**: 84
identity **29**: 269
imagination and art **3**: 365, 371, 381, 402, 412, 417, 421, 423, 441, 459, 468, 506, 516, 520; **22**: 39
language and imagery **3**: 397, 401, 410, 412, 415, 432, 453, 459, 468, 494; **22**: 23, 39, 93, 378; **28**: 9; **29**: 263; **45**: 96, 126, 136, 147; **45**: 143, 169, 175; **48**: 23, 32
male domination **3**: 483, 520; **13**: 19; **25**: 36; **29**: 216, 225, 243, 256, 269; **42**: 46; **45**: 84
marriage **3**: 402, 423, 450, 483, 520; **29**: 243, 256; **45**: 136, 143; **48**: 32; **51**: 1, 30, 44
metadramatic elements **3**: 427, 468, 477, 516, 520; **29**: 190, 225, 243; **50**: 86
Metamorphoses (Golding translation of Ovid) **16**: 25
Minotaur, myth of **3**: 497, 498; **29**: 216
music and dance **3**: 397, 400, 418, 513; **12**: 287, 289; **25**: 36
Oberon as controlling force **3**: 434, 459, 477, 502; **29**: 175
Ovid, influence of **3**: 362, 427, 497, 498; **22**: 23; **29**: 175, 190, 216
parent-child relations **13**: 19; **29**: 216, 225, 243
passionate or romantic love **3**: 372, 389, 395, 396, 402, 408, 411, 423, 441, 450, 480, 497, 498, 511; **29**: 175, 225, 263, 269; **45**: 126, 136; **51**: 44
Pauline doctrine **3**: 457, 486, 506
Platonic elements **3**: 368, 437, 450, 497; **45**: 126
politics **29**: 243
power **42**: 46; **45**: 84
psychoanalytic interpretations **3**: 440, 483; **28**: 15; **29**: 225; **44**: 1; **45**: 107, 117
Puck **45**: 96, 158
Pyramus and Thisbe interlude **3**: 364, 368, 379, 381, 389, 391, 396, 408, 411, 412, 417, 425, 427, 433, 441, 447, 457, 468, 474, 511; **12**: 254; **13**: 27; **16**: 25; **22**: 23; **29**: 263; **45**: 107, 175; **50**: 74
race **53**: 1, 32
reason versus imagination **3**: 381, 389, 423, 441, 466, 506; **22**: 23; **29**: 190; **45**: 96
reconciliation **3**: 412, 418, 437, 459, 468, 491, 497, 502, 513; **13**: 27; **29**: 190
reversal **29**: 225
Romeo and Juliet, compared with **3**: 396, 480
rustic characters **3**: 376, 397, 432; **12**: 291, 293; **45**: 147, 160
sexuality **22**: 23, 93; **29**: 225, 243, 256, 269; **42**: 46; **45**: 107 **53**: 32
sources **29**: 216
staging issues **3**: 364, 365, 371, 372, 377; **12**: 151, 152, 154, 158, 159, 280, 284, 291, 295; **16**: 34; **19**: 21; **29**: 183, 256; **48**: 23
structure **3**: 364, 368, 381, 402, 406, 427, 450, 513; **13**: 19; **22**: 378; **29**: 175; **45**: 126, 175
textual issues **16**: 34; **29**: 216
Theseus **51**: 1
  characterization **3**: 363
  Hippolyta, relationship with **3**: 381, 412, 421, 423, 450, 468, 520; **29**: 175, 216, 243, 256; **45**: 84
  as ideal **3**: 379, 391
"lovers, lunatics, and poets" speech (Act V, scene i) **3**: 365, 371, 379, 381, 391, 402, 411, 412, 421, 423, 441, 498, 506; **29**: 175
  as representative of institutional life **3**: 381, 403
Titania **29**: 243
tragic elements **3**: 393, 400, 401, 410, 445, 474, 480, 491, 498, 511; **29**: 175; **45**: 169
unity **3**: 364, 368, 381, 402, 406, 427, 450, 513; **13**: 19; **22**: 378; **29**: 175, 263
unnatural ordering **22**: 378

Much Ado about Nothing (Volumes 8, 18, 31)

appearance versus reality **8**: 17, 18, 48, 63, 69, 73, 75, 79, 88, 95, 115; **31**: 198, 209
battle of the sexes **8**: 14, 16, 19, 48, 91, 95, 111, 121, 125; **31**: 231, 245
Beatrice and Benedick
  Beatrice's femininity **8**: 14, 16, 17, 24, 29, 38, 41, 91; **31**: 222, 245
  Beatrice's request to "kill Claudio" (Act IV, scene i) **8**: 14, 17, 33, 41, 55, 63, 75, 79, 91, 108, 115; **18**: 119, 120, 136, 161, 245, 257
  Benedick's challenge of Claudio (Act V, scene i) **8**: 48, 63, 79, 91; **31**: 231
  Claudio and Hero, compared with **8**: 19, 28, 29, 75, 82, 115; **31**: 171, 216
  marriage and the opposite sex, attitudes toward **8**: 9, 13, 14, 16, 19, 29, 36, 48, 63, 77, 91, 95, 115, 121; **16**: 45; **31**: 216
  mutual attraction 8: 13, 14, 19, 24, 29, 33, 41, 75
  nobility **8**: 13, 19, 24, 29, 36, 39, 41, 47, 82, 91, 108
  popularity **8**: 13, 38, 41, 53, 79
  transformed by love **8**: 19, 29, 36, 48, 75, 91, 95, 115; **31**: 209, 216
  unconventionality **8**: 48, 91, 95, 108, 115, 121
  vulgarity **8**: 11, 12, 33, 38, 41, 47
  wit and charm **8**: 9, 12, 13, 14, 19, 24, 27, 28, 29, 33, 36, 38, 41, 47, 55, 69, 95, 108, 115; **31**: 241
Borachio and Conrade **8**: 24, 69, 82, 88, 111, 115
Christian elements **8**: 17, 19, 29, 55, 95, 104, 111, 115; **31**: 209
church scene (Act IV, scene i) **8**: 13, 14, 16, 19, 33, 44, 47, 48, 58, 63, 69, 75, 79, 82, 91, 95, 100, 104, 111, 115; **18**: 120, 130, 138, 145, 146, 148, 192; **31**: 191, 198, 245
Claudio
  boorish behavior **8**: 9, 24, 33, 36, 39, 44, 48, 63, 79, 82, 95, 100, 111, 115; **31**: 209
  credulity **8**: 9, 17, 19, 24, 29, 36, 41, 47, 58, 63, 75, 77, 82, 95, 100, 104, 111, 115, 121; **31**: 241; **47**: 25
  mercenary traits **8**: 24, 44, 58, 82, 91, 95
  noble qualities **8**: 17, 19, 29, 41, 44, 58, 75
  reconciliation with Hero **8**: 33, 36, 39, 44, 47, 82, 95, 100, 111, 115, 121
  repentance **8**: 33, 63, 82, 95, 100, 111, 115, 121; **31**: 245

sexual insecurities **8:** 75, 100, 111, 115, 121
courtship and marriage **8:** 29, 44, 48, 95, 115, 121, 125; **31:** 191, 231; **51:** 33, 44
deception, disguise, and duplicity **8:** 29, 55, 63, 69, 79, 82, 88, 108, 115; **31:** 191, 198
Dogberry and the Watch **8:** 9, 12, 13, 17, 24, 28, 29, 33, 39, 48, 55, 69, 79, 82, 88, 95, 104, 108, 115; **18:** 138, 152, 205, 208, 210, 213, 231; **22:** 85; **31:** 171, 229; **46:** 60
Don John **8:** 9, 12, 16, 17, 19, 28, 29, 36, 39, 41, 47, 48, 55, 58, 63, 82, 104, 108, 111, 121
Don Pedro **8:** 17, 19, 48, 58, 63, 82, 111, 121
eavesdropping scenes (Act II, scene iii and Act III, scene i) **8:** 12, 13, 17, 19, 28, 29, 33, 36, 48, 55, 63, 73, 75, 82, 121; **18:** 120, 138, 208, 215, 245, 264; **31:** 171, 184
egotism or narcissism **8:** 19, 24, 28, 29, 55, 69, 95, 115
Elizabethan culture, relation to **8:** 23, 33, 44, 55, 58, 79, 88, 104, 111, 115; **51:** 15
Friar **8:** 24, 29, 41, 55, 63, 79, 111
genre **8:** 9, 18, 19, 28, 29, 39, 41, 44, 53, 63, 69, 73, 79, 82, 95, 100, 104; **48:** 14
Hero **8:** 13, 14, 16, 19, 28, 29, 44, 48, 53, 55, 82, 95, 104, 111, 115, 121; **31:** 231, 245; **47:** 25
implausibility of plot, characters, or events **8:** 9, 12, 16, 19, 33, 36, 39, 44, 53, 100, 104
irony **8:** 14, 63, 79, 82; **28:** 63
justice and mercy **22:** 85
language and imagery **8:** 9, 38, 43, 46, 55, 69, 73, 88, 95, 100, 115, 125; **19:** 68; **25:** 77; **28:** 63; **31:** 178, 184, 222, 241, 245; **48:** 14
law versus passion for freedom **22:** 85
love **8:** 24, 55, 75, 95, 111, 115; **28:** 56; **51:** 30
Messina **8:** 19, 29, 48, 69, 82, 91, 95, 108, 111, 121, 125; **31:** 191, 209, 229, 241, 245
misgovernment **22:** 85
music and dance **19:** 68; **31:** 222
"nothing," significance of **8:** 17, 18, 23, 55, 73, 95; **19:** 68
performance issues **18:** 173, 174, 183, 184, 185, 186, 187, 188, 189, 190, 191, 192, 193, 195, 197, 199, 201, 204, 206, 207, 208, 209, 210, 254
power **22:** 85; **25:** 77; **31:** 231, 245
repentance or forgiveness **8:** 24, 29, 111
resurrection, metamorphosis, or transformation **8:** 88, 104, 111, 115
romance or chivalric tradition, influence of **8:** 53, 125; **51:** 15
self-knowledge **8:** 69, 95, 100
setting **18:** 173, 174, 183, 184, 185, 186, 187, 188, 189, 190, 191, 192, 193, 195, 197, 199, 201, 204, 206, 207, 208, 209, 210, 254
slander or hearsay, importance of **8:** 58, 69, 82, 95, 104
sources **8:** 9, 19, 53, 58, 104
staging issues **8:** 18, 33, 41, 75, 79, 82, 108; **16:** 45; **18:** 245, 247, 249, 252, 254, 257, 261, 264; **28:** 63

structure **8:** 9, 16, 17, 19, 28, 29, 33, 39, 48, 63, 69, 73, 75, 79, 82, 115; **31:** 178, 184, 198, 231
virginity or chastity, importance of **8:** 44, 75, 95, 111, 121, 125; **31:** 222
wit **8:** 27, 29, 38, 69, 79, 91, 95; **31:** 178, 191
works by Shakespeare or other authors, compared with **8:** 16, 19, 27, 28, 33, 38, 39, 41, 53, 69, 79, 91, 104, 108; **31:** 231

Othello (Volumes 4, 11, 35, 53)

autobiographical elements **4:** 440, 444; **53:** 324
Brabantio **25:** 189
Cassio **25:** 189
Clarissa (Samuel Richardson), compared with **48:** 277
consummation of marriage **22:** 207; **53:** 246, 333
contrasts and oppositions **4:** 421, 455, 457, 462, 508; **25:** 189; **53:** 268
Desdemona
    as Christ figure **4:** 506, 525, 573; **35:** 360
    culpability **4:** 408, 415, 422, 427; **13:** 313; **19:** 253, 276; **35:** 265, 352, 380
    innocence **35:** 360; **47:** 25; **53:** 310, 333
    as mother figure **22:** 339; **35:** 282; **53:** 324
    passivity **4:** 402, 406, 421, 440, 457, 470, 582, 587; **25:** 189; **35:** 380
    spiritual nature of her love **4:** 462, 530, 559
    staging issues **11:** 350, 354, 359; **13:** 327; **32:** 201
dramatic structure **4:** 370, 390, 399, 427, 488, 506, 517, 569; **22:** 207; **28:** 243; **53:** 261
Duke **25:** 189
Emilia **4:** 386, 391, 392, 415, 587; **35:** 352, 380
evil **52:** 78
gender issues **32:** 294; **35:** 327; **53:** 255, 268, 310, 315, 324
handkerchief, significance of **4:** 370, 384, 385, 396, 503, 530, 562; **35:** 265, 282, 380; **53:** 333
Hercules Furens (Seneca) as source **16:** 283
Iago
    affinity with Othello **4:** 400, 427, 468, 470, 477, 500, 506; **25:** 189; **44:** 57
    as conventional dramatic villain **4:** 440, 527, 545, 582; **53:** 288
    as homosexual **4:** 503; **53:** 275
    Machiavellian elements **4:** 440, 455, 457, 517, 545; **35:** 336, 347
    motives **4:** 389, 390, 397, 399, 402, 409, 423, 424, 427, 434, 451, 462, 545, 564; **13:** 304; **25:** 189; **28:** 344; **32:** 201; **35:** 265, 276, 310, 336, 347; **42:** 278; **53:** 246, 275, 324
    revenge scheme **4:** 392, 409, 424, 451
    as scapegoat **4:** 506
    as victim **4:** 402, 409, 434, 451, 457, 470
idealism versus realism **4:** 457, 508, 517; **13:** 313; **25:** 189; **53:** 350
implausibility of plot, characters, or events **4:** 370, 380, 391, 442, 444; **47:** 51
jealousy **4:** 384, 488, 527; **35:** 253, 265, 282, 301, 310; **44:** 57, 66; **51:** 30
justice **35:** 247; **53:** 288, 350

language and imagery **4:** 433, 442, 445, 462, 493, 508, 517, 552, 587, 596; **13:** 304; **16:** 272; **22:** 378; **25:** 189, 257; **28:** 243, 344; **42:** 278; **47:** 51; **53:** 261
love **4:** 412, 493, 506, 512, 530, 545, 552, 569, 570, 575, 580, 591; **19:** 253; **22:** 207; **25:** 257; **28:** 243, 344; **32:** 201; **35:** 261, 317; **51:** 25, 30; **53:** 315
love and reason **4:** 512, 530, 580; **19:** 253
madness **35:** 265, 276, 282
marriage **35:** 369; **51:** 44; **53:** 315
Marxist criticism **42:** 234
Measure for Measure, compared with **25:** 189
medieval dramatic conventions, influence of **4:** 440, 527, 545, 559, 582
Merchant of Venice, compared with **53:** 288, 255, 268, 298
military and sexual hierarchies **16:** 272; **53:** 324
moral corruption **52:** 78
Othello
    affinity with Iago **4:** 400, 427, 468, 470, 477, 500, 506; **25:** 189; **35:** 276, 320, 327
    as conventional "blameless hero" **4:** 445, 486, 500; **53:** 233, 288, 298, 304
    credulity **4:** 384, 385, 388, 390, 396, 402, 434, 440, 455; **13:** 327; **32:** 302; **47:** 25, 51
    Desdemona, relationship with **22:** 339; **35:** 301, 317; **37:** 269; **53:** 315
    divided nature **4:** 400, 412, 462, 470, 477, 493, 500, 582, 592; **16:** 293; **19:** 276; **25:** 189; **35:** 320; **53:** 268, 289, 343
    egotism **4:** 427, 470, 477, 493, 522, 536, 541, 573, 597; **13:** 304; **35:** 247, 253
    self-destructive anger **16:** 283; **53:** 324
    self-dramatizing or self-deluding **4:** 454, 457, 477, 592; **13:** 313; **16:** 293; **35:** 317
    self-knowledge **4:** 462, 470, 477, 483, 508, 522, 530, 564, 580, 591, 596; **13:** 304, 313; **16:** 283; **28:** 243; **35:** 253, 317; **53:** 233, 343
    spiritual state **4:** 483, 488, 517, 525, 527, 544, 559, 564, 573; **28:** 243; **35:** 253; **53:** 298
perception **19:** 276; **25:** 189, 257; **53:** 246, 289
poetic justice, question of **4:** 370, 412, 415, 427
pride and rightful self-esteem **4:** 522, 536, 541; **35:** 352
psychoanalytic interpretations **4:** 468, 503; **35:** 265, 276, 282, 301, 317, 320, 347; **42:** 203; **44:** 57; **53:** 275, 343
racial issues **4:** 370, 380, 384, 385, 392, 399, 401, 402, 408, 427, 564; **13:** 327; **16:** 293; **25:** 189, 257; **28:** 249, 330; **35:** 369; **42:** 203; **37:** 336; **53:** 1, 233, 238, 246, 255, 261, 268, 275, 289, 298, 304
religious, mythic, or spiritual content **4:** 483, 517, 522, 525, 559, 573; **22:** 207; **28:** 330; **53:** 289
revenge **35:** 261
Romeo and Juliet, compared with **32:** 302
sexuality **22:** 339; **28:** 330, 344; **35:** 352, 360; **37:** 269; **44:** 57, 66; **51:** 44; **53:** 275, 310, 315
sources **28:** 330
staging issues **11:** 273, 334, 335, 339, 342, 350, 354, 359, 362; **53:** 233, 304
structure **22:** 378; **28:** 325

time scheme **4:** 370, 384, 390, 488; **22:** 207; **35:** 310; **47:** 51; **53:** 333
'Tis Pity She's a Whore (John Ford), compared with
unnatural ordering **22:** 378
Venetian politics **32:** 294; **53:** 350
violence **22:** 12; **43:** 32
The Winter's Tale, compared with **35:** 310
women, role of **19:** 253; **28:** 344; **53:** 310

Pericles (Volumes 2, 15, 36, 51)

archetypal structure **2:** 570, 580, 582, 584, 588; **25:** 365; **51:** 71, 79
art and nature **22:** 315; **36:** 233
audience perception **42:** 359; **48:** 364
authorship controversy **2:** 538, 540, 543, 544, 545, 546, 548, 550, 551, 553, 556, 558, 564, 565, 568, 576, 586; **15:** 132, 141, 148, 152; **16:** 391, 399; **25:** 365; **36:** 198, 244
autobiographical elements **2:** 551, 554, 555, 563, 581
brothel scenes (Act IV, scenes ii and vi) **2:** 548, 550, 551, 553, 554, 586, 590; **15:** 134, 145, 154, 166, 172, 177; **36:** 274; **51:** 118
composition date **2:** 537, 544
Deconstructionist interpretation of **48:** 364
Diana, as symbol of nature **22:** 315; **36:** 233; **51:** 71
doubling of roles **15:** 150, 152, 167, 173, 180
Gower chorus **2:** 548, 575; **15:** 134, 141, 143, 145, 149, 152, 177; **36:** 279; **42:** 359
incest, motif of **2:** 582, 588; **22:** 315; **36:** 257, 264; **51:** 110, 97
as inferior or flawed plays **2:** 537, 546, 553, 563, 564; **15:** 139, 143, 156, 167, 176; **36:** 198; **51:** 79
innocence **36:** 226, 274
Jacobean culture, relation to **37:** 361; **51:** 110, 86
language and imagery **2:** 559, 560, 565, 583; **16:** 391; **19:** 387; **22:** 315; **36:** 198, 214, 233, 244, 251, 264; **51:** 86, 99
Marina **37:** 361; **51:** 118
as miracle play **2:** 569, 581; **36:** 205; **51:** 97
nature as book **22:** 315; **36:** 233
oaths, importance of **19:** 387
patience **2:** 572, 573, 578, 579; **36:** 251
Pericles
  characterization **36:** 251; **37:** 361
  patience **2:** 572, 573, 578, 579
  suit of Antiochus's daughter **2:** 547, 565, 578, 579; **51:** 126
  Ulysses, compared with **2:** 551
politics **37:** 361
popularity **2:** 536, 538, 546; **37:** 361
recognition scene (Act V, scene i) **15:** 138, 139, 141, 145, 161, 162, 167, 172, 175
reconciliation **2:** 555, 564, 584, 586, 588; **36:** 205
religious, mythic, or spiritual content **2:** 559, 561, 565, 570, 580, 584, 588; **22:** 315; **25:** 365; **51:** 97
riddle motif **22:** 315; **36:** 205, 214
Shakespeare's other romances, relation to **2:** 547, 549, 551, 559, 564, 570, 571, 584, 585; **15:** 139; **16:** 391, 399; **36:** 226, 257; **51:** 71, 79
spectacle **42:** 359
sources **2:** 538, 568, 572, 575; **25:** 365; **36:** 198, 205; **51:** 118, 126

staging issues **16:** 399; **48:** 364; **51:** 99
suffering **2:** 546, 573, 578, 579; **25:** 365; **36:** 279
textual revisions **15:** 129, 130, 132, 134, 135, 136, 138, 152, 155, 167, 181; **16:** 399; **25:** 365; **51:** 99

The Phoenix and Turtle (Volumes 10, 38, 51)

allegorical elements **10:** 7, 8, 9, 16, 17, 48; **38:** 334, 378; **51:** 138, 188
art and nature **10:** 7, 42
authenticity **10:** 7, 8, 16
autobiographical elements **10:** 14, 18, 42, 48; **51:** 155
bird imagery **10:** 21, 27; **38:** 329, 350, 367; **51:** 145, 181, 184
Christian elements **10:** 21, 24, 31; **38:** 326; **51:** 162, 171, 181
complex or enigmatic nature **10:** 7, 14, 35, 42; **38:** 326, 357; **51:** 145, 162
consciously philosophical **10:** 7, 21, 24, 31, 48; **38:** 342, 378
constancy and faithfulness **10:** 18, 20, 21, 48; **38:** 329
Court of Love **10:** 9, 24, 50
Donne, John, compared with **10:** 20, 31, 35, 37, 40; **51:** 143
satiric elements **10:** 8, 16, 17, 27, 35, 40, 45, 48
love **10:** 31, 37, 40, 50; **38:** 342, 345, 367; **51:** 145, 151, 155
as metaphysical poem **10:** 7, 8, 9, 20, 31, 35, 37, 40, 45, 50; **51:** 143, 171, 184
Neoplatonism **10:** 7, 9, 21, 24, 40, 45, 50; **38:** 345, 350, 367, 184
as "pure" poetry **10:** 14, 31, 35; **38:** 329
Scholasticism **10:** 21, 24, 31; **51:** 188
Shakespeare's dramas, compared with **10:** 9, 14, 17, 18, 20, 27, 37, 40, 42, 48; **38:** 342; **51:** 151, 155
sources **10:** 7, 9, 18, 24, 45; **38:** 326, 334, 350, 367; **51:** 138
structure **10:** 27, 31, 37, 45, 50; **38:** 342, 345, 357; **51:** 138, 143
style **10:** 8, 20, 24, 27, 31, 35, 45, 50; **38:** 334, 345, 357, 171; **51:** 188

The Rape of Lucrece (Volumes 10, 33, 43)

allegorical elements **10:** 89, 93
Brutus **10:** 96, 106, 109, 116, 121, 125, 128, 135
Christian elements **10:** 77, 80, 89, 96, 98, 109
Collatine **10:** 98, 131; **43:** 102
Elizabethan culture, relation to **33:** 195; **43:** 77;
gender **53:** 1
irony or paradox **10:** 93, 98, 128
language and imagery **10:** 64, 65, 66, 71, 78, 80, 89, 93, 116, 109, 125, 131; **22:** 289, 294; **25:** 305; **32:** 321; **33:** 144, 155, 179, 200; **43:** 102, 113, 141
Lucrece
  chastity **33:** 131, 138; **43:** 92
  as example of Renaissance virt[0097] **22:** 289; **43:** 148
  heroic **10:** 84, 93, 109, 121, 128
  patriarchal woman, model of **10:** 109, 131; **33:** 169, 200
  self-responsibility **10:** 89, 96, 98, 106, 125; **33:** 195; **43:** 85, 92, 158

unrealistic **10:** 64, 65, 66, 121
verbose **10:** 64, 81, 116; **25:** 305; **33:** 169
  as victim **22:** 294; **25:** 305; **32:** 321; **33:** 131, 195; **43:** 102, 158
male/female relationships **10:** 109, 121, 131; **22:** 289; **25:** 305; **43:** 113, 141
narrative strategies **22:** 294
race **53:** 1
Roman history, relation to **10:** 84, 89, 93, 96, 98, 109, 116, 125, 135; **22:** 289; **25:** 305; **33:** 155, 190
Shakespeare's dramas, compared with **10:** 63, 64, 65, 66, 68, 71, 73, 74, 78, 80, 81, 84, 98, 116, 121, 125; **43:** 92
sources **10:** 63, 64, 65, 66, 68, 74, 77, 78, 89, 98, 109, 121, 125; **25:** 305; **33:** 155, 190; **43:** 77, 92, 148
structure **10:** 84, 89, 93, 98, 135; **22:** 294; **25:** 305, **43:** 102, 141
style **10:** 64, 65, 66, 68, 69, 70, 71, 73, 74, 77, 78, 81, 84, 98, 116, 131, 135; **43:** 113, 158
Tarquin **10:** 80, 93, 98, 116, 125; **22:** 294; **25:** 305; **32:** 321; **33:** 190; **43:** 102
tragic elements **10:** 78, 80, 81, 84, 98, 109; **43:** 85, 148
the Troy passage **10:** 74, 89, 98, 116, 121, 128; **22:** 289; **32:** 321; **33:** 144, 179; **43:** 77, 85
Venus and Adonis, compared with **10:** 63, 66, 68, 69, 70, 73, 81; **22:** 294; **43:** 148
violence **43:** 148, 158

Richard II (Volumes 6, 24, 39, 52)

abdication scene (Act IV, scene i) **6:** 270, 307, 317, 327, 354, 359, 381, 393, 409; **13:** 172; **19:** 151; **24:** 274, 414; **52:** 141, 144
acting and dissimulation **6:** 264, 267, 307, 310, 315, 368, 393, 409; **24:** 339, 345, 346, 349, 352, 356
allegorical elements **6:** 264, 283, 323, 385
audience perception **24:** 414, 423; **39:** 295
Bolingbroke
  comic elements **28:** 134
  guilt **24:** 423; **39:** 279
  language and imagery **6:** 310, 315, 331, 347, 374, 381, 397; **32:** 189
  as Machiavellian figure **6:** 305, 307, 315, 331, 347, 388, 393, 397; **24:** 428
  as politician **6:** 255, 263, 264, 272, 277, 294, 364, 368, 391; **24:** 330, 333, 405, 414, 423, 428; **39:** 256; **52:** 124
  Richard, compared with **6:** 307, 315, 347, 374, 391, 393, 409; **24:** 346, 349, 351, 352, 356, 395, 419, 423, 428; **52:** 108, 124
  his silence **24:** 423
  structure, compared with **39:** 235
  usurpation of crown, nature of **6:** 255, 272, 289, 307, 310, 347, 354, 359, 381, 385, 393; **13:** 172; **24:** 322, 356, 383, 419; **28:** 178; **52:** 108, 124
Bolingbroke and Richard as opposites **24:** 423
Bolingbroke-Mowbray dispute **22:** 137
carnival elements **19:** 151; **39:** 273
censorship **24:** 260, 261, 262, 263, 386; **42:** 120; **52:** 141, 144

ceremonies, rites, and rituals, importance of **6:** 270, 294, 315, 368, 381, 397, 409, 414; **24:** 274, 356, 411, 414, 419
comic elements **24:** 262, 263, 395; **39:** 243
contractual and economic relations **13:** 213; **49:** 60
costumes **24:** 274, 278, 291, 304, 325, 356, 364, 423
deposition scene (Act III, scene iii) **24:** 298, 395, 423; **42:** 120
Elizabethan attitudes, influence of **6:** 287, 292, 294, 305, 321, 327, 364, 402, 414; **13:** 494; **24:** 325; **28:** 188; **39:** 273; **42:** 120; **52:** 141, 144
Essex Rebellion, relation to **6:** 249, 250; **24:** 356
family honor, structure, and inheritance **6:** 338, 368, 388, 397, 414; **39:** 263, 279
fate **6:** 289, 294, 304, 352, 354, 385
garden scene (Act III, scene iv) **6:** 264, 283, 323, 385; **24:** 307, 356, 414
Gaunt **6:** 255, 287, 374, 388, 402, 414; **24:** 274, 322, 325, 414, 423; **39:** 263, 279
gender issues **25:** 89; **39:** 295
historical sources, compared with **6:** 252, 279, 343; **28:** 134; **39:** 235; **49:** 60
irony **6:** 270, 307, 364, 368, 391; **24:** 383; **28:** 188
King of Misrule **19:** 151; **39:** 273
kingship **6:** 263, 264, 272, 277, 289, 294, 327, 354, 364, 381, 388, 391, 402, 409, 414; **19:** 151, 209; **24:** 260, 289, 291, 322, 325, 333, 339, 345, 346, 349, 351, 352, 356, 395, 408, 419, 428; **28:** 134; **39:** 235, 243, 256, 273, 279, 289; **42:** 175
language and imagery **6:** 252, 282, 283, 294, 298, 315, 323, 331, 347, 368, 374, 381, 385, 397, 409; **13:** 213, 494; **24:** 269, 270, 298, 301, 304, 315, 325, 329, 333, 339, 356, 364, 395, 405, 408, 411, 414, 419; **28:** 134, 188; **39:** 243, 273, 289, 295; **42:** 175; **52:** 154, 157, 169, 174, 183
Marlowe's works, compared with **19:** 233; **24:** 307, 336; **42:** 175
medievalism and chivalry, presentation of **6:** 258, 277, 294, 327, 338, 388, 397, 414; **24:** 274, 278, 279, 280, 283; **39:** 256
mercantilism and feudalism **13:** 213
mirror scene (Act IV, scene i) **6:** 317, 327, 374, 381, 393, 409; **24:** 267, 356, 408, 414, 419, 423; **28:** 134, 178; **39:** 295
mythological elements **52:** 154, 157, 169
negative assessments **6:** 250, 252, 253, 255, 282, 307, 317, 343, 359
Northumberland **24:** 423
Richard
    artistic temperament **6:** 264, 267, 270, 272, 277, 292, 294, 298, 315, 331, 334, 347, 368, 374, 393, 409; **24:** 298, 301, 304, 315, 322, 390, 405, 408, 411, 414, 419; **39:** 289
    Bolingbroke, compared with **24:** 346, 349, 351, 352, 356, 419; **39:** 256; **52:** 108, 124
    characterization **6:** 250, 252, 253, 254, 255, 258, 262, 263, 267, 270, 272, 282, 283, 304, 343, 347, 364, 368; **24:** 262, **263, 267, 269, 270, 271, 272, 273, 274, 278, 280, 315, 322, 325, 330, 333, 390, 395, 402, 405, 423; 28:** 134; **39:** 279, 289; **52:** 169
    dangerous aspects **24:** 405
delusion **6:** 267, 298, 334, 368, 409; **24:** 329, 336, 405
homosexuality **24:** 405
kingship **6:** 253, 254, 263, 272, 327, 331, 334, 338, 364, 402, 414; **24:** 278, 295, 336, 337, 339, 356, 419; **28:** 134, 178; **39:** 256, 263; **52:** 169
loss of identity **6:** 267, 338, 368, 374, 381, 388, 391, 409; **24:** 298, 414, 428
as martyr-king **6:** 289, 307, 321; **19:** 209; **24:** 289, 291; **28:** 134
nobility **6:** 255, 258, 259, 262, 263, 391; **24:** 260, 263, 274, 280, 289, 291, 402, 408, 411
political acumen **6:** 263, 264, 272, 292, 310, 327, 334, 364, 368, 374, 388, 391, 397, 402, 409; **24:** 405; **39:** 256
private versus public persona **6:** 317, 327, 364, 368, 391, 409; **24:** 428
role-playing **24:** 419, 423; **28:** 178
role in Gloucester's death **52:** 108, 124
seizure of Gaunt's estate **6:** 250, 338, 388; **49:** 60
self-dramatization **6:** 264, 267, 307, 310, 315, 317, 331, 334, 368, 393, 409; **24:** 339; **28:** 178
self-hatred **13:** 172; **24:** 383; **39:** 289
self-knowledge **6:** 255, 267, 331, 334, 338, 352, 354, 368, 388, 391; **24:** 273, 289, 411, 414; **39:** 263, 289
spiritual redemption **6:** 255, 267, 331, 334, 338, 352, 354, 368, 388, 391; **24:** 273, 289, 411, 414; **52:** 124
Shakespeare's other histories, compared with **6:** 255, 264, 272, 294, 304, 310, 317, 343, 354, 359; **24:** 320, 325, 330, 331, 332, 333; **28:** 178
Shakespeare's sympathies, question of **6:** 277, 279, 287, 347, 359, 364, 391, 393, 402
Sicilian Usurper (Nahum Tate adaptation) **24:** 260, 261, 262, 263, 386, 390
staging issues **13:** 494; **24:** 273, 274, 278, 279, 280, 283, 291, 295, 296, 301, 303, 304, 310, 315, 317, 320, 325, 333, 338, 346, 351, 352, 356, 364, 383, 386, 395, 402, **405, 411, 414, 419, 423, 428; 25:** 89
structure **6:** 282, 304, 317, 343, 352, 359, 364, 39; **24:** 307, 322, 325, 356, 395
textual arrangement **24:** 260, 261, 262, 263, 271, 273, 291, 296, 356, 390
time **22:** 137
usurpation **6:** 263, 264, 272, 287, 289, 315, 323, 331, 343, 354, 364, 381, 388, 393, 397; **24:** 383; **52:** 108, 141, 154
York **6:** 287, 364, 368, 388, 402, 414; **24:** 263, 320, 322, 364, 395, 414; **39:** 243, 279

Richard III (Volumes 8, 14, 39, 52)

allegorical elements **52:** 5
ambivalence and ambiguity **44:** 11; **47:** 15
conscience **8:** 148, 152, 162, 165, 190, 197, 201, 206, 210, 228, 232, 239, 243, 252, 258; **39:** 341; **52:** 5, 196, 205
Elizabethan politics, relation to **22:** 395; **25:** 141; **37:** 144; **39:** 345, 349; **42:** 132 **52:** 201, 214, 257
evil **52:** 78
family honor, structure and inheritance **8:** 177, 248, 252, 263, 267; **25:** 141; **39:** 335, 341, 349, 370
flattery **22:** 395
gender issues **25:** 141; **37:** 144; **39:** 345; **52:** 223, 239
genre **8:** 181, 182, 197, 206, 218, 228, 239, 243, 252, 258; **13:** 142; **39:** 383; **52:** 239
ghost scene (Act V, scene iii) **8:** 152, 154, 159, 162, 163, 165, 170, 177, 193, 197, 210, 228, 239, 243, 252, 258, 267
Henry VI, relation to **8:** 159, 165, 177, 182, 193, 201, 210, 213, 218, 228, 243, 248, 252, 267; **25:** 164; **39:** 370
historical accuracy **8:** 144, 145, 153, 159, 163, 165, 168, 213, 223, 228, 232; **39:** 305, 308, 326, 383
historical principles **39:** 308, 326, 387
language and imagery **8:** 159, 161, 165, 167, 168, 170, 177, 182, 184, 186, 193, 197, 201, 206, 218, 223, 243, 248, 252, 258, 262, 267; **16:** 150; **25:** 141, 245; **39:** 360, 370, 383; **47:** 15; **52:** 285, 290
Margaret **8:** 153, 154, 159, 162, 163, 170, 193, 201, 206, 210, 218, 223, 228, 243, 248, 262; **39:** 345
Christopher Marlowe's works, compared with **19:** 233
minor characters **8:** 154, 159, 162, 163, 168, 170, 177, 184, 186, 201, 206, 210, 218, 223, 228, 232, 239, 248, 262, 267
modernization **14:** 523
moral corruption of English society **8:** 154, 163, 165, 177, 193, 201, 218, 228, 232, 243, 248, 252, 267; **39:** 308; **52:** 78, 201
morality **52:** 5, 78
plot and incident **8:** 146, 152, 159; **25:** 164
popularity **8:** 144, 146, 154, 158, 159, 162, 181, 228; **39:** 383
rebellion **22:** 395
retribution **8:** 163, 170, 177, 182, 184, 193, 197, 201, 206, 210, 218, 223, 228, 243, 248, 267
Richard III
    ambition **8:** 148, 154, 165, 168, 170, 177, 182, 213, 218, 228, 232, 239, 252, 258, 267; **39:** 308, 341, 360, 370, 383; **52:** 201, 223
    attractive qualities **8:** 145, 148, 152, 154, 159, 161, 162, 165, 168, 170, 181, 182, 184, 185, 197, 201, 206, 213, 228, 243, 252, 258; **16:** 150; **39:** 370, 383; **52:** 272, 280, 285
    credibility, question of **8:** 145, 147, 154, 159, 165, 193; **13:** 142
    death, decay, and nature's destructiveness **8:** 145, 148, 154, 159, 165, 168, 170, 177, 182, 197, 210, 223, 228, 232, 243, 248, 252, 258, 267
    deformity as symbol **8:** 146, 147, 148, 152, 154, 159, 161, 165, 170, 177, 184, 185, 193, 218, 248, 252, 267; **19:** 164
    inversion of moral order **8:** 159, 168, 177, 182, 184, 185, 197, 201, 213, 218, 223, 232, 239, 243, 248, 252, 258, 262, 267; **39:** 360; **52:** 205, 214
    as Machiavellian villain **8:** 165, 182, 190, 201, 218, 232, 239, 243, 248; **39:** 308, 326, 360, 387; **52:** 201, 205, 257, 285
    as monster or symbol of diabolic **8:** 145, 147, 159, 162, 168, 170, 177, 182, 193, 197, 201, 228, 239, 248, 258; **13:** 142; **37:** 144; **39:** 326, 349; **52:** 227, 272

other literary villains, compared with **8:** 148, 161, 162, 165, 181, 182, 206, 213, 239, 267
role-playing, hypocrisy, and dissimulation **8:** 145, 148, 154, 159, 162, 165, 168, 170, 182, 190, 206, 213, 218, 228, 239, 243, 252, 258, 267; **25:** 141, 164, 245; **39:** 335, 341, 387; **52:** 257, 267
as scourge or instrument of God **8:** 163, 177, 193, 201, 218, 228, 248, 267; **39:** 308
as seducer **52:** 223
self-esteem **52:** 196
shamelessness **52:** 196
as Vice figure **8:** 190, 201, 213, 228, 243, 248, 252; **16:** 150; **39:** 383, 387; **52:** 223, 267
Richmond **8:** 154, 158, 163, 168, 177, 182, 193, 210, 218, 223, 228, 243, 248, 252; **13:** 142; **25:** 141; **39:** 349; **52:** 214, 257, 285
settings **14:** 516, 528; **52:** 263
Shakespeare's artistic growth, Richard III's contribution to **8:** 165, 167, 182, 193, 197, 206, 210, 228, 239, 267; **25:** 164; **39:** 305, 326, 370
Shakespeare's political sympathies **8:** 147, 163, 177, 193, 197, 201, 223, 228, 232, 243, 248, 267; **39:** 349; **42:** 132
sources **52:** 263, 290
chronicles **8:** 145, 165, 193, 197, 201, 206, 210, 213, 228, 232
Marlowe, Christopher **8:** 167, 168, 182, 201, 206, 218
morality plays **8:** 182, 190, 201, 213, 239
Seneca, other classical writers **8:** 165, 190, 201, 206, 228, 248
staging issues **14:** 515, 527, 528, 537; **16:** 137; **52:** 263, 272
structure **8:** 154, 161, 163, 167, 168, 170, 177, 184, 193, 197, 201, 206, 210, 218, 223, 228, 232, 243, 252, 262, 267; **16:** 150
The Tragical History of King Richard III (Colley Cibber adaptation), compared with **8:** 159, 161, 243
traditional values **39:** 335
Tudor myth **8:** 163, 165, 177, 184, 193, 201, 218, 228, 232, 243, 248, 252, 267; **39:** 305, 308, 326, 387; **42:** 132
Wars of the Roses **8:** 163, 165, 177, 184, 193, 201, 218, 228, 232, 243, 248, 252, 267; **39:** 308
wooing scenes (Act I, scene ii and Act IV, scene iv) **8:** 145, 147, 152, 153, 154, 159, 161, 164, 170, 190, 197, 206, 213, 218, 223, 232, 239, 243, 252, 258, 267; **16:** 150; **19:** 164; **25:** 141, 164; **39:** 308, 326, 360, 387; **52:** 227, 249, 280

Romeo and Juliet (Volumes 5, 11, 33, 51)

accident or chance **5:** 418, 444, 448, 467, 470, 487, 573
adolescence **33:** 249, 255, 257
amour-passion or Liebestod myth **5:** 484, 489, 528, 530, 542, 550, 575; **32:** 256; **51:** 195, 219, 236
androgyny **13:** 530
anxiety **13:** 235
balcony scene **32:** 276; **51:** 219
Caius Marius (Thomas Otway adaptation) **11:** 377, 378, 488, 495
comic and tragic elements, combination of **46:** 78
contradiction, paradox, and opposition **5:** 421, 427, 431, 496, 509, 513, 516, 520, 525, 528, 538; **33:** 287; **44:** 11
costuming **11:** 505, 509
courtly love tradition, influence of **5:** 505, 542, 575; **33:** 233
desire **51:** 227, 236
detention of Friar John **5:** 448, 467, 470
divine will, role of **5:** 485, 493, 505, 533, 573
dramatic shortcomings or failure **5:** 416, 418, 420, 426, 436, 437, 448, 464, 467, 469, 480, 487, 524, 562
Elizabethan poetics, influence of **5:** 416, 520, 522, 528, 550, 559, 575
evil **5:** 485, 493, 505
as experimental play **5:** 464, 509, 528
fate **5:** 431, 444, 464, 469, 470, 479, 480, 485, 487, 493, 509, 530, 533, 562, 565, 571, 573; **33:** 249
feud **5:** 415, 419, 425, 447, 458, 464, 469, 479, 480, 493, 509, 522, 556, 565, 566, 571, 575; **25:** 181; **51:** 245
Friar Lawrence
contribution to catastrophe **5:** 437, 444, 470; **33:** 300; **51:** 253
philosophy of moderation **5:** 427, 431, 437, 438, 443, 444, 445, 458, 467, 479, 505, 538
as Shakespeare's spokesman **5:** 427, 431, 437, 458, 467
ideal love **5:** 421, 427, 431, 436, 437, 450, 463, 469, 498, 505, 575; **25:** 257; **33:** 210, 225, 272; **51:** 25, 44, 195, 203, 219
gender issues **32:** 256; **51:** 253
lamentation scene (Act IV, scene v) **5:** 425, 492, 538
language and imagery **5:** 420, 426, 431, 436, 437, 456, 477, 479, 489, 492, 496, 509, 520, 522, 528, 538, 542, 550, 559; **25:** 181, 245, 257; **32:** 276; **33:** 210, 272, 274, 287; **42:** 271; **51:** 203, 212, 227
love versus fate **5:** 421, 437, 438, 443, 445, 458; **33:** 249
medieval influence **5:** 480, 505, 509, 573
Mercutio
bawdy **5:** 463, 525, 550, 575
death, decay, and nature's destructiveness **5:** 415, 418, 419, 547; **33:** 290
as worldly counterpoint to Romeo **5:** 425, 464, 542; **33:** 290; **51:** 195
comic and tragic elements, combination of **5:** 496, 524, 528, 547, 559
Neoclassical rules **5:** 416, 418, 426
Nurse **5:** 419, 425, 463, 464, 575; **33:** 294
Othello, compared with **32:** 302
Petrarchan poetics, influence of **5:** 416, 520, 522, 528, 550, 559, 575; **32:** 276; **51:** 212, 236
prose adaptations of Juliet's character **19:** 261
psychoanalytic interpretation **5:** 513, 556; **51:** 253
public versus private worlds **5:** 520, 550; **25:** 181; **33:** 274
reconciliation **5:** 415, 419, 427, 439, 447, 480, 487, 493, 505, 533, 536, 562
rhetoric **42:** 271
rival productions **11:** 381, 382, 384, 385, 386, 487
Romeo and Juliet
death-wish **5:** 431, 489, 505, 528, 530, 538, 542, 550, 566, 571, 575; **32:** 212
first meeting (Act I, scene v) **51:** 212
immortality **5:** 536
Juliet's epithalamium speech (Act III, scene ii) **5:** 431, 477, 492
Juliet's innocence **5:** 421, 423, 450, 454; **33:** 257
maturation **5:** 437, 454, 467, 493, 498, 509, 520, 565; **33:** 249, 257
rebellion **25:** 257
reckless passion **5:** 419, 427, 431, 438, 443, 444, 448, 467, 479, 485, 505, 533, 538, 542; **33:** 241
Romeo's dream (Act V, scene i) **5:** 513, 536, 556; **45:** 40; **51:** 203
Rosaline, Romeo's relationship with **5:** 419, 423, 425, 427, 438, 498, 542, 575
sexuality **25:** 181; **33:** 225, 233, 241, 246, 274, 300; **51:** 227, 236
source of tragic catastrophe **5:** 418, 427, 431, 448, 458, 469, 479, 480, 485, 487, 493, 509, 522, 528, 530, 533, 542, 565, 571, 573; **33:** 210; **51:** 245
sources **5:** 416, 419, 423, 450; **32:** 222; **33:** 210; **45:** 40
staging issues **11:** 499, 505, 507, 514, 517; **13:** 243; **25:** 181; **32:** 212
structure **5:** 438, 448, 464, 469, 470, 477, 480, 496, 518, 524, 525, 528, 547, 559; **33:** 210, 246
tomb scene (Act V, scene iii) **5:** 416, 419, 423; **13:** 243; **25:** 181, 245; **51:** 219
triumph over death or fate **5:** 421, 423, 427, 505, 509, 520, 530, 536, 565, 566; **51:** 219
Verona society **5:** 556, 566; **13:** 235; **33:** 255; **51:** 245
wordplay **32:** 256

Sonnets (Volumes 10, 40, 51)

ambiguity **10:** 251, 256; **28:** 385; **40:** 221, 228, 268
audience **51:** 316
authenticity **10:** 153, 154, 230, 243; **48:** 325
autobiographical elements **10:** 159, 160, 166, 167, 175, 176, 182, 196, 205, 213, 215, 226, 233, 238, 240, 251, 279, 283, 302, 309, 325, 337, 377; **13:** 487; **16:** 461; **28:** 363, 385; **42:** 303; **48:** 325
beauty **10:** 247; **51:** 288
Christian elements **10:** 191, 256
composition date **10:** 153, 154, 161, 166, 196, 217, 226, 270, 277; **28:** 363, 385
Dark Lady **10:** 161, 167, 176, 216, 217, 218, 226, 240, 302, 342, 377, 394; **25:** 374; **37:** 374; **40:** 273; **48:** 346; **51:** 284, 288, 292, 321
deception, disguise, and duplicity **25:** 374; **40:** 221
dramatic elements **10:** 155, 182, 240, 251, 283, 367
editorial and textual issues **28:** 363; **40:** 273; **42:** 303
Elizabeth, audience of **48:** 325
the Friend **10:** 279, 302, 309, 379, 385, 391, 394; **51:** 284, 288, 292, 300, 304, 316, 321
friendship **10:** 185, 279; **28:** 380; **51:** 284
gender issues **37:** 374; **40:** 238, 247, 254, 264, 268, 273; **53:** 1

homoerotic elements **10:** 155, 156, 159, 161, 175, 213, 391; **16:** 461; **28:** 363, 380; **37:** 347; **40:** 254, 264, 273; **51:** 270, 284
identities of persons **10:** 154, 155, 156, 161, 166, 167, 169, 173, 174, 175, 185, 190, 191, 196, 218, 226, 230, 233, 240; **40:** 238
Ireland, William Henry, forgeries of **48:** 325
irony or satire **10:** 256, 293, 334, 337, 346; **51:** 300
Italian influences **28:** 407
language and imagery **10:** 247, 251, 255, 256, 290, 353, 372, 385; **13:** 445; **28:** 380, 385; **32:** 327, 352; **40:** 228, 247, 284, 292, 303; **51:** 270, 304
love **10:** 173, 247, 287, 290, 293, 302, 309, 322, 325, 329, 394; **28:** 380; **37:** 347; **51:** 270, 284, 288, 292
love versus reason **10:** 329
A Lover's Complaint (the Rival Poet) **10:** 243, 353
   gender issues **48:** 336
     pastoral tradition, compared with **48:** 336
     sonnets, compared with **48:** 336
lust **51:** 292
lust versus reason **51:** 288
magic **48:** 346
Mr. W. H. **10:** 153, 155, 161, 169, 174, 182, 190, 196, 217, 218, 377
Montaigne's Essais, relation to **42:** 382
mutability, theme of **42:** 382
Neoplatonism **10:** 191, 205
occult **48:** 346
other sonnet writers, Shakespeare compared with **10:** 247, 260, 265, 283, 290, 293, 309, 353, 367; **28:** 380, 385, 407; **37:** 374; **40:** 247, 264, 303; **42:** 303
pedagogy **37:** 374
performative issues **48:** 352
poet-patron relationship **48:** 352
poetic style **10:** 153, 155, 156, 158, 159, 160, 161, 173, 175, 182, 214, 247, 251, 255, 260, 265, 283, 287, 296, 302, 315, 322, 325, 337, 346, 349, 360, 367, 385; **16:** 472; **40:** 221, 228; **51:** 270
procreation **10:** 379, 385; **16:** 461;
race **53:** 1
rhetoric of consolation **42:** 382
the Rival Poet **10:** 169, 233, 334, 337, 385; **48:** 352
self-love **10:** 372; **25:** 374; **51:** 270, 300, 304
selfishness versus self-knowledge **51:** 292
sexuality **25:** 374
as social action **48:** 352
sonnet arrangement **10:** 174, 176, 182, 205, 226, 230, 236, 315, 353; **28:** 363; **40:** 238
sonnet form **10:** 255, 325, 367; **37:** 347; **40:** 284, 303; **51:** 270
sonnets (individual):
  3 **10:** 346
  12 **10:** 360
  15 **40:** 292
  18 **40:** 292
  20 **10:** 391; **13:** 530
  21 **32:** 352
  26 **10:** 161
  30 **10:** 296
  35 **10:** 251
  49 **10:** 296
  53 **10:** 349; **32:** 327, 352
  54 **32:** 352
  55 **13:** 445
  57 **10:** 296
  59 **16:** 472
  60 **10:** 296; **16:** 472
  64 **10:** 329, 360
  65 **10:** 296; **40:** 292
  66 **10:** 315
  68 **32:** 327
  71 **10:** 167
  73 **10:** 315, 353, 360
  76 **10:** 334
  79 **32:** 352
  82 **32:** 352
  86 **32:** 352
  87 **10:** 296; **40:** 303
  93 **13:** 487
  94 **10:** 256, 296; **32:** 327
  95 **32:** 327
  98 **32:** 352
  99 **32:** 352
  104 **10:** 360
  105 **32:** 327
  107 **10:** 270, 277
  116 **10:** 329, 379; **13:** 445
  117 **10:** 337
  119 **10:** 337
  121 **10:** 346
  123 **10:** 270
  124 **10:** 265, 270, 329
  126 **10:** 161
  129 **10:** 353, 394; **22:** 12
  130 **10:** 346
  138 **10:** 296
  144 **10:** 394
  145 **10:** 358; **40:** 254
  146 **10:** 353
sonnets (groups):
  1-17 **10:** 296, 315, 379, 385; **16:** 461; **40:** 228
  1-21 **40:** 268
  1-26 **10:** 176
  1-126 **10:** 161, 176, 185, 191, 196, 205, 213, 226, 236, 279, 309, 315, 372
  18-22 **10:** 315
  18-126 **10:** 379
  23-40 **10:** 315
  27-55 **10:** 176
  33-9 **10:** 329
  56-77 **10:** 176
  76-86 **10:** 315
  78-80 **10:** 334, 385
  78-101 **10:** 176
  82-6 **10:** 334
  100-12 **10:** 337
  102-26 **10:** 176
  123-25 **10:** 385
  127-52 **10:** 293, 385
  127-54 **10:** 161, 176, 185, 190, 196, 213, 226, 236, 309, 315, 342, 394
  151-52 **10:** 315
sources **10:** 153, 154, 156, 158, 233, 251, 255, 293, 353; **16:** 472; **28:** 407; **42:** 382
structure **10:** 175, 176, 182, 205, 230, 260, 296, 302, 309, 315, 337, 349, 353; **40:** 238
subjectivity **37:** 374
time **10:** 265, 302, 309, 322, 329, 337, 360, 379; **13:** 445; **40:** 292
visual arts, relation to **28:** 407
voice **51:** 316
  apparent inconsistencies in **51:** 321

The Taming of the Shrew (Volumes 9, 12, 31)

  appearance versus reality **9:** 343, 350, 353, 365, 369, 370, 381, 390. 430; **12:** 416; **31:** 326
  Baptista **9:** 325, 344, 345, 375, 386, 393, 413
  Bianca **9:** 325, 342, 344, 345, 360, 362, 370, 375
  Bianca-Lucentio subplot **9:** 365, 370, 375, 390, 393, 401, 407, 413, 430; **16:** 13; **31:** 339
  Catherine and Petruchio (David Garrick adaptation) **12:** 309, 310, 311, 416
  class distinctions, conflict, and relations **31:** 300, 351; **50:** 64, 74
  deception, disguise, and duplicity **12:** 416
  Elizabethan culture, relation to **31:** 288, 295, 300, 315, 326, 345, 351
  as farce **9:** 330, 337, 338, 341, 342, 365, 381, 386, 413, 426
  folk elements **9:** 381, 393, 404, 426
  gender issues **28:** 24 **31:** 261, 268, 276, 282, 288, 295, 300, 335, 351
  genre **9:** 329, 334, 362, 375; **22:** 48; **31:** 261, 269, 276
  induction **9:** 320, 322, 332, 337, 345, 350, 362, 365, 369, 370, 381, 390, 393, 407, 419, 424, 430; **12:** 416, 427, 430, 431, 441; **19:** 34, 122; **22:** 48; **31:** 269, 315, 351
  irony or satire **9:** 340, 375, 398, 407, 413; **13:** 3; **19:** 122
  Kate
    characterization **32:** 1
    final speech (Act V, scene ii) **9:** 318, 319, 329, 330, 338, 340, 341, 345, 347, 353, 355, 360, 365, 381, 386, 401, 404, 413, 426, 430; **19:** 3; **22:** 48
    love for Petruchio **9:** 338, 340, 353, 430; **12:** 435
    portrayals of **31:** 282
    shrewishness **9:** 322, 323, 325, 332, 344, 345, 360, 365, 370, 375, 386, 393, 398, 404, 413
    transformation **9:** 323, 341, 355, 370, 386, 393, 401, 404, 407, 419, 424, 426, 430; **16:** 13; **19:** 34; **22:** 48; **31:** 288, 295, 339, 351
  Kiss Me, Kate (Cole Porter adaptation) **31:** 282
  language and imagery **9:** 336, 338, 393, 401, 404, 407, 413; **22:** 378; **28:** 9; **31:** 261, 288, 300, 326, 335, 339; **32:** 56
  Lucentio **9:** 325, 342, 362, 375, 393
  marriage **9:** 322, 325, 329, 332, 329, 332, 334, 341, 342, 343, 344, 345, 347, 353, 360, 362, 375, 381, 390, 398, 401, 404, 413, 426, 430; **13:** 3; **19:** 3; **28:** 24; **31:** 288; **51:** 44
  metadramatic elements **9:** 350, 419, 424; **31:** 300, 315
  metamorphosis or transformation **9:** 370, 430
  pedagogy **19:** 122
  performance history **31:** 282
  performance issues **12:** 313, 314, 316, 317, 337, 338; **31:** 315
  Petruchio
    admirable qualities **9:** 320, 332, 341, 344, 345, 370, 375, 386
    as lord of misrule **50:** 64
    audacity or vigor **9:** 325, 337, 355, 375, 386, 404

characterization **32:** 1
coarseness or brutality **9:** 325, 329, 365, 390, 393, 398, 407; **19:** 122
as lord of misrule **9:** 393
love for Kate **9:** 338, 340, 343, 344, 386; **12:** 435
portrayals of **31:** 282
pragmatism **9:** 329, 334, 375, 398, 424; **13:** 3; **31:** 345, 351
taming method **9:** 320, 323, 329, 340, 341, 343, 345, 355, 369, 370, 375, 390, 398, 407, 413, 419, 424; **19:** 3, 12, 21 **31:** 269, 295, 326, 335, 339
popularity **9:** 318, 338, 404
role-playing **9:** 322, 353, 355, 360, 369, 370, 398, 401, 407, 413, 419, 424; **13:** 3; **31:** 288, 295, 315
romantic elements **9:** 334, 342, 362, 375, 407
Shakespeare's other plays, compared with **9:** 334, 342, 360, 393, 426, 430; **31:** 261; **50:** 74
Sly **9:** 320, 322, 350, 370, 381, 390, 398, 430; **12:** 316, 335, 416, 427, 441; **16:** 13; **19:** 34, 122; **22:** 48; **37:** 31; **50:** 74
sources
  Ariosto **9:** 320, 334, 341, 342, 370
  folk tales **9:** 332, 390, 393
  Gascoigne **9:** 370, 390
  Old and New Comedy **9:** 419
  Ovid **9:** 318, 370, 430
  Plautus **9:** 334, 341, 342
  shrew tradition **9:** 355; **19:** 3; **32:** 1, 56
structure **9:** 318, 322, 325, 332, 334, 341, 362, 370, 390, 426; **22:** 48, 378; **31:** 269
play-within-a-play **12:** 416; **22:** 48
The Taming of a Shrew (anonymous), compared with **9:** 334, 350, 426; **12:** 312; **22:** 48; **31:** 261, 276, 339
textual issues **22:** 48; **31:** 261, 276; **31:** 276
violence **43:** 61

The Tempest (Volumes 8, 15, 29, 45)

allegorical elements **8:** 294, 295, 302, 307, 308, 312, 326, 328, 336, 345, 364; **42:** 327
Antonio and Sebastian **8:** 295, 299, 304, 328, 370, 396, 429, 454; **13:** 440; **29:** 278, 297, 343, 362, 368, 377
Ariel **8:** 289, 293, 294, 295, 297, 304, 307, 315, 320, 326, 328, 336, 340, 345, 356, 364, 420, 458; **22:** 302; **29:** 278, 297, 362, 368, 377
art versus nature **8:** 396, 404; **29:** 278, 297, 362
autobiographical elements **8:** 302, 308, 312, 324, 326, 345, 348, 353, 364, 380
Caliban **8:** 286, 287, 289, 292, 294, 295, 297, 302, 304, 307, 309, 315, 326, 328, 336, 353, 364, 370, 380, 390, 396, 401, 414, 420, 423, 429, 435, 454; **13:** 424, 440; **15:** 189, 312, 322, 374, 379; **22:** 302; **25:** 382; **28:** 249; **29:** 278, 292, 297, 343, 368, 377, 396; **32:** 367; **45:** 211, 219, 226, 259; **53:** 45, 64
characterization **8:** 287, 289, 292, 294, 295, 308, 326, 334, 336; **28:** 415; **42:** 339; **45:** 219
classical influence and sources **29:** 278, 343, 362, 368

colonialism **13:** 424, 440; **15:** 228, 268, 269, 270, 271, 272, 273; **19:** 421; **25:** 357, 382; **28:** 249; **29:** 343, 368; **32:** 338, 367, 400; **42:** 327; **45:** 200, 280; **53:** 11, 21, 45, 67
compassion, theme of **42:** 346
conspiracy or treason **16:** 426; **19:** 357; **25:** 382; **29:** 377
dreams **45:** 236, 247, 259
education or nurturing **8:** 353, 370, 384, 396; **29:** 292, 368, 377
exposition scene (Act I, scene ii) **8:** 287, 289, 293, 299, 334
Ferdinand **8:** 328, 336, 359, 454; **19:** 357; **22:** 302; **29:** 362, 339, 377
freedom and servitude **8:** 304, 307, 312, 429; **22:** 302; **29:** 278, 368, 377; **37:** 336
gender **53:** 64, 67
Gonzalo **22:** 302; **29:** 278, 343, 362, 368
Gonzalo's commonwealth **8:** 312, 336, 370, 390, 396, 404; **19:** 357; **29:** 368; **45:** 280
good versus evil **8:** 302, 311, 315, 370, 423, 439; **29:** 278, 297
historical content **8:** 364, 408, 420; **16:** 426; **25:** 382; **29:** 278, 339, 343, 368; **45:** 226; **53:** 21, 53
the island **8:** 308, 315, 447; **25:** 357, 382; **29:** 278, 343
language and imagery **8:** 324, 348, 384, 390, 404, 454; **19:** 421; **29:** 278; **29:** 297, 343, 368, 377
love **8:** 435, 439; **29:** 297, 339, 377, 396
magic or supernatural elements **8:** 287, 293, 304, 315, 340, 356, 396, 401, 404, 408, 435, 458; **28:** 391, 415; **29:** 297, 343, 377; **45:** 272
the masque (Act IV, scene i) **8:** 404, 414, 423, 435, 439; **25:** 357; **28:** 391, 415; **29:** 278, 292, 339, 343, 368; **42:** 339; **45:** 188
Miranda **8:** 289, 301, 304, 328, 336, 370, 454; **19:** 357; **22:** 302; **28:** 249; **29:** 278, 297, 362, 368, 377, 396; **53:** 64
Montaigne's Essais, relation to **42:** 346
morality **52:** 43
music **8:** 390, 404; **29:** 292; **37:** 321; **42:** 339
nature **8:** 315, 370, 390, 408, 414; **29:** 343, 362, 368, 377
Neoclassical rules **8:** 287, 292, 293, 334; **25:** 357; **29:** 292; **45:** 200
politics **8:** 304, 307, 315, 353, 359, 364, 401, 408; **16:** 426; **19:** 421; **29:** 339; **37:** 336; **42:** 327; **45:** 272, 280; **52:** 43
Prospero
  characterization **8:** 312, 348, 370, 458; **16:** 442; **22:** 302; **45:** 188, 272
  as God or Providence **8:** 311, 328, 364, 380, 429, 435
  magic, nature of **8:** 301, 340, 356, 396, 414, 423, 458; **25:** 382; **28:** 391; **29:** 278, 292, 368, 377, 396; **32:** 338, 343
  psychoanalytic interpretation **45:** 259
  redemptive powers **8:** 302, 320, 353, 370, 390, 429, 439, 447; **29:** 297
  as ruler **8:** 304, 308, 309, 420, 423; **13:** 424; **22:** 302; **29:** 278, 362, 377, 396
  self-control **8:** 312, 414, 420; **22:** 302; **44:** 11
  self-knowledge **16:** 442; **22:** 302; **29:** 278, 292, 362, 377, 396
  as Shakespeare or creative artist **8:** 299, 302, 308, 312, 320, 324, 353, 364, 435, 447

as tragic hero **8:** 359, 370, 464; **29:** 292
providential order **52:** 43
race **53:** 11, 21, 45, 53, 64, 67
realism **8:** 340, 359, 464
reality and illusion **8:** 287, 315, 359, 401, 435, 439, 447, 454; **22:** 302; **45:** 236, 247
reconciliation **8:** 302, 312, 320, 334, 348, 359, 370, 384, 401, 404, 414, 429, 439, 447, 454; **16:** 442; **22:** 302; **29:** 297; **37:** 336; **45:** 236
religious, mythic, or spiritual content **8:** 328, 390, 423, 429, 435; **45:** 211, 247
romance or pastoral tradition, influence of **8:** 336, 348, 396, 404; **37:** 336
sexuality **53:** 45
Shakespeare's other plays, compared with **8:** 294, 302, 324, 326, 348, 353, 380, 401, 464; **13:** 424
spectacle versus simple staging **15:** 206, 207, 208, 210, 217, 219, 222, 223, 224, 225, 227, 228, 305, 352; **28:** 415
sources **45:** 226
staging issues **15:** 343, 346, 352, 361, 364, 366, 368, 371, 385; **28:** 391, 415; **29:** 339; **32:** 338, 343; **42:** 339; **45:** 200
Stephano and Trinculo, comic subplot of **8:** 292, 297, 299, 304, 309, 324, 328, 353, 370; **25:** 382; **29:** 377; **46:** 14, 33
structure **8:** 294, 295, 299, 320, 384, 439; **28:** 391, 415; **29:** 292, 297; **45:** 188
subversiveness **22:** 302
The Tempest; or, The Enchanted Island (William Davenant/John Dryden adaptation) **15:** 189, 190, 192, 193
The Tempest; or, The Enchanted Island (Thomas Shadwell adaptation) **15:** 195, 196, 199
time **8:** 401, 439, 464; **25:** 357; **29:** 278, 292; **45:** 236
tragic elements **8:** 324, 348, 359, 370, 380, 408, 414, 439, 458, 464
trickster, motif of **22:** 302; **29:** 297
usurpation or rebellion **8:** 304, 370, 408, 420; **25:** 357, 382; **29:** 278, 362, 377; **37:** 336
utopia **45:** 280

Timon of Athens (Volumes 1, 20, 27, 52)

Alcibiades **25:** 198; **27:** 191
alienation **1:** 523; **27:** 161
Apemantus **1:** 453, 467, 483; **20:** 476, 493; **25:** 198; **27:** 166, 223, 235
appearance versus reality **1:** 495, 500, 515, 523; **52:** 311, 329
Athens **27:** 223, 230
authorship controversy **1:** 464, 466, 467, 469, 474, 477, 478, 480, 490, 499, 507, 518; **16:** 351; **20:** 433
autobiographical elements **1:** 462, 467, 470, 473, 474, 478, 480; **27:** 166, 175
Elizabethan culture, relation to **1:** 487, 489, 495, 500; **20:** 433; **27:** 203, 212, 230; **50:** 13; **52:** 320, 354
as inferior or flawed plays **1:** 476, 481, 489, 499, 520; **20:** 433, 439, 491; **25:** 198; **27:** 157, 175; **52:** 338, 349
genre **1:** 454, 456, 459, 460, 462, 483, 492, 499, 503, 509, 511, 512, 515, 518, 525, 531; **27:** 203
King Lear, relation to **1:** 453, 459, 511; **16:** 351; **27:** 161; **37:** 222

language and imagery **1:** 488; **13:** 392; **25:** 198; **27:** 166, 184, 235; **52:** 329, 345, 354
language and philosophy **52:** 311
as medieval allegory or morality play **1:** 492, 511, 518; **27:** 155
mixture of genres **16:** 351; **25:** 198
nihilistic elements **1:** 481, 513, 529; **13:** 392; **20:** 481
pessimistic elements **1:** 462, 467, 470, 473, 478, 480; **20:** 433, 481; **27:** 155, 191
Poet and Painter **25:** 198; **52:** 320
politics **27:** 223, 230; **50:** 13
religious, mythic, or spiritual content **1:** 505, 512, 513, 523; **20:** 493
satirical elements **27:** 155, 235
self-knowledge **1:** 456, 459, 462, 495, 503, 507, 515, 518, 526; **20:** 493; **27:** 166
Senecan elements **27:** 235
Shakespeare's other tragedies, compared with **27:** 166; **52:** 296
sources **16:** 351; **27:** 191; **52:** 301
staging issues **20:** 445, 446, 481, 491, 492, 493
structure **27:** 191; **52:** 338, 345, 349
Timon
  comic traits **25:** 198
  as flawed hero **1:** 456, 459, 462, 472, 495, 503, 507, 515; **16:** 351; **20:** 429, 433, 476; **25:** 198; **27:** 157, 161
  misanthropy **13:** 392; **20:** 431, 464, 476, 481, 491, 492, 493; **27:** 161, 175, 184, 196; **37:** 222; **52:** 296, 301
  as noble figure **1:** 467, 473, 483, 499; **20:** 493; **27:** 212
wealth and social class **1:** 466, 487, 495; **25:** 198; **27:** 184, 196, 212; **50:** 13

Titus Andronicus (Volumes 4, 17, 27, 43)

Aaron **4:** 632, 637, 650, 651, 653, 668, 672, 675; **27:** 255; **28:** 249, 330; **43:** 176; **53:** 86, 92
amputations, significance of **48:** 264
authorship controversy **4:** 613, 614, 615, 616, 617, 619, 623, 624, 625, 626, 628, 631, 632, 635, 642
autobiographical elements **4:** 619, 624, 625, 664
banquet scene **25:** 245; **27:** 255; **32:** 212
ceremonies, rites, and rituals, importance of **27:** 261; **32:** 265; **48:** 264
characterization **4:** 613, 628, 632, 635, 640, 644, 647, 650, 675; **27:** 293; **43:** 170, 176
Christian elements **4:** 656, 680
civilization versus barbarism **4:** 653; **27:** 293; **28:** 249; **32:** 265
Clarissa (Samuel Richardson), compared with **48:** 277
Elizabethan culture, relation to **27:** 282
Euripides, influence of **27:** 285
evil **53:** 86, 92
language and imagery **4:** 617, 624, 635, 642, 644, 646, 659, 664, 668, 672, 675; **13:** 225; **16:** 225; **25:** 245; **27:** 246, 293, 313, 318, 325; **43:** 186, 222, 227, 239, 247, 262,
language versus action **4:** 642, 644, 647, 664, 668; **13:** 225; **27:** 293, 313, 325; **43:** 186
Lavinia **27:** 266; **28:** 249; **32:** 212; **43:** 170, 239, 247, 255, 262

marriage as political tyranny **48:** 264
medieval literary influence **4:** 646, 650; **27:** 299
order versus disintegration **4:** 618, 647; **43:** 186, 195
Ovid, influence of **4:** 647, 659, 664, 668; **13:** 225; **27:** 246, 275, 285, 293, 299, 306; **28:** 249; **43:** 195, 203, 206
partiarchy 50: 13
political content **43:** 262
politics **27:** 282; **48:** 264
primogeniture 50: 13
race **53:** 86, 92
rape **43:** 227, 255; **48:** 277
rightful succession **4:** 638
Roman elements **43:** 206, 222
Romans versus Goths **27:** 282
Senecan or revenge tragedy elements **4:** 618, 627, 628, 636, 639, 644, 646, 664, 672, 680; **16:** 225; **27:** 275, 318; **43:** 170, 206, 227
Shakespeare's canon, place in **4:** 614, 616, 618, 619, 637, 639, 646, 659, 664, 668; **43:** 195
Shakespeare's other tragedies, compared with **16:** 225; **27:** 275, 325
staging issues **17:** 449, 452, 456, 487; **25:** 245; **32:** 212, 249
structure **4:** 618, 619, 624, 631, 635, 640, 644, 646, 647, 653, 656, 659, 662, 664, 668, 672; **27:** 246, 285
Tamora **4:** 632, 662, 672, 675; **27:** 266; **43:** 170
Titus **4:** 632, 637, 640, 644, 647, 653, 656, 662; **25:** 245; **27:** 255
Vergil, influence of **27:** 306; **28:** 249
violence **13:** 225; **25:** 245; **27:** 255; **28:** 249; **32:** 249, 265; **43:** 1, 186, 203, 227, 239, 247, 255, 262

Troilus and Cressida (Volumes 3, 18, 27, 43)

allegorical elements **52:** 5
ambiguity **3:** 544, 568, 583, 587, 589, 599, 611, 621; **27:** 400; **43:** 365
ambivalence **43:** 340
assignation scene (Act V, scene ii) **18:** 442, 451
autobiographical elements **3:** 548, 554, 557, 558, 574, 606, 630
body, role of **42:** 66
characterization **3:** 538, 539, 540, 541, 548, 566, 571, 604, 611, 621; **27:** 381, 391
Chaucer's Criseyde, compared with **43:** 305
chivalry, decline of **16:** 84; **27:** 370, 374
communication, failure of **43:** 277
conclusion **3:** 538, 549, 558, 566, 574, 583, 594
comedy vs. tragedy **43:** 351
contradictions **43:** 377
costumes **18:** 289, 371, 406, 419
courtly love **22:** 58
Cressida
  as ambiguous figure **43:** 305
  inconsistency **3:** 538; **13:** 53; **16:** 70; **22:** 339; **27:** 362
  individual will versus social values **3:** 549, 561, 571, 590, 604, 617, 626; **13:** 53; **27:** 396
  infidelity **3:** 536, 537, 544, 554, 555; **18:** 277, 284, 286; **22:** 58, 339; **27:** 400; **43:** 298
  lack of punishment **3:** 536, 537
  as mother figure **22:** 339

objectification of **43:** 329
as sympathetic figure **3:** 557, 560, 604, 609; **18:** 284, 423; **22:** 58; **27:** 396, 400; **43:** 305
cynicism **43:** 298
desire **43:** 317, 329, 340
disillusioned or cynical tone **3:** 544, 548, 554, 557, 558, 571, 574, 630, 642; **18:** 284, 332, 403, 406, 423; **27:** 376
disorder **3:** 578, 589, 599, 604, 609; **18:** 332, 406, 412, 423; **27:** 366
double plot **3:** 569, 613
Elizabeth I
  waning power **43:** 365
Elizabethan culture, relation to **3:** 560, 574, 606; **25:** 56
food imagery **43:** 298
genre **3:** 541, 542, 549, 558, 566, 571, 574, 587, 594, 604, 630, 642; **27:** 366
Greece **43:** 287
inaction **3:** 587, 621; **27:** 347
language and imagery **3:** 561, 569, 596, 599, 606, 624, 630, 635; **22:** 58, 339; **27:** 332; 366; **42:** 66
love and honor **3:** 555, 604; **27:** 370, 374
love versus war **18:** 332, 371, 406, 423; **22:** 339; **27:** 376; **43:** 377
male/female relationships **16:** 70; **22:** 339; **27:** 362
marriage **22:** 339; **51:** 44
master-slave relationship **22:** 58
medieval chivalry **3:** 539, 543, 544, 555, 606; **27:** 376
moral corruption **3:** 578, 589, 599, 604, 609; **18:** 332, 406, 412, 423; **27:** 366; **43:** 298
morality **52:** 5
Neoclassical rules **3:** 537, 538; **18:** 276, 278, 281
nihilistic elements **27:** 354
patriarchy **22:** 58
politics **3:** 536, 560, 606; **16:** 84
as "problem play" **3:** 555, 566
  lack of resolution **43:** 277
psychoanalytical criticism **43:** 287
rape **43:** 357
satirical elements **3:** 539, 543, 544, 555, 558, 574; **27:** 341
sexuality **22:** 58, 339; **25:** 56; **27:** 362; **43:** 365
sources **3:** 537, 539, 540, 541, 544, 549, 558, 566, 574, 587; **27:** 376, 381, 391, 400
staging issues **16:** 70; **18:** 289, 332, 371, 395, 403, 406, 412, 419, 423, 442, 447, 451
structure **3:** 536, 538, 549, 568, 569, 578, 583, 589, 611, 613; **27:** 341, 347, 354, 391
Thersites **13:** 53; **25:** 56; **27:** 381
time **3:** 561, 571, 583, 584, 613, 621, 626, 634
Troilus
  contradictory behavior **3:** 596, 602, 635; **27:** 362
  Cressida, relationship with **3:** 594, 596, 606; **22:** 58
  integrity **3:** 617
  opposition to Ulysses **3:** 561, 584, 590
  as unsympathetic figure **18:** 423; **22:** 58, 339; **43:** 317
  as warrior **3:** 596; **22:** 339
Troilus and Cressida, or Truth Found too late (John Dryden adaptation) **18:** 276, 277, 278, 280, 281, 283

Trojan versus Greek values **3:** 541, 561, 574, 584, 590, 596, 621, 638; **27:** 370
Trojan War
   as myth **43:** 293
Troy **43:** 287
Ulysses's speech on degree (Act I, scene iii) **3:** 549, 599, 609, 642; **27:** 396
value systems **3:** 578, 583, 589, 602, 613, 617; **13:** 53; **27:** 370, 396, 400
violence **43:** 329, 351, 357, 365, 377
   through satire **43:** 293

Twelfth Night (Volumes 1, 26, 34, 46)

ambiguity **1:** 554, 639; **34:** 287, 316
Antonio **22:** 69
appetite **1:** 563, 596, 609, 615; **52:** 57
autobiographical elements **1:** 557, 561, 599; **34:** 338
bear-baiting **19:** 42
characterization **1:** 539, 540, 543, 545, 550, 554, 581, 594; **26:** 257, 337, 342, 346, 364, 366, 371, 374; **34:** 281, 293, 311, 338; **46:** 286, 324
Christian elements **46:** 338
comic elements **26:** 233, 257, 337, 342, 371; **51:** 1; **52:** 57
composition date **37:** 78
credibility **1:** 540, 542, 543, 554, 562, 581, 587
dark or tragic elements **46:** 310
Elizabethan culture, relation to **1:** 549, 553, 555, 563, 581, 587, 620; **16:** 53; **19:** 42, 78; **26:** 357; **28:** 1; **34:** 323, 330; **46:** 291; **51:** 15
ethical or moral issues **52:** 57
fancy **1:** 543, 546
Feste
   characterization **1:** 558, 655, 658; **26:** 233, 364; **46:** 1, 14, 18, 33, 52, 60, 303, 310
   role in play **1:** 546, 551, 553, 566, 570, 571, 579, 635, 658; **46:** 297, 303, 310
   song **1:** 543, 548, 561, 563, 566, 570, 572, 603, 620, 642; **46:** 297
festive or folklore elements **46:** 338; **51:** 15
gender issues **19:** 78; **34:** 344; **37:** 59; **42:** 32; **46:** 347, 362, 369
homosexuality **22:** 69; **42:** 32; **46:** 362
language and imagery **1:** 570, 650, 664; **22:** 12; **28:** 9; **34:** 293; **37:** 59
love **1:** 543, 546, 573, 580, 587, 595, 600, 603, 610, 660; **19:** 78; **26:** 257, 364; **34:** 270, 293, 323; **46:** 291, 333, 347, 362; **51:** 30; **52:** 57
madness **1:** 554, 639, 656; **26:** 371
Malvolio
   characterization **1:** 540, 544, 545, 548, 550, 554, 558, 567, 575, 577, 615; **26:** 207, 233, 273; **46:** 286
   forged letter **16:** 372; **28:** 1
   punishment **1:** 539, 544, 548, 549, 554, 555, 558, 563, 577, 590, 632, 645; **46:** 291, 297, 338
   as Puritan **1:** 549, 551, 555, 558, 561, 563; **25:** 47
   role in play **1:** 545, 548, 549, 553, 555, 563, 567, 575, 577, 588, 610, 615, 632, 645; **26:** 337, 374; **46:** 347
music **1:** 543, 566, 596
Olivia **1:** 540, 543, 545; **46:** 286, 333, 369; **47:** 45
order **1:** 563, 596; **34:** 330; **46:** 291, 347

Orsino **46:** 286, 333; **47:** 45
philosophical elements **1:** 560, 563, 596; **34:** 301, 316; **46:** 297
Puritanism **1:** 549, 553, 555, 632; **16:** 53; **25:** 47; **46:** 338
psychoanalytic criticism **46:** 333
Saturnalian elements **1:** 554, 571, 603, 620, 642; **16:** 53
self-deception **1:** 554, 561, 591, 625; **47:** 45
self-indulgence **1:** 563, 615, 635
sexual ambiguity and sexual deception **1:** 540, 562, 620, 621, 639, 645; **22:** 69; **34:** 311, 344; **37:** 59; **42:** 32
Shakespeare's canon, place in **1:** 543, 548, 557, 569, 575, 580, 621, 635, 638
Shakespeare's other plays, relation to **34:** 270; **46:** 303
sources **1:** 539, 540, 603; **34:** 301, 323, 344; **46:** 291
staging issues **26:** 219, 233, 257, 337, 342, 346, 357, 359, 360, 364, 366, 371, 374; **46:** 310, 369
structure **1:** 539, 542, 543, 546, 551, 553, 563, 570, 571, 590, 600, 660; **26:** 374; **34:** 281, 287; **46:** 286
time **37:** 78; **46:** 297
tragic elements **1:** 557, 569, 572, 575, 580, 599, 621, 635, 638, 639, 645, 654, 656; **26:** 342
Viola **26:** 308; **46:** 286, 324, 347, 369

The Two Gentlemen of Verona (Volumes 6, 12, 40)

absurdities, inconsistencies, and shortcomings **6:** 435, 436, 437, 439, 464, 507, 541, 560
appearance versus reality **6:** 494, 502, 511, 519, 529, 532, 549, 560
audience versus character perceptions **6:** 499, 519, 524
authorship controversy **6:** 435, 436, 437, 438, 439, 449, 466, 476
characterization **6:** 438, 442, 445, 447, 449, 458, 462, 560; **12:** 458; **40:** 312, 327, 330, 365
Christian elements **6:** 438, 494, 514, 532, 555, 564
education **6:** 490, 494, 504, 526, 532, 555, 568
Elizabethan setting **12:** 463, 485
forest **6:** 450, 456, 492, 514, 547, 555, 564, 568
genre **6:** 460, 468, 472, 516; **40:** 320
identity **6:** 494, 511, 529, 532, 547, 560, 564, 568; **19:** 34
ironic or parodic elements **6:** 447, 472, 478, 484, 502, 504, 509, 516, 529, 549; **13:** 12
Julia or Silvia **6:** 450, 453, 458, 476, 494, 499, 516, 519, 549, 564; **40:** 312, 327, 374
language and imagery **6:** 437, 438, 439, 445, 449, 490, 504, 519, 529, 541; **28:** 9; **40:** 343
Launce and Speed, comic function of **6:** 438, 439, 442, 456, 458, 460, 462, 472, 476, 478, 484, 502, 504, 507, 509, 516, 519, 549; **40:** 312, 320
love **6:** 442, 445, 456, 479, 488, 492, 494, 502, 509, 516, 519, 549; **13:** 12; **40:** 327, 335, 343, 354, 365; **51:** 30, 44

love versus friendship **6:** 439, 449, 450, 458, 460, 465, 468, 471, 476, 480; **40:** 354, 359, 365
marriage **48:** 32
mimetic rivalry **13:** 12; **40:** 335
morality **6:** 438, 492, 494, 514, 532, 555, 564
Proteus **6:** 439, 450, 458, 480, 490, 511; **40:** 312, 327, 330, 335, 359; **42:** 18
repentance and forgiveness **6:** 450, 514, 516, 555, 564
resolution **6:** 435, 436, 439, 445, 449, 453, 458, 460, 462, 465, 466, 468, 471, 476, 480, 486, 494, 509, 514, 516, 519, 529, 532, 541, 549; **19:** 34
romantic and courtly conventions **6:** 438, 460, 472, 478, 484, 486, 488, 502, 507, 509, 529, 541, 549, 560, 568; **12:** 460, 462; **40:** 354, 374
setting **12:** 463, 465, 485
sources **6:** 436, 460, 462, 468, 476, 480, 490, 511, 547; **19:** 34; **40:** 320
staging issues **12:** 457, 464; **42:** 18
structure **6:** 445, 450, 460, 462, 504, 526
youth **6:** 439, 450, 464, 514, 568

The Two Noble Kinsmen (Volumes 9, 41, 50)

amorality, question of **9:** 447, 460, 492
authorship controversy
   Shakespeare not a co-author **9:** 445, 447, 455, 461
   Shakespearean portions of the text **9:** 446, 447, 448, 455, 456, 457, 460, 462, 463, 471, 479, 486; **41:** 308, 317, 355
   Shakespeare's part in the overall conception or design **9:** 444, 446, 448, 456, 457, 460, 480, 481, 486, 490; **37:** 313; **41:** 326; **50:** 326
ceremonies, rites, and rituals, importance of **9:** 492, 498
characterization **9:** 457, 461, 471, 474; **41:** 340, 385; **50:** 305, 326
chivalry **50:** 305, 348
class distinctions, conflict and relations **50:** 295, 305, 310
Emilia **9:** 460, 470, 471, 479, 481; **19:** 394; **41:** 372, 385; **42:** 368
free will versus fate **9:** 474, 481, 486, 492, 498
friendship **9:** 448, 463, 470, 474, 479, 481, 486, 490; **19:** 394; **41:** 355, 363, 372; **42:** 368
gender issues **42:** 368; **50:** 310
innocence to experience **9:** 481, 502; **19:** 394
irony or satire **9:** 463, 481, 486; **41:** 301; **50:** 348
the jailer's daughter **9:** 457, 460, 479, 481, 486, 502; **41:** 340; **50:** 295, 305, 310, 348, 361
language and imagery **9:** 445, 446, 447, 448, 456, 461, 462, 463, 469, 471, 498, 502; **41:** 289, 301, 308, 317, 326; **50:** 310
love **9:** 479, 481, 490, 498; **41:** 289, 301, 363, 372, 385; **50:** 295, 361
masque elements **9:** 490
Palamon and Arcite **9:** 474, 481, 490, 492, 502; **50:** 295, 305, 348, 361
sexuality **50:** 361
sources **19:** 394; **41:** 289, 301, 363, 385; **50:** 326, 348
structure **37:** 313; **50:** 326, 361

Venus and Adonis (Volumes 10, 33, 51)

Adonis **10**: 411, 420, 424, 427, 429, 434, 439, 442, 451, 454, 459, 466, 473, 489; **25**: 305, 328; **28**: 355; **33**: 309, 321, 330, 347, 352, 357, 363, 370, 377; **51**: 345, 377
allegorical elements **10**: 427, 434, 439, 449, 454, 462, 480; **28**: 355; **33**: 309, 330
ambiguity **10**: 434, 454, 459, 462, 466, 473, 480, 486, 489; **33**: 352; **51**: 368, 377, 388
beauty **10**: 420, 423, 427, 434, 454, 480; **33**: 330, 352
the boar **10**: 416, 451, 454, 466, 473; **33**: 339, 347, 370; **51**: 359, 368
comic elements **51**: 377
the courser and the jennet **10**: 418, 439, 466; **33**: 309, 339, 347, 352
death, decay, and nature's destructiveness **10**: 419, 427, 434, 451, 454, 462, 466, 473, 480, 489; **25**: 305; **33**: 309, 321, 347, 352, 363, 370
dramatic elements **10**: 459, 462, 486
domesticity **51**: 359
eroticism or sensuality **10**: 410, 411, 418, 419, 427, 428, 429, 442, 448, 454, 459, 466, 473; **25**: 305, 328; **28**: 355; **33**: 321, 339, 347, 352, 363, 370; **51**: 345, 352, 359, 368
Faerie Queene (Edmund Spenser), compared with **33**: 339
forgiveness **51**: 377
Hero and Leander (Christopher Marlowe), compared with **10**: 419, 424, 429; **33**: 309, 357; **51**: 345, 377
comic elements **10**: 429, 434, 439, 442, 459, 462, 489; **33**: 352
hunt motif **10**: 434, 451, 466, 473; **33**: 357, 370
imagery **10**: 414, 415, 416, 420, 429, 434, 449, 459, 466, 473, 480; **25**: 328; **28**: 355; **33**: 321, 339, 352, 363, 370, 377; **42**: 348; **51**: 335, 388
love versus lust **10**: 418, 420, 427, 434, 439, 448, 449, 454, 462, 466, 473, 480, 489; **25**: 305; **28**: 355; **33**: 309, 330, 339, 347, 357, 363, 370; **51**: 359
morality **10**: 411, 412, 414, 416, 418, 419, 420, 423, 427, 428, 439, 442, 448, 449, 454, 459, 466; **33**: 330
negative appraisals **10**: 410, 411, 415, 418, 419, 424, 429
Ovid, compared with **32**: 352; **42**: 348; **51**: 335, 352
pictorial elements **10**: 414, 415, 419, 420, 423, 480; **33**: 339
popularity **10**: 410, 412, 418, 427; **25**: 328
procreation **10**: 439, 449, 466; **33**: 321, 377
reason **10**: 427, 439, 449, 459, 462, 466; **28**: 355; **33**: 309, 330
rhetoric **33**: 377; **51**: 335, 345, 352
Shakespeare's plays, compared with **10**: 412, 414, 415, 434, 459, 462
Shakespeare's sonnets, compared with **33**: 377
sources **10**: 410, 412, 420, 424, 429, 434, 439, 451, 454, 466, 473, 480, 486, 489; **16**: 452; **25**: 305; **28**: 355; **33**: 309, 321, 330, 339, 347, 352, 357, 370, 377; **42**: 348; **51**: 335
structure **10**: 434, 442, 480, 486, 489; **33**: 357, 377
style **10**: 411, 412, 414, 415, 416, 418, 419, 420, 423, 424, 428, 429, 439, 442, 480, 486, 489; **16**: 452
Venus **10**: 427, 429, 434, 439, 442, 448, 449, 451, 454, 466, 473, 480, 486, 489; **16**: 452; **25**: 305, 328; **28**: 355; **33**: 309, 321, 330, 347, 352, 357, 363, 370, 377; **51**: 335, 352, 377, 388
Wat the hare **10**: 424, 451

The Winter's Tale (Volumes 7, 15, 36, 45)

Antigonus
  characterization **7**: 394, 451, 464
  death scene (Act III, scene iii) **7**: 377, 414, 464, 483; **15**: 518, 532; **19**: 366
appearance versus reality **7**: 429, 446, 479
art versus nature **7**: 377, 381, 397, 419, 452; **36**: 289, 318; **45**: 329
audience perception, Shakespeare's manipulation of **7**: 394, 429, 456, 483, 501; **13**: 417; **19**: 401, 431, 441; **25**: 339; **45**: 374
autobiographical elements **7**: 395, 397, 410, 419
Autolycus **7**: 375, 380, 382, 387, 389, 395, 396, 414; **15**: 524; **22**: 302; **37**: 31; **45**: 333; **46**: 14, 33; **50**: 45
Christian elements **7**: 381, 387, 402, 410, 417, 419, 425, 429, 436, 452, 460, 501; **36**: 318
counsel **19**: 401
court society **16**: 410
dramatic structure **7**: 382, 390, 396, 399, 402, 407, 414, 429, 432, 473, 479, 493, 497, 501; **15**: 528; **25**: 339; **36**: 289, 295, 362, 380; **45**: 297, 344, 358, 366
ethnicity **37**: 306
folk drama, relation to **7**: 420, 451
forgiveness or redemption **7**: 381, 389, 395, 402, 407, 436, 456, 460, 483; **36**: 318
fusion of comic, tragic, and romantic elements **7**: 390, 394, 396, 399, 410, 412, 414, 429, 436, 479, 483, 490, 501; **13**: 417; **15**: 514, 524, 532; **25**: 339; **36**: 295, 380; **45**: 295, 329
grace **7**: 420, 425, 460, 493; **36**: 328
Hermione
  characterization **7**: 385, 395, 402, 412, 414, 506; **15**: 495, 532; **22**: 302, 324; **25**: 347; **32**: 388; **36**: 311; **47**: 25; **49**: 18
  restoration (Act V, scene iii) **7**: 377, 379, 384, 385, 387, 389, 394, 396, 412, 425, 436, 451, 452, 456, 464, 483, 501; **15**: 411, 412, 413, 518, 528, 532; **49**: 18
  supposed death **25**: 339; **47**: 25
  trial of **49**: 18
as historical allegory **7**: 381; **15**: 528
homosexuality **48**: 309
hospitality **19**: 366
irony **7**: 419, 420
Jacobean culture, relation to **19**: 366, 401, 431; **25**: 347; **32**: 388; **37**: 306
language and imagery **7**: 382, 384, 417, 418, 420, 425, 460, 506; **13**: 409; **19**: 431; **22**: 324; **25**: 347; **36**: 295; **42**: 308; **45**: 297, 333, 344; **50**: 45

Leontes
  characterization **19**: 431; **45**: 366
  jealousy **7**: 377, 379, 382, 383, 384, 387, 389, 394, 395, 402, 407, 412, 414, 425, 429, 432, 436, 464, 480, 483, 497; **15**: 514, 518, 532; **22**: 324; **25**: 339; **36**: 334, 344, 349; **44**: 66; **45**: 295, 297, 344, 358; **47**: 25
  Othello, compared with **7**: 383, 390, 412; **15**: 514; **36**: 334; **44**: 66; **47**: 25
  repentance **7**: 381, 389, 394, 396, 402, 414, 497; **36**: 318, 362; **44**: 66
love **7**: 417, 425, 469, 490; **51**: 30, 33, 44
Mamillius **7**: 394, 396, 451; **22**: 324
metadramatic elements **16**: 410
myth of Demeter and Persephone, relation to **7**: 397, 436
nationalism and patriotism **32**: 388
nature **7**: 397, 418, 419, 420, 425, 432, 436, 451, 452, 473, 479; **19**: 366; **45**: 329
Neoclassical rules **7**: 376, 377, 379, 380, 383, 410; **15**: 397
Ovid's Metamorphoses, relation to **42**: 308
Pandosto, compared with **7**: 376, 377, 390, 412, 446; **13**: 409; **25**: 347; **36**: 344, 374
Paulina **7**: 385, 412, 506; **15**: 528; **22**: 324; **25**: 339; **36**: 311
Perdita
  characterization **7**: 395, 412, 414, 419, 429, 432, 452, 506; **22**: 324; **25**: 339; **36**: 328
  reunion with Leontes (Act V, scene ii) **7**: 377, 379, 381, 390, 432, 464, 480
plot **7**: 376, 377, 379, 382, 387, 390, 396, 452; **13**: 417; **15**: 518; **45**: 374
rebirth, regeneration, resurrection, or immortality **7**: 397, 414, 417, 419, 429, 436, 451, 452, 456, 480, 490, 497, 506; **25**: 339 452, 480, 490, 497, 506; **45**: 366
sheep-shearing scene (Act IV, scene iv) **7**: 379, 387, 395, 396, 407, 410, 412, 419, 420, 429, 432, 436, 451, 479, 490; **16**: 410; **19**: 366; **25**: 339; **36**: 362, 374; **45**: 374
staging issues **7**: 414, 425, 429, 446, 464, 480, 483, 497; **13**: 409; **15**: 518; **48**: 309
statue scene (Act V, scene iii) **7**: 377, 379, 384, 385, 387, 389, 394, 396, 412, 425, 436, 451, 456, 464, 483, 501; **15**: 411, 412, 518, 528, 532; **25**: 339, 347; **36**: 301
subversiveness **22**: 302
symbolism **7**: 425, 429, 436, 452, 456, 469, 490, 493
textual issues **19**: 441; **45**: 333
Time-Chorus **7**: 377, 380, 412, 464, 476, 501; **15**: 518
time **7**: 397, 425, 436, 476, 490; **19**: 366; **36**: 301, 349; **45**: 297, 329, 366, 374
trickster, motif of **22**: 302; **45**: 333
Union debate, relation to **25**: 347
violence **43**: 39
witchcraft **22**: 324
women, role of **22**: 324; **36**: 311; **42**: 308; **51**: 30